Ward 1—Precinct 1

City of Boston

List of Residents 20 years of Age and Over

(Non-Citizens Indicated by Asterisk)

(Females Indicated by Dagger) as of January 1, 1941

Unknown

Alpha Editions

This edition published in 2020

ISBN : 9789354027857

Design and Setting By
Alpha Editions
email - alphaedis@gmail.com

Ward 18—Precinct 1

CITY OF BOSTON

LIST OF RESIDENTS
20 YEARS OF AGE AND OVER

(NON-CITIZENS INDICATED BY ASTERISK)
(FEMALES INDICATED BY DAGGER)

AS OF

JANUARY 1, 1941

JOSEPH F. TIMILTY, *Chairman*
FREDERIC E. DOWLING, *Secretary*
WILLIAM A. MOTLEY, JR.
FRANCIS B. McKINNEY
HILDA HEDSTROM QUIRK
Listing Board.

CITY OF BOSTON PRINTING DEPARTMENT

Page.	Letter	Full Name	Residence, Jan. 1, 1941	Occupation	Supposed Age.	Reported Residence, Jan. 1, 1940. Street and Number.
1		**Avander Court**				
	A	Moran Alberta A—†	3	housewife	24	11 Caton
	B	Moran Walter	3	laborer	31	30 Monponset
	C	Hubley Catherine B—†	4	operator	49	11 Caton
	D	Hubley Catherine E—†	4	housewife	28	11 "
	E	Hubley Daniel J	4	porter	27	11 "
	F	Hammond Cora—†	5	housewife	58	here
	G	Hammond George A	5	laborer	63	"
		Babson Street				
	H	Regan John J	119	tel worker	36	here
	K	Regan Mary—†	119	housewife	35	"
	L	Regan Barbara—†	119	"	75	"
	M	Regan Lawrence	119	clerk	37	"
	O	Detert John E	121	"	23	"
	P	Detert John H	121	sexton	53	"
	R	Detert Mary E—†	121	housewife	43	"
	S	Detert William H	121	sexton	22	"
	T	Gibbs William A	127–129	janitor	56	894 Cummins H'way
	U	Ward Annie E—†	127–129	housekeeper	66	894 "
	V	Putman Ellen A—†	127–129	"	74	here
	X	Burgess Mary H—†	130	teacher	69	"
	Y	Hunt Anna L—†	130	housewife	58	"
	Z	Hunt Ernest R	130	caretaker	63	"
2		**Blue Hill Avenue**				
	B	Hichens Richard	1548	clergyman	35	here
	C	Keefe Daniel J	1548	"	49	"
	D	Kittridge Beatrice—†	1548	domestic	34	"
	E	Ryan Francis J	1548	clergyman	81	"
	F	Walsh Edwin W	1548	"	48	"
	G	Butler Beatrice—†	1550	waitress	31	"
	H	Butler Clifford	1550	salesman	29	"
	K	Giles Clifford L	1550	painter	64	"
	L	Giles Janice—†	1550	manager	58	"
	M	Goldman Deborah—†	1550	teacher	43	"
	N	Guild Grace A—†	1550	housekeeper	67	"
	O	Holm Ingvard N	1550	R F D	54	"
	P	Mikolajewski Caesar M	1550	"	44	"

Page	Letter	Full Name	Residence, Jan. 1, 1941	Occupation	Supposed Age	Reported Residence, Jan. 1, 1940. Street and Number

Blue Hill Avenue—Continued

Page	Letter	Full Name	Residence	Occupation	Age	Reported Residence
	R	Norton Doris †	1550	teacher	40	here
	S	Sliney Leo J	1550	clerk	36	22 Birchcroft rd

Cookson Terrace

Page	Letter	Full Name	Residence	Occupation	Age	Reported Residence
4						
	G	Coughlan Charles L	38	policeman	38	here
	H	Coughlan James T	38	clerk	45	"
	K	Coughlan John J	38	retired	71	"
	L	Coughlan Margaret—†	38	housewife	68	"
	M	Coughlan Thomas D	38	chauffeur	39	"
	N	Connolly Anna N—†	41	teacher	23	"
	O	Connolly Daniel S	41	messenger	21	"
	P	Connolly Garrett	41	engineer	50	"
	R	Connolly John T	41	clerk	25	"
	S	Connolly Mary G—†	41	stenographer	24	"
	T	Connolly Nora M—†	41	housewife	50	"
	U	Hutchinson Alice—†	47	clerk	26	35 Tremont
	V	Martin John F	47	janitor	55	here
	W	*Martin Violet A—†	47	housewife	44	"
	X	Bell Esther—†	49	"	23	54 Copeland
	Y	Bell Norman	49	chauffeur	28	54 "
	Z	Coffin Everett	49	clerk	27	48 Sherman
5						
	A	Coffin Mary T—†	49	housewife	24	48 "
	B	Jordan Howard L	51	laborer	50	here
	C	Jordan Lillian M—†	51	clerk	48	"
	D	Reid Annie—†	51	housekeeper	74	"
	E	Guerini Andrew	53	clerk	52	"
	G	*Remondi John	53	mechanic	34	"
	F	*Remondi Lena—†	53	housewife	34	"

Dania Street

Page	Letter	Full Name	Residence	Occupation	Age	Reported Residence
	H	Bolle Johanna—†	19	housewife	78	here
	L	Durup Helene—†	19	"	25	Hingham
	K	Durup Johan	19	salesman	53	"

Doone Avenue

Page	Letter	Full Name	Residence	Occupation	Age	Reported Residence
	M	Dreiker Arthur	16	salesman	33	74 Lucerne
	N	Dreiker Sadie—†	16	housewife	34	74 "

Page.	Letter.	Full Name.	Residence, Jan. 1, 1941.	Occupation.	Supposed Age.	Reported Residence, Jan. 1, 1940. Street and Number.

Doone Avenue—Continued

Page	Letter	Full Name	Residence	Occupation	Age	Reported Residence
	O	Erickson Emil	17	machinist	50	here
	P	Erickson Gertrude—†	17	housewife	46	"
	R	Erickson Robert	17	machinist	24	"
	S	Erickson Victor	17	clerk	21	"
	T	Fienn Charles F	20	accountant	39	"
	U	Fienn Mildred—†	20	housewife	47	"
	V	Peters Elizabeth—†	20	"	34	"
	W	Peters Philip	20	clerk	35	"
	X	Johansen Gladys E—†	24	housewife	35	"
	Y	Johansen Leif	24	mechanic	46	"
	Z	Hanley Allan	24	signalman	25	"
6						
	A	Hanley Donald	24	mechanic	23	"
	B	Hanley Florence—†	24	saleswoman	21	"
	C	Hanley Hugh	24	blacksmith	52	"
	D	Hanley Mary—†	24	housewife	50	"
	E	Schell Frank J	25	compositor	73	330 W Fourth
	F	Schell Magdaline—†	25	housewife	70	330 "
	G	Schell Pauline M—†	25	clerk	32	330 "
	H	Holderried Charles J	25	retired	65	here
	K	Holderried Maude B—†	25	housewife	56	"
	L	Perry Margaret E—†	25	housekeeper	77	"

Duxbury Road

Page	Letter	Full Name	Residence	Occupation	Age	Reported Residence
	M	*McGrath Catherine M—†	3	housewife	50	here
	N	McGrath Patrick J	3	operator	45	"
	O	Botti Joseph L	4	contractor	30	"
	P	Botti Veronica C—†	4	housewife	28	"
	R	Robbins Alice K—†	4	"	34	"
	S	Robbins Elmer M	4	clerk	34	"
	T	Daly Catherine E—†	5	housewife	44	"
	U	Daly John M	5	clerk	47	"
	V	Sullivan Evelyn J—†	5	typist	21	61 Waldeck
	W	Sullivan John W	5	clerk	26	61 "
	X	Sullivan Marguerite B—†	5	typist	22	61 "
	Y	Sullivan Mary L—†	5	housewife	51	61 "
	Z	Sullivan Timothy J	5	carpenter	27	61 "
7						
	A	Campbell Catherine F—†	6	housewife	28	here
	B	Campbell Charles F	6	plater	31	"

Page	Letter	Full Name	Residence Jan. 1, 1941	Occupation	Supposed Age	Reported Residence Jan. 1, 1940 Street and Number

Duxbury Road Continued

Page	Letter	Full Name	Residence Jan. 1, 1941	Occupation	Supposed Age	Reported Residence Jan. 1, 1940
	C	Donovan James	7	chauffeur	32	here
	D	Donovan Mildred †	7	housewife	29	"
	E	Desmond Arthur F	7	fitter	45	"
	F	Desmond Catherine A †	7	housewife	42	"
	G	Nagle Anna E †	8	"	38	"
	H	Nagle David F	8	mechanic	39	"
	K	Thomson Archibald W	10	photographer	30	"
	L	Thomson Lillian C †	10	housewife	55	"
	M	Thomson Marguerite L †	10	cashier	29	"
	N	Thomson Richard V	10	clerk	22	"
	O	Waters Emma T †	10	at home	68	400 Columbus av
	P	Desmond Leo C	11	contractor	38	here
	R	Desmond Margaret H †	11	housewife	35	"
	S	*Windedal Astrid M †	14	"	45	"
	T	Windedal Martin B	14	painter	42	"

Faunce Road

Page	Letter	Full Name	Residence Jan. 1, 1941	Occupation	Supposed Age	Reported Residence Jan. 1, 1940
	U	Mahoney Henry S	11–13	mechanic	37	here
	V	Mahoney Marie E †	11–13	housewife	33	"
	W	Powers John F	11–13	salesman	40	"
	X	Powers Joseph B	11–13	postal clerk	36	"
	Y	Powers Thomas T	11–13	actor	38	"
	Z	McCusker James	15	retired	68	"
8						
	A	McCusker Ruth E †	15	stenographer	26	"
	B	McCusker Winifred M †	15	housewife	58	"
	C	Keating Alfred	15	welder	50	"
	D	Keating Anna †	15	housewife	49	"
	E	*Carrara Andrew	17	laborer	60	"
	F	Noris Guido	17	clerk	21	"
	G	*Noris Lena †	17	housewife	53	"
	H	*Noris Louis	17	laborer	54	"
	K	MacArthur Mary M †	19	housewife	30	"
	L	MacArthur William H	19	painter	43	"
	M	Sullivan Pauline H †	19	seamstress	60	53 Rosewood
	N	Gillis Clara M †	27	housewife	27	here
	O	Gillis John L	27	laborer	32	"
	P	Gibbs Jeanette †	27	clerk	61	"
	R	Johnson Annie †	27	housekeeper	56	"
	S	Stappen Elizabeth †	27	at home	73	"

Page.	Letter.	Full Name.	Residence, Jan. 1, 1941	Occupation.	Supposed Age.	Reported Residence Jan. 1, 1940. Street and Number.

Faunce Road—Continued

Page	Letter	Full Name	Residence	Occupation	Age	Reported Residence
	V	Hutchinson Bradford G	35	salesman	29	here
	W	Hutchinson Irving B	35	"	27	8 Akron
	X	Kennedy Caroline—†	37	housewife	65	here
	Y	Kennedy James A	37	steelworker	36	"
	Z	Kennedy John F	37	clerk	35	"

Freeland Street

Page	Letter	Full Name	Residence	Occupation	Age	Reported Residence
9	A	Sullivan Ellen E—†	7	housewife	57	here
	B	Sullivan John P	7	salesman	60	"
	C	Cannon Frank E	10	painter	50	"
	D	Cannon Joseph F	10	draftsman	21	"
	E	Cannon Lillian M—†	10	housewife	45	"
	F	Cronin James J	12	clerk	40	"
	G	Haverty John J	12	mechanic	46	"
	H	Haverty Sheila—†	12	housewife	47	"
	K	Lancaster Hannah—†	16	"	20	Delaware
	L	Lancaster Vernon	16	attendant	21	"
	M	Sullivan Margaret—†	16	housewife	43	here
	N	Sullivan Timothy V	16	carpenter	44	"
	O	Kirk Peter F	18	fireman	36	"
	P	Kirk Ruth M—†	18	housewife	33	"
	R	Murphy Arthur F	20	supervisor	49	"
	S	Murphy Catherine D—†	20	housewife	44	"
	T	Stuart Margaret M—†	23	operator	44	"
	U	Stuart Peter M	23	retired	77	"
	V	*Hegarty Mary P—†	27	housewife	28	"
	W	Hegarty Peter A	27	policeman	33	"
	X	Rabbitt Margaret A—†	29	housewife	59	"
	Y	Rabbitt Michael A	29	mechanic	63	"
	Z	Galvin Patrick J	35	retired	69	"
10	A	Galvin Robert F	35	carpenter	33	"
	B	Galvin Theresa A—†	35	housewife	68	"
	C	Galvin Thomas J	35	clerk	42	"
	D	Howard Joseph F	39	retired	69	"
	E	Kerins Lillian R—†	39	housewife	38	"
	F	Kerins William J	39	manager	41	"
	G	*Russo Graziano	41	tailor	45	"
	H	*Russo Josephine—†	41	housewife	38	"
	K	*Russo Marguerite—†	41	seamstress	54	"

Page	Letter	Full Name	Residence, Jan. 1, 1941	Occupation	Supposed Age	Reported Residence, Jan. 1, 1940. Street and Number

Freeland Street—Continued

Page	Letter	Full Name	Residence, Jan. 1, 1941	Occupation	Supposed Age	Reported Residence, Jan. 1, 1940. Street and Number
	L	*Russo Santa—†	41	at home	88	here
	M	Woodward Clarence E	43	operator	56	"
	N	Woodward Eleanor E—†	43	housewife	52	"
	O	Woodward Myrtle—†	43	clerk	20	"
	P	*Russo Alphonsa—†	45	housewife	57	"
	R	*Russo Joseph	45	retired	61	"
	S	Galvin Jennie—†	47	housewife	58	"
	T	Galvin William	47	operator	63	"
	U	McCarthy Anne T—†	57	housewife	48	"
	V	McCarthy Jeremiah	57	bricklayer	46	"

Fremont Street

Page	Letter	Full Name	Residence, Jan. 1, 1941	Occupation	Supposed Age	Reported Residence, Jan. 1, 1940. Street and Number
	X	Oprandi Carlo J	47	cabinetmaker	47	here
	Y	Oprandi Elizabeth—†	47	housewife	47	"
	Z	Oprandi Lawrence T	47	mechanic	28	"
11						
	A	Merlino Josephine—†	50	housewife	33	23 Lawrence av
	B	Merlino Nicholas	50	barber	45	23 "
	C	Lee Anna J—†	56	housewife	46	here
	D	Lee Bartholomew	56	manufacturer	52	"
	E	Lee Francis J	56	clerk	20	"
	F	Folsom Mary A—†	59	housewife	33	6 Freeport
	G	Folsom Richard J	59	chauffeur	36	6 "
	H	Yocco Angelo	59	laborer	45	41 Malta
	K	*Yocco Maria H—†	59	housewife	30	41 "
	L	DelSignore Angelo D	60	machinist	23	here
	M	DelSignore Joseph	60	bookkeeper	25	"
	N	DelSignore Josephine—†	60	housewife	61	"
	O	DelSignore Marie—†	60	operator	37	"
	P	DelSignore Matilda A—†	60	"	20	"
	R	DelSignore Rocco	60	painter	32	"

Glenhill Road

Page	Letter	Full Name	Residence, Jan. 1, 1941	Occupation	Supposed Age	Reported Residence, Jan. 1, 1940. Street and Number
	S	Johnson Amelia D—†	2	housewife	49	here
	T	Johnson Frank H	2	chauffeur	47	"
	U	Burke John F	4	clerk	41	"
	V	Burke Margaret J—†	4	housewife	63	"
	W	Hanley Mary E—†	4	clerk	65	Framingham
	X	Murphy Jeremiah	4	contractor	60	here

Page.	Letter.	Full Name.	Residence, Jan. 1, 1941.	Occupation.	Supposed Age.	Reported Residence, Jan. 1, 1940. Street and Number.
		Glenhill Road—Continued				
	Y	Murphy Mary A—†	4	housewife	58	here
	Z	Weiner Anna—†	10	"	28	"
12						
	A	Weiner Hyman	10	merchant	37	"
	B	McCarthy Annie F—†	14	typesetter	65	"
	C	McCarthy Catherine C—†	14	at home	70	"
	D	McManus Claire—†	18	housewife	46	"
	E	McManus Terrance	18	policeman	44	"
	F	Ribeck Alice—†	22	beautician	21	"
	G	Ribeck Henry	22	plumber	24	"
	H	*Ribeck May—†	22	housewife	50	"
	K	Ribeck Nathan	22	carpenter	57	"
	L	Ribeck Sarah—†	22	beautician	27	"
	M	Braverman Albert	30	floor sander	21	"
	N	*Braverman Bessie—†	30	housewife	46	"
	O	Braverman Theodore	30	mechanic	49	"
	P	Hayes Frances—†	33–35	housekeeper	84	948 Morton
	R	West Rose W—†	33–35	clerk	42	50 Peacevale rd
	S	Barth Harry H	33–35	salesman	43	948 Morton
	T	Barth Irene—†	33–35	housewife	41	948 "
	U	*Adams Harry	34	shoemaker	46	here
	V	*Adams Nettie—†	34	housewife	39	"
	W	Bowman Ella—†	37	"	29	"
	X	Bowman Fred W	37	mason	31	"
	Y	O'Neil Louise P—†	37	clerk	33	3 Holmfield av
13						
	A	Gorman John P	104	water inspector	47	here
	B	McQuaide Alice E—†	104	housewife	48	"
	C	McQuaide Francis J	104	clerk	22	"
	D	McQuaide James W	104	fireman	46	"
	E	Jenness Herman A	104	engraver	63	"
	F	Walsh Archie K	104	clerk	51	"
	G	Walsh Frances B—†	104	housewife	46	"
		Groveland Street				
	H	Galvin Helen M—†	14	housewife	25	here
	K	Galvin William T	14	collector	30	"
	L	Galvin Catherine E—†	14	housewife	29	"
	M	Galvin John G	14	salesman	30	"
	N	Downey James B	14	clerk	24	"

Page	Letter	Full Name	Residence, Jan. 1, [illegible]	Occupation	Supposed Age	Reported Residence, Jan. 1, [illegible] Street and Number

Groveland Street—Continued

Page	Letter	Full Name	Residence	Occupation	Supposed Age	Reported Residence
	o	Downey Margaret M—†	14	housewife	64	here
	P	Downey Maurice J	14	teacher	33	"
	R	*Curran Eileen J—†	30	housewife	24	"
	S	Curran John J	30	mechanic	34	"
	T	Costello Ellen J—†	30	housewife	62	"
	U	Costello John R	30	dispatcher	27	"
	V	Costello Michael W	30	engineer	68	"
	W	Curran Michael	30	bartender	29	"
	X	*Botti Elizabeth—†	48	housewife	58	"
	Y	Botti Joseph	48	mason	60	"
	Z	Botti Onorina—†	48	cashier	24	"
14						
	A	Rota Celeste	48	laborer	42	"

Hopkins Place

Page	Letter	Full Name	Residence	Occupation	Supposed Age	Reported Residence
	B	Bouffard Albert	1	machinist	67	here
	C	Bouffard Mary—†	1	housewife	62	"
	D	Doyle Annie—†	2	"	65	"
	E	Doyle Edna—†	2	waitress	27	"
	F	Doyle Raymond	2	clerk	32	"
	G	Munroe Donald	2	chauffeur	36	8 Fremont
	H	Munroe Mary A—†	2	housewife	28	8 "
	K	Trenholm Martha M—†	2	housekeeper	67	here
	M	McDonald James A	4	roofer	47	"
	N	McDonald Mary M—†	4	housewife	35	"
	O	Murphy Lillian—†	4	waitress	37	4 Market
	P	Viecelli Enrico	5	chauffeur	28	here
	R	*Viecelli Genoveffa—†	5	housewife	53	"
	S	Viecelli Louis	5	clerk	24	"
	T	McGuire James	6	chauffeur	52	"
	U	McGuire Mary—†	6	housewife	53	"
	V	Lombardi Delia—†	6	"	28	56 Cedar
	W	Lombardi Dominic	6	laborer	30	56 "

Liversidge Way

Page	Letter	Full Name	Residence	Occupation	Supposed Age	Reported Residence
	Z	Draper Lena O—†	6	housekeeper	35	here
15						
	A	Ryan Ethel M—†	7	housewife	40	"
	B	Ryan Ruth B—†	7	operator	22	"

Page	Letter	Full Name	Residence, Jan. 1, 1941	Occupation	Supposed Age	Reported Residence, Jan. 1, 1940. Street and Number.

Liversidge Way—Continued

Page	Letter	Full Name	Residence, Jan. 1, 1941	Occupation	Supposed Age	Reported Residence, Jan. 1, 1940. Street and Number.
	C	Ryan Walter C	7	chauffeur	42	here
	D	Ryan Charles	8	papermaker	24	"
	E	Ryan Mary—†	8	housewife	54	"
	F	Martin Joseph P	9	clerk	34	"
	G	Dowley George W	10	retired	81	"
	H	Elliott Irving	10	painter	65	"

Lorna Road

Page	Letter	Full Name	Residence, Jan. 1, 1941	Occupation	Supposed Age	Reported Residence, Jan. 1, 1940. Street and Number.
	K	Waters Freda F—†	4	housewife	32	here
	L	Waters Max	4	manager	38	"
	M	Persh Hyman	4	manufacturer	41	5 Nazing ct
	N	Persh Sadie—†	4	housewife	38	here
	O	Mason Hyman	5-7	storekeeper	34	"
	P	Mason Lena—†	5-7	housewife	32	"
	R	Slavet Anna—†	5-7	"	39	"
	S	Slavet Daniel	5-7	manager	44	"
	T	Slavet Joseph S	5-7	student	21	"
	U	Santer Bertha E—†	6	housewife	34	"
	V	Santer Herman	6	agent	36	"
	W	Selden Bessie—†	6	housewife	35	"
	X	Selden Irving M	6	salesman	39	"
	Y	Kupperstein Barney	9-11	pharmacist	37	"
	Z	Kupperstein Benjamin R	9-11	"	42	"
16						
	A	Kupperstein Charlotte—†	9-11	housewife	35	"
	B	Shuman Annette—†	9-11	buyer	25	732 Morton
	C	Shuman Barnet	9-11	retired	56	732 "
	D	Shuman Betty—†	9-11	laborer	26	732 "
	E*	Shuman Eva—†	9-11	housewife	47	732 "
	F	Shuman Sidney	9-11	contractor	23	732 "
	G	Starr Edith—†	15-17	housewife	30	here
	H	Starr Nathan	15-17	boxmaker	40	"
	K*	Braverman Mollie—†	15-17	housewife	37	"
	L	Braverman Morris	15-17	storekeeper	42	"
	M	Ganz Lawrence	19-21	tire dealer	33	"
	N	Ganz Minnie—†	19-21	housewife	32	"
	O	Berks Gloria—†	19-21	"	44	"
	P	Berks Harry	19-21	artist	44	"
	R*	Flashner Ida—†	36-38	housewife	33	"
	S	Flashner Israel	36-38	clerk	39	"

Page	Letter	Full Name	Residence, Jan. 1, 1941	Occupation	Supposed Age	Reported Residence, Jan. 1, 1940. Street and Number

Lorna Road Continued

Page	Letter	Full Name	Residence, Jan. 1, 1941	Occupation	Supposed Age	Reported Residence, Jan. 1, 1940. Street and Number
	U	Flashner Celia †	36-38	housewife	60	here
	V	Flashner Esther †	36-38	operator	30	"
	T	Flashner William	36-38	salesman	32	"
	W	Weinbaum Dora †	37	housewife	47	"
	X	Weinbaum Leonide J	37	laborer	24	"
	Y	Weinbaum Morris J	37	manufacturer	52	"
	Z	Silverstein Ida †	37	housewife	51	"
17						
	A	Silverstein Nathan	37	salesman	27	"
	B	Silverstein Samuel	37	cabinetmaker	47	"
	C	Santis Frances †	40	housewife	37	"
	D*	Santis Joseph M	40	salesman	38	"
	E	Bronstein Bessie †	40	housewife	40	"
	F	Bronstein Harry	40	merchant	43	"
	G	Cooper Annette E †	41	housewife	44	"
	H	Cooper Annette H †	41	saleswoman	26	"
	K	Cooper Irwin	41	student	22	"
	L	Cooper Joseph	41	accountant	46	"
	M	Glover Florence G †	41	domestic	27	"
	N	Breger Louis	41	metalworker	55	"
	O	Breger May †	41	housewife	52	"
	P	Lerner Abraham	45	merchant	38	"
	R*	Lerner Stella †	45	housewife	32	"
	S	Russell Lavina †	45	domestic	44	"
	T	Goldberg Morris	45	cutter	47	"
	U	Goldberg Sarah †	45	housewife	46	"
	V	Cohen Alice †	46	saleswoman	26	"
	W	Cohen Ethel †	46	housewife	47	"
	X	Cohen Jacob	46	tailor	49	"
	Y	Cohen Marion †	46	saleswoman	23	"
	Z	Hesson Joseph E	48	engineer	38	"
18						
	A	Hesson Martin T	48	retired	75	"
	B	Hesson Mary †	48	housewife	73	"
	C	Hesson Mary F †	48	operator	40	"
	D	Fierman Beatrice †	49	housewife	46	"
	E	Fierman William E	49	accountant	46	"
	F	Snyder Israel	49	storekeeper	47	"
	G	Snyder Myron	49	manager	21	"
	H	Snyder Sarah †	49	housewife	44	"
	K	Levine Hannah †	55	"	30	"

Page	Letter	Full Name	Residence, Jan. 1, 1941	Occupation	Supposed Age	Reported Residence, Jan. 1, 1940. Street and Number.

Lorna Road—Continued

Page	Letter	Full Name	Residence, Jan. 1, 1941	Occupation	Supposed Age	Reported Residence, Jan. 1, 1940. Street and Number.
	L	Levine Morris	55	salesman	32	here
	M	Boule Armand	55	guard	34	"
	N	Boule Lillian—†	55	housewife	36	"
	O	Zola Fay—†	59–61	"	27	72 Lorna rd
	P	Zola Peter	59–61	printer	33	72 "
	R	Blacker Leo	59–61	fruit	26	here
	S	Blacker Sylvia—†	59–61	secretary	23	"
	T	Markell Elizabeth—†	59–61	housewife	62	"
	U	Markell Hyman	59–61	retired	73	"
	W	Budd Joseph	60	mechanic	40	33 Stow rd
	X	Budd Zelda—†	60	housewife	38	33 "
	Y	Potash Ida—†	60	maid	35	here
	Z	Grosser Albert	64	electrician	31	120 Brainerd rd
19						
	A	Grosser Sarah—†	64	housewife	30	120 "
	B	*Grosser Frances—†	64	"	34	here
	C	Grosser Maxwell	64	pharmacist	42	"
	D	*Freeman Etta M—†	68	housewife	40	"
	E	Freeman William S	68	carpenter	47	"
	F	Perlis Ada—†	69	housewife	41	"
	G	Perlis Maurice	69	mechanic	44	"
	H	Shoolman Jessie—†	69	housewife	30	Milton
	K	Shoolman Meyer	69	salesman	32	"
	L	Lerner Abraham I	71	"	29	here
	M	Lerner Mildred—†	71	housewife	27	"
	N	O'Leary Margaret—†	71	domestic	24	262 Broadway
	O	Weinberg Abraham	71	operator	36	here
	P	Weinberg Ida—†	71	housewife	34	"
	R	Denner Abraham	72–74	entertainer	26	"
	S	Denner Rose—†	72–74	housewife	25	"
	T	*Reback Celia—†	72–74	"	34	"
	U	*Reback Harry	72–74	manager	36	"
	W	Poley Frances—†	72–74	housewife	40	"
	V	Poley Joseph	72–74	presser	43	"
	Y	*Zola Joseph	72–74	retired	66	"
	X	*Zola Rose—†	72–74	housewife	66	"
	Z	Rabatsky Philip	76–78	manufacturer	25	"
20						
	A	Rabatsky Sylvia—†	76–78	housewife	24	"
	B	Cohen Jacob	76–78	clerk	27	"
	C	Cohen Morris	76–78	tailor	58	"

Page	Letter	Full Name	Residence, Jan. 1, 1941.	Occupation	Supposed Age.	Reported Residence, Jan. 1, 1940. Street and Number.

Lorna Road—Continued

Page	Letter	Full Name	Residence, Jan. 1, 1941.	Occupation	Supposed Age.	Reported Residence, Jan. 1, 1940. Street and Number.
	D	*Cohen Sadie—†	76–78	housewife	56	here
	E	Isgur Ida—†	80–82	"	32	"
	F	Isgur Jacob	80–82	constable	34	"
	G	Flax Annie—†	80–82	housewife	40	"
	H	Flax Benjamin	80–82	salesman	50	"
	K	Flax Sidney	80–82	student	20	"
	L	Cechario Frank J	86	merchant	46	"
	M	Cechario Mary E—†	86	housewife	40	"

Manchester Street

Page	Letter	Full Name	Residence, Jan. 1, 1941.	Occupation	Supposed Age.	Reported Residence, Jan. 1, 1940. Street and Number.
	N	McLellan Malcolm P	241	inspector	42	here
	O	McLellan Ronaldsa—†	241	housewife	37	"
	P	Downey Eleanore F—†	241	clerk	24	"
	R	Downey Ellen—†	241	housewife	63	"
	S	Downey Maurice	241	retired	75	"
	T	Fraser Francis L	245	salesman	32	"
	U	Fraser Mildred M—†	245	housewife	30	"
	V	Mathey Annie—†	249	"	60	"
	W	Mathey John	249	gardener	68	"
	X	Mathey Richard L	249	salesman	24	"
	Y	Doherty Daniel F	252	agent	47	"
	Z	Doherty Rachel S—†	252	housewife	42	"
21						
	B	Byrne Margaret—†	256	"	80	"
	A	Byrne Michael	256	retired	80	"

Menton Street

Page	Letter	Full Name	Residence, Jan. 1, 1941.	Occupation	Supposed Age.	Reported Residence, Jan. 1, 1940. Street and Number.
	C	Durkin Bridget M—†	9	housewife	48	here
	D	Durkin John T	9	laborer	53	"
	E	Milloy Anna R—†	9	housewife	42	"
	F	Milloy John T	9	splicer	43	"

Morton Street

Page	Letter	Full Name	Residence, Jan. 1, 1941.	Occupation	Supposed Age.	Reported Residence, Jan. 1, 1940. Street and Number.
	G	Levine Albert	939	physician	31	here
	H	Levine Bette—†	939	housewife	70	"
	K	Levine Harry	939	retired	71	"
	L	Goff Leon	939	jeweler	31	"
	M	Goff Muriel—†	939	clerk	23	"

Page.	Letter.	Full Name.	Residence, Jan. 1, 1941.	Occupation.	Supposed Age.	Reported Residence, Jan. 1, 1940. Street and Number.

Morton Street—Continued

Page.	Letter.	Full Name.	Residence, Jan. 1, 1941.	Occupation.	Supposed Age.	Reported Residence, Jan. 1, 1940. Street and Number.
	N	Goff Rose—†	939	housewife	53	here
	O	Goff Sidney	939	jeweler	27	"
	P	Leventhal Bernard	939	manager	38	"
	R	Leventhal Faye—†	939	housewife	31	"
	S	Rosenthal Lillian—†	941	"	27	"
	T	Rosenthal Myron R	941	physician	35	"
	U	*Rosenthal Rose—†	941	housewife	58	"
	V	Damie Anna—†	941	clerk	32	"
	W	Fliegelman Ada—†	941	housewife	40	"
	X	Fliegelman Samuel	941	pharmacist	45	"
	Y	Cohen Benjamin	941	mechanic	52	"
	Z	*Cohen Jennie—†	941	housewife	46	"
22						
	A	*Getz Rebecca—†	941	"	47	"
	B	*Getz Samuel	941	merchant	45	"
	C	Sorkin Joseph	943	physician	42	"
	D	Sorkin Minnie—†	943	housewife	38	"
	E	Solomon Ida—†	943	"	47	"
	F	Solomon Saul	943	mechanic	47	"
	G	Walker Frances—†	943	housewife	21	"
	H	Walker Irving	943	musician	23	"
	K	Kravitz William	943	chauffeur	45	"
	L	Szathmary Adolph	943	clerk	50	"
	M	Szathmary Nellie—†	943	housewife	50	"
	N	Szathmary William	943	plumber	20	"
	O	Lapidus Charles	947	student	20	"
	P	Lapidus Frank E	947	dentist	40	"
	R	Lapidus Rahmel	947	shipper	70	110 Holland
	S	Lapidus Rose—†	947	housewife	36	here
	T	*Castaline Anna—†	947	"	40	"
	U	Castaline Arnold H	947	student	20	"
	V	*Castaline Henry D	947	merchant	47	"
	W	Gelles Charles S	947	manufacturer	51	"
	X	Gelles Pauline—†	947	housewife	47	"
	Y	Gelles Sidney S	947	salesman	24	"
	Z	Meyers Bernice G—†	947	housewife	23	"
23						
	A	Meyers David	947	teacher	27	56 Nelson
	B	Samuelson Clare—†	949	housewife	35	here
	C	Samuelson Edward	949	auditor	39	"
	D	Sperling Jacob	949	retired	68	"

Page	Letter	Full Name	Residence Jan. 1 1941	Occupation	Supposed Age	Reported Residence Jan. 1, 1940 Street and Number

Morton Street Continued

Page	Letter	Full Name	Residence Jan. 1 1941	Occupation	Supposed Age	Reported Residence Jan. 1, 1940 Street and Number
	E	Levine Bernard	951	printer	40	here
	F	Levine Ruth †	951	housewife	35	"
	G	Marcus Etta †	953	"	35	"
	H	Marcus Harry M	953	salesman	41	"
	K	Datz David	955	furrier	57	"
	L	Datz Esther †	955	housewife	54	"
	M	Biederman David	957	painter	45	952 Morton
	N	*Biederman Ida †	957	housewife	43	952 "
	O	Biederman Jerome	957	student	20	952 "
	P	*Orkin Rachael †	957	housekeeper	75	952 "
	R	*Geller Anne †	957	clerk	26	here
	S	*Geller Benjamin	957	"	24	"
	T	*Geller Mollie †	957	housewife	49	"
	U	*Geller Morris	957	tailor	22	"
	V	*Neidle Aaron	957	retired	66	35 Mora
	W	Neidle Bessie †	957	saleswoman	32	35 "
	X	Neidle Dorothy †	957	teacher	25	35 "
	Y	*Neidle Mary †	957	housewife	65	35 "
	Z	*Neidle Morris	957	paperhanger	37	35 "
24						
	A	Neidle Sarah †	957	saleswoman	27	35 "
	B	Hodge Gertrude V †	959	housewife	39	here
	C	Hodge Robert J	959	shipper	39	"
	D	Logan Edward P	959	policeman	40	"
	E	Logan Mary A †	959	housewife	39	"
	F	McCrensky David	965	salesman	40	"
	G	McCrensky Etta †	965	housewife	36	"
	H	Manning Catherine †	965	clerk	23	"
	K	Manning Francis	965	"	34	"
	L	Manning John J	965	"	39	"
	M	Manning Michael J	965	retired	74	"
	N	Doran Frank	969	salesman	42	"
	O	Doran Lillian †	969	housewife	39	"
	P	Ambuter David	969	manufacturer	55	"
	R	Ambuter Jeanne †	969	housewife	32	"
	S	Gazzo Elizabeth †	969	housekeeper	70	"
	T	O'Reilly Patrick J	973	policeman	39	"
	U	O'Reilly Sarah E †	973	housewife	27	"
	V	Atkinson Ainsley	973	operator	65	"
	W	Atkinson Alfreda †	973	housewife	60	"
	X	Atkinson Charles	973	merchant	35	"

Page	Letter	Full Name.	Residence, Jan. 1, 1941.	Occupation.	Supposed Age.	Reported Residence, Jan. 1, 1940. Street and Number.

Morton Street—Continued

Page	Letter	Full Name.	Residence, Jan. 1, 1941.	Occupation.	Supposed Age.	Reported Residence, Jan. 1, 1940. Street and Number.
	Y	*Epstein Jacob	977	retired	70	here
	Z	Morris Charles	977	merchant	43	"
25						
	A	*Morris Jennie—†	977	housewife	40	"
	B	Gettleman Harry	977	painter	23	"
	C	Gettleman Isaac	977	"	44	"
	D	*Gettleman Lillian—†	977	housewife	43	"
	E	Senders Florence—†	981	clerk	26	33 Hopkins
	F	Senders Joseph H	981	salesman	28	33 "
	G	Senders Joshua	981	retired	64	33 "
	H	Senders Maurice	981	salesman	35	Oklahoma
	K	Smith Dorothy—†	981	clerk	25	here
	L	Smith Jacob	981	meatcutter	34	"
	M	Smith Minnie M—†	981	housewife	67	"
	N	Hill Jean—†	981	"	30	203 St Botolph
	O	Hill John	981	clerk	37	203 "
	P	O'Meara Daniel	993	mechanic	49	here
	R	O'Meara Grace—†	993	housewife	50	"
	S	O'Meara Louise—†	993	clerk	25	"
	T	O'Meara Martha—†	993	"	21	"
	U	*Collins Josephine—†	1057	housekeeper	80	"
	W	Kerwin Antoinette—†	1057	housewife	37	"
	V	Kerwin Thomas G	1057	electrician	42	"

Owen Street

Page	Letter	Full Name.	Residence, Jan. 1, 1941.	Occupation.	Supposed Age.	Reported Residence, Jan. 1, 1940. Street and Number.
	X	Baritz Bessie—†	10	housewife	43	here
	Y	Baritz Morris	10	carpenter	45	"
	Z	Miller Beatrice—†	10	clerk	24	"
26						
	A	Ullian Ida—†	10	housewife	28	"
	B	Ullian Jonas	10	pharmacist	29	"
	C	Ullian Nathan L	10	"	25	35 Corey rd
	D	Christodoulelis John	11	restaurateur	37	here
	E	Christodoulelis Penelope—†	11	housewife	28	"
	F	Christodoulelis Irene—†	15	"	24	"
	G	Christodoulelis James	15	merchant	35	"
	H	Moskos Despina—†	15	housewife	50	"
	K	Moskos William	15	manager	27	"
	L	Kelly Grace—†	18	housewife	29	"
	M	Kelly Robert M	18	engineer	34	"

Page	Letter	Full Name	Residence, Jan. 1, 1941	Occupation	Supposed Age	Reported Residence, Jan. 1, 1940. Street and Number

Owen Street—Continued

Page	Letter	Full Name	Residence, Jan. 1, 1941	Occupation	Supposed Age	Reported Residence, Jan. 1, 1940. Street and Number
	N	Currie John H	18	tel worker	25	here
	O	Currie Loretta H—†	18	housewife	45	"
	P	Currie Martin H	18	policeman	49	"
	R	*Schwartz Annie—†	19	housewife	61	"
	S	Suvalle Esther—†	19	"	38	"
	T	Suvalle Jerome	19	constable	41	"
	U	Schauer Frank F	22	conductor	63	"
	V	Schauer Josephine L—†	22	housewife	63	"
	W	Heins Clara—†	23	"	40	"
	X	Heins Louis	23	restaurateur	48	"

River Street

Page	Letter	Full Name	Residence, Jan. 1, 1941	Occupation	Supposed Age	Reported Residence, Jan. 1, 1940. Street and Number
	Z	Foley Grace M—†	108	clerk	21	here
27						
	A	Foley Grace M—†	108	housewife	50	"
	B	Foley Henry J	108	superintendent	51	"
	C	Dynan John	108	chauffeur	24	37 Neponset av
	D	Dynan Mary H—†	108	housewife	23	37 "
	E	Grimes Anna R—†	108	"	29	here
	F	Grimes Thomas F	108	chauffeur	40	"
	G	Murphy Johanna A—†	108	housewife	54	"
	H	Murphy William J	108	mechanic	26	"
	K	Cushing Daniel L	rear 108	retired	70	"
	L	Cushing Edward J	" 108	painter	28	"
	M	Cushing Joseph G	" 108	student	23	"
	N	Cushing Madelynne L—†	" 108	housewife	31	"
	O	Ashenden Edith B—†	110	"	28	12 Sanford
	P	Ashenden Lawrence E	110	technician	24	12 "
	R	Harrington Dorothy—†	110	housewife	29	here
	S	Harrington John A	110	cook	31	"
	U	Murphy Henry P	116	carpenter	50	"
	V	Murphy Mary T—†	116	housewife	48	"
	X	Hannafin Joseph	118	chauffeur	32	"
	Y	Hannafin Wilhelmina—†	118	housewife	31	"
	W	Fallon Helen L—†	118	housekeeper	49	"
	Z	Ego Gertrude—†	124	"	39	"
28						
	A	Ego Marguerite F—†	124	clerk	41	"
	B	Ego Mary J—†	124	housewife	82	"
	C	Bellamy Gladys J—†	148	"	46	"

Page	Letter	Full Name	Residence, Jan. 1, 1941.	Occupation	Supposed Age	Reported Residence, Jan. 1, 1940. Street and Number.

River Street—Continued

Page	Letter	Full Name	Residence, Jan. 1, 1941.	Occupation	Supposed Age	Reported Residence, Jan. 1, 1940. Street and Number.
	D	Bellamy Harold M	148	salesman	50	here
	E	Gilbert Emily M—†	148	housewife	55	27 Greenbrier
	F	Gilbert Joseph H	148	operator	61	27 "
	G	McGowan Margaret E—†	153	housekeeper	64	here
	H	McGowan Mary E—†	153	"	58	"
	M	Dowling Catherine—†	154	housewife	55	"
	N	Dowling Parker	154	fireman	58	"
	O	Hathaway Julia F—†	155	housewife	30	58 Torrey
	P	Hathaway Martin H	155	teacher	31	58 "
	R	Hathaway Martin R	155	chauffeur	57	58 "
	S	Sullivan George F	155	clerk	47	here
	T	Sullivan Mary A—†	155	housewife	45	"
	U	Pokrierka Bertha M—†	155	"	44	"
	V	Pokrierka John L	155	machinist	56	"
	W	Drummey Maurice	156	laborer	46	"
	X	Drummey Richard D	156	"	45	"
	Y	Murphy Annie—†	156	housekeeper	55	"
	Z	Schofield Annie—†	157	operator	23	"
29						
	A	Schofield Hilton	157	assembler	60	"
	B	Schofield Martha—†	157	housewife	60	"
	C	Savoy David A	157	retired	64	"
	D	Savoy Marcella R—†	157	operator	22	"
	E	Savoy Mary L—†	157	housewife	62	"
	F	Savoy Thomas G	157	clerk	29	"
	G	Juracek Helen—†	157	housewife	51	"
	H	Juracek Joseph	157	tailor	63	"
	K	Gustafson Dora—†	162	manager	40	"
	L	Cahill Anna G—†	164	housewife	58	"
	M	Cahill Cornelius J	164	merchant	58	"
	N	Cahill Francis A	164	clerk	22	"
	O	Dennison Edward	168	retired	73	"
	P	Durham Madelyn M—†	168	beautician	33	"
	R	Lewis Thomas	168	laborer	60	"
	S	McIntyre Isabelle C—†	168	teacher	66	"
	T	Palmer Violet M—†	168	housewife	52	"
	U	Palmer Walter B	168	foreman	52	"
	V	Connell James J	168	weigher	24	"
	W	Deagle Margaret—†	168	stenographer	33	"
	X	Deagle Maria I—†	168	at home	72	"
	Y	Durham Albert J	168	clerk	31	"

River Street Continued

Page	Letter	Full Name	Residence, Jan. 1, 1941	Occupation	Supposed Age	Reported Residence, Jan. 1, 1940. Street and Number
	Z	Durham Margaret V †	168	housewife	27	here
30						
	A	Ramsdell Lucy J †	168	nurse	45	"
	B	Allen William P	208	checker	36	8 Butler
	C	Herget Joseph F	208	engraver	45	here
	D	Herget Mary T †	208	housewife	48	"
	E	Toone Thomas L	208	optician	23	8 Butler
	F	Herget Anthony C	212	polisher	53	here
	G	Kelly Beatrice A †	212	saleswoman	21	47 Fremont
	H	Kelly Florence C †	212	attendant	26	47 "
	K	Kelly Florence M †	212	housewife	52	47 "
	L	Kelly Lillian M †	212	operator	25	47 "
	M	Kelly William F	212	clerk	24	47 "
	N	Cahill Edmund J	218	salesman	28	here
	O	Cahill Marian B †	218	housewife	28	"
	P	Freeman Katherine L †	218	"	39	"
	R	Freeman Leslie J	218	clerk	41	"
	S	Spring Bessie W †	220	housewife	49	"
	T	Spring Frank S	220	welder	51	"
	U	Spring Richard S	220	student	20	"
	V	Spring Wilfred E	220	machinist	27	"
	W	Hickey Julia M †	220	housekeeper	60	"
	X	Hickey Margaret A †	220	domestic	57	"
	Y	Calnan Daniel W	224	laborer	37	153 River
	Z	Calnan Theresa M †	224	housewife	37	153 "
31						
	A	Burke Edward W	224	attorney	32	23 Idaho
	B	Burke John J	224	clerk	35	here
	C	Burke Rose †	224	housewife	69	"
	D	Chiehetto Christine M †	232	"	30	"
	E	Chiehetto Frank A	232	manager	36	"
	F	Corcoran Hazel †	232	housewife	30	"
	G	Corcoran William P	232	salesman	28	"
	H	Kenney Annie †	236	housewife	58	"
	K	Kenney Frank R	236	laborer	64	"
	L	Carroll Alice †	236	housekeeper	70	"
	M	Duffley Gladys †	236	housewife	30	"
	N	Duffley Robert	236	shipper	35	"
	O	Ahern John J	249	physician	41	"
	P	Ahern Louise M †	249	housewife	43	"
	R	Andosia John B	249	physician	34	"

Page.	Letter.	Full Name.	Residence, Jan. 1, 1941.	Occupation.	Supposed Age.	Reported Residence, Jan. 1, 1940. Street and Number.

River Street—Continued

Page.	Letter.	Full Name.	Residence, Jan. 1, 1941.	Occupation.	Supposed Age.	Reported Residence, Jan. 1, 1940. Street and Number.
	S	Barr Catherine E—†	249	domestic	48	here
	T	Barr Sarah V—†	249	"	50	"
	U	Barttell Rachel W—†	249	nurse	37	"
	V	Bogan Frederick B	249	physician	65	"
	W	Bogan Frederick B, jr	249	student	22	"
	X	Boucher Alfred	249	nurse	29	"
	Y	Brady Lydia F—†	249	domestic	45	"
	Z	Bresnahan Della E—†	249	"	29	"
32						
	A	Carney Margaret T—†	249	"	52	"
	C	Casey Mary E—†	249	nurse	32	"
	B	Cauley Jennie B—†	249	"	50	"
	D	Chapdelaine Ruth A—†	249	"	35	"
	E	Dempsey Mary E—†	249	"	35	"
	F	Denning Mary L—†	249	"	31	"
	G	Derrah Bernice—†	249	"	35	"
	H	Dillon Catherine—†	249	domestic	48	"
	[1]H	Duncan Ann—†	249	nurse	40	"
	K	Eagles Alice L—†	249	"	33	"
	L	Ellis Margaret—†	249	dieitian	39	"
	M	Fitzgibbons Mary E—†	249	waitress	53	"
	N	Fitzpatrick Georgia A—†	249	nurse	40	"
	O	Gallagher Genevieve—†	249	"	21	"
	P	Garrity Sarah D—†	249	domestic	61	"
	R	Gaunt Gladys—†	249	nurse	31	"
	S	Gavin Bridget—†	249	domestic	65	"
	T	Grady Florence I—†	249	nurse	63	"
	U	Greene Delia F—†	249	domestic	58	"
	V	Hammond Irene—†	249	nurse	35	"
	W	Hirtle Ethel G—†	249	domestic	44	"
	X	Hodnett Frances—†	249	"	21	"
	Y	Karklin Emma—†	249	cook	52	"
	Z	Kelliher Marie—†	249	domestic	55	"
33						
	A	Linehan Mary A—†	249	nurse	64	"
	B	Linn Sadie C—†	249	"	50	"
	C	Lowder Mary—†	249	domestic	45	"
	D	Lynch Ann—†	249	"	24	Beverly
	E	Malone Josephine M—†	249	nurse	30	here
	F	Manning Thomas G	249	"	31	"

Page	Letter	Full Name	Residence Jan. 1, 1941	Occupation	Supposed Age	Reported Residence, Jan. 1, 1940. Street and Number

River Street Continued

Page	Letter	Full Name	Residence Jan. 1, 1941	Occupation	Supposed Age	Reported Residence, Jan. 1, 1940. Street and Number
	G	McCabe Eleanor R—†	249	domestic	26	here
	H	McDonald Bridie—†	249	"	38	"
	K	McDonald Margaret—†	249	"	25	"
	M	McInnis Charles C	249	attendant	36	"
	L	McLean Margaret L—†	249	technician	41	"
	N	Mullin Olive—†	249	nurse	30	"
	O	Murphy Helen J—†	249	dietitian	41	"
	P	Ney Martha V—†	249	domestic	68	"
	R	Nicholson Catherine G—†	249	nurse	56	"
	S	Nugent Clara—†	249	"	35	"
	T	O'Brien Alice—†	249	"	39	"
	U	O'Neil Cora—†	249	"	35	"
	V	Pender Catherine E—†	249	"	54	"
	W	Penner Charles F	249	attendant	30	"
	X	Pizer Lillian B—†	249	waitress	45	"
	Y	Powell Arthur A	249	laborer	50	"
	Z	Reese Annette—†	249	student	21	"
34						
	A	Reese Charles A	249	physician	60	"
	B	Reese Helen R—†	249	housewife	45	"
	C	Roach Mary A—†	249	nurse	44	"
	D	Romakaite Anna—†	249	"	45	"
	E	Slavin Anna—†	249	domestic	35	"
	F	Spellacy Thomas W	249	chef	50	"
	G	Stewart Florence G—†	249	nurse	26	"
	H	Sullivan Celia A—†	249	"	35	"
	K	Sullivan Helen M—†	249	domestic	44	"
	L	Talty Nellie S—†	249	housekeeper	60	"
	M	Taylor Beulah—†	249	nurse	49	"
	N	Thornell Edythe G—†	249	"	44	"
	O	Upton Laurence A	249	waiter	62	"
	P	Tibbetts Helen A—†	291	housewife	62	"
	R	Tibbetts Howard M	291	caretaker	37	157 Hemenway
	S	Tibbetts Julia—†	291	saleswoman	23	here
	T	Tibbetts Marguerite—†	291	housewife	38	157 Hemenway
	U	O'Brien Joseph G	413	mailer	52	here
	V	O'Brien Theresa P—†	413	housewife	44	"
	W	Shedd Myrtie A—†	421	at home	73	"
	X	Connors Edward A	422	woodworker	73	"
	Y	Gibbs James	422	stagehand	62	"

Page	Letter	Full Name.	Residence, Jan. 1, 1941.	Occupation.	Supposed Age.	Reported Residence, Jan. 1, 1940. Street and Number.

River Street—Continued

Page	Letter	Full Name.	Residence, Jan. 1, 1941.	Occupation.	Supposed Age.	Reported Residence, Jan. 1, 1940. Street and Number.
	Z	Belanger Mary J—†	430	cashier	27	here
35						
	A	Silva Delphine E—†	430	teacher	30	"
	B	Flahive Ernestine N—†	430	housewife	37	"
	C	Flahive Thomas J	430	clerk	36	"
	D	Meany Eileen G—†	438	"	33	"
	E	Meany Mary M—†	438	housewife	69	"
	F	Meany Michael A	438	retired	70	"
	G	Gerales Esther—†	438	housewife	50	"
	H	Gerales Peter	438	shoeworker	56	"
	K	Torgersen Eva—†	438	housewife	36	"
	L	Torgersen Thor J	438	contractor	46	"
	M	Curtis Bessie R—†	442	housewife	47	"
	N	Curtis Royden W	442	carpenter	48	"
	O	Martin Ida D—†	443	housekeeper	69	"
	P	Goff Bertha B—†	445	housewife	21	Canton
	R	Goff William C	445	welder	22	"
	S	Walsh Anna M—†	447	housewife	30	46 Rexford
	T	Walsh John R	447	machinist	31	46 "
	U	Hughes Charles F	449	welder	26	8 Malta
	V	Hughes Lillian B—†	449	housewife	26	8 "
	W	Hughes Stephen L	449	student	24	8 "
	X	McNeil Mary—†	449	at home	67	11 Mattakeeset
	Y	Garfinkle Bessie—†	459	"	79	9 Ruxton rd
	Z	Kirkpatrick Ida L—†	459	housekeeper	53	9 "
36						
	A	Wentworth Charles H	459	pharmacist	66	Milton
	B	Hurd Mira—†	461	at home	73	here
	C	Carey John E	463	fireman	39	"
	D	Carey Rosalie M—†	463	housewife	34	"
	E	Field Harvey A	465	physician	65	"
	G	Colligan Henry T	466	chauffeur	34	"
	H	Colligan Kathleen E—†	466	housewife	23	"

Riverside Place

Page	Letter	Full Name.	Residence, Jan. 1, 1941.	Occupation.	Supposed Age.	Reported Residence, Jan. 1, 1940. Street and Number.
	R	Bixby Carrie M—†	7	housekeeper	79	here
	S	Cox Addie F—†	7	housewife	76	"
	T	Cox Joseph W	7	retired	82	"
	U	Turner Florence B—†	7	housekeeper	76	"
	V	Beck Myrtle J—†	21	clerk	56	"

Page	Letter	Full Name	Residence, Jan. 1, 1941	Occupation	Supposed Age	Reported Residence, Jan. 1, 1940. Street and Number

Riverside Place—Continued

Page	Letter	Full Name	Residence, Jan. 1, 1941	Occupation	Supposed Age	Reported Residence, Jan. 1, 1940. Street and Number
	W	Eldredge Jessie M—†	21	clerk	26	here
	X	Parr Francis C	21	"	23	"
	Y	Parr Mary E—†	21	housewife	49	"
	Z	Parr Thomas J	21	clerk	21	"
37						
	A	Parr Thomas P	21	shipper	50	"
	B	Meadows John A	23	waiter	31	"
	C	Meadows Patricia—†	23	housewife	25	"
	D	McDermott Delia A—†	29	"	60	"
	E	McDermott George A	29	chauffeur	29	"
	F	McDermott William E	29	foreman	62	"
	G	McDermott William E, jr	29	printer	35	"

Standard Street

Page	Letter	Full Name	Residence, Jan. 1, 1941	Occupation	Supposed Age	Reported Residence, Jan. 1, 1940. Street and Number
	H	Wahlstedt Eugene H	4	mechanic	53	Milton
	K	Wahlstedt Mary E—†	4	housewife	47	"
	L	Burke Catherine A—†	4	"	46	here
	M	Burke Mary M—†	4	chemist	26	"
	N	McManus George J	8	packer	30	"
	O	McManus Margaret E—†	8	housewife	30	"
	P	Butler Estelle M—†	8	"	45	"
	R	Butler Walter J	8	painter	46	"
	S	Minden Ralph	8	chauffeur	41	"
	T	Minden Susie A—†	8	housewife	32	"
	U	Sullivan John L	19	salesman	65	"
	V	Sullivan Margaret E—†	19	clerk	32	"
	W	Sullivan Margaret V—†	19	housewife	60	"
	X	Sullivan Mary B—†	19	clerk	22	"
	Y	White Catherine A—†	21	housekeeper	68	"
	Z	Burke Marie A—†	26	housewife	47	"
38						
	A	Burke Walter E	26	manager	49	"
	B	Byrne Cecelia E—†	30	housewife	43	"
	C	Byrne Edmund J—†	30	letter carrier	47	"
	D	*Gannon Nora C—†	31	housewife	29	Somerville
	E	Gannon Thomas F	31	mechanic	36	"
	F	Sullivan Daniel A	31	"	40	here
	G	Sullivan May D—†	31	housewife	38	"
	H	Henderson Mary C—†	31	"	68	"
	K	Henderson Robert H	31	retired	31	"

Page	Letter	Full Name	Residence, Jan. 1, 1941.	Occupation	Supposed Age.	Reported Residence, Jan. 1, 1940. Street and Number

Standard Street—Continued

Page	Letter	Full Name	Residence, Jan. 1, 1941.	Occupation	Supposed Age.	Reported Residence, Jan. 1, 1940. Street and Number
	L	*Savage Catherine—†	31	at home	70	21 Chestnut
	M	Peatfield Charles R	35	electrician	38	here
	N	Peatfield Jessie D—†	35	housewife	37	"
	O	Koppelman Robert	44	florist	45	"
	P	Koppelman Sarah B—†	44	housewife	45	"
	R	Jones Etta A—†	56	operator	50	"
	S	Fitzgerald Delia J—†	58	housekeeper	54	"
	T	Lynch Mark L	58	letter carrier	30	"
	U	Lynch Mary P—†	58	housewife	28	"
	V	Ronayne Helen A—†	58	"	28	"
	W	Ronayne John F, jr	58	salesman	30	"
	X	Laffan Dorothy E—†	62	housewife	26	"
	Y	Laffan John J	62	clerk	28	"
	Z	Lee Lillian—†	62	housewife	34	"
39						
	A	Lee Walter E	62	watchman	38	"
	B	Willard Ralph	62	mechanic	26	28 Sturbridge
	C	Willard Rita—†	62	housewife	24	90 Park
	D	Kenney Annie A—†	63	at home	70	here
	E	Kenney James F	63	fireman	54	"
	F	Kenney James F, jr	63	draftsman	26	"
	G	Kenney Joseph V	63	accountant	22	"
	H	Kenney Mary F—†	63	housewife	47	"
	K	Broderick Elizabeth—†	63	at home	69	"
	L	McKay Phoebe—†	63	"	59	"
	M	Doherty Eugene J	67	fireman	50	"
	N	Dionne Henry H	67	"	47	"
	O	Dionne Sarah T—†	67	housewife	49	"
	P	Sherman Catherine I—†	70	housekeeper	52	"
	R	Vandette Edward A	70	plasterer	52	"
	S	Drummond Kathryne M—†	74	housewife	60	"
	T	Drummond William J	74	engineer	61	"
	U	Dannahy Margaret M—†	77	housewife	55	"
	V	Dannahy Ruth M—†	77	teacher	25	"
	W	Brennan Bartholomew J	78	salesman	48	"
	X	Brennan Helena M—†	78	housewife	48	"
	Y	Brennan John B	78	student	21	"
	Z	Brennan Robert D	78	salesman	23	"
40						
	A	Kebler Fred T	83	engineer	51	"
	B	Kebler Lois E—†	83	chemist	21	"

Page	Letter	Full Name	Residence, Jan. 1, 1941	Occupation	Supposed Age	Reported Residence, Jan. 1, 1940, Street and Number

Standard Street—Continued

Page	Letter	Full Name	Residence	Occupation	Age	Reported Residence
	C	Kebler Mary M—†	83	housewife	50	here
	D	Kebler Virginia M—†	83	clerk	23	"
	E	Sarjeant Elizabeth F—†	86	teacher	43	"
	F	Sarjeant Joseph J	86	attorney	46	"
	G	Sarjeant Julia A—†	86	housewife	46	"
	H	Martino Josephine A—†	87	"	37	"
	K	Martino Philip A	87	manufacturer	50	"
	L	Dole Ella F—†	94	bookkeeper	53	"
	M	Young Elizabeth V—†	94	student	20	"
	N	Young Helen F—†	94	clerk	22	"
	O	Young Mary E—†	94	housewife	63	"
	P	Young William J	94	architect	65	"
	R	Conley Bernard J	95	superintendent	57	"
	S	Conley Frances C—†	95	housewife	57	"
	T	Conley Frances M—†	95	teacher	30	"
	U	Conley Joseph B	95	investigator	29	"

Stow Road

Page	Letter	Full Name	Residence	Occupation	Age	Reported Residence
	V	*Ashman Minnie—†	5	at home	70	here
	W	Gomberg Benjamin A	5	proprietor	59	"
	X	Gomberg Ida—†	5	housewife	49	"
	Y	Gomberg Edith—†	6	"	25	5 Stow rd
	Z	Gomberg Herman	6	attendant	27	5 "
41						
	A	*Goldsmith Gertrude—†	9	clerk	35	here
	B	*Shapiro Anna—†	9	housewife	56	"
	C	Shapiro Isaac	9	retired	65	"
	D	Cohen Abraham	17 19	agent	32	"
	E	Cohen Sylvia—†	17 19	housewife	25	"
	F	*Slavet Dora—†	17 19	"	42	"
	G	*Slavet Harry H	17 19	plumber	46	"
	H	Slavet Murray	17 19	"	20	"
	K	Slavet Ralph	17 19	cutter	22	"
	L	Slavet Sidney	17 19	plumber	23	"
	M	Kleinberg Mitchell	21 23	mechanic	31	"
	N	Kleinberg Rose—†	21 23	housewife	26	"
	O	Budd Jean—†	21 23	saleswoman	27	"
	P	Budd Louis	21 23	constable	40	"
	R	*Gunderson Emil	25	mechanic	48	"
	S	Gunderson Mina—†	25	housewife	51	"

Page	Letter	Full Name	Residence, Jan. 1, 1941	Occupation	Supposed Age	Reported Residence, Jan. 1, 1940. Street and Number

Stow Road Continued

Page	Letter	Full Name	Residence, Jan. 1, 1941	Occupation	Supposed Age	Reported Residence, Jan. 1, 1940. Street and Number
	T	Gunderson Paul M	25	laborer	22	here
	U	Rogers James	25	conductor	55	"
	V	Ahern Clifford C	28	painter	48	"
	W	Ahern Irma—†	28	housewife	43	"
	X	Forest Charles H	30	plumber	33	"
	Y	Forest Louise P—†	30	housewife	32	"
	Z	Meerowiz Bella—†	31–33	"	30	"
42						
	A	*Meerowiz Louis H	31–33	merchant	32	"
	C	O'Donnell Dorothea H—†	34	housewife	34	"
	D	O'Donnell Walter F	34	clerk	40	"
	E	Dargie Lillian—†	37	nurse	53	"
	F	Hamilton James	37	retired	59	"
	G	Thompson Lesley	45	chauffeur	40	"
	H	Thompson Renforth	45	operator	65	"
	K	Thompson Rita—†	45	housewife	63	"
	L	Pugsley Elizabeth M—†	46	"	50	"
	M	Pugsley George R	46	rigger	50	"
	N	Winters Cyril	48	carpenter	47	"
	O	Winters Cyril, jr	48	student	23	"
	P	Winters Douglas	48	clerk	20	"
	R	Winters Isabella—†	48	"	22	"
	S	Winters Jessie—†	48	housewife	47	"
	T	Brymer Douglass	51	conductor	58	"
	U	Brymer Jane—†	51	housewife	58	"

Tiverton Road

Page	Letter	Full Name	Residence, Jan. 1, 1941	Occupation	Supposed Age	Reported Residence, Jan. 1, 1940. Street and Number
	V	Rubin Jennie—†	2	housewife	38	here
	W	Rubin Simon	2	merchant	42	"
	X	Wilson David H	2	engineer	33	"
	Y	Wilson Ethel—†	2	housewife	29	"
	Z	Howitt Annie R—†	3–5	"	45	"
43						
	A	Howitt Thomas	3–5	bricklayer	45	"
	B	*Wilson Jane—†	3–5	at home	77	"
	C	Chorofsky Rose—†	3–5	housewife	37	51 Hiawatha rd
	D	Silverman Carl	3–5	salesman	23	here
	E	*Silverman Daniel	3–5	tailor	62	"
	F	Silverman Edward	3–5	salesman	31	"
	G	*Silverman Sarah—†	3–5	housewife	55	"

Tiverton Road Continued

Page	Letter	Full Name	Residence, Jan. 1, 1941	Occupation	Supposed Age	Reported Residence, Jan. 1, 1940. Street and Number
	H	*Clerico Severina †	4	housewife	38	here
	K	Clerico Victor	4	waiter	45	"
	L	*Tonetti Dante	4	busboy	28	Italy
	M	*Bianchetti Felix	4	retired	72	here
	N	Cerruti Enrico	4	cook	51	"
	O	Cerruti Lorena †	4	housewife	53	"
	P	Bean Coral C †	7	"	45	"
	R	Bean Harold	7	chauffeur	21	"
	S	*Schneiderman Fannie †	10	housewife	51	"
	T	Schneiderman Harold	10	student	21	"
	U	*Schneiderman Julius	10	tailor	54	"
	V	Simches Pearl †	11	housewife	26	"
	W	Simches Victor	11	merchant	34	"
	X	Swartz Anna †	11	housewife	35	"
	Y	Swartz Jacob	11	merchant	36	"
	Z	*Feinberg Mary †	14	housewife	45	"
44						
	A	Feinberg Max	14	manufacturer	48	"
	B	Feinberg Samuel	14	student	22	"
	C	Bovarnick Lillian K †	15–17	housewife	31	"
	D	Bovarnick Max	15–17	manager	34	"
	E	Kolpack Max	15–17	retired	70	"
	F	*Slavet Esther †	15–17	housewife	34	"
	G	Slavet Samuel	15–17	plumber	36	"
	H	Nelson Karin †	25	housewife	60	"
	K	Nelson Nils A	25	sexton	59	"
	L	Nelson Roy L	25	seaman	24	"
	M	Nelson Vincent E	25	mechanic	28	"
	N	Flax Annie †	29	housewife	54	60 Lorna rd
	O	Flax Edith †	29	secretary	28	here
	P	Flax Lillian †	29	"	23	"
	R	Eichorn Frank W	35	machinist	52	"
	S	Eichorn Marie †	35	housewife	50	"

West Selden Street

Page	Letter	Full Name	Residence, Jan. 1, 1941	Occupation	Supposed Age	Reported Residence, Jan. 1, 1940. Street and Number
	T	Abrams Esther †	6	housewife	40	35 Goodale rd
	U	Abrams Samuel S	6	cutter	45	35 "
	V	Naigles Gladys †	6	housewife	31	911 Morton
	W	Naigles Horace	6	musician	31	911 "
	X	Naigles Minnie †	6	merchant	51	here

Page	Letter	Full Name	Residence, Jan. 1, 1941	Occupation	Supposed Age	Reported Residence, Jan. 1, 1940. Street and Number.

West Selden Street Continued

Page	Letter	Full Name	Residence, Jan. 1, 1941	Occupation	Supposed Age	Reported Residence, Jan. 1, 1940. Street and Number.
	Y	Courlang Jacques	10	director	32	here
	Z	Courlang Ruth †	10	housewife	33	"
45						
	A	Berkowitz Abraham	10	manager	35	"
	B	Berkowitz Reva †	10	housewife	33	"
	C	Hart Samuel B	10	manager	63	"
	D	Landsman Fay †	14	housewife	29	"
	E	Landsman Jacob	14	manufacturer	35	"
	G	Kleinberg Frances †	18	housewife	32	"
	H	Kleinberg Irving	18	metalworker	34	"
	K	Rich Barnet	18	buyer	34	"
	L	Rich Esther †	18	housewife	29	"
	M	Rich Irving	18	salesman	25	"
	N	Rich Robert	18	operator	57	"
	O	Rich Sarah †	18	housewife	55	"
	P	Karp Freida †	22	"	37	"
	R	Karp Samuel	22	proprietor	43	"
	S	Daitch Ruth †	22	housewife	40	"
	T	Daitch Samuel	22	salesman	42	"
	U	Strumph Herman	26	florist	38	"
	V	Strumph Rose †	26	housewife	38	"
	W	Bloomberg Bessie †	26	housekeeper	56	"
	X	Bloomberg Nellie †	26	clerk	40	"
	Y	Shneider Esther †	30	housewife	29	"
	Z	Shneider Irving I	30	manager	30	"
46						
	A	Goldberg Abraham	30	mechanic	47	"
	B	Goldberg Philip	30	student	20	"
	C	Goldberg Rose †	30	housewife	42	"
	D	Abelson David	34	jeweler	50	"
	E	Abelson Esther †	34	housewife	39	"
	F	Abelson Lillian †	34	student	20	"
	G	Tomas Helen †	34	milliner	34	"
	H	Bossie Louis	38	clerk	43	"
	K	Bossie Marion B †	38	housewife	33	"
	L	Leonard Edward J	42	buyer	24	"
	M	Leonard Mary T †	42	housewife	48	"
	N	Lyons Owen E	42	laborer	47	48 Allston
	O	Levine Helen †	46	bookkeeper	22	here
	P	Levine Hyman	46	expressman	48	"
	R	Levine Rose †	46	housewife	46	"

Page	Letter	Full Name	Residence Jan. 1, 1941	Occupation	Supposed Age	Reported Residence Jan. 1, 1940. Street and Number

West Selden Street—Continued

Page	Letter	Full Name	Residence Jan. 1, 1941	Occupation	Supposed Age	Reported Residence Jan. 1, 1940. Street and Number
	S	Diamond Kate †	46	housewife	40	here
	T	Diamond Myer	46	merchant	38	"
	U	Stoller Bessie †	48	housewife	40	"
	V	Stoller Maurice A	48	pharmacist	42	"
	W	Jerome Florence L †	48	housewife	42	"
	X	Jerome Frank J	48	salesman	42	"
	Y	Jerome Lena †	48	housewife	66	24 Lorne
	Z	Rubin Agnes †	50	"	28	51 Colonial av
47						
	A	Rubin Benjamin	50	salesman	31	51 "
	D	Leonard Frances M †	56	saleswoman	25	here
	E	Leonard Mary K †	56	housewife	55	"
	F	Leonard Maurice	56	watchman	55	"
	G	Donahue Doris G †	58	housewife	29	"
	H	Donahue Joseph W	58	operator	40	"
	K	Gulesian George	60	coppersmith	62	"
	L	Gulesian Georgiana †	60	housewife	56	"
	M	Gulesian Mellen	60	repairman	27	"
	N	Killeen James F	62	salesman	26	10 Dennis
	O	Killeen Louise M †	62	housewife	25	64 W Selden
	P	*Maher Mary D †	64	"	52	here
	R	Maher William H	64	porter	62	"
	S	Plonsky Irma M †	66	housewife	47	"
	T	Plonsky Louis M	66	buyer	46	"
	U	Waldman Anna †	74	housewife	31	"
	V	Waldman Joseph	74	merchant	36	"
	W	Rissman Edith †	74	saleswoman	20	"
	X	Rissman Morris	74	salesman	27	"
	Y	*Rissman Rose †	74	housewife	50	"
	Z	Seidel Helen P †	76	"	31	"
48						
	A	Seidel Maurice P	76	manager	39	"
	B	Grosser Mary †	76	housewife	35	"
	C	Grosser Philip	76	pharmacist	37	"
	D	Finn Benjamin	78	foreman	32	"
	E	Finn Dorothy †	78	housewife	32	"
	F	*Shapiro Leah †	78	housekeeper	56	"
	G	Silver Sadie †	78	housewife	39	"
	H	Silver Samuel	78	merchant	40	"
	K	*Blaustein Goldie †	80	housewife	42	"
	L	Blaustein Harry A	80	painter	42	"

Page	Letter	Full Name	Residence, Jan. 1, 1941.	Occupation	Supposed Age.	Reported Residence, Jan. 1, 1940. Street and Number.

West Selden Street—Continued

Page	Letter	Full Name	Residence, Jan. 1, 1941.	Occupation	Supposed Age.	Reported Residence, Jan. 1, 1940. Street and Number.
	M	Kaiser David	80	accountant	41	here
	N	Kaiser Herbert	80	clerk	22	"
	O	Kaiser Minnie—†	80	housewife	40	"
	P*	Menzer Isadore	88	salesman	33	"
	R	Menzer Jeanette H—†	88	housewife	29	"
	S	DeCola Joseph W	88	U S N	23	"
	T*	DeCola Mary—†	88	housewife	45	"
	U	DeCola Mary E—†	88	stenographer	24	"
	V	DeCola Simon	88	barber	47	"
	W	Anderson Amanda—†	92	housewife	60	"
	X	Anderson Charles	92	engineer	63	"
	Y	Anderson Helen—†	92	nurse	23	"
	Z	Armstrong James H	94	chemist	43	"
49						
	A	Armstrong Lillian M—†	94	housewife	40	"
	B	Blagdon Frances L—†	100	"	42	40 North av
	C	Blagdon John S	100	estimator	66	40 "
	D	Sullivan Frances L—†	100	teacher	26	here
	E	Sullivan Francis R	100	merchant	52	"
	F	Sullivan Lillian A—†	100	housewife	51	"
	G*	Silevsky Anna—†	106	"	47	151 H
	H	Silevsky David	106	student	20	151 "
	K	Silevsky Jacob	106	builder	61	151 "
	L	Witten Frances—†	114	housewife	27	here
	M	Witten Max	114	manager	30	"
	N*	Fritz Carl	116	mechanic	39	38 Mascot
	O	Fritz Sarah—†	116	housewife	36	38 "
	P	Swardlick Bertha—†	118	"	36	here
	R	Swardlick Edward J	118	salesman	43	"
	S	Crosby Marion—†	120	housewife	30	"
	T	Crosby Nathan	120	merchant	36	"
	U	Yassen Nathan	122	chauffeur	25	81 Lucerne
	V	Yassen Victoria—†	122	housewife	20	81 "
	W	Grocer Edward	124	salesman	34	here
	X	Grocer Ida—†	124	housewife	33	"
	Y	Opper Fannie—†	126	"	54	"
	Z	Opper Philip	126	merchant	50	"
50						
	A	Schiller Gussie—†	128	housewife	53	"
	B	Schiller Irving P	128	salesman	25	"
	C	Schiller Louis B	128	furrier	57	"

Page.	Letter	Full Name	Residence Jan. 1, 1941	Occupation	Supposed Age	Reported Residence Jan. 1, 1940 Street and Number

West Selden Street—Continued

Page.	Letter	Full Name	Residence Jan. 1, 1941	Occupation	Supposed Age	Reported Residence Jan. 1, 1940 Street and Number
	D	Schiller Milton S	128	attorney	26	here
	E	Goldstein Charles	130	musician	30	1630 Com av
	F	Goldstein Irene †	130	housewife	30	1630 "
	G	*Cohen Rose †	132	"	30	102 Talbot av
	H	Cohen Samuel	132	electrician	30	102 "
	K	Simons Harry	132	conductor	46	here
	L	Simons Mollie †	132	housewife	46	"
	M	Maybury Margaret †	138	at home	85	"
	N	Coulsey Margaret †	160	housewife	47	"
	O	Coulsey William C	160	papermaker	58	"
	P	Malone Clinton	160	porter	65	159 W Selden
	R	Armstrong Arthur	164	fireman	31	here
	S	Armstrong Ellen †	164	teacher	28	"
	T	Armstrong Harold D	164	pharmacist	39	"
	U	Armstrong James H	164	retired	70	"
	V	Armstrong May E †	164	teacher	35	"
	W	Armstrong Sarah †	164	housekeeper	41	"
	X	Armstrong William L	164	teacher	25	"
	Y	Fleming Arthur T	178	baker	23	"
	Z	Fleming Barbara †	178	clerk	20	"
51						
	A	Fleming Marcella †	178	housewife	43	"
	B	Fleming Stephen	178	manager	44	"
	C	Noller Erwin	180	proprietor	26	11 Baird
	D	Noller Mildred †	180	housewife	21	11 "
	E	Bourne Catherine †	184–186	housekeeper	60	here
	F	Withington Alice †	184–186	housewife	40	"
	G	Withington John	184–186	retired	45	"
	H	Palmer Elphine †	184–186	housewife	35	"
	K	Palmer Rodman	184–186	salesman	34	"
	L	Green Edith †	188	housewife	29	"
	M	Green Nathan	188	manager	38	"
	N	Fahey Frederick F	198	seaman	30	"
	O	Fahey John F	198	supervisor	43	"
	P	Fahey John H	198	retired	69	"
	R	Fahey Louis X	198	clerk	35	"
	S	Fahey Margaret E †	198	housewife	70	"
	T	Fahey Raymond C	198	mechanic	38	"
	U	Lennox Blanche †	202	housewife	27	Springfield
	V	Lennox John E	202	baker	30	"
	X	Proctor Nathan I	206	clerk	31	here

Page.	Letter.	Full Name.	Residence Jan. 1, 1941	Occupation.	Supposed Age.	Reported Residence, Jan. 1, 1940. Street and Number.

West Selden Street Continued

Page.	Letter.	Full Name.	Residence Jan. 1, 1941	Occupation.	Supposed Age.	Reported Residence, Jan. 1, 1940.
	Y	Proctor Zelda—†	206	housewife	32	here
	Z	Morse Benjamin L	206	collector	38	"
52						
	A	Morse Esther—†	206	housewife	32	"
	B	Lindroff Carl	210	bookbinder	41	"
	C	Lindroff Madge D—†	210	housewife	36	"
	D	Seary Althea C—†	210	operator	36	"
	E	Seary Doris K—†	210	teacher	29	"
	F	Seary Mary J—†	210	housewife	69	"
	G	Seary Reuben B	210	retired	79	"
	H	Forsyth Alexander	218	painter	58	"
	K	Forsyth Blanche M—†	218	housewife	57	"
	L	Forsyth Carol—†	218	mechanic	23	"
	M	Hauswirth Charles B	222	clerk	41	"
	N	Hauswirth Ethel V—†	222	housewife	36	"
	O	Fitzsimmons Catherine—†	232	"	54	"
	P	Fitzsimmons Clarence T	232	policeman	52	"
	R	Fitzsimmons Kenneth	232	laborer	26	"
	S	Kelly Miriam W—†	234	student	25	"
	T	Kelly Richard E	234	foreman	61	"
	U	Kelly Susan—†	234	housewife	61	"
	V	Cannon Jennie—†	234	"	69	"
	W	Cannon Mildred—†	234	secretary	30	"
	X	Gordon Harry	244	clerk	31	"
	Y	Gordon Jennie—†	244	housewife	73	"
	Z	Gordon Max	244	retired	73	"

Ward 18—Precinct 2

CITY OF BOSTON

LIST OF RESIDENTS
20 YEARS OF AGE AND OVER

(NON-CITIZENS INDICATED BY ASTERISK)
(FEMALES INDICATED BY DAGGER)

AS OF

JANUARY 1, 1941

JOSEPH F. TIMILTY, *Chairman*
FREDERIC E. DOWLING, *Secretary*
WILLIAM A. MOTLEY, JR.
FRANCIS B. McKINNEY
HILDA HEDSTROM QUIRK
Listing Board.

CITY OF BOSTON PRINTING DEPARTMENT

Page	Letter	Full Name	Residence, Jan. 1, 1941	Occupation	Supposed Age	Reported Residence, Jan. 1, 1940. Street and Number.

200

Astoria Street

Page	Letter	Full Name	Residence, Jan. 1, 1941	Occupation	Supposed Age	Reported Residence, Jan. 1, 1940. Street and Number.
200	A	Caggiula Daniel E	60	tailor	57	here
	[1]A	Caggiula Emma—†	60	bookkeeper	32	"
	B	Caggiula Rita D—†	60	clerk	24	"
	C	Caggiula Sarah—†	60	housewife	54	"
	D	Caggiula Vincent E	60	manager	26	"
	E	Flagg Elizabeth D—†	62	housewife	30	Hingham
	F	Flagg Elmer A	62	carpenter	26	"
	G	Luhrman Julia—†	62	housekeeper	65	here
	H	Spry Elizabeth S—†	62	housewife	67	"
	K	Spry Joseph	62	mover	71	"
	L	Mulhall Catherine A—†	66	housewife	70	"
	M	Mulhall Charles P	66	welder	35	"
	N	Mulhall Frances W—†	66	hairdresser	32	"
	O	Mulhall John F	66	salesman	47	"
	P	Mulhall Marion E—†	66	clerk	41	"
	R*	Sturn Frances—†	67	housewife	38	28 Wellington Hill
	S	Sturn Frederick	67	salesman	44	28 "
	T	Horwitz David E	67	U S A	25	here
	U	Horwitz Philip	67	salesman	59	"
	V	Horwitz Rose—†	67	housewife	54	"
	W	Horwitz Sumner L	67	student	23	"
	X*	Baker Ethel—†	67	housewife	48	"
	Y	Baker Oscar	67	tailor	52	"
	Z	Baker Toby—†	67	clerk	20	"
201	A	Spencer David	67	pharmacist	28	71 Devon
	B	Spencer Sarah—†	67	housewife	24	here
	C	Chuker Anna—†	71	"	46	"
	D	Chuker Jacob J	71	salesman	50	"
	E	Chuker Melvin S	71	student	20	"
	F	Stern Arthur F	71	physician	26	38 Fessenden
	G	Stern Sylvia F—†	71	housewife	25	here
	H	Beresnack Elsie M—†	71	secretary	21	"
	K	Beresnack Ida F—†	71	housewife	43	"
	L	Beresnack Samuel M	71	butcher	47	"
	M	Furman Harry A	71	merchant	30	"
	N	Furman Manya—†	71	housewife	25	"
	O	Wexler Harry J	71	baker	58	"
	P	Wexler Jack	71	physician	28	Virginia
	R	Wexler Max	71	waiter	24	here

Page	Letter	Full Name	Residence, Jan. 1, 1941	Occupation	Supposed Age	Reported Residence, Jan. 1, 1940. Street and Number

Astoria Street Continued

Page	Letter	Full Name	Residence, Jan. 1, 1941	Occupation	Supposed Age	Reported Residence, Jan. 1, 1940. Street and Number
	S	*Wexler Sophie †	71	housewife	56	here
	T	*Modell Helen †	72	"	39	"
	U	Modell Manuel	72	chauffeur	40	"
	V	*Belkin Anna †	72	housewife	57	"
	W	Belkin Frank	72	shipper	27	"
	X	*Belkin Ida †	72	bookkeeper	34	"
	Y	Davis Annie †	72	housewife	61	"
	Z	Davis Philip	72	realtor	65	"
202						
	A	Weiner Benjamin	72	salesman	31	"
	B	Weiner Jean †	72	housewife	30	"
	C	Castaline Harry	72	butcher	40	"
	D	Castaline Leah †	72	housewife	36	"
	E	Goodis Martha †	72	bookkeeper	38	"
	F	Tate Julius	72	atorney	29	36 Goodale rd
	G	Tate Norma †	72	housewife	26	36 "
	H	Pritzker Bernice †	74	bookkeeper	20	here
	K	Pritzker Morris	74	contractor	48	"
	L	Pritzker Sadie F †	74	housewife	44	"
	M	*Small Beatrice †	74	"	51	"
	N	Small David T	74	student	23	"
	O	Small Meyer	74	tailor	51	"
	P	Small Rose †	74	bookkeeper	25	"
	R	Small Theresa †	74	saleswoman	22	"
	S	Figur Ida †	75	housewife	26	"
	T	Figur Samuel	75	baker	36	"
	U	Abelow Sadie †	75	housewife	31	"
	V	Abelow Samuel	75	salesman	35	"
	W	Brickman Helen P †	78	housewife	36	"
	X	Brickman Herbert P	78	electrician	41	"
	Y	Glaskin Louis	78	metalworker	50	"
	Z	Glaskin Norman	78	chemist	25	"
203						
	A	*Glaskin Sarah †	78	housewife	48	"
	B	*Stone Mollie †	78	"	40	"
	C	Stone Peter	78	shipper	20	"
	D	*Stone Samuel	78	plasterer	44	"
	E	Moore Christine A †	79	housewife	64	"
	F	Moore George	79	retired	66	"
	G	Smith Gladys †	79	housewife	26	"
	H	Smith Lewis	79	printer	27	"

Page	Letter	Full Name.	Residence, Jan. 1, 1941.	Occupation.	Supposed Age	Reported Residence, Jan. 1, 1940. Street and Number.

Astoria Street—Continued

Page	Letter	Full Name.	Residence, Jan. 1, 1941.	Occupation.	Supposed Age	Reported Residence, Jan. 1, 1940. Street and Number.
	K	Kahn Samuel	81	draftsman	38	here
	L	*Kahn Sarah—†	81	housewife	35	"
	M	Lieter Alfred L	82	metalworker	27	33 Nelson
	N	*Lieter Bessie—†	82	housewife	53	33 "
	O	Lieter Charlotte R—†	82	bookkeeper	23	33 "
	P	Lieter Samuel	82	metalworker	54	33 "
	R	Soll Anna D—†	82	housewife	50	here
	S	Soll Eleanor P—†	82	student	22	"
	T	Soll Robert D	82	physician	25	"
	U	Soll William W	82	merchant	48	"
	V	Stone Iola—†	85	housewife	40	"
	W	Stone Nathan	85	mover	40	"
	X	Stone William R	85	chauffeur	20	"
	Y	Ferris James J	86	retired	70	"
	Z	Ferris Ralph G	86	toolmaker	33	"
204						
	A	Ogilvie Vera B—†	86	housekeeper	56	"
	B	Boyle Melita A—†	86	saleswoman	55	"
	C	Glasco John J	86	engineer	53	"
	D	Glasco Mary J—†	86	housewife	53	"

Babson Street

Page	Letter	Full Name.	Residence, Jan. 1, 1941.	Occupation.	Supposed Age	Reported Residence, Jan. 1, 1940. Street and Number.
	E	Leong George	4	laundryman	47	here
	G	Maxwell Allen B	7	painter	46	"
	H	Maxwell Allen B, jr	7	shipper	21	"
	K	Maxwell Beatrice M—†	7	housewife	46	"
	L	Maxwell Robert H	7	machinist	23	"
	M	Savage Lawrence E	7	clerk	52	"
	N	Savage Madeline M—†	7	housewife	43	"
	O	Savage Mary E—†	7	nurse	24	"
	P	Savage Patricia A—†	7	clerk	21	"
	R	Webber Edward F	7	garageman	38	1422 Blue Hill av
	S	Ryan Katherine G—†	9	housewife	55	here
	T	Ryan Mary E—†	9	domestic	30	"
	U	Ryan Thomas M	9	clerk	20	"
	V	Cook Garrett N	10	messenger	24	"
	W	Haven Elizabeth A—†	10	housewife	26	"
	X	Haven George R	10	clerk	28	"
	Y	Kimball Albert S	14	starter	64	"

Page.	Letter.	Full Name.	Residence, Jan. 1, 1941.	Occupation.	Supposed Age.	Reported Residence, Jan. 1, 1940. Street and Number.

Babson Street—Continued

Page.	Letter.	Full Name.	Residence, Jan. 1, 1941.	Occupation.	Supposed Age.	Reported Residence, Jan. 1, 1940. Street and Number.
	Z	Kimball Myra—†	14	housewife	63	here
205						
	A	Chesler Freda—†	18	"	30	"
	B	Chesler Louis J	18	designer	40	"
	C	Higgins Delia E—†	22	housewife	50	"
	D	Higgins John J	22	salesman	50	"
	E	Cassford Madeline—†	22	housewife	35	"
	F	Cassford Theodore R	22	chauffeur	36	"
	H	Fried Frances—†	26	clerk	29	"
	G	Fried Joseph	26	salesman	23	"
	K	Fried Rose—†	26	housewife	62	"
	L	Breger Joseph	26	leatherworker	45	"
	M	Breger Lillian—†	26	housewife	40	"
	N	Fineberg Charles	26	painter	52	"
	O	Fineberg Louis	26	merchant	49	"
	P	Meehan Mary—†	72	housekeeper	40	"
	R	Meehan Thomas	72	caretaker	42	"
	T	Gavin Elizabeth M—†	98	dressmaker	45	"
	U	Gavin Jacquelene M—†	98	clerk	20	"
	V	Gavin James T	98	chauffeur	20	"
	W	Gavin John F	98	policeman	43	"
	X	Callon George	100	laborer	38	20 Cedar
	Y	Cloutier Leona—†	100	presser	25	here
	Z	Whitehead Charles E	100	retired	79	"
206						
	A	Whitehead Charles E, jr	100	cleaner	54	"
	B	Whitehead Mary—†	100	housewife	43	"
	C	Hart Marguerite—†	100	"	21	"
	D	Hart Thomas	100	dyeworker	25	"
	G	Tosi Blaise	116	mechanic	30	"
	H	Tosi Frances—†	116	housewife	26	"
	K	Aicardi Gertrude R—†	116	"	49	91 Babson
	L	Aicardi John	116	manager	28	91 "
	M	Aicardi Katherine M—†	116	clerk	21	506 E Sixth

Banfield Avenue

Page.	Letter.	Full Name.	Residence, Jan. 1, 1941.	Occupation.	Supposed Age.	Reported Residence, Jan. 1, 1940. Street and Number.
	N	Wyman Delia T—†	35	housewife	55	here
	O	Wyman Lloyd D	35	plumber	52	"

Page.	Letter.	Full Name.	Residence, Jan. 1, 1941.	Occupation.	Supposed Age.	Reported Residence, Jan. 1, 1940. Street and Number.

Blue Hill Avenue

Page.	Letter.	Full Name.	Residence, Jan. 1, 1941.	Occupation.	Supposed Age.	Reported Residence, Jan. 1, 1940. Street and Number.
	V	*Gusin Anna—†	1290	housewife	26	here
	W	*Gusin Morris	1290	butcher	30	"
	X	Rosenthal Lillian—†	1290	saleswoman	22	"
	Y	Rosenthal Samuel	1290	painter	49	"
	Z	Rosenthal Sophie—†	1290	housewife	42	"
207						
	A	*Galler Rose—†	1290	"	51	"
	H	Palner William	1310	janitor	55	36 Oak
	K	Libin Jacob	1310	pharmacist	48	here
	L	Libin Muriel—†	1310	student	20	"
	M	*Libin Sarah—†	1310	housewife	46	"
	N	Gold Adelaide—†	1310	"	29	"
	O	Simons Benjamin	1310	clerk	45	"
	P	Simons Freida—†	1310	housewife	43	"
	R	Orenstein Jacob	1310	merchant	55	50 W Walnut pk
	S	Orenstein Joseph	1310	pharmacist	27	50 "
	T	Orenstein Louis	1310	"	24	50 "
	U	*Millman Ida—†	1314	housewife	50	16 Clarkwood
	V	Selett Rose—†	1314	"	39	16 "
	W	Selett Samuel	1314	merchant	42	45 Fottler rd
	X	Speyer Joseph	1314	chauffeur	26	here
	Y	Speyer Marion—†	1314	housewife	23	"
	Z	Luftman Gussie—†	1314	clerk	30	"
208						
	A	Luftman Sarah—†	1314	housewife	60	"
	B	Sheinberg Rae—†	1314	"	36	"
	C	Sheinberg Samuel	1314	merchant	44	"
	D	Bornstein Florence—†	1314	housewife	28	"
	E	Bornstein Ida—†	1314	"	48	"
	F	Bornstein Milton	1314	teacher	27	"
	G	*Pollinow Esther—†	1314	housewife	36	"
	H	*Pollinow Louis	1314	chauffeur	39	"
	K	Stone Goldie—†	1314	housewife	32	86 Deering rd
	L	Stone Henry	1314	salesman	39	86 "
	M	Richstein Matilda—†	1314	housewife	35	here
	N	Richstein Max	1314	salesman	45	"
	O	Greenfield Frances L—†	1314	housewife	41	"
	P	Greenfield Moses M	1314	salesman	43	"
	R	Saltman Louis	1314	"	29	241 Woodrow av
	S	Saltman Sally—†	1314	housewife	26	241 "
	T	Kadish Ida—†	1314	"	54	here

Page	Letter	Full Name.	Residence, Jan. 1, 1941.	Occupation.	Supposed Age.	Reported Residence, Jan. 1, 1940. Street and Number.

Blue Hill Avenue—Continued

Page	Letter	Full Name	Residence	Occupation	Age	Reported Residence
	U	Kadish Mary—†	1314	clerk	25	here
	V	Shuman Helen—†	1314	"	23	"
	W	Kramer Nathaniel	1314	realtor	21	17 Fairmount
	X	Kramer Ruth—†	1314	housewife	23	17 "
	Y	*Snyder Annie—†	1326	"	54	here
	Z	Snyder Esther—†	1326	"	28	"
209						
	A	*Snyder Hyman	1326	tailor	56	"
	B	Snyder Morris L	1326	dentist	30	"
	C	Mitchell Abraham	1326	merchant	58	"
	D	Mitchell Louis	1326	accountant	28	"
	E	Mitchell Rebecca—†	1326	clerk	23	"
	F	Mitchell Sarah—†	1326	housewife	55	"
	G	Simons Arthur	1326	salesman	43	20 Vesta rd
	H	Simons Bertha—†	1326	housewife	40	20 "
	K	Zamon Anna—†	1326	"	54	here
210						
	C	Laneta George L	1368	laborer	34	"
	D	Rota Florence—†	1368	housewife	37	"
	E	Rota John C	1368	laborer	45	"
	F	Penniman Gladys—†	1368	housewife	43	"

Cookson Terrace

Page	Letter	Full Name	Residence	Occupation	Age	Reported Residence
	M	Higgins James J	11	fireman	58	here
	N	Higgins Jennie E—†	11	housewife	54	"
	O	Higgins Robert E	11	clerk	23	"
	R	MacDonald Jennie—†	15	housewife	65	"
	S	MacDonald Rudolph	15	retired	70	"
	T	Aspessi Chesar	17	fireman	47	"
	U	Aspessi Francis	17	toolmaker	20	"
	V	Aspessi William	17	printer	23	"
	W	Lane Catherine A—†	17	housewife	42	"
	X	Lane Catherine A—†	17	clerk	20	"
	Y	Lane Richard J	17	fireman	49	"
	Z	Lane Richard J, jr	17	electrician	22	"
211						
	A	Barron Marie J—†	21	housewife	48	"
	B	Barron Thomas E	21	policeman	46	"
	C	Barron Annie C—†	23	clerk	21	"
	D	Fox John F	23	fireman	55	"

Page	Letter	Full Name	Residence, Jan. 1, 1941	Occupation	Supposed Age	Reported Residence, Jan. 1, 1940. Street and Number.

Cookson Terrace—Continued

Page	Letter	Full Name	Residence, Jan. 1, 1941	Occupation	Supposed Age	Reported Residence, Jan. 1, 1940. Street and Number.
	E	Fox Theresa E—†	23	housewife	50	here
	F	Grant Fairy L—†	27	"	56	"
	G	Knight Hartwell J	27	candyworker	29	"
	H	Knight Hazel L—†	27	saleswoman	37	"

Crossman Street

Page	Letter	Full Name	Residence, Jan. 1, 1941	Occupation	Supposed Age	Reported Residence, Jan. 1, 1940. Street and Number.
	M	*Goldberg Rebecca—†	6–8	housekeeper	60	here
	K	Novack Irving	6–8	machinist	34	"
	L	Novack Jean—†	6–8	housewife	30	"
	N	Goldstein Benjamin	6–8	carpenter	39	"
	O	Goldstein Sophie—†	6–8	housewife	38	"
	P	Anderson Herbert E	10–12	pipefitter	37	"
	R	Anderson Lucia—†	10–12	housewife	32	"
	S	Donahue Edna—†	10–12	"	40	"
	T	Donahue William	10–12	plumber	42	"
	U	Trever Marion—†	10–12	clerk	40	"
	V	Jackson Hazel—†	14–16	housewife	32	Brockton
	W	Jackson Robert	14–16	accountant	22	"
	X	O'Sullivan Alice—†	14–16	housewife	27	here
	Y	O'Sullivan Patrick	14–16	operator	31	"
212						
	A	Carter Adeline G—†	18	housekeeper	71	"
	B	Shea Margeanna C—†	18	nurse	50	"

Delhi Street

Page	Letter	Full Name	Residence, Jan. 1, 1941	Occupation	Supposed Age	Reported Residence, Jan. 1, 1940. Street and Number.
	C	O'Leary Bridget W—†	149	housewife	64	here
	D	O'Leary Gertrude—†	149	clerk	37	"
	E	O'Leary Timothy	149	operator	28	"
	F	Butterworth Ida—†	153	housewife	43	"
	G	Butterworth Walter	153	policeman	45	"
	H	Veale Emma L—†	200	housewife	43	"
	K	Veale John S	200	clerk	46	"
	L	Hill Anna L—†	200	housewife	55	"
	M	Hill James J	200	chauffeur	32	"
	N	Beskosty Alec	200	clerk	22	"
	O	*Beskosty Mary—†	200	housekeeper	47	"
	P	Beskosty Paul	200	laborer	22	"
	R	Beskosty Peter	200	clerk	24	"
	S	Hill Andrew F	200	chauffeur	34	"
	T	Hill Anna—†	200	sealer	26	"

Page	Letter	Full Name	Residence Jan. 1 1941	Occupation	Supposed Age	Reported Residence, Jan. 1, 1940 Street and Number

Delhi Street—Continued

Page	Letter	Full Name	Residence Jan. 1 1941	Occupation	Supposed Age	Reported Residence, Jan. 1, 1940 Street and Number
	U	Porter Dorothea †	204	housewife	36	here
	V	Porter Robert S	204	machinist	40	"
	W	Mathisen Irving O	204	photographer	40	"
	X	Neagle Charles H	204	operator	27	"
	Y	Neagle Dorothy †	204	housewife	25	"
	Z	Maclay John	204	chef	48	1885 Hyde Park av
213						
	A	Maclay Lillian P †	204	housewife	46	1885 "
	B	Ahlberg Florence †	211	"	59	here
	C	Ahlberg Mary C †	211	secretary	22	"
	D	Ahlberg Oliver D	211	retired	69	"
	E	Carver Ida †	211	housekeeper	50	"
	F	Flynn George A	211	buyer	45	"
	G	Findley John W	220	salesman	77	"
	H	Nelson Berna †	228	clerk	20	"
	K	*Nelson Ellen †	228	housewife	42	"
	L	Nelson Eric	228	carpenter	52	"
	M	Nelson Lisa †	228	nurse	23	"
	N	Albertelli Lawrence	230	laborer	50	"
	O	McKay Michael	230	guard	47	"
	P	McKay Teresa †	230	clerk	20	"
	R	McKay Tina †	230	housewife	47	"
	S	Campbell Anna †	232	"	45	"
	T	Campbell Charles	232	machinist	47	"
	U	Giggey George A	234	carpenter	84	"
	V	Harvey Marion L †	234	housewife	47	"
	W	Harvey William L	234	salesman	48	"
	X	Burke Emma †	235	housewife	43	"
	Y	Burke James	235	lather	49	"
	Z	Burke John R	235	"	23	"
214						
	A	Wolfe Louise †	235	housekeeper	66	"
	B	Doolin Anna †	237	housewife	39	"
	C	Doolin Francis	237	laborer	37	"
	D	Flood Thomas	237	shipper	70	"
	E	Barrett Mary †	239	housekeeper	33	"

Elizabeth Street

Page	Letter	Full Name	Residence Jan. 1 1941	Occupation	Supposed Age	Reported Residence, Jan. 1, 1940 Street and Number
	G	*Borges Harry	5	tailor	70	here
	H	*Borges Sarah †	5	housewife	65	"
	K	Gilbert Eli	7	manager	32	"

Page	Letter	Full Name.	Residence, Jan. 1, 1941.	Occupation.	Supposed Age.	Reported Residence, Jan. 1, 1940. Street and Number.

Elizabeth Street—Continued

Page	Letter	Full Name.	Residence, Jan. 1, 1941.	Occupation.	Supposed Age.	Reported Residence, Jan. 1, 1940. Street and Number.
	L	Gilbert Hyman	7	furrier	59	here
	M	Gilbert Minnie—†	7	housewife	55	"
	N	Gilbert Saul	7	musician	27	"
	O	Schachter Minnie—†	9	housewife	29	"
	P	Schachter Sydney	9	manager	32	"
	R	*Simon Rose—†	11	housewife	57	"
	S	Simon Samuel	11	clerk	25	"
	T	Simon Sophie—†	11	secretary	33	"
	U	Patlock Ida—†	17	housewife	52	"
	V	Patlock Jacob	17	tailor	53	"
	W	Kerwin Gertrude—†	27	housewife	52	"
	X	Kerwin Virginia G—†	27	stenographer	20	"
	Y	Kerwin Walter	27	chauffeur	32	"

Evelyn Street

Page	Letter	Full Name.	Residence, Jan. 1, 1941.	Occupation.	Supposed Age.	Reported Residence, Jan. 1, 1940. Street and Number.
	Z	Glassman Harry	15	carpenter	58	here
215						
	A	Glassman Lena—†	15	housewife	52	"
	B	Glassman Philip	15	salesman	33	41 Hiawatha rd
	C	Glassman Rose—†	15	housewife	29	41 "
	D	Finn Edith—†	15	"	24	560 Walk Hill
	E	Finn Hyman	15	proprietor	28	here
	F	Finn Morris	15	retired	67	"
	G	Finn Rose—†	15	housewife	69	"
	H	Finn Sylvia—†	15	saleswoman	23	"
	K	Finkelstein Annie—†	15	housewife	50	"
	L	Finkelstein Gertrude—†	15	hairdresser	20	"
	M	Finkelstein Israel	15	tailor	56	"
	N	Silverman Harry	15	mechanic	26	346 Norfolk
	O	Silverman Ruth—†	15	housewife	26	here
	P	*Kolton Albert	17	shoeworker	51	"
	R	*Kolton Etta—†	17	leatherworker	51	"
	S	White Anna—†	17	housewife	65	"
	T	White Samuel	17	presser	58	"
	U	Goldman Nathan	17	salesman	25	"
	V	Goldman Rebecca E—†	17	housewife	31	"
	W	Levinsky Betty—†	19	saleswoman	25	"
	X	*Levinsky Hilda—†	19	housewife	57	"
	Y	*Levinsky Louis	19	tailor	57	"
	Z	*Sachs Bertha—†	19	housewife	32	"

Page	Letter	Full Name	Residence, Jan. 1, 1941	Occupation	Supposed Age	Reported Residence, Jan. 1, 1940. Street and Number

216

Evelyn Street Continued

Page	Letter	Full Name	Residence, Jan. 1, 1941	Occupation	Supposed Age	Reported Residence, Jan. 1, 1940. Street and Number
216	A	Sachs Louis	19	merchant	35	here
	B	Borison Irving	19	musician	31	"
	C	*Borison Thelma †	19	housewife	29	"
	D	Fogelnest Dorothy †	21	"	37	"
	E	Fogelnest Louis	21	manager	40	"
	F	*Katz Ida †	21	housewife	36	"
	G	Katz Nathan	21	plumber	39	"
	H	Finkelstein Abraham	21	salesman	60	"
	K	Finkelstein Harry	21	"	60	"
	L	*Lewis Frances †	21	housewife	46	"
	M	*Lewis Sam	21	salesman	50	"
	N	Blander Abraham	23	manager	54	"
	O	Blander Fred J	23	attorney	23	"
	P	Blander Iola †	23	housewife	49	"
	R	*Polsky Ida †	23	"	44	"
	S	Polsky Joseph	23	tailor	46	"
	T	Polsky Melvin	23	student	20	"
	U	Weinberg Ida †	23	dressmaker	21	"
	V	*Weinberg Joseph	23	merchant	49	"
	W	*Weinberg Rebecca †	23	housewife	54	"
	X	Kaufman Abraham	27	presser	53	"
	Y	Kaufman Grace †	27	saleswoman	24	"
	Z	Kaufman Rebecca †	27	housewife	54	"
217	A	Milner Abraham	27	presser	32	"
	B	Milner Rose †	27	housewife	26	"
	C	Rubinovitz Bessie †	27	"	75	51 Deering rd
	D	Rubinovitz Celia †	27	stenographer	40	51 "
	E	Strumph Sarah †	27	housekeeper	72	here
	F	Berson Annie †	27	"	62	"
	G	Berson Jean †	27	housewife	28	"
	H	Berson Max	27	chauffeur	29	"
	K	Meltzer Maurice	27	salesman	41	California
	L	Meltzer Sadie †	27	housewife	27	"
	M	Fagin Israel	29	laborer	62	235 W Selden
	N	Seifer Agusta †	29	housewife	29	235 "
	O	Seifer Matthew	29	pharmacist	32	235 "
	P	*Yelovitz Anna †	29	housekeeper	22	here
	R	Young Frederick	29	carpenter	24	"
	S	Young Judith †	29	saleswoman	22	"

Page	Letter	Full Name	Residence, Jan. 1, 1941.	Occupation	Supposed Age	Reported Residence, Jan. 1, 1940. Street and Number.

Evelyn Street—Continued

Page	Letter	Full Name	Residence, Jan. 1, 1941.	Occupation	Supposed Age	Reported Residence, Jan. 1, 1940. Street and Number.
	T	Young Leo	29	merchant	28	here
	U	*Gitlin John J	29	"	41	"
	V	Rubin Adele—†	29	secretary	20	"
	W	Rubin Harry	29	repairman	46	"
	X	Rubin Ida R—†	29	housewife	43	"
	Y	*Volkin Annie—†	31	"	59	"
	Z	Volkin Dora—†	31	saleswoman	26	"
218						
	A	*Volkin Max	31	manufacturer	58	"
	B	Volkin Mildred—†	31	clerk	22	"
	C	*Kaplan Rubin	31	plasterer	48	"
	D	Kaplan Sophie—†	31	housewife	45	"
	E	Cidulka Leo	31	student	21	"
	F	Cidulka Mollie—†	31	housewife	57	"
	G	Clevenson Gershon	31	clerk	29	"
	H	Clevenson Ruth—†	31	housewife	28	"
	K	Elfman Abraham J	33	painter	42	"
	L	Elfman Dora E—†	33	housewife	39	"
	M	Rosenblatt Bertha—†	33	"	44	"
	N	Rosenblatt David	33	presser	50	"
	O	Rosenblatt Sylvia—†	33	saleswoman	21	"
	P	Cohen Blanche—†	33	housewife	30	274 Walnut av
	R	Cohen Jacob	33	salesman	32	274 "
	S	*Gordon Barnett	33	tailor	62	403 Warren
	T	*Gordon Gussie—†	33	housewife	57	403 "
	U	Gordon Jacob	33	chauffeur	21	403 "
	V	Chiten Elizabeth—†	37	housewife	36	here
	W	Chiten William A	37	agent	38	"
	X	Carpenter Edward M	37	student	21	"
	Y	Carpenter Jennie—†	37	clerk	26	"
	Z	Carpenter Joseph	37	student	24	"
219						
	A	Carpenter Morris	37	salesman	28	"
	B	Carpenter Pearl S—†	37	secretary	23	"
	C	Goldberg Harry I	37	manager	40	"
	D	Goldberg Ida C—†	37	housewife	35	"
	E	Richmond Fannie—†	37	"	43	"
	F	Richmond Herbert B	37	student	20	"
	G	Richmond Joseph W	37	salesman	23	"
	H	*Richmond Louis	37	operator	48	"
	K	Wanberg Claus E	41	retired	72	"

Page	Letter	Full Name	Residence, Jan. 1, 1941.	Occupation	Supposed Age	Reported Residence, Jan. 1, 1940. Street and Number.

Evelyn Street—Continued

Page	Letter	Full Name	Residence, Jan. 1, 1941.	Occupation	Supposed Age	Reported Residence, Jan. 1, 1940. Street and Number.
	L	Wanberg Ida †	41	housewife	72	here
	M	Berch Bernard	41	shipper	24	"
	N	Berch Bessie †	41	housewife	45	"
	O	Berch Isadore	41	carpenter	22	"
	P	Berch Rose—†	41	artist	26	"
	R	Bergling Carl E	41	operator	62	"
	T	Peterson Josephine—†	41	housewife	67	"
	S	Peterson Philip	41	machinist	67	"
	U	Snyder Elsie W †	45	housewife	45	"
	V	Snyder Joseph S	45	policeman	53	"
	W	Cohen Doris †	45	housewife	39	100 Ormon
	X	Cohen Joseph G	45	agent	42	100 "
	Y	*Orenberg Bessie †	45	housewife	71	78 Capen
	Z	*Orenberg David	45	retired	84	78 "
220						
	A	Silverstein Bella †	45	housewife	48	78 "
	B	Silverstein Jacob	45	jeweler	52	78 "
	C	Fineberg Morris	51	photographer	48	Lynn
	D	Obshatkin Rosalie—†	51	housekeeper	25	here
	E	Price David H	51	clerk	27	"
	F	Price Henry S	51	U S A	32	"
	G	Price Louis N	51	merchant	60	"
	H	Raskind Benjamin	53	salesman	45	"
	K	Raskind Bessie †	53	housewife	44	"
	L	Becker Leo	55	manager	33	"
	M	Becker Minna †	55	housewife	33	"
	N	Kauffman Charles C	55	agent	38	83 Erie
	O	*Kauffman Dora †	55	housekeeper	71	83 "
	P	Trebub George	55	inspector	24	here
	R	Trebub Rose †	55	housekeeper	42	"

Faunce Road

Page	Letter	Full Name	Residence, Jan. 1, 1941.	Occupation	Supposed Age	Reported Residence, Jan. 1, 1940. Street and Number.
	S	Kenney John J	8	painter	46	here
	T	Kenney Margaret †	8	housewife	42	"
	U	McNab Eric L	8	gardener	37	"
	V	McNab Mary A †	8	housewife	33	"
	W	Meehan Emily K—†	20	"	33	15 Larchmont
	X	Meehan John J	20	inspector	36	15 "
	Y	Densmore Alice †	22	housewife	42	here
	Z	Densmore William J	22	fireman	51	"

Page.	Letter.	Full Name.	Residence, Jan. 1, 1941.	Occupation.	Supposed Age.	Reported Residence, Jan. 1, 1940. Street and Number.
221						
		Faunce Road—Continued				
	A	Fitzgerald Gertrude—†	22	housewife	21	24 W Cedar
	B	Fitzgerald John	22	carpenter	21	here
	C	Jones Richard	22	clerk	20	"
	D	Herman Belle—†	26	housewife	35	"
	E	Herman Charles	26	laborer	40	"
	F	Williams Elmer	26	papermaker	31	"
	G	Williams Mary—†	26	housewife	26	"
	H	Jennings Margaret M—†	26	operator	26	"
	K	Lockney Mary V—†	26	domestic	60	"
	L	Porter Arthur	26	finisher	56	32 Milford
	M	Porter Charles I	26	manager	63	here
	N	Porter Ellen—†	26	housewife	56	"
	O	Porter Gerald W	26	attendant	24	"
	P	Murphy Jeremiah	34	engineer	40	"
	R	Murphy Winifred—†	34	housewife	38	"
	S	Spring Edward	34	steamfitter	35	"
	T	Spring Eleanor—†	34	housewife	33	"
	U	Higgins James E	44	printer	30	"
	V	Higgins Mary E—†	44	housewife	32	"
	W	Clifford Anna M—†	50	clerk	29	"
	X	Hayes Alfred W	50	chauffeur	28	"
	Y	Hayes Eileen C—†	50	housewife	27	"
	Z	Tirrell George H	52	clerk	30	"
222						
	A	Tirrell Helen S—†	52	housewife	27	"
		Fessenden Street				
	B	Shane Edith—†	5	housewife	20	484 Blue Hill av
	C	Shane Theodore	5	physician	24	51 Woolson
	D	Lieberman Anna C—†	5	housewife	33	here
	E	Lieberman Samuel	5	broker	36	"
	F	*Gall Esther—†	5	housewife	45	Cuba
	G	*Gall Nathan	5	mechanic	43	"
	H	Gorman May—†	5	housewife	28	here
	K	Gorman Morris	5	salesman	34	"
	L	Goldberg Charles C	5	"	50	"
	M	*Krasnow Anna—†	5	housewife	31	102 Columbia rd
	N	*Krasnow Samuel	5	proprietor	37	102 "
	O	Wolff Abraham	5	merchant	33	here

Page	Letter	Full Name	Residence, Jan. 1, 1941.	Occupation	Reported Age	Reported Residence, Jan. 1, 1940. Street and Number

Fessenden Street—Continued

Page	Letter	Full Name	Residence, Jan. 1, 1941.	Occupation	Reported Age	Reported Residence, Jan. 1, 1940. Street and Number
	P	Wolff Edith—†	5	housewife	31	here
	R	*Tankel Celia—†	8	"	37	1372 Blue Hill av
	S	Tankel Leonard	8	electrician	39	1372 "
	T	*Tolman Fanny—†	8	at home	60	1372 "
	U	Tolman Lillian—†	8	bookkeeper	20	1372 "
	V	Darman Annie M—†	8	housewife	36	here
	W	Darman Hyman N	8	mechanic	45	"
	X	*Sussman Rebecca—†	8	at home	59	"
	Y	Weiner Evelyn—†	8	saleswoman	26	"
	Z	*Weiner Peter S	8	merchant	47	"
223						
	A	*Weiner Polly—†	8	housewife	46	"
	B	Hyman Ann—†	10	"	54	"
	C	Hyman Philip	10	cleaner	55	"
	D	Kravitz Hyman	10	upholsterer	21	61 Elmhurst
	E	Slotnick Frank	10	laborer	24	28 Litchfield
	F	Slotnick Jean—†	10	housewife	22	here
	G	Kaplan Etta—†	10	"	62	"
	H	Kaplan Jack	10	chemist	28	"
	K	Kaplan Louis	10	butcher	62	"
	L	Kaplan Milton	10	student	21	"
	M	Witt Harry	10	tailor	42	"
	N	Witt Mildred—†	10	housewife	36	"
	O	Dubrow Dorothy—†	14	hairdresser	24	"
	P	Dubrow Edith—†	14	saleswoman	22	"
	R	*Dubrow Mary—†	14	at home	63	"
	S	Dubrow Sally—†	14	agent	29	"
	T	Brown Bertha—†	14	housewife	45	"
	U	Brown Louis	14	ironworker	47	"
	V	Cohen Abraham	14	"	23	"
	W	Cohen Frances—†	14	at home	20	"
	X	*Dukst Albert	14	clerk	39	"
	Y	*Dukst Bertha—†	14	"	22	"
	Z	*Dukst Molly—†	14	housewife	60	2 Creston
224						
	A	*Taperon Esther—†	14	"	32	24 Magnolia
	B	Gold Charles	15	manager	37	Malden
	C	Gold Charlotte—†	15	housewife	26	"
	D	Gold Israel	15	realtor	72	1330 Blue Hill av
	E	Becker Abraham	15	salesman	49	here
	F	Becker Miriam—†	15	bookkeeper	20	"

Page.	Letter.	Full Name.	Residence, Jan. 1, 1941.	Occupation.	Supposed Age.	Reported Residence, Jan. 1, 1940. Street and Number.

Fessenden Street—Continued

Page.	Letter.	Full Name.	Residence, Jan. 1, 1941.	Occupation.	Supposed Age.	Reported Residence, Jan. 1, 1940. Street and Number.
	G	Becker Rose—†	15	housewife	49	here
	H	Caplan David	15	clerk	23	"
	K	Friedlander Ida—†	15	housewife	53	"
	L	*Zimmerman Sarah—†	15	"	80	"
	M	Olansky Abraham	15	manager	43	"
	N	*Olansky Dora—†	15	housewife	38	"
	O	Weinstein Fanny—†	15	"	46	"
	P	Weinstein Nathan	15	salesman	55	"
	R	*Israel Benjamin	15	butcher	33	9 Wales
	S	*Israel Rose—†	15	saleswoman	28	9 "
	V	Brown Harry S	19	merchant	43	here
	W	Brown May—†	19	housewife	40	"
	X	Moskowitz Jacob	19	merchant	55	"
	Y	Moskowitz Sophie—†	19	housewife	53	"
	Z	Saks Helen—†	19	"	30	"
225						
	A	*Saks Philip	19	salesman	32	"
	B	Jacobs Flora—†	19	housewife	43	"
	C	Jacobs Harold L	19	student	22	"
	D	Jacobs John E	19	chauffeur	46	"
	E	Mayerson Betty—†	21	bookkeeper	33	"
	F	Mayerson Deby—†	21	housewife	63	"
	G	Mayerson Ethel—†	21	secretary	37	"
	H	Mayerson Harold	21	shipper	25	"
	K	*Rothman Benjamin	21	tailor	62	"
	L	Rothman Jeannette—†	21	bookkeeper	21	"
	M	*Rothman Rebecca—†	21	housewife	56	"
	N	Rothman Sarah—†	21	saleswoman	24	"
	O	Nider Fanny—†	21	milliner	44	"
	P	Nider Harris	21	tailor	74	"
	R	Nider Lena—†	21	housewife	61	"
	S	Hyman Charles S	22	salesman	36	"
	T	Hyman Molly—†	22	housewife	34	"
	U	Goodman Isaac	22	realtor	53	"
	V	Goodman Lillian—†	22	housewife	51	"
	W	Abelow Aaron	23	salesman	37	26 Evelyn
	X	Abelow Emma—†	23	housewife	30	26 "
	Y	*Mappen Fanny—†	23	"	55	682 Walk Hill
	Z	*Mappen Morris	23	cleanser	61	682 "
226						
	A	Winer Joseph	23	manufacturer	31	682 "

Page	Letter	Full Name	Residence, Jan. 1, 1941	Occupation	Supposed Age	Reported Residence, Jan. 1, 1940. Street and Number

Fessenden Street Continued

Page	Letter	Full Name	Residence, Jan. 1, 1941	Occupation	Supposed Age	Reported Residence, Jan. 1, 1940. Street and Number
	B	Winer Sarah †	23	housewife	28	682 Walk Hill
	C	Shuman Elsie †	23	"	30	here
	D	Shuman Irving	23	salesman	35	"
	E	Greenberg Samuel	24	"	36	"
	F	Greenberg Sophie †	24	housewife	24	"
	G	*Pearlmutter Eva †	24	"	75	"
	H	Pearlmutter Irving	24	manager	42	"
	K	*Solomon Katie †	24	housewife	46	"
	M	Solomon Peter	24	merchant	57	"
	L	Solomon Philip	24	bookkeeper	20	"
	N	Bernstein Harry I	24	tailor	39	"
	O	Bernstein Rose †	24	housewife	38	"
	P	Cheredman Charles	24	chauffeur	30	"
	R	Shapiro Hyman	25	retired	65	"
	S	Shapiro Isabelle †	25	clerk	27	"
	T	Shapiro Louis	25	musician	31	"
	U	Zahler Leo	25	salesman	36	"
	V	Zahler Ruth †	25	housekeeper	36	"
	W	Cohen Minnie †	25	clerk	28	16 Havelock
	X	Cohen Pearl †	25	housewife	24	29 Tucker
	Y	Cohen Samuel	25	operator	25	29 "
	Z	*Schwartz Annie †	26	housewife	50	here
227						
	A	Schwartz Charlotte †	26	clerk	20	"
	B	Schwartz Hyman	26	butcher	57	"
	C	Schwartz Sadie †	26	saleswoman	23	"
	D	Rosenstein Rose †	26	housekeeper	45	"
	E	Sheinberg Abraham	26	salesman	46	"
	F	*Sheinberg Israel	26	retired	78	"
	G	Sheinberg Sarah †	26	dressmaker	43	"
	H	Levine Bernard	26	salesman	50	"
	K	Levine Eva †	26	housewife	49	"
	L	Levine Morris	26	pharmacist	27	"
	M	Bazar Benjamin	27	tailor	54	"
	N	Bazar Rose †	27	housewife	50	"
	O	Dillon Dorothy †	27	"	26	"
	P	Dillon Eli	27	proprietor	26	Chelsea
	R	*Richmond Ada †	27	housewife	50	247 Wash'n
	S	Richmond Max	27	tailor	59	247 "
	T	Katz Benjamin	27	shoeworker	58	here
	U	Katz Elsie †	27	proprietor	34	"

Page	Letter	Full Name	Residence, Jan. 1, 1941	Occupation	Supposed Age	Reported Residence, Jan. 1, 1940. Street and Number

Fessenden Street—Continued

Page	Letter	Full Name	Residence, Jan. 1, 1941	Occupation	Supposed Age	Reported Residence, Jan. 1, 1940. Street and Number
	V	Katz Martin	27	proprietor	34	here
	W	Katz Rose—†	27	housewife	56	"
	X	Alpert Anna L—†	29	"	37	"
	Y	Alpert Morris H	29	salesman	38	"
	Z	Goldman Bessie—†	29	housewife	34	"
228						
	A	Goldman Mitchell	29	butcher	39	"
	B	Kofman Mollie—†	29	housewife	55	Chelsea
	C	*Levine Eli	29	butcher	36	here
	D	Levine Sarah—†	29	housewife	26	"
	E	Palmbaum Gabriel	30	salesman	33	New York
	F	Perlmutter Esther—†	30	manicurist	27	here
	G	*Perlmutter Yetta—†	30	housewife	52	"
	H	*Willner Bernhard	30	laborer	24	New York
	K	Baker Joseph	30	broker	34	here
	L	Baker Lillian—†	30	housewife	29	"
	M	*Wasserman Eva—†	30	"	54	"
	N	*Wasserman Louis	30	tailor	58	"
	O	*Richman Ruth—†	30	housewife	36	"
	P	*Richman Samuel	30	manager	46	"
	R	Powell Harry	31	barber	31	"
	S	Powell Shirley—†	31	housewife	31	"
	T	*Francer Anna—†	31	"	38	"
	U	Francer Jacob	31	roofer	43	"
	V	Strasbourg Louis	31	salesman	42	"
	W	Bloom Abraham L	31	proprietor	46	"
	X	Bloom Anna C—†	31	housewife	35	"
	Y	Spiegel Alfred J	31A	clerk	24	71 Walnut pk
	Z	Francer Arthur	31A	roofer	51	here
229						
	A	Francer Cecelia—†	31A	housewife	40	"
	B	Ballace Ada L—†	31A	"	40	"
	C	Ballace Harry A	31A	plumber	43	"
	D	Ballace Howard J	31A	salesman	22	"
	E	Pederson Mary—†	31A	domestic	26	"
	F	Kimball Ethel—†	33	librarian	40	"
	G	Levin Gussie—†	33	housewife	72	"
	H	Levin Robert	33	retired	72	"
	K	Segal Betty—†	33	housewife	31	"
	L	Segal Charles	33	salesman	31	"
	M	Stock Moses S	33	manager	34	"

Page	Letter	Full Name	Residence Jan. 1, 1941	Occupation	Supposed Age	Reported Residence Jan. 1, 1940, Street and Number

Fessenden Street Continued

Page	Letter	Full Name	Residence Jan. 1, 1941	Occupation	Supposed Age	Reported Residence Jan. 1, 1940
	N	Norwood Hyman	33	proprietor	59	here
	O	Norwood Robert	33	salesman	45	"
	P	Norwood Rose †	33	housewife	45	"
	R	Natanson Simon	34	retired	64	"
	S	Shuman Esther †	34	housewife	32	"
	T	Shuman Saul	34	merchant	30	"
	U	Cohen Arnold	34	student	30	"
	V	Cohen Lillian †	24	housewife	43	"
	W	*White Max	34	butcher	54	"
	X	*White Sarah †	34	housewife	50	"
	Y	Strock Frances †	35	"	32	"
	Z	Strock Fred	35	barber	63	"
230						
	B	Polansky George	35	accountant	24	"
	C	Polansky Harry	35	tailor	58	"
	D	Polansky Rose †	35	housewife	50	"
	E	*Waxman Esther †	35	at home	74	"
	F	*Gershkovitz Helen †	36	housewife	61	"
	G	Gershkovitz Max	36	roofer	61	"
	H	Sigel Ida †	36	housewife	28	"
	K	Sigel Sydney	36	salesman	30	"
	L	Koren Philip W	36	decorator	37	"
	M	Koren Sophie †	36	housewife	37	"
	N	Wynne Roberta †	36	"	35	Illinois
	O	Ainbender Gertrude †	36	"	48	here
	P	Ainbender Isadore	36	clerk	22	"
	R	Ainbender Morris	36	painter	29	"
	S	Ainbender Samuel	36	"	50	"
	T	Canner Irving	38	salesman	43	"
	U	Canner Isabelle †	38	housewife	42	"
	V	*Stern Maurice	38	salesman	50	"
	W	*Stern Mollie †	38	housewife	48	"
	X	Stern Myrtle †	38	bookkeeper	20	"

Fremont Street

Page	Letter	Full Name	Residence Jan. 1, 1941	Occupation	Supposed Age	Reported Residence Jan. 1, 1940
	Y	Gavin John J	36	retired	78	here
	Z	Chalmers Ellen †	46	housewife	60	"
231						
	A	Chalmers Hugh	46	chauffeur	26	"
	B	Chalmers Leo E	46	"	24	"

Page	Letter	Full Name	Residence, Jan. 1, 1941	Occupation	Supposed Age	Reported Residence, Jan. 1, 1940. Street and Number.

Fremont Street—Continued

Page	Letter	Full Name	Residence, Jan. 1, 1941	Occupation	Supposed Age	Reported Residence, Jan. 1, 1940. Street and Number.
	C	Chalmers Robert M	46	shipper	58	here
	D	Foley Julia—†	46	clerk	36	"
	E	*Brugnetti Adele—†	48	housewife	52	"
	F	Brugnetti Serafino	48	mason	52	"

Halborn Street

Page	Letter	Full Name	Residence, Jan. 1, 1941	Occupation	Supposed Age	Reported Residence, Jan. 1, 1940. Street and Number.
	G	Beal Rena—†	7	housewife	38	90 Milton av
	H	Beal William	7	salesman	49	90 "
	K	Sorensen Elmer	7	clerk	25	here
	L	Sorensen Magda—†	7	housewife	70	"
	M	Sorensen Nils A	7	salesman	35	"
	N	Sorensen Soren P	7	"	73	"
	O	McCarthy Anna—†	7	housewife	81	"
	P	McCarthy John	7	salesman	72	"
	R	Clarke Kathryn—†	8	bookkeeper	43	"
	S	McGuire Edna—†	8	housekeeper	30	"
	T	Anderson Gustave	10–12	painter	39	"
	U	*Anderson Ruth—†	10–12	housewife	44	"
	V	Lee Bartholomew	10–12	baker	53	"
	W	Lee Jane—†	10–12	housewife	47	"
	X	*Gordon Charles	14–16	salesman	36	"
	Y	Gordon Frances—†	14–16	housewife	33	"
	Z	O'Brien Esther—†	14–16	"	27	27 Halborn
232						
	A	O'Brien James M	14–16	salesman	30	27 "
	D	Levine Adah—†	18–20	housewife	31	here
	E	Levine Louis	18–20	bartender	32	"
	F	Gusenoff Joseph D	18–20	salesman	30	Winthrop
	G	Gusenoff Lillian—†	18–20	housewife	28	"
	H	Tidemann Christian	19–21	painter	68	here
	K	Tidemann Gudreun—†	19–21	housewife	54	"
	L	Willard Helga—†	19–21	clerk	30	"
	M	Rimer Anna—†	19–21	housewife	38	"
	N	Rimer Joseph	19–21	baker	40	"
	O	Rimer Manuel	19–21	clerk	21	"
	P	Rimer Samuel	19–21	"	20	"
	R	Tenney Edna—†	22–24	housewife	25	"
	S	Tenney Harold	22–24	machinist	29	"
	T	Davis Esther—†	22–24	housewife	29	20 Halborn

Page	Letter	Full Name	Residence, Jan. 1, 1941	Occupation	Supposed Age	Reported Residence, Jan. 1, 1940. Street and Number

Halborn Street—Continued

Page	Letter	Full Name	Residence, Jan. 1, 1941	Occupation	Supposed Age	Reported Residence, Jan. 1, 1940. Street and Number
	U	Davis Jacob	22–24	salesman	40	20 Halborn
	V	Harriman Florence E †	26–28	housewife	33	35 Edson
	W	Harriman William B	26–28	mechanic	32	35 "
	X	Webber Edward	26–28	baker	53	here
	Y	Weber Juliana †	26–28	housewife	37	"
	Z	McLaughlin Joseph	27	chauffeur	27	46 Wood av
233						
	A	McLaughlin Margaret †	27	housewife	26	46 "

Henrici Street

Page	Letter	Full Name	Residence, Jan. 1, 1941	Occupation	Supposed Age	Reported Residence, Jan. 1, 1940. Street and Number
	B	Ebbs Edna †	4	housewife	38	here
	C	Ebbs Vernon	4	chauffeur	39	"

Mildred Avenue

Page	Letter	Full Name	Residence, Jan. 1, 1941	Occupation	Supposed Age	Reported Residence, Jan. 1, 1940. Street and Number
	D	Benatuil Leo	10	electrician	38	here
	E	Benatuil Rose †	10	housewife	36	"
	F	Beckerman Evelyn †	10	clerk	21	"
	G	Beckerman Frank	10	salesman	29	Chelmsford
	H	Beckerman Hazel †	10	housewife	27	"
	K	*Beckerman Hyman	10	coppersmith	57	here
	L	Bartoloni Josephine †	14	housewife	42	"
	M	Bartoloni Louis	14	machinist	46	"
	N	Bartoloni Paul	14	"	35	"
	O	*Bartoloni Virginia †	14	housewife	65	"
	P	Riordan Catherine †	14	"	24	"
	R	Riordon Paul	14	operator	25	"
	S	Driscoll Agnes G †	18	packer	21	"
	T	Driscoll Alice L †	18	typist	23	"
	U	Driscoll Mary C †	18	housewife	58	"
	V	Evans Mary A †	18	"	88	"
	W	Bartoloni Catherine †	18	"	31	"
	X	Bartoloni Charles	18	manager	30	"
	Y	Gordon Mary †	18	housewife	76	"
	Z	Peters Dora †	20	packer	41	"
234						
	A	Reinstein Louis	20	retired	82	"
	B	Reinstein Mary †	20	housewife	67	"
	C	O'Brien John	20	chauffeur	23	"

Page	Letter	Full Name	Residence, Jan. 1, 1941.	Occupation.	Supposed Age.	Reported Residence, Jan. 1, 1940. Street and Number.

Mildred Avenue—Continued

Page	Letter	Full Name	Residence, Jan. 1, 1941.	Occupation.	Supposed Age.	Reported Residence, Jan. 1, 1940. Street and Number.
	D	O'Brien Mary—†	20	housewife	47	here
	E	O'Brien William	20	laborer	21	"
	F	Demetri Mary—†	20	housewife	35	"
	G	Demetri Simon	20	clerk	36	"
	H	Allen Harry S	22	caretaker	46	Maine
	K	Allen Sara P—†	22	housewife	38	"
	L*	O'Reilly Elsie—†	22	"	25	15 Oakwood
	M*	O'Reilly Louis	22	salesman	29	15 "
	N	Dole Edward J	22	"	31	16 Carson
	O	Dole Eileen T—†	22	housewife	26	16 "
	P	Spain Frances C—†	24	"	43	36 Rockdale
	R	Spain Frederick G	24	packer	21	36 "
	S*	Cohen Esther—†	24	housewife	38	here
	T	Cohen Louis	24	baker	39	"
	U	Duncan Elmer	24	chauffeur	35	"
	V	Duncan Helen—†	24	housewife	33	"
	W	McLaughlin Joseph F	26	chauffeur	34	"
	X	McLaughlin Mary E—†	26	housewife	58	"
	Y	McLaughlin Mary I—†	26	operator	36	"
	Z	McLaughlin Paul W	26	clerk	39	"
235						
	A	Bittman Anna—†	26	housewife	63	"
	B	Bittman George	26	foreman	38	"
	C	Driscoll Agnes T—†	26	housewife	35	"
	D	Driscoll John J	26	watchman	45	"
	E*	Jenson Carla—†	28	housewife	37	"
	F	Bohnfeldt Arthur E	28	machinist	38	"
	G	Bohnfeldt Margaret G—†	28	housewife	40	"
	H	Lapidas Julius	28	storekeeper	38	"
	K	Lapidas Sophie—†	28	housewife	35	"
	L	Somers Geraldine—†	30	clerk	20	"
	M	Somers Guy	30	chauffeur	47	"
	N*	Campbell Eliza—†	30	housewife	74	"
	O	Gillis Francis	30	salesman	32	"
	P	Gillis Mary—†	30	housewife	32	"
	R	Garmache Herman	30	steelworker	46	"
	S	Garmache Mary A—†	30	housewife	40	"
	T*	Natkus Gabriel—†	32	wireworker	55	"
	U*	Natkus Mary—†	32	housewife	42	"
	V	Lowe Edith—†	32	"	38	"

Mildred Avenue Continued

Page	Letter	Full Name	Residence Jan. 1 1941	Occupation	Supposed Age	Reported Residence, Jan. 1, 1940 Street and Number
	W	Driscoll Gladys †	32	housewife	32	8 Mulvey
	X	Driscoll John E	32	janitor	34	8 "
	Y	Slaney Frank L	34	knitter	40	here
	Z	Slaney Margaret †	34	housewife	41	"
236						
	A	Overson Ida M †	34	"	30	40 Colorado
	B	Overson John O	34	painter	36	40 "
	D	Fay Agnes A †	36	clerk	40	here
	E	McLaughlin David L	36	chauffeur	31	"
	F	McLaughlin Phyllis M †	36	housewife	32	"
	G	Leveroni Albert	36	expressman	29	"
	H	Leveroni Alice †	36	housewife	26	"
	K	Farrell Michael	36	salesman	37	"
	L*	Farrell Nora †	36	housewife	32	"
	M	Sheridan Pauline †	38	"	35	"
	N	Baxter Paul C	38	electrician	37	"
	O	Baxter Viola M †	38	housewife	35	"
	P	Baxter Mary A †	38	"	35	"
	R	Baxter Warren A	38	painter	35	"
	S	Purtell Anna A †	40	domestic	40	"
	T	Purtell Cecelia C †	40	housewife	45	"
	U	Purtell Edward J	40	packer	46	"
	V	Purtell Margaret M †	40	housewife	35	"
	W	Hefferman Dorothy E †	40	"	25	5 Warren pl
	X	Hefferman Russell J	40	counterman	26	5 "
	Y	Wine Eva †	40	housewife	43	here
	Z*	Wine Harry	40	tailor	45	"
237						
	A	Richards Anna †	42	housewife	49	"
	B	Richards Dorothy †	42	clerk	21	"
	C	Richards George	42	mechanic	46	"
	D	Richards Helen †	42	clerk	23	"
	E	Kimball Gertrude M †	42	housewife	33	"
	F	Kimball Victor M	42	operator	48	"
	G	Kimball Virginia F †	42	packer	26	"
	K	Lindgren Pontus A	44	painter	40	"
	L	Lindgren Wilhelmina L †	44	housewife	38	"
	M	Rabinovitz Celia †	44	"	62	"
	N	Rabinovitz Harry	44	upholsterer	34	"
	O*	Rabinovitz Minnie †	44	housewife	34	"

Page.	Letter	Full Name.	Residence, Jan. 1, 1941.	Occupation.	Supposed Age.	Reported Residence, Jan. 1, 1940. Street and Number.

Mildred Avenue—Continued

Page.	Letter	Full Name.	Residence, Jan. 1, 1941.	Occupation.	Supposed Age.	Reported Residence, Jan. 1, 1940.
	P	Bohnfeldt Charles	44	retired	70	here
	R	Bohnfeldt George	44	machinist	22	"
	S	Bohnfeldt Louise—†	44	housewife	64	"

Morton Street

Page.	Letter	Full Name.	Residence, Jan. 1, 1941.	Occupation.	Supposed Age.	Reported Residence, Jan. 1, 1940.
	T	Daner Haskell	883	salesman	28	here
	U	*Daner Ida—†	883	housewife	60	"
	V	*Daner Joseph	883	tailor	65	"
	W	Daner Lorna—†	883	bookkeeper	28	"
	X	*Ravreby Leah—†	883	at home	65	"
	Y	*Aronson Anna—†	883	housewife	39	"
	Z	*Aronson Irving	883	chauffeur	42	"
238						
	A	Wolper Arthur	883	clerk	26	"
	B	Wolper Edith D—†	883	"	24	"
	C	*Wolper Ida—†	883	housewife	61	"
	D	*Wolper Nathan	883	tailor	60	"
	E	Wolper Shirley R—†	883	clerk	21	"
	F	Parad Gertrude—†	887	housewife	41	"
	G	Parad Maurice	887	merchant	48	"
	H	Fleitman David	887	barber	47	"
	K	Fleitman Fannie—†	887	housewife	44	"
	L	Wolf David	887	tailor	45	"
	M	Wolf Gussie—†	887	clerk	22	"
	N	Wolf Ida—†	887	housewife	44	"
	O	Wolf Marion—†	887	saleswoman	24	"
	P	Goodsnyder Nathan	891	clerk	32	"
	R	Goodsnyder Rose—†	891	housewife	27	"
	S	Chudnovsky Bessie—†	891	"	41	"
	T	Chudnovsky William	891	proprietor	42	"
	U	*Swartz Benjamin	891	merchant	68	"
	V	*Swartz Ida—†	891	housewife	65	"
	W	Dopkeen Anna—†	891	"	48	"
	X	Dopkeen Isaiah	891	guard	53	"
	Y	Dopkeen Leo	891	clerk	32	"
	Z	Dopkeen Rose—†	891	housewife	27	"
239						
	A	Agger Leah—†	895	"	38	"
	B	Agger Oscar	895	salesman	36	"
	C	Elman Daisy—†	895	housewife	29	"

Page	Letter	Full Name	Residence Jan. 1, 1941	Occupation	Age	Reported Residence Jan. 1, 1940 Street and Number

Morton Street Continued

Page	Letter	Full Name	Residence	Occupation	Age	Reported Residence
	D	Elman Samuel	895	manager	31	here
	E	Greenbaum Bertha †	895	housewife	70	"
	F	Greenbaum Bessie †	895	clerk	35	"
	G	Kosky Julius	895	cleaner	50	"
	H	Kosky Rebecca †	895	housewife	47	"
	K	*Dockser Annie †	895	"	70	"
	L	Green Edward	895	merchant	38	"
	M	Green Elizabeth †	895	housewife	30	"
	N	*Harris Beatrice †	899	"	37	33 Michigan av
	O	Lander Harry	899	merchant	48	here
	P	*Lander Sadie †	899	housewife	46	"
	R	*Parad Eli	899	plumber	48	"
	S	*Malkiel Rebecca †	899	housewife	65	15 Greendale rd
	T	Shepard Leah †	899	"	35	15 "
	U	Shepard Morris	899	furrier	38	15 "
	V	Kraus Arthur	899	engraver	21	here
	W	Kraus Dora †	899	housewife	43	"
	X	Kraus Simon	899	salesman	43	"
	Y	*Polatnick Ida †	903	housewife	68	"
	Z	Wallace Anna †	903	"	38	"
240						
	A	Wallace Irving	903	painter	41	"
	B	Sirota Harry	903	butcher	44	16 W Selden
	C	*Sirota Lillian †	903	housewife	41	16 "
	D	Sirota Melvin	903	chemist	22	16 "
	E	Horowitz Jacob H	903	merchant	50	787 Morton
	F	Horowitz Milton	903	clerk	20	787 "
	G	Horowitz Sadie †	903	housewife	49	787 "
	H	Horowitz Sylvia †	903	clerk	23	787 "
	K	Goldberg Anna †	907	housewife	32	here
	L	Goldberg Harry	907	mechanic	40	"
	M	Schwartz Isaac	907	butcher	43	"
	N	Schwartz Rachel †	907	housewife	32	"
	O	Ford Hyman	907	pharmacist	32	7 Landor rd
	P	Ford Lilian †	907	housewife	30	7 "
	R	Zimmerman Anne †	907	"	65	7 "
	S	Silverman Abraham	911	manufacturer	44	here
	T	*Silverman Frances †	911	housewife	43	"
	U	Silverman Victor	911	clerk	22	"
	V	Shulman Alice †	911	artist	26	11 Lorne
	W	Shulman Benjamin	911	accountant	28	here

Page.	Letter.	Full Name.	Residence, Jan. 1, 1941.	Occupation.	Supposed Age.	Reported Residence, Jan. 1, 1940. Street and Number.

Morton Street—Continued

Page.	Letter.	Full Name.	Residence, Jan. 1, 1941.	Occupation.	Supposed Age.	Reported Residence, Jan. 1, 1940. Street and Number.
	X	Shulman Jack	911	laborer	23	here
	Y	*Shulman Max	911	metalworker	58	"
	Z	*Shulman Samuel	911	plumber	32	"
241						
	A	*Shulman Sarah—†	911	housewife	55	"
	B	Stern Etta—†	911	"	48	"
	C	*Stern Nathan	911	carpenter	52	"
	D	Gaffer Bertha F—†	915	housewife	29	"
	E	Gaffer Samuel W	915	attorney	29	"
	F	*Horowitz Louis—†	915	electrician	50	"
	G	*Horowitz Molly—†	915	housewife	53	"
	H	Horowitz Susan—†	915	clerk	20	"
	K	Hamberg Celia—†	915	housewife	50	"
	L	Hamberg Isadore	915	tailor	63	"
	M	*Dorfman Edward	915	printer	40	"
	N	*Dorfman Jean—†	915	housewife	34	"
	O	Rossman Dorothy—†	915	"	27	"
	P	Rossman Nathan	915	engineer	29	"
	R	Lown Harry	915	pharmacist	38	"
	S	Lown Jean—†	915	housewife	40	"
	T	Dantowitz Isaac	915	operator	54	"
	U	Dantowitz Pearl—†	915	housewife	53	"
	V	Green Bernard	915	collector	35	29 Babson
	W	Green Ruth—†	915	housewife	31	29 "
	X	Raverby Jacob	915	pharmacist	29	here
	Y	Raverby Sophia E—†	915	housewife	27	"
	Z	Margolis Abraham	915	pharmacist	43	"
242						
	A	Margolis Frances—†	915	housewife	46	"
	B	Margolis Herman L	915	clerk	21	"
	C	Gilbert Harry L	915	agent	42	"
	D	Gilbert Rose—†	915	housewife	42	"
	E	Delaney Florence G—†	915	"	41	"
	F	Delaney Francis C	915	clerk	22	"
	G	Delaney John J	915	cabel splicer	49	"
	H	Abrams Bernice—†	915	housewife	21	16 Westview
	K	Abrams George	915	machinist	21	92 Devon
	L	*Weinberg Ann—†	915	housewife	24	23 Evelyn
	M	Weinberg Jacob	915	merchant	24	23 "

Page	Letter	Full Name	Residence, Jan. 1, 1941	Occupation	Supposed Age	Reported Residence, Jan. 1, 1940. Street and Number

Norfolk Street

Page	Letter	Full Name	Residence, Jan. 1, 1941	Occupation	Supposed Age	Reported Residence, Jan. 1, 1940. Street and Number
	N	Goldstein Eva †	480	housewife	45	41 Fabyan
	O	Goldstein Samuel	480	manager	44	41 "
	P	Goldstein Saul	480	student	23	41 "
	R	Shapiro Bessie †	482	housewife	53	here
	S	Shapiro Samuel	482	clerk	59	"
	T	Fainzin Norman	482	salesman	25	80 Mountain av
	U	Fainzin Sarah †	482	housewife	50	80 "
	V	Fainzin Seymour	482	pharmacist	54	80 "
	W	Hoffman Eva †	486	housewife	48	578 Blue Hill av
	X	Hoffman Martin	486	clerk	28	578 "
	Y	Hoffman Samuel	486	salesman	50	578 "
	Z	Hoffman Sylvia †	486	housewife	21	578 "
243						
	A	Cunningham Oscar	486	retired	67	here
	B	Levin Anna †	486	housewife	65	"
	C	Levin Sophia †	486	clerk	42	"
	D	Spitz Morris	486	salesman	44	305 Fuller
	E	Spitz Sadie †	486	housewife	38	305 "
	F	Ingall Rebecca †	484	"	45	here
	G	Ingall Samuel M	494	pharmacist	51	"
	H	Cohen Gertrude †	494	housewife	43	595 Morton
	K	Cohen Joseph L	494	merchant	43	595 "
	L	Boyle Archibald	498	clerk	32	here
	M	Boyle Margaret †	498	housewife	71	"
	N	Boyle Murdock	498	carpenter	71	"
	O	MacDonald John P	498	"	60	"
	P	MacDonald Margaret A †	498	housewife	60	"
	R	Clayman Annie †	502	forewoman	29	"
	S	Clayman Benjamin	502	clerk	65	"
	T	Clayman Rebecca †	502	housewife	65	"
	U	Hershoff Blanche †	502	saleswoman	28	"
	V	Hershoff Dora †	502	housewife	58	"
	W	Hershoff Samuel	502	jeweler	58	"
	X	Hershoff Simon	502	"	57	"
	Y	Salata Ida †	502	housewife	66	Peabody
	Z	Kaslosky Elinor †	502	"	27	here
244						
	A	Kaslosky Stanley	502	mechanic	27	"
	B	Blanchette Joseph E	506	ironworker	42	"

Page	Letter	Full Name.	Residence, Jan. 1, 1941.	Occupation.	Supposed Age.	Reported Residence, Jan. 1, 1940. Street and Number.

Norfolk Street Continued

Page	Letter	Full Name	Residence	Occupation	Age	Reported Residence
	C	Blanchette Lily †	506	housewife	39	here
	D	Rosenbloom Ethel A †	506	"	32	"
	E	Rosenbloom Morris	506	bookkeeper	37	"
	F	Seidler Daniel	506	entertainer	28	"
	G	Seidler Hannah †	506	housewife	64	"
	H	Seidler Lillian †	506	clerk	34	"
	K	Seidler Leo	506	artist	65	"
	L	Coffey Helen †	510	nurse	32	"
	M	Coffey May †	510	housewife	70	"
	N	Frechette Nellie †	510	"	23	"
	O	Frechette Ralph	510	chef	31	"
	P	Lynds Anna †	510	housewife	42	"
	R	Lynds Elgin	510	clerk	46	"
	S	Furman Anne †	526	housewife	29	"
	T	Furman Jacob	526	merchant	33	"
	U	Weinberg Charlotte †	529	housewife	35	25 Astoria
	V	Weinberg Harry	529	tailor	58	25 "
	W	Weinberg Mary †	529	housewife	58	25 "
	X	Weinberg Maurice A	529	agent	37	25 "
	Y	Kramer Abraham	530	foreman	54	here
	Z	Kramer Dora †	530	housewife	53	"
245						
	A	Kramer Sidney	530	clerk	32	"
	B	Pasquantonio Albert	530	salesman	22	"
	C	Pasquantonio Muriel †	530	clerk	22	"
	D	Milch Annie †	533	housewife	38	"
	E	Milch Norbert	533	electrician	37	"
	F	*Taylor Annie †	533	housewife	60	"
	G	*Taylor Ernest	533	retired	59	"
	H	Ginsburg Jean †	533	housewife	32	Rhode Island
	K	Ginsburg Samuel I	533	salesman	34	"
	L	Silverstein Anne †	533	housewife	34	here
	M	Silverstein Julius	533	painter	35	"
	N	Gilman Louis	537	"	45	"
	O	Gilman Sarah †	537	housewife	43	"
	P	Fishgal Abraham	537	merchant	60	"
	R	Fishgal Sadie †	537	housewife	53	"
	S	Lawrence Albert T	537	salesman	46	"
	T	Lawrence Lena †	537	housewife	43	"
	U	Lawrence Maxine †	537	secretary	20	"
	V	Levine Isaac	541	realtor	63	"

Page	Letter	Full Name	Residence, Jan. 1, 1941	Occupation	Supposed Age	Reported Residence, Jan. 1, 1940. Street and Number

Norfolk Street Continued

Page	Letter	Full Name	Residence, Jan. 1, 1941	Occupation	Supposed Age	Reported Residence, Jan. 1, 1940. Street and Number
	W	Levine Mary †	541	housewife	62	here
	X	Cohen Dora †	541	"	68	"
	Y	Cohen Harry	541	salesman	36	"
	Z	Cohen Morris	541	chef	47	"
246						
	A	Freeman Esther †	541	housewife	43	"
	B	Freeman Nathan	541	plumber	47	"
	C	*Ostrofsky Barney	551	laborer	36	"
	D	Ostrofsky I Robert	551	attorney	35	"
	E	Ostrofsky Ralph	551	student	27	"
	F	*Ostrofsky Sarah †	551	housewife	71	"
	G	*Ostrofsky Solomon	551	retired	72	"
	H	Ginsberg Esther †	551	housewife	33	29 Wyoming
	K	Ginsberg George	551	agent	37	29 "
	L	Schlager Dora †	551	housewife	68	here
	M	Schlager Samuel	551	retired	71	"
	N	*Kramer Bluma †	555	housewife	52	"
	O	Kramer Louis	555	clerk	26	"
	P	Kramer Morris	555	jeweler	54	"
	R	Kramer Tillie †	555	clerk	21	"
	S	*Binder Abraham	555	manufacturer	46	"
	T	Binder Arthur	555	salesman	25	"
	U	Binder Herbert	555	clerk	21	"
	V	*Binder Pauline †	555	housewife	42	"
	W	Weiner Esther †	555	"	38	"
	X	Weiner Morris	555	jeweler	41	"
	Y	*Rosen Anna †	557	clerk	25	"
	Z	*Spiegel Louis	557	foreman	32	"
247						
	A	*Spiegel Ruth †	557	housewife	30	"
	B	Jacobs Annie †	557	"	59	31 Gayland
	C	Jacobs Myer	557	retired	61	31 "
	D	Jacobs Yetta †	557	clerk	27	31 "
	E	*Astrachan Anna †	557	housewife	74	here
	F	*Rubin Elizabeth †	557	"	46	"
	G	Rubin Melvin	557	student	20	"
	H	Rubin Samuel	557	mechanic	17	"
	K	Goodkin Gertrude †	563	housewife	23	55 Hawthorne rd
	L	Goodkin Harry	563	salesman	27	55 "
	M	Arbit Jacob	563	pedler	24	46 Astoria
	N	Arbit Muriel †	563	housewife	23	46 "

Page	Letter	Full Name.	Residence, Jan. 1, 1941.	Occupation.	Supposed Age.	Reported Residence, Jan. 1, 1940. Street and Number.

Norfolk Street—Continued

Page	Letter	Full Name.	Residence, Jan. 1, 1941.	Occupation.	Supposed Age.	Reported Residence, Jan. 1, 1940. Street and Number.
	O	Weisberg Edna—†	563	housewife	32	here
	P	Weisberg Maurice J	563	furrier	35	"
	R	Corman Ann—†	563	housewife	29	54 Johnston rd
	S	Corman George	563	lithographer	29	54 "
	T	Hamlin Abraham	563	clerk	45	here
	U	Hamlin Israel B	563	"	22	"
	V	Hamlin Jennie—†	563	housewife	43	"
	W	Aronson Harry	563	salesman	53	"
	X	Aronson Nathan	563	clerk	20	"
	Y	Aronson Sonia—†	563	housewife	43	"
	Z	Kelton Bertha—†	563	"	43	"
248						
	A	Kelton Robert V	563	janitor	44	"
	D	Goldberg Samuel	565	clerk	38	4 Vinal
	E	Goldberg Shirley—†	565	housewife	37	4 "
	B	Koffman Harry	565	merchant	40	here
	C	Koffman Mildred—†	565	housewife	35	"
	F	Cohen Lena—†	565	"	41	"
	G	Cohen Samuel	565	finisher	40	"
	H	*Green Fannie—†	565	housewife	45	"
	K	Green Reuben	565	salesman	52	"
	L	*Rubinovitz Rose—†	565	clerk	56	"
	O	Moldau Bertha—†	565	housewife	46	"
	P	Moldau Oscar	565	pharmacist	46	"
	R	Goldman Nathan	566	manufacturer	48	"
	S	*Sittig Albert	566	salesman	43	England
	T	*Sittig Elsa—†	566	housewife	41	"
	U	Lampert Charles	566	chauffeur	45	here
	V	Lampert Mary—†	566	housewife	39	"
	X	Noon Elsie—†	568	"	42	387 Norfolk
	Y	Noon Julius	568	buyer	48	387 "
	Z	Lief Benjamin	568	watchmaker	36	here
249						
	A	Lief Evelyn—†	568	clerk	21	"
	B	Lief Louis	568	watchmaker	49	"
	C	*Lief Rose—†	568	housewife	49	"
	D	Lief Sarah—†	568	clerk	22	"
	E	Cherner Bella—†	569	"	22	"
	F	Cherner Myer	569	tailor	36	"
	G	*Cherner Peter	569	"	60	"
	H	*Cherner Rebecca—†	569	housewife	55	"

Page	Letter	Full Name	Residence, Jan. 1, 1941	Occupation	Supposed Age	Reported Residence Jan. 1, 1940 Street and Number

Norfolk Street Continued

Page	Letter	Full Name	Residence	Occupation	Age	Reported Residence
	K	Cherner Samuel	569	bartender	30	here
	L	Koster David	569	broker	64	"
	M	Koster Deborah †	569	housewife	65	"
	N	Koster Leah †	569	clerk	31	"
	O	Koster Mildred †	569	"	37	"
	P	Koster William	569	upholsterer	34	"
	R	Berzon Eli	569	blacksmith	60	"
	S	Berzon Esther †	569	housewife	48	"
	T	*Spiegel Max	569	stitcher	43	"
	U	Chamish Alice †	570	housewife	34	"
	V	Chamish George J	570	auditor	35	"
	W	Sadwin Belle †	570	housewife	38	1333 Blue Hill av
	X	Sadwin Morton	570	manufacturer	40	1333 "
	Y	Dronsick Alice †	571	clerk	43	here
	Z	Dronsick Edward	571	pharmacist	48	"
250						
	A	Gordon Martin	571	student	20	"
	B	Green Rose †	571	housewife	65	"
	C	Goldman Hyman	571	tailor	53	745 Morton
	D	Goldman Samuel	571	bookkeeper	26	745 "
	E	Goldman Sophie †	571	housewife	52	745 "
	F	Lidman Edward	571	salesman	46	here
	G	Lidman Grace †	571	clerk	22	"
	H	Lidman Rebecca †	571	housewife	42	"
	K	Romer Sidney	571	salesman	38	"
	L	Shepard Eileen †	573	housewife	39	32 Marcella
	M	Shepard John W	573	laborer	58	32 "
	N	Norwood Margaret C †	573	housewife	62	here
	O	Norwood Roy H	573	salesman	62	"
	P	Berggren Constance †	574	housewife	34	84 Shepton
	R	Berggren Karl	574	electrician	40	84 "
	S	Jacobs Abraham	574	packer	56	here
	T	Jacobs Marie †	574	clerk	26	"
	U	Jacobs Meta †	574	housewife	54	"
	V	Tischler Maurice	574	chef	44	"
	W	Berkowitz Alice †	577	housewife	26	27 Greendale rd
	X	Berkowitz Benjamin	577	manager	29	27 "
	Y	*Flom Jennie †	577	housewife	56	27 "
	Z	*Flom Joseph	577	carpenter	53	27 "
251						
	A	Flom Sylvia †	577	clerk	23	27 "

Page	Letter	Full Name	Residence, Jan. 1 1941	Occupation	Supposed Age	Reported Residence, Jan. 1, 1940. Street and Number.
		Norfolk Street—Continued				
	B	Landy Dora—†	577	housewife	50	here
	C	Landy Frank	577	salesman	54	"
	D	Landy Minnie—†	577	clerk	25	"
	E	Landy Rose—†	577	teacher	31	"
	F	Cohen Adelaide—†	577	bookkeeper	30	"
	G	Cohen Amelia—†	577	housewife	56	"
	H	Cohen John J	577	student	21	"
	L	Cohen S Julia—†	577	attorney	31	"
	K	Cohen Samuel	577	cigarmaker	59	"
	M	Martini Frank	578	clerk	55	"
	N	Martini John	578	retired	60	"
	O	Martini John F	578	student	20	"
	P	Martini Paul J	578	engineer	34	"
	R	Martini Rose J—†	578	teacher	31	"
	S	*Wienberg Max	578	tailor	58	"
	T	Wienberg Nathan	578	florist	26	"
	U	Zaltzman Benjamin	578	butcher	43	"
	V	Zaltzman Bessie—†	578	housewife	38	"
	W	*Green Anna—†	581	"	33	"
	X	*Green Bessie—†	581	"	61	"
	Y	Green Irving	581	manager	35	"
	Z	Green Max	581	musician	65	"
252						
	A	Cline Grace E—†	581	housewife	47	"
	B	Cline Jacob	581	optician	51	"
	C	Swartz David J	581	merchant	49	"
	D	Swartz Rose S—†	581	clerk	52	"
	E	Kogos Joseph	585	salesman	64	"
	F	Kogos Minnie—†	585	housewife	64	"
	G	Spector Aaron	585	engineer	45	"
	H	Spector Myrtle S—†	585	housewife	45	"
	K	Godefroi Clara—†	585	"	53	"
	L	Godefroi Harry J	585	manufacturer	55	"
	M	*Spyer Cornelia—†	585	housewife	85	"
	N	Mamuchin Abe	586	designer	29	"
	O	Mamuchin Anna—†	586	housewife	46	"
	P	Mamuchin Mildred—†	586	"	29	"
	R	Mamuchin Nathan	586	designer	54	"
	S	Ribok Daniel	586	carpenter	51	"
	T	Ribok Helen—†	586	clerk	21	"
	U	*Ribok Rose—†	586	housewife	50	"

Norfolk Street—Continued

Page	Letter	Full Name	Residence, Jan. 1, 1941	Occupation	Reported Age	Reported Residence, Jan. 1, 1940. Street and Number
	V	Ribok Samuel	586	carpenter	25	here
	W	English J George	589	farmer	67	"
	X	English Lillian W—†	589	housewife	63	"
	Y	English Lucile—†	589	secretary	36	"
	Z	Barnes Mary O—†	589	at home	69	"
253						
	A	St George Christine—†	589	stenographer	22	45 Mattapan
	B	Cangiona Archie	589	baker	21	here
	C	Grello Pasquale	589	"	42	"
	D	Grello Sussie—†	589	housewife	26	"
	E	Isaacs Flora—†	600	"	36	"
	F	Isaacs Louis H	600	manager	40	"
	G	Uminsky Edward	600	contractor	57	"
	H	Uminsky Jennie—†	600	housewife	47	"
	K	Uminsky Nathan	600	clerk	28	"
	L	Uminsky Norman	600	"	22	"
	M	*Goldstein Dora—†	604	housewife	51	"
	N	Goldstein Jacob	604	merchant	52	"
	O	Goldstein Nathan	604	clerk	25	"
	P	Goldstein Rose—†	604	"	23	"
	R	Blake Lillian E—†	604	housekeeper	38	"
	S	McGrath John F	604	mechanic	36	"
	T	McGrath Michael F	604	teamster	64	"
	U	Lurraine Harry	604	salesman	35	"
	V	Lurraine Mildred—†	604	housewife	29	"
	W	Deagle Herbert J	608	carpenter	53	"
	X	MacDonald Evelyn—†	608	clerk	25	"
	Y	MacDonald Linus	608	carpenter	66	"
	Z	MacDonald Marion—†	608	housekeeper	28	"
254						
	A	MacDonald Mary L—†	608	housewife	51	"
	B	Owens Mary M—†	612	"	37	"
	C	Owens Philip J	612	salesman	40	"
	D	Boyle Helen J—†	612	clerk	27	"
	E	Boyle Mary A—†	612	housewife	65	"

Rich Street

Page	Letter	Full Name	Residence, Jan. 1, 1941	Occupation	Reported Age	Reported Residence, Jan. 1, 1940. Street and Number
	F	Smith Frederick H	11	jeweler	74	here
	G	Smith Gordon	11	salesman	46	"
	H	Smith Mary G—†	11	housewife	70	"

Page.	Letter	Full Name	Residence, Jan. 1, 1941.	Occupation.	Supposed Age.	Reported Residence, Jan. 1, 1940. Street and Number.

Rich Street—Continued

Page.	Letter	Full Name	Residence, Jan. 1, 1941.	Occupation.	Supposed Age.	Reported Residence, Jan. 1, 1940. Street and Number.
	K	Fish Clarence L	12	salesman	75	here
	L	Hall Angus	14	painter	67	"
	M	Hall Lena—†	14	housewife	63	"
	N	Anderson John A	17	baker	22	"
	O	Anderson John M	17	carpenter	49	"
	P	Anderson Margaret—†	17	housewife	39	"
	R	Cummings Dorothy E—†	18	"	24	"
	S	Cummings John J	18	electrician	27	"
	T	Preen David	18	laborer	48	"
	U	Preen Margaret—†	18	housewife	48	"
	V	Fahey Joseph R	19	operator	38	"
	W	Fahey Mary M—†	19	housewife	40	"
	X	Halstock Henry J	20	upholsterer	75	55 Wilcock
	Y	Halstock Mary—†	20	housewife	74	55 "
	Z	Axelson Pearl—†	21	"	47	here
255						
	A	Axelson Sidney	21	salesman	45	"
	B	Ralston John E	22	U S N	45	"
	C	Ralston Justine—†	22	housewife	43	"
	D	Holte Agnes—†	24	"	42	"
	E	Holte John	24	painter	45	"
	F	Holte Paul	24	machinist	23	"

West Selden Street

Page.	Letter	Full Name	Residence, Jan. 1, 1941.	Occupation.	Supposed Age.	Reported Residence, Jan. 1, 1940. Street and Number.
	G	Maister Frieda—†	11	saleswoman	30	here
	H	*White Rebecca—†	11	housewife	40	"
	K	White Samuel	11	salesman	40	"
	L	Datz Jacob	11	"	25	955 Morton
	M	Datz Pauline—†	11	housewife	24	here
	N	Gaffer Morris	11	manufacturer	48	"
	O	*Gaffer Sadie—†	11	housewife	48	"
	P	Gaffer Sarah—†	11	student	22	"
	R	Werner Bessie E—†	17	housewife	51	"
	S	Werner Joseph J	17	salesman	55	"
	T	Bloomberg Philip L	17	"	35	"
	U	Bloomberg Sally R—†	17	housewife	35	"
	V	Goldstein Celia—†	17	"	63	"
	W	Goldstein David M	17	manufacturer	77	"
	X	King Matthew	21	attorney	39	"
	Y	King Winifred—†	21	housewife	26	"

West Selden Street Continued

Page	Letter	Full Name	Residence, Jan. 1, 1941	Occupation	Supposed Age	Reported Residence, Jan. 1, 1940. Street and Number
	Z	Goodman Esther †	21	housewife	37	here
256						
	A	Goodman Herman	21	printer	42	"
	B	Jersky Evelyn F †	25	housewife	23	"
	C	Jersky Irving	25	salesman	27	"
	D	Rogoff Abraham M	25	foreman	56	"
	E	Rogoff Joseph S	25	artist	24	"
	F	Rogoff Sarah C †	25	housewife	49	"
	G	Issenberg David	25	salesman	23	"
	H	*Issenberg Pearl †	25	housewife	54	"
	K	Issenberg Solomon	25	salesman	56	"
	L	Goldberg Israel	29	"	58	"
	M	Goldberg Mollie †	29	housewife	57	"
	N	Goldberg Rae R †	29	dietitian	26	"
	O	Porter Louis	29	glazier	58	"
	P	*Porter Sarah †	29	housewife	58	"
	R	Wilson Abraham	29	glazier	29	Worcester
	S	Wilson Esther †	29	housewife	28	"
	T	Manin Ida †	33	"	39	here
	U	Manin Joseph	33	jeweler	46	"
	V	Manin Milton	33	shipper	23	"
	X	Covall Hyman	33	jobber	44	"
	W	Covall Mildred †	33	housewife	38	"
	Y	Krips Jennie †	37	"	54	"
	Z	Krips Leah †	37	clerk	32	"
257						
	A	Krips Max	37	tailor	59	"
	B	Sorota Benjamin	37	"	45	9 Theodore
	C	*Sorota Dora †	37	housewife	40	9 "
	D	Sorota George	37	student	20	9 "
	E	Weitzner Alice †	41	housewife	38	here
	F	Weitzner Morris	41	engineer	42	"
	G	Fieldman Ethel †	41	housewife	40	"
	H	Fieldman William	41	furrier	42	"
	K	Coblentz Abraham S	45	salesman	22	"
	L	Coblentz Harry	45	"	54	"
	M	Coblentz Lucy †	45	housewife	47	"
	N	*Melnick Gussie †	45	stitcher	50	815 Morton
	O	Prensky Abraham	45	gasfitter	46	here
	P	Prensky Seldo †	45	housewife	44	"
	R	Linsky Annie †	49	"	60	"

Page	Letter	Full Name	Residence, Jan. 1, 1941.	Occupation	Supposed Age.	Reported Residence, Jan. 1, 1940. Street and Number.

West Selden Street—Continued

Page	Letter	Full Name	Residence, Jan. 1, 1941.	Occupation	Supposed Age.	Reported Residence, Jan. 1, 1940. Street and Number.
	S	Linsky Jacob	49	tailor	60	here
	T	Manecopsky Bella—†	49	housewife	35	"
	U	Manecopsky Joseph	49	salesman	39	"
	V	Pransky Abraham	49	electrician	46	"
	W	Pransky Edith—†	49	housewife	44	"
	X	Davis Hyman W	55	bookkeeper	36	"
	Y	Davis Jacob	55	salesman	31	"
	Z	Davis Mary—†	55	housewife	33	"
258						
	A	Leahy Annie A—†	55	"	60	"
	B	Leahy Edward M	55	fireman	67	"
	C	Leahy John P	55	clerk	26	"
	D	Leahy Joseph W	55	electrician	23	"
	E	Murphy Catherine G—†	55	housekeeper	53	"
	F	Arno Constance—†	59	housewife	28	101 Maxwell
	G	Arno Samuel	59	attorney	32	101 "
	H	Cassarino Frank	59	laborer	22	here
	K	Cassarino Mary—†	59	housewife	48	"
	L	Cassarino Santo	59	student	30	"
	M	Ginsberg Jeannette—†	59	clerk	30	"
	N	*Ginsberg Lena—†	59	housewife	68	"
	O	*Ginsberg Max	59	retired	63	"
	P	Sheltry Anna—†	63	housewife	39	96 Burrell
	R	Sheltry Joseph	63	laborer	33	96 "
	S	Hanlon Charles W	63	caretaker	27	here
	T	Hanlon Florence W—†	63	housewife	33	"
	V	Silverman Abraham	65	tailor	58	"
	W	Silverman Irving	65	student	21	"
	X	Silverman Jennie—†	65	housewife	47	"
	Y	Kingsberg Benjamin	65	plumber	46	"
	Z	*Kingsberg Eva—†	65	housewife	44	"
259						
	A	*Lunchick Esther—†	67	"	42	"
	B	Lunchick Hyman	67	cleaner	41	"
	C	Horowitz Clara—†	67	housewife	35	"
	D	Horowitz Morris	67	attorney	42	"
	E	Goldberg Faye—†	71	housewife	31	"
	F	Goldberg Louis	71	salesman	35	"
	G	Weiner Morris	71	manager	29	"
	H	Weiner Rose—†	71	housewife	28	"
	M	Merrill Ruth—†	71	housekeeper	43	"

Page.	Letter.	Full Name.	Residence, Jan. 1, 1941.	Occupation.	Supposed Age.	Reported Residence, Jan. 1, 1940. Street and Number

West Selden Street—Continued

Page.	Letter.	Full Name.	Residence, Jan. 1, 1941.	Occupation.	Supposed Age.	Reported Residence, Jan. 1, 1940. Street and Number
	K	Newman Barney	71	salesman	37	here
	L	Newman Minnie—†	71	housewife	30	"
	N	*Raverby Bernard	71	merchant	29	20 Dyer
	O	Raverby Pearl—†	71	housewife	27	20 "
	P	Cohen Philip	71	steamfitter	40	here
	R	*Cohen Sonia—†	71	housewife	35	"
	S	Mendler Bertha—†	71	"	29	"
	T	Mendler Milton J	71	salesman	40	"
	U	Davis Arthur I	75–77	merchant	34	37 Peacevale rd
	V	Davis Edith L—†	75–77	housewife	33	37 "
	W	*Soltz Annie—†	75–77	"	48	here
	X	Soltz Jacob	75–77	merchant	48	"
	Y	Soltz Joseph	75–77	salesman	22	"
	Z	Sandler Charles	79–81	carpenter	24	80 Walnut av
260						
	A	*Sandler Fannie—†	79–81	housewife	57	80 "
	B	*Sandler Louis	79–81	clerk	27	80 "
	C	*Sandler Max	78–81	merchant	60	80 "
	D	Sandler Mildred—†	79–81	secretary	30	80 "
	E	Cristadora John	79–81	baker	43	here
	F	Cristadora Mary—†	79–81	housewife	40	"
	G	Duchin Philip	83	merchant	22	"
	H	*Duchin Rose—†	83	housewife	43	"
	K	*Duchin Samuel	83	tailor	45	"
	L	Stern Abraham M	85	operator	41	"
	M	Stern Katherine—†	85	housewife	40	"
	N	Stanley Cletus C	87	salesman	34	"
	O	Stanley Dorothy—†	87	housewife	33	"
	P	Brown Margaret—†	87	housekeeper	71	Watertown
	R	Sullivan Ann—†	87	teacher	56	here
	S	Sullivan Margaret—†	87	"	45	"
	T	Slotnick Harry	91	salesman	39	79 W Selden
	U	Slotnick Marion—†	91	housewife	36	79 "
	V	Zola Edna S—†	91	clerk	21	here
	W	*Zola Mollie—†	91	housewife	44	"
	X	Zola Rose—†	91	clerk	23	"
	Y	Zola Simon	91	designer	48	"
	Z	Baker Catherine—†	93	housewife	38	"
261						
	A	Baker Joseph	93	pressman	40	"
	B	Holland Joseph M	93	retired	76	"

Page.	Letter.	Full Name.	Residence, Jan. 1, 1941.	Occupation.	Supposed Age.	Reported Residence, Jan. 1, 1940. Street and Number.

West Selden Street—Continued

Page.	Letter.	Full Name.	Residence, Jan. 1, 1941.	Occupation.	Supposed Age.	Reported Residence, Jan. 1, 1940.
	C	Holland Mary—†	93	secretary	51	here
	D	Holland Teresa—†	93	teacher	30	"
	E	Green George J	97	salesman	31	"
	F	Green Josephine—†	97	housewife	30	"
	G	Molloy John	97	porter	42	"
	H	Stewart Elizabeth M—†	97	housekeeper	44	"
	K	*Lewis Frances—†	105	housewife	40	"
	L	*Lewis Fred	105	salesman	44	"
	M	Miller David F	105	"	50	"
	N	Miller Elizabeth D—†	105	housewife	50	"
	O	Miller Ruth M—†	105	entertainer	22	"
	P	Levenson Arthur A	109–111	jeweler	29	"
	R	Levenson Lillian—†	109–111	housewife	29	"
	S	Kuttner Annie H—†	109–111	saleswoman	29	"
	T	Kuttner Elizabeth—†	109–111	housewife	60	"
	U	Kuttner Lazarus	109–111	retired	64	"
	V	Fraser Jennie L—†	115	teacher	58	"
	W	Fraser Wendell H	115	builder	46	"
	X	Lauwers Henry P	119	mechanic	40	"
	Y	Lauwers Mary R—†	119	housewife	38	"
	Z	Kent John S	119	foreman	44	"
262						
	A	Kent Mary R—†	119	housewife	37	"
	B	Sullivan Anita E—†	125	clerk	23	"
	C	Sullivan Edward	125	custodian	66	6 Woodlawn av
	D	Sullivan Florence—†	125	housewife	50	6 "
	E	Sullivan Robert L	125	B F D	25	here
	F	Sullivan Wilfred J	125	clerk	23	"
	G	Kent Alfred T	133	carpenter	73	"
	H	Kent Alma S—†	133	housewife	76	"
	K	Roode Eva—†	133	"	35	"
	L	Roode Lloyd E	133	accountant	35	"
	M	Rockman Aaron H	137	salesman	31	"
	N	*Rockman Alice—†	137	housewife	30	"
	O	Hart Albert C	137	plasterer	36	"
	P	Hart Charles J	137	"	39	"
	R	Hart Delia M—†	137	housewife	75	"
	S	Hart Ellen T—†	137	seamstress	37	"
	T	Hart Michael J	137	retired	75	"
	U	MacRae Catherine—†	141	housewife	44	"
	V	MacRae John F	141	welder	44	"

Page	Letter	Full Name	Residence, Jan. 1, 1941	Occupation	Supposed Age	Reported Residence Jan. 1, 1940, Street and Number

West Selden Street—Continued

Page	Letter	Full Name	Residence, Jan. 1, 1941	Occupation	Supposed Age	Reported Residence Jan. 1, 1940, Street and Number
	W	MacRae Agnes—†	141	housewife	68	here
	X	MacRae Alexander	141	engineer	70	"
	Y	Weinert Esther—†	145–147	housewife	48	"
	Z	Weinert Joseph	145–147	teacher	49	"
263						
	A	Trachtenberg Esther—†	145–147	housewife	47	"
	B	Trachtenberg Frances—†	145–147	entertainer	22	"
	C	Trachtenberg Philip	145–147	jeweler	56	"
	D	Flynn Mary J—†	149	housewife	68	"
	E	Flynn William J	149	retired	68	"
	F	Cazanove Max	149	"	67	"
	G	Davidson Albert D	149	clerk	38	"
	H	Davidson Elizabeth—†	149	housewife	36	"
	L	Walsh Alice—†	179	"	45	"
	M	Walsh Alice A—†	179	operator	24	"
	N	Walsh John J	179	salesman	29	"
	O	Walsh Patrick J	179	laborer	51	"
	P	Walsh Philip P	179	salesman	27	"
	R	Walsh Thomas V	179	seaman	22	"
	S	Leahy David D	181	mechanic	40	"
	T	Leahy John D	181	salesman	52	"
	U	Leahy John F	181	retired	74	"
	V	Peterson John A	189	mechanic	29	"
	W	Peterson Laura J—†	189	housewife	61	"
	X	Peterson Rose L—†	189	"	27	10 Whitney pk
	Y	Herrett Esther—†	189	"	30	here
	Z	Herrett Leonard	189	salesman	34	"
264						
	A	Crowley James F	191	mechanic	20	"
	B	Richards George E	191	"	42	"
	C	Richards Olive M—†	191	housewife	39	"
	D	Burke Gertrude—†	191	"	38	17 Halborn
	E	Burke James	191	laborer	40	17 "
	F	Logue Hannah—†	rear 191A	housekeeper	52	here
	G	Madden Josephine T—†	" 191A	housewife	27	"
	H	Madden Stephen F	" 191A	tree surgeon	29	"
	K	Kent Eunice—†	197	housewife	29	62 W Selden
	L	Kent Ralph	197	repairman	34	62 "
	M	Shea Gerald	203	seaman	20	here
	N	Shea James A	203	plumber	44	"
	O	Shea James J	203	U S N	22	"

Page.	Letter.	Full Name.	Residence, Jan. 1, 1941.	Occupation.	Supposed Age.	Reported Residence, Jan. 1, 1940. Street and Number.

West Selden Street—Continued

Page.	Letter.	Full Name.	Residence, Jan. 1, 1941.	Occupation.	Supposed Age.	Reported Residence, Jan. 1, 1940.
	P	Shea Sarah J—†	203	housewife	44	here
	R	Smith Alice E—†	211	stenographer	34	"
	S	Smith Edward C	211	retired	68	"
	T	Smith Mary L—†	211	stenographer	31	"
	U	Smith Mildred R—†	211	teacher	37	"
	V	Smith Ruth V—†	211	"	25	"
	W	Smith Walter E	211	electrician	28	"
	X	Beamfield Charles	215	retired	72	4 Lester pl
	Y	Coulter Elizabeth J—†	215	housewife	73	here
	Z	Coulter Theodore	215	chauffeur	28	"
265						
	A	Dahl Freeman	219	laborer	23	"
	B	Dahl Gladys—†	219	housewife	23	60 Newburg
	C	Dahl Marjorie—†	219	"	51	here
	D	Hoff Ole	219	retired	83	"
	E	Dooley Dorothy A—†	225	secretary	23	"
	F	Dooley Gertrude C—†	225	teacher	35	"
	G	Dooley Henry F	225	salesman	30	"
	H	Dooley Joseph	225	retired	70	"
	K	Dooley Pauline C—†	225	housewife	61	"
	L	Schell Anna C—†	229	"	65	"
	M	Schell William J	229	printer	63	"
	N	Schell William J, jr	229	machinist	25	"
	O	Taggart Margaret M—†	229	housewife	30	"
	P	Taggart Maurice J	229	clerk	33	"
	R	*Steinberg Bessie—†	231	housewife	48	"
	S	*Steinberg Hyman	231	tailor	49	"
	T	Steinberg Saul	231	salesman	23	"
	U	Steinberg Sylvia—†	231	student	20	"
	V	Shuman David W	231	butcher	36	36 Mountain av
	W	Shuman Minnie—†	231	housewife	33	36 "
	X	Isenberg Anna—†	233	"	37	here
	Y	Isenberg Bernard	233	agent	38	"
	Z	Nadler Charlotte L—†	233	stenographer	21	683 Walk Hill
266						
	A	Nadler Henry	233	housewife	53	683 "
	B	Nadler Samuel	233	salesman	54	683 "
	E	Haley Frances L—†	239	housewife	29	87 Centre
	F	Haley Joseph	239	reporter	37	87 "
	G	Himmelfart David	239	ropemaker	35	here
	H	Himmelfart Leah—†	239	housewife	30	"

Page.	Letter.	Full Name	Residence Jan. 1, 1941.	Occupation	Supposed Age	Reported Residence Jan. 1, 1940. Street and Number

West Selden Street—Continued

	K	Levy Ida—†	243	housewife	33	here
	L	Levy Nathan	243	clerk	37	"
	M	Myers Albert	243	manager	22	"
	N	Myers Bessie—†	243	housewife	46	"
	O	Myers Louis	243	electrician	23	"
	P	Myers Samuel J	243	chauffeur	49	"

Wilmore Street

	R	Hyman Eleanor—†	6	clerk	20	here
	S	*Hyman Fannie—†	6	housewife	54	"
	T	Hyman Samuel	6	tailor	56	"
	U	Markowitz Aura	6	merchant	27	28 Whitman
	V	Markowitz Sarah—†	6	saleswoman	28	here
	W	Wasserman Anna—†	6	housewife	44	"
	X	Wasserman Harry	6	foreman	47	"
	Y	Corman Alice—†	6	housewife	32	"
	Z	*Corman Anna—†	6	"	60	"
267						
	A	*Corman Herman	6	cutter	40	"
	B	Corman Israel	6	merchant	39	"
	C	Cohen Alice—†	7	saleswoman	23	"
	D	Cohen Elizabeth—†	7	housewife	58	"
	E	Cohen Melvin B	7	salesman	26	"
	F	Appel Annie—†	7	housewife	53	"
	G	Appel Bernard	7	student	20	"
	H	Appell Jacob	7	foreman	55	"
	K	Mofchun Israel	7	retired	76	"
	L	Mofchun Jeannette—†	7	housewife	68	"
	M	Webber Bernice—†	10	teacher	20	"
	[1]M	Webber Eva—†	10	housewife	45	"
	N	Webber Harry	10	manufacturer	45	"
	O	Cohen Alfred	10	electrician	37	"
	P	Cohen Jacob	10	operator	25	"
	R	Cohen Joseph	10	salesman	55	New York
	S	Cohen Michael	10	shoemaker	66	here
	T	Cohen Rachel—†	10	housewife	61	"
	U	Cohen William	10	shipper	24	"
	V	Fine Esther—†	10	housewife	32	"
	W	Sussman Eva—†	10	"	42	"
	X	Sussman Ruth—†	10	bookkeeper	20	"

Page	Letter	Full Name	Residence, Jan. 1, 1941	Occupation	Supposed Age	Reported Residence, Jan. 1, 1940. Street and Number

Wilmore Street—Continued

Page	Letter	Full Name	Residence, Jan. 1, 1941	Occupation	Supposed Age	Reported Residence, Jan. 1, 1940. Street and Number
	Y	Sussman Saul	10	foreman	41	here
	Z	Obsbaum Viola—†	11	housewife	38	"
268						
	A	Obsbaum William	11	electrician	38	"
	B	Silverman Robert	11	retired	62	"
	C	Weener Beatrice—†	11	student	21	"
	[1]C	Weener Isaac	11	proprietor	52	"
	D*	Weener Rose—†	11	housewife	50	"
	E*	Sandman Daniel	11	chauffeur	59	"
	F	Sandman Irving	11	shipper	24	"
	G*	Sandman Rose—†	11	housewife	55	"
	H	Miller Harold H	14	salesman	40	20 Bowdoin av
	K	Miller Lillian—†	14	housewife	35	20 "
	L*	Simon Esther—†	14	"	53	here
	M	Simon Joseph	14	carpenter	57	"
	N	Simon Max	14	merchant	26	"
	O	Simon Morris	14	"	23	"
	P	Stern Lilly—†	14	housewife	43	"
	R	Stern Morris	14	merchant	44	"
	S*	Rudkin Fannie—†	15	housewife	55	"
	T	Rudkin Frank	15	tailor	65	"
	U	Rudkin Irene—†	15	saleswoman	21	"
	V	Rudkin Louis	15	accountant	32	"
	W	Siegel Esther—†	15	housewife	33	"
	X	Siegel Harry	15	manager	34	"
	Y*	Wittenberg Delia—†	15	housewife	59	"
	Z	Wittenberg Edward	15	salesman	31	"
269						
	A	Greenberg Libby—†	15	housewife	40	"
	B	Greenberg Myer	15	merchant	42	"
	[1]B	Fox Morris	18	salesman	43	"
	C	Fox Sophia—†	18	housewife	42	"
	D	Weiner Benjamin	18	retired	85	"
	E	Manosky Julia—†	18	housewife	25	"
	F	Manosky Philip	18	butcher	31	"
	G	Obsbaum Rebecca—†	18	housewife	69	"
	H*	Glassman Elizabeth—†	18	"	78	"
	K*	Glassman Samuel	18	retired	76	"
	L*	Engelson Ida—†	19	housewife	58	"
	M	Engelson Jacob	19	merchant	57	"
	N	Engelson Joseph	19	"	27	"

Page	Letter	Full Name	Residence Jan. 1, 1941	Occupation	Supposed Age	Reported Residence, Jan. 1, 1940. Street and Number

Wilmore Street Continued

Page	Letter	Full Name	Residence Jan. 1, 1941	Occupation	Supposed Age	Reported Residence, Jan. 1, 1940. Street and Number
	O	Raines Ethel †	19	housewife	33	here
	P	Raines Max	19	jeweler	34	"
	R	Seigel Bessie—†	19	housewife	60	"
	S	Shuman Celia—†	19	"	42	"
	T	Shuman Louie	19	chauffeur	45	"
	U	Fleishman Annie—†	19	housewife	44	"
	V	Fleishman Julius	19	tailor	49	"
	W	Blender Aida L—†	22	housewife	31	"
	X	Blender Louis J	22	attorney	33	"
	Y*	Fishman Eva—†	22	housewife	65	"
	Z	Fishman Ida—†	22	"	33	"
270						
	A	Fishman Isreal	22	retired	68	"
	B	Alpert Anna—†	22	stenographer	30	9 Courtland
	C	Alpert Esther—†	22	"	28	9 "
	D*	Alpert Jacob	22	merchant	68	9 "
	E*	Alpert Sarah—†	22	housewife	66	9 "
	F	Kauffman Irene—†	23	"	28	here
	G*	Kauffman Joseph	23	butcher	35	"
	H	Jacobson Ida—†	23	housewife	32	"
	K	Jacobson Manuel	23	contractor	32	"
	L	Nomerosky Mary—†	23	housewife	72	"
	M*	Hurwitz Goldie—†	23	"	72	"
	N	Rosenfield Bessie—†	23	"	37	"
	O	Rosenfield Hyman	23	mason	52	"
	P	Carver Sophie—†	26	housewife	65	"
	R	Wolfe Bessie—†	26	"	28	"
	S	Wolfe Charles	26	accountant	29	"
	T	Newman Etta—†	26	housewife	37	"
	U	Newman Joseph	26	salesman	34	"
	V	Stern David	26	merchant	43	"
	W	Stern Elizabeth—†	26	housewife	48	"
	X*	Isaacson Gertrude—†	27	"	53	"
	Y*	Isaacson Morris	27	butcher	58	"
	Z*	Saltzberg Leah—†	27	housewife	54	"
271						
	A	Binder Geraldine—†	27	secretary	22	"
	B	Binder Israel	27	manufacturer	49	"
	C	Binder Mary—†	27	housewife	45	"
	D*	Binder Bessie—†	27	"	50	"
	E*	Binder Nathan	27	manufacturer	54	"

Page	Letter	Full Name	Residence, Jan. 1, 1941	Occupation	Supposed Age	Reported Residence, Jan. 1, 1940. Street and Number

Wilmore Street—Continued

Page	Letter	Full Name	Residence, Jan. 1, 1941	Occupation	Supposed Age	Reported Residence, Jan. 1, 1940. Street and Number
	F	Isaacson Geraldine—†	27	housewife	21	here
	G	Isaacson Samuel	27	manager	23	"
	H	Brooks Annie—†	30	saleswoman	31	"
	K	Brooks Benjamin	30	laborer	28	"
	L	Moshin Ella—†	30	saleswoman	30	"
	M*	Moshin Mary—†	30	housewife	59	"
	N	Mitchell Edna—†	30	clerk	21	"
	O	Mitchell Morris	30	"	43	"
	P	Mitchell Rose—†	30	housewife	45	"
	R	Goldstein Fay—†	30	saleswoman	32	"
	S	Kaplan Kalman	30	tailor	66	"
	T	Kaplan Sarah—†	30	housewife	65	"
	U	Shanfield Evelyn—†	30	salesman	34	"

Woodlawn Avenue

Page	Letter	Full Name	Residence, Jan. 1, 1941	Occupation	Supposed Age	Reported Residence, Jan. 1, 1940. Street and Number
	V	Ladd Catherine—†	5	housewife	31	here
	W	Ladd George F	5	salesman	32	"
	X	LeBlanc John F	6	"	50	"
	Y	LeBlanc Mary—†	6	housewife	45	"
	Z	LeBlanc Robert J	6	custodian	22	"
272						
	A	Stanley Adoniram J	6	engineer	32	244 Almont
	B	Stanley Julia—†	6	housewife	32	244 "
	C	Cochran Angeline—†	7	operator	29	29 Nelson
	D	Cochran Margaret—†	7	housekeeper	66	29 "
	E	Francis Mary M—†	7	housewife	34	here
	F	Francis Philipp	7	clerk	31	"
	G	Driscoll John J	10	shipper	38	"
	H	Driscoll Marguerite—†	10	housewife	45	"
	K	Dixon Doris M—†	10	teacher	50	"
	L	Quinn Agustus	10	cook	74	"
	M	Quinn Nellie H—†	10	housewife	63	"
	N	Wishart M Emelene—†	10	teacher	40	"
	O	Hovey Dorothy—†	14	housewife	26	63 Rockdale
	P	Hovey Paul K	14	salesman	26	898 Cummins H'way
	R	O'Leary John C	16	electrician	35	149 Delhi
	S	O'Leary Vivian—†	16	housewife	26	149 "
	T	Durbin Francis W	16	clerk	21	here
	U	Durbin Leon F	16	chauffeur	47	"
	V	Durbin Mary—†	16	housewife	45	"

Page	Letter	Full Name	Residence, Jan. 1, 1941	Occupation	Supposed Age	Reported Residence, Jan. 1, 1940. Street and Number

Woodlawn Avenue—Continued

Page	Letter	Full Name	Residence, Jan. 1, 1941	Occupation	Supposed Age	Reported Residence, Jan. 1, 1940
	W	Richards Joseph	17	salesman	45	here
	X	Richards Marion G—†	17	housewife	43	"
	Y	Richards Rosemary—†	17	nurse	23	"
	Z	Smith Harold P	17	inspector	47	"
273						
	A	Smith Harriet M—†	17	housewife	45	"
	B	Smith Joseph T	17	carpenter	23	"
	C	Peterson Anna L—†	17	housewife	34	"
	D	Peterson Robert	17	roofer	51	"
	E	Urquhart Catherine—†	26	housewife	54	"
	F	Urquhart James L	26	clerk	33	"
	G	Urquhart Lorenzo	26	electrician	67	"
	H	Urquhart Thomas G	26	clerk	26	"
	K	Green Walter J	30	laborer	32	"
	L	Green Winifred—†	30	housewife	31	"
	M	Meehan Dorothy—†	30	cashier	28	"
	N	Meehan John J	30	printer	52	"
	O	Meehan Leonard F	30	clerk	24	"
	P	Meehan Mary A—†	30	housewife	42	"
	R	MacQuarrie Artemas	31	janitor	73	"
	S	MacQuarrie Sara—†	31	housewife	72	"
	T	Jacobsen Solomon	31	fisherman	59	"
	U	Jensen Anna—†	31	housewife	31	"
	V	Jensen Henry	31	carpenter	40	"

Ward 18—Precinct 3

CITY OF BOSTON

LIST OF RESIDENTS
20 YEARS OF AGE AND OVER

(NON-CITIZENS INDICATED BY ASTERISK)
(FEMALES INDICATED BY DAGGER)

AS OF

JANUARY 1, 1941

CITY OF BOSTON PRINTING DEPARTMENT

Page.	Letter	Full Name.	Residence, Jan. 1, 1941.	Occupation	Supposed Age	Reported Residence, Jan. 1, 1940. Street and Number.

300

Alabama Street

Page.	Letter	Full Name.	Residence, Jan. 1, 1941.	Occupation	Supposed Age	Reported Residence, Jan. 1, 1940.
300	A	Witt Edith—†	18	housewife	29	244 Almont
	B	Witt Nelson	18	chauffeur	31	244 "
	C*	Fredericksen Carley—†	18	housewife	43	here
	D*	Fredericksen John A	18	machinist	44	"
	E	Hayes Josephine T—†	19	housewife	28	"
	F	Hayes William D	19	repairman	27	"
	G	Sullivan Alice M—†	19	housewife	51	"
	H	Sullivan William J	19	instructor	51	"
	K	Sullivan William J	19	clerk	22	"
	L	Hayes Alice M—†	23	stenographer	23	"
	M	Hayes Josephine M—†	23	housewife	55	"
	N	Hayes Margaret J—†	23	clerk	26	"
	O	Hayes Thomas J	23	engineer	67	"
	P	Scully Walter	23	clerk	23	"
	R	Kimball Archie	25	leatherworker	30	"
	S	Kimball Dorothy—†	25	housewife	29	"
	T	Hohmann Charles F	25	fireman	55	"
	U	Hohmann Elizabeth F—†	25	housewife	56	"
	V	Monarch Katherine F—†	26	"	45	"
	W	Monarch Lester W	26	merchant	49	"
	X*	Johnson Annie L—†	30	housewife	64	187 Almont
	Y	Johnson Mildred—†	30	"	37	187 "
	Z	Johnson Walter E	30	clerk	36	187 "
301						
	A	Moran Augusta N—†	34	housewife	63	here
	B	Moran Thomas A	34	engineer	74	"
	C	Carlsen Anna—†	37	stenographer	31	"
	D	Carlsen Elsie—†	37	"	29	"
	E	Carlsen Helen—†	37	housekeeper	25	"
	F	Carlsen Marie—†	37	housewife	59	"
	G	Kocen May B—†	54	"	54	"
	H	Kocen William	54	letter carrier	56	"
	K	Fitton William	59	rubberworker	33	"
	L	Aronoff Bertha M—†	67	housewife	36	"
	M	Aronoff William	67	attorney	43	"
	N	DeSisto Angelo	95	laborer	54	"
	O	DeSisto Elvira—†	95	housewife	39	"
	P	Delcorso Angelo	101	clerk	59	"
	R	Delcorso Carmino	101	baker	20	"
	S	Delcorso Fred	101	clerk	21	"

Page.	Letter.	Full Name.	Residence, Jan. 1, 1944.	Occupation.	Supposed Age.	Reported Residence, Jan. 1, 1943. Street and Number.

Alabama Street—Continued

Page.	Letter.	Full Name.	Residence, Jan. 1, 1944.	Occupation.	Supposed Age.	Reported Residence, Jan. 1, 1943. Street and Number.
	T*	Decloroso Mary †	101	housewife	59	here
	U	Murphy Mary T †	111	"	42	"
	V	Murphy Patrick T	111	carpenter	42	"

Almont Street

Page.	Letter.	Full Name.	Residence, Jan. 1, 1944.	Occupation.	Supposed Age.	Reported Residence, Jan. 1, 1943. Street and Number.
	W	Teplitz Harvey	4	clerk	20	here
	X	Teplitz Hyman S	4	salesman	44	"
	Y	Teplitz Mae W †	4	housewife	44	"
	Z	Goodman Joseph	4	furrier	40	"
302						
	A	Goodman Shirley †	4	housewife	37	"
	B	Weiner Lillian †	4	"	27	17 Homestead
	C	Weiner Max	4	salesman	32	17 "
	D	Sullivan Cornelius D	6–8	inspector	58	here
	E	Sullivan Dorothy †	6–8	clerk	22	"
	F	Sullivan Jereome J	6–8	"	28	"
	G	Sullivan Mary C †	6–8	"	26	"
	H	Sullivan Mary J †	6–8	housewife	54	"
	K	Fried Charles	6–8	policeman	37	"
	L	Fried Edith †	6–8	housewife	28	"
	M	Mathey Sophie †	12	"	31	"
	N	Mathey T Joseph	12	salesman	28	"
	O	Quinlan Annie J †	12	housewife	71	"
	P	Quinlan John J	12	machinist	42	"
	R	Quinlan M Catherine †	12	secretary	44	"
	S	Broderick Clarence	12	messenger	33	"
	T	Broderick Dorothy †	12	housewife	31	"
	U	Barsky Albert	16	metalworker	43	"
	V	Barsky Esther †	16	housewife	39	"
	W	Borkow Edward H	16	salesman	20	"
	X	Borkow Sydney	16	manufacturer	49	"
	Y	Grossman Bernard L	16	attorney	34	20 Waumbeck
	Z	Ross David	16	chauffeur	57	here
303						
	A	Ross Rose †	16	housewife	52	"
	B	Driben Cecelia †	19	"	33	12 Tennis rd
	C	Driben Harry	19	merchant	35	12 "
	D	Goodale William	19	retired	53	here
	E	Shechman Barney	19	merchant	45	"
	F*	Shechman Lillian †	19	housewife	44	"

Page	Letter	Full Name	Residence, Jan. 1, 1941	Occupation	Supposed Age	Reported Residence, Jan. 1, 1940. Street and Number

Almont Street Continued

Page	Letter	Full Name	Residence, Jan. 1, 1941	Occupation	Supposed Age	Reported Residence, Jan. 1, 1940. Street and Number
	G	Sheehman Paul	19	chauffeur	23	here
	H	*Feingold Fannie †	20	housewife	46	"
	K	*Feingold Samuel	20	pedler	48	"
	L	Feingold Tillie †	20	clerk	21	"
	M	Harris Pearl †	20	"	24	"
	N	Harris Philip	20	carpenter	50	"
	O	*Harris Rebecca †	20	housewife	51	"
	P	Roomgeiler Annie †	20	"	48	"
	R	Roomgeiler Morris	20	painter	46	"
	S	Davis Edna †	21	pharmacist	24	"
	T	Davis Ella †	21	clerk	27	"
	U	Davis Fannie †	21	housewife	50	"
	V	Davis Frank	21	foreman	50	"
	W	Fleisher Gertrude †	21	clerk	35	"
	X	Fleisher Jacob	21	merchant	60	"
	Y	Grover Aaron	23	tailor	63	"
	Z	Grover Bessie †	23	housewife	60	"
304						
	A	Grover Frances †	23	clerk	25	"
	B	Zatsky Gertrude †	23	beautician	28	"
	C	Zatsky Israel	23	laborer	50	"
	D	Zatsky Max	23	barber	27	"
	E	Zatsky Sarah †	23	housewife	48	"
	F	O'Connor Margaret R †	24	"	49	"
	G	O'Connor William E	24	teacher	49	"
	H	Goldstein Ida †	25	housewife	65	"
	K	Kravetz David	25	tailor	43	"
	L	Kravetz Reva †	25	housewife	40	"
	M	Slishman Dorothy †	25	clerk	29	"
	N	Slishman Ida †	25	housewife	52	"
	O	Slishman Milton	25	clerk	22	"
	P	Slishman Samuel	25	metalworker	54	"
	R	O'Neill Elizabeth V †	26	physician	46	"
	S	O'Neill James W	26	salesman	43	"
	T	O'Neill Margaret A †	26	housewife	84	"
	U	Wiener Israel	27	manufacturer	47	"
	V	Wiener Rose †	27	housewife	40	"
	W	*Trachtenberg Anna †	27	"	60	"
	X	Trachtenberg Irving	27	accountant	34	18 Hildreth
	Y	Trachtenberg Leah †	27	housewife	33	here
	Z	*Glassman Clara †	29	"	32	15 Marden av

305

Almont Street Continued

Letter	Full Name	Residence, April 1, 1941	Occupation	Reputed Age	Reported Residence, April 1, 1940. Street and Number
A	Glassman Herman	29	merchant	40	15 Marden av
B	*Bryer David T	29	mech dentist	43	here
C	*Bryer Emma †	29	housewife	42	"
D	*Chernes Rebecca †	31	"	83	"
E	Helper Herbert	31	pharmacist	30	706 Walk Hill
F	Limansky Diana †	31	clerk	27	here
G	*Limansky Isaac	31	tailor	66	"
H	Limansky Rose †	31	housewife	55	"
K	Scotch Lillian †	31	"	50	"
L	Scotch Max	31	bricklayer	52	"
M	Scotch Norman	31	student	20	"
N	Goldberg John	33	tailor	40	"
O	Goldberg Max	33	broker	36	"
P	Goldberg Mollie †	33	housewife	65	"
R	Shaw Sophie †	33	"	25	"
S	Morris Harry	33	salesman	37	"
T	Morris Rose †	33	clerk	30	"
U	Olem Florence †	35	"	20	"
V	*Olem Hattie †	35	housewife	46	"
W	*Olem Leo	35	mover	47	"
X	Olem Sylvia †	35	clerk	22	"
Z	Gorfinkle Evelyn †	35	saleswoman	23	"
Y	*Gorfinkle Rebecca †	35	housewife	54	"
306					
A	Gorfinkle Samuel	35	tailor	63	"
B	*Katz Anna †	35	housewife	65	"
C	*Katz Casper	35	retired	65	"
D	*Klein Estelle †	37	housewife	40	"
E	Klein Max	37	salesman	45	"
F	*Rosenthal Rebecca †	37	housewife	68	"
G	Hazen Morris	37	tailor	50	"
H	Hazen Rebecca †	37	housewife	50	"
K	Pollack Carl	39	salesman	24	"
L	Pollack Rachel †	39	housewife	54	"
M	Pollack Robert	39	accountant	[illegible]	
N	Pollack Sydney S	39	[illegible]	[illegible]	
O	Brooks Frieda †	39	housewife	[illegible]	
P	Brooks Louis	39	[illegible]	[illegible]	
R	Brooks Mildred †	39	[illegible]		
S	Kessler Benjamin	41	[illegible]		

Page	Letter	Full Name	Residence, Jan. 1, 1941	Occupation	Supposed Age	Reported Residence, Jan. 1, 1940. Street and Number.

Almont Street—Continued

Page	Letter	Full Name	Residence, Jan. 1, 1941	Occupation	Supposed Age	Reported Residence, Jan. 1, 1940. Street and Number.
	T	Kessler Louis	41	merchant	50	here
	U	Kessler Rebecca †	41	housewife	49	"
	V	Bayley Abraham	41	merchant	42	"
	W	Bayley Frances †	41	housewife	41	"
	X	Ezrin Edna G †	43	"	40	"
	Y	Ezrin Joseph	43	manager	40	"
	Z	Bresnick Nathan T	43	physician	37	"
307						
	A	Bresnick Rose †	43	housewife	36	"
	B	Cohen Matthew	45	attorney	34	133 Columbia rd
	C	Cohen Rose †	45	housewife	30	133 "
	D	Allen Gladys †	45	housekeeper	29	46 Lamartine
	E	Cohen Lena †	45	housewife	40	here
	F	Cohen Monte	45	salesman	41	"
	G	Cohen Bertha †	47	housewife	40	"
	H	Cohen Charles	47	clerk	40	"
	K	Kurhan Harry	47	plumber	40	"
	L	Kurhan Julia †	47	housewife	40	"
	M	Weeks Mary †	47	houseworker	21	Everett
	N	Kirshen Edward	49	printer	44	here
	O	Kirshen Gertrude †	49	housewife	44	"
	P	Richmond Frances †	49	"	41	"
	R	Richmond George	49	attorney	44	"
	S	Cohen Alfred	55	manufacturer	37	"
	T	*Cohen Gladys †	55	housewife	35	"
	U	Baitler Bessie †	55	clerk	27	"
	V	Baitler Hyman	55	builder	62	"
	W	*Baitler Lena †	55	housewife	60	"
	X	Katz Morris	55	carpenter	55	"
	Y	Delory Dorothy †	115	housewife	24	"
	Z	Delory Joseph	115	tree surgeon	38	"
308						
	A	Cook Arthur	115	machinist	30	"
	B	Cook Frances H †	115	housewife	30	"
	C	*Fairweather Annie †	115	"	80	"
	D	Fairweather Dorothy †	115	"	23	"
	E	*Fairweather William	115	millwright	36	"
	F	Johnson Frank	117	manager	24	"
		Johnson Mary †	117	housewife	22	"
	H	*Panton Lottie †	117	"	50	"
		Panton William	117	baker	59	"

Page	Letter	Full Name	Residence	Occupation	Age	Reported Residence
		Almont Street Continued				
	L	Panton William, jr	117	chauffeur	22	here
	M	Wipler John	117	mechanic	23	"
	N	Wipler Marjorie †	117	housewife	25	"
	O	Taranto Esther †	117	"	26	"
	P	Taranto Joseph	117	merchant	41	"
	R	Lindstrom Richard	118	asbestos worker	50	"
	S	Danehy A Josephine †	150	clerk	37	"
	T	Danehy Edward	150	"	34	"
	U	Danehy John J	150	retired	74	"
	V	Danehy Katherine J †	150	housewife	70	"
	W	Danehy Mary A †	150	secretary	39	"
	X	Danehy T Francis	150	teacher	31	"
	Y	Toronto Edwina M †	187	secretary	22	199 Almont
	Z	Toronto Katherine L †	187	housewife	55	199 "
309						
	A	Toronto Joseph R	187	musician	51	199 "
	B	Toronto Joseph R, jr	187	"	24	199 "
	C	Hanley John J	190	fireman	45	here
	D	Hanley Lucy †	190	housewife	31	"
	E	Hanley Mary †	190	domestic	48	"
	F	Beniers Henry	196	machinist	39	"
	G	Beniers Mary †	196	housewife	39	"
	H	*DeCorte Emma †	196	"	70	"
	K	Farrell Marie M †	199	"	19	299 Forest Hills
	L	Farrell Walter J	199	repairman	27	299 "
	M	Kelley Jerome L	199	pipefitter	38	15 Palmer
	N	Wells Ellen †	204	housewife	27	Rhode I[illegible]
	O	Wells Frank	204	chauffeur	28	"
	P	Wells Ida G †	204	housewife	67	here
	R	Wells John	204	engineer	69	"
	S	Donovan Edward V	208	foreman	45	"
	T	Donovan Katherine M †	208	housewife	42	"
	U	Lynch John L	215	clerk	[illegible]	"
	V	Lynch Mary A †	215	housewife	[illegible]	"
	W	Lynch Thomas	215	laborer	[illegible]	"
	X	Lynch Walter	215	clerk	[illegible]	"
	Y	O'Neill Daniel P	216	attendant	64	"
	Z	O'Neill Nellie B †	216	housewife	64	"
310						
	A	O'Neill Mary A †	216	artist	[illegible]	[illegible]
	B	Drews Frank E	220	[illegible]	[illegible]	[illegible]

Page	Letter	Full Name	Residence, Jan. 1, 1941.	Occupation	Supposed Age.	Reported Residence, Jan. 1, 1940. Street and Number.

Almont Street—Continued

Page	Letter	Full Name	Residence, Jan. 1, 1941.	Occupation	Supposed Age.	Reported Residence, Jan. 1, 1940. Street and Number.
	C	Drews Helen E †	220	secretary	23	here
	D	Drews Irene R †	220	clerk	22	"
	E	Drews Marie †	220	housewife	52	"
	F	Hynes James J	220	postal clerk	58	"
	G	Flynn Gertrude J †	224	housewife	47	449 River
	H	Flynn James A	224	rigger	25	449 "
	K	Flynn James M	224	tool grinder	49	449 "
	L	Flynn Robert J	224	printer	21	449 "
	M	Sjoquist Alfhild †	224	housewife	55	here
	N	Sjoquist Carl J	224	drawtender	60	"
	O	Voight Anna †	224	housewife	32	"
	P	Brown Margaret †	234	"	47	"
	R	Brown Rufus E	234	shipper	27	"
	S	Brown Rufus P	234	chauffeur	46	"
	T	Mulligan Margaret †	240	clerk	38	"
	U	Stevenson Cora A †	240	housewife	68	"
	V	Walsh Ethel †	244	"	41	"
	W	Walsh Evelyn †	244	clerk	21	"
	X	Walsh William	244	painter	42	"
	Y	Flynn Francis	244	laborer	20	62 Torrey
	Z	Richards Mary †	244	housewife	25	62 "
311						
	A	Richards William	244	merchant	31	62 "

Babson Street

Page	Letter	Full Name	Residence, Jan. 1, 1941.	Occupation	Supposed Age.	Reported Residence, Jan. 1, 1940. Street and Number.
	B	Litchfield Eben S	15	salesman	48	here
	C	Litchfield Minnie †	15	housewife	78	"
	D	Forsyth Joseph B	17	clerk	65	"
	E	Forsyth Mabel F †	17	housewife	60	"
	F	Stewart Arthur E	19	electrician	78	"
	G	Stewart Maud †	19	housekeeper	55	"
	K	Byrne Joseph F	23-25	brakeman	57	"
	L	Saxon John	23-25	clerk	75	"
	M	Saxon Mary †	23-25	housewife	72	"
	N	*Wyman Edna †	23-25	"	39	"
	O	Wyman George E	23-25	machinist	42	"
	P	Lynsky Beatrice †	23-25	housewife	50	"
	R	Lynsky Frank	23-25	clerk	57	"
	S	Lynsky Harold	23-25	laborer	31	"
	T	Paretsky Fannie †	29	housewife	51	"

Page.	Letter.	Full Name.	Residence, Jan. 1, 1941.	Occupation.	[illegible]	[illegible]

Babson Street Continued

Page.	Letter.	Full Name.	Residence, Jan. 1, 1941.	Occupation.	[illegible]	[illegible]
	U	Paretsky Harry	29	cutter	51	here
	V	Paretsky Samuel I	29	student	21	"
	W	Hurwitz Frances †	29	housewife	63	"
	X	Hurwitz Hyman	29	reporter	30	"
	Y	Hurwitz Philip	29	salesman	66	"
	Z	Hurwitz Samuel	29	chauffeur	34	"
312						
	A	Rabinovitz Anna †	29	bookkeeper	21	115 Wa
	B	Rabinovitz Ida †	29	"	23	115 "
	C	Rabinovitz Irving	29	student	24	115 "
	D	Rabinovitz Minnie †	29	housewife	52	115 "
	E	Rabinovitz Philip	29	laborer	53	115 "
	F	Stella Charles	33	"	73	here
	G	Stella John	33	"	26	"
	H	Stella Pasquale	33	"	43	"
	K	Stella Rosemary †	33	saleswoman	22	"
	L	Stella Sadie †	33	housewife	59	"
	N	Martellino Barbara †	37	"	78	"
	O	Martellino Barbara A †	37	clerk	24	"
	P	Martellino Joseph	37	laborer	86	"
	R	Martellino Rose †	37	clerk	35	"
	S	Gatta Annie †	37	housewife	34	"
	T	Gatta Emidio	37	baker	19	"

Blue Hill Avenue

Page.	Letter.	Full Name.	Residence, Jan. 1, 1941.	Occupation.	[illegible]	[illegible]
	Z	Eckert Henry D	1387	clerk	57	here
313						
	A	Reeves Edith G †	1387	saleswoman	52	"
	B	Spurr Jennie B †	1387	at home	85	"
	C	McComiskey Charles	1393	busboy	25	"
	D	McComiskey Elizabeth †	1393	housewife	59	"
	E	Stone Elmer	1393	agent	66	[illegible]
	F	Stone Isabelle J †	1393	housewife	64	[illegible]
	G	Gibson Doris †	1393	clerk	22	[illegible]
	H	Gibson Ellen †	1393	housewife	[illegible]	[illegible]
	K	Gibson Thomas J	1393	engineer	[illegible]	[illegible]
	L	Cohen Bessie †	1395	housewife	[illegible]	[illegible]
	M	Cohen Harry	1395	[illegible]	[illegible]	[illegible]
	N	Rudin Doris †	1395	clerk	[illegible]	[illegible]
	O	Rudin Harry	1395	[illegible]	[illegible]	[illegible]

Page	Letter	Full Name	Residence, Jan. 1, 1941	Occupation	Supposed Age	Reported Residence, Jan. 1, 1940. Street and Number.

Blue Hill Avenue Continued

Page	Letter	Full Name	Residence, Jan. 1, 1941	Occupation	Supposed Age	Reported Residence, Jan. 1, 1940. Street and Number.
	P	Rudin Michael	1395	electrician	45	here
	R	Rudin Sadie †	1395	housewife	40	"
	S	Savage Christine †	1395	"	57	"
	T	Savage Harry N	1395	hotel captain	62	"
	U	Savage Miriam †	1395	clerk	28	"
	V	Savage Rita †	1395	"	21	"
	W	Rosen Maurice	1405	florist	60	"
	X	Rosen Miriam †	1405	housewife	59	"
	Y	Rosen Wilhelmina M †	1405	clerk	32	"
	Z	Rosen William M	1405	U S A	20	"
314						
	A	Bloom Morris	1405	merchant	46	"
	B	Bloom Sarah †	1405	housewife	46	"
	C	Fine Annie †	1405	"	53	"
	D	Fine Frances †	1405	clerk	20	"
	E	Fine Rebecca †	1405	saleswoman	28	"
	F	Fine William	1405	usher	22	"
	G	Goldman Rebecca †	1405	librarian	24	"
	H	Hazlett Edward A	1407	clerk	22	"
	K	Hazlett Sarah †	1407	housewife	56	"
	L	Hazlett William L	1407	seaman	23	"
	M	Hazlett William S	1407	clerk	58	"
	N	Leary Anna D †	1407	teacher	45	"
	O	Leary Margaret A †	1407	clerk	70	"
	P	Leary Mary A †	1407	"	47	"
	R	Kaitz Saul	1407	"	25	"
	S	Kaufman Jacob	1407	operator	48	"
	T	Kaufman Mildred J †	1407	teacher	22	"
	U	Kaufman Sadie †	1407	housewife	45	"
	V	O'Leary Mary E †	1410	"	23	591 Park
	W	O'Leary Nellie V †	1410	"	60	here
	X	O'Leary Vincent J	1410	chauffeur	27	591 Park
	Y	O'Leary William E	1410	compositor	63	here
	Z	O'Leary William E, jr	1410	carpenter	29	"
315						
	A	Getch Patricia †	1410	operator	42	"
	B	Orgonek Frances †	1410	"	31	"
	C	[illegible] Susan †	1410	housewife	40	"
	D	[illegible] Anna †	1410	housekeeper	70	"
	E	[illegible] George	1410	clerk	42	20 Evelyn
	F	[illegible] Aaron	1411	welder	50	here

Page	Letter	Full Name	Residence	Occupation	Age	Reported Residence

Blue Hill Avenue Continued

Letter	Full Name	Residence	Occupation	Age	Reported Residence
G	*Beiff Annie †	1411	housewife	48	here
H	Beiff Bertha †	1411	bookkeeper	23	"
K	*Erlich Anna †	1411	saleswoman	27	112 W[illegible]
L	*Erlich Emma †	1411	housewife	53	112 "
M	Wixon Irene †	1412	bookkeeper	25	here
N	Wixon Joseph T	1412	laborer	24	"
O	Wixon Orin	1412	seaman	67	"
P	Wixon Theresa †	1412	housewife	49	"
R	Allen Elizabeth †	1412	housekeeper	28	[illegible]
S	Sutherland Josephine †	1412	clerk	30	1372 "
T	Sutherland William	1412	electrician	35	1372 "
V	*Azanow John J	1414	tailor	18	here
W	*Azanow Lillian †	1414	housewife	47	"
X	Blumberg Agnes †	1414	"	21	"
Y	Blumberg Arthur	1414	welder	24	"
316					
A	Watson James B	1414	sexton	70	"
B	Watson Margaret †	1414	housewife	66	"
C	Feely Anna †	1414	"	46	"
D	Feely Maurice	1414	cook	56	"
E	Klayman Benjamin	1416	tailor	62	"
F	Klayman David	1416	clerk	25	"
G	Klayman Sadie †	1416	housewife	60	"
H	Aaron Rose †	1416	clerk	62	[illegible]
K	Beck Sadie †	1416	nurse	62	[illegible]
L	Cohen Harvey E	1416	salesman	21	here
M	Cohen John S	1416	"	58	"
N	Cohen Phylis †	1416	housewife	57	"
O	Durst Alice M †	1416	"	18	[illegible]
P	Durst Frank J	1416	pharmacist	52	[illegible]
R	Durst Frank J, jr	1416	social worker	29	[illegible]
S	Cohan Louis	1420	pedler	65	[illegible]
T	Cohan Rose †	1420	housewife	64	[illegible]
U	Bagelman Goldie †	1420	"	[illegible]	[illegible]
V	Bagelman Joseph	1420	clerk	50	[illegible]
W	Gerson Freida †	1420	housewife	30	[illegible]
X	Gerson Perry	1420	salesman	30	[illegible]
Y	*Manolis Diana †	1420	housewife	42	[illegible]
Z	Manolis Louis	1420	[illegible]	[illegible]	[illegible]
317					
A	Mattiaccia Filomena A †	1422	[illegible]	[illegible]	[illegible]

Page	Letter	Full Name	Residence, Jan. 1, 1941	Occupation	Supposed Age	Reported Residence, Jan. 1, 1940. Street and Number.

Blue Hill Avenue Continued

Page	Letter	Full Name	Residence, Jan. 1, 1941	Occupation	Supposed Age	Reported Residence, Jan. 1, 1940. Street and Number.
	B	Mattiaccia James	1422	laborer	40	here
	D	Hanley Edward F	1422	operator	59	"
	E	Hanley Margaret †	1422	housewife	40	"
	F	Hanley Mary A †	1422	clerk	22	"
	G	Wall Annie †	1422	housekeeper	28	"
	H	Patz Joseph	1424	salesman	29	"
	K	Patz Sarah †	1424	housewife	24	"
	L	Richmond Harry	1424	clerk	33	"
	M	Richmond Isaac	1424	tailor	63	"
	N	Richmond Mary †	1424	housewife	58	"
	O	Becovsky Hyman	1424	painter	49	"
	P	Becovsky Mary †	1424	housewife	42	"
	R	Wolk Alice †	1428	"	38	"
	S	Wolk Herman L	1428	printer	39	"
	T	Hurley Charles P	1428	clerk	21	"
	U	Hurley Elsie †	1428	housewife	41	"
	V	Hurley Michael T	1428	policeman	51	"
	W	*Barto Mary †	1428	housewife	56	"
	X	Barto Theodore	1428	barber	25	"
	Y	*Barto Thomas	1428	"	62	"
	Z	*Smookler Lena †	1430	housewife	43	"
318						
	A	Smookler Louis	1430	furrier	53	"
	B	Lewis Edward	1430	clerk	20	"
	C	Lewis Rose †	1430	housewife	54	"
	D	*Price Jennie †	1430	"	48	"
	E	Price Samuel	1430	spotter	48	"
	F	Hansen Alfred H	1434	ironworker	42	"
	G	Hansen Kaia E †	1434	housewife	40	"
	H	Becker Fannie †	1434	"	68	"
	K	Becker Joseph	1434	cabinetmaker	68	"
	L	Clark Ann L †	1434	housekeeper	54	"
	M	Clark William C	1434	shipper	30	"
	N	Amundsen Lars	1436	engineer	60	"
	O	*Amundsen Lucy †	1436	housewife	48	"
	P	*Wood Jean †	1436	"	21	"
	R	Wood Raymond E	1436	salesman	23	"
	S	Ey Frederick	1436	accountant	30	Pennsylvania
	T	Ey Hazel N †	1436	housewife	31	"
	U	McHugh Charles W	1438	starter	41	9 Tokio
	V	McHugh Helena †	1438	housekeeper	47	9 "

Page	Letter	Full Name	Residence, Jan. 1, 1941	Occupation	Age	Reported Residence

Blue Hill Avenue—Continued

Page	Letter	Full Name	Residence	Occupation	Age	Reported Residence
	W	Stanton Helena G †	1438	waitress	21	9 [illegible]
	X	Johnson Elinor †	1438	housekeeper	70	here
	Y	Proud Elinor †	1438	housewife	30	"
	Z	Proud Harry	1438	laborer	31	"
319						
	A	Delory Mary †	1438½	housewife	70	"
	B	Delory Thomas	1438½	laborer	78	"
	C	Regan Sarah †	1438½	clerk	40	"
	D	Kessler Samuel	1439	pedler	69	"
	E*	Kessler Sarah †	1439	housewife	56	"
	F	Mlinash Harry	1439	tailor	48	"
	G*	Mlinash Iola †	1439	housewife	46	"
	H	Mlinash Lillian †	1439	clerk	21	"
	K	Milender Rose †	1439	housewife	66	"
	L	Milender William	1439	merchant	67	"
	M	Finer Harry	1439	clerk	30	[illegible]
	N	Finer Shirley †	1439	housewife	31	17 "
	O	Baimel Ida †	1439	"	55	here
	P	Baimel Nathan	1439	merchant	64	"
	R	Shienfeld Charles H	1439	attorney	33	"
	S	Shienfeld Rose B †	1439	housewife	32	"
	T	Weiner Gertrude †	1439	"	29	"
	U	Weiner Louis	1439	barber	28	"
	V	Leppo Hazel †	1439	housewife	24	Chelsea
	W	Leppo Nathan	1439	salesman	25	79 [illegible]
	X	Rubin Irene †	1439	housewife	26	122 [illegible]
	Y	Rubin Irving	1439	salesman	27	122 "
	Z	Cohen Anna †	1439	housewife	42	here
320						
	A	Cohen Louis	1439	fireman	[illegible]	[illegible]
	B	Cohen Max	1439	chauffeur	47	[illegible]
	C*	Cohen Mollie †	1439	housewife	70	[illegible]
	D	Goldberg Ethel †	1439	housekeeper	[illegible]	[illegible]
	E	Goldberg Hyman	1439	druggist	[illegible]	[illegible]
	F	Goldberg Jacob	1439	shipper	[illegible]	[illegible]
	G	Klebanow Benjamin	1439	merchant	40	[illegible]
	H	Klebanow Dora †	1439	housewife	40	[illegible]
	K*	Goffin Rebecca †	1439	"	[illegible]	[illegible]
	L	Goffin Samuel	1439	retired	[illegible]	[illegible]
	M	Mednick Lena C †	1439	housewife	[illegible]	[illegible]
	N	Mednick Louis	1439	[illegible]	[illegible]	[illegible]

Page	Letter	Full Name	Residence, Jan. 1, 1941.	Occupation.	Supposed Age.	Reported Residence, Jan. 1, 1940. Street and Number.

Blue Hill Avenue Continued

Page	Letter	Full Name	Residence, Jan. 1, 1941.	Occupation.	Supposed Age.	Reported Residence, Jan. 1, 1940. Street and Number.
	O	Klebanow Frances D †	1443	housewife	30	here
	P	Klebanow Louis M	1443	salesman	32	"
	R	Shack Helen M †	1443	housewife	21	Quincy
	S	Shack Jacob F	1443	optometrist	26	14 Fessenden
	T	Segal Mildred †	1443	housewife	28	here
	U	Segal Ralph	1443	salesman	29	"
	V	Sacon Nathan	1443	accountant	31	"
	W	Sacon Yetta †	1443	housewife	28	"
	X	Brasslow Blanche †	1443	bookkeeper	20	"
	Y	Brasslow Ida †	1443	dressmaker	56	"
	Z	Brasslow Lillian †	1443	bookkeeper	25	"
321						
	A	Goldstein Frances †	1443	beautician	23	"
	B	*Goldstein Ida †	1443	housewife	52	"
	C	Goldstein Israel	1443	tailor	57	"
	D	*Heller Annie †	1443	housewife	50	48 Charlotte
	E	Heller Harry	1443	plumber	51	48 "
	F	Goldman Abram I	1443	druggist	28	here
	G	Goldman Rose G †	1443	housewife	28	"
	H	Kaufman Eli G	1443	shipper	31	"
	K	*Kaufman Fannie †	1443	housekeeper	57	"
	L	Kaufman Margaret †	1443	bookkeeper	29	"
	M	Gootner Anne †	1443	housewife	34	"
	N	Gootner Samuel	1443	merchant	41	"
	O	Koven Frances S †	1443	housewife	32	"
	P	Koven Jerome	1443	druggist	36	"
	R	Talisman Charlotte †	1443	housewife	27	"
	S	Talisman Samuel	1443	merchant	33	"
	T	Siders Max	1443	salesman	43	"
	U	Siders Nellie †	1443	housewife	39	"
	V	Feinburg Sarah †	1447	"	32	"
	W	Feinburg William	1447	clerk	32	"
	X	Epstein Martha †	1447	housewife	21	Woburn
	Y	Epstein Morris L	1447	shipper	25	177 Fairmount
	Z	Shockett Katherine †	1447	housewife	31	here
322						
		Shockett Nathan	1447	salesman	36	"
	B	Ginsburg Annie †	1447	housewife	75	65 Westminster av
	C	Ginsburg Sallie †	1447	clerk	31	65 "
	D	Maltz Benjamin	1447	salesman	34	24 Crawford
	E	Maltz Ida †	1447	housewife	29	24 "

Page.	Letter.	Full Name.	Residence	Occupation		

Blue Hill Avenue (Continued)

Page	Letter	Full Name	Residence	Occupation	Age	Former residence
	G	Weinberger Benjamin Z	1447	salesman	30	[illegible]
	F	Weinberger Elise †	1447	housekeeper	26	1451
	H	Weinberger Gertrude †	1447	student	22	1451
	K	Kleiman Esther †	1447	bookkeeper	32	here
	L	Kleiman Sophie †	1447	housewife	60	"
	M	Dinsen Albertine †	1447	beautician	51	"
	N	Greenberg Frances †	1447	saleswoman	33	"
	O	Leahy Irene †	1447	housekeeper	28	"
	P*	Grasfield Sarah †	1447	"	64	"
	R	Wolf Goldie †	1447	housewife	32	"
	S	Wolf Joseph	1447	carpenter	30	"
	T	Feinberg Rose †	1447	housewife	34	"
	U	Feinberg Victor	1447	manager	40	"
	V	Rosenbloom Burnett	1447	electrician	26	128 W [illegible]
	W	Rosenbloom Charlotte †	1447	housewife	24	128 "
	X*	Needle Fannie †	1447	"	55	here
	Y	Needle William	1447	salesman	26	"
	Z	McDonald Eunice †	1450	housewife	28	70 Neponset [illegible]
323						
	A	McDonald Gerald	1450	clerk	32	70 "
	B	Gavin Florence †	1450	housewife	31	here
	C	Gavin William	1450	salesman	31	"
	D	Seeley Dorothy †	1450	clerk	20	"
	E	Seeley Fred	1450	plumber	55	"
	F	Seeley Frederick	1450	clerk	21	"
	G*	Seeley Lena †	1450	housewife	51	"
	H	Schlossberg Annette †	1451	"	24	"
	K	Schlossberg Louis	1451	undertaker	24	"
	L	Greenberg Harry	1451	pharmacist	30	"
	M	Greenberg Sarah †	1451	housewife	29	"
	N	Brittan Alfred	1451	salesman	27	"
	O	Brittan Evelyn †	1451	housewife	[illegible]	1447
	P	Seltzer Celia †	1451	"	[illegible]	[illegible]
	R	Seltzer Dorothy †	1451	saleswoman	[illegible]	[illegible]
	S	Seltzer Mary †	1451	"	[illegible]	[illegible]
	T	Davis Beatrice F †	1451	housewife	[illegible]	[illegible]
	U	Davis Isadore	1451	salesman	[illegible]	[illegible]
	V	Bloomenberg Mary †	1451	housewife	[illegible]	[illegible]
	W	Bloomenberg Samuel	1451	[illegible]	[illegible]	[illegible]
	X	Newman Jacob	1451	"	[illegible]	[illegible]
	Y	Anderson Elizabeth †	1451	[illegible]	[illegible]	[illegible]

Page	Letter	Full Name	Residence, Jan. 1, 1941	Occupation	Supposed Age	Reported Residence, Jan. 1, 1940. Street and Number.

Blue Hill Avenue—Continued

Page	Letter	Full Name	Residence, Jan. 1, 1941	Occupation	Supposed Age	Reported Residence, Jan. 1, 1940. Street and Number.
	Z	Finnegan Miriam †	1451	housewife	33	698 Walk Hill
324						
	A	Finnegan William	1451	salesman	39	698 "
	B	Walpe Ida †	1451	housewife	46	here
	C	Walpe Samuel	1451	accountant	40	"
	D	Fair Allen	1451	pharmacist	30	108 Maple
	E	Fair Ethel †	1451	housewife	28	108 "
	F	Wineapple Irving	1451	machinist	25	here
	G	Wineapple Maurice	1451	manager	56	"
	H	Wineapple Rae †	1451	housewife	56	"
	K*	Chiklis Goldie †	1451	"	27	"
	L*	Chiklis Louis	1451	counterman	28	"
	M	Schlosberg Edward	1451	salesman	38	45 Stanwood
	N	Schlosberg Emma †	1451	housewife	34	45 "
	O	McCarthy Mary †	1454	"	44	here
	P	McCarthy Robert	1454	chauffeur	44	"
	R*	Belyea Hilda †	1454	housewife	24	Milton
	S*	Belyea Robert	1454	salesman	24	670 Cummins H'way
	T	McCarthy Margaret †	1454	nurse	45	here
	U	Connolly Mary †	1454	housewife	41	"
	V	Redington Malachi	1454	B F D	46	"
	W*	Barlas Demetra †	1458	housewife	36	"
	X	Barlas Philip	1458	shoemaker	46	"
	Y	Goldstein Ella †	1458	housewife	51	1412 Blue Hill av
	Z	Goldstein Harry	1458	upholsterer	51	1412 "
325						
	A	Mandrakos Christopher	1458	salesman	46	here
	B*	Mandrakos Dovla †	1458	housewife	28	"
	C*	Mandrakos Mary †	1458	"	33	"
	D	Mandrakos Peter	1458	laborer	45	"
	E	Cook Catherine †	1460	housewife	48	"
	F	Cook Kathryn †	1460	clerk	25	"
	G	Hughes Dorothy †	1460	"	27	"
	H	Giovannucci Anna †	1460	housewife	40	"
	K	Giovannucci Sando	1460	clerk	42	"
	L	Frongello Dora †	1460	housewife	40	"
	M	Frongello John	1460	carpenter	45	"
	N	Sanderson Morris	1461	clerk	33	643 Walk Hill
	O	Taub Bertha †	1461	housewife	69	25 Fessenden
	P	Taub David	1461	salesman	73	25 "
	R	Granberg Justin S	1461	"	44	here

Letter	Full Name	Residence	Occupation	Age	Reported Residence

Blue Hill Avenue (Continued)

Letter	Full Name	Residence	Occupation	Age	Reported Residence
S	Oranburg Reba †	1461	housewife	44	here
T	Zola Harriett †	1461	clerk	25	125 [illegible]
U	*Lilenfield Celia †	1461	housewife	62	here
V	*Lilenfield Henry	1461	tailor	65	"
W	Lilenfield Rose †	1461	clerk	36	"
X	Rosenstein Bertha †	1461	housewife	32	"
Y	Rosenstein Irving	1461	clerk	34	"
Z	Hackel Ethel †	1463	"	27	"
326					
A	Hackel Harry	1463	"	28	"
B	*Hackel Helen †	1463	housewife	63	"
C	*Rosen Mollie †	1463	"	37	"
D	Rosen Rubin	1463	salesman	38	"
E	Nason Fannie †	1463	housewife	39	683 [illegible]
F	Nason Harry	1463	postal clerk	41	683 "
G	Levenson Bernard	1463	salesman	20	here
H	Levenson Harry	1463	"	17	"
K	Levenson Mildred †	1463	secretary	24	"
L	Levenson Sophia †	1463	housewife	43	"
M	Smart Fannie †	1465	"	63	"
N	Smart Silas E	1465	machinist	64	"
O	Ohrenberger Frederick J	1465	custodian	64	"
P	Ohrenberger Katherine †	1465	housewife	61	"
R	Ohrenberger William J	1465	chauffeur	31	"
S	McGuiggan Catherine †	1465	housewife	58	[illegible]
T	McGuiggan Doris †	1465	clerk	28	[illegible]
U	McGuiggan James F	1465	operator	[illegible]	[illegible]
V	McGuiggan Mary A †	1465	saleswoman	[illegible]	[illegible]
W	McGuiggan Paul	1465	clerk	21	[illegible]
X	McGuiggan William	1465	"	[illegible]	[illegible]
Y	Lane Ann T †	1466	[illegible]	[illegible]	[illegible]
Z	Lane John J	1466	[illegible]	[illegible]	[illegible]
327					
A	Lane John J, jr	1466	clerk	[illegible]	[illegible]
B	Goldman Annie †	1467	[illegible]	[illegible]	[illegible]
C	Goldman Michael	1467	[illegible]	[illegible]	[illegible]
D	Kahn Albert	1467	[illegible]	[illegible]	[illegible]
E	Kahn Rose †	1467	[illegible]	[illegible]	[illegible]
F	Rosenthal Ottillie †	1467	[illegible]	[illegible]	[illegible]
G	Rosenthal Ruben	1467	[illegible]	[illegible]	[illegible]
H	Rosenthal Sarah †	1467	[illegible]	[illegible]	[illegible]

Page	Letter	Full Name	Residence, Jan. 1, 1941	Occupation	Supposed Age	Reported Residence, Jan. 1, 1940. Street and Number.

Colorado Street

Page	Letter	Full Name	Residence, Jan. 1, 1941	Occupation	Supposed Age	Reported Residence, Jan. 1, 1940
	K	Daly Catherine †	5	housewife	44	here
	N	Trapni Antonio	12	fishcutter	28	"
	L*	Trapni Frances †	12	housewife	40	"
	M	Trapni Frank	12	carpenter	50	"
	O	Hansen Charlotte †	19	housewife	71	"
	P	Hansen George	19	superintendent	75	"
	R	Forsyth Bella †	28	housewife	60	"
	S	Forsyth Isabella M †	28	cook	33	"
	T	Forsyth Margaret L †	28	nurse	27	"
	U	Forsyth Wallace R	28	painter	61	"
	V	Bancroft Charles A	32	retired	72	"
	W	Bancroft Emma C †	32	housewife	68	"
	X	Kilby David E	32	clerk	58	"
	Y	Kilby Lenora S †	32	housewife	65	"
	Z	Pitcher Frederick E	32	clerk	67	"
328						
	C	Fahey Nora T †	130	housekeeper	70	"
	D	Iverson Ernest M	130	clerk	39	"
	E	Iverson John P	130	retired	71	"
	F	Iverson Margaret F—†	130	clerk	34	"
	G	Iverson Othilie S †	130	housewife	66	"
	H	Flint Elizabeth †	143	"	46	"
	K	Flint Harry G	143	pressman	49	"
	L*	Hansen David	143	blacksmith	69	"
	M	Belyea Catherine †	158	housewife	49	"
	N	Belyea Margaret †	158	clerk	23	"
	O	Belyea Mina †	158	"	20	"
	P	Belyea Robert W	158	carpenter	46	"
	R*	MacIntosh Mary †	158	housekeeper	65	"
	S*	MacIntosh Stewart	158	carpenter	46	"

Culbert Street

Page	Letter	Full Name	Residence, Jan. 1, 1941	Occupation	Supposed Age	Reported Residence, Jan. 1, 1940
		Poverman Josephine †	7	housewife	31	here
	U	Poverman Julius	7	manufacturer	38	"
	V	Barenberg Harry	7	"	36	"
	W	Barenberg Marcia †	7	housewife	29	"
	X	Baron Leonard	8	laborer	45	"
	Y	Baron Mildred †	8	student	20	"
	Z	Baron Sarah †	8	housewife	40	"

Page / Letter	Full Name	[illegible]	[illegible]	[illegible]	[illegible]
329					

Culbert Street (Continued)

Letter	Full Name				
A	Kaplan Ida †	8	housewife	42	here
B	Kaplan Israel	8	cutter	50	"
C	Kaplan Sydney	8	student	22	"
D	Manzoli Leo	9	merchant	35	"
E	Manzoli Nora †	9	housewife	29	"
F	*Verrinoldi Helen †	9	"	30	"
G	Verrinoldi Peter J	9	salesman	42	1159 [illegible]
H	Spring Dorothy †	9	housewife	32	here
K	Spring Frank L	9	mechanic	31	"
L	Jackson Phyllis V †	11	operator	31	5070 W[illegible]
M	McEntee Alice †	11	housewife	27	61 Adams
N	McEntee John A	11	special police	25	5070 W[illegible]
O	McEntee Mary A †	11	housewife	55	5070 "
P	McEntee Norman F	11	steward	30	61 Adams
R	McEntee Phillip J	11	installer	58	5070 W[illegible]
S	Manzoli Alfonso	11	clerk	47	here
T	*Manzoli Lucia †	11	at home	79	"
U	Jones Alice †	11	forewoman	26	"
V	Jones Edwin F †	11	salesman	27	"
W	Jones Theresa †	11	housewife	33	"
X	Jones William J	11	salesman	38	"
Y	McEntee Edward A	12	retired	65	"
Z	McEntee James	12	shipper	52	"
330					
A	Ennis Lillian †	12	waitress	21	[illegible]
B	McCarthy Agnes L †	12	housewife	49	here
C	McCarthy Thomas	12	leathercutter	51	[illegible]

Elene Street

Letter	Full Name				
D	Gould Margaret †	8	housewife	[illegible]	[illegible]
E	Gould William F	8	policeman	[illegible]	[illegible]
F	Scott Elizabeth G †	23	housewife	[illegible]	[illegible]
G	Scott Wallace J	23	rigger	[illegible]	[illegible]

Fottler Road

Letter	Full Name				
H	Ajemian Charles	25	[illegible]	[illegible]	[illegible]
K	Ajemian Louise K †	25	[illegible]	[illegible]	[illegible]

Page	Letter	Full Name	Residence, Jan. 1, 1941	Occupation	Supposed Age	Reported Residence, Jan. 1, 1940. Street and Number.

Fottler Road Continued

Page	Letter	Full Name	Residence, Jan. 1, 1941	Occupation	Supposed Age	Reported Residence, Jan. 1, 1940. Street and Number.
	L	Sullivan John E	25	retired	55	20 Westglow
	M	Sullivan Louise V †	25	housewife	54	20 "
	N	Granville Mary †	29	"	68	here
	O	MacDonald Harry	29	salesman	47	"
	P	MacDonald Marie †	29	housewife	46	"
	R	Crawford Charlotte †	33	"	64	"
	S	Crawford John E	33	chef	60	"
	T	Currier Doreen F †	33	saleswoman	35	"
	U	Napoleon Bessie †	41	housewife	34	"
	V	Napoleon Boris	41	abstractor	38	"
	W	Chernov Anna †	41	housewife	32	"
	X	Chernov Paul	41	salesman	34	"
	Y	Goodman Frances †	41	housewife	34	94 Ballou av
	Z	Goodman Max	41	chauffeur	38	94 "
331						
	A	Wiseberg Rose †	41	at home	44	here
	B	Goldberg Freida †	41	housewife	36	"
	C	Goldberg William	41	agent	42	"
	D	Talcofsky Morton	41	clerk	27	48 Fottler rd
	E	Talcofsky Rita †	41	housewife	27	48 "
	F	Salutsky Harry	45	cutter	45	here
	G	Salutsky Nathan	45	retired	76	"
	H	Salutsky Rebecca †	45	housewife	70	"
	K	Berman Betty †	45	"	30	"
	L	Berman Isadore	45	agent	35	"
	M	Barron Joseph	45	contractor	37	"
	N	Barron Sadie †	45	housewife	36	"
	O	Aronson Goldie †	45	"	34	"
	P	Aronson Louis	45	salesman	40	"
	R	Doodlesack Louis	45	pharmacist	28	"
	S	Fox Abraham J	45	restaurateur	42	"
	T	Fox Minnie †	45	housewife	39	"
	U	Goodwin Jeannette †	48	"	22	Natick
		Goodwin Sidney	48	chauffeur	27	"
	W	Gart Freida †	48	housewife	39	here
	X	Gart John	48	machinist	42	"
		Brown Albert	48	tailor	46	"
	Z	Brown Rose †	48	housewife	37	"
332						
	A	Goldsmith Lillian †	49	"	37	"

Fottler Road Continued

Page	Letter	Full Name	Residence, April 1, 1940	Occupation	Age	Reported Residence, April 1, 1939
	B	Goldsmith Mitchell	49	manager	39	[illegible]
	C	Kreponitsky Betty †	49	housewife	31	[illegible]
	D	Kreponitsky Irving	49	clerk	31	[illegible]
	E	Baker Anna—†	49	housewife	27	[illegible]
	F	Baker Louis	49	restaurateur	32	[illegible]
	G	Berish Henry	49	ironworker	25	[illegible]
	H	Berish Pearl—†	49	housewife	22	[illegible]
	K	Davis Etta—†	49	"	40	[illegible]
	L	Davis Harry	49	salesman	40	"
	M	Shair Eva—†	49	housewife	33	[illegible]
	N	Shair Joseph	49	salesman	35	"
	O	Jacobson Rose—†	50	seamstress	38	"
	P	*Shapiro Barnett	50	mason	37	"
	R	*Shapiro Sara—†	50	housewife	34	"
	S	Cohen Ida—†	50	"	38	[illegible]
	T	Cohen Isidore	50	letter carrier	39	1117 [illegible]
	U	Glass Marion—†	53	housewife	40	1314 [illegible]
	V	Glass Myer	53	printer	41	1314 [illegible]
	W	Kaplan Jeanette—†	53	housewife	40	[illegible]
	X	Kaplan Morris	53	tailor	50	"
	Y	Goldman Abraham	53	chauffeur	28	M[illegible]
	Z	Goldman Sally—†	53	housewife	2[illegible]	"
333						
	A	Limonsky Frances—†	53	"	32	[illegible]
	B	Limonsky Louis	53	[illegible]	[illegible]	[illegible]
	C	Israel Pearl—†	53	housewife	[illegible]	[illegible]
	D	Israel Samuel	53	ironworker	[illegible]	[illegible]
	E	Lindman Phillip	53	[illegible]	[illegible]	[illegible]
	F	Lindman Rose—†	53	housewife	[illegible]	[illegible]
	G	Sorofman Benjamin	57	[illegible]	[illegible]	[illegible]
	H	Sorofman Frances—†	57	[illegible]	[illegible]	[illegible]
	K	Sorofman Stanley	57	[illegible]	[illegible]	[illegible]
	L	Charm Ann—†	57	[illegible]	[illegible]	[illegible]
	M	Charm Samuel	57	[illegible]	[illegible]	[illegible]
	N	Sklaver Evelyn—†	57	[illegible]	[illegible]	[illegible]
	O	Sklaver Goldie—†	57	[illegible]	[illegible]	[illegible]
	P	Sklaver Harry	57	[illegible]	[illegible]	[illegible]
	R	Shapiro Sarah—†	57	[illegible]	[illegible]	[illegible]
	S	Tattleman Goldie—†	57	[illegible]	[illegible]	[illegible]
	T	Tattleman Nathan	57	[illegible]	[illegible]	[illegible]

Letter	Full Name	Residence, Jan. 1, 1941.	Occupation.	Supposed Age.	Reported Residence, Jan. 1, 1940. Street and Number.
	Hebron Street				
U	Hanson Bernard	75	painter	44	here
V	Hanson Mabel I †	75	housewife	39	"
W	Yakminski John A	75	carpenter	45	"
X*	Yakminski Rose †	75	housewife	47	"
	Hiawatha Road				
Y	Sandberg Max	2	physician	32	here
Z	Sandberg Sarah †	2	housewife	31	"
	334				
A	Liebster Anna †	2	"	36	"
B	Liebster Simon	2	salesman	52	"
C	Ginsberg Henry †	2	"	40	"
D	Ginsberg Mabel †	2	housewife	35	"
E	Smith Abraham	4	mechanic	42	"
F	Smith Sarah †	4	housewife	40	"
G	Cohen Julius	4	tailor	60	"
H	Cohen Mildred †	4	bookkeeper	28	"
K	Cohen Rose †	4	housewife	55	"
L	Koplow Lillian †	4	"	36	"
M	Koplow Sigmund	4	postal worker	39	"
N	Raphael Esther †	8	housewife	35	"
O	Raphael Samuel	8	attorney	39	"
P	Ezrin Lillian †	8	housewife	30	"
R	Ezrin Thomas	8	manager	33	"
S	Finneran Elizabeth †	8	housewife	37	"
T	Finneran Joseph	8	fireman	39	"
U*	Ruboy Mary †	8	housewife	48	"
V	Ruboy Samuel	8	cabinetmaker	48	"
W	Bennett Samuel	8	salesman	34	"
X	Bennett Sarah †	8	housewife	30	"
Y	Mendel Samuel	8	salesman	30	"
Z	Mendel Sarah †	8	housewife	28	"
	335				
	Connell Agnes †	12	"	60	"
	Connell Elizabeth †	12	"	72	"
	Connell Helen V †	12	clerk	62	"
D	Connell James J	12	retired	76	"
	Connell Mary A †	12	housewife	75	"
	Bergstein Louis	12	merchant	60	"
	Bergstein Rebecca †	12	housewife	58	"
	Bergstein Selma †	12	saleswoman	21	"

Hiawatha Road Continued

Page	Letter	Full Name	[illegible]	[illegible]	[illegible]	[illegible]
	K	Fleishman Sarah †	12	housewife	62	35 W[illegible]
	L	Onigman Benjamin	12	clerk	29	53 [illegible]
	M	Onigman Gertrude †	12	housewife	29	53 "
	N	Starr Ethel †	12	stenographer	24	35 W[illegible]
	O	Fendell Aleck	16	salesman	40	here
	P	Fendell Sarah †	16	housewife	40	"
	R	Gussenoff Cynthia †	16	stenographer	28	"
	S	Gussenoff David	16	merchant	62	"
	T	*Gussenoff Ida †	16	housewife	60	"
	U	Rosemark Dorothy †	16	stenographer	33	Somerville
	V	Marr Arthur E	16	photographer	63	here
	W	Semans Gertrude †	17	housewife	38	"
	X	Semans Maurice	17	bookkeeper	42	"
	Y	Atkins Eve †	17	clerk	28	20 Old [illegible]
	Z	Atkins Isaac	17	laborer	60	20 "
336						
	A	Atkins Jacob	17	student	20	20 "
	B	Atkins Jennie †	17	housewife	50	20 "
	C	Yorra Henry	17	attorney	31	20 "
	D	Packer Benjamin	17	letter carrier	42	20 M[illegible]
	E	Packer Bessie †	17	housewife	38	20 "
	F	Durham Helena †	19	operator	54	here
	G	Durham John F	19	packer	58	"
	H	Callahan Daniel	22	retired	71	"
	K	Callahan Sarah †	22	housekeeper	[illegible]	"
	L	Doonan Catherine †	22	housewife	[illegible]	"
	M	Goodnough Grace N †	27	clerk	23	"
	N	Littlewood Lillian L †	27	teacher	18	"
	O	Rolfe Charles F	27	retired	75	"
	P	Rolfe Grace E †	27	housewife	[illegible]	"
	R	Dowling Annie L †	28	housekeeper	[illegible]	"
	S	Dowling Daniel P	28	retired	[illegible]	"
	T	Dowling Mary C †	28	operator	[illegible]	"
	U	Hurst Bessie †	30	housewife	52	[illegible]
	V	*Hurst Max	30	cobbler	[illegible]	[illegible]
	W	Katz Benjamin	30	druggist	[illegible]	[illegible]
	X	Katz Michael	30	retired	[illegible]	[illegible]
	Y	Wesolo Alice †	30	[illegible]	[illegible]	[illegible]
	Z	*Brother Celia †	31	housewife	[illegible]	[illegible]
337						
	A	Brother Sidney	31	[illegible]	[illegible]	[illegible]
	B	Brother Sylvia †	31	[illegible]	[illegible]	[illegible]

Page	Letter	Full Name	Residence, Jan. 1, 1941	Occupation	Supposed Age	Reported Residence, Jan. 1, 1940. Street and Number.

Hiawatha Road Continued

Page	Letter	Full Name	Residence	Occupation	Age	Reported Residence
	c	Cohen Benjamin	31	laborer	27	here
	d	Cohen Eva †	31	housewife	27	"
	e	Weinberg Mary †	31	"	28	"
	f	Weinberg Morris	31	laborer	28	"
	g	Shapiro Esther †	31	housewife	40	"
	h	Shapiro Samuel	31	machinist	42	"
	k	Liverfarb Anna †	31	housewife	54	"
	l	Liverfarb Benjamin	31	teacher	29	"
	m	Liverfarb Jacob	31	furrier	55	"
	n	Liverfarb Lillian †	31	bookkeeper	22	"
	o	Liverfarb Sidney	31	clerk	25	"
	p	Block Henry	32	cigarmaker	64	"
	r	Block Rose †	32	housewife	62	"
	s	Okun Abraham	32	agent	43	"
	t	Okun Viola †	32	housewife	41	"
	u	Fried Shirley †	35	bookkeeper	32	20 Wilcock
	v	Kadushin Miriam †	35	saleswoman	28	20 "
	w	Kadushin Nathan	35	machinist	68	20 "
	x	Kadushin Yetta †	35	housewife	59	25 "
	y	Selden Bessie †	35	"	38	486 Norfolk
	z	Selden Joseph	35	salesman	40	486 "
338						
	a	Halper Fannie †	35	housewife	54	here
	b	Halper Samuel	35	student	20	"
	c	Halper Solomon	35	merchant	59	"
	d	Keller Lillian †	35	housewife	36	"
	e	Keller Solomon	35	clerk	37	"
	f	Karp Albert	35	accountant	37	"
	g	Karp Sally †	35	housewife	33	"
	h	Gordon Celia †	35	"	30	"
	k	Gordon Samuel	35	laundryman	32	"
	l	Gordon Jacob	38	chauffeur	29	Lynn
	m	Gordon Rachel †	38	housewife	24	"
	n	Goldberg Hyman	40	painter	32	here
	o	Goldberg Minnie †	40	housewife	35	"
	p	Peltz Bessie †	40	saleswoman	25	"
	r	Peltz Elizabeth †	40	housewife	55	"
		[illegible]	40	"	52	1232 Blue Hill av
		[illegible]	40	shoeworker	53	1232 "
		[illegible]	40	chauffeur	21	1232 "
		[illegible]	41	clerk	24	here

Page	Letter	Full Name	Residence	Occupation	Age	

Hiawatha Road (Cont'd)

Page	Letter	Full Name	Residence	Occupation	Age	
	W	Seltzer Esther †	11	saleswoman	27	
	X	Seltzer Joseph	11	clerk	[illegible]	
	Y	*Seltzer Rose †	11	housewife	[illegible]	
	Z	Rosen Charlotte †	11	"	[illegible]	
339						
	A	Rosen William	11	salesman	27	
	B	Schwartz Elsie †	11	housewife	[illegible]	[illegible] W
	C	Schwartz Joseph	11	agent	25	[illegible]
	D	Rosen Beatrice †	11	saleswoman	22	[illegible] W
	E	Rosen Bessie †	11	housewife	[illegible]	[illegible]
	F	Rosen William	11	tailor	[illegible]	[illegible]
	G	Lewis Augustus L	11	merchant	[illegible]	[illegible]
	H	Lewis Helen †	11	housewife	[illegible]	
	K	Harmon William	11	salesman	[illegible]	
	L	Harmon Yvette †	11	housewife	[illegible]	
	M	Bloomberg Arthur	12	salesman	[illegible]	
	N	Bloomberg Blumah †	12	housewife	[illegible]	
	O	Sidman Lillian †	12	"	[illegible]	[illegible]
	P	Sidman Phillip	12	adjuster	[illegible]	[illegible]
	R	Kerman Barney	12	tailor	[illegible]	
	S	Kerman Bessie †	12	housewife	[illegible]	
	T	Kerman Harold	12	[illegible]	[illegible]	
	U	Kerman Milton	12	[illegible]	[illegible]	
	V	Lamke Haskill	16	[illegible]	[illegible]	
	W	Lamke Ruth †	16	[illegible]		[illegible] W
	X	Miller Bessie †	16	[illegible]	[illegible]	
	Y	Miller David	16	[illegible]	[illegible]	[illegible]
	Z	Sherman Barney	17	[illegible]	[illegible]	
340						
	A	Sherman Irving	17	[illegible]	[illegible]	
	B	Sherman Rose †	17	[illegible]		
	C	Salon Charlotte K †	17			[illegible]
	D	Salon Emanuel	17	[illegible]		[illegible]
	E	Salon Esther †	17	[illegible]		
	F	Salon Julius	17	[illegible]		
	G	Salon Samuel	17	[illegible]		
	H	Asarkof Albert	17			
	K	Asarkof Rose †	17	[illegible]		
	L	*Smolett Arthur	17			
	M	*Solomon Goldie †	17	[illegible]	[illegible]	[illegible]
	N	*Solomon Maurice	17		[illegible]	

Page	Letter	Full Name	Residence, Jan. 1, 1941	Occupation	Supposed Age	Reported Residence, Jan. 1, 1940. Street and Number.

Hiawatha Road—Continued

Page	Letter	Full Name	Residence, Jan. 1, 1941	Occupation	Supposed Age	Reported Residence, Jan. 1, 1940. Street and Number.
	O	Stone Leah †	47	housewife	76	here
	P	Spivack Frank	50	electrician	42	"
	R	Spivack Tillie †	50	housewife	41	"
	S	Benjamin Joseph	50	clerk	51	"
	T	Benjamin Maurice	50	chauffeur	59	"
	U	Benjamin Rachel †	50	housewife	50	"
	V	Benjamin Sadie †	50	"	49	"
	W	Richards Leo H	50	clerk	30	"
	X	Richards Pauline †	50	housewife	27	"
	Y	Wolfe Abraham	50	laborer	60	"
	Z	Wolfe Pauline †	50	housewife	55	"
341						
	A	Britchky Anna †	51	saleswoman	40	"
	B	Britchky Joseph	51	tailor	63	"
	C	Sokolov Benjamin	51	cleaner	29	"
	D	Sokolov Celia †	51	housewife	27	"
	E	Breen Bessie †	51	"	44	"
	F	Breen Maurice	51	agent	44	"
	G	Meltzer Myer	51	retired	80	"
	H	Olem Anna †	51	housewife	85	"
	K	Slavin Evelyn †	51	saleswoman	26	"
	L	Steinberg Anna †	51	housewife	51	"
	M	Steinberg Barnet	51	salesman	28	"
	N	Steinberg Isadore	51	furrier	52	"
	O	Steinberg Rose †	51	stenographer	31	"
	P	Alexander Esther †	55	secretary	34	"
	R	Alexander Fannie †	55	housewife	57	"
	S	Alexander Frederick	55	machinist	23	"
	T	Alexander Henrietta †	55	saleswoman	25	"
	U	Alexander Morris	55	clerk	28	"
	V	Richmond Anna †	55	housewife	22	"
	W	Richmond Harry	55	salesman	25	"
	X	Shapiro Abraham	55	mason	50	"
		Shapiro Fannie †	55	housewife	48	"
	Z	Feinberg Rose †	55	"	48	"
342						
		Feinberg Victor	55	plumber	50	"
		Krozy Charles	58	merchant	37	24 Donald rd
		Krozy Rose †	58	housewife	31	24 "
		Sedersky Bessie †	58	"	48	here
		Sedersky Irving	58	merchant	22	"

Page	Letter	Full Name	Residence	Occupation	Age	Reported Residence

Hiawatha Road (Continued)

Page	Letter	Full Name	Residence	Occupation	Age	Reported Residence
	F	Sedersky Joseph	58	merchant	50	here
	G	Franklin Abraham	58	"	47	"
	H	Franklin David	58	clerk	21	"
	K	Franklin Gertrude †	58	housewife	44	"
	L	Franklin Mildred †	58	clerk	20	"
	M	Leone Guy	61	"	36	"
	N	Mattaliano Angela †	61	housewife	44	"
	O	Mattaliano Joseph	61	chauffeur	50	"
	P	Saho Arthur	63	salesman	28	15 [illegible]
	R	Saho Mary †	63	housewife	23	15 "
	S	*Rubin Herman	63	cutter	38	here
	T	*Rubin Rose †	63	housewife	32	17 [illegible]
	U	*Hurst David	63	cobbler	58	here
	V	Hurst Gertrude †	63	clerk	26	"
	W	Hurst Mildred †	63	saleswoman	23	"
	X	Waitze Eva †	63	housewife	28	"
	Y	Waitze Jacob	63	merchant	30	"
	Z	Leefe Ruth †	69	bookkeeper	22	"
343						
	A	Wooll Benjamin	69	laundryman	54	"
	B	Wooll David	69	merchant	20	"
	C	*Wooll Leana †	69	housewife	51	"
	D	Wooll Sarah †	69	clerk	29	"
	E	Wooll Saul	69	student	24	"
	F	Berg John T	72	retired	82	"
	G	Curley Lillian E †	72	housewife	59	"
	H	Curley Walter C	72	broker	48	"
	K	Hawkins Catherine †	76	housekeeper	40	"
	L	Singer Ida †	76	housewife	58	
	M	Singer Max	76	retired	59	

Itasca Street

Page	Letter	Full Name	Residence	Occupation	Age	Reported Residence
	N	Brunke Charles	9	clerk	20	[illegible]
	O	*Brunke Katherine †	9	[illegible]	[illegible]	[illegible]
	S	Savakian Haig	9	[illegible]	[illegible]	[illegible]
	R	Savakian Surpoohy †	9	[illegible]	[illegible]	[illegible]
	P	*Tarbassin Shoushanig †	9	[illegible]	[illegible]	[illegible]
	T	Anderson Carl	9	[illegible]	[illegible]	[illegible]
	U	*Anderson Marie †	9	[illegible]	[illegible]	[illegible]
	V	Katz Fannie †	10	[illegible]	[illegible]	[illegible]

Page	Letter	Full Name	Residence, Jan. 1, 1941	Occupation	Supposed Age	Reported Residence, Jan. 1, 1940. Street and Number.

Itasca Street—Continued

Page	Letter	Full Name	Residence, Jan. 1, 1941	Occupation	Supposed Age	Reported Residence, Jan. 1, 1940. Street and Number.
	W	Morrison Goodwin	10	machinist	35	here
	X	Morrison Pauline †	10	housewife	35	"
	Y	Morrison Hilda †	10	"	26	"
	Z	Morrison Theodore	10	electrician	29	"
344						
	A	Sager Bertha †	10	housewife	60	41 Fottler rd
	B	Sager Joseph	10	clerk	60	41 "
	C	Morrison Annie †	10	housewife	51	here
	D	Morrison Gertrude †	10	clerk	28	"
	E	Morrison Harry	10	tailor	53	"
	F	Leonard Gladys †	33	housewife	48	"
	G	Leonard William	33	investigator	50	"
	H	Wilson Esther E †	37	clerk	27	"
	K	Wilson Janet †	37	housewife	60	"
	L	Wilson Robert	37	painter	57	"
	M	Wilson Robert D	37	machinist	21	"
	N	Wahlstrom Alma C †	85	housekeeper	23	"
	O	Wahlstrom Arvid J	85	teacher	57	"
	P	Wahlstrom Sven A	85	student	21	"
	R	Anderson Albert	88	clerk	30	"
	S	Peterson Emma †	88	housewife	52	"
	T	Peterson Oscar	88	machinist	52	"
	U	Higgins Nettie F †	104	housewife	48	170 Colorado
	V	Higgins Wilmer L	104	machinist	63	170 "
	W	Welch Timothy J	104	retired	67	170 "
	X	Rudenauer Catherine †	104	housewife	46	here
	Y	Rudenauer John L	104	chauffeur	47	"

Kennebec Street

Page	Letter	Full Name	Residence, Jan. 1, 1941	Occupation	Supposed Age	Reported Residence, Jan. 1, 1940. Street and Number.
	Z	Whalen Stephen	10	carpenter	39	24 Dearborn
345						
	A	Whalen Theresa †	10	housewife	27	24 "
	B	Krause Augusta †	10	"	39	here
	C	Krause John	10	carpenter	49	"
	D	Gargiulo Annie †	11	housewife	40	"
	E	Gargiulo Anthony	11	clerk	27	"
	F	Gargiulo Carmela †	11	housewife	59	"
	G	Gargiulo Frank	11	candymaker	57	"
	H	Gargiulo Gerardo	11	chauffeur	33	"
	K	[illegible]	21	"	33	"

Page	Letter	Full Name				

Kennebec Street (Continued)

Page	Letter	Full Name				
	L	Carlton Jennie M †	21	housewife	39	[illegible]
	M	Pino Catherine †	33	"	63	"
	N	Pino Charles	33	clerk	21	"
	O	Pino Elizabeth †	33	housekeeper	25	"
	P	Pino Frank	33	papermaker	58	"
	R	Bernhardt Mary †	33	housekeeper	56	"
	S	Schillig Anne †	33	housewife	52	"
	T	Schillig Francis W	33	clerk	27	"

Livermore Street

Page	Letter	Full Name				
	U	Carrara Alice †	24	housewife	26	here
	V	Carrara Frank	24	shipper	22	"
	W	Carrara Louis	24	clerk	23	"
	X	*Carrara Margaret †	24	housewife	57	"
	Y	*Carrara Muriel †	24	housekeeper	21	Cambridge
	Z	Carrara Richard	24	carpenter	35	here
346						
	A	Toffoloni Erminia †	26	housewife	53	"
	B	Toffoloni Joseph	26	carpenter	51	"

Mattapan Street

Page	Letter	Full Name				
	C	Needle Joseph	17	tailor	64	[illegible]
	D	Stein Rose †	17	housewife	56	[illegible]
	E	White Dora †	17	at home	77	"
	F	Resnick Arthur	17	metalworker	44	"
	G	Resnick Rose †	17	housewife	43	"
	H	Blum Joseph B	20	carpenter	45	"
	K	Blum Mary M †	20	housewife	44	"
	L	Blum Ruth E †	20	beautician	20	"
	M	Gordon Anna †	20	bookkeeper	[illegible]	[illegible]
	N	Gordon Isadore	20	"	[illegible]	[illegible]
	O	Gordon Joseph L	20	"	23	[illegible]
	P	*Gordon Rose †	20	housewife	50	[illegible]
	R	Brown Belle †	21	"	[illegible]	[illegible]
	S	Brown Isaac R	21	[illegible]	[illegible]	[illegible]
	T	Benatuil Bella †	21	[illegible]	[illegible]	[illegible]
	U	Benatuil Holla †	21	[illegible]	[illegible]	[illegible]
	V	Benatuil Moses	21	[illegible]	[illegible]	[illegible]
	W	*Pill Blume †	21	[illegible]	[illegible]	[illegible]

Page	Letter	FULL NAME	Residence, Jan. 1, 1941.	Occupation	Supposed Age.	Reported Residence, Jan. 1, 1940. Street and Number.

Mattapan Street—Continued

Page	Letter	FULL NAME	Residence, Jan. 1, 1941.	Occupation	Supposed Age.	Reported Residence, Jan. 1, 1940. Street and Number.
	X	Weiss Murray E	24	salesman	36	136 Callender
	Y	*Weiss Ruth †	24	housewife	36	136 "
	Z	Freedman Jacob S	24	electrician	35	here
347						
	A	Freedman Mollie †	24	housewife	29	"
	B	Goldman Frank	24	manager	32	50 Winston rd
	C	Goldman Harriet †	24	housewife	28	50 "
	D	*Hittel Joseph	24	designer	57	50 "
	E	*Bricker Eva †	25	at home	78	here
	F	Masters Robert S	25	clerk	27	"
	G	Masters Sara †	25	housewife	61	"
	H	Berman Annie †	25	"	48	"
	K	Berman Hyman	25	salesman	55	"
	L	Gold Hyman	25	merchant	45	"
	M	*Gold Jennie †	25	housewife	43	"
	N	Goldenberg Morris	29	retired	75	"
	O	Goldenberg Sara †	29	housewife	69	"
	P	Lincoln Arthur H	29	retired	70	"
	R	Goldman Frances †	29	housewife	37	"
	S	Goldman Joseph	29	salesman	38	"
	T	Brown Ida †	29	housewife	31	"
	U	Brown Morris	29	engineer	35	"
	V	Grob Harry	32	manager	34	"
	W	Grob Winnifred †	32	housewife	30	"
	X	Teplitz Arthur I	32	carpenter	25	1633 Com av
	Y	Teplitz Helen †	32	housewife	22	1633 "
	Z	Teplitz Joseph	32	retired	66	here
348						
	A	Teplitz Leo	32	salesman	38	140 Capen
	B	Teplitz Rebecca †	32	at home	43	here
	C	Teplitz Rose †	32	housewife	66	"
	D	Werldoff Max	32	carpenter	45	"
	E	Werldoff Sophie †	32	bookkeeper	40	"
	F	White Clara E †	33	at home	76	"
	G	Vernon Bernard	33	letter carrier	39	52 Columbia rd
	H	Vernon Sarah †	33	housewife	29	52 "
	K	Kimball Charlotte †	37	"	38	here
	L	Kimball Donald T	37	cleaner	42	"
	M	*Krinsky Edith †	38	housewife	48	"
	N	Krinsky Max	38	chauffeur	49	"
	O	White [illegible]	38	nurse	23	"

Page.	Letter	Full Name	Residence	Occupation	Age	Reported Residence

Mattapan Street—Continued

Page.	Letter	Full Name	Residence	Occupation	Age	Reported Residence
	P	Appel Joseph	38	manufacturer	44	here
	R	Appel Sara—†	38	housewife	34	"
	S	Finn Arlene—†	38	clerk	20	"
	T	Finn Joseph	38	factoryhand	26	"
	U	Finn Mary—†	38	teacher	32	"
	V	Finn Sarah—†	38	housewife	57	"
	W	Baker Eva—†	40	saleswoman	24	"
	X*	Baker Jacob	40	carpenter	48	"
	Y*	Baker Rose—†	40	housewife	47	"
	Z	Baker Yetta—†	40	clerk	22	"
349						
	A	Rosen Celia—†	40	housewife	40	"
	B	Rosen Morris	40	salesman	43	"
	C	Rosen Ruth—†	40	saleswoman	20	"
	D	Prager Adele—†	40	secretary	28	"
	E	Prager Bella—†	40	nurse	24	"
	F	Prager Gussie—†	40	housewife	52	"
	G	Prager Rose—†	40	clerk	30	"
	H	Prager Samuel	40	ironworker	52	"
	K	Sharff Anna—†	41	housewife	35	Chelsea
	L	Sharff Benjamin	41	merchant	40	"
	M	Brass Jennie—†	41	housewife	50	here
	N	Brass Max	41	merchant	56	"
	O	Brass Sidney	41	student	22	"
	P	Leventhal Bessie—†	45	clerk	32	"
	R	Leventhal Fannie—†	45	housewife	64	"
	S	Leventhal Mary—†	45	clerk	30	"
	T	Leventhal Morris	45	retired	73	"
	U	Leventhal Rose—†	45	clerk	28	"
	V	Tobin Ida—†	45	housewife	56	"
	W	Tobin Samuel	45	chauffeur	57	"
	X	Budlong Lucy—†	45	housewife	55	[illegible]
	Y	Farrar Arthur L	45	laborer	50	[illegible]
	Z	Fitton Ira	45	"	56	[illegible]
350						
	A	Fitton Mildred—†	45	housewife	26	[illegible]
	B	Damiano Dominic	46	fireman	48	[illegible]
	C	Damiano Mary—†	46	housewife	47	[illegible]
	D	Sangiorgio Angelina—†	46	"	40	[illegible]
	E	Sangiorgio Christina—†	46	stenographer	32	[illegible]
	F	Sangiorgio Giuseppe	46	barber	45	[illegible]

Page	Letter	Full Name	Residence, Jan. 1, 1941.	Occupation	Supposed Age	Reported Residence, Jan. 1, 1940. Street and Number.

Mattapan Street—Continued

Page	Letter	Full Name	Residence, Jan. 1, 1941.	Occupation	Supposed Age	Reported Residence, Jan. 1, 1940. Street and Number.
	G	Sangiorgio Maria G †	46	nurse	20	here
	H	*Rubin Celia †	47	housewife	57	"
	K	Rubin Nathan	47	tailor	63	"
	L	Kredenser Frances †	48	housewife	38	"
	M	Kredenser Hyman	48	salesman	37	"
	N	Fishman Ida †	48	housewife	32	"
	O	Fishman Morris	48	merchant	40	"
	P	Shuman Hyman	48	cutter	61	"
	R	Shuman Joseph D	48	merchant	29	"
	S	Shuman Lizzie †	48	housewife	61	"
	T	Gilbert Lewis	48	constable	35	"
	U	*Gilbert Minnie V †	48	housewife	30	"
	V	Barker Mildred †	48	"	34	"
	W	Barker Nathan	48	mech dentist	39	"
	X	Dantowitz Diana †	48	housewife	20	"
	Y	Dantowitz Samuel	48	manufacturer	25	"
	Z	Baker Anne S †	49	clerk	21	"
351						
	A	Baker Henry B	49	mechanic	24	"
	B	Baker Mary M †	49	housewife	48	"
	C	Baker Victor A	49	baker	50	"
	D	Caswell Anna †	49	factoryhand	20	Malden
	E	*Caswell Morris	49	shoeworker	52	"
	F	*Caswell Rebecca †	49	housewife	49	"
	G	Feeney Andrew J	52	electrician	36	here
	H	Feeney Helena A †	52	housewife	35	"
	K	Small Catherine †	52A	"	42	"
	L	Russo Cecile †	52A	"	22	"
	M	Russo Thomas	52A	foreman	28	"
	N	Goode James A	54	chauffeur	28	"
	O	Goode Marie J †	54	housewife	26	"
	P	Cimyk Catherine †	54A	"	23	2 Dimock
	R	Cimyk Joseph	54A	baker	26	2 "
	S	Little George	54A	millman	26	here
	T	Little Marie †	54A	housewife	24	"
	U	*Proctor Claude O	55	salesman	31	"
	V	Proctor Elizabeth E †	55	housewife	28	"
	W	*Mougholian Mildred †	55	"	33	"
	X	Mougholian Stephen	55	repairman	38	"
	Y	Dean Ashley	56	mechanic	49	"
	Z	Dean Demaron L	56	retired	85	"

352

Mattapan Street (Continued)

Page	Letter	Full Name	Residence, Jan. 1, 1941	Occupation	Age	Reported Residence
352	A	Dean Lorraine †	56	housewife	50	here
	B	Burke Anna †	56A	"	37	"
	C	Burke Joseph E	56A	janitor	41	"
	D	Tansey Margaret M †	56A	packer	45	"
	E	Burke Elizabeth A †	56A	domestic	31	"
	F	Burke Ethel †	56A	housewife	30	32 George
	G	Burke James A	56A	salesman	30	32 "
	H	Burke Margaret †	56A	saleswoman	29	here
	K	Burke Walter E	56A	metalworker	38	"
	L	Welsh Irene †	56A	housewife	42	"
	M	Welsh John E	56A	chauffeur	42	"
	N	Lowney Adelaide G †	59	beautician	20	"
	O	Lowney Alice L †	59	nurse	31	"
	P	Lowney Alice M †	59	housewife	58	"
	R	Lowney Marjorie A †	59	student	24	"
	S	Lowney Mary L †	59	teacher	33	"
	T	Lowney William H	59	retired	66	"
	U	Lowney William J	59	clerk	30	"
	V	Buck Arlene S †	62	housewife	30	"
	W	Buck David M	62	accountant	27	"
	X	Buck Frank A	62	manufacturer	69	"
	Y	Buck Mary E †	62	housewife	64	"
353	A	Wood Emanuel C	74	machinist	55	"
	B	Wood Martha I †	74	housewife	55	"
	C	Yaeger Albert J	74A	mechanic	26	"
	D	Yaeger Margaret E †	74A	housewife	24	"
	E	Weger Abraham	74A	merchant	31	"
	F	Weger Harry	74A	clerk	27	"
	G	Weger Louis	74A	merchant	58	"
	H	*Weger Minnie †	74A	housewife	58	"
	K	Bemister Clare M †	75	"	31	Q[illegible]
	L	Bemister Frank S	75	mechanic	[illegible]	[illegible]
	M	Lane Beverley C	75A	"	[illegible]	[illegible]
	N	Lane Cecile M †	75A	housewife	[illegible]	[illegible]
	O	McFayden Helen †	75A	[illegible]	[illegible]	[illegible]
	P	Killion Albert M	75A	[illegible]	[illegible]	W[illegible]
	R	Killion Doris †	75A	[illegible]	[illegible]	[illegible]
	S	*Forbes Firth †	77	[illegible]	[illegible]	[illegible]
	T	*Forbes Wilfred E	77	[illegible]	[illegible]	[illegible]

Page	Letter	Full Name	Residence, Jan. 1, 1941	Occupation	Supposed Age	Reported Residence, Jan. 1, 1940. Street and Number.

Mattapan Street Continued

Page	Letter	Full Name	Residence, Jan. 1, 1941	Occupation	Supposed Age	Reported Residence, Jan. 1, 1940. Street and Number.
	U	Jardine Gertrude A †	77	housewife	31	here
	V	Jardine Willis B	77	supervisor	36	"
	W	Cross Myrtle †	77A	housewife	39	"
	X	Cross Stanley J	77A	caretaker	46	"
	Y	Gart Anna †	78	housewife	55	"
	Z	Gart Bertha †	78	student	25	"
354						
	A	Gart Frieda †	78	clerk	25	"
	B	Gart Louis	78	plumber	61	"
	C	Gedrich Helen †	78	housewife	24	22 Arcola
	D	Gedrich Walter V	78	electrician	26	Cambridge
	E	Gillis Roderick J	78A	porter	48	here
	F	Gillis Sadie †	78A	housewife	41	"
	G	Buttomer Andrew	133	retired	74	"
	H	Buttomer Ellen †	133	housewife	44	"
	K	Smart William M	133	painter	54	"
	L	Johnson Edith †	137	teacher	43	"
	M	Johnson Knute	137	toolmaker	45	"

Messinger Street

Page	Letter	Full Name	Residence, Jan. 1, 1941	Occupation	Supposed Age	Reported Residence, Jan. 1, 1940. Street and Number.
	N	*Signori Eugene	171	mechanic	56	here
	O	Signori Lena †	171	housekeeper	21	"
	P	Signori Mario	171	papermaker	27	"
	R	*Signori Theresa †	171	housewife	52	"

Mulvey Street

Page	Letter	Full Name	Residence, Jan. 1, 1941	Occupation	Supposed Age	Reported Residence, Jan. 1, 1940. Street and Number.
	S	Taylor Ernest J	3	engineer	63	here
	T	Taylor Ernest J, jr	3	weigher	21	"
	U	Taylor Mabel W †	3	housewife	58	"
	V	Sullivan Helen F †	3	stenographer	29	"
	W	Sullivan Sarah E †	3	housewife	62	"
	X	Sullivan William P	3	retired	61	"
	Y	Murphy John F	4	meatcutter	70	"
	Z	Murphy John F	4	clerk	40	"
355						
	A	Murphy Mary A	4	housewife	64	"
	B	Schiavina Alphonse	4	painter	28	"
	C	Schiavina Mary [illegible]	4	housewife	30	"
	D	Root Bernard	4	salesman	20	"

Page	Letter	Full Name	Residence, Jan. 1	Occupation		

Mulvey Street Continued

Page	Letter	Full Name	Residence	Occupation	Age	Reported Residence
	E	Root Joseph H	4	salesman	46	here
	F	Root Rose †	4	housewife	43	"
	G	Moore Alice †	5	"	31	[illegible]
	H	Caristi Joseph	6	manager	44	5 Mulvey
	K	Caristi Mary †	6	housewife	45	5 "
	M	Booris Albert	7	musician	24	474 Col[illegible]
	N	Booris Constance †	7	housewife	23	474 "
	O	Gibbons John F	8	meatcutter	46	9 Mulvey
	P	Gibbons Mary E †	8	housewife	47	9 "
	R	Powell Gladys †	8	"	39	11 "
	S	Powell Thomas A	8	machinist	41	11 "
	T	Kelly Ethel J †	9	housewife	23	Milton
	U	Kelly F Russell	9	factoryhand	25	40 Burgess
	V	Lentini Frank C	10	policeman	32	here
	W	Lentini Jean †	10	housewife	29	"
	X	Phipps Joseph A	11	chauffeur	48	28 Pond
	Y	Phipps Teresa J †	11	housewife	45	28 "
356						
	A	Collins Grace †	11A	"	39	Vermont
	B	Collins Hobart	11A	operator	40	"
	C	Doyle Catherine †	12	housewife	51	here
	D	Doyle Edward	12	watchman	57	"
	E	Doyle George	12	clerk	21	"
	F	Murphy James J	12	manager	53	58 Norfolk
	G	*Murphy Mary T †	12	housewife	51	58 "
	H	Murphy Richard S	12	student	22	58 "
	K	*Knell Arthur T	14	carpenter	39	here
	L	*Knell Marjorie L †	14	housewife	33	"

Norfolk Street

Page	Letter	Full Name	Residence	Occupation	Age	Reported Residence
	M	Goldman Gertrude †	620	housewife	41	here
	N	Goldman William	620	jeweler	[illegible]	[illegible]
	O	Silver Gussie †	620	housewife	[illegible]	[illegible]
	P	Silver Wolf	620	[illegible]	[illegible]	[illegible]
	R	Fishman Abraham	620	florist	[illegible]	[illegible]
	S	Fishman Benjamin	620	[illegible]	[illegible]	[illegible]
	T	Fishman Minnie †	620	housewife	[illegible]	[illegible]
	U	Fishman Nathan	620	[illegible]	[illegible]	[illegible]
	V	Segal Jennie †	620	[illegible]	[illegible]	[illegible]
	W	Segal Samuel	620	[illegible]	[illegible]	[illegible]

Page	Letter	Full Name	Residence, Jan. 1, 1941.	Occupation.	Supposed Age.	Reported Residence, Jan. 1, 1940. Street and Number.

Norfolk Street—Continued

Page	Letter	Full Name	Residence, Jan. 1, 1941.	Occupation.	Supposed Age.	Reported Residence, Jan. 1, 1940. Street and Number.
	X	Kravetz Charles	620	tailor	59	here
	Y	Kravetz David	620	"	25	"
	Z	Kravetz Esther—†	620	clerk	24	Brookline
357						
	A	Kravetz Fannie—†	620	housewife	53	here
	B	Kravetz Nelson E	620	clerk	21	"
	C	Kravetz Sydney	620	U S A	24	"
	D	Goldberg Clara—†	624	bookkeeper	23	"
	E	Goldberg Frank	624	presser	59	"
	F	Goldberg Ida—†	624	housewife	56	"
	G	Leven David	624	salesman	31	"
	H	Leven Sari—†	624	housewife	31	"
	K	Silberberg Harry	624	salesman	41	"
	L	Silberberg Lena—†	624	housewife	39	"
	M	*Zolloto Bessie—†	624	"	69	"
	N	*Zolloto Samuel	624	tailor	69	"
	O	Greenberg Frances—†	624	clerk	27	"
	P	Greenberg Max	624	student	25	"
	R	Greenberg Rose—†	624	housewife	48	"
	S	Greenberg Saul	624	meatcutter	53	"

Savannah Avenue

Page	Letter	Full Name	Residence, Jan. 1, 1941.	Occupation.	Supposed Age.	Reported Residence, Jan. 1, 1940. Street and Number.
	T	Davis Lillian—†	45	housewife	45	here
	U	Davis Michael	45	salesman	50	"
	V	*Levine Tillie—†	45	housekeeper	70	"
	W	Taylor Arthur S	49	clerk	22	"
	X	Taylor Samuel	49	builder	52	"
	Y	Taylor Sarah—†	49	housewife	51	"
	Z	Taylor Stanley J	49	clerk	20	"
358						
	A	Winsloe Agnes M—†	53	housewife	62	"
	B	Winsloe John	53	engineer	63	"
	C	Winsloe Mildred A—†	53	teacher	36	"
	D	Hartford Irene—†	57	operator	44	"
	E	Hartford J Warren	57	salesman	22	"

Tennis Road

Page	Letter	Full Name	Residence, Jan. 1, 1941.	Occupation.	Supposed Age.	Reported Residence, Jan. 1, 1940. Street and Number.
	F	Wolfson Joseph	3	grocer	30	here
	G	Wolfson Max	3	salesman	54	"
	H	Wolfson Rae—†	3	housewife	49	"

Tennis Road—Continued

Page.	Letter	Full Name	Residence	Occupation	Age	
	K	Wolfson Rita—†	3	clerk	22	here
	L	*Singer Mollie—†	3	housewife	50	5 W[illegible]
	M	*Singer Samuel	3	merchant	50	5 "
	N	Golan Bessie—†	6	at home	66	here
	O	Wallace Abraham	6	manager	45	"
	P	*Wallace Lillian—†	6	housewife	41	"
	R	Goldstein Louis	6	meatcutter	43	"
	S	Goldstein Mollie—†	6	housewife	40	"
	T	Saperstein Joseph	6	manager	38	"
	U	Saperstein Morris	6	"	37	"
	V	Lepore Albert	7	counterman	49	"
	W	Lepore Rose—†	7	housewife	35	"
	X	*Weiner Edith—†	7	at home	51	"
	Y	Cohen Esta—†	7	housewife	32	"
	Z	Cohen Oscar	7	manufacturer	34	"
359						
	A	Plotinsky Gladys—†	7	stenographer	21	35 Hav[illegible]
	B	Plotinsky Ida—†	7	housewife	50	35 "
	C	Gordon Abraham H	8	superintendent	38	here
	D	Gordon Ruth—†	8	housewife	38	"
	E	Wenetsky Evelyn—†	8	secretary	20	"
	F	Wenetsky Helen—†	8	"	23	"
	G	Wenetsky Rose—†	8	housewife	58	"
	H	Wenetsky Selma—†	8	teacher	30	"
	K	Wenetsky Solomon O	8	chemist	60	"
	L	Bronstein Lillian—†	11	housewife	29	63 H[illegible]
	M	Shiffman Celia—†	11	"	34	here
	N	Shiffman Isadore	11	salesman	42	"
	O	Berly Charlotte—†	11	stenographer	21	"
	P	Berly Louis	11	retired	64	"
	R	Berly Rebecca—†	11	housewife	58	[illegible]
	S	Rothberg Annie—†	12	"	[illegible]	[illegible]
	T	Stone Lena—†	12	typist	[illegible]	[illegible]
	U	Ross Henry	12	chauffeur	[illegible]	6 A[illegible]
	V	Ross Jessie—†	12	housewife	[illegible]	[illegible]
	W	Finn Ida—†	15	"	[illegible]	[illegible]
	X	Finn Joseph	15	salesman	[illegible]	[illegible]
	Y	Winick Ester B—†	15	housewife	[illegible]	[illegible]
	Z	Winick Ida—†	15	"	[illegible]	[illegible]
360						
	A	Winick Louis	15	[illegible]	[illegible]	[illegible]
	B	Shulkin Arnold	16	[illegible]	[illegible]	[illegible]

Page	Letter	Full Name	Residence, Jan. 1, 1941	Occupation	Supposed Age	Reported Residence, Jan. 1, 1940. Street and Number

Tennis Road Continued

Page	Letter	Full Name	Residence, Jan. 1, 1941	Occupation	Supposed Age	Reported Residence, Jan. 1, 1940. Street and Number
	C	Shulkin Rose †	16	housewife	27	here
	D	White Philip	16	retired	56	"
	E	Epstein Ida †	16	housewife	32	202 W Selden
	F	Epstein Joseph H	16	printer	32	202 "
	G	Oenoff Abraham	19	manager	50	here
	H	Oenoff Anna †	19	housewife	47	"
	K	Oenoff Miriam †	19	teacher	22	"
	L	Bindman Emma †	20	housewife	48	"
	M	Bindman Samuel	20	factoryhand	48	"
	N	Horace Celia H †	20	at home	21	"
	O	Horace Lena †	20	housewife	46	"
	P	Horace William	20	salesman	50	"
	R	Simberg Harry	23	merchant	43	"
	S	Simberg Jennie †	23	housewife	41	"
	T	Orenstein Jennie †	23	"	50	"
	U	Orenstein Max	23	merchant	52	"
	V	Weiner Louis	23	laborer	27	"
	W	Weiner Sylvia †	23	housewife	23	"
	X	Averbuck Allen	24	salesman	30	"
	Y	Averbuck Celia †	24	housewife	27	"
	Z	Crawford Jacob	24	manufacturer	51	"
361						
	A	Crawford Minnie †	24	housewife	52	32 Linwood sq
	B	Tobias Nathan	24	retired	81	here
	C	Gashin Abraham	27	watchmaker	48	"
	D	Gashin Annie †	27	housewife	41	"
	E	Gashin Irving	27	attorney	22	"
	F	Finklestein Lillian M †	27	housewife	39	58 Hutchings
	G	Finklestein Paul	27	druggist	39	58 "
	H	Weitz Joseph	28	proprietor	30	here
	K	Weitz Rose †	28	housewife	28	"
	L	Kass Sophie †	28	"	45	"
	M	Abrams Annie †	31	"	46	"
	N	Abrams Beatrice †	31	bookkeeper	27	"
	O	Abrams Benjamin	31	salesman	23	"
	P	Abrams Jeannette †	31	teacher	21	"
	R	Abrams Morris	31	marketman	48	"
	S	Levine Bernard	31	manufacturer	38	36 Tennis rd
	T	Levine Sonia †	31	housewife	36	36 "
	U	Rittenburg Fannie †	32	"	65	here

Tennis Road Continued

Letter	Full Name		Residence	Occupation	Age	Reported Residence
V	Rittenburg Gertrude	†	32	bookkeeper	35	here
W	Rittenburg Jacob H		32	salesman	65	"
X	Rittenburg Ralph B		32	engineer	21	"
Y	Daniels Benjamin		32	dentist	43	"
Z	Daniels Hesse	†	32	housewife	41	"
362						
A	Davidson Jacob		35	salesman	41	"
B	Davidson Ruth	†	35	housewife	39	"
C	Lipson Augusta	†	35	"	45	"
D	Lipson Nathan I		35	salesman	50	"
E	*Kelliher Ann	†	35	housekeeper	31	"
F	Neustadt Bella	†	35	merchant	42	"
G	Neustadt Herman J		35	salesman	22	"
H	Neustadt Roland I		35	"	21	"
K	Neustadt Samuel		35	merchant	45	"
L	Kaplan Celia	†	36	housewife	33	35 Wal
M	Kaplan Morris M		36	salesman	36	35 "
N	*Tatelbaum Mary	†	36	housewife	40	here
O	Tatelbaum Mildred	†	36	at home	20	"
P	Tatelbaum Morris		36	leatherworker	43	"
R	Berman Lillian	†	39	housewife	68	"
S	Lipson Augusta	†	39	"	45	"
T	Lipson Nathan I		39	merchant	50	"
U	Daniels Jennie	†	39	housewife	52	"
V	Daniels Norman		39	manufacturer	24	"
W	Daniels Shirley	†	39	housewife	20	82 Ballou av
X	Robinson Albert		40	salesman	39	here
Y	Robinson Kate	†	40	housewife	31	"
Z	Wernon Louis		40	salesman	64	"
363						
A	Levine Henry		40	"	39	"
B	Levine Rose	†	40	housewife	34	"
C	*Curran Mary	†	43	housekeeper	48	54 Lessard
D	Sidman Annabelle	†	43	housewife	40	here
E	Sidman Manuel		43	merchant	44	"
F	Kline Abbot A		43	salesman	25	"
G	Kline Bessie H	†	43	housewife	[illegible]	"
H	Kline Harriet	†	43	secretary	20	"
K	Karas Ann	†	44	student	23	[illegible]
L	Karas Mary	†	44	[illegible]	[illegible]	[illegible]

Page	Letter	Full Name	Residence, Jan. 1, 1941.	Occupation	Supposed Age.	Reported Residence, Jan. 1, 1940. Street and Number.

Tennis Road—Continued

Page	Letter	Full Name	Residence, Jan. 1, 1941.	Occupation	Supposed Age.	Reported Residence, Jan. 1, 1940. Street and Number.
	M	Karas Myer	44	merchant	47	here
	N	Gordon Rose †	47	housewife	37	"
	O	Sriberg Samuel	47	merchant	67	"
	P	Oppenheim Anna W—†	47	housewife	44	"
	R	Oppenheim Mathew	47	student	20	"
	S	Kravitz Ida †	48	at home	28	"
	T	Shuman Fannie †	48	housewife	50	"
	U	Shuman Franklin	48	student	23	"
	V	Shuman Harry	48	salesman	54	"
	W	Lukatch Dora †	51	housewife	61	"
	X	Lukatch Harry	51	retired	63	"
	Y	Lukatch Maurice H	51	salesman	33	"
	Z	Soreff Esther †	52	housewife	35	"
364						
	A	Soreff Max	52	salesman	43	"
	B	Kravetz Pearl †	55	housewife	40	"
	C	Kravetz Philip	55	marketman	44	"
	D	Weinstein Miriam A—†	55	housewife	41	"
	E	Weinstein Samuel	55	manufacturer	45	"
	F	Belder Benjamin	56	salesman	27	"
	G	Belder Fannie †	56	housewife	50	"
	H	Belder Louis	56	salesman	53	"
	K	Gutlian David	59	marketman	24	"
	L	Gutlian Sylvia †	59	housewife	20	"
	M	Karas Elia †	60	glazier	54	"
	N	Karas Fannie †	60	housewife	54	"
	O*	Yanofsky Ida †	64	"	40	"
	P*	Yanofsky Jacob	64	ironworker	42	"
	R	Gulesian Adelaide †	67	bookkeeper	38	"
	S	Gulesian Henrietta †	67	housewife	33	"
	T	Gulesian Mark	67	retired	71	"

Wabash Street

Page	Letter	Full Name	Residence, Jan. 1, 1941.	Occupation	Supposed Age.	Reported Residence, Jan. 1, 1940. Street and Number.
	U	Joyce Austin	5	painter	36	here
	V	Joyce Josephine †	5	housewife	36	"
	W	Hahn Walter H	10	clerk	32	Milton
	X	Torgersen Fritz O	10	supervisor	42	here
	Y	Torgersen Louise M †	10	housewife	31	"

Walk Hill Street

Page	Letter	Full Name	Residence	Occupation		
	Z	Coffey Cornelius	591	shipper	47	here
365						
	A	Coffey Eileen †	591	housewife	20	"
	B	Coffey Susan †	591	secretary	24	"
	C	Killam Christine †	605	housewife	36	"
	D	Killam Harold	605	manager	44	"
	E	Hadjian Eugenia †	605	housewife	58	"
	F	Hadjian Louis	605	merchant	59	"
	G	Hadjian Victoria †	605	student	21	"
	H	Olson Harold E	605	bartender	45	"
	K	Olson Margaret †	605	housewife	43	"
	M	Rosen Jennie †	643	"	60	"
	N	Rosen Samuel	643	grocer	65	"
	O	Freeman Annie †	649	housewife	48	32 Hosmer
	P	Freeman Louis	649	merchant	48	32 "
	R	Freeman Saul B	649	student	20	32 "
	S	White Beatrice †	623	housewife	38	here
	T	White Louis	623	salesman	39	"
	U	Burke Mary A †	625	housekeeper	49	"
	V	Burke Sarah A †	625	clerk	42	"
	W	Burke Thomas F	625	policeman	44	"
	X	Green Katie †	627	housewife	44	[illegible]
	Y	Green Max H	627	agent	44	961 "
	Z	Denat Samuel	627	retired	73	here
366						
	A	Rosen Christina †	627	housewife	39	"
	B	Rosenston Diana †	629	"	44	"
	C	Rosenston Morris	629	lawyer	44	"
	D	Mishara Bessie †	629	housewife	43	"
	E	Mishara Diana †	629	secretary	22	"
	F	Connell Ellen M †	631	housewife	64	"
	G	Fitzgerald James J	631	plumber	49	"
	H	Fitzgerald James J, jr	631	clerk	20	"
	K	Sullivan Lillian G †	631	housewife	54	"
	L	Sullivan Patrick J	631	engineer	55	"
	M	Sullivan Paul J	631	clerk	21	"
	N	Fennessy Mary E †	635	housewife	58	"
	O	Fennessy Theodore	635	salesman	62	"
	P	Flax Lillian L †	637	housewife	53	[illegible]
	R	Flax Max	637	[illegible]	[illegible]	[illegible]

Page	Letter	Full Name	Residence, Jan. 1, 1941.	Occupation.	Supposed Age.	Reported Residence, Jan. 1, 1940. Street and Number.

Walk Hill Street—Continued

Page	Letter	Full Name	Residence, Jan. 1, 1941.	Occupation.	Supposed Age.	Reported Residence, Jan. 1, 1940. Street and Number.
	S	Rosenthal Lawrence	637	accountant	33	here
	T	Rosenthal Rose †	637	housewife	29	"
	U	Nanes Goldie †	637	"	28	12 Am Legion H'way
	V	Nanes Paul	637	salesman	28	12 "
	W	Zaff Benjamin	637	manager	32	here
	X	Zaff Ida †	637	housewife	32	"
	Y	Rosenberg Gertrude—†	637	"	32	62 Am Legion H'way
	Z	Rosenberg Myer	637	salesman	35	62 "
367						
	A	White Charles	637	manager	32	12 Roxton
	B	White Gertrude †	637	housewife	30	12 "
	C	Wides Ann †	637	housekeeper	58	77 Mattapan
	D	Goode Ellen L †	639	housewife	55	12 Mulvey
	E	Goode Margaret †	639	attendant	24	12 "
	F	Goode Stephen	639	gardener	59	12 "
	G	Lewis Merton C	639	counterman	64	here
	H	Sladen Frank E	639	gardener	55	Milton
	K	Ward Alvah E	639	barber	57	here
	L	Ward Elsie J †	639	housewife	50	"
	N	Sapienza Frank	641	barber	26	"
	O	Sapienza Margaret—†	641	housewife	23	"
	T	Sarnie Barbara S—†	641A	"	31	"
	U	Sarnie William J	641A	manager	31	"
	V	Feinberg Anne †	643	housewife	35	28 Dyer
	W	Kolow Katherine—†	643	"	36	here
	X	Kolow Morris	643	druggist	37	"
	Y	Fitzgerald Teresa A—†	645	housewife	25	"
	Z	Fitzgerald William B	645	salesman	25	"
368						
	A	Hutchings Cleonice—†	645	housewife	32	30 Groveland
	B	Hutchings Lionel B	645	baker	37	30 "
	C	Jardine Robert F	645	laborer	62	16 Woodlawn av
	D	Jardine Ross	645	garageman	20	16 "
	E	Wood Carrie A †	645	housewife	28	16 "
	F	Wood Charles E	645	manager	29	16 "
	G	*Cohen Paula †	647	housewife	32	here
	H	Cohen Philip	647	salesman	34	"
	K	Hayett Max	647	"	39	"
	L	*Hayett Rose †	647	housewife	36	"
	M	Arbit Annette †	647A	clerk	21	574 Norfolk
	N	Arbit George	647A	manager	25	33 Hazleton

Page	Letter	Full Name	Residence	Occupation		

Walk Hill Street—Continued

O	Malitz Lillian—†	647A	bookkeeper	20	here
P	Silverstein Beatrice—†	647A	housewife	25	"
R	Silverstein George	647A	manager	27	"
S	Mayer Charles A	649	machinist	47	"
T	Mayer Elsie L—†	649	nurse	22	"
U	Mayer Elsie W—†	649	housewife	49	"
V	Watkinson Rose E—†	649	"	71	"
W	Harris Anna—†	651	"	21	"
X	Harris Kenneth	651	cutter	25	"
Y*	Romanko Peter	651	caretaker	49	95 Poplar
Z*	Romanko Tatitiana—†	651	housewife	45	95 "
369					
A	Romanko Theresa—†	651	waitress	21	95 "
B	Greenberg Leo C	653	manufacturer	37	524 E Seventh
C	Greenberg Sara—†	653	housewife	28	Connecticut
D	Finnigan Mary J—†	661	"	30	here
E	Finnigan Richard A	661	foreman	34	"
F	Killion Thomas	661	retired	68	"
G	Gould Carleton	665	machinist	26	21 Belden
H	Gould Edna—†	665	housewife	21	21 "
K	White John F	665	retired	63	here
L	McDermott Daniel J	669	inspector	63	"
M	McDermott Freda—†	669	housewife	56	"
N	McDermott George E	669	U S N	28	"
O	McDermott William H	669	manager	34	"
P	Kaplan Harry	671	projectionist	44	"
R	Kaplan Ida—†	671	housewife	44	"
S	Lennon David	671	merchant	67	"
T	Lennon Sophie—†	671	housewife	63	"
U	Satter Charlotte—†	671	secretary	22	"
V	Satter Ida—†	671	housewife	49	"
W	Satter John J	671	superintendent	49	"
X	Shriber Abraham	671	manufacturer	28	"
Y*	Shriber Mary—†	671	housewife	54	"
Z	Shriber Max	671	plumber	52	"
370					
A	Shriber Ruth—†	671	housewife	[illegible]	[illegible]
B	Kalus Lena—†	683	"	58	[illegible]
C	Barkin Albert	683	attorney	[illegible]	[illegible] Morton
D*	Barkin Eva—†	683	housewife	[illegible]	[illegible] "
E*	Barkin Samuel	683	[illegible]	[illegible]	[illegible] "

Page	Letter	Full Name	Residence, Jan. 1, 1941.	Occupation.	Supposed Age.	Reported Residence, Jan. 1, 1940. Street and Number.

Walk Hill Street Continued

Page	Letter	Full Name	Residence, Jan. 1, 1941.	Occupation.	Supposed Age.	Reported Residence, Jan. 1, 1940. Street and Number.
	F	Levenson Bertha †	683	housewife	39	here
	G	Levenson Harold	683	mechanic	40	"
	H	Gillis Margaret †	687	housekeeper	46	"
	K	Sawdy Annie †	687	housewife	50	"
	L	Sawdy Archie	687	chauffeur	20	"
	M	Welsh Sarah †	687	at home	66	"
	N	Buckley Alice †	687	"	69	"
	O	Donald Elizabeth †	687	"	83	552 Centre
	P	Gillis John A	687	painter	48	here
	R	Gillis Mary †	687	clerk	44	"
	S	Lane Mary K †	687	at home	81	"
	T	Lees Mary †	687	"	81	"
	U	MacInnis Josephine †	687	housewife	40	"
	V	Snyder Frank	687	retired	50	"
	W	Walsh Annie †	687	at home	79	"
	X	Alpert David	689	barber	52	41 Fottler rd
	Y	Alpert Zelda †	689	housewife	41	41 "
	Z	Showstack Nathaniel	689	physician	28	49 Browning av
371						
	A	Showstack Paul J	689	photographer	24	49 "
	B	*Showstack Philip	689	retired	66	49 "
	C	Rutstein Anne †	691	housewife	24	here
	D	Rutstein Nathan	691	baker	26	"
	E	Cohen Elaine †	691	housewife	25	"
	F	Cohen Robert	691	salesman	30	"
	G	Boylan Andrew G	695	retired	82	New York
	H	Hubbard Clifford W	695	painter	54	here
	K	Hubbard Ella A †	695	housewife	51	"
	L	Allen Edith L †	695	"	36	"
	M	Allen Howard	695	repairman	36	"
	N	Arthur Frank E	695	retired	77	"
	O	Meyer Henry S	699	"	79	"
	P	Meyer Mary B †	699	housewife	77	"
	R	Koplow Albert	701	merchant	40	"
	S	Koplow Jennie †	701	housewife	37	"
	T	Goodman Alice †	701	clerk	43	"
	U	Kaplan Mendal	701	pedler	70	"
	V	Mathews Mabel †	701	housekeeper	29	"
	W	Dreyfus Bessie †	701	housewife	40	"
	X	Dreyfus George	701	musician	20	"
	Y	Dreyfus Harry	701	cutter	45	"

Page.	Letter.	Full Name.	Residence Jan. 1 [illegible]	Occupation	[illegible]	[illegible]

Walk Hill Street (Continued)

Page.	Letter.	Full Name.	Residence	Occupation	Age	Reported Residence
	Z	Mindes Louis	701	retired	71	here
372						
	A	Brown Dora †	703	housewife	32	
	B	Brown Samuel	703	salesman	42	"
	C	Roberts Celia †	703	housewife	33	"
	D	Roberts Charles	703	upholsterer	37	"
	E	Danis Aaron	703	tailor	52	"
	F	*Danis Esther †	703	housewife	51	"
	G	Danis Helen †	703	bookkeeper	22	"
	H	Danis Israel	703	accountant	26	"
	K	Danis Joseph	703	attorney	24	"
	L	Galarneaux Alexander W	711	merchant	50	"
	M	Galarneaux Rae †	711	housewife	50	"
	N	McCray Clyde	715	clerk	21	"
	O	McCray Harry A	715	marker	51	"
	P	McCray Mary A †	715	housewife	40	"
	R	Nelson Ethel M †	715	"	40	21 Corbet
	S	Nelson Lewin	715	engineer	37	21 "
	T	Minot Dorothy L †	715	saleswoman	22	here
	U	Minot Evelyn E †	715	clerk	23	"
	V	Minot Helen R †	715	secretary	20	"
	W	Minot Jessie R †	715	housewife	51	"
	X	Martin Raymond	717	carpenter	41	"
	Y	Martin Vera R †	717	housewife	36	"
	Z	Smith Doris L †	717	"	32	"
373						
	A	Smith Thomas E	717	manager	38	"
	B	Galvin Joseph	717	chauffeur	23	"
	C	Galvin Mary F †	717	housewife	69	"
	D	Smith Louise †	717	"	27	"

Woodhaven Avenue

Page.	Letter.	Full Name.	Residence	Occupation	Age	Reported Residence
	E	Deshler Alice †	23	housewife	53	here
	F	Deshler Charles	23	salesman	52	"
	G	Hovey Alice †	23	housewife	35	"
	H	Hovey Frank	23	manager	36	"
	K	*Gorelick Fannie †	31	housewife	48	"
	L	Gorelick Jacob	31	student	21	"
	M	*Gorelick Nathan	31	tailor	[illegible]	"
	N	Singer Benjamin H	31	[illegible]	[illegible]	

Page	Letter	Full Name	Residence, Jan. 1, 1941.	Occupation	Supposed Age	Reported Residence, Jan. 1, 1940. Street and Number.

Woodhaven Avenue—Continued

Page	Letter	Full Name	Residence, Jan. 1, 1941.	Occupation	Supposed Age	Reported Residence, Jan. 1, 1940. Street and Number.
	O	Singer Selma R †	31	housewife	33	here
	P	Melnick Claire †	35	"	38	"
	R	Melnick Samuel	35	engineer	39	"
	S	Kogos Evelyn †	35	housewife	42	"
	T	Kogos Irving J	35	salesman	45	"
	U	Nemrow Abraham	35	attorney	35	"
	V	Myers Anne †	38	housewife	23	"
	W	Myers Elizabeth E †	38	"	44	"
	X	Myers Melvin M	38	manager	23	"
	Y	Myers Samuel A	38	merchant	45	"
	Z	Myers Sidney D	38	chauffeur	20	"
374						
	A	Perlman Clara †	39	at home	21	"
	B	Perlman Jacob	39	printer	50	"
	C	Perlman Lester	39	U S A	23	Philippine Islands
	D	Perlman Rose †	39	housewife	47	here
	E	Perlman Wilfred	39	U S A	23	Philippine Islands
	F	Sorofman Marion †	39	clerk	27	here
	G	Sorofman Tillie †	39	at home	68	"
	H	Rybier Harry	47	tailor	45	"
	K	Rybier Sadie †	47	housewife	41	"
	L	Handel Frances †	51	"	41	"
	M	Handel Myer	51	printer	44	"
	N	Myers Anne †	51	at home	23	"
	O	Myers Elizabeth E †	51	housewife	44	"
	P	Myers Melvin M	51	manager	23	"
	R	Myers Samuel A	51	salesman	45	"
	S	Myers Sidney D	51	chauffeur	20	"

Ward 18 Precinct 4

CITY OF BOSTON

LIST OF RESIDENTS
20 YEARS OF AGE AND OVER

(NON-CITIZENS INDICATED BY ASTERISK)
(FEMALES INDICATED BY DAGGER)

AS OF

JANUARY 1, 1941

CITY OF BOSTON PRINTING DEPARTMENT

Page	Letter	Full Name	Residence, Jan. 1, 1941	Occupation	Supposed Age	Reported Residence, Jan. 1, 1940. Street and Number.
400						

Burmah Street

Page	Letter	Full Name	Residence, Jan. 1, 1941	Occupation	Supposed Age	Reported Residence, Jan. 1, 1940. Street and Number.
	A	LeLacheur Guild A	24	chauffeur	33	here
	B	LeLacheur Mary H †	24	housewife	33	"
	C	Donovan Timothy	25	retired	84	"
	D	Degan John J	28	clerk	32	"
	E	Degan Mildred A †	28	housewife	29	"
	F	Mathiasen Carl	29	painter	57	"
	G	Mathiasen Elizabeth M †	29	housewife	53	"
	H	Mathiasen Esther M †	29	clerk	22	"
	K	Day Catherine B †	30	housewife	42	"
	L	Day Harold W	30	custodian	42	"
	M	Griffiths Bessie D †	31	housewife	49	"
	N	Griffiths William J	31	policeman	54	"
	O	Griffiths William J, jr	31	accountant	21	"
	P	Toland Charlotte A †	33	clerk	21	"
	R	Toland Christine M †	33	housewife	44	"
	S	Toland John F	33	U S A	22	"
	T	Toland Rita M †	33	clerk	20	"
	U	Toland William P	33	custodian	47	"
	V	Jackson Dorothy B †	35	physician	25	"
	W	Jackson Ida B †	35	housewife	58	"
	X	Jackson Walter	35	superintendent	60	"
	Y	*LeLacheur Angus M	36	carpenter	68	"
	Z	LeLacheur Lauretta A †	36	nurse	24	"
401						
	A	MacDonald Iris J	37	clerk	31	1112 Hyde Park av
	B	McSherry George F	37	"	36	here
	C	McSherry Lillian M †	37	housewife	32	"

Cummins Highway

Page	Letter	Full Name	Residence, Jan. 1, 1941	Occupation	Supposed Age	Reported Residence, Jan. 1, 1940. Street and Number.
	D	O'Connell Helen F †	821	housewife	31	here
	E	O'Connell Joseph P	821	fireman	36	"
	F	Cuddy Rita A †	821	housewife	37	"
	G	Cuddy William J	821	agent	38	"
	H	O'Leary Margaret †	821	housekeeper	67	"
	K	Alexander Margaret V †	825	housewife	76	"
	L	Cushman Lotta †	825	housekeeper	54	"
	M	Pratt Arthur	825	laborer	55	"
	N	Pratt Walter K	825	clerk	24	"
	O	McKenna Bessie D †	827	housewife	50	"

Cummins Highway (Continued)

Page	Letter	Full Name	Residence, Jan. 1	Occupation	Age	Reported Residence
	P	McKenna Joseph	827	printer	54	[illegible]
	R	Herman Joan I †	833	secretary	22	[illegible]
	S	*Herman Cytlia S †	833	housewife	45	[illegible]
	T	Herman Stephen	833	furrier	54	[illegible]
	U	Kidney Bessie M †	833	housewife	49	104 [illegible]
	V	Kidney Philip F	833	watchman	47	104
	W	Kidney Philip F, jr	833	porter	20	104
	X	*Nicholson Alice †	833	operator	17	104
	Y	Bowman Josephine †	833	housekeeper	73	[illegible]
	Z	Pagle Charles	833	mechanic	49	[illegible]
402						
	A	Pagle Lillian M †	833	housewife	48	[illegible]
	B	Lyons Catherine †	837	"	67	
	C	Lyons James W	837	retired	68	
	D	Wilson George A	837	compositor	69	
	E	Wilson Jennie L †	837	housewife	69	
	F	Erhard Mary G †	837	"	53	
	G	Erhard Thomas J	837	machinist	54	
	H	MacKenzie Annie †	837	at home	76	
	N	O'Hare Bella M †	849	housewife	31	
	O	O'Hare James H	849	letter carrier	39	
	P	MacKenzie Alice L †	849	housewife	35	
	R	MacKenzie Thomas H	849	forester	39	
	S	*Papastathis Mary †	849	housewife	16	
	T	Sanborn Jesse A	853	salesman	68	
	U	Sanborn Mabel F †	853	housewife	74	
	V	Sanborn Raymond A	853	salesman	39	
	W	*Brown Charles	853	watchman	60	
	X	*Brown Jessie †	853	housewife	60	
	Y	*Brown Leslie G	853	operator	58	
	Z	Nichols Ada B †	853	housewife	69	
403						
	A	Nichols Elmer L	853	mechanic	62	
	C	Buckley John D	889	agent	46	
	D	Welsh Alice G †	889	typist	[illegible]	
	E	Welsh Joseph A	889	machinist	[illegible]	
	F	Welsh Martin A	889	engineer	[illegible]	
	G	Welsh Mary K †	889	housewife	[illegible]	
	H	Welsh William H	889	[illegible]	[illegible]	
	K	Hinchliffe Robert L	891	[illegible]	[illegible]	
	L	McGrath James H	891	[illegible]		

Page	Letter	Full Name	Residence, Jan. 1, 1941.	Occupation	Supposed Age.	Reported Residence, Jan. 1, 1940. Street and Number.

Cummins Highway—Continued

Page	Letter	Full Name	Residence, Jan. 1, 1941.	Occupation	Supposed Age.	Reported Residence, Jan. 1, 1940. Street and Number.
	M	McGrath Mary L †	891	housewife	51	here
	N	McGrath Virginia L †	891	typist	27	"
	O	Yee Ling Hung	901	laundryman	43	"

Edgewater Drive

Page	Letter	Full Name	Residence, Jan. 1, 1941.	Occupation	Supposed Age.	Reported Residence, Jan. 1, 1940. Street and Number.
	W	Hoeffner Charles W	19	mechanic	43	here
	X	Hoeffner Lillian W †	19	housewife	43	"
	Y	Bruce Edwin J	21	plasterer	42	"
	Z	Bruce Martha †	21	housewife	47	"
404						
	A	Coppell Dorothy J †	21	clerk	22	"
	B	Partelow Charles T	33	watchman	63	"
	E	Barnes Dorothy M †	49	stenographer	20	"
	F	Barnes Ethel M †	49	housewife	43	"
	G	Barnes Stephen A	49	engineer	46	"
	H	Roberts James A	51	laborer	48	"
	K	Roberts Josephine A †	51	housewife	67	N Reading
	L	Roberts Mary F †	51	"	38	here
	M	Roberts William J	51	machinist	49	N Reading
	N	DeProfio Frank	69	laborer	46	here
	O	DeProfio Rose †	69	housewife	39	"
	P	Allen M Marie †	69	"	33	"
	R	Allen Raymond T	69	chauffeur	33	43 Malta
	S	Celli Blanche †	69	housewife	23	here
	T	Celli Joseph G	69	retired	74	"
	U	Celli Joseph V	69	painter	29	"
	V	Tebbetts Harry E	89	operator	48	"
	W	Tebbetts Harry E, jr	89	chauffeur	28	"
	X	Tebbetts Viola G †	89	housewife	46	"
	Y	Carey Katherine H †	91	"	48	"
	Z	Carey Patrick J	91	laborer	59	"
405						
	A	Bailey Elizabeth R †	93	housewife	55	"
		Bailey Frank A	93	retired	55	"
		Bailey Frank J	93	clerk	25	"
		Bailey Lillian J †	93	"	21	"
		Dinezio Domenica †	95	housewife	54	"
		Dinezio Joseph	95	chauffeur	50	"
		Dinezio Nicholas	95	laborer	27	"
		Dinezio Ralph H	95	salesman	32	"

Page	Letter	Full Name	Residence	Occupation	Age

Edgewater Drive (Continued)

Letter	Full Name	Residence	Occupation	Age
K	Fioravante Nicola †	95	laborer	[illegible]
L	*Clementi Maria †	97	at home	62
M	Guerra Celia †	97	housewife	40
O	Guerra Melinda †	97	student	20
N	Guerra Michael	97	laborer	52
P	Hall Edward W	99	agent	57
R	Hall Helen F †	99	housewife	53
S	Stoddard Helen E †	99	at home	89
T	MacKinnon Joan V †	123	beautician	35
U	Roberts Arthur H	123	baker	59
V	Roberts Masie †	123	housewife	58

Hollingsworth Street

Letter	Full Name	Residence	Occupation	Age
W	Welch Edward F	4	retired	82
X	Welch Elizabeth R †	4	operator	30
Y	Welch Margaret E †	4	clerk	33
Z	Cogan John J	4	"	31
	406			
A	MacKinnon Alberta D †	4	housewife	38
B	MacKinnon Windsor G	4	clerk	39
C	Spry Irma M †	8	housewife	52
D	Spry Walter	8	mason	61
E	Bailey Mabel O †	11	waitress	[illegible]
F	Bailey Winifred F †	11	cashier	[illegible]
G	Nispel Carsten H	11	clerk	[illegible]
H	Nispel Dorothy C †	11	stenographer	28
K	Nispel James C	11	cashier	[illegible]
L	Nispel Margaret M †	11	housewife	[illegible]
M	Nispel Mary L †	11	stenographer	[illegible]
N	Harris Efrosine †	11	housewife	[illegible]
O	Harris George	11	bartender	48
P	Milch Edmund J	12	[illegible]	[illegible]
R	Milch Erna L †	12	[illegible]	[illegible]
S	Milch Joseph	12	[illegible]	[illegible]
T	Milch Josephine A †	12	housewife	[illegible]
U	Milch Leona M †	12	clerk	[illegible]
V	Brown Alice S †	15	[illegible]	[illegible]
W	Brown Nathan J	15	[illegible]	[illegible]
X	Goodale Marion E †	15	[illegible]	[illegible]
Y	Goodale William H	15	[illegible]	[illegible]

Page	Letter	Full Name	Residence, Jan. 1, 1941.	Occupation.	Supposed Age.	Reported Residence, Jan. 1, 1940. Street and Number

Hollingsworth Street—Continued

Page	Letter	Full Name	Residence, Jan. 1, 1941.	Occupation.	Supposed Age.	Reported Residence, Jan. 1, 1940. Street and Number
	Z	Kiriacopoulos Bessie †	15	housewife	33	here
407						
	A	Kiriacopoulos James	15	shoemaker	53	"
	B	Whipple Henry W	16	mechanic	69	"
	C	Whipple Nancy †	16	housewife	69	"
	D	Amendola Joseph P	19	teamster	41	"
	E	Amendola Louise †	19	housewife	36	"
	F	Binda Enrico	19	retired	76	"
	G	Kelly Helen J †	20	housewife	39	"
	H	Kelly Terence E	20	electrician	41	"
	K	Freeman Hazel G †	23	clerk	40	"
	L	Freeman Mary A †	23	"	45	"
	M	Copell Evelyn †	24	cashier	30	Milton
	N	Lyon Gordon	24	electrician	47	here
	O	Wood Blanche H †	24	housekeeper	62	"
	P	McNerny Anna T †	27	social worker	30	"
	R	McNerny Charlotte F †	27	stenographer	39	"
	S	McNerny Charlotte J †	27	housewife	67	"
	T	McNerny James F	27	laborer	69	"
	U	Heaney Arthur G	28	accountant	33	"
	V	*Heaney Jessie †	28	housewife	55	"
	W	Collins Anna †	30	"	49	"
	X	Collins Timothy J	30	clerk	49	"
	Y	Gallagher Anna M †	31	housewife	47	"
	Z	Gallagher Joseph J	31	salesman	47	"
408						
	A	Gallagher Rita V †	31	clerk	23	"
	B	Foster Howard F	34	engineer	67	"
	C	Foster Irene M †	34	teacher	43	"
	D	Foster Mabel F †	34	housewife	65	"
	E	Nolan Edith M †	35	"	46	"
	F	Nolan Thomas E	35	engineer	45	"
	G	Cronin Eugene W	38	"	63	"
	H	Cronin Francis J	38	"	37	"
	K	Cronin Helen R †	38	stenographer	24	"
	L	Cronin Mary A †	38	housewife	61	"
	M	Quinn Ellen †	38	operator	54	"
	O	Lynch James J	42	chauffeur	56	"
	P	Lynch Johanna †	42	housewife	44	"
	R	Lynch Martin J	42	guard	54	"
	S	Lynch Nellie E †	42	housewife	50	"

Hollingsworth Street Continued

Letter	Full Name	Residence	Occupation	Age	Former Residence
T	Lynch Patrick J	42	storekeeper	48	here
U	Montague James J	46	contractor	51	"
V	Montague Margaret E †	46	housewife	49	"
W	Ingalls Dorothy A †	48	clerk	20	Brookline
X	Ingalls Howard S	48	manager	40	here
Y	Ingalls Minnie J †	48	housewife	42	Brookline
Z	Wallace John T	48	baker	34	here
409					
A	Cheney Catherine †	54	housewife	79	"
B	Cheney William J	54	shipper	79	"
C	Lancaster Mary F †	54	stenographer	39	"
D	Castendyk Fritz C	62	chemist	33	"
E	Worton Anne †	62	housewife	67	"
F	Worton William	62	retired	77	"
G	Simpson Alice †	62	housewife	67	"
H	Simpson David	62	accountant	67	"
K	Lee Mabel F †	65	housewife	54	"
L	Lee Martin R	65	packer	56	"
M	Losordo John J	65	carpenter	26	"
N	Losordo Mabel L †	65	housewife	23	"
O	Little Elizabeth C †	65	clerk	25	"
P	Little James	65	bricklayer	51	"
R	Little Mabel E †	65	housewife	51	"
S	Newton Bernice I †	67	secretary	42	"
T	Benson Mabel I †	67	housewife	41	"
U	Benson Nils W	67	patternmaker	43	"
V	Hutchinson Bessie A †	70	housewife	63	"
W	Hutchinson Percy L	70	carpenter	62	"
X	Haskett Caroline C †	71	housewife	50	"
Y	Haskett Samuel W	71	mechanic	50	"
Z	Petersen Anna C †	72	clerk	24	"
410					
A	Petersen Emil T †	72	salesman	54	"
B	Petersen Mary E †	72	housewife	47	"
C	Petersen Mildred P †	72	saleswoman	22	"
D	Roberts Austin E	74	foreman	34	"
E	Roberts Hazel A †	74	housewife	32	"
F	Kent Alice E †	74	"	25	155 Park [illegible]
G	Kent Charles P	74	accountant	23	155 "
H	Kent Edna L †	74	nurse	21	here
K	Kent Estella M †	74	[illegible]	52	"

Page	Letter	Full Name	Residence, Jan. 1, 1941	Occupation	Supposed Age	Reported Residence, Jan. 1, 1940. Street and Number

Hollingsworth Street—Continued

Page	Letter	Full Name	Residence, Jan. 1, 1941	Occupation	Supposed Age	Reported Residence, Jan. 1, 1940. Street and Number
	L	Kent Louis W	74	contractor	60	here
	M	Whalen Grace †	75	housewife	45	"
	N	Whalen William T	75	fireman	52	"
	O	Martin Hazel A †	80	housewife	33	4 Violante
	P	Martin Joseph M	80	clerk	36	4 "
	R	Maier Edna M †	80	housewife	40	here
	S	Maier Francis P	80	fireman	46	"
	T	Pearson Albert	81	inspector	49	"
	U	Pearson Mabelle H †	81	housewife	49	"
	V	Sweet Charles E	82	draftsman	37	"
	W	Sweet Marie K †	82	housewife	31	"
	X	Hayes Eugene F	82	clerk	65	"
	Y	Hayes Katherine F †	82	housewife	65	"
	Z	Eklund Laura L †	83	stenographer	40	"
411						
	A	Keene Charles F	83	teacher	24	63 Providence
	B	Keene Elizabeth C †	83	housewife	23	Cambridge
	C	Clark Alice M †	84	"	55	here
	D	Clark Dorothy C †	84	musician	30	"
	E	Clark Frank E	84	repairman	54	"
	F	Colgan Madeline V †	85	clerk	21	138 Hunt'n av
	G	Kimpel Alice E †	85	housewife	40	138 "
	H	Kimpel George J	85	storekeeper	50	138 "
	K	Cohen Albert	86	salesman	39	here
	L	Cohen Loretta †	86	housewife	39	"
	M	Roycroft Agnes M †	87	secretary	21	"
	N	Roycroft Gertrude L †	87	housewife	45	"
	O	Roycroft Louise G †	87	teacher	24	"
	P	Roycroft Richard F	87	B F D	56	"
	R	Leahy Joseph P	88	policeman	44	"
	S	Leahy Margaret F †	88	housewife	42	"
	T	Leahy Margaret J †	88	clerk	22	"
	U	Ahearn Ellen †	88	at home	77	Dedham
	V	Ahearn Emma F †	88	housewife	33	"
	W	Ahearn John J	88	groom	36	"
	X	McDonald Arthur J	88	bartender	43	here
		McDonald Dorothy E †	88	operator	22	"
	Z	McDonald Mary E †	88	housewife	44	"
412						
		Mulcahy Mary J †	89	teacher	48	"
		Dunphy Alice E †	90	clerk	25	"

Letter	Full Name					

Hollingsworth Street—Continued

Letter	Full Name					
C	Dunphy John J		90	superintendent	64	[illegible]
D	Murray James	91	93	tel worker	38	
E	Murray Mae †	91	93	housewife	37	
F	Waite John J	91	93	decorator	39	
G	Waite Margaret J †	91	93	housewife	29	"
H	Barry Charles E		92	fireman	57	"
K	Barry Josephine L †		92	housewife	57	"
L	Barry Marie A †		92	stenographer	23	"
M	Dillon Mary A †		94	housewife	62	"
N	Leadbetter Ella G †		94	"	23	77 Hol[illegible]
O	Leadbetter Raymond O		94	engineer	25	Rhode I[illegible]
P	Fogarty Donald T		95	student	22	here
R	Fogarty Elizabeth F †		95	secretary	25	"
S	Fogarty Michael S		95	engineer	18	"
T	Fogarty Sarah E †		95	housewife	55	"
U	Buckley William J		96	fireman	43	"
V	Lovell Irva M †		97	housewife	26	Ded[illegible]
W	Lovell James G		97	salesman	26	"
X	Kelly Katherine T †		98	housewife	38	here
Y	Kelly Thomas J		98	butler	44	"
Z	Marshall Edna M †		100	housewife	32	"
413						
A	Marshall Frank P, jr		100	merchant	37	"
B	Drury Augusta E †	102	104	housewife	55	"
C	Drury Frederick F	102	104	clerk	56	"
D	Drury Gardner F	102	104	polisher	22	"
E	Drury Warren E	102	104	student	21	"
F	O'Keefe Alice M †	102	104	housewife	72	"
G	O'Keefe Arthur J	102	104	secretary	44	"
H	O'Keefe Genevieve J †	102	104	housewife	33	"
K	Smith Esther G †		119	housekeeper	60	[illegible]

Malta Street

Letter	Full Name					
L	Carlson Mary E †		5	housewife	[illegible]	[illegible]
M	Davis Milton W		5	salesman	[illegible]	[illegible]
N	Davis Thelma G †		5	housewife	28	[illegible]
O	Sabath Helen †		5	[illegible]	[illegible]	[illegible]
P	Sabath John		5	[illegible]	[illegible]	[illegible]
R	Sabath Mollie †		5	[illegible]	[illegible]	[illegible]
S	Lane Mary E †		[illegible]	[illegible]	[illegible]	[illegible]

Page	Letter	Full Name	Residence, Jan. 1, 1941	Occupation	Supposed Age	Reported Residence, Jan. 1, 1940. Street and Number.

Malta Street—Continued

Page	Letter	Full Name	Residence, Jan. 1, 1941	Occupation	Supposed Age	Reported Residence, Jan. 1, 1940. Street and Number.
	T	Lane William J	8	shipper	47	18 Pinewood
	U	Kelliher Elizabeth †	8	at home	73	here
	V	Warren Anna S †	8	"	72	"
	W	Kennedy Joseph L	8	laborer	32	"
	X	Kennedy Rose L †	8	housewife	25	"
	Y	May Mildred G †	8	clerk	39	100 Hamilton
	Z	Pearson Eleanor R †	9	housewife	25	841 River
414						
	A	Pearson Frederick C	9	laborer	30	841 "
	B	Field Dorothy M †	9	housewife	38	here
	C	Field William A	9	painter	58	"
	D	Myers George D	10	welder	28	Falmouth
	E	Myers Juanita I †	10	housewife	22	"
	F	Hodgdon Flora J †	10	at home	83	here
	G	Hodgdon Harriet V †	10	housewife	60	"
	H	Curley Bernard J	10	clerk	29	"
	K	Curley Mary E †	10	housewife	26	"
	L	Liz Ignacy	15	laborer	45	"
	M	Liz Mary †	15	housewife	38	"
	N	Dromdek Frank P	15	merchant	34	558 River
	O	Dromdek Helen T †	15	housewife	24	558 "
	P	Brett Elizabeth M †	15	"	45	here
	R	Brett John H	15	draftsman	21	"
	S	Brett John M	15	metalworker	56	"
	T	Brett Thomas A	15	attorney	26	"
	U	Brett Thomas F	15	constable	49	"
	V	Cushing Amelia L †	18–20	housewife	28	"
	W	Cushing Howard F	18–20	salesman	34	"
	X	Trocki Adam	18–20	machinist	54	"
	Y	Trocki Frank A	18–20	manager	37	"
	Z	Trocki Joseph J	18–20	inspector	34	"
415						
	A	Trocki Mary †	18–20	housewife	63	"
	B	Trocki Mary E †	18–20	chemist	35	"
	C	Trocki Stella D †	18–20	clerk	27	"
	D	Putnam Martin T	19	salesman	32	"
	E	Putnam Sabina I †	19	housewife	31	"
	F	Foley Catherine A †	19	student	20	"
	G	Foley Edmund D	19	metalworker	45	"
	H	Foley Mary E †	19	housewife	44	"
	K	Foley Mary J †	19	student	21	"

Malta Street Continued

Letter	Full Name				
L	Kelley Catherine N †	25	clerk	35	Maldeu[illegible]
M	Kelley Margretta †	25	housewife	58	"
N	Kelley Marion E †	25	"	31	"
O	Kelley Ralph J	25	inspector	34	"
P	McLean Margaret B †	25	at home	72	here
R	McGrath Evelyn C †	25	housewife	41	"
S	McGrath John J	25	roofer	43	103 [illegible]
T	Wipfler Joseph B	25	operator	24	here
U	Youngelaus Albert T	26	manager	37	"
V	Youngelaus Winifred F †	26	housewife	36	"
W	Kelliher Mary †	26	at home	62	"
X	McKinnon Catherine M †	26	housewife	41	"
Y	McKinnon John R	26	foreman	41	"
Z	Golden Helen E †	39	housewife	26	"
	416				
A	Golden Richard J	39	operator	33	640 [illegible]
B	Golden William H	39	chauffeur	25	here
C	Languirand Jeanette †	41	housewife	25	"
D	Languirand Joseph	41	manager	26	"
E	Allen Robert J	43	policeman	34	"
F	Allen Timothy C	43	chauffeur	32	"
G	Ridge John J	43	engineer	36	"
H	Ridge Mildred M †	43	housewife	35	"
K	Stewart Elizabeth P †	43	laundryworker	44	"

Mattakeeset Street

Letter	Full Name				
L	Fulton Martin A	8	auditor	44	here
M	Fulton Robert E	8	clerk	20	"
N	Fulton Sarah E †	8	housewife	40	"
O	Levine Benjamin	10	foreman	[illegible]	[illegible]
P	McNaught Elizabeth †	10	clerk	45	here
R	Kamison Abraham A	12	foreman	[illegible]	[illegible]
S	Kamison Mary E †	12	housewife	[illegible]	[illegible]
T	Bowser Edna M †	14	"	[illegible]	[illegible]
U	Bowser William E	14	[illegible]	[illegible]	[illegible]
V	McKeon Maude F †	14	attendant	[illegible]	[illegible]
W	Gallivan Marion J †	16 18	housewife	[illegible]	[illegible]
X	Gallivan Patrick	16 18	chauffeur	[illegible]	[illegible]
Y	Willard Christine F †	16 18	housewife	[illegible]	[illegible]
Z	Willard Francis I	16 18	[illegible]	[illegible]	[illegible]

Page	Letter	Full Name	Residence Jan. 1, 1941	Occupation	Supposed Age	Reported Residence, Jan. 1, 1940. Street and Number.

417
Mattakeeset Street Continued

	Letter	Full Name	Residence	Occupation	Age	Reported Residence
	A	Peterson Elizabeth A †	22	housewife	48	here
	B	Peterson George H	22	jeweler	47	"
	C	Peterson Muriel E †	22	clerk	25	"
	D	Moore Frederick T	26	"	31	"
	E	Moore John J	26	retired	74	"
	F	Moore Thomasine F †	26	housewife	72	"
	G	Moore William H	26	clerk	42	"
	H	Lynch Loretta M †	30	housekeeper	54	"
	K	Olson Emma M †	30	clerk	21	"
	L	Olson John L	30	machinist	62	"
	M	Olson John L, jr	30	student	23	"
	N	Olson Lisa C †	30	housewife	52	"
	O	Olson Stena L †	30	waitress	24	"
	P	Edler Caroline S †	34	housewife	68	"
	R	Edler Ernest L	34	merchant	35	"
	S	Dronzek Lucy †	36	proprietor	35	"
	T	Diemer Anna E †	40	at home	83	"
	U	Diemer Carl F	40	attorney	51	"
	V	Diemer Eleanor L †	40	housewife	40	"
	W	Pineo Isaiah B	44	salesman	50	"
	X	Pineo Jean M †	44	housewife	51	"
	Y	Haydostian Martin	48	realtor	46	Malden
	Z	Haydostian Mary †	48	housewife	44	"

418 Rector Road

	Letter	Full Name	Residence	Occupation	Age	Reported Residence
	A	McIntosh George E	9	clerk	43	here
	B	McIntosh Mary E †	9	housewife	37	"
	C	Clark Doris G †	11	bookkeeper	20	"
	D	Clark Gertrude C †	11	housewife	43	"
	E	Clark William F	11	chauffeur	23	"
	F	Belanger Georgia M †	15	housewife	58	"
	G	Belanger John F	15	foreman	36	"
	H	MacKinnon Wilson M	15	superintendent	50	43 Lexington
	K	Andersen Frederick E	15	machinist	63	here
	L	Andersen Laura A †	15	housewife	56	"
	M	Chippindale Frank G	17	clerk	30	"
	N	Chippindale John F	17	"	65	"
	O	Chippindale Thomas J	17	physician	32	"
	P	Clark Mary T †	17	beautician	41	"

Page	Letter	Full Name	Residence			

Rector Road Continued

Page	Letter	Full Name	Residence	Occupation	Age	
	R	Ralston Alice †	19	housewife	38	here
	S	Ralston Frederick R	19	foreman	31	"
	T	Appleblad Gustaf L	21	machinist	72	"
	U	Appleblad Helen A †	21	at home	32	"
	V	Appleblad Hilda †	21	housewife	71	"
	W	Appleblad Hilda J †	21	stenographer	43	"
	X	Marks Margaret M †	27	housewife	47	"
	Y	Marks Thomas E	27	superintendent	47	"
	Z	Agnew Catherine F †	33	housewife	42	"
419						
	A	Agnew Edwin J	33	clerk	46	"
	B	Kelm Agnes M †	35	operator	35	"
	C	Kelm Mary A †	35	housewife	66	"
	D	Kelm Max P	35	cabinetmaker	71	"
	E	Martell Dorothea J †	35	housewife	27	"
	F	Martell Vincent J	35	carpenter	25	7 Dana
	G	Applegate Annie †	37	housewife	80	here
	H	Applegate Richard	37	plasterer	82	"
	K	Conboy Julia G †	39	housewife	70	"
	L	Conboy Thomas P	39	letter carrier	74	"
	M	Bossinger Catherine N †	41	housewife	47	"
	N	Bossinger Harry A	41	salesman	50	"

420 River Street

Page	Letter	Full Name	Residence	Occupation	Age	
	E	McDonald Lewis D	546	carpenter	52	[illegible]
	F	McDonald Mary L †	546	housewife	56	[illegible] "
	G	Celli Adelina †	548	"	50	here
	H	Celli Elsie J †	548	secretary	29	"
	K	Celli Warren M	548	steamfitter	52	"
	P	Duca Frances R †	558	housewife	22	11 [illegible]
	R	Duca James P	558	shipper	22	11 "
	S	Rowe Doris M †	558	housewife	31	here
	T	Rowe John J	558	[illegible]	32	"
	U	Richards Clarence	560	[illegible]	[illegible]	[illegible]
	V	Richards Medina O †	560	housewife	[illegible]	[illegible]
	W	Stacey Evelyn R †	562	"	42	[illegible]
	X	Stacey Robert H	562	[illegible]	[illegible]	[illegible]
	Y	Logie George S	562	[illegible]	[illegible]	[illegible]
	Z	Logie Grace M †	562	housewife	[illegible]	[illegible]

Page	Letter	Full Name	Residence, Jan. 1, 1941	Occupation	Supposed Age	Reported Residence, Jan. 1, 1940. Street and Number.
421		**River Street—Continued**				
	A	Vosburg Alfred M	564	mechanic	43	here
	B	Vosburg Pearl F †	564	housewife	41	"
	C	*Mulhern Delia T †	565	housekeeper	70	"
	D	Yee Howard	565	laundryman	36	"
	E	Larsen Frank V	565	longshoreman	47	48 Sherman
	F	*Larsen Margaret M †	565	housewife	50	48 "
	G	Orcutt Blanche E †	565	"	56	here
	H	Orcutt Daniel C	565	meatcutter	67	"
	K	Orcutt Irvin A	565	clerk	21	"
	L	McCarthy Catherine †	566	housewife	51	"
	M	McCarthy Charles	566	laborer	24	"
	N	McCarthy Daniel F	566	"	65	"
	O	Archdeacon Francis J	568	welder	25	Lynn
	P	Phinney Alice L †	568	housewife	30	"
	R	Phinney Walter D	568	mechanic	30	"
	S	*Brennan Margaret †	569	housewife	31	here
	T	*Brennan Patrick T	569	rubberworker	31	"
	U	Norton Francis J	569	pipefitter	47	"
	V	Baker Richard H	569	retired	69	"
	W	Hayes Jeremiah	569	"	68	"
	X	Hurley James F	569	upholsterer	48	"
	Y	Jensen Soven P	569	chauffeur	48	60 Davison
	Z	Amolini Joseph	569	laborer	48	Milton
422						
	A	Bacon Altena M †	569	housewife	40	here
	B	Bacon Augustine W	569	foreman	39	"
	C	Cantwell George A	569	baker	39	"
	D	Cantwell Michael H	569	carpenter	75	"
	E	Spillane Daniel	569	painter	42	"
	F	Morse Gertrude E †	571	housewife	25	27 Elmont
	G	Morse Leslie S	571	electrician	28	27 "
	H	Herman Stanley	575	machinist	60	here
	K	Sullivan Eileen J †	575	housewife	34	31 Rugby rd
	L	Sullivan John W	575	agent	35	31 "
	M	Herman Anna †	575	housewife	55	here
	N	Herman Edward H	575	teacher	34	"
	O	Herman Rosanna †	575	stenographer	35	"
	P	Sneedy Alice M †	575	housewife	68	"
	R	Sneedy Edward F	575	retired	69	"
	S	Jules Annie †	576	laundryworker	56	"

Page	Letter	Full Name	Residence, April 1, 1941	Occupation	Reported Age	Reported Residence, April 1, 1940

River Street—Continued

Page	Letter	Full Name	Residence	Occupation	Age	Reported Residence
	T	Jackson Francis J	576	cooper	24	here
	U	Jackson George J	576	metalworker	56	"
	V	Jackson Harriet T †	576	secretary	33	"
	W	Jackson Theresa A †	576	housewife	53	"
	X	Lawler Helen F †	576	"	55	"
	Y	Lawler Henry W	576	clerk	56	"
	Z	Lawler Marjorie H †	576	secretary	24	"
423						
	C	Alexander Anna B †	580	housewife	31	"
	D	Alexander John J	580	chauffeur	35	"
	E	Ruane John J	582	"	30	"
	F	Ruane Katherine M †	582	secretary	36	"
	G	Ruane Margaret A †	582	clerk	34	"
	H	Santospirito Jennie †	584	housewife	44	"
	K	Santospirito Lawrence	584	merchant	47	"
	L	Santospirito Anthony	586	"	52	"
	M	Santospirito Mary C †	586	housewife	49	"
	N	Thompson Doris L †	588	"	25	54 [illegible]
	O	Thompson Walter L	588	clerk	31	54 "
	P	Bransdon Charlotte B †	590	housewife	32	[illegible]
	R	Sanborn Frances M †	591	secretary	20	"
	S	Sanborn Gerald J	591	salesman	45	"
	T	Sanborn Geraldine J †	591	typist	22	"
	U	Sanborn Mary E †	591	housewife	44	"
	V	Quinn John E	591	plumber	63	"
	W	Quinn Mary E †	591	housewife	59	"
	X	*Luthman Astrid K †	591	"	29	"
	Y	*Luthman Harold W	591	mechanic	45	"
	Z	Dwyer Audrey F †	592	housewife	36	"
424						
	A	Dwyer William E	592	chauffeur	39	"
	B	Crofton Jane G †	594	housewife	54	"
	C	Crofton Mary L †	594	waitress	24	118
	D	Crofton Thomas A	594	laborer	22	118
	E	Ellis James E	594	chauffeur	54	[illegible]
	F	Ellis Thomas J	594	retired	74	[illegible]
	G	Moran Ethel M †	594	at home	[illegible]	[illegible]
	H	Forbes Edwin J	595	[illegible]	[illegible]	[illegible]
	K	Forbes Edwin L	595	[illegible]	[illegible]	[illegible]
	L	Forbes Frances L †	595	[illegible]	[illegible]	[illegible]
	M	*Serena Philomena †	595	[illegible]	[illegible]	[illegible]

River Street—Continued

Page	Letter	Full Name	Residence, Jan. 1, 1941	Occupation	Supposed Age	Reported Residence, Jan. 1, 1940. Street and Number.
	N	Glantz John A	595	clerk	27	here
	O	Glantz Madeline M †	595	housewife	27	"
	P	Glantz Maude E †	595	"	57	"
	R	Glantz William A	595	machinist	58	"
	S	Noble Joseph R	596	retired	70	"
	T	Noble Mabel E †	596	housewife	64	"
	U	Short Esther B †	599	secretary	23	24 Ufford
	V	Short Max	599	merchant	49	24 "
	W	Short Philip	599	engineer	25	California
	X	Short Sadie †	599	housewife	47	24 Ufford
	Y	Orrok Henry D	599	buyer	68	here
	Z	Orrok Theresa F †	599	housewife	58	"
425						
	A	Fitzgerald William F	599	machinist	25	"
	B	White Edward P	599	foreman	44	"
	C	White Viola M †	599	housewife	47	"
	D	Johnson Albert	600	retired	72	"
	E	Johnson Hilda †	600	housewife	75	"
	F	Fairbanks Henry G	601	teacher	23	19 Baldwin
	G	Fairbanks Mary G †	601	housewife	53	19 "
	H	Fairbanks Nelson A	601	clerk	53	19 "
	K	Fairbanks Walter F	601	"	25	19 "
	L	Tilley Eugene	601	"	22	here
	M	Tilley Helen M †	601	teacher	30	"
	N	Tilley John W	601	shipper	25	"
	O	Tilley Margaret E †	601	housewife	58	"
	P	Tilley Margaret R †	601	student	20	"
	R	Tilley William F	601	salesman	60	"
	S	Tolland James	601	superintendent	56	"
	T	Tolland Margaret †	601	clerk	22	"
		Tolland Mary †	601	housewife	52	"
		Moore Charles	603	millwright	30	8 St Charles
	W	Obert Francis J	603	retired	80	here
	X	Obert Margaret E †	603	housewife	70	"
	Z	Jacob Robert E	605	operator	31	Milton
426						
		Obert Francis J	605	constructor	49	here
		Obert Mary M †	605	clerk	21	"
		Obert Sadie B †	605	housewife	49	"
		Sullivan Ann G †	605	saleswoman	38	"
		Blomquist Amanda J †	607	housewife	62	"

Page	Letter	Full Name	Residence	Occupation	Age	Reported Residence

River Street—Continued

Page	Letter	Full Name	Residence	Occupation	Age	Reported Residence
	F	*Blomquist Axel	607	retired	6[illegible]	[illegible]
	G	*Blomquist Carl	607	papermaker	54	"
	H	Scanlon Edward P	608	seaman	21	"
	K	Scanlon Genevieve H †	608	housewife	57	"
	L	Scanlon Paul J	608	salesman	57	"
	M	Scanlon Paul L	608	clerk	25	"
	N	Scanlon Thomas A	608	instructor	21	"
	O	Deasy Nora †	609	at home	65	"
	P	McEleney Beatrice †	609	waitress	35	"
	R	O'Keefe Catherine †	609	housewife	71	"
	S	Raines Reuben	609	janitor	71	"
	V	Williams Edward A	609	steamfitter	42	"
	T	Williams John	609	operator	22	"
	U	Williams Margaret †	609	housewife	42	"
	W	Geisel Ethel P †	610	clerk	37	"
	X	Geisel Fred G	610	"	59	"
	Y	*Perry George A	610	foreman	34	"
427						
	A	Perry Ruth M †	610	housewife	33	"
	B	Lagadimos Arthur	611	clerk	21	10 Bl[illegible]
	C	Lagadimos Flora †	611	waitress	23	10 "
	D	*Lagadimos Vera †	611	housewife	50	10 "
	E	*Johnson Nora †	611	"	62	[illegible]
	F	*Johnson Peter	611	chef	6[illegible]	"
	G	Walker Elmer R	611	inspector	59	"
	H	Walker Margaret E †	611	housewife	[illegible]	"
	K	Antonia Alice L †	614	"	[illegible]	"
	L	Antonia Gerald S	614	clerk	[illegible]	"
	M	Martin Claire R †	614	operator	[illegible]	"
	N	Martin James W	614	[illegible]	[illegible]	"
	O	Martin John B	614	[illegible]	[illegible]	"
	P	Martin Mary G †	614	[illegible]	[illegible]	"
	R	Martin Rita J †	614	[illegible]	[illegible]	"
	S	*Backlund Augusta †	615	[illegible]	[illegible]	[illegible]
	T	Backlund Oscar	615	[illegible]	[illegible]	[illegible]
	U	Backlund Sigurd	615	[illegible]	[illegible]	[illegible]
	V	*Backlund Steven	615	[illegible]	[illegible]	[illegible]
	W	Kelm Helen L †	615	[illegible]	[illegible]	[illegible]
	X	Kelm Robert H	615	[illegible]	[illegible]	[illegible]
	Y	Gallant Edmond J	619	[illegible]	[illegible]	[illegible]
	Z	Gallant Marie E †	619	[illegible]	[illegible]	[illegible]

River Street—Continued

Page	Letter	Full Name	Residence, Jan. 1, 1941	Occupation	Supposed Age	Reported Residence, Jan. 1, 1940. Street and Number
428						
	A	Gallant Mary A †	619	housewife	53	here
	B	Kane Emily †	619	"	60	"
	C	Kane Thomas J	619	bartender	54	"
	D	Kenney James	620	retired	76	"
	E	Kenney Mary F †	620	clerk	41	"
	F	Morris George C	620	janitor	54	25 Hamilton
	G	Morris George C, jr	620	student	20	25 "
	H	Morris Lucy B †	620	housewife	47	25 "
	K	Harrington Margaret V †	620	"	54	here
	L	Harrington Winifred F †	620	operator	20	"
	M	Fairbanks Edna E †	621	housewife	29	"
	N	Fairbanks Robert W	621	mechanic	31	"
	O	Brennen Alice F †	624	clerk	37	"
	P	Brennan Arthur H	624	policeman	35	"
	R	Brennan Arthur S	624	retired	65	"
	S	Brennan Marion L †	624	clerk	33	"
	T	Brennan Mary F †	624	housewife	65	"
	U	Ainslie Janet H †	625	operator	35	"
	V	*Fisher Ethel G †	625	stenographer	47	"
	W	Wilkinson James	625	barber	75	"
	X	Wilkinson Jemima †	625	housewife	71	"
	Y	Crean Christine †	628	housekeeper	44	"
	Z	Dominico Charles	628	chauffeur	41	"
429						
	A	Dominico Josephine †	628	housewife	32	"
	B	Hitchings Margaret B †	629	"	51	"
	C	Hitchings Ruth †	629	clerk	25	"
	D	Hitchings William C	629	"	31	"
	E	Pitman Jessie T †	629	operator	32	"
	F	Boody Matilda J †	629	at home	77	"
	G	Kellsey Carrie A †	629	"	77	17 Hiawatha rd
	H	Lord Helen E †	629	housewife	49	here
	K	Lord Helen E †	629	dressmaker	25	"
	L	Alexander George	629	merchant	40	"
	M	Cook Jacob	629	retired	83	"
	N	Leslie Mary †	629	at home	66	10 Tesla
	O	Magee Elizabeth †	629	housekeeper	53	here
	P	Bottai Eva †	633	housewife	24	1589 Blue Hill av
	R	Bottai Louis A	633	cook	34	1589 "
	S	Grandy Mary E †	633	housewife	40	here

Page	Letter	Full Name	Residence, April 1	Occupation	Age	Reported Residence
	T	*Grundy Robert	633	carpenter	40	here
	U	Demers Emily †	633	housewife	26	82 W[illegible]
	V	Demers James A	633	polisher	29	82 "
	W	Spear Cecelia B †	633	housewife	26	here
	X	Spear Joseph E	633	salesman	30	"
	Y	Nicholson Florence L †	633	housewife	42	"
	Z	Nicholson Frank E	633	electrician	18	"
430						
	A	Nicholson George E	633	chemist	20	"
	B	Oprandi Grace †	633	housewife	25	"
	C	Oprandi Frank	633	clerk	27	"
	D	Ryan Eva C †	636	housekeeper	60	"
	E	Wilbur Helen T †	636	housewife	42	"
	F	Wilbur Reginald L	636	clerk	18	"
	G	Barry Francis D	640	"	35	"
	H	Barry Helen M †	640	housewife	31	"
	K	Morad Mary A †	640	"	27	"
	L	Morad Raymond	640	manager	29	"
	M	Rathjen Marion E †	640	housewife	27	"
	N	Rathjen William F	640	manager	27	"
	O	Pierce Edwin F	640	salesman	30	[illegible]
	P	Pierce Eileen M †	640	housewife	23	[illegible]
	R	Daly Arthur	640	electrician	31	here
	S	Daly Ethel †	640	housewife	28	"
	T	Crouse Eldredge	640	salesman	33	"
	U	Crouse Marguerite L †	640	housewife	31	"
	V	Broderick Helen †	644	"	28	"
	W	Broderick James A	644	pipefitter	32	"
	X	Hawkins Francis J	644	salesman	32	"
	Y	Powers Robert C	644	draftsman	45	"
	Z	Powers Sabina †	644	housewife	43	"
431						
	A	*McMonagle Mary E †	644	at home	78	"
	B	*Morse Mary E †	644	baker	58	"
	C	Fergie David	644	machinist	49	[illegible]
	D	Fergie Louise O †	644	housewife	[illegible]	[illegible]
	E	Bradshaw Mildred J †	644	"	[illegible]	[illegible]
	F	Bradshaw Robert R	644	salesman	[illegible]	[illegible]
	G	Charrier Albert	644	[illegible]	[illegible]	[illegible]
	H	*Charrier Isabel †	644	[illegible]	[illegible]	[illegible]

Page	Letter	Full Name	Residence, Jan. 1, 1947	Occupation	Supposed Age	Reported Residence, Jan. 1, 1946. Street and Number.

Rockdale Street

Page	Letter	Full Name	Residence	Occupation	Age	Reported Residence
	K	Berkonert Frank E	7	metalworker	65	here
	L	Fandel Anastasia M †	7	clerk	41	"
	M	Fandel Annie M †	7	housewife	70	"
	N	Fandel Clotilda †	7	bookkeeper	60	Milton
	O	Fandel George M	7	metalworker	71	here
	P	Ryan Alice E †	8	housewife	39	"
	R	Ryan John F	8	inspector	42	"
	S	Ryan Pauline A †	8	student	21	"
	T	Byrne Amapara †	11	housewife	53	"
	V	Byrne David J	11	pharmacist	55	"
	W	Byrne David J, jr	11	clerk	25	"
	X	Byrne Priscilla A †	11	student	21	"
	Y	O'Connor Eleanor V †	14	teacher	26	"
	Z	O'Connor Ellen V †	14	housewife	54	"
432						
	A	O'Connor Patrick J	14	letter carrier	62	"
	B	Cunnally Jeannette M †	14	housewife	30	"
	C	Cunnally Thomas F	14	clerk	33	"
	D	Cook Elizabeth B †	15	stenographer	20	"
	E	Cook Henry C	15	salesman	57	"
	F	Cook Henry C, jr	15	carpenter	24	"
	G	Cook Marjorie M †	15	stenographer	22	"
	H	Cook Nina B †	15	housewife	54	"
	K	White Emma R †	15	at home	77	"
	L	Hooper Frederick W	16	retired	69	"
	M	Hooper Garrett	16	chauffeur	43	"
	N	Hooper Marline †	16	housewife	65	"
	O	Hart Josephine T †	16	"	70	"
	P	Hart Mary B †	16	teacher	29	"
	R	Parkin Aretta M †	19	housekeeper	44	"
	S	Lee Edward N	20	clerk	41	"
		Lee Evelyn C †	20	housewife	38	"
		Macdonald Charles W	20	salesman	60	132 Summit
		Macdonald Etta L †	20	clerk	61	132 "
	X	Macdonald Katherine A †	20	housewife	63	132 "
		Quinlan Arthur F	22	salesman	63	here
		Quinlan Catherine C †	22	telegrapher	24	"
		Quinlan Catherine E †	22	housewife	61	"
433						
		Quinlan John H	22	engineer	35	"
		[illegible] Marie †	22	housewife	76	"

Page	Letter	Full Name	Residence				

Rockdale Street (Continued)

Page	Letter	Full Name					
	C	Henrici Sylvia M †		22	clerk	17	[illegible]
	D	Flaherty Michael F		23	retired	71	"
	E	Maney Maurice M		23	laborer	23	"
	F	Maney Robert		23	decorator	20	"
	G	Shedd Frank		23	baker	65	"
	H	Shedd Julia S †		23	housewife	63	"
	K	Spaulding Catherine W †		24	"	48	"
	L	Spaulding Fred T		24	clerk	22	"
	M	Spaulding Ruth E †		24	typist	20	"
	N	Spaulding Walter W		24	cashier	53	"
	O	Badger Roland J		25	millwright	48	Quincy
	P	Currie Benjamin M		25	retired	76	here
	R	Kimball Carolyn R †		25	housewife	38	"
	S	Kimball Harry E		25	plumber	47	"
	T	Northup Patience †		25	housekeeper	79	"
	U	Powers Patience M †		25	clerk	20	"
	V	Powers Phyllis I †		25	"	31	"
	W	Powers Sadie N †		25	housewife	59	"
	X	Powers Stillman J		25	photographer	60	"
	Y	Fay Helen L †		26	clerk	50	"
	Z	Fay Irene N †		26	secretary	54	"
434							
	A	Fay Thomas J		26	clerk	48	"
	B	Jenkins Alice L †		28	housewife	67	"
	C	Jenkins Francis T		28	manager	33	"
	D	Jenkins George T		28	retired	69	"
	E	Jenkins Sarah †		28	nurse	29	"
	F	Fenton John F		28	adjustor	43	"
	G	Fenton Madeline G †		28	housewife	41	"
	H	Orcutt Albert C		32	retired	86	"
	K	Williams Samuel		32	bookkeeper	59	"
	L	Laughlin Anna M †		32	housewife	58	"
	M	Laughlin Francis J		32	inspector	38	"
	N	Laughlin Joseph W		32	cashier	65	"
	O	Hackel Jean L †	33	35	housewife	30	New Y[illegible]
	P	Hackel Stanley J	33	35	manager	31	"
	R	Young Anita P †	33	35	housewife	50	[illegible]
	S	Young Edward F	33	35	salesman	60	[illegible]
	T	White John J		36	forester	[illegible]	[illegible]
	U	White Pauline R †		36	housewife	47	[illegible]
	V	Coppola Angelo R		36	[illegible]	[illegible]	[illegible]

Page	Letter	Full Name	Residence, Jan. 1, 1941	Occupation	Supposed Age	Reported Residence, Jan. 1, 1940. Street and Number.

Rockdale Street—Continued

Page	Letter	Full Name	Residence, Jan. 1, 1941	Occupation	Supposed Age	Reported Residence, Jan. 1, 1940.
	W	Coppola Margaret R †	36	housewife	38	5 Penryth
	X	Ronan James P	36	janitor	26	Braintree
	Y	Grant Frank	39	engineer	74	here
	Z	Grant Frank E	39	clerk	31	"
435						
	A	Grant Margaret †	39	housewife	73	"
	B	Grant Margaret M †	39	hostess	28	"
	C	Peters Mary L †	40	at home	76	"
	D	Peters Rose M †	40	clerk	45	"
	E	Ware Helen J †	40	"	43	"
	F	Long Josephine A †	40	"	50	32 Rexford
	G	O'Connor John J	40	"	47	here
	H	O'Connor Mary A †	40	housewife	77	"
	K	O'Connor Monica T †	40	housekeeper	43	"
	L	Cornyn Delia C †	43	housewife	47	10 Rockdale
	M	Cornyn William	43	superintendent	49	10 "
	N	Delaney Catherine M †	44	housewife	76	here
	O	Delaney Lester L	44	electrician	35	"
	P	Delaney Mildred V †	44	saleswoman	41	"
	R	Razzeto Catherine L †	44	clerk	35	"
	S	Razzeto Rose †	44	housewife	64	"
	T	Curley Edna J †	47	bookkeeper	39	"
	U	Cusack George J	47	watchman	76	"
	V	Cusack Susan †	47	housewife	68	"
	W	West Grace †	47	clerk	39	"
	X	Moffett Mary †	47	cashier	79	"
	Y	Daddario Alice B †	48	instructor	31	18 Rector rd
	Z	Daddario Louis	48	contractor	42	here
436						
	A	Daddario Virginia †	48	housewife	70	"
	B	Kelley Constance B †	48	"	30	48 Lyndhurst
	C	Kelley John F	48	tel worker	32	48 "
	D	Crawley Andrew E	51	superintendent	70	here
	E	Crawley Clara M †	51	housewife	59	"
	F	Neagle Bridget A †	51	"	79	"
	G	Neagle Sarah A †	51	secretary	39	"
	H	O'Hara Sarah A †	51	housekeeper	80	"
	K	Hoelscher Annie M †	52	housewife	52	"
	L	Hoelscher Henry H	52	electrician	60	"
	M	Duggan Frank J	52	policeman	36	"
	N	Duggan Mary E †	52	housewife	34	"

Page	Letter	Full Name	Residence, April 1, 1940	Occupation	Supposed Age	Reported Residence, April 1, 1939

Rockdale Street *Continued*

Page	Letter	Full Name	Residence, April 1, 1940	Occupation	Supposed Age	Reported Residence, April 1, 1939
	O	Keegan Thomas J	52	retired	77	here
	P	Ruggiero Anthony	55	clerk	22	"
	R	Ruggiero Eleanor R †	55	housewife	23	"
	S	Ruggiero Lawrence J	55	chauffeur	30	"
	T	*Ruggiero Mary †	55	housewife	59	"
	U	Carlson Gertrude A †	55	secretary	22	"
	V	Carlson Hulda V †	55	housewife	53	"
	W	*Carlson Wilhelm T	55	painter	32	"
	X	Piatelli Anthony	56	contractor	47	"
	Y	Piatelli Leon	56	student	20	"
	Z	Piatelli Mary †	56	housewife	47	"
437						
	A	Ballerino Emily M †	56	"	35	"
	B	Ballerino Salvatore E	56	manager	37	"
	C	Adelberg Fannie †	59	housewife	70	"
	D	Adelberg Jeannette †	59	"	33	12 Floyd
	E	Adelberg Simon	59	plumber	43	here
	F	Fieldstad Olga †	60	nurse	60	"
	G	Breen John G	60	auditor	48	"
	H	Breen Mary A †	60	housewife	48	"
	K	Stack Sarah A †	60	housekeeper	80	"
	L	Campbell Geraldine L †	63	housewife	28	22 Ellison
	M	Campbell Lawrence J	63	electrician	28	22 "
	N	Westlund Carl E	63	molder	65	Somerville
	O	Westlund Hilda L †	63	housewife	68	"
	P	Samuelson Abraham	64	retired	63	here
	R	Smith Lillian †	64	housewife	61	"
	S	Smith Louis	64	merchant	68	"
	T	Doxer Anna †	64	housewife	40	"
	U	Doxer Louis	64	agent	46	"
	V	McIntosh Catherine J †	68	housewife	32	15 Regent rd
	W	McIntosh Robert L	68	glazier	33	15 "
	X	Aglio Esther L †	68	housewife	35	"
	Y	Aglio Thomas A	68	salesman	34	"
	Z	Mahoney Jeremiah J	68	retired	75	"
438						
	A	Tighe Charlotte M †	69	clerk	25	here
	B	Tighe Lillian G †	69	housewife	59	"
	C	Tighe William J	69	clerk	[illegible]	"
	D	Murphy David L	69	merchant	29	"
	E	Murphy Dorothy L †	69	housewife	28	"

Page	Letter	Full Name	Residence, Jan. 1, 1941.	Occupation	Supposed Age.	Reported Residence, Jan. 1, 1940. Street and Number.

Rockdale Street Continued

Page	Letter	Full Name	Residence	Occupation	Age	Reported Residence
	F	LaRocco Rose †	71	janitress	50	here
	G	McGuire Francis P	71	policeman	44	"
	H	McGuire Irene G †	71	housewife	43	"
	K	Morrison Archie S	79	salesman	64	656 River
	L	Morrison Emma J †	79	housewife	58	656 "
	M	Burnhardt Charles	79	collector	53	here
	N	Burnhardt Emma B †	79	housewife	52	"
	O	Wilder Lillian G †	79	housekeeper	79	"
	P	Mee Francis T	81	agent	24	"
	R	Mee Frank J	81	motorman	50	"
	S	Mee Hannah M †	81	housewife	48	"
	T	Mee Margaret T †	81	at home	21	"
	U	Mee William J	81	laborer	20	"
	V	Toy Elizabeth A †	85	housewife	63	"
	W	Toy Joseph B	85	superintendent	62	"
	X	Durant William L	91	retired	90	"
	Y	Hackley Ada M †	91	housewife	63	"
	Z	Hackley Charles J	91	operator	27	"
439						
	A	Lang Christina M †	92	housewife	43	"
	B	Lang Jean M †	92	nurse	21	"
	C	Lang Johannes H	92	policeman	50	"
	D	McNeil Cornelius J	94	"	39	"
	E	McNeil Frances E †	94	housewife	37	"
	F	Shaughnessey Annie †	94	housekeeper	76	"
	G	Daiey Elmer R	94	molder	34	"
	H	Daiey Doris L †	94	housewife	40	"
	K	Roberts Chester I	94	molder	33	"
	L	Carlson Hilda A †	95	at home	80	"
	M	Lundberg Anna L †	95	housekeeper	76	"
	N	Nothelfer Emilie †	98	housewife	59	"
	O	Nothelfer Rene M	98	bookkeeper	39	"
	P	Sexton Agnes M †	99	housewife	40	"
	R	Sexton John W	99	accountant	43	"
	S	Reynolds Margaret T †	99	collector	60	"
	T	Sullivan Daniel	100	retired	61	"
	U	Sullivan Georgina †	100	housewife	60	"
	V	Healy James	103	iceman	45	624 Cummins H'way
	W	Mitchell Francis X	103	clerk	30	here
	X	Mitchell Mary I †	103	housewife	68	"
	Y	Carlson Alice I †	103	"	40	"

Page	Letter	Full Name	Residence	Occupation	Age	[illegible]

Rockdale Street (Continued)

Page	Letter	Full Name	Residence	Occupation	Age	[illegible]
	Z	Carlsen Carl M	103	mechanic	40	here
440						
	A	Helmsdorff Hannah M †	103	housekeeper	67	"
	B	Holt Stephen O	106	electrician	34	[illegible]
	C	O'Day Katherine E †	106	housewife	59	here
	D	O'Day Thomas	106	laborer	61	"
	E	O'Day Thomas F	106	reporter	30	"
	F	Dunn Alice †	108	housewife	31	562 R[illegible]
	G	Dunn William	108	tinsmith	31	562 "
	H	Sullivan Rose A †	108	housekeeper	46	here
	K	O'Gorman Gaynor	109	salesman	51	"
	L	O'Gorman Gaynor, jr	109	clerk	27	"
	M	O'Gorman Kathleen †	109	stenographer	23	"
	N	O'Gorman Mary C †	109	housewife	52	"
	O	O'Gorman Vincent	109	student	21	"
	P	Donohoe John J	115	retired	55	611 So[illegible]
	R	Donohoe Mary F †	115	housewife	50	611 "
	S	Higgins Catherine A †	115	housekeeper	50	611 "
	T	Huestis Fannie I †	115	housewife	67	here
	U	Huestis George R	115	retired	65	"

Rosewood Street

Page	Letter	Full Name	Residence	Occupation	Age	[illegible]
	V	*Rosvall Carl A	7	metalworker	40	here
	W	*Rosvall Ebba B †	7	housewife	[illegible]	"
	X	Burwell Arthur M	7	bookbinder	50	"
	Y	Burwell Herbert A	7	messenger	[illegible]	"
	Z	Burwell Marian M †	7	housewife	[illegible]	[illegible]
441						
	A	Foster Helena R †	7	housekeeper	[illegible]	[illegible]
	B	Tanner Walter D	7	paperhanger	[illegible]	[illegible]
	C	Mahoney Margaret G †	8	at home	[illegible]	[illegible]
	D	Myers Wesley L	8	manager	30	[illegible]
	E	*Thorson Alma †	8	[illegible]	[illegible]	[illegible]
	F	Thorson John A	8	retired	[illegible]	[illegible]
	G	Wilkinson Louetta †	8	[illegible]	[illegible]	[illegible]
	H	Crowe Charles F	11	[illegible]	[illegible]	[illegible]
	K	Crowe Drusilla M †	11	[illegible]	[illegible]	[illegible]
	L	Crowe Jonathan A	11	[illegible]	[illegible]	[illegible]
	M	Crowe Wesley B	11	[illegible]	[illegible]	[illegible]
	N	Broughal Eleanor L †	11	[illegible]	[illegible]	[illegible]

Rosewood Street Continued

Page	Letter	Full Name	Residence, Jan. 1, 1941	Occupation	Supposed Age	Reported Residence, Jan. 1, 1940. Street and Number.
	O	Barry Phyllis M †	12	nurse	35	1139 Com av
	P	Hennebery Anne L †	12	technician	22	here
	R	Hennebery Delia J †	12	housewife	55	"
	S	Hennebery Mary C †	12	secretary	24	"
	T	Hennebery Philip A	12	dentist	55	"
	U	Hennebery Phyllis E †	12	technician	28	"
	V	Hennebery Richard F	12	clerk	26	"
	W	Martin Dorothy P †	15	housewife	34	"
	X	Martin Paul E	15	printer	31	"
	Y	*Dawyskiba Anna †	15	housewife	48	"
	Z	*Dawyskiba Peter	15	cook	52	"
442						
	A	Dawyskiba Peter J	15	instructor	21	"
	B	Dawyskiba Walter	15	laborer	25	"
	C	Barry Lillian J †	16	dressmaker	61	"
	D	Choate Arthur F	16	clerk	55	"
	E	Choate Elizabeth M †	16	housewife	54	"
	F	Choate Francis X	16	draftsman	21	"
	G	Taft Joseph	19	retired	86	"
	H	Taft Mary E †	19	housewife	71	"
	K	Soper Agnes M †	20	"	40	"
	L	Soper Charles B	20	manager	42	"
	M	Handy Annie E †	21	housekeeper	66	"
	N	Henderson Margaret E †	21	housewife	22	40 Pond
	O	Henderson Robert E	21	chauffeur	22	40 "
	P	Stackpole Fred H	21	electrician	65	here
	R	Cogan Edward C	24	clerk	33	"
	S	Cogan Ella C †	24	housewife	56	"
	T	Cogan Mildred E †	24	secretary	27	"
	U	Cogan Thomas E	24	salesman	60	"
	V	Kirby Helen F †	25	teacher	38	"
	W	McDonough Elizabeth J †	26	housewife	39	63 Ridlon rd
	X	McDonough Patrick J	26	longshoreman	39	63 "
	Y	Gay Charles H	27	retired	74	here
	Z	Gay Mabel A †	27	nurse	40	"
443						
	A	Gay Sarah A †	27	housewife	73	"
	B	[illegible] Archer L	31	teacher	69	"
	C	[illegible] Florence M †	31	housewife	55	"
	D	[illegible] Elizabeth C †	34 36	"	33	"
	E	[illegible] Frederick J	34 36	manager	36	"

Page	Letter	Full Name		Residence, April 1, 1944	Occupation	Age	Residence, April 1, 1943

Rosewood Street Continued

Page	Letter	Full Name		Residence	Occupation	Age	Residence 1943
	F	Dever Esther C	†	34–36	housewife	58	here
	G	Dever Grace A	†	34–36	houseworker	52	"
	H	Dever John F		34–36	clerk	59	"
	K	DeFlurin Grace A	†	37	housewife	46	18 Rosa
	L	DeFlurin William C		37	painter	47	18 "
	M	DeFlurin William F		37	clerk	27	18 "
	N	Margolin Philip		37	agent	48	Revere
	O	Margolin Rebecca	†	37	housewife	43	"
	P	Wheeler Julia C	†	37	saleswoman	38	"
	R	O'Malley James P		38–40	policeman	43	here
	S	O'Malley Mabel M	†	38–40	housewife	30	"
	T	Carabbio John		38–40	retired	69	"
	U	Carabbio Lillia	†	38–40	saleswoman	27	"
	V	Carabbio Victoria	†	38–40	housewife	65	"
	W	Fortini Ella	†	38–40	secretary	35	"
	X	Marshall Eleanor	†	39	housewife	25	"
	Y	Marshall Joseph C		39	broker	30	"
	Z	Ruchione John L		39	salesman	39	"
444							
	A	Ruchione Margaret M	†	39	housewife	38	"
	B	Rushlow Alice M	†	39	houseworker	68	"
	C	Hunt Gertrude P	†	41	housewife	75	"
	D	Hunt Ira J		41	engineer	75	"
	E	Dawyskiba Mary	†	41	housewife	43	"
	F	Dawyskiba Nicholas		41	chef	45	"
	G	Dobbins Eva H	†	43	housewife	49	"
	H	Dobbins Thomas S		43	manager	52	"
	K	Dawyskiba Andrew		43	cook	41	"
	L	Dawyskiba Michael		43	"	49	"
	M	Dawyskiba Sadie	†	43	housewife	47	"
	N	Lourie Albert B		44	manager	38	"
	O	Lourie Ruth L	†	44	housewife	34	"
	P	Sullivan Josephine M	†	44	housekeeper	50	"
	R	Picard Anna	†	44	housewife	45	"
	S	Picard Charlotte	†	44	secretary	20	"
	T	Picard Morris		44	agent	50	"
	U	Powers Edward J		48	merchant	58	"
	V	Powers Evelyn L	†	48	housewife	52	"
	W	Bradshaw Elizabeth G	†	48	clerk	[illegible]	
	X	Bradshaw R Theresa	†	48	[illegible]	[illegible]	
	Y	Bradshaw Stephen J		48	[illegible]	[illegible]	

Page	Letter	Full Name	Residence, Jan. 1, 1941	Occupation	Supposed Age	Reported Residence, Jan. 1, 1940. Street and Number.

Rosewood Street—Continued

Page	Letter	Full Name	Residence, Jan. 1, 1941	Occupation	Supposed Age	Reported Residence, Jan. 1, 1940. Street and Number.
	Z	Grogan Stephen M	48	painter	52	here
445						
	A	Steele John M	50	manager	38	1 Carmen
	B	Steele Marie C †	50	housewife	33	1 "
	C	Walsh Margaret M †	50	"	70	here
	D	Walsh Mary L †	50	teacher	34	"
	E	Walsh William J	50	retired	74	"
	F	Laughlin Francis R	53	salesman	29	138 Chittick rd
	G	Laughlin Mary T †	53	housewife	34	25 Claymoss rd
	H	Long John S	53	engraver	44	here
	K	Long Mildred G †	53	housewife	42	"
	L	Powers James J	54	retired	44	"
	M	Powers Marion T †	54	housewife	41	"
	N	Gallagher Charles J	54	carpenter	74	"
	O	Gallagher Margaret M †	54	stenographer	29	"
	P	Gallagher Mary A †	54	housewife	71	"
	R	LaCroix Henry J	57–59	policeman	43	"
	S	LaCroix Rose E †	57–59	housewife	42	"
	T	Moore Eleanor M †	57–59	cashier	24	Milton
	U	Moore Emily M †	57–59	housewife	48	"
	V	Moore R Claire †	57–59	secretary	22	"
	W	Moore William F	57–59	accountant	48	"
	X	Garland Catherine M †	58	housewife	29	here
	Y	Garland Herbert A	58	sales manager	36	"
	Z*	Mendes John C	58	manufacturer	37	"
446						
	A	Mendes Medora Y †	58	housewife	37	"
	B	Kelly John	61	laborer	35	10 O'Connell rd
	C	Kelly Mary †	61	housewife	31	10 "
	D	Rossi Joseph	61	barber	56	10 "
	E	Rossi Olympia †	61	housewife	52	10 "
	F	Coughlin Kathleen T †	62	"	33	48 Hampstead rd
	G	Coughlin Thomas F	62	lineman	36	48 "
	K	Burke Margaret G †	63	stenographer	38	here
	L	Burke Mary E †	63	housewife	76	"
	M	Burke Thomas A	63	carpenter	40	"
	N	Clayton Fred	65	retired	89	"
	O	Hopcroft Ella M †	65	housekeeper	53	"
	P	Taylor James W	65	chauffeur	45	"
	R	Clark Jessie M †	65	housekeeper	59	"
	S	Hughes Joseph J	65	U S A	33	"

Page	Letter	Full Name	Residence, April 1, 1943	Occupation	Age	Reported Residence

Rosewood Street Continued

Letter	Full Name	Residence	Occupation	Age	Reported Residence
T	Hughes Pauline E †	65	housewife	28	here
U	Shea Ellen L †	66	"	18	"
V	Shea Joseph B	66	drawtender	55	"
W	Morganstern Elizabeth †	66	housewife	78	"
X	Morganstern Frank	66	clerk	68	"
Y	Morganstern M Ethel †	66	housekeeper	38	"
Z	Morganstern Marion E †	66	clerk	35	"
447					
A	Morganstern Ruth †	66	housekeeper	41	"
B	Stevens Carlysle R	67	appraiser	39	"
C	Stevens Virginia W †	67	housewife	30	"
D	Wakefield John J	67	shipper	63	"
E	Wakefield Lula M †	67	housewife	59	"
F	Minehan Anna C †	71	teacher	26	"
G	Minehan Annie M †	71	housewife	65	"
H	Minehan Frank	71	buyer	31	"
K	Minehan Michael F	71	fireman	65	"
L	Tangney Anna M †	75	housewife	39	"
M	Tangney Michael R	75	engineer	42	"
N	Calpin Evelyn †	76	housekeeper	36	"
O	Calpin Frank	76	operator	40	"
P	Calpin Robert	76	chauffeur	34	"
R	Calpin Sarah †	76	housekeeper	66	"
S	Honywill Evalda P †	78	housewife	57	"
T	Honywill Frederick B	78	salesman	63	"
U	Honywill Charles W	78A	retired	85	"
V	Trenoweth Howard G	78A	salesman	49	"
W	Trenoweth Susie M †	78A	housewife	49	"
X	MacDonald Hazel W †	82	teacher	35	"
Y	MacDonald Marion M †	82	"	[illegible]	"
Z	MacDonald Wilhelmina †	82	housewife	[illegible]	[illegible]
448					
A	Bullard Eliza †	83	"	[illegible]	[illegible]
C	Knutson Anna †	88	"	[illegible]	[illegible]
D	Knutson Elna M †	88	[illegible]	[illegible]	[illegible]
E	Burckhart Ellen R †	91	[illegible]	[illegible]	[illegible]
F	Burckhart John A	91	[illegible]	[illegible]	[illegible]
G	Flanagan Catherine B †	91	[illegible]	[illegible]	[illegible]
H	Flanagan Thomas A	91	[illegible]	[illegible]	[illegible]
K	Simmons Eugene W	95	[illegible]	[illegible]	[illegible]
L	Simmons Eva A †	95	[illegible]	[illegible]	[illegible]

Page	Letter	Full Name	Residence, Jan. 1, 1941	Occupation	Supposed Age	Reported Residence, Jan. 1, 1940. Street and Number.
		Rosewood Street Continued				
	M	Congdon Esther †	96	receptionist	38	here
	N	Congdon John P	96	woodworker	69	"
	O	Congdon Mary F †	96	housewife	65	"
	P	Congdon Miriam †	96	technician	35	"
	R	Coughlin Grace M †	99	housewife	46	"
	S	Coughlin Joseph M	99	electrician	45	"
	T	Currant Edward L	103	clerk	61	"
	U	Currant Florence M †	103	housewife	49	"
	V	Stevens Barbara †	104	teacher	23	"
	W	Stevens Clarence	104	signalman	65	"
	X	Stevens Paul	104	engineer	27	"
	Y	Ardini Barbara V †	108	housewife	50	46 Seminole
	Z	Ardini Gertrude M †	108	housekeeper	23	46 "
449						
	A	Ardini James A	108	machinist	51	46 "
	B	Ardini Joseph L	108	tester	21	46 "
	C	Kilduff Elizabeth E †	110	saleswoman	23	62 Rosewood
	D	Knauber Jessie V †	110	housewife	50	62 "
	E	Knauber William L	110	bartender	58	62 "
	F	MacIver Donald	110A	shipfitter	55	1132 Wash'n
	G	MacIver Donald, jr	110A	electrician	21	1132 "
	H	MacIver Margaret R †	110A	housewife	51	1132 "
		Tesla Street				
	K	Darling Harold R	1	repairman	40	here
	L	Darling Sarah H †	1	housewife	35	"
	M	Haskell David G	10	operator	55	"
	N	Haskell Edward G	10	laborer	22	"
	O	Haskell Mary I †	10	housewife	59	"
	P	Clark Elizabeth M †	10	at home	75	12 Whitney pk
	R	Sundell Ida A †	10	housekeeper	63	here
	S	Nyquist Berne E †	10	housewife	57	"
	T	Nyquist Hilda K †	10	bookkeeper	34	"
	V	Lanata Clara J †	11	housewife	46	"
	W	Lanata Emanuel J	11	student	21	"
	X	Lanata John A	11	realtor	44	"
	Y	Lanata Joseph L	11	student	22	"
	Z	Cox Sarah C	11	housewife	51	"
450						
	A	Cox Thomas F	11	tel worker	53	"

Page	Letter	Full Name	[illegible]	[illegible]	[illegible]	[illegible]

Tesla Street Continued

Letter	Full Name				
B	Winchenbaugh Marie †	14	housewife	21	[illegible]
C	Winchenbaugh Vincent	14	clerk	22	356 [illegible]
D	Wendel Elizabeth H †	14	housewife	19	here
E	Wendel Iver J	14	engineer	19	"
F	Couture Catherine W †	23	housewife	24	[illegible]
G	Couture Edward C	23	engineer	27	3 W[illegible]
H	Howard Esther †	23	housewife	45	here
K	Howard Leon	23	engineer	23	"

Tokio Street

Letter	Full Name				
L	McNay James L	9	machinist	56	here
M	*McNay Jennie †	9	housewife	55	"
N	Mitton Clara A †	9	"	32	"
O	Mitton Warren A	9	salesman	32	"
P	*Green Agnes B †	9	housewife	29	"
R	Green Edgar	9	salesman	36	"
S	Murphy Frederick	9	operator	28	"
T	Murphy Mary †	9	housewife	30	"
U	McGovern Mary G †	9	"	38	352 Riv[illegible]
V	McGovern William L	9	salesman	35	352 "
W	White James F	9	chauffeur	30	[illegible]
X	*White Rosanna †	9	housewife	29	Milto[illegible]
Y	Brown John J	21	fireman	58	here
Z	Cleary Catherine A †	21	housewife	66	"
451					
A	Cleary William J	21	salesman	69	"
B	Hubbell Emma †	25	housewife	78	
C	Hubbell Frank E	25	mechanic	78	

Violante Street

Letter	Full Name				
E	Cantwell Michael H	1	manager	[illegible]	[illegible]
F	Cantwell Sarah A †	1	housewife	[illegible]	[illegible]
G	McGrane Sarah A †	1	at home	60	[illegible]
H	Norris Clara M †	1	housewife	[illegible]	[illegible]
K	Norris Thomas F	1	locksmith	[illegible]	[illegible]
L	Sheridan Catherine M †	1	housewife	[illegible]	[illegible] W
M	Sheridan Peter T	1	chauffeur	[illegible]	[illegible]
N	Crawford Dewey H	6	[illegible]	[illegible]	[illegible]
O	Crawford June †	6	[illegible]	[illegible]	[illegible]

Page	Letter	Full Name	Residence, Jan. 1, 1941	Occupation	Supposed Age	Reported Residence, Jan. 1, 1940. Street and Number.

Violante Street—Continued

Page	Letter	Full Name	Residence, Jan. 1, 1941	Occupation	Supposed Age	Reported Residence, Jan. 1, 1940. Street and Number.
	P	Stern Gertrude †	6	musician	33	here
	R	Harris Catherine G †	6	housewife	38	"
	S	Harris Thomas J	6	supervisor	44	"
	T	Leonardi Florence C †	8	housewife	27	42 Regent
	U	Leonardi Thomas	8	engineer	29	42 "
	V	Monoco Antonio	8	baker	60	here
	W	Monoco Josephine †	8	housewife	50	"
	X	Praino Anthony F	15	pharmacist	48	"
	Y	Praino Catherine A †	15	housewife	48	"
	Z	MacGaregill Mary T †	15	"	53	"
452						
	A	MacGaregill William A	15	foreman	51	"
	B	Milk Edna T †	19	housewife	71	599 River
	C	Milk Herbert A	19	accountant	43	599 "
	D	Milk Katherine †	19	housewife	37	599 "
	E	Weller Edward W	19	chauffeur	73	599 "
	G	Donabed John	19	hairdresser	30	here
	F	Donabed Juanita M †	19	housewife	24	"
	H	Gibson Alice M †	25	printer	51	"
	K	Gibson Cora A †	25	"	53	"
	L	Gibson Michael J	25	retired	94	"
	M	Ferullo Mary †	29	housewife	80	"
	N	Franceschi Richard	29	clerk	21	"
	O	Siblo Mary †	29	housewife	57	"
	P	Siblo Michael W	29	laborer	30	"
	R	Siblo Ralph A	29	metalworker	28	"

Whitney Park

Page	Letter	Full Name	Residence, Jan. 1, 1941	Occupation	Supposed Age	Reported Residence, Jan. 1, 1940. Street and Number.
	S	McDonough Margaret F †	3	housewife	64	here
		McDonough Robert B	3	clerk	25	"
		McDonough William A	3	carpenter	28	"
		McDonough William J	3	retired	76	"
	V	Burchfield Bertha P †	8	housewife	48	"
		Burchfield William M	8	salesman	48	"
		[illegible] Marie †	8	housekeeper	73	"
		[illegible] Ernest C	9	patternmaker	68	"
453						
		[illegible] Florence K †	9	housewife	60	"
		[illegible] R	10	proprietor	35	"

Page	Letter	Full Name	Residence			

Whitney Park—Continued

Page	Letter	Full Name	Residence			
	C	Donabed Margaret †	10	housewife	56	here
	D	Donabed Yeghia	10	shoecutter	58	"
	E	Fish Phyllis S †	11	housekeeper	58	"
	F	Fitzpatrick Daniel E	11	packer	29	"
	G	Sullivan Anne G †	11	housewife	45	"
	H	Sullivan Edmund R	11	engineer	43	"
	K	Sullivan Estelle P †	11	clerk	23	"
	L	Alward Mary A †	12	housekeeper	56	"
	M	Schindler James A	12	laborer	36	Milton
	N	Schindler Jane C †	12	housewife	31	67 [illegible] rd
	O	Metcalfe Ethel M †	14	housekeeper	51	here
	P	Metcalfe Margaret M †	14	clerk	53	"
	R	Clancy Mary M †	15	housekeeper	60	"
	S	Reiley James B	15	towerman	54	"
	T	Moreland Alice F †	16	clerk	40	"
	U	Ward Henry L	16	retired	74	"
	V	Doherty Alice †	16	housewife	67	"
	W	Doherty Peter J	16	operator	34	"
	X	Richards Katherine J †	16	"	36	"
	Y	Martin Bertram	16	painter	33	"
	Z	Martin Katherine D †	16	housewife	39	"
454						
	A	DeSantis Lillian A †	17	"	23	7 Pa[illegible]
	B	DeSantis Victor F	17	machinist	27	7 "
	C	*McKay Helen G †	17	housewife	36	here
	D	McKay Joseph	17	steamfitter	33	"
	E	McGilvray Joseph A	17	carpenter	38	"
	F	McGilvray Mary C †	17	housewife	34	"
	G	Johnson Carl G	18	carpenter	50	"
	H	Johnson Ernest P	18	machinist	22	"
	K	Johnson Harriet E †	18	stenographer	25	"
	L	Johnson Hulda †	18	housewife	51	"
	M	Johnson Vincent T	18	U S A	23	"
	N	*Swanson Nils	18	spinner	50	"
	O	*Ryan Katherine S †	18	housewife	40	"
	P	Ryan Stephen	18	laborer	41	
	R	Bitsikas Hiro	18	shoemaker	57	H[illegible]
	S	Bitsikas Jennie †	18	housewife	50	
	T	Buckley James H	19	porter	[illegible]	
	U	Buckley Katherine A †	19	housewife	[illegible]	
	V	Horigan John J	19	[illegible]	[illegible]	

Page	Letter	Full Name	Residence, Jan. 1, 1941	Occupation	Supposed Age	Reported Residence, Jan. 1, 1940. Street and Number.

Whitney Park Continued

Page	Letter	Full Name	Residence, Jan. 1, 1941	Occupation	Supposed Age	Reported Residence, Jan. 1, 1940. Street and Number.
	w	Horigan Mary A †	19	housewife	32	here
	x	George James L	19	waiter	49	"
	y	Phelopoulos James	19	bartender	38	"
	z	*Phelopoulos Stella †	19	housewife	29	"
455						
	A	Christensen Marie †	22	at home	78	"
	B	Kolb Esther C †	22	housewife	39	"
	C	Kolb Jacob C	22	clergyman	39	"

Ward 18—Precinct 5

CITY OF BOSTON

LIST OF RESIDENTS
20 YEARS OF AGE AND OVER

(NON-CITIZENS INDICATED BY ASTERISK)
(FEMALES INDICATED BY DAGGER)

AS OF

JANUARY 1, 1941

CITY OF BOSTON PRINTING DEPARTMENT

Page	Letter	Full Name	Residence, Jan. 1, 1941	Occupation	Supposed Age	Reported Residence, Jan. 1, 1940. Street and Number.

500

Agnes Avenue

A	Rohan Catherine J †	1	housewife	68	here
B	Rohan Harriet V †	1	clerk	32	"
C	Rohan Margaret M †	1	teacher	26	"
D	Walsh John C	1	machinist	48	"
E	Walsh Mary A †	1	housewife	42	"
F	Scioletti Elizabeth †	15	"	31	"
G	*Scioletti Nicholas	15	operator	34	"
H	Daddario Attilio	15	contractor	51	"
K	Daddario Bernice †	15	housewife	25	New York
L	Daddario Emilio Q	15	student	22	here
M	Daddario Francis E	15	engineer	23	"

Alpine Street

N	Quinlan Genevieve M †	9–11	housewife	24	here
O	Quinlan Pierce F	9–11	salesman	27	"
P	Cowan Amos E	9–11	clerk	49	"
R	Cowan Everett J	9–11	"	21	"
S	Cowan Mary C †	9–11	housewife	48	"
T	Cowan Ruth C †	9–11	stenographer	23	"

Baldwin Street

U	Harnden Ethel D †	11	housewife	34	here
V	Harnden George J	11	policeman	40	"
W	*Green Maria †	15	at home	68	"
X	MacDonald Agatha T †	15	operator	38	"
Y	Ruddick Albert E	15	packer	25	"
Z	Ruddick Jane M †	15	housewife	25	"

501

A	Thimot Agnes M †	15	"	37	"
B	Hicks Clifford M	19–21	chauffeur	63	"
C	Hicks Josephine G †	19–21	housewife	62	"
E	Burke Clara J †	23–25	"	49	"
F	Burke Louis W	23–25	chauffeur	49	"
G	Nelson Doris †	23–25	housewife	26	"
H	Nelson George	23–25	stenographer	30	"
K	Cella Mary R †	27–29	packer	33	"
L	Clough Emma R †	27–29	housewife	29	"
M	Clough George H	27–29	salesman	29	"

Page	Letter	Full Name				Occupation		

Baldwin Street (Continued)

	Full Name				Occupation		
N	Sollitto Catherine	†	27	29	housewife	35	here
O	Sollitto Joseph E		27	29	accountant	37	"
P	Jones Gabrielle N	†	31	33	housewife	38	"
R	Jones William P		31	33	rigger	41	"
S	Long Albert D		31	33	laundryman	41	"
T	*Long Belle	†	31	33	housewife	38	"
U	Webb Chester J		31	33	manager	26	"
V	Webb Goldie R	†	31	33	housewife	48	"
W	Webb Samuel L		31	33	attorney	56	"
X	Webb Stanley L		31	33	manager	24	"
Y	O'Leary Dennis N		35	37	accountant	40	19 [illegible]
Z	O'Leary Josephine V	†	35	37	housewife	39	19 "

502

	Full Name				Occupation		
A	Feltquate Eva B	†	35	37	"	34	[illegible]
B	Feltquate Phillip		35	37	manager	46	880 "
C	O'Brien Frank A		39	41	salesman	41	here
D	O'Brien Helen F	†	39	41	housewife	36	"
E	*Gray Mary A	†	39	41	"	89	"
F	*Hamilton Catherine	†	39	41	"	82	"
G	Hamilton Joseph H		39	41	chauffeur	45	"
H	Hamilton Rose A	†	39	41	stenographer	46	"

Belnel Road

	Full Name				Occupation		
K	Harrington Catherine	†	5	7	housewife	39	here
L	Harrington John J		5	7	laborer	43	"
M	Cameron Malcolm E		5	7	electrician	50	"
N	*Cameron Rose J	†	5	7	housewife	40	"
O	*Stanley Amelia	†	9	11	"	52	"
P	Stanley Frank G		9	11	foreman	52	"
R	Allen Muriel F	†	9	11	housewife	31	7 [illegible]
S	Allen William B		9	11	rigger	33	7 "
T	Crichton Jessie E	†	13	15	cutter	41	here
U	Leahy Annie E	†	13	15	housewife	39	"
V	Leahy Francis A		13	15	proprietor	40	"
W	Lynch Edward J		13	15	chauffeur	31	"
X	Lynch Ellen	†	13	15	housewife	62	"
Y	Lynch Patrick F		13	15	clerk	27	"
Z	McLaughlin Gertrude M	†	13	15	housewife	31	"

503

	Full Name				Occupation		
A	McLaughlin Robert F		13	15	clerk	34	215 Wood [illegible]

Belnel Road Continued

Page	Letter	Full Name	Residence, Jan. 1, 1941	Occupation	Supposed Age	Reported Residence, Jan. 1, 1940. Street and Number.
	B	Harding Dorothy F †	19-21	housewife	29	22 Osceola
	C	Harding Edward H	19-21	printer	32	Cambridge
	D	Gottbald Frederick	19-21	retired	40	here
	E	Gottbald Grace M †	19-21	housewife	35	"
	F	O'Toole Ellen M †	31	"	65	"
	G	O'Toole Theresa M †	31	stenographer	31	"
	H	Hanson Harold	35	molder	23	"
	K	Hanson Ralph E	35	manager	21	"
	L	Smith Catherine L †	35	housewife	74	"
	M	Smith Harold R	35	clerk	51	"
	N	Smith Lawton W	35	laborer	40	"
	O	*Olsen Anna L †	39	housewife	44	"
	P	Olsen Peter H	39	toolmaker	50	"
	S	O'Neill Florence J †	43-45	housewife	27	"
	T	O'Neill Forrest A	43-45	chauffeur	26	"
	U	LeLacheur Ernest L	47-49	"	28	"
	V	LeLacheur Rita C †	47-49	housewife	25	"
	W	Will John A	47-49	chauffeur	26	"
	X	*Will Marguerite I †	47-49	housewife	22	"
	Y	Gulick Bessie E †	51-53	"	24	Brookline
	Z	Gulick Max V	51-53	laborer	28	"
504						
	A	Martinson Laura F †	51-53	housewife	27	N Hampshire
	B	Martinson William O	51-53	baker	30	"
	C	Daner Louis	55-57	salesman	35	here
	D	Daner Sarah †	55-57	housewife	31	"
	E	Matheson George W	55-57	machinist	40	"
	F	Matheson Gertrude C †	55-57	housewife	36	"
	G	*Wilder Jean B †	59-61	"	36	"
	H	Wilder Raymond J	59-61	steward	32	"
	K	Gregory Boniface	59-61	welder	25	52 Garfield av
	L	Gregory Dorothea E †	59-61	housewife	23	42 Milton
	M	Peacock Rose M †	63-65	"	41	here
	N	Peacock William R	63-65	custodian	41	"
	O	Burke John H	63-65	watchman	61	807 Hyde Park av
	P	Fillbin Alice M †	63-65	housewife	27	807 "
	R	Fillbin John T	63-65	clerk	26	807 "
	S	Shea Helen L †	67-69	typist	34	21 Tesla
		Shea Margaret †	67-69	housewife	66	21 "
		Gean Anna M †	67-69	"	26	here
		Gean William C	67-69	shoeworker	29	"

Belnel Road Continued

Letter	Full Name		Residence		Occupation	Age	
W	*Johansen Johannah	†	79	81	housewife	38	38 Hopewell
X	Johansen John A		79	81	carpenter	36	38 "
Y	Childs Ada F	†	79	81	housewife	71	here
Z	Childs Walter A		79	81	clerk	70	"
	505						
A	Gover Esther F	†	83	85	housewife	27	86 Brainerd [illegible]
B	Gover John T		83	85	chauffeur	32	86 "
C	LaVene Gertrude C	†	83	85	housewife	65	here
D	LaVene Helen	†	83	85	operator	35	"
E	LaVene Paul A		83	85	mechanic	31	"
F	LaVene Rita J	†	83	85	waitress	24	"
G	Goode Catherine V	†		120	housewife	48	"
H	Goode Lillian V	†		120	clerk	23	"
K	Johnson John			124	policeman	49	"
L	Johnson Mary M	†		124	housewife	39	"
M	Dingwell Arthur R			126	dentist	50	Somerville
N	O'Sullivan Gertrude M	†		126	supervisor	35	here
O	O'Sullivan James M			126	clerk	63	"
P	O'Sullivan Lula M	†		126	housewife	60	"

Blake Street

Letter	Full Name		Residence	Occupation	Age	
R	Toomey Daniel F		7	retired	73	here
S	Toomey James E		7	student	21	
T	Toomey John J		7	laborer	24	
U	Ryan Herbert		11	B F D	13	
V	Ryan Margaret	†	11	housewife	57	
W	Lalor Abbie M	†	11	bookkeeper	19	
X	Lalor Thomas F		11	clerk	41	
Y	Lyons Beatrice	†	13	housewife	58	
Z	Lyons Margaret T	†	13	clerk	21	
	506					
A	Grimley Irene E	†	15	stenographer	20	
B	Grimley John		15	policeman	54	
C	Grimley Katherine T	†	15	secretary	27	
D	Grimley Mary A	†	15	housewife	[illegible]	
E	Corbett Anna M	†	17	"	31	[illegible]
F	Corbett John J		17	clerk	32	[illegible]
G	Hoppe Gerard T		17	salesman	[illegible]	[illegible]
H	Hoppe Margaret A	†	17	housewife	[illegible]	

Page	Letter	Full Name	Residence, Jan. 1, 1941	Occupation	Supposed Age	Reported Residence, Jan. 1, 1940. Street and Number.

Blake Street—Continued

Page	Letter	Full Name	Residence, Jan. 1, 1941	Occupation	Supposed Age	Reported Residence, Jan. 1, 1940. Street and Number.
	K	Crowe Daisy †	19	supervisor	55	here
	L	Hackett Kathleen I †	19	housekeeper	51	"
	M	Currier Geraldine M †	19	saleswoman	23	"
	N	Currier Gertrude M †	19	"	43	"
	O	Currier Herman H	19	chauffeur	47	"
	P	Troy Margaret E †	21	at home	77	"
	R	Troy Mary E †	21	"	79	"
	S	DeLory John H	25	policeman	49	"
	T	DeLory Mary J †	25	housewife	40	"
	V	Devine John J	29	B F D	53	"
	W	Devine John J, jr	29	pipefitter	22	"
	X	Devine Leo F	29	student	21	"
	Y	Devine Rose A †	29	housewife	50	"
	Z	Westwood May M †	31	"	43	"
507						
	A	Westwood Walter J	31	salesman	45	"
	B	Hall Andrew M	31	metalworker	63	"
	C	Hall Dorothy M †	31	supervisor	28	"
	D	Hall Lillian M †	31	artist	24	"
	E	Hall Minnie †	31	housewife	60	"
	F	Elliot Gerald S	33	draftsman	35	"
	G	Elliot Helen V †	33	housewife	29	"
	H	Janitschke Christina I †	33	nurse	36	"
	K	Janitschke Helena I †	33	housewife	72	"
	L	Janitschke Hortense S †	33	stenographer	30	"
	M	Janitschke John B	33	retired	80	"
	N	Janitschke Mina A †	33	bookkeeper	34	"
	O	Bates Mary A †	35	housekeeper	70	"
	P	Loudin Catherine †	35	at home	80	"
	R	Miller Lillian M †	35	bookkeeper	42	"
	S	Simpson Mildred C †	35	housekeeper	29	"
	T	Gillcrist Allan M	37	carpenter	52	"
	U	Gillcrist Edna R †	37	stenographer	23	"
	V	Gillcrist Minnie F †	37	housewife	51	"
	W	Corbett George T	47	shipper	20	"
	X	Corbett John A	47	"	22	"
	Y	Corbett Margaret A †	47	housewife	62	"
	Z	Shea George	47	clerk	28	"
508						
	A	Shea Marie A †	47	housewife	27	"

Caton Street

Page	Letter	Full Name		Residence	Occupation	Age	Reported Residence
	B	*Cunniff Peter B		4	retired	71	[illegible]
	C	Schoepplein Irene A †		4	housewife	45	here
	D	Schoepplein Raymond W		4	machinist	50	"
	E	Grant John H		7	electrician	33	"
	F	Grant Violet M †		7	housewife	29	"
	G	Smith Edward P		7	clerk	35	"
	H	Smith Mary G †		7	housewife	28	"
	K	Eichorn Charles R		7	salesman	32	"
	L	Eichorn Dolores M †		7	housewife	31	"
	M	McNealy Alice T †	S	10	"	58	"
	N	McNealy Alice T †	S	10	clerk	23	"
	O	McNealy Ann T †	S	10	stenographer	22	"
	P	McNealy James L	S	10	manager	26	"
	R	McNealy John P	S	10	policeman	59	"
	S	McNealy John E	S	10	teacher	30	"
	T	McNealy Mary A †	S	10	housewife	29	"
	U	Tobin Ann F †	S	10	cashier	63	"
	V	Whiting Dorothy M †		9	cook	22	Brockton
	W	Whiting Edward L		9	printer	19	"
	X	Whiting George S		9	"	25	"
	Y	Whiting Margaret T †		9	housewife	45	"
	Z	Burns Mary A †		9	"	60	11 M[illegible]
569							
	A	Burns Theresa M †		9	packer	25	11 [illegible]
	C	Maynard George		11	machinist	29	994 R[illegible]
	D	Maynard Norine †		11	housewife	49	994 [illegible]
	E	Maynard Rita M †		11	saleswoman	27	994 [illegible]
	F	O'Brien Mary C †		11	housewife	28	12 V[illegible]
	G	*O'Brien William M		11	shipper	31	12 "
	H	Curtis Charles L		11	"	31	here
	K	Curtis Genevieve †		11	housewife	22	[illegible]
	L	Rachiborski Anna †		11	waitress	24	[illegible]
	M	*Perry Emma L †		12	housewife	60	[illegible]
	N	*Perry Waitstill W		12	fishcutter	62	[illegible]
	O	Elworthy Ruth F †		12	housewife	32	[illegible]
	P	Elworthy Wilmot		12	foreman	37	[illegible]
	R	Harwood Catherine G †		16	housewife	42	[illegible]
	S	Harwood Edward G		16	accountant	46	[illegible]
	T	Flynn Dorothy M †		16	teacher	27	[illegible]
	U	Flynn Florence L †		16	housewife	54	[illegible]
	V	Flynn Helen G †		16	clerk	28	"

Page	Letter	Full Name	Residence, Jan. 1, 1941	Occupation	Supposed Age	Reported Residence, Jan. 1, 1940. Street and Number

Caton Street—Continued

Page	Letter	Full Name	Residence, Jan. 1, 1941	Occupation	Supposed Age	Reported Residence, Jan. 1, 1940. Street and Number
	W	Flynn Joseph A	16	carpenter	59	here
	X	*Burt Evelyn J †	17	housewife	33	"
	Y	Burt Melvin R	17	engineer	34	"
	Z	Munroe Ernest J	17	electrician	31	640 River
510						
	A	Parcheski Catherine N †	17	housewife	30	640 "
	B	Wilkes Catherine E †	17	"	54	640 "
	C	Wilkes Robert W	17	baker	67	640 "
	D	Murray Margaret A †	18	housekeeper	43	here
	E	Ross Roxanna J †	18	housewife	31	"
	F	Ross Thomas S	18	clerk	36	"
	G	*Matthews Benjamin M	18	carpenter	67	"
	H	*Matthews Mary E †	18	housewife	71	"
	K	Russell Charles W	19	custodian	68	"
	L	Russell Pauline M †	19	housewife	44	"
	M	Russell William E	19	clerk	44	"
	N	Shelley Anna T †	19	housewife	59	"
	O	Shelley James A	19	shoecutter	55	"
	P	Shelley Veronica A †	19	teacher	22	"
	R	Baldwin Anna F †	20	housewife	36	"
	S	Baldwin Frank W	20	contractor	36	"
	T	Baldwin Albert F	20	lather	69	"
	U	Baldwin Lillian T †	20	housewife	55	"
	V	Antonia Francis J	21	fireman	27	"
	W	Antonia Mary J †	21	packer	25	"
	X	Antonia Nancy M †	21	housewife	22	"
	Y	Poulson Jeanette B †	26	"	70	837 River
	Z	Poulson Richard H	26	engineer	71	837 "
511						
	A	Kennedy Henry J	26	shoeworker	48	here
	B	Kennedy Mildred †	26	housewife	49	"
	C	*Drane Catherine †	26	at home	91	"
	D	Drane John W	26	retired	63	"
	E	McIsaac Ellen †	30	housewife	63	"
	F	McIsaac James	30	foreman	61	"

Coronado Road

Page	Letter	Full Name	Residence, Jan. 1, 1941	Occupation	Supposed Age	Reported Residence, Jan. 1, 1940. Street and Number
	G	Carroll Mary C †	4	housewife	46	here
	H	Carroll William F	4	chauffeur	46	"
	K	DeSoto Bessie †	8	housewife	52	"
	L	DeSoto Harry	8	salesman	35	"

Page	Letter	Full Name	[illegible]	[illegible]	[illegible]	[illegible]

Coronado Road (Continued)

Page	Letter	Full Name				
	M	DeSoto Robert	8	student	26	here
	N	Woodman Alice E †	9	hygienist	27	"
	O	Woodman Geraldine M †	9	housewife	23	"
	P	Woodman Katherine M †	9	"	67	"
	R	Glynn Katherine J †	15	"	45	"
	S	Glynn William F	15	engineer	42	"
	T	MacNeil Alexander J	19	chauffeur	28	"
	U	MacNeil Hugh C	19	cook	26	"
	V	MacNeil Michael	19	engineer	55	"

Friendship Road

Page	Letter	Full Name				
	W	Legg James T	8	proprietor	47	here
	X	Legg Olga I †	8	housewife	42	"
	Y	Davenport Harwood A	9	salesman	56	"
	Z	Davenport Ida C †	9	housewife	49	"
512						
	A	Hill Geraldine †	9	"	31	Rock[illegible]
	B	Hill William	9	molder	35	"
	C	Piper Edward E	9	retired	84	here
	D	Anderson Oscar T	11	carpenter	51	16 Fr[illegible]
	E	Anderson Ruth I †	11	cashier	22	16 "
	F*	Anderson Victoria †	11	housewife	50	16 "
	G	Gale Francis X	12	clerk	27	16 O[illegible]
	H	Gale Helen E †	12	housewife	28	16 "
	K	Gale John J	12	auditor	32	16 "
	L	Davis Alice †	16	housewife	38	[illegible]
	L[1]	Davis Andrew L	16	inspector	43	[illegible]
	M	Flaherty Herbert J	17	collector	46	[illegible]
	N	Flaherty Iola M †	17	housewife	43	"
	O	Machain George	20	butler	55	[illegible]
	P	Machain Mary T †	20	housewife	60	[illegible]
	R	Marshall Henry F	21	salesman	25	104 B[illegible]
	S	Marshall Marjorie G †	21	housewife	24	104 [illegible]
	T	Kinnear Alfhild S †	21	"	41	[illegible]
	U	Kinnear Artie S	21	machinist	4[illegible]	[illegible]

Greenfield Road

Page	Letter	Full Name				
	V	Barnes Annie C †	66	housewife	64	[illegible]
	W	McDermott Marie F †	70	"	23	R[illegible]
	X	McDermott Thomas J	70	[illegible]	[illegible]	[illegible]

Page	Letter	Full Name	Residence, Jan. 1, 1941	Occupation	Supposed Age	Reported Residence, Jan. 1, 1940, Street and Number

Greenfield Road—Continued

Page	Letter	Full Name	Residence, Jan. 1, 1941	Occupation	Supposed Age	Reported Residence, Jan. 1, 1940, Street and Number
	Y	Wilson Anna M †	70	secretary	21	here
	Z	Wilson Charles F	70	clerk	57	"
513						
	A	Wilson Margaret A †	70	housewife	55	"
	B	Forrest Elenor F †	72	"	21	708 Parker
	C	Forrest John E	72	ironworker	22	708 "
	D	Burke Clara L †	72	housewife	43	here
	E	Burke Edward M	72	shipper	20	"
	F	Camozzi Peter	78	laborer	41	114 Woodhaven
	G	*Camozzi Teresa †	78	operator	37	114 "
	H	Levezi John	78	bricklayer	54	here
	K	King Ada V †	80	stenographer	24	"
	L	King Barbara E †	80	auditor	20	"
	M	King Joseph A	80	shipper	22	"
	N	King Leroy S	80	forester	51	"
	O	King Pauline C †	80	housewife	54	"
	P	Block Lillian †	84	clerk	32	"
	R	Block Ralph S	84	photographer	35	"
	S	Land Ruth †	84	housekeeper	37	184 Walnut av
	T	Knox Louise †	84	housewife	33	here
	U	Knox Richard W	84	painter	37	"
	V	Flaherty Sarah C †	86	housewife	52	"
	W	Flaherty William J	86	stockman	50	"
	X	Madden John J	86	teamster	58	"
	Y	Waple Bernadette C †	86	at home	22	"
	Z	Waple Bert L	86	chauffeur	47	"
514						
	A	Waple Katherine J †	86	housewife	51	"

Hollingsworth Street

Page	Letter	Full Name	Residence, Jan. 1, 1941	Occupation	Supposed Age	Reported Residence, Jan. 1, 1940, Street and Number
	B	McDermott Mary R †	129	housewife	37	here
	C	McDermott Raymond C	129	manager	37	"
	D	Bilodeau John A	131	accountant	36	"
	E	Bilodeau Wilma E †	131	housewife	29	"
	F	Deegan Teresa †	131	"	60	"
	G	Deegan Viola M †	131	bookkeeper	33	"
	H	*Fulton Bridget †	135	housewife	70	"
	K	Fulton Catherine E †	135	stenographer	47	"
	L	*Fulton James A	135	retired	79	"
	M	Fulton John J	135	mechanic	31	"

Hollingsworth Street (Continued)

Page	Letter	Full Name	Residence	Occupation	Age	Reported Residence
	N	Fulton Mary M †	135	at home	11	here
	O	Soule Nicholas B	140	retired	81	"
	P	Straus Elsie M †	140	housewife	59	"
	R	Bamberg Aina C †	141	"	57	"
	S	Bamberg Daniel G	141	carpenter	62	"
	T	Bamberg Linnea V †	141	teacher	37	"
	U	Briggeman Florence E †	142	housewife	57	"
	V	Fitzwilliam Alice J †	144	buyer	21	"
	W	Fitzwilliam Frank J	144	clerk	32	"
	X	Fitzwilliam Frank M	144	policeman	63	"
	Y	Fitzwilliam Mary J †	144	housewife	62	"
	Z	Nolan Alma F †	145	"	11	"
515						
	A	Nolan John L	145	custodian	52	"
	B	Stephens Edward	149	salesman	46	"
	C	Stephens Pearl †	149	housewife	38	"
	D	O'Connor John J	151	teacher	26	"
	E	O'Connor Margaret M †	151	bookkeeper	28	"
	F	O'Connor Nellie M †	151	housewife	58	"
	G	O'Connor Thomas A	151	clerk	21	"
	H	O'Connor Timothy J	151	foreman	60	"
	K	O'Connor Timothy J, jr	151	laborer	24	"

Holmfield Avenue

Page	Letter	Full Name	Residence	Occupation	Age	Reported Residence
	L	Crehan Frank P	3	proprietor	49	[illegible]
	M	Crehan Mark H	3	laborer	44	[illegible]
	N	Crehan Mary C †	3	clerk	36	[illegible]
	O	Flanagan Arthur J	3A	salesman	50	here
	P	Flanagan Catherine M †	3A	housewife	47	"
	R	Woods Jeanne A †	5	"	34	"
	S	Woods John A	5	chauffeur	31	"
	T	Card Joseph G	5A	salesman	23	"
	U	Card Martha M †	5A	superintendent	47	"
	V	Card Pierce L	5A	chauffeur	47	"
	W	Spry Margaret E †	5A	clerk	36	"
	X	Spry Ruth †	5A	"	32	"
	Y	Bates Elizabeth B †	7	housewife	48	"
	Z	Bates Joseph F	7	[illegible]	50	"
516						
	A	Bates Joseph H	7	[illegible]	24	

Page	Letter	Full Name	Residence, Jan. 1, 1941.	Occupation	Supposed Age.	Reported Residence, Jan. 1, 1940. Street and Number.

Holmfield Avenue Continued

Page	Letter	Full Name	Residence, Jan. 1, 1941.	Occupation	Supposed Age.	Reported Residence, Jan. 1, 1940. Street and Number.
	B	Bates Patricia J †	7	clerk	22	here
	C	Bates Robert J	7	solderer	20	"
	D	Olsson Dorothy G †	9	nurse	32	"
	E	Olsson Gertrude A †	9	cook	38	"
	F	Olsson Gustaf A	9	retired	80	"
	G	Olsson Signe †	9	housewife	65	"
	H	Ivarson Alvera J †	10	housekeeper	45	Hudson
	K	Steere Constance W †	10	housewife	24	Milton
	L	Steere Ivaliew †	10	"	60	here
	M	Steere Sherwood W	10	physician	27	"
	N	Steere William W	10	exterminator	67	"
	N¹	Drummond Alexander	11	retired	67	"
	O	Drummond Mary †	11	housewife	67	"
	P	Carlson Eskel O	12	teacher	46	"
	R	Carlson Leta W †	12	housewife	48	"
	S	Forbes Anna D †	13	"	41	"
	T	Forbes Charles A	13	retired	76	"
	U	Zachrisson Anders Z	15	cabinetmaker	66	"
	V	Zachrisson Sanna †	15	proofreader	29	"
	W	Zachrisson Sanna M †	15	housewife	63	"
	X	Zachrisson Carroll	15	photographer	36	"
	Y	Zachrisson Lillian E †	15	housewife	37	"
	Z	Lynch Frances K †	16	"	55	"
517						
	A	Lynch Frances K †	16	stenographer	21	"
	B	Lynch Joseph P	16	retired	64	"
	C	Lynch Joseph P, jr	16	salesman	23	"
	D	Mullin John F	16	inspector	62	"
	E	White Dorothy F †	20	at home	21	"
	F	White Frank A	20	policeman	50	"
	G	White Herbert G	20	salesman	30	"
	H	White Marie C †	20	housewife	48	"
	K	Daly Rose †	21	housekeeper	70	"
	L	Quirk George	21	inspector	42	"
	M	Quirk Irene M †	21	housewife	41	"
	O	Hannaford Mary E †	23	milliner	59	"
	P	Colson Ralph H	24	supervisor	38	40 Hamilton
	R	Colson Svea †	24	housewife	38	40 "
	S	Lidh Careen †	26	clerk	25	here
	T	Lidh Hulda M †	26	housewife	67	"

Holmfield Avenue Continued

Page	Letter	Full Name				
	U	Nunes Mary †	26	housekeeper	50	here
	V	Moran Lillian M †	26	housewife	36	"
	W	Moran Richard L	26	salesman	36	"
	X	Marshall James	27	retired	71	"
	Y	Marshall Pauline M †	27	housewife	68	"
	Z	Rich Ella F †	35	"	49	"
518						
	A	Rich Lewis A	35	exterminator	49	"
	B	Stewart Sarah L †	35	at home	88	"

Hopewell Road

Page	Letter	Full Name				
	C	Gedies Alfred H	7	machinist	40	here
	D	Gedies Henrietta †	7	housewife	68	"
	E	Gedies Ruth E †	7	nurse	36	"
	F	Gifford Helen M †	8	housewife	40	"
	G	Gifford Winfred B	8	clerk	42	"
	H	Robinette Lenore C †	10	housewife	37	87 [illegible]
	K	Robinette William	10	optician	46	87 "
	L	Horton Frederick W	11	clerk	51	here
	M	Horton Frederick W, jr	11	laborer	29	"
	N	Horton Mary V †	11	housewife	45	"
	O	Davidson Bernice †	14	"	31	"
	P	Davidson John P	14	salesman	34	"
	R	Rhodes Charlotte †	14	at home	65	"
	S	Hogan Anna A †	15	housewife	31	"
	T	Hogan William E	15	plumber	32	"
	V	*DeRoche Cleveland S	19	mechanic	47	11 [illegible]
	W	DeRoche Margaret A †	19	housewife	47	11 "
	X	Seavey Andrew H	24	repairman	49	here
	Y	Seavey Mildred E †	24	housewife	50	"
	Z	Magnussen Elsa D †	38	"	20	[illegible]
519						
	A	Magnussen Henry W	38	rigger	25	[illegible]
	B	Mulcahey Juliette S †	38	housewife	26	28 [illegible]
	C	Lee Christopher F	38	agent	32	here
	D	Lee Mary T †	38	housewife	31	"
	E	*Hadden David P	38	engraver	36	[illegible]
	F	*Hadden Elizabeth M †	38	housewife	[illegible]	[illegible]

Page.	Letter.	Full Name.	Residence, Jan. 1, 1941.	Occupation.	Supposed Age.	Reported Residence, Jan. 1, 1940. Street and Number.
		Le Fevre Street				
	G	Dionne Janet I †	12	clerk	25	here
	H	Dionne Leona M †	12	typist	20	"
	K	Dionne Odile C †	12	housewife	53	"
	L	Dionne Peter J	12	bookkeeper	59	"
		Linden Avenue				
	M	Asack Louis A	2	foreman	29	80 Appleton
	N	Asack Toini L †	2	housewife	28	66 "
	O	Poly Angelo A	2	manufacturer	42	30 Stellman rd
	P	Poly Betty A †	2	housewife	24	30 "
	R	Madden Anna B †	3	bookkeeper	36	here
	S	Madden Bridget †	3	housewife	68	"
	T	Madden Catherine C †	3	bookkeeper	42	"
	U	Robinson Annie D †	4	housewife	70	"
	V	Robinson John W	4	retired	74	"
	W	*McPhee Margaret †	5	at home	91	"
	X	McPhee Mildred †	5	saleswoman	61	"
	Y	Williams Evelyn I †	5	housewife	35	"
	Z	Williams Henry R	5	salesman	42	"
520						
	A	Topham Marion I †	6	stitcher	58	"
		Massasoit Street				
	B	Fox Mary †	6	housekeeper	66	here
	C	Killilea Claire H †	6	housewife	36	"
	D	Killilea John P	6	laundryman	40	"
	F	Bendoni Joseph	14	carpenter	55	690 Cummins H'way
	G	Bendone Louisa †	14	housewife	43	690 "
	H	Galvin Edward D	15	freighthandler	61	here
	K	Galvin Grace E †	15	clerk	30	"
	L	Galvin Grace M †	15	housewife	56	"
	M	Galvin Jean P †	15	student	20	"
	N	Galvin Ruth M †	15	clerk	27	"
	O	Galvin William F	15	machinist	26	"
	R	*Teare Bertha M †	17	housewife	52	88 Florida
	S	*Teare William A	17	superintendent	50	88 "
	T	Shanks Anna L †	18	housewife	57	here
	U	Shanks Esther M †	18	clerk	32	"
	V	Shanks Florence F †	18	housewife	27	242 Kennebec

Page / Letter	Full Name	[illegible]	[illegible]	[illegible]	[illegible]

Massasoit Street (Continued)

Letter	Full Name	No.	Occupation	Age	Residence
W	Shanks John J	18	laundryman	57	here
X	Shanks Joseph M	18	millwright	32	212 K[illegible]
Y	Shanks Virginia M †	18	clerk	21	here
Z	Hayes Catherine A †	19	housewife	63	"
521					
A	Hayes Daniel W	19	chauffeur	63	"
B	Hayes William F	19	laborer	22	"
D	Erickson Erling D	23	painter	29	"
E	Erickson Helen E †	23	at home	21	"
F	*Erickson Inga B †	23	housewife	59	"
G	*Erickson John E	23	retired	66	"
H	Erickson Ralph	23	painter	33	"
K	Tosi John	23	rigger	31	"
L	Tosi Lorraine F †	23	housewife	21	"
M	Stevens Lillian O †	26	"	25	1060 R[illegible]
N	Stevens Sidney A	26	chauffeur	42	1060 "
O	Lindfors Anna E †	26	housewife	50	Brookline
P	Lindfors Victor E	26	shipper	53	"
R	Hargreaves Albert G	27	clerk	32	here
S	Hargreaves Fred H	27	agent	31	"
T	Hargreaves George A	27	chauffeur	28	"
U	Hargreaves Louise W †	27	housewife	60	"
V	Hargreaves Robert W	27	clerk	22	"
W	Hargreaves Walter A	27	student	23	"
X	Kammler Agnes †	27	housekeeper	16	"
Y	Schaeper Anne †	27	"	52	"
Z	Conway Annie F †	30	at home	66	[illegible]
522					
A	Conway Catherine M †	30	"	81	886 [illegible]
B	Cunningham Catherine L †	30	housewife	36	here
C	Cunningham Edward L	30	leatherworker	37	[illegible]
D	Hinchey Margaret M †	31	housekeeper	56	[illegible]
E	Vaughan Charles F	31	leather sorter	25	"
F	Vaughan Leo S	31	salesman	34	[illegible]
G	Vaughan Mary E †	31	teacher	38	[illegible]
H	Vaughan Mary R †	31	housewife	62	[illegible]
K	Swanson Hannah †	33	"	81	[illegible]
L	Swanson Loretta F †	33	bookkeeper	44	[illegible]
M	Craft John C	34	superintendent	[illegible]	[illegible]
N	Craft Mary L †	34	housewife	71	[illegible]
O	Dickinson Anna R †	34	[illegible]	59	[illegible]

Page	Letter	Full Name	Residence, Jan. 1, 1941	Occupation	Supposed Age	Reported Residence, Jan. 1, 1940. Street and Number.

Massasoit Street Continued

Page	Letter	Full Name	Residence, Jan. 1, 1941	Occupation	Supposed Age	Reported Residence, Jan. 1, 1940.
	P	Benson Gertrude I †	35	nurse	24	here
	R	Benson Nannie †	35	housewife	59	"
	S	Benson Richard W	35	laborer	21	"
	T	Benson Thurston I	35	teller	27	"
	U	Gillian Fred W	38	exterminator	49	"
	V	Gillian Mabel L †	38	housewife	47	"
	W	Lindsay Clara L †	38	at home	79	"
	X	Forsyth Neil M	39	painter	65	"
	Y	Forsyth Nettie †	39	housewife	58	"
	Z	Green Albert A	41	manager	36	"
523						
	A	Green Rose A †	41	housewife	34	"
	B	Lewis Florence M †	42	"	44	"
	C	Lewis Ira	42	painter	39	"
	D	McLellan Robert N	42	retired	73	"
	E	Broderick Florence †	43	housewife	37	"
	F	Broderick James	43	plumber	59	"
	G	Zoehler Sarah †	43	housewife	65	"
	H	Barter Charles M	46	exterminator	56	"
	K	Barter Elizabeth †	46	housewife	51	"
	L	Coffin Nancy J †	46	clerk	56	"
	M	Roush Anne M †	47	housewife	55	"
	N	Roush Dorothy M †	47	operator	25	"
	O	Shea Jeremiah J	47	porter	62	"
	P	Shea John F	47	agent	27	"
	R	Shea Joseph J	47	student	22	"
	S	Shea Mary E †	47	nurse	25	"
	T	Shea Mary J †	47	housewife	61	"
	U	Ambrose Norman	50	mechanic	22	"
	V	*Kasey Anna †	50	housewife	48	"
	W	Kasey Jeremiah	50	printer	26	"
	X	*Kasey Joseph	50	stitcher	51	"

Mattakeeset Street

Page	Letter	Full Name	Residence, Jan. 1, 1941	Occupation	Supposed Age	Reported Residence, Jan. 1, 1940.
	Z	Brownell Arthur D	9	fireman	43	here
524						
	A	Brownell Etta †	9	housewife	41	"
	B	Hunnefeld Louise M †	9	housekeeper	65	"
	C	*Zetterquist Gunhild M †	9	housewife	45	"
	D	Zetterquist Olaf W	9	machinist	46	"

Page	Letter	Full Name		Occupation	Age	

Mattakeeset Street (Continued)

Page	Letter	Full Name		Occupation	Age	
	E	Clark Blanche †	11	housewife	46	6 Ashland
	F	Clark Evelyn E †	11	inspector	23	6 "
	G	Clark Frank C	11	plumber	49	6 "
	H	Wiswell Andrew G	13	clerk	42	here
	K	Wiswell Hilda A †	13	housewife	53	"
	L	Wiswell John T	13	electrician	26	Westwood
	M	Wiswell Mabel A †	13	operator	32	here
	N	Wiswell Martha M †	13	clerk	31	"
	O	Doyle Mary D †	15	housewife	22	"
	P	Doyle Robert B	15	manager	24	"
	R	Rubin Louis	17	manufacturer	39	"
	S	Rubin Rosa †	17	housewife	33	"
	T	Scott Ernest W	17	meatcutter	70	"
	U	Scott Fannie H †	17	housewife	76	"
	V	McKay Alice B †	19	"	63	"
	W	McKay William B	19	retired	71	"
	X	McWade Dorothy M †	19	at home	21	35 Norton
	Y	McWade Georgianna †	19	housewife	51	35 "
	Z	McWade Michael J	19	engineer	58	35 "
525						
	A	McWade Russell J	19	"	21	35 "
	B	Delano Julia H †	21	housewife	38	17 Blake
	C	Delano Richard W	21	chauffeur	39	17 "
	D	Hoppe Margaret †	21	housewife	65	here
	E	Spear Daniel B	25	policeman	55	"
	F	Spear Gerard D	25	mechanic	27	"
	G	Spear James A	25	clerk	25	"
	H	Spear Margaret A †	25	housewife	55	"
	K	Spear Marion A †	25	clerk	22	New York
	L	Hackel Emil	29	salesman	56	here
	M	Hackel Melvin H	29	U S A	25	"
	N	Hackel Rose †	29	housewife	52	[illegible]
	O	Lichtenstein Matilda †	29	at home	79	[illegible]
	P	Burrows Joseph C	39	cleanser	33	[illegible]
	R	Burrows Vera E †	39	housewife	31	[illegible]
	S	Siwicki Florian	39	retired	58	[illegible]
	T	Siwicki Frances S †	39	beautician	25	[illegible]
	U	Siwicki John S	39	stripper	23	[illegible]
	V	Siwicki Joseph S	39	superintendent	27	[illegible]
	W	Siwicki Mary A †	39	restaurateur	52	[illegible]
	X	Dever John J	43	policeman	54	[illegible]

18—5

	Full Name		Occupation		Reported Residence, Jan. 1, 1940. Street and Number

Mattakeeset Street—Continued

	Full Name		Occupation		Reported Residence
Y	Dever John J, jr	43	shipper	21	here
Z	Dever Margaret T †	43	housewife	47	"

526

	Full Name		Occupation		Reported Residence
A	Dever Margaret T †	43	inspector	23	"
B	Magnuson Anna C †	47	housewife	70	"
C	Magnuson Carl G	47	machinist	68	"
D	Magnuson Ruth M †	47	teacher	29	"
E	Bonner Owen J	51	inspector	64	"
F	Bonner Rose A †	51	housewife	55	"

Mercer Street

	Full Name		Occupation		Reported Residence
G	Boucher Catherine F †	5	housewife	36	here
H	Boucher Joseph P	5	installer	40	"
K	Walsh Mary A †	9	housewife	32	"
L	Walsh Richard A	9	manager	32	"
M	Locke Ruth E †	11	housewife	34	"
N	Locke William A	11	bartender	34	"
O	Wideberk Christine E †	17	housewife	54	"
P	Wideberk Thomas K	17	painter	53	"
R	Stevens Ethel E †	21	housewife	28	"
S	Stevens Frederick J	21	salesman	36	"

Monponset Street

	Full Name		Occupation		Reported Residence
T	Burt George L	6	laborer	53	here
U	Quinn Christine C †	6	housewife	54	"
V	Quinn James K	6	attendant	24	"
W	Quinn Richard F	6	guard	56	"
X	Chambers Alice E †	7	housewife	36	"
Y	Chambers Charles O	7	draftsman	36	"
Z	Cronin Mary P †	7	housewife	26	"

527

	Full Name		Occupation		Reported Residence
A	Cronin Raymond E	7	salesman	30	"
B	Alger Chester	10	laborer	34	Milton
C	Martin Doris B †	10	waitress	28	here
D	Rancourt Henry R	10	bartender	27	274 Kennebec
E	Rancourt Jacqueline †	10	housewife	49	274 "
F	Rancourt Zephir W	10	carpenter	55	274 "
G	Murphy Helen R †	11	housewife	32	here
H	Murphy Thomas C	11	B F D	45	"

Monponset Street—Continued

Page	Letter	Full Name		Occupation		
	K	Sullivan Lillian E †	11	housewife	27	24 [illegible]
	L	Sullivan Thomas F	11	mechanic	33	[illegible]
	N	Cameron Catherine A †	18	housewife	51	here
	O	Cameron Daniel F	18	machinist	26	"
	P	Cameron Paul B	18	agent	23	"
	R	Clark David S	19	salesman	57	"
	S	Clark Mary D †	19	housewife	57	"
	T	*Curry Geraldine L †	22	"	49	"
	U	*Curry Guy S	22	painter	51	"
	V	Grace Adrian R	26	B F D	57	"
	W	Grace Mary F †	26	housewife	57	"
	X	Grace William J	26	usher	21	"
	Y	Hanrahan Esther C †	26	nurse	55	"
	Z	Moran Edward F	30	plumber	45	"
528						
	A	Moran Jennie E †	30	housewife	68	"
	B	Moran John J	30	chauffeur	28	"
	C	Moran Mary E †	30	housewife	25	26 Monponset
	D	Moran Michael F	30	plumber	70	here
	E	Fox Arthur C	31	chauffeur	24	[illegible]
	F	Fox Hazel M †	31	housewife	21	124 [illegible]
	G	Redmond Cora B †	31	"	57	here
	H	Redmond John A	31	salesman	59	"
	K	Redmond Marion B †	31	stenographer	21	"
	L	Gray Dorothy E †	31	housewife	48	"
	M	Gray Dorothy E †	31	clerk	23	"
	N	Gray Ernest M	31	salesman	49	"
	O	MacDonald George M	38	manager	65	"
	P	MacDonald George R	38	salesman	30	"
	R	MacDonald Louisa A †	38	housewife	65	"
	S	MacDonald Norman M	38	engineer	24	"
	T	Halloran Henry G	42	chemist	60	"
	U	Halloran Mary E †	42	housewife	70	"
	V	Halloran Robert S	42	accountant	34	"
	W	Johnson Anders G	43	retired	75	"
	X	Johnson Anna E †	43	housewife	78	"
	Y	Johnson Ruth C †	43	clerk	36	"
	Z	Cotton Marie L †	46	"	[illegible]	"
529						
	A	Phelps Archie G	46	[illegible]	49	"
	B	Phelps Ethel E †	46	housewife	45	"

Page	Letter	Full Name	Residence, Jan. 1, 1941.	Occupation	Supposed Age	Reported Residence, Jan. 1, 1940. Street and Number.

Monponsett Street Continued

Page	Letter	Full Name	Residence, Jan. 1, 1941.	Occupation	Supposed Age	Reported Residence, Jan. 1, 1940. Street and Number.
	C	Fischbach Henry F	47	carpenter	73	here
	D	Fischbach Martha †	47	housewife	72	"

Osceola Street

Page	Letter	Full Name	Residence, Jan. 1, 1941.	Occupation	Supposed Age	Reported Residence, Jan. 1, 1940. Street and Number.
	E	Grady Edward C	3	salesman	38	Milton
	F	Grady Katherine F †	3	housewife	38	"
	G	MacRitchie Dorothy C †	5	"	34	here
	H	MacRitchie Henry D	5	yardman	32	"
	K	Aronne Cora M †	7 9	housewife	36	"
	L	Aronne Edward F	7 9	operator	33	"
	M	Aronne John B	7 9	clerk	31	"
	N	Aronne Patrick J	7 9	printer	40	"
	O	Sullivan Dorothy L †	7 9	housewife	33	"
	P	Sullivan James J	7 9	repairman	36	"
	R	Clark Edward B	10	manager	45	"
	S	Clark Theresa †	10	housewife	43	"
	T	Lundberg Gina †	10	housekeeper	77	"
	U	O'Connell Agnes E †	11 11A	housewife	35	356 Cummins H'way
	V	O'Connell Joseph	11 11A	inspector	37	29 W Milton
	W	Noble Elizabeth M †	11 11A	housewife	41	here
	X	Noble Thomas W	11 11A	policeman	45	"
	Y	Swan Gladys M †	12	housewife	41	"
	Z	Swan Herman G	12	watchman	41	"
530						
	A	Smerage A Marion †	15	housewife	25	"
	B	Smerage Robert G	15	salesman	26	"
	C	Devine Michael F	15	policeman	41	"
	D	Devine Sarah M †	15	housewife	40	"
	E	Leahy Margaret F †	18	"	40	121 Rossiter
	G	Leahy William M	18	clerk	44	121 "
	H	MacKnight Carolyn M †	19 21	teacher	44	here
	K	MacKnight Margaret †	19 21	forewoman	56	"
	L	MacKnight Mary E †	19 21	housewife	58	"
	M	Lacey Jane R †	19 21	"	40	"
	N	Lacey Neil F	19 21	electrician	43	"
	O	Jennings Margaret †	22	housewife	36	Wollaston
	P	Jennings Thomas J	22	chef	36	"
	R	Waters James J	23 25	accountant	41	52 Bailey
	S	Waters Hazel C †	23 25	housewife	26	Wash'n D C
	T	Pelletier Ann A †	23 25	"	41	here

Osceola Street Continued

Page / Letter	Full Name					
U	Pelletier Paul J	23	25	accountant	39	here
V	Hedtler Christine E †		26	clerk	69	"
W	Hedtler Henrietta †		26	housewife	39	"
X	Hedtler Irving		26	manager	39	"
Y	Hedtler James		26	carpenter	71	"
Z	Swain Gina †		26	housekeeper	71	589 Norfolk
531						
A	Kelliher Josephine C †	27	29	housewife	29	106 Lorenzo
B	Kelliher Patrick J	27	29	clerk	31	106 "
C	Bruen Anne L †	27	29	"	25	here
D	*Feeney Edward J	27	29	shipper	60	"
E	*Feeney Mary A †	27	29	housewife	63	"
F	Shea Leo J	27	29	clerk	34	"
G	Shea Margaret M †	27	29	housewife	31	Newton [illegible]
H	Shaughnessy Anna †	31	33	saleswoman	35	here
K	Shaughnessy John E	31	33	plumber	40	"
L	Kennedy Mary †	31	33	housekeeper	52	"
M	McNeill Mildred R †	31	33	waitress	25	"
N	McNeill William H	31	33	porter	28	11 [illegible]
O	Clay Alexander E		34	proprietor	25	here
P	Clay Gustavus A		34	retired	73	"
R	Clay Lillian M †		34	waitress	34	"
S	Clay Thomas R		34	freighthandler	31	"
T	Wilcox Charles E	35	37	timekeeper	40	"
U	*Wilcox Grace R †	35	37	housewife	31	"
V	Wilcox Jennie G †	35	37	at home	60	[illegible]
W	Wingfield Carroll B	35	37	stagehand	16	[illegible]
X	Wingfield Margaret A †	35	37	accountant	20	[illegible]
Y	Wingfield Mary A †	35	37	housewife	46	[illegible]
Z	Porter Grace E †		38	"	43	[illegible]
532						
A	Porter John D		38	contractor	45	[illegible]
B	Porter John D, jr		38	clerk	20	[illegible]
C	Finnegan Martin A	39	41	steamfitter	45	[illegible]
D	Finnegan Mary T †	39	41	housewife	39	[illegible]
E	Mitchell Patrick	39	41	laborer	56	[illegible]
F	Behrens Henry F	39	41	retired	50	[illegible]
G	Behrens Marie S †	39	41	housewife	45	[illegible]
H	*Walsh Catherine †		43	"	42	[illegible]
K	Walsh Richard		43	[illegible]	44	[illegible]
L	McGrath Francis J		45	[illegible]	49	[illegible]

	Full Name	Residence, Jan. 1, 1941	Occupation	Supposed Age	Reported Residence, Jan. 1, 1940. Street and Number.

Osceola Street—Continued

	Full Name	Residence	Occupation	Age	Reported Residence
M	McGrath Grace L †	45	housewife	45	here
N	McGrath Ruth E †	45	clerk	20	"
O	Meade Alice M †	47	housewife	31	"
P	Meade William L	47	shipper	31	"
R	Rund Alfred P	49	polisher	39	"
S	Rund Estelle M †	49	housewife	42	"
T	Son Anna F †	50	hairdresser	29	"
U	Son Anthony J	50	machinist	56	"
V	Son Michelina †	50	housewife	51	"
W	Hazelwood Claire P †	51	waitress	25	"
X	Hazelwood Frank H	51	accountant	22	"
Y	*Hazelwood Margaret †	51	stitcher	49	"
Z	Higginson Edward L	53	inspector	37	"
	533				
A	Higginson Mildred C †	53	housewife	38	"
B	Williamson Alberta F †	55	"	35	"
C	Williamson Payton R	55	mechanic	40	"
D	*Thomson Arthur G	57	retired	69	Brookline
E	Thomson Elizabeth C †	57	clerk	32	"
F	Thomson Stuart W	57	salesman	30	"

Poydras Street

	Full Name	Residence	Occupation	Age	Reported Residence
G	Kullberg Warren A	5	welder	23	here
H	Nilsen Agnes C †	5	housewife	45	"
K	Nilsen Hjalmar M	5	painter	36	"
L	Rabbitt Agnes G †	7	housewife	22	"
M	Rabbitt James J	7	operator	23	"
N	Ryan Mary A †	7	housekeeper	50	"
O	Young Anna E †	80	forewoman	29	"
P	Young Ernest M	80	carpenter	33	"
R	Young Mary A †	80	housewife	73	"
S	Young Mary A †	80	laundress	35	"
T	Young Natalie E †	80	housekeeper	31	"
U	Young William J	80	papermaker	34	"

Radcliffe Road

	Full Name	Residence	Occupation	Age	Reported Residence
V	Pickup Florence †	76	housewife	50	here
W	Pickup George E	76	clerk	20	Wyoming
X	Rooney Helen J †	76	housewife	29	25 Lockwood

Radcliffe Road (Continued)

Page	Letter	Full Name		Residence	Occupation	Age	Previous Residence
	Y	Rooney John F, jr		76	plumber	30	84 [illegible]
	Z	*MacFarlane Jenny	†	76	housewife	41	here
534							
	A	MacFarlane John		76	patternmaker	40	"
	B	Williams Alice E	†	80	housewife	40	"
	C	Williams Henry J, jr		80	policeman	40	"
	D	Robert Louis J		82	inspector	30	"
	E	Robert Rose L	†	82	housewife	31	"
	F	Dacko Peter		82	baker	21	"
	G	Dacko Selma	†	82	operator	23	87 [illegible]
	H	*Kravetz Harry		82	waiter	55	here
	K	*Kravetz Mary	†	82	cook	53	"
	L	Saffian Peter		82	laborer	29	"
	M	Eastman Helen G	†	92	housewife	32	"
	N	Eastman John C		92	artist	30	"
	O	Cruickshank Albert A		92	engineer	39	"
	P	Cruickshank Alice V	†	92	housewife	36	"
	R	Yanushis Francis J		96	shipfitter	27	"
	S	Yanushis Stella	†	96	housewife	27	"
	T	*Rajunas Michaelina	†	96A	"	51	"
	U	Rajunas Paul V		96A	roofer	22	"
	V	Rajunas Stanley		96A	"	21	"
	W	*Rajunas Stanley J		96A	janitor	57	"
	X	Rajunas Veronica	†	96A	cashier	26	"

Raleigh Road

Page	Letter	Full Name		Residence	Occupation	Age	Previous Residence
	Y	*Gettins John P		21	retired	75	here
	Z	Gettins Lawrence C		21	roofer	51	"

Ransom Road

Page	Letter	Full Name		Residence	Occupation	Age	Previous Residence
535							
	C	Kram Joseph E		15	guard	19	here
	D	Kram Leokadia B	†	15	housewife	17	"
	E	Zarsinski Helen M	†	15	clerk	21	"
	F	Zarsinski John P		15	engineer	24	"
	G	Bogie John		23	[illegible]	29	[illegible]
	H	Koutrouba Evan P		23	carpenter	21	187[illegible]
	K	Kukuruza Nicholas		23	[illegible]	55	21 Middlesex

Page	Letter	Full Name	Residence, Jan. 1, 1941	Occupation	Supposed Age	Reported Residence, Jan. 1, 1940. Street and Number.

Ransom Road—Continued

	L	Kukuruza Olga †	23	housewife	49	21 Middlesex
	M	McCarthy Anna M †	27	stenographer	20	here
	N	McCarthy Mary M †	27	housewife	44	"
	O	McCarthy Thomas J	27	plumber	43	"

Rector Road

	P	Lawler Annie M †	8	housewife	71	Westwood
	R	Lawler Catherine F †	8	"	74	12 Rector rd
	S	Lawler Joseph D	8	clerk	32	12 "
	T	Lawler Marie G †	8	housewife	38	12 "
	U	Forbes Lawrence G	8	watchman	22	here
	V	*Forbes Walter E	8	engineer	65	"
	W	Pickering Bertha M †	8	housewife	32	"
	X	Pickering Samuel W	8	upholsterer	35	"
	Y	Garber Bella †	8	housekeeper	74	"
	Z	Parker Georgina †	8	housewife	35	"
536						
	A	Parker Rex A	8	inspector	41	"
	B	Lewis Edward F	12	laborer	37	Medford
	C	Lewis Irene C †	12	housewife	32	"
	E	Goodspeed Ardath C †	12	saleswoman	41	here
	F	Goodspeed Manley J	12	inspector	42	"
	G	Jones Mina †	12	housekeeper	74	"
	H	Spallone Joseph	14	architect	34	"
	K	Spallone Yole †	14	housewife	30	"
	L	Rocheleau Joseph O	14	lineman	55	"
	M	Rocheleau Mary J †	14	housewife	57	"
	N	Morin Antoinette M †	14	"	47	"
	O	Morin Fred P	14	welder	45	"
	P	Duffey John C	16	engineer	52	"
	R	Duffey Mary C †	16	housewife	51	"
	S	Ford Anne †	16	housekeeper	34	Brookline
	T	Jones Anna †	16	housewife	40	324 Center
	U	Jones Henry J	16	bartender	45	324 "
	V	Woods James	16	laborer	34	324 "
	W	Ardini Elizabeth A †	16	housewife	33	here
	X	Ardini James M	16	engineer	31	"
	Y	Boran Florence M †	18	housewife	43	"
	Z	Boran John L	18	salesman	48	"

Page	Letter	Full Name	Residence	Occupation	Age	Reported Residence

537

Rector Road Continued

Letter	Full Name	Residence	Occupation	Age	Reported Residence
A	Cuthbert Arthur J	18	mechanic	57	here
B	Cuthbert Arthur J, jr	18	"	20	"
C	Cuthbert Edna G †	18	housewife	50	"
D	Johnson Albert H	18	agent	39	"
E	Johnson Gwendolyn A †	18	housewife	40	"
F	*Dymowski Bronislaw	20	laborer	53	"
G	Dymowski Genevieve B †	20	operator	25	"
H	*Dymowski Stephanie †	20	housewife	48	"
K	Sweeney Charles	20	chauffeur	29	"
L	Sweeney Sarah †	20	housewife	28	"
M	Kenney Edward C	20	accountant	24	63 [illegible]
N	Kenney Mary V †	20	housewife	22	18 O'C[illegible]
O	Keenan Agnes G †	24	"	56	here
P	Keenan Thomas M	24	retired	63	"
R	Montgomery Philip J	24	letter carrier	47	"
S	Garofalo Katherine M †	24	housewife	51	"
T	Garofalo Louis	24	confectioner	60	"
U	Patterson Allan C	30	plasterer	57	"
V	Patterson Davina M †	30	housewife	55	"
W	Patterson Walter S	30	operator	25	"
X	Starratt Charles F	30	salesman	32	"
Y	Starratt Mildred D †	30	clerk	26	"
Z	Voye Catherine E †	34	housewife	55	"

538

Letter	Full Name	Residence	Occupation	Age	Reported Residence
A	Voye Charles G	34	auditor	30	"
B	Voye George W	34	clerk	59	"
C	Voye Gladys E †	34	stenographer	26	"
E	Quinn Eileen M †	36	housewife	44	"
F	Quinn Joseph W	36	supervisor	48	"
D	Sheahan Peter	36	laborer	44	"
G	Burnett Lucy H †	38	housewife	63	
H	Burnett William C	38	retired	75	"
K	Parker Freda B †	38	housewife	36	"
P	Parker George	38	janitor	40	
M	Mitton Charles R	38	bookkeeper	43	
N	Mitton Ethel A †	38	stenographer	46	
O	Mitton George M	38	carpenter	69	
P	Fontes Anthony D	40 42	cook	58	
R	Fontes Marion †	40 42	housewife	34	
S	Rose Cecil	40 42	clergyman	37	New York

25

Page Letter	Full Name	Residence Jan. 1, 1941	Occupation	Supposed Age	Reported Residence Jan. 1, 1940. Street and Number.

River Street

X	Stanford Catherine E †	654	housewife	74	here
Y	Stanford Eveline M †	654	secretary	35	"
Z	Stanford Gorham E	654	retired	76	"
539					
A	Stanford Helen G †	654	secretary	37	"
B	Hanrahan John J	656	mariner	33	91 Gordon
C	Hanrahan Pearl A †	656	housewife	35	91 "
D	Cunniff Ethel G †	658	"	41	here
E	Cunniff William F	658	policeman	49	"
F	Leary Madeline E †	658	saleswoman	21	"
G	LaBarbera Agnes †	659	at home	42	"
H	LaBarbera Annette †	659	saleswoman	43	"
K	LaBarbera Lydia †	659	"	34	"
L	Adduci Arthur A	659	manager	41	"
M	Adduci Marie A †	659	housewife	37	"
N	Trovato Ellen †	662	"	30	"
O	Trovato John	662	barber	34	"
P	Trovato Josephine †	662	housewife	43	"
R	Trovato Peter	662	barber	49	"
S	Russo Gaetana †	662	dressmaker	54	"
T	White Catherine B †	663	housewife	28	"
U	White Charles F	663	chauffeur	30	"
V	Brennan Catherine M †	663	housewife	38	"
W	Brennan John F	663	proprietor	38	"
X	Natter Josephine M †	663	clerk	39	"
Y	Cobb Thelma L †	666	maid	21	"
Y	Haskard Grace †	666	housewife	58	"
Z	Haskard Roger B	666	salesman	62	"
540					
A	Haynes Grace †	666	at home	70	"
B	Winters Harriett †	666	"	71	22 Hiawatha rd
C	Fallen Bella R †	670	housewife	63	here
D	Fallen Ellis C	670	student	20	"
E	Fallen Morton L	670	merchant	27	"
F	Fallen Myrtle B †	670	housewife	27	"
G	Altshuler Abe	670	salesman	65	"
H	Althsuler Frances E †	670	housewife	63	"
K	Korb Charles	670	physician	41	"
L	Korb Cynthia E †	670	housewife	34	"
M	Murphy Daniel L	674	salesman	40	"
N	Murphy Margaret B †	674	housewife	40	"

River Street—Continued

Page	Letter	Full Name			Occupation	Age	Residence
	O	Coffey Madeline †		671	clerk	12	[illegible]
	P	Coffey May †		671	"	15	"
	R	Briggs Clara †	675	677	housewife	76	"
	S	Briggs Dorothy L †	675	677	typist	33	"
	T	Davis Hazel I †	675	677	housewife	35	"
	U	Davis Herbert J	675	677	salesman	39	"
	V	Middleton Jane R †	675	677	bookkeeper	21	"
	W	Middleton Janet †	675	677	housewife	53	"
	X	Middleton John	675	677	engineer	57	"
	Y	Lydon Mary C †	675	677	at home	75	"
	Z	Wright Elizabeth †	675	677	nurse	34	"
541							
	A	Wright George J	675	677	bookbinder	36	"
	B	O'Brien Cornelius J		679	motorman	63	
	C	O'Brien Mary T †		679	housewife	51	25 "
	D	O'Brien Thomas C		679	chauffeur	23	25 "
	E	Sheridan William F		679	metalworker	30	25 "
	F	Gross Alfred		679	manager	34	here
	G	Gross Ruth P †		679	housewife	37	"
	H	McPhee Elizabeth M †		679	"	47	"
	K	McPhee John K		679	machinist	50	"
	L	McPhee Kilburn L		679	papermaker	25	"
	M	Shedd Ella V †		679	at home	65	Somerville
	N	Barrett Edna G †		684	housewife	32	here
	O	Barrett John H		684	engineer	37	"
	P	McCoy Eleanor C †	685	687	housewife	36	"
	R	McCoy John H	685	687	chauffeur	39	"
	S	Schumacher Albert D	685	687	operator	53	"
	T	Schumacher Kathleen A †	685	687	at home	21	"
	U	Schumacher Marion E †	685	687	clerk	29	"
	V	Schumacher Mary †	685	687	housewife	51	"
	W	Ryan Dorothy M †	685	687	stenographer	24	"
	X	Ryan Margaret B †	685	687	housewife	55	"
	Y	Barrett Edward F		686	retired	72	"
	Z	Barrett Mary S †		686	housewife	71	"
542							
	A	Martin Elliot V		688	agent	36	"
	B	Martin Evelyn †		688	housewife	34	"
	C	Donovan Catherine M †		691	"	30	"
	D	Donovan Simon J		691	window dresser	32	"
	E	Carnes Ada M †		691	[illegible]	21	34 [illegible]

Page	Letter	Full Name	Residence, Jan. 1, 1941	Occupation	Supposed Age	Reported Residence, Jan. 1, 1940. Street and Number.
		River Street Continued				
	F	Carnes Henry D	691	meterman	22	19 Rosa
	G	Adler Joseph	691	salesman	40	here
	H	Adler Sadie †	691	housewife	36	"
	K	Scanlon James	691	chauffeur	38	"
	L	Dasey Mildred B †	691	housewife	25	"
	M	Dasey Roland F	691	salesman	28	"
	N	Lewis Annette E †	691	dressmaker	47	"
	O	Lewis Walter K	691	salesman	48	"
	P	McInis Frances J †	691	housewife	55	63 Rockdale
	R	Wright Alfred F	698	clerk	20	here
	S	Wright Harriett L †	698	"	24	"
	T	Wright Harriett †	698	housewife	50	"
	U	Wright John J	698	clerk	58	"
	V	Wright Margaret E †	698	librarian	28	"
	W	Wright Richard H	698	student	24	"
	X	Wright Robert G	698	buyer	27	"
	Y	Bergman Ernest	702	carpenter	62	"
	Z	Bergman Julia M †	702	housewife	66	"
543						
	A	Bergman Lilly J †	702	secretary	27	"
	B	Labelle Ivy A †	705	housewife	41	"
	C	Labelle Maurice M	705	chemist	41	"
	D	Ray Elizabeth E †	705	at home	70	"
	E	Ray Ella †	705	housewife	57	"
	F	Ray Frederick A	705	clerk	51	"
	G	Costello Margaret L †	706	"	42	"
	H	Costello Theresa A †	706	secretary	40	"
	K	Eagan Lillian F †	706	housewife	34	"
	L	Eagan Walter F	706	broker	34	"
	M	Ray Ella M †	713	housewife	71	"
	N	Ray John G	713	storekeeper	68	"
	O	Bangs Mary A †	713	housewife	46	"
	P	Bangs Paul P	713	fireman	46	"
	R	Recchia Angelo	714	carpenter	50	"
	S	Recchia Minerva †	714	housewife	45	"
	T	Petta Olinda †	714	at home	75	"
	U	Recchia Croce	714	mason	60	"
	V	Recchia Flora †	714	housewife	52	"
544						
	B	Shapiro Lillian †	738	"	31	"
	C	Shapiro S Charles	738	attorney	32	"

Page	Letter	Full Name	Residence	Occupation	Age	Reported Residence

River Street—Continued

Page	Letter	Full Name	Residence	Occupation	Age	Reported Residence
	D	Graham Joseph W	738	salesman	25	here
	E	Graham Marion A †	738	housewife	28	"
	F	Sahl G Esther †	738	student	21	"
	G	Sahl Harold	738	electrician	27	"
	H	Sahl Louise †	738	saleswoman	25	"
	K	Sahl Sarah †	738	housewife	57	"
	L	Sheer Pauline †	738	"	29	"
	M	Sheer Samuel	738	salesman	31	"
	N	McNeil Martha E †	738	housewife	25	9 Reddy av
	O	McNeil Warren V	738	operator	28	9 "
	P	Landry Albert J	738	chauffeur	21	19 Peterboro
	R	Landry Cecilia M †	738	housewife	27	19 "
	S	Sullivan Wesley J	742	waiter	27	here
	T	Sullivan Winifred C †	742	housewife	22	"
	U	LeBlanc Irene †	742	"	33	"
	V	*LeBlanc Louis	742	carpenter	38	"
	W	Dalton Irene K †	742	housewife	37	"
	X	Dalton William J	742	waterproofer	36	"
	Y	Fall Esther M †	742	housewife	26	"
	Z	Fall Henry B	742	accountant	29	"
545						
	A	Filbin Mildred L †	742	saleswoman	16	"
	B	Filbin Robert	742	student	21	"
	C	Filbin Thomas S	742	machinist	16	"
	D	Murphy John T	742	blacksmith	36	101 Draper
	E	Murphy Mary J †	742	housewife	34	101 "
	F	Nichols Eva M †	746	nurse	40	706 River
	G	Nichols Howard M	746	engineer	51	here
	H	Perry Charles	746	salesman	29	706 River
	K	Perry Rhoda †	746	housewife	29	706 "
	L	*Tupper Carrie M †	746	at home	62	706 "
	M	Hayes James	807	packer	26	19 Mass[illegible]
	N	Hayes Ruth †	807	clerk	22	[illegible]
	O	Viola Peter	807	brickmaker	47	here
	P	Viola Rose †	807	housewife	37	"
	R	*Ialenti Angelina †	807	"	54	"
	S	Ialenti Lena †	807	saleswoman	21	"
	T	Ialenti Marcello	807	shoemaker	52	"
	V	Conway Amy L †	811A	housewife	27	"
	W	Conway William H	811A	carpenter	35	[illegible]
	X	McCaffrey Frances B †	812	bookkeeper	58	[illegible]

Page	Letter	Full Name	Residence, Jan. 1, 1941	Occupation	Supposed Age	Reported Residence, Jan. 1, 1940. Street and Number.

River Street—Continued

Page	Letter	Full Name	Residence	Occupation	Age	Reported Residence
	Y	Rooney Anna V †	812	housewife	61	here
	Z	Rooney Anne V †	812	stenographer	26	"
546						
	A	Rooney John F	812	plumber	68	"
	B	Rooney Joseph F	812	"	23	"
	C	Rooney Mary F †	812	typist	21	"
	D*	Denardo Amelia †	816	housewife	48	"
	E	Denardo Joseph	816	laborer	45	"
	F	Forcillo Ida †	816	dressmaker	22	"
	G	Forcillo Mary †	816	"	24	"
	H	Rose Anthony	818	clerk	22	17 Copley
	K	Rose Elizabeth †	818	housewife	39	17 "
	L	Rose Elizabeth J †	818	checker	20	17 "
	M	O'Hearn Alice V †	820	housewife	58	here
	N	O'Hearn Eleanor C †	820	stenographer	41	"
	O	O'Hearn James A	820	manager	57	"
	P	MacLeod Colin J	822	chauffeur	25	"
	R	MacLeod Duncan	822	merchant	48	"
	S	MacLeod Margaret S †	822	operator	24	"
	T*	MacLeod Marie A †	822	housewife	47	"
	U	MacLeod Melba M †	822	waitress	22	"
	V	Johnson Johanna †	822	at home	79	"
	W	Diemer Elizabeth †	824	housewife	27	"
	X	Diemer Robert	824	riveter	29	"
	Y	O'Neill Agnes M †	824	laundryworker	25	"
	Z	O'Neill Elizabeth †	824	housewife	54	"
547						
	A	O'Neill James J	824	clerk	57	"
	B	O'Neill John F	824	"	22	"
	C	O'Neill William P	824	"	28	"
	D	Haley Cornelius J	826	chauffeur	47	"
	E	Haley Margaret T †	826	housewife	46	"
	F	Williams Henry J	826	papermaker	71	"
	G	Green Anna M †	828	at home	28	"
	H	Green Joseph E	828	painter	31	"
	K	Green Lena C †	828	housewife	66	"
	L	Green Mary L †	828	operator	33	"
	M	Green Stephen C	828	carpenter	61	"
	N	Peterson Helen S †	828	housewife	28	"
	O	Peterson Lester D	828	installer	30	"
	P	Fleming John F	830	finisher	35	"

Page	Letter	Full Name	Residence	Occupation	Age	Former Residence

River Street—Continued

Page	Letter	Full Name	Residence	Occupation	Age	Former Residence
	R	Fleming Lillian H †	830	housewife	[illegible]	[illegible]
	S	*Horan Anna C †	830	"	[illegible]	[illegible]
	T	Warren Robert F	830	finisher	[illegible]	[illegible]
	U	McCarthy Edith †	830	housewife	28	[illegible]
	V	McCarthy Paul	830	operator	26	[illegible]

Rosebery Road

Page	Letter	Full Name	Residence	Occupation	Age	Former Residence
	W	Pierce Grace V †	12 14	housewife	[illegible]	here
	X	Pierce Stanley B	12 14	salesman	31	"
	Y	Pettingell Allison P †	12 14	housewife	30	15 [illegible]
	Z	Pettingell Clarence L	12 14	salesman	27	15 "
548						
	A	Pettingell Maude L †	12 14	papercutter	51	15 "
	B	Fernands Mary A †	16	housewife	41	here
	C	Fernands Richard E	16	steamfitter	[illegible]	"
	D	Sheehan Jennie L †	16	housewife	73	"
	E	Sheehan Patrick A	16	retired	[illegible]	"
	F	Johnstone Eleanor D †	20	housewife	[illegible]	"
	G	Johnstone William G	20	instructor	36	"
	H	Cloonan Mary A †	24	housewife	78	"
	K	Riley Edward F	24	clerk	[illegible]	"
	L	Riley George E	24	diecutter	56	"
	M	Riley Mary A †	24	housewife	47	"
	N	Pinert Eva M †	42	"	27	15 [illegible]
	O	Pinert Frederic R	42	clerk	25	[illegible]
	P	Waugh Hedley T	42	painter	22	here
	R	Waugh Martha †	42	housewife	55	"
	S	Waugh Martha H †	42	cashier	25	"
	T	*Lockhart Bertha M †	16	housewife	71	"
	U	*Lockhart Walter S	16	retired	[illegible]	[illegible]

Rosemont Street

Page	Letter	Full Name	Residence	Occupation	Age	Former Residence
	V	Welch Edward K	20	student	[illegible]	[illegible]
	W	Welch Lawrence W	20	guard	[illegible]	[illegible]
	X	Welch Lawrence W, jr	20	clerk	[illegible]	[illegible]
	Y	Welch Margaret T †	20	housewife	[illegible]	[illegible]
	Z	Welch Marion J †	20	teacher	[illegible]	[illegible]

Page	Letter	Full Name	Residence, Jan. 1, 1941	Occupation	Supposed Age	Reported Residence, Jan. 1, 1940. Street and Number.
549						

Rosemont Street—Continued

Page	Letter	Full Name	Residence, Jan. 1, 1941	Occupation	Supposed Age	Reported Residence, Jan. 1, 1940. Street and Number.
	A	Welch Ruth L †	20	secretary	26	here
	B	Shamon Mary M †	24	housewife	40	"
	C	Shamon Michael J	24	B F D	45	"
	D	Nevins Alice F †	28	housewife	37	"
	E	Nevins Martin J	28	policeman	40	"
	F	Scannell Gertrude C †	28	clerk	32	"
	G	Scannell Mary J †	28	at home	72	"
	H	Foley Frank T	35	clerk	59	"
	K	Foley Marcella A †	35	housewife	30	"
	L	Burke Catherine †	44 46	"	43	"
	M	Burke William	44 46	carpenter	50	"
	N	Fitzgerald Bartholomew	44 46	chauffeur	55	"
	O	Fitzgerald John C	44 46	student	21	"
	P	Fitzgerald Nora M †	44 46	housewife	51	"
	R	Morse Charles R	44 46	repairman	35	"
	S	Morse Hazel †	44 46	housewife	33	"

Royal Road

Page	Letter	Full Name	Residence, Jan. 1, 1941	Occupation	Supposed Age	Reported Residence, Jan. 1, 1940. Street and Number.
	T	Shea Joseph P, jr	9	manager	31	here
	U	Shea Margaret F †	9	housewife	32	"
	V	Kamis Eva †	9	hygienist	21	"
	W*	Kamis Nellie †	9	housewife	45	"
	X*	Kamis Peter	9	butcher	51	"
	Y	Hagarty Frances †	9	housewife	27	"
	Z	Hagarty John	9	clerk	29	"
550						
	A	White Estelle J †	11	housewife	21	"
	B	White Roger T	11	machinist	27	"
	C	Lubach Alexander	11	cook	42	"
	D	Lubach Helen †	11	dietitian	24	"

Ruskindale Road

Page	Letter	Full Name	Residence, Jan. 1, 1941	Occupation	Supposed Age	Reported Residence, Jan. 1, 1940. Street and Number.
	F	[illegible] †	176 178	housewife	40	here
	G	Canavan Thomas R	176 178	B F D	39	"
	H	Dow Bertha †	176 178	housewife	61	"
	K	Dow Frank	176 178	retired	72	"

Page	Letter	Full Name					

Ruskindale Road—Continued

Page	Letter	Full Name				Age	
	L	Simmons William	176	178	salesman	23	here
	M	McGee Bernard J		181	stereotyper	34	"
	N	McGee Mary †		181	housewife	33	"
	O	*Nichols Constantina †		181	at home	66	"
	P	Nichols James		181	merchant	46	"
	R	Nichols Philomina †		181	housewife	33	"
	S	McNulty Eugene F		185	janitor	46	54 Alexander
	T	McNulty Margaret A †		185	housewife	41	54 "
	U	Smith Isabelle H †		185	folder	31	54 "
	V	Smith James H		185	engineer	37	here
	W	Smith Mary R †		185	housewife	26	"
	X	Stone Rita †		185	"	38	"
	Y	Stone Robert		185	merchant	41	"
	Z	Stewart Catherine C †		193	stenographer	37	"
551							
	A	Stewart John R		193	chauffeur	35	"

Taunton Avenue

Page	Letter	Full Name				Age	
	B	Morrison Gertrude †		85	housewife	53	here
	C	Morrison Howard W		85	clerk	55	"
	D	Tarutz Anna †		93	stenographer	30	"
	E	Tarutz Ida †		93	housewife	62	"
	F	Tarutz Max		93	junk dealer	68	"
	G	Tarutz Ruth †		93	bookkeeper	24	"
	H	Tarutz Sarah †		93	stenographer	31	"
	K	Tarutz Simon E		93	salesman	34	"
	L	Donahue Louis N		100	painter	65	"
	M	Donahue Louise T †		100	nurse	29	"
	N	Donahue Mary A †		100	housewife	61	"
	O	Horigan Anna †		104	"	32	"
	P	Horigan George T		104	teacher	34	"
	R	Anderson Alfred		109	engineer	34	"
	S	Anderson Ruth †		109	stenographer	30	"
	T	Carr Minnie †		109	housekeeper	72	"
	U	Miller Lester		109	salesman	31	"
	V	Miller Louise †		109	housewife	32	"
	W	Yee Eva †		112	"	51	"
	X	Yee Mabel †		112	nurse	24	"
	Y	Yee Raymond		112	clerk	34	"

Page	Letter	Full Name	Residence, Jan. 1, 1941	Occupation	Supposed Age	Reported Residence, Jan. 1, 1940. Street and Number.

Tchapitoulas Street

Page	Letter	Full Name	Residence, Jan. 1, 1941	Occupation	Supposed Age	Reported Residence, Jan. 1, 1940. Street and Number.
	Z	Hurley Mary G †	1	housekeeper	70	here
552						
	A	McCarthy Dorothy R †	1	housewife	41	"
	B	McCarthy Helen J †	1	teacher	34	"
	C	McCarthy Margaret C †	1	wigmaker	48	"

Tileston Street

Page	Letter	Full Name	Residence, Jan. 1, 1941	Occupation	Supposed Age	Reported Residence, Jan. 1, 1940. Street and Number.
	E	Fedrico Domenic	28	operator	42	here
	D	Fedrico Marie †	28	housewife	37	"
	F	Day Marjorie S †	28	clerk	31	"
	G	Day Muriel A †	28	"	25	"
	H	Abazorius Alphonso	41	machinist	23	"
	K*	Abazorius Anna †	41	housewife	49	"
	L*	Abazorius Anthony	41	watchman	55	"
	M*	Abazorius Kostantas	41	tailor	57	"

Tracton Avenue

Page	Letter	Full Name	Residence, Jan. 1, 1941	Occupation	Supposed Age	Reported Residence, Jan. 1, 1940. Street and Number.
	N	Price Anna T †	1	housewife	41	here
	O	Price George E	1	spinner	43	"
	P	Harrington Dorothy F †	3	housewife	22	42 Rosebery rd
	R	Harrington Joseph D	3	clerk	27	42 "
	S	Corbett Hugh	3	packer	41	here
	S*	Corbett Margaret †	3	housewife	34	"
	T	Larson Arline M †	4	"	24	249 Savannah av
	U	Larson John N	4	chauffeur	32	249 "
	V	White Mary J †	4	housewife	45	here
	W	White Richard F	4	policeman	40	"

Wachusett Street

Page	Letter	Full Name	Residence, Jan. 1, 1941	Occupation	Supposed Age	Reported Residence, Jan. 1, 1940. Street and Number.
	X	Berry M Herbert	3	safe expert	67	here
	Y	Berry Mary A †	3	housewife	65	"
	Z	Lawrence Dorothy R †	3	housekeeper	42	"
553						
	A	Lundberg Carl G	7	investigator	46	"
	B	Lundberg Marion C †	7	housewife	47	"
	C	Southwick Sarah E †	7	at home	73	"
	D	Trow Mildred F †	7	housewife	56	"
	E	Trow Ralph H	7	custodian	54	"

Page / Letter	Full Name				
Wachusett Street—Continued

F	Wadsworth Irene J †	7	librarian	29	here
G	MacKenzie Ensley	11	carpenter	56	"
H	Webster Fred H	11	serviceman	29	"
K	Webster Helen L †	11	housewife	29	"
L	Hackley Ruth W †	12	"	42	"
M	Budge Olga F †	15	housekeeper	57	"
N	Starke Henrietta C †	15	teacher	54	"
O	Budge Louise †	19-21	housewife	41	"
P	Budge Norman D	19-21	accountant	39	"
R	Bowering Gertrude A †	19-21	housewife	42	"
S	Bowering Nathaniel H	19-21	engineer	51	"
T	Hoefer Bernard C	20	salesman	53	"
U	Smith Frederica †	20	housewife	67	"
V	Rogers Arthur V	23	chauffeur	35	"
W	Rogers Ethel †	23	housewife	32	"
X	Saunders Bruce E	23	printer	24	"
Y	Saunders Joseph C	23	draftsman	18	"
Z	Saunders Mela H †	23	housewife	51	"
554					
A	Sinclair Christina †	24	"	58	"
B	Sinclair J Robert	24	messenger	20	"
C	Sinclair Stanley L	24	engineer	32	"
D	Sinclair William M	24	machinist	59	"
E	MacLean Doris M †	24	housewife	26	31 Wachusett
F	MacLean Duncan C	24	secretary	27	31 "
G	Sivertsen Warren R	24	"	25	31 "
H	Thorpe Edwin T	24	student	29	7 [illegible]
K	Gillespie Helen J †	24	housewife	50	here
L	Gillespie Thomas	24	foreman	53	"
M	Gillespie Thomas M	24	biller	21	"
N	Cantwell Dennis J	28	salesman	75	[illegible]
O	Hassan Edward D	28	attorney	51	[illegible]
P	Hassan Edward D, jr	28	clerk	24	[illegible]
R	Hassan Marguerite G †	28	housewife	50	[illegible]
S	Hassan William J	28	investigator	29	[illegible]
T	Cronin John J	31	agent	28	[illegible]
V	Cronin Margaret †	31	housewife	[illegible]	[illegible]
W	Andruszkiwiez Edna C †	39	"	[illegible]	[illegible]
X	Andruszkiwiez Stephen	39	[illegible]	[illegible]	[illegible]
Y	Bilodeau Henry L	39	[illegible]	[illegible]	[illegible]
Z	Bilodeau Katherine C †	39	[illegible]	[illegible]	[illegible]

Page	Letter	FULL NAME	Residence, Jan. 1, 1941	Occupation	Supposed Age	Reported Residence, Jan. 1, 1940. Street and Number
555		**Wachusett Street**—Continued				
	A	Bilodeau Ruth †	39	saleswoman	25	here
	B	Holland Mary L †	39	housekeeper	63	"
	C	Griffin Harry J	40	clerk	35	"
	D	Griffin Louise M †	40	housewife	35	"
	E	Kiernan Mary K †	40	bookkeeper	37	"
	F	Cohen Mark E	40	retired	70	"
	G	Archibald Dorothy †	44	housewife	30	"
	H	Archibald Warren	44	agent	36	"
	K	Myers Earl P	44	exterminator	36	"
	L	Myers Gladys T †	44	housewife	25	"
		Windsor Street				
	M	Gulezynski Anna †	8	dressmaker	25	here
	N	Gulezynski Karol	8	welder	22	"
	O*	Gulezynski Lottie †	8	housewife	45	"
	P*	Gulezynski Stephen	8	blacksmith	49	"
	R	Campbell Pearl †	11	maid	41	28 Richmere rd
	S	MacAuley Daniel A	11	printer	44	28 "
	T	MacAuley Donald C	11	machinist	20	28 "
	U	MacAuley Ethel M †	11	housewife	42	28 "
	V	McCarthy Francis R	12	policeman	31	here
	W	McCarthy Helen F †	12	laundress	27	"
	X	McCarthy Josephine E †	12	clerk	32	"
	Y	McCarthy Julia T †	12	housewife	58	"
	Z	McCarthy Mary F †	12	boxmaker	34	"
556						
	A	McCarthy Mildred R †	12	seamstress	24	"
	B	McCarthy William A	12	laborer	29	"
	C	Cannift Edward T	15	stonecutter	32	"
	D	Cannift Mary A †	15	housewife	30	"
	E	Gorman Rose M †	16	"	34	"
	F	Gorman William T	16	policeman	38	"
	G	Hastings John V	19	installer	48	"
	H	Hastings Mary F †	19	housewife	49	"
	K	McAvoy Celia A †	20	at home	82	"
	L	McAvoy Delia †	20	"	69	"
	M	McAvoy Walter J	20	U S A	28	"
	N	Winn Agnes E †	20	housewife	39	"
	O	Winn Robert B	20	letter carrier	42	"

Page.	Letter.	Full Name.					
		Windsor Street—Continued					
	P	Lynch Hannah M †	23	housewife	70	here
	R	Lynch Helen M †	23	teacher	28	"
	S	Lynch Mary E †	23	"	37	"
	T	Lynch Thomas D	23	retired	71	"
	U	Cahill Michael J	24	salesman	19	"
	V	Cassell Doris M †	24	housewife	26	"
	W	Cassell Henry J	24	salesman	31	"
	X	McGinnis Cecelia T †	27	housewife	43	"
	Y	McGinnis Walter W	27	clerk	41	"
	Z	Morrissey Mary F †	28	housewife	35	"
557						
	A	Morrissey Nicholas P	28	clerk	37	"
	B	Widebeck Carl T	31	machinist	29	"
	C	Widebeck Olga G †	31	housewife	31	"

Woodland Road

Page.	Letter.	Full Name.				
	D	Cronin Jennie E †	50	housewife	50	here
	E	Cronin John J	50	clerk	31	"
	F	Hagerty Margaret †	50	housekeeper	19	"
	G	Patterson Annie †	55	waitress	45	"
	H	Strom Florence P †	55	housewife	52	"
	K	Strom Harold R	55	machinist	52	"
	L	Strom William A	55	shipper	20	"

Ward 18—Precinct 6

CITY OF BOSTON

LIST OF RESIDENTS
20 YEARS OF AGE AND OVER

(NON-CITIZENS INDICATED BY ASTERISK)
(FEMALES INDICATED BY DAGGER)

AS OF

JANUARY 1, 1941

CITY OF BOSTON PRINTING DEPARTMENT

Page	Letter	Full Name	Residence, Jan. 1, 1941.	Occupation	Supposed Age.	Reported Residence, Jan. 1, 1940. Street and Number.

Annafran Street

Page	Letter	Full Name	Residence, Jan. 1, 1941.	Occupation	Supposed Age.	Reported Residence, Jan. 1, 1940. Street and Number.
600						
	A	Kelly John F	11	retired	65	Everett
	B	Regan John F	11	policeman	39	here
	C	Regan Mary E †	11	housewife	35	"
	D	DeAmelio Catherine †	24	"	26	"
	E	DeAmelio William	24	shipper	27	"
	F	Spoon Albert	24	laborer	31	"
	G	Spoon Mary †	24	housewife	29	"
	H	Sarno Leo	24	pressman	33	"
	K	Sarno Rose †	24	housewife	31	"
	L	Kostecki Anne †	37	cook	26	"
	M	*Kostecki Mary †	37	housewife	46	"
	N	*Kostecki Matro	37	machinist	48	"
	O	Kostecki Michael	37	laborer	23	"
	P	Bachyn Anna †	42	housewife	45	"
	R	Bachyn Marie †	42	hairdresser	25	"
	S	Bachyn Natalie †	42	saleswoman	23	"
	T	Bachyn Peter	42	cleaner	54	"
	U	Bartko Bohdon	43	mechanic	22	"
	V	Bartko Theodore F	43	cleaner	47	"
	W	Bartko Theodore S	43	"	23	"
	X	Weremey Catherine †	50	housewife	31	"
	Y	Weremey John	50	B F D	43	"
	Z	Voye Vivian R †	55	housewife	29	"
601						
	A	Voye William E	55	clerk	32	"
	B	Mazur Mary †	55	housewife	34	"
	C	Mazur Michael	55	custodian	44	"
	D	Curran Catherine M †	74	housewife	30	28 Rossmore rd
	E	Curran Phillip J	74	laborer	30	28 "
	F	Demaso James	75	shoeworker	33	here
	G	Demaso Mary †	75	housewife	31	"
	H	Magliarditi Frank	78	salesman	64	"
	K	Magliarditi Josephine †	78	housewife	60	"
	L	Nelson Carl F	79	accountant	33	"
	M	Nelson Julia M †	79	housewife	26	"
	N	Stone Anna †	79	"	55	"
	O	Stone Victor	79	carpenter	59	"
	P	Holmberg Hannah †	81	housewife	60	"
	R	Holmberg John	81	carpenter	45	"
	S	Trenholm E Anna †	83	housewife	27	83 Wood av

Page	Letter	Full Name	Residence, Jan. 1, 1941	Occupation	Reputed Age	Reported Residence, Jan. 1, 1940. Street and Number
		Annafran Street Continued				
	T	Trenholm Floyd W	83	carpenter	58	here
	U	Trenholm Floyd W, jr	83	laborer	24	83 Wood av
	V	Howland Doris O †	87	housewife	36	83 Annafran
	W	Howland George A, jr	87	painter	40	83 "
	X	*Krumin Elizabeth †	88	housewife	86	here
	Y	Krumin Henry F	88	bookbinder	53	"
	Z	Mohr Elizabeth R †	91-97	housewife	49	"
602						
	A	Mohr Peter	91-97	laborer	48	"
	B	Reardon Leo A	109	carpenter	39	"
	C	Reardon Mary J †	109	housewife	43	"
		Birchcroft Road				
	D	McGrann Mae D †	5	housewife	36	here
	E	McGrann William J	5	policeman	35	"
	F	Carey Ethel M †	8	housewife	32	"
	G	Carey Francis L	8	electrotypist	37	"
	H	Riordan Helen B †	9	housewife	40	"
	K	Riordan John J	9	fireman	41	"
	L	Brooker John P	10	inspector	45	"
	M	Brooker Virginia M †	10	housewife	45	"
	N	Thomas Reginald J	10	compositor	25	"
	O	O'Hea Catherine M †	14	entertainer	52	"
	P	O'Hea Evelyn M †	14	"	25	"
	R	O'Hea Katherine B †	14	"	23	"
	S	O'Hea Marguerite M †	14	"	21	"
	T	Patts Alice M †	14	housewife	49	"
	U	Patts Margaret T †	14	housekeeper	78	"
	V	Patts Michael J	14	clerk	49	"
	W	Zuckerman Albert J	18	artist	31	19 Bismarck
	X	Zuckerman Maizie G †	18	housewife	32	19 "
	Y	McCue Catherine A †	22	saleswoman	60	here
603						
	A	O'Brien Edward F	22	serviceman	43	"
	B	O'Brien Esther M †	22	housewife	38	"
	C	Shea Veronica M †	22	teacher	22	"
	D	Dunlea Anna C †	26	housewife	32	32 Pierce av
	E	Dunlea Joseph M	26	clerk	33	32 "
	F	Dooley Catherine V †	34	"	24	726 Parker
	G	Dooley Elizabeth F †	34	saleswoman	20	726 "

Page	Letter	Full Name	Residence, Jan. 1, 1941	Occupation	Supposed Age	Reported Residence, Jan. 1, 1940. Street and Number.

Birchcroft Road—Continued

Page	Letter	Full Name	Residence, Jan. 1, 1941	Occupation	Supposed Age	Reported Residence, Jan. 1, 1940. Street and Number.
	H	Dooley Margaret E †	34	housewife	48	726 Parker
	K	Dooley Rita H †	34	saleswoman	22	726 "
	L	Dooley William P	34	shipper	51	726 "
	M	Lanigan Albert E	35	supervisor	45	191 Sycamore
	N	Lanigan Harriet A †	35	housewife	44	191 "
	O	Aho Augustus H	38	repairman	35	5 Moody
	P	Aho Marion O †	38	housewife	33	5 "
	R	Buckley Ada F †	42	housekeeper	61	Quincy
	S	Ingram Jessie S †	52	housewife	36	7 Alleyne
	T	Ingram William R	52	manager	35	7 "
	U	Simpson Edith M †	54	bookeeper	24	14 Egleston
	V	Simpson LeBaron	54	longshoreman	49	14 "
	W	Simpson Margaret †	54	housewife	48	14 "
	X	George Joseph E	56	laborer	55	746 E Eighth
	Y	George Sarah E †	56	clerk	48	746 "
	Z	Cinecotti Eleanor C †	59	housewife	28	Cambridge
604						
	A	Cincotti Henry J	59	plumber	31	Belmont

Blake Street

Page	Letter	Full Name	Residence, Jan. 1, 1941	Occupation	Supposed Age	Reported Residence, Jan. 1, 1940. Street and Number.
	C	Stewart Charles N	8	chef	43	here
	D	Stewart Nellie Y †	8	housewife	41	"
	E	Bennett Elizabeth †	10	clerk	41	"
	F	Bennett Mabel B †	10	teacher	45	"
	G	Hurley Mary J †	10	housewife	26	207 Savannah av
	H	Hurley Timothy J	10	clerk	31	207 "
	K	O'Lalor David R	14	armorer	44	here
	L	O'Lalor Margaret F †	14	housewife	42	"
	M	Frangioso Gentelina †	16	"	38	"
	N	Frangioso Larry	16	engineer	43	"
	O	Bonarrigo Catherine †	16	housewife	50	"
	P	Bonarrigo Francis J	16	presser	22	"
	R	Bonarrigo Joseph	16	laborer	54	"
	S	Milne Charles H	24	policeman	55	"
	T	Milne Lucy †	24	housewife	58	"
	U	Hoppe Edith D †	28	"	40	"
	V	Hoppe John T	28	B F D	48	"
	W	Corboy James J	30	fireman	45	"
	X	Corboy Mary M †	30	housewife	50	"
	Y	Lynch Edward R	30	proprietor	54	"

Page	Letter	Full Name	Residence, Jan. 1, 1941	Occupation	Supposed Age	Reported Residence, Jan. 1, 1940. Street and Number

Blake Street—Continued

Page	Letter	Full Name	Residence, Jan. 1, 1941	Occupation	Supposed Age	Reported Residence, Jan. 1, 1940. Street and Number
	Z	Lynch Joseph F	30	realtor	52	here
605						
	A	Brown Ernest	36	proprietor	64	13 Savin Hill av
	B	Brown Penelope †	36	housewife†	63	13 "
	C	Janises Alice M †	36	"	33	25 Dillingham
	D	*Janises Gustas	36	hatter	41	25 "
	E	Rosenthal Monto	40	proprietor	40	here
	F	Rosenthal Rose †	40	housewife	62	"
	G	Rosenthal Sadie E †	40	"	33	"
	H	Coombs Agnes E †	44	"	54	"
	K	Coombs Harold W	44	repairman	28	"
	L	Coombs Lillian M †	44	housewife	21	30 Bradlee
	M	Coombs Robert W	44	operator	54	here
	N	Shuman Amelia †	48	housewife	59	"
	O	Shuman David	48	salesman	55	"
	P	Trafton George N	50	bartender	40	"
	R	*Trafton Rita †	50	housewife	34	"
	S	Briggs George S	52	salesman	61	"
	T	Maguire Daniel C	52	clerk	55	131 Perham
	U	Maguire Margaret G †	52	housewife	58	131 "
	V	Leavitt Catherine V †	56	"	41	here
	W	Leavitt John O	56	foreman	46	"
	X	Fitzpatrick Mary T †	57	housewife	26	"
	Y	Fitzpatrick Robert F	57	shipper	30	"
	Z	Morgan Anna L †	57	housewife	32	"
606						
	A	Morgan Arthur F	57	clerk	32	"
	B	Barnard Edwin F	61	retired	76	"
	C	Barnard Wilfred E	61	janitor	41	"
	D	Brauneis Cecelia M †	61	housewife	47	"
	E	Brauneis Joseph J	61	carpenter	52	"
	F	*Walner Bessie †	62	housewife	50	"
	G	Walner Edward	62	mechanic	47	"
	H	Wallace Catherine F †	65	housewife	68	24 Egleston
	K	Wiley Edith E †	65	"	34	Milton
	L	Wiley Robert C	65	salesman	34	"
	M	Johnson Mary A †	66	housewife	44	29 Blake
	N	Johnson Richard S	66	attendant	43	29 "
	O	Freeman Edmund F	67	agent	43	Waltham
	P	Freeman Lucy A †	67	housewife	40	"
	R	Sweeney George V	71	manager	30	Milton

Page	Letter	Full Name	Residence, Jan. 1, 1941	Occupation.	Supposed Age.	Reported Residence, Jan. 1, 1940. Street and Number.

Blake Street—Continued

Page	Letter	Full Name	Residence, Jan. 1, 1941	Occupation.	Supposed Age.	Reported Residence, Jan. 1, 1940. Street and Number.
	S	Sweeney Mary A †	71	housewife	28	Milton
	T	Alexander Anna E †	73	"	39	here
	U	Alexander Harold F	73	letter carrier	41	"
	V	Alexander Mildred E †	73	inspector	20	"
	W	Bretanus George	78	tailor	65	"
	X	Bretanus Madaline †	78	housewife	34	"
	Y	Bretanus Paul	78	machinist	36	"
	Z	DeCelles John B	79	manager	42	"
607						
	A	DeCelles Mary L †	79	housewife	36	"
	B	Asmus John F	80–82	machinist	23	"
	C	Asmus Zita C †	80–82	housewife	21	"
	D	Fuller Ann M †	80–82	"	31	"
	E	Fuller Frank M	80–82	salesman	64	"
	F	Fuller George R	80–82	machinist	20	"
	G	Fuller Mabel A †	80–82	housewife	53	"
	H	Fuller Robert A	80–82	meatcutter	27	"
	K	Pezznola Guy R	83	merchant	32	"
	L*	Pezznola Jessie †	83	housewife	33	"
	M	Corboy Ann M †	89	receptionist	25	136 Blake
	N	Corboy Anna †	89	stewardess	50	136 "
	O	Corboy Elizabeth L †	89	clerk	27	136 "
	P	Heavey Evelyn †	90	housewife	34	here
	R	Heavey John F	90	agent	44	"
	S	MacPhail Helen C †	90	bookkeeper	52	"
	T	McCulloch Margaret W †	90	housewife	44	"
	U	McCulloch William B	90	laborer	42	"
	V	Fundin Aurora †	91	housewife	67	"
	W	Fundin Oscar	91	retired	73	"
	X	Mathisen Lillian G †	91	housewife	34	"
	Y	Mathisen Wilfred H	91	mechanic	33	"
	Z	Higgins Harold T	94	inspector	37	"
608						
	A	Higgins Rose M †	94	housewife	33	"
	B	Thomas John J	94	steamfitter	38	"
	C	Thomas Margaret I †	94	housewife	35	"
	D	Toffoloni Kathryn N †	94	"	24	293 Wood av
	E	Toffoloni Luciano	94	toolmaker	26	26 Livermore
	F	MacCartney Helen J †	95	housewife	46	130 Blake
	G	MacCartney James D	95	clerk	50	130 "
	H	Albani Catherine M †	95	housewife	27	Salem

Page	Letter	Full Name	Residence, Jan. 1, 1941	Occupation	Supposed Age	Reported Residence, Jan. 1, 1940. Street and Number

Blake Street—Continued

Page	Letter	Full Name	Residence, Jan. 1, 1941	Occupation	Supposed Age	Reported Residence, Jan. 1, 1940. Street and Number
	K	Albani Peter E	95	draftsman	28	Salem
	L	Hill Gertrude L †	103	housewife	57	here
	M	Hill Harriett L †	103	clerk	23	"
	N	Hill Leon F	103	mechanic	60	"
	P	Johansen John B	105	inspector	53	"
	R	Johansen Lena M †	105	housewife	42	"
	S	Ellis Abraham	106	musician	49	"
	T	Ellis Anna †	106	housewife	43	"
	U	Clouherty Mary E †	107	at home	70	"
	V	Clougherty Paul E	107	inspector	22	"
	W	Gleason Joseph A	107	supervisor	15	"
	X	Gleason Julia A †	107	housewife	43	"
	Y	Winquist Carl J	108	machinist	53	"
	Z	Winquist Esther M †	108	housewife	52	"
609						
	A	Madden Mary F †	115	at home	23	31 Brainard
	B	Moran Frank A	115	fireman	47	31 "
	C	Moran Mary E †	115	housewife	51	31 "
	D	*Peters Jane †	115A	"	35	here
	E	Peters Theme	115A	proprietor	39	"
	F	Fallon Ethel K †	117	housewife	28	"
	G	Fallon Frederick E	117	chauffeur	31	"
	H	Foster Eileen M †	118	housewife	24	21 Hopewell rd
	K	Foster Gerald B	118	technician	25	here
	L	Foster Sofie †	118	housewife	60	"
	M	Brown Alice R †	119	clerk	33	"
	N	Brown Elinor C †	119	"	26	"
	O	Brown James L	119	mechanic	38	"
	P	Brown Mary E †	119	housewife	63	"
	R	Hiltz Emma †	120	"	63	"
	S	Hiltz George W	120	machinist	64	"
	T	Apelgren Fannie †	120	housewife	57	"
	U	Apelgren Frank O	120	boilermaker	53	"
	V	Apelgren Helga I †	120	at home	35	"
	W	Hanson Norman C	120	accountant	23	Woburn
	X	Norton Joseph E	121	superintendent	49	here
	Y	Norton Kathleen †	121	housewife	40	"
	Z	Anderson Peter	124	papermaker	68	"
610						
	A	Anderson Ruth †	124	secretary	38	"
	B	Geick Harold	124	chauffeur	38	"

Blake Street Continued

Page	Letter	Full Name	Residence, Jan. 1, 1941	Occupation	Supposed Age	Reported Residence, Jan. 1, 1940. Street and Number.
	C	Bragdon Clavin W	125	engineer	62	here
	D	Bragdon Marie E †	125	saleswoman	28	"
	E	Bragdon Myra A †	125	housewife	63	"
	F	Pellegrini Erma †	128	"	25	Vermont
	G	Pellegrini Robert	128	painter	26	150 Hyde Hark av
	H	LaFleur May A †	128	at home	61	California
	K	Walsh Frank E	128	operator	60	here
	L	Connors Anna L †	130	housewife	32	297 Wood av
	M	Connors John J	130	superintendent	42	297 "
	N	O'Brien Ellen A †	131	secretary	40	here
	O	O'Brien Grace E †	131	hairdresser	38	"
	P	O'Brien Thomas	131	retired	75	"
	R	O'Brien Thomas R	131	steelworker	23	"
	S	Kimball Keith F	132	electrician	38	"
	T	Kimball Marjorie E †	132	housewife	30	"
	U	Sullivan Mary L †	133	"	37	"
	V	O'Donnell Edward F	134	clerk	30	"
	W	O'Donnell Ellen T †	134	housewife	48	"
	X	O'Donnell John R	134	waiter	28	"
	Y	O'Donnell Richard D	134	salesman	23	"
	Z	Wentworth Julia F †	134	secretary	33	"
611						
	A	Hanaway Elinor G †	136	housewife	26	134 Blake
	B	Hanaway Paul E	136	supervisor	36	Quincy
	C	Stiles Charles H	138	salesman	50	here
	D	Stiles Henrietta A †	138	housewife	47	"
	E	O'Connell Julia †	140	maid	50	"
	F	O'Connell Mary †	140	housewife	58	"
	G	O'Connell Thomas	140	operator	61	"
	H	Ashmore Charles F	143	stagehand	44	"
	K	Ashmore Hannah A †	143	housewife	75	"
	L	Ashmore Thomas F	143	fireman	53	"
	M	Walsh Ellen I †	144	housewife	37	"
	N	Walsh William G	144	clerk	40	"
	O	Woodward Mary †	144	housewife	57	"
	P	Woodward Roy R	144	operator	60	"
	R	Pettingill Alton H	146	policeman	40	"
	S	Pettingill Elizabeth J †	146	housewife	34	"
	T	Donovan Charles S	146	manager	43	"
	U	Donovan Pauline L †	146	housewife	31	"

Page	Letter	Full Name	Residence, Jan. 1, 1941	Occupation	Reputed Age	Reported Residence, Jan. 1, 1940. Street and Number
		Brockton Street				
	V	Carey Daniel F	33	weigher	33	12 Ashley
	W	Carey Mary J †	33	housewife	28	22 Dalrymple
612		**Cummins Highway**				
	D	Lattie Blanche E †	571	housewife	51	here
	E	Lattie Blanche M †	571	nurse	21	"
	F	Lattie Kenneth	571	salesman	25	New York
	G	Lattie Thomas	571	clerk	51	here
	H	Marinelli Ann M †	571	packer	24	"
	K	Marinelli John	571	laborer	53	"
	L	Marinelli Louis J	571	clerk	22	"
	M	Marinelli Peter J	571	machinist	26	"
	N	*Marinelli Theresa †	571	housewife	53	"
	O	Salvoni Alfred A	571	plumber	26	"
	P	Salvoni Candida †	571	housewife	47	"
	R	McKenna George E	615 617	salesman	31	186 W Seventh
	S	McKenna Wanda F †	615 617	housewife	33	186 "
	T	*Organek Cecelia †	615 617	"	65	here
	U	Organek Edward	615 617	musician	39	"
	V	*Jankowski Jean M †	615 617	housewife	41	226 Kennebec
	W	Jankowski Walter	615 617	baker	46	226 "
	X	*Kowolski Mary L †	615 617	housewife	39	245 "
	Y	Kowolski Paul B	615 617	machinist	42	245 "
613						
	C	Faiella Helen M †	635	housewife	28	here
	D	Faiella Nicholas P	635	machinist	28	"
	E	Farinella Julio M	635	laborer	33	"
	F	Farinella Rose M †	635	housewife	27	"
	G	Sullivan Charles P	635	laborer	24	10 Colorado
	H	Wright Mary E †	635	housewife	39	10 "
	K	Wright William A	635	salesman	45	10 "
	M	Eno Dominic A	639	printer	30	here
	N	Eno Marie M †	639	housewife	29	"
	O	*Faiella Anthony	639	shoemaker	51	"
	P	*Faiella Mary †	639	housewife	51	"
		Danbury Road				
	S	Stelzer George A	5	policeman	40	here
	T	Stelzer Mary L †	5	housewife	38	"

Page	Letter	Full Name	Residence, Jan. 1, 1941	Occupation	Supposed Age	Reported Residence, Jan. 1, 1940. Street and Number.

Danbury Road—Continued

Page	Letter	Full Name	Residence, Jan. 1, 1941	Occupation	Supposed Age	Reported Residence, Jan. 1, 1940. Street and Number.
	U	Fitzgerald John F	6	inspector	24	here
	V	Gray Annie †	6	"	59	"
	W	Harrington Daniel J	6	agent	51	"
	X	Harrington Florence F †	6	housewife	51	"
	Y	Collins Agnes C †	9	"	30	"
	Z	Collins Patrick A	9	fireman	33	"
614						
	A	Doyle Daniel T	10	policeman	43	"
	B	Doyle Rose B †	10	housewife	38	"
	C	Erwin Anna G †	14	"	30	"
	D	Erwin John E	14	salesman	56	"
	E	Erwin Pearl R †	14	housewife	59	"
	F	Erwin Richard W	14	clerk	29	"
	G	Hocknell Albert F	15	manager	56	"
	H	Hocknell Albert F	15	collector	28	"
	K	Hocknell Dorothy C †	15	teacher	26	"
	L	Hocknell Irene M †	15	student	22	"
	M	Hocknell Irene M †	15	housewife	52	"
	N	Connor Alice M †	18	"	50	"
	O	Connor James L	18	clerk	26	"
	P	Connor John E	18	welder	51	"
	R	Connor Rita M †	18	student	21	"
	S	Connor Ruth E †	18	nurse	28	"
	T	Donahue John A	19	accountant	36	33 Favre
	U	Donahue Ruth C †	19	housewife	35	33 "

George Street

Page	Letter	Full Name	Residence, Jan. 1, 1941	Occupation	Supposed Age	Reported Residence, Jan. 1, 1940. Street and Number.
	V	MacPherson John L	7	trainman	43	140 Howard av
	W	MacPherson Margaret C †	7	housewife	41	140 "
	X	Barme Elise M †	9	clerk	56	here
	Y	Shedd Albert P	9	manager	45	"
	Z	Shedd Charlotte B †	9	housewife	44	"
615						
		Drake Francis O	11	clergyman	28	Michigan
		Drake Marjorie E †	11	housewife	24	"
	C	Pigott Edna A †	11	housekeeper	29	here
	D	Pigott George H	11	carpenter	56	"
	E	Pigott Mary I †	11	teacher	26	"
	F	Pigott Wendell D	11	chauffeur	21	"

Page	Letter	Full Name	Residence Jan. 1, 1941	Occupation	Supposed Age	Reported Residence Jan. 1, 1940 Street and Number

George Street—Continued

Page	Letter	Full Name	Residence Jan. 1, 1941	Occupation	Supposed Age	Reported Residence Jan. 1, 1940 Street and Number
	G	Jones Alfred H	12	agent	41	837 River
	H	Jones Jeanne E †	12	housewife	42	837 "
	K	Piveronus Anna M †	14	"	33	here
	L	*Piveronus John G	14	mechanic	36	"
	M	*Piveronus Anthony	14	laborer	65	"
	N	*Piveronus Josephine †	14	housewife	61	"
	O	Piveronus Peter J	14	shipfitter	25	"
	P	Piveronus Rose C †	14	housewife	23	23 Blanchard
	R	Lalor Catherine M †	15	"	27	946 Wash'n
	S	Lalor Edward T	15	accountant	21	here
	T	Lalor Henrietta M †	15	housewife	46	"
	U	Lalor Richard H	15	foreman	48	"
	V	Lalor Richard H, jr	15	clerk	28	"
	W	Lalor Robert A	15	mechanic	27	"
	X	McEvoy Esther M †	17	housewife	58	"
	Y	McEvoy Evelyn M †	17	houseworker	24	"
	Z	McEvoy Isaac W	17	shoeworker	66	"
616						
	A	Burke John J	18	retired	82	"
	B	Burke Richard F	18	painter	52	"
	C	Donovan Margaret L †	18	housekeeper	44	"
	D	*Walsh Mary C †	18	clerk	42	"
	E	Gould Bertha E †	19	housewife	67	"
	F	Gould William F	19	salesman	71	"
	G	Ormond Isabelle †	21	housewife	62	"
	H	Ormond John J	21	designer	63	"
	K	Ormond John J, jr	21	printer	27	"
	L	Ormond Loretta V †	21	stenographer	22	"
	M	Ormond Louise M †	21	secretary	21	"
	N	MacDougall Margaret †	23	housekeeper	75	"
	O	Spence John L	23	chauffeur	37	"
	P	Spence Mary I †	23	housewife	35	"
	R	Hayer Alfred C	25	accountant	37	"
	S	Hayer Gertrude A †	25	stenographer	27	"
	T	Hayer Margaret †	25	housewife	62	"
	U	Hayer Thomas E	25	bookkeeper	21	"
	V	Hayer William F	25	checker	31	"
	W	McDonnell John	26	fireman	38	273 [illegible]
	X	McDonnell Margaret †	26	housewife	29	273 "
	Y	McIntire Beatrice H †	27	"	37	here
	Z	McIntire William D	27	clerk	36	"

Page	Letter	Full Name	Residence, Jan. 1, 1941.	Occupation	Supposed Age	Reported Residence, Jan. 1, 1940. Street and Number.

617

George Street—Continued

Page	Letter	Full Name	Residence, Jan. 1, 1941.	Occupation	Supposed Age	Reported Residence, Jan. 1, 1940. Street and Number.
617	A	Linskey John F	27	letter carrier	41	here
	B	Linskey Katherine V †	27	housewife	40	"
	C	Danner John W	28	carpenter	50	"
	D	Danner Mary †	28	housewife	43	"
	E	Danner Mary F †	28	student	20	"
	F	Holden Jane A †	29	housewife	52	"
	G	Holden Joseph A	29	engineer	53	"
	H	Strack Edward H	29	machinist	28	"
	K	Augherton Charles S	31	foreman	67	"
	L	Augherton Mary C †	31	housewife	67	"
	M	Augherton Rita E †	31	bookkeeper	23	"
	N	Duffy Barbara E †	32	clerk	22	48 Mattakeeset
	O	Duffy Ethel E †	32	housewife	42	48 "
	P	Duffy Francis W	32	furrier	50	48 "
	R	Higgins Donald A	35	laborer	20	here
	S	Higgins Frances R †	35	housewife	44	"
	T	Higgins Nathan A	35	foreman	47	"
	U	Losordo Frank	35	carpenter	54	"
	V	Losordo Joseph J	35	"	22	"
	W	*Losordo Lena †	35	housewife	50	"
	X	Losordo Phyllis †	35	bookkeeper	23	"
	Y	Murphy Arthur R	39	clerk	26	"
	Z	Murphy Catherine M †	39	housewife	34	"
618						
	A	Murphy Edward F	39	clerk	30	"
	B	Murphy Ella J †	39	housewife	65	"

Greenfield Road

Page	Letter	Full Name	Residence, Jan. 1, 1941.	Occupation	Supposed Age	Reported Residence, Jan. 1, 1940. Street and Number.
	C	MacKenzie Mary C †	92	housewife	43	here
	D	Groves John E	96 98	meter reader	31	"
	E	Groves Marion E †	96 98	housewife	29	"
	F	Groves Dorothy E †	96 98	secretary	29	"
	G	Groves Mildred E †	96 98	housewife	61	"
	H	Groves Ruth E †	96 98	clerk	33	"
	K	Duffey Florence †	104	housekeeper	45	"
	L	Gallagher Abbie †	104	housewife	73	"
	M	Gallagher Helen F †	104	stenographer	34	"
	N	Gallagher Margaret E †	104	"	36	"
	O	Gallagher Patrick	104	retired	73	"

Page	Letter	Full Name	Residence Jan. 1	Occupation	Supposed Age	Reported Residence Jan. 1 — Street and Number

Greenfield Road Continued

Page	Letter	Full Name	Residence	Occupation	Age	Reported Residence
	P	*Joyce Annie †	104	housekeeper	67	here
	R	Ford Alma L †	108	housewife	30	"
	S	Ford Paul F	108	engineer	31	"
	T	*Kutny Andrew	108	chef	55	"
	U	*Kutny Anna †	108	housewife	48	"
	V	Kutny Theodore	108	clerk	21	"
	W	Rush Georgie B †	112	housewife	42	"
	X	Rush Roger J	112	shipper	42	"
	Y	*Swidzinski Frank	112	chef	46	"
	Z	*Swidzinski Rose †	112	housewife	44	"
619						
	A	Bartoloni Joseph F	124	shipper	35	"
	B	Bartoloni Phyllis E †	124	housewife	35	"
	C	Bowditch Bertha †	124	stitcher	64	"
	D	L'Heureux Charles E, jr	126	manager	27	41 Burt
	E	L'Heureux Edith B †	126	housewife	23	55 Bailey
	F	Hood Jessica †	126	"	27	here
	G	Hood Leo	126	manager	29	"
	H	Anderson Bertil	128	welder	47	14 Tesla
	K	Anderson Elfrida †	128	housekeeper	64	Quincy
	L	Anderson Eva †	128	housewife	44	14 Tesla
	M	Sawyer Sarah F †	128	"	60	12 Fenelon
	N	Sundell Carl E	130	undertaker	37	here
	O	Sundell Dorothy M †	130	housewife	33	"
	P	Grundy Joseph H	130	chauffeur	34	264 Wood av
	R	Grundy Louise F †	130	waitress	28	264 "
	S	Holden Alice M †	132	housewife	33	here
	T	Holden William H	132	engineer	43	"
	U	McAdams Edward R	132	letter carrier	34	[illegible]
	V	McAdams Eleanor C †	132	housewife	26	264 "
	W	Brennan Mary A †	146	clerk	49	here
	X	Foran Mary F †	149	proprietor	55	"
	Y	Foran Mary G †	149	inspector	26	"
	Z	Byrnes Ethel C †	150	housewife	33	91 Greenfield
620						
	A	Byrnes Martin J	150	policeman	35	91 "
	B	Byrnes Alice M †	150	stenographer	27	here
	C	Byrnes Florence M †	150	"	10	"
	D	Byrnes George W	150	plumber	71	"
	E	Byrnes Mary A †	150	housewife	66	"
	F	Byrnes Walter J	150	clerk	33	"

Page	Letter	Full Name	Residence, Jan. 1, 1941	Occupation	Supposed Age	Reported Residence, Jan. 1, 1940. Street and Number.

Greenfield Road—Continued

Page	Letter	Full Name	Residence, Jan. 1, 1941	Occupation	Supposed Age	Reported Residence, Jan. 1, 1940. Street and Number.
	G	Wier Alfred M	157	retired	72	here
	H	Baker Carl	158	patternmaker	68	"
	K	Baker George	158	"	47	"
	L	Baker Maria S †	158	housewife	70	"
	M	Larsen Ethel †	163	secretary	24	"
	N*	Larsen Kristian	163	painter	53	"
	O	Larsen Lloyd	163	"	27	"
	P*	Larsen Petra †	163	housewife	53	"
	R	Davis George P	165	painter	41	"
	S	Davis Katherine C †	165	housewife	40	"
	T	Gately Bessie †	165	housekeeper	32	"
	U	Smith James F	166	mechanic	55	"
	V	Smith Mary A †	166	housewife	53	"
	W	Smith Virginia M †	166	stenographer	20	"
	X	Noyes Edward	170	gardener	70	"
	Y	Towner David J	170	electrician	42	"
	Z	Towner Helen E †	170	inspector	41	"
621						
	A	Towner Helena J †	170	stenographer	20	"
	B	Benson Hannah †	171	housekeeper	67	Connecticut
	C	Carlson Christina †	171	housewife	64	here
	D	Ohlin Agnes †	171	housekeeper	69	"
	E	Bangs Edith L †	174	secretary	42	"
	F	Bangs Louisa G †	174	housewife	72	"
	G	Bangs Revere W	174	foreman	46	"
	H	Sheridan Charlotte M †	178	housewife	52	"
	K	Sheridan Rita M †	178	secretary	20	"
	L	Harke Belle †	184	housewife	32	"
	M	Harke Harry A	184	butcher	39	"

Hebron Street

Page	Letter	Full Name	Residence, Jan. 1, 1941	Occupation	Supposed Age	Reported Residence, Jan. 1, 1940. Street and Number.
	N*	Carlson Emilie †	198	at home	69	here
	O*	Holm Einar	198	painter	48	"
	P*	Holm Judith †	198	housewife	42	"
	R	Larson John A	202	engineer	64	"
	S	Larson Signe E †	202	housewife	60	"
	T	Filip Alice G †	249	at home	26	"
	U	Filip Anthony	249	manager	52	"
	V	Filip Chester K	249	foreman	27	"
	W	Filip Sophie †	249	housewife	50	"

Page	Letter	Full Name	Residence, Jan. 1, 1941	Occupation	Supposed Age	Reported Residence, Jan. 1, 1940. Street and Number

Hebron Street—Continued

Page	Letter	Full Name	Residence, Jan. 1, 1941	Occupation	Supposed Age	Reported Residence, Jan. 1, 1940. Street and Number
	X	*DiSciullo Annie †	261	housewife	37	here
	Y	DiSciullo John	261	cook	48	"
	Z	Castracane Ida †	261	examiner	20	"
622						
	A	*DeSciullo Domenica †	261	housewife	42	"
	B	DiSciullo Silvio	261	cook	40	"

Kennebec Street

Page	Letter	Full Name	Residence, Jan. 1, 1941	Occupation	Supposed Age	Reported Residence, Jan. 1, 1940. Street and Number
	C	Paciotti Nazzareno	220	mason	44	here
	D	*Romaniuk Julia †	224	housewife	48	"
	E	Romaniuk Teresa †	224	waitress	21	"
	F	Romaniuk William	224	cleaner	48	"
	G	Taylor Sadie †	225	housewife	32	"
	H	Taylor Timothy	225	chauffeur	36	"
	K	*Kosticki Agnes †	225	maid	44	"
	L	Kosticki George	225	bartender	46	"
	M	Holmes Elsie E †	226	housewife	25	196 Austin
	N	Holmes Gustav S	226	mechanic	33	196 "
	O	Gettings Delia C †	226	housewife	38	here
	P	Gettings John P	226	gardener	42	"
	R	McCarthy Charles H	234	buffer	20	"
	S	McCarthy Joseph F	234	assembler	24	"
	T	McCarthy Joseph J	234	painter	54	"
	U	McCarthy Margaret †	234	at home	21	"
	V	McCarthy Margaret T †	234	housewife	49	"
	X	Mercer Arrietta V †	rear 242	"	27	222 Westville
	Y	Mercer Earl C	" 242	machinist	29	222 "
	Z	Wilezewski John F	244	clerk	24	here
623						
	A	*Wilezewski Julia †	244	housewife	54	"
	B	Wilezewski Stella C †	244	operator	33	"
	C	Wilezewski Stephen	244	adjuster	30	"
	D	Wilezewski Walter	244	cabinetmaker	64	"
	E	Wilezewski Walter, jr	244	installer	32	"
	F	Baker Bertha †	244	at home	52	"
	G	Coolbrith George J	244	chauffeur	34	"
	H	Coolbrith Olive †	244	housewife	34	"
	K	Anderson John A	245	cashier	34	"
	L	*Tukis Annie W †	245	housewife	67	"
	M	Tukis Blanche M †	245	at home	29	"

Page	Letter	Full Name	Residence, Jan. 1, 1941.	Occupation.	Supposed Age.	Reported Residence, Jan. 1, 1940. Street and Number.

Kennebec Street—Continued

Page	Letter	Full Name	Residence, Jan. 1, 1941.	Occupation.	Supposed Age.	Reported Residence, Jan. 1, 1940. Street and Number.
	N	Tukis Leopold B	245	cashier	37	here
	O	Yarrow Alphonse G	245	clerk	28	Wash D C
	P	Healy John F	245	salesman	31	15 Malta
	R	Healy Mary C †	245	clerk	26	15 "
	S	Callahan Helen †	247	housewife	29	186 Wood av
	T	Callahan Joseph	247	draftsman	35	186 "
	U	*Villani Carmilla †	247	housekeeper	77	here
	V	Villani John	247	mechanic	39	"
	W	Nocero Anthony	247	laborer	42	"
	X	Nocero Mary †	247	dressmaker	35	"
	Y	*Duggan Catherine †	255	housewife	30	"
	Z	*Duggan James	255	engineer	38	"
624						
	A	Thompson Amelia A †	259	stenographer	26	"
	B	Thompson George	259	carpenter	58	"
	C	Thompson Janet K †	259	at home	31	"
	D	Thompson Jessie O †	259	housewife	59	"
	E	Colcord Phyllis P †	274	at home	20	11 Delnore pl
	F	Hooper Herbert W	274	salesman	49	11 "
	G	Hooper Mildred †	274	housewife	40	11 "
	H	Carrabes Ida †	275	"	53	here
	K	Carrabes Rocco	275	laborer	64	"
	L	Carrabes Mary †	275	housewife	24	"
	M	Carrabes Michael	275	carpenter	34	"

Mariposa Street

Page	Letter	Full Name	Residence, Jan. 1, 1941.	Occupation.	Supposed Age.	Reported Residence, Jan. 1, 1940. Street and Number.
	N	O'Brien Bernard L	16	steamfitter	21	here
	O	O'Brien Francis P	16	plumber	20	"
	P	O'Brien James A	16	mechanic	22	"
	R	O'Brien Nora A †	16	housewife	53	"
	S	Lamb Ellen M †	19	"	41	"
	T	Lamb Frederick D	19	salesman	42	"
	U	Belyea John H	20–22	laborer	27	"
	V	Belyea Rose M †	20–22	housewife	24	"
	W	O'Brien Anna G †	20–22	secretary	26	19 Grant pl
	X	O'Brien Clifford T	20–22	chauffeur	24	19 "
	Y	O'Brien Elizabeth M †	20–22	housewife	50	19 "
	Z	O'Brien Joseph J	20–22	mechanic	22	19 "
625						
	A	O'Brien Joseph M	20–22	caretaker	52	19 "

Page	Letter	Full Name	Residence, April 1, 1924	Occupation	Supposed Age	Reported Residence, April 1, 1923. Street and Number

Mariposa Street Continued

Page	Letter	Full Name	Residence	Occupation	Age	Reported Residence
	B	Berestecki Andrew	31	porter	55	here
	C	Berestecki Caroline †	31	housewife	33	"
	D	Berestecki Katherine †	31	"	50	"
	E	Berestecki Teofil	31	cleaner	40	"
	F	Berestecki Nicholas	33	cook	41	"
	G	*Berestecki Sally †	33	counter girl	35	"
	H	*Grabowic Anna †	33	housekeeper	62	"
	K	Geoghegan Alice L †	33	housewife	27	"
	L	Geoghegan Thomas P	33	inspector	27	"
	M	Civalina Francis	34	milkman	31	58 Sefton
	N	Civalina Lottie †	34	housewife	32	58 "
	O	Domurat Blanche †	34	dressmaker	30	here
	P	*Domurat Rose †	34	housewife	60	"
	R	Domurat Stanley	34	papercutter	25	"
	S	*Domurat Wojciech	34	"	62	"
	T	Johnson Emily †	36	housewife	29	"
	U	Johnson Eric	36	electrician	30	"
	V	Rodin Edwin A	36	machinist	81	"
	W	Rodin Emilia †	36	housewife	76	"
	X	Rodin Ralph E	36	salesman	50	"
	Y	Moriarty Isabelle †	38	housewife	30	3 Huckins
	Z	*Moriarty Joseph	38	floorlayer	32	3 "
626						
	A	Dabrowski Caroline †	38	housewife	59	here
	B	Dabrowski Michael	38	bricklayer	63	"
	C	Gurlan Frank	40	chauffeur	52	"
	D	Gurlan Helen R †	40	housewife	48	"
	E	Sayce Catherine F †	42	"	25	64 Weybosset
	F	Sayce John W	42	salesman	26	64 "
	G	*Yarushites Petronella †	42	housekeeper	59	here
	H	Kukuruza Henry	46	electrician	27	"
	K	Kukuruza Michael	46	chauffeur	29	"
	L	Kukuruza Robert	46	U S A	22	"
	M	Milch Alwin K	62	teacher	37	"
	N	Milch Eleanor A †	62	housewife	37	"
	O	Redden Ellen L †	66	stenographer	28	"
	P	Redden Gladys M †	66	"	30	"
	R	Redden Grant A	66	glazier	56	"
	S	Redden Katherine M †	66	housewife	58	"
	T	Hesselbarth Catherine †	83 85	clerk	23	"
	U	Hesselbarth Paul	83 85	cook	28	"

Page	Letter	Full Name	Residence Jan. 1 1941	Occupation	Supposed Age	Reported Residence, Jan. 1, 1940. Street and Number.
		Mariposa Street—Continued				
	V	Darrigo Gaetano	83 85	boilermaker	52	here
	W	Darrigo Joseph J	83 85	machinist	23	"
	X	Darrigo Mary A †	83 85	housewife	26	"
	Y	Boratti Paul	88	laborer	62	"
	Z	Boratti Teresa †	88	housewife	60	"
627						
	A	*Pozzi Aida †	88	"	57	"
	B	Pozzi Mary †	88	typist	23	"
		Oakwood Street				
	C	Muzyka Anna †	8	clerk	22	here
	D	Muzyka Mary †	8	housewife	45	"
	E	Muzyka Peter	8	chef	45	"
	F	Mogan Katherine A †	10	operator	51	"
	G	Krawczuk Anna †	11	housewife	54	"
	H	Morawski Winnie C †	11	teacher	26	"
	K	Jaeger Elizabeth B †	20	housekeeper	71	"
	L	Russell Pauline E †	20	"	36	"
	M	Donlan Catherine A †	32	housewife	46	"
	N	Donlan William H	32	painter	46	"
	O	Thomson Bessie M †	42	housewife	30	90 Florence St East
	P	Thomson George	42	teacher	33	90 "
	R	Nilsen Abel	46	carpenter	41	here
	S	Nilsen Dorothy †	46	operator	20	"
	T	Nilsen Sophie †	46	housewife	42	"
		Orchard Street				
	U	Thompson Andrew T	26	carpenter	37	here
	V	Thompson Margaret R †	26	housewife	37	"
	W	Petelle Dorothy V †	27	"	21	27 Delnore pl
	X	Petelle Ernest J	27	chauffeur	23	Worcester
	Y	Thompson Kittel A	30	carpenter	44	here
	Z	Thompson Sigrid K †	30	housewife	34	"
628						
	A	Andersen Andrew E	31	patternmaker	20	"
	B	Andersen Esther C †	31	clerk	22	"
	C	Andersen Jennie H †	31	housewife	44	"
	D	Andersen Knute E	31	painter	46	"

Page	Letter	Full Name	Residence, Jan. 1, 1941	Occupation	Supposed Age	Reported Residence, Jan. 1, 1940. Street and Number
		Parker Street				
	E	Krumin Flora — †	7	housewife	21	132 Wood av
	F	Krumin Harold	7	bookbinder	25	88 Annafran
	G	*Brink Jennie — †	7	housewife	52	here
	H	*Brink Mary — †	7	housekeeper	75	"
	K	*Brink Mitchell	7	stitcher	55	"
	L	Leavey Emily G — †	14	housewife	29	"
	M	Leavey Walter J	14	brakeman	29	"
	N	*Burdulis Rose A — †	14	housewife	47	"
	O	Burdulis William	14	machinist	49	"
	P	Williams Charles F	14	clerk	20	"
	R	Shaw Joseph	18	carpenter	55	136 Dana av
	S	*Dorofi Margaret — †	20	housewife	42	here
	T	Dorofi William	20	baker	44	"
	U	Muzyka Michael	20	machinist	23	8 Oakwood
		Pinewood Street				
	V	Amos George	18-20	mechanic	28	Westwood
	W	Amos Helen — †	18-20	housewife	25	"
	X	Drohan Emma M — †	18-20	housekeeper	68	here
	Y	Samuels Marguerite E — †	18-20	housewife	35	"
	Z	Samuels Milton J	18-20	electrician	36	"
629		**Pleasantview Street**				
	A	Flynn Chester W	26	baker	23	here
	B	Iverson Mary A — †	26	housewife	41	"
	C	Iverson Thomas S	26	chauffeur	41	"
	D	*Karpowich Sophia — †	26	at home	66	"
	E	Armata Baldassare	36	mason	60	"
	F	Armata Leonis	36	chauffeur	29	"
	G	*Armata Mary — †	36	housewife	60	"
	H	*Armata Annie — †	38	"	54	"
	K	Armata Bertha A — †	38	"	21	"
	L	Armata Giacomo	38	laborer	58	"
	M	Armata Louis	38	"	23	"
	N	McCaffrey Ann K — †	52	clerk	20	"
	O	McCaffrey Annie C — †	52	housewife	64	"
	P	McCaffrey Forrest B	52	reporter	24	"
	R	McCaffrey William J	52	retired	67	"
	S	McCaffrey William J, jr	52	laborer	21	"

Page	Letter	Full Name	Residence, Jan. 1, 1941.	Occupation	Supposed Age.	Reported Residence, Jan. 1, 1940. Street and Number.

Pleasantview Street—Continued

Page	Letter	Full Name	Residence, Jan. 1, 1941.	Occupation	Supposed Age.	Reported Residence, Jan. 1, 1940. Street and Number.
	T	Addesa Irene †	80	housewife	23	here
	U	Addesa Michael	80	boilermaker	24	"
	V*	Addesa Grace †	80	housewife	50	"
	W	Addesa Pasquali	80	laborer	60	"
	X	Grande James	86	"	30	"
	Y	Grande Virginia †	86	housewife	30	"
	Z*	Raffeale Christine †	86	"	60	"
630						
	A*	Raffeale Joseph	86	laborer	69	"
	B	Taromino James	86	"	30	"
	C	Taromino Philomena †	86	housewife	27	"

Radcliffe Road

Page	Letter	Full Name	Residence, Jan. 1, 1941.	Occupation	Supposed Age.	Reported Residence, Jan. 1, 1940. Street and Number.
	D	Lynch Margaret T †	10–12	housewife	64	951 Hyde Park av
	E	Lynch Mark L	10–12	retired	62	951 "
	F	Lynch Mary M †	10–12	stenographer	27	951 "
	G*	McCary Mary A †	10–12	at home	64	951 "
	H	Doherty Bridget M †	10–12	housewife	58	here
	K	Doherty Daniel J	10–12	U S A	24	"
	L	Doherty Frank H	10–12	laborer	23	"
	M	Doherty John F	10–12	engineer	54	"
	N	Doherty Margaret M †	10–12	secretary	31	"
	O	Doherty Rita E †	10–12	waitress	21	"
	P	Canon Charles H	11	letter carrier	44	"
	R	Canon Katherine D †	11	housewife	42	"
	S	Canon L Grace †	11	"	61	"
	T	Wolski Michael B	16	machinist	53	"
	U	Wolski Stella †	16	at home	28	"
	W	McCormick George	19	waiter	39	"
	X	McCormick John	19	cutter	37	"
	Y	Sullivan Mae A †	19	sealer	42	"
	Z	Buntin Anne C †	21	housewife	53	"
631						
	A	Buntin Margaret L †	21	secretary	26	"
	B	Buntin Wallace A	21	buffer	52	"
	C	Lang Francis J	25	merchant	33	"
	D	Lang Mary E †	25	housewife	33	"
	E	Browne Alice M †	27	stenographer	22	"
	F	Browne Frank E	27	clerk	52	"
	G	Browne Mary C †	27	housewife	52	"

Page	Letter	Full Name	Residence, Jan. 1, 1941	Occupation	Supposed Age	Reported Residence, Jan. 1, 1940. Street and Number

Radcliffe Road—Continued

Page	Letter	Full Name	Residence	Occupation	Age	Reported Residence
	H	Browne Paul G	27	clerk	21	here
	K	McNeil Arthur R	28	plumber	31	694 River
	L	McNeil Edna M †	28	housewife	31	694 "
	M	Matheson Anna M †	28	"	42	Milton
	N	Matheson Francis H	28	clerk	20	"
	O	Matheson William F	28	chauffeur	43	"
	P	Browne Alice G †	29 29A	housewife	25	27 Radcliffe rd
	R	Browne Frank X	29 29A	shoecutter	25	27 "
	S	Lynch Gertrude V †	29 29A	housewife	35	here
	T	Lynch William F	29 29A	gasfitter	35	"
	U	Sutcliffe Ellen †	31	housewife	55	"
	V	Sutcliffe John A	31	machinist	58	"
	W	Sutcliffe John H	31	"	21	"
	X	Larsen Aagot O †	35	housewife	47	"
	Y	Larsen Arthur	35	electrician	47	"
	Z	Larsen Harry A	35	draftsman	22	"
632						
	A	Davies Esther R †	47	clerk	21	"
	B	Davies Jessie C †	47	housewife	48	"
	C	Davies Thomas	47	foreman	52	"
	D	McAdam Mary M †	47	clerk	39	10 Park
	E	McAdam Stephen A	47	operator	32	10 "
	F	Fenton Charles F	65	salesman	42	here
	G	Fenton Gertrude A †	65	housewife	41	"
	H	Martin Edward B	101	investigator	32	28 Lockwood
	K	Martin Louise F †	101	housewife	32	28 "
	L	*Kunegett Charles J	105	laborer	50	here
	M	*Lazarowich Lena †	105	housewife	45	"
	N	Lazarowich Mae †	105	stamper	20	"

Ridlon Road

Page	Letter	Full Name	Residence	Occupation	Age	Reported Residence
	O	Hamilton May H †	2	at home	84	here
	P	Holdridge Jessie I †	2	housewife	53	"
	R	Holdridge Warren E	2	contractor	51	"
	S	Rau Albert	6	baker	26	"
	T	Rau Edna †	6	clerk	24	"
	U	Rau Elsie †	6	"	35	"
	V	Rau Jacob	6	baker	63	"
	W	White John	12	carpenter	34	"
	X	White Marion †	12	housewife	36	"

Page	Letter	Full Name	Residence, Jan. 1, 1941	Occupation	Supposed Age	Reported Residence, Jan. 1, 1940. Street and Number.

Ridlon Road—Continued

Page	Letter	Full Name	Residence, Jan. 1, 1941	Occupation	Supposed Age	Reported Residence, Jan. 1, 1940. Street and Number.
	Y	Dolan Alice V—†	12	saleswoman	42	here
	Z	Philbrick Ann E—†	12	housewife	39	"
633						
	A	Philbrick William A	12	policeman	40	"
	B	McIver Frances A—†	15	factoryhand	23	Dedham
	C	McIver Garvin R	15	tinsmith	20	here
	D	McIver Ruth E—†	15	housewife	46	"
	E	McIver Samuel J	15	clerk	56	"
	F	McIver Samuel J	15	"	22	"
	G	Warren Corey G	16	welder	48	615 River
	H	Warren Gertrude E—†	16	housewife	46	615 "
	K	Warren Marion G—†	16	clerk	21	615 "
	L	Weissent Frederick N	18	salesman	53	here
	M	Weissent Frederick W	18	student	25	"
	N	Weissent Helen E—†	18	stenographer	22	"
	O	Weissent Sarah—†	18	housewife	51	"
	P	Aznive Anna L—†	21	"	45	"
	R	Aznive John R	21	inspector	48	"
	S	Nicholson Ellsworth A	21	seaman	23	"
	T	Tosi Adelmo	21	machinist	26	"
	U	Tosi Georgianna—†	21	housewife	20	"
	V	Olsen Olaf G	22	machinist	41	"
	W	Olsen Ruth—†	22	housewife	42	"
	X	Creighton Charles R	26–28	manager	33	76 Claybourne
	Y	Creighton Hope R—†	26–28	housewife	32	76 "
	Z	Rooney Frances F—†	26–28	clerk	21	here
634						
	A	Rooney Frederick W	26–28	chauffeur	26	"
	B	Rooney Margaret V—†	26–28	housewife	60	"
	C	Hayes Edith—†	30	housekeeper	48	"
	D	Finch James H	31	metalworker	78	"
	E	Grant Anna R—†	32	stenographer	24	"
	F	Grant Charles A	32	optometrist	64	"
	G*	Grant Mary H—†	32	housewife	55	"
	H	Tapley Doris M—†	32	stenographer	26	"
	K*	Bulger Catherine—†	32A	cashier	34	"
	L	Malone John L	32A	salesman	31	"
	M*	Malone Mary I—†	32A	housewife	34	"
	N	Griffin Joseph A	34	agent	44	"
	O	Griffin Lillian—†	34	housewife	43	"
	P	Hyde Helen J—†	34	"	54	"

Page	Letter	Full Name	Residence, Jan. 1, 1940	1941	Occupation	Age	Reported Residence, Jan. 1, 1940. Street and Number

Ridlon Road—Continued

Page	Letter	Full Name			Occupation	Age	Reported Residence
	R	Legendre Alma L †		37	stenographer	20	here
	S	Legendre Anna M †		37	housewife	50	"
	T	Legendre Paul N		37	painter	61	"
	U	Legendre William L		37	factoryhand	22	"
	V	Bulger Genevieve E †		38	stenographer	22	"
	W	Bulger Jennie I †		38	housewife	60	"
	X	Bulger Patrick J		38	printer	63	"
	Y	Pedersen Rebecca B †		41	housewife	43	"
	Z	*Petersen Clara K †		41	"	64	"
635							
	A	Petersen Ole K		41	mehainist	65	"
	B	Abbott Albert L		42	student	22	"
	C	Gertsen George L		42	seaman	21	"
	D	Gertsen Gerda A †		42	housewife	61	"
	E	Gertsen John D		42	seaman	27	"
	F	Gertsen Susanne †		42	housewife	28	"
	G	Kelly Ann C †		50	clerk	20	"
	H	Kelly Ellen E †		50	housewife	52	"
	K	Kelly John J		50	guard	51	"
	L	Sloan Adeline M †	52	54	housewife	39	"
	M	Sloan John A	52	54	policeman	38	"
	N	Carroll Catherine R †	52	54	housewife	39	"
	O	Carroll Mary †	52	54	at home	80	"
	P	Carroll William E	52	54	chauffeur	46	"
	R	*Bliznuk Konditt		55	meatcutter	54	"
	S	*Bliznuk Mary †		55	housewife	58	"
	T	Casilli Mary †		55	clerk	24	69 Pierce
	U	Casilli Richard		55	seaman	29	[illegible]
	V	McCann Lucille E †		55	housewife	33	here
	W	McCann Paul L		55	salesman	33	"
	X	Balicki Anna †		58	waitress	26	"
	Y	Balicki Anthony		58	watertender	50	"
	Z	Balicki Lillian †		58	factoryhand	20	"
636							
	A	Balicki Michael		58	machinist	22	"
	B	*Balicki Paska †		58	housewife	47	"
	C	*Eschuk Mary †		60	"	50	"
	D	*Eschuk Michael		60	presser	52	"
	E	Eschuk Pauline †		60	nurse	24	Worcester
	F	Eschuk Philip		60	factoryhand	21	here
	G	Thompson John H		60	salesman	33	"

Page	Letter	Full Name	Residence, Jan. 1, 1941.	Occupation.	Supposed Age.	Reported Residence, Jan. 1, 1940. Street and Number.

Ridlon Road—Continued

Page	Letter	Full Name	Residence, Jan. 1, 1941.	Occupation.	Supposed Age.	Reported Residence, Jan. 1, 1940. Street and Number.
	H	Thompson Madeline A †	60	housewife	31	here
	K	Barthel Charlotte A †	60	"	46	"
	L	Barthel John F	60	policeman	47	"
	M	Sheehan Jeremiah	60	clerk	44	"
	O	Richard Anna M †	64	housewife	57	"
	P	Richard James F	64	weigher	59	"
	R	Richard Joseph F	64	longshoreman	21	"

River Street

Page	Letter	Full Name	Residence, Jan. 1, 1941.	Occupation.	Supposed Age.	Reported Residence, Jan. 1, 1940. Street and Number.
	S	*McGuiness Adelaide M †	823	housewife	30	here
	T	McGuiness Albert J	823	chauffeur	35	"
	U	Sullivan John F	823	painter	49	"
	V	Sullivan Madeline F †	823	housewife	40	"
	W	Bean Cecil R	827	mechanic	43	"
	X	Bean Herman A	827	machinist	69	"
	Y	Grigsby Lillian T †	827	housewife	41	"
	Z	Schwartz Mildred B †	837	"	22	38 Hosmer
637						
	A	Schwartz Robert	837	physician	24	New York
	B	Perkins Edward A	837	engineer	46	155 Florence
	C	Perkins Eleanor E †	837	secretary	20	155 "
	D	Perkins Mae V †	837	housewife	42	155 "
	E	Rosenberg Lillian B †	841	"	38	here
	F	Rosenberg Louis H	841	electrician	48	"
	G	Brennan Helen L †	841	housewife	26	11 Minden
	H	Brennan Paul J	841	furrier	29	11 "
	L	English Barbara A †	845	waitress	23	63 Westminster
	M	English Frank V, jr	845	shipper	26	63 "
	N	Lawrence Sarah W †	845	secretary	22	63 "
	O	Koza John S	845	salesman	29	here
	P	Koza Mary C †	845	housewife	28	"
	R	Chaharyn Katie †	845	cook	22	Dedham
	S	Chaharyn William	845	machinist	23	14 City Point ct
	T	Germano Carmilo	847	barber	49	here

Roanoke Road

Page	Letter	Full Name	Residence, Jan. 1, 1941.	Occupation.	Supposed Age.	Reported Residence, Jan. 1, 1940. Street and Number.
	[illegible]	Wilson Alice P †	67	stenographer	28	here
	[illegible]	Wilson Elizabeth F †	67	nurse	32	"

Page	Letter	Full Name	Residence, Jan. 1, 1944	Occupation	Reputed Age	Reported Residence, Jan. 1, 1943. Street and Number

Roanoke Road Continued

Page	Letter	Full Name	Residence, Jan. 1, 1944	Occupation	Reputed Age	Reported Residence, Jan. 1, 1943. Street and Number
	Z	Wilson George	67	electrician	60	here
638						
	A	Wilson Mary J †	67	housewife	60	"

Rock Road

Page	Letter	Full Name	Residence, Jan. 1, 1944	Occupation	Reputed Age	Reported Residence, Jan. 1, 1943. Street and Number
	B	Lamb Anna M †	2	saleswoman	57	here
	C	Lamb Harriett O †	2	clerk	52	"
	D	Dyke Evelyn G †	3	housewife	47	"
	E	Dyle John P	3	supervisor	47	"
	F	James Eben	3	retired	79	"
	G	Hook Elizabeth †	6	housekeeper	72	"
	H	Spencer Allen P	6	laborer	44	"
	K	Spencer Edna G †	6	housewife	48	"
	L	McRae Irene C †	6	"	40	37 Rosewood
	M	McRae Joseph W	6	retired	42	37 "
	N	Feeney Catherine A †	7	laundress	22	101 Decatur
	O	Feeney James F	7	printer	21	101 "
	P	Feeney Katherine †	7	housewife	54	101 "
	R	Feeney William G	7	engineer	63	101 "
	S	Feeney William G, jr	7	laborer	24	101 "
	T	Byrnes Christine G †	10	housekeeper	37	here
	U	Byrnes Mary E †	10	housewife	40	[illegible]
	V	Byrnes Walter T	10	superintendent	36	here
	W	Gifford Alice M †	11	housekeeper	66	"
	X	Wachtler George C	11	manager	69	"

Rosebery Road

Page	Letter	Full Name	Residence, Jan. 1, 1944	Occupation	Reputed Age	Reported Residence, Jan. 1, 1943. Street and Number
	Y	Webster Edna E †	7	housewife	51	Milton
	Z	Webster Russell E	7	welder	25	"
639						
	A	MacNeill Anna †	7	nurse	25	Vermont
	B	MacNeill Donald	7	baker	25	"
	C	Westhaver Alice V †	7	housekeeper	58	here
	D	Andersen Adolf	15	carpenter	51	"
	E	Andersen Marie †	15	housewife	53	"
	F	Andersen Reidar F	15	student	21	"
	G	*Olson Josephine †	15	at home	82	"
	H	Blackwell James	33	retired	60	"

Page	Letter	Full Name	Residence, Jan. 1, 1941	Occupation	Supposed Age	Reported Residence, Jan. 1, 1940. Street and Number.
		Rosebery Road Continued				
	K	Blackwell Jeannette †	33	housewife	60	here
	L	Thompson Ida †	33	maid	64	"
	M	Fehrm Hugo B	33	patternmaker	58	"
	N	Fehrm Marion W †	33	housewife	38	"
		Rugby Road				
	O	Duggan Helen E †	25	housekeeper	32	here
	P	Woloschuk Elias	25	foreman	48	"
	R	Woloschuk Mary †	25	housewife	45	"
	S	Woloschuk Sophie †	25	clerk	23	"
	T	Woloschuk Walter	25	student	22	"
	U	Bailey Annie T †	29	housewife	53	"
	V	Bailey Joseph L	29	engraver	54	"
	W	Early Nellie E †	29	clerk	49	"
	X	Nolan Ruth E †	31	housewife	28	46 Rugby rd
	Y	Nolan Valentine B, jr	31	letter carrier	31	46 "
	Z	Adams Agnes M †	31	housewife	51	6 Biltmore
640						
	A	Adams Fred W	31	machinist	60	6 "
	B	Adams Hazel B †	31	clerk	22	6 "
		Ruskindale Road				
	C	*Carroll Daniel	27	retired	80	here
	D	Conley Catherine †	27	housekeeper	77	"
	E	Conley Edward L	27	engraver	31	"
	F	Conley Elizabeth F †	27	housewife	27	8 Marine rd
	G	Conley Frank M	27	fireman	50	here
	H	Conley Joseph A	27	retired	44	8 Marine rd
	K	Conley Anna E †	31	housewife	40	here
	L	Conley James B	31	repairman	46	"
	M	Becherer Frederick J	35	policeman	45	"
	N	Becherer Frederick R	35	student	20	"
	O	Becherer Mabel L †	35	housewife	40	"
	P	Helmsdorff Marthea †	43	housekeeper	67	"
	R	Nielsen Ernest T	43	painter	30	"
	S	Nielsen Esther M †	43	housewife	28	"
		Edwards Esther R †	43	"	43	"
		Edwards Harold G	43	foreman	44	"
		Halatyn Alexander	44	repairman	29	"

Ruskindale Road (Continued)

Page	Letter	Full Name	Residence, Jan. 1, [illegible]	Occupation	Age	Reported Residence, Jan. 1, [illegible]. Street and Number
	W	Halatyn Demiter	44	repairman	51	here
	X	Halatyn Tinia †	44	housewife	51	"
	Z	Nychay Anna H †	56	"	44	"
641						
	A	Nychay Joseph	56	carpenter	47	"
	B	Nychay Olga I †	56	saleswoman	21	"
	C	*Nychay Barbara †	64	housewife	46	"
	D	Nychay Maurice M	64	machinist	22	"
	E	Nychay Michael	64	cleaner	52	"
	F	*Bodnar Anna †	68	housewife	49	"
	G	Bodnar Walter	68	mechanic	22	"
	H	Parelius Eva I †	72	housewife	44	19 Pevear pl
	K	Parelius Robert L	72	machinist	57	19 "
	L	Edwards Elizabeth J †	91	housewife	55	here
	M	Edwards Herbert H	91	retired	65	"
	N	Albion Hulda K †	103	housewife	50	"
	O	Albion Stanley	103	machinist	23	"
	P	Albion Thure A	103	painter	50	"
	R	*Stewart Florence †	104	housewife	76	"
	S	Stewart Pearl L †	104	"	40	"
	T	Stewart Silas C	104	inspector	41	"
	U	Gallant Charles A	111	policeman	42	"
	V	Gallant Svea N †	111	housewife	42	"
	W	Fields Anne F †	112	secretary	47	"
	X	Hanscom Albert	112	broker	55	"
	Y	Hanscom Mabelle F †	112	housewife	55	"
	Z	*Balchunas Mary †	116	housekeeper	57	"
642						
	A	Bareikis Anna †	116	housewife	38	"
	B	Bareikis James Z	116	grocer	50	"
	C	McGonagle Agnes M †	119	presser	25	"
	D	McGonagle Evelyn G †	119	stenographer	30	"
	E	McGonagle Michael J	119	fireman	53	"
	F	Christiansen Arthur E	120	repairman	27	"
	G	Christiansen Carl H	120	carpenter	63	"
	H	Christiansen Clarence W	120	instructor	28	"
	K	Christiansen Ellen M †	120	secretary	29	"
	L	Christiansen Kiai A †	120	housewife	56	"
	M	Jacobson Edwina W †	127	"	57	"
	N	Jacobson Frederick	127	tailor	57	"
	O	Whiton Eleanor I †	127	housewife	31	"

Page	Letter	Full Name	Residence, Jan. 1, 1941.	Occupation	Supposed Age.	Reported Residence, Jan. 1, 1940. Street and Number.

Ruskindale Road—Continued

	P	Whiton Robert H	127	chauffeur	34	here
	R	Andrews Alice M †	140	housewife	42	"
	S	Andrews George H	140	paperhanger	42	"
	T	Lyon Harriett L †	140	saleswoman	44	"
	U	Maines Eleanor W †	145	housewife	59	"
	V	Maines James R	145	retired	72	"

Ruxton Road

	Y	McDermott Eugene F	6	machinist	34	here
	Z	McDermott Mary M †	6	housewife	30	"
643						
	A	Holland Alfred C	6	manager	38	224 Almont
	B	Holland Alice M †	6	housewife	36	224 "
	C	Matheson Elizabeth †	10	"	63	here
	D	Matheson John	10	operator	60	"
	E	Rowley Jane M †	10	clerk	38	"
	F	McCarthy Annie †	22	housewife	72	"
	G	McCarthy Edward	22	retired	73	"

Sefton Street

	H	Hooton Ethel M †	58	saleswoman	23	38 Mariposa
	K	Hooton Warren F	58	machinist	24	38 "
	L	Miglin Carl A	58	conductor	48	here
	M	Miglin Julia H †	58	housewife	44	"
	N	Arsenault Beatrice V †	63	operator	24	"
	O	Arsenault Edward	63	shipper	27	"
	P	Howland Betty †	63	waitress	22	"
	R	Haugh John	63	machinist	47	"
	S	Haugh Ruth O †	63	housewife	45	"

Seminole Street

	T	Akermark Anna S †	12	housewife	63	here
	U	Akermark Harry S	12	painter	59	"
	V	Wisniewski Stanley	17	chauffeur	29	"
	W	Wisniewski Wanda M †	17	housewife	30	"
	X	Marek Frances †	17	"	49	"
	Y	Marek Helen H †	17	operator	23	"
	Z	Marek Thomas A	17	cabinetmaker	55	"

Page	Letter	Full Name	Residence, Jan. 1, 1941	Occupation	Reported Age	Reported Residence, Jan. 1, 1940. Street and Number
644						

Seminole Street—Continued

Page	Letter	Full Name	Residence, Jan. 1, 1941	Occupation	Reported Age	Reported Residence, Jan. 1, 1940. Street and Number
644	A	Akermark Alice M †	20	secretary	22	here
	B	Akermark Marie E †	20	housewife	54	"
	C	Akermark Thorsten	20	painter	54	"
	D	Sunde Marie †	29	housewife	25	4373 Wash'n
	E	Sunde Torger	29	operator	27	4373 "
	F	Tsetsi Effie †	31	housewife	25	Southbridge
	G	*Tsetsi Heraklis	31	proprietor	48	181 Ruskindale rd
	H	Ryder David C	42	chauffeur	33	here
	K	Ryder Dorothy M †	42	housewife	32	"
	L	Frangioso Benjamin	42	chauffeur	28	32 Mildred av
	M	Frangioso Frances †	42	housewife	25	32 "
	N	*Goscinak Anna †	46	"	46	40 Etonia
	O	Goscinak Henry	46	welder	22	40 "
	P	Goscinak Joseph	46	operator	53	40 "
	R	Anderson Ebba A †	50	dressmaker	60	here
	S	Magnuson Axel B	50	retired	71	"
	T	*Magnuson Ruth S †	50	housewife	64	"
	U	*Careano Charles	54	retired	72	"
	V	Careano Clara †	54	housewife	60	"
	W	Careano Louis A	54	bricklayer	35	"
	X	Crowley Sarah E †	62	housewife	40	"
	Y	Crowley William F	62	policeman	44	"
	Z	Esposito Angelo	72	painter	20	"
645	A	Esposito Elizabeth †	72	housekeeper	22	"
	B	*Esposito Phyllis †	72	housewife	44	"
	C	Esposito Rocco	72	cook	50	"
	D	Carlin Anna F †	76	housewife	33	"
	E	Carlin John F	76	splicer	34	"
	F	Pond Anna G †	76	housewife	65	"
	G	Noll Heinrich	78	retired	73	"
	H	Noll Henrietta L †	78	housewife	77	"

Tampa Street

Page	Letter	Full Name	Residence, Jan. 1, 1941	Occupation	Reported Age	Reported Residence, Jan. 1, 1940. Street and Number
645	K	DeLuca Anthony V	10	letter carrier	37	31 Seminole
	L	DeLuca Margaret M †	10	housewife	31	31 "
	M	Mello Beatrice N †	10	"	36	here
	N	Mello John E	10	fireman	40	"
	O	*Amico Angeline †	11	housewife	53	"

Page	Letter	Full Name	Residence, Jan. 1, 1941.	Occupation.	Supposed Age.	Reported Residence, Jan. 1, 1940. Street and Number.

Tampa Street Continued

Page	Letter	Full Name	Residence, Jan. 1, 1941.	Occupation.	Supposed Age.	Reported Residence, Jan. 1, 1940. Street and Number.
	P	Amico Antonio	11	laborer	57	here
	R	Bobkin Alyce †	15	housewife	22	“
	S	Bobkin John	15	salesman	27	“
	T	Wolochka Jean A †	15	clerk	21	9 Wordsworth
	U	DeAngelis Josephine †	20	housewife	38	here
	V	DeAngelis Nazzareno	20	proprietor	45	“
	W	Healey John F	20	mechanic	41	“
	X	Healey Katherine D †	20	housewife	30	“
	Z	Guzevicus Albert	27	electrician	24	“
	Y	Guzevicus Anna †	27	housewife	43	“
646						
	A	Guzevicus Joseph	27	molder	48	“
	B	Guzevicus Vitautas J	27	clerk	22	“
	C	Damish Charles	41	carpenter	48	“
	D*	Damish Madeline †	41	housewife	45	“
	F	Naczas Michael	54	inspector	51	“
	G*	Naczas Sophie †	54	housewife	52	“
	H	Sopp Henry	54	machinist	33	Norwood
	K	Sopp Nellie †	54	housewife	26	here
	L	Grant Rachel †	57	domestic	55	“
	M	MacDonald George A	57	chauffeur	24	“
	N	MacDonald Margaret J †	57	housewife	24	“
	O*	Naczas Barbara †	58	“	41	“
	P	Naczas Joseph	58	operator	42	“
	R	Naczas William	58	student	20	“
	S	Ford John	59	plumber	69	“
	T	Ford Katherine J †	59	clerk	38	“
	U	Ford Mary C †	59	waitress	28	“
	V	Ford Sarah E †	59	housewife	64	“
	W	Brooks Alice E †	63	“	31	“
	X	Brooks Charles R	63	chauffeur	35	“
	Y	Angeloni Anna †	66	teacher	25	“
	Z	Angeloni Joseph	66	chauffeur	23	“
647						
	A	Angeloni Loretta †	66	housewife	45	“
	B	Angeloni Louis	66	carpenter	27	“
	C	Jones Catherine †	73	housewife	71	“
	D	Jones Richard	73	retired	70	“
	E	McCabe Helena †	73	housewife	35	“
	F	McCabe Joseph A	73	clerk	35	“
	G	Kowalski Agnes †	77	housewife	65	“

Page.	Letter	Full Name	Residence, Jan. 1, 1941	Occupation	Supposed Age	Reported Residence, Jan. 1, 1940. Street and Number

Tampa Street Continued

Page.	Letter	Full Name	Residence, Jan. 1, 1941	Occupation	Supposed Age	Reported Residence, Jan. 1, 1940. Street and Number
	H	Kowalski Frank	77	retired	69	here
	K	Murphy Daniel J	77	manager	33	"
	L	Murphy Helen A †	77	housewife	34	"

Taunton Avenue

Page.	Letter	Full Name	Residence, Jan. 1, 1941	Occupation	Supposed Age	Reported Residence, Jan. 1, 1940. Street and Number
	M	Nielsen Elsie C †	5	housewife	36	here
	N	Nielsen Milton A	5	electrician	36	"
	O	Wheeler Ernest H	6	carpenter	58	"
	P	Wheeler Mabelle E †	6	housewife	50	"
	R	Carey Helen T †	8	packer	24	"
	S	Gillen Dorothy B †	8	"	20	"
	T	Kennelly John F	8	janitor	47	"
	U	Kennelly Nora T †	8	housewife	47	"
	V	Manfra Vera †	10	packer	27	"
	W	Viscione Anthony	10	candymaker	32	"
	X	Viscione Rose S †	10	housewife	29	"
	Y	Weckbacher George F	11	policeman	45	"
	Z	Weckbacher Sarah M †	11	housewife	40	"
648						
	A	Heuser Agnes E †	12	"	39	"
	B	Heuser Arthur E	12	broker	39	"
	C	Heuser Olga A †	12	clerk	45	"
	D	*Holmlin Elsa M †	15	housewife	36	"
	E	*Holmlin Knute I	15	printer	39	"
	F	Torgesen Anna M †	16	housewife	62	"
	G	Torgersen Carl F	16	painter	67	"
	H	Torgersen Carl T	16	"	36	"
	K	Buckley Mildred C †	17	housewife	24	"
	L	Norton Francis C	17	manager	23	"
	M	Norton John F	17	mechanic	51	"
	N	Norton Margaret V †	17	housewife	53	"
	O	Stapleton Annie J †	18	"	67	"
	P	Stapleton Frank F	18	retired	64	"
	R	Stapleton Henry P	18	houseman	68	"
	T	Kullen Arthur A	19	machinist	28	65 Bethel
	U	Kullen Frances K †	19	housewife	29	65 "
	S	Kulberg Annette †	19	housekeeper	66	here
	V	Blakely Dorothy W †	22	stenographer	25	"
	W	Blakely Ellen †	22	housewife	59	"

Taunton Avenue Continued

Page	Letter	Full Name	Residence, Jan. 1, 1941	Occupation	Supposed Age	Reported Residence, Jan. 1, 1940. Street and Number.
	X	Blakely Thomas H	22	foreman	28	here
	Y	Blakely William G	22	retired	71	"
	Z	Atkinson Francis R	23	engineer	47	"
649						
	A	Atkinson Marion U †	23	housewife	47	"
	B	Atkinson Richard	23	retired	83	"
	C	Farren Eleanor P †	24	clerk	22	"
	D	Farren James J	24	letter carrier	24	"
	E	Farren Mary †	24	housewife	58	"
	F	Kelliher Margaret M †	25	"	53	"
	G	Kelliher Michael J	25	fireman	53	"
	H	Donnellan Catherine E †	27	housewife	28	"
	K	Donnellan Paul B	27	foreman	28	"
	L	Sullivan James J	28	chauffeur	44	"
	M	Sullivan Mary T †	28	housewife	40	"
	N	Forsyth Frances S †	30	"	28	"
	O	Forsyth Joseph F	30	manager	34	"
	P	Armata Alice E †	30	housewife	28	"
	R	Armata Vito	30	chauffeur	27	"
	S	Love Susan V †	33	housewife	48	"
	T	Love William R	33	machinist	56	"
	U	Drohan Harold J	38	clerk	31	"
	V	Lynch Marion F †	38	housewife	37	"
	W	Lynch Peter J	38	registrar	43	"
	X	Shorrock Ernest S	40	machinist	24	"
	Y	Shorrock Harry	40	proprietor	60	"
	Z*	Shorrock Lettie †	40	housewife	62	"
650						
	A	Shorrock Louise †	40	saleswoman	33	"
	B*	Magnussen Olaf H	43	painter	53	"
	C*	Magnussen Olga W †	43	housewife	63	"
	D	Bennett Marion S †	45	"	39	"
	E	Bennett Reginald N	45	accountant	45	"
	F	Lockhart Beatrice R †	49	artist	34	"
	G	Lockhart Celeste A †	49	housewife	62	"
	H	Lockhart Clinton D	49	carpenter	60	"
	K	MacPherson Dorothy S †	52	clerk	29	"
	L	MacPherson Kathryn M †	52	stenographer	33	"
	M	MacPherson Malcolm A	52	carpenter	65	"
	N	O'Neil James D	56	plumber	50	"
	O	O'Neil Margaret J †	56	housewife	50	"

Taunton Avenue—Continued

Page	Letter	Full Name	Residence, Jan. 1, 1941	Occupation	Supposed Age	Reported Residence, Jan. 1, 1940, Street and Number
	P	Twohig Mary E †	56	housekeeper	79	here
	R	Stevens Daniel P	60	retired	75	"
	S	Wyman Adrian A	60	"	72	"
	T	Wyman Mary A †	60	housewife	73	"
	U	Eichorn Joseph H, jr	64	foreman	28	12 Brainard
	V	Eichorn Mary E †	64	housewife	26	12 "
	W	Ryan Frank C	65	salesman	35	22 Lockwood
	X	Ryan Mary T †	65	housewife	31	22 "
	Y	Killion Elizabeth J †	67	housekeeper	55	here
	Z*	Yanuski Mary N †	79	clerk	34	"
651						
	A	Yanuski Vincent G	79	chauffeur	27	"
	B*	Kinches Ann G †	79	domestic	57	"
	C	Kinches Jane G †	79	"	27	"
	D*	Kinches Joseph	79	retired	67	"

Tina Avenue

Page	Letter	Full Name	Residence, Jan. 1, 1941	Occupation	Supposed Age	Reported Residence, Jan. 1, 1940, Street and Number
	E	Zoller Gustafe	3	electrician	59	here
	F	Zoller Hulda †	3	housewife	59	"
	G	Zoller Robert E	3	machinist	25	"
	H*	Twerago Molly †	16	housewife	45	"
	K*	Twerago Stephen	16	papermaker	52	"
	L	Twerago Stephen, jr	16	operator	22	"
	M	Sebetes Joseph P	16	clerk	23	"
	N	Sebetes Mildred E †	16	housewife	26	"

Vanderbilt Avenue

Page	Letter	Full Name	Residence, Jan. 1, 1941	Occupation	Supposed Age	Reported Residence, Jan. 1, 1940, Street and Number
	O	O'Connor Debora †	1	housekeeper	49	here
	P	O'Connor John J	1	laborer	49	"
	R	O'Connor Mary †	1	housewife	55	"
	S*	O'Connor Nellie †	1	"	63	"
	T	Bengtson August	4	retired	74	"
	U	Bengtson Francis B	4	agent	40	"
	V	Charron Mary E †	5	housewife	42	"
	W	Charron Paul	5	installer	47	"
	X	Kelley Andrew	6	chauffeur	50	"
	Y	Kelley Henrietta †	6	housewife	48	"

Page.	Letter.	Full Name.	Residence, Jan. 1, 1941.	Occupation.	Supposed Age.	Reported Residence, Jan. 1, 1940. Street and Number.

Weybosset Street

Page.	Letter.	Full Name.	Residence, Jan. 1, 1941.	Occupation.	Supposed Age.	Reported Residence, Jan. 1, 1940. Street and Number.
	Z	*Fedirka Ann †	21	housewife	40	here
652						
	A	*Fedirka Stanley	21	chef	46	"
	B	Baeigalupo Fortuna †	21	clerk	32	Abington
	C	Baeigalupo John S	21	chauffeur	27	49 Cook ter
	D	*Baeigalupo Lynda †	21	housewife	57	49 "
	E	Wilkening Lillian M †	22-24	"	25	Brookline
	F	Wilkening Paul	22-24	clerk	27	"
	G	*Buchan Ina †	22-24	housewife	47	here
	H	*Buchan William	22-24	gardener	65	"
	K	Violandi Charles V	25	foreman	36	"
	L	Violandi Josephine H †	25	housewife	28	"
	M	Angelone Anne N †	25	"	31	Swampscott
	N	Angelone Leo	25	laborer	36	"
	O	Melnyk Mary M †	29	housewife	34	here
	P	Melnyk Michael	29	proprietor	49	"
	R	Kennedy Agnes M †	29	saleswoman	36	263 Fuller
	S	Buccari Joseph	32	student	24	here
	T	Buccari Salvatore	32	carpenter	66	"
	U	*Buccari Theresa †	32	housewife	66	"
	V	Smith Frederick J	32	manager	44	21 Weybosset
	W	Smith Mary A †	32	housewife	43	21 "
	X	Walsh Evelyn A †	33	"	34	here
	Y	Walsh Warner W	33	painter	36	"
	Z	*Harmatiuk Anthony J	52	"	53	"
653						
	A	Staruski Anthony	52	student	24	"
	B	*Staruski Eva A †	52	housewife	54	"
	C	Staruski Michael	52	laborer	24	"
	D	Staruski Stephanie †	52	clerk	22	"
	E	*Staruski Stephen	52	laborer	63	"
	F	Knecht Frederick	52	carpenter	40	"
	G	Knecht Nathalie T †	52	housewife	43	"
	H	Campbell Elizabeth J †	53	maid	54	"
	K	Williams Anna B †	53	housewife	59	"
	L	Williams Dorothy †	53	stenographer	23	"
	M	Williams Edmund C	53	carpenter	65	"
	N	Williams Florence †	53	biller	21	"
	O	Malone Thomas W	53	clerk	66	730 Metropolitan av
	P	Malone William L	53	investigator	52	730 "
	R	Neilson James R	55	teacher	33	here

Page	Letter	Full Name.	Residence, Jan. 1, 1941.	Occupation.	Supposed Age.	Reported Residence, Jan. 1, 1940. Street and Number.

Weybosset Street—Continued

Page	Letter	Full Name.	Residence, Jan. 1, 1941.	Occupation.	Supposed Age.	Reported Residence, Jan. 1, 1940. Street and Number.
	T	Nielsen Ruth A †	55	housewife	30	here
	S	Nielsen Karen F †	55	"	65	"
	U	*Pankevitch Alex	58	laborer	45	"
	V	*Pankevitch Mary †	58	housewife	43	"
	W	*Colery Mary †	58	at home	54	197 Savannah
	X	Kantaros Asimo	58	student	25	197 "
	Y	Kantaros Louis W	58	clerk	25	197 "
	Z	Philopoulos John	58	"	47	197 "
654						
	A	Yachniewicz Ignacy	64	machinist	59	here
	B	Yachniewicz Josephine †	64	housewife	45	"
	C	Kowalski Benjamin A	64	agent	48	37 Bullard
	D	Kowalski Mary F †	64	housewife	35	37 "

Wood Avenue

Page	Letter	Full Name.	Residence, Jan. 1, 1941.	Occupation.	Supposed Age.	Reported Residence, Jan. 1, 1940. Street and Number.
	E	Tack Emily †	8-10	housewife	37	here
	F	Tack Maurice	8-10	printer	37	"
	G	*Spoon Catherine †	8-10	housewife	53	"
	H	Spoon Catherine M †	8-10	operator	24	"
	K	Spoon Frank	8-10	laborer	58	"
	L	Spoon Lena M †	8-10	typist	22	"
	M	Keough Anna J †	18	housewife	50	"
	N	Keough James F	18	painter	43	"
	O	Keough Ruth C †	18	clerk	33	"
	P	Williams Margaret E †	21	housewife	51	"
	R	Williams Walter R	21	laborer	51	"
	S	Hoey Elizabeth †	21	maid	36	Brookline
	T	Mueller Bessie L †	21	housewife	49	here
	U	Mueller Charles A	21	cook	59	"
	V	Arvidson Karin †	28	photographer	70	654 Tremont
	W	Gran Elin †	28	housewife	62	here
	X	Gran Ethel C †	28	stenographer	24	"
	Y	Gran Karl A	28	printer	37	"
	Z	Westhaver George B	28	salesman	36	"
655						
	A	Westhaver Martha G †	28	housewife	35	"
	B	Dunican Belinda †	32	"	45	"
	C	Dunican Patrick	32	sorter	48	"
	D	Mulhern Leo H	36	supervisor	28	"

Page	Letter	Full Name	Residence, Jan. 1, 1941	Occupation	Supposed Age	Reported Residence, Jan. 1, 1940. Street and Number.
	E	Mulhern Ruth G †	36	housewife	28	here
	F	Costello John J	36	printer	67	"
	G	Costello Margaret E †	36	secretary	33	"
	H	Costello William F	36	clerk	24	"
	K	Walsh Gertrude †	36	shoeworker	41	"
	L	Shindul Anna †	40	housewife	46	"
	M	Shindul Arnold J	40	carpenter	20	"
	N	Shindul August J	40	"	52	"
	O	Shindul Lillian E †	40	nurse	23	"
	P*	Gagnon Mary A †	41	housewife	38	"
	R*	Gagnon William F	41	laborer	38	"
	S*	Rosata Annie †	41	housewife	54	"
	T	Rosata Bonnie	41	mechanic	24	"
	U	Rosata Marco	41	laborer	20	"
	V	Piotrowski Florence M †	42	housekeeper	20	"
	W	Piotrowski Frank	42	barber	49	"
	X	Piotrowski Lucille C †	42	checker	21	"
	Y*	Piotrowski Stella †	42	housewife	42	"
	Z	Murphy Margaret E †	48	copyist	25	"
656						
	A	Murphy Mary E †	48	housewife	52	"
	B	Murphy Peter J	48	bookkeeper	53	"
	C*	Rufo Carmela †	51	housewife	53	"
	D	Rufo Ida †	51	waitress	29	"
	E	Yule Marion R †	59	housewife	47	"
	F	Yule Russell J	59	laborer	26	"
	G	Yule Walter	59	"	24	"
	K	Clark Marguerite P †	79	teacher	22	"
	L	Clark Olive B †	79	housewife	47	"
	M	Clark Raymond S	79	installer	46	"
	N	MacDonald Albert J	80	engineer	34	"
	O	MacDonald Barbara †	80	housewife	30	"
	P	MacDonald John J	80	retired	62	"
	R*	Peters Angelina †	80	housewife	56	"
	S	Peters Charles	80	proprietor	31	"
	[illegible]	Peters James	80	clerk	22	"
	U	Peters Stephen	80	teacher	34	"
	[illegible]	Peters Thelma †	80	"	21	"
	W	Wright Mary C †	82 84	housewife	30	"
	X	Wright Stephen A	82 84	foreman	38	"
	Y	[illegible] Wanda †	82 84	housekeeper	57	"

Page	Letter	Full Name	Residence, Jan. 1, 1941	Occupation	Supposed Age	Reported Residence, Jan. 1, 1940. Street and Number
657		**Wood Avenue**—Continued				
	A	Neros Petra †	82 84	at home	67	here
	B	Solbjor Birger	82 84	engineer	53	"
	C	Solbjor Edith N †	82 84	bookkeeper	24	"
	D	Solbjor Olive †	82 84	housewife	56	"
	E	Conrod Alice F †	83	"	32	Cambridge
	F	*Conrod Frank C	83	shipper	32	"
	G	Kelly Celia B †	83	housewife	48	here
	H	Kelly Francis G	83	operator	22	"
	K	Kelly Frank J	83	policeman	50	"
	L	Kelly Rita N †	83	clerk	20	"
	M	Davis Annie T †	85	housekeeper	50	"
	N	Davis Catherine A †	85	"	72	"
	O	Davis Catherine S †	85	housewife	43	"
	P	Davis James J	85	mechanic	49	"
	R	Berestecki Peter	85	chef	40	"
	S	*Berestecki Stacia †	85	housewife	27	"
	T	Bernard Henry	86	cook	33	Cambridge
	U	Rapes William	86	"	26	here
	V	*Zasimoridge Alice C †	86	housewife	70	"
	W	Zasimoridge Alice V †	86	clerk	30	"
	X	Zasimoridge Anna A †	86	"	38	"
	Y	Zasimoridge Catherine F †	86	"	32	"
	Z	Zasimoridge Walter	86	guard	34	"
658						
	A	Bunker Louise E †	88	housewife	27	Mansfield
	B	Bunker William N	88	draftsman	26	"
	C	Thompson Alfred R	89	fireman	55	here
	D	Thompson Devona †	89	housewife	56	"
	E	Thompson William	89	steamfitter	52	"
	F	Blackburn Alice M †	90	dressmaker	45	"
	G	Parsons Frances M †	90	at home	65	"
	H	McDonough Constance M †	90	housewife	20	Weymouth
	K	McDonough Francis M	90	chauffeur	24	"
	L	Fowler Florence E †	93	stenographer	36	here
	M	Fowler Mabel †	93	housewife	66	"
	N	Driscoll Carrie †	94	"	33	"
	O	Driscoll William H	94	draftsman	34	"
	P	Santosuosso Lenore †	95	housewife	21	Newton
	R	Santosuosso Vincent	95	collector	25	33 Thatcher
	S	Ward George	96	retired	68	here

Page	Letter	Full Name	Residence, Jan. 1, 1941	Occupation	Supposed Age	Reported Residence, Jan. 1, 1940. Street and Number.

Wood Avenue—Continued

Page	Letter	Full Name	Residence, Jan. 1, 1941	Occupation	Supposed Age	Reported Residence, Jan. 1, 1940. Street and Number.
	T	Ward Gertrude F †	96	housewife	54	here
	U	Fitzwilliams Alice F †	97	"	28	"
	V	Fitzwilliams Edward P	97	milkman	28	"
	W	*Mielaika Victoria †	97	housewife	69	"
	X	Cavanagh Joseph F	99	operator	40	776 Broadway
	Y	Cavanagh Louise V †	99	housewife	42	here
	Z	Cook Ivy V †	122	"	36	"
659						
	A	Cook Roger C	122	printer	34	"
	B	Drozdick Catherine †	122	housewife	44	"
	C	Drozdick Michael	122	blacksmith	48	"
	D	Culpin Joseph	124	policeman	43	"
	E	Culpin Monica V †	124	housewife	41	"
	F	Ryan Frederick J	124	mechanic	42	Brookline
	G	Ryan Margaret V †	124	housewife	38	"
	H	Pitts Joseph C	128	meter reader	40	here
	K	Pitts Lillian †	128	housewife	40	"
	L	Baxter Ella H †	128	at home	65	471 E Eighth
	M	McNeil Dorothy E †	128	housewife	29	471 "
	N	McNeil Oliver E	128	chauffeur	31	471 "
	O	Biagi Elizabeth H †	132	housewife	36	here
	P	Biagi Guido	132	policeman	40	"
	R	White Pauline M †	132	at home	67	"
	S	Begin Alice E †	132	housewife	38	"
	T	Walper Harry J	132	machinist	65	239 Centre
	U	Ward William	132	stockman	21	here
	V	Lang Catherine †	168	housewife	70	"
	W	Lang Michael J	168	retired	70	"
	X	*Holman Clifford J	178	operator	42	"
	Y	Holman Mary E †	178	housewife	40	"
	Z	*Kozlowska Fedora †	186	"	73	"
660						
	A	Kozlowska Peter	186	fireman	69	"
	B	Day Frank J	186	realtor	40	23 Foster
	C	Day Marion G †	186	housewife	33	23 "
	D	Taylor Charles E	186	draftsman	39	110 Westminster
	E	Taylor Irene L †	186	housewife	29	110 "
	F	Klucken Alice J †	196	stitcher	40	722 Metropolitan av
	G	Kuman Alvina †	196	operator	48	here
	H	Silling Suzanna †	196	housewife	65	"
	K	*Johnson Alfred M	196	ironworker	51	"

Page	Letter	Full Name	Residence, Jan. 1, [illegible]	Occupation	Reputed Age	Reported Residence, Jan. 1, [illegible] Street and Number

Wood Avenue—Continued

Page	Letter	Full Name	Residence	Occupation	Age	Reported Residence
	L	*Johnsen Lilly B †	196	housewife	50	here
	M	McDonald Anna M †	196	"	44	"
	N	McDonald Daniel J	196	carpenter	43	"
	O	McDonald Mary †	196	at home	57	"
	P	Klarich Irene C †	200 202	operator	21	"
	R	Klarich William B	200 202	boilermaker	47	"
	S	Feldman Horace W	200 202	research work'r	41	37 Warren av
	T	Feldman Margaret E †	200 202	housewife	37	37 "
	U	Nevinski Anna †	206	"	65	here
	V	Nevinski Mary A †	206	bookkeeper	42	"
	W	Nevinski Nellie G †	206	at home	45	"
	X	Glancy Francis J	206	clerk	64	"
	Y	Jasionis Harriet B †	210	housewife	31	427 E Seventh
	Z	Jasionis John P	210	superintendent	34	427 "
661						
	A	*Rimkus Catherine †	210	housewife	47	here
	B	Rimkus Mary C †	210	waitress	20	"
	C	*Rimkus Stanley	210	tailor	51	"
	D	Rimkus Stanley C, jr	210	instruments	22	"
	E	Geoghegan Catherine †	216	stenographer	24	"
	F	Geoghegan Mary †	216	housewife	55	"
	G	Geoghegan Mary R †	216	stenographer	21	"
	H	Geoghegan Patrick F	216	installer	55	"
	K	Kiewicz Chester	220	clerk	29	"
	L	Kiewicz Jennie †	220	housewife	67	"
	M	Kiewicz John	220	designer	77	"
	N	Boyd Catherine V †	230	housewife	34	"
	O	Boyd Lucy †	230	at home	70	"
	P	Boyd Norman J	230	policeman	35	"
	R	Curtis Lillian †	230	housewife	34	"
	S	Curtis William F	230	clerk	35	"
	T	Zubrinsky Edmund	230	laborer	60	"
	U	Zubrinsky Mary †	230	housewife	55	"
	V	Myers Bessie †	260	housekeeper	72	"
	W	Page Mary J †	260	at home	75	"
	X	*Savill Arthur	262	manager	51	"
	Y	*Savill Rebecca †	262	housewife	51	"
	Z	Suskin Emanuel	262	operator	21	"
662						
	A	Pickering James H, jr	264	repairman	22	18 Capen
	B	Pickering Marjorie †	264	housewife	24	18 "

Page	Letter	Full Name	Residence, Jan. 1, 1941	Occupation	Supposed Age	Reported Residence, Jan. 1, 1940. Street and Number

Wood Avenue—Continued

Page	Letter	Full Name	Residence, Jan. 1, 1941	Occupation	Supposed Age	Reported Residence, Jan. 1, 1940. Street and Number
	C	Foley Sarah †	264	at home	75	here
	D	Notini Louis	266	cook	27	78 E Cottage
	E	Notini Marjorie E †	266	stitcher	26	270 Wood av
	F*	Martin Harriett M †	266	housewife	34	here
	G	Martin Joseph F	266	finisher	35	"
	H	Lufkin Eugene	268	chauffeur	48	"
	K	Lufkin Gladys †	268	housewife	43	"
	L	MacCabe Evelyn †	268	"	20	Dedham
	M	MacCabe James F	268	chauffeur	22	"
	N	Corsi Joseph	270	laborer	62	here
	O*	Corsi Pia †	270	housewife	63	"
	P	LaSota John H	270	operator	27	"
	R*	Maybroda Anna †	270	charwoman	47	"
	S	Maybroda Mary †	270	secretary	23	"
	T	Maybroda Stephanie †	270	packer	21	"
	U*	Maybroda Sofron	270	porter	52	"
	V	Battles Mary A †	272	housewife	72	961 River
	W	Battles Patrick J	272	chauffeur	65	961 "
	X	Williams Doris †	272	housewife	22	Dedham
	Y	Williams Thomas	272	upholsterer	30	7 Webster
	Z	Kenney Curtis	274	laborer	20	here
663						
	A	Kenney Edith M †	274	housewife	59	"
	B	Kenney Florence E †	274	maid	26	"
	C	Kenney Minot M	274	laborer	60	"
	D	Pulgini Rosina †	274	housekeeper	51	"
	E	Barme Helen G †	276	housewife	45	"
	F	Barme William T	276	machinist	57	"
	H	Weinberg Reuben	288	laborer	39	3 Baird
	K	Weinberg Sarah †	288	housewife	37	3 "
	L*	Acorn Laura E †	292	"	30	here
	M*	Acorn Sherman S	292	boilermaker	34	"
	N*	Pegurri Leo	292	laborer	52	"
	O	Pegurri Palma †	292	housewife	49	"
	P*	Baxter Elizabeth †	304	"	59	"
	R	Baxter John J	304	laborer	29	"
	S	Squillante Gertrude †	304	housewife	28	"
	T	Squillante Henry	304	chauffeur	32	"
	U	Cushman Elizabeth †	310	at home	53	"
	V	Hill Mary †	310	housekeeper	55	"
	W	Richards Florence J †	314	housewife	72	"

Page	Letter	Full Name	Residence, Jan. 1, 1941	Occupation	Supposed Age	Reported Residence, Jan. 1, 1940. Street and Number

Wood Avenue Continued

Page	Letter	Full Name	Residence, Jan. 1, 1941	Occupation	Supposed Age	Reported Residence, Jan. 1, 1940. Street and Number
	Y	Richards John J	314	retired	85	here
	Z	*Purdy Anna F †	314	housewife	28	W Virginia
664						
	A	Purdy Stanley E	314	machinist	28	"
	B	Anderson Ena W †	320	housewife	45	here
	C	Anderson William H	320	fireman	46	"
	D	*Fernandez Marcello J	324	chef	34	10 Malta
	E	Fernandez Marjorie †	324	housewife	29	10 "
	F	Hume Thomas	324	buyer	69	10 "

Ward 18—Precinct 7

CITY OF BOSTON

LIST OF RESIDENTS
20 YEARS OF AGE AND OVER

(NON-CITIZENS INDICATED BY ASTERISK)
(FEMALES INDICATED BY DAGGER)

AS OF

JANUARY 1, 1941

CITY OF BOSTON PRINTING DEPARTMENT

Page.	Letter.	Full Name.	Residence, Jan. 1, 1941.	Occupation.	Supposed Age.	Reported Residence, Jan. 1, 1940. Street and Number.
700		**American Legion Highway**				
	A	*Russo Louise M †	611	housewife	40	here
	B	Russo Anthony	611	laborer	49	"
	C	Tamboni John	611	barber	40	Somerville
	D	Murphy Catherine †	615	housewife	35	here
	E	Murphy James M	615	lineman	40	"
	F	Conway Alphonse L	619	painter	37	"
	G	Conway Catherine T †	619	housewife	73	"
	H	Conway Esther T †	619	clerk	32	"
	K	Lynch Evelyn F †	619	housekeeper	35	"
	L	McDonald Patrick	619	laborer	35	"
	M	*DelSignori Joseph	717	"	68	"
	O	Raimo Florence †	721	housewife	79	"
	P	Raimo Joseph	721	carpenter	40	"
	R	Moccia John A	721	laborer	55	"
	S	Moccia Lena †	721	housewife	47	"
	T	Cardillo Anthony	725	laborer	25	"
	U	Cardillo Harry E	725	painter	24	"
	V	*Cardillo Rose †	725	housewife	51	"
	W	*Cardillo William	725	laborer	54	"
	X	Orrall Arthur D	725	"	35	"
	Y	Orrall Doris †	725	housewife	34	"
	Z	*Cardillo Benjamin	729	laborer	55	"
701						
	A	*Cardillo Coletta †	729	housewife	49	"
	B	Cardillo Guy C	729	laborer	24	"
	C	Cardillo Louise M †	729	inspector	22	"
	D	Cardillo Samuel J	729	laborer	21	"
	E	DeAngelis John	729	"	30	"
	F	DeAngelis Mildred †	729	housewife	29	"
	G	*Monaco Angelina †	729	"	56	"
	H	Monaco Thomas	729	presser	27	"
	K	Cassano Charles	733	cutter	26	"
	L	Cassano Jennie †	733	housewife	21	"
	M	Ricci Albert F	733	cutter	26	"
	N	Ricci Angelina †	733	housewife	49	"
	O	Lavin Alice G †	737	seamstress	37	"
	P	Lavin Anna T †	737	housewife	45	"
	R	Lavin George P	737	plasterer	44	"
	S	Lavin Joseph W	737	B F D	51	"

Page	Letter	Full Name	Residence, April 1, 1941	Occupation	Supposed Age	Reported Residence, April 1, 1940. Street and Number

American Legion Highway—Continued

Page	Letter	Full Name	Residence, April 1, 1941	Occupation	Supposed Age	Reported Residence, April 1, 1940. Street and Number
	T	Lavin Margaret M †	737	housewife	40	here
	U	Pierce Ida C †	741	"	23	2 Way pl
	V	Pierce Joseph A	741	chauffeur	25	2 "
	W	Emmett Agnes J †	745	housewife	21	1 Madison
	X	Emmett William	745	laborer	28	1 "
	Z	Femino Dominick	755	cutter	54	here
702						
	A*	Femino Jennie †	755	housewife	53	"
	B	Femino Peter G	755	salesman	21	"
	C	Glynn John J	761	B F D	44	"
	D	Glynn Mary J †	761	housewife	43	"
	F	Luke Anna M †	765	"	40	"
	G	Luke Charles	765	clerk	44	"
	K	Bixby Ella H †	771	housekeeper	66	"
	L	Cummings Cleone A †	771	teacher	23	"
	M	Cummings George H	771	retired	69	"
	N	Cummings Seavour B †	771	housewife	56	"
	O	Shaw Frank E	775	printer	46	"
	P	Shaw Margaret †	775	housewife	45	"
	R	DeMatteo Anna †	806	"	31	"
	S	DeMatteo John	806	contractor	31	"
	T*	Capaldo Domonic	809	foreman	66	"
	U	Cataldi Anthony	809	laborer	55	"
	V	Cataldi Maria †	809	housewife	37	"
	W	Coppenrath Frederick W	810	wheelwright	32	3828 Wash'n
	X	Coppenrath Margaret G †	810	housewife	70	3828 "
	Y	Coppenrath Margaret M †	810	"	36	3828 "
	Z	Civitarese Etta M †	810	"	34	here
703						
	A	Civitarese Nicholas J	810	engineer	34	"
	B	Cardillo Anna †	810	housewife	27	"
	C	Cardillo Charles	810	laborer	27	"
	D	Fitzsimmons Bernard J	814	mechanic	38	[illegible]
	E	Fitzsimmons Caroline J †	814	cleanser	42	215 "
	F	Fitzsimmons Josephine E †	814	housewife	33	253 "
	G	Fitzsimmons Thomas	814	mechanic	46	253 "
	H	Terrano Elizabeth A †	819	housewife	41	here
	K	Terrano Rocco J	819	hairdresser	42	"
	L	Kinnaly Daniel J	821	clerk	42	"
	M	Kinnaly Emily F †	821	housewife	37	"
	N	Kinnaly Katherine V †	821	clerk	39	"

Page	Letter	Full Name	Residence, Jan. 1, 1941.	Occupation	Supposed Age.	Reported Residence, Jan. 1, 1940. Street and Number.

Bradstreet Avenue

Page	Letter	Full Name	Residence, Jan. 1, 1941.	Occupation	Supposed Age.	Reported Residence, Jan. 1, 1940. Street and Number.
	O	Callahan Albert G	11	student	25	here
	P	Callahan Eleanor G †	11	clerk	29	"
	R	Callahan Elizabeth F †	11	housewife	64	"
	S	Callahan John A	11	laborer	27	"
	T	Callahan John F	11	electrician	67	"
	U	Callahan Mary A †	11	clerk	30	"
	V	*Kelleher Ellen †	12	housewife	38	62 Mt Hope
	W	Kelleher John F	12	machinist	41	62 "
	X	Lundberg Ida †	19	clerk	39	here
	Y	Spataro Amelia J †	19	hairdresser	32	"
	Z	Tulliani Caroline E †	19	housewife	43	"
704						
	A	Tulliani Cesidio J	19	gardener	44	"
	B	*Moschello Mary C †	19	housekeeper	77	"
	C	Crognale Carmela †	19	housewife	32	"
	D	*Crognale Sabatino	19	operator	39	"
	E	Coppola Helen J †	21	housewife	24	72 Walworth
	F	Coppola Michael A	21	clerk	25	72 "
	G	Moschella Frances M †	23	housewife	38	here
	H	Moschella Michael	23	carpenter	47	"
	K	Cunningham Bertha E †	24	bookkeeper	58	"
	L	Cunningham Gertrude J †	24	saleswoman	41	"
	M	Cunningham Mabel A †	24	housekeeper	46	"
	N	Cunningham Mary J †	24	clerk	27	"
	O	Stacho Emily †	42	housewife	42	"
	P	Stacho George E	42	upholsterer	43	"
	R	Donovan Anna M †	46	secretary	21	"
	S	Donovan Edward J	46	machinist	24	"
	T	Donovan Katherine J †	46	housewife	48	"
	U	Donovan Kathleen R †	46	secretary	20	"
	V	Donovan Philip J	46	gardener	50	"

Bridge Street

Page	Letter	Full Name	Residence, Jan. 1, 1941.	Occupation	Supposed Age.	Reported Residence, Jan. 1, 1940. Street and Number.
	W	Manning Elizabeth K †	30	housewife	49	here
	X	Manning John J	30	counterman	22	"
	Y	Manning Thomas	30	dyesetter	23	"
	Z	Manning Thomas F	30	grocer	55	"
705						
	A	Kannegieser Frank	30	inspector	40	"
	B	Kannegieser Katherine †	30	housewife	38	"

Byrd Avenue

Page	Letter	Full Name	Residence, Jan. 1, 1941	Occupation	Supposed Age	Reported Residence, Street and Number
	C	Kennedy Agnes †	7	nurse	65	here
	D	Kennedy Agnes †	7	housewife	34	"
	E	Kennedy David	7	machinist	36	"
	F	Leeber Frank F	9	knitter	30	"
	G	Leeber Helen T †	9	housewife	29	"
	H	Boudreau Henri L	11	salesman	37	"
	K	Boudreau Margaret E †	11	housewife	35	"
	L	Nicholson Olive A †	13	"	31	"
	M	Nicholson Walter F	13	packer	38	"
	N	Swenson Nils	13	retired	76	"

Canterbury Street

Page	Letter	Full Name	Residence, Jan. 1, 1941	Occupation	Supposed Age	Reported Residence, Street and Number
	O	Houle Leon	574	chauffeur	23	here
	P	Sullivan Blanche M †	574	housewife	23	"
	R	Sullivan Dennis J	574	attendant	26	"
	S	Buhlman Inez †	578	housewife	55	"
	T	Buhlman Louis	578	cabinetmaker	57	"
	U	DePalma Joseph	582	laborer	47	"
	V	DePalma Rosa †	582	housewife	29	"
	W	Howley Catherine †	586	"	46	"
	X	Howley Joseph J	586	operator	45	"
	Y	Sinacola Nellie †	594	housekeeper	41	5 Meyer
	Z	Christian Amenda †	594	housewife	60	here
706						
	A	Christian Emil	594	laborer	37	"
	B	Christian Ernest	594	student	26	"
	C	Clementi Jeanette †	594	housewife	25	"
	D	Walsh Frances L †	598	"	35	"
	E	Walsh Peter F	598	chauffeur	36	"
	F	Morey Helen †	602	housewife	37	"
	G	Morey Thomas H	602	attendant	45	"
	H	Walsh Estelle R †	602	housewife	23	Porto Rico
	K	Walsh Martin L	602	engineer	40	"
	L	Hamilton Arthur	620	retired	64	here
	M	Hamilton Catherine †	620	housewife	60	"
	N	Hamilton Mary †	620	housekeeper	33	"
	O	Hamilton Walter	620	salesman	30	"
	P	Arenda John	620	shoemaker	46	"
	R	Arenda Rose †	620	housewife	38	"
	S	Babstock Catherine †	628	"	53	"

Page	Letter	Full Name	Residence, Jan. 1, 1941	Occupation	Supposed Age	Reported Residence, Jan. 1, 1940. Street and Number.

Canterbury Street—Continued

Page	Letter	Full Name	Residence, Jan. 1, 1941	Occupation	Supposed Age	Reported Residence, Jan. 1, 1940. Street and Number.
	T	Babstock Mary C †	628	attendant	20	here
	U	*Fiore Louis	630	retired	77	19 Greenwood av
	V	*Lombardi Adalgisa †	630	housewife	45	here
	W	Lombardi Anthony	630	chauffeur	21	"
	X	Lombardi Carmen	630	"	22	"
	Y	Lombardi John B	630	contractor	51	"
	Z	Lombardi Silviano	630	chauffeur	23	"
707						
	A	Lombardi Theresa †	630	beautician	24	"
	C	Berg Carl E	678	machinist	31	"
	D	Berg Gertrude L †	678	housewife	23	"
	E	Nolan Charles S	679	salesman	22	"
	F	Nolan Mary E †	679	housewife	59	"
	G	Nolan Mary E †	679	housekeeper	24	"
	H	Nolan William	679	rubberworker	26	"
	K	Nolan William E	679	electrician	53	"
	L	O'Brien John A	679	chauffeur	57	"
	M	O'Brien Marguerite M †	679	bookkeeper	20	"
	N	O'Brien Rose C †	679	housewife	42	"
	O	O'Brien Rose C †	679	clerk	21	"
	P	Walsh Mary E †	680	at home	70	"
	R	Mullen Agnes T †	684	housewife	54	"
	S	Mullen John F	684	retired	64	"
	T	Herron Arthur	688	machinist	37	"
	U	Herron Louise †	688	housewife	31	"
	V	Power Olando F	698	retired	64	"
	W	Smith Elmer J	698	clerk	20	"
	X	Smith Mary †	698	housewife	49	"
	Y	Smith Philip F	698	policeman	47	"
	Z	Smith Phyllis F †	698	at home	26	"
708						
	A	Mason Dorothy †	760	nurse	44	43 Metropolitan av
	B	Regan Cornelius	760	porter	40	43 "
	C	*Regan Elizabeth †	760	housewife	39	43 "
	D	Flynn James J	764	laborer	65	here
	E	Flynn Mary E †	764	housewife	63	"
	F	Buchanan Madeline †	772	"	37	"
	G	Buchanan William R	772	inspector	40	"
	H	Lawrence James E	776	clerk	36	"
	K	Lawrence Jane A †	776	housewife	29	"
	L	McCauley Francis J	776A	bricklayer	39	"

Canterbury Street Continued

Page	Letter	Full Name	Residence Jan. 1, 1941	Occupation	Age	Reported Residence Jan. 1, 1940 Street and Number
	M	McCauley Helen F †	776A	housewife	38	here
	N	Hester Elizabeth C †	778	"	39	68 Day
	O	Hester Roderick E	778	clerk	43	68 "
	P	*Buechieri Paulina †	780	housewife	47	784 [illegible]
	R	Buechieri Salvatore	780	laborer	50	784 "
	S	Brooks Anna C †	784	housewife	62	here
	T	Brooks Frank D	784	clerk	28	"
	U	Brooks George P	784	retired	69	"
	V	Brooks George P	784	mechanic	30	"
	W	Esmond Gertrude A †	784	housewife	46	"
	X	Esmond Leo J	784	chauffeur	21	"
	Y	McElaney Daniel E	788	retired	73	"
	Z	Munns Grace †	788	housekeeper	40	"
709						
	B	Newton Clifford A	788	beveler	33	"
	C	Newton Margaret M †	788	housewife	26	"
	D	Mahoney Daniel J	800	retired	73	"
	E	Mahoney George E	800	salesman	38	"
	F	Mahoney Mary †	800	housewife	73	"
	G	O'Rourke Mary A †	804	"	34	"
	H	O'Rourke Peter F	804	mechanic	34	"
	K	McKeon Evelyn A †	806	housewife	37	Worcester
	L	McKeon Philip J	806	supervisor	34	"
	M	Stevens George H	812	chauffeur	54	here
	N	Stevens Josephine †	812	housewife	54	"
	O	Stevens Roland	812	U S A	24	"
	P	Brissenden Edward E	817	chauffeur	25	41 Westwood
	R	Brissenden Elsie D †	817	housewife	22	41 "
	S	Brissenden Mattie M †	817	"	61	Worcester
	T	Cameron Elbridge H	817	accountant	33	597 Dudley
	U	Mulrey Helen R †	818	stenographer	52	here
	V	Mulrey John E	818	clerk	61	"
	W	Mulrey Mary V †	818	housekeeper	55	"
	X	Mulrey Thomas F	818	policeman	61	"
	Y	Maginnis Frank B	819	retired	67	"
	Z	Maginnis Robert J	819	guard	30	"
710						
	A	Morton Frances M †	819	housewife	29	"
	B	Morton George R	819	chauffeur	37	"
	C	Herbert Anne C †	821	bookkeeper	50	"
	D	Wetzler Eugene J	821	retired	73	"

Canterbury Street—Continued

Page	Letter	Full Name	Residence, Jan. 1, 1941	Occupation	Supposed Age	Reported Residence, Jan. 1, 1940. Street and Number.
	E	*Lindstrom Lisa L †	823	housewife	32	here
	F	Lindstrom Thor R	823	painter	37	"
	G	Wentsel Elsa M †	823	cook	48	"
	H	Duenges Elizabeth †	824	housekeeper	67	"
	K	Reynolds Bridget M †	825	at home	70	"
	L	Reynolds Francis E	827	teacher	40	"
	M	Reynolds Rose K †	827	housewife	34	"
	N	*Renzi Caroline †	836	"	42	"
	O	Renzi Domenic	836	laborer	52	"
	P	Doyle Mary M †	836	housewife	26	"
	R	Doyle Mary †	836	"	25	"
	S	Hale George C	836	mechanic	29	"
	T	Hale Wanda †	836	housewife	26	"
	U	Vegonoli Joseph A	842	painter	46	844 Canterbury
	V	Vegonoli Victor L	842	"	26	844 "
	W	*Pagnotta Celia †	842	housewife	35	here
	X	Pagnotta John	842	leatherworker	27	"
	Y	Pagnotta Mildred †	842	wrapper	25	"
	Z	Pagnotta Patrick	842	carpenter	35	"
711						
	A	Brait Albina †	844	housewife	26	7 Filomena rd
	B	Brait Robert	844	supervisor	33	7 "
	C	*Scaccia Columbia †	844	housewife	62	here
	D	Scaccia Joseph	844	retired	68	"
	E	Bernasconi Helen †	844	housewife	25	"
	F	Bernasconi William	844	leatherworker	26	"
	H	Paone Gaetano	847	jeweler	53	"
	K	Paone Julia L †	847	clerk	22	"
	L	Paone Mary F †	847	housewife	48	"
	M	*Cook Agnes E †	849	"	36	"
	N	*Cook George W	849	carman	37	"
	O	Kerregan Francis J	850	starter	46	"
	P	Kerregan Mattie †	850	housewife	33	"
	S	Manning Francis T	850	gardener	55	"
	T	Manning Mary D †	850	housewife	36	"
	U	Israelson August G	864	janitor	72	"
	V	Olson Charles S	864	retired	80	"
	W	Olson Lena A †	864	housewife	75	"
	X	Freeley Austin J	866	mechanic	39	264 Roslindale av
	Y	Freeley Helen L †	866	housewife	38	264 "
	Z	Tirrell Marion A †	866	operator	39	Dedham

Page.	Letter	Full Name	Residence, Jan. 1, 1941	Occupation	Supposed Age	Reported Residence, Jan. 1, 1940. Street and Number
712		**Canterbury Street** Continued				
	A	Sullivan Elizabeth M †	868	housekeeper	60	here
	B	Kinlin Anita E †	868	housewife	29	66 Boynton
	C	Kinlin George H	868	chauffeur	28	66 "
	D	Greszat Gustaf	870	ironworker	52	160 Boston
	E	*Greszat Ida †	870	housewife	49	160 "
	F	Goldstein Lillian M †	873	"	36	here
	G	Goldstein Martin M	873	salesman	39	"
	H	Arini John	873	barber	42	"
	K	Arini Josephine M †	873	housewife	39	"
	L	Scandurra Mary †	873	leatherworker	22	"
	M	Hardy Lloyd W	875	painter	33	"
	N	Scherber Anita C †	875	stenographer	37	"
	O	Moran Catherine A †	875	nurse	21	"
	P	Moran Joseph F	875	laborer	20	"
	R	Moran Mary J †	875	housewife	49	"
	S	Moran William F	875	hostler	53	"
	T	Moran William F, jr	875	proofreader	24	"
	U	Klose Paul	880	court officer	50	"
	V	Klose Paul C	880	student	26	"
	W	Klose Sarah E †	880	housewife	48	"
	X	McEachern Anna J †	886	"	38	"
	Y	McEachern Daniel S	886	boxmaker	50	"
	Z	Cullinane Teresa A †	890	housekeeper	36	"
713						
	A	Freeley Catherine M †	890	secretary	41	"
	B	Freeley James F	890	mechanic	49	"
	C	Keller Cornelius T	894	salesman	30	"
	D	Keller Ellen G †	894	housewife	48	"
	E	Keller Gertrude E †	894	stenographer	24	"
	F	Keller Kathleen †	894	clerk	22	"
	G	Keller Mary T †	894	secretary	26	"
	H	Keller Thomas C	894	salesman	55	"
	K	Devlin Sarah †	895	clerk	55	[illegible]
	L	Ryan Annie M †	895	housewife	85	199 "
	M	Ryan Daniel F	895	collector	58	199 "
	N	Ryan Elizabeth †	895	maid	53	199 "
	O	Berman Marjorie E †	897	housewife	40	here
	P	Berman Maurice	897	printer	42	"
	R	Jenkins Annie E †	897	housekeeper	71	"
	S	Jensen Petra †	898	at home	65	"

Page	Letter	Full Name	Residence, Jan. 1, 1941	Occupation	Supposed Age	Reported Residence, Jan. 1, 1940. Street and Number.

Canterbury Street Continued

Page	Letter	Full Name	Residence, Jan. 1, 1941	Occupation	Supposed Age	Reported Residence, Jan. 1, 1940. Street and Number.
	T	Rieman Augusta †	898	housekeeper	75	here
	U	Burns Robert J	907	electrician	50	"
	V	Gebhardt Catherine F †	907	housekeeper	54	"
	W	Gebhardt Frances C †	907	clerk	25	"
	X	Smith Emmett R	907	"	34	"
	Y	Smith Gladys G †	907	instructor	31	"
	Z	Graham Vera M †	911	housewife	24	60 Seymour
714						
	A	Graham Walter H	911	electrician	29	60 "
	B	Donovan Mary T †	911	housewife	42	here
	C	Donovan Patrick J	911	chauffeur	42	"
	D	McGuinness Anna M †	914	housewife	32	"
	E	McGuinness William P	914	laborer	43	"
	F	O'Rourke Francis T	914	clerk	31	8 Granfield av
	G	O'Rourke Ruth M †	914	housewife	31	8 "
	H	Page Mae †	914	"	32	here
	K	Page Raoul G	914	diemaker	46	"
	L	Halligan Christine A †	915	housewife	43	"
	M	Halligan Russell W	915	electrician	23	"
	N	Halligan William E	915	operator	46	"
	O	Gundal Marie B †	915	housewife	42	"
	P	Gundal Peter H	915	granite cutter	68	"
	R	Smith George S	918	operator	36	"
	S	Smith Lucy B †	918	housewife	34	"
	T	McSweeney Margaret G †	918	"	46	"
	U	McSweeney Timothy J	918	electrician	46	"
	V	Challis Esther M †	922	housewife	35	94 Mt Hope
	W	Challis John D	922	merchant	39	94 "
	X	Hafferty Walter T	922	printer	43	here
	Y	Ralph Alice M †	922	housekeeper	41	"

Charme Avenue

Page	Letter	Full Name	Residence, Jan. 1, 1941	Occupation	Supposed Age	Reported Residence, Jan. 1, 1940. Street and Number.
	Z	Rando Angelina †	6	housewife	38	here
715						
	A	Rando Joseph	6	barber	45	"
	B	Kindamo Anthony M	7	shipfitter	20	"
	C	Kindamo Joseph	7	riveter	48	"
	D	Kindamo Mary T †	7	housewife	37	"
	E	Conrad Bernard W	7	pressman	43	"
	F	Conrad Fanny †	7	housewife	39	"

Charme Avenue Continued

Page	Letter	Full Name	Residence, Jan. 1, 1941	Occupation	Reported Age	Reported Residence, Jan. 1, 1940. Street and Number
	G	Falcone Frances †	8	housewife	41	here
	H	Falcone Frank V	8	B F D	41	"
	K	Ceruti Anthony	10	waiter	34	New York
	L	Julio John J	10	"	33	97 Neponset av
	M	Julio Louise M †	10	housewife	25	97 "
	N	Glissler Frederick E	11	operator	44	here
	O	Glissler Inez D †	11	housewife	39	"
	P	Schormann Charles C	11	plumber	56	"
	R	Schormann Elizabeth P †	11	housewife	54	"
	S	Waterman John P	12	stockman	34	"
	T	Waterman Minnie T †	12	housewife	28	"
	U	Pease Catherine E †	14	"	46	"
	V	Pease Clarence W	14	laborer	48	"
	W*	Domiano Michael	15	"	50	"
	X*	Domiano Rose †	15	housewife	42	"
	Y	Manley Joseph H	15	manager	41	"
	Z	Manley Mary C †	15	housewife	43	"
716						
	A	Kilduff James F	16	salesman	29	335 Hyde Park av
	B	Kilduff Josephine E †	16	housewife	28	335 "
	C*	Buckley Nora F †	18	operator	40	here
	D	Hallisey Catherine †	18	housewife	42	"
	E	Hallisey John J	18	teamster	42	"
	F	Hallisey Mary M †	18	clerk	20	"
	G	Manley Edward J	19	"	36	"
	H	Manley Eva †	19	housewife	35	"
	K	Colamaria Andrew	19	bartender	25	"
	L	Colamaria Carmela †	19	housewife	44	"
	M*	Colamaria Joseph	19	retired	59	"
	N	Colamaria Sabino T	19	student	24	"
	O	Reissfelder Frederick	20	chauffeur	37	"
	P	Reissfelder Marie E †	20	housewife	36	"
	R	MacDonald Sarah F †	22	"	29	"
	S	MacDonald William J	22	lineman	30	"
	T	Cleary Harriett E †	23	housewife	39	"
	U	Cleary Michael W	23	operator	42	"
	V	Kenny Catherine A †	24	housewife	51	"
	W	Kenny Patrick J	24	salesman	54	"
	X	Kenny Rose E †	24	secretary	25	"
	Y	Kenny William P	24	checker	27	"
	Z	Kenny Winifred J †	24	stenographer	28	"

Page	Letter	Full Name	Residence, Jan. 1, 1941	Occupation	Supposed Age	Reported Residence, Jan. 1, 1940. Street and Number

717

Charme Avenue—Continued

Letter	Full Name	Residence, Jan. 1, 1941	Occupation	Supposed Age	Reported Residence, Jan. 1, 1940
A	Clark Lettie B †	25	housewife	50	99 Wellsmere rd
B	Clark Norman C	25	porter	24	99 "
C	Clark Raymond W	25	"	49	99 "
D	McDevitt Elizabeth †	26	at home	52	here
E	McDevitt John J	26	chauffeur	28	"
F	McDevitt Josephine E †	26	housewife	24	"
G	MacEachern Charles I	27	salesman	41	"
H	*MacEachern Olga †	27	housewife	37	"
K	Powers Erma W †	28	"	31	"
L	Powers James F	28	chauffeur	37	"
M	Jones Louise A †	29	housewife	39	"
N	Jones Stanley R	29	mechanic	46	"
O	McIntyre Elizabeth †	30	housewife	68	"
P	McIntyre Marguerite E †	30	bookkeeper	26	"
S	McCarthy Barbara †	34	housewife	49	"
T	McCarthy John J	34	clerk	56	"
U	Donlon Margaret †	36	coatmaker	31	Cambridge
V	Donlon Thomas	36	U S N	38	Portugal
W	Fahey Bartholomew L	36	"	40	99 Alexander
X	Fahey Mary A †	36	coatmaker	40	99 "
Y	Bryant Frank S	38	salesman	46	14 Wortham pk
Z	Bryant Juliette E †	38	housewife	36	14 "

718

Letter	Full Name	Residence, Jan. 1, 1941	Occupation	Supposed Age	Reported Residence, Jan. 1, 1940
A	*Rando Rose †	39	"	34	here
B	Rando Vincent	39	barber	44	"
C	Boutiette Leo H	40	cooper	30	245 Lamartine
D	Boutiette Marie F †	40	housewife	28	245 "
E	Padovano Anthony	42	metalworker	38	26 Charme av
F	Padovano Rose M †	42	housewife	29	26 "
G	*Faehy Mary †	43	"	38	here
H	*Faehy Victor	43	grinder	45	"
K	Scandura John	43	barber	48	"
L	Donovan Joseph J	44	salesman	47	"
M	Donovan Joseph J	44	optician	21	"
N	Donovan Rose A †	44	housewife	44	"
O	McDermott Elsie L †	46	"	24	278 Roslindale av
P	McDermott Joseph T	46	attorney	30	278 "
R	Harmon Louise A †	48	housewife	45	here
S	Harmon Ray A	48	accountant	40	"
T	Holub Florence C †	50	housewife	51	"

Page	Letter	Full Name	Residence, Jan. 1, 1941	Occupation	Reputed Age	Reported Residence, Jan. 1, 1940. Street and Number

Charme Avenue Continued

Page	Letter	Full Name	Residence, Jan. 1, 1941	Occupation	Reputed Age	Reported Residence, Jan. 1, 1940
	U	Holub Rudolph F	50	musician	49	here
	V	Giamnone Louis F	52	chauffeur	21	"
	W	Giamnone Louise V †	52	housewife	22	"

Cummins Highway

Page	Letter	Full Name	Residence, Jan. 1, 1941	Occupation	Reputed Age	Reported Residence, Jan. 1, 1940
	X	Luscomb Rachel †	260	at home	59	here
	Y	Silber Bernard	260	salesman	40	"
	Z	Silber Etta †	260	housewife	40	"
719						
	A	McDougall Duncan	260	carpenter	50	"
	B	*McDougall Gwendolyn †	260	housewife	47	"
	C	Rush Arthur F	260	clerk	30	"
	D	Rush Elizabeth B †	260	housewife	24	"
	E	*Sebago John	260	laborer	62	"
	F	*Chee Ning	262	laundryman	53	"
	H	Deichert Barbara K †	290	housewife	80	"
	K	Deichert Elsie E †	290	hairdresser	40	"
	L	Thompson Howard S	290	attendant	44	"
	M	Giroux Albert H	304 306	retired	58	"
	N	Giroux Florence E †	304 306	housewife	50	"
	O	Donovan John J	304 306	baker	32	868 Canterbury
	P	*Donovan Marie R †	304 306	housewife	33	868 "
	R	*Cantwell Mary F †	304 306	"	48	here
	S	Cantwell Peter D	304 306	chauffeur	45	"
	T	Cortez Dorothy †	308 310	housewife	34	920 Hyde Park av
	U	Cortez Harry	308 310	salesman	36	920 "
	V	Welsh Florence †	308 310	housewife	30	here
	W	Welsh Herbert	308 310	operator	33	"
	X	O'Connor Mary T †	308 310	clerk	27	"
	Y	O'Connor Michael	308 310	janitor	62	"
	Z	O'Connor Teresa M †	308 310	housewife	59	"
720						
	B	Blois James W	312 314	chauffeur	37	"
	C	Blois Louise A †	312 314	housewife	36	"
	D	Peterson Hulda V †	312 314	"	65	"
	E	Peterson John E	312 314	draftsman	35	"
	F	McLean Albert M	316	collector	53	1045 Wash'n
	G	McLean Mildred M †	316	housewife	42	1045 "
	H	Conlon Margaret M †	318	"	43	here
	K	Conlon Thomas	318	B F D	42	"

Page.	Letter.	FULL NAME.	Residence, Jan. 1, 1941.	Occupation.	Supposed Age.	Reported Residence, Jan. 1, 1940. Street and Number.

Cummins Highway—Continued

Page.	Letter.	FULL NAME.	Residence, Jan. 1, 1941.	Occupation.	Supposed Age.	Reported Residence, Jan. 1, 1940.
	L	Meely Alice †	318	nurse	45	here
	M	*Meely Margaret †	318	housekeeper	78	"
	N	Meely Mary A †	318	supervisor	46	"
	O	Meely William	318	clerk	34	"
	P	Sutherland Margaret F †	342	laundryworker	47	"
	R	Sutherland Walter	342	knitter	56	"
	S	Sutherland Walter J	342	shipper	21	"
	T	Carver Mary L †	346	housewife	35	"
	U	Carver Reginald G	346	laborer	37	"
	V	Kohler Ernest	346	watchman	70	"
	W	Kenney Elizabeth N †	350	clerk	26	"
	X	Kenney Herbert A	350	chauffeur	23	"
	Y	Kenney Mary A †	350	housewife	56	"
	Z	Kenney Michael B	350	printer	57	"
721						
	A	*Hamer Ernest	354	watchmaker	41	"
	B	*Hamer Margaret A †	354	housewife	40	"
	C	Hickey Anna M †	356	clerk	26	"
	D	Hickey Dennis J	356	meatbuyer	64	"
	E	Hickey Margaret J †	356	housewife	68	"
	F	Burwell John E	356	technician	23	7 Rosewood
	G	Burwell Marguerite E †	356	housewife	23	7 "
	H	Lampro Evelyn M †	360	"	42	here
	K	Lampro George W	360	selector	39	"
	L	Saunders Esther A †	360	teacher	22	Oak Bluffs
	M	Saunders Harriet S †	360	clerk	27	here
	N	Saunders Rose E †	360	nurse	26	"

Curley Street

Page.	Letter.	FULL NAME.	Residence, Jan. 1, 1941.	Occupation.	Supposed Age.	Reported Residence, Jan. 1, 1940.
	R	Antetomaso Frances †	12	marker	28	here
	S	Antetomaso Nancy †	12	housewife	45	"
	T	Antetomaso Nancy †	12	marker	21	"
	U	Antetomaso Peter	12	attendant	57	"

Gilman Street

Page.	Letter.	FULL NAME.	Residence, Jan. 1, 1941.	Occupation.	Supposed Age.	Reported Residence, Jan. 1, 1940.
	V	Lenz Ernest	9	gardener	48	here
	W	*Lenz Lillian L †	9	housewife	43	"
	X	Lenz Louise †	9	seamstress	54	Hopkinton
	Y	Benson Arnold L	10	shipper	27	here

Page	Letter	Full Name	Residence, Jan. 1, 1941	Occupation	Reputed Age	Reported Residence, Jan. 1, 1940. Street and Number

Gilman Street—Continued

Page	Letter	Full Name	Residence, Jan. 1, 1941	Occupation	Reputed Age	Reported Residence, Jan. 1, 1940. Street and Number
	Z	Benson Arthur R	10	machinist	27	here
722						
	A	Benson Martina C †	10	housewife	61	"
	B	Benson Olof	10	gardener	64	"
	C	Callaghan Emma T †	11	housewife	46	"
	D	Callaghan Hugh P	11	watchman	54	"
	E	Hunzelman Mary J †	11	stitcher	56	"
	F	Archibald Thomas R	16	pipefitter	40	44 Colberg av
	G	Moon Annie J †	16	housekeeper	52	44 "
	H	Iovinelli Harry	18	musician	40	553 Hyde Pk av
	K	Iovinelli Susie †	18	housewife	34	553 "
	L	Dosch Bertha M †	19	"	66	here
	M	Dosch Konrad	19	retired	72	"
	N	Schmid John	19	contractor	58	"
	O	Little Christina †	20	housewife	25	"
	P	Little Ralph M	20	clerk	26	"
	R	Heaney Bridget †	20	housewife	65	"
	S	Clegg Catherine E †	22	clerk	38	"
	T	Clegg John F	22	rigger	44	"
	U	Clegg Nora T †	22	housekeeper	70	"
	V	Tarby Anna G †	27	buyer	36	"
	W	Tarby Maxine †	27	operator	34	"

Hadwin Way

Page	Letter	Full Name	Residence, Jan. 1, 1941	Occupation	Reputed Age	Reported Residence, Jan. 1, 1940. Street and Number
	X	Carlson Edith M †	7	clerk	21	here
	Y	Carlson Gladys M †	7	operator	24	"
	Z	Carlson John S	7	plumber	54	"
723						
	A	Carlson Lillian M †	7	housewife	52	"
	B	Kuppens Henrietta †	8	"	72	"
	C	Carty Helen †	8	"	43	3968 Wash'n
	D	Carty Thomas P	8	conductor	46	3968 "
	E	Heneghan Mary R †	8	housewife	30	1179 Boylston
	F	Heneghan Patrick	8	laborer	31	3968 Wash'n
	G	Manley Frances M †	9	clerk	21	here
	H	Manley Gertrude M †	9	housewife	42	"
	K	Manley John C	9	agent	46	"
	L	Brodin Albin F	10	architect	60	"
	M	Brodin Helen L †	10	secretary	25	"
	N	Brodin Olga E †	10	housewife	61	"

Page	Letter	Full Name	Residence, Jan. 1, 1941	Occupation	Supposed Age	Reported Residence, Jan. 1, 1940. Street and Number.
		Hadwin Way—Continued				
	O	Everts Carl	10	machinist	34	Worcester
	P	Everts Elsie M †	10	receptionist	32	here
	R	Sweeney Ellen F †	11	housewife	77	"
	S	Sweeney Thomas F	11	machinist	81	"
	T	Madden Anna L †	12	secretary	38	"
	U	Madden Mary C †	12	bookkeeper	42	"
	V	Madden Nora A †	12	housewife	80	"
	W	Madden Richard	12	laborer	37	"
	X	Kelly Marie L †	12	housewife	57	"
	Y	Kelly Marion J †	12	clerk	21	"
	Z	MacLachlin Archibald	12	"	25	"
724						
	A	MacLachlin Hazel M †	12	typist	26	"
		Hammatt Road				
	B	Petrini Francis	9	proprietor	28	109 Redlands rd
	C	Petrini Primina †	9	housewife	26	N Hampshire
	D	Cerutta Albena †	9	"	52	here
	E	Cerutta Margaret V †	9	clerk	22	"
	F	Doyle Francis X	9	salesman	28	21 Rockwell
	G	Doyle Rena †	9	bookkeeper	27	here
	H	Piekarski Bolasle	11	toolmaker	58	"
	K	Piekarski Gladys †	11	housewife	54	"
	L	*Damant Theodore †	11	"	79	"
	M	Kadeg Elizabeth †	11	"	62	22 Union ter
	N	Legsdin Betty G †	11	"	21	294 Poplar
	O	Legsdin Edward A	11	patternmaker	29	294 "
	P	Witol Adolph	11	machinist	22	here
	R	Witol Rudolph	11	candymaker	22	"
	S	Witol Virginia †	11	houseworker	25	"
	T	Berentsen Anna †	15	housewife	76	"
	U	Berentsen Johannes C	15	retired	76	"
	V	Nelson Hannah C †	15	housewife	44	"
	W	Nelson Sivert E	15	machinist	45	"
	X	Sherman Frederick H	19	salesman	70	"
	Y	Sherman Lida J †	19	housewife	79	"
	Z	Wearner Carl O	21	carpenter	52	"
725						
	A	Wearner Elma †	21	housewife	48	"
	B	Sullivan Catherine V †	22	"	54	"

Page	Letter	Full Name	Residence, Jan. 1, 1941.	Occupation	Supposed Age	Reported Residence, Jan. 1, 1940. Street and Number

Hammatt Road Continued

Page	Letter	Full Name	Residence, Jan. 1, 1941.	Occupation	Supposed Age	Reported Residence, Jan. 1, 1940. Street and Number
	C	Sullivan Charles A	22	serviceman	58	here
	D	Sullivan Edward C	22	chauffeur	30	"
	E	Sullivan Richard J	22	adjuster	26	"
	F	Dick Bertha E—†	24	housewife	59	"
	G	Dick William F	24	coffee roaster	60	"
	H	Van Lier Hubert	27	rodman	21	"
	K	Van Lier John P	27	policeman	47	"
	L	Van Lier Wilhelmina A—†	27	housewife	57	"

Hyde Park Avenue

Page	Letter	Full Name	Residence, Jan. 1, 1941.	Occupation	Supposed Age	Reported Residence, Jan. 1, 1940. Street and Number
	N	*Ricci Anthony	420	laborer	56	6 Dana av
	O	*Ricci Concetta J—†	420	housewife	50	6 "
	P	Ricci Domonic	420	laborer	24	6 "
	R	Ricci Jean—†	420	factoryhand	29	6 "
	S	Ricci Paul	420	bottler	26	6 "
	T	Land Frederick J	420	electrician	41	here
	U	Land Margaret A—†	420	housewife	72	"
	V	Land Ruth I—†	420	laundress	43	"
	W	Ahern Elizabeth E—†	424	housewife	45	"
	X	Ahern Evelyn J—†	424	saleswoman	27	"
	Y	Ahern Joseph	424	painter	62	"
	Z	Piciulo Minnie—†	424	dressmaker	40	"
726						
	A	Piciulo Palmira—†	424	librarian	37	"
	B	Kelly Daniel J	426	steamfitter	22	16 Hawthorne
	C	*Kelly Ellen—†	426	housewife	65	16 "
	D	Kelly Patrick M	426	rigger	55	16 "
	E	Biscoe Allen W	428	salesman	27	here
	F	Biscoe Estelle M—†	428	housewife	50	"
	G	Biscoe Frances J—†	428	"	27	"
	H	Biscoe Gerald A	428	chauffeur	22	"
	K	Biscoe Harold A	428	counterman	50	"
	L	Biscoe Harold B	428	clerk	30	"
	M	Biscoe Henry R	428	laborer	24	"
	N	LaCourse Grace—†	428	housewife	38	25 Pinedale rd
	O	Crafts Harold H	430	steamfitter	40	here
	P	Crafts Marjorie G—†	430	housewife	36	"
	W	Massimino Anna—†	440	"	43	"
	X	Massimino Mario P	440	bartender	22	"
	Y	McCarthy Christine M—†	440	secretary	26	"

Page	Letter	Full Name	Residence, Jan. 1, 1941	Occupation	Supposed Age.	Reported Residence, Jan. 1, 1940. Street and Number.

Hyde Park Avenue—Continued

Page	Letter	Full Name	Residence, Jan. 1, 1941	Occupation	Supposed Age.	Reported Residence, Jan. 1, 1940.
	Z	McCarthy Francis J	440	musician	33	here
727						
	A	McCarthy John W	440	retired	63	"
	B	McCarthy Julia S †	440	housewife	63	"
	C	McCarthy Richard A	440	machinist	23	"
	D	Pelkus Henry L	444	physician	34	"
	E	Pelkus Theresa M †	444	housewife	28	"
	F	DiCicco Charles	444	contractor	47	"
	G	*DiCicco Rose G †	444	housewife	38	"
	H	Chesbro Ethel †	444	laundryworker	26	"
	K	Chesbro Robert J	444	salesman	27	"
	T	Scholz Christine †	457	housewife	57	"
	U	Scholz John A	457	carpenter	65	"
	V	Kocen Rosina J †	rear 457	housewife	25	10 Wash'n
	W	Kocen William J	" 457	welder	28	10 "
	X	Moccaldi Luigi	" 457	laborer	58	here
728						
	G	John Soo H	467	laundryman	65	"
	H	Coulthurst Thomas E	480	proprietor	60	"
	K	Grainger Catherine C— †	480	housewife	52	"
	L	Grainger Henry B	480	student	24	"
	M	Grainger Henry J	480	superintendent	52	"
	N	Costa Catherine †	485	housewife	39	"
	O	Costa John	485	merchant	44	"
	P	*Musto Amelia †	485	housewife	50	50 Jewett
	R	Musto Carmen	485	chauffeur	26	50 "
	S	Musto John	485	laborer	24	50 "
	T	Musto Joseph	485	"	22	50 "
	U	Musto Lawrence	485	proprietor	29	50 "
	V	*Musto Ralph	485	retired	63	50 "
	W	McKenna Mary A †	485	housewife	74	33 Mt Hope
	Y	DeStefano Anthony	488	laborer	52	here
	Z	*DeStefano Raffaela †	488	housewife	50	"
729						
	A	DeStefano Augustine	488	printer	24	"
	B	Cunningham Cora M †	494	housewife	44	"
	C	Cunningham John F	494	yardman	52	"
	D	Athridge Katherine †	494	clerk	42	"
	E	Athridge Thomas P	494	agent	43	"
	G	Lynch Evelyn V †	496	saleswoman	24	"
	H	Lynch James J	496	paver	69	"

Page.	Letter	Full Name	Residence, Jan. 1, 1941	Occupation	Reputed Age	Reported Residence, Jan. 1, 1940. Street and Number

Hyde Park Avenue Continued

Page.	Letter	Full Name	Residence, Jan. 1, 1941	Occupation	Reputed Age	Reported Residence, Jan. 1, 1940. Street and Number
	K	Lynch Jennie J †	496	housewife	69	here
	L	Lynch Thomas J	496	steamfitter	37	"
	M	Marena Ethel M †	497	housewife	26	"
	N	Marena Harold B	497	attendant	30	"
	O	Skjold Chester R	497	operator	28	2 Regent sq
	P	Skjold Olive J †	497	housewife	28	2 "
	R	Clark Anna I †	497	housekeeper	53	here
	S	Holland Joseph E	497	bookkeeper	25	"
	T	Holland Mary E †	497	housewife	24	"
	U	Flynn John F	498	laborer	69	"
	V	Flynn Mary F †	498	housewife	58	"
	W	Flynn Mary I †	498	stenographer	29	"
	X	Clinton Doris M †	500	"	21	"
	Y	Clinton James E	500	printer	50	"
	Z	Clinton Mary H †	500	housewife	49	"
730						
	A	Mullins Thomas F	500	machinist	51	"
	B	Mullins William J	502	printer	35	"
	C	Seegraber Alice H †	502	winder	37	"
	E	Clinton Charles F	510	machinist	46	"
	F	Clinton Charles F	510	printer	21	"
	G	Clinton James F	510	machinist	23	"
	H	Clinton Margaret F †	510	housewife	43	"
	K	McTomney Rita †	510	"	27	"
	L*	McTomney William M	510	salesman	27	"
	M	Powers Edward F	510	machinist	57	"
	N	Powers Mary L †	510	housewife	52	"
	O	Brogan Elizabeth R †	512	"	34	"
	P	Brogan Bernard F	512	janitor	36	"
	R	Doyle Agnes C †	512	housewife	46	"
	S	Doyle Dorothy T †	512	factoryhand	20	"
	T	Doyle Robert F	512	clerk	21	"
	U	Doyle Thomas J	512	carman	51	"
	V	Doyle Thomas P	512	chauffeur	26	"
	W	Doyle Warren P	512	boilermaker	23	"
	Y*	Davison George C	520	attendant	34	"
	Z	Davison Mary G †	520	housewife	30	"
731						
	A	Bowden Amy †	520	"	41	189 Bourne
	B	Bowden John E	520	janitor	43	189 "
	C	Holt Emma †	520	at home	61	[illegible] Hyde Park av

Page	Letter	Full Name	Residence, Jan. 1, 1941	Occupation	Supposed Age	Reported Residence, Jan. 1, 1940. Street and Number.

Hyde Park Avenue Continued

Page	Letter	Full Name	Residence, Jan. 1, 1941	Occupation	Supposed Age	Reported Residence, Jan. 1, 1940. Street and Number.
	D	*Costa Mary †	524	housewife	60	35 Glendale
	E	Costa Sarina †	524	teacher	26	35 "
	F	White Anna G †	524	housewife	32	here
	G	White George B	524	lineman	32	"
	H	Bialobreski Edward J	524	clerk	26	"
	K	Bialobreski Julia †	524	housewife	24	"
	L	DeBiasi Domenic	524	engineer	34	"
	M	DeBiasi Theresa †	524	housewife	32	"
	O	Gulski Mary †	524	"	27	"
	P	Gulski Stephen	524	welder	28	"
	R	Pescatore Carmelia †	528	operator	25	"
	S	Pescatore Cosimo	528	laborer	48	"
	T	Pescatore Josephine †	528	dressmaker	24	"
	U	*Pescatore Raffeala †	528	housewife	48	"
	V	McGrath Agnes L †	528	"	26	30 Stellman rd
	W	McGrath John J	528	salesman	27	30 "
	X	*Aruda Louise †	528	stitcher	49	188 Durnell av
	Y	Collins Frances B †	528	marker	26	188 "
	Z	Collins Joseph W	528	photographer	26	Bay State rd
732						
	A	McDermott Francis J	531	steamfitter	62	here
	B	McDermott Margaret E †	531	housewife	52	"
	C	Moran Mary A †	531	housekeeper	41	"
	D	Peterson Edna J †	531	housewife	27	5 Blanvon rd
	E	Peterson John J	531	shipfitter	31	5 "
	F	Anderson Grace E †	531	housewife	37	here
	G	Anderson John J	531	laborer	46	"
	K	Curtain David J	532	manager	20	"
	L	Curtain Frances M †	532	housewife	45	"
	M	Curtain Frances M †	532	clerk	23	"
	N	Curtain Timothy J	532	"	50	"
	O	Kenfield Sylvia †	532	teacher	27	"
		Cassidy Elizabeth †	532	housewife	23	"
	R	Cassidy Raymond L	532	clerk	27	"
	S	Bench Elizabeth F †	535	housewife	50	"
		Bench Frank S	535	retired	65	"
		Bench Kathryn F †	535	clerk	27	"
		Vozzella Annibale	536	blacksmith	37	"
	W	Vozzella Carmelia †	536	housewife	30	"
		Szydlik Jennie †	536	"	21	"
		Szydlik Joseph	536	factoryhand	26	"

Page.	Letter.	FULL NAME	Residence, Jan. 1, 1941	Occupation	Supposed Age.	Reported Residence, Jan. 1, 1940. Street and Number

Hyde Park Avenue (Continued)

Page.	Letter.	FULL NAME	Residence, Jan. 1, 1941	Occupation	Supposed Age.	Reported Residence, Jan. 1, 1940. Street and Number
	Z	Donley James T	539	retired	82	here
733						
	A	Donley Margaret M—†	539	housewife	46	"
	B	Donley Stephen H	539	printer	47	"
	C	DeAngelis Anthony	539	chauffeur	31	62 Mt Hope
	D	DeAngelis Margaret—†	539	housewife	30	543 Hyde Park av
	E	Marque Harold M	540	optician	46	here
	F	Marque Mary H—†	540	housewife	38	"
	G	Spinelli Caroline—†	540	"	34	"
	H	Spinelli Philip	540	laborer	36	"
	K	Hughes Kathleen H—†	543	housewife	41	25 Seymour
	L	Hughes Lawrence A	543	chauffeur	43	25 "
	M	Wadels Andrew P	543	machinist	51	here
	N	Wadels Mary S—†	543	housewife	41	"
	O	Donehey Albert E	543	supervisor	39	"
	P	Donehey Sarah J—†	543	housewife	39	"
	R	Doherty Helen—†	544	housekeeper	61	"
	S	McLaughlin John J	544	B F D	51	"
	T	McLaughlin Mary J—†	544	housekeeper	62	"
	U	Ritchie Annabelle—†	544	saleswoman	63	"
	V*	Hines Mary M—†	547	housewife	39	"
	W	Hines Thomas J	547	carpenter	41	"
	X	Boston Frank G	547	merchant	60	"
	Y	Little Barbara C—†	547	seamstress	59	"
	Z	Beaupre Archie	547	B F D	43	"
734						
	A	Beaupre Ernestine—†	547	housewife	46	"
	B*	Foley Mary J—†	551	housekeeper	54	"
	C	Barry Adelle G—†	551	housewife	26	"
	D	Barry Joseph V	551	bookkeeper	24	"
	E	Doyle Dorothy F—†	551	housewife	31	"
	F	Doyle Edward C	551	plumber	36	88 High
	G	Doyle Joseph G	551	B F D	42	here
	H	Civitarese Don	552	mechanic	26	"
	K	McKenna Helen M—†	552	housewife	32	"
	L	McKenna Thomas J	552	technician	36	"
	M	McKeon Grace A—†	552	nurse	39	"
	N	McKeon James T	552	machinist	18	"
	O	McKeon Mary A—†	552	housewife	39	"
	P	Sharkey Joseph T	552	shoeworker	52	"
	R	McHugh Eleanor P—†	553	housewife	28	177 School

Page	Letter	Full Name.	Residence, Jan. 1, 1941.	Occupation.	Supposed Age.	Reported Residence, Jan. 1, 1940. Street and Number.

Hyde Park Avenue—Continued

Page	Letter	Full Name.	Residence, Jan. 1, 1941.	Occupation.	Supposed Age.	Reported Residence, Jan. 1, 1940. Street and Number.
	S	McHugh Frank J	553	photographer	31	177 School
	T	Pagliuca Catherine E—†	553	housewife	25	16 Charme av
	U	Pagliuca Charles J	553	manager	26	16 "
	V	Murphy Hugh J	553	carpenter	47	here
	W	Murphy Isabelle—†	553	housewife	44	"
	X	Murphy Kathleen D—†	553	stenographer	23	"
	Y	Puleo Anna B—†	559	housewife	50	"
	Z	Puleo Edmund J	559	laborer	21	"
735						
	A	Puleo Joseph	559	draftsman	52	"
	B	Cummins Annie—†	559	at home	75	"
	C	Downey Catherine—†	559	matron	55	"
	D	Turley Ellen—†	559	housewife	65	"
	F	Goode James R	563	repairman	44	"
	G	Goode Margaret E—†	563	housewife	44	"
	H	Assmus Carl F	563	machinist	43	"
	K	Assmus Catherine J—†	563	winder	20	"
	L	Assmus Gretchen E—†	563	clerk	46	"
	M	Assmus Mary J—†	563	housewife	43	"
	N	Goode Bridget—†	563	at home	79	250 Arborway
	O	Goode William	563	machinist	46	250 "
	P	O'Hara Della—†	563	dressmaker	51	250 "
	R	Colantuoni Theresa—†	564	housewife	49	here
	S	Lacey Catherine A—†	564	"	46	6 Meyer
	T	Lacey Edward J	564	chauffeur	21	6 "
	U	Lacey John P	564	machinist	53	6 "
	V	Hackenson Walter	566	manager	47	here
	W	Cornell John F	568	cook	46	Westfield
	X	Curley Anna M—†	568	housewife	43	here
	Y	Curley Walter R	568	clerk	21	"
736						
	A	O'Donnell Gertrude L—†	570	at home	54	43 Ainsworth
	B	Sheehan Gertrude V—†	570	housewife	25	43 "
	C	Sheehan Leo F	570	machinist	25	43 "
	D	Powers Rita T—†	570	housewife	27	here
	E	Powers William E	570	chauffeur	27	"
	F	Bremner Helen—†	571	housewife	33	"
	G	Bremner Nathan	571	physician	37	"
	H	Wilson Stella—†	571	housekeeper	36	"
	K	Riley Charles	571	painter	66	3 Kensington

Page	Letter	Full Name	Residence, Jan. 1, 1941.	Occupation	Reputed Age.	Reported Residence, Jan. 1, 1940. Street and Number.

Hyde Park Avenue—Continued

Page	Letter	Full Name	Residence, Jan. 1, 1941.	Occupation	Reputed Age.	Reported Residence, Jan. 1, 1940. Street and Number.
	L	Riley Frances †	571	operator	40	3 Kensington
	M	Cogan Mary †	571	at home	66	here
	N	Costello Grace C †	571	housewife	33	"
	O	Costello James M	571	carpenter	33	"
	P	Pulver Benjamin	572	chauffeur	52	"
	R	Pulver Eva G †	572	housewife	59	"
	S	*Costello Anna †	572	"	38	"
	T	Costello Peter	572	laborer	43	"
	U	Coffey Gertrude M †	574	housewife	42	29 Centre
	V	Coffey William P	574	laborer	45	29 "
	W	Schnurr Bertha A †	574	housewife	71	here
	X	Schnurr William R	574	machinist	41	"
	Y	Bean Anna T †	575	housewife	57	"
	Z	Andrea Eugene J	575	baker	64	"
737						
	A	Andrea Helen H †	575	bookkeeper	34	"
	B	Andrea Louise †	575	housewife	64	"
	C	Andrea Mary L †	575	"	26	"
	D	Andrea Raymond L	575	mechanic	25	"
	E	*Lahage Pauline †	575	clerk	31	"
	F	*Lahage Richard	575	shoeworker	45	"
	G	Norsigian George B	578	machinist	54	"
	H	Norsigian George F	578	clerk	20	"
	K	Norsigian Lougret †	578	housewife	45	"
	L	Norsigian Veronica †	578	housekeeper	22	"
	M	*Damiano Marie †	578	housewife	49	"
	N	Damiano Savino	578	laborer	54	"
	O	Dahill Harriet F †	578	housewife	45	"
	P	Dahill John J	578	chauffeur	43	"
	S	Pistorio Esther †	580	housewife	30	"
	T	Pistorio Joseph L	580	musician	31	"
	U	Shields Rose †	580	housewife	65	"
	V	DiMarzio Catherine G †	580	"	23	"
	W	DiMarzio Victor P	580	clothing cutter	25	"
738						
	E	Stamoulis George E	596	proprietor	46	"
	F	*Stamoulis Mary K †	596	housewife	49	"
	G	Sylvestro Antonio S	596	clerk	31	923 Hyde Park av
	H	Sylvestro Mary R †	596	housewife	28	923 "
	L	*Cossette Armance †	602	"	42	1368 Wash'n

Page	Letter	Full Name	Residence, Jan. 1, 1941.	Occupation	Supposed Age	Reported Residence, Jan. 1, 1940. Street and Number.

Hyde Park Avenue—Continued

Page	Letter	Full Name	Residence	Occupation	Age	Reported Residence
	M	*Cossette Roch	602	carpenter	40	4368 Wash'n
	N	Todd Harris H	602	bookbinder	51	here
	O	Todd Madeline C—†	602	housewife	49	"

Jewett Street

Page	Letter	Full Name	Residence	Occupation	Age	Reported Residence
	R	Sexton Albert W	7	decorator	44	here
	S	Sexton Arthur J	7	guard	40	"
	T	Sexton Marion F—†	7	housewife	39	"
	U	Sexton Pauline F—†	7	"	40	"
	V	McCarthy Annie F—†	10	"	49	"
	W	McCarthy Edna L—†	10	student	21	"
	X	McCarthy Elinor A—†	10	operator	23	"
	Y	McCarthy John F	10	checker	27	"
	Z	McCarthy John J	10	foreman	56	"
739						
	A	McCarthy M Joan—†	10	waitress	20	"
	B	McCarthy Mary C—†	10	operator	25	"
	C	Walsh Mary T—†	10	housekeeper	52	"
	D	Finneran Cecelia F—†	12	housewife	33	"
	E	Finneran Peter F	12	B F D	34	"
	F	Williams Alice M—†	12	packer	36	43 Metropolitan av
	G	Williams James E	12	laborer	34	43 "
	H	Conroy Mary—†	15	housekeeper	67	here
	K	Conroy Thomas P	15	salesman	28	"
	L	*Walsh Delia M—†	15	maid	63	"
	M	Healy James E	15	mechanic	42	"
	N	Healy Joseph P	15	chauffeur	38	"
	O	Healy Mary M—†	15	housekeeper	47	"
	P	Healy Thomas E	15	retired	82	"
	R	Ieneaelli Anna R—†	16	assembler	23	"
	S	Ieneaelli Domenica—†	16	housewife	48	"
	T	Ieneaelli Nicola	16	laborer	57	"
	U	*Swanson Douglas	16	machinist	51	"
	V	*Swanson Edith—†	16	housewife	53	"
	W	*Connolly Helena—†	18	"	29	31 Millmont
	X	Connolly John J	18	chauffeur	32	31 "
	Y	Dolan Bridie M—†	18	housewife	45	here
	Z	Dolan John J	18	plasterer	59	"
740						
	A	Jenness E Margaret—†	18	housewife	37	N Hampshire

Page.	Letter.	Full Name.	Residence, Jan. 1, 1941.	Occupation.	Supposed Age.	Reported Residence, Jan. 1, 1940. Street and Number.

Jewett Street Continued

Page.	Letter.	Full Name.	Residence, Jan. 1, 1941.	Occupation.	Supposed Age.	Reported Residence, Jan. 1, 1940. Street and Number.
	B	Patchett Irma L—†	20	housewife	35	here
	C	Patchett John N	20	plasterer	36	"
	D	*Downey Catherine M—†	20	housewife	78	"
	E	Downey Josephine A—†	20	stenographer	36	"
	F	Downey Michael J	20	laborer	69	"
	G	*Scully Thomas J	20	"	71	"
	H	Nicotera Batista	22	"	47	"
	K	Nicotera Domenic	22	"	22	"
	L	Nicotera Eleanora R—†	22	assembler	21	"
	M	*Nicotera Mary—†	22	housewife	41	"
	N	Robinson Annie I—†	32	"	50	"
	O	Robinson Harry W	32	plasterer	60	"
	P	Ardolino Emilio	32	laborer	55	"
	R	*Ardolino Sigrid A—†	32	housewife	62	"
	S	Boyd Anna—†	46	housekeeper	63	"
	T	Starke Anna E—†	50	clerk	20	518 Hyde Park av
	U	Starke Harold E	50	chauffeur	44	518 "
	V	Starke Maude E—†	50	housewife	44	518 "
	W	Elworthy Ernest A	50	painter	40	here
	X	Elworthy Teresa M—†	50	housewife	40	"
	Y	Antonelli Angelo R	50	welder	37	"
	Z	Antonelli Frances—†	50	housewife	28	"
741						
	A	Amico Angelo	54	clerk	30	"
	B	Amico Margaret M—†	54	housewife	30	"
	C	DiBiasi Anthony	54	laborer	56	"
	D	Welch Eileen M—†	54	waitress	22	"
	E	Welch Francis J	54	ironworker	46	"
	F	Welch Mary E—†	54	housewife	46	"
	G	Sheehan Joseph	54	meatcutter	55	"
	H	Sheehan Katherine F—†	54	typist	21	"
	K	Sheehan Rachel K—†	54	housewife	52	"

Manning Street

Page.	Letter.	Full Name.	Residence, Jan. 1, 1941.	Occupation.	Supposed Age.	Reported Residence, Jan. 1, 1940. Street and Number.
	L	Solari Andrew J	21	inspector	29	180 E Seventh
	M	Solari Anne T—†	21	housewife	25	180 "
	N	Falk Arthur C	28	florist	47	here
	O	Falk Mary L—†	28	housewife	47	"
	P	Connolly Dorothy F—†	29	clerk	25	"
	R	Connolly Martin W	29	carpenter	48	"

Page	Letter	Full Name	Residence, Jan. 1, 1941.	Occupation.	Supposed Age.	Reported Residence, Jan. 1, 1940. Street and Number.

Manning Street—Continued

Page	Letter	Full Name	Residence, Jan. 1, 1941.	Occupation.	Supposed Age.	Reported Residence, Jan. 1, 1940. Street and Number.
	S	Connolly Mary E—†	29	housewife	44	here
	T	Gordon Kathryn R—†	31	housekeeper	42	"
	U	Gordon Mae E—†	31	typist	40	"
	V	O'Brien William H	31	investigator	49	"
	W	Adie Pauline E—†	32	housewife	37	"
	X	Adie Robert S	32	manager	37	"
	Y	Carmichael Katherine—†	32	housewife	47	"
	Z	Carmichael Mary C—†	32	finisher	20	"
742						
	A	Carmichael Patrick W	32	manager	48	"
	B	*Grahn Bertha M—†	35	housewife	31	"
	C	Grahn Thorsten	35	metalworker	33	"
	D	Chase Ballard M	35	chauffeur	40	"
	E	Chase Grace E—†	35	housewife	47	"
	F	MacCallum John	36	operator	46	"
	G	MacCallum Marion B—†	36	housewife	42	"
	H	Foley Agnes H—†	36	secretary	33	"
	K	Foley Charles A	36	retired	86	"
	L	Foley Nora A—†	36	operator	37	"
	M	Flynn Arthur L	40	repairman	35	"
	N	Flynn Cecelia C—†	40	housewife	35	"
	O	O'Malley Austin F	40	clerk	47	"
	P	O'Malley Kathleen E—†	40	housewife	45	"

Mount Calvary Road

Page	Letter	Full Name	Residence, Jan. 1, 1941.	Occupation.	Supposed Age.	Reported Residence, Jan. 1, 1940. Street and Number.
	S	McCarthy Annie L—†	15	housewife	56	here
	T	McCarthy Charles	15	carpenter	32	"
	U	McCarthy Joseph J	15	cook	22	"
	V	Dorr Christine—†	16	waitress	42	"
	W	Dorr Emma—†	16	housekeeper	49	"
	X	Dorr Frederick	16	tree surgeon	50	"
	Y	Dorr Frederick	16	mechanic	22	"
	Z	Walsh Joseph	16	policeman	42	"
743						
	A	Dorr Elizabeth—†	16	collector	65	"
	B	Falk Helene E—†	35	florist	73	"
	C	Stolpner Clara A—†	35	housekeeper	68	"
	D	Stolpner Max F	35	florist	56	"
	E	Worms Beatrice M—†	37	housewife	38	"
	G	Worms Jesse	37	policeman	46	"

Mount Calvary Road—Continued

Page	Letter	Full Name	Residence, Jan. 1, 1941	Occupation	Age	Reported Residence, Jan. 1, 1940. Street and Number
	H	Stolpner Clara H †	43	bookkeeper	34	here
	K	Stolpner Paul	43	retired	63	"
	L	Stolpner Walter	43	boilermaker	27	"
	M	Cronin Sarah O †	45	housewife	47	"
	N	Cronin William M	45	papercutter	58	"
	O	Diese Mary A †	45	at home	77	361 Wash'n
	P	Leary Cornelius P	49	painter	50	here
	R	Leary Josephine C †	49	housewife	41	"
	S	Zoppo Thomas F	49	electrician	23	"
	T	McHugh Florence R †	53	housewife	39	"
	U	McHugh Francis J	53	electrician	43	"
	V	Tierney Agnes †	57	housewife	42	"
	W	*Bradwin Gladys C †	61	"	45	"
	X	Bradwin Herbert A	61	butler	50	"
	Y	Newton Charles J	65	woodworker	36	"
	Z	Newton Estes H	65	"	70	"
744						
	A	Newton Margaret †	65	housewife	60	"
	B	Newton Maude B †	65	nurse	31	"

Mount Hope Street

Page	Letter	Full Name	Residence, Jan. 1, 1941	Occupation	Age	Reported Residence, Jan. 1, 1940. Street and Number
	D	Golden Charles J	1	steeple jack	23	here
	E	Golden Francis V	1	manager	48	"
	F	Golden Francis V, jr	1	clerk	21	"
	G	Golden Josephine C †	1	housewife	44	"
	H	McNeff Bernard	1	mechanic	39	"
	K	McNeff Mary †	1	housewife	33	"
	L	Grady Dorothy C †	1	"	20	"
	M	Grady Thomas F	1	lamplighter	25	"
	N	Hughson Catherine E †	1	saleswoman	40	"
	O	Morrison Charles E	1	laborer	52	"
	P	Morrison Ottilia E †	1	housewife	54	"
	R	Brine Ethel L †	6	"	41	"
	S	Brine James W	6	packer	20	"
	T	Brine John T	6	mailer	18	"
	U	Sutherland Elizabeth C †	6	laundryworker	20	"
	V	Sutherland Jane J †	6	housewife	47	"
	W	Sutherland John W	6	finisher	46	"
	X	Sutherland Kenneth W	6	chauffeur	21	"
	Y	Sutherland Ralph T	6	manager	22	"

Page	Letter	Full Name	Residence, Jan. 1, 1941.	Occupation.	Supposed Age.	Reported Residence, Jan. 1, 1940. Street and Number.

Mount Hope Street—Continued

Page	Letter	Full Name	Residence, Jan. 1, 1941.	Occupation.	Supposed Age.	Reported Residence, Jan. 1, 1940. Street and Number.
	Z	Cane Gone T	6	laborer	59	here
745						
	A	*Cane Hope †	6	housekeeper	25	"
	B	Cane Ralph	6	clerk	28	"
	C	*Cane Sophie †	6	housewife	58	"
	D	Brogna Allessandro	15	reporter	25	"
	E	Brogna Carmela †	15	housewife	49	"
	F	Brogna Felix	15	machinist	62	"
	G	Brogna Raffela	15	factoryhand	23	"
	H	Trullo Aida †	15	laundryworker	27	"
	K	Trullo Antoinette †	15	factoryhand	25	"
	L	Hughes Alfred A	15	painter	29	"
	M	Hughes Louise †	15	housewife	26	"
	N	Bastianelli Enis E †	15	"	26	"
	O	Bastianelli Frank B	15	mechanic	27	"
	P	Axt Anna E †	19	stenographer	29	"
	R	Axt William J, jr	19	inspector	27	"
	S	DeRosa Daniel J	19	plasterer	49	"
	T	DeRosa Marie A †	19	housewife	48	"
	U	Drew Charles H	22	clerk	58	"
	V	Drew Curtis C	22	laborer	25	"
	W	Drew Phyllis M †	22	clerk	23	"
	X	Drew Ruth I †	22	housewife	46	"
	Y	Smiley John F	22	policeman	40	"
	Z	Smiley Mary B †	22	housewife	40	"
746						
	A	Chase Cornelius B	23	retired	70	"
	B	Downey Elizabeth †	23	housewife	47	"
	C	Kepple Edward B	23	packer	26	"
	D	Kepple Francis B	23	bellboy	22	"
	E	Kepple John H	23	U S A	24	"
	F	Kepple Joseph C	23	captain	28	"
	G	Cameron Cassie †	27	housekeeper	72	"
	H	Cameron John	27	shipper	30	"
	K	Cameron Lawrence	27	laborer	35	"
	L	Cameron Rebecca †	27	factoryhand	41	"
	M	Power John	28	mechanic	36	"
	N	Power Mary †	28	housewife	25	"
	O	Scopa Mary F †	28	"	49	"
	P	Scopa Nicholas	28	mechanic	52	"
	R	Scopa Ralph F	28	laborer	23	"

Mount Hope Street (Continued)

Page	Letter	Full Name	Residence, Jan. 1, 1941	Occupation	Reputed Age	Reported Residence, Jan. 1, 1940. Street and Number
	S	Clarke George D	30	laundryworker	32	here
	T	Clarke Mary—†	30	housewife	32	"
	U	Heeney Anna—†	30	"	38	"
	V	Heeney William	30	machinist	40	"
	W	DeAngelis Anna—†	33	housewife	27	40 Mt Hope
	X	DeAngelis Frederick	33	laborer	34	40 "
	Y	DeStefano Charles A	33	chauffeur	30	488 Hyde Park
	Z	DeStefano Victoria T—†	33	housewife	27	488 "
747						
	A	*O'Regan Irene—†	34	"	43	47 Dewey
	B	*O'Regan Wilbur F	34	operator	57	47 "
	C	*Petitto Andrew F	34	laborer	36	here
	D	Petitto Antoinette—†	34	housewife	32	"
	E	Panico Anthony	34	chauffeur	22	4309 Wash'n
	F	Panico Eleanor C—†	34	seamstress	20	4309 "
	G	Panico Emilia—†	34	housewife	51	4309 "
	H	Panico Ralphael	34	laborer	59	4309 "
	K	*Kally Bridget—†	37	housekeeper	65	568 Hyde Park
	L	Kally John J	37	mechanic	40	568 "
	M	Cataldo Helen—†	37	housewife	36	here
	N	Cataldo Henry R	37	painter	36	"
	O	Marpaux Bertrand	38	U S A	22	"
	P	Marpaux George	38	patternmaker	54	"
	R	Marpaux Rose—†	38	housewife	44	"
	S	*DeAngelis Elizabeth—†	40	"	65	"
	T	*DeAngelis Thomas	40	retired	65	"
	U	DeAngelis Charles	40	painter	39	"
	V	DeAngelis Louise—†	40	housewife	40	"
	W	Curley Annie E—†	41	"	70	"
	X	Curley Edward F	41	retired	72	"
	Y	Curley Edward F, jr	41	salesman	37	[illegible]
	Z	Curley William J	41	policeman	48	here
748						
	A	Bastianelli Catherine—†	45	forewoman	25	"
	B	Bastianelli Lawrence	45	chauffeur	25	"
	C	Cataldo Dorothy—†	45	clerk	21	"
	D	Cataldo John	45	operator	23	"
	E	Cataldo Joseph	45	janitor	52	"
	F	Cataldo Mary—†	45	housewife	46	"
	G	Cataldo Ralph	45	wrapper	27	"
	H	Foisy Maurice J	47	policeman	47	"

Page	Letter	Full Name	Residence, Jan. 1, 1941.	Occupation	Supposed Age	Reported Residence, Jan. 1, 1940. Street and Number.

Mount Hope Street—Continued

Page	Letter	Full Name	Residence, Jan. 1, 1941.	Occupation	Supposed Age	Reported Residence, Jan. 1, 1940. Street and Number.
	K	Foisy Yvonne B †	47	housewife	45	here
	L	Dolan James	55	retired	72	"
	M	Carver Henry R	55	"	76	"
	N	Carver Joseph H	55	draftsman	35	"
	O	Carver Mathilda †	55	housewife	77	"
	P	Callahan Elizabeth F †	58	operator	43	"
	R	Hiatt Frederick W, jr	58	mattressmaker	54	"
	S	Hiatt Mary R †	58	housewife	52	"
	T	Hiatt Mary V †	58	secretary	23	"
	U	Robinson Anna K †	62	cleaner	55	"
	V	Kelleher Bessie †	62	teacher	45	11 Bradstreet av
	W	Kelleher Thomas	62	examiner	43	11 "
	X	Donely Edith M †	65	housewife	60	here
	Y	Donely William J	65	gardener	65	"
	Z	Egar Mary M †	66	teacher	53	"
749						
	A	Egar William F	66	salesman	26	"
	B	Doyle Evelyn †	66	operator	22	"
	C	Doyle Lena C †	66	housewife	48	"
	D	Doyle William	66	chauffeur	55	"
	E	McKernan Elizabeth V † r	66	housewife	51	"
	F	McKernan James H "	66	salesman	51	"
	G	McKernan Katherine F † "	66	student	20	"
	H*	McKernan Catherine A †	68	housewife	68	"
	K*	McKernan John	68	merchant	62	"
	L	McKernan Mary E †	68	stenographer	39	"
	M	Murry Edward F	71	tollman	62	"
	N	Murry Margaret †	71	housewife	50	"
	O	Goodwin Mary J †	73	"	76	"
	P	Goodwin Thomas J	73	retired	81	"
	R	Woodard Herbert C	76	meatcutter	61	"
	S	Woodard Marion E †	76	housewife	51	"
	T	Chisholm Margaret J †	76	at home	68	"
	U	McCormack Nellie J †	76	housekeeper	74	"
	V	Gutowski Andrew	79	florist	48	Springfield
	W*	Gutowski Sophie †	79	housewife	51	Brookline
	X	Gutowski Stephen	79	florist	50	here
	Y	Kuntz August L	80	waiter	47	"
	Z	Kuntz Emma C †	80	housewife	50	"
750						
	A	Pottier James	80	retired	80	"

Page	Letter	Full Name	Residence, Jan. 1, 1941	Occupation	Reputed Age	Reported Residence, Jan. 1, 1940. Street and Number
Mount Hope Street (Continued)

Page	Letter	Full Name	Residence, Jan. 1, 1941	Occupation	Reputed Age	Reported Residence, Jan. 1, 1940. Street and Number
	B	*Pottier Rose †	80	housewife	78	here
	D	Rourke Frank J, jr	94	plumber	21	"
	E	Rourke Gertrude E †	94	housewife	45	"
	F	Norton Gertrude M †	94	clerk	34	"
	G	Norton Mary G †	94	housewife	66	"
	H	Norton Thomas F	94	plumber	32	"
	K	Norton Thomas J	94	retired	72	"
	L	Mulrean Annie †	94	operator	45	18 Summit
	M	Leonard Bernard V	99	merchant	37	here
	N	*Leonard Margaret †	99	housewife	31	"
	O	Melia John B	99	carpenter	35	"
	P	Melia Rita C †	99	housewife	32	"
	R	O'Malley Mary F †	117	"	32	"
	S	O'Malley Peter F	117	steamfitter	34	"
	T	Thompson Bridget M †	117	housekeeper	65	"
	U	Cataldo Alfred	119	chauffeur	26	"
	V	Cataldo Guy	119	cook	22	"
	W	Cataldo Ida †	119	housewife	23	"
	X	*Cataldo Josephine †	119	"	56	"
	Y	*Cataldo Ralph	119	laborer	58	"
	Z	Cataldo Anthony	119	chauffeur	32	"
751						
	A	Cataldo Mary †	119	housewife	29	"
	B	Balzano Mary †	119	"	30	"
	C	Balzano Vincent	119	barber	39	"
	D	Barrett Lora B †	135	housekeeper	41	Natick
	E	Small Estelle H †	135	housewife	66	here
	F	Small Walter B	135	carpenter	55	"
	G	Williams Walter J	135	cook	34	"
	H	Kennedy John M	137	mechanic	54	"
	K	Kennedy Mary B †	137	housewife	52	"
	L	Fornauf Frank	158	machinist	31	"
	M	Fornauf Katherine †	158	housewife	31	"
	N	Lucia Anglina R †	158	clerk	20	"
	O	Lucia Joseph A	158	buffer	45	"
	P	Lucia Mary V †	158	saleswoman	21	"
	R	*Lucia Rose †	158	housewife	44	"
	T	Fravassi Angela E †	162	"	32	"
	U	Fravassi Eugene S	162	florist	33	"
	W	Jenkins Eric H	168	manager	39	"
	X	Jenkins Mildred B †	168	housewife	44	"
	Y	Buchanan Jessie †	176	saleswoman	42	"

Page	Letter	Full Name	Residence, Jan. 1, 1941.	Occupation.	Supposed Age.	Reported Residence, Jan. 1, 1940. Street and Number.

Mount Hope Street—Continued

Page	Letter	Full Name	Residence, Jan. 1, 1941.	Occupation.	Supposed Age.	Reported Residence, Jan. 1, 1940. Street and Number.
	Z	Buchanan Madeline †	176	housewife	38	here
752						
	A	Buchanan Margaret †	176	operator	26	"

Neponset Avenue

Page	Letter	Full Name	Residence, Jan. 1, 1941.	Occupation.	Supposed Age.	Reported Residence, Jan. 1, 1940. Street and Number.
	B	Bogardus Emma C †	7	housewife	43	here
	C	Bogardus Fred H	7	policeman	53	"
	D	Balkin William	7	retired	74	British Columbia
	E	Walsh James M	19	"	69	here
	F	Geissler Ernest F	27	"	73	24 Paul Gore
	G	Geissler Johanna †	27	housewife	68	24 "
	H	Fitzgibbons Maurice G	27	laborer	41	here
	K	Paterson Jean I †	27	housewife	21	Ohio
	L	Paterson Stewart W	27	clerk	29	Hingham
	M	Carosella Carmen	43	laborer	52	here
	N	*Carosella Concetta †	43	housewife	52	"
	O	Hobart Catherine †	45	housekeeper	61	"
	P	Hobart Estella L †	45	manager	40	"
	R	Hobart Kathleen V †	45	clerk	27	"
	S	Lawrence Harry	45	"	36	285 Dudley
	T	Lawrence Mary C †	45	"	34	here
	U	Skillings Margaret R †	45	saleswoman	30	"
	V	Campbell Hector J	53	blacksmith	23	91 Sanborn av
	W	Campbell Mildred M †	53	housewife	23	91 "
	X	Waechter Fritz H	53	foreman	49	here
	Y	Waechter Philippine †	53	housewife	50	"
	Z	Bridgeo May †	53	housekeeper	45	"
753						
	A	Morris Margaret A †	57	housewife	26	"
	B	Morris Thomas F	57	clerk	28	"
		Costello Mary A †	59	housewife	42	"
	D	Costello Patrick	59	chauffeur	49	"
	E	Scarlata Joseph	61	clerk	47	"
	F	Scarlata Rose †	61	housewife	35	"
	G	Joseph Mary †	63	"	35	"
	H	Joseph Phillip T	63	foreman	41	"
	K	Long Bernard L	67	shipper	34	"
	L	Long Michelina M †	67	housewife	24	"
	M	Ciccio Grace †	69	"	44	"

Page	Letter	Full Name	Residence, April 1, 1940	Occupation	Supposed Age	Reported Residence, April 1, 1939. Street and Number

Neponset Avenue—Continued

Page	Letter	Full Name	Residence	Occupation	Age	Reported Residence
	N	Ciccio Joseph P	69	engraver	24	here
	O	Ciccio Salvatore	69	barber	50	"
	P	Doyle Catherine D—†	71	housewife	35	"
	R	Doyle Frederick C	71	policeman	32	"
	S	Ammendolia Anthony	73	laborer	56	"
	T	Ammendolia Gasper	73	machinist	22	"
	U	Ammendolia Jennie—†	73	seamstress	25	"
	V	Ammendolia Joseph	73	machinist	20	"
	W	*Ammendolia Rose—†	73	housewife	48	"
	X	Finneran Helen J—†	75	clerk	29	"
	Y	O'Connor Joseph M	75	electrician	34	"
	Z	O'Connor Mary L—†	75	housewife	31	"
754						
	A	Pedranti Elna A—†	77	"	22	124 Peters
	B	Pedranti George A	77	tinsmith	23	101 Neponset av
	C	Roger Estelle M—†	79	housewife	24	here
	D	Roger Spencer W	79	rug cutter	27	"
	E	Cadigan Arthur W	81	foreman	36	"
	F	Cadigan Stella E—†	81	housewife	34	"
	G	Ryba Viola M—†	81	inspector	29	"
	H	Healey Laurel E—†	83	housewife	36	"
	K	Healey William A	83	installer	44	"
	L	Daly Ellen M—†	85	housewife	44	"
	M	Daly William F	85	chauffeur	43	"
	N	Daly William F	85	assembler	21	"
	O	*Bates Mary C—†	87	housewife	44	"
	P	Bates William J	87	painter	44	"
	R	Andrews George E	89	laborer	45	"
	S	Finnell Francis A	89	operator	26	"
	T	Finnell George E	89	laborer	26	"
	U	Finnell Joseph	89	letter carrier	60	"
	V	Finnell Joseph R	89	laborer	27	"
	W	Finnell Julia L—†	89	housewife	54	"
	X	Finnell Margaret E—†	89	clerk	24	"
	Y	Angelini Albert	95	laborer	50	"
	Z	Angelini Margaret D—†	95	glazier	21	"
755						
	A	Angelini Peter	95	sorter	24	"
	B	Barone Charles	97	salesman	36	1379 Com av
	C	Barone Ethel Q—†	97	housewife	32	1379 "
	D	Cataldo Alfred F	99	letter carrier	41	here

Page	Letter	Full Name	Residence, Jan. 1, 1941	Occupation	Supposed Age	Reported Residence, Jan. 1, 1940. Street and Number

Neponset Avenue—Continued

Page	Letter	Full Name	Residence, Jan. 1, 1941	Occupation	Supposed Age	Reported Residence, Jan. 1, 1940. Street and Number
	E	Cataldo Ruth A—†	99	housewife	40	here
	F	Walsh Ellen F—†	101	"	35	"
	G	Walsh Martin F	101	salesman	36	"
	H	DePietro Catherine—†	103	housewife	40	"
	K	DePietro Salvatore	103	policeman	44	"
	L	Lionetto Grace—†	105	dressmaker	44	79 Lubec
	M	Lionetto John	105	laborer	50	79 "

Paine Street

Page	Letter	Full Name	Residence, Jan. 1, 1941	Occupation	Supposed Age	Reported Residence, Jan. 1, 1940. Street and Number
	N	Flynn Barbara—†	27	beautician	24	here
	O	Flynn Leo	27	salesman	24	50 Rosemont
	P	Simpson Alden E	27	welder	27	here
	R	Simpson Margaret—†	27	housewife	44	"
	S	Perry Florence—†	35	"	36	"
	T	Perry Frank	35	electrician	36	"
	U	*Hawkes Charles M	41	machinist	54	"
	V	Hawkes Helen E—†	41	housewife	49	"
	W	*Cossette Jules	51	carpenter	36	"
	X	*Cossette Rachael—†	51	housewife	33	"
	Y	McNulty Francis P	55	laborer	50	"
	Z	McNulty Paul	55	loamworker	25	"
756						
	A	McNulty Sarah—†	55	housewife	50	"
	B	McNulty Winifred—†	55	nurse	22	"
	C	Curran Agnes R—†	59	housewife	32	"
	D	Curran Leonard E	59	engineer	33	"
	E	DeAngelis George	59	toolmaker	26	"
	F	DeAngelis Mary—†	59	housewife	26	"
	G	Geraci John	89	chauffeur	38	"
	H	Geraci Mary—†	89	housewife	28	"
	K	Greenwood Francis W	89	packer	25	69 Water
	L	Greenwood Mary—†	89	housewife	21	69 "
	M	Farrar Clarence	93	publisher	42	here
	N	Farrar Karla—†	93	housewife	34	"
	O	Nielsen Ada—†	93	artist	30	"
	P	Nielsen Anna N—†	93	housewife	58	"
	R	Nielsen Arnold	93	shipwright	29	"
	S	Norris James	93	mechanic	36	"
	T	Norris Mary—†	93	housewife	41	"

Page	Letter	Full Name	Residence Jan. 1, 1941	Occupation	Supposed Age	Reported Residence Jan. 1, 1940. Street and Number

Paine Street—Continued

Page	Letter	Full Name	Residence Jan. 1, 1941	Occupation	Supposed Age	Reported Residence Jan. 1, 1940
	U	Lynch Edward J	97	merchant	46	here
	V	Lynch Margaret C—†	97	housekeeper	54	"

Peters Street

Page	Letter	Full Name	Residence Jan. 1, 1941	Occupation	Supposed Age	Reported Residence Jan. 1, 1940
	W	Bianchetto Ernest E	124	dresscutter	24	here
	X*	Bianchetto Linda—†	124	housewife	47	"
	Y*	Bianchetto Peter	124	cook	51	"
	Z*	Drago Federica—†	124	housekeeper	78	"
757						
	A	Gulio Celestina—†	124	housewife	50	"
	B	Gulio Eda E—†	124	bookkeeper	20	"
	C	Gulio Joseph	124	waiter	54	"

Philbrick Street

Page	Letter	Full Name	Residence Jan. 1, 1941	Occupation	Supposed Age	Reported Residence Jan. 1, 1940
	D	Clerken Elizabeth—†	21	housekeeper	76	here
	E	Ranahan John J	21	retired	63	"
	F	Russell Mary A—†	21	nurse	54	"
	G	Hendsbee Robertina—†	22	housekeeper	33	Cambridge
	H	Sedgwick Elizabeth S—†	22	housewife	66	here
	K	Sedgwick Watkin	22	retired	82	"
	L*	Murphy Mary—†	25	housewife	33	"
	M*	Murphy Patrick J	25	chauffeur	40	"
	N*	Sedgewick Ruby M—†	25	housewife	32	"
	O	Sedgewick Wendell W	25	samplemaker	29	"
	R	Johnston Bickford R	29	meatcutter	28	"
	S	Johnston Christine C—†	29	checker	28	"
	T	Billings Annie G—†	29	housewife	65	"
	U	Billings Franklin L	29	retired	73	"
	V	McManus James F	29	shipper	36	"
	W*	Saldwalk Louise—†	33	housewife	72	"
	X	Saldwalk Ernest W	33	painter	42	"
	Y	Taylor Anna J—†	33	housewife	73	"
	Z	Taylor Eleanor G—†	33	seamstress	35	"
758						
	A	Farmer Glenice K—†	33	librarian	24	"
	B	Farmer Noyes D, jr	33	student	23	"
	C*	Manning Annie—†	35	housekeeper	66	"
	D*	McGuire John J	35	salesman	31	"
	E	McGuire Mary E—†	35	housewife	34	"

Page	Letter	Full Name	Residence, Jan. 1, 1941	Occupation	Supposed Age	Reported Residence, Jan. 1, 1940. Street and Number

Philbrick Street—Continued

Page	Letter	Full Name	Residence, Jan. 1, 1941	Occupation	Supposed Age	Reported Residence, Jan. 1, 1940. Street and Number
	F	McGowan John	35	operator	64	here
	G	McGowan Mary †	35	housewife	58	"
	H	Malone Joseph	41	machinist	25	958 River
	K	Malone Mildred—†	41	stenographer	24	1041 Hyde Park av
	L	Murray Catherine E—†	41	housewife	38	here
	M	Murray George L	41	operator	42	"
	N	Young Frederick	47	sander	42	"
	O	Young Grace	47	waitress	40	"
	P	Brady Helen C—†	49	housekeeper	31	"
	R	Doyle Joseph F	51	policeman	24	"
	S	Doyle Joseph P	51	B F D	48	"
	T	MacQuarrie Ann J—†	53	housewife	35	"
	U	MacQuarrie Neil J	53	chauffeur	39	"
	V	Cataldo Lawrence	54	florist	33	"
	W	Cataldo Virginia †	54	housewife	28	"
	X	Isbriglio Aurelia—†	54	"	59	"
	Y	Isbriglio Nicola	54	cook	55	"
	Z	Wallace Ellen A †	54	housekeeper	69	"
759						
	A	MacDonald Emily C—†	57	housewife	33	"
	B	MacDonald Ronald J	57	chauffeur	35	"
	C	Cataldo Joseph	58	"	28	119 Mt Hope
	D	Cataldo Rose M—†	58	housewife	23	119 "
	E	Dobrikowski Julius	58	metalworker	63	here
	F	Dobrikowski Mabel L—†	58	housewife	61	"
	G	Starkey Catherine V—†	59	"	46	"
	H	Starkey Ervin F	59	upholsterer	47	"
	K	Starkey Phyllis V †	59	clerk	20	"
	L	Murray Ann C †	61	housewife	62	"
	M	Murray Edward T	61	pressman	36	"
	N	Perkins Alfred H	63	policeman	51	"
	O	Perkins Eula B †	63	housewife	48	"

Stella Road

Page	Letter	Full Name	Residence, Jan. 1, 1941	Occupation	Supposed Age	Reported Residence, Jan. 1, 1940. Street and Number
	P	Callahan Catherine J †	20	housewife	69	here
	R	Maloney Joseph A	20	clerk	58	"
	S	DeMatteo Martin	55	contractor	61	"
	T	DeMatteo Martin, jr	55	"	21	"
	U	DeMatteo Pasqualina †	55	housekeeper	28	"
	V	DeMatteo Stella †	55	housewife	55	"

Page.	Letter.	Full Name.	Residence, Jan. 1, 1941.	Occupation.	Reputed Age.	Reported Residence, Jan. 1, 1940. Street and Number.

Stella Road—Continued

Page.	Letter.	Full Name.	Residence, Jan. 1, 1941.	Occupation.	Reputed Age.	Reported Residence, Jan. 1, 1940. Street and Number.
	W	Peterson Elsie D—†	60	housewife	43	5 Aldwin rd
	X	Peterson Eric E	60	machinist	48	5 "
	Y	Peterson John O	60	"	24	5 "
	Z	Sardella Carmella—†	60	housewife	31	here
760						
	A	Sardella Paul	60	contractor	30	"

Walk Hill Street

Page.	Letter.	Full Name.	Residence, Jan. 1, 1941.	Occupation.	Reputed Age.	Reported Residence, Jan. 1, 1940. Street and Number.
	B	Tannaro Frank S	289	laborer	32	here
	C	Tannaro John C	289	"	28	"
	D	Tannaro Nicholas	289	retired	74	"
	E	Tannaro Rose C—†	289	housekeeper	29	"
	F	Brahany Thomas H	321	retired	79	"
	G	Fopiano Emilio J	327	proprietor	53	"
	H	Mahoney Ella J—†	335	operator	48	"
	K	Williams John J	335	clerk	72	"

Ward 18—Precinct 8

CITY OF BOSTON

LIST OF RESIDENTS
20 YEARS OF AGE AND OVER

(NON-CITIZENS INDICATED BY ASTERISK)
(FEMALES INDICATED BY DAGGER)

AS OF

JANUARY 1, 1941

CITY OF BOSTON PRINTING DEPARTMENT

Page.	Letter	Full Name	Residence, Jan. 1, 1941	Occupation	Supposed Age.	Reported Residence, Jan. 1, 1940. Street and Number.

800

Bradlee Street

Page.	Letter	Full Name	Residence, Jan. 1, 1941	Occupation	Supposed Age.	Reported Residence, Jan. 1, 1940. Street and Number.
800	A	Anderson Herbert C	3	machinist	48	here
	B	Melin Carl	3	"	68	"
	C	Melin Hilda A †	3	housewife	67	"
	D	Colwell Ida J †	8	"	63	"
	E	Colwell William V	8	gardener	71	"
	F	Jewett George M	8	machinist	51	144 Beaver
	G	Jewett Grace E †	8	housewife	50	144 "
	H	Jewett Phyllis M †	8	"	22	Maine
	K	Jewett Richard G	8	clerk	25	"
	L	Degnan Helen †	9	attorney	32	here
	M	Degnan Lucy †	9	housewife	74	"
	N	Degnan Thomas E	9	textileworker	36	Pennsylvania
	O	Sessler Margaret L †	9	papermaker	38	here
	P	Warren Marion †	10	housekeeper	71	"
	R	Shire Marie A †	14	housewife	35	"
	S	Shire Towfick E	14	mechanic	42	"
	T	McKinnon Alice V †	18	housewife	27	"
	U	McKinnon Raymond	18	carpenter	26	"
	V	Toti Philip	22	welder	45	"
	W	*Toti Theresa †	22	housewife	34	"
	Y	Kretschmer Edith B †	26	stenographer	34	"
	Z	Kretschmer Ernest M	26	baker	29	"
801	A	Kretschmer Max	26	retired	74	"
	B	Pistorio James P	30	machinist	26	"
	C	Pistorio John B	30	barber	64	"
	D	Pistorio Lillian L †	30	housewife	63	"
	E	Pistorio Mary V †	30	beautician	38	"
	F	Michel Catherine †	36	housewife	32	"
	G	Michel Hugo	36	plumber	32	"
	H	Michel William	36	printer	34	"
	K	Smith Julia A †	36	housewife	43	"
	L	Smith Walter H	36	loomfixer	49	"
	M	*Blake Christine A †	44	at home	74	"
	N	Blake Herman	44	policeman	37	"
	O	*Blake Samuel	44	retired	74	Maine
	P	*Grant Annie V †	44	housewife	51	here
	R	*Grant Charles T	44	engineer	25	"

Page	Letter	Full Name	Residence, Jan. 1, 1941	Occupation	Supposed Age	Reported Residence, Jan. 1, 1940. Street and Number

Canterbury Street

Page	Letter	Full Name	Residence, Jan. 1, 1941	Occupation	Supposed Age	Reported Residence, Jan. 1, 1940. Street and Number
	T	Bryan Mary C †	951	housewife	45	here
	U	Bryan Thomas E	951	contractor	49	"
	V	Wylie Catherine †	951	at home	77	"
	W	*Leckie Sadie F †	961	housewife	71	"
	X	Leckie William L	961	retired	79	"
	Y	McLaughlin Mary †	rear 961	housekeeper	45	"
	Z	Pretorius Josephine †	965	housewife	40	"
802						
	A	Pretorius Olaf	965	painter	40	"
	B	Pretorius Victoria R †	965	housewife	65	"
	C	Welch Ellen A †	969	"	50	"
	D	Welch John B	969	painter	24	"
	E	McCusker Dorothy M †	969	operator	26	Newton
	F	McCusker Mary C †	969	housewife	57	here
	G	McCusker William	969	lineman	64	"
	H	Ayan Albert J	973	machinist	23	"
	K	Ayan George E	973	coremaker	21	"
	L	Ayan Solveig †	973	housewife	43	"
	M	*Hanley Ann M †	975	"	31	"
	N	Hanley John F	975	chauffeur	34	"
	O	*Paglinca Carmella †	975	housewife	47	"
	P	Paglinca James	975	laborer	21	"
	R	Paglinca Joseph	975	"	18	"
	S	Paglinca Josephine †	975	at home	25	"
	T	Casey Margaret †	977	housewife	33	[illegible]
	U	*Merola Mary †	977	"	41	here
	V	Merola William	977	mason	41	"
	W	Nagle Ralph S	1002	chauffeur	38	"
	X	Nagle Theresa R †	1002	housewife	35	"

Clare Avenue

Page	Letter	Full Name	Residence, Jan. 1, 1941	Occupation	Supposed Age	Reported Residence, Jan. 1, 1940. Street and Number
	Y	Rich Edwin A	2	engineer	61	5 Leniston
	Z	Rich Ina E †	2	housewife	53	5 "
803						
	A	Bowman Mary †	2	housekeeper	42	here
	B	Kent Astra A †	4	housewife	20	57 Prospect
	C	Kent George A	4	clerk	24	57 "
	D	Kundert Caroline L †	6	housewife	71	here
	E	Kundert Christine C †	6	"	51	"
	F	Mulkern Agnes F †	8	housekeeper	50	"

Page	Letter	Full Name	Residence, Jan. 1, 1941	Occupation	Supposed Age	Reported Residence, Jan. 1, 1946. Street and Number.

Clare Avenue—Continued

Page	Letter	Full Name	Residence, Jan. 1, 1941	Occupation	Supposed Age	Reported Residence, Jan. 1, 1946
	G	Mulkern Cecelia M †	8	clerk	42	here
	H	Mulkern Margaret †	8	housewife	82	"
	K	*Ryan Gertrude M †	12 14	"	48	"
	L	Ryan John F	12 14	salesman	54	"
	M	MacDonald Edwin	12 14	metalworker	30	11 Pitsmoor rd
	N	*MacDonald Jeanette †	12 14	housewife	30	11 "
	O	Flaherty Delia M †	15	"	45	here
	P	Flaherty John J	15	laborer	46	"
	R	Burns Virginia M †	15	housewife	30	"
	S	Burns William F	15	clerk	30	"
	T	Stukas Albert J	16	meatcutter	22	"
	U	Stukas Ernest J	16	clerk	24	"
	V	Stukas Joseph D	16	chef	65	"
	W	Stukas Joseph G	16	musician	20	"
	X	Stukas Martha D †	16	housewife	45	"
	Y	*Bartlett Daisy G †	17	"	42	"
	Z	Bartlett John L	17	salesman	43	"
804						
	A	Watson Ernest	17	watchman	55	"
	B	Watson Mary H †	17	housewife	55	"
	C	Martin Mary E †	20	"	56	"
	D	Martin Thomas F	20	custodian	54	"
	E	Dolan Ernest D	20	clerk	47	"
	F	Dolan Gertrude A †	20	housewife	44	"
	G	Murray James T	21	painter	32	"
	H	Murray Ruth M †	21	housewife	30	"
	K	Uriot Carl H	21	retired	69	"
	L	Uriot Ida E †	21	housewife	66	"
	M	Carlson John A	25	patternmaker	80	"
	N	Anderson Goodwin F	28	chauffeur	41	"
	O	*Anderson Pauline †	28	housewife	44	"
	P	McRae James F	28	foreman	48	457 Cummins H'way
	R	McRae Katherine F †	28	housewife	46	457 "
	S	Anderson Annie †	29	"	53	here
	T	Anderson Hans L	29	machinist	65	"
	U	*Wickberg Bertie G	29	estimator	36	"
	V	Wickberg Ruth I †	29	housewife	37	"
	V	Devitt Mary A †	32	housekeeper	81	"
	W	Erlandson Edward C	32	upholsterer	52	"
	X	Erlandson Nina G †	32	housewife	48	"
	Z	*Mayo Lottie †	32	waitress	36	"

Page	Letter	Full Name	Residence Jan. 1, 1941	Occupation	Supposed Age	Reported Residence, Jan. 1, 1940. Street and Number

805

Clare Avenue Continued

Letter	Full Name	Residence	Occupation	Age	Reported Residence
A	*Mayo Stanley	32	porter	33	here
B	*Perrin Janetta —†	33	housewife	44	"
C	Perrin Thomas	33	machinist	46	"
D	Alexander Lettie P —†	33	housekeeper	83	"
E	Johnson Bertha G —†	36	housewife	33	"
F	Johnson Harold V	36	machinist	31	"
G	Erlandson Henry A	36	clerk	44	"
H	Phinney Charles A	37	cutter	75	"
K	Phinney Elizabeth —†	37	housewife	72	"
L	Troy Elizabeth C —†	37	"	31	"
M	Troy Francis A	37	engineer	34	"
N	Peters Robert G	38	operator	67	"
O	Greenberg Anna N —†	38	housekeeper	55	"
P	Lawson Carl E	38	retired	70	"
R	Lawson Selma M —†	38	housewife	60	"
S	Picozzi Constance —†	43	"	40	"
T	Picozzi Elvira M —†	43	waitress	29	"
U	Picozzi Emilio	43	shoemaker	47	"
V	Picozzi James	43	painter	40	"
W	Picozzi Joseph	43	barber	44	"
X	Civitarese Anthony	62	contractor	37	"
Y	Civitarese Margaret —†	62	housewife	34	"
Z	Avellino Innocenzo	62	engineer	54	"

806

Letter	Full Name	Residence	Occupation	Age	Reported Residence
A	Avellino Louise R —†	62	housewife	46	"
B	Avellino Sebastian	62	student	25	"
C	Avellino Silvio	62	salesman	26	"
D	Barnes Garrett H	65	retired	73	"
E	Barnes Gertrude M —†	65	housewife	68	"
F	Erickson Betty —†	66	"	70	"
G	Erickson Henning	66	finisher	67	"
H	Laverie Emily I —†	69	housewife	32	"
K	Laverie James F	69	manager	31	"
L	Withers Edward H	69	retired	72	"
M	Palmborg Hilda J —†	70	housewife	64	"
N	Palmborg Peter A	70	janitor	70	"
O	Wikman John	73	painter	61	"
P	Wikman Pauline S —†	73	housewife	52	"
R	Wikman Caroline P —†	73	"	30	"
S	Wikman Wilfred R	73	salesman	29	"

Page	Letter	Full Name	Residence, Jan. 1, 1941	Occupation.	Supposed Age.	Reported Residence, Jan. 1, 1940. Street and Number.

Clare Avenue Continued

Page	Letter	Full Name	Residence	Occupation	Age	Reported Residence
	T	Fleming George L	74-76	manager	52	here
	U	Fleming Honora T—†	74-76	housewife	85	"
	V	Fleming Martin J	74-76	installer	54	"
	W	Lundell Axel	78	blacksmith	51	"
	X	Lundell Signe D—†	78	housewife	51	"
	Y	Nelson Christina—†	78	housekeeper	71	"
	Z	Olson Frederick	81	printer	24	"
807						
	A	Olson Ingeborg A—†	81	housewife	72	"
	B	Olson Olaf	81	machinist	72	"
	C	Kincannon Moses M	85	repairman	41	"
	D	Schlecht John	85	florist	41	"
	E	Schlecht Mary—†	85	housewife	47	"
	F	DiMartino Camillo	86	contractor	47	"
	G	DiMartino Mary—†	86	housewife	31	"
	H	Oser Anna—†	93	housekeeper	81	"
	K	Warren Ivy A—†	93	housewife	35	"
	L	Warren Joseph P	93	electrician	36	"
	M	Fagnano Carmen	94	operator	59	"
	N	Ventola Jennie—†	94	housewife	55	"
	O	Delaconte Frances—†	94	"	28	"
	P	Delaconte James	94	printer	29	"
	R	Ventola Joseph	94	upholsterer	28	"
	S	Ventola Rose—†	94	housewife	25	"
	T	Quigley Edward C	97	hygienist	20	"
	U	Quigley John B	97	student	21	"
	V	Quigley John D	97	U S N	50	"
	W	Quigley Mary—†	97	housewife	45	"
	X	Hebb Ann E—†	99	"	28	"
	Y	Hebb Earl A	99	mechanic	32	"
	Z	Gleason John B	105	U S N	36	"
808						
	A	Schneider Apollonia—†	105	housewife	74	"
	B	Schneider Elizabeth B—†	105	technician	39	"
	C	Schneider John	105	retired	75	"
	D	Reardon John J	106	operator	21	28 Custer
	E	Smith Mary E—†	106	housekeeper	68	here
	F	LaDue Lillian—†	109	seamstress	44	656 E Eighth
	G	Zinke August C	109	retired	76	here
	H	Zinke Augusta—†	109	housewife	69	"
	K	Zinke Bertha—†	109	operator	32	"

Clare Avenue Continued

Page	Letter	Full Name	Residence, Jan. 1, 1941	Occupation	Age	Reported Residence, Jan. 1, 1940. Street and Number
	L	Zinke Herman W	109	breweryworker	39	here
	M	Zinke Johanna C—†	109	packer	42	"
	N	Zinke Louise—†	109	operator	37	"
	O	Zinke Walter A	109	salesman	34	"
	P	Zinke William E	109	clerk	35	"
	R	Murphy Ellen M—†	115	housewife	54	"
	S	Murphy James P	115	machinist	57	"
	T	Hanson Helen J—†	117	bookkeeper	42	"
	U	Hanson William O	117	pipefitter	41	"
	V	McCarthy Alice V—†	117	bookbinder	40	"
	W	Nulick Margaret L—†	118	housewife	36	14 W Dedham
	X	Nulick Richard E	118	U S N	41	14 "
	Y	Wightman James E	119	policeman	40	911 Hyde Park av
	Z	Wightman Margaret—†	119	housewife	35	911 "
809						
	A	MacNaught Florence L—†	121	"	45	43 Lexington
	B	MacNaught William C	121	clerk	45	43 "
	C	Howard Albert J	123	"	42	563 Hyde Park av
	D	Howard Katherine A—†	123	housewife	40	563 "
	E	Andrews Harry O	126	laborer	20	here
	F	Andrews Mary A—†	126	housewife	42	"
	G	Andrews Oliver C	126	painter	52	"
	H	Weider Alice J—†	127	accountant	28	Winthrop
	K	Weider Edward B	127	shipper	33	"
	L	Costello Alice M—†	129	housewife	31	85 Moreland
	M	Costello James D	129	clerk	31	85 "
	N	Gallagher Robert E	130	operator	31	724 Saratoga
	O	Kane Kathleen E—†	130	housewife	38	724 "
	P	Kane William J	130	machinist	45	724 "
	R	Dunn Eleanor B—†	133	housewife	34	19 Roseway
	S	Dunn Reginald F	133	chef	42	19 "
	T	Feehan Amy L—†	134	housewife	28	51 Stanley
	U	Feehan Joseph W	134	bellhop	32	51 "
	V	Guilford Alice—†	138	housewife	35	43 Beverly Circle
	W	Guilford Joseph H	138	manager	36	43 "
	X	Moore Edith V—†	178	housewife	30	here
	Y	Moore Thomas	178	machinist	40	"
	Z	Haering Edna—†	178	operator	27	Avon
810						
	A	Sander Hugo	178	clerk	48	here
	B	Sander Irene—†	178	operator	22	"

Page.	Letter	Full Name	Residence, Jan. 1, 1941	Occupation	Supposed Age	Reported Residence, Jan. 1, 1940. Street and Number.

Clare Avenue—Continued

Page.	Letter	Full Name	Residence, Jan. 1, 1941	Occupation	Supposed Age	Reported Residence, Jan. 1, 1940.
	C	Allsop Ethel M—†	189	housewife	52	here
	D	Allsop John	189	fireman	59	"
	E	Knecht Jacob F	189	barber	68	"
	F	O'Reilly Helen E—†	189	housewife	24	"
	G	O'Reilly William F	189	meatcutter	34	"
	H	Broadbent Barbara M—†	190	secretary	29	"
	K	Zaugg Ernest L	190	journalist	27	"
	L	Zaugg Marguerite K—†	190	housewife	59	"
	M	Zaugg Otto E	190	merchant	59	"
	N	Pardo Antonio	193	retired	63	"
	O*	Pardo Caroline—†	193	housewife	53	"
	P	Pardo Josephine—†	193	embroiderer	26	"
	R	Pardo Margaret—†	193	"	23	"
	S*	Pardo Richard	193	retired	60	"
	T	Pardo Salvatore	193	plater	20	"
	U	Wood Theresa—†	193	housekeeper	55	"
	V*	Simpson Edith M—†	201	housewife	25	71 Sunnyside
	W	Simpson Kenneth S	201	clerk	25	71 "
	X	O'Connor Dennis A	201	laborer	35	here
	Y	O'Connor Ellen—†	201	housewife	62	"
	Z	O'Connor Joseph G	201	conductor	23	"

811 Collins Street

Page.	Letter	Full Name	Residence, Jan. 1, 1941	Occupation	Supposed Age	Reported Residence, Jan. 1, 1940.
811	A	DeFilippo Dominic	15	machinist	51	here
	B*	DeFilippo Rose—†	15	housewife	43	"
	C*	Sveistys Frances—†	15	"	48	"
	D	Sveistys Joseph	15	watchman	48	"
	E	Sveistys Josephine—†	15	saleswoman	29	"
	F	Alberto Felicia—†	21	housewife	32	"
	G	Alberto Frank	21	foreman	35	"
	H*	Alberto Veneranda—†	21	housewife	65	"
	K	Alberto Alfred L	21	agent	40	"
	L	Alberto Florence M—†	21	housewife	45	"
	M	DiStefano Anthony S	21	plasterer	31	708 Com av
	N	DiStefano Edna J—†	21	housewife	22	708 "

Cummins Highway

Page.	Letter	Full Name	Residence, Jan. 1, 1941	Occupation	Supposed Age	Reported Residence, Jan. 1, 1940.
	O	Moccea Angela—†	291	housewife	39	here
	P	Moccea Joseph	291	shoemaker	45	"

Page	Letter	Full Name	Residence Jan. 1, 1941	Occupation	Supposed Age	Reported Residence Jan. 1, 1940. Street and Number

Cummins Highway—Continued

Page	Letter	Full Name	Residence Jan. 1, 1941	Occupation	Supposed Age	Reported Residence Jan. 1, 1940. Street and Number
	R	*Mussi Elizabeth †	291	housewife	30	here
	S	Mussi Pompeo	291	painter	47	"
	T	*Gudelis Jennie M †	295	housewife	39	"
	U	*Gudelis John	295	baker	47	"
	V	Donnellan Bridget A †	297	housewife	55	"
	W	Donnellan Daniel B	297	painter	63	"
	X	Murphy Helen †	301–303	housewife	39	"
	Y	Murphy Raymond	301–303	machinist	41	"
	Z	Dillon Edward M	301–303	engineer	32	36 Symmes
812						
	A	Dillon Loretta M †	301–303	housewife	32	36 "
	B	Dillon Margaret A †	301–303	"	57	36 "
	C	Hogan Doris M †	301–303	saleswoman	21	here
	D	Zaman Doris M †	301–303	housewife	38	"
	E	Zaman Michael	301–303	shipper	38	"
	F	*Picozzi Assunta †	305–307	housewife	45	"
	G	Picozzi Rosindo	305–307	operator	44	"
	H	McCarthy Emma †	305–307	housewife	40	"
	K	McCarthy Martin E	305–307	inspector	43	"
	L	Oberst Lawrence	305–307	gardener	40	"
	M	Oberst Marie †	305–307	housewife	40	"
	N	Morris Margaret M †	305–307	"	37	"
	O	Morris Melville A	305–307	painter	40	"
	P	Grant Alice †	305–307	housewife	40	"
	R	Grant William	305–307	agent	37	"
	S	Fischer Christopher	305–307	plumber	70	"
	T	Fischer Meta †	305–307	housewife	59	"
	U	Hermitage George T	305–307	operator	31	"
	V	Hermitage Kathleen L †	305–307	housewife	26	"
	W	*Magnuson Katherine C †	309	"	35	"
	X	Magnuson William O	309	carpenter	42	"
	Y	November Elizabeth L †	309	housewife	31	"
	Z	November Samuel H	309	painter	41	"
813						
	A	Lehan Anna †	309	housewife	70	1586 Tremont
	B	Lehan David J	309	shipper	26	here
	C	*Lehan Sarah V †	309	housewife	30	"
	F	Martin Delia †	343	"	78	"
	G	Martin Edward I	343	chauffeur	32	"
	H	Martin Harold G	343	laborer	43	"
	K	Cook Mary E †	433	housekeeper	38	131 Grange

Page	Letter	Full Name	Residence Jan. 1 1941	Occupation	Supposed Age	Reported Residence, Jan. 1, 1940. Street and Number.

Cummins Highway—Continued

Page	Letter	Full Name	Residence	Occupation	Age	Reported Residence
	L	Mullaney Francis J	433	clerk	37	1516 Blue Hill av
	M	Mullaney Rose E—†	433	"	42	1516 "
	N	Wittekind Julius	433	watchman	65	here
	O	Baasner Gustave H	457	chauffeur	65	"
	P	Ridley Chester	457	blacksmith	35	27 Glendower
	R	Ridley Myrtle—†	457	housewife	32	27 "
	S	DelCorsa John	495	tinsmith	35	here
	T	DelCorsa Ruth—†	495	housewife	32	"
	U	Mulcahy Helen G—†	495	"	41	"
	V	Mulcahy Thomas J, jr	495	starter	41	"

Farrar Avenue

Page	Letter	Full Name	Residence	Occupation	Age	Reported Residence
	X	McGonagle John	11	ironworker	43	here
	Y	McGonagle Sarah E—†	11	housewife	35	"
	Z	O'Neil Carlye M—†	15	demonstrator	45	"
814						
	A	O'Neil Lawrence F	15	installer	50	"
	B	Tierney Francis J	16	foreman	51	"
	C	Tierney Francis P	16	manager	23	"
	D	Tierney Mary A—†	16	housewife	50	"
	E	Tierney Roger T	16	cashier	22	"
	F	Falvey John J	19	policeman	43	65 Dewey
	G	Falvey Marion V—†	19	housewife	41	65 "
	H	Bellew Joseph F	20	blacksmith	42	249 River
	K	Gioiosa Catherine C—†	20	housewife	37	here
	L	Gioiosa Salvatore L	20	salesman	37	"
	M	Moore Harry F	21	draftsman	21	88 Wood av
	N	Moore Mary M—†	21	housewife	40	88 "
	O	Moore Murray W	21	guard	49	88 "
	P	MacDonald Edna—†	24	housekeeper	47	here
	R	Roth Edward L	24	machinist	38	"
	S	Carlson Esther G—†	25	housewife	28	50 Rosewood
	T	Carlson Harold E	25	optician	27	50 "
	U	Johnson Adolph E	26	manager	48	here
	V	Johnson Marie S—†	26	housewife	46	"
	W	Martin Dorothy L—†	72	"	30	"
	X	Martin Francis T	72	teacher	31	"
	Y	Gartland Helen F—†	76	housewife	29	"
	Z	Gartland John J	76	attorney	34	"

Page	Letter	Full Name	Residence Jan. 1, 1941	Occupation	Supposed Age	Reported Residence Jan. 1, 1940 Street and Number

815

Farrar Avenue—Continued

	A	Powers Linda E—†	80	housewife	37	here
	B	Powers Pearson J	80	B F D	47	"
	C	Mullen Blanche—†	84	housewife	33	"
	D	Mullen Joseph A	84	teacher	36	"
	E	O'Malley Helen A—†	87	housewife	31	"
	F	O'Malley Patrick L	87	manager	31	"
	G	Duncan Annie B—†	88	housewife	35	"
	H	Duncan Harvey P	88	engineer	35	"
	K	Nugent Christine M—†	91	attendant	24	"
	L	Nugent Mary E—†	91	secretary	27	"
	M	Nugent Sarah P—†	91	housewife	52	"
	N	Nugent Thomas D	91	machinist	23	"
	O	Nugent Thomas H	91	chauffeur	53	"
	P	Forsell Herbert G	92	teacher	38	19 Grayson
	R	Forsell John	92	retired	64	19 "
	S	Forsell Sofia—†	92	housewife	62	19 "
	T	Hokenson Alfred P	92	machinist	35	19 "
	U	Hokenson Edna D—†	92	housewife	34	19 "
	V	Sweetland Myra H—†	95	"	62	here
	W	Sweetland Samuel J	95	policeman	67	"
	X	White Archibald L	96	painter	58	"
	Y	White Mary L—†	96	housewife	57	"
	Z	Devereux James T	99	policeman	38	"
816						
	A	Devereux Pauline E—†	99	housewife	35	"

Huntington Avenue

	B	Berry Emily H—†	214	bookbinder	54	here
	C	Holzer Albert	214	"	57	"
	D	Holzer Bertha—†	214	"	60	"
	F	Pautzsch Arthur B	222	salesman	24	"
	G	Pautzsch Margaret A—†	222	housewife	62	"
	H	Pautzsch Richard O	222	student	21	"
	K	*Fleiger Caroline—†	222	housewife	74	"
	L	Hill Dorothy M—†	230	"	31	"
	M	Hill Leonard F	230	engineer	36	"
	N	Morley Mary W—†	230	bookkeeper	40	42 Rosa
	O	Bliss Louise W—†	234	housewife	79	here

Page	Letter	Full Name	Residence, Jan. 1, 1941.	Occupation	Supposed Age	Reported Residence, Jan. 1, 1940. Street and Number.

Huntington Avenue—Continued

Page	Letter	Full Name	Residence, Jan. 1, 1941.	Occupation	Supposed Age	Reported Residence, Jan. 1, 1940. Street and Number.
	P	Bliss Walter B	234	clerk	75	here
	R	Malcolm Ellen J †	240	housewife	58	"
	S	Shea Corinne E †	240	"	22	"
	T	Shea John G	240	laborer	25	"
	U	Hennessey Alice R †	248	housewife	33	"
	V	Hennessey James L	248	clerk	37	"
	W	*Hennessey Julia M †	248	at home	73	"
	X	Cadogan James J	248	laborer	27	114 Winthrop
	Y	Cadogan Mary R †	248	stenographer	26	20 Holmfield av
	Z	Cox Eleanor †	260	waitress	23	992 River
817						
	A	Cox George	260	laborer	25	Dedham
	B	McLeod Lillian F †	260	housewife	32	here
	C	*McLeod Roderick A	260	retired	86	"
	D	McLeod Tucker S	260	foreman	45	"
	E	Held John	320	retired	76	"
	F	Lynch Anna M †	320	housewife	51	"
	G	Lynch Edward J	320	printer	21	"
	H	Lynch Mary G †	320	stenographer	23	"
	K	Lynch Thomas J	320	laborer	26	"
	L	Bogle Esther †	320	housewife	45	"
	M	Bogle John	320	foreman	46	"
	N	Anderson Anton S	327–329	manager	43	596 Metropolitan av
	O	Anderson Gertrude †	327–329	housewife	30	596 "
	P	Bogan Alice H †	327–329	waitress	24	here
	R	Bogan Alta H †	327–329	housewife	66	"
	S	Bogan Floyd	327–329	machinist	39	"
	T	Bogan Kathleen †	327–329	housewife	29	"
	U	Murphy Hazel †	327–329	clerk	24	"
	V	Paine Alice C †	328	housewife	25	"
	W	Paine Harold E	328	mechanic	26	"
	X	Brauneis Alice G †	328	housewife	42	"
	Y	Brauneis Frederick C	328	policeman	46	"
	Z	Carr Prentice O	331	retired	82	"
818						
	A	Paulsen Harold	331	machinist	45	"
	B	Paulsen Isabel B †	331	housewife	31	"
	C	Strachan Adelaide †	332	"	70	"
	D	Strachan William D	332	pipefitter	60	"
	E	Cochrane Edith M †	332	clerk	28	"
	F	Cochrane Helen D †	332	housewife	64	"

Page	Letter	Full Name	Residence, Jan. 1, 1941	Occupation	Supposed Age	Reported Residence, Jan. 1, 1940. Street and Number

Huntington Avenue *Continued*

Page	Letter	Full Name	Residence, Jan. 1, 1941	Occupation	Supposed Age	Reported Residence, Jan. 1, 1940. Street and Number
	G	Cochrane Joseph	332	retired	66	here
	H	Broders Harold	335	installer	47	"
	K	Broders Helen L †	335	housewife	31	"
	L	Murray James A	339	repairman	50	"
	M	Murray Margaret H †	339	housewife	45	"
	N	Wilson Elizabeth J †	340	"	53	Milton
	O	Wilson Harold W	340	linotyper	36	"
	P	Wilson Phyllis E †	340	housewife	37	"
	R	O'Leary Arthur J	340	teacher	33	here
	S	O'Leary Catherine T †	340	housewife	62	"
	T	O'Leary Ellen I †	340	clerk	30	"
	U	O'Leary James F	340	chauffeur	32	"
	V	O'Leary Margaret C †	340	stenographer	23	"
	W	Smith Florence B †	343	housewife	44	"
	X	Smith John W	343	engineer	53	"
	Y	Cibotti Nicholas	347–349	contractor	48	"
	Z	Cibotti Philomena †	347–349	housewife	35	"
819						
	A	D'Alessandro Antonio	347–349	bricklayer	33	"
	B	*D'Alessandro Lucy †	347–349	housewife	33	"
	C	MacDonald Geraldine P †	348	inspector	26	"
	D	MacDonald Leonard J	348	chauffeur	26	"
	E	Ford Everett J	348	teacher	40	"
	F	Ford Genevieve †	348	housewife	73	"
	G	Ford Jeremiah A	348	clerk	76	"
	H	McDonough Veronica †	348	saleswoman	68	"
	K	*Mariano Angelo	351–353	housewife	42	"
	L	Mariano Vincent	351–353	cook	41	"
	M	Galeota Elsie R †	351–353	housewife	28	"
	N	Galeota Nicholas F	351–353	draftsman	32	"
	O	Corbett Andrew D	352	spinner	61	"
	P	Corbett Charles F	352	brass finisher	70	"
	R	Corbett George T	352	salesman	47	"
	S	Corbett Laura E †	352	at home	63	"
	T	Corbett Walter E	352	finisher	66	"
	U	Corbett William C	352	printer	55	"
	V	Faulkner Daniel M	357	retired	78	"
	W	Faulkner Julia M †	357	housewife	64	"
	X	Margeson Charles	357	carpenter	76	Milton
	Y	Margeson Ella †	357	housewife	72	"
	Z	Chase Beulah M †	359	"	46	here

Page	Letter	Full Name	Residence Jan. 1, 1941.	Occupation	Supposed Age.	Reported Residence, Jan. 1, 1940. Street and Number.
820		**Huntington Avenue**—Continued				
	A	Chase Walter E	359	B F D	55	here
	B	Troland Concettina †	360–362	housewife	41	"
	C	Troland James D	360–362	engineer	42	"
	D	Cibotti Jennie V †	360–362	housewife	39	"
	E	Cibotti Louis	360–362	metalworker	43	"
	F	Monahan Catherine A †	363	housewife	67	"
	G	Monahan John F	363	retired	75	"
	H	Monahan Marguerite L †	363	at home	36	"
	K	Monahan Richard F	363	agent	26	"
	L	White Armand	364–366	tailor	35	"
	M	White Doris †	364–366	housewife	25	"
	N	DiGironimo Rose †	364–366	"	38	"
	O	DiGironimo Sabatino	364–366	cook	44	"
	P	Fawcett Christinia †	368–370	housewife	34	"
	R	Fawcett Frederick J	368–370	milkman	41	"
	S	Salvatore Camille †	368–370	clerk	20	"
	T	Salvatore Philip	368–370	cook	45	"
	U	*Salvatore Philipina †	368–370	housewife	43	"
	V	Ryan Aloysius R	371	leatherworker	33	"
	W	Ryan Catherine V †	371	housewife	60	"
	X	Ryan Florence T †	371	stenographer	26	"
	Y	Ryan Henry	371	meter reader	22	"
	Z	Ryan Joseph F	371	shoeworker	59	"
821						
	A	Ryan Margaret L †	371	stenographer	20	"
	B	Bleakney Keith D	372	chauffeur	50	"
	C	Bleakney Minerva †	372	housewife	52	"
	D	Crockett Beatrice †	372	"	31	"
	E	Crockett John	372	buffer	34	"
	F	Cruzan Dorothy †	372	milliner	30	"
	G	Hamilton Donald F	375	baker	35	"
	H	Hamilton Dorothy G †	375	housewife	33	"
	K	Lewis Ralph H	375	baker	21	"
	L	Quattrucci Louise M †	375	housewife	44	"
	M	Quattrucci Ralph	375	fireman	44	"
	N	Barra Joseph	376	cook	49	"
	O	*Barra Serafina †	376	housewife	38	"
	P	DiSciullo Carmello	376	laborer	49	"
	R	DiSciullo Catherine †	376	housewife	46	"
	S	DiSciullo John	376	machinist	20	"

Page	Letter	Full Name	Residence, Jan. 1, 1941	Occupation	Supposed Age	Reported Residence, Jan. 1, 1940. Street and Number
		Huntington Avenue—Continued				
	T	Kinsman Frederick W	381	timekeeper	21	here
	U	Kinsman Herbert	381	clerk	20	"
	V	Kinsman Herbert W	381	metalworker	48	"
	W	Kinsman Marguerite M †	381	housewife	48	"
	Y	Aliberti Andrew	384	laborer	52	"
	Z	Aliberti Anna †	384	housewife	48	"
822						
	A	Aliberti Lucy †	384	operator	21	"
	B	Aliberti Nicholas	384	laborer	24	"
	C	Ryan John A	387	salesman	65	"
	D	Ryan Mary M †	387	housewife	64	"
	E	Ryan Edward J	387	clerk	35	"
	F	Ryan Lillian A †	387	"	34	102 Mt Pleasant av
	G	Schlichting Margaret †	388	housewife	45	here
	H	Schlichting Walter	388	freighthandler	45	"
	K	Bohmiller August	388	metalworker	62	"
	L	Bohmiller Marie M †	388	housewife	61	"
	M	*Frattasio Lucia †	392–394	"	41	"
	N	Frattasio Vincent	392–394	cook	42	"
	R	Corbett Alexander W	396	retired	68	"
	S	Corbett Margaret J †	396	housewife	66	"
	T	Trask Henry A	396	clerk	29	"
	U	Trask Margaret E †	396	housewife	34	"
		Hyde Park Avenue				
	Z	Claffey Anna C †	613	secretary	20	here
823						
	A	Claffey Catherine A †	613	housewife	63	"
	B	D'entremont Arlene M †	613A	"	23	307 Harvard
	C	*D'entremont Augustine A	613A	cutter	39	307 "
	D	D'entremont Elmer A	613A	foreman	30	213 Lexington
	E	O'Brien Catherine †	614	housewife	72	here
	F	Wahl George E	614	machinist	47	"
	G	Wahl Mary A †	614	housewife	48	"
	K	Cassidy Edmund L	617	timekeeper	32	"
	L	Cassidy Mary B †	617	housewife	67	"
	M	Cassidy William J	617	salesman	34	"
	N	Rumpf Annie †	617	housewife	71	"
	O	Rumpf Charlotte C †	617	housekeeper	44	"
	P	Rumpf Henry	617	musician	71	"

Page	Letter	Full Name	Residence, Jan. 1, 1941	Occupation	Supposed Age	Reported Residence, Jan. 1, 1940. Street and Number.

Hyde Park Avenue—Continued

Page	Letter	Full Name	Residence, Jan. 1, 1941	Occupation	Supposed Age	Reported Residence, Jan. 1, 1940. Street and Number.
	R	Rumpf Henry, jr	617	musician	43	here
	S	Robichaud Agnes M †	617	bookkeeper	31	"
	T	Robichaud Catherine M †	617	operator	34	"
	U	Robichaud Eugenie M †	617	stenographer	29	"
	V	Robichaud Leonis J	617	chauffeur	27	"
	W	Sorenson Edward	618	"	39	"
	X	Sorenson Gustav	618	retired	82	"
	Y	Sorenson Louise †	618	housewife	82	"
	Z	Sorenson Ruth E †	618	"	37	"
824						
	A	Chisholm William B	621	mechanic	64	"
	B	Sweeney Edward G	621	agent	24	"
	C	Sweeney Mary F †	621	housewife	63	"
	D	Sweeney Owen F	621	barber	65	"
	E	Morgan Mary J †	621	housekeeper	62	"
	F	Konetsky Elmer W	624	supervisor	24	"
	G	Konetsky Marie D †	624	housewife	63	"
	H	Konetsky Rosa E †	624	stenographer	34	"
	L	*Cataldo Alexandre †	628	housewife	60	20 Pheasant
	M	*Cataldo Augustine	628	laborer	55	20 "
	Y	Larson Carl W	641	salesman	39	here
	Z	Larson Helen M †	641	housewife	76	"
825						
	A	Larson Helen S †	641	"	39	"
	B	MacDonald William	641	laborer	25	632 Hyde Park av
	D	Swanbom Albert H	644	machinist	40	here
	E	Swanbom Irene R †	644	housewife	38	"
	F	Balicki Sophie V †	644	"	27	"
	G	Balicki William	644	chauffeur	27	"
	H	Cobb John F	644	clerk	30	"
	K	Krasnoff Eva †	644	housewife	59	"
	L	Krasnoff Harold J	644	clerk	26	"
	M	Krasnoff Samuel	644	storekeeper	62	"
	N	Pekan Corinne L †	644	housewife	56	"
		Pekan William H	644	patternmaker	72	"
		Hines Edward A	644	chauffeur	30	"
		Hines Mary E †	644	housewife	28	"
	S	Driscoll James J	644	chauffeur	29	"
		Driscoll Mary †	644	hairdresser	29	"
		Hotz Gertrude M †	648	housewife	39	"
	W	Hotz Lester C	648	mechanic	41	"

Page	Letter	Full Name	Residence, Jan. 1, 1941	Occupation	Supposed Age	Reported Residence, Jan. 1, 1940. Street and Number

Hyde Park Avenue—Continued

Page	Letter	Full Name	Residence, Jan. 1, 1941	Occupation	Supposed Age	Reported Residence, Jan. 1, 1940. Street and Number
	X	O'Neil Michael P	648	manager	38	here
	Y	O'Neil Rose A—†	648	housewife	38	"
	Z	Sherwood Mary M—†	648	operator	24	"
826						
	A	Sherwood Samuel H	648	machinist	27	"
	B	Feist Alfred E	651	mechanic	44	"
	C	Feist Edith M—†	651	housewife	46	"
	D	Mullen Margaret C—†	651	"	42	"
	E	Mullen William M	651	chauffeur	45	"
	F	Bowler Edmund F	651	B F D	51	"
	G	Bowler Grace E—†	651	housewife	42	"
	H	Salvoni Joseph	652	repairman	27	"
	K	Salvoni Mary—†	652	housewife	26	"
	L	Payne Dorothy E—†	652	"	34	"
	M	Payne John J, jr	652	mechanic	36	"
	N	Daniels Agatina L—†	652	clerk	27	"
	O	Daniels Joseph J	652	machinist	24	"
	P	Costa Angelina R—†	652	saleswoman	27	135 Rowe
	R	Costa Mario J	652	artist	34	35 Glendale
	S	Lyons Augustus J	652	B F D	28	142 Paul Gore
	T	Lyons Helen C—†	652	housewife	25	142 "
	U	Carlo Barbara D—†	652	"	33	here
	V	Carlo Francis C	652	pipefitter	34	"
	W	Gray Ellen—†	655	housewife	65	"
	X	Gray Florence E—†	655	supervisor	42	"
	Y	Lambert John J	655	machinist	42	"
	Z	Lambert Mabel R—†	655	housewife	36	"
827						
	A	Lambert Thomas A	655	chauffeur	40	"
	B	Canavan Edith E—†	655	housewife	39	"
	C	Canavan Philip	655	meter reader	45	"
	D	*Anderson Augusta—†	659	housewife	56	"
	E	*Anderson Oscar	659	garmentmaker	54	"
	F	O'Neil Florence V—†	659	packer	21	"
	G	O'Neil Mary E—†	659	housewife	46	"
	H	O'Neil Peter J	659	chauffeur	46	"
	K	Kearney John P	659	policeman	42	"
	L	Kearney Mary S—†	659	housewife	42	"
	M	Columbare Giovannina—†	663	"	52	"
	N	Columbare Grenier	663	engineer	57	57 Sumner
	O	*Bown Flora M—†	663	housewife	62	here

Page	Letter	Full Name	Residence, Jan. 1, 1941	Occupation	Supposed Age	Reported Residence, Jan. 1, 1940. Street and Number.

Hyde Park Avenue Continued

Page	Letter	Full Name	Residence, Jan. 1, 1941	Occupation	Supposed Age	Reported Residence, Jan. 1, 1940.
	P	Bown Mary E †	663	stenographer	29	here
	R	Jordan Evelyn A †	663	housewife	25	"
	S	Jordan Philip J	663	laborer	29	"
	T	Every Catherine A †	663	housewife	52	"
	U	Every Evelyn M †	663	clerk	24	"
	V	Every Frederick W	663	steward	54	"
	W	Every Frederick W, jr	663	attendant	25	"
	X	Britton Lee	668	student	23	"
	Y	Weimer Hermine †	668	housewife	79	"
	Z	Weimar Walter A	668	salesman	56	"
828						
	A	Sullivan Helen E †	669	teacher	45	"
	B	Sullivan Mary R †	669	"	39	"
	C	Suck Julius A	670	retired	64	"
	D	Buhlman Ann G †	677	housewife	30	44 Winthrop
	E	Buhlman Robert I	677	janitor	32	44 "
	F	Martin Dorothy E †	680	stenographer	33	here
	G	Martin John H	680	machinist	55	"
	H	Martin Mary E †	680	housewife	54	"
	K	Martin Walter H	680	laborer	31	"
	L*	Cataldo Joseph	687	"	57	"
	M	Cataldo Julia †	687	dressmaker	22	"
	N	Cataldo Raffaele	687	shipper	25	"
	O*	Cataldo Virginia †	687	housewife	52	"
	P	Cataldo Virginia †	687	clerk	20	"
	R*	Ippolito Edward	687	tailor	42	"
	S	Ippolito Ida †	687	housewife	38	"
	T	Dolan Francis T	687	bartender	48	"
	U	Dolan Margaret C †	687	housewife	48	"
	V	McMahon Frances M †	687	waitress	26	"
	W	Gerrard George W	699	operator	34	"
	X	Gerrard Mary †	699	housewife	28	"
	Y	Slade Joseph	699	custodian	30	"
	Z	Slade Margaret M †	699	housewife	27	"
829						
	A	Wickes Chester	699	laborer	35	"
	B	Wickes Josephine †	699	housewife	35	"
	C	Burke Emma F †	699	"	35	"
	D	Burke George B	699	clerk	37	"
	E	Bedugnis Benjamin	699	laborer	20	"
	F	Bedugnis Mary †	699	housewife	52	"

Page.	Letter.	FULL NAME.	Residence, Jan. 1, 1941.	Occupation.	Reputed Age.	Reported Residence, Jan. 1, 1940. Street and Number.

Hyde Park Avenue—Continued

Page.	Letter.	FULL NAME.	Residence, Jan. 1, 1941.	Occupation.	Reputed Age.	Reported Residence, Jan. 1, 1940. Street and Number.
	G	Bown Edward F	699	bookkeeper	33	here
	H	Bown Loretta M †	699	housewife	30	"
	K	*Caruso Concetta †	700	"	64	"
	L	Caruso Sabato	700	clerk	38	"
	M	*Polvere Florinda †	700	housewife	35	"
	N	Polvere Giovanni A	700	laborer	50	"
	O	Burke Clara L †	700	housewife	50	"
	P	Burke Louise Z †	700	teacher	22	"
	R	Burke William A	700	agent	50	"
	S	Green Walter	700	machinist	48	"
	T	Nania Dorothea †	700	housekeeper	70	505 Cummins H'way
	U	Keating Elizabeth I †	703	housewife	36	here
	V	Keating Thomas E	703	superintendent	43	"
	W	Donlan Katherine M †	703	housewife	45	"
	X	Donlan Patrick J	703	mechanic	48	"
	Y	Harrington Audrey †	703	secretary	21	"
	Z	Harrington Mary C †	703	housewife	43	"
830						
	A	Gangemi Anna A †	706	"	23	"
	B	Gangemi Anthony J	706	machinist	27	"
	C	Amara Joseph	706	laborer	47	"
	D	Amara Sarah †	706	housewife	30	"
	E	*McLean Mary M †	714	housekeeper	85	"
	F	Atkinson Bessie L †	714	housewife	46	"
	G	Atkinson James H	714	plumber	40	"
	H	Bruce Elizabeth †	721	housewife	72	"
	K	Bruce John A	721	janitor	75	"
	L	Bruce Robert A	721	salesman	36	"
	M	Hubbard Cecelia †	721	housewife	77	"
	N	Hubbard Frederick T	721	usher	22	"
	O	Hubbard Mary F †	721	housewife	45	"
	P	Hubbard William T	721	laborer	43	"
	R	Forrest Ann E †	721	housewife	34	"
	S	Forrest George J	721	foreman	39	"
	T	Eames Marie †	722	housewife	46	"
	U	Eames Maximilian	722	clerk	45	"
	V	Costello Ellen †	722	at home	72	"
	W	Costello William J	722	retired	72	"
	X	Rein John A	722	agent	43	"
	Y	Rein Mary J †	722	housewife	40	"
	Z	Rein Mary J †	722	student	20	"

831

Hyde Park Avenue—Continued

Page	Letter	Full Name	Residence, Jan. 1, 1941	Occupation	Supposed Age	Reported Residence, Jan. 1, 1940. Street and Number.
831	A	St Cyr Dorothy E †	723	housewife	25	here
	B	St Cyr Hervey A	723	contractor	31	"
	C	Webber Anita †	723	housewife	28	"
	D	Webber Blaine B	723	laborer	28	"
	E	Webber George	723	operator	25	"
	F	Havey Edith †	726	cashier	28	"
	G	Havey Ruth †	726	clerk	25	"
	H	Mack Mary †	726	housewife	73	"
	K	Mack Michael	726	retired	75	"
	L	Mack Thomas	726	laborer	42	"
	M	Copp Albert	730	welder	31	"
	N	Copp Catherine †	730	housewife	65	"
	O	Copp Margaret—†	730	"	28	"
	P	Gibson Edith G †	730	"	25	"
	R	Gibson Francis J	730	salesman	35	"
	S	*Constantino Catherine—†	731	housewife	53	"
	T	Constantino Nancy E—†	731	clerk	28	"
	U	Constantino Vito J	731	chauffeur	26	"
	V	McKeeman Annie B †	731	housewife	65	"
	W	McKeeman Marion L—†	731	"	29	"
	X	McKeeman Samuel H	731	laborer	73	"
	Y	McKeeman Samuel H, jr	731	salesman	31	"
	Z	Pagliuso Michael A	731	engineer	27	"
832						
	A	Pagliuso Santina M †	731	housewife	31	"
	B	Stone Eva M †	733	"	25	"
	C	Stone Walter C, jr	733	manager	26	"
	D	Costello Delia A †	733	housewife	69	"
	E	Curley Catherine †	733	dietitian	33	"
	F	Curley William F	733	chauffeur	36	"
	G	Kirchgassner Eugene J	734	assembler	45	"
	H	Kirchgassner Mary B †	734	housewife	50	"
	K	Bannon James F	734	yardman	36	797 Hyde Park av
	L	Bannon Theresa †	734	housewife	37	797 "
	M	Carroll Elizabeth M †	734	"	42	here
	N	Carroll John J	734	mechanic	48	"
	O	VanPutten Elizabeth †	735	housewife	47	"
	P	VanPutten Rudolph	735	painter	48	"
	R	Gilson Carrie C †	738	housewife	57	"
	S	Gilson Edward L	738	electrician	58	"

Page	Letter	Full Name	Residence Jan. 1, 1941	Occupation	Supposed Age	Reported Residence Jan. 1, 1940. Street and Number

Hyde Park Avenue (Continued)

Page	Letter	Full Name	Residence Jan. 1, 1941	Occupation	Supposed Age	Reported Residence Jan. 1, 1940. Street and Number
	U	Gilson Edward L, jr	738	repairman	22	here
	V	Gilson Ruth C †	738	stenographer	26	"
	W	Steinbrenner Elizabeth †	742	housewife	65	"
	X	Johnson Charlotte A †	743	"	43	"
	Y	Johnson John G	743	foreman	38	"
	Z	Bentson Carl J	743	cabinetmaker	75	"
833						
	A	Carty Ethel M †	747	housewife	52	"
	B	Ferson Frances V †	747	bookbinder	46	"
	C	Ferson Harriet F †	747	housekeeper	48	"
	F	Manardo Anthony	758	operator	21	"
	G	*Manardo Joseph	758	laborer	59	"
	H	Taplin James W	758	foreman	25	"
	K	Taplin Josephine C †	758	housewife	24	"
	L	*Thompson Ingrid J †	760	"	50	"
	M	Thompson John R	760	salesman	27	"
	N	Nichols Anna B †	762	housewife	47	46 Rossmore rd
	O	Nichols William J	762	shipper	44	46 "
	P	Alaimo Ida †	766	housewife	53	15 Maywood
	R	Alaimo Joseph	766	presser	55	15 "
	S	Beal Annie †	770	housewife	48	89 E Canton
	T	Beal Oscar A	770	clerk	55	89 "
	U	Hurley Anna M †	774	secretary	38	312 Cummins H'way
	V	Hurley Mary †	774	housewife	76	312 "
	W	Johnson Margaret T †	774	clerk	39	312 "
	X	Roper Albert E	774	plumber	41	46 Hancock
	Y	Roper Mary A †	774	housewife	42	46 "
	Z	Tonnesen Barney	797 799	shipfitter	36	Onset
834						
	A	Tonnesen Marie †	797 799	housewife	31	"
	B	Domohowski Anna S †	797 799	"	25	here
	C	Domohowski Theodore B	797 799	proprietor	25	"
	D	Donohue Elizabeth †	797 799	housewife	28	34 Vose av
	E	Donohue Robert A	797 799	machinist	28	34 "
	F	*Hall Mary N †	797 799	housewife	32	here
	G	*Hall Patrick J	797 799	warehouseman	41	"
	H	Donohue Edward K	797 799	chauffeur	32	"
	K	Donohue Margaret †	797 799	housewife	25	"
	L	Walsh Edmond J	797 799	compositor	34	20 Parker
	M	Walsh Katherine S †	797 799	housewife	32	20 "
	N	Connolly Herbert J	798	florist	26	here

Page	Letter	Full Name	Residence, Jan. 1, 1941	Occupation	Supposed Age	Reported Residence, Jan. 1, 1940. Street and Number

Hyde Park Avenue—Continued

Page	Letter	Full Name	Residence, Jan. 1, 1941	Occupation	Supposed Age	Reported Residence, Jan. 1, 1940. Street and Number
	O	Connolly James	798	machinist	63	here
	P	O'Callaghan Angus	798	optician	35	"
	R	O'Callaghan Virginia R †	798	housewife	28	"
	S	Barry Catherine M †	803–805	"	31	"
	T	Barry Francis J	803–805	leatherworker	33	"
	U	Sears Florence L †	803–805	housewife	29	"
	V	Sears Godfrey W	803–805	ropemaker	31	"
	W	MacDonald John P	803–805	chauffeur	21	96 La Grange
	X	MacDonald Mary E †	803–805	housewife	53	96 "
	Y	Cox Helen E †	803–805	"	43	here
	Z	Cox Thomas W	803–805	packer	40	"
835						
	A	Cahill John W	803–805	machinist	42	Warren
	B	Cahill Rose B †	803–805	housewife	39	"
	C	*Peckham Jessie †	803–805	"	39	here
	D	*Peckham John C	803–805	carpenter	40	"
	E	Laskey Vera L †	807	housewife	30	234 Austin
	F	Laskey William F	807	mechanic	40	234 "
	H	Cummings Charles J	807	engineer	33	here
	K	Cummings Mary †	807	housewife	28	"
	L	Iannello Carmelo C	811	photographer	27	"
	M	Iannello Sarah E †	811	housewife	25	"
	N	Cullinan Nora M †	811	"	51	"
	O	Cullinan William L	811	boilermaker	53	"
	P	Cullinan William N	811	pipefitter	20	"
	R	Howarth Louise C †	811	housekeeper	57	"
	S	Potts Alice E †	811	housewife	35	"
	T	Potts William A	811	washer	37	"
	U	Bartlett Mary E †	819	housewife	33	"
	V	Bartlett Robert	819	machinist	42	"
	X	Sullivan Agnes B †	819	housewife	46	"
	Y	Sullivan Ernest J	819	mechanic	49	"
	Z	Crapo Rae C †	823	housewife	39	"
836						
	A	McKenney Theodora R †	823	"	30	"
	B	McKenney William J	823	operator	30	"
	C	Blomquist Beatrice M †	823	housewife	31	452 Beech
	D	Blomquist Donald W	823	pipefitter	33	452 "
	E	Flaherty Frank J	823	laborer	37	here
	F	Flaherty Margaret V †	823	housewife	31	"
	G	Welles Amelia †	823	"	45	"

Page	Letter	Full Name	Residence Jan. 1, 1941	Occupation	Age	Reported Residence Jan. 1, 1940 Street and Number

Hyde Park Avenue Continued

Page	Letter	Full Name	Residence	Occupation	Age	Reported Residence
	H	Welles Richard	823	engineer	45	here
	K	*Solitro Anna †	823	housewife	47	"
	L	Solitro Frances J †	823	bookbinder	21	"
	M	Solitro Peter	823	manufacturer	50	"
	N	Spinzola Mildred C †	827	housewife	32	24 Cornell
	O	Spinzola William	827	painter	49	24 "
	P	Strom Marion R †	827	housewife	24	here
	R	Strom Stanley C	827	operator	34	"
	S	*Duggan Catherine M †	827	housewife	34	"
	T	*Duggan Patrick	827	laborer	40	"
	U	Hager Joseph G	829	"	50	340 Hyde Park av
	V	Hager Ruth C †	829	housewife	47	340 "
	W	Hager Ruth C †	829	clerk	22	340 "
	X	Barme Florence A †	829	housewife	54	here
	Y	Barme Joseph B	829	machinist	62	"
	Z	Lewis George A	829	salesman	35	"
837						
	A	Lewis Rose H †	829	housewife	30	"
	B	Ryder Alvin C	846	retired	80	"
	C	Ryder Ruth E †	846	housewife	80	"
	D	Slocum Israel H	846	retired	78	"
	E	Slocum Leroy H, jr	846	manager	23	"
	F	Slocum Marie M †	846	housewife	72	"
	G	VanWart Alice L †	854	"	67	"
	H	VanWart Benjamin M	854	retired	68	"
	L	Felsch Jeannette A †	858	stenographer	22	"
	M	Felsch Martha H †	858	housewife	50	"
	N	Mulligan Margaret L †	858	secretary	40	"
	O	Wheeler Ellen E †	858	housewife	22	"
	P	Wheeler Ernest B	858	mechanic	24	"
	R	Williams Doris D †	858	housewife	28	427 Metropolitan av
	S	Williams Robert A	858	engineer	31	427 "
	T	Schwinn Edna M †	862	housewife	49	here
	U	Schwinn John J	862	metalworker	49	"
	V	Schwinn Louise M †	862	clerk	22	"
	W	Pulster Emma A †	862	housekeeper	78	Lawrence
	X	DeAngelis Antoinette J †	870	housewife	28	here
	Y	DeAngelis Dominic	870	laborer	49	"
	Z	McDermott Veronica †	870	housekeeper	35	"
838						
	A	Gerbrands Louise †	871	housewife	39	821 E Second

Page	Letter	Full Name	Residence, Jan. 1, 1941	Occupation	Supposed Age	Reported Residence, Jan. 1, 1940. Street and Number.

Hyde Park Avenue—Continued

Page	Letter	Full Name	Residence, Jan. 1, 1941	Occupation	Supposed Age	Reported Residence, Jan. 1, 1940. Street and Number.
	B	*Gerbrands Richard	871	chauffeur	37	821 E Second
	C	Keppler Amelia G †	871	housewife	30	here
	D	Keppler Arthur E	871	mechanic	29	"
	E	Keppler Elizabeth †	871	housewife	60	"
	F	Keppler Elizabeth L †	871	clerk	22	"
	G	Daggett Myrtle B †	871	housewife	43	"

Jalleison Street

Page	Letter	Full Name	Residence, Jan. 1, 1941	Occupation	Supposed Age	Reported Residence, Jan. 1, 1940. Street and Number.
	H	Chapski Edith E †	5	housewife	35	here
	K	Chapski Peter F	5	chauffeur	38	"

James Street

Page	Letter	Full Name	Residence, Jan. 1, 1941	Occupation	Supposed Age	Reported Residence, Jan. 1, 1940. Street and Number.
	L	Kelly Elsie †	11	housewife	55	here
	M	Kelly Elsie M †	11	at home	26	"
	N	Kelly Catherine B †	11	housewife	23	"
	O	Kelly John R	11	blacksmith	33	"

Lockwood Street

Page	Letter	Full Name	Residence, Jan. 1, 1941	Occupation	Supposed Age	Reported Residence, Jan. 1, 1940. Street and Number.
	P	Geyer Albert H	5	salesman	46	here
	R	Geyer Anna H †	5	housewife	74	"
	S	Seifert Annie E †	5	"	39	"
	T	Seifert Max	5	repairman	52	"
	U	McGuire Ethel M †	11	clerk	20	"
	V	McGuire Margaret A †	11	housewife	55	"
	W	McGuire Margaret L †	11	saleswoman	23	"
	X	McGuire Thomas J	11	watchman	71	"
	Y	Blomberg Anne M †	15	housewife	30	83 Gordon
	Z	Blomberg Frederick R	15	salesman	27	83 "
839						
	A	Lugton Alexander H	15	repairman	73	here
	B	Lugton Ella †	15	housewife	61	"
	C	Chanonhouse Lucy S †	22	housekeeper	60	630 Metropolitan av
	D	Schlichting Bernard W	22	foreman	47	630 "
	E	Schlichting Ruth C †	22	housewife	42	630 "
	F	Finamore Frank	22	chef	36	here
	G	Finamore Lucy †	22	housewife	37	"
	H	Ryder Annie C †	23 25	"	40	87 Newburg
	K	Ryder Leroy L	23 25	chemist	45	87 "

Page	Letter	Full Name	Residence, Jan. 1, 1941	Occupation	Supposed Age	Reported Residence Jan. 1, 1940 Street and Number

Lockwood Street—Continued

Page	Letter	Full Name	Residence, Jan. 1, 1941	Occupation	Supposed Age	Reported Residence Jan. 1, 1940 Street and Number
	L	Juzukonis Helen E †	23 25	packer	23	261 Wood[illegible]
	M	*Juzukonis Rose E †	23 35	housewife	45	261 "
	N	Juzukonis Walter S	23 25	cabinetmaker	45	261 "
	O	DeCosta Anthony	24 26	fireman	41	here
	P	DeCosta Doris C †	24 26	housewife	37	"
	R	Covill Clarence R	24 26	clerk	28	"
	S	Covill Elliott R	24 26	agent	25	"
	T	Craig Jeannette C †	24 26	housekeeper	52	"

Metropolitan Avenue

Page	Letter	Full Name	Residence, Jan. 1, 1941	Occupation	Supposed Age	Reported Residence Jan. 1, 1940 Street and Number
	U	Tarrant Emily F †	464	housekeeper	72	here
	V	Marque Wilhelmina †	464	"	79	"
	W	Gaglio Anna †	468	operator	23	"
	X	Gaglio Mildred †	468	dressmaker	23	"
	Y	Gaglio Paul	468	barber	50	"
	Z	Gaglio Peter	468	machinist	21	"
840						
	C	*Lanzi Anthony	472	baker	21	9 Wilton
	D	Lanzi Josephine R †	472	floorwalker	22	11 A
	E	Trementozzi Dominic	472	blacksmith	43	1502 Hyde P[illegible]
	F	*Trementozzi Mary †	472	housewife	44	1502 "
	G	Murray Gerard	476	chauffeur	29	here
	H	Murray Mary †	476	housewife	24	"
	K	Campisi Joseph	476	laborer	45	"
	L	Campisi Josephine †	476	housewife	37	"
	M	Civitarese Joseph	480	operator	25	"
	N	*Civitarese Raffaella †	480	housewife	60	"
	O	Civitarese Ralph	480	contractor	57	"
	P	DiMartino Rocco	480	driller	53	New York
	R	Andreasse Carrie †	480	housewife	32	here
	S	Andreasse John	480	contractor	39	"
	T	McClellan Donald F	484	electrician	23	"
	U	McClellan George R	484	student	21	"
	V	McClellan Gertrude H †	484	housewife	53	"
	W	Bitz Annie I †	484	"	36	"
	X	Bitz William H	484	repairman	41	"
	Y	*MacKenzie Sadie M †	484	domestic	34	New York
	Z	Richard David	488	policeman	44	here
841						
	A	Richard Rosanna †	488	housewife	70	"

Page	Letter	Full Name	Residence, Jan. 1, 1941	Occupation	Supposed Age	Reported Residence, Jan. 1, 1940. Street and Number

Metropolitan Avenue Continued

Page	Letter	Full Name	Residence, Jan. 1, 1941	Occupation	Supposed Age	Reported Residence, Jan. 1, 1940. Street and Number
	B	DelloCono Albert	488	welder	31	here
	C	*DelloCono Antoinette †	488	housewife	54	"
	D	*DelloCono Carmino	488	laborer	55	"
	E	DelloCono Lena †	488	laundress	26	"
	F	DelloCono Mary †	488	nurse	21	"
	G	*Apone Adelina †	492	housewife	40	"
	H	Apone Michael	492	laborer	44	"
	K	*Apone Maria †	492	housewife	51	"
	L	*Apone Thomas	492	papermaker	44	"
	M	MacMorrow Ernest	496	student	25	"
	N	May Glee †	496	housewife	42	"
	O	May Harry L	496	painter	62	"
	P	Taylor Minnie E †	496	housekeeper	67	"
	R	*Cunniff Mabel C †	500	housewife	31	"
	S	Cunniff Thomas S	500	laborer	34	"
	T	Hoag Charles E	500	meatcutter	36	"
	U	*Hoag Madeline V †	500	housewife	35	"
	V	Strang Russell J	500	salesman	39	"
	W	*Russo Jennie—†	508	housewife	43	"
	X	Russo Joseph	508	laborer	46	"
	Y	Snow Ernest W	564	electrician	56	"
	Z	Snow Linda A †	564	housewife	55	"
842						
	A	Linden John J	564	clerk	30	"
	B	Linden Theresa F †	564	housewife	30	"
	C	Mills Mary J †	564	nurse	20	"
	D	Mills U Katherine †	564	secretary	21	"
	F	Arno Clara †	580	entertainer	25	"
	G	*Arno Josephine †	580	housewife	46	"
	H	Arno Santo	580	machinist	22	"
	K	*Battaglia Catherine †	580	housewife	43	"
	L	Battaglia Santo	580	merchant	55	"
	M	*Gangemi Catherine †	580	at home	83	"
	N	MacPherson Alexander D	592	carpenter	89	"
	O	MacPherson Catherine †	592	housewife	76	"
	P	Carle Alice M †	592	"	41	"
	R	Carle Harold A	592	salesman	40	"
	S	Hitchings Frederick H	596	lineman	31	"
	T	Hitchings Helen V †	596	housewife	29	"
	U	Kilduff Eleanor A †	596	"	53	"
	V	Kilduff Henry E	596	machinist	22	"

Page	Letter	Full Name	Residence Jan. 1, 1941	Occupation	Supposed Age	Reported Residence, Jan. 1, 1940 Street and Number

Metropolitan Avenue (Continued)

Page	Letter	Full Name	Residence	Occupation	Age	Reported Residence
	W	Kilduff Paul M	596	machinist	26	here
	X	Morin Eleanor M †	596	housewife	32	18 Hillside
	Y	Morin Francis X	596	meatcutter	64	18 "
	Z	Morin Frederick J	596	"	31	18 "
843						
	A	Cass Helen L †	600	operator	40	here
	B	Cass Walter M	600	electrician	46	"
	D	Bauer Elizabeth E †	626	housewife	36	"
	E	Bauer Louis M	626	baker	38	"
	F	Nietzel Martha M †	626	housewife	60	"
	G	Nietzel Oscar H	626	harnessmaker	63	"
	H	Cleminson John R	630	retired	51	"
	K	Cleminson Mary A †	630	housewife	57	"
	L	Marshall Ethel †	630	"	49	"
	M	Marshall James H	630	U S A	22	"
	N	Marshall John W	630	pressman	50	"
	O	Roberts Annie C †	630	housewife	52	694 Metropolitan av
	P	Roberts Edwin J	630	mechanic	55	694 "
	R	Roberts Ruth D †	630	secretary	23	694 "
	S	*Walantas Charlotte †	630	housewife	48	here
	T	Walantas John	630	boilermaker	52	"
	U	Walantas John	630	draftsman	21	"
	V	Covell Edith C †	634	housewife	43	109 Peterboro
	W	Covell George P	634	salesman	44	109 "
	X	*Ekstrand Alfred	634	painter	41	109 "
	Y	Ekstrand Grace †	634	housewife	41	109 "
	Z	Sears Susan A †	634	housekeeper	84	here
844						
	A	Chandler William J	638	plasterer	49	"
	B	Chandler Winifred E †	638	housewife	50	"
	C	Huggins Frances L †	638	at home	96	"

Navarre Street

Page	Letter	Full Name	Residence	Occupation	Age	Reported Residence
	D	Reagan Margaret G †	25	housewife	45	here
	E	Reagan Philip J, jr	25	inspector	44	"
	F	Saunders Susan J †	25	housekeeper	80	"
	G	*Zokas Anna †	33	housewife	38	"
	H	Zokas Frank	33	carpenter	48	"
	K	Nordling Ernest	34	mechanic	65	"
	L	Nordling Karin M †	34	housewife	58	"

Page	Letter	Full Name	Residence, Jan. 1, 1941	Occupation	Supposed Age	Reported Residence, Jan. 1, 1940. Street and Number

Navarre Street—Continued

Page	Letter	Full Name	Residence, Jan. 1, 1941	Occupation	Supposed Age	Reported Residence, Jan. 1, 1940. Street and Number
	M	McManus Margaret M—†	35	housewife	41	here
	N	McManus Thomas J	35	librarian	52	"
	O	Salerno Angelina—†	38	housewife	49	"
	P	Salerno Carmella S—†	38	clerk	23	"
	R	Salerno Eleanor M—†	38	at home	20	"
	S	Salerno Mary E—†	38	stitcher	26	"
	T	Kutny Ann—†	38B	clerk	25	"
	U	Kutny Eva—†	38B	housewife	45	"
	V	Kutny Nicholas	38B	machinist	20	"
	W	O'Connor Catherine—†	38B	housewife	22	204 Warren
	X	O'Connor John P	38B	carpenter	28	204 "
	Y	Johnson Alice E—†	39	operator	30	here
	Z	Johnson Leo V	39	mailer	27	"
845						
	A	Johnson Mary E—†	39	housewife	59	"
	B	McDonough Ethel V—†	39	housekeeper	28	"
	C	Bonino Joseph C	43	laborer	20	"
	D	Bonino Josephine—†	43	housewife	41	"
	E	Bonino Samuel C	43	mechanic	47	"
	F	Hogan Anna M—†	43	housekeeper	22	59 Oak
	G	*Wortman Davis	47	painter	47	here
	H	Wortman Joseph	47	laborer	20	"
	K	Wright Eliza—†	47	housekeeper	68	"
	L	McDonald Margaret L—†	51	"	30	"
	M	Mohan Anna C—†	51	housewife	67	"
	N	Mohan James F	51	retired	71	"
	O	McAuliffe Adeline—†	51	housewife	35	"
	P	McAuliffe Joseph	51	carpenter	39	"
	R	Walters Eugene L	51	retired	74	"
	S	Weekesser Elizabeth—†	51	housewife	28	"
	T	Weekesser Francis	51	mechanic	28	"
	U	Weekesser George	51	laborer	62	"
	V	Weekesser Gertrude—†	51	housewife	60	"
	W	Burke Mary A—†	55	nurse	43	"
	X	Conlon Agnes T—†	55	housewife	67	"
	Y	Conlon Bernard L	55	cutter	37	"
	Z	Anderson Helen N—†	64	bookkeeper	25	"
846						
	A	Anderson Lillian S—†	64	waitress	24	"
	B	Anderson Louise B—†	64	housewife	58	"
	C	Anderson Sander D	64	inspector	64	"

Page.	Letter.	FULL NAME.	Residence, Jan. 1, 1941.	Occupation.	Supposed Age.	Reported Residence, Jan. 1, 1940. Street and Number.

Navarre Street—Continued

Page.	Letter.	FULL NAME.	Residence, Jan. 1, 1941.	Occupation.	Supposed Age.	Reported Residence, Jan. 1, 1940. Street and Number.
	D	Anderson Walter V	64	laborer	30	here
	E	Estes Elsie V—†	64	housewife	57	"
	F	Estes William A	64	watchman	52	"
	G	Estes William J	64	shipper	31	"
	H	Kerle Alphonse G	72	retired	76	"
	K	Kerle Katherine—†	72	housewife	72	"
	L	*Kerle Louis	72	machinist	53	"

Newburn Street

Page.	Letter.	FULL NAME.	Residence, Jan. 1, 1941.	Occupation.	Supposed Age.	Reported Residence, Jan. 1, 1940. Street and Number.
	M	O'Brien Agnes T—†	83	housewife	50	here
	N	O'Brien Leo H	83	installer	52	"
	O	Felsch Olga—†	84	housewife	59	"
	P	Felsch Robert	84	weaver	60	"
	R	Arena Frank	90	pedler	37	1010 Hyde Park av
	S	*Arena Josephine—†	90	housewife	30	here
	T	Drislane Dorothy A—†	91	student	21	"
	U	Drislane Elizabeth A—†	91	housewife	55	"
	V	Drislane Richard L	91	inspector	57	"
	W	Drislane Richard L, jr	91	clerk	23	"
	X	Drislane Ruth E—†	91	secretary	22	"
	Y	Olson Ethel M—†	95	stenographer	20	"
	Z	Olson Hilma W—†	95	housewife	46	"
847						
	A	Olson Richard V	95	finisher	52	"
	B	Sandell Anna W—†	95	housekeeper	66	"
	C	*Oliver Jennie—†	96	housewife	48	"
	D	*Oliver John	96	storekeeper	50	"
	E	Camelio Susan—†	100	housekeeper	66	"
	F	Furlong Fred J	100	mechanic	40	"
	G	McCarthy Myra—†	104	clerk	55	"
	H	Moschera Salvatore	111	printer	42	"
	K	Welch Edith M—†	111	housekeeper	32	"
	L	Hart Carl S	115	salesman	51	"
	M	Hart Marguerite E—†	115	housewife	46	"
	N	Hart Robert B	115	counterman	21	"
	O	Gardner Clarence A	115	installer	43	"
	P	Gardner Madeline D—†	115	housewife	42	"
	R	Dwan Isabella A—†	119	"	69	"
	S	Dwan Leon A	119	clerk	28	"
	T	Dwan Peter	119	carpenter	71	"

Newburn Street Continued

Page	Letter	Full Name	Residence, Jan. 1, 1941.	Occupation	Supposed Age.	Reported Residence, Jan. 1, 1940. Street and Number.
	U	Dewar Herbert E	123	plumber	62	here
	V	Dewar Isabelle C †	123	secretary	24	"
	W	Dewar Mary M †	123	attendant	21	"
	X	Dewar Mary V †	123	housewife	58	"
	Y	Miller Julia E †	123	housekeeper	52	"
	Z	Capulli Antoinette †	127	stitcher	24	"
848						
	A	*Capulli Elizabeth †	127	housewife	46	"
	B	*Capulli Ernest	127	laborer	50	"
	C	Capulli Louise †	127	operator	25	"
	D	Capulli Mario	127	machinist	21	"
	E	Capulli Matilda †	127	operator	23	"

Pleasantview Street

Page	Letter	Full Name	Residence, Jan. 1, 1941.	Occupation	Supposed Age.	Reported Residence, Jan. 1, 1940. Street and Number.
	F	Hassey Gladys M †	11	housewife	43	here
	G	Hassey Gladys M †	11	at home	22	"
	H	Hassey John A	11	superintendent	43	"
	K	*D'Ambrosio Jennie †	15	housewife	51	"
	L	D'Ambrosio Mary †	15	tailoress	23	"
	M	D'Ambrosio Rose T †	15	laundryworker	21	"
	N	D'Ambrosio Sabato	15	supervisor	56	"
	O	Trenholm Leroy I	65	carpenter	34	75 Pleasantview
	P	Trenholm Mary E †	65	housewife	27	75 "
	R	Mace Madeline E †	75	"	28	14 Woodlawn av
	S	Mace William G	75	chauffeur	30	14 "
	T	Colander Charles A	87	machinist	62	here
	U	Colander Sophie †	87	housewife	61	"
	V	*Olson James	91	salesman	55	29 Seminole
	W	*Olson Lena †	91	laundress	54	29 "
	X	*Sullivan Emma J †	91	housekeeper	63	here
	Y	Johnson William	121	mechanic	60	"
	Z	Elliott Charlotte E †	124	housewife	40	"
849						
	A	Elliott Robert	124	blacksmith	68	"
	B	Elliott William D	124	painter	35	"

Ramsdell Avenue

Page	Letter	Full Name	Residence, Jan. 1, 1941.	Occupation	Supposed Age.	Reported Residence, Jan. 1, 1940. Street and Number.
	C	Ohlson Elizabeth P †	5	housewife	36	here
	D	Ohlson Eric A	5	painter	40	"

Page.	Letter	Full Name	Residence Jan. 1 1941	Occupation	Supposed Age	Reported Residence Jan. 1, 1940 Street and Number

Ramsdell Avenue Continued

Page.	Letter	Full Name	Residence Jan. 1 1941	Occupation	Supposed Age	Reported Residence Jan. 1, 1940 Street and Number
	E	Grenham Joseph M	7	salesman	27	Quincy
	F	Grenham Margaret A †	7	housewife	57	here
	G	Grenham Matthew	7	foreman	57	"
	H	Grenham Thomas J	7	carpenter	24	"
	K	Hurley Albert C	rear 7	B F D	42	"
	L	Hurley Frances M †	" 7	housewife	40	Randolph
	M	Erlandson Helen E †	11	housekeeper	42	here
	N	Johnson Matilda †	11	"	72	"
	O	Engdahl Elmer T	15	operator	32	"
	P	Engdahl Viola E †	15	housewife	26	"
	R	Nordahl Elfriede D †	17	"	30	"
	S	Nordahl Eric H	17	bookkeeper	29	"
	T	Koppe Hans	24	foreman	49	"
	U	Koppe Lillian H †	24	housewife	48	"
	V	Ericson Alfrieda †	24	"	58	"
	W	Ericson Frans O	24	woodworker	55	"
	X	Hanson Annette M †	24	housekeeper	58	"
	Y	Mulcahy Daniel	28	operator	54	"
	Z	Mulcahy Margaret †	28	housewife	54	"
850						
	A	Rooney Henry J	28	printer	61	"
	B	Rooney Lucy J †	28	housewife	61	"
	C	Rooney Thomas E	28	printer	37	"
	D	Chisholm Colin E	32	repairman	55	"
	E	Chisholm Margaret M †	32	stenographer	21	"
	F	Chisholm Mary J †	32	housewife	54	"
	G	Chisholm Paul W	32	manager	27	"
	H	Hines Benedict T	32	salesman	27	"
	K	Hines Margaret A †	32	stenographer	25	"
	L	Hines Mary C †	32	"	31	"
	M	Wyman Mary †	32	housekeeper	66	"
	N	*Jones Edward	35	carpenter	73	"
	O	*Jones Harriet †	35	housewife	76	"
	P	Jones Marjorie H †	35	operator	42	"
	R	Civitarese Dorothea †	36	housewife	24	"
	S	Civitarese Louis J	36	laborer	24	"
	T	Civitarese Rita †	36	housewife	50	"
	U	Walsh Mary M †	37	"	43	"
	V	Walsh Thomas	37	guard	50	"
	W	Walsh Thomas J	37	attendant	21	"
	X	Spoon Celia †	39	housewife	28	"

Page	Letter	Full Name	Residence, Jan. 1, 1941	Occupation	Supposed Age	Reported Residence, Jan. 1, 1940. Street and Number

Ramsdell Avenue—Continued

Page	Letter	Full Name	Residence, Jan. 1, 1941	Occupation	Supposed Age	Reported Residence, Jan. 1, 1940. Street and Number
	Y	Spoon Peter	39	laborer	26	here
	Z	Smigliano Dominic	39	"	49	"
851						
	A*	Smigliano Michelina †	39	housewife	43	"
	B	Zoppo Elizabeth †	44	"	33	"
	C	Zoppo Rocco	44	contractor	44	"

Roanoke Road

Page	Letter	Full Name	Residence, Jan. 1, 1941	Occupation	Supposed Age	Reported Residence, Jan. 1, 1940. Street and Number
	D	Morrison John A	50	salesman	46	here
	E*	Morrison Katherine J †	50	housewife	43	"
	F	Morrison Thomas C	50	meatcutter	35	"
	G	Casanova Emilio R	62	decorator	55	"
	H	Casanova John B	62	model	57	"
	K	Carew Michael J	76	upholsterer	61	86 Roanoke rd
	L	Carew Susan †	76	housewife	58	86 "
	M	Mullen Frederick D	76	painter	40	86 "
	N	Elliott Margaret M †	82	housewife	45	here
	O	Elliott Robert	82	painter	40	"
	R	Dacko Hylko	92	chef	48	"
	S	Dacko Michael	92	baker	21	"
	T*	Dacko Stella †	92	housewife	48	"
	U	Dacko Walter	92	baker	23	"
	V	Dacko William	92	"	25	"
	W*	Arsenault Annie F †	104	housewife	52	"
	X	Arsenault John H	104	carpenter	23	"
	Y	Arsenault Marie C †	104	at home	21	"
	Z*	Arsenault Mark O	104	carpenter	58	"
852						
		Connelly Arthur J	114	chauffeur	26	"
		Connelly Edith G †	114	housewife	26	"

Ruskin Road

Page	Letter	Full Name	Residence, Jan. 1, 1941	Occupation	Supposed Age	Reported Residence, Jan. 1, 1940. Street and Number
		[illegible]le Mary A †	9	housewife	36	212 River
		[illegible]le William L	9	engineer	35	212 "
		[illegible]hn Jennie †	10	housewife	44	here
		[illegible]hn Joseph	10	chauffeur	45	"
	[illegible]	[illegible]nagel Bridget M †	14	housewife	43	"

Page	Letter	Full Name	Residence, Jan. 1, 1941	Occupation	Reported Age	Reported Residence, Jan. 1, 1940. Street and Number

Ruskin Road—Continued

Page	Letter	Full Name	Residence, Jan. 1, 1941	Occupation	Reported Age	Reported Residence, Jan. 1, 1940. Street and Number
	H	Hufnagel Francis J	14	operator	46	here
	K	Murphy Edward F	18	teacher	34	"
	L	Murphy Ethel V—†	18	housewife	37	"

Safford Street

Page	Letter	Full Name	Residence, Jan. 1, 1941	Occupation	Reported Age	Reported Residence, Jan. 1, 1940. Street and Number
	M	Cass Annabelle G—†	10	housewife	51	here
	N	Cass Beatrice A—†	10	stenographer	21	"
	O	Cass John F	10	carpenter	53	"
	P	Cass Mary A—†	10	housewife	79	"
	R	Sheehan Charles W	12	teacher	37	"
	S	Sheehan Helen W—†	12	housewife	33	"
	T	Neelon Florence E—†	16	clerk	22	"
	U	Neelon John J	16	plasterer	46	"
	V	Neelon Katherine E—†	16	housewife	44	"
	W	Neelon Kenneth W	16	shoeworker	23	"
	X	Godfrey Carl D	17	engineer	55	"
	Y	Godfrey David M	17	lineman	25	"
	Z	Godfrey Katherine C—†	17	secretary	23	"
853						
	A	Godfrey Katherine G—†	17	housewife	55	"
	B	Godfrey Robert B	17	laborer	20	"
	C	Murray Helen J—†	18	operator	54	"
	D	Murray Mary A—†	18	housewife	79	"
	E	Conlin Charles H	19	salesman	46	"
	F	Conlin Florence M—†	19	housewife	44	"
	G	Chisholm Alice F—†	20	"	29	11 Monponset
	H	Scanlon Helen A—†	20	clerk	39	here
	K	Scanlon Margaret E—†	20	proofreader	35	"
	L	Scanlon Margaret M—†	20	housewife	66	"
	M	Scanlon Mary C—†	20	secretary	37	"
	N	Scanlon Michael J	20	retired	66	"
	O	Blaher Lawrence J	21–23	U S N	21	"
	P	Blaher Vincetta M—†	21–23	housewife	63	"
	R	Blaher William G	21–23	bookbinder	63	"
	S	Blaher Esther—†	21–23	housewife	32	"
	T	Blaher Francis W	21–23	bookbinder	33	"
	U	Kelly Mary F—†	24–26	housewife	32	"
	V	Kelly Maurice F	24–26	clerk	32	"
	W	Occhiolini Pasquale	24–26	toolmaker	45	"
	X	Occhiolini Theresa—†	24–26	housewife	32	"

Page	Letter	Full Name.	Residence Jan. 1, 1941.	Occupation.	Supposed Age.	Reported Residence, Jan. 1, 1940. Street and Number.

Safford Street—Continued

	Y	Riley Marguerite M †	99	housewife	40	here
	Z	Riley Matthew G	99	clerk	42	"

854 Tacoma Street

	A	Larsson Elna C †	3	housewife	35	here
	B	Larsson G George	3	instructor	40	"
	C	*Johanson Carl	7	ironworker	38	"
	D	*Johanson Helga B †	7	housewife	42	"
	E	Brown Francis E	11	agent	48	"
	F	Brown Helen M †	11	housewife	35	"
	G	Holden Annie C †	15	"	47	"
	H	Holden Walter D	15	B F D	47	"
	K	Larson Amanda †	16	housewife	55	"
	L	Larson John A	16	machinist	59	"
	M	Larson Roy D	16	laborer	20	"
	N	Kind Celia M †	19	housewife	50	"
	O	Kind George L	19	manager	52	"
	P	Kind George M	19	clerk	28	"
	R	Kind Lydia C †	19	housewife	27	"
	S	Larkin Rose A †	23	"	44	"
	T	Larkin Thomas S	23	machinist	44	"
	U	Ansel Mabel M †	24	hairdresser	47	"
	V	Ansel Philip P	24	merchant	42	"
	W	Fahey Julia †	27	housewife	49	"
	X	Fahey Nicholas E	27	laborer	51	"
	Y	Fahey Winifred M †	27	stenographer	24	"
	Z	Beaton Violet †	28	domestic	50	Ohio
855						
	D	MacAndrews Mae †	28	housekeeper	60	128 Wood av
	A	*MacIntosh Elexie †	28	housewife	50	here
	B	*MacIntosh John D	28	plasterer	51	"
	C	*MacQueen Hugh N	28	carpenter	48	"
	E	Hughes Charles A	32	teacher	35	"
	F	Hughes Mary M †	32	housewife	30	"
	G	Maloney Helen J †	35	"	51	"
	H	Maloney Joseph P	35	policeman	49	"
	K	Maher George F	40	engineer	42	"
	L	Maher Gertrude P †	40	housewife	49	"
	M	Allen Arthur W	48	carpenter	44	"
	N	Allen Emma E †	48	housewife	51	"

Page	Letter	Full Name	Residence, Jan. 1	Occupation	Supposed Age	Reported Residence, Jan. 1 — Street and Number

Tacoma Street Continued

Page	Letter	Full Name	Residence, Jan. 1	Occupation	Supposed Age	Reported Residence, Jan. 1 — Street and Number
	O	Miller Camille F—†	51	housewife	36	here
	P	Miller Roy A	51	ironworker	35	"
	R	Dexter Phyllis H—†	52	housewife	47	"
	S	Moore Elizabeth M—†	52	"	58	"
	T	Moore Frank A	52	salesman	57	"
	U	Cheverie Eleanor P—†	55	housewife	44	"
	V	Cheverie James S	55	manager	47	"
	X	Cronan Edward V	63	agent	51	"
	Y	Cronan Edward V, jr	63	inspector	28	"
	Z	Cronan Gertrude V—†	63	housewife	48	"
856						
	A	Cronan Helena M—†	63	clerk	23	"
	B	Johanson Gertrude C—†	64	"	33	"
	C	Johanson Tage L	64	machinist	31	"
	E	Weigel Evelyn A—†	67	nurse	27	"
	D	Weigel Evelyn L—†	67	housewife	55	"
	F	Weigel Frederick A	67	salesman	56	"
	H	Chisholm Margaret R—†	71	housekeeper	69	"
	K	Deneen Bernadette J—†	71	housewife	61	"
	L	Deneen Charles E	71	welder	27	"
	M	Deneen George C	71	student	21	"
	N	Olofsson Bror L	75	supervisor	44	"
	O	Olofsson Estelle P—†	75	housewife	43	"
	P	Olofsson Herbert L	75	clerk	22	"
	R	Erickson Eola C—†	79	housewife	37	"
	S	Erickson Eric L	79	salesman	38	"
	T	Olson Hilma A—†	79	housekeeper	62	"
	U	Harris Cleora L—†	83	housewife	40	"
	V	Harris Raymond J	83	salesman	40	"
	W	Bannon James L	89	electrician	44	"
	X	Bannon Mary A—†	89	housewife	45	"
	Y	Johnson Hillary J	93	custodian	61	"
	Z	Johnson Marie A—†	93	housewife	41	"

857 Thatcher Street

Page	Letter	Full Name	Residence, Jan. 1	Occupation	Supposed Age	Reported Residence, Jan. 1 — Street and Number
	A	Conlin Helen R—†	50	housewife	43	here
	B	Conlin James A	50	chauffeur	46	"
	C	Hawley Frank E	50	machinist	24	"
	D	Hawley Ruth L—†	50	stenographer	20	"
	E	Lauterbach Ernest G	50	machinist	52	"

Page.	Letter.	Full Name.	Residence, Jan. 1, 1941.	Occupation.	Supposed Age.	Reported Residence, Jan. 1, 1940. Street and Number.

Thatcher Street—Continued

	F	Lauterbach Florence M—†	50	housewife	44	here
	G	Watson Harry H	54	machinist	58	"
	H	Watson Penzy—†	54	housewife	59	"
	K	Miller Carl A	57	printer	52	"
	L	Miller Lily W—†	57	housewife	65	"
	M	MacDonald Annie—†	58	"	73	"
	N	MacDonald Michael	58	machinist	61	"
	O	MacDonald Sarah—†	58	housewife	63	"
	P	Astramskas Barbara H—†	60	"	24	"
	R	Astramskas John J	60	merchant	26	"
	S	Argraves Clara L—†	62	housewife	33	"
	T	Argraves Newman E	62	engineer	35	"
	V	Falk Estella—†	72	housewife	40	48 Sunnyside
	W	Falk William	72	painter	41	48 "
	Y	Senger Pauline—†	74	housewife	70	here
	Z	Senger Pauline A—†	74	secretary	21	"
858						
	A	Senger Theodore	74	breweryworker	71	"
	B	Burke Eugenia—†	78	cashier	23	"
	C	Burke Mary E—†	78	housewife	63	"
	D	Burke Mary T—†	78	saleswoman	38	"
	E	Burke Patrick H	78	plumber	66	"
	F	Dodge Clarence C	79	screenmaker	63	"
	G	Dodge Emily A—†	79	housewife	59	"
	H	Dodge Emily A—†	79	clerk	26	"
	K	Dodge Etta H—†	79	bookkeeper	32	"
	L	Dodge James B	79	mechanic	33	"
	M	Muller Bertha H—†	79	housewife	33	5 Glenvale ter
	N	Muller William C	79	chauffeur	44	5 "

Westminster Street

	O	Sheehan Edmond J	88	gardener	60	here
	P	Sheehan Katherine T—†	88	housewife	58	"
	R	Sheehan Katherine T—†	88	secretary	25	"
	S	Kleindienst Alice G—†	90	housewife	36	"
	T	Kleindienst Frederick C	90	bookbinder	37	"
	U	Kleindienst Max F	90	retired	69	"
	V	Campbell David T	92	operator	62	"
	W	Campbell Ethel M—†	92	housewife	56	"
	X	Campbell Kenneth T	92	welder	28	"

Page	Letter	Full Name	Residence Jan. 1 1941	Occupation	Supposed Age	Reported Residence [illegible] Street and Number

Westminster Street (Continued)

Page	Letter	Full Name	Residence	Occupation	Age	Reported Residence
	Y	Hatfield Justus A	92	mechanic	47	here
	Z	Suck Gertrude B—†	92	stenographer	32	Somerville
859						
	A	Colsch Elizabeth W—†	94	housewife	24	here
	B	Colsch Frederick J	94	porter	37	"
	C	Hultberg Anna—†	94	housekeeper	73	"
	D	Keough Esther G—†	94	housewife	41	Malden
	E	Keough Peter E	94	steelworker	48	"
	F	Topham Arthur H	98	student	21	here
	G	Topham Madeline—†	98	housewife	44	"
	H	Topham Richard A	98	carpenter	55	"
	K	Topham Robert C	98	clerk	23	"
	L	Mahler Florence M—†	98	housewife	39	"
	M	Mahler Henry S	98	B F D	47	"
	N	Ransom Charlotte—†	98	housewife	56	"
	O	Ransom Paul A	98	clerk	23	"
	P	Talanian Mary—†	106	housewife	32	[illegible]
	R	Talanian Michael K	106	proprietor	43	953 "
	S	Peterson Doris S—†	108	housewife	38	[illegible]
	T	Peterson Herbert F	108	contractor	43	106 "
	U	Anthony Barnaby D	110	dairyman	34	7 Rock rd
	V	Anthony Hilda M—†	110	housewife	32	7 "
	W	Mitchell Arthur E	112	engineer	38	here
	X	Mitchell Evelyn L—†	112	housewife	34	"
	Y	McGuiness Mary E—†	114–116	"	40	"
	Z	McGuiness Thomas J	114–116	chauffeur	50	"
860						
	A	McGuire Dorothy—†	114–116	housewife	45	"
	B	McGuire Loftus C	114–116	printer	59	"

Wilmot Street

Page	Letter	Full Name	Residence	Occupation	Age	Reported Residence
	C	Miller Chester A	4	compositor	56	here
	D	Miller Hazel L—†	4	housewife	57	"

Wood Avenue

Page	Letter	Full Name	Residence	Occupation	Age	Reported Residence
	E	Johansen Fred L	129	laborer	26	[illegible]
	F	Johansen Ludwig	129	molder	63	"
	G	*Johansen Maren—†	129	housewife	64	"
	H	Johansen Stanley N	129	patternmaker	23	"

Page	Letter	Full Name	Residence, Jan. 1, 1941	Occupation	Supposed Age	Reported Residence, Jan. 1, 1940. Street and Number.

Wood Avenue—Continued

Page	Letter	Full Name	Residence, Jan. 1, 1941	Occupation	Supposed Age	Reported Residence, Jan. 1, 1940
	K	Beckwith Charles R	133	salesman	40	here
	L	Beckwith Helen C †	133	housewife	33	"
	M	Crowley James	137	clerk	26	"
	N	Crowley Ruth M †	137	housewife	24	"
	O	Leonard Michael L	137	cabinetmaker	54	"
	P	O'Brien John A	137	printer	60	"
	R	O'Brien Maria A †	137	housewife	56	"
	S	O'Brien Zoe †	137	clerk	23	"
	T*	O'Loughlin James C	141	retired	82	"
	U	O'Loughlin Margaret G †	141	housewife	40	"
	V	O'Loughlin Thomas A	141	teacher	40	"
	W	Reeves Arthur C	149	typist	23	"
	X	Reeves Arthur E	149	policeman	49	"
	Y	Reeves Violet M †	149	housewife	45	"
	Z	Carrigan James E	155	agent	28	9 Ruskin rd
861						
	A	Carrigan Mildred A †	155	housewife	28	9 "
	B	Nelson Dorothy S †	165	"	39	here
	C	Nelson Hilmar	165	laborer	50	"
	D	Schieber Ethel H †	165	clerk	58	"
	E	Sumner Edith L †	165	salesman	62	"
	F	Gokey Mary E †	203–205	clerk	54	"
	G	Maloney Evelyn M †	203–205	stenographer	33	"
	H*	Sandstrom Magnus	203–205	salesman	45	210 Wood av
	K*	Sandstrom Margaret †	203–205	housewife	36	210 "
	L	Leon Dorothy †	207–209	"	50	here
	M	Leon Peter H	207–209	mechanic	40	"
	N	Freeman Eleanor M †	207–209	housewife	30	13 Water
	O	Freeman Frederick A	207–209	engineer	45	13 "
	P*	Dow Lottie †	211–213	housewife	39	here
	R	Dow Percy M	211–213	salesman	43	"
	S	Jackson William P	211–213	mechanic	63	6 Clarendon
	T	Neely Alice E †	211–213	housewife	36	6 "
	U	Neely James H	211–213	policeman	40	6 "
	V	Caron Esther C †	215–217	housewife	40	here
	W	Caron Omer F	215–217	salesman	40	"
	Y	McLean Elizabeth †	219–221	housewife	45	"
	Z	McLean William E	219–221	instructor	50	"
862						
	A	Howland James J	219–221	papermaker	28	27 Osceola
	B*	Howland Margaret †	219–221	housewife	26	27 "

Ward 18—Precinct 9

CITY OF BOSTON

LIST OF RESIDENTS
20 YEARS OF AGE AND OVER

(NON-CITIZENS INDICATED BY ASTERISK)
(FEMALES INDICATED BY DAGGER)

AS OF

JANUARY 1, 1941

JOSEPH F. TIMILTY, *Chairman*
FREDERIC E. DOWLING, *Secretary*
WILLIAM A. MOTLEY, JR.
FRANCIS B. McKINNEY
HILDA HEDSTROM QUIRK
Listing Board.

CITY OF BOSTON PRINTING DEPARTMENT

Page	Letter	Full Name	Residence, Jan. 1, 1941.	Occupation.	Supposed Age.	Reported Residence, Jan. 1, 1940. Street and Number.
900		**Alpheus Road**				
	A	Pedersen Bertha—†	16	housewife	43	here
	B	Pedersen Neil A	16	clerk	52	"
	C	Pedersen Vernon	16	"	20	"
	D	Merrill Clarke B	20	manager	45	"
	E	Merrill Lillian V—†	20	saleswoman	45	"
	F	Lawrence Eugene M	24	watchman	57	"
	G	Lawrence Isabel V—†	24	saleswoman	57	"
	H	Ryder Lillian S—†	24	housewife	75	"
	K	Valencia Muriel G—†	24	housekeeper	26	"
	L	Dowler Frank A	25	custodian	42	"
	M	Dowler Violet F—†	25	housewife	34	"
	N	Vietze Emma—†	76	"	59	"
	O	Vietze Joseph	76	mechanic	66	"
	P	Adair Clark D	84	policeman	43	"
	R	Adair Marguerite C—†	84	housewife	43	"
	S	Swett Mabel I—†	84	at home	50	Dedham
	T	Landers Joseph F	86	inspector	43	here
	U	Landers Mary A—†	86	housewife	41	"
	V	MacEwan Daphne L—†	88	"	45	"
	W	MacEwan Robert	88	carpenter	44	"
		Asheville Road				
	X	Crossen John J	14	policeman	47	here
	Y	Crossen Mary C—†	14	housewife	47	"
	Z	Forbes Donald S	32	operator	28	"
901						
	A	Forbes Edith R—†	32	housewife	25	"
	B	Wahlstedt Elmer G	32	machinist	57	"
	C	Wahlstedt Ida C—†	32	housewife	56	"
		Augustus Avenue				
	D	Kelly Louise M—†	6	cashier	23	38 Pinehurst
	E	Kelly William L	6	clerk	24	Somerville
	F	Jones Anna V—†	8	stenographer	22	35 Rossmore rd
	G	Jones Clinton A	8	salesman	27	Cambridge
	H	Marshall Charles H	32	engineer	30	here
	K	Marshall Dorothy M—†	32	housewife	30	"
	L	Arena Carmina—†	32	"	48	"

Page.	Letter.	Full Name.	Residence, Jan. 1	Occupation.	Reputed Age.	Reported Residence, Jan. 1 Street and Number.

Augustus Avenue (Continued)

Page	Letter	Full Name	Residence	Occupation	Age	Reported Residence
	M	Arena Max	32	barber	58	here
	N	Goetz Albert E	34	electrician	33	"
	O	Goetz Helen R †	34	housewife	37	"
	P	Cunningham Julia T—†	38	"	53	"
	R	Cunningham Michael F	38	operator	53	"
	S	Collins Catherine V—†	38	housewife	29	58 Oak rd
	T	Collins James P	38	clerk	29	8 Mt Vernon
	U	*Semerjian Alice †	42	housewife	27	here
	V	Semerjian Nubar	42	engraver	39	"
	W	*Siracusa Concetta—†	42	housewife	42	"
	X	*Siracusa Frances—†	42	"	44	"
	Y	Siracusa Joseph	42	cabinetmaker	46	"
	Z	Siracusa Salvatore	42	"	44	"
902						
	A	Nugent Margaret †	44	housewife	30	"
	B	Nugent Robert A	44	clerk	34	"
	C	Crimmins Bertha M—†	44	teacher	33	"
	D	Crimmins Francis L	44	laborer	27	"
	E	Crimmins Joseph A	44	clerk	22	"
	F	Crimmins Theresa †	44	housewife	60	"
	G	Crimmins Thomas J	44	clerk	31	"
	H	Crimmins Timothy J	44	"	64	"
	K	Wurtz Maxwell D	48	operator	44	"
	L	Wurtz Olga †	48	housewife	45	"
	M	Wurtz Ruth L †	48	at home	20	"
	N	Schwartz Catherine †	48	"	71	"
	O	Wurtz Alfred	48	salesman	38	"
	P	Wurtz Anna †	48	clerk	45	"
	R	Wurtz William	48	"	36	"
	S	Odiorne Helen T †	52	housewife	52	"
	T	Odiorne Ralph L	52	clerk	55	"
	U	Schwartz Joseph	52	shoeworker	53	"
	V	Schwartz Marie †	52	housewife	55	"
	W	McEleney Anna C †	56	"	38	"
	X	McEleney John P	56	teacher	53	"
	Y	Barry Louis	56	meatcutter	55	"
	Z	Hourigan Mary †	56	housewife	65	"
903						
	A	Hourigan Mary V †	56	clerk	28	"
	B	DeFerrari Helen F †	60	housewife	41	"
	C	DeFerrari Vincent L	60	clerk	43	"

Page	Letter	Full Name	Residence, Jan. 1, 1941	Occupation	Supposed Age	Reported Residence, Jan. 1, 1940. Street and Number.

Augustus Avenue—Continued

Page	Letter	Full Name	Residence	Occupation	Age	Reported Residence
	D	Harney Catherine J—†	60	housewife	53	here
	E	Harney James F	60	operator	56	"

Austin Street

Page	Letter	Full Name	Residence	Occupation	Age	Reported Residence
	F	Howden Herbert R, jr	196	salesman	31	here
	G	Howden Madeline E—†	196	housewife	30	"
	H	Thomas Elizabeth—†	196	seamstress	20	160 Beaver
	K	Thomas George	196	retired	65	160 "
	L	Thomas Mary—†	196	housewife	59	160 "
	M	Deprey Alphie	204	clerk	31	here
	N	Deprey Theresa B—†	204	housewife	28	"
	O	Mahoney Christine—†	204	"	28	70 Aldrich
	P	Mahoney Edward	204	shipper	31	70 "
	R	Carlson Ada V—†	212	housewife	32	here
	S	Carlson Nils O	212	carpenter	32	"
	T	Koury Elizabeth—†	212	teacher	22	624 Harris'n av
	U	Koury Frederick	212	chemist	25	624 "
	V	Koury Mary—†	212	housewife	50	624 "
	W	Koury Paul K	212	shipfitter	55	624 "
	X	Koury Philip	212	electrician	20	624 "
	Y	Toffoloni Dorothy—†	232–234	housewife	23	here
	Z	Toffoloni John	232–234	welder	25	"
904						
	B	Walsh Alma V—†	236–238	housewife	38	"
	C	Walsh John A	236–238	operator	40	"
	D	Crehan Francis	236–238	chauffeur	43	"
	E	Crehan Theresa—†	236–238	housewife	40	"
	F	Nee Eileen I—†	240–242	"	51	"
	G	Nee Joseph P	240–242	superintendent	52	"
	H	Nee Joseph W	240–242	agent	26	"
	K	Flister Carl	240–242	clerk	64	"
	L	Flister Florence I—†	240–242	housewife	53	"
	M	Flister Roy M	240–242	shipper	24	"
	N	Allen Mildred A—†	244–246	housewife	34	Brockton
	O	Allen Neal	244–246	inspector	45	39 Minot
	P	Black Esther C—†	244–246	housewife	32	here
	R	Black Richard	244–246	policeman	32	"
	S	Kilburn Eleanor—†	244–246	nurse	30	Everett
	T	Newton George R	248–250	machinist	36	2969 Wash'n
	U	Newton Grace M—†	248–250	housewife	33	2969 "
	V	Peterson Augusta—†	248–250	at home	75	here

Page	Letter	Full Name	Residence, Jan. 1, 194[illegible]	Occupation	Supposed Age	Reported Residence, Jan. 1, 194[illegible]. Street and Number

Austin Street Continued

Page	Letter	Full Name	Residence	Occupation	Supposed Age	Reported Residence
	W	Peterson Rune	248 250	cleaner	31	here
	X	Schelin Ethel †	248 250	housewife	34	"
	Y	Schelin Joseph	248 250	shipper	49	"
	Z	Richenburg Alice †	252 254	housewife	33	"
905						
	A	Richenburg Ernest	252 254	mechanic	42	"
	B	Perry George D	252 254	bartender	55	"
	C	Perry George D, jr	252 254	attendant	28	"
	D	Perry Helen M †	252 254	housewife	50	"
	E	Perry Helen V †	252 254	waitress	25	"

Bateman Street

Page	Letter	Full Name	Residence	Occupation	Supposed Age	Reported Residence
	F	Clarke George	9 11	mechanic	31	here
	G	Clarke Grace †	9 11	housewife	27	"
	H	Steeger Charles H	9 11	painter	55	"
	K	Steeger Olive L †	9 11	housewife	48	"
	L	Brook Avis †	15	"	33	"
	M	Brook Perry	15	salesman	35	"
	N	O'Malley Gertrude C †	15	housewife	42	"
	O	O'Malley Harry H	15	collector	46	"
	P	Scollins Kathleen R †	16	housewife	36	23 Jetters
	R	Scollins William R	16	pharmacist	36	23 "
	S*	Anderson Clara J †	35	housekeeper	56	here
	T	Leaf Grace C †	35	housewife	33	"
	U	Leaf Oscar K	35	painter	40	"
	V*	Anders Dolina †	41	housewife	44	"
	W	Anders Frederick W	41	baker	40	"
	X	Ellis Albert E	65	policeman	43	"
	Y	Ellis Irene A †	65	housewife	43	"
	Z	French Aubrey M	81	retired	70	"
906						
	A	French Susan †	81	housewife	60	"
	B	Benson Gustaf O	104	engineer	54	"
	C	Benson Helga O †	104	housewife	54	"
	D	Benson Ralph G	104	engineer	24	"

Beech Street

Page	Letter	Full Name	Residence	Occupation	Supposed Age	Reported Residence
	E	Donahue Dorothy E †	587	housewife	37	here
	F	Donahue Leo J	587	laborer	42	"
	G*	Donahue Mary A †	587	housewife	64	"

Page	Letter	Full Name	Residence, Jan. 1, 1941	Occupation	Supposed Age	Reported Residence, Jan. 1, 1940. Street and Number

Beech Street—Continued

Page	Letter	Full Name	Residence, Jan. 1, 1941	Occupation	Supposed Age	Reported Residence, Jan. 1, 1940. Street and Number
	H	Dolan Mildred E—†	588	stenographer	36	here
	K	Favor Eugene G	588	gasfitter	51	"
	K	Favor Evelyn A—†	588	housewife	56	"
	L*	Archambault Evangeline—†	588	"	63	"
	M	Archambault Fernande—†	588	binder	31	"
	N	Archambault Henriette—†	588	"	40	"
	O*	Archambault Ubald	588	manager	32	"
	P	Archambault Ulric A	588	painter	68	"
	R	Rosecaln Henry	589	chemist	30	18 Reddy av
	S	Rosecaln Sophie C—†	589	housewife	25	943 Hyde Park av
	T	Bumpus Frederick W	591	clerk	47	55 Northbourne rd
	U	Bumpus Gertrude N—†	591	housewife	43	55 "
	V	Power Joseph W	592	engineer	40	here
	W	Power Mary T—†	592	housewife	36	"
	X	Yeadon Foster A	594	mechanic	37	"
	Y*	Yeadon Nettie A—†	594	housewife	37	"
	Z	Gavin Ellen M—†	596	"	31	743 Parker
907						
	A	Gavin John T	596	laborer	42	743 "
	B	Brooker George G	598	engineer	37	here
	C	Brooker Thelma M—†	598	housewife	33	"
	D	Hargbal Dagmar—†	600	"	42	"
	E	Hargbal Wagn H	600	accountant	43	"
	F	Burke Jessie E—†	601	housewife	40	"
	G	Burke John F	601	policeman	39	"
	H	Harrington Edward F	603	"	39	"
	K	Harrington Marion H—†	603	housewife	39	"
	L	Sawyer James	605	lineman	45	"
	M*	Sawyer Sarah M—†	605	housewife	39	"
	N	Sullivan Mildred M—†	607	"	34	"
	O	Sullivan Timothy P	607	chauffeur	35	"
	P	Downey Constance B—†	608	stenographer	24	"
	R*	Downey Isabelle M—†	608	housewife	48	"
	S	Downey James T	608	plumber	48	"
	T	Downey Lloyd J	608	"	21	"
	U*	Yeadon Carl H	608	painter	42	Hopkinton
	V	Balod Ernest	620	carpenter	56	here
	W	Balod Mildred M—†	620	stenographer	30	"
	X	Lueth Charles H	622	salesman	39	"
	Y	Lueth Minnie A—†	622	housewife	41	"
	Z	MacLean Murdock N	622	shoeworker	40	"

Page	Letter	Full Name	Residence Jan. 1, 1941	Occupation	Supposed Age	Reported Residence Jan. 1, 1940. Street and Number
908						
		Beech Street Continued				
	A	Short Robertina F †	624	housewife	35	12 Atherton
	B	Short William H	624	policeman	39	12 "
	C	Nocca Gaetano	626	clerk	39	here
	D	Nocca Rose †	626	housewife	31	"
	E	Flanagan Albert J	656	operator	60	"
	F	Flanagan Helen G †	656	housewife	50	"
	G	Flanagan Helen R †	656	bookkeeper	24	"
	H	Flanagan Laura M †	656	clerk	22	"
	K	Flanagan Mary G †	656	"	26	"
	L	Noble Albert L	656	carpenter	24	"
		Burley Street				
	M	Falconer Mary E †	14	housewife	41	here
	N	Falconer William J	14	accountant	41	"
	O	Hopkins Edward J	14	attendant	66	33 Austin
	P	Hopkins Francis P	14	shipper	34	33 "
	R	Hopkins Veronica M †	14	housewife	27	33 "
	S	Karcher Ella C †	17	"	73	here
	T	Karcher John E	17	engineer	40	"
	U	Ringdahl Margaret P †	21	housewife	32	"
	V	Ringdahl Wilhelm	21	painter	43	"
	W	Anderson Albert B	27	salesman	28	"
	X	Anderson Margaret I †	27	housewife	27	"
		Canterbury Street				
	Y	Deely Joseph M	1022	bookkeeper	44	here
	Z	Deely Margaret I †	1022	housewife	44	"
909						
	A	Andrews Annie L †	1024	"	44	31 Rodman
	B	Andrews Henry C	1024	painter	44	31 "
	C	Power Anna F †	1024	housewife	37	here
	D	Power John G	1024	chauffeur	43	"
	E	Celata Carmela †	1036	housewife	39	"
	F	Celata Joseph M	1036	florist	45	"
	G	Hallisey Mary †	1038	housewife	36	"
	H	Hallisey Michael J	1038	laborer	38	"
	K	Townsend Ethel M †	1038	housewife	30	"
	L	Townsend Gertrude M †	1038	"	63	"

Page	Letter	Full Name	Residence, Jan. 1, 1941.	Occupation	Supposed Age.	Reported Residence, Jan. 1, 1940. Street and Number.

Canterbury Street—Continued

Page	Letter	Full Name	Residence, Jan. 1, 1941.	Occupation	Supposed Age.	Reported Residence, Jan. 1, 1940. Street and Number.
	M	Townsend Luther G	1038	draftsman	30	here
	N	Townsend Raymond E	1038	machinist	22	"
	O	Doria Angelina—†	1038	housewife	42	"
	P	Walsh Delia A—†	1048	"	41	"
	R	Walsh Michael J	1048	pipefitter	41	"
	T*	Marinaccio Josephine—†	1048	housewife	52	"
	U	Marinaccio Mary R—†	1048	clerk	20	"
	V	Crateau Joseph	1054	engineer	40	"
	W	Crateau Mary A—†	1054	housewife	38	"
	X	Kilroy Catherine—†	1054	"	73	"
	Y	Butterworth John R	1058	watchman	60	"
	Z	Ganong Mary A—†	1058	housewife	70	"
910						
	A	Ganong Seth	1058	retired	79	"
	B	Morris Catherine A—†	1058	housewife	60	"
	C	Morris Dorothea V—†	1058	clerk	21	"
	D	Morris John J	1058	repairman	25	"
	E	Morris Mary C—†	1058	stenographer	22	"
	F	Morris Patrick J	1058	laborer	57	"
	G	Clausen Carl G	1062	policeman	28	"
	H	Clausen Marie M—†	1062	housewife	29	"
	K	Richenburg Eleanor M—†	1062	"	28	"
	L	Richenburg Frederick H	1062	salesman	27	"
	M	Borges Alfred J	1066	clerk	43	"
	N	Borges Josephine A—†	1066	housewife	39	"
	O	Butler Catherine E—†	1066	"	34	36 Whitford
	P	Butler Ralph A	1066	stereotyper	38	36 "
	R	Sheehan Annie F—†	1066	housewife	62	here
	S	Sheehan Jeremiah C	1066	retired	68	"
	T	Sheehan Marie G—†	1066	secretary	32	"
	U	Sheehan Thomas J	1066	attorney	28	"
	V	Duby James J	1070	manager	31	"
	W	Duby Kathryn M—†	1070	housewife	31	"
	X	Walsh Daniel P	1070	manager	52	"
	Y	Walsh Thomas V	1070	"	58	"
	Z	Denzler Mary—†	1074	housewife	46	"
911						
	A	Denzler Walter	1074	clerk	47	"
	B	Denzler Walter, jr	1074	"	28	"
	C	Gibbons Alice E—†	1074	teacher	36	"
	D	Gibbons Helena J—†	1074	housewife	70	"
	E	Gibbons Patrick J	1074	retired	76	"

Page.	Letter	Full Name	Residence, Jan. 1, 1941.	Occupation	Supposed Age	Reported Residence, Jan. 1, 1940. Street and Number

Canterbury Street—Continued

Page.	Letter	Full Name	Residence, Jan. 1, 1941.	Occupation	Supposed Age	Reported Residence, Jan. 1, 1940. Street and Number
	F	Gibbons Theresa M—†	1074	clerk	44	here
	G	Peterson Joseph G	1078	chauffeur	39	"
	H	Peterson Lillian B—†	1078	housewife	41	"
	K	Mahoney Andrew J	1078	clerk	33	"
	L	Mahoney Clara F—†	1078	housewife	24	"
	M	Martin Catherine A—†	1082	"	55	"
	N	Dooley Edgar P	1082	cable splicer	44	"
	O	Dooley Mary E—†	1082	housewife	43	"
	P	Gallant Florence R—†	1086	stenographer	26	"
	R	Gallant Louise—†	1086	"	23	"
	S	Gallant William I	1086	retired	65	"
	T	Claus August	1086	storekeeper	50	"
	U	Claus Catherine E—†	1086	clerk	20	"
	V	Claus Emma J—†	1086	housewife	48	"
	W	Glockner Madeline C—†	1086	"	25	"

Clarendon Court

Page.	Letter	Full Name	Residence, Jan. 1, 1941.	Occupation	Supposed Age	Reported Residence, Jan. 1, 1940. Street and Number
	X	Blume Catherine L—†	2	beautician	20	here
	Y	Blume David W	2	freighthandler	56	"
	Z	Blume Mary S—†	2	housewife	50	"
912						
	A	Harrington Helen J—†	4	"	32	14 Quarley rd
	B	Harrington Thomas L	4	retired	39	14 "
	C	Ruth Mary E—†	4	at home	65	14 "

Clarendon Park

Page.	Letter	Full Name	Residence, Jan. 1, 1941.	Occupation	Supposed Age	Reported Residence, Jan. 1, 1940. Street and Number
	D	Childinidos James	60	salesman	42	here
	E	Childinidos John	60	"	45	"
	F	Greggotte Eva—†	60	dressmaker	47	"
	G	*Arnold Anna L—†	67	at home	63	"
	H	Arnold Gerda R—†	67	secretary	26	"
	K	Stopp Hildegard L—†	67	housewife	44	"
	L	Stopp Reinhard M	67	designer	45	"

Cliffmont Street

Page.	Letter	Full Name	Residence, Jan. 1, 1941.	Occupation	Supposed Age	Reported Residence, Jan. 1, 1940. Street and Number
	M	Ahearn Dolores C—†	11	housewife	40	here
	N	Ahearn William A	11	policeman	40	"
	O	Tuohy Catherine—†	11	housewife	65	"
	P	Tuohy Margaret M—†	11	teacher	34	"

Page	Letter	Full Name	Residence, Jan. 1, 1941	Occupation	Supposed Age	Reported Residence, Jan. 1, 1940. Street and Number

Cliffmont Street—Continued

Page	Letter	Full Name	Residence, Jan. 1, 1941	Occupation	Supposed Age	Reported Residence, Jan. 1, 1940. Street and Number
	R	Tuohy Marie C—†	11	operator	24	here
	S	Dorman Rosemond L—†	19	"	50	"
	T	Dolan Arlene A—†	33	housewife	48	"
	U	Dolan Timothy J	33	printer	58	"
	V	Anderson Carl T	33	retired	74	"
	W	Anderson Hildur S—†	33	stenographer	50	"
	X	*Camp Ida H—†	41	domestic	62	"
	Y	Leuthy Anna E—†	41	at home	22	"
	Z	Leuthy Antoine	41	retired	82	"
913						
	A	Leuthy Christina M—†	41	housewife	50	"
	B	*Moore Mary A—†	57	at home	73	"
	C	Rietzl Ella—†	57	"	80	"
	D	Turner Alice M—†	57	housewife	32	"
	E	Turner Thomas	57	welder	43	"
	F	Kenny Helen P—†	61	housewife	31	"
	G	Kenny John H	61	teacher	39	"
	H	*Keady Martin	61	molder	40	"
	K	Lyons Delia—†	61	at home	43	"
	L	*McDonough James	61	laborer	55	"
	M	Mulkern Timothy	61	"	40	"
	N	Greenlow John D	69	retired	80	"
	O	Greenlow Kate—†	69	housewife	69	"
	P	Tibbetts Flora—†	69	"	44	"
	R	Tibbetts Robert A	69	salesman	45	"
	S	Tibbetts Russell A	69	U S A	20	"
	T	Harris George W	73	draftsman	46	"
	U	Harris Mary R—†	73	housewife	47	"
	V	Northam John	73	electrician	37	"
	W	Sumberg Edward	73	"	36	"
	X	Sumberg John	73	engineer	68	"
	Y	O'Rourke Mary J—†	81	instructor	45	"
	Z	Sandock Anna M—†	81	housewife	43	"
914						
	A	Sandock John J	81	custodian	43	"
	B	Maier Emil H	85	machinist	40	"
	C	Maier Mina—†	85	housewife	37	"

Crandall Street

Page	Letter	Full Name	Residence, Jan. 1, 1941	Occupation	Supposed Age	Reported Residence, Jan. 1, 1940. Street and Number
	D	Connor Mary A—†	1	beautician	26	here
	E	Gorman Catherine E—†	1	housewife	59	"

Page	Letter	Full Name	Residence, Jan. 1, 1941	Occupation	Supposed Age	Reported Residence, Jan. 1, 1940. Street and Number

Crandall Street—Continued

Page	Letter	Full Name	Residence, Jan. 1, 1941	Occupation	Supposed Age	Reported Residence, Jan. 1, 1940. Street and Number
	F	Gorman Margaret E—†	1	clerk	27	here
	G	Gerhardt Clara L—†	2	housewife	58	"
	H	Gerhardt Edward P	2	manager	64	"
	L	Amirault Louis T	6	upholsterer	70	Braintree
	M	D'Entremont Charles J	6	stenographer	20	here
	N	D'Entremont Mary M—†	6	housewife	63	"
	O	D'Entremont Oliver	6	retired	70	"
	P	Thompson Robert	6	laborer	29	"
	R	Greim Erna F—†	9	bookkeeper	20	"
	S	Greim Lena F—†	9	housewife	52	"
	T	Greim Robert J	9	salesman	54	"
	U	Greim Robert W	9	clerk	22	"
	V	Smith Emilia H—†	10	housewife	57	"
	W	Smith Paul W	10	accountant	58	"
	X	Smith Paul W, jr	10	electrician	21	"
	Y	Devlin Frances J—†	14	clerk	20	"
	Z	Devlin James M	14	salesman	23	"
915						
	A	Devlin Louise E—†	14	artist	29	"
	B	Devlin Mary L—†	14	teacher	27	"
	C	Devlin Nora L—†	14	housewife	60	"
	D	Devlin Thomas M	14	retired	66	"
	E	Gagen Elizabeth V—†	14	domestic	58	"
	F	Hunter May S—†	15	housewife	47	"
	G	Hunter William M	15	salesman	47	"
	H	*Hebb Ella P—†	20	housekeeper	82	"
	K	Caffrey Ruth C—†	21	beautician	45	"
	L	Hoskin Eva R—†	21	"	30	"
	M	Oberacker Wilhelmina—†	24	housewife	65	50 Lasell
	N	Oberacker William E	24	foreman	66	here
	O	Oberacker Lawrence W	24	salesman	42	"
	P	Oberacker Pearl E—†	24	housewife	42	"
	R	Douglas George C	26	clerk	21	"
	S	Douglas Helen C—†	26	nurse	25	"
	T	Douglas Nancy M—†	26	secretary	18	"
	U	Ladd Philip H	26	engineer	56	"

Dale Street

Page	Letter	Full Name	Residence, Jan. 1, 1941	Occupation	Supposed Age	Reported Residence, Jan. 1, 1940. Street and Number
	V	Lundquist Alma W—†	16	housewife	67	here
	W	Lundquist John A	16	tailor	73	"
	X	Thurston Henry G	20	laborer	21	"

Page	Letter	Full Name	Residence, Jan. 1, 1941	Occupation	Supposed Age.	Reported Residence, Jan. 1, 1940. Street and Number.

Dale Street—Continued

Page	Letter	Full Name	Residence, Jan. 1, 1941	Occupation	Supposed Age.	Reported Residence, Jan. 1, 1940. Street and Number.
	Y	Thurston Louise A—†	20	housewife	50	here
	Z	Thurston Richard M	20	attendant	20	"
916						
	A	*Canale Mary G—†	25	housewife	37	"
	B	*Canale Pasquale	25	mason	49	"
	C	Foster John W	38	chauffeur	63	"
	D	Foster Mildred E—†	38	clerk	28	"
	E	Foster Susette F—†	38	housewife	44	"
	F	Day Ann E—†	40	housekeeper	34	"
	G	Day Eleanor J—†	40	stenographer	37	"
	H	Murray Bessie G—†	40	at home	72	"
	K	Ziegler Arnold U	40	salesman	41	"
	L	Berglund Alice G—†	45	housewife	49	"
	M	Berglund John W	45	superintendent	46	"
	N	Balerma Mark	49	laborer	43	"
	O	Balerma Mary F—†	49	housewife	40	"
	P	Megliola Gaetano F	50	carpenter	20	"
	R	Megliola Joseph	50	contractor	45	"
	S	Megliola Mary L—†	50	inspector	21	"
	T	Megliola Melisse—†	50	housewife	39	"
	U	Weitzel Earl H	62	steamfitter	53	"
	V	Weitzel Helen F—†	62	housewife	50	"
	W	Weitzel Helen F—†	62	student	20	"
	X	*Buttewitz Emily—†	66	housewife	50	"
	Y	*Buttewitz Karl	66	machinist	50	"
	Z	Eibye Carl, jr	66	painter	29	"
917						
	A	Eibye Mary—†	66	housewife	27	"
	B	*Rae James F	68	salesman	52	"
	C	*Rae Jean D—†	68	milliner	48	"
	D	*Rae Margaret D—†	68	photographer	50	"
	E	*Rae Mary H—†	68	housewife	64	"

Deforest Street

Page	Letter	Full Name	Residence, Jan. 1, 1941	Occupation	Supposed Age.	Reported Residence, Jan. 1, 1940. Street and Number.
	F	Cotton Edith M—†	11	housekeeper	20	here
	G	Cotton Everett	11	foreman	50	"
	H	Lockhart Harry D, jr	14	chemist	34	"
	K	Lockhart Ruth A—†	14	housewife	34	"
	L	O'Connell Bridget E—†	15	at home	70	"
	M	O'Connell Lila F—†	15	housewife	31	"

Page	Letter	Full Name	Residence, Jan. 1, 1941	Occupation	Age	Reported Residence, Jan. 1, 1940. Street and Number

Deforest Street—Continued

Page	Letter	Full Name	Residence	Occupation	Age	Reported Residence
	N	O'Connell Thomas J	15	clerk	41	here
	O	Gerraughty Olive—†	19	housewife	35	"
	P	Gerraughty Raymond	19	manager	35	"
	R	Bamberg Mildred A—†	25	teacher	40	"
	T	Gustafson Charlotte A—†	37	housewife	48	"
	U	Gustafson Eric	37	machinist	45	"
	V	Mattson Corinne E—†	37	housewife	40	"
	W	Mattson William W	37	carpenter	45	"
	X*	Maloney Bridie F—†	45	housewife	36	5 Osceola
	Y	Maloney Jeremiah	45	clerk	38	5 "
	Z	Darling E Muriel—†	49	student	21	here
918						
	A	Darling Ethel M—†	49	housewife	47	"
	B	Darling James T	49	dispatcher	50	"
	C	Bamberg Henry F	52	accountant	49	"
	D	Bamberg Marie R—†	52	operator	20	"
	E	Bamberg Mary E—†	52	housewife	45	"
	F	McGeever Francis H	57	policeman	43	"
	G	McGeever Helen L—†	57	housewife	41	"
	H	Murphy Bernice M—†	61	"	29	"
	K	Murphy Joseph O	61	policeman	45	"
	L	Burum Thelma A—†	65	housewife	27	"
	M	Burum Walter J	65	salesman	34	"

Delano Park

Page	Letter	Full Name	Residence	Occupation	Age	Reported Residence
	N	Carrigan Edith H—†	1	housewife	26	here
	O	Carrigan James J	1	clerk	30	"
	P	Ryan Annie T—†	1	at home	65	"
	R	Ryan Catherine G—†	1	"	71	"
	S	Tierney Alice M—†	4	housewife	34	"
	T	Tierney John L	4	mechanic	43	"
	U	Weider Louis F	4	at home	52	"
	V	Weider Mary C—†	4	housewife	51	"
	W	Cox Joseph H	5	carpenter	35	"
	X	Cox Mildred L—†	5	housewife	34	"
	Y	Cokely Arthur E	5	clerk	47	"
	Z	Cokely Margaret G—†	5	maid	21	"
919						
	A	Cokely Veronica M—†	5	housewife	47	"
	B	Sullivan Daniel J	8	chauffeur	46	"

Page.	Letter.	Full Name.	Residence, Jan. 1, 1941.	Occupation.	Supposed Age.	Reported Residence, Jan. 1, 1940. Street and Number.

Delano Park Continued

Page.	Letter.	Full Name.	Residence, Jan. 1, 1941.	Occupation.	Supposed Age.	Reported Residence, Jan. 1, 1940. Street and Number.
	C	Sullivan Mary J—†	8	housewife	43	here
	D	Donlon Henry M	10	agent	44	"
	E	Donlon Mary L—†	10	housewife	36	"
	F	Ruane Katherine G—†	10	operator	35	"
	G	Ruane Michael J	10	mason	63	"
	H	Fernekees Anna G—†	11	waitress	30	"
	K	Fernekees Charles L	11	cashier	33	"
	L	Bachofner Catherine L—†	11	housewife	36	70 Weld Hill
	M	Bachofner Fred	11	fireman	40	70 "
	N	Flynn Esther G—†	12	housewife	39	here
	O	Flynn Joseph G	12	clerk	43	"
	P	Williams Mary B—†	15	housewife	34	"
	R	Williams Richard H	15	manager	35	"
	S	Nevin Lawrence	15	carpenter	64	"
	T	Nevin Lawrence F	15	salesman	20	"
	U	Nevin Margaret B—†	15	clerk	25	"
	W	Nevin Theresa M—†	15	stenographer	22	"
	X	Nevin Theresa T—†	15	housewife	56	"
	V	Nevin Thomas L	15	accountant	21	"
	Y	Thompson Alan M	16	secretary	39	"
	Z	Thompson Amanda M—†	16	at home	74	"
920						
	A	Thompson Isabelle R—†	16	housewife	37	"
	B	Glynn Anna J—†	17	operator	27	"
	C	Glynn James G	17	laborer	24	"
	D	Glynn John J	17	carpenter	31	"
	E	Glynn Margaret F—†	17	housewife	63	"
	F	Glynn Margaret F—†	17	operator	32	"
	G	Glynn Mary L—†	17	stenographer	34	"
	H	Little Dorothy M—†	19	secretary	25	"
	K	Little John P	19	"	25	"
	L	*McNeil Joseph H	21	retired	93	"
	M	*McNeil Margaret J—†	21	housewife	75	"
	N	Curley Lillian L—†	26	"	36	29 Bromley
	O	Nilson Anna C—†	26	"	71	here
	P	Nilson Carl D	26	painter	71	"
	R	Nelson Harry E	30	mechanic	39	"
	S	Nelson Johanna C—†	30	housewife	65	"
	T	Patterson Edward J	35	superintendent	53	"
	U	Patterson Edward J, jr	35	clerk	24	"

Page	Letter	Full Name	Residence, Jan. 1	Occupation	Reported Age	Reported Residence, Street and Number

Delano Park Continued

Page	Letter	Full Name	Residence, Jan. 1	Occupation	Reported Age	Reported Residence, Street and Number
	v	Patterson Mary †	35	housewife	54	here
	w	Patterson Mary M †	35	stenographer	22	"
	x	Rooney John L	35	artist	50	"
	y	Nilson Elvira M †	38	housewife	31	"
	z	Nilson George A	38	painter	38	"
921						
	a	Delaney Margaret J †	39	housewife	36	"
	b	Delaney Timothy J	39	clerk	36	"
	c	Surplass Mary L †	40	housewife	36	"
	d	Surpluss Warren R	40	clerk	40	"
	e	Surpluss William H	40	retired	71	"
	f	Duffey Walter J	42	welder	21	Pennsylvania
	g	Quirk Sarah †	42	housewife	38	here
	h	Quirk William O	42	inspector	40	"
	k	Pickett Helen A †	43	housewife	47	"
	l	Pickett William M	43	compositor	51	"
	m	Kenny Nora †	44	housewife	48	"
	n	Kenny Peter J	44	conductor	48	"
	o	Bowser Mary J †	47	housewife	63	"
	p	Bowser William H	47	photographer	63	"

Doncaster Street

Page	Letter	Full Name	Residence, Jan. 1	Occupation	Reported Age	Reported Residence, Street and Number
	r	Murphy Lawrence E	24	accountant	31	here
	s	Murphy Mabel A †	24	housewife	28	"
	t	Bottari Anthony	24	laborer	41	578 Hyde Park av
	u	Bottari Lillian †	24	housewife	33	578 "
	v*	DePaulis Alice M †	5	"	32	here
	w	DePaulis Yneve E	5	carpenter	38	"
	x	Roche David	5	chauffeur	24	805 Hyde Park av
	y	Roche Jane †	5	housewife	24	805 "
	z	Bartlett Dorothy E †	10	"	38	here
922						
	a	Bartlett Elizabeth L †	10	at home	75	"
	b	Bartlett Harold I	10	broker	40	"
	c	White Leslie R	20	clerk	38	"
	d	White Mary G †	20	housewife	35	"
	e	Higgins Edna R †	21	"	47	"
	f	Higgins Warren A	21	manager	63	"
	g	Richardson Earl E	22	painter	41	"

Page	Letter	Full Name	Residence, Jan. 1, 1941	Occupation	Supposed Age	Reported Residence, Jan. 1, 1940. Street and Number

Doncaster Street—Continued

Page	Letter	Full Name	Residence, Jan. 1, 1941	Occupation	Supposed Age	Reported Residence, Jan. 1, 1940. Street and Number
	H	Richardson Madge B—†	22	housewife	44	here
	K	Bennett Ethel R—†	23	"	54	"
	L	Bennett Wardell L	23	retired	71	"
	M	Lowell Muriel E—†	23	teacher	47	"
	N	Whitehead Edna S—†	23	housekeeper	44	"
	O	Upham Alice R—†	27	housewife	55	"
	P	Upham Charles W	27	proprietor	57	"
	R	Parker Eleanore T—†	30	housewife	43	"
	S	Parker John J	30	machinist	46	"
	T	Schriftgiesser Anna—†	30	at home	72	"
	U	Matson Anna M—†	33	housewife	54	"
	V	Matson Victor S	33	foreman	47	"
	W	Noxon George D	34	bookkeeper	44	"
	X	Noxon Hazel C—†	34	housewife	46	"
	Y	Ledbury Harry J	37	salesman	50	"
	Z	Ledbury Marion L—†	37	housewife	52	"
923						
	A	Pataillot Earle A	38	printer	37	289 Metropolitan av
	B	Pataillot Virginia H—†	38	housewife	31	289 "
	C	Doyle Anna L—†	42	"	60	here
	D	Doyle Edward L	42	engineer	60	"

Grew Avenue

Page	Letter	Full Name	Residence, Jan. 1, 1941	Occupation	Supposed Age	Reported Residence, Jan. 1, 1940. Street and Number
	F	Attaya Arthur V	14	student	25	here
	G	Attaya James E	14	U S A	21	"
	H	Attaya Joseph	14	salesman	27	"
	K	Attaya Joseph N	14	"	55	"
	L	Attaya Mary E—†	14	housewife	53	"
	M	Attaya Mary L—†	14	secretary	23	"
	N	Geisbecker Edward J	18	manager	56	"
	O	Geisbecker Eleanor R—†	18	teacher	22	"
	P	Geisbecker Johanna A—†	18	housewife	51	"
	R	DeRoma Catherine A—†	32	"	44	"
	S	DeRoma Florindo	32	contractor	51	"
	T	DeRoma Frederick J	32	chauffeur	22	"
	U	Doyle Ambrose F	34	clerk	38	"
	V	Lesha Joseph R	34	bottler	39	"
	W	Lesha Nora G—†	34	housewife	36	"
	X	Lesha Raymond M	34	retired	65	"

Page	Letter	Full Name	Residence, Jan. 1, 1941	Occupation	Supposed Age	Reported Residence, Jan. 1, 1940, Street and Number

Gwinnett Street

Page	Letter	Full Name	Residence, Jan. 1, 1941	Occupation	Supposed Age	Reported Residence, Jan. 1, 1940, Street and Number
	Y	Little Doris E †	1	saleswoman	22	90 Kenrick
	Z	Little Edward J	1	molder	43	90 "
924						
	A	Little Marie C †	1	housewife	41	90 "
	D	Mannion Madeline M †	5	"	30	43 Royal
	E	Mannion Martin M	5	brakeman	39	43 "
	F	Lambert Catherine R †	6	housewife	34	Medford
	G	Lambert Harry	6	foreman	39	"
	H	Lambert Herbert	6	clerk	22	"
	K	Murphy Elizabeth R †	9	housewife	48	300 Hyde Park av
	L	Murphy George F	9	custodian	50	300 "
	M	O'Toole Mary C †	9	operator	65	300 "
	N	Ouellette Elizabeth M †	9	clerk	27	300 "
	O	Anthony Evelyn A †	10	housewife	26	Norwood
	P	Anthony Olney P	10	machinist	28	"
	R	Pettersen Ethel F †	14	housewife	27	67 Homer
	S	Pettersen Harold	14	engineer	43	67 "
	T	Ryan Edward J	15	operator	32	37 Brown av
	U	Ryan Mildred C †	15	housewife	28	37 "
	V	Snow Clarence W	18	B F D	34	39 Webster
	W	Snow Loretta †	18	housewife	30	39 "
	X	Flanagan Delia †	19	"	62	10 Rowe
	Y	Flanagan Gertrude A †	19	clerk	28	10 "
	Z	Flanagan Helen M †	19	typist	32	10 "
925						
	A	Honiker Carroll J	19	operator	25	1000 River
	B	Honiker Theresa M †	19	housewife	21	1000 "
	C	O'Brien Mary J †	22	"	33	37 Brown av
	D	O'Brien Robert F	22	teacher	34	37 "
	E	McFadden Charlotte I †	25	housewife	39	458 E Eighth
	F	McFadden Stephen J	25	policeman	39	458 "
	G	Clark Catherine †	26	housewife	30	117 Williams
	H	Clark Walter F	26	chauffeur	42	117 "
	K	Frederick Marion M †	29	housewife	36	Watertown
	L	Frederick Theodore E	29	inspector	31	"
	M	Anderson James F	30	laborer	40	105 W[illegible] rd
	N	Jordan James W	30	salesman	41	105 "
	O	Jordan Loretta F †	30	housewife	39	105 "
	P	Powers Albert J	31	chauffeur	31	14 Olmstead
	R	Powers Bridget †	31	housewife	72	14 "

Page	Letter	Full Name	Residence, Jan. 1, 1941.	Occupation.	Supposed Age.	Reported Residence, Jan. 1, 1940. Street and Number.

Gwinnett Street—Continued

Page	Letter	Full Name	Residence, Jan. 1, 1941.	Occupation.	Supposed Age.	Reported Residence, Jan. 1, 1940. Street and Number.
	S	Powers Mary C †	31	housewife	31	14 Olmstead
	T	Powers Thomas J	31	retired	72	14 "
	U	Abbott Albert L	34	manager	43	Brookline
	V	Abbott Katherine M †	34	housewife	36	"
	W	O'Connor Mary E †	34	operator	38	13 Newbern
	X	Brown Louise M †	35	housekeeper	65	35 Colgate rd
	Y	Harnois George F	35	policeman	38	35 "
	Z	Harnois Mary F †	35	housewife	36	35 "

926 Hilburn Street

Page	Letter	Full Name	Residence, Jan. 1, 1941.	Occupation.	Supposed Age.	Reported Residence, Jan. 1, 1940. Street and Number.
926	A	Jolin Cora H †	7	housewife	59	here
	B	Jolin Eli V	7	foreman	65	"
	C	Barrett Annie M †	12	housewife	68	"
	D	Barrett Mary A †	12	supervisor	40	"
	E	Barrett Rose †	12	clerk	42	"
	F	Crellen R Ollivett †	21	housewife	41	"
	G	Crellen Walter R	21	manager	37	"
	H	Field Alma E †	25	housewife	36	"
	K	Field Frank C	25	repairman	36	"
	L	Winshman Alfred O	27	adjuster	34	"
	M	Winshman Josephine S †	27	housewife	32	"
	N	Winshman Louise B †	27	"	60	"
	O	Winshman Otto	27	proprietor	61	"
	P	Murphy Helen T †	31	stenographer	24	"
	R	Murphy Laura H †	31	housewife	59	"
	S	Murphy William L	31	accountant	61	"
	T	MacLeod Emma †	32	housewife	44	"
	U	MacLeod Oliver C	32	manager	44	"
	V	Kollmeyer August	36	printer	60	"
	W	Kollmeyer August, jr	36	"	26	"
	X	Kollmeyer Rosa A †	36	housewife	58	"
	Y	Emmel Chris A	40	decorator	56	"
	Z	Emmel Doris F †	40	teacher	27	"
927	A	Emmel Madeline R †	40	clerk	22	"
	B	Emmel Rose E †	40	housewife	50	"
	C	Roth Frances M †	40	clerk	50	"
	D	Worth Grace E †	41	housewife	52	"
	E	MacLeod Alexander	46	retired	70	"
	F	MacLeod Izabel E †	46	secretary	40	"

Page	Letter	Full Name	Residence, Jan. 1, 1941	Occupation	Supposed Age	Reported Residence, Jan. 1, 1940. Street and Number

Hilburn Street—Continued

Page	Letter	Full Name	Residence, Jan. 1, 1941	Occupation	Supposed Age	Reported Residence, Jan. 1, 1940. Street and Number
	G	Shackley Elmer F	47	salesman	47	here
	H	Shackley Margaret A †	47	housewife	54	"
	K	Lally Edith †	50	"	45	Revere
	L	Lally Patrick J	50	estimator	56	here
	M	Lally Walter	50	clerk	22	"
	N	Williams Carrie M †	51	housewife	58	"
	O	Williams Frederick H	51	salesman	52	"
	P	Harrington John J	54	clerk	37	"
	R	Harrington Mildred M †	54	housewife	31	"
	S	Joyce Mary J †	54	matron	63	"
	T	Fish Josephine A †	55	housewife	44	"
	U	Fish Louis J	55	supervisor	51	"
	V	Tobin Helen M †	59	housewife	37	"
	W	Tobin Walter F	59	proprietor	40	"
	X	Adair Bertha B †	70	at home	71	"
	Y	Adair Eldred	70	policeman	40	"
	Z	Adair Ruth A †	70	housewife	26	Medford
928						
	A	Downing John J	71	mechanic	51	here
	B	Downing John J, jr	71	clerk	24	"
	C	Downing Mary F †	71	secretary	20	"
	D	Downing Nora A †	71	housewife	48	"
	E	Stedman Charles F	71	chauffeur	43	"
	F	Stedman John P	71	accountant	22	"
	G	Stedman Virginia E †	71	housewife	43	"
	H	Mullen Frances J †	74	"	39	"
	K	Mullen Joseph J	74	clerk	39	"
	L	Simpson Emily T †	77	housewife	54	"
	M	Simpson Norman J	77	accountant	52	"
	N	Simpson Norman J	77	clerk	20	"

Hillview Avenue

Page	Letter	Full Name	Residence, Jan. 1, 1941	Occupation	Supposed Age	Reported Residence, Jan. 1, 1940. Street and Number
	O	Scherniff Eileen †	1	housewife	24	here
	P	Scherniff John C	1	chauffeur	27	"
	R	Driscoll Ellen M †	2	housewife	40	"
	S	Driscoll Francis F	2	clerk	40	"
	T	Britton Edward	3	engraver	48	"
	U	Britton Jeannette †	3	housewife	46	"
	V	Britton William	3	engraver	23	"
	W	Haggman Adle †	4	stenographer	23	"

Page	Letter	Full Name.	Residence, Jan. 1, 1941.	Occupation.	Supposed Age.	Reported Residence, Jan. 1, 1940. Street and Number.

Hillview Avenue—Continued

Page	Letter	Full Name.	Residence, Jan. 1, 1941.	Occupation.	Supposed Age.	Reported Residence, Jan. 1, 1940. Street and Number.
	X	Haggman George	4	contractor	48	here
	Y	Shepherd John J	5	teacher	38	"
	Z	Shepherd Lena M †	5	housewife	36	"
929						
	A	Sorenson Ida M †	6	"	38	"
	B	Sorenson William	6	chauffeur	46	"
	C	Carey Francis	6	manager	33	1463 Centre
	D	Carey Mary †	6	housewife	28	1463 "
	E	McCarrick Bridget †	7	"	70	here
	F	McCarrick James J	7	clerk	32	"
	G	McCarrick Loretta F †	7	operator	33	"
	H	McCarrick Peter J	7	examiner	72	"
	K	Deninger Maria †	8	housewife	65	"
	L	Deninger Martin	8	waiter	59	"
	M	Blake Charles M	8	foreman	51	"
	N	Blake George M	8	clerk	24	"
	O	Blake Mary G †	8	housewife	46	"
	P	McGuckian Elizabeth D †	9	"	28	12 Courtney rd
	R	McGuckian John W	9	teacher	31	12 "
	S	Breheney Michael	9	operator	46	here
	T	Breheney Winifred †	9	housewife	39	"
	U	Bowers Edward F	11	salesman	24	"
	V	Bowers Mary V †	11	housewife	25	"
	W	Dinsmore Amy L †	11	buyer	48	"
	X	Dinsmore Henry N	11	retired	86	"
	Y	Dinsmore Louise †	11	housewife	80	"
	Z	Khouri Angela M †	12	"	28	35 Peter Parley rd
930						
	A	Khouri Frederick G	12	merchant	28	Florida
	B	Monello Ann V †	14	housewife	23	Brookline
	C	Monello Ferrar	14	contractor	30	"
	D	Bouzan Johanna †	15	housewife	44	here
	E	Bouzan Michael J	15	mechanic	48	"
	F	Ihley Charles O	15	carpenter	48	"
	G	Ihley Irene E †	15	operator	24	"
	H	Rourke Mary †	15	housekeeper	60	Watertown
	K	Ryan Joseph A	16	porter	30	here
	L	Ryan Mary T †	16	housewife	66	"
	M	Ryan Thomas F	16	clerk	41	"
	N	Ryan Thomas J	16	porter	66	"
	O	MacLean Joseph M	17	mechanic	41	74 Chesbrough rd

Page	Letter	Full Name	Residence, Jan. 1, 1941	Occupation	Supposed Age	Reported Residence, Jan. 1, 1940. Street and Number

Hillview Avenue Continued

Page	Letter	Full Name	Residence, Jan. 1, 1941	Occupation	Supposed Age	Reported Residence, Jan. 1, 1940. Street and Number
	P	MacLean Mae L †	17	housewife	38	[illegible]
	R	Ryan Grace R †	17	"	37	here
	S	Ryan James E	17	chauffeur	39	"
	T	McGurl James	18	cashier	44	"
	U	McGurl Mary A †	18	housewife	33	"
	V	Kelley Bernard	21	student	21	"
	W	Kelley John J	21	carpenter	53	"
	X	Kelley Mary A †	21	housewife	52	"
	Y	McKay Cecelia B †	21	"	42	"
	Z	McKay William	21	mechanic	46	"
931						
	A	Wilson Mary S †	25	housewife	45	"
	B	Wilson William C	25	chemist	46	"

Jeffers Street

Page	Letter	Full Name	Residence, Jan. 1, 1941	Occupation	Supposed Age	Reported Residence, Jan. 1, 1940. Street and Number
	C	Dowling Ida M †	14	housewife	46	here
	D	Dowling Thomas	14	clerk	56	"
	E	MacGregor Archibald	19	upholsterer	57	"
	F	MacGregor Homer M	19	"	24	"
	G	MacGregor Marion †	19	housewife	42	"
	H	MacGregor Robert O	19	upholsterer	21	"
	K	Pick Owen	19	retired	78	"
	N	Amelotte Mildred T †	26	housewife	40	"
	O	Amelotte Napoleon R	26	policeman	47	"
	P	Jodoin Lionel A	26	U S A	24	Ludlow
	R	Olson Adolph G	31	finisher	56	here
	S	Olson Marie †	31	housewife	56	"

Littledale Street

Page	Letter	Full Name	Residence, Jan. 1, 1941	Occupation	Supposed Age	Reported Residence, Jan. 1, 1940. Street and Number
	T	Kalsh John E	5	accountant	30	here
	U	Kalsh Marguerite †	5	housewife	30	"
	V	Kleinberg Andrew	5	engineer	69	"
	W	Kleinberg Clara †	5	housewife	55	"
	X	Stenberg Belinda V †	6	at home	81	"
	Y	Stokinger Catherine V †	6	housewife	42	"
	Z	Stokinger Frederick J	6	salesman	43	"
932						
	A	Stokinger Frederick J, jr	6	clerk	20	"
	B	Pittman Corbett	9	carpenter	51	"

Page	Letter	Full Name	Residence, Jan. 1, 1941	Occupation	Supposed Age	Reported Residence, Jan. 1, 1940. Street and Number

Littledale Street—Continued

Page	Letter	Full Name	Residence, Jan. 1, 1941	Occupation	Supposed Age	Reported Residence, Jan. 1, 1940. Street and Number
	C	Pittman Elfreda †	9	housewife	48	here
	D	*Pittman Emma †	9	bookkeeper	21	"
	E	Smith Edwin	10	carpenter	55	"
	F	Smith Mary F †	10	housewife	47	"
	G	Grother Anna E †	14	"	62	"
	H	Grother John H	14	trimmer	66	"
	K	*Moore Catherine †	15	clerk	32	"
	L	*Moore Margaret †	15	housewife	71	"
	M	*Moore William	15	retired	71	"
	N	*Thomson Elizabeth M †	15	housewife	35	"
	O	Thomson William H	15	laborer	40	"
	P	Donahue Euphemia B †	17	housewife	37	"
	R	Donahue Joseph F	17	finisher	42	"
	S	White Emma †	18	housewife	45	8 Romar ter
	T	White Fritz	18	machinist	57	here
	U	White Robert	18	tilelayer	31	"

Lodge Hill Road

Page	Letter	Full Name	Residence, Jan. 1, 1941	Occupation	Supposed Age	Reported Residence, Jan. 1, 1940. Street and Number
	V	Cacciagrani Frances H †	5	housewife	26	56 Warren av
	W	Cacciagrani Vincent B	5	merchant	30	56 "
	X	Erickson Carl E	14	molder	51	here
	Y	Erickson Carl W	14	clerk	21	"
	Z	*Erickson Naomi C †	14	housewife	51	"
933						
	A	Jansky Eva †	17	"	40	"
	B	Jansky John	17	carpenter	52	"
	C	Jansky Richard	17	mechanic	22	"
	D	McCarthy Gertrude E †	22	housekeeper	39	"
	E	Oberlander Ralph	22	optician	47	"
	F	Oberlander Winifred A †	22	housewife	42	"
	G	O'Brien Mary †	22	clerk	30	"

Magee Street

Page	Letter	Full Name	Residence, Jan. 1, 1941	Occupation	Supposed Age	Reported Residence, Jan. 1, 1940. Street and Number
	H	White Olive N †	37	housewife	36	here
	K	White William M	37	salesman	35	"
	L	Raymond M Frances †	37	at home	76	"
	M	Sprague Bessie A †	37	"	72	"

Page	Letter	Full Name	Residence, Jan. 1, 1941	Occupation	Supposed Age	Reported Residence, Jan. 1, 1940. Street and Number.

Mansfield Street

Page	Letter	Full Name	Residence, Jan. 1, 1941	Occupation	Supposed Age	Reported Residence, Jan. 1, 1940. Street and Number.
	N	Holleran Elizabeth A †	3	housewife	39	here
	O	Holleran Joseph E	3	inspector	43	"
	P	Green Edith †	20	housewife	41	"
	R	Green Jacob	20	proprietor	37	"

Mansur Street

Page	Letter	Full Name	Residence, Jan. 1, 1941	Occupation	Supposed Age	Reported Residence, Jan. 1, 1940. Street and Number.
	S	Aubrey Dorothy S †	3	housewife	34	here
	T	Aubrey Howard W	3	advertising	33	"

Maynard Street

Page	Letter	Full Name	Residence, Jan. 1, 1941	Occupation	Supposed Age	Reported Residence, Jan. 1, 1940. Street and Number.
	U	Mooney Catherine M †	15	housewife	30	87 Roseclair
	V	Mooney James E	15	policeman	31	87 "
	W	Donlan Fred J	19	custodian	46	here
	X	Donlan Violet C †	19	housewife	40	"
	Y	Burke John M	20	B F D	26	"
	Z	Burke Marie F †	20	housewife	25	"
934						
	A	McLaughlin Dennis J	20	B F D	45	"
	B	McNamara Angela B †	22	housewife	35	"
	C	McNamara Edward J	22	policeman	38	"
	D	Reddington John J	22	clerk	28	"
	E	Reddington Madeline †	22	housewife	32	Malden
	F	Reddington Mary B †	22	"	66	here
	G	Jones George E	24	clerk	30	"
	H	Jones Mary E †	24	housewife	30	"
	K	Geha Joseph	26	clerk	29	"
	L	*Geha Selma †	26	housewife	46	"
	M	Rosenberg Augusta †	28	"	46	"
	N	Rosenberg Hyman	28	salesman	56	"
	O	*Hannes Gertrude F †	30	housewife	42	18 Marbury ter
	P	*Hannes Julius H	30	cabinetmaker	46	18 "
	R	Blackburn Roy C	32	secretary	47	here
	S	Sill Alice E †	32	housewife	73	"
	T	Sill Louise †	32	clerk	36	"
	U	Coakley Catherine N †	34	housewife	63	"
	V	Coakley Dennis J	34	clerk	58	"
	W	Jones Catherine M †	34	housewife	27	"
	X	Jones Joseph E	34	operator	29	14 Schuyler

Page.	Letter.	Full Name.	Residence, Jan. 1, 1941.	Occupation.	Supposed Age.	Reported Residence, Jan. 1, 1940. Street and Number.

Maynard Street—Continued

Page.	Letter.	Full Name.	Residence, Jan. 1, 1941.	Occupation.	Supposed Age.	Reported Residence, Jan. 1, 1940. Street and Number.
	Y	Carney George F	36	operator	39	61 Kittredge
	Z	Carney Helen C †	36	housewife	40	61 "
935						
	A	Hogan Frank J	38	investigator	33	here
	B	Hogan Margaret M †	38	housewife	33	"
	C	*Frantzen Amelia R †	40	"	46	29 Wenham
	D	Frantzen Peter A	40	laborer	23	29 "
	E	Hagerty Jeremiah J	67	"	61	here
	F	Hagerty Margaret M †	67	housewife	63	"
	G	Hagerty Thomas C	67	clerk	21	"
	H	McInerney James W	67	chauffeur	29	New York
	K	McInerney Margaret E †	67	housewife	22	Mansfield
	L	*Cossette Hermine †	73	"	61	here
	M	*Cossette Napoleon	73	clerk	29	"
	N	*Cossette Pauline †	73	"	25	"
	O	*Cossette Urbain	73	retired	66	"
	P	Chaberek Walter W	76	mechanic	37	"
	R	Chaberek Wanda V †	76	housewife	33	"
	S	Puzia Jacob M	76	retired	68	"
	T	Clark Olive M †	76	housekeeper	47	"
	U	Baxter Arthur R	80	shipper	37	"
	V	Baxter Phyllis E †	80	housewife	28	"
	W	Haigh Mary J †	80	housekeeper	66	"
	X	Gaffney Mary F †	83	housewife	52	"
	Y	Gaffney Mary F †	83	clerk	21	"
	Z	Gaffney Rita M †	83	"	20	"
936						
	A	O'Leary Edward F	83	letter carrier	46	"
	B	Lyons Eileen A †	87	clerk	27	"
	C	Lyons Kathleen T †	87	teacher	25	"
	D	Lyons Marjorie M †	87	clerk	29	"
	E	Lyons Sarah T †	87	housewife	53	"
	F	Lyons Thaddeus J	87	inspector	53	"
	G	Lyons Thaddeus J, jr	87	student	21	"
	H	*Avelino Constance M †	95	housewife	32	"
	K	Avellino Michael A	95	engineer	30	"

Metropolitan Avenue

Page.	Letter.	Full Name.	Residence, Jan. 1, 1941.	Occupation.	Supposed Age.	Reported Residence, Jan. 1, 1940. Street and Number.
	L	Sybertz Adeline M †	130	housewife	39	here
	M	Sybertz Henry C	130	R F D	43	"

Page	Letter	Full Name	Residence, Jan. 1, 1941	Occupation	Supposed Age	Reported Residence, Jan. 1, 1940. Street and Number

Metropolitan Avenue (Continued)

Page	Letter	Full Name	Residence, Jan. 1, 1941	Occupation	Supposed Age	Reported Residence, Jan. 1, 1940. Street and Number
	N	Nickerson Annie †	130	housewife	54	here
	O	Nickerson Francis	130	manager	26	"
	P	Nickerson Ralph	130	student	21	"
	R	Nickerson Shurben	130	chef	52	"
	S	Nickerson Vera †	130	saleswoman	28	"
	T	Lang George H	134	manager	60	"
	U	Lang Mabel C †	134	housewife	50	"
	V	Callowhill Adell †	142	"	63	"
	W	Stanley Anna M †	142	at home	70	N Hampshire
	X	Kleinberg Elizabeth †	146	"	72	here
	Y	Kleinberg Mildred L †	146	stenographer	33	"
	Z	Warner Jennie M †	146	housewife	40	"
937						
	A	Warner Walter	146	electrician	43	"
	B	Yardumian Dickranouhie	154	druggist	43	"
	C	Yardumian John	154	clerk	56	"
	D	Yardumian Rose J †	154	student	21	"
	E	Varteresian Avedis	154	mechanic	46	"
	F	Varteresian Esther †	154	housewife	39	"
	G	Adams Andrew L	154	printer	32	[illegible] Metropolitan av
	H	Adams Lena A †	154	stitcher	30	190 "
	K	Scoff Alfred J	162	salesman	31	here
	L	Scoff Elias M	162	merchant	66	"
	M	Scoff Theodora †	162	librarian	39	"
	N	Perry Aristotle	166	manager	41	"
	O	Perry Janet †	166	housewife	39	"
	P	Menton Anna M †	166	"	40	"
	R	Menton Thomas J	166	clerk	44	"
	S	Doherty Marion P †	178	teacher	37	"
	T	Parmelee Clayton H	178	retired	79	"
	U	Rossetti Lena †	190	housewife	45	"
	V	Rossetti Michael	190	mechanic	48	"
	W	Borman Martha †	190	housewife	48	"
	X	Borman William	190	watchmaker	49	"
	Y	Bergin Edward J	198	mechanic	45	"
	Z	Bergin Mary C †	198	housewife	42	"
938						
	A	Kremer Anthony M	202	clerk	40	"
	B	Kremer Emma S †	202	housewife	67	"
	C	Kremer Hilda B †	202	clerk	33	"
	D	Kremer Paul J	202	printer	36	"

Page	Letter	Full Name	Residence, Jan. 1, 1941	Occupation	Supposed Age	Reported Residence, Jan. 1, 1940. Street and Number.

Metropolitan Avenue—Continued

Page	Letter	Full Name	Residence, Jan. 1, 1941	Occupation	Supposed Age	Reported Residence, Jan. 1, 1940. Street and Number.
	E	Mugar Arthur A	206	clerk	50	here
	F	Mugar Rose G †	206	housewife	45	"
	G	Rush Kathleen †	206	"	31	"
	H	Rush William M	206	policeman	43	"
	K	Bigwood Alton	206	clerk	24	"
	L	Bigwood Edith †	206	housewife	53	"
	M	Bigwood Frederick	206	clerk	54	"
	N	Bigwood Winton	206	salesman	23	"
	O	Eilertson Olaf	214	retired	79	1 Vesta
	P	Loescher Blanche E †	214	housewife	28	here
	R	Loescher Carl B	214	instructor	29	"
	S	Morgan Johanna E †	214	housewife	35	"
	T	Morgan Merrill R	214	electrician	38	"
	U	Krim Josephine †	218	housewife	32	"
	V	Krim William A	218	engineer	34	"
	W	Kratzer Elizabeth D †	218	housewife	36	"
	X	Kratzer Raymond	218	instructor	46	"
	Y	Faunce Catherine A †	226	teacher	27	"
	Z	Faunce Mary F †	226	housewife	67	"
939						
	A	Faunce Walter J	226	inspector	30	"
	B	Lynch Anne R †	238	housewife	63	"
	C	Lynch Barbara A †	238	teacher	30	"
	D	Lynch Patricia R †	238	stenographer	27	"
	E	Lynch Patrick J	238	manager	67	"
	F	Lynch Ruth E †	238	teacher	31	"
	G	Mirabile Annie †	250	housewife	38	"
	H	Mirabile Gaspare	250	chauffeur	47	"
	K	Mirabile Josephine †	250	operator	35	"
	M	Gundal Carl	273	stonecutter	65	"
	N	Gundal Carl A	273	carpenter	27	"
	O	Gundal Elizabeth H †	273	stenographer	24	"
	P	Gundal Evelyn C †	273	"	34	"
	R	Gundal Katherine J †	273	housewife	60	"
	S	Wessling Anna C †	273	"	30	"
	T	Wessling Edward A	273	clerk	33	"
	U	Ciarlone Emily †	274	housewife	45	"
	V	Ciarlone Gaetano	274	manager	46	"
	W	Colarossi Ernestine †	274	examiner	40	"
	X	Galassi Emma †	274	secretary	32	"
	Y	*Galassi Victoria †	274	housewife	51	"

Metropolitan Avenue—Continued

Page	Letter	Full Name	Residence, Jan. 1, 1941	Occupation	Supposed Age	Reported Residence, Jan. 1, 1940, Street and Number
	Z	Shaw Emily K †	289	housewife	31	here
940						
	A	Shaw Thomas C	289	plumber	32	"
	B	Dunne John J	289	machinist	24	"
	C	Dunne Marion L †	289	housewife	21	"
	D	Oakes George F	290	broker	34	949 Hyde Park av
	E	Oakes Mildred B †	290	housewife	34	949 "
	F	MacDonald Isabelle †	294	"	30	here
	G	MacDonald Ronald J	294	salesman	29	"
	H	Klippel Anna †	294	housekeeper	55	"
	K	Klippel Mary †	294	"	40	"
	L	Schmitt Carl L	304	clerk	28	"
	M	Schmitt Emilia †	304	artist	37	"
	N	Schmitt Erma †	304	housewife	60	"
	O	Schmitt Ludwig	304	confectioner	62	"
	P	Yeames George H	311	retired	69	"
	R	Yeames Isabelle E †	311	housewife	59	"
	S	Yeames Margaret C †	311	bookkeeper	28	"
	T	Kramer Charles C	331	butcher	48	"
	V	Kramer Nora A †	331	housewife	50	"
	X	Hendsby Daisy †	336	"	46	"
	Y	Hendsby John T	336	chef	50	"
	Z	Hicks Edgar C	338	machinist	41	"
941						
	A	Hicks Marion J †	338	housewife	37	"
	B	Ochs Harriet E †	338	"	43	11 McBride
	C	Ochs Joseph P	338	shoecutter	49	11 "
	D	*Weiler Marie Y †	338	housekeeper	68	Brookline
	E	Whidden Arthur W	344	electrician	51	here
	F	Whidden Margaret W †	344	housewife	51	"
	G	Gleason Charles W	345	teacher	39	5 Austin
	H	Gleason Mary J †	345	housewife	34	5 "
	K	Olson Agnes M †	345	domestic	46	75 Glendower
	L	Mosley Herbert	345	clerk	26	Dedham
	M	Mosley Martha Q †	345	housewife	24	"
	N	LaRosa Charles	348	bartender	39	here
	O	LaRosa Mary †	348	housewife	38	"
	P	Smith Harold R	352	nurse	52	"
	R	Anderson Edith M †	355	clerk	20	"
	S	Anderson Emil H	355	patternmaker	54	"
	T	Anderson Signe W †	355	housewife	55	"

Page	Letter	Full Name	Residence, Jan. 1, 1941	Occupation	Supposed Age	Reported Residence, Jan. 1, 1940. Street and Number

Metropolitan Avenue Continued

Page	Letter	Full Name	Residence	Occupation	Age	Reported Residence
	U	Joyce John J	356	clerk	42	here
	V	Joyce John J, jr	356	laborer	21	"
	W	Joyce Sarah E †	356	housewife	43	"
	X	Girvan Agnes C †	366	"	46	"
	Y	Girvan George W	366	policeman	51	"
	Z	Girvan Georgia J †	366	housekeeper	20	"
942						
	A	McGuinness Edward M	366	retired	70	"
	B	Nelson Henry R	371	mechanic	26	1330 Com av
	C	Nelson Virginia W †	371	housewife	25	1330 "
	D	*Sano Angelina †	371	laundress	47	here
	E	Sano Anthony	371	packer	28	"
	F	Sano Rosario	371	laundryman	25	"
	G	King Dorothy L †	372	housewife	33	"
	H	King James A	372	welder	28	"
	K	MacDonald John B	372	fitter	24	"
	L	MacDonald Margaret M †	372	housewife	47	"
	M	Tanfield Charles W	377	caretaker	71	"
	N	McIver Elizabeth M †	389	housewife	80	"
	O	McIver Isabella L †	389	housekeeper	49	"
	P	Holzer Emma G †	393	housewife	62	"
	R	Holzer Henry N	393	bookbinder	67	"
	S	Wessel Carl	398	guard	70	"
	T	Wessel Carl, jr	398	clerk	39	"
	U	Wessel Goldie M †	398	housewife	35	"
	V	Dauphinee Adele E †	427	"	60	"
	W	Dauphinee Bernard R	427	engineer	61	"
	X	Norton Mary F †	427	housewife	29	"
	Y	Norton Robert J	427	shipper	32	"

Pinedale Road

Page	Letter	Full Name	Residence	Occupation	Age	Reported Residence
	Y	Mahoney John M	2	gardener	33	here
	Z	Mahoney Margaret T †	2	housewife	26	"
943						
	A	Carlezon Edward J	2	inspector	52	"
	B	Carlezon Mary E †	2	housewife	40	"
	C	Canavan Anna †	2	packer	22	"
	D	Canavan John T	2	clerk	29	"
	E	Canavan Martin	2	retired	64	"
	F	Canavan Mary E †	2	housewife	62	"

Page	Letter	Full Name.	Residence, Jan. 1, 1941.	Occupation.	Supposed Age.	Reported Residence, Jan. 1, 1940. Street and Number.

Pinedale Road—Continued

Page	Letter	Full Name.	Residence, Jan. 1, 1941.	Occupation.	Supposed Age.	Reported Residence, Jan. 1, 1940. Street and Number.
	G	Walsh Agnes †	6	housewife	66	here
	H	Walsh Edward J	6	carpenter	43	"
	K	Walsh Mary C †	6	housewife	38	"
	L	Lyons Agnes G †	6	"	26	"
	M	Lyons William	6	chef	33	"
	N	Walsh Dennis	6	mechanic	34	"
	O	Walsh Helen I †	6	housewife	27	"
	P	O'Malley Edward J	8	laborer	66	"
	R	O'Malley Mary †	8	housewife	65	"
	S	Kilroy James J	10	engineer	42	"
	T	Kilroy Mary A †	10	housewife	43	"
	U	Malia Patrick	10	retired	70	"
	V	Richardson Alva L	11	engineer	59	"
	W	Tinker George K	11	machinist	25	"
	X	Tinker Margaret F †	11	housewife	56	"
	Y	Orsi Amedeo	11	meatcutter	56	"
	Z	Orsi Joseph M	11	cashier	20	"
944						
	A	Orsi Leonetta †	11	housewife	50	"
	B	Orsi Rita T †	11	packer	22	"
	D	Connelly Elizabeth †	19	dressmaker	27	"
	E	Connelly Nora †	19	housewife	68	"
	F	*Molyneaux Rachael †	25	"	36	"
	G	Molyneaux Wilfred G	25	carpenter	42	"
	H	O'Brien Bridget E †	25	housewife	52	24 Walden
	K	O'Brien Edward	25	mechanic	54	24 "
	L	O'Brien Margaret †	28	housewife	77	here
	M	O'Brien Michael F	28	policeman	35	"
	N	O'Brien Nicholas W	28	manager	42	"
	O	Walsh Margaret M †	28	domestic	47	"
	P	Armington Agnes H †	28	housewife	44	"
	R	Armington Ralph	28	mechanic	44	"
	S	Kenny Della †	28	housewife	31	"
	T	Kenny John T	28	manager	31	"
	U	Hammer Anna †	32	housewife	77	"
	V	Hammer Elsie V †	32	"	50	"
	W	Hammer Ralph R	32	engineer	56	"
	X	Hammer Ruth M †	32	stenographer	25	"
	Z	O'Toole Catherine †	52	housewife	31	"
945						
	A	O'Toole John	52	salesman	35	"

Page	Letter	Full Name.	Residence, Jan. 1, 1941.	Occupation.	Supposed Age.	Reported Residence, Jan. 1, 1940. Street and Number.

Poplar Street

Page	Letter	Full Name.	Residence, Jan. 1, 1941.	Occupation.	Supposed Age.	Reported Residence, Jan. 1, 1940. Street and Number.
	B	Thompson Elizabeth M †	181	housewife	32	6 Augustus av
	C	Thompson William H	181	clerk	31	6 "
	D	Costello Gertrude C †	183	housewife	32	here
	E	Costello John J	183	inspector	34	"
	F	Anderson Mary †	185	housewife	37	"
	G	Anderson Oscar	185	auditor	45	"
	H	Stueber Elizabeth B †	185	housewife	44	"
	K	Steuber Ralph	185	agent	43	"
	L	Savill Agnes M †	185	housewife	25	"
	M	*Savill Albert A	185	clerk	24	"
	N	Stewart George A	191	B F D	43	"
	O	Stewart Rose †	191	housewife	44	"
	P	Aeres Margaret R †	191	"	35	Malden
	R	Aeres Walter B	191	compositor	48	Medford
	S	Hennessey Catherine M †	195	housewife	35	here
	T	Hennessey Francis P	195	teacher	36	"
	U	O'Connell George L	195	"	32	"
	V	O'Connell Mary C †	195	housewife	31	"
	W	Breed Emily E †	209	"	63	"
	X	Breed Fred C	209	machinist	67	"
	Y	Morrison Ella A †	209	housewife	37	"
	Z	Morrison John	209	foreman	49	"
946						
	A	Hener Charles F	213	clerk	46	"
	B	Hener Emelie †	213	at home	78	"
	C	Hener Joseph W	213	shoecutter	54	"
	D	Donigan Mary A †	221	at home	70	"
	E	Fallon Martin F	221	barber	40	"
	F	Fallon Martin J	221	U S N	30	"
	G	Fallon Winifred B †	221	bookkeeper	41	"
	H	Pinner Phyllis I †	221	saleswoman	28	"
	K	Savage John T	229	B F D	46	"
	L	Savage Theresa M †	229	housewife	46	"
	M	Schroeder Ethel †	229	"	36	103 Kilsyth rd
	N	Schroeder Kurt F	229	painter	34	103 "
	O	Murray George D	229	salesman	36	here
	P	Murray Helen E †	229	housewife	34	"
	R	Bazin Frank A	233	salesman	32	"
	S	Bazin Harry H	233	shoecutter	65	"
	T	Bazin Sabina J †	233	housewife	63	"
	U	Polk Astrid I †	233	"	46	"

Page	Letter	Full Name	Residence, Jan. 1, 1941	Occupation	Supposed Age	Reported Residence, Jan. 1, 1940. Street and Number

Poplar Street—Continued

Page	Letter	Full Name	Residence, Jan. 1, 1941	Occupation	Supposed Age	Reported Residence, Jan. 1, 1940
	V	Polk Hadley G	233	repairman	48	here
	W	McManus Caroline E †	233	housewife	45	"
	X	McManus Patrick	233	policeman	45	"
	Y	Keyes Anna M †	279	housewife	40	"
	Z	Keyes James J	279	guard	45	"
947						
	A	Guittarr Eva M †	281	dressmaker	51	"
	B	Maillet Edgar P	281	plasterer	48	"
	C	Maillet Ella K †	281	housewife	47	"
	D	Warren Frances M †	285	"	33	"
	E	Warren Thomas F	285	engineer	33	"
	F	Lawrie Jane M †	289	saleswoman	25	"
	G	Lawrie Jeannie M †	289	housewife	51	"
	H	Lawrie William E	289	dispatcher	52	"
	K	Lawrence Almyra M †	293	housewife	49	"
	L	Cushing Sarah E †	297	clerk	52	"
	M	Doherty Charlotte †	297	secretary	45	24 Virgil rd
	N	Roberts Eliza C †	297	housekeeper	69	here
	O	Berg Francis J	301	engineer	47	"
	P	Bohmiller Bertha †	301	clerk	40	"
	R	Bohmiller Sophie †	301	housewife	38	"
	S	Ammidown Helene T †	301	"	32	526 Newbury
	T	Ammidown Raymond L	301	clerk	41	36 Mora
	U	Shea Mary †	301	"	52	here
	V	Cook Everett R	307	"	20	"
	W	Cook Malcolm A	307	accountant	22	"
	X	Cook Marion F †	307	housewife	52	"
	Y	Cook William A	307	ironmolder	56	"
	Z	Brown John L	309	investigator	31	"
948						
	A	Brown Nora C †	309	saleswoman	50	"
	B	Silva Anna M †	309	housewife	44	"
	C	Silva Frank E	309	broker	45	"
	D	Silva Frank E, jr	309	student	21	"
	E	Rogers Everett C	325	florist	62	"
	F	Rogers Helen A †	325	at home	56	"
	G	Rogers Margaret †	325	housewife	51	"
	H	Mahoney Daniel	331	clerk	49	"
	K	Mahoney Elsie M †	331	housewife	46	"
	L	Lawson Dorothy †	335	clerk	28	"
	M	Sellers Gertrude L †	335	housewife	44	"

Page.	Letter.	Full Name.	Residence, Jan. 1, 1941.	Occupation.	Supposed Age.	Reported Residence, Jan. 1, 1940. Street and Number.

Poplar Street—Continued

Page.	Letter.	Full Name.	Residence, Jan. 1, 1941.	Occupation.	Supposed Age.	Reported Residence, Jan. 1, 1940.
	N	Sellers William E	335	policeman	44	here
	O	Shehadi Edna †	363	housewife	23	"
	P	Shehadi Henry	363	factoryhand	26	"
	R	Shehadi Joseph	363	"	28	"
	S	*Shehadi Sadie †	363	housewife	53	"
	T	Shehadi Sarah †	363	seamstress	22	"
	U	Allen George H	387	retired	71	"
	V	Jaworski Cora E †	387	housewife	37	"
	W	Jaworski Paul	387	salesman	41	"
	X	French Benjamin H	387	engineer	36	"
	Y	French Grace C †	387	housewife	34	"
	Z	Metcalfe Mary †	390	"	68	"
949						
	A	Metcalfe William	390	gardener	74	"
	B	Howalt F Harvey	391	attorney	42	"
	C	Howalt Gertrude F †	391	housewife	43	"
	D	*Crocker Ada D †	391	"	53	831 South
	E	Crocker Catherine N †	391	secretary	23	831 "
	F	Crocker Florence V †	391	clerk	25	831 "
	G	Crocker William N	391	millworker	55	831 "
	H	Dorion Donald E	393	policeman	38	257 Highland
	K	Dorion Ruth H †	393	housewife	33	257 "
	L	Mack John H	393	letter carrier	40	here
	M	Mack Lois C †	393	housewife	36	"
	N	McLeod Catherine M †	399	"	53	"
	O	McLeod James H	399	compositor	60	"
	P	McLeod Katherine H †	399	social worker	30	"
	R	McLeod Margaret R †	399	"	28	"
	S	Kremer Frank G	408	machinist	38	"
	T	Kremer Lillian J †	408	housewife	35	"
	U	Sweet Mary E †	408	"	74	"
	V	Malmquist Carl W	412	machinist	68	"
	W	Malmquist Olga G †	412	clerk	42	"
	X	Malmquist Signe H †	412	stenographer	35	"
	Y	Malmquist Sofia †	412	housewife	64	"
	Z	Gniod Grace K †	419	"	24	"
950						
	A	Gniod Joseph J	419	machinist	29	"
	B	Tripp Harriet J †	430	housewife	64	"
	C	Tripp Oliver W	430	salesman	36	"

Page	Letter	Full Name	Residence, Jan. 1, 1941	Occupation	Supposed Age	Reported Residence, Jan. 1, 1940. Street and Number
		Poplar Street—Continued				
	D	Tripp Wayland F	430	retired	66	here
	F	Carlson Agda M †	490	housewife	45	"
	G	Carlson Gustav H	490	pipefitter	43	"
	H	Lundquist Robert E	492	clerk	29	"
	K	Lundquist Ruth M †	492	housewife	26	"
	L	Sheehan Mary D †	494	"	37	"
	M	Sheehan Timothy F	494	inspector	40	"
	N	Cassidy Elizabeth †	496	housewife	29	"
	O	Cassidy Thomas	496	chauffeur	32	"
	P	Harrison Helen L †	500	housewife	34	265 Roslindale av
	R	Harrison William H	500	clerk	32	265 "
	S	Ogryzek Bernard	502	chef	22	20 Amory av
	T	Ogryzek Catherine †	502	housewife	51	20 "
	U	Ogryzek John	502	chauffeur	27	20 "
	V	Ogryzek Joseph	502	baker	51	20 "
	W	Ogryzek Mary †	502	clerk	20	20 "
	X	Ogryzek Stanley	502	chauffeur	25	180 Boylston
	Y	Ogryzek Thomas	502	laborer	24	20 Amory av
	Z	Simonian Edward J	508	accountant	35	here
951						
	A	Simonian Mary †	508	housewife	67	"
	B	Simonian Mary A †	508	hairdresser	31	"
	C	Simonian Violet †	508	seamstress	35	"
	D	Mooney George S	510	chauffeur	42	"
	E	Mooney Mary D †	510	housewife	44	"
	F	Soeldner Gertrude K †	516	cutter	46	"
	G	Soeldner Mary R †	516	operator	40	"
	H	Soeldner Michael	516	carpenter	70	"
	K	Kenny Grace †	518	operator	25	236 Kittredge
	L	Soeldner Adolph M	518	estimator	31	236 "
	M	Soeldner Irene T †	518	housewife	29	236 "
		Ruffing Street				
	N	Newton Anna B †	18–20	housewife	31	here
	O	Newton Victor J	18–20	social worker	35	"
	P	Gade Daniel H	18–20	B F D	41	"
	R	Gade Elsie A †	18–20	housewife	34	"
	S	Gade Emily A †	18–20	"	68	"
	T	*Ferazzi Eda †	26	"	40	"

Page	Letter	Full Name	Residence Jan. 1, 1941	Occupation	Supposed Age	Reported Residence, Jan. 1, 1940. Street and Number.

Ruffing Street—Continued

Page	Letter	Full Name	Residence Jan. 1, 1941	Occupation	Supposed Age	Reported Residence, Jan. 1, 1940. Street and Number.
	U	Ferazzi John	26	barber	44	here
	V	Ferazzi John, jr	26	operator	20	"

Weeks Avenue

Page	Letter	Full Name	Residence Jan. 1, 1941	Occupation	Supposed Age	Reported Residence, Jan. 1, 1940. Street and Number.
	W	*Moore Edna S †	1	housewife	68	here
	X	Moore John A	1	machinist	48	"
	Y	Moore John A	1	student	21	"
	Z	Kirkland James T	19	mechanic	54	"
952						
	A	Kirkland Mary S †	19	housewife	52	"
	B	Kane Gladys M †	20	"	37	95 Blake
	C	Kane John J	20	chauffeur	37	95 "
	D	Miachle Frederick L	30	inspector	44	here
	E	Maichle Sophie †	30	housewife	43	"
	F	Kueffner Barbara †	30	housekeeper	69	"
	G	Stanley Margaret †	30	"	61	"

West Street

Page	Letter	Full Name	Residence Jan. 1, 1941	Occupation	Supposed Age	Reported Residence, Jan. 1, 1940. Street and Number.
	H	*Toloczko Frank	223-225	laborer	60	here
	K	Toloczko John	223-225	"	26	"
	L	*Toloczko Mary †	223-225	housewife	50	"
	M	Toloczko Sophie †	223-225	clerk	24	"
	N	Connell Katherine T †	223-225	saleswoman	34	"
	O	*Connell Mary L †	223-225	housewife	28	"
	P	Connell Michael J	223-225	policeman	50	"
	R	Skogstrom Ruth †	223-225	housekeeper	53	"
	S	Anderson Oscar T	231	laborer	51	"
	T	Musumeci Lucio	231	merchant	53	"
	V	Smith Agnes †	239	housewife	52	280 Nep Valley P'way
	W	Smith Andrew R	239	policeman	54	280 "
	X	Morrison Daniel H	239	retired	66	here
		Morrison Louise E †	239	housewife	62	"
	Z	Kendricken Agnes A †	279	"	58	"
953						
	A	Kendricken Mary A †	279	stenographer	26	"
	B	Grace Edna †	309	housekeeper	26	"
	C	McCleary Gladys M †	309	housewife	38	"
	D	McCleary Joseph W	309	policeman	41	"
	E	Roche Catherine E †	311	housewife	38	"

Page	Letter	Full Name	Residence, Jan 1, 1941	Occupation	Supposed Age	Reported Residence Jan 1, 1940. Street and Number

West Street Continued

Page	Letter	Full Name	Residence, Jan 1, 1941	Occupation	Supposed Age	Reported Residence Jan 1, 1940. Street and Number
	F	Roche Dorothea M †	311	student	20	here
	G	Roche Michael J	311	policeman	40	"

Whitford Street

Page	Letter	Full Name	Residence, Jan 1, 1941	Occupation	Supposed Age	Reported Residence Jan 1, 1940. Street and Number
	H	Nilson Edward G	25	painter	39	here
	K	Nilson Gertrude L †	25	housewife	34	"
	L	Nilson Mabel L †	25	cook	62	"
	M	Nilson Mabel M †	25	stenographer	29	"
	N	Baronie Anna L †	28	social worker	39	15A Walk Hill
	O	Baronie Mary E †	28	at home	20	15A "
	P	Brooks Joseph E	30	policeman	44	here
	R	Kelley Isaac	32	retired	78	1140 Com av
	S	Kelley Martha †	32	housewife	68	1140 "
	T	O'Brien Charles M	32	superintendent	41	1140 "
	U	O'Brien Laura L †	32	housewife	33	1140 "
	V	Diamond Daniel A	34	B F D	66	here
	W	Diamond Margaret E †	34	housewife	65	"
	X	Diamond Rita M †	34	clerk	20	"
	Y	Carnes Elvira †	36	housewife	23	103 Redlands rd
	Z	Carnes George	36	chauffeur	26	103 "
954						
	A	Dinneen Catherine T †	38	housewife	48	here
	B	Dinneen Helen M †	38	clerk	20	"
	C	Dinneen Joseph F	38	steamfitter	29	"
	D	Sexton John T	40	policeman	41	"
	E	Sexton Mary A †	40	housewife	34	"
	F	Metcalf Frederick F	41	mechanic	45	7 Vera
	G	Metcalf Madeline M †	41	housewife	42	7 "
	H	Reed Hilda M †	41	"	21	7 "
	K	Reed Morris E, jr	41	assembler	35	7 "
	L	Reed Paul V	41	"	24	7 "
	O	Lorenzoni Inez †	45	housewife	27	here
	P	Lorenzoni Primo	45	teacher	31	"
	R	Palmieri Domenic A	53	shoemaker	21	"
	S	Palmieri James I	53	shoecutter	50	"
	P	Palmieri James J	53	shoemaker	26	"
	U	Palmieri Vincenza †	53	housewife	47	"
	V	Bonner Elmer W	61	machinist	24	73 Wenham
	W	Bonner Margaret M †	61	housewife	20	73 "
	X	Murray John A	61	draftsman	27	here

Page	Letter	Full Name.	Residence, Jan. 1, 1941.	Occupation.	Supposed Age.	Reported Residence, Jan. 1, 1940. Street and Number.

Whitford Street—Continued

Page	Letter	Full Name	Residence	Occupation	Age	Reported Residence
	Y	Murray Nora T †	61	housewife	62	here
	Z	Kinney Elizabeth †	64	"	43	"
955						
	A	Kinney Oliver C	64	clerk	48	"
	B	Murray Richard	64	social worker	45	"
	C	Smith John C	65	electrician	37	"
	D	*Smith Nora †	65	housewife	37	"
	F	Coppinger Angela †	69	"	36	"
	G	Coppinger Michael	69	laborer	36	"
	H	*Bishop Isabella J †	70	housewife	26	Wayland
	K	Bishop Orville A	70	operator	31	"
	L	Carmichael James T	74	machinist	46	here
	M	Carmichael Mary T †	74	housewife	41	"
	N	O'Brien Genevieve †	98	"	42	"
	O	O'Brien John J	98	inspector	47	"
	P	Busch Mildred L †	100	housewife	37	"
	R	Busch Winfred T	100	seaman	40	"
	S	MacLachlan Edna J †	103	stenographer	46	"
	T	MacLachlan Sarah J †	103	housewife	71	"
	U	Smith Agnes L †	103	teacher	49	"
	V	Eldridge John B	105	freighthandler	36	"
	W	Eldridge Neil B	105	retired	71	"
	X	Loree Mary E †	105	housewife	42	"
	Y	Simpson Charles H	129	mechanic	22	"
	Z	Simpson Dorothy †	129	housewife	48	"
956						
	A	Simpson Harold	129	machinist	55	"
	B	Simpson John A	129	shipper	20	"
	D	Frederick Carl	131	mechanic	35	24 Stellman rd
	E	Frederick Irene L †	131	housewife	35	24 "
	F	Schuler Emil	133	printer	30	here
	G	Schuler Muriel B †	133	housewife	32	"
	H	Carrierie Earl M	134	contractor	43	66 Wellsmere rd
	K	Carrierie Rose A †	134	housewife	43	66 "
	L	Mathieson George H	135	chauffeur	34	here
	M	Mathieson Isabelle G †	135	housewife	35	"

Woodland Street

Page	Letter	Full Name	Residence	Occupation	Age	Reported Residence
	N	Wight Eda L †	67	housewife	55	here
	O	Wight Marjorie A †	67	student	21	"

Ward 18—Precinct 10

CITY OF BOSTON

LIST OF RESIDENTS
20 YEARS OF AGE AND OVER

(NON-CITIZENS INDICATED BY ASTERISK)
(FEMALES INDICATED BY DAGGER)

AS OF

JANUARY 1, 1941

CITY OF BOSTON PRINTING DEPARTMENT

Page	Letter	Full Name	Residence, Jan. 1, 1941	Occupation	Supposed Age	Reported Residence, Jan. 1, 1940. Street and Number

1000

Albano Street

Page	Letter	Full Name	Residence, Jan. 1, 1941	Occupation	Supposed Age	Reported Residence, Jan. 1, 1940
	A	Sullivan George L	4	engraver	33	here
	B	Sullivan Margaret—†	4	housewife	34	"
	C	Pearson Edna—†	4	clerk	21	"
	D	Pearson Edward	4	student	25	"
	E	Pearson Matilda—†	4	housewife	54	"
	F	Pearson Oscar	4	carpenter	55	"
	G	Schmidt Charles F	6	machinist	48	"
	H	Schmidt Florence E—†	6	housewife	48	"
	K	Tabraham Adelaide—†	10	at home	58	"
	L	*Foote Edith L—†	11	housewife	53	"
	M	Foote Percy L	11	cutter	54	"
	N	Clayton Carl	11	"	40	"
	O	Clayton Julia A—†	11	housewife	42	"
	P	Nichols Irma—†	12	"	39	"
	R	Nichols William	12	laborer	47	"
	S	*Johnson Johannah—†	15	housekeeper	61	"
	T	Larson Clarence	15	clerk	32	"
	U	Larson Marion—†	15	housewife	63	"
	V	Larson Nils	15	superintendent	64	"
	W	Rommelfanger Else—†	19	clerk	41	"
	X	Stenzel Frederick	19	salesman	37	"
	Y	Stenzel Olga—†	19	housewife	31	"
	Z	Burnham Frederick	20	salesman	68	"
1001						
	A	Burnham Gertrude—†	20	secretary	34	"
	B	Yardumian Frank	20	tailor	45	"
	C	Cowley Charles F	28	manager	59	"
	D	Cowley Ernest W	28	photographer	24	"
	E	Cowley Eva E—†	28	housewife	56	"
	F	Anderson Carl H	29	foreman	24	"
	G	Anderson Ruth—†	29	housewife	24	"
	H	Frost Barbara C—†	29	"	25	"
	K	Frost Leslie E	29	manager	30	"
	L	Hagberg Charles E	29	rigger	41	"
	M	Hagberg Dorothy—†	29	housewife	37	"
	N	Fandel Francis J	32	laborer	31	"
	O	Fandel Margaret—†	32	housewife	70	"
	P	Fandel Paul J	32	porter	24	"
	R	Fandel Theodore F	32	janitor	67	"
	S	McKebitt Ethel B—†	32	nurse	51	"

Albano Street—Continued

Page	Letter	Full Name	Residence, Jan. 1, 1941	Occupation	Supposed Age	Reported Residence, Jan. 1, 1940. Street and Number
	T	Davis Olga †	36	nurse	46	here
	U	Murphy Norah †	36	checker	40	"
	W	Spiegel Jennie †	42	housewife	65	"
	X	Spiegel Joseph	42	bartender	60	"
	Y	Dordoni Joseph	45	attendant	51	"
	Z	Dordoni Linda †	45	housewife	41	"
1002						
	A	Dordoni Peter	45	retired	75	"
	B	Dordoni Victoria †	45	housewife	70	"
	C	Carey Alice †	46	"	47	"
	D	Carey Gordan	46	clergyman	50	"
	E	Schnabel Daniel	50	retired	69	"
	F	Schnabel Emma †	50	housewife	67	"
	G	Schnabel Ruth †	50	at home	22	"
	H	Patterson Alfred M	54	salesman	39	"
	K	Patterson Thelma †	54	beautician	30	"
	L	Bryant Evelyn †	54	housewife	69	"
	M	Bryant Iva †	54	teacher	39	"
	N	Bryant Matthias	54	carpenter	74	"

Atherton Avenue

Page	Letter	Full Name	Residence, Jan. 1, 1941	Occupation	Supposed Age	Reported Residence, Jan. 1, 1940. Street and Number
	O	Fasanello Angela †	6	manager	38	here
	P	Fasanello Carmello	6	shoeworker	35	"
	R	Fasanello Frank	6	engineer	32	"
	S	Fasanello Laura †	6	clerk	25	"
	T	Fasanello Marion †	6	dressmaker	33	"
	U*	Fasanello Theresa †	6	housewife	62	"
	V	Hancock Henry J	6	mechanic	39	40 Quint av
	W	Hancock Mildred O †	6	clerk	36	40 "
	X	Brough Marie T †	6	housewife	48	here
	Y	Brough William T	6	engraver	54	"
	Z	Pofcher Abraham	6	tailor	63	"
1003						
	A	Pofcher Mamie †	6	housewife	62	"
	B	Pofcher Philip E	6	agent	31	"
	C	Yanchuck Alice †	10	housewife	39	"
	D	Yanchuck Michael	10	clerk	47	"
	E	Davis Hazel H †	18	housewife	57	"
	F	Corea Edward V	24	draftsman	27	"
	G	Corea Eleanor T †	24	stenographer	28	"

Page.	Letter.	Full Name.	Residence, Jan. 1, 1941.	Occupation.	Supposed Age.	Reported Residence, Jan. 1, 1940. Street and Number.

Atherton Avenue—Continued

	H	Corea Genoveffa—†	24	housewife	53	here
	K	Corea Genoveffa—†	24	teacher	24	"
	L	Corea Nicholas A	24	chauffeur	30	"
	M	Corea Vitaliano	24	shoeworker	62	"
	N	Bowers Emma J—†	25	at home	73	"
	O	Dexter Edwin	25	U S N	23	"
	P	Dexter Marion—†	25	housewife	47	"
	R	Dexter Philip S	25	laborer	51	"

Augustus Avenue

	S	Burke Florence E—†	15	housewife	56	here
	T	Burke John J	15	trainman	63	"
	U	Olander Marie—†	17	housewife	30	"
	V	Olander O Karl	17	clergyman	30	"
	W	Edlund Charles A	19	teacher	32	"
	X	Edlund Elinor G—†	19	housewife	26	Dighton
	Y	Edlund Gertrude M—†	19	"	70	here
	Z	Johnson Frank A	19	retired	72	"
1004						
	A	Burge Elizabeth A—†	21	housewife	52	"
	B	Burge William S	21	engineer	70	"
	C	Gilman Arnold W	23	salesman	24	"
	D	Gilman Bertha M—†	23	housewife	48	"
	E	Marz Frederick W	23	clerk	29	"
	F	Marz Muriel C—†	23	"	28	"
	G	Doyle Annie M—†	25	housewife	64	"
	H	Doyle Thomas J	25	clerk	29	"
	K	Doyle Timothy C	25	"	66	"
	L	Reinhardt Augustus J	29	meter reader	41	"
	M	Reinhardt Florence G—†	29	housewife	60	"
	N	Reinhardt Florence M—†	29	bookkeeper	32	"
	O	Reinhardt Grace L—†	29	housewife	27	"
	P	Reinhardt Peter J	29	engraver	64	"
	R	Hailer Frederick C	35	druggist	41	7 Furnival rd
	S	Hailer Theresa K—†	35	housewife	36	7 "
	T	Murray Mary A—†	35	laundress	52	39 Folsom
	U	Hooper Herbert J	39	manager	58	here
	V	Hooper Mabel H—†	39	secretary	28	"
	W	Hooper Mary E—†	39	housewife	56	"
	X	McNamee Catherine A—†	53	"	62	"

Page.	Letter.	Full Name.	Residence, Jan. 1, 1941.	Occupation.	Supposed Age.	Reported Residence, Jan. 1, 1940. Street and Number.

Augustus Avenue—Continued

Page.	Letter.	Full Name.	Residence, Jan. 1, 1941.	Occupation.	Supposed Age.	Reported Residence, Jan. 1, 1940. Street and Number.
	Y	McNamee Edith M †	53	teacher	35	here
	Z	McNamee George F	53	laborer	27	"
1005						
	A	McNamee John E	53	"	32	"
	B	McNamee Joseph	53	freighthandler	66	"
	C	McNamee Joseph J	53	electrician	37	"
	D	Morris Katherine †	71	beautician	32	"
	E	Morris Robert	71	laborer	25	"
	F	Dyer Walter G	71	executive	28	"
	G	Dyer Marion J †	71	housewife	27	"
	H	Ramos Walter A	71	machinist	22	40 Warren av
	K	Richenburg Frederick H	75	architect	54	here
	L	Richenburg Robert B	75	artist	22	"
	M	Richenburg Spray E—†	75	housewife	52	"
	N	Doherty Dennis	77	engineer	49	"
	O	Doherty Mary E —†	77	housewife	44	"
	P	DeVeuve Ernest A	77	student	21	"
	R	DeVeuve Eugene	77	salesman	44	"
	S	DeVeuve Jennie L—†	77	housewife	41	"
	T	Martin Catherine M—†	77	"	35	254 Rosedale av
	U	Martin John H	77	ropemaker	35	254 "
	V	Martin Joseph A	77	lense grinder	32	254 "

Cliftondale Street

Page.	Letter.	Full Name.	Residence, Jan. 1, 1941.	Occupation.	Supposed Age.	Reported Residence, Jan. 1, 1940. Street and Number.
	X	Otto Mae C †	11	at home	57	here
	Y	Ryan Anna J †	11	"	64	"
	Z	Ryan Claire H †	11	comptometrist	24	"
1006						
	A	Brayton Hattie E †	14	at home	66	"
	B	Brayton Warren H	14	upholsterer	66	"
	C	Finch Hilda †	18	housewife	44	"
	D	Finch Horatio	18	auditor	47	"
	E	Stanley Christina †	18	at home	71	"
	F	Enos Anna M †	18	housewife	43	"
	G	Enos John F	18	manager	47	"
	H*	Sienkiewicz Eva †	22	housewife	48	"
	K	Sienkiewicz Helen †	22	clerk	23	"
	L	Sienkiewicz Joseph	22	"	28	"
	M	Sienkiewicz Martin	22	"	57	"
	N	Sienkiewicz Michael	22	machinist	26	"

Page.	Letter	Full Name	Residence, Jan. 1, 1941	Occupation	Supposed Age	Reported Residence, Jan. 1, 1940. Street and Number

Cliftondale Street—Continued

Page.	Letter	Full Name	Residence, Jan. 1, 1941	Occupation	Supposed Age	Reported Residence, Jan. 1, 1940. Street and Number
	P	Chapman Bertha L—†	27	at home	66	here
	R	Chapman Myrtle A—†	27	housewife	39	"
	S	Chapman Willard M	27	salesman	39	"
	T	Ebbeson Anna—†	29	housewife	59	50 Child
	U	Ebbeson George	29	clerk	22	50 "
	V	Ebbeson Herbert	29	"	27	50 "
	W	Anderson Edla N—†	31	housewife	56	here
	X	Anderson John R	31	painter	26	"
	Y	Rauhaut Catherine M—†	42	at home	60	"
	Z	Rauhaut Julia—†	42	housewife	25	"
1007						
	A	Rauhaut Paul H	42	clerk	31	"
	B	Kirk Francis A	43	roofer	32	17 St Lukes rd
	C	Kirk Mary J—†	43	clerk	32	8 Mt Vernon
	D	Quinn Leopold F	43	assessor	52	57 Hobart
	E	Grimes Dorothy—†	43	clerk	23	here
	F	Reichert Carl	43	painter	58	"
	G	Reichert Elizabeth—†	43	housewife	43	"
	H	Wheeler Fred	43	clerk	21	"
	K	Sullivan Genevieve A—†	46	secretary	40	"
	L	Trethewey Alberta M—†	46	at home	69	"
	M	Trethewey Robert P	46	salesman	31	"
	N	Calden Francis X	47	U S N	21	"
	O	Calden Jane—†	47	housewife	58	"
	P	Calden Jeremiah F	47	machinist	60	"
	R	Calden Joseph L	47	U S N	23	"
	S	Stuck Anna M—†	51	housewife	71	"
	T	Stuck Julius J	51	retired	71	"
	U	Karchenes Arthur	56	florist	28	98 Blue Hill av
	V	*Karchenes Athena—†	56	housewife	48	98 "
	W	Karchenes Efthemios	56	florist	56	98 "
	X	Karchenes Lucille—†	56	at home	21	98 "
	Y	Karchenes Persefon—†	56	housewife	21	Worcester
	Z	Karchenes William	56	florist	23	98 Blue Hill av
1008						
	A	Grottendeck Frank A	57	watchman	65	here
	B	Grottendeck Mary E—†	57	housewife	60	"
	C	Cranshaw Evelyn M—†	59	"	39	"
	D	Cranshaw William G	59	clerk	48	"
	E	Cruickshank Emma G—†	61	housewife	35	"
	F	Cruickshank George P	61	manager	28	"

Page	Letter	FULL NAME	Residence, Jan. 1, 1941	Occupation	Supposed Age	Reported Residence, Jan. 1, 1940. Street and Number

Cliftondale Street—Continued

Page	Letter	FULL NAME	Residence, Jan. 1, 1941	Occupation	Supposed Age	Reported Residence, Jan. 1, 1940. Street and Number
	G	Aitken Clifford C	64	pressman	42	here
	H	Aitken Jeanette—†	64	housewife	42	"
	K	Grady Thomas	65	B F D	46	"
	L	O'Brien Catherine—†	68	housewife	39	14 Glenside av
	M	O'Brien Joseph P	68	chauffeur	36	14 "
	N	Davenport Frank A	72	retired	71	here
	O	Davenport Louise W—†	72	housewife	64	"

Cornell Street

Page	Letter	FULL NAME	Residence, Jan. 1, 1941	Occupation	Supposed Age	Reported Residence, Jan. 1, 1940. Street and Number
	P	Ledlie Agnes—†	153	housewife	39	here
	R	Brymer Alfred	153	electrician	62	"
	S	Brymer Ellen—†	153	housewife	60	"
	T	Brymer Kathryn I—†	153	teacher	27	"
	U	Brymer Marjorie H—†	153	"	21	"
	V	McLeod Annabelle—†	153	housewife	56	"
	W	McLeod John A	153	carpenter	55	"
	X	Bruno Joseph	155	painter	36	"
	Y	Bruno Josephine—†	155	housewife	32	"
	Z*	Menna Camillo	155	laborer	55	"
1009						
	A	Earley Ellen A—†	157	housewife	66	"
	B	Earley James F	157	brakeman	70	"
	C	Earley James F, jr	157	cleaner	25	"
	D	Earley Ruth M—†	157	operator	30	"
	E	DeAngeli Edward	159	letter carrier	28	4069 Wash'n
	F	DeAngeli Margaret E—†	159	housewife	30	82 Hancock
	G	Iorio Alba—†	161	beautician	25	here
	H*	Iorio Erminia—†	161	housewife	63	"
	K	Iorio Pasqualina—†	161	secretary	30	"
	L	Doppler Hilda—†	163	housewife	41	"
	M	Doppler Paul	163	lather	36	"
	N	Runci Andrew	165	retired	76	"
	O	Runci Anna—†	165	housewife	63	"
	P	Runci Domenica—†	165	at home	27	"
	R	Runci Joseph	165	laborer	25	"
	S	Runci Michael	165	clerk	32	"
	T	Santamaria Mary—†	165	bookkeeper	33	"
	U	Venti Frank	167	engineer	30	50 Neptune rd
	V	Venti Sylvia M—†	167	housewife	22	8 Whipple
	W	Coolidge Elizabeth A—†	169	"	73	141 Welles av

Cornell Street—Continued

Page	Letter	Full Name	Residence, Jan. 1, 1941.	Occupation.	Supposed Age.	Reported Residence, Jan. 1, 1940. Street and Number.
	X	Coolidge William A	169	watchman	60	141 Welles av
	Y	LaBlanc Margaret—†	169	at home	25	Arlington
	Z	Pantano Anna C—†	173	housewife	35	here
1010						
	A	Pantano John	173	hairdresser	39	"
	B	*Armano Carmela—†	175	housewife	53	"
	C	Armano Michael	175	shoeworker	58	"
	D	Puccia Frank	175	merchant	23	64 Pinehurst
	E	Puccia Sadie—†	175	housewife	23	here
	F	Healy Joseph F	177	clerk	30	"
	G	Healy Madelyn M—†	177	housewife	30	"
	H	Erskine Philip	179	clerk	36	"
	K	Erskine Rose—†	179	housewife	28	"
	L	Quigley Helen M—†	179	"	37	"
	M	Quigley Joseph M	179	jeweler	38	"
	N	Tessier Alexander	179	retired	75	"
	O	Tessier Mary M—†	179	at home	40	"
	P	*Nuzzola Angelina—†	181	housewife	60	"
	R	Nuzzola Gerardo	181	bricklayer	29	"
	S	*Nuzzola Nicholas	181	"	60	"
	T	Nuzzola Stella—†	181	stitcher	24	"
	U	Burns Lillian—†	183	dietitian	26	"
	V	Nuzzola Barbara E—†	183	housewife	23	"
	W	Nuzzola Frank	183	shipper	27	"
	X	Weed Eleanor L—†	183	stitcher	26	"
	Y	Weed Lena A—†	183	forewoman	46	"
	Z	DeMatteo Antonio	185	laborer	42	"
1011						
	A	DeMatteo Jennie—†	185	housewife	41	"
	B	Hoepfner Henry	185	salesman	47	"
	C	*Hoepfner Margaret—†	185	housewife	43	"
	D	DiRienzo Daniel	185	chauffeur	40	"
	E	DiRienzo Emily—†	185	housewife	40	"
	F	Cameron Daniel F	187	clerk	55	"
	G	Cameron Mary O—†	187	housewife	51	"
	K	Drab Laura—†	191	packer	22	"
	L	Iantosca Anna B—†	191	housewife	22	"
	M	Iantosca Emilio D	191	manager	27	"
	N	Iantosca Angelina C—†	193	waitress	22	"
	O	Iantosca Anthony	193	bartender	30	"
	P	Iantosca James F	193	retired	66	"

Page	Letter	Full Name	Residence, April 1, 1937	Occupation	Supposed Age	Reported Residence, April 1, 1936. Street and Number

Cornell Street Continued

Page	Letter	Full Name	Residence	Occupation	Age	Reported Residence
	R	*Iantosca Marie C †	193	housewife	58	here
	S	Iantosca Palmorino	193	bartender	24	"
	T	Iantosca Rose E †	193	waitress	22	"
	U	Ford James P	195	installer	54	66 Albano
	V	Mahoney Joseph J	195	chauffeur	46	66 "
	W	Mahoney Lillian G †	195	housewife	43	66 "
	X	Bevilacqua Felice	195	laborer	57	here
	Y	McDermott Alice †	195	housewife	58	"
	Z	McDermott Herbert	195	broker	28	"

1012 Denton Terrace

Page	Letter	Full Name	Residence	Occupation	Age	Reported Residence
	A	Kunze Meta E †	3	clerk	62	here
	B	Swangren Elsa O †	3	housekeeper	36	"
	C	Miller Frederick C	3	merchant	74	"
	D	Miller Herman C	3	adjustor	24	"
	E	Miller Olga B †	3	housewife	60	"
	F	Hammerlee John	5	laborer	66	"
	G	Hammerlee Mary †	5	housewife	66	"
	H	Davies Bertha †	5	"	59	"
	K	Davies George	5	inspector	58	"
	L	Lynch Anna G †	6	housewife	50	"
	M	Lynch J Harry	6	salesman	63	"
	N	Lynch J Harry, jr	6	student	22	"
	O	Brunck Elizabeth †	7	housewife	72	"
	P	Brunck Emily †	7	operator	36	"
	R	Brunck John	7	carpenter	70	"
	S	Brunck Louise †	7	operator	45	"
	T	Donovan Anna J †	8	housewife	53	"
	U	Donovan Arthur H	8	printer	27	"
	V	Donovan William J	8	clerk	62	"
	W	Munz Theresa C †	8	at home	60	"
	X	Killion Mary T †	9	bookkeeper	47	"
	Y	Meek Elizabeth R †	9	housewife	45	"
	Z	Meek George	9	clerk	50	"
1013						
	A	Stanley John J	10	painter	45	"
	B	Stanley Sophie †	10	housewife	43	"
	D	Josephson Augusta A †	12	"	76	"
	E	Josephson Carl G	12	retired	76	"
	F	Josephson Ella N †	12	stenographer	45	"

Page	Letter	Full Name	Residence, Jan. 1, 1941	Occupation	Supposed Age	Reported Residence, Jan. 1, 1940. Street and Number.

Denton Terrace Continued

Page	Letter	Full Name	Residence, Jan. 1, 1941	Occupation	Supposed Age	Reported Residence, Jan. 1, 1940. Street and Number.
	G	Josephson Eva E †	12	stenographer	44	here
	H	Josephson Helen N †	12	at home	36	"
	K	Ferrari Elizabeth †	14	housewife	60	"
	L	Ferrari Louis F	14	salesman	60	"
	M	Nairn George A	15	printer	52	"
	N	Nairn May †	15	housewife	50	"
	O	Bleriot Camile	16	chef	58	"
	P	Decot Gabrielle—†	16	supervisor	37	"
	R	Decot Geoffrey	16	clerk	23	"
	S	Decot Marie—†	16	housewife	61	"
	T	Caradonna Ruth C—†	17	"	34	"
	U	Caradonna William G	17	salesman	29	"
	V	Daley Charles	17	chef	55	Milton
	W	Hastings Edith—†	17	housewife	36	62 Walworth
	X	Hastings Robert	17	broker	38	62 "
	Y	Kelley Frances †	17	at home	75	8 Dever
	Z	Weiscopf Edwin L	18	attorney	57	here
1014						
	A	Weiscopf Jeanne F †	18	teacher	23	"
	B	Weiscopf Louise R—†	18	librarian	25	"
	C	Weiscopf Minnie—†	18	housewife	57	"
	D	Falcone Joseph V	19	mechanic	25	"
	E	Falcone Julia †	19	housewife	44	"
	F	Falcone Louis T	19	accountant	23	"
	G	Falcone Rose †	19	student	20	"
	H	Falcone Vincent J	19	merchant	45	"
	K	Keaney Bartholomew	20	retired	69	"
	L	Keaney Frank	20	seaman	20	"
	M	Keaney Mary †	20	housewife	57	"
	N	Keaney Robert	20	clerk	22	"
	O	Nichols Eva †	20	saleswoman	66	"
	P	Parker Alice †	20	"	30	"
	R	Parker Lorraine †	20	"	27	"
	S	Robie Irene V †	21	at home	72	"
	T	Boyd Grace E †	22	"	48	"
	U	Boyd Mabelle M †	22	manager	50	"
	V	Boyd Margaret †	22	at home	80	"
	W	Boyd Olive L †	22	statistician	46	"
	X	Jonah George H	23	retired	86	"
	Y	Fallon Gerard E	24	painter	43	"
	Z	Fallon James	24	decorator	33	"

1015

Denton Terrace Continued

Page	Letter	Full Name	Residence, Jan. 1, 1941	Occupation	Reported Age	Reported Residence, Jan. 1, 1940. Street and Number
1015	A	Fallon Louis	24	carpenter	39	here
	B	Fallon Michael	24	laborer	76	"
	C	MacIsaac Archie	25	bookkeeper	23	"
	D	MacIsaac Christine †	25	housewife	45	"
	E	MacIsaac Duncan	25	engineer	53	"
	F	Maloney Helena †	26	housewife	28	Needham
	G	Young Alfred H	26	accountant	42	here
	H	Young Ethel R †	26	fitter	34	"
	K	Young Mary A †	26	housewife	56	"
	L	Cassidy Elizabeth †	27	secretary	37	"
	M	Cassidy Margaret †	27	clerk	35	"
	N	Cassidy Patrick	27	retired	81	"
	O	Adams Edward E	28	manager	57	"
	P	Adams Elizabeth M †	28	housewife	53	"
	R	Adams Elizabeth M †	28	secretary	23	"
	S	Foley Helen D †	29	bookkeeper	22	156 Dorchester
	T	Foley Helen E †	29	housewife	55	156 "
	U	Foley Francis P	29	salesman	24	156 "
	V	Foley Patrick F	29	printer	57	156 "

Kittredge Street

Page	Letter	Full Name	Residence, Jan. 1, 1941	Occupation	Reported Age	Reported Residence, Jan. 1, 1940. Street and Number
1015	W	Williams Clarence	8	custodian	60	here
	X	Lento Josephine †	10	housewife	41	"
	Y	Lento Theresa P †	10	stenographer	22	"
	Z	Christoforo Joseph	10	floorlayer	55	"
1016	A	Clark Charles O	10	engineer	39	"
	B	Clark Edward F	10	salesman	36	"
	C	Clark Jennie G †	10	housewife	64	"
	D*	Scaramuzzo Felicia †	10	"	43	"
	E	Scaramuzzo Joseph	10	shoeworker	44	"
	F	Benersani Augustus	11	watchman	62	"
	G	Cunningham Frances P †	11	clerk	23	34 Catherine
	H	Cunningham Ida M †	11	housewife	45	here
	K	Cunningham Thomas J	11	letter carrier	44	"
	L	DeMinico Mariano	11	manager	65	"
	M*	DeMinico Rose †	11	housewife	60	"
	N*	Schwarz Ella †	11	"	38	"
	O	Schwarz Ludwig	11	fisherman	38	"

Page.	Letter	Full Name	Residence, Jan. 1, 1941.	Occupation	Supposed Age.	Reported Residence, Jan. 1, 1940. Street and Number.

Kittredge Street Continued

Page.	Letter	Full Name	Residence, Jan. 1, 1941.	Occupation	Supposed Age.	Reported Residence, Jan. 1, 1940. Street and Number.
	P	Connolly Catherine T —†	14	stenographer	24	here
	R	Connolly Delia —†	14	housewife	54	"
	S	Connolly Margaret M —†	14	stenographer	26	"
	T	Connolly Mary E —†	14	clerk	21	"
	U	Gummeson Gustave A	14	electrician	43	"
	V	Gummeson Helen V —†	14	housewife	44	"
	W	Huberman Frank	14	salesman	55	"
	X*	McNeil Alphonsus M	14	attendant	50	"
	Y*	McNeil Laura —†	14	housewife	37	"
	Z	Torrey Margaret —†	17	"	74	New York
1017						
	A	Torrey Ralph J	17	carpenter	41	Needham
	B	Torrey Sadie —†	17	housewife	40	"
	C*	Scaramuzzo Esther —†	17	"	34	here
	D	Scaramuzzo Louis	17	shoemaker	36	"
	E*	Schouten Gerardus H	18	cigarmaker	46	"
	F*	Schouten Maria W —†	18	housewife	42	"
	G	Hogan Frank	18	laborer	45	"
	H	Hogan Marion —†	18	housewife	38	"
	K	Schramm Anna K —†	21	at home	47	"
	L	Schramm John	21	watchman	72	"
	M	Schramm John F	21	electrician	37	"
	N	Schramm John M	21	carpenter	41	"
	O	Schramm Edna M —†	21	housewife	38	"
	P	Schramm Herman F	21	machinist	46	"
	R	Mooney Helen M —†	21	housewife	43	"
	S	Mooney Joseph F	21	chauffeur	44	"
	T	Atkinson Charles A	22	policeman	43	"
	U	Atkinson Charles T	22	bellhop	20	"
	V	Atkinson Maud F —†	22	housewife	41	"
	W	DeForest Lillian —†	25	"	31	"
	X	Genson William J	25	painter	65	"
	Y	Paraschos Anna —†	26	housewife	38	"
	Z	Paraschos John J	26	shoemaker	37	"
1018						
	A	Rossi Amando A	26	clerk	20	"
	B	Rossi Anthony V	26	draftsman	28	"
	C	Rossi Louis S	26	"	29	"
	D	Rossi Raffaella —†	26	housewife	49	"
	E	Rossi Theresa M —†	26	"	28	"
	F	McDonough Catherine —†	26	"	75	"

Kittredge Street Continued

Letter	Full Name	Residence Jan. 1, 1941	Occupation	Age	Reported Residence, Jan. 1, 1940 Street and Number
G	Allgaier George	28	salesman	68	here
H	Allgaier Katherine E †	28	housewife	64	"
K	Bonang Catherine †	28	"	51	"
L	Bonang Robert J	28	fireman	47	"
M	Mathews Theresa A †	28	housekeeper	58	"
N	Pettipas Henry L	28	nurse	55	"
O	Foster Herbert J	29	motorman	63	"
P	Foster Marjorie †	29	housewife	67	"
R	Walter Frank J	29	butcher	35	"
S	Walter Marjorie †	29	housewife	35	"
T	Daly Catherine †	29	"	42	"
U	Buckroth Charles F	32	clergyman	56	"
V	Buckroth Lydia †	32	housewife	46	"
W	Goodwin Irene E †	32	"	56	"
X	Goodwin Thomas W	32	printer	21	"
Y	Goodwin William H	32	custodian	57	"
Z	Scannell Elizabeth T †	34	housewife	50	"
	1019				
A	Scannell John J	34	attendant	53	"
B	Wipperman Charles A	36	decorator	57	"
C	Wipperman Elizabeth F †	36	housewife	56	"
D	Wipperman Elizabeth G †	36	saleswoman	24	"
E	Wipperman Herbert F	36	decorator	23	"
F	Blume Catherine C †	38	housewife	24	2 Clarendon et
G	Blume Thomas E	38	salesman	27	2 "
H	Cameron Edmund L	38	retired	87	31 Aldrich
K	Graves Dora M †	38	housewife	48	31 "
L	Graves George J	38	custodian	38	31 "
M	Graves Winifred M †	38	teacher	21	31 "
N	Inch Margaret G †	42	housewife	35	4349 Wash'n
O	Inch William T	42	agent	40	4349 "
P	MacLeod George R	42	purchaser	29	here
R	MacLeod Norman R	42	retired	69	"
T	LaBadessa Elizabeth †	44	housewife	33	"
S	LaBadessa Salvatore F	44	draftsman	40	"
U	Kimball Charles E	52	inspector	73	Milton
V	Kimball Charlotte A †	52	housewife	73	"
W	Rehwaldt Edward A	52	engineer	56	here
X	Rehwaldt Mary K †	52	housewife	55	"
Y	Rehwaldt Sidonia T †	52	therapist	29	"
Z	Lawrence Alberta †	55	housewife	37	"

Page	Letter	Full Name	Residence, Jan. 1, 1941	Occupation	Supposed Age	Reported Residence, Jan. 1, 1940. Street and Number

1020
Kittredge Street Continued

Page	Letter	Full Name	Residence, Jan. 1, 1941	Occupation	Supposed Age	Reported Residence, Jan. 1, 1940. Street and Number
	A	Lawrence Charles W	55	painter	57	here
	B	Pfeiffer John F	55	clergyman	62	"
	C	Schwenzfeier Elizabeth †	56	clerk	23	"
	D	Schwenzfeier Roy	56	packer	23	18 Cypress
	E	Weigold Emma †	56	housewife	50	here
	F	Weigold Milton V	56	machinist	56	"
	G	Davidson Margaret I †	57	housewife	77	"
	H	Gadsby Margaret †	57	"	54	"
	K	Gadsby Walter F	57	clerk	56	"
	L	Rauding Frederick A	60	printer	22	"
	M	Rauding John A	60	laborer	66	"
	N	*Rauding Lucy A †	60	housewife	54	"
	O	*Randolph Frederick W	60	manager	47	"
	P	*Randolph Lucille A †	60	teacher	41	"
	R	Meldrum Doris †	61	housewife	26	193 Belgrade av
	S	Meldrum John	61	machinist	31	193 "
	T	Hansen Edwin B	63	letter carrier	39	here
	U	Hansen Grace E †	63	housewife	39	"
	V	MacDonald Colin J	65	lineman	38	"
	W	MacDonald Helen E †	65	housewife	33	"
	Y	Fenton Edward E	67	shipper	33	"
	Z	Fenton Elizabeth M †	67	housewife	28	"
1021						
	B	Edge Doris †	69	clerk	53	"
	C	Halloran John D	69	lineman	33	38 Larchmont
	D	Halloran Kathleen †	69	housewife	31	38 "
	E	Wagner Minnie †	69	"	63	here
	G	Andrews Edmund	71	salesman	23	"
	H	Andrews Mary †	71	housewife	59	"
	K	O'Connor Nora †	71	"	43	2 Barry pk
	L	Powers John E	71	chauffeur	49	16 Bradbury
	N	Spyridakis Manuel	75	chef	43	7 Irvington
	O	Spyridakis Stella †	75	housewife	40	7 "
	P	*Kay Gurney V	78	mechanic	39	here
	R	*Kay Lillian W †	78	housewife	39	"
	S	Grant Florence L †	78	"	54	"
	T	Grant John E	78	carpenter	59	"
	U	Smith Bessie †	78	housewife	83	"
	V	Smith Herbert F	78	retired	81	"
	W	D'Entremont Claire M †	80	at home	26	"

Page.	Letter.	Full Name	Residence, Jan. 1, 1941.	Occupation.	Age	Reported Residence, Jan. 1, 1940. Street and Number.

Kittredge Street Continued

Page.	Letter.	Full Name	Residence, Jan. 1, 1941.	Occupation.	Age	Reported Residence, Jan. 1, 1940. Street and Number.
	X	D'Entremont Edith M †	80	clerk	24	here
	Y	D'Entremont F Robert	80	"	21	"
	Z	D'Entremont Mary M †	80	housewife	63	"
1022						
	A	Paul Jeanette M †	80	"	28	5 Marion
	B	Paul Jesse J	80	baker	34	5 "
	C	Johnson Arthur L	82	repairman	48	here
	D	Johnson Mary H †	82	housewife	50	"
	E	Johnson Robert R	82	plumber	21	"
	F	Coffin Eileen G †	86	housewife	22	288 Beech
	G	Coffin Robert	86	accountant	24	559 Weld
	H	Whittemore Evelyn J †	86	housewife	22	here
	K	Whittemore Ralph G	86	dealer	24	"
	L*	Brooks Catherine A †	90	housewife	42	"
	M	Brooks Charles	90	dispatcher	23	"
	N	Brooks William	90	"	21	"
	O	Brooks William E	90	chauffeur	49	"
	P	Frykstrand Emil P	96	retired	86	"
	R	Frykstrand Frank E	96	treasurer	55	"
	S	Chellman Lillian O †	100	housewife	63	"
	T	Sinquefield Ruth L †	100	secretary	43	"
	U	Dumaine Helen H †	101	at home	65	32 [illegible]
	V	Grottendieke Louise †	101	bookkeeper	40	32 "
	W	Shaw Bronzelia †	101	at home	58	32 "
	X	Meehan Garrett J	101	accountant	38	here
	Y	Meehan Hilda B †	101	housewife	38	"
	Z*	Hansen Serine †	101	domestic	60	"
1023						
	A	Kelland Harold A	101	carpenter	28	"
	B	Richardson Anna †	101	at home	79	Lakeville
	C	Fichtner Alice M †	105	housewife	51	53 Sycamore
	D	Fichtner Joseph S	105	inspector	53	53 "
	E	McManus John E	105	clerk	32	here
	F	McManus Margaret †	105	housewife	72	"
	G	McManus Patrick	105	retired	72	"
	H	Swanson Mary †	105	housewife	36	35 Bradeen
	K	Coutoulakis Emmanuel	106	bartender	31	here
	L*	Coutoulakis Rose †	106	housewife	32	"
	M*	Vaselarakes Anthousa †	106	"	58	"
	N	Vaselarakes George	106	salesman	26	"
	O	Vaselarakes Louis	106	chef	52	"

Page	Letter	Full Name	Residence, Jan. 1, 1941	Occupation	Supposed Age	Reported Residence, Jan. 1, 1940. Street and Number

Kittredge Street—Continued

Page	Letter	Full Name	Residence, Jan. 1, 1941	Occupation	Supposed Age	Reported Residence, Jan. 1, 1940. Street and Number
	P	Johnson William B	110	mechanic	47	here
	R	Jones Carroll A	110	clerk	62	"
	S	Jones Ethel F—†	110	housewife	57	"
	T	Spriano Albert	111	agent	35	144 Roslindale av
	U	Spriano Vera—†	111	housewife	34	144 "
	W	Angland Loretta V—†	118	pianist	45	here
	X	Angland Maurice J	118	retired	79	"
	Y	Angland Raymond A	118	clerk	42	"
	Z	Angland Thomas	118	student	20	"
1024						
	A	Pinkham Marcus F	123	engineer	63	"
	B	Pinkham Sadie M—†	123	housewife	51	"
	C	Raftery Margaret E—†	123	clerk	22	"
	D	Raftery Mary J—†	123	housewife	56	"
	E	Raftery Michael J	123	laborer	64	"
	F	McMahon Alice C—†	130	at home	48	"
	G	McMahon Edward P	130	letter carrier	38	"
	H	McMahon Helen F—†	130	housewife	38	"
	K	McMahon James F	130	B F D	45	"
	L	Bryan Dorothy G—†	136	bookkeeper	22	"
	M	Bryan John F	136	contractor	46	"
	N	Bryan Margaret E—†	136	housewife	45	"
	O	Crotty Catherine G—†	136	at home	68	"
	P	Sargent Henrietta—†	137	saleswoman	64	"
	R	Sargent Joseph	137	electrician	65	"
	S	Schwender Eugene	137	architect	61	"
	T	Schwender Laura B—†	137	housewife	59	"
	U	Sherwood Florence—†	137	saleswoman	58	"
	V	LaValle Anna—†	139	clerk	21	"
	W	LaValle Antonette—†	139	housewife	72	"
	X	LaValle Egidio L	139	attorney	37	"
	Y	LaValle Leo	139	student	23	"
	Z	Lee Martin J	140	metalworker	51	"
1025						
	A	Lee Winnetta A—†	140	housewife	50	"
	B	Raschke Louise—†	140	"	50	"
	C	Wiengarten Joseph	140	salesman	65	"
	D	Minichiello Albert A	146	engineer	32	"
	E	Minichiello Elsie—†	146	housewife	28	"
	F	Johnson Hulda—†	146	"	61	"
	G	Johnson Johan L	146	retired	76	"

Page	Letter	Full Name	Residence, Jan. 1, 1941	Occupation	Reputed Age	Reported Residence, Jan. 1, 1940. Street and Number

Kittredge Street Continued

Page	Letter	Full Name	Residence, Jan. 1, 1941	Occupation	Reputed Age	Reported Residence, Jan. 1, 1940. Street and Number
	H	Rossi Dorothy E †	147	housewife	31	98 W[illegible]
	K	Rossi Orpheus J	147	operator	32	98 "
	L	Balboni Henry J	149	"	33	78 Metropolitan av
	M	Balboni Julia M †	149	housewife	52	78 "
	N	Balboni Marion A †	149	"	23	Orange
	O	Rossi Mildred R †	149	"	29	78 Metropolitan av
	P	Rossi Romeo G	149	mechanic	30	78 "
	R	Cameron Laura †	151	clerk	45	here
	S	McCarthy Charles	151	"	32	"
	T	McCarthy Dorothea †	151	"	25	"
	U	McCarthy Geraldine †	151	saleswoman	30	"
	V	Urbsho Josephine †	152	housewife	46	"
	W	Urbsho Paul H	152	tailor	49	"
	X	Urbsho Virginia A †	152	technician	22	"
	Y	Maddox James R	152	machinist	50	"
	Z	Maddox Laura R †	152	housewife	55	"
1026						
	A	Begley Edmund J	209	student	20	"
	B	Begley Helen †	209	clerk	30	"
	C	Begley James G	209	plumber	22	"
	D	Begley John F	209	bricklayer	63	"
	E	Begley John F, jr	209	shipper	24	"
	F	Begley Margaret †	209	housewife	56	"
	G	Begley Margaret M †	209	clerk	32	"
	H	Begley Martin	209	laborer	58	"
	K	Begley Martin J	209	"	26	"
	L	*Sullivan Ellen F †	209	housekeeper	72	"
	M	Gavin Irene H †	215	housewife	41	"
	N	Gavin Thomas P	215	policeman	41	"
	O	Jacob Emma C †	219	manager	46	"
	P	McGrory John E	219	agent	25	"
	R	McGrory Mary C †	219	housewife	51	"
	S	McGrory Mary D †	219	student	22	"
	T	Goguen Celina A †	225	housewife	44	"
	U	Goguen Oscar J	225	plasterer	49	"
	V	Goguen Paul L	225	mechanic	20	"
	W	*Lavoie Marie A †	225	nurse	47	"
	X	Lykora Louise A †	225	houseworker	50	"
	Y	Breen Adelaide J †	229	organist	36	"
	Z	Breen Alice M †	229	stenographer	25	"

Page.	Letter.	Full Name	Residence, Jan. 1, 1941	Occupation	Supposed Age.	Reported Residence, Jan. 1, 1940. Street and Number.

1027
Kittredge Street—Continued

Page.	Letter.	Full Name	Residence, Jan. 1, 1941	Occupation	Supposed Age.	Reported Residence, Jan. 1, 1940.
1027	A	Breen John P	229	retired	70	here
	B	Breen Rose A—†	229	housewife	61	"
	C	McGoldrich Frances—†	231	receptionist	25	"
	D	Thies Frank R	231	butcher	38	"
	E	Thies Gerard E	231	clerk	32	"
	F	Thies Marjorie V—†	231	housewife	34	"
	G	Thies Melbourne R	231	clerk	40	"
	H	Kavoukjian Alice—†	233	bookkeeper	21	"
	K	Kavoukjian Catherine—†	233	housewife	45	"
	L	Kavoukjian Karnig	233	tailor	59	"
	M	Kavoukjian Mary—†	233	clerk	26	"
	N	Kavoukjian Rose—†	233	bookkeeper	25	"
	O	Spenazzolo Antonette—†	235	housewife	37	"
	P	Spenazzolo Daniel	235	retired	49	"
	R	Falcone Louis F	235	manager	43	"
	S	Falcone Rose M—†	235	housewife	34	"
	T	Padula Frances—†	235	"	58	"
	U	Padula Michael	235	salesman	39	"
	V	Padula Vincent	235	retired	73	"
	W	Padula Vincent P	235	clerk	22	"
	X	Keenan Jennie V—†	237	"	46	"
	Y	Keenan Mary—†	237	housewife	63	"
	Z	Keenan Tennyson	237	operator	43	"
1028	A	Keenan Walter D	237	clerk	50	"
	B	Daisy George W	239	accountant	37	New York
	C	Daisy Mada—†	239	housewife	35	"
	D	Graham Bertha P—†	241	"	46	here
	E	Graham Mary—†	241	at home	68	"
	F	Graham William J	241	draftsman	46	"
	G	Graham William J, jr	241	clerk	20	"
	H	Stock Edward A	241	retired	78	"
	K	Cunningham Helen—†	243	housewife	47	"
	L	Cunningham Patrick J	243	carpenter	53	"
	M	Campiglia Joseph T	245	instructor	22	"
	N	Campiglia Mary F—†	245	housewife	47	"
	O	Campiglia Savirio	245	musician	54	"
	P	Campiglia Lenora—†	247	clerk	38	"
	R	Sbraccia Bernard V	247	mason	55	"
	S	Sbraccia Vincenza—†	247	housewife	46	"

Page.	Letter.	Full Name.	Residence, Jan. 1, 1941.	Occupation.	Reported Age.	Reported Residence, Jan. 1, 1940. Street and Number.

Kittredge Street—Continued

Page.	Letter.	Full Name.	Residence	Occupation	Age	Reported Residence
	T	Haggerty James E	249	retired	35	here
	U	Haggerty Leo J	249	clerk	29	"
	V	Haggerty Lillian M †	249	teacher	35	"
	W	White Hannah †	249	housekeeper	78	"
	X	Keefe Annie J †	251	supervisor	61	"
	Y	McDonald Elizabeth M †	251	clerk	41	"
	Z	McDonald Lucy A †	251	housewife	64	"
1029						
	A	McDonald Michael J	251	operator	66	"

Kittredge Terrace

Page.	Letter.	Full Name.	Residence	Occupation	Age	Reported Residence
	B	Finley Charles F	1	metalworker	22	43 Stellman rd
	C	Jackson Dorothy †	1	housewife	22	23 Vista
	D	Jackson Howard T	1	clerk	22	here
	E	Jackson Jennie †	1	housewife	58	"
	F	Costello Francis	2	painter	25	Dedham
	G	Crotty James F	2	"	60	423 Mass av
	H	Ahearn Robert	2	laborer	34	here
	K	Arnold George	2	painter	45	36 LaSalle
	L	Choppas Peter	2	retired	69	60 Clarendon pk
	M	Galvin William	2	machinist	42	here
	N	*Goddard John	2	janitor	65	"
	O	Grimes Arthur	2	plumber	37	"
	P	Savage George A	2	draftsman	60	"
	R	Zakos Nicholas	2	chef	46	"

Metropolitan Avenue

Page.	Letter.	Full Name.	Residence	Occupation	Age	Reported Residence
	S	O'Brien Mary E †	42	housewife	49	here
	T	O'Brien Peter C	42	operator	55	"
	V	Wenners Edward B	43	agent	24	12 Colberg av
	W	Wenners Helen E †	43	housewife	22	12 "
	X	Donaruma Ernest	46	designer	47	here
	Y	Donaruma Generoso	46	retired	82	"
	Z	Donaruma Natalie †	46	housewife	35	"
1030						
	A	Claus Ambrose J	46	proprietor	44	"
	B	Claus Anna G †	46	housewife	44	"
	C	Dowd Blanche G †	46	at home	50	"
	D	Dowd Daniel F	46	"	86	"

Page	Letter	Full Name.	Residence, Jan. 1, 1941.	Occupation.	Supposed Age.	Reported Residence, Jan. 1, 1940. Street and Number.

Metropolitan Avenue—Continued

Page	Letter	Full Name	Residence	Occupation	Age	Reported Residence
	E	Evans Nora T—†	47	at home	45	here
	F	Pennie Elizabeth F—†	47	secretary	47	"
	G	Pennie Louis F	47	electrician	58	"
	H	Jellison Leonard T	49	manager	73	"
	K	Jellison Nellie E—†	49	housewife	65	"
	L	Clark Grace—†	50	saleswoman	51	"
	M	Serues Edward A	50	tailor	49	"
	N	Serues Fred J	50	carpenter	70	"
	O	Serues Mary J—†	50	housewife	71	"
	P	Claus Charles L	50	salesman	47	"
	R	Claus Rose P—†	50	housewife	48	"
	S	Kaufman Charles J	50	retired	75	"
	T	Piekarski Roman	51	manager	61	"
	U	Piekarski Victoria I—†	51	secretary	34	"
	V	Piekarski Wladys—†	51	housewife	55	"
	W	Fogerty Dorothy G—†	52	"	31	"
	X	Fogerty Eugene W	52	teacher	32	"
	Y	Fogerty Clarence H	52	clerk	65	"
	Z	Fogerty Ella F—†	52	housewife	65	"
1031						
	A	Fogerty Richard E	52	clerk	27	"
	B	Maier Ferdinand R	55	manager	66	"
	C	Maier Mabel M—†	55	housewife	60	"
	D	Maier Robert W	55	engineer	31	"
	E	Fernekees Anne T—†	56	housewife	66	198 Cornell
	F	Fernekees Mildred L—†	56	clerk	37	198 "
	G	Parker Frederick C	56	retired	70	here
	H	Parker Mabel F—†	56	housewife	65	"
	K	Parker Marjorie E—†	56	secretary	42	"
	L	Parker Walter C	56	clerk	34	"
	M	Donnelly Mary A—†	57	stenographer	50	"
	N	Stewart James W	58	engineer	38	"
	O	Stewart Margaret—†	58	housewife	36	"
	P	Cronin Charles W	58	chauffeur	39	"
	R	Cronin Gertrude C—†	58	housewife	34	"
	S	Cronin Mary A—†	58	at home	72	"
	T	Dolle Frank T	60	engraver	46	"
	U	Dolle Helen A—†	60	housewife	43	"
	V	Kharibian Alice—†	60	"	33	"
	W	Kharibian Krikor M	60	shoemaker	48	"
	X	Ryan Edward B	60	clerk	31	"

Page	Letter	Full Name	Residence, Jan. 1, 1941	Occupation	Supposed Age	Reported Residence, Jan. 1, 1940. Street and Number

Metropolitan Avenue—Continued

Page	Letter	Full Name	Residence, Jan. 1, 1941	Occupation	Supposed Age	Reported Residence, Jan. 1, 1940. Street and Number
	Y	Ryan Mary C †	60	housewife	32	here
	Z	Gleason Ellen M †	61	"	64	"
1032						
	A	Gleason Frederick L	61	meter reader	33	"
	B	Gleason Mildred †	61	housewife	30	"
	C	Poblenz Annie †	63	"	68	"
	D	Poblenz Oscar	63	retired	74	"
	E	*Genco Angelina †	65	housewife	47	"
	F	Genco Angelina F †	65	dressmaker	23	"
	G	Genco Giuseppe	65	laborer	52	"
	H	Genco Mary †	65	dressmaker	25	"
	K	Genco Tina †	65	at home	21	"
	L	Crimmins Alice L †	69	clerk	32	"
	M	Crimmins Ann M †	69	"	26	"
	N	Crimmins George F	69	salesman	30	"
	O	Crimmins John S	69	retired	70	"
	P	Crimmins John S, jr	69	clerk	22	"
	R	Crimmins Julia G †	69	housewife	64	"
	S	Crimmins Marion V †	69	secretary	42	"
	T	Morgan Mary A †	71	housewife	65	"
	U	Morgan Mary A †	71	clerk	36	"
	V	Ohlen Alma †	73	housewife	70	"
	W	Ohlen Andrew	73	carpenter	73	"
	X	Ferrari Abby M †	78	housewife	24	Dedham
	Y	Ferrari Edwin G	78	machinist	24	14 Denton ter
	Z	Ward Catherine †	79	housewife	58	here
1033						
	A	Ward James M	79	clerk	23	"
	B	Ward John J	79	inspector	56	"
	C	Dempsey Frederick	83	clerk	30	"
	D	Dempsey Gertrude S †	83	housewife	56	"
	E	Walsh Mary A †	83	at home	66	"
	F	Connolly Annie T †	92	"	63	"
	G	Wilson Mary E †	92	housewife	44	"
	H	Wilson Thomas	92	policeman	47	"
	K	Campbell Lena S †	92	housewife	55	"
	L	Campbell William W	92	salesman	54	"
	M	Lydon Marguerite †	92	housewife	36	109 Williams
	N	Lydon Richard J	92	chauffeur	38	109 "
	O	McCabe Helen J †	96	housewife	53	here
	P	McCabe John J	96	guard	63	"

Page.	Letter.	Full Name.	Residence, Jan. 1, 1941.	Occupation.	Supposed Age.	Reported Residence, Jan. 1, 1940. Street and Number.

Metropolitan Avenue—Continued

Page.	Letter.	Full Name.	Residence, Jan. 1, 1941.	Occupation.	Supposed Age.	Reported Residence, Jan. 1, 1940. Street and Number.
	R	Henningson Sigrid—†	96	housewife	68	here
	S	Jute Ann—†	96	clerk	34	"
	T	Pearson Lawrence	96	"	53	"
	U	Munsell George L	100	decorator	28	71 Wellsmere rd
	V	Munsell Mildred A—†	100	housewife	26	71 "
	W	Clason August H	100	manager	57	here
	X	Eck Anna S—†	100	housewife	50	"
	Y	Eck Carl A	100	manager	65	"
	Z	Eck Mildred A—†	100	secretary	26	"
1034						
	A	Frazee Heber	104	retired	82	"
	B	Maddox Dorothy F—†	104	housewife	48	"
	C	Maddox Frederick W	104	collector	55	"
	D	Maddox Evelyn E—†	106	at home	89	"
	E	Maddox Evelyn L—†	106	stenographer	53	"
	F	MacDonald Helen M—†	110	operator	41	119 Montclair av
	G	MacDonald John W	110	chauffeur	29	119 "
	H	MacDonald Mary L—†	110	teacher	37	119 "
	K	MacDonald Raymond K	110	chauffeur	40	119 "
	L	Jones Harold F	110	salesman	49	here
	M	Jones John H	110	clerk	21	"
	N	Jones Marion L—†	110	director	25	"
	O	Jones Rebecca—†	110	housewife	49	"

Otis Place

Page.	Letter.	Full Name.	Residence, Jan. 1, 1941.	Occupation.	Supposed Age.	Reported Residence, Jan. 1, 1940. Street and Number.
	P	Otto George A	3	electrician	45	here
	R	Otto Julia J—†	3	housewife	70	"
	S	Otto Mary A—†	3	"	37	"
	T	Beaumont Katherine—†	6	at home	76	"
	U	White Annie E—†	6	housewife	45	"
	V	White James A	6	machinist	45	"
	W	Sullivan Mary G—†	8	teacher	42	"
	X	Sullivan Timothy J	8	electrician	66	"
	Y	Lynch Grace V—†	10	housewife	57	"
	Z	Lynch William	10	engineer	60	"
1035						
	A	Kenney Lena R—†	12	at home	62	"
	B	Somes Abbie L—†	12	"	73	"
	C	Somes Evan C	12	printer	73	"

Page	Letter	Full Name.	Residence, Jan. 1, 1941.	Occupation.	Supposed Age.	Reported Residence, Jan. 1, 1940. Street and Number.

Poplar Street

Page	Letter	Full Name.	Residence, Jan. 1, 1941.	Occupation.	Supposed Age.	Reported Residence, Jan. 1, 1940. Street and Number.
	G	Gile Harry N	79	optometrist	75	here
	H	Gile Lula F †	79	housewife	74	"
	K	Cobleigh Charlotte E †	79	"	62	"
	L	Haskell Frances E †	87	at home	85	"
	M	Spofford Florence K †	87	domestic	56	"
	N	Watkins Mary S †	87	secretary	53	"
	O	Chisholm Anne C †	95	housewife	50	"
	P	Chisholm Earl H	95	foreman	53	"
	R	Donahue James T	99	retired	74	"
	S	Donahue Marion F †	99	housewife	31	"
	T	Donahue Paul F	99	contractor	33	"
	U	O'Brien Edward S	99	collector	46	"
	V	O'Brien Ellen M †	99	housewife	66	"
	W	O'Brien William G	99	retired	75	"
	X	McLaughlin Edward P	103	mechanic	21	"
	Y	McLaughlin May †	103	housewife	39	"
	Z	McLaughlin Patrick	103	clerk	49	"
1036						
	A	*Amirault Edith E †	103	domestic	47	"
	B	Amirault Jeanne E †	103	clerk	22	"
	C	*Amirault Michael J	103	retired	83	"
	D	*LeBlanc Evelyn J †	103	engineer	44	"
	E	*LeBlanc Genevieve C †	103	housewife	49	"
	F	*LeBlanc Madeline †	103	operator	35	"
	G	*LeBlanc Ralph E	103	clerk	39	"
	H	Callaghan Daniel J	107	foreman	62	"
	K	Callaghan John J	107	houseman	22	"
	L	Tyldesley Mary C †	107	housewife	36	"
	M	Tyldesley Walter	107	policeman	38	"
	N	Bates Emily L †	113	secretary	45	"
	O	Williams Nathaniel W	113	decorator	54	"
	P	Williams Rose B †	113	housewife	54	"
	R	Slayter Isabella B †	121	"	80	"
	S	Slayter Jeane M †	121	typist	22	"
	T	Slayter John W	121	salesman	26	"
	U	Slayter Malcolm F	121	U S A	20	"
	V	Slayter Robert	121	florist	22	"
	W	Murphy John T	129	fireman	53	"
	X	Murphy Mary A †	129	housewife	44	"
	Y	Sullivan Florence M	129	retired	85	"

Page.	Letter	Full Name	Residence, Jan. 1, 1941	Occupation.	Supposed Age.	Reported Residence, Jan. 1, 1940. Street and Number.

Poplar Street—Continued

Page.	Letter	Full Name	Residence, Jan. 1, 1941	Occupation.	Supposed Age.	Reported Residence, Jan. 1, 1940.
	Z	Connor Gertrude M †	133	stenographer	25	here
1037						
	A	Connor Henry J	133	operator	63	"
	B	Connor Mary G †	133	housewife	65	"
	C	Boylan Hazel J †	137	"	26	38 Mt Vernon
	D	Boylan Robert L	137	salesman	28	38 "
	E	Johnson Marie L †	137	domestic	48	892 Hunt'n av
	F	Sullivan John L	137	retired	70	156 Mt Vernon
	G	Mulkern Geraldine M †	137	housewife	44	here
	H	Mulkern William F	137	foreman	47	"
	K	Blest Barbara M †	137	housewife	42	17 Newbury
	L	Blest William	137	guard	44	17 "
	M	Mosel Lawrence	137	mechanic	72	17 "
	N	Halligan Nora †	139	cook	45	362 Marlboro
	O	*Halligan Winifred †	139	"	55	754 W Roxbury P'kway
	P	Munroe Hugh	139	B F D	40	here
	R	Munroe Mary H †	139	housewife	35	"
	S	Waldron Joseph F	139	policeman	39	"
	T	Waldron Margaret B †	139	housewife	34	"
	U	D'Entremont Clarisse F †	143	"	40	"
	V	*D'Entremont Melbourne S	143	painter	44	"
	W	Manning Anna M †	143	clerk	20	46 Guernsey
	X	Manning Mary L †	143	housewife	49	46 "
	Y	Manning Thomas P	143	superintendent	50	46 "
	Z	Manning William T	143	clerk	23	46 "
1038						
	A	Leyland Aaron T	149	shoeworker	51	here
	B	Leyland Doris M †	149	housewife	43	"
	C	Leyland Florence V †	149	clerk	24	"
	D	*Hughes Eva E †	149	housewife	40	"
	E	*Hughes Milton K	149	clerk	49	"
	F	Lawson Charles, jr	155	gasfitter	46	"
	G	Lawson Vivian †	155	housewife	34	"
	H	Newman Almira J †	155	"	51	"
	K	Newman Harry J	155	engineer	52	"
	L	Newman Theresa A †	155	clerk	21	"
	M	Trask Raymond G	155	cleaner	43	"
	N	Trask Vivian H †	155	housewife	44	"
	O	Morrison Florence R †	155	"	35	"
	P	Morrison George W	155	chauffeur	38	"
	R	Patterson Joseph H	155	salesman	45	28 Stellman rd

Page	Letter	Full Name	Residence, Jan. 1, 1941	Occupation	Reputed Age	Reported Residence, Jan. 1, 1940. Street and Number
		Poplar Street Continued				
	S	Patterson Sarah V †	155	housewife	49	28 Stellman rd
	T	Fitzgerald Cecelia H †	155	"	44	here
	U	Fitzgerald Paul J	155	typist	17	"
	Y	*Brener Mae R †	175	housewife	34	"
	Z	Brener Marcus A	175	attorney	36	"
1039						
	A	Doyle Elizabeth J †	175	stitcher	36	"
	B	Doyle Louisa †	175	housewife	54	"
	C	Doyle Richard J	175	proprietor	58	"
	D	Gale Alvin P	175	manager	31	Weymouth
	E	Gale Margaret S †	175	housewife	28	"
	F	Devenney Charlotte †	175	"	50	here
	G	Devenney Cyril J	175	clerk	28	"
	H	Devenney Joan V †	175	"	21	"
		Rosecliff Street				
	K	Brogren Olga E †	10	photographer	42	here
	L	Holmes Ellen M †	10	housewife	46	"
	M	Holmes Eugene L	10	photographer	42	"
	N	Kannegieser Agnes †	15	housewife	42	"
	O	Kannegieser George	15	laborer	36	"
	P	Kannegieser Jacob	15	"	41	"
	R	*Kress Gertrude †	15	at home	33	"
	S	McKinney Robert E	16	dealer	56	"
	T	Wayne Karah P †	16	housewife	53	"
	U	Cox Rosalie I †	19	"	59	"
	V	Cox William H	19	architect	60	"
	W	Mulholland George A	20	salesman	40	"
	X	Mulholland Irene †	20	housewife	39	"
	Y	Waterman Edith H †	24	"	53	"
	Z	Waterman Roland O	24	electrician	57	"
1040						
	A	Dunkerly Albert M	25	letter carrier	45	"
	B	Dunkerly Louise A †	25	housewife	45	"
	C	Dunkerly Paul A	25	student	21	"
	D	Maher Francis B	29	salesman	52	"
	E	Maher John B	29	clerk	22	"
	F	Frasca Anthony R	29	"	20	"
	G	Frasca Clementina †	29	housewife	44	"
	H	Frasca Ralph	29	newsdealer	45	"

Page	Letter	Full Name.	Residence, Jan. 1, 1941.	Occupation.	Supposed Age.	Reported Residence, Jan. 1, 1940. Street and Number.

Rosecliff Street—Continued

Page	Letter	Full Name	Residence	Occupation	Age	Reported Residence
	K	Grilli Joseph	29	foreman	57	here
	L	Morse Charles H	34	clerk	32	25 Ashfield
	M	Morse Mildred E—†	34	housewife	30	25 "
	N	Schmidt Clara M—†	35	"	67	here
	O	Schmidt Otto H	35	retired	68	"
	P	McMorrow John F	38	clerk	56	"
	R	McMorrow Lena E—†	38	housewife	50	"
	S	McMorrow Richard H	38	student	21	"
	T	Sullivan Catherine M—†	39	housewife	41	"
	U	Sullivan John J	39	custodian	45	"
	V	White Harriett A—†	40	teacher	34	"
	W	White John K	40	clerk	37	"
	X	White Mary J—†	40	housewife	67	"
	Y	*Rogan Ella J—†	44	"	41	"
	Z	Rogan Henry J	44	investigator	58	"
1041						
	A	Wadsten Augusta W—†	44	housewife	68	"
	B	Wadsten Carl B	44	machinist	62	"
	C	Ackman Tyra C—†	48	housewife	40	"
	D	Ackman Walter G	48	metalworker	44	"
	E	Ivan Francis P	48	baker	23	"
	F	Ivan Frank	48	"	50	"
	G	Ivan Theaphila—†	48	housewife	49	"

Struzziery Terrace

Page	Letter	Full Name	Residence	Occupation	Age	Reported Residence
	H	*Sammartino Angelica—†	9	housewife	75	here
	K	Struzziery Charles	9	contractor	47	"
	L	Struzziery Charles F	9	chauffeur	21	"
	M	Struzziery Frances—†	9	housewife	45	"
	N	Struzziery Joseph J	9	timekeeper	24	"
	O	McClellan Gilbert	10	manager	37	"
	P	McClellan Julia—†	10	housewife	38	"
	R	McNeil Dowell P	14	musician	36	"
	S	McNeil Jennie—†	14	housewife	39	"
	T	McSweeney Blandine—†	15	"	40	"
	U	McSweeney Edward	15	engineer	44	"

Sycamore Street

Page	Letter	Full Name	Residence	Occupation	Age	Reported Residence
	V	Casey George F	10	retired	72	here
	W	Curran Anna M—†	10	housewife	33	"

Page	Letter	Full Name	Residence, Jan. 1, 1941	Occupation	Reported Age	Reported Residence, Jan. 1, 1940. Street and Number

Sycamore Street—Continued

Page	Letter	Full Name	Residence, Jan. 1, 1941	Occupation	Reported Age	Reported Residence, Jan. 1, 1940
	X	Curran Charles W	10	clerk	36	here
	Y	Chisholm Frederick I	10	mechanic	28	"
	Z	Chisholm Irene B †	10	housewife	30	"
1042						
	A	Aghjayan Ramella †	12	"	35	"
	B	Aghjayan Yezagiel	12	proprietor	48	"

Washington Street

Page	Letter	Full Name	Residence, Jan. 1, 1941	Occupation	Reported Age	Reported Residence, Jan. 1, 1940
	T	*Tellier Ellen M †	4280A	housewife	33	here
	U	*Tellier Gaston J	4280A	clerk	35	"
1043						
	B	Petruzzo Alphonso	4292	stitcher	53	"
	C	Petruzzo Annie †	4292	housewife	43	"
	D	Schwarz Josephine V †	4292	"	21	24 Broadway
	E	Schwarz Paul F	4292	musician	26	Dedham
	F	*Urban Anthony J	4292	steamfitter	43	here
	G	*Urban Helen A †	4292	housewife	39	"
	H	*Nigohosian Mary †	4294	"	37	"
	K	Nigohosian Michael	4294	cobbler	52	"
	L	Ivan Frances †	4294	stenographer	22	"
	M	*Ivan Mary †	4294	housewife	48	"
	N	Ivan William	4294	laborer	52	"
	O	Pozerski Blanche †	4294	housewife	27	"
	P	Pozerski Felix	4294	baker	32	"
	W	Kiessling C Herman	4320	retired	91	"
	X	Kiessling Martha †	4320	housewife	59	"
	Y	Byrnes Margaret †	4324	clerk	35	"
	Z	Harbert Mary †	4324	housekeeper	60	"
1044						
	A	Hill Eleanor †	4324	clerk	21	"
	B	Hill Lulu †	4324	nurse	55	"
	D	Dinn Beatrice †	4344	housewife	29	"
	E	Dinn Ronald	4344	receiver	34	"
	F	Foley Audrey P †	4344	housewife	30	"
	G	Foley Bernard J	4344	salesman	36	"
	H	Parentin Amelia †	4344	secretary	54	"
	K	Weisner Allegra F †	4344	saleswoman	30	"
	L	Weisner Frances †	4344	buyer	49	"
	M	*Ruggiero Angeline †	4346	housewife	48	"
	N	Ruggiero Antonio	4346	foreman	57	"

Page	Letter	Full Name	Residence Jan. 1, 1941.	Occupation	Supposed Age.	Reported Residence, Jan. 1, 1940. Street and Number.

Washington Street Continued

Page	Letter	Full Name	Residence	Occupation	Age	Reported Residence
	O	Ruggiero Louis	4346	musician	26	here
	P	Ruggiero Patricia †	4346	clerk	24	"
	R	Ruggiero Phyllis †	4346	"	20	"
	S	Parrish Helen M †	4346	housewife	40	"
	T	Peterson Walter L	4346	clerk	39	"
	U	Catalano Alice †	4346	housewife	33	"
	V	Catalano Fedele	4346	bartender	41	"
	W	Caprera Jennie †	4350	housewife	42	"
	X	Caprera Josephine †	4350	bookkeeper	22	"
	Y	Caprera Mario	4350	laborer	46	"
	Z	Milone Antonio P	4354	physician	31	957 South
1045						
	A	Milone Margaret R †	4354	housewife	31	957 "
	B	Curelli Biagio	4354	waiter	47	here
	C	*Curelli Fausta †	4354	housewife	47	"
	D	Curelli Rocco	4354	attorney	21	"
	E	Alfano Frances M †	4354	housewife	41	"
	F	Alfano Frank	4354	merchant	47	"
	G	Guglielmino Giuseppe	4356	laborer	57	"
	H	*Guglielmino Louise †	4356	housewife	55	"
	K	Milling Angelina †	4356	"	25	"
	L	Milling William	4356	waiter	26	"
	M	Verdoia Pio	4356	clerk	41	"
	N	Floreskul Onufry	4360	baker	46	"
	O	Floreskul Rose †	4360	housewife	46	"
	P	Floreskul Stanley	4360	radioman	21	"
	R	Lothrop Annabel E †	4360	housewife	25	163 Williams av
	S	Lothrop John W	4360	teacher	22	157 Stanwood
	T	Frasca Anna †	4362	saleswoman	21	here
	U	Frasca Charles	4362	salesman	54	"
	V	Frasca Lillian E †	4362	housewife	44	"
	W	Frasca Louise A †	4362	stenographer	26	"
	X	Polito Anthony	4362	salesman	44	"
	Y	Polito Louis A	4362	clerk	21	"
	Z	Polito Margaret †	4362	housewife	41	"
1046						
	A	Sarnie Eugene J	4362	salesman	43	"
	B	Sarnie Jennie †	4362	housewife	40	"
	C	Grasso John	4368	salesman	25	4313 Wash'n
	D	Grasso Mary †	4368	housewife	25	4313 "
	E	Barnaby Catherine †	4368	"	20	384 Amory

Washington Street—Continued

Page	Letter	Full Name	Residence, Jan. 1, 1941	Occupation	Supposed Age	Reported Residence, Jan. 1, 1940. Street and Number
	F	Barnaby Frederick	4368	salesman	26	384 Amory
	G	Casale Ella †	4368	housewife	39	here
	H	Casale Joseph	4368	bookbinder	50	"
	K	Casale Joseph	4368	laborer	20	"
	L	Broughton Charles S	4370	engineer	60	2993 Wash'n
	M	Broughton Henrietta J †	4370	housewife	55	88 Blue Hill av
	N	Sharpe Michael B	4370	fireman	50	2993 Wash'n
	O	Lang Lewis	4370	riveter	51	here
	P	Dickie Alice E †	4374	housewife	33	"
	R	*Dickie Ralph B	4374	laborer	33	"
	S	Stehle Cora G †	4374	housewife	50	"
	T	Stehle Mabel E †	4374	operator	29	"
	U	Stehle William C	4374	baker	55	"
	V	Stehle Mabel J †	4374	operator	52	"
	W	Stehle Walter J	4374	baker	50	"
	X	Bartlett Grace M †	4380	at home	65	"
	Y	Lincoln Clara E †	4380	"	70	"
	Z	Bowser Roy J	4386	chauffeur	47	"
1047						
	A	David Blanche M †	4386	stenographer	56	"
	B	David Ellen H †	4386	at home	91	"
	C	Dick John S	4390	shipper	55	149 Orange
	D	Dick Rose P †	4390	housewife	53	149 "
	E	Mulligan Margaret L †	4390	operator	28	187 Cornell
	F	Mulligan Thomas A	4390	timekeeper	27	187 "
	G	Brooks John E	4394	salesman	37	here
	H	Brooks Mildred W †	4394	housewife	41	"
	K	Brooks Pauline C †	4394	"	39	"
	L	Childs Alice M †	4394	nurse	40	"
	M	Feely James J	4398	retired	87	"
	N	O'Gorman Laura G †	4398	housewife	42	"
	O	O'Gorman Patrick W	4398	clerk	42	"
	P	Bullens Charles F	4398	lather	63	"
	R	Bullens Jennie T †	4398	housewife	70	"
	S	Brooks Martha E †	4398	"	61	"
1048						
	A	*Hasekian Alice †	4410	"	45	"
	B	Hasekian Charles	4410	clerk	21	"
	C	Hasekian Harry	4410	musician	52	"
	D	Tankar Adam	4410	tailor	36	"
	E	Tankar Catherine †	4410	housewife	61	"

Page.	Letter.	Full Name.	Residence, Jan. 1, 1941	Occupation.	Supposed Age.	Reported Residence, Jan. 1, 1940. Street and Number.

Washington Street—Continued

Page.	Letter.	Full Name.	Residence, Jan. 1, 1941	Occupation.	Supposed Age.	Reported Residence, Jan. 1, 1940. Street and Number.
	F	Kenney Elizabeth J—†	4410	housewife	47	645 Walk Hill
	G	Kenney John H	4410	supervisor	49	645 "
	H	Kenney Joseph L	4410	"	25	645 "
	K	Kenney Peter E	4410	clerk	23	645 "
	L	O'Brien Albert M	4412	mechanic	49	here
	M	MacDonald Elizabeth—†	4412	housewife	65	"
	N	MacDonald Joseph R	4412	clerk	66	"
	O	Crawford Beatrice M—†	4412	housewife	40	"
	P	Crawford Chester L	4412	testman	40	"
	R	Rowland Mary R—†	4412	housewife	26	"
	S	Rowland Sumner C	4412	caretaker	35	"
	T	Maginot Emil J	4416	merchant	43	"
	U	Maginot Ruth M—†	4416	housewife	43	"
	V	Maginot Marie—†	4416	"	71	"
	W	Bemis Doris M—†	4416	stenographer	22	"
	X	Bemis Frank	4416	shoeworker	60	"
	Y	Bemis Wilhelmina—†	4416	stenographer	21	"
	Z	Eichwald Alice—†	4420	housewife	59	"
1049						
	A	Eichwald Theodore	4420	machinist	60	"
	B	McAllister Ann—†	4420	housewife	56	"
	C	McAllister Henry	4420	machinist	58	"
	D	McAllister Thomas F	4420	chauffeur	26	"
	E	Hillberg Edwin T	4420	clerk	32	"
	F	Hillberg Ruth V—†	4420	housewife	29	"
	G	Tedesco A Charles	4428	clerk	26	"
	H	Tedesco Albert	4428	merchant	49	"
	K	Tedesco Josephine—†	4428	housewife	49	"
	L	Capone Anna—†	4430	"	29	"
	M	Capone George	4430	chauffeur	29	"
	R	Boyce Anna M—†	4436	housewife	34	96 Harriet
	S	Maroney Agnes—†	4436	cashier	24	here
	T	Maroney Alice—†	4436	bookkeeper	30	"
	U	Maroney Marion—†	4436	stenographer	32	"
	V	Maroney Nora—†	4436	housewife	65	"
	W	Fitzgerald Michael	4436	bookkeeper	30	"
	X	Healy Timothy	4436	retired	74	"
	Y	Long Johanna—†	4436	housewife	50	"
	Z	Keenan Annie J—†	4436	"	57	"
1050						
	A	Keenan Daniel F	4436	engineer	64	"

Washington Street Continued

Page	Letter	Full Name	Residence, Jan. 1, 1941	Occupation	Supposed Age	Reported Residence, Jan. 1, 1940. Street and Number
	B	Tedesco Roger	4438	laborer	30	here
	C	Sola Guy	4438	manager	24	34 Averton
	D	Sola Stella †	4438	housewife	24	181 Cornell
	E	Meloni Charles	4438	laborer	27	314 Kittredge
	F	Meloni Concetta †	4438	housewife	23	314 "
	G	Pendleton Lawrence M	4438	fireman	29	here
	H	Pendleton Ruth †	4438	housewife	26	"
	K	Merigan Grace H †	4438	"	37	"
	L	Slater Madeline †	4438	operator	46	"
	M	*Shea Esther P †	4438	housewife	27	"
	N	Shea Michael J	4438	painter	36	"
	O	Lawton Celia †	4440	at home	56	"
	P	Rowe Josephine A †	4440	housewife	34	"
	R	Rowe Wesley J	4440	decorator	37	"
	S	Farley James A	4440	watchman	69	"
	T	Farley Walter F	4440	laborer	28	"
	U	Hicks Anna G †	4440	housewife	35	"
	V	Hicks Frank E	4440	chauffeur	38	"
	W	Morris Christopher F	4440	salesman	37	"
	X	Morris Marie †	4440	housewife	35	"
	Y	Harvey Kathryn †	4440	teacher	37	"
	Z	Norley Mary M †	4440	housewife	46	"
	1Z	Norley Richard	4440	clerk	59	"
1051						
	A	Foley Helen M †	4442	operator	28	"
	B	Foley James J	4442	cashier	29	1431 Centre
	C	*Grankewicz Adolf	4442	longshoreman	56	here
	D	*Grankewicz Mary †	4442	housewife	49	"
	E	Bergquist Anna C †	4442	"	53	"
	F	Bergquist David E	4442	finisher	55	"
	G	Timilty Gerard J	4444	mechanic	28	10 Jamaicaway
	H	Timilty Grace F †	4444	clerk	30	here
	K	Timilty Joseph T	4444	foreman	35	"
	L	Timilty Mary †	4444	housewife	68	"
	M	Molla Albina J †	4446	attorney	47	"
	N	Molla Mary A †	4446	student	24	"
	O	Keenan Alexander	4448	laborer	55	"
	P	Keenan Eleanor S †	4448	cashier	22	"
	R	Keenan Mary †	4448	housewife	52	"
	S	*Sullivan Agnes †	4448	"	20	"
	T	Sullivan Daniel	4448	engineer	53	"

Page.	Letter.	Full Name.	Residence, Jan. 1, 1941.	Occupation.	Supposed Age.	Reported Residence, Jan. 1, 1940. Street and Number.

Welles Park

Page	Letter	Full Name	Residence, Jan. 1, 1941	Occupation	Supposed Age	Reported Residence, Jan. 1, 1940
	V	Hancotte Camille	10	musician	69	here
	W	Hancotte John J	10	policeman	42	"
	X	Hancotte Margaret M †	10	housewife	43	"
	Y	Hancotte Palmyra †	10	"	67	"
	Z	Haskey Elida †	14	"	44	"
1052						
	A	Haskey John	14	carpenter	46	"
	B	O'Neill Emily R †	18	housekeeper	42	"

Wellsmere Road

Page	Letter	Full Name	Residence, Jan. 1, 1941	Occupation	Supposed Age	Reported Residence, Jan. 1, 1940
	C	Page Ernest W	60–62	merchant	30	27 Bradfield av
	D	Page Madeline †	60–62	housewife	29	here
	E	Gavin Rose M †	60–62	"	40	"
	F	Gavin Walter A	60–62	B F D	41	"
	G	Ierardi Beatrice †	61–63	teacher	21	"
	H	Ierardi John F	61–63	manager	47	"
	K	Ierardi Regina †	61–63	housewife	43	"
	L	Bell Dorothy †	61–63	instructor	20	"
	M	Bell Rita †	61–63	operator	21	"
	N	Bell Rose †	61–63	housewife	39	"
	O	Bell William H	61–63	B F D	39	"
	P	McFaden Delbert	61–63	chauffeur	36	"
	R	McFaden James	61–63	laborer	32	"
	S	McFaden Rose †	61–63	at home	63	"
	T	Fay Francis J	64–66	registrar	40	"
	U	Fay Marie J †	64–66	housewife	37	"
	V	Brady James J	64–66	chauffeur	35	205 Webster
	W	Brady Marie J †	64–66	housewife	31	205 "
	X	Penza James F	65–67	manager	32	here
	Y	Penza Mary J †	65–67	housewife	36	"
	Z	Consolian Anthony	65–67	student	20	"
1053						
	A	Consolian Charles	65–67	shoemaker	41	"
	B	Consolian Mary †	65–67	housewife	41	"
	C	Wishart Alice M †	69–71	"	50	"
	D	Wishart Edna C †	69–71	operator	24	"
	E	Wishart William T	69–71	installer	51	"
	F	Fraser Caroline †	69–71	at home	80	"
	G	Hacklin Arnold	69–71	salesman	40	"
	H	Hacklin Marion †	69–71	housewife	37	"

Wellsmere Road Continued

Page	Letter	Full Name	Residence Jan. 1, 1941		Occupation	Reputed Age	Reported Residence, Jan. 1, 1940. Street and Number
	K	Mazzei Edith †	72	74	housewife	37	here
	L	Mazzei Frank J	72	74	starter	48	"
	M	Parnagian Anna †	72	74	housewife	47	"
	N	Parnagian Lulu †	72	74	"	47	"
	O	Parnagian Oscar	72	74	barber	44	"
	P	Parnagian Richard	72	74	"	55	"
	R	Greene Dorothy †	73	75	stenographer	20	"
	S	Greene Frank J	73	75	technician	46	"
	T	Greene Hazel †	73	75	housewife	44	"
	U	Allen Annie E †	73	75	"	60	"
	V	Allen Charles M	73	75	painter	60	"
	W	Allen James C	73	75	messenger	36	"
	X	Vozzella Jennie †	76	78	housewife	35	"
	Y	Vozzella Joseph	76	78	stonecutter	42	"
	Z	Palmer Frank V	76	78	barber	40	"
1054							
	A	Palmer Mildred †	76	78	housewife	38	"
	B	Albertazzi Joseph P	77	79	agent	38	"
	C	Albertazzi Kathleen F †	77	79	housewife	35	"
	D	Sullivan Catherine F †	77	79	"	76	"
	E	Sullivan John F	77	79	barber	69	"
	F	Schattgen Gertrude M †	77	79	clerk	20	"
	G	Schattgen Hansine †	77	79	housewife	44	"
	H	Schattgen Joseph L	77	79	retired	80	"
	K	Schattgen Ludwig	77	79	carpenter	46	"
	L	*Connell Ann T †	80	82	housewife	48	"
	M	Connell John J	80	82	gardener	48	"
	N	Wynn Celena M †	80	82	housewife	31	[illegible]
	O	Wynn Thomas J	80	82	manager	31	100 "
	P	Bernardo Frank S	81	83	chauffeur	27	here
	R	Bernardo Geneva E †	81	83	housewife	28	"
	S	Bernardo Bernard	81	83	contractor	40	"
	T	Bernardo Etta †	81	83	housewife	36	"
	U	O'Malley Margaret M †	84	86	"	43	"
	V	O'Malley Thomas F	84	86	policeman	43	"
	W	Brennan Catherine †	84	86	housewife	50	"
	X	Brennan Francis	84	86	molder	53	"
	Y	Brennan Rose †	84	86	operator	28	"
	Z	Cohen Muriel †	85	87	housewife	34	"
1055							
	A	Waffle Martha †	85	87	housekeeper	43	"

Page	Letter	Full Name.	Residence, Jan. 1, 1941.	Occupation.	Supposed Age.	Reported Residence, Jan. 1, 1940. Street and Number.

Wellsmere Road—Continued

Page	Letter	Full Name.	Residence, Jan. 1, 1941.	Occupation.	Supposed Age.	Reported Residence, Jan. 1, 1940. Street and Number.
	B	Kelleher Annie—†	85–87	housewife	64	here
	C	Kelleher Edna F—†	85–87	operator	24	"
	D	Kelleher Edward F	85–87	shipper	61	"
	E	Kelleher James J	85–87	B F D	62	"
	F	Kelleher Lillian E—†	85–87	nurse	27	"
	G	Kelleher Mary L—†	85–87	student	23	"
	H	Kelleher Patricia F—†	85–87	teacher	29	"
	K	Buckley Anna A—†	88–90	housewife	52	"
	L	Buckley Claire R—†	88–90	stenographer	25	"
	M	Buckley William J	88–90	B F D	50	"
	N	Martin Catherine V—†	88–90	at home	50	19 Highland av
	O	Bentz Augustine—†	88–90	housewife	67	here
	P	Bentz Victor	88–90	retired	74	"
	R	Tournour Louis	88–90	waiter	54	"
	S	Tournour Louise—†	88–90	housewife	48	"
	T	Laninger Josephine L—†	89–91	stenographer	30	"
	U	Laninger Katherine—†	89–91	operator	26	"
	V	Laninger Veronica—†	89–91	housewife	57	"
	W	Bohlin Iris—†	89–91	"	30	"
	X	Bohlin Sven	89–91	machinist	31	"
	Y	Grinnell Margaret M—†	93–95	housewife	36	"
	Z	Grinnell Raymond J	93–95	manager	37	"
1056						
	A	Fitzpatrick John F	93–95	draftsman	42	"
	B	Fitzpatrick Rose E—†	93–95	housewife	38	"
	C	Mahoney Arthur J	96–98	supervisor	45	"
	D	Mahoney Florence—†	96–98	housewife	36	"
	E	Mahoney Martin J	96–98	watchman	42	"
	F	Carlton Charles L	96–98	engineer	57	18 Kingsboro pk
	G	Carlton Charlotte—†	96–98	housewife	52	18 "
	H	Catarius Charlotte—†	96–98	stenographer	22	18 "
	K	Singer Charles A	97–99	manager	47	here
	L	Singer Irene—†	97–99	milliner	20	"
	M	Singer Pauline—†	97–99	housewife	42	"
	N	Singer Phillip	97–99	chauffeur	20	"
	O	Knarr Charles A	97–99	clerk	33	71 Parkton rd
	P	Knarr Emily—†	97–99	stenographer	29	71 "
	R	Knarr Fred W	97–99	salesman	35	71 "
	S	Knarr Helen G—†	97–99	teacher	27	71 "
	T	Knarr Margaret—†	97–99	housewife	65	71 "
	U	Knarr Otto A	97–99	machinist	31	71 "

Page	Letter	Full Name.	Residence, Jan. 1, 1941.	Residence, Jan. 1, 1940.	Occupation.	Supposed Age.	Reported Residence, Jan. 1, 1940. Street and Number.

Wellsmere Road—Continued

Page	Letter	Full Name	1941	1940	Occupation	Age	Reported Residence
	V	Higgins Catherine †	100	102	housewife	46	here
	W	Higgins John C	100	102	salesman	55	"
	X	Hynes James J	100	102	manager	45	"
	Y	Hynes Kathleen †	100	102	housewife	47	"
	Z	DeSimone Anna—†	101	103	"	26	"
1057							
	A	DeSimone Louis	101	103	chauffeur	32	"
	B	Cherkezian Edward	101	103	druggist	30	"
	C	Cherkezian Mary—†	101	103	housewife	21	"
	D	Benedetti Alfred	105	107	chef	51	Missouri
	E	Benedetti Zofia—†	105	107	housewife	48	"

Wellsmere Terrace

Page	Letter	Full Name	1941	1940	Occupation	Age	Reported Residence
	G	Colskie Julia J—†		8	housewife	46	here
	H	Colskie Stephen		8	gardener	47	"
	K	Skordos Carmen—†		11	housewife	42	"
	L	Skordos Christopher		11	chef	47	"
	M	Cleary Margaret G—†		12	housewife	49	"
	N	Cleary Thomas J		12	chauffeur	49	"
	O	Milano Stella M—†		16	housewife	35	"

Whitford Street

Page	Letter	Full Name	1941	1940	Occupation	Age	Reported Residence
	P	Hersee Charles		3	retired	87	here
	R	Hersee Grace D—†		3	stenographer	36	"
	S	*Worthylake Maud A—†		3	housekeeper	62	Somerville
	T	Topham Mary E—†		7	housewife	67	here
	U	Topham William H		7	custodian	66	"
	V	Wakefield Helen L—†		7	at home	37	"
	W	Wakefield Marion L—†		7	nurse	31	"
	X	Marden George F		10	inspector	36	Brockton
	Y	Marden Lucy M—†		10	housewife	34	77 Arlington
	Z	Kunze Dorothea—†		11	"	32	here
1058							
	A	Kunze Paul G		11	shipper	32	"
	B	Getchell Clara M—†		11	nurse	30	"
	C	Kehling George H		11	laborer	26	"
	D	Schirmer F Herman		11	upholsterer	79	"
	E	Walejora Julia—†		11	housekeeper	68	"
	F	Wood Anne R—†		12	housewife	34	"

Page.	Letter.	Full Name.	Residence, Jan. 1, 1941.	Occupation.	Supposed Age.	Reported Residence, Jan. 1, 1940. Street and Number.

Whitford Street—Continued

Page.	Letter.	Full Name.	Residence, Jan. 1, 1941.	Occupation.	Supposed Age.	Reported Residence, Jan. 1, 1940. Street and Number.
	G	Wood George D	12	manager	37	here
	H	Ryan Catherine—†	14	housewife	59	"
	K	Ryan George J	14	clerk	26	"
	L	Ryan Joseph A	14	student	24	"
	M	Cooper Chester J	15	engineer	43	"
	N	Cooper Mary R—†	15	beautician	35	"
	O	Miller Ethel G—†	15	at home	68	"

Wyman Street

Page.	Letter.	Full Name.	Residence, Jan. 1, 1941.	Occupation.	Supposed Age.	Reported Residence, Jan. 1, 1940. Street and Number.
	P	Guyette George H	6	carpenter	56	here
	S	Guyette Roger W	6	clerk	28	"
	R	Guyette Winifred B—†	6	housewife	55	"
	T	Knudsen Dorothy P—†	7	"	26	8 Cotton
	U	Knudsen Harold E	7	carpenter	31	8 "
	V	Wikstrom Agnar B	11	toolmaker	54	here
	W	Wikstrom Ida S—†	11	housewife	54	"
	X	Reilly Patrick	11	operator	54	"
	Y	Grueter Leo H	14	teacher	46	"
	Z	Grueter Marguerite—†	14	housewife	45	"
1059						
	A	Anderson Helen C—†	15	"	26	"
	B	Anderson Richard E	15	clerk	28	"
	C	Lannon Edith—†	15	housewife	54	"

Ward 18—Precinct 11

CITY OF BOSTON

LIST OF RESIDENTS
20 YEARS OF AGE AND OVER

(NON-CITIZENS INDICATED BY ASTERISK)
(FEMALES INDICATED BY DAGGER)

AS OF

JANUARY 1, 1941

CITY OF BOSTON PRINTING DEPARTMENT

Page.	Letter.	Full Name.	Residence, Jan. 1, 1941.	Occupation.	Supposed Age.	Reported Residence, Jan. 1, 1940. Street and Number.

1100

Augustus Avenue

	A	McCarter Grace H—†	107	housewife	37	here
	B	McCarter Harry L	107	retired	72	"
	C	McCarter Howard R	107	superintendent	39	"
	D	Nolfi Bambina—†	111	housewife	65	"
	E	Nolfi George J	111	superintendent	31	"
	F	Nolfi John	111	retired	76	"
	G	Nolfi Rose S—†	111	housewife	24	"
	H	Pruyne Ethel M—†	115	"	35	"
	K	Pruyne Howard G	115	operator	35	"
	L	Bleiler Henry C	117	contractor	31	"
	M	Bleiler Marvinna R—†	117	housewife	30	"
	N	*Kiszkan John	119	cleaner	57	"
	O	Kiszkan Pauline—†	119	housewife	52	"
	P	Campbell Archibald M	121	clerk	61	"
	R	Campbell Emily—†	121	housewife	56	"
	S	Leveridge Florence M—†	123	housekeeper	71	"
	T	Shepherd Mary E—†	123	clerk	65	"
	U	Shepherd Rose J—†	123	housekeeper	76	"

Beech Street

	V	Raftery Anna L—†	380	housewife	53	here
	W	Raftery Thomas E	380	laborer	56	"
	X	Capone Antonetta—†	380	housewife	41	"
	Y	Capone Joseph	380	contractor	50	"
	Z	Capone Virginia—†	380	packer	22	"
1101						
	A	*Christoforo Concetta—†	384	at home	87	"
	B	Sarni Alvisa—†	384	packer	30	"
	C	Sarni Celia—†	384	housewife	58	"
	D	DeGregorio Louis	384	foreman	45	"
	E	DeGregorio Louise—†	384	student	20	"
	F	DeGregorio Rose—†	384	housewife	40	"
	G	Ciampa Domenic	388	fireman	54	"
	H	Ciampa Edward L	388	operator	21	"
	K	Ciampa Julia—†	388	housewife	56	"
	L	Ciampa Lydia—†	388	at home	23	"
	M	Ciampa Pasquale	388	welder	28	"
	O	Lawson Otto F	392	retired	72	"
	N	Lawson Ruth E—†	392	cashier	35	"

Page	Letter	Full Name	Residence Jan. 1 1941	Occupation	Supposed Age	Reported Residence Jan. 1, 1940 Street and Number

Beech Street Continued

Page	Letter	Full Name	Residence Jan. 1 1941	Occupation	Supposed Age	Reported Residence Jan. 1, 1940 Street and Number
	P	Regan Cornelius J	392	bartender	28	here
	R	Regan Helen E †	392	housewife	27	"
	S	Melillo Adelaide †	392	saleswoman	51	"
	T	Melillo Emanuel	392	laborer	28	"
	U	Melillo Lillian †	392	stenographer	30	"
	V	Piper Emma A †	396	housewife	56	"
	W	Piper Lloyd F	396	superintendent	56	"
	X	Piper Lloyd R	396	carpenter	24	"
	Y	Gardella Fredrick	396	letter carrier	34	"
	Z	Ghirardelli Frank	396	superintendent	41	"
1102						
	A	Ghirardelli John	396	retired	74	"
	B	Ghirardelli Lillian †	396	housewife	41	"
	C	Ghirardelli Theresa †	396	"	63	"
	D	Tassinari Fred	417	carpenter	62	"
	E	Tassinari Mary †	417	housewife	56	"
	F	Delaney Jennie C †	419	"	70	"
	G	Delaney Margaret M †	419	clerk	30	"
	H	Malaguti Evelyn †	421	housewife	36	"
	K	Malaguti Lionel	421	salesman	38	"
	L	Valinote Esther M †	423	housewife	40	"
	M	Valinote Nicholas T	423	mechanic	44	"
	N	Marseglia Angelo	425	retired	65	"
	O	Marseglia Angelo J	425	baker	22	"
	P	Marseglia Antonette †	425	clerk	27	"
	R	McKenzie James D	425	roofer	57	"
	S	Rollins Margaret M †	425	housewife	31	"
	T	Rollins Theodore E	425	engineer	35	"
	U	Costello Elizabeth R †	429	housewife	41	"
	V	Costello John W	429	laborer	43	"
	W	Gunther Jessie L †	432	stenographer	25	"
	X	Gunther Mary M †	432	housewife	64	"
	Y	Gunther Emma †	432	"	59	"
	Z	Gunther Gertrude †	432	stenographer	24	"
1103						
	A	Gunther Hilda †	432	"	24	"
	B	Gunther John R	432	retired	61	"
	C	Viofara Anthony	433	laborer	47	"
	D	*Viofara Frank	433	retired	82	"
	E	*Viofara Marie †	433	housewife	79	"
	F	Arntz Irvin	433	policeman	25	"

Page.	Letter.	FULL NAME.	Residence, Jan. 1, 1941.	Occupation.	Supposed Age.	Reported Residence, Jan. 1, 1940. Street and Number.

Beech Street—Continued

Page.	Letter.	FULL NAME.	Residence, Jan. 1, 1941.	Occupation.	Supposed Age.	Reported Residence, Jan. 1, 1940. Street and Number.
	G	Arntz Leona—†	433	housewife	29	here
	H	Richard Beatrice—†	433	housekeeper	51	"
	L	Hockman Angelique B—†	437	clerk	25	"
	M	Hockman Earl A	437	printer	27	"
	N	Hockman Earl E	437	janitor	54	"
	O	Hockman Elizabeth C—†	437	housewife	53	"
	P	Carey Abraham	437	laborer	22	"
	R	*Carey Annie—†	437	housewife	50	"
	S	Carey Edward	437	painter	26	"
	T	Carey John	437	carpenter	25	"
	U	Carey Moses	437	molder	49	"
	V	Caracasis Ariathne—†	437	at home	56	"
	W	Caracasis Nicholas	437	restaurateur	32	"
	X	Caracasis Stephen	437	manager	26	"
	Y	Manousos Demetra—†	437	housewife	28	"
	Z	Manousos George	437	manager	29	"
1104						
	A	Ricchia Nunzio	444	salesman	48	68 Middle
	B	*Ricchia Rose—†	444	housewife	30	68 "
	C	Moccia Joseph	444	salesman	26	here
	D	Moccia Sophie—†	444	housewife	25	"
	E	*Petrillo Angelina—†	445	"	59	"
	F	*Petrillo Antonio	445	shoeworker	47	"
	G	Polcari Mary G—†	445	housewife	30	"
	H	Polcari Nicholas	445	dresscutter	30	"
	L	Grady Mary W—†	447	at home	71	"
	M	Young Catherine M—†	447	"	46	"
	N	*Fiore John J	447	machinist	38	"
	O	Fiore Marie—†	447	housewife	38	"
	P	Marchese Antonio	447	janitor	65	"
	R	Blasenak Catherine—†	451	housewife	35	417 Beech
	S	Blasenak Fredrick	451	grocer	34	417 "
	T	McCann Emma—†	451	housewife	47	here
	U	McCann Helen—†	451	at home	21	"
	V	McCann William F	451	boilermaker	50	"
	W	Tassinari Lawrence	451	builder	32	"
	X	Tassinari Ruth—†	451	housewife	30	"
	Y	Bernard Joseph	452	cook	34	14 Prospect av
	Z	Bernard Marguerite—†	452	housewife	25	14 "
1105						
	A	Carulli Angelo	452	baker	25	338 Metropolitan av

Page	Letter	Full Name	Residence, Jan. 1, 1941	Occupation	Supposed Age	Reported Residence, Jan. 1, 1940. Street and Number

Beech Street—Continued

Page	Letter	Full Name	Residence, Jan. 1, 1941	Occupation	Supposed Age	Reported Residence, Jan. 1, 1940. Street and Number
	B	Carulli Carmelo	452	baker	22	338 Metropolitan av
	C	*Carulli Grace—†	452	housewife	50	338 "
	D	Carulli Guy	452	laborer	21	338 "
	E	*Carulli Salvatore	452	factoryhand	59	338 "
	F	Cirone Luigi	454	laborer	54	here
	G	Cirone Mario	454	clerk	20	"
	H	*Cirone Rose—†	454	housewife	52	"
	K	*Cirone Annie—†	454	"	55	"
	L	*Cirone Thomas	454	laborer	61	"
	M	Tibari Henry	454	"	52	"
	N	Young Donald J	460	student	20	"
	O	Young Hilda M—†	460	bookkeeper	56	"
	P	Young Margaret A—†	460	housewife	77	"
	R	Geppert Carl O	461	woodcarver	66	"
	S	Holm Elina—†	461	housewife	63	"
	T	Holm Gothard	461	tailor	68	"
	U	Holm Vincent	461	shipper	28	"
	V	Fish Annie D—†	461	housewife	39	"
	W	Fish Charles L	461	engineer	43	"
	X	Amoling Claire—†	466	housewife	27	"
	Y	Wright John	466	foreman	29	"
	Z	Wright Josephine—†	466	housewife	27	"
1106						
	A	Wengenroth Edith V—†	466	"	61	"
	B	Wengenroth William E	466	machinist	58	"
	C	Feeney Edward C	471	bookkeeper	31	"
	D	Feeney Joseph F	471	clerk	65	36 Charme av
	E	Feeney Mary J—†	471	housewife	63	36 "
	F	Claus Charles F	471	retired	76	here
	G	May Anna M—†	471	housewife	44	"
	H	May August	471	mechanic	47	"
	K	Mendenhall Ernest P	471	cabinetmaker	22	461 Beech
	L	Mendenhall Marion F—†	471	housewife	20	461 "
	M	Fettig Doris—†	472	cashier	22	here
	N	Fettig Elizabeth C—†	472	housewife	55	"
	O	Fettig Emma—†	472	maid	30	"
	P	Scott Dorothy—†	475	housewife	45	"
	R	Scott Francis W	475	janitor	51	"
	S	Ryan John	475	clerk	28	140 Birch
	T	Ryan Mary—†	475	social worker	28	140 "
	U	Johnson Frieda G—†	475	housewife	25	here

Page.	Letter	Full Name.	Residence, Jan. 1, 1941	Occupation.	Supposed Age.	Reported Residence, Jan. 1, 1940. Street and Number.

Beech Street—Continued

Page.	Letter	Full Name.	Residence, Jan. 1, 1941	Occupation.	Supposed Age.	Reported Residence, Jan. 1, 1940.
	v	Johnson Parker W	475	designer	24	here
	w	Dunn Esther—†	477	housewife	28	"
	x	Dunn Robert L	477	meatcutter	30	"
	y	Ledbury Dorothy B—†	477	housewife	25	"
	z	Ledbury Walter	477	clerk	27	"
1107						
	B	Meyer Elizabeth A—†	478	housewife	33	"
	C	Meyer Henry F	478	investigator	38	"
	D	Barman Adolph	479	assembler	76	"
	E	Barman Lillian—†	479	housekeeper	46	"
	F	Wagner Alfred	481	chauffeur	33	"
	G	Wagner Helen—†	481	housewife	29	"
	H	Ritscher Emma—†	482	"	68	"
	K	Ritscher Franklin	482	superintendent	42	"
	L	Ritscher Juliet C—†	482	saleswoman	44	"
	M	Ritscher Myrtle—†	482	housewife	35	"
	N	*Stengel Martha R—†	483	"	61	"
	O	Stengel Richard B	483	retired	72	"
	P	O'Niel Felicia—†	484	housewife	38	"
	R	O'Niel George F	484	lineman	39	"
	S	Tobin Anna T—†	484	housewife	34	"
	T	Tobin James J	484	collector	39	"
	U	Schultheis Joseph	484	steward	38	"
	V	Schultheis Marie A—†	484	waitress	39	"
	W	Ciccolo Rose K—†	485	housewife	32	"
	X	Ciccolo Santo	485	roofer	40	"
	Y	Rothfuchs Amelia—†	495	saleswoman	59	"
	Z	Rothfuchs Catherine—†	495	at home	86	"
1108						
	A	Rothfuchs Mathilda—†	495	dressmaker	49	"
	B	Koch Ernest F	496	hostler	50	"
	C	Koch Fred	496	woodworker	43	"
	D	Koch Gottlieb	496	retired	77	"
	E	Koch Gottlieb W	496	shoeworker	52	"
	F	Koch Harold	496	clerk	30	"
	G	Koch Mabel—†	496	operator	34	"
	H	Collassi Domenic	498	engineer	31	"
	K	Collassi Louise—†	498	housewife	31	"
	L	Baer George	498	painter	52	"
	M	Baer Lillian—†	498	housewife	40	"
	N	Russo Carman	499	contractor	49	"

Page	Letter	Full Name	Residence, Jan. 1, 1941	Occupation	Supposed Age	Reported Residence, Jan. 1, 1940, Street and Number

Beech Street—Continued

Page	Letter	Full Name	Residence, Jan. 1, 1941	Occupation	Supposed Age	Reported Residence, Jan. 1, 1940, Street and Number
	O	Russo Fred	499	storekeeper	38	here
	P	Russo Grace A—†	499	housewife	42	"
	R	Christoforo Charles	502	bricklayer	40	"
	S	Christoforo Josephine—†	502	housewife	33	"
	T	Miller Gertrude—†	502	"	35	"
	U	Miller Irwin	502	storekeeper	35	"
	V	Bauman Mathilda—†	504	at home	65	170 Amory
	W	Brandli Gottlieb	504	retired	71	here
	X	Brandli Rebecca—†	504	housewife	55	"
	Y	Glidden Gertrude—†	511	"	40	"
1109						
	A	Steinbaeker Charles M	543	machinist	47	"
	B	Steinbaeker Frank M	543	chauffeur	33	"
	C	Steinbaeker Mary T—†	543	housewife	42	"
	D	Wiedemann Carl H	550	clerk	20	"
	E	Wiedemann Carl P	550	foreman	49	"
	F	Wiedemann Katherine H—†	550	housewife	45	"
	G	McEachern Benjamin	555	policeman	48	"
	H	McEachern Margaret—†	555	housewife	37	"
	K	Rose Arthur	571	retired	79	"
	L	Rose Emma—†	571	housewife	73	"
	M	Dolle Helen L—†	573	saleswoman	26	"
	N	Dolle Lanchen M—†	573	housewife	57	"
	O*	Dolle William	573	machinist	58	"
	P	Vriot Berthold V	573	electrician	50	"
	R	Vriot John L	573	painter	64	"
	S	Pelech Mary—†	574	housewife	54	"
	T	Pelech Paul J	574	cleaner	55	"
	U	Galandzy June P—†	574	housewife	30	"
	V	Galandzy Leon	574	painter	38	"

Cedrus Avenue

Page	Letter	Full Name	Residence, Jan. 1, 1941	Occupation	Supposed Age	Reported Residence, Jan. 1, 1940, Street and Number
	W	Abizaid Nella—†	22	housewife	31	here
	X	Abizaid Roger J	22	physician	34	"
	Y	Walnie Anna—†	22	at home	60	"
	Z	Grassia Elvira—†	25	housewife	30	"
1110						
	A	Grassia Frank	25	waiter	38	"
	B	Margnetti Anthony	25	"	51	"
	C	Margnetti Carmella—†	25	housewife	47	"

Page.	Letter.	Full Name.	Residence, Jan. 1, 1941.	Occupation.	Supposed Age.	Reported Residence, Jan. 1, 1940. Street and Number.

Cedrus Avenue—Continued

Page.	Letter.	Full Name.	Residence, Jan. 1, 1941.	Occupation.	Supposed Age.	Reported Residence, Jan. 1, 1940. Street and Number.
	D	Margnetti Charles	25	student	23	here
	E	*Crusco Antonette—†	26–28	housewife	66	"
	F	*Crusco Concetta—†	26–28	"	31	"
	G	*Crusco Louis	26–28	retired	74	"
	H	*Crusco Michael A	26–28	lithographer	33	"
	K	Bligh Edna—†	26–28	housewife	35	30 Granfield av
	L	Bligh Isabelle—†	26–28	housekeeper	72	20 Creighton
	M	Bligh Raymond E	26–28	paperhanger	43	30 Granfield av
	N	Bensusan Nathan	30–32	glazier	47	here
	O	Bensusan Olive—†	30–32	housewife	42	"
	P	Bensusan Rayner	30–32	clerk	21	"
	R	Pennini Fannie—†	30–32	housekeeper	62	"
	S	Pennini Helen—†	30–32	saleswoman	26	"
	T	Pennini Louis	30–32	clerk	36	"
	U	Pennini Rose—†	30–32	hairdresser	30	"
	V	Margnetti Mary—†	34–36	housewife	44	"
	W	Margnetti Peter	34–36	cook	51	"
	X	Margnetti Tina—†	34–36	saleswoman	22	"
	Y	Margnetti Virginia—†	34–36	stenographer	25	"
	Z	Crosby John W	34–36	engraver	46	"
1111						
	A	Crosby Martha M—†	34–36	housewife	43	"
	B	Andrews Athans P	37–39	manager	42	"
	C	Andrews Frances A—†	37–39	housewife	33	"
	D	MacDonald James R	37–39	engineer	49	"
	E	MacDonald Margaret M—†	37–39	housewife	43	"
	F	Ross Harry J	38	chauffeur	45	"
	G	Ross Matilda—†	38	housewife	29	"
	H	Caponetti Lucy—†	40	"	51	"
	K	Caponetti Michael	40	cobbler	55	"
	L	Caponetti Michael	40	instructor	22	"
	M	Haddigan Edward J	41–43	foreman	45	"
	N	Haddigan Madeline J—†	41–43	housewife	36	"
	O	Concannon James F	41–43	chauffeur	22	"
	P	Concannon Michael	41–43	lineman	53	"
	R	Concannon Nora—†	41–43	housewife	53	"
	S	Concannon Rita—†	41–43	student	26	"
	T	Concannon Thomas	41–43	repairman	23	"
	U	Gaeta Jennie—†	42–44	candyworker	47	"
	V	Grilli Margaret—†	42–44	housewife	49	"
	W	Grilli Rocco	42–44	builder	52	"

Page	Letter	Full Name	Residence Jan. 1, 1941	Occupation	Supposed Age	Reported Residence Jan. 1, 1940. Street and Number

Cedrus Avenue Continued

Page	Letter	Full Name	Residence Jan. 1, 1941	Occupation	Supposed Age	Reported Residence Jan. 1, 1940. Street and Number
	X	Mondini Eugene	42-44	packer	42	here
	Y	Mondini Laura †	42-44	housewife	35	"
	Z	*Rho Caroline †	42-44	"	56	"
1112						
	A	*Rho Peter	42-44	retired	69	"
	B	*Apkarian Arvedis	45	merchant	49	"
	C	Apkarian Mary †	45	clerk	24	"
	D	Apkarian Rita †	45	housewife	46	"
	E	Kalunian Karekian	47	merchant	49	"
	F	Kalunian Sarah †	47	housewife	38	"
	G	Verrochi Antonio	50	contractor	48	"
	H	Verrochi Evelyn †	50	stenographer	21	"
	K	Verrochi Lucy E †	50	"	25	"
	L	Verrochi Mary R †	50	housewife	45	"
	M	McIntyre Susan †	52	housekeeper	72	"
	N	McIntyre Wallace J	52	bookkeeper	31	"
	O	Santosuosso Artenza †	58	housewife	42	"
	P	Santosuosso John	58	student	21	"
	R	Santosuosso Joseph	58	letter carrier	46	"
	S	Gibbons Agnes †	64	housewife	51	"
	T	Gibbons Edward	64	retired	67	"
	U	Susi Angelina †	68	housewife	43	"
	V	Susi Angelo	68	foreman	51	"
	W	Susi Eleanor †	68	stenographer	21	"
	X	Susi Joseph	68	operator	23	"
	Y	Davenport Marion †	70	housewife	42	"
	Z	Davenport Stephen	70	salesman	42	"
1113						
	A	Lynn Ellen †	70	at home	72	"
	B	Lynn Louise †	70	stenographer	38	"
	C	Lynn Ruth †	70	bookkeeper	36	"

Chisholm Road

Page	Letter	Full Name	Residence Jan. 1, 1941	Occupation	Supposed Age	Reported Residence Jan. 1, 1940. Street and Number
	D	Graumann Charles	1	cigarmaker	61	here
	E	Graumann Julia M †	1	housewife	58	"
	F	Graumann Matilda J †	1	teacher	50	"
	G	Herlihy Anne F †	2	housewife	42	"
	H	Herlihy Frank J	2	teacher	49	"
	K	Leesam Charlotte M †	5	at home	80	"
	L	Row Alfred E	5	collector	44	"

Page.	Letter.	Full Name.	Residence Jan. 1 1941	Occupation.	Supposed Age.	Reported Residence, Jan. 1, 1940. Street and Number.

Chisholm Road—Continued

Page.	Letter.	Full Name.	Residence Jan. 1 1941	Occupation.	Supposed Age.	Reported Residence, Jan. 1, 1940. Street and Number.
	M	Row Susan E—†	5	housewife	41	here
	N	Kilroy Edith F—†	8	"	48	"
	O	Kilroy John F	8	letter carrier	48	"
	P	Dreist Edwin H	9	"	45	"
	R	Dreist Frank E	9	student	20	"
	S	Dreist Ruth H—†	9	housewife	45	"
	T	Foster Elizabeth—†	12	"	46	8 Seymour
	U	Foster Ernest H	12	engineer	45	here
	V	Higgins George P	15	clerk	35	"
	W	Higgins Mary G—†	15	housewife	36	"
	X	Dawson Alice J—†	16	"	42	"
	Y	Dawson Charles J	16	buyer	42	"
	Z	Morse John J	19	repairman	57	"
1114						
	A	Morse Patrick T	19	"	53	"
	B	Morse William J	19	shipper	45	"
	D	Benson Kathleen—†	24	housewife	40	"
	E	Benson Warren	24	director	43	"
	F	Cantony Esther—†	28	housewife	50	"
	G	Cantony John	28	buyer	57	"
	H	Lovetere Anthony	28	chauffeur	32	"
	K	Lovetere Christine—†	28	housewife	28	"
	L	Daston Elizabeth—†	31	clerk	22	"
	M	Daston George P	31	chef	52	"
	N	Daston Phillip G	31	clerk	23	"
	O	Daston Zenobea—†	31	housewife	47	"
	R	MacFaden James J	34	promoter	41	"
	S	MacFaden Thelma—†	34	housewife	33	"

Clarendon Avenue

Page.	Letter.	Full Name.	Residence Jan. 1 1941	Occupation.	Supposed Age.	Reported Residence, Jan. 1, 1940. Street and Number.
	V	Hansen Arthur H	5	machinist	25	here
	W	Hansen Henry L	5	clerk	26	"
	X	Hansen Irene—†	5	housewife	25	"
	Y	Capobianco Charles	5	boilermaker	37	"
	Z	Capobianco Helen L—†	5	housewife	30	"
1115						
	A	Gustafson Eric K	14	carpenter	41	"
	B*	Gustafson Esther—†	14	housewife	41	"
	C	Wittenauer Anna W—†	14	"	69	"
	D	Wittenauer Constance—†	14	dressmaker	34	"

Clarendon Avenue Continued

Page	Letter	Full Name	Residence, Jan. 1, 1941	Occupation	Supposed Age	Reported Residence, Jan. 1, 1940. Street and Number
	E	Anderson Carl J	15	retired	68	here
	F	Anderson Clara †	15	housewife	57	"

Cornell Street

Page	Letter	Full Name	Residence, Jan. 1, 1941	Occupation	Supposed Age	Reported Residence, Jan. 1, 1940. Street and Number
	G	Mahony Francis D	7	mechanic	41	here
	H	Mahony Mary R †	7	housewife	38	"
	K	Mitchell George L	11	inspector	54	"
	L	Mitchell Margaret J †	11	housewife	49	"
	M	Ambrose Margaret M †	15	"	36	"
	N	Ambrose William E	15	drawtender	46	"
	O	Kelsey Sarah E †	19	housekeeper	72	"
	P	McCarthy Charles F	23	salesman	55	"
	R	O'Brien Dennis	23	retired	93	"
	S	O'Brien William M	23	laborer	51	"
	T	Pagliazzo Mary †	24	housewife	28	Waltham
	U	Pagliazzo Salvatore	24	painter	28	"
	V	*DeStefano Antonetta M †	24	housewife	36	here
	W	DeStefano Carmine	24	laborer	41	"
	Y	Poretsky Evelyn D †	27	stenographer	24	96 Wellsmere rd
	Z	Poretsky Normand R	27	shipper	28	97 "
1116						
	A	Benker Charles	27	painter	43	here
	B	Benker John N	27	retired	77	"
	C	Benker John N, jr	27	machinist	55	"
	D	Fabbrucci Dina †	28	housewife	50	"
	E	Fabbrucci Floria †	28	clerk	25	"
	F	Fabbrucci Mario	28	"	24	"
	G	Fabbrucci William	28	carpenter	53	"
	H	Cummins Helena T †	32	housewife	44	"
	K	Cummins James J	32	salesman	36	"
	L	Cummins Albert	34	"	31	"
	M	Cummins Bernice M †	34	housewife	30	"
	N	Guba Helen C †	35	"	25	"
	O	Guba Theodore E	35	optician	27	"
	P	Young Arthur H	35	laborer	34	"
	R	Young Katherine †	35	housewife	34	"
	S	Panska Anna R †	48	operator	37	"
	T	Panska Augusta †	48	housewife	75	"
	U	Panska Bernard	48	carpenter	42	"
	V	Panska Conrad	48	optician	51	"

Page.	Letter.	Full Name.	Residence, Jan. 1, 1941.	Occupation.	Supposed Age.	Reported Residence, Jan. 1, 1940. Street and Number.

Cornell Street—Continued

Page.	Letter.	Full Name.	Residence, Jan. 1, 1941.	Occupation.	Supposed Age.	Reported Residence, Jan. 1, 1940. Street and Number.
	W	Carlson Arthur	52	machinist	44	here
	X	Connor Blanche M—†	53	housewife	42	88 Hemman
	Y	Connor Edward J	53	electrician	43	88 "
	Z	McDermott Ethel M—†	53	housewife	28	here
1117						
	A	McDermott Paul D	53	photographer	28	"
	B	Smith John J	53	foreman	26	"
	C	Smith Mary J—†	53	housewife	49	"
	D	Carmichael Christina—†	57	"	45	132 Greenfield rd
	E	Carmichael James A	57	operator	50	132 "
	F	Dindio Antonio	60	pressman	50	here
	G	Dindio Antonio, jr	60	student	21	"
	H	Dindio Maria—†	60	housewife	48	"
	K	Dindio Rosario	60	mechanic	22	"
	L	DeVasto Mary—†	62	housewife	29	"
	M	DeVasto Raymond	62	meatcutter	33	"
	N	Spear Emma G—†	68	housewife	53	"
	O	Spear Frank H	68	inspector	55	"
	P	Haller John	72	retired	67	"
	R	Haller Louise K—†	72	clerk	46	"
	S	*Lentini Biaggio	82	mechanic	48	"
	T	*Lentini Catherine—†	82	housewife	49	"
	U	Lentini Earl	82	clerk	25	"
	V	*Fetters Peter	83	laborer	55	"
	W	*Johnson Martha—†	83	housewife	56	"
	X	Johnson Robert	83	machinist	22	"
	Y	Johnson Rudolph	83	"	28	"
	Z	Dillon John S	83	salesman	37	"
1118						
	A	Dillon Lucille M—†	83	housewife	37	"
	B	Renner John	83	carpenter	61	"
	C	Kretchman Johanna—†	86	housewife	50	"
	D	Kretchman Otto	86	shipper	49	"
	E	Leadbetter Anna T—†	86	operator	49	"
	F	Lavery Francis W	89	electrician	31	"
	G	Lavery Veronica J—†	89	housewife	27	"
	H	Caruso Grace—†	89	"	47	"
	K	Caruso Joseph	89	barber	53	"
	L	Caruso Joseph J	89	engineer	25	"
	M	Caruso Nancy C—†	89	secretary	24	"
	N	Susi James A	90	contractor	42	"

Page	Letter	Full Name.	Residence, Jan. 1, 1941.	Occupation.	Supposed Age.	Reported Residence, Jan. 1, 1940. Street and Number.

Cornell Street—Continued

Page	Letter	Full Name.	Residence, Jan. 1, 1941.	Occupation.	Supposed Age.	Reported Residence, Jan. 1, 1940. Street and Number.
	O	Susi Rose †	90	housewife	34	here
	P	Gallinetti Annibale	90	waiter	39	"
	R	Gallinetti Theresa †	90	housewife	32	"
	S	Mercantonio Antonetta †	91	"	50	"
	T	Mercantonio James V	91	bartender	50	"
	U	Sinopoli Leo	91	agent	28	"
	V	Sinopoli Rose †	91	housewife	28	"
	W	Eagan Margaret T †	91	"	38	"
	X	Eagan Raymond S	91	printer	44	"
	Y	Mooney George A	91	tinsmith	71	"
	Z	Mooney John P	91	clerk	36	"
1119						
	A	Mooney Theresa †	91	housewife	70	"
	B	Weider Charles	92	carpenter	45	"
	C	Weider Elizabeth †	92	housewife	43	"
	D	Grace Lawrence	92	chauffeur	30	266 Centre
	E	Grace Ruth †	92	housewife	23	266 "
	F	Fanning Anna M †	93	"	30	here
	G	Fanning Robert W	93	clerk	32	"
	H	DeSisto Eleanor M †	93	housewife	33	"
	K	DeSisto James J	93	contractor	34	"
	L	Galvin Clara A †	94	housewife	21	2 Clare av
	M	Galvin Robert F	94	clerk	24	2 "
	N	Demling Elizabeth †	95	at home	73	here
	O	Nickerson Bessie †	95	housewife	47	"
	P	Nickerson Earl	95	clerk	25	"
	R	Maxwell Elizabeth †	95	housewife	50	"
	S	Maxwell Joseph M	95	laborer	52	"
	T	Maxwell Mildred R †	95	stenographer	21	"
	U	Bridges Henry A	98	carpenter	28	Cohasset
	V	Costello Jeremiah F	98	chauffeur	39	here
	W	Costello Mary H †	98	housewife	38	"
	X	Taylor Joseph S	100	laborer	36	"
	Y	McDermott Cecelia A †	102	secretary	31	"
	Z	McDermott Frances C †	102	artist	35	"
1120						
	A	McDermott Mary C †	102	stenographer	36	"
	B	Mahoney Alice H †	103	housewife	28	688½ E Fifth
	C	Mahoney Robert H	103	operator	26	Sharon
	D	Andersen Catherine †	105	housewife	37	here
	E	Andersen Einar B	105	letter carrier	37	"

Page.	Letter.	FULL NAME.	Residence, Jan. 1, 1941.	Occupation.	Supposed Age.	Reported Residence, Jan. 1, 1940. Street and Number.

Cornell Street—Continued

Page.	Letter.	FULL NAME.	Residence, Jan. 1, 1941.	Occupation.	Supposed Age.	Reported Residence, Jan. 1, 1940. Street and Number.
	F	Sheehy Elizabeth H—†	106	housewife	39	here
	G	Sheehy John J	106	custodian	56	"
	H	Sheehy Joseph J	106	stagehand	39	"
	K	*Balukonis Ann—†	106	clerk	21	"
	L	*Balukonis Eva—†	106	housewife	47	"
	M	*Yocos Joseph	106	meatcutter	48	"
	N	Yocos Joseph W	106	laborer	23	"
	O	Weed Louis	rear 108	electrician	25	183 Cornell
	P	Weed Mary—†	" 108	housewife	23	Quincy
	R	Hulbig Mildred G—†	" 108	"	21	here
	S	Hulbig William J	" 108	realtor	22	"
	T	*Salonen Charles A	109	carpenter	43	"
	U	*Salonen Elvi S—†	109	housewife	43	"
	V	*Skenderian George	109	shoemaker	65	Watertown
	W	Skenderian Joseph	109	bookkeeper	34	"
	X	Skenderian Josephine—†	109	housewife	28	"
	Y	Frey Edward G	110	letter carrier	32	62 Hemman
	Z	*Frey Hilda L—†	110	housewife	31	62 "
1121						
	A	Anderson Anton	110	laborer	67	here
	B	Anderson Elmer A	110	clerk	32	"
	C	Anderson Karen E—†	110	housewife	64	"
	D	Fleet Margaret—†	114	nurse	34	69 Paul Gore
	E	Paley Alexander J	114	machinist	25	69 "
	F	Paley Alice—†	114	clerk	28	69 "
	G	Paley Alice A—†	114	housewife	64	69 "
	H	Paley Mary D—†	114	operator	36	69 "
	K	Paley Percy J	114	clerk	24	69 "
	L	Paley Ruth—†	114	operator	30	69 "
	M	Holzman Elizabeth L—†	115	housewife	32	83 Aldrich
	N	Holzman Paul J	115	manager	31	83 "
	O	Holzman William H	115	U S A	21	here
	P	Mutch James R	115	mason	48	"
	R	Mutch Violet H—†	115	housewife	45	"
	S	St Laurant Bessie—†	117	housekeeper	65	"
	T	Fisher Dorothy T—†	118	stenographer	26	"
	U	Fisher Frederick A	118	steamfitter	56	"
	V	Fisher Helen L—†	118	nurse	23	"
	W	Fisher Leonora G—†	118	housewife	55	"
	X	Fisher Mildred P—†	118	nurse	21	"
	Y	Fisher Vincent C	118	operator	29	"

1122

Cornell Street Continued

Page	Letter	Full Name	Residence Jan. 1 1941	Occupation	Supposed Age	Reported Residence Jan. 1 1940 Street and Number
1122	A	Seidel Erwin	119	laborer	27	here
	B	Seidel Wilhelmina A †	119	housewife	69	"
	C	Miller John	122	painter	55	"
	D	Miller Lena L †	122	housewife	48	"
	E	Stevens Edward R	124	chauffeur	34	"
	F	Stevens Jeanette M †	124	housewife	29	"
	G	Fegan Chester A	125	janitor	47	"
	H	Fegan Elizabeth L †	125	housewife	44	"
	K	McGrath Cornelius	127	watchman	73	"
	L	McGrath Cornelius F	127	chauffeur	42	"
	M	McGrath Elizabeth M †	127	housewife	42	"
	N	Clark Charles H	128	inspector	40	"
	O	Clark Ethel S †	128	housewife	37	"
	P	Clark Irene M †	128	operator	46	"
	R	Craig Jennie †	128	at home	69	"
	S	*Robinson Mildred †	128	operator	22	"
	U	Adams George	130	research worker	36	"
	V	Adams George J	130	woodcarver	70	"
	W	Adams Johanna †	130	housewife	60	"
	X	Adams Louise M †	130	countergirl	32	"
	Y	Knibb Clarence E	130	floorman	42	22 Cumberland
	Z	Knibb Julia M †	130	housewife	36	22 "
1123	A	Bracy Herbert I	130	attendant	47	73 Bradwood
	B	Bracy May C †	130	housekeeper	57	73 "
	D	*Biehler Louise †	133	housewife	36	here
	E	*Sillaber Anna †	133	at home	71	"
	F	Selby Nora A †	133	housewife	42	"
	G	Selby Paul N	133	shipper	40	"
	H	Holmes William	137	machinist	44	"
	K	Holmes William B	137	clerk	21	"
	L	Desautelle Edith †	137	housewife	58	"
	M	Desautelle Joseph T	137	mortician	64	"
	N	Groh George M	141	attorney	36	"
	O	Groh Rosalie M †	141	housewife	36	"
	P	McLeod Alice C †	148	"	38	"
	R	McLeod Douglas	148	policeman	45	"
	S	Carlson Helen †	152	housewife	29	"
	T	Poggie Angeline †	152	"	38	"
	U	*Poggie Fred	152	salesman	43	"

Page.	Letter.	Full Name.	Residence, Jan. 1, 1941.	Occupation.	Supposed Age.	Reported Residence, Jan. 1, 1940. Street and Number.

Cornell Street—Continued

Page.	Letter.	Full Name.	Residence, Jan. 1, 1941.	Occupation.	Supposed Age.	Reported Residence, Jan. 1, 1940. Street and Number.
	V	DeChristoforo Carmella—†	152	boxmaker	32	here
	W	DeChristoforo John	152	laborer	65	"
	X*	DeChristoforo Julia—†	152	housewife	65	"
	Y	Ordile Anthony	162	barber	23	"
	Z	Ordile John	162	"	53	"
1124						
	A	Ordile Patrina—†	162	housewife	47	"
	B	Pessa Marie—†	164	housekeeper	42	"
	C	Bevilacqua Celestino	166	contractor	49	"
	D	Bevilacqua James	166	chauffeur	20	"
	E	Bevilacqua John	166	"	23	"
	F*	Bevilacqua Mary—†	166	housewife	45	"
	G	Doherty Mary A—†	168	at home	66	18 Weld Hill
	H	Lynch Daniel J	168	chauffeur	39	18 "
	K	Lynch Margaret A—†	168	housewife	41	18 "
	L	Tradd Alexander C	174	operator	34	here
	M	Tradd Isabelle—†	174	housewife	23	"
	N	Hibbard Caroline—†	174	"	50	"
	O	Hibbard James	174	mechanic	25	"
	P	Hibbard William	174	chef	53	"
	R	Hibbard William, jr	174	printer	23	"
	S	Waff Dorothy H—†	178	housewife	37	"
	T	Waff William H	178	photographer	45	"
	U	Shirar Margaret K—†	178	housewife	45	"
	V	Shirar William	178	policeman	47	"
	W	Riley Emily J—†	184	housewife	30	Quincy
	X	Riley Joseph J	184	machinist	38	"
	Y	Crowley Alice M—†	184	housewife	26	255 Chestnut av
	Z	Crowley Thomas F	184	clerk	28	255 "
1125						
	A	Murphy Edward F	188	"	35	here
	B	Murphy Johanna A—†	188	housewife	32	"
	C	McIntyre Gladys—†	188	housekeeper	36	"
	D	McIntyre Mary J—†	188	at home	76	"
	E	Boyle Helen—†	190	housewife	30	38 Dalrymple
	F	Boyle Thomas	190	policeman	31	38 "
	G*	Cahill John	190	janitor	23	38 "
	H	Richmond Charles H	190	carpenter	51	here
	K	Richmond Katherine—†	190	housewife	49	"
	L	Lenzi Alfred	194	laborer	28	"

Page	Letter	Full Name	Residence, Jan. 1, 1941	Occupation	Supposed Age	Reported Residence, Jan. 1, 1940. Street and Number

Cornell Street—Continued

Page	Letter	Full Name	Residence, Jan. 1, 1941	Occupation	Supposed Age	Reported Residence, Jan. 1, 1940. Street and Number
	M	Lenzi Caroline—†	194	housewife	64	here
	N	Lenzi Gaetano	194	cook	65	"
	O	DeRiggi Peter	196	merchant	50	"
	P	*DeRiggi Susan—†	196	housewife	45	"
	R	Zerrien Edmund	198	welder	27	"
	S	Zerrien Gilda—†	198	housewife	24	"
	T	Garcia Felicia—†	198	"	32	Rhode Island
	U	Garcia Joseph L	198	engineer	40	"
	V	Brambilla Eva—†	202	housewife	30	here
	W	Brambilla Mario	202	merchant	35	"
	X	Fasciano James	204	laborer	57	"
	Y	*Fasciano Providence—†	204	housewife	52	"

Ethel Street

Page	Letter	Full Name	Residence, Jan. 1, 1941	Occupation	Supposed Age	Reported Residence, Jan. 1, 1940. Street and Number
	Z	Bauch Emilie—†	1	bookkeeper	62	here
1126						
	A	Bauch Emma L—†	1	housewife	66	"
	B	Bauch Marie A—†	1	stenographer	64	"
	C	Bauch Robert E	1	machinist	68	"
	D	O'Neil Mary A—†	2	housewife	57	"
	E	O'Neil Patrick J	2	retired	63	"
	F	Welch Ellen J—†	2	housewife	60	"
	G	Welch Mary D—†	2	clerk	25	"
	H	Jordan Catherine V—†	4	housewife	74	"
	K	Jordan Leverett H	4	retired	78	"
	L	Keating Ethel M—†	4	housewife	48	"
	M	Keating William H	4	signalman	48	"
	N	Keating William J	5	photographer	22	"
	O	Ungroska Bertha A—†	5	nurse	70	"
	P	Moran Anna—†	6	housekeeper	58	"
	R	Welch Ethel M—†	6	housewife	63	"
	S	Welch Michael J	6	retired	66	"
	T	Welch William L	6	laborer	24	"
	U	Nolan George W	8	"	20	"
	V	Schultz Herbert E	8	policeman	49	"
	W	Schultz Herbert F	8	student	21	"
	X	Schultz Ruth D—†	8	housewife	45	"
	Y	Shea Mary L—†	8	stenographer	43	94 Florida
	Z	Gruseck Anton	10	barber	61	here

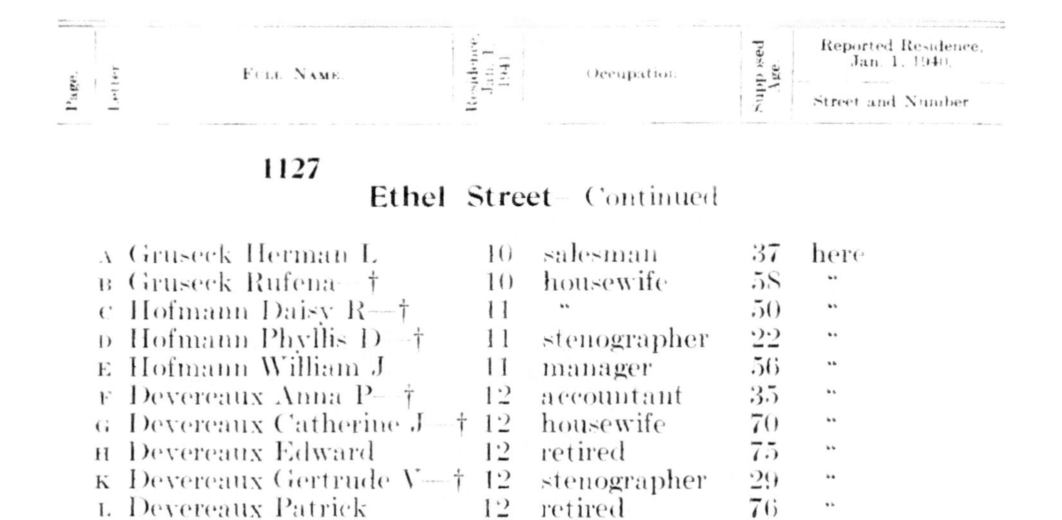

Page	Letter	Full Name	Residence, Jan. 1, 1941	Occupation	Supposed Age	Reported Residence, Jan. 1, 1940. Street and Number

1127
Ethel Street—Continued

Page	Letter	Full Name	Residence, Jan. 1, 1941	Occupation	Supposed Age	Reported Residence, Jan. 1, 1940. Street and Number
1127	A	Gruseck Herman L	10	salesman	37	here
	B	Gruseck Rufena—†	10	housewife	58	"
	C	Hofmann Daisy R—†	11	"	50	"
	D	Hofmann Phyllis D—†	11	stenographer	22	"
	E	Hofmann William J	11	manager	56	"
	F	Devereaux Anna P—†	12	accountant	35	"
	G	Devereaux Catherine J—†	12	housewife	70	"
	H	Devereaux Edward	12	retired	75	"
	K	Devereaux Gertrude V—†	12	stenographer	29	"
	L	Devereaux Patrick	12	retired	76	"
	M	Jones Catherine J—†	12	housewife	36	"
	N	Jones Douglas R	12	welder	39	"
	O	Baker Harry S	16	draftsman	32	"
	P	Doherty James	16	retired	68	"
	R	Doherty Josephine F—†	16	housewife	61	"
	S	Vey Charles J	17	roofer	41	73 Glendower
	T	Vey Elizabeth—†	17	housewife	35	73 "
	U	Schofield James B	17	artist	40	here
	V	Schofield Mary C—†	17	housewife	38	"
	W	Chartrand Elinor W—†	18	"	28	"
	X	Chartrand Gerard S	18	machinist	30	"
	Y	Cooper Hattie E—†	18	housewife	75	"
	Z	Waterman Charlotte—†	18	secretary	26	"
1128	A	Waterman Charles A	18	salesman	60	"
	B	Waterman Gertrude—†	18	housewife	55	"
	C	MacCuspie Marjorie W—†	19	"	31	"
	D	MacCuspie Norman E	19	chemist	34	"
	E	Johnson Albert G	19	engineer	38	"
	F	Johnson Hilda M—†	19	housewife	33	"
	G	Peluso Benjamin	23	retired	54	"
	H	Peluso Mary—†	23	housewife	50	"
	K	Gerardi Bertina R—†	23	"	39	"
	L	Gerardi Gennaro V	23	musician	46	"

Glendower Road

Page	Letter	Full Name	Residence, Jan. 1, 1941	Occupation	Supposed Age	Reported Residence, Jan. 1, 1940. Street and Number
	M	Kenney Charles C	12	B F D	40	12 Blackwood
	N	Kenney Marie F—†	12	housewife	35	12 "
	O	Sekore Anna—†	16	clerk	21	here

Page	Letter	Full Name	Residence, Jan. 1, 1941	Occupation	Supposed Age	Reported Residence, Jan. 1, 1940. Street and Number

Glendower Road (Continued)

Page	Letter	Full Name	Residence, Jan. 1, 1941	Occupation	Supposed Age	Reported Residence, Jan. 1, 1940. Street and Number
	P	Sekore Catherine †	16	clerk	25	here
	R	*Sekore Pauline †	16	housewife	43	"
	S	Kennedy Agnes †	20	"	39	"
	T	Kennedy Edward J	20	operator	60	"
	U	Shaughnessy Mary E †	20	at home	33	"
	V	Shaughnessy Veronica M †	20	"	32	"
	W	Jackson Gladys E †	21	housewife	34	"
	X	Jackson Roy W	21	tender	41	"
	Y	Spiller Dorothy †	21	clerk	24	"
	Z	Eichwald Herbert M	23	chauffeur	30	"
1129						
	A	Eichwald Margaret A †	23	housewife	30	"
	B	Murray John J	25	operator	51	"
	C	Murray John J, jr	25	clerk	23	"
	D	Murray Mary A †	25	housewife	45	"
	E	Blanchard Arthur S	27	chauffeur	32	524 [illegible]
	F	Blanchard Catherine T †	27	housewife	32	524 "
	G	Topping Anna †	27	"	63	133 Cornell
	H	Topping Richard	27	clerk	24	133 "
	K	Bowley Etta M †	29	housewife	63	here
	L	Bowley William A	29	foreman	64	"
	M	Lafon George L	29	salesman	40	California
	N	Lafon Lillian C †	29	housewife	36	"
	O	Casey Hazel J †	31	"	33	here
	P	Casey Henry M	31	clerk	42	"
	R	Hamilton Anna R †	33	housewife	38	"
	S	Hamilton Henry H	33	tester	42	"
	T	Johnson Augusta †	35	housewife	60	"
	U	Johnson Gustave	35	bookkeeper	65	"
	V	DeCristoforo Pasquale	38	contractor	44	"
	W	*DeCristoforo Pasqualina †	38	housewife	47	"
	X	Eibye Carl	39	machinist	60	"
	Y	Eibye Emma F †	39	housewife	51	"
	Z	Eibye Helen †	39	hairdresser	25	"
1130						
	A	Landers John H	41	supervisor	55	"
	B	Landers Margaret †	41	housewife	45	"
	C	Fitzgerald Thomas J	44	engineer	60	"
	D	Fitzgerald William P	44	chauffeur	52	"
	E	Burke Joseph V	45	electrician	48	"
	F	Burke Winifred E †	45	housewife	45	"

Page.	Letter.	Full Name.	Residence, Jan. 1, 1941	Occupation.	Supposed Age.	Reported Residence, Jan. 1, 1940. Street and Number.

Glendower Road Continued

Page.	Letter.	Full Name.	Residence, Jan. 1, 1941	Occupation.	Supposed Age.	Reported Residence, Jan. 1, 1940. Street and Number.
	G	Chisholm Catherine C †	45	housewife	44	here
	H	Chisholm John J	45	engraver	45	"
	K	Gray Anna E †	48	housewife	44	"
	L	Gray Bernard T	48	policeman	42	"
	M	Coar Christopher	48	lineman	49	"
	N	Coar Ellen †	48	housewife	85	"
	O	Coar Ernest	48	repairman	36	"
	P	Coar Joseph P	48	carpenter	46	"
	R	Coar William J	48	"	51	"
	S	*Maloof Alexander	49	manager	50	"
	T	Shayeb Joseph	49	retired	57	"
	U	*Shayeb Kabra—†	49	housewife	49	"
	V	Meissner Dorothy E—†	52	"	25	Newton
	W	Meissner Herbert N	52	pressman	28	248 Hunt'n av
	X	Nawrocki Helen †	52	housewife	63	here
	Y	Nawrocki Joseph	52	retired	62	"
	Z	Brenner Albert	55	bookbinder	48	"
1131						
	A	*Brenner Poldi—†	55	housewife	40	"
	B	Walkat Charles	57	retired	78	"
	C	Walkat Mary—†	57	housewife	65	"
	D	Walkat Mary L—†	57	clerk	34	"
	E	Lynch Frances D—†	60	housewife	32	"
	F	Lynch Mark H	60	contractor	38	"
	G	*Schroeder Emil	62	painter	49	"
	H	Schroeder Gerda—†	62	clerk	20	"
	K	*Schroeder Sophie—†	62	housewife	49	"
	L	Sutterlin Angelina—†	63	"	51	"
	M	Sutterlin Arnold	63	clerk	56	"
	N	Shabowski Joseph	63	chef	48	"
	O	*Shabowski Philomena—†	63	housewife	45	"
	P	Dittmar Elizabeth—†	64	"	72	"
	R	Glasheen George L	64	messenger	22	"
	S	Glasheen June E—†	64	nurse	20	"
	T	Hagelstein Edward M	65	machinist	41	"
	U	Hagelstein Theresa V—†	65	housewife	38	"
	V	Seale Estelle A †	66	"	33	"
	W	Seale Lawrence M	66	policeman	34	"
	X	Griffin Margaret E †	68	housewife	55	"
	Y	Griffin Paul E	68	student	23	"
	Z	Griffin Thomas F	68	chauffeur	58	"

Page	Letter	Full Name	Residence Jan. 1 1941	Occupation	Supposed Age	Reported Residence Jan. 1 1940 Street and Number
1132						

Glendower Road Continued

Page	Letter	Full Name	Residence Jan. 1 1941	Occupation	Supposed Age	Reported Residence Jan. 1 1940 Street and Number
	A	*Kostigan Edive —†	73	housewife	43	19 Decatur
	B	Kostigan William J	73	manager	43	19 "
	C	Kharibian Melek —†	73	housewife	32	here
	D	Kharibian Setrak	73	manager	36	"
	E	Lynch Harriet P —†	75	housewife	33	"
	F	Lynch Hugh W	75	B F D	36	"
	G	Johnson Martin J	75	"	47	4593 Wash'n
	H	Johnson Mary M —†	75	housewife	38	4593 "
	K	Magrath Catherine F—†	75	"	39	here
	L	Magrath Robert D	75	chauffeur	43	"
	M	Wilson Alexander W	76	B F D	43	"
	N	Wilson Johanna F—†	76	housewife	42	"
	O	Barry Elizabeth L —†	76	"	42	"
	P	Barry Lawrence D	76	B F D	43	"
	R	*Edwards Alfred	78	machinist	41	"
	S	Edwards Christina B—†	78	housewife	36	"
	T	Giblin Julia M —†	78	"	36	110 Knoll
	U	Giblin Paul R	78	draftsman	34	110 "
	V	Denner John	79	shipper	67	here
	W	Denner Mary —†	79	housewife	60	"
	X	Maguire Bertram A	79	machinist	39	"
	Y	Maguire Theresa —†	79	housewife	40	"
	Z	Fortier Arthur	79	clerk	37	"
1133						
	A	Fortier Rose —†	79	housewife	31	"
	B	Burns Marjorie V —†	83	at home	57	"
	C	Ridley Florence —†	83	housewife	62	"
	D	Ridley Fred	83	foreman	64	"
	E	Weider Anna L —†	86	housewife	46	"
	F	Weider Otto G	86	contractor	47	"
	K	Hakanson Axel J	89	foreman	53	"
	L	Hakanson Berthel H	89	salesman	24	"
	M	Hakanson Hilda —†	89	housewife	53	"
	N	Fisher Henrietta M —†	89	"	46	"
	O	Fisher Henry H	89	policeman	46	"
	P	Griem George	89	retired	69	"
	R	Griem Marguerite —†	89	housewife	66	"
	S	Swanson Adolf	89	polisher	43	"
	T	Swanson Harold	89	clerk	25	"
	U	Swanson Ingeborg —†	89	secretary	27	"

Page	Letter	Full Name.	Residence, Jan. 1, 1941.	Occupation.	Supposed Age.	Reported Residence, Jan. 1, 1940. Street and Number.

Glendower Road—Continued

Page	Letter	Full Name.	Residence, Jan. 1, 1941.	Occupation.	Supposed Age.	Reported Residence, Jan. 1, 1940.
	V	Swanson Karstin—†	89	housewife	50	here
	W	Densmore Frank H	92	plumber	45	"
	X	Densmore Marie A—†	92	housewife	32	"
	Y	Heald Henry	96	wireman	63	"
	Z	Heald John	96	clerk	23	"
1134						
	A	Heald Mary—†	96	housewife	61	"
	B	Lento Helen M—†	97	"	30	11 Haydn
	C	Lento Nicholas	97	machinist	30	11 "
	D	Norton Irene M—†	97	operator	21	263 Roslindale av
	E	Norton James J	97	carpenter	29	263 "
	F	Norton James S	97	machinist	56	263 "
	G	Spiegel Emma C—†	97	housewife	53	here
	H	Hatcher Louis H	97	welder	30	"
	K	Hatcher Ruth H—†	97	housewife	29	"
	L	Weider Rose M—†	rear 97	at home	43	"
	M	Weider Willibald	" 97	retired	81	"
	N	Weider Edward M	" 97	steamfitter	43	"
	O	Weider Theresa J—†	" 97	housewife	46	"
	P	Yngve Enoch R	" 97	cabinetmaker	23	"
	R	Yngve Evelyn C—†	" 97	housewife	22	"
	S	Skane Eva R—†	99	"	36	"
	T	Skane John J	99	chauffeur	41	"
	U	Lucas Alfred D	101	"	35	"
	V	Lucas Louise E—†	101	housewife	33	"
	W	Wieland Fred	101	machinist	59	"
	X	Haslam Evelyn B—†	105	housewife	32	"
	Y	Haslam Robert W	105	manager	34	"
1135						
	A	Haigh Alfred	107	engineer	54	"
	B	Haigh Laura C—†	107	at home	81	"
	C	Haigh William	107	clerk	46	"
	D	McNulty John F	107	social worker	33	"
	E	McNulty Mary V—†	107	housewife	31	"
	F	Weber Anastasia—†	109	"	41	"
	G	Weber Ernest L	109	wireman	46	"
	H	Helgren Dorothy L—†	110	stenographer	28	"
	K	Ryberg Sigrid E—†	110	housewife	62	"
	L	Fyfe John	110	clerk	30	21 Wenham
	M	Fyfe Madeline A—†	110	housewife	29	21 "
	N	Carlson Arvid K	111	manufacturer	59	here

Glendower Street Continued

Page.	Letter	Full Name	Residence, Jan. 1, 1941	Occupation	Reputed Age	Reported Residence, Jan. 1, 1940. Street and Number
	O	Carlson Ralph	111	repairman	24	here
	P	Carlson Sarah M †	111	housewife	48	"
	R	Emberg Albin	114	machinist	58	"
	S	Emberg Albin S	114	shipper	25	"
	T	Emberg Ellen C †	114	housewife	48	"
	U	Emberg Ernest S	114	machinist	61	"
	V	Clayton Bertha †	115	housewife	64	7 Grandview
	W	Clayton William	115	machinist	65	7 "
	X	Erhardt John M	115	welder	52	here
	Y	Erhardt John M, jr	115	mechanic	21	"
	Z	Erhardt Theresa †	115	housewife	48	"
1136						
	A	Chessman Marie †	118	"	62	"
	B	Chessman William J	118	steamfitter	63	"
	C	Ryan Ann T †	119	housewife	71	"
	D	Ryan Lawrence W	119	clerk	34	"
	E	Ryan William J	119	decorator	67	"
	F	Gahn Arthur	119	shipper	28	"
	G	*Gahn Ella †	119	housewife	42	"
	H	Gahn John	119	baker	55	"
	K	Blank August	119	shipper	53	"
	L	Blank Emma C †	119	housewife	50	"
	M	Kreutel Bernice E †	121	operator	25	"
	N	Kreutel Martha A †	121	housewife	64	"
	O	Thalin Hilda M †	121	waitress	39	"
	P	LeShane Albert A	121	machinist	45	"
	R	LeShane Alma H †	121	housewife	41	"
	S	Connelly Bridget A †	121	"	50	"
	T	Connelly John T	121	guard	61	"
	U	*Ward Mary †	121	maid	30	Brookline
	V	Dansrow Frank	123	mechanic	48	here
	W	Dansrow Hilda †	123	housewife	43	"
	X	Lee Gertrude A †	123	"	40	"
	Y	Lee William B	123	policeman	47	"
	Z	Meisel Anna †	123	housewife	69	"
1137						
	A	Meisel George	123	retired	78	"
	B	Arzomanian Asdour	123	photographer	52	"
	C	Arzomanian Zumohe †	123	housewife	43	"
	D	Devlin Anthony	124	shipper	66	"
	E	Devlin Katherine †	124	stenographer	30	"

Page.	Letter	FULL NAME.	Residence, Jan. 1, 1941.	Occupation.	Supposed Age.	Reported Residence, Jan. 1, 1940. Street and Number.

Glendower Road—Continued

Page.	Letter	FULL NAME.	Residence, Jan. 1, 1941.	Occupation.	Supposed Age.	Reported Residence, Jan. 1, 1940. Street and Number.
	F	Devlin Marcella—†	124	stenographer	20	here
	G*	Devlin Mary—†	124	housewife	58	"
	H	Doherty Charles F	124	ironworker	31	"
	K	Doherty Mary F—†	124	housewife	27	"

Granada Avenue

Page.	Letter	FULL NAME.	Residence, Jan. 1, 1941.	Occupation.	Supposed Age.	Reported Residence, Jan. 1, 1940. Street and Number.
	L	Carlson Carl A	5	retired	74	here
	M	Carlson Clara L—†	5	housewife	64	"
	P	Pierce John J	6	retired	70	"
	N	Pierce Margaret V—†	6	housewife	67	"
	O	Pierce Marguerite V—†	6	teacher	35	"
	R	Guilderson Hugh	7	roofer	66	"
	T	Doyle Mary F—†	10	housewife	65	"
	U	Doyle William	10	toolmaker	70	"
	V	Vasil Aldona—†	11	housewife	47	"
	W	Vasil George C	11	chauffeur	23	"
	X	Vasil Roman J	11	broker	53	"
	Y	VanHam Andrew	14	retired	71	"
	Z	VanHam Jennie—†	14	housewife	71	"
1138						
	A	VanHam Nettie—†	14	stenographer	47	"
	B	Derr Clarence M	16	clerk	56	"
	C	Derr Ida E—†	16	housewife	56	"
	D	Garrabrant Elizabeth M—†	16	secretary	27	"
	E	Mahoney Alice H—†	17	housewife	32	"
	F	Mahoney James	17	truant officer	49	"
	G	Claffy Catherine T—†	18	housewife	68	"
	H	Claffy Charles G	18	printer	73	"
	K	Savage Francis J	19	installer	35	"
	L	Savage Mary M—†	19	housewife	31	"
	M	Story Gordon L	20	agent	36	"
	N	Story Marjorie W—†	20	housewife	30	"
	O	Horan Claire S—†	23	clerk	20	42 Mt Ida rd
	P	Horan Doris J—†	23	bookkeeper	24	42 "
	R	Horan Grace A—†	23	stenographer	26	42 "
	S	Horan Isabelle F—†	23	clerk	22	42 "
	T	Horan Sarah A—†	23	housewife	53	42 "

Page	Letter	Full Name	Residence Jan. 1 1941	Occupation	Age	Reported Residence Jan. 1 1941 Street and Number
		Grandview Street				
	U	Schmidt Elizabeth †	7	housewife	38	here
	V	Schmidt Harold	7	clerk	40	"
	W	*Thulender Astrid †	7	housewife	34	Sweden
	X	*Thulender Harry	7	painter	34	Everett
	Y	Uriot Anna W †	11	housewife	55	here
	Z	Uriot Fred G	11	engraver	62	"
1139						
	A	Benson Einar R	12	carpenter	35	"
	B	Benson Mildred T †	12	housewife	34	"
	C	Lucy George A	12	plasterer	34	"
	D	Lucy Pauline E †	12	housewife	34	"
	E	Garvey Helen M †	12	"	20	884 E B'way
	F	Getch Charles	12	ironworker	30	here
	G	Getch Katherine †	12	housewife	26	"
	H	Huber Amelia †	26	at home	72	"
	K	Huber Edward C	26	supervisor	53	"
	L	Huber Gertrude I †	26	housewife	59	"
	M	Gross Anna †	30	"	64	"
	N	*Swanson Alma V †	36	"	39	"
	O	Swanson Carl A	36	assembler	41	"
		Granville Street				
	P	Deichert Julius	8	clerk	54	here
	R	Walsh Frank	9	policeman	24	[illegible]
	S	Walsh Marjorie †	9	housewife	23	257 "
	T	Walsh Florence †	9	"	45	here
	U	Walsh Florence A †	9	typist	20	"
	V	Dempster Louise C †	12	housewife	43	"
	W	Dempster Walter E	12	agent	45	"
	X	Sharp Arthur F	23	clerk	38	"
	Y	Sharp Loretta G †	23	housewife	35	"
	Z	Fuller Hilda T †	23	"	35	"
1140						
	A	Fuller James W	23	metalworker	36	"
	B	Schultheis Alphonse	27	assembler	40	"
	C	Schultheis Grace E †	27	housewife	40	"
	D	Schultheis Caroline M †	27	clerk	36	"
	E	Schultheis Louise A †	27	housewife	63	"

Page	Letter	Full Name	Residence, Jan. 1, 1941	Occupation	Supposed Age	Reported Residence, Jan. 1, 1940. Street and Number.

Granville Street—Continued

Page	Letter	Full Name	Residence, Jan. 1, 1941	Occupation	Supposed Age	Reported Residence, Jan. 1, 1940
	F	Kuphal Julius E	31	clerk	40	here
	G	Kuphal Margaret L—†	31	housewife	34	"
	H	Oser Christabel—†	31	"	60	"
	K	Oser Joseph G	31	machinist	64	"
	L	Munchbach Albert W	35	farmer	45	"
	M	Munchbach Frank	35	"	48	"
	N	Munchbach Rose—†	35	housewife	67	"
	O	Munchbach Sophie—†	35	"	35	"

Hautevale Street

Page	Letter	Full Name	Residence, Jan. 1, 1941	Occupation	Supposed Age	Reported Residence, Jan. 1, 1940
	P	Steinbacher Charles, jr	19	carpenter	23	543 Beech
	R	Steinbacher Myrtle—†	19	housewife	29	242 Cornell
	S	Urbeshak John	19	retired	71	here
	T	*Urbashek Marie S—†	19	housewife	64	"
	U	Weigold Catherine—†	23	at home	79	"
	V	Weigold George J	23	decorator	57	"
	W	Weigold Mary B—†	23	housewife	55	"
	X	Deininger Caroline P—†	28	saleswoman	55	"
	Y	Reinhart Alice A—†	28	housewife	37	"
	Z	Reinhart Edward A	28	metalworker	40	"
1141						
	A	Schulz Emil	32	upholsterer	39	"
	B	Schulz Margaret—†	32	housewife	31	"
	C	*Howard Kathleen—†	32	"	21	"
	D	Howard Wallace	32	clerk	24	"
	E	Hawes Dorothy—†	34	saleswoman	28	"
	F	Ricker Ella—†	34	housewife	56	"
	G	Ricker Henry W	34	guard	62	"
	K	Vozzella Elizabeth L—†	67	housewife	38	"
	L	Vozzella Pellegrino	67	blacksmith	40	"

Hemman Street

Page	Letter	Full Name	Residence, Jan. 1, 1941	Occupation	Supposed Age	Reported Residence, Jan. 1, 1940
	M	Gaffney Timothy M	2	physician	58	here
	N	Krug Robert A	2	clerk	51	"
	O	Krug Vera G—†	2	housewife	49	"
	P	Luzio Dorothy N—†	5	stenographer	21	"
	R	Luzio Louis T	5	bricklayer	63	"
	S	Luzio Mary B—†	5	housewife	60	"
	T	Schacht Hilda—†	9	"	50	"

Page	Letter	Full Name	Residence Jan. 1 1941	Occupation	Supposed Age	Reported Residence Jan. 1, 1940. Street and Number

Hemman Street Continued

Page	Letter	Full Name	Residence	Occupation	Age	Reported Residence
	U	Schacht William	9	bookbinder	54	here
	V	Fondacaro Anita †	14	seamstress	33	"
	W	Fondacaro Lydia †	14	operator	30	"
	X	Fondacaro Vincent	14	tailor	73	"
	Y	Bachofner Gustave A	15	motorman	49	"
	Z	Bachofner Gustave E	15	clerk	22	"
1142						
	A	Bachofner Irma L †	15	housewife	43	"
	B	Anderer Henry C	18	electrician	50	70 Florence
	C	Brodbeck Bertha E †	18	housewife	66	here
	D	Dipersio Alfred	19	chauffeur	29	"
	E	Pirozzi Eugene A	19	clerk	22	"
	F	Pirozzi Matilda †	19	housewife	44	"
	G	Pirozzi William L	19	barber	56	"
	H	Susi Ernest	21	mechanic	21	"
	K	Susi Julia †	21	housewife	44	"
	L	Joyce Mary A †	22	"	34	"
	M	Joyce Thomas A	22	engineer	39	"
	N	Bernardo Joseph A	23	chauffeur	34	"
	O	Bernardo Margaret J †	23	housewife	31	"
	P	Maguire Francis F	34	painter	46	"
	R	Maguire Margaret M †	34	housewife	45	"
	T	Nagel Carl T	45	painter	42	"
	U	Nagel Josephine B †	45	housewife	41	"
	V	Barrie Catherine C †	45	"	56	9 Thatcher
	W	Barrie Peter L	45	chauffeur	27	9 "
	X	Barrie Warren M	45	machinist	22	9 "
	Y	Bath Elizabeth C †	49	housekeeper	59	159 Cornell
	Z	Kelley Catherine M †	49	housewife	38	159 "
1143						
	A	Kelley Christopher	49	inspector	38	159 "
	B	Manfre Frank	50	manager	41	here
	C	Manfre Vincenza G †	50	housewife	33	"
	G	Zappala Charles	58	barber	55	"
	H	Zappala Helen C †	58	cashier	26	"
	K	Zappala John W	58	barber	22	"
	L	Zappala Mary †	58	housewife	50	"
	M	Noyd Dorothy †	62	"	28	Arlington
	N	Noyd Edwin O	62	salesman	31	"
	O	Moberg Arvid L	62	tailor	33	17 Kimball
	P	Moberg Phyllis N †	62	housewife	21	17 "

Page.	Letter	Full Name.	Residence, Jan. 1, 1941.	Occupation.	Supposed Age.	Reported Residence, Jan. 1, 1940. Street and Number.

Hemman Street—Continued

Page.	Letter	Full Name.	Residence, Jan. 1, 1941.	Occupation.	Supposed Age.	Reported Residence, Jan. 1, 1940.
	R	Coleman Catherine H—†	62	housewife	34	here
	S	Coleman Michael J	62	porter	40	"
	U	Skudra Annie—†	70	housewife	60	"
	V	Skudra John	70	carpenter	70	"
	W	Bersin Emma—†	76	housewife	72	"
	X	Bersin Jacob J	76	painter	73	"
	Y	Krumin Amalie D—†	76	housewife	49	"
	Z	Krumin Peter B	76	printer	55	"
1144						
	A	Frame John	88	chauffeur	29	Maine
	B	Frame Margaret—†	88	housewife	30	"
	C	Manzoni Eleanor—†	88	"	30	here
	D	Manzoni Peter	88	foreman	32	"

Kittredge Street

Page.	Letter	Full Name.	Residence, Jan. 1, 1941.	Occupation.	Supposed Age.	Reported Residence, Jan. 1, 1940.
	E	Reid Bella M—†	172	bookkeeper	52	here
	F	Reid Janet—†	172	at home	82	"
	G	Robinson Albert J	172	salesman	67	"
	H	Robinson Eunice T—†	172	housewife	67	"
	K	Schirmer Adelbert F	172	physician	35	"
	L	Schirmer Eunice R—†	172	housewife	30	"
	M	Robinson Agnes M—†	176	"	43	"
	N	Robinson Dexter T	176	salesman	41	"
	O	McCarthy Anna J—†	180	housewife	31	"
	P	McCarthy James B	180	salesman	24	"
	R	Seena Adam	180	foreman	59	"
	S	Seena Arthur A	180	engraver	36	"
	T	Seena Delia D—†	180	saleswoman	23	"
	U	Seena Elizabeth—†	180	housewife	56	"
	V	Seena Ernest J	180	presser	29	"
	W	Seena Galindia E—†	180	teacher	27	"
	X	Seena Thomas E	180	clerk	25	"
	Y	Lodge Catherine R—†	188	housewife	34	"
	Z	Lodge George F	188	manager	35	"
1145						
	A	Borghols Jacob	192	carpenter	35	"
	B	Borghols Martha J—†	192	housewife	41	"
	C	Mealey Margaret H—†	196	"	38	"
	D	Mealey Patrick J	196	foreman	49	"

Page	Letter	Full Name	Residence, Jan. 1, 1941	Occupation	Supposed Age	Reported Residence, Jan. 1, 1940. Street and Number

Kittredge Street—Continued

Page	Letter	Full Name	Residence, Jan. 1, 1941	Occupation	Supposed Age	Reported Residence, Jan. 1, 1940. Street and Number
	E	Lamont Jane M †	200	cook	55	here
	F	MacMillan Anna M †	200	nurse	53	"
	G	Marshalsea Dorothy R †	200	secretary	22	"
	H	Marshalsea Mary E †	200	at home	30	"
	K	Marshalsea Sarah A †	200	housewife	49	"
	L	Marshalsea Theophilus	200	agent	55	"
	M	Nagle George F	230	lineman	39	"
	N	Nagle Sarah C †	230	housewife	30	"
	O	Morrell Betty H—†	236	typist	26	246 Cornell
	P	Morrell Frank	236	oiler	68	246 "
	R	Morrell Mary E—†	236	housewife	61	246 "
	S	Brannelly James J	236	merchant	33	here
	T	Geraghty Elizabeth M—†	236	housewife	33	"
	U	Geraghty John J	236	bartender	33	"
	V	Dewan John J, jr	240	chauffeur	34	"
	W	Dewan Mary E—†	240	housewife	33	"
	X	Navoy Anthony	240	manager	50	46 Poplar
	Y	Navoy Leocadia J—†	240	stenographer	20	Medford
	Z	Navoy Stella—†	240	housewife	40	"
1146						
	A	Wurtz Frank D	242	engineer	35	here
	B	Wurtz Janet W—†	242	housewife	34	"
	C	Farrell Helen J—†	244	"	48	"
	D	Farrell John	244	ironworker	48	"
	E	Farrell Mary F—†	244	secretary	21	"
	F	Fox Edith E—†	292	"	23	"
	G	Fox Emilie M †	292	housewife	52	"
	H	Fox Marion A †	292	secretary	21	"
	K	Fox Victor J	292	steamfitter	52	"
	L	MacLean Agnes A †	292A	housewife	63	"
	M	MacLean Frank G	292A	carpenter	66	"
	N	Carlson Margaret K †	294	housewife	40	"
	O	Carlson Phillip G	294	cutter	42	"
	P	Miley Catherine T †	294	laundress	66	"
	S	West Florence E †	297	housewife	40	"
	T	West Maurice E	297	policeman	43	"
	U	Falcone Joseph T	297	chauffeur	20	"
	V	Falcone Mabel V †	297	housewife	39	"
	W	Falcone Salvatore F	297	barber	44	"
	Y	Young Dorothy E †	298	housewife	27	"
	Z	Young George E	298	merchant	37	"

Page	Letter	Full Name	Residence, Jan. 1, 1941.	Occupation	Supposed Age.	Reported Residence, Jan. 1, 1940. Street and Number.

1147
Kittredge Street Continued

Page	Letter	Full Name	Residence, Jan. 1, 1941.	Occupation	Supposed Age.	Reported Residence, Jan. 1, 1940.
1147	A	Bonnell Donald C	305	laborer	22	here
	B	Bonnell Frances A †	305	clerk	25	"
	C	Bonnell Margaret †	305	housewife	57	"
	D	Crass Elizabeth †	305	"	68	"
	E	Crass Henry	305	retired	77	"
	F	MacKinnon Donald A	306	superintendent	29	246 Cornell
	G	MacKinnon Edith M †	306	housewife	30	246 "
	H	Ziegler Emily †	306	"	70	here
	K	Dota Angelina L †	307	laundress	34	97 Walworth
	L	Dota Mario J	307	barber	41	97 "
	M	Tate Alexina †	307	housewife	32	here
	N	Tate William J	307	lineman	40	"
	O	Bertram Frederick	309	jeweler	37	"
	P	Bertram Margaret †	309	housewife	37	"
	S	Diemer Matilda †	311	housekeeper	65	"
	T	Smith Louise †	311	housewife	51	"
	U	Viafora Angela †	314	"	32	"
	V	Viafora Richard D	314	treasurer	35	"
	W	Christy Dorothy J †	314	housewife	23	"
	X	Christy Harry	314	laborer	27	"
	1X	*Shea Michael	314	retired	75	"
	2X	*Wrenn Abbie M †	314	housewife	37	"
	Y	Wrenn Mildred †	314	"	44	"
	Z	Dellaki Hilda †	314	"	31	"
1148	A	Dellaki Joseph A	314	laborer	40	"
	C	*DiGiovanna Lucy †	314	housekeeper	53	Weymouth

Malverna Road

Page	Letter	Full Name	Residence, Jan. 1, 1941.	Occupation	Supposed Age.	Reported Residence, Jan. 1, 1940.
	E	Beigbeder Louise S †	6	housewife	61	here
	F	Beigbeder Marie E †	6	student	20	"
	G	Beigbeder Paul	6	builder	65	"
	H	Pretat William H	6	retired	80	"
	K	Crump Beatrice H †	8	teacher	29	"
	1K	Crump Loretta B †	8	stenographer	26	"
	L	Crump Norbert P	8	student	20	"
	M	Crump Thomas J	8	meatcutter	57	"
	N	Henchon Annie G †	10	housewife	53	"
	O	Henchon James D	10	special officer	57	"

Page	Letter	Full Name	Residence, Jan. 1, 1941	Occupation	Supposed Age	Reported Residence, Jan. 1, 1940. Street and Number

Malverna Road Continued

Page	Letter	Full Name	Residence, Jan. 1, 1941	Occupation	Supposed Age	Reported Residence, Jan. 1, 1940
	P	Stowers Albert E	12	retired	71	here
	R	Stowers Ernestine A †	12	housewife	71	"
	S	Bagnall Clara C †	14	housekeeper	83	"
	T	Bagnall Verna G †	14	stenographer	45	"
	U	Davidson Dorothy W †	16	housewife	26	"
	V	Davidson William J	16	accountant	28	"
	W	Hughes Anthony	16	plumber	71	"
	X	Hughes Dorothy A †	16	bookkeeper	29	"
	Y	Hughes Elizabeth A †	16	housewife	71	"
	Z	Hughes William L	16	plumber	42	"
1149						
	A	Patterson George J	16	clerk	23	"
	B	Crowe Beatrice M †	18	housekeeper	52	"
	C	Crowe William J	18	shipper	26	"
	D	Glynn John J	18	clerk	45	"
	E	Kane Mary M †	20	matron	53	"
	F	Manning Elizabeth A †	20	clerk	20	"
	G	Manning Michael F	20	retired	53	"
	H	Manning Patrick J	20	B F D	55	"
	K	Manning Sarah A †	20	housewife	54	"

Metropolitan Avenue

Page	Letter	Full Name	Residence, Jan. 1, 1941	Occupation	Supposed Age	Reported Residence, Jan. 1, 1940
	L	Sugden Elizabeth M †	101	housewife	56	here
	M	Sugden James W	101	artist	54	"
	N	Swanson Charles	103	metalworker	60	"
	O	Swanson Sarah †	103	housewife	59	"
	P	Hunter Mabel A †	111	housekeeper	68	"
	R	Muir Robert B	111	retired	40	"
	S	Muir William E	111	"	40	"
	T	Mullaney Anna †	117	housewife	41	"
	U	Mullaney Richard F	117	salesman	44	"
	V	Lykos Calliope †	121	bookkeeper	30	"
	W	*Lykos Christopher	121	merchant	68	"
	X	*Lykos Helen †	121	housewife	50	"
	Y	Lykos Minnie †	121	bookkeeper	25	"
	Z	Bieber Louis	125	plumber	63	"
1150						
	A	Bieber Sophie M †	125	saleswoman	60	"
	B	MacRitchie Agnes M †	129	housewife	45	"
	C	MacRitchie John J	129	chauffeur	49	"

Page	Letter	Full Name	Residence, Jan. 1, 1941	Occupation	Supposed Age	Reported Residence, Jan. 1, 1940. Street and Number.

Metropolitan Avenue—Continued

Page	Letter	Full Name	Residence, Jan. 1, 1941	Occupation	Supposed Age	Reported Residence, Jan. 1, 1940. Street and Number.
	D	Kiessling Elizabeth—†	129	housewife	57	here
	E	Kiessling Homer	129	architect	58	"
	F	Diettrich Albert R	133	clerk	25	"
	G	Diettrich Arthur B	133	shipper	55	"
	H	Diettrich Frederick J	133	laborer	22	"
	K	Diettrich Hazel B—†	133	clerk	31	"
	L	Diettrich Helen C—†	133	stenographer	24	"
	M	Diettrich Katherine A—†	133	at home	29	"
	N	Diettrich Katherine K—†	133	housewife	55	"
	O	Scannell Francis X	137	student	23	"
	P	Scannell Geraldine D—†	137	librarian	28	"
	R	Scannell Helen G—†	137	housewife	58	"
	S	Scannell William J	137	salesman	58	"
	T	Khouri Albert G	145	"	26	"
	U	*Khouri Esma J—†	145	housewife	47	"
	V	Khouri George J	145	merchant	52	"
	W	Khouri Selma E—†	145	saleswoman	23	"
	X	Nelson Lulu M—†	149	librarian	24	"
	Y	Nelson Ulrica A—†	149	housewife	60	"
	Z	Nelson Victor E	149	cutter	61	"
1151						
	A	Carroll Henry L	149	clerk	33	"
	B	Carroll Katherine J—†	149	housewife	28	"
	C	Crump Charles	153	salesman	23	"
	D	Crump George V	153	clerk	26	"
	E	Crump John J	153	merchant	34	"
	F	Bellows Florence L—†	157	housewife	44	"
	G	Bellows Fred E	157	clerk	44	"
	H	Bellows Irma M—†	157	accountant	22	"
	K	Sink Phillip J	157	shipper	41	"
	L	Murphy Albina B—†	161	housewife	41	"
	M	Murphy Louise M—†	161	nurse	23	"
	N	Murphy Timothy C	161	secretary	60	"
	O	Garland Clarence H	165	draftsman	49	"
	P	Garland Florence M—†	165	housewife	44	"
	R	Walsh Alice E—†	165	housekeeper	59	"
	S	Slone Dorothy E—†	169	housewife	26	"
	T	Slone Gilbert E	169	photographer	24	"
	U	Goode Frances C—†	169	secretary	25	"
	V	Goode James J	169	watchman	64	"
	W	Goode Mary E—†	169	housewife	62	"

Metropolitan Avenue Continued

Page	Letter	Full Name	Residence, Jan. 1, 1941	Occupation	Reported Age	Reported Residence, Jan. 1, 1940. Street and Number
	X	Goode Patricia †	169	clerk	21	here
	Y	Goode Thomas	169	"	29	"
	Z	Barry Alice E †	173	housewife	51	"
1152						
	A	Barry Daniel A	173	compositor	53	"
	B	Barry Daniel A	173	student	23	"
	C	Barry Lawrence F	173	salesman	24	"
	D	Barry William J	173	laborer	51	"
	E	Zepp Anita D †	177	teacher	23	"
	F	Zepp Emil W	177	"	56	"
	G	Zepp Josephine †	177	housewife	57	"
	H	Galvin John	181	clerk	46	"
	K	Galvin Margaret †	181	housewife	45	"
	L	Gullanti Frank	181	waiter	52	"
	M	Gullanti Mary †	181	housewife	49	"
	N	Boettcher Anna B †	185	"	40	"
	O	Boettcher Eliza †	185	at home	75	"
	P	Boettcher Ernest E	185	compositor	51	"
	R	Goldenbaum Florence B †	185	secretary	46	"
	S	Stillings Arthur A	189	foreman	39	50 Linwood
	T	Stillings Muriel D †	189	housewife	35	50 "
	U	McLaughlin Catherine A †	189	"	72	here
	V	McLaughlin Frances M †	189	cashier	34	"
	W	McLaughlin Mary M †	189	secretary	36	"
	X	McLaughlin Mildred C †	189	bookkeeper	32	"
	Y	Frost Alfred J	189	machinist	32	"
	Z	Frost Bertha I †	189	housewife	32	"
1153						
	A	Dunn Edward J	221	editor	60	"
	B	Dunn Sarah M †	221	housewife	60	"
	C	Dunn Sheila C †	221	student	22	"
	D	Natale Hilda A †	229	housewife	32	3318 Wash'n
	E	Natale Joseph F	229	electrician	29	3318 "
	F	Towers Selendy M †	229	housewife	32	here
	G	Towers William L	229	chauffeur	32	"
	H	Blenus Janet A †	233	housewife	58	"
	K	Blenus Stanley C	233	guard	69	"
	L	Handel Carl H	233	brewer	37	"
	M	Handel Esther K †	233	housewife	34	"
	N	Payne Raymond A	243	clerk	35	11 Havana
	O	Payne Wilda †	243	housewife	32	11 "

Page	Letter	Full Name.	Residence, Jan. 1, 1941.	Occupation.	Supposed Age.	Reported Residence, Jan. 1, 1940. Street and Number.

Metropolitan Avenue—Continued

	P	Ferguson Harry	243	student	22	here
	R	Ferguson Maude—†	243	housewife	46	"
	S	Ferguson William E	243	carpenter	46	"
	T	Barry Daisy L—†	253	housewife	55	"
	U	Barry Walter J	253	engraver	57	"
	V	Richenberg Gertrude C—†	257	housewife	43	"
	W	Richenberg Phillip	257	attorney	46	"
	X	McGrath John M	261	salesman	50	"
	Y	McGrath Margaret T—†	261	at home	35	"
	Z	McGrath Nora A—†	261	housewife	74	"

1154 Metropolitan Terrace

	A	Gould Harry W	3	carpenter	54	here
	B	Gould Lillian M—†	3	housewife	48	"
	C	Gould Ralph E	3	clerk	23	"
	D	Cerello James	4	painter	51	"
	E	Cerello Margaret M—†	4	housewife	42	"
	F	Schmitt Helen L—†	5	clerk	29	"
	G	Schmitt Henry J	5	"	54	"
	H	Schmitt Louise C—†	5	housewife	53	"
	K	Schmitt Marguerite E—†	5	clerk	22	"
	L	Piranian Alexander	6	laborer	70	"
	M	Piranian Dorothy—†	6	housewife	60	"
	N	Piranian Penron—†	6	"	36	"
	O	Piranian Richard	6	merchant	41	"
	P	Hovey Thomas E	7	contractor	77	"
	R	Borghols Jacob	8	carpenter	60	"
	S	Borghols Wilhelmina C—†	8	housewife	42	"

Poplar Street

	T	Rooney Hugh J	439	salesman	46	here
	U	Rooney Theresa M—†	439	housewife	43	"
	V	Denehy James	443	mechanic	38	"
	W	Denehy Margaret—†	443	housewife	39	"
	X	Grant Angus J	447	foreman	41	"
	Y	Grant Sarah J—†	447	housewife	43	"
	Z	Grant Mary C—†	451	housekeeper	58	"
1155						
	A	Adolph Agnes—†	455	housewife	58	"
	B	Adolph August	455	diemaker	60	"

Page	Letter	Full Name	Residence Jan. 1, 1941	Occupation	Supposed Age	Reported Residence Jan. 1, 1940 Street and Number

Poplar Street Continued

Page	Letter	Full Name	Residence Jan. 1, 1941	Occupation	Supposed Age	Reported Residence Jan. 1, 1940 Street and Number
	C	Harring George W	459	manufacturer	69	here
	D	Harring Lily P †	459	housewife	70	"
	E	Keeney Esther †	463	"	38	"
	F	Keeney Frank	463	policeman	48	"
	G	Langenfield Mary—†	467	housewife	42	"
	H	Langenfield William	467	cabinetmaker	52	"
	K	Burchill William	475	salesman	22	"
	L	Richenberg Caroline P—†	475	housewife	48	"
	M	Richenberg Opal—†	475	"	22	"
	N	Richenberg Paul J	475	merchant	51	"
	O	Richenberg Paul J, jr	475	salesman	26	"
	P	Richenberg George	485	clerk	23	475 Poplar
	R	Richenberg Mildred R—†	485	housewife	20	here
	S	Schoen Herbert O	485	foreman	41	"
	T	Schoen Rose C—†	485	housewife	40	"
	V	Benson Florence E—†	493	"	28	"
	U	Benson O Clarence	493	engineer	27	"
	W	Clausen Jans P	493	carpenter	55	"
	X	Clausen Kirsten A—†	493	housewife	49	"
	Y	Steffens Clara—†	497	decorator	64	"
	Z	Steffens Mary—†	497	"	59	"
1156						
	A	Scocozza Angela—†	519	at home	67	"
	B	Scocozza Antonette—†	519	clerk	31	"
	C	Sodano Camilla—†	519	"	22	"
	D	Sodano Madeline—†	519	housewife	46	"
	E	Sodano Santos	519	musician	47	"
	F	Grivetto Anthony	521	waiter	50	"
	G	Merlo Irene—†	521	housekeeper	63	"
	H	Stefano Carnetta—†	521	housewife	26	76 W Cedar
	K	Stefano Edward	521	waiter	30	76 "
	L	Stefano George	521	candymaker	20	76 "

Rawston Road

Page	Letter	Full Name	Residence Jan. 1, 1941	Occupation	Supposed Age	Reported Residence Jan. 1, 1940 Street and Number
	M	Henderson Caroline L—†	6	housewife	52	here
	N	Henderson Francis F	6	serviceman	25	"
	O	Henderson Lillian S—†	6	examiner	23	"
	P	Henderson Ralph M	6	foreman	52	"
	R	Luippold Henrietta M—†	9	housewife	55	"
	T	Luippold William	9	salesman	59	"
	S	Luippold William E	9	attendant	22	"

Page.	Letter.	Full Name.	Residence, Jan. 1, 1941.	Occupation.	Supposed Age.	Reported Residence, Jan. 1, 1940. Street and Number.

Rawston Road—Continued

Page.	Letter.	Full Name.	Residence, Jan. 1, 1941.	Occupation.	Supposed Age.	Reported Residence, Jan. 1, 1940. Street and Number.
	U	Roeber Alfred K	9	machinist	46	here
	V	Roeber Johanna—†	9	housewife	43	"
	W	Parker Leon A	10	manager	35	"
	X	Parker Mary A—†	10	housekeeper	63	"
	Y	Haley Nora E—†	11	"	82	"
	Z	Reidy John J	11	inspector	50	"
1157						
	A	Reidy John J, jr	11	student	23	"
	B	Reidy Margaret J—†	11	housewife	53	"
	C	Kelley Edwin J	12	accountant	46	"
	D	Kelley Frances—†	12	housewife	46	"
	E	Murphy James	12	letter carrier	50	"
	F	Fullerton Albert L	14	estimator	43	"
	G	Fullerton Marjorie D—†	14	housewife	44	"
	H	Luippold George	15	clerk	54	"
	K	Luippold Mary A—†	15	housewife	51	"
	L	Flynn Claire M—†	16	nurse	26	"
	M	Flynn Mary A—†	16	housewife	58	"
	N	Flynn Robert J	16	investigator	29	"
	O	Flynn Thomas F	16	porter	58	"
	P	Flint Alice M—†	17	at home	77	"
	R	Flint Ernest M	17	manager	58	"
	S	Flint Ida—†	17	housewife	56	"
	T	Greene Ada—†	18	housekeeper	65	"
	U	Greene Frank	18	retired	84	"
	V	Harrigan Alice M—†	20	housewife	42	"
	W	Harrigan Francis J	20	supervisor	41	"
	X	Murphy Annie—†	20	at home	71	"

Summit Street

Page.	Letter.	Full Name.	Residence, Jan. 1, 1941.	Occupation.	Supposed Age.	Reported Residence, Jan. 1, 1940. Street and Number.
	Y	Sarnie Annette D—†	12	clerk	22	here
	Z	Sarnie Antonio	12	retired	72	"
1158						
	A	Sarnie Ethel C—†	12	housewife	43	"
	B	Sarnie Mary—†	12	dressmaker	39	"
	C	Sarnie Peter	12	carpenter	47	"
	D	Sarnie George	12	tilesetter	35	"
	E	Sarnie Gladys—†	12	housewife	31	"
	F	VanDam Arie	16	chauffeur	39	"
	G	VanDam Blanche—†	16	housewife	37	"

Summit Street—Continued

Page	Letter	Full Name	Residence, Jan. 1, 1941	Occupation	Supposed Age	Reported Residence, Jan. 1, 1940. Street and Number
	H	Spognardi Nancy—†	20	saleswoman	23	here
	K	*Spognardi Ruggiero	20	carpenter	48	"
	L	VanDam Clara—†	20	housewife	21	"
	M	VanDam Matyse	20	laborer	21	16 Summit
	N	Brabazon Edward R	24	cook	24	9 Whitten
	O	Brabazon Veronica—†	24	housewife	25	9 "
	P	*Sammartino Erminia—†	24	"	48	here
	R	Sammartino Joseph	24	teacher	23	"
	S	Sammartino Lillian—†	24	student	20	"
	T	Sammartino Pasquale A	24	tailor	50	"
	U	Sammartino William	24	laborer	22	"
	W	Garmory Florence—†	26	housewife	26	1 Day
	V	Garmory Harold	26	optician	29	Somerville
	X	Franzosa Emily T—†	26	housewife	24	here
	Y	Franzosa Louis N	26	constable	27	39 Bruce
	Z	Moulton Eva C—†	26	nurse	64	here
1159						
	A	Palmer Beatrice V—†	26	housewife	38	"
	B	Palmer Charles W	26	painter	44	"
	C	Russell Alice A—†	32	housewife	72	"
	D	Russell Ethel M—†	32	secretary	43	"
	E	Russell Florence A—†	32	bookkeeper	46	"
	F	Gustavsen Carl	32	chauffeur	40	"
	G	Gustavsen Greta—†	32	housewife	35	"
	H	Winters William K	32	toolmaker	41	"
	K	Fisher Bradford T	32	engineer	24	Rhode Island
	L	Fisher Elizabeth J—†	32	housewife	23	"

Vista Street

Page	Letter	Full Name	Residence, Jan. 1, 1941	Occupation	Supposed Age	Reported Residence, Jan. 1, 1940. Street and Number
	M	Essery Gladys R—†	1	housewife	31	here
	N	*Essery W Ralph	1	salesman	31	Brookline
	O	Tennyson Theodore H	1	superintendent	63	here
	P	Mullowney Elise J—†	1	housewife	60	"
	R	Mullowney Elise M—†	1	stenographer	28	"
	S	Mullowney Henry	1	retired	65	"
	T	Mullowney Henry G	1	clerk	22	"
	U	Linton Margaret J—†	2	housewife	69	"
	V	Linton Thomas R	2	retired	67	"
	W	Driscoll Dennis J	4	clerk	47	"
	X	Driscoll Lillian F—†	4	housewife	45	"

Page	Letter	Full Name	Residence, Jan. 1, 1941	Occupation	Supposed Age	Reported Residence, Jan. 1, 1940. Street and Number.

Vista Street—Continued

Page	Letter	Full Name	Residence, Jan. 1, 1941	Occupation	Supposed Age	Reported Residence, Jan. 1, 1940. Street and Number.
	Y	Driscoll Margaret F—†	4	secretary	21	here
	Z	Barrett Anna J—†	5	housewife	55	"
1160						
	A	Barrett George T	5	teacher	57	"
	B	Roche Agnes E—†	6	housewife	44	"
	C	Roche David A, jr	6	policeman	49	"
	D	Galway Elizabeth R—†	8	housewife	52	"
	E	Galway James M	8	bookbinder	58	"
	F	Galway Murray J	8	clerk	21	"
	G	Scannell Josephine V—†	8	stenographer	42	"
	H	Scannell Mary A—†	8	clerk	46	"
	K	Bonnyeastle Grace S—†	9	housekeeper	65	"
	L	Maxey John P	9	retired	72	"
	M	Maxey Mary F—†	9	housewife	70	"
	N	Brown Chester K	10	dentist	43	"
	O	Crowley Katherine J—†	10	housewife	72	"
	P	Crowley Marion F—†	10	stenographer	35	"
	R	Alsterlund Auguste H—†	11	housewife	66	"
	S	Rowe Catherine L—†	12	"	64	"
	T	Rowe Helen B—†	12	stenographer	36	"
	U	Rowe Katherine L—†	12	secretary	38	"
	V	Rowe Lillian I—†	12	clerk	42	"
	W	Rowe Walter H	12	retired	68	"
	X	Rowe Walter H, jr	12	clerk	41	"
	Y	Teahan Katherine F—†	14	housewife	80	"
	Z	Ferrari Joseph L	16	policeman	57	"
1161						
	A	Ferrari Marion E—†	16	teacher	29	"
	B	Ferrari Mary L—†	16	housewife	57	"
	C	Fraser Daniel J	17	retired	61	"
	D	Fraser Mary A—†	17	housewife	64	"
	E	Calabro Horatio J	18	teacher	38	"
	F	Calabro Mary M—†	18	housewife	34	"
	G	Conroy Anna M—†	19	clerk	32	"
	H	Conroy Helen V—†	19	housewife	39	"
	K	Conroy Mary A—†	19	"	62	"
	L	Conroy Thomas J	19	engineer	37	"
	M	Ralph Nora H—†	19	clerk	38	"
	O	Mulligan Alice T—†	21	housewife	56	"
	P	Mulligan Thomas A	21	inspector	57	"
	R	Colpitts Mary M—†	23	housewife	64	"
	S	Colpitts Melburn W	23	buyer	66	"

Page	Letter	Full Name	Residence, Jan. 1, 1941	Occupation	Supposed Age	Reported Residence, Jan. 1, 1940. Street and Number

Washington Street

Page	Letter	Full Name	Residence, Jan. 1, 1941	Occupation	Supposed Age	Reported Residence, Jan. 1, 1940. Street and Number
	T	Marijanian Dorothy †	4464	clerk	28	here
	U	Marijanian Helen †	4464	housewife	53	"
	V	Marijanian Martin	4464	machinist	59	"
	W	Ciampa Domenic	4466	shoemaker	43	"
	X	Ciampa Jennie †	4466	housewife	29	"
	Y	Ajemian Joseph	4466	realtor	53	"
	Z*	Ajemian Maritza †	4466	housewife	47	"
1162						
	A	Rechnagel Carl	4566	retired	77	"
	C	Feist Ernest E	rear 4566	machinist	42	"
	D	Feist Florence B †	" 4566	housewife	46	"
	H	McAvoy Kevin J	" 4648	manager	28	"
	K	Sawyer Cecil H	" 4648	mechanic	42	"
	L	Sawyer Eva M †	" 4648	housewife	39	"
	M	Minnich Freda †	" 4648	"	35	"
	N	Minnich John	" 4648	mechanic	38	"
	O	Barlow William	" 4648	entertainer	20	Canada
	P	Case Marvin	" 4648	"	34	Florida
	R	Powell Albert	" 4648	manager	73	Canada
	S	Powell Marie †	" 4648	housewife	65	"
	T	Greene Belle †	" 4648	"	38	here
	U	Greene Percy	" 4648	decorator	42	"
	V	Pimental George	" 4648	machinist	24	37 Dromey av
	W	Vigneur Bessie †	" 4648	housewife	22	Waltham
	X	Vigneur Wilfred	" 4648	tree surgeon	28	"
	Y	Donato Harold	" 4648	machinist	27	Worcester
	Z	Donato Vida †	" 4648	housewife	25	"
1163						
	A	Galvin Nellie M †	4740	"	71	here

Winton Street

Page	Letter	Full Name	Residence, Jan. 1, 1941	Occupation	Supposed Age	Reported Residence, Jan. 1, 1940. Street and Number
	B	Sevenson Anna †	9	housewife	71	here
	C	Sevenson Edward	9	operator	77	"
	D	Sevenson Edward, jr	9	"	36	"
	E	Sevenson John	9	"	38	"
	F	Livingston Estella M †	9	statistician	25	"
	G	Livingston Gordon M	9	superintendent	56	"
	H	Livingston Sadie M †	9	housewife	50	"
	K	McCarthy Charles P	10	agent	37	"
	L	McCarthy Harriet A †	10	housewife	43	"
	N	Handel Herman	15	R F D	68	"

Page	Letter	Full Name	Residence Jan. 1, 1941.	Occupation	Supposed Age.	Reported Residence, Jan. 1, 1940. Street and Number.

Winton Street—Continued

Page	Letter	Full Name	Residence Jan. 1, 1941.	Occupation	Supposed Age.	Reported Residence, Jan. 1, 1940. Street and Number.
	O	Smith Charles E	15	electrician	40	393 Poplar
	P	Smith Elvira E—†	15	housewife	41	393 "
	R	Kenney John J	18	builder	73	here
	S	Kenney Mary A—†	18	housewife	70	"
	T	Ray Ruth—†	18	waitress	29	"
	U	Strain John L	22	druggist	35	"
	V	Strain Mary A—†	22	housewife	34	"
	W	Menier Rose—†	23	"	71	"
	X	Menier William	23	retired	67	"
	Y	Brandli Helen L—†	23	housewife	32	"
	Z	Brandli Henry W	23	painter	35	"
1164						
	A	Cohen Joseph D	23	letter carrier	36	"
	B	Cohen Mary—†	23	housewife	29	"
	C	Homer Joseph	26	laborer	39	"
	D	Homer Viola—†	26	housewife	38	"
	E	O'Donnell Charles	26	laborer	30	"
	F	O'Donnell Mary—†	26	housewife	31	"
	G	Walsh Ellen—†	26	at home	71	"
	H	Homer Kasper	26	retired	75	"
	K	Zweeker Bertha—†	27	housewife	72	"
	L	Zweeker Fredrick J	27	retired	78	"
	M	*Stennes Inga—†	34	housewife	45	18 Neponset av
	N	*Stennes John	34	laborer	49	18 "
	O	*Stennes John S	34	inspector	22	18 "
	P	Sund Bernard E	36	cleaner	31	43 Fenwood rd
	R	Sund Valberg L—†	36	housewife	24	43 "
	S	Olson Eric O	38	patternmaker	68	here
	T	*Olson Olga—†	38	housewife	69	"
	U	Singer Emily—†	40	"	27	1750 Centre
	V	Singer John T	40	chauffeur	33	1750 "
	W	Soderlund Edwin J	50	machinist	63	here
	X	Soderlund Elise—†	50	housewife	57	"
	Y	Soderlund Gustaf A	50	machinist	58	"

Ward 18—Precinct 12

CITY OF BOSTON

LIST OF RESIDENTS

20 YEARS OF AGE AND OVER

(NON-CITIZENS INDICATED BY ASTERISK)
(FEMALES INDICATED BY DAGGER)

AS OF

JANUARY 1, 1941

JOSEPH F. TIMILTY, *Chairman*
FREDERIC E. DOWLING, *Secretary*
WILLIAM A. MOTLEY, JR.
FRANCIS B. McKINNEY
HILDA HEDSTROM QUIRK
Listing Board.

CITY OF BOSTON PRINTING DEPARTMENT

Page.	Letter.	FULL NAME.	Residence, Jan. 1, 1941.	Occupation.	Supposed Age.	Reported Residence, Jan. 1, 1940. Street and Number.

1200 Arnold Street

Page.	Letter.	FULL NAME.	Residence, Jan. 1, 1941.	Occupation.	Supposed Age.	Reported Residence, Jan. 1, 1940.
	A	Feeney Bernard J	11	timekeeper	29	42 Dana av
	B	Feeney Catherine—†	11	factoryhand	37	42 "
	C	Feeney Mary A—†	11	at home	78	42 "
	D	Feeney Mary E—†	11	housekeeper	48	42 "
	E	Feeney Nicholas	11	laborer	56	42 "
	F	Feeney Patrick	11	retired	82	42 "
	G	Stack Nona R—†	11	housewife	44	here
	H	Stack Thomas P	11	dentist	51	"
	K	Carroll Katharine F—†	15	housekeeper	52	"
	L	McDonald Margaret E—†	15	stenographer	48	"
	M	*Benson Hilda T—†	15	housewife	57	30 Dalrymple
	N	*Benson Otto	15	painter	50	30 "
	O	Benson Theodore R	15	clerk	21	30 "
	P	Hubley Gordon J	19	"	33	7 Rock rd
	R	Hubley Minnie D—†	19	housewife	58	7 "
	S	Hubley Walter C	19	carpenter	58	1074 River
	T	Fisher Alvin H	22	chauffeur	36	here
	U	Fisher Florence V—†	22	housewife	36	"
	V	Tinkham Stanley	22	merchant	31	"
	W	*Kovatsi Demetre	24	restaurateur	24	Lexington
	X	Nika Frank	24	"	26	"
	Y	*Ward Annie—†	24	housewife	52	here
	Z	Ward Robert	24	clerk	21	"

1201 Austin Street

Page.	Letter.	FULL NAME.	Residence, Jan. 1, 1941.	Occupation.	Supposed Age.	Reported Residence, Jan. 1, 1940.
	A	Cummings Carrie C—†	5	housewife	61	here
	B	Cummings Earl F	5	clerk	65	"
	C	Danahy Anna E—†	7	teacher	42	"
	D	White Grace L—†	7	"	50	"
	E	Jepson Anna—†	7	housewife	55	"
	F	Jepson Emil M	7	machinist	56	"
	G	Nordlund Arva A	7	gearcutter	25	"
	H	Nordlund Maxine L—†	7	housewife	24	"
	K	Weddleton Doris A—†	8-10	"	32	"
	L	Weddleton Gordon W	8-10	teller	30	"
	M	Koshivos Anthony	8-10	clerk	20	"
	N	*Koshivos Helen—†	8-10	housewife	48	"
	O	Koshivos John N	8-10	clerk	56	"
	P	Koshivos Nicholas	8-10	student	24	"

Page	Letter	Full Name	Residence, Jan. 1, 1941	Occupation	Supposed Age	Reported Residence, Jan. 1, 1940. Street and Number

Austin Street Continued

Page	Letter	Full Name	Residence, Jan. 1, 1941	Occupation	Supposed Age	Reported Residence, Jan. 1, 1940. Street and Number
	R	Espinola Catherine M †	11	housewife	71	here
	S	Espinola Mary P †	11	teacher	41	"
	T	Espinola Victor M	11	retired	71	"
	V	Makar Helen †	12 14	saleswoman	23	"
	W	Zebrowski Francis E	12 14	draftsman	25	"
	X	Zebrowski Helen †	12 14	clerk	30	"
	Y	Zebrowski Stanley J	12 14	U S A	27	"
	Z	Wightman Anna †	12 14	housewife	32	"
1202						
	A	Wightman William E	12 14	salesman	37	"
	B	Jank Anna L †	13	housewife	43	"
	C	Jank Herbert W	13	superintendent	46	"
	D	Jank Herbert W, jr	13	clerk	22	"
	E	Jank Roger W	13	"	20	"
	F	Clogston Florence E †	15	housewife	55	"
	G	Clogston Mark B	15	custodian	57	"
	H	Keith Mowry W	15	chemist	27	"
	K	Stark Cecil	15	"	29	"
	L	Bain James	16	retired	69	"
	M	White Flora M †	16	accountant	48	"
	N	White Mary R †	16	operator	56	"
	O	Goodwin Alice G †	19	housewife	76	70 Child
	P	Goodwin William T	19	retired	78	70 "
	R	Brown Doris M †	19	clerk	24	here
	S	Brown Gertrude D †	19	housewife	55	"
	T	Brown H Lockwood	19	toolmaker	55	"
	U	Neelon John J, jr	21	clerk	25	16 Safford
	V	Neelon Teresa M †	21	housewife	21	16 Gordon av
	W	Griffin Isabelle N †	21	housekeeper	69	here
	X	Cassidy Charlotte S †	22	housewife	36	"
	Y	Cassidy Morton H	22	teacher	12	"
	Z	Holland Joseph E	25	retired	83	"
1203						
	A	McDermott Florence H †	25	housewife	53	"
	B	McDermott Marian H †	25	bookkeeper	27	"
	C	Murray Mildred L †	25	clerk	29	"
	D	Marsh Charles E	26	chauffeur	45	30 Lexington av
	E	Marsh Ruth E †	26	housewife	39	30 "
	G*	Zorn Bertha M †	26	"	47	here
	H	Zorn Gustave C	26	mechanic	57	"
	K	Zorn Melvin G	26	"	21	"

Page	Letter	Full Name.	Residence, Jan. 1, 1941.	Occupation.	Supposed Age.	Reported Residence, Jan. 1, 1940. Street and Number.

Austin Street—Continued

Page	Letter	Full Name.	Residence, Jan. 1, 1941.	Occupation.	Supposed Age.	Reported Residence, Jan. 1, 1940. Street and Number.
	L	Downing Viola E—†	30	housewife	33	here
	M	Downing William T	30	inspector	35	"
	N	*Wuosmaa Frank J	30	tinsmith	53	"
	O	*Wuosmaa Saimi M—†	30	housewife	52	"
	P	Leonard Alice M—†	31	"	53	"
	R	Leonard Dorothy M—†	31	waitress	22	"
	S	Leonard Michael J	31	chauffeur	54	"
	T	Leonard Mildred J	31	shoeworker	25	"
	U	Marston Alice M—†	31	housewife	60	"
	V	Marston George H	31	janitor	61	"
	W	Stevens Raymond W	32	contractor	38	"
	X	Stevens Sylvia E—†	32	housewife	37	"
	Y	Cheverie John J	32	clothcutter	36	26 Austin
	Z	Cheverie Ruth A—†	32	housewife	28	26 "
1204						
	A	Murray Joseph L	33	salesman	33	330 Hyde Park av
	B	Murray Mary G—†	33	housewife	32	330 "
	C	Hill Samuel C	33	salesman	64	here
	D	Young Charles R	33	machinist	40	"
	E	Young Sarah H—†	33	housewife	42	"
	F	Estey Willard G	36	machinist	67	"
	G	Guerin Ethel K—†	36	at home	75	"
	H	Wood Hattie C—†	36	housewife	72	"
	K	Wood Leonard A	36	coremaker	71	"
	L	*Kowalski Catherine—†	38	housewife	47	"
	M	Kowalski Joseph P	38	clerk	24	"
	N	Kowalski Leona J—†	38	student	22	"
	O	Kowalski Stasia C—†	38	clerk	27	"
	P	Kowalski William M	38	laborer	51	"
	R	Gonski Frances R—†	38	housewife	24	"
	S	Gonski Stanley T	38	machinist	32	"
	T	Herring Alexander J	39	retired	80	"
	U	Herring Annie E—†	39	housewife	80	"
	V	Seery Michael T	39	retired	66	"
	W	Wagner Edith—†	40	housewife	64	"
	X	Wagner John T	40	laborer	24	"
	Y	Langley Albert J	41	"	65	"
	Z	Langley Bessie—†	41	housewife	53	"
1205						
	A	Langley Eleanor—†	41	clerk	30	"
	B	Langley William J	41	"	25	"

Page.	Letter.	Full Name.	Residence, Jan. 1, 1941.	Occupation.	Supposed Age.	Reported Residence, Jan. 1, 1940. Street and Number.
		Austin Street Continued				
	C	Smith Margaret A †	41	housewife	38	here
	D	Smith Thomas W	41	agent	42	"
	E	Szablewicz John H	46	student	22	"
	F*	Szablewicz Josephine †	46	housewife	45	"
	G	Szablewicz Paul	46	upholsterer	48	"
	H	O'Brien Dorothy C †	46	housewife	37	"
	K	O'Brien Frederick J	46	maint'n'ce man	40	"
	L	Suprenovich Jane †	49	clerk	23	"
	M*	Suprenovich Josephine †	49	housewife	48	"
	N	Suprenovich Nicholas	49	laborer	55	"
	O	Trask Janet †	49	dressmaker	25	"
	P	Trask Rose M †	49	housewife	45	"
	R	Trask William M	49	machinist	23	"
	S	Brown Elenora †	50	housewife	46	1144 River
	T	Brown Leo J	50	mechanic	42	1144 "
	U	Borsari Alice E †	50	housewife	28	29 Readville
	V	Borsari Amedio	50	chauffeur	33	29 "
	W	Borsari Evo	50	shipper	21	29 "
	X	Brown Delmar A	50	laborer	52	29 "
	Y*	Brown Laura A †	50	housewife	57	29 "
	Z*	Rachalski Anna †	51	"	46	here
1206						
	A	Rachalski John	51	molder	48	"
	B	Rachalski Phillip	51	painter	22	"
	C	Sesko Victor	51	butcher	45	"
	D	Hurley Frederick T	51	clerk	27	"
	E	Hurley Margaret M †	51	"	27	"
	F	Hurley Timothy H	51	letter carrier	56	"
	G	Pagington John S	52	plumber	69	"
	H	Pagington Lillian †	52	housewife	65	"
	K	Loughlin Agnes L †	53	stenographer	40	"
	L	Nickerson Mary J †	53	housewife	65	"
	M	Nickerson Thomas H	53	janitor	64	"
	N	McMahon Mary A †	53	housewife	70	"
	O	McMahon Thomas F	53	retired	71	"
	P	Crompton Albert H	54	merchant	59	"
	R	Crompton Margaret E †	54	housewife	58	"
	S	Roche Martin J	54	custodian	44	"
	T	Roche Thelma M †	54	housewife	36	"
	V	Aubin Emma F †	56	"	56	"
	W	Aubin Oscar S	56	salesman	54	"

Page.	Letter.	Full Name.	Residence, Jan. 1, 1941.	Occupation.	Supposed Age.	Reported Residence, Jan. 1, 1940. Street and Number.

Austin Street—Continued

Page.	Letter.	Full Name.	Residence, Jan. 1, 1941.	Occupation.	Supposed Age.	Reported Residence, Jan. 1, 1940. Street and Number.
	X	Sullivan Margaret †	56	nurse	24	here
	Y	Ziergiebel Agnes B †	57	housewife	54	"
	Z	Ziergiebel Max B	57	machinist	63	"
1207						
	A	Ziergiebel Myrtle A—†	57	teacher	27	"
	B	Picone Joseph L	57	mechanic	36	102 Austin
	C	Picone Katherine R—†	57	housewife	30	102 "
	D	Giunti Guy	57	machinist	26	Dedham
	E	Timperi Alfredo	57	welder	53	"
	F	*Timperi Rose—†	57	housewife	52	"
	G	Russo Alma A †	58	"	45	here
	H	Russo Patrick F	58	plumber	47	"
	K	Scigliano Claire A—†	58	stenographer	21	"
	M	Benn Gordon L	59	manager	27	91 Bynner
	N	Benn Rita J †	59	housewife	24	91 "
	O	MacWhinnie Elizabeth M †	59	housekeeper	43	91 "
	P	Gregory Loretta †	59	"	61	here
	R	Russo Brunelda †	59	housewife	38	"
	S	Russo Henry	59	plumber	45	"
	T	Gregory Areline	61	laborer	41	"
	U	Gregory Jennie E—†	61	housewife	33	"
	V	Marsh Frances G—†	61	saleswoman	23	"
	W	Marsh Louis H	61	engineer	50	"
	X	Marsh Marie G †	61	housewife	44	"
	Y	Veno Daniel J	66 68	fireman	46	"
	Z	Veno Mary A †	66 68	housewife	77	"
1208						
	A	Veno Simon A	66 68	investigator	44	"
	B	Lang Eugene E	66 68	shipper	39	"
	C	Lang Irene R †	66 68	housewife	39	"
	D	Strout Bertha E †	70 72	"	47	"
	E	Strout Edwin H	70 72	electrician	57	"
	F	Conley Joseph J	70 72	painter	33	"
	G	Conley Rita M †	70 72	housewife	27	"
	H	Whitcher Ellen L †	70 72	housekeeper	59	"
	K	Donelan Anita M †	74 76	housewife	47	"
	L	Donelan William J	74 76	motorman	46	"
	M	Felekos Mary †	74 76	housewife	28	"
	N	Felekos Michael	74 76	proprietor	40	"
	O	Johnson Albert T	78 80	operator	33	"
	P	Johnson Mathilde A †	78–80	housewife	34	"

Page	Letter	Full Name	Residence, Jan. 1, 1941	Occupation	Supposed Age	Reported Residence, Jan. 1, 1940. Street and Number

Austin Street—Continued

Page	Letter	Full Name	Residence, Jan. 1, 1941	Occupation	Supposed Age	Reported Residence, Jan. 1, 1940. Street and Number
	R	Spicer George H	78–80	conductor	54	1066 Hyde Park av
	S	Spicer George W	78–80	salesman	24	1066 "
	T	Spicer Katherine V—†	78–80	housewife	51	1066 "
	U	Spicer Mary C—†	78–80	"	25	27 Harmon
	V	Palano Dominic	79	manager	42	68 E Lenox
	W	Palano Jennie—†	79	housewife	28	68 "
	X	Johanson Carol P	82–84	carpenter	34	15 Coleman
	Y	Johanson Ruth C—†	82–84	housewife	34	15 "
	Z	Olson Lillian S—†	82–84	"	23	Pennsylvania
1209						
	A	Olson Robert F	82–84	blacksmith	24	50 Prescott
	D	Nelson Albert V	102–104	machinist	40	here
	E	Nelson Grace W—†	102–104	housewife	37	"
	G	Brady Ann J—†	106–108	"	69	"
	H	Brady Elizabeth A—†	106–108	saleswoman	31	"
	K	Brady Isabelle E—†	106–108	stenographer	35	"
	L	Brady Thomas G	106–108	U S A	28	"
	M	Hull Eleanor J—†	106–108	housewife	31	"
	N	Hull Roland A	106–108	surveyor	32	"
	O	Claflin James W	110–112	engineer	29	"
	P	Claflin Margaret M—†	110–112	housewife	29	"
	R	Claflin Donald F	110–112	adjuster	24	82 Moss Hill rd
	S	Claflin Eileen P—†	110–112	housewife	21	47 Arborough rd
	V	Sarandrea Giovanna—†	118–120	"	55	here
	W	Sarandrea Nazareno	118–120	laborer	61	"
	X	McPherson Daniel A	118–120	pressman	30	"
	[1]X	McPherson Mary J—†	118–120	housewife	52	"
	Y	McPherson Peter	118–120	mechanic	55	"
	Z	Blomstrom Eleanor M—†	122	housewife	26	72 W Milton
1210						
	A	Blomstrom Gustav W	122	metalworker	31	72 "

Beaver Street

Page	Letter	Full Name	Residence, Jan. 1, 1941	Occupation	Supposed Age	Reported Residence, Jan. 1, 1940. Street and Number
	B	*Kolodko Frank V	29	weaver	49	here
	C	Kolodko Joseph	29	laborer	20	"
	D	Kolodko Theresa H—†	29	housewife	45	"
	E	Samsevich Eleanor—†	29	factoryhand	22	"
	F	Samsevich Elias	29	laborer	47	"
	G	Samsevich Mary—†	29	factoryhand	20	"
	H	*Samsevich Natalie—†	29	housewife	45	"

Page.	Letter.	Full Name.	Residence, Jan. 1, 1941.	Occupation.	Supposed Age.	Reported Residence, Jan. 1, 1940. Street and Number.

Beaver Street—Continued

Page.	Letter.	Full Name.	Residence, Jan. 1, 1941.	Occupation.	Supposed Age.	Reported Residence, Jan. 1, 1940.
	K	Iacurto Henrietta—†	30	housewife	33	here
	L	Iacurto Nicholas	30	laborer	40	"
	M	McNulty Agnes L—†	31	saleswoman	23	"
	N	McNulty Constance P—†	31	"	20	"
	O	McNulty Helen C—†	31	housewife	53	"
	P	McNulty James T	31	salesman	53	"
	R	Narciso Mary—†	35	housewife	49	"
	S	Narciso Pasquale	35	metalworker	56	"
	T	Haskell John	42	retired	81	"
	U	Haskell Sarah E—†	42	housewife	76	"
	V	Ryan Bartlett	42	laborer	21	"
	W	Haskell Benjamin R	42	electrician	38	"
	X	Haskell Helen W—†	42	housewife	34	"
	Y	Bruun Anders H	46	machinist	43	"
	Z	Hanson Edith A—†	46	housewife	49	"
1211						
	A	Hanson Robert H	46	machinist	51	"
	B	Simpson Agnes K—†	53	housewife	51	"
	C	Simpson Anna V—†	53	nurse	29	"
	D	Simpson David B, jr	53	pressman	53	"
	E	Simpson Jeanette A—†	53	clerk	24	"
	F	Frank Blanche R—†	107	manager	50	"
	G	Frank Ellsworth H	107	musician	56	"
	K	Sweeney Elwin J	115	reporter	20	"
	L	Sweeney John L	115	bricklayer	26	"
	M	Sweeney Margaret T—†	115	clerk	24	"
	N	Sweeney Mary I—†	115	housewife	64	"
	O	Sweeney Thomas F	115	tinsmith	29	"
	P	Sweeney Thomas P	115	laborer	62	"
	R	Duggan Ellen A—†	124	housekeeper	71	"
	S	Noon Edward F	132	chauffeur	43	"
	T	Noon Mary J—†	132	housewife	31	"
	U	Noon Raymond W	132	mechanic	41	"
	V	Noon Sarah J—†	132	housewife	72	"
	W	O'Keefe Catherine G—†	132	"	45	"
	X	O'Keefe Harold A	132	investigator	52	"
	Y	Boe Boleslaw S	137–139	carpenter	45	"
	Z	Boe Julia D—†	137–139	housewife	43	"
1212						
	A	Bush Chester W	137–139	student	20	"
	B	Burgess Elsie M—†	137–139	teacher	65	"

Page	Letter	Full Name	Residence, Jan. 1, 1941	Occupation	Supposed Age	Reported Residence, Jan. 1, 1940. Street and Number

Beaver Street Continued

Page	Letter	Full Name	Residence, Jan. 1, 1941	Occupation	Supposed Age	Reported Residence, Jan. 1, 1940. Street and Number
	C	Neill Edwin N	137–139	machinist	60	here
	D	Neill Helen B †	137–139	housewife	57	"
	E	Hughey Carl W	140	instruments	40	79 Sprague
	F	Hughey Mary †	140	sewer	63	79 "
	G	Hughey Mary A †	140	housewife	34	79 "
	H	Swank William F	140	contractor	52	79 "
	K	Belanger Phillip T	140	machinist	22	here
	L	Morin Alexaeena M †	140	housewife	42	"
	M	Morin Francis X	140	laborer	43	"
	N	Crowley John J	141–143	"	46	"
	O	Crowley Julia J †	141–143	housewife	46	"
	P	Burke Catherine H †	141–143	"	60	"
	R	Burke Catherine H †	141–143	nurse	29	"
	S	Burke Michael H	141–143	laborer	62	"
	T	Angelli Frank C	142	cook	39	"
	U	*Angelli Marguerite C †	142	housewife	34	"
	V	Dray Grace H †	144	housekeeper	30	18 [illegible]
	W	Hilliard Leonard P	144	salesman	27	18 "
	X	Molinari Chester J	144	chauffeur	33	here
	Y	Molinari Rebecca B †	144	housewife	33	"
1213						
	A	Branagan Martha †	148	"	47	122 Austin
	B	Branagan Walter R	148	carpenter	42	122 "
	C	Turchetta Albert	150	machinist	25	here
	D	*Turchetta Frances †	150	housewife	72	"
	E	Turchetta Francesico A	150	laborer	74	"
	F	Aliberti John	151	electrician	19	"
	G	*Aliberti Mary †	151	housewife	36	"
	H	Arcinoli Joseph	151	laborer	21	"
	K	Bondarek Adolph J	151	machinist	23	"
	L	Bondarek Albina J †	151	housewife	23	"
	M	Bondarek James J	151	machinist	29	"
	N	LeClair George A	152	steelworker	26	211 [illegible]
	O	LeClair Ruth A †	152	housewife	22	211 "
	P	Taylor Anna A †	152	"	33	here
	R	Taylor William F	152	metalworker	34	"
	S	Haskell George R	153	retired	78	"
	T	Gray Harland D	155	mechanic	55	"
	U	Gray Lillian M †	155	housewife	54	"
	V	Smith Helen O †	155	"	43	"
	W	Smith Ralph P	155	superintendent	50	"

Page	Letter	Full Name	Residence, Jan. 1, 1941.	Occupation	Supposed Age	Reported Residence, Jan. 1, 1940. Street and Number.

Beaver Street—Continued

Page	Letter	Full Name	Residence, Jan. 1, 1941.	Occupation	Supposed Age	Reported Residence, Jan. 1, 1940. Street and Number.
	X	Glowick Adolph	157	carpenter	51	here
	Y	Glowick Blanche—†	157	hairdresser	24	"
	Z*	Glowick Esla—†	157	housewife	46	"
1214						
	A	DiMarzio Americo	157	chauffeur	22	"
	B	DiMarzio Angela—†	157	housewife	46	"
	C	DiMarzio Frank	157	machinist	50	"
	D	DiMarzio Ida M—†	157	clerk	24	"
	E*	Fraioli Elizabeth—†	159	housewife	44	1092 Hyde Park av
	F	Fraioli Salvatore	159	mechanic	47	1092 "
	H	Bennett Elizabeth K—†	162	housekeeper	55	here
	K	Skelly Daniel J	162	paintmaker	68	"
	L	Skelly Daniel P	162	welder	29	"
	M	Skelly Edmund B	162	ropemaker	25	"
	N	Skelly Francis G	162	draftsman	32	"
	O	Grinnell Arthur W, jr	163	chauffeur	27	W Hanover
	P	Grinnell Sophie N—†	163	housewife	28	here
	R*	Shibley Helen—†	163	"	48	"
	S	Shibley Marion B—†	163	operator	21	"
	T	Shibley Peter	163	carpenter	52	"
	U	Shibley Peter, jr	163	"	21	"
	V	Sweeney Anna L—†	166	housewife	48	"
	W	Sweeney James H	166	clerk	58	"
	X	Sweeney Rita J—†	166	stenographer	22	"
	Y	Hatch Elmer P	167	chauffeur	37	"
	Z	Hatch Ruth H—†	167	housewife	31	"
1215						
	A	Aylward Gertrude—†	167	"	33	"
	B	Aylward Joseph N	167	laborer	42	"
	C	Budkus Henry	170	"	37	"
	D*	Budkus Stella E—†	170	housewife	40	"
	E	Graham Alice L—†	170	housekeeper	27	"

Braeburn Road

Page	Letter	Full Name	Residence, Jan. 1, 1941.	Occupation	Supposed Age	Reported Residence, Jan. 1, 1940. Street and Number.
	F	Canty Elinor—†	1	housewife	28	106 Hemenway
	G	Canty Joseph	1	attorney	42	106 "
	K	Bowe James L	5	policeman	42	7 Speedwell
	L	Bowe Mary E—†	5	housewife	40	7 "
	O	Eagan Frances M—†	11	"	37	309 Kittredge
	P	Eagan Thomas A	11	policeman	41	309 "

Page	Letter	Full Name	Residence, Jan. 1, 1941	Occupation	Supposed Age	Reported Residence, Jan. 1, 1940, Street and Number

Braeburn Road Continued

Page	Letter	Full Name	Residence, Jan. 1, 1941	Occupation	Supposed Age	Reported Residence, Jan. 1, 1940, Street and Number
	S	Suszinski Bernard E	15	policeman	38	6 Mercer
	T	Suszinski Helen I †	15	housewife	36	6 "

1216 Brainard Street

Page	Letter	Full Name	Residence, Jan. 1, 1941	Occupation	Supposed Age	Reported Residence, Jan. 1, 1940, Street and Number
1216	H	Mahoney Mary H †	9	clerk	28	here
	K	Mahoney Nellie †	9	housewife	55	"
	L	Mahoney Timothy J	9	agent	55	"
	M	Mahoney Veronica P †	9	clerk	21	"
	N	Long Alice F †	11	housewife	49	"
	O	Long Austin L	11	policeman	47	"
	P	Eichorn Edward F	12	chauffeur	26	"
	R	Eichorn Joseph H	12	foreman	61	"
	S	Eichorn Lillian M †	12	housewife	54	"
	U	Schultz Alma S †	13	governess	26	"
	V	Schultz Nellie G †	13	housewife	58	"
	W	Schultz Richard M	13	toolmaker	60	"
	X	Annis Fred H	15	operator	62	"
	Y	Annis Lillian R †	15	housewife	60	"
	Z	Bixby Agnes E †	17	"	80	"
1217	A	Feeney James F	19	operator	41	"
	B	Feeney Margaret C †	19	housewife	41	"
	C	Funk Bertha S †	19	"	42	"
	D	Funk Edna M †	19	typist	23	"
	E	Funk Edward M	19	retired	69	"
	F	Funk Lillian B †	19	housewife	21	"
	G	Funk Raymond L, jr	19	guard	24	"
	H	Funk Raymond M	19	instructor	46	"
	K	Suket Henry R	21	merchant	46	"
	M	Suket Leonore R †	21	stenographer	24	"
	L	Suket Leonore S †	21	housewife	44	"
	N	Woodworth Ernest H	23	machinist	46	"
	O	Woodworth Ernest H, jr	23	coppersmith	23	"
	P	Woodworth Gladys P †	23	housewife	47	"
	R	Woodworth Marion P †	23	clerk	21	"
	S	Davenport Elizabeth †	25	housewife	70	"
	T	Davenport Harry F	25	chauffeur	71	"
	U	Richardson John W	27	papermaker	21	"
	V	Richardson Leslie	27	mason	55	"
	W	Richardson Leslie, jr	27	papermaker	22	"

Page.	Letter.	Full Name.	Residence Jan. 1, 1941.	Occupation.	Supposed Age.	Reported Residence, Jan. 1, 1940. Street and Number.

Brainard Street—Continued

Page.	Letter.	Full Name.	Residence Jan. 1, 1941.	Occupation.	Supposed Age.	Reported Residence, Jan. 1, 1940. Street and Number.
	X	Richardson Louise F—†	27	housewife	54	here
	Y	Meas Bridget G—†	29–31	"	61	"
	Z	Meas Francis J	29–31	operator	25	"
1218						
	A	Meas Helen T—†	29–31	clerk	20	"
	B	Meas Margaret E—†	29–31	"	31	"
	C	Meas Ruth V—†	29–31	"	27	"
	D*	McEntee Alice E—†	29–31	housewife	33	48 Maple
	E	McEntee Phillip	29–31	mechanic	39	48 "
	F	Wiezel Joseph	33–35	bartender	46	here
	G	Wiezel Nellie—†	33–35	housewife	48	"
	H	Gordan Jean—†	33–35	"	22	"
	K	Gordan Thomas	33–35	watchman	22	65 Empire
	L	Noonan Mary—†	33–35	housewife	24	65 "
	M	Noonan Morris	33–35	mechanic	26	65 "
	N	Colsch Herman L	37–39	optician	40	here
	O	Colsch Josephine M—†	37–39	housewife	33	"
	P	Dinnington Christina E—†	37–39	"	43	"
	R	Dinnington Louise W—†	37–39	clerk	20	"
	S	Miller Robert	37–39	machinist	37	"

Chestnut Street

Page.	Letter.	Full Name.	Residence Jan. 1, 1941.	Occupation.	Supposed Age.	Reported Residence, Jan. 1, 1940. Street and Number.
	T	Julian Mary C—†	3	housewife	63	here
	U	Julian Robert A	3	retired	68	"
	V	Doyle Ellen G—†	3	housewife	68	"
	W	Doyle Gerard B	3	accountant	30	"
	X	Doyle James J	3	fireman	68	"
	Y	Findlen Anne P—†	3	housewife	30	Cohasset
	Z	Findlen Austin M	3	carpenter	27	Dedham
1219						
	A*	MacDonald Irene—†	8	housewife	39	45 Webster
	B*	MacDonald Roderick J	8	carpenter	44	45 "
	C	Carr Joseph T	19	manager	29	here
	D	Shea Bertha—†	19	housewife	33	"
	E	Shea Harold	19	machinist	36	"
	F	Sullivan Mary E—†	19	housekeeper	60	"
	G	Hagman Gustav A	21	metalworker	44	"
	H	Hagman Theresa N—†	21	housewife	39	"
	M	Devery Frances—†	22	"	48	"
	N	Devery William J	22	gardener	49	"

Page.	Letter.	Full Name.	Residence, Jan. 1, 1941.	Occupation.	Supposed Age.	Reported Residence, Jan. 1, 1940. Street and Number.

Chestnut Street—Continued

Page.	Letter.	Full Name.	Residence, Jan. 1, 1941.	Occupation.	Supposed Age.	Reported Residence, Jan. 1, 1940. Street and Number.
	K	Dacey Mabel E—†	22	housewife	33	Newton
	L	Dacey William J	22	milkman	29	Milton
	O	Holmer Harry V	23	machinist	41	104 Arlington
	P	Holmer Isabel—†	23	housewife	40	104 "
	R	Mattson Hilda—†	25	"	60	here
	S	Mattson Ivar W	25	machinist	57	"

Child Street

Page.	Letter.	Full Name.	Residence, Jan. 1, 1941.	Occupation.	Supposed Age.	Reported Residence, Jan. 1, 1940. Street and Number.
	T	Tryder James W	6	laborer	67	here
	U	Tryder Margaret A—†	6	housewife	57	"
	V	McDonough Daniel J	8	shipper	22	"
	W	McDonough Joseph F	8	custodian	57	"
	X	McDonough Sarah—†	8	housewife	48	"
	Y	Burke Alice E—†	14	"	30	16 Child
	Z	Burke Edward J	14	roofer	31	16 "
1220						
	A	Tobin Evelyn—†	16	housewife	39	107 Arlington
	B	Tobin Francis	16	painter	35	107 "
	C	Bertram Joseph L	22	tree surgeon	28	50 Austin
	D	Gaines Maida I—†	22	checker	23	50 "
	E	Gaines Ruth C—†	22	housewife	57	50 "
	F	Augusta Albion R	24	policeman	46	here
	G	Augusta Ruth E—†	24	housewife	43	"
	H	Campbell Anna M—†	30	"	37	"
	K	Campbell William D	30	carpenter	42	"
	L	Morrissey Martina—†	30	housekeeper	55	10 Beaufort rd
	M	Hutton Frances M—†	32	"	36	here
	N	Greenwood Catherine H—†	45	housewife	34	"
	O	Greenwood Oscar J	45	mechanic	33	"
	P	McCarron Albert J	45	carpenter	50	"
	R	Simmons Montford C	47	engineer	49	"
	S	Simmons Rose A—†	47	housewife	44	"
	T	Cashman Miriam F—†	48	merchant	59	"
	U	Fisher Josephine—†	48	"	50	"
	V	Anderson Helen C—†	49	secretary	29	"
	W	Daly Frank H	49	B F D	42	"
	X	Daly Sarah A—†	49	housewife	39	"
	Y	Schlosser Ann M—†	50	"	38	Connecticut
	Z	Schlosser William E	50	salesman	38	"

Page	Letter	Full Name	Residence, Jan. 1, 1941.	Occupation	Supposed Age.	Reported Residence, Jan. 1, 1940. Street and Number.

1221
Child Street—Continued

Page	Letter	Full Name	Residence, Jan. 1, 1941.	Occupation	Supposed Age.	Reported Residence, Jan. 1, 1940. Street and Number.
	A	Spencer Mary L—†	52	housewife	71	here
	B	Spencer Timothy	52	retired	76	"
	C	Wragg Lydia A—†	55	housekeeper	66	"
	D	Pray Jennie R—†	58	secretary	72	"
	E	Perry Catherine E—†	58	housewife	61	"
	F	Perry Charles E	58	salesman	61	"
	G	Perry Elinor L—†	58	clerk	29	"
	H	Perry George L	58	mechanic	25	"
	K	Fourtellotte Emma S—†	59	housekeeper	82	"
	L	Fourtellotte Mabel E—†	59	"	53	"
	M	Layton Grace E—†	62	saleswoman	37	"
	N	Leason Emily B—†	62	housekeeper	78	"
	O	Hoitt Alfred W	63	bookkeeper	64	"
	P	Hoitt Ellen G—†	63	housewife	62	"
	R	Bass Hattie G—†	63	housekeeper	85	"
	S	Fellows George F	66	clerk	65	"
	T	Fellows Sadie G—†	66	housewife	59	"
	U	Leason Charlotte P—†	67	"	46	"
	V	Leason Edwin E	67	advertising	47	"
	W	Pickard Mary E—†	67	housekeeper	69	"
	X	Carr Mary J—†	68	"	65	"
	Y	McCormack Rose C—†	68	"	59	"
	Z	O'Brien Mary R—†	68	"	30	Buzzards Bay
1222						
	A	O'Brien William J	68	retired	73	here
	B	Holmes Edgar F	69	teller	58	"
	C	Willard Florence H—†	69	housekeeper	66	"
	D	Hartmann George K	70	retired	80	56 Central av
	E	Ruggles Caroline—†	70	at home	80	Quincy
	F	Scott Louise E—†	70	housewife	50	97 Beacon
	G	Scott Samuel J	70	attorney	56	97 "
	K	Simpson Dana P	75	merchant	66	here
	L	Simpson Maud E—†	75	housewife	63	"
	M	Simpson Phillip N	75	buyer	37	"
	N	Rothwell Albert J	76	shipper	21	"
	O	Rothwell Richard J	76	clerk	51	"
	P	Rothwell Thomas A	76	laborer	22	"
	R	Robinson Pearl C—†	81	housekeeper	60	"
	S	Schwalb Benjamin L	82	attorney	38	"
	T	Schwalb Lucy D—†	82	housewife	31	"

Page	Letter	Full Name	Residence, Jan. 1, 1944	Occupation	Supposed Age	Reported Residence, Jan. 1, 1943. Street and Number

Child Street—Continued

Page	Letter	Full Name	Residence	Occupation	Age	Reported Residence
	U	Burnaby M Gertrude †	87	teacher	56	here
	V	Facht Amy M †	87	"	57	"
	W	Farnsworth Alice B †	87	"	60	"
	X	Murphy William F	91	clerk	37	"
	Y	Reilly Alice E †	91	housewife	32	"
	Z	Reilly Francis K	91	reporter	37	"
1223						
	A	Pieczkowski Alvin J	96	contractor	39	"
	B	Pieczkowski Mary A †	96	housewife	38	"
	C	Larsson Charles	97	merchant	64	"
	D	Larsson Elizabeth A †	97	housewife	66	"
	G	Howard Helen W †	101	"	36	"
	H	Howard Richard J	101	constructor	35	"
	E	Lyons Harold S	101	metalworker	29	"
	F	Lyons Mary J—†	101	housewife	29	"
	K	Whittier Sarah J—†	101	housekeeper	68	"
	L	LeClair Alma N—†	104	clerk	22	"
	M	LeClair Edward J	104	"	26	"
	N	LeClair Ernest J	104	U S A	23	"
	O	LeClair Jacqueline—†	104	housewife	55	"
	P	LeClair Joseph F	104	butcher	50	"
	R	Dacey Albert P	105	welder	43	"
	S	Dacey Anna A †	105	housewife	40	"
	T	Nicholson Nelson D	107	clerk	33	"
	U	Nicholson Ruth V †	107	housewife	32	"
	V	McGowan Charles M	115	mechanic	66	"
	W	McGowan Helen M †	115	student	20	"
	X	McGowan Marie A †	115	housewife	60	"
	Y	O'Connor Alice L †	117	clerk	38	"
	Z	O'Connor Emma R †	117	housewife	68	"
1224						
	A	O'Connor William E	117	retired	68	"
	B	Shea Dennis	119 121	blacksmith	53	"
	C	Shea Dennis, jr	119 121	chauffeur	33	"
	D	Shea Francis J	119 121	painter	24	"
	E	Shea Sarah T †	119 121	housewife	51	"
	F	McKenna James A	119 121	clerk	51	"
	G	McKenna Mary J—†	119 121	housewife	48	"
	H	McKenna William F	119 121	salesman	53	"
	K	Gildea Florence L—†	123 125	stenographer	23	"
	L	Gildea James E	123 125	foreman	58	"

Page.	Letter.	Full Name.	Residence, Jan. 1, 1941.	Occupation.	Supposed Age.	Reported Residence, Jan. 1, 1940. Street and Number.

Child Street Continued

Page.	Letter.	Full Name.	Residence, Jan. 1, 1941.	Occupation.	Supposed Age.	Reported Residence, Jan. 1, 1940.
	M	Gildea Mary E—†	123–125	housewife	55	here
	N	Gildea Robert F	123–125	clerk	22	"
	O	Sullivan John F	123–125	B F D	54	"
	P	Sullivan John F, jr	123–125	electrician	22	"
	R	Sullivan Mary A—†	123–125	housewife	52	"
	S	Gutowski Adam	127	woodworker	20	"
	T	*Gutowski Helen—†	127	housewife	46	"
	U	Gutowski Leon	127	mechanic	54	"
	V	Gutowski Leona—†	127	clerk	23	"
	W	*Valente Jeannette—†	127	housewife	44	"
	X	Valente Joseph	127	laborer	50	"
	Y	Sears Alfred F	128	painter	30	"
	Z	Sears Marguerite S—†	128	housewife	28	"
1225						
	A	Carveale Patrick	128	laborer	27	"
	B	Carveale Raphaella—†	128	entertainer	24	"
	C	*DeFrauze Camella—†	128	housewife	53	"
	D	*Cook Mary M—†	131	"	30	"
	E	Cook Paul H	131	machinist	35	"
	F	*Meede Olive M—†	131	housewife	25	8 Wash'n
	G	*Meede Paul	131	upholsterer	34	8 "
	H	Cacciagrani Antoinette—†	131	housewife	31	here
	K	Cacciagrani Mario	131	candymaker	45	"
	L	Fusco Anthony	132	laborer	45	"
	M	Graneri Frank	132	"	62	"
	N	*Graneri Maria—†	132	housewife	59	"
	O	*Prada Anthony	132	polisher	20	"
	P	Prada Benedict	132	"	46	"
	R	*Cook Mildred M—†	133	housewife	30	"
	S	*Cook Stephen E	133	installer	31	"
	T	*Arena Antonia—†	133	housewife	43	25 Readville
	U	Arena Joseph	133	laborer	44	25 "
	V	Manning Ella E—†	135	housewife	61	here
	W	Manning John P	135	plumber	21	"
	X	*Pinchieri John B	136	laborer	63	"
	Y	*Pinchieri Teresa—†	136	housewife	60	"
	Z	Piacentini Chester	136	metalworker	38	"
1226						
	A	*Piacentini Sadie—†	136	housewife	35	"
	B	Karpowicz Alexander	139	laborer	53	"
	C	Karpowicz Alexander	139	clerk	22	"

Page	Letter	Full Name	Residence, Jan. 1, 1941	Occupation	Supposed Age	Reported Residence, Jan. 1, 1940. Street and Number.

Child Street Continued

Page	Letter	Full Name	Residence, Jan. 1, 1941	Occupation	Supposed Age	Reported Residence, Jan. 1, 1940. Street and Number.
	D	*Karpowicz Stella †	139	housewife	48	here
	E	Fitzhenry Lawrence C	139	packer	56	"
	F	Fitzhenry Mary E †	139	housewife	53	"
	G	Piolunek Anna V †	140	seamstress	23	"
	H	*Piolunek Mary C †	140	housewife	51	"
	K	Piolunek Walter F	140	mechanic	50	"
	L	Piolunek William R	140	assembler	22	"
	M	Baggett Helen †	140	housewife	27	"
	N	Dudovich Loraine †	141	"	24	"
	O	Dudovich Stanley	141	machinist	25	"
	P	Brown Loretta G †	144	housewife	26	"
	R	Brown William K	144	clerk	38	"
	S	Jennette Henry L	144	factoryhand	23	"
	T	Jennette Joseph D	144	"	33	"
	U	Jennette William	144	"	27	"
	V	Brown Cornelius G	153	plumber	40	"
	W	Brown Mary A †	153	housewife	36	"
	X	McCormack Mary E †	153	"	33	"
	Y	Crivellaro Diego J	153	machinist	40	"
	Z	Crivellaro Yvonne M †	153	housewife	37	"

1227 Cleveland Street

Page	Letter	Full Name	Residence, Jan. 1, 1941	Occupation	Supposed Age	Reported Residence, Jan. 1, 1940. Street and Number.
	A	Rudy Michael	2	mattresses	43	here
	B	Rudy Sophie M †	2	housewife	36	"
	C	Fuller Allan W	2	laborer	28	1004 Hyde Park av
	D	Fuller Blanche D †	2	saleswoman	26	96 West
	E	Fuller Lucille E †	2	housewife	25	1004 Hyde Park av
	F	Fuller Russell G	2	laborer	25	1004 "
	G	Kimball Robert	9	salesman	60	here
	H	*Phelan Elizabeth M †	9	housewife	25	"
	K	Phelan Joseph J	9	receiver	26	"
	L	Wipperman Edmund L	9	inspector	32	119 Birch
	M	Wipperman Virginia C †	9	housewife	27	119 "
	N	Hurley Ina B †	10	"	76	here
	O	Hurley John F	10	attorney	75	"
	P	Hurley Ruth L †	10	stenographer	31	"
	R	Forguites Clyde H	13	laborer	47	"
	S	Forguites Cora †	13	housewife	44	"
	T	Forguites Richard	13	guard	23	"
	U	McDonough Rose A †	13	housekeeper	85	"

Page.	Letter.	Full Name.	Residence, Jan. 1, 1941.	Occupation.	Supposed Age.	Reported Residence, Jan. 1, 1940. Street and Number.

Cleveland Street—Continued

Page.	Letter.	Full Name.	Residence, Jan. 1, 1941.	Occupation.	Supposed Age.	Reported Residence, Jan. 1, 1940.
	V	Morrison Alice G—†	13	clerk	53	here
	W	Morrison Mary A—†	13	housewife	75	"
	X	Brehm Elizabeth—†	17	housekeeper	82	"
	Y	Hamm Elwin C	17	painter	45	"
	Z	Hamm Mary J—†	17	housewife	42	"
1228						
	A	Wisnesky Helena S—†	17	housekeeper	72	"
	B	Morrison Annie M—†	19	housewife	64	"
	C	Morrison Harriet A—†	19	adjuster	39	"
	D	Morrison Margaret G—†	19	secretary	33	"
	E	Morrison William J	19	retired	73	"
	F	Ivens Cornelius	20–22	cigarmaker	61	"
	G	Ivens Mary—†	20–22	housewife	60	"
	H	Ivens Peter J	20–22	machinist	25	"
	K	Collins Alice M—†	20–22	clerk	32	"
	L	Collins Francis A	20–22	pharmacist	37	"
	M	Collins Frederick D	20–22	clerk	29	"
	N	Hickey Gladys V—†	21	housewife	44	"
	O	Hickey John J	21	installer	45	"
	P	Houston Albert A	23	gardener	45	"
	R	Houston Thomas E	23	teacher	38	"
	S	Houston Thomas J	23	retired	80	"
	T	Uzdavinis Joseph	24–26	laborer	22	"
	U*	Uzdavinis Mary—†	24–26	housewife	44	"
	V*	Uzdavinis William	24–26	laborer	46	"
	W	Punis Alexander	24–26	gatetender	23	190 D
	X	Punis Annie—†	24–26	housewife	24	here
	Y	Pitman Bernice M—†	25–27	"	44	"
	Z	Pitman Ephraim W	25–27	policeman	50	"
1229						
	A	Soley Edna C—†	25–27	clerk	33	"
	B*	Soley Josephine—†	25–27	housewife	72	"
	C	Soley Theodora—†	25–27	clerk	31	"
	D	Corcoran Catherine M—†	28–28A	housewife	33	"
	E	Corcoran Michael J	28–28A	gardener	36	"
	F	Sharp Eileen T—†	28–28A	housewife	36	"
	G	Sharp Walter	28–28A	clerk	34	"
	H	Kaminski Joseph	29–31	welder	45	"
	K*	Kaminski Mary—†	29–31	housewife	37	"
	L	Alimenti Frank	29–31	artist	29	"
	M*	Alimenti Josephine—†	29–31	housewife	63	"

Page	Letter	Full Name	Residence, Jan. 1, 1941	Occupation	Supposed Age	Reported Residence, Jan. 1, 1940. Street and Number

Cleveland Street—Continued

Page	Letter	Full Name	Residence	Occupation	Age	Reported Residence
	N	Alimenti Raymond	29-31	mechanic	26	here
	O	*Alimenti Tina †	29-31	saleswoman	31	"
	P	Sikora Alice †	30	housewife	24	"
	R	Sikora John J	30	machinist	30	"
	S	Phinney Chandler D	30	operator	34	"
	T	Phinney Mary C—†	30	housewife	35	"
	U	Nolan Alcide	34	designer	31	"
	V	Nolan Dorena—†	34	housewife	53	"
	W	Nolan Eugene B	34	statistician	29	"
	X	Nolan Ovidas P	34	cabinetmaker	52	"
	Y	Lawrence Frank A	34	machinist	54	"
	Z	Lawrence George H	34	accountant	28	"
1230						
	A	Lawrence Grace E—†	34	housewife	50	"
	B	Lawrence John R	34	laborer	21	"
	C	Foley Catherine J—†	35	housewife	60	"
	D	Foley Charles J	35	B F D	66	"
	E	Foley Phillip M	35	laborer	33	"
	F	O'Callaghan John P	36	manager	38	"
	G	O'Callaghan Winifred T—†	36	housewife	33	"
	H	Laughlin Catherine M—†	36	saleswoman	22	"
	K	Laughlin Mary E—†	36	housewife	44	"
	L	Laughlin Richard F	36	shipper	20	"
	M	Laughlin Thomas J	36	boilermaker	47	"
	N	Daly Margaret F—†	37	stenographer	23	"
	O	Johnson George	37	bricklayer	63	"
	P	Johnson Margaret—†	37	housewife	57	"
	R	Graniere Dominic	38	laborer	53	"
	S	*Graniere Maria—†	38	housewife	43	"
	T	Garabedian Mary—†	38	"	27	"
	U	Garabedian Robert	38	laundryworker	31	"
	V	Tacey Anna M—†	39	housewife	44	"
	W	Tacey George R	39	painter	44	"
	X	*Mattaliano Harriet—†	40	housewife	38	"
	Y	Mattaliano Pasquale J	40	chauffeur	38	"
	Z	Martin Elizabeth G—†	42	housewife	44	"
1231						
	A	Martin William J	42	policeman	44	"
	B	Mahoney Joseph T	44	chauffeur	33	"
	C	Mahoney Norah C—†	44	bookkeeper	35	"
	D	Gustowski Anna F—†	44	housekeeper	20	"

Page	Letter	Full Name	Residence, Jan. 1, 1941	Occupation	Supposed Age	Reported Residence, Jan. 1, 1940. Street and Number.

Cleveland Street—Continued

Page	Letter	Full Name	Residence, Jan. 1, 1941	Occupation	Supposed Age	Reported Residence, Jan. 1, 1940. Street and Number.
	E	*Gustowski Frances M—†	44	housewife	50	here
	F	Gustowski Mary H—†	44	secretary	27	"
	G	Gustowski Peter M	44	machinist	57	"
	H	Gustowski Stella J—†	44	secretary	23	"
	K	*Conopka Anthony	45	repairman	54	"
	L	Conopka Antoinette F—†	45	housekeeper	23	"
	M	*Conopka Julia—†	45	housewife	53	"
	N	Conopka Sophia C—†	45	clerk	30	"
	O	Conopka Stephen A	45	electrician	28	"
	P	Hall Catherine—†	46–48A	housewife	39	"
	R	Hall Walter E	46–48A	collector	40	"
	S	Hall Gertrude M—†	46–48A	housewife	28	"
	T	Hall Henry E	46–48A	chauffeur	36	"
	U	Jenkins Annie E—†	50	housewife	64	"
	V	Jenkins Irene M—†	50	stenographer	30	"
	W	Jenkins John H	50	laborer	27	"
	Y	Breen Elizabeth—†	52	at home	76	233 West
	Z	Connell Alice F—†	52	housewife	40	233 "
1232						
	A	Connell Alice P—†	52	stenographer	23	233 "
	B	Connell George F	52	instructor	46	233 "
	C	McMillan Margaret R—†	52	hairdresser	24	233 "
	D	Cox Gertrude M—†	52	housewife	28	693 Metropolitan av
	E	Cox Robert P	52	chauffeur	31	693 "
	F	Higgins John J	54–56	welder	34	here
	G	Moore Delia A—†	54–56	housewife	37	"
	H	Moore Matthew A	54–56	steward	36	"
	K	Burns Helen M—†	54–56	housewife	39	"
	L	Burns John C	54–56	letter carrier	41	"

Coleman Street

Page	Letter	Full Name	Residence, Jan. 1, 1941	Occupation	Supposed Age	Reported Residence, Jan. 1, 1940. Street and Number.
	M	Rolfing Albert	9	laborer	36	here
	N	Rolfing Mary E—†	9	housewife	36	"
	O	Stahl Alice L—†	9	"	53	"
	P	Stahl Harold E	9	upholsterer	50	"
	R	Wysocki Edward B	15	machinist	27	"
	S	Wysocki Henry	15	"	21	"
	T	Wysocki Mary M—†	15	stitcher	26	5 Margin
	U	Osuchowski Peter	15	operator	46	here
	V	*Osuchowski Stella—†	15	housewife	50	"

Coleman Street—Continued

Page	Letter	Full Name	Residence, Jan. 1, 1941	Occupation	Supposed Age	Reported Residence, Jan. 1, 1940. Street and Number
	W	*Reppo Stanley	15	carpenter	62	here
	X	Couture Christine C †	15	housewife	33	26 Austin
	Y	Couture Paul	15	carpenter	40	26 "

Cottage Place

Page	Letter	Full Name	Residence, Jan. 1, 1941	Occupation	Supposed Age	Reported Residence, Jan. 1, 1940. Street and Number
	Z	Cusick Francis J	9	machinist	34	2600 Centre
1233						
	A	Cusick Mabel I †	9	housewife	34	2600 "
	B	Richards Angus A	12	machinist	51	here
	C	*Richards Lulu B †	12	housewife	45	"
	D	Stepanovitch Elsa †	14	"	40	"
	E	*Stepanovitch Fred A	14	carpenter	45	"

Emmet Street

Page	Letter	Full Name	Residence, Jan. 1, 1941	Occupation	Supposed Age	Reported Residence, Jan. 1, 1940. Street and Number
	F	Gilmartin Agnes T †	15	stenographer	33	here
	G	Gilmartin Bridget M †	15	housewife	76	"
	H	Gilmartin Helen F †	15	secretary	36	"
	K	Gilmartin Joseph E	15	constable	38	"
	L	Gilmartin Katherine M †	15	bookkeeper	40	"
	M	Gilmartin Mary E †	15	"	42	"
	N	Gilmartin William J	15	retired	80	"
	O	Morris Thomas F	16	laborer	40	"
	P	O'Brien Robert T	16	teacher	39	"
	R	O'Brien Susan V †	16	housewife	70	"
	S	*Johnson Hulda †	20	"	49	"
	T	Johnson Lillian E †	20	attendant	20	"
	U	Johnson Robert R	20	metalworker	23	"
	V	Johnson William O	20	carpenter	52	"
	W	Barrett Anne J †	20	housekeeper	68	"
	X	Barrett Thomas J	20	retired	66	"
	Y	Canning Mary L †	20	clerk	32	"
	Z	O'Brien Erline L †	25	housewife	26	"
1234						
	A	O'Brien Paul S	25	clerk	28	"
	B	Pagington Kenneth W	25	laborer	28	"
	C	Pagington Valerie C †	25	housewife	27	"
	D	Barrett Mary J †	rear 25	"	63	"
	E	Barrett Michael W	" 25	gardener	73	"
	F	Barrett John	33	retired	73	"

Page	Letter	Full Name	Residence, Jan. 1, 1941	Occupation	Supposed Age	Reported Residence, Jan. 1, 1940. Street and Number.

Emmet Street—Continued

Page	Letter	Full Name	Residence, Jan. 1, 1941	Occupation	Supposed Age	Reported Residence, Jan. 1, 1940. Street and Number.
	G	Barrett John F	33	mechanic	28	here
	H	Barrett Nellie E—†	33	housewife	53	"
	K	Catarius Francis R	33	salesman	31	"
	L	Catarius Helen E—†	33	housewife	30	"
	M	Morin Delvina—†	42	"	62	"
	N	Morin Ovid	42	retired	65	"

Gordon Avenue

Page	Letter	Full Name	Residence, Jan. 1, 1941	Occupation	Supposed Age	Reported Residence, Jan. 1, 1940. Street and Number.
	S	Kelly Nellie—†	7	matron	56	here
	T	Laurie Evelyn M—†	7	waitress	32	"
	U	Lincoln Annie L—†	7	housewife	60	"
	V	Lincoln Doris E—†	7	checker	20	"
	W	Lincoln Harriet L—†	7	stitcher	23	"
	X	Lincoln Harry E	7	carpenter	64	"
	Y	Carroll Robert E	7	painter	23	"
	Z	Kumme Hilda E—†	7	stitcher	55	"
1235						
	A	Munroe Helene E—†	7	"	27	"
	B	Munroe Helene O—†	7	housewife	60	"
	C	*Strickland Kathleen H—†	7	"	35	1398 River
	D	Strickland William B	7	chauffeur	34	1398 "
	F	Chin Toy	9	laundryman	62	here
	L	*Chludzinski Nellie—† rear	11	housewife	35	"
	M	Chludzinski William "	11	laborer	45	"
	N	Burnham Eleanor—† "	11	housewife	45	"
	O	Burnham Elmer A "	11	printer	39	"
	P	*Zatrib Julian "	11	merchant	74	"
	R	*Zatrib Victoria—† "	11	housewife	74	"
	T	Clement Doris C—†	13	clerk	22	5 Gardner ter
	U	Clement Evelyn A—†	13	saleswoman	20	5 "
	V	Clement Margaret J—†	13	nurse	23	5 "
	W	Clement Paul R	13	salesman	49	5 "
	X	LoVuolo Eleanor F—†	13	packer	21	here
	Y	LoVuolo Mary V—†	13	housewife	40	"
	Z	LoVuolo Samuel N	13	machinist	45	"
1236						
	B	Baker Warren C	15	laborer	24	Dedham
	C	Coarr Charles V	15	clerk	20	15 Woodman
	D	Coarr John J	15	"	21	15 "
	E	Coarr Michael J	15	painter	51	15 "

Page	Letter	Full Name	Residence, Jan. 1, 1941	Occupation	Supposed Age	Reported Residence Jan. 1, 1940. Street and Number

Gordon Avenue—Continued

Page	Letter	Full Name	Residence, Jan. 1, 1941	Occupation	Supposed Age	Reported Residence Jan. 1, 1940. Street and Number
	F	Coarr Rose H †	15	housewife	46	15 Woodman
	G	Hanson Lester E	15	draftsman	24	here
	H	Oliver Charles E	15	engineer	24	27 Lincoln
	K	Carroll Charles L	16	shipper	49	9 Atherton av
	L	Carroll Clara L †	16	housewife	49	9 "
	M	Brown George E	16	clerk	57	here
	N	Peterson Teckla †	16	dressmaker	51	"
	O	Pitts Rose O †	16	housekeeper	82	"
	P	Thayer Helen M—†	16	"	56	"
	R	Gaudet Ernest J	16	bricklayer	55	"
	S	Gaudet Margaret E—†	16	housewife	62	"
	T	*Langlois Mary L—†	16	"	50	"
	U	Langlois Peter J	16	laborer	52	"
	V	Ferry Arthur W	16	salesman	57	"
	W	Ferry Etta M—†	16	housewife	56	"
	X	*Waitkemus Matilda—†	16	"	57	"
	Y	Waitkemus Paul	16	tailor	63	"
	Z	*Waitkemus Robert	16	retired	68	"
1237						
	A	White Joseph	16	salesman	24	"
	B	White Victoria—†	16	packer	23	"
	C	*Burns Mary E †	16	housewife	39	56 Charlesgate East
	D	*Burns William B	16	painter	41	56 "
	E	Butler Annie L †	19	housewife	64	709 Metropolitan av
	F	Butler Melvin E	19	toolmaker	67	709 "
	G	Butler Russell E	19	clerk	35	709 "
	H	Iapicca Guy	20	shoeworker	38	Reading
	K	*Iapicca Josephine—†	20	housewife	32	"
	L	Bowman Jane †	20	"	72	here
	M	Bowman Janet R †	20	clerk	44	"
	N	Bowman Malcolm A	20	salesman	41	19 Summer
	O	Bowman William H	20	sexton	72	here
	P	Houston Francis J	21	clerk	52	"
	R	Houston Margaret T †	21	housewife	47	"
	S	Avery Bessie L †	24	"	42	"
	T	Avery Guy F	24	surveyor	46	"
	U	Knapp Carrie I †	24	housewife	83	"
	V	Knapp George F	24	milkman	62	"
	W	Wesolowski Alice †	26	housewife	49	"
	X	Wesolowski Joseph F	26	machinist	51	"
	Y	Scully Frances †	29	housewife	27	11 Prospect

Gordon Avenue Continued

Page	Letter	Full Name	Residence, Jan. 1, 1941	Occupation	Supposed Age	Reported Residence, Jan. 1, 1940. Street and Number.
	Z	Scully Thomas	29	machinist	30	11 Prospect
1238						
	A	Tarallo Amelia †	29	clerk	26	here
	B	Tarallo Anna †	29	housewife	52	"
	C	Tarallo Bertha †	29	clerk	31	"
	D	Tarallo George	29	"	30	"
	E	Tarallo William	29	machinist	28	"
	F	Stone Minnie B †	31	housekeeper	80	"
	H	Goodwin Ella M †	50	"	57	"
	K	Pearson Amy L †	50	housewife	55	"
	L	Pearson Florence R †	50	clerk	32	240 Kelton
	M	Pearson Norman R	50	mortician	29	here
	N	Maddalena Assunta †	53	housewife	44	"
	O	Maddalena Salvatore	53	metalworker	50	"
	P	Fermano Alphonse	54	conductor	41	"
	R	Fermano Matilda †	54	housewife	35	"
	S	Fermano Ferdinand	54	clerk	20	"
	T	Fermano Mary †	54	housewife	52	"
	U	Fermano Nicola	54	retired	67	"
	V*	Shuman David	55–57	merchant	45	"
	W*	Shuman Mary †	55–57	clerk	43	"
	X	Shuman Myer H	55–57	salesman	23	"
	Y	Andonian Margaret †	55–57	housewife	45	"
	Z	Andonian Sarkis	55–57	merchant	48	"
1239						
	A	Craig Ann M †	59–61	housewife	45	Reading
	B	Craig James H	59–61	guard	51	"
	C*	Croteau Jean	59–61	mechanic	36	here
	D	Fillion Germaine †	59–61	housewife	35	"
	E	Fillion Omer	59–61	carpenter	33	"
	F	Chapman Georgina †	63–65	saleswoman	39	"
	G	Musgrave Alice G †	63–65	housekeeper	71	"
	H	Glennon Joseph T	63–65	steamfitter	36	"
	K*	Glennon Kathleen M †	63–65	housewife	35	"
	L	Creamer Hazel †	67–69	"	40	"
	M	Creamer Morgan	67–69	supervisor	47	"
	O	Olese Blanche †	76	coilwinder	29	47 Dana av
	P	Olese Peter	76	attendant	31	47 "
	R	McDougall Daniel A	78	molder	50	here
	S	McDougall Margaret M †	78	housewife	41	"
	T	Andrews Olga M †	79	"	29	"

Page	Letter	Full Name	Residence	Occupation	Reported Age	Reported Residence, Street and Number
		Gordon Avenue Continued				
	U	Andrews William J	79	laborer	30	here
	W	*Rogers Sophia †	79	housewife	53	"
	X	*Modano Eileen F †	80	"	35	"
	Y	Modano Michael	80	merchant	42	"
	Z	Wright Edgar H, jr	82	retired	59	"
1240						
	A	Wright George A	82	electrician	35	"
	B	Wright Nellie J †	82	housewife	70	"
	C	*Wilson Constance †	88	"	33	"
	D	Wilson Walter	88	chauffeur	34	"
	E	Quinlan Mary F †	88	housewife	55	"
	F	Quinlan Maurice F	88	manager	36	"
	G	*Quinlan Vera †	88	housewife	30	"
	H	McLellan Alexander J	92	cabinetmaker	50	"
	K	McLellan Doris †	92	housewife	46	"
	L	Fisher Eleanor L †	92	clerk	22	"
	M	Fisher James A	92	"	25	Milton
	N	Cherrington Mary E †	96	teacher	67	here
	O	Allen Alice †	100	at home	63	24 Chittick rd
	P	Bennett Myrtle M †	100	nurse	43	Melrose
	R	Bugbee Jennie †	100	at home	81	here
	S	*Ditullio Camillio	100	retired	86	"
	T	Dodd E Gladys †	100	housewife	48	"
	U	Dodd Percy L	100	chauffeur	48	"
	V	Dodd Richard P	100	U S A	22	"
	W	Glazier Evelina †	100	at home	95	"
	X	Patten Sarah L †	100	"	84	"
	Y	Ridley Madora B †	100	housekeeper	65	"
	Z	Towner Ellen †	100	at home	84	118 Dana av
1241						
	A	Bonanno Andrew	103	laborer	51	here
	B	*Bonanno Anna †	103	housewife	48	"
	C	Tosi Augusto	103	clerk	64	"
	D	Tosi Warren	103	laborer	36	"
	E	Tosi Zenaide †	103	housewife	63	"
	F	*Chisholm Mary B †	106	"	65	"
	G	Chisholm Mary D †	106	stenographer	34	"
	H	*Chisholm Roderick R	106	conductor	69	"
	K	Chisholm Rose L †	106	boxmaker	41	"
	L	Hoar Gladys M †	112	clerk	41	"
	M	Hoar Katherine E †	112	housewife	59	"

Page	Letter	Full Name.	Residence, Jan. 1, 1941.	Occupation.	Supposed Age.	Reported Residence, Jan. 1, 1940. Street and Number.

Gordon Avenue—Continued

Page	Letter	Full Name	Residence	Occupation	Age	Reported Residence
	N	Hoar William M	112	retired	76	here
	O	Heath Alice—†	112	clerk	52	Watertown
	P	Heath Henry	112	salesman	47	"
	S	Aykroyd Ida M—†	117	housewife	56	here
	T	Aykroyd Thomas	117	teacher	57	"
	U	Aykroyd Thomas E	117	"	23	"
	V	Aykroyd Winifred G—†	117	nurse	21	"
	W	Rooney Katherine M—†	127	clerk	42	"
	X	Rooney Mary—†	127	housekeeper	45	"
	Y	Rooney Susan G—†	127	clerk	39	"
	Z	Brown Amos L	128	mechanic	40	Needham
1242						
	A	Brown Christine—†	128	housewife	40	"
	B	*McLeod Mary—†	128	at home	72	"

Hale Street

Page	Letter	Full Name	Residence	Occupation	Age	Reported Residence
	C	Blaszkiewicz Antoinette—†	29	teacher	32	here
	D	Dabrowski Francis S	29	clergyman	38	Salem
	E	Dec Stella—†	29	teacher	22	here
	F	Gajewski Blanche—†	29	"	40	"
	G	Kaminski Ladisla—†	29	"	34	"
	H	Kuczynski Stephanie—†	29	"	37	"
	K	Mocium Ladisla—†	29	"	38	"
	L	Mroz Helen—†	29	"	25	"
	M	Ostrowski Veronica—†	29	"	35	Pennsylvania
	N	*Szczecinski Felixa—†	29	"	52	New Jersey
	O	*Totos Josephine—†	29	"	35	here
	P	*Walas Agnes—†	29	"	49	"
	R	*Wendolouski Veronica—†	29	"	36	"
	S	*Wojtas Catherine—†	29	"	50	"
	T	Wozniak Mary—†	29	"	29	"
	U	Costello Martin J	31	laborer	35	"
	V	Costello Mary R—†	31	housewife	62	"
	W	Costello Thomas	31	laborer	66	"
	X	Costello Thomas P	31	clerk	23	"
	Y	Stancar John A	33	policeman	46	"
	Z	Stancar Mildred E—†	33	housewife	41	"
1243						
	A	Lockhart Gertrude A—†	35	clerk	27	"
	B	Lockhart Harry D	35	exterminator	59	"

Page	Letter	Full Name	Residence, Jan. 1, 1941	Occupation	Supposed Age	Reported Residence, Jan. 1, 1940. Street and Number

Hale Street—Continued

Page	Letter	Full Name	Residence, Jan. 1, 1941	Occupation	Supposed Age	Reported Residence, Jan. 1, 1940. Street and Number
	C	Lockhart Mary J—†	35	housewife	59	here
	D	Lockhart Robert F	35	exterminator	23	"

Linwood Street

Page	Letter	Full Name	Residence, Jan. 1, 1941	Occupation	Supposed Age	Reported Residence, Jan. 1, 1940. Street and Number
	E	Bergman Leo E	3	manager	38	here
	F	Bergman Mildred G—†	3	housewife	42	"
	G	Peterson Charles A	7	machinist	62	"
	H	Peterson Ellen C—†	7	librarian	36	"
	K	Peterson Ellen O—†	7	housewife	59	"
	L	Galvin George J	8	salesman	30	12 Austin
	M	Hayes Anna F—†	8	housewife	33	12 "
	N	Hayes Bessie A—†	8	"	61	12 "
	O	Hayes Henry M	8	cashier	34	12 "
	P	King Clara K—†	10	housewife	62	here
	R	King George M	10	treasurer	63	"
	S	Howe Kittie M—†	11	housewife	80	1188 River
	T	Savage Bridget—†	11	clerk	52	1060 "
	U	Strickland Annie J—†	11	mattresses	43	1060 "
	V	Sullivan Anna J—†	11	housewife	54	17 Linwood
	W	Sullivan John F	11	molder	56	17 "
	X	Chesley Marion—†	14	housewife	69	here
	Y	Lung Clara I—†	14	"	80	"
	Z	Macker Anna F—†	14	"	62	"
1244						
	A	Macker Melvin A	14	operator	65	"
	B	Crichton Andrew W	17	foreman	63	"
	C	Crichton Sarah A—†	17	housewife	64	"
	D	Appleton Carrie G—†	17	"	68	Somerville
	E	Appleton Francis H	17	clerk	65	"
	F	Johnson Anders	18	boilermaker	33	"
	G	Johnson Phillip B	18	welder	37	here
	H	*Johnson Selma V—†	18	housewife	33	"
	K	Mitchell David H	18	watchman	56	Everett
	L	Swanstrom Helen H—†	22	housewife	64	here
	M	Swanstrom John A	22	accountant	67	"
	N	Conroy Mary J—†	24	housewife	60	"
	O	McDonough Lillian J—†	24	"	60	"
	P	Dodge Lillian M—†	26	"	40	22 Arnold
	R	Groves Joseph P	26	retired	70	here
	S	Groves Margaret L—†	26	stenographer	30	"

Page.	Letter.	Full Name.	Residence, Jan. 1, 1941.	Occupation.	Supposed Age.	Reported Residence, Jan. 1, 1940. Street and Number.

Linwood Street—Continued

Page.	Letter.	Full Name.	Residence, Jan. 1, 1941.	Occupation.	Supposed Age.	Reported Residence, Jan. 1, 1940. Street and Number.
	T	Ford Irene D—†	28	housewife	27	here
	U	Lowell Delcie D—†	28	"	62	"
	V	Lowell Dorothy B—†	28	"	30	"
	W	Lowell Herbert S	28	clerk	30	"
	X*	Campia Giovanna—†	30	housewife	60	"
	Y	Campia Jennie M—†	30	clerk	20	"
	Z	Campia Michael A	30	salesman	22	"
1245						
	A	Campia Oscar J	30	engineer	29	"
	B	Campia Theodore A	30	salesman	27	"
	C	Lattanzio Bambina M—†	34	housewife	35	"
	D	Lattanzio Joseph J	34	salesman	33	"
	E	Kruhmin Emilie A—†	53	housewife	46	"
	F	Kruhmin Ernest	53	draftsman	50	"
	G	O'Reilly Bridget M—†	59	housewife	29	"
	H	O'Reilly Patrick J	59	bartender	32	"
	K	Turner Carl J	61	court officer	48	"
	L	Turner Carl W	61	clerk	20	"
	M	Turner Emma L—†	61	housewife	48	"

Myopia Road

Page.	Letter.	Full Name.	Residence, Jan. 1, 1941.	Occupation.	Supposed Age.	Reported Residence, Jan. 1, 1940. Street and Number.
	P	Williams Lawrence P	16	manager	42	94 Hunt'n av
	R	Williams Lolita—†	16	housewife	29	94 "
	S	Huguenard Albert T	17	clerk	46	19 Lindall
	T	Huguenard Lillian F—†	17	housewife	43	19 "
	U	Reagan Helen M—†	17	"	65	19 "
	V	Short Albert W	20	shipfitter	43	26 Fox
	W	Short Alicetta—†	20	housewife	48	26 "
	X	Botting Mary—†	21	"	67	1429 River
	Z	Croke Joseph T	21	accountant	38	1429 "
	Y	Croke Louise P—†	21	housewife	38	1429 "
1246						
	A	Howard Helen E—†	24	"	43	469 Ashmont
	B	Howard Robert F	24	policeman	41	469 "
	C	MacNaught James	25	carpenter	72	57 Austin
	D	Rooney Francis B	25	inspector	40	57 "
	E	Rooney Gladys—†	25	housewife	33	57 "
	F	Feldman Harry	28	pharmacist	30	36 Deforest
	G	Feldman Libby—†	28	housewife	28	36 "

Page	Letter	Full Name	Residence, Jan. 1, 1941.	Occupation	Supposed Age	Reported Residence, Jan. 1, 1940. Street and Number

Myopia Road—Continued

Page	Letter	Full Name	Residence, Jan. 1, 1941.	Occupation	Supposed Age	Reported Residence, Jan. 1, 1940. Street and Number
	K	Cahill Helen—†	34	housewife	38	here
	L	Cahill John A	34	jeweler	42	"
	M	Norton A David	34	physician	41	"
	N	Norton Clement A	34	superintendent	44	"
	O	Norton Harold F	34	physician	39	"
	P	Norton Richard	34	embalmer	34	"
	R	Ryan John J, jr	40	fireman	47	1 Jones av
	S	Ryan Sarah A—†	40	housewife	48	1 "
	T*	Grant Edith E—†	44	"	53	393 Ashmont
	U*	Grant Edward	44	main'n'ce man	56	393 "
	V	Grant Elizabeth A—†	44	housewife	30	385 "
	W	Grant Eric	44	jeweler	31	385 "
	X	Shea Joseph J	45	B F D	46	1275 Mass av
	Y	Shea Madeline R—†	45	housewife	38	1275 "
	Z	Doody Albert E	48	adjuster	41	Revere
1247						
	A	Doody Margaret—†	48	housewife	35	"
	B	Whittredge Anna H—†	52	"	29	Belmont
	C	Whittredge Edgar S	52	compositor	30	"
	D	Whittredge Harry T	52	retired	65	"
	E	Addison Harold	56	newsdealer	35	73 Fowler
	F	Addison Mary C—†	56	housewife	34	3 O'Callaghan way
	G	Cassidy Alexander	59	blacksmith	59	172 Orange
	H	Cassidy Annie—†	59	housewife	58	172 "
	K	Reardon Bridget J—†	59	saleswoman	28	172 "
	L	Casey Mary M—†	60	bookbinder	36	Arlington
	M	McCoy Anna M—†	60	housewife	31	"
	N	McCoy Frederick J	60	investigator	40	"
	O	Dooley James F	63	policeman	46	393 Ashmont
	P	Dooley Mary M—†	63	housewife	47	393 "
	R	Mulcahy John J	63	steamfitter	39	393 "
	S	Mulcahy Thomas J	63	retired	73	393 "
	T	Mulcahy William F	63	laborer	35	393 "
	U*	Adams Bessie E—†	66	housewife	35	12 George
	V	Adams James W	66	printer	36	12 "
	W	Mikita Frank A	67	shoeworker	43	4 Longwood ter
	X	Mikita Rita P—†	67	housewife	37	4 "
	Y*	Haines Effie—†	75	housekeeper	72	16 Hopewell rd
	Z	MacBain DeWitt S	75	chauffeur	38	16 "
1248						
	A	MacBain Mildred M—†	75	librarian	33	16 "

Page	Letter	Full Name	Residence, Jan. 1, 1941	Occupation	Supposed Age	Reported Residence, Jan. 1, 1940. Street and Number.

Parrott Street

Page	Letter	Full Name	Residence, Jan. 1, 1941	Occupation	Supposed Age	Reported Residence, Jan. 1, 1940. Street and Number.
	B	Johnson Elof	2	machinist	71	here
	C	Litzen Axel	2	"	60	"
	D	Litzen Selma †	2	housewife	55	"
	E	Gustafson Irene †	2	"	38	"
	F	Gustafson Oscar	2	electrician	43	"

Perkins Avenue

Page	Letter	Full Name	Residence, Jan. 1, 1941	Occupation	Supposed Age	Reported Residence, Jan. 1, 1940. Street and Number.
	G	O'Brien Frederick F	8	steamfitter	50	here
	H	O'Brien Mary A—†	8	at home	81	"
	K	O'Brien Mary L—†	8	stenographer	46	"
	L	O'Brien Sarah M—†	8	operator	55	"
	M	O'Brien William F	8	compositor	43	"
	N	Lappin Albert S	9	physician	38	"
	O	Lappin Pearl S—†	9	housewife	31	"
	P	Godfrey Marion E—†	11	teacher	42	"
	R	Godfrey Mary E—†	11	housewife	71	"
	S	Godfrey Mildred H—†	11	bookkeeper	45	"
	T	Godfrey Robert W	11	engineer	40	"
	U	Carlton Grace L—†	12	housewife	51	"
	V	Carlton Walter E	12	bookkeeper	51	"
	W	Faille Edna S—†	16	housewife	34	"
	X	Faille Edward S	16	inspector	38	"
	Y	Klosowski Henry	17	milkman	26	Lynn
	Z	Mills Clinton	17	salesman	33	here
1249						
	A	Mills Ina C—†	17	housewife	29	"
	B	Gruberski Antoinette—†	17	clerk	26	"
	C	Gruberski Frances M—†	17	inspector	20	"
	D	Gruberski John	17	mechanic	23	"
	E	Gruberski Julia V—†	17	stitcher	45	"
	F	Gruberski Michael J	17	molder	52	"
	G	Gruberski Walter M	17	mechanic	25	"
	H	Smith Bernice M—†	19	housewife	50	"
	K	Smith Carroll V	19	thermo tester	25	"
	L	Smith Chellis V	19	clergyman	53	"
	M	Smith Frances M—†	19	nurse	22	"
	N	Outlaw Guy D, jr	19	clergyman	44	"
	O	Outlaw Jean M—†	19	receptionist	20	"
	P	Outlaw Juanita A—†	19	nurse	22	"
	R	Outlaw Lilly L—†	19	housewife	44	"

Page.	Letter.	Full Name.	Residence, Jan. 1, 1941.	Occupation.	Supposed Age.	Reported Residence, Jan. 1, 1940. Street and Number.

Perkins Avenue—Continued

Page.	Letter.	Full Name.	Residence, Jan. 1, 1941.	Occupation.	Supposed Age.	Reported Residence, Jan. 1, 1940. Street and Number.
	S	Beaulieu George L	20	proprietor	42	here
	T	*Beaulieu Rose B †	20	housewife	35	"
	U	Walsh Fred J	21	compositor	35	"
	V	Walsh Margaret M †	21	housewife	34	"
	W	Wood Sarah T †	21	at home	69	"

Reservation Road

Page.	Letter.	Full Name.	Residence, Jan. 1, 1941.	Occupation.	Supposed Age.	Reported Residence, Jan. 1, 1940. Street and Number.
	X	Abramczyk Edward P	201	painter	23	61 Sunnyside
	Y	Abramczyk Lillian S †	201	housewife	23	44 "
	Z	Baker George J	201	laundryworker	37	here
1250						
	A	Baker Lillian H †	201	operator	33	"
	B	McKelligan Cassie E †	203	housewife	51	"
	C	McKelligan John E	203	clerk	21	"
	D	McKelligan William J	203	dyer	56	"
	E	Olson Anna J †	203	housewife	69	"
	F	Olson Nils G	203	machinist	73	"
	G	Newland Cecil C	205	painter	37	"
	H	Newland Mary E †	205	housewife	35	"
	K	Newland Sarah J †	205	housekeeper	62	"
	L	Powers James J	211	retired	69	"
	M	Powers Margaret I †	211	housewife	69	"
	N	McCabe Esther M †	213	"	41	"
	O	McCabe James L	213	foreman	44	"
	P	Smith Mary E †	213	housekeeper	79	"
	R	Jones Leo F	215	woodworker	37	"
	S	Jones Mary A †	215	housewife	35	"
	T	O'Hare Elsie N †	215	"	39	"
	U	O'Hare Michael E	215	merchant	43	"
	V	Tarallo Eleanor †	221	hairdresser	31	"
	W	Tarallo Gaetana †	221	housewife	55	"
	X	*Benfante Lydia †	221	housekeeper	39	1384 River
	Y	Trocchio Guido	221	agent	25	here
	Z	Trocchio Iola †	221	housewife	20	"
1251						
	B	Cwalina Edward P	225	presser	26	46 Winthrop
	C	Cwalina Estelle B †	225	operator	22	here
	D	Slobogen Caroline †	225	housewife	51	"
	E	Slobogen Marion †	225	operator	54	"
	F	Slobogen Stanley J	225	"	26	"

Page	Letter	Full Name	Residence, Jan. 1, 1941	Occupation	Supposed Age	Reported Residence, Jan. 1, 1940. Street and Number.

Reservation Road—Continued

Page	Letter	Full Name	Residence	Occupation	Age	Reported Residence
	G	Brown Emma—†	225	housewife	66	here
	H	Brown William	225	laborer	42	"
	L	*Colageo Carmella—†	229	housewife	48	"
	M	Colageo Lazzareno	229	mason	51	"
	N	Sulinski Charlotte—†	231	housewife	35	"
	O	Sulinski William	231	machinist	33	"
	P	Ames Gertrude M—†	231	housekeeper	51	Dedham
	R	Wentzell Ross L	231	rigger	51	here
	S	West Karl	247	salesman	42	"
	T	West Louise—†	247	housewife	40	"
	U	Gilmartin Albert J	249	bookbinder	27	"
	V	Gilmartin Gladys G—†	249	housekeeper	29	"
	X	Gilmartin Julia T—†	249	bookkeeper	31	"
	W	Gilmartin Katherine F—†	249	housewife	60	"
	Y	Gilmartin Patrick J	249	melter	66	"
	Z	Lengevich Helen K—†	251	teacher	27	"
1252						
	A	Lengevich Joseph W	251	clerk	25	"
	B	Lengevich Phillip J	251	machinist	23	"
	C	*Lengevich Stella—†	251	housewife	61	"
	D	*Lengevich William	251	laborer	61	"
	E	McCarthy Alice T—†	253	bookkeeper	35	"
	F	McCarthy Frances I—†	253	operator	22	"
	G	McCarthy James J	253	maint'nce man	32	"
	H	*McCarthy Margaret—†	253	housewife	63	"
	K	McCarthy Mary E—†	253	clerk	32	"

River Street

Page	Letter	Full Name	Residence	Occupation	Age	Reported Residence
	M	Stack Charles F	1315	physician	70	here
	N	Stack Charles F, jr	1315	clerk	36	"
	O	Stack Grace L—†	1315	housekeeper	23	"
	P	Hicks John J	1319	chauffeur	39	"
	R	Hicks Mary J—†	1319	housewife	70	"
	S	Gaudet Clara M—†	1319	"	39	1197 Hyde Park av
	T	Gaudet Earle E	1319	laborer	44	1197 "
	V	Dodge Addie L—†	1335	housewife	70	here
	W	Dodge Frederick W	1335	physician	75	"
	X	Kennedy Jessie A—†	1335	maid	32	"
	Y	Alden Augustus E	1339	physician	52	"
	Z	Alden Doris P—†	1339	housewife	42	"

Page	Letter	Full Name	Residence Jan. 1, 1941	Occupation	Supposed Age	Reported Residence Jan. 1, 1940. Street and Number.
1253						

River Street Continued

Page	Letter	Full Name	Residence Jan. 1, 1941	Occupation	Supposed Age	Reported Residence Jan. 1, 1940.
	A	DeMarzio Celtib R †	1351	bookkeeper	30	111 Readville
	B	DeMarzio Francis J	1351	draftsman	36	111 "
	C	DeMarzio Raphael F	1351	machinist	26	111 "
	D	Femino Dominic	1353	merchant	44	1351 River
	E	Femino Susan M †	1353	housewife	35	1351 "
	F	Dench Joseph J	1355–1357	policeman	41	here
	G	Dench Katherine L †	1355–1357	housewife	39	"
	H	Dwyer William F	1355–1357	laborer	43	"
	L	Richardson Amelia M †	1369	housewife	55	"
	M	Richardson Wallace A	1369	floorman	61	"
	N	Childs George S	1369	draftsman	40	"
	O	Childs Louise B †	1369	housewife	66	"
	P	Childs William G	1369	mechanic	65	"
	R	English Ettie E †	1377	housekeeper	75	"
	T	Travers Mary A †	1385	"	66	"
	U	McIntosh Florence N †	1385	housewife	63	"
	V	McIntosh William R	1385	foreman	61	"
	X	Mamaty Albert G	1399	clerk	46	130 Bird
	Y	Mamaty Alice E †	1399	housewife	40	130 "
	Z	Mamaty Frances A †	1399	housekeeper	20	130 "
1254						
	A	Bloom Louis	1399	salesman	33	16 Fenelon
	B	Bloom Sally †	1399	housewife	29	16 "
	C	Paradis Albert J	1399	draftsman	29	N Hampshire
	D	Sanborn Irene M †	1403	clerk	43	here
	E	Sanborn Mary E †	1403	housewife	71	"
	F	Sanborn William E	1403	electrician	40	"
	G	McGeough Catherine †	1409	housewife	70	"
	H	McGeough Frank X	1409	salesman	45	"
	K	McGeough Gerard W	1409	letter carrier	30	"
	L	McGeough John F	1409	retired	74	"
	M	McGeough John J	1409	laborer	44	"
	N	McGeough Joseph P	1409	plumber	42	"
	O	Norton Edward J	1415	maint'nce man	53	"
	P	Norton Eleanor E †	1415	counter girl	27	"
	R	Norton James T	1415	papermaker	24	"
	S	Norton John R	1415	maint'nce man	24	"
	T	Norton Joseph E	1415	papermaker	31	"
	U	Norton Mary M †	1415	counter girl	32	"
	V	*Sikora Frank	1417	laborer	62	"

Page.	Letter.	Full Name.	Residence, Jan. 1, 1941.	Occupation.	Supposed Age.	Reported Residence, Jan. 1, 1940. Street and Number.

River Street—Continued

Page.	Letter.	Full Name.	Residence, Jan. 1, 1941.	Occupation.	Supposed Age.	Reported Residence, Jan. 1, 1940. Street and Number.
	W	Sikora Frank	1417	laborer	22	here
	X	Sikora Joseph	1417	clerk	32	"
	Y	*Sikora Lena †	1417	housewife	60	"
	Z	Sikora Mary †	1417	operator	26	"
1255						
	A	Sikora Walter	1417	painter	24	"
	B	Brown Marjorie H †	1421	housewife	36	"
	C	Brown Walter J	1421	chauffeur	36	"
	D	Hewitt George W	1421	guard	63	"
	E	Picott Ruth †	1421	housekeeper	30	"
	F	Grenier Flora M †	1421	housewife	28	"
	G	Grenier Leo J	1421	machinist	31	"
	K	Moriarty Harriet F †	1433	housewife	55	"
	L	Moriarty James E	1433	retired	65	"
	M	Amback Charles A	1433	"	75	"
	N	Amback Minnie †	1433	housewife	75	"
	O	Czarnowski Joachim	1437	laborer	57	"
	P	Czarnowski John	1437	"	23	"
	R	Czarnowski Mary †	1437	operator	26	"
	S	*Czarnowski Theodosia †	1437	housewife	57	"
	T	Gookin John A	1437	clerk	58	21 Mt Vernon
	U	Gookin John A, jr	1437	laborer	21	21 "
	V	Gookin Margaret M †	1437	housewife	53	21 "
	W	*Mullane Catherine †	1441	housekeeper	77	here
	X	Jamgochian George	1441	merchant	47	39 King
	Y	*Jamgochian Mary †	1441	housewife	33	39 "
	Z	Healey Lucy A †	1445	housekeeper	65	here
1256						
	A	Kenney Dorothy M †	1445	stenographer	21	"
	B	Kenney Francis E	1445	mortician	46	"
	C	Kenney Grace N †	1445	housewife	42	"

Shepard Court

Page.	Letter.	Full Name.	Residence, Jan. 1, 1941.	Occupation.	Supposed Age.	Reported Residence, Jan. 1, 1940. Street and Number.
	D	Kiessling Fred C	7	custodian	41	here
	E	Kiessling Winifred C †	7	housewife	37	"
	F	Hatch Charles E	9	plumber	66	"
	G	Hatch Mary A †	9	housewife	65	"
	H	Visnor John J	9	operator	32	225 Reservation rd
	K	Visnor Lena V †	9	housewife	29	225 "

Page	Letter	Full Name	Residence, Jan. 1, 1941	Occupation	Supposed Age	Reported Residence, Jan. 1, 1940. Street and Number

Summer Street

Page	Letter	Full Name	Residence, Jan. 1, 1941	Occupation	Supposed Age	Reported Residence, Jan. 1, 1940. Street and Number
	L	Curran Catherine †	3	clerk	23	here
	M	Curran Delia †	3	housewife	65	"
	N	Curran Francis	3	timekeeper	25	"
	O	Condon Catherine †	4	sorter	26	"
	P	Condon Margaret †	4	housewife	56	"
	R	Condon Michael J	4	watchman	64	"
	S	Condon Rita †	4	clerk	23	"
	T	Grison Bertha L †	4	housewife	70	"
	U	*Grison Gabriel A	4	molder	67	"
	V	Grison John	4	laborer	30	"
	W	Williams Marie G †	4	beautician	42	"
	X	Grendle Nathan T	4	painter	50	Somerville
	Y	Jewett Fred O	4	machinist	23	"
	Z	Nason Florence †	4	seamstress	44	here
1257						
	A	Barbarish John	4	machinist	37	"
	B	Berube Joseph	4	polisher	37	"
	C	*Berube Marie A †	4	housewife	34	"
	D	Jackson Florence E †	4	entertainer	23	"
	E	Jackson Harold B	4	manager	21	"
	F	Jackson Louisa B †	4	housewife	65	"
	G	Jackson Samuel	4	molder	63	"
	H	Alexieff Olga P †	4	housewife	57	"
	K	Alexieff Stephen T	4	toolmaker	66	"
	L	Concannon Sarah †	6	housewife	45	"
	M	Kerwin Frank W	6	teacher	30	15 Gordon av
	N	Kerwin Sadie L †	6	matron	50	15 "
	O	*Decker Jenny M †	8	housewife	38	here
	P	Decker Joseph	8	brewer	51	"
	S	Morrison Ellen V †	9	houseworker	61	"
	T	Morrison Grace E †	9	"	60	"
	U	Morrison Hannah M †	9	"	77	"
	V	Rooney Frances M †	9	housewife	68	"
	W	*Donabed Avgin	10	retired	76	"
	X	*Donabed Youghaber †	10	housewife	65	"
	Y	McGillivrey James	10	carpenter	54	"
	Z	McGillivrey Jessie A †	10	maid	48	"
1258						
	A	Deinha Barsam	10	clerk	30	"
	B	Deinha Joseph	10	waiter	29	"

Page.	Letter.	Full Name.	Residence, Jan. 1, 1941.	Occupation.	Supposed Age.	Reported Residence, Jan. 1, 1940. Street and Number.

Summer Street—Continued

Page	Letter	Full Name	Residence	Occupation	Age	Reported Residence
	C	Clark Cora A †	13	secretary	50	here
	D	Clark Thomas A	13	retired	84	"
	E	McVinney Frances P †	15	clerk	31	"
	F	McVinney George J	15	machinist	26	"
	G	McVinney Joseph F	15	engineer	60	"
	H	McVinney Margaret A †	15	housewife	60	"
	K	McVinney Mary M †	15	stenographer	20	"
	L	Scribner Elizabeth A †	15	housewife	68	"
	M	Scribner Frederick P	15	retired	70	"
	N	Scribner William J	15	student	22	"
	P	Rando Joseph	18	serviceman	33	"
	R	Rando Mary †	18	housewife	34	"
	S	*Cedrone Ralph	19	gardener	45	1433 Hyde Park av
	T	Chamberlain James D	19	clerk	28	here
	U	Drummey John L	19	"	23	17 Pine
	V	Ewen John J	19	painter	66	1144 River
	W	Hanson Arthur H	19	upholsterer	47	28 Davison
	X	Robinson Christine C †	19	housewife	72	here
	Y	Scherber Harry J	19	shipper	33	Dedham
	Z	Stomski Gideon	19	weaver	45	here
1259						
	A	Wright Alvin H	19	clerk	27	"
	B	Ruzzo Antonio	20	plumber	51	"
	C	Ruzzo Maria †	20	housewife	47	"
	D	Ruzzo Raphaela †	20	boxmaker	25	"
	E	Ruzzo Rosina †	20	"	20	"
	F	Palombo Edward J	22	welder	44	"
	G	Palombo Josephine M †	22	housewife	35	"
	H	Richards John F	23	retired	80	"
	K	Richards Lila B †	23	housewife	74	"
	L	Lavoie Arthur	23	rubberworker	33	"
	M	Lavoie Marie †	23	operator	31	"
	N	Ascolese Anthony	24	manager	40	"
	O	Ascolese Josephine †	24	housewife	34	"
	P	*Ascolese Michael	24	retired	75	95 N Margin
	S	Marini Benjamin	24	laborer	60	here
	T	Marini Frances †	24	housewife	55	"
	U	Marini Mary †	24	hairdresser	34	"
	V	Duggan Kathryn M †	25	housewife	38	49 Williams av
	W	McCarthy Edmond H	25	student	22	here
	X	McCarthy Elizabeth B †	25	housewife	54	"

Page	Letter	Full Name	Residence, Jan. 1, 1941	Occupation	Supposed Age	Reported Residence, Jan. 1, 1940. Street and Number

Summer Street—Continued

Page	Letter	Full Name	Residence, Jan. 1, 1941	Occupation	Supposed Age	Reported Residence, Jan. 1, 1940. Street and Number
	Y	McCarthy Kathleen M †	25	nurse	32	here
	Z	McCarthy Michael E	25	proprietor	36	"
1260						
	A	Gibson Esther J †	26	bookkeeper	22	"
	B	Gibson Frederick H	26	plumber	55	"
	C	Gibson Frederick J	26	welder	24	"
	D	Gibson Mary E †	26	housewife	58	"
	E	Gibson Robert L	26	laborer	21	"
	F	Whitney Elroy E	26	welder	28	"
	G	Whitney Irene K †	26	housewife	28	"
	H	Donaruma Dominic	28	boilermaker	52	53 Summer
	K	Donaruma Josephine F †	28	finisher	23	53 "
	L	Donaruma Ralph	28	machinist	21	53 "
	M*	Donaruma Susie †	28	housewife	51	53 "
	N	Saccardo Grace †	28	"	35	95 N Margin
	O	Tobin Cecilia M †	29	stenographer	21	here
	P	Tobin Francis P	29	"	24	"
	R	Tobin Mary G †	29	housewife	42	"
	S	Whelan Mary E †	29	"	44	"
	T	Whelan William R	29	machinist	47	"
	U	Guevin Alfred A	29	mechanic	41	32 Garfield av
	V	Guevin Annette G †	29	housewife	38	32 "
	W	Domonawski Anita †	32	stitcher	21	here
	X	Domonawski Anthony	32	molder	45	"
	Y*	Domonawski Peter	32	spinner	53	"
	Z*	Domonawski Victoria †	32	housewife	53	"
1261						
	A	Connick Alfred J	34	accountant	47	"
	B	Connick James A	34	retired	79	"
	C	Downey Elizabeth C †	34	housewife	45	"
	D	Downey Fred A	34	carpenter	55	"
	E	Downey Joseph A	34	laborer	26	"
	F	Downey Margaret M †	34	beautician	27	"
	G	Ciccarelli Alfred	35	foreman	43	"
	H	Ciccarelli Angelina M †	35	housewife	38	"
	K	Cleary Ethel M †	35	houseworker	25	"
	L	Cleary John D	35	mason	38	"
	M	Cleary Mae V †	35	stenographer	40	"
	N	Cleary Nora A †	35	housewife	61	"
	O	Cleary Ralph A	35	mason	24	"
	P	Carty Thomas	37	policeman	52	"

Page.	Letter.	Full Name.	Residence, Jan. 1, 1941.	Occupation.	Supposed Age.	Reported Residence, Jan. 1, 1940. Street and Number.

Summer Street—Continued

Page.	Letter.	Full Name.	Residence, Jan. 1, 1941.	Occupation.	Supposed Age.	Reported Residence, Jan. 1, 1940. Street and Number.
	R	James Charles L	37	watchman	59	here
	S	James Clifford F	37	harnessmaker	55	"
	T	James Mabel A †	37	housewife	82	"
	U	James William H	37	retired	85	"
	V	Galvin Edward L	38	freighthandler	37	"
	W*	Galvin Mary A †	38	housewife	70	"
	X	Whitman Alice L †	38	stenographer	31	"
	Y	Whitman Joseph F	38	welder	31	"
	Z	Jordan Martin A	41	painter	61	"
1262						
	A	Jordan Sadie A †	41	housewife	61	"
	B	Conroy Arthur J	41	grinder	34	"
	C	Conroy Dorothea W †	41	housewife	35	"
	D	Barron Frederick J	43	gasfitter	44	"
	E	Barron Frederick R	43	chauffeur	22	"
	F	Barron Mabel R †	43	housewife	41	"
	G	Jenkins Burton W	46	policeman	43	"
	H	Jenkins Marie J †	46	housewife	41	"
	K	Lampron Louis	46	retired	69	"
	L	Foley Anthony	47	clerk	23	"
	M	Foley Charles	47	salesman	51	"
	N	Foley Geraldine M †	47	stenographer	21	"
	O	Foley Kathleen †	47	housewife	46	"
	P	Foley Vincent H	47	clerk	22	"
	R	Dalesandro Clement	48	chauffeur	21	"
	S*	Dalesandro Mary †	48	housewife	38	"
	T	Dalesandro Pasquale	48	molder	42	"
	U	Moore Margaret A †	49	housewife	36	"
	V	Moore William	49	cabinetmaker	38	"
	W	Hall Dorothy M †	49	cashier	22	"
	X*	Hall Gertrude L †	49	housewife	42	"
	Y	Hall Gertrude L †	49	clerk	20	"
	Z	Hall Helen L †	49	packer	23	"
1263						
	A	Lynch Frances †	49	housewife	63	"
	B	Lynch Michael F	49	foreman	64	"
	C	Stapleton Helen F †	50	housewife	48	Wollaston
	D	Stapleton James A	50	engineer	51	"
	E	Laconte Antonio	51	laborer	48	here
	F	Laconte Virginia †	51	housewife	37	"

Page	Letter	Full Name.	Residence, Jan. 1, 1941.	Occupation.	Supposed Age.	Reported Residence, Jan. 1, 1940. Street and Number.

Summer Street—Continued

Page	Letter	Full Name.	Residence, Jan. 1, 1941.	Occupation.	Supposed Age.	Reported Residence, Jan. 1, 1940. Street and Number.
	G	Giddings Clara L †	51	clerk	40	here
	H	Tranfaglia James	51	laborer	43	"
	K	DeFuria Mary †	51	stenographer	23	"
	L	Giammito Phillip	51	laborer	54	"
	M	Giammito Rose †	51	housewife	54	"
	N	Christy Alice V †	52	clerk	42	"
	O	Welsh Edward J	52	retired	68	"
	P	Welsh Helen V †	52	stenographer	28	"
	R	Gaita Angelo	53	draftsman	42	"
	S	Gaita Rose M †	53	housewife	37	"
	T	Carey Francis J	53	pipefitter	38	Mansfield
	U	Carey Hazel L †	53	housewife	29	"
	V	Durant Edward G	53	chauffeur	40	127 West
	W	Durant Helen M †	53	housewife	35	127 "
	X	Carroll John	55	porter	37	15 Areola
	Y	Carroll Julia †	55	housewife	25	15 "
	Z	James George D	57	painter	42	here
1264						
	A	James Mary E †	57	housewife	43	"
	B	Fitzmaurice Donald	57	cook	27	165 Hunt'n av
	C	Fitzmaurice Genevieve M †	57	waitress	21	165 "
	D	Guard Constance †	57	"	24	165 "
	E	O'Brien Jennie †	57	housekeeper	58	165 "
	F	Shellmer Beatrice †	58	housewife	42	here
	G	Shellmer Walter	58	clerk	44	"
	H	*Montanaro Angelina †	58	housewife	40	"
	K	*Montanaro Joseph	58	mechanic	43	"
	L	Welch John J	59	machinist	40	42 West
	M	Welch Mary K †	59	housewife	35	42 "
	N	Brown Helen E †	60	"	27	1000 Hyde Park av
	O	Brown Warren B	60	clerk	27	1000 "
	P	Moran Helen M †	60	housewife	47	here
	R	Moran James H	60	clerk	19	"
	S	*Borey Elizabeth †	60	housewife	47	"
	T	Borey Mary †	60	stenographer	21	"
	U	Stefaniak Edward	61	machinist	23	"
	V	*Stefaniak Joseph	61	painter	60	"
	W	Stefaniak Olga †	61	housewife	21	27A Bellflower
	X	Stefaniak Stella †	61	papercutter	28	here
	Y	*Stefaniak Valeria †	61	housewife	52	"

Page.	Letter.	Full Name.	Residence, Jan. 1, 1941.	Occupation.	Supposed Age.	Reported Residence, Jan. 1, 1940. Street and Number.

Summer Street—Continued

Page.	Letter.	Full Name.	Residence, Jan. 1, 1941.	Occupation.	Supposed Age.	Reported Residence, Jan. 1, 1940. Street and Number.
	Z	Haley Hazel †	63	housewife	32	here
1265						
	A	Haley Herman	63	carpenter	35	"
	B	*MacInnes Helen J †	65	housewife	49	"
	C	MacInnes John A	65	machinist	36	"
	D	McCarthy Dennis H	65	repairman	43	"
	E	McCarthy Mary T †	65	housewife	46	"
	F	*Acconcia Anna †	67	"	36	"
	G	Acconcia Peter	67	clerk	33	"
	H	Mancini Mary †	69	housewife	33	"
	K	Mancini Serafino	59	laborer	47	"
	L	Fermanio Frances †	69	housewife	38	"
	M	Fermanio Francis	69	clerk	20	"
	N	Fermanio Louis	69	foreman	42	"
	O	*Bevilacqua Ann †	70	housewife	34	"
	P	Bevilacqua Gaetano	70	driller	37	"
	R	*Perisi Theresa †	70	housekeeper	63	"
	S	Grogan Henry D	71–73	clerk	45	"
	T	Grogan Margaret C †	71–73	housewife	47	"
	U	Lynch Alice L †	71–73	"	33	"
	V	Lynch Francis D	71–73	clerk	38	"
	W	Cleary Arthur	75–77	mason	35	"
	X	Cleary Kathleen †	75–77	housewife	33	"
	Y	Doherty John E	75–77	retired	68	"
	Z	*Martin Anna M †	75–77	housewife	41	"
1266						
	A	Martin James F	75–77	auditor	40	"
	B	MacDonald Elizabeth C †	95	housewife	45	"
	C	MacDonald John F	95	machinist	57	"
	D	Thompson Mary E †	95	stitcher	62	"
	E	DiBartolomeo Adelaide †	97	housewife	47	"
	F	DiBartolomeo Pasquale	97	blacksmith	47	"

West Street

Page.	Letter.	Full Name.	Residence, Jan. 1, 1941.	Occupation.	Supposed Age.	Reported Residence, Jan. 1, 1940. Street and Number.
	G	Holland John	252	retired	77	here
	H	Ricci Catherine T †	252	housewife	40	"
	K	Ricci Luigi	252	B F D	40	"
	L	Jenkins Emma D †	290	housewife	66	"
	M	Jenkins Ulric B	290	decorator	63	"
	N	Dickers Hannah M †	294	housewife	31	"

Page	Letter	Full Name	Residence Jan. 1, 1941	Occupation	Supposed Age	Reported Residence, Jan. 1, 1940. Street and Number

West Street—Continued

Page	Letter	Full Name	Residence	Occupation	Age	Reported Residence
	O	Dickers John	294	salesman	30	here
	P	Dickers Magdalena J—†	294	housewife	57	"
	R	Dickers Peter J	294	operator	59	"
	S	DeHont Della T—†	298	housewife	43	"
	T	DeHont Peter	298	merchant	39	"
	U	Stevens Fred E	310	registrar	31	Arlington
	V	Stevens Winifred E—†	310	housewife	23	"
	W	Mains Harriett W—†	310	"	50	96 West
	X	Mains Walter R	310	salesman	60	96 "

Winslow Street

Page	Letter	Full Name	Residence	Occupation	Age	Reported Residence
	Y	Stack Joseph A	11	policeman	40	here
	Z	Stack Therese C—†	11	housewife	36	"
1267						
	A	Dooley Aurella—†	12	"	55	"
	B	Dooley Charles F	12	retired	66	"
	C	Dooley Grace M—†	12	stenographer	30	"
	D	Feeney Anna M—†	13	packer	27	50 Austin
	E	Waugh Francis P	13	mechanic	26	50 "
	F	Waugh Josephine G—†	13	housewife	56	50 "
	G	Butler John A	14	printer	42	here
	H	Butler Mary C—†	14	housewife	42	"
	K	Gudaitis Charles	15	machinist	52	"
	L	Gudaitis Eva—†	15	housewife	46	"
	M	Gudaitis Francis	15	bartender	27	"
	N	Anusewicz Joseph	16	mechanic	48	"
	O	Anusewicz Victoria—†	16	housewife	44	"
	P*	Bielawski Nellie—†	16	"	46	"
	R	Bielawski Peter	16	machine tender	48	"
	S*	Ylanda John	16	laborer	58	"
	T	Taylor George F	17	retired	61	"
	U	Taylor Ida A—†	17	housewife	59	"
	V	Anusewicz Edna B—†	17	"	23	132 Brook av
	W	Anusewicz Joseph M	17	cleaner	23	132 "
	X	Flaherty Roger J, jr	19	winder	55	here
	Y	Flaherty Rose A—†	19	housewife	55	"
	Z	Gonski Helen C—†	19	"	31	"
1268						
	A	Gonski John H	19	retired	73	"
	B	Gonski John J	19	laborer	30	"

Page	Letter	Full Name	Residence Jan. 1 1941	Occupation	Supposed Age	Reported Residence, Jan. 1, 1940. Street and Number.

Winslow Street Continued

Page	Letter	Full Name	Residence Jan. 1 1941	Occupation	Supposed Age	Reported Residence, Jan. 1, 1940.
	C	Gonski Julia †	19	housewife	67	here
	D	Kowalezk Stanley A	19	clerk	23	"
	E	Ozier Charles L	20	"	59	"
	F	Ozier Charles N	20	"	27	"
	G	Ozier Margaret A †	20	housewife	58	"
	H	Neal Wallace I	24	retired	72	"
	K	Bent George P	24	carpenter	47	11 Reddy av
	L	Bent George P	24	laborer	26	11 "
	M	Bent Mary L †	24	housewife	53	11 "
	N	Nessar Nasema A †	29	"	35	here
	O*	Nessar Toufie	29	proprietor	46	"
	P	Haley Jeremiah J	29	tree surgeon	31	Brockton
	R	Haley Rose E †	29	housewife	25	"
	S	Moraski Eugenia †	33	"	22	here
	T	Moraski Merritt	33	waiter	25	"
	U*	Wojciechowiez Barbara †	33	housewife	47	"
	V	Wojciechowiez John	33	bartender	44	"
	W	Pinchieri Nellie P †	33	housewife	25	136 Child
	X	Pinchieri Rocco P	33	metalworker	28	136 "
	Y	Slyva Apolonia †	35	housewife	46	here
	Z	Slyva John A	35	painter	57	"
1269						
	A	Slyva John S	35	toolmaker	22	"
	B	Slyva Joseph W	35	teacher	26	"
	C	Sisti Rose M †	36	housewife	23	1518 Hyde Park av
	D	Sisti Victor	36	cabinetmaker	25	1518 "
	E	Toti Guy	36	laborer	56	here
	F*	Toti Victoria †	36	housewife	51	"
	G	Leufgren Gertrude E †	38	librarian	55	"
	H	Leufgren Harold L	38	photographer	46	"
	K	Leufgren Lilly M †	38	housewife	46	Sandwich

Ward 18—Precinct 13

CITY OF BOSTON

LIST OF RESIDENTS
20 YEARS OF AGE AND OVER

(NON-CITIZENS INDICATED BY ASTERISK)
(FEMALES INDICATED BY DAGGER)

AS OF

JANUARY 1, 1941

CITY OF BOSTON PRINTING DEPARTMENT

Page.	Letter	Full Name.	Residence, Jan. 1, 1941	Occupation	Supposed Age.	Reported Residence, Jan. 1, 1940. Street and Number.

1300
Central Avenue

Page.	Letter	Full Name.	Residence, Jan. 1, 1941	Occupation	Supposed Age.	Reported Residence, Jan. 1, 1940. Street and Number.
	D	Goodwin George W	21	sexton	65	here
	E	Leonard Elizabeth T †	21	domestic	84	"
	F	Terry Sarah M—†	21	housekeeper	67	"
	H	Horn David Y	25	foreman	46	"
	K	*Horn Isa M—†	25	housewife	39	"
	L	Perry Charles E	25	clerk	29	"
	M	Perry Florence M—†	25	housewife	62	"
	N	Perry Louis H	25	draftsman	61	"
	O	Perry Vivian C—†	25	housewife	30	"
	P	Lord Doris W—†	27	"	34	"
	R	Lord Lemuel K	27	clergyman	34	"
	S	Briggs Elizabeth M—†	31	physician	63	"
	T	Briggs Merton L	31	"	62	"
	U	George Elizabeth L—†	31	teacher	32	"
	V	George Forrest W	31	extractmaker	33	"
	X	Clarke James E	44	retired	78	"
	Y	Harlfinger Richard L	44	machinist	33	"
	Z	Harlfinger Signe M—†	44	housewife	28	"
1301						
	A	Safford Irene M—†	44	housekeeper	61	Malden
	B	Reynolds Esther—†	49	typist	33	142 West
	C	Reynolds Henrietta—†	49	housewife	54	142 "
	D	Reynolds John L	49	laborer	30	142 "
	E	Reynolds John J	49	letter carrier	58	142 "
	F	Reynolds Joseph M	49	laborer	27	142 "
	G	Foster Effie H—†	49	typist	22	here
	H	Foster George A	49	reporter	23	"
	K	Foster Marion W—†	49	housewife	50	"
	L	Goodwin Estella G—†	55	"	32	"
	M	Goodwin Morrell P	55	broker	36	"
	N	Hartman Frederick A	55	mechanic	36	"
	O	Hartman Walter A	55	"	34	"
	P	*Munroe Donald	56	cutter	30	689 Metropolitan av
	R	Munroe Mildred T—†	56	bookkeeper	29	7 Vose av
	S	Erickson Erick G	56	instructor	47	78 Pierce
	T	Erickson Esther C—†	56	housewife	50	78 "
	V	Marshall Edwin L	58	salesman	66	here
	W	Marshall Edwin L, jr	58	clerk	24	"
	X	Marshall Grace E—†	58	housewife	61	"
	Y	Marshall Louis C	58	salesman	34	"

Page	Letter	Full Name	Residence, Jan. 1, 1941	Occupation	Supposed Age	Reported Residence, Jan. 1, 1940. Street and Number

Central Avenue Continued

Page	Letter	Full Name	Residence, Jan. 1, 1941	Occupation	Supposed Age	Reported Residence, Jan. 1, 1940. Street and Number
	Z	Radell Emma L †	58	housekeeper	79	here
1302						
	A	Beaumont Clara E †	58	housewife	76	"
	B	Beaumont John	58	retired	75	"
	C	Niver Grace B †	58	housewife	41	"
	D	Niver John D	58	chauffeur	43	"
	E	Greenwood Helen P †	60	housekeeper	87	"
	F	Dann Harry K	61	steamfitter	21	"
	G	Dann Margaret E †	61	housewife	49	"
	H	Dann Sumner H	61	manager	53	"
	K	Hurlbert Ethel M †	62	housewife	54	"
	L	Hurlbert Hartley A	62	agent	53	"
	M	Merritt Elizabeth J †	62	housekeeper	76	"
	N	Wadsworth Christina †	68	housewife	81	"
	O	Wadsworth Mary E †	68	teacher	53	"
	P	Wadsworth William W	68	clerk	55	"
	R	Macaskill Kenneth A	69	salesman	56	"
	S	Macaskill Marion D †	69	housewife	49	"
	T	Boyd Joseph T	71	foreman	33	"
	U	Boyd Virginia R †	71	housewife	34	"
	V	Boyd Elsie W †	71	housekeeper	44	"
	W	Boyd Muriel E †	71	operator	42	"
	X	Dunbar Albert	71	clerk	57	"
	Y	Beaupre Augustus J	74	B F D	46	"
	Z	Beaupre Marie E †	74	student	20	"
1303						
	A	Beaupre Mary T †	74	housewife	46	"
	B	Leonard Mary E †	75	"	41	"
	C	Leonard Thomas C	75	clerk	36	"
	D	Leonard William F	75	"	20	"
	E	Leonard William H	75	B F D	42	"
	F	*Pacewicz Amelia †	75	housekeeper	70	"
	G	Hanson B Catherine †	76	secretary	23	"
	H	*Hanson Lillian E †	76	housewife	70	"
	K	House Howard L	76	clerk	28	97 Arlington
	L	House Mildred E †	76	stenographer	27	97 "
	M	Stevens Evelyn B †	77	housewife	63	here
	N	Stevens Frederick B	77	physician	73	"
	O	Earle George W	79	retired	77	"
	P	Hyde Beatrice E †	80	housewife	41	"
	R	Hyde Marshall A	80	packer	43	"

Page	Letter	Full Name.	Residence, Jan. 1, 1941.	Occupation.	Supposed Age.	Reported Residence, Jan. 1, 1940. Street and Number.

Central Avenue—Continued

Page	Letter	Full Name	Residence	Occupation	Age	Reported Residence
	S	Gleason Nellie G—†	80	housekeeper	84	here
	T	Russell Annie—†	80	"	73	22 Glenarm
	U	Russell Mary A—†	80	"	65	22 "
	V	Hartmann Helen C—†	82	housewife	28	1002 River
	W	Hartmann Karl	82	machinist	28	55 Central av
	X	Derry Armanda R—†	82	housekeeper	78	16 Park
	Y	*Taper Jeanette—†	82	"	67	7 Elm

Davison Street

Page	Letter	Full Name	Residence	Occupation	Age	Reported Residence
	Z	Caccigrani Albert	8	laborer	22	here
1304						
	A	Hurd Catherine E—†	8	waitress	21	"
	B	Hurd Gladys I—†	8	housewife	41	"
	C	Hurd Henry C	8	repairman	20	"
	D	Hurd Henry F	8	clerk	39	"
	E	*McCormack Katherine A—†	8	"	21	"
	F	*Meagher Clara W—†	8	housekeeper	38	"
	G	Brennon George	10	machinist	27	72 Neponset av
	H	*Dolce Frank	10	laborer	47	here
	K	Holmes Arthur W	10	salesman	28	Weymouth
	L	Klucker Frank H	10	printer	31	722 Metropolitan av
	M	*Landy Patrick	10	laborer	57	59 Dana av
	N	Liljestrand Axel A	10	boilermaker	64	here
	O	Liljestrand Ellen—†	10	housewife	63	"
	P	Liljestrand Phillip A	10	musician	24	"
	R	Liljestrand Richard G	10	laborer	25	"
	S	McWhinney Robert F	10	retired	67	"
	T	Moran Edward	10	laborer	64	29 Business
	U	Stack John T	10	machinist	55	11 Winslow
	V	Stanion Edward	10	laborer	52	here
	W	Walsh John J	10	"	55	"
	X	Moran Grace A—†	13–15	housekeeper	50	"
	Y	Maxwell Edwin	13–15	tree surgeon	23	"
	Z	Maxwell Elsie M—†	13–15	housewife	46	"
1305						
	A	Maxwell Ruth E—†	13–15	saleswoman	21	"
	B	Kearns Mary M—†	14	housewife	36	212 Austin
	C	Kearns Thomas J	14	letter carrier	42	212 "
	D	Hicks George	14	carpenter	34	here
	E	Hicks Margaret—†	14	operator	34	"

Page	Letter	Full Name	Residence, Jan. 1, 1941	Occupation	Supposed Age	Reported Residence, Jan. 1, 1940, Street and Number

Davison Street Continued

Page	Letter	Full Name	Residence	Occupation	Age	Reported Residence
	F	O'Brien Isabella E †	14	housekeeper	58	here
	G	Sandgren William R	14	engineer	53	"
	H	Barrett Gertrude L †	14	housewife	38	"
	K	Barrett Jeremiah A	14	policeman	38	"
	L	Camara John L	14	engineer	23	"
	M	Manson Mildred †	16	housewife	35	"
	N	Manson William J	16	manager	35	"
	O	Taylor Elizabeth G †	16	housewife	31	"
	P	Taylor Francis P	16	clerk	38	"
	R	McDonald Lawrence P	16	woolworker	36	102 Austin
	S	McDonald Mary E †	16	housekeeper	40	102 "
	T	Wills Helen G †	16	housewife	27	here
	U	Wills Wallace D	16	bookkeeper	33	"
	V	Lucyk Flora M †	16	housewife	39	"
	W	Lucyk Nicholas J	16	stockman	37	"
	X	Mitchell Bridget †	17	housewife	73	"
	Y	Mitchell John A	17	retired	74	"
	Z	Mitchell William J	17	clerk	29	"
1306						
	A	Buchanan Robert J	17	assembler	35	"
	B	Buchanan Susan †	17	housewife	34	"
	C	Button Margaret R †	17	clerk	21	"
	D	Carle Lillian M †	17	housewife	50	"
	E	Carle Maynard K	17	salesman	43	"
	F	Holst Victoria †	17	clerk	56	6 Everett
	G	Quinlan Joseph P	18	salesman	47	here
	H	Hewitt Arthur W	19	laborer	43	"
	K	MacNeal Catherine H †	19	housewife	54	"
	L	MacNeal Edward H	19	welder	31	"
	M	MacNeal Helen M †	19	beautician	24	"
	N*	MacNeal Pauline V †	19	nurse	31	"
	O	Yusavitch John	19	machinist	30	"
	P	Tingos Effie P †	20	housewife	32	"
	R	Tingos Peter	20	clerk	42	"
	S*	Lanetin Anna E †	21	housewife	47	"
	T	Lanetin Julian L	21	machinist	52	"
	U	Lanetin Leonce M †	21	secretary	22	"
	V	Downing Annie †	22	housewife	75	"
	W	Downing Gertrude H †	22	typist	33	"
	X	Downing Joseph H	22	clerk	37	"
	Y	Downing Michael	22	retired	75	"

Page	Letter	Full Name	Residence, Jan. 1, 1941	Occupation	Supposed Age	Reported Residence, Jan. 1, 1940. Street and Number

Davison Street—Continued

Page	Letter	Full Name	Residence, Jan. 1, 1941	Occupation	Supposed Age	Reported Residence, Jan. 1, 1940
	Z	Carpenter Harold E	24	optician	46	here
1307						
	A	Carpenter Mildred M—†	24	stenographer	20	"
	B	Carpenter Zorah E—†	24	housewife	40	"
	C	Buckley Margaret—†	27	at home	70	841 River
	D	Devlin John J	27	retired	81	66 Maple
	E	Dunn Grace M—†	27	housewife	67	here
	F	Dunn William T	27	manager	69	"
	G	McGillis William R	27	lens grinder	20	1035 South
	H	*Hannon Elsie E—†	29	housewife	47	here
	K	Hannon Joseph J	29	laborer	45	"
	L	Hannon Mary E—†	29	clerk	20	"
	M	Steckelman Alexander A	29	"	26	23 Ransom rd
	N	Steckelman Joseph P	29	papermaker	22	23 "
	O	*Steckelman Mary M—†	29	housewife	53	23 "
	P	*Steckelman Stanley J	29	laborer	56	23 "
	R	Steckelman Veronica A—†	29	wrapper	26	23 "
	S	Abbott Mary A—†	30	housewife	55	here
	T	Abbott Ruth A—†	30	operator	31	"
	U	Alward Beatrice—†	30	housewife	47	"
	V	Alward Harry V	30	baker	50	"
	W	Frederick Alice E—†	30	housewife	72	"
	X	Frederick Forrest	30	retired	71	"
	Y	O'Brien Edward F	31	attorney	35	"
	Z	O'Brien Mary A—†	31	housewife	65	"
1308						
	A	O'Brien Mary M—†	31	"	34	"
	B	Walters Marion J—†	31	housekeeper	58	"
	C	Wheeler Florence E—†	31	"	56	"
	D	Bliss Earl L	33	carpenter	51	"
	E	Bliss Celia A—†	33	housewife	51	"
	F	Bliss Eleanor L—†	33	clerk	27	"
	G	*Richards Charles A	33	laborer	23	965 Hyde Park av
	H	Richards Helen M—†	33	housewife	23	965 "
	K	Armour Joseph G	33	machinist	22	45 W Milton
	L	Armour Josephine C—†	33	housewife	55	45 "
	M	Armour Josephine C—†	33	clerk	26	45 "
	N	Goddard Julia D—†	35	housewife	35	here
	O	Goddard Samuel	35	attendant	39	"
	P	Negrini Jennie B—†	35	housewife	26	Dedham
	R	Negrini Libero L	35	bartender	30	"

Page	Letter	Full Name	Residence, Jan. 1, 1941.	Occupation.	Supposed Age.	Reported Residence, Jan. 1, 1940. Street and Number.

Davison Street—Continued

Page	Letter	Full Name	Residence, Jan. 1, 1941.	Occupation.	Supposed Age.	Reported Residence, Jan. 1, 1940. Street and Number.
	S	Johnson Eula C †	35	housewife	53	here
	T	Johnson Irving C	35	electrician	23	"
	U	Shea Mary J †	36	housewife	71	"
	V	Casey Agnes M †	36	"	41	"
	W	Casey Lester W	36	printer	38	"
	X	Brown Henry A	38	retired	72	29 Dana av
	Y	Copeland Euphemia H †	38	housewife	72	here
	Z	Mulhern Anna M †	39	"	38	"
1309						
	A	Mulhern Joseph T	39	custodian	50	"
	B	*O'Reilly Ellen †	55	housewife	70	Milford
	C	*O'Reilly Margaret M †	55	saleswoman	34	here
	D	Huffan Archie T	55	salesman	23	"
	E	*Huffan Harold H	55	painter	58	"
	F	*Huffan Margaret B †	55	housewife	50	"
	G	Goodale Evan G	55	pharmacist	65	"
	H	*Kelly Patrick J	56	papermaker	31	"
	K	*Kofskey John	56	mechanic	67	"
	L	*Kofskey Nellie †	56	housewife	50	"
	M	Moore James J	56	papermaker	43	"
	N	McLean Austin W	56	retired	69	"
	O	McLean Elinor M †	56	housewife	34	"
	P	McLean Henry A	56	clerk	35	"
	R	Jenkins Anne A †	56	at home	72	"
	S	Hayes Michael J	59	laborer	68	"
	T	Quartley Isabella L †	59	housekeeper	67	"
	U	O'Neil Frank A	59	clerk	40	"
	V	O'Neil Mary M †	59	housewife	39	"
	W	McMahon Alice M †	60	"	49	"
	X	McMahon Irene M †	60	hygienist	25	"
	Y	McMahon John T	60	plumber	51	"
	Z	McMahon Marguerite †	60	clerk	20	"
1310						
	A	*Lombard Evelyn †	60	at home	71	293 Paris
	B	Carey Charles A	62	clerk	33	here
	C	Carey John J	62	manager	40	"
	D	Carey Veronica E †	62	secretary	35	"
	E	Sawyer Albert C	62	electrician	47	"
	F	Sawyer Elizabeth J †	62	housewife	47	"
	G	Neilsen Anton	63	retired	84	"
	H	Neilson Hanssine P †	63	at home	85	"

Page.	Letter.	Full Name.	Residence, Jan. 1, 1941.	Occupation.	Supposed Age.	Reported Residence, Jan. 1, 1940. Street and Number.

Davison Street Continued

Page	Letter	Full Name	Residence	Occupation	Age	Reported Residence
	K	Nielsen Jorgine E †	63	at home	50	here
	L	Crudgington Amos	65	retired	75	"
	M	Crudgington Arthur A	65	"	80	"
	N	Crudgington Fanny M †	65	housewife	73	"
	O	McMahon Helen H †	66	"	35	"
	P	McMahon Thomas A	66	manager	37	"
	R	Martell Margaret B †	67	housewife	64	"
	S	Martell Margaret G †	67	stenographer	30	"
	T	Martell Simon A	67	porter	76	"
	U	Strachan Caroline E †	69	housewife	47	"
	V	Strachan Douglas	69	patternmaker	48	"
	W	Strachan Jessie L †	69	at home	70	"
	X	Lockhart Anna L †	70	housewife	55	"
	Y	Lockhart Edna M †.	70	supervisor	35	"
	Z	Crook John E	70	superintendent	69	"
1311						
	A	*Crook Verna K †	70	housewife	31	Canada
	B	Sheffield Coretta †	71	"	42	108 Hyde Park av
	C	McDermott Cornelius F	71	papermaker	31	here
	D	McDermott Louise A †	71	housewife	30	"
	E	Cataloni Nora C †	71	"	23	"
	F	Cataloni Ralph B	71	machinist	24	"
	G	Calcagni Anthony F	74	carpenter	28	"
	H	*Calcagni Frank	74	watchman	67	"
	K	*Calcagni Jennie †	74	housewife	30	"
	L	*Calcagni Marie †	74	"	67	"
	M	Calcagni Stephen	74	chauffeur	32	"
	N	Ferris Dorothy P †	75	housewife	46	"
	O	Ferris Joseph W	75	bookkeeper	21	"
	P	Keegan Margaret C †	75	nurse	56	"
	R	Keegan Mary J †	75	stenographer	58	"
	S	Keegan Thomas F	75	machinist	53	"
	T	*Swagher Julia D †	77	housewife	52	"
	U	Swagher Sabino	77	shoemaker	59	"
	V	*Zanoni Peter	77	mason	52	"
	W	Speranza James V	77	manager	32	"
	X	Speranza Theresa S †	77	housewife	28	"
	Y	Doughty Edgar W	77	clerk	27	"
	Z	Doughty Frederick W	77	retired	72	"
1312						
	A	Doughty Grace L †	77	housewife	56	"

Page	Letter	Full Name	Residence, Jan. 1, 1941	Occupation	Supposed Age	Reported Residence, Jan. 1, 1940. Street and Number

Davison Street Continued

Page	Letter	Full Name	Residence, Jan. 1, 1941	Occupation	Supposed Age	Reported Residence, Jan. 1, 1940. Street and Number
	B	Coullahan Eliza †	78	housewife	62	here
	C	Coullahan Malachi	78	engineer	56	"

Dell Avenue

Page	Letter	Full Name	Residence, Jan. 1, 1941	Occupation	Supposed Age	Reported Residence, Jan. 1, 1940. Street and Number
	C	Tuckerman Bertha E †	3	housewife	58	here
	E	Tuckerman Edna E †	3	musician	30	"
	F	Tuckerman William O	3	salesman	62	"
	G	Daly Alice L †	7	saleswoman	25	"
	H	Daly Eleanor T †	7	secretary	20	"
	K	Daly Elizabeth V †	7	bookkeeper	26	"
	L	Daly Frank	7	retired	69	"
	M	Daly James A	7	clerk	23	"
	N	Daly Margaret E †	7	secretary	27	"
	O	Daly Mary F †	7	librarian	31	"
	P	Daly Mary T †	7	housewife	60	"
	R	Zwicker George H	10	salesman	58	Milton
	S	Zwicker Leon P	10	student	21	"
	T	Zwicker Mabel D †	10	housewife	47	"
	U	Bradley Alice †	11	teacher	65	here
	V	Bradley Kate E †	11	at home	87	"
	W	Bradley Mabel C †	11	registrar	61	"
	X	Smith Margaret E †	11	housekeeper	60	"
	Y	Day John H	12	bookkeeper	72	"
	Z	Payne Dorothy L †	12	housewife	45	"
1313						
	A	Payne Hildreth L	12	manager	44	"
	B	*Ballagh Allen B	15	student	21	Canada
	C	Daly Agnes †	15	housewife	46	here
	D	Daly Arthur J	15	supervisor	49	"
	E	Rattigan Grace E †	15	secretary	23	"
	F	Rattigan John P	15	physician	30	"
	G	Rattigan Margaret F †	15	housewife	64	"
	H	Rattigan Margaret F †	15	teacher	31	"
	K	Strachan Elmer W	15	student	21	Nebraska
	M	Teachout Edna L †	19	housewife	71	here
	N	Teachout Hattie C †	19	secretary	37	"
	O	Thatcher Evangeline †	19	musician	50	"
	P	Farlin Kate †	19	teacher	64	"
	R	Buckley Charlotte B †	20	housewife	31	"
	S	Buckley John J	20	teacher	35	"

Page	Letter	Full Name	Residence, Jan. 1, 1941	Occupation	Supposed Age	Reported Residence, Jan. 1, 1940. Street and Number

Dell Avenue Continued

Page	Letter	Full Name	Residence, Jan. 1, 1941	Occupation	Supposed Age	Reported Residence, Jan. 1, 1940. Street and Number
	T	Scott Herbert W	21	engineer	53	here
	U	Scott Margaret H †	21	housewife	50	"
	V	Scott Vera E †	21	stenographer	21	"
	W	Metcalf Elsie R †	24	teacher	58	7 Elm
	X	Munster Bertha †	24	"	60	7 "
	Y	Wright Florence †	24	secretary	52	here
	Z	Nichols Bela	27	retired	75	"
1314						
	A	Nichols Lavinia C †	27	housewife	72	"
	B	Wagner Jane †	27	clerk	60	"
	C	Dean Gertrude M †	28	secretary	21	Cambridge
	D	Quealy Emma M †	28	physician	48	here
	E	Quealy Robert W	28	student	25	"
	F	Quealy William H	28	clerk	52	"
	G	Reardon Catherine E †	29	housewife	48	"
	H	Reardon Edward D	29	laborer	22	"
	K	Reardon Harold F	29	machinist	48	"
	L	Reardon Harold F	29	mechanic	25	"
	M	Reardon Robert T	29	clerk	20	"
	N	MacRae John	31	welder	40	"
	O	McSharry William	31	policeman	44	"
	P	O'Leary Margaret †	31	housekeeper	48	"
	R	O'Leary Nellie J †	31	at home	82	"
	Z	White David D	31	chauffeur	35	"
	T	White Mary E †	31	housewife	34	"
	U	Lemay Jessie M †	32	"	49	"
	V	Lemay Mabel K †	32	operator	21	"
	W	Lemay Victor J	32	teacher	45	"
	X	Waltz Charles S	32	retired	88	"
	Y	Conley Bridget A †	35	housewife	65	"
	Z	Conley Helen G †	35	teacher	31	"
1315						
	A	Conley Mary M †	35	clerk	24	"
	B	Conley Michael M	35	operator	65	"
	C	Conley Robert J	35	laborer	22	"
	D	Conley Walter J	35	painter	26	"

Dell Terrace

Page	Letter	Full Name	Residence, Jan. 1, 1941	Occupation	Supposed Age	Reported Residence, Jan. 1, 1940. Street and Number
	E	Holtham Sarah E †	3	housewife	63	here
	F	Holtham William E	3	salesman	63	"

Page	Letter	Full Name	Residence, Jan. 1, 1941	Occupation	Supposed Age	Reported Residence, Jan. 1, 1940. Street and Number

Dell Terrace—Continued

Page	Letter	Full Name	Residence, Jan. 1, 1941	Occupation	Supposed Age	Reported Residence, Jan. 1, 1940. Street and Number
	G	Macaskill John S	3	salesman	60	here
	H	*Dewhirst Kenneth	6	student	23	Canada
	M	Harding Ada L †	6	housekeeper	81	here
	K	Henderson Mabel L †	6	housewife	63	"
	L	Henderson William J	6	retired	69	"
	N	Morse Elwin	6	student	23	New York
	O	Topham Chester	6	architect	50	Milton
	P	Taylor Dorothy R †	7	housewife	43	here
	R	Taylor George E	7	supervisor	43	"
	S	Henderson Marvette E †	7	housewife	23	6 Dell ter
	T	Henderson Richard B	7	shipper	24	6 "

Everett Street

Page	Letter	Full Name	Residence, Jan. 1, 1941	Occupation	Supposed Age	Reported Residence, Jan. 1, 1940. Street and Number
	U	Hogberg Oscar	5	machinist	59	here
	V	Hogberg Sarah †	5	housewife	49	"
	W	Koganian Geragos	5	retired	59	"
	X	Tominey Catherine E †	5	clerk	29	6 Sunnyside
	Y	Tominey Harry	5	machinist	29	1073 River
	Z	Mercer Annie A †	9	housewife	63	56 Central av
1316						
	A	Mercer Frank L	9	machinist	68	56 "
	B	Bunker Mabel †	9	housewife	52	here
	C	Bunker Phillip	9	professor	45	"
	E	Leach Annie M †	16	housewife	54	"
	F	Leach Willis H	16	machinist	59	"
	G	Pagington Annie †	16	housewife	53	"
	H	Pagington George	16	plumber	57	"
	K	McCarthy Isabel †	32	buyer	40	"
	L	McCarthy Mary †	32	housekeeper	44	"
	M	Palmer Kathleen †	32	housewife	39	1078 River
	N	Palmer Thomas H	32	welder	44	1078 "
	O	Corrigan Anna M †	34	at home	31	here
	P	Corrigan Helen K †	34	teacher	36	"
	R	Corrigan Louise T †	34	secretary	26	"
	S	Corrigan Mary S †	34	housewife	56	"
	T	Corrigan William E	34	chauffeur	68	"
	U	Corrigan William E, jr	34	clerk	29	"
	V	Marchankeviez Chester	35	upholsterer	23	"
	W	Marchankeviez Joseph	35	stitcher	24	"
	X	*Marchankeviez Julia †	35	housewife	49	"

Page.	Letter	FULL NAME.	Residence, Jan. 1, 1941.	Occupation.	Supposed Age.	Reported Residence, Jan. 1, 1940. Street and Number.

Everett Street—Continued

Page.	Letter	FULL NAME.	Residence, Jan. 1, 1941.	Occupation.	Supposed Age.	Reported Residence, Jan. 1, 1940.
	Y	Marchankeviez Mary—†	35	packer	26	here
	Z	Marchankeviez Sophie—†	35	"	20	"
1317						
	A	*Marchankeviez Stanley	35	machinist	55	"
	B	Colby Gerald	36	chauffeur	32	"
	C	Colby Mildred R—†	36	housewife	31	"
	D	Currie James A	36	clerk	28	"
	E	Currie John R	36	packer	64	"
	F	Currie Rose M—†	36	housewife	64	"

Fairmount Avenue

Page.	Letter	FULL NAME.	Residence, Jan. 1, 1941.	Occupation.	Supposed Age.	Reported Residence, Jan. 1, 1940.
	O	Bruun Nils G	8	janitor	44	here
	P	Cox Josephine—†	8	chiropodist	53	"
	R	Gerrish Mary—†	8	housekeeper	68	1188 River
	S	Johnson Karen A—†	8	hairdresser	51	here
	T	Brown Raymond	8	machinist	38	1188 River
	U	Channell Carleton	8	seaman	40	here
	V	Ellis Albina—†	8	housekeeper	57	"
	W	Jackson William P	8	painter	45	"
	X	Leporte Henry	8	barber	57	"
	Y	McMorrow Catherine—†	8	housekeeper	65	29 Business
	Z	Montgomery Alexander P	8	machinist	65	here
1318						
	A	Montgomery Elizabeth—†	8	housekeeper	72	"
	B	O'Connor James	8	janitor	65	"
	C	Waker Nettie B—†	8	papermaker	54	"
	D	Cox Elizabeth—†	8	at home	68	"
	E	Kellam Katherine—†	8	operator	54	"
	F	MacDonald Alice—†	8	housekeeper	71	"
	G	Shedd Sadie—†	8	"	54	"
	N	Marino Anthony	24	metalworker	23	3 Nelson
	O	Marino Mabel T—†	24	housewife	23	here
	P	Dimmick Bessie—†	24	clerk	49	"
	R	Walsh Catherine—†	24	housekeeper	76	"
	T	Lawler Rita E—†	28	housewife	22	5 Knight
	U	Lawler William J	28	operator	24	5 "
	V	Hollenbeck Loie M—†	28	seamstress	44	here
	W	Minnick Kathryn—†	28	"	63	"
	Y	Bogen Caroline L—†	32	housewife	30	"
	Z	Bogen Einar I	32	machinist	37	"

Page	Letter	Full Name	Residence, Jan. 1, 1941	Occupation	Reported Age	Reported Residence, Jan. 1, 1940. Street and Number
1319		**Fairmount Avenue**—Continued				
	A	D'Amato Henry	32	chauffeur	29	here
	B	D'Amato Mary M—†	32	housewife	25	"
	P	Vertullo Pasquale	78	cobbler	48	"
	R	Vertullo Saveria—†	78	housewife	43	"
	S	Powers Richard	78	laborer	47	Cambridge
	T	Wilson Grace—†	78	housewife	42	here
	U	Wilson Joseph K	78	operator	43	"
	V	Sparks Fred B	78	retired	69	"
	W	Sparks Mary A—†	78	housewife	58	"
		Harvard Avenue				
	Z	Boucher Alfred	36	painter	56	here
1320						
	A	Hicks Albira L—†	36	housewife	36	"
	B	Hicks Eugene	36	janitor	39	"
	C	Royds Caroline A—†	38	housewife	47	"
	D	Royds Charles E	38	laborer	58	"
	E	Royds Fred	38	"	56	"
	F	Archibald Edward S	40	barber	70	"
	G	Chatfield Helen W—†	40	proofreader	47	"
	H	Whitman Annetta M—†	40	housekeeper	71	"
	K	Whitman Marion A—†	40	bookkeeper	40	"
	L	Congdon Mildred G—†	42	housewife	51	"
	M	Graham Lilla C—†	42	at home	83	"
	N	Corrigan Helen F—†	48	housekeeper	59	"
	O	Doyle Frances M—†	48	at home	86	"
	P	Doyle Frances M—†	48	instructor	46	Dedham
	R	Soulnier Agnes M—†	50	housewife	52	here
	S	Soulnier Edmund J	50	chauffeur	54	"
	T	Johnson Anna E—†	56	secretary	35	"
	U	Johnson Arthur C	56	artist	43	"
	V	Johnson Marion—†	56	secretary	41	"
	W	Johnson Sarah P—†	56	housewife	76	"
	X	Mounce Buford R	56	student	24	Texas
	Y	Sinclair Alexander	62	boilermaker	59	here
	Z	Sinclair Ellen N—†	62	housewife	53	"
1321						
	A	Sinclair Henry M	62	clerk	24	"
	B	Sinclair Robert P	62	molder	31	"

Page.	Letter.	Full Name.	Residence, Jan. 1, 1941.	Occupation.	Supposed Age.	Reported Residence, Jan. 1, 1940. Street and Number.

Harvard Avenue—Continued

Page.	Letter.	Full Name.	Residence, Jan. 1, 1941.	Occupation.	Supposed Age.	Reported Residence, Jan. 1, 1940. Street and Number.
	C	Sinclair William M	62	dishwasher	33	here
	D	*Greenwood Mabel B—†	66	housewife	36	203 Fairmount av
	E	Greenwood William	66	estimator	40	203 "
	F	Coughlin Ellen W—†	66	housekeeper	69	here
	G	Reynolds Bernadette F—†	66	housewife	35	"
	H	Reynolds James F	66	chauffeur	36	"
	M	McDonough Helen J—†	74	at home	33	"
	N	McDonough Louise C—†	74	clerk	21	"
	O	McDonough Lucy A—†	74	housewife	63	"
	P	McDonough Rita J—†	74	hairdresser	24	"
	R	McDonough Thomas E	74	machinist	63	"
	S	McDonough Thomas E	74	merchant	26	"
	U	McMasters Clarendon H	76	proprietor	48	"
	V	Wilson Camilla F—†	76	clerk	30	"
	W	Wilson Catherine A—†	76	housewife	57	"
	X	Wilson John H	76	retired	72	"
	Y	Bilodeau Wilfred J	77	machinist	33	"
	Z	Bilodeau Yvonne E—†	77	housewife	36	"
1322						
	A	Brackett Alfreda C—†	77	housekeeper	46	70 Childs
	B	Hennessey Helen D—†	78	housewife	32	here
	C	Hennessey Henry M	78	salesman	40	"
	D	Hennessey John L	78	boilermaker	50	"
	E	Allendorf George P	79	attendant	35	"
	F	Allendorf Gertrude A—†	79	housewife	33	"
	G	Perchard Agnes T—†	79	housekeeper	62	"
	H	Keating Anna R—†	83	technician	24	"
	K	Keating Helen G—†	83	secretary	27	"
	L	Keating John L	83	student	21	"
	M	Keating Mary E—†	83	housewife	57	"
	N	Keating Nicholas M	83	merchant	54	"
	O	Alley Evelyn—†	83	teacher	53	"
	P	Pellicani Peter J	85	draftsman	31	13 Gordon av
	R	Pellicani Sarah M—†	85	housewife	29	13 "
	S	Rubino Mary—†	85	"	30	52 Lincoln
	T	Rubino Nicholas	85	boilermaker	31	52 "
	U	Fahey Francis I	88	chauffeur	34	here
	V	Fahey Margaret L—†	88	housewife	73	"
	W	Fahey Mary M—†	88	bookkeeper	42	"
	X	O'Connor Catherine T—†	90	housewife	27	389 Adams
	Y	O'Connor Joseph M	90	salesman	25	here

Harvard Avenue (Continued)

Page	Letter	Full Name	Residence Jan. 1, 1941	Occupation	Age	Reported Residence Jan. 1, 1940 Street and Number
	Z	O'Connor Mary C †	90	housekeeper	64	here
1323						
	A	Ellison George R	90	machinist	63	"
	B	Ellison Hilda C †	90	housewife	65	"
	C	King Arthur J	92	embalmer	69	"
	D	King Edith L †	92	housewife	74	"
	E	King Gladys E †	92	at home	48	"

Hyde Park Avenue

Page	Letter	Full Name	Residence Jan. 1, 1941	Occupation	Age	Reported Residence Jan. 1, 1940 Street and Number
	F	Petelle Theodore	1111A	machinist	56	33 Davison
	G	Ross James A	1111A	"	59	33 "
	H	Ross Virginia A †	1111A	housewife	57	33 "
	K	Cann George L	1111A	assembler	26	here
	L	Hart Helen T †	1111A	housewife	52	"
	M	Hart John J	1111A	tinsmith	57	"
	N	McNair Agnes M †	1112	housewife	39	"
	O	McNair Alexander J	1112	foreman	44	"
	P	Beals William	1112	clerk	39	55 Ottawa
	R	Fisher Harry	1112	machinist	61	55 "
	S	Fisher Helen †	1112	housewife	65	55 "
	T	Wilson Edna A †	1115	"	30	55 "
	U	Wilson Ervin C	1115	seaman	35	55 "
	V	*MacLean Clark	1115	chauffeur	32	here
	W	MacLean Elizabeth A †	1115	housewife	57	"
	X	*MacLean Hector A	1115	painter	59	"
	Y	*MacLean John W	1115	chauffeur	21	"
	Z	Thompson Everett	1116	clerk	20	"
1324						
	A	Thompson Mabel †	1116	housewife	43	"
	B	Hill Delia F †	1116	"	35	"
	C	Hill Margaret †	1116	clerk	20	"
	D	Brown Edith †	1119	housewife	50	"
	E	Brown William	1119	tailor	53	"
	F	Ravida Anna †	1119	saleswoman	24	"
	G	Ravida Filippa †	1119	housewife	53	"
	H	Ravida Joseph	1119	barber	56	"
	K	Horn Henry D	1120	machinist	70	[illegible] Hyde Park av
	L	Horn Mary †	1120	housewife	70	1011 "
	M	*Kent Norman	1120	watchman	19	1011 "
	N	*Pow Elizabeth †	1120	housewife	15	1011 "

Page.	Letter.	Full Name.	Residence, Jan. 1, 1941.	Occupation.	Supposed Age.	Reported Residence, Jan. 1, 1940. Street and Number.

Hyde Park Avenue—Continued

Page.	Letter.	Full Name.	Residence, Jan. 1, 1941.	Occupation.	Supposed Age.	Reported Residence, Jan. 1, 1940. Street and Number.
	O	*Pow Mary V—†	1120	saleswoman	26	1011 Hyde Park av
	P	Kowal Walter M	1123	machinist	46	here
	R	Shpakofski Frank	1123	policeman	48	"
	S	Shpakofski Jennie—†	1123	housewife	38	"
	T	Brennan Edward F	1123	mechanic	63	"
	U	Brennan Edward J	1123	welder	28	"
	V	Brennan Frances A—†	1123	at home	30	"
	W	Brennan Mary E—†	1123	housewife	62	"
	X	Brennan Mary T—†	1123	beautician	33	"
	Y	Brennan Paul W	1123	chemist	23	"
	Z	Coveney James D	1124	salesman	32	"
1325						
	A	Coveney Mary L—†	1124	at home	68	"
	B	Corcoran Mary E—†	1125	housekeeper	68	"
	C	Wise Hannah—†	1125	housewife	58	"
	D	Wise Robert H	1125	physician	28	"
	E	Olsen Charles A	1125	clerk	27	"
	F	Olsen Henry M	1125	machinist	59	"
	G	Olsen Marjorie M—†	1125	nurse	24	"
	H	Olsen Wilhelmina—†	1125	housewife	59	"
	K	McDonald James J	1125	B F D	56	"
	L	McDonald James P	1125	retired	80	"
	M	McDonald Pauline V—†	1125	housewife	55	"
	N	Murphy George L	1127	merchant	53	"
	O	Murphy George L, jr	1127	student	23	"
	P	Murphy Rosamond—†	1127	at home	25	"
	R	Murphy Theresa R—†	1127	housewife	52	"
	S	Mullen John F	1127	engineer	59	"
	T	McKenna James	1128	retired	71	"
	U	Perry David	1128	metalworker	58	"
	V	Perry Dorothy V—†	1128	clerk	28	"
	W	Perry Ethel F—†	1128	"	32	"
	X	Perry Sarah R—†	1128	housewife	59	"
	Y	Miles Elizabeth M—†	1128	"	69	"
	Z	Miles William C	1128	retired	67	"
1326						
	A	Colburn Frederick W	1129	physician	70	"
	B	Colburn Prentis S	1129	salesman	38	"
	C	Colburn Ruth—†	1129	secretary	41	"
	D	Hayes Alfred J	1131	clerk	45	"
	E	Hayes James B	1131	retired	81	"

Hyde Park Avenue (Continued)

Page	Letter	Full Name	Residence, Jan. 1, 1941	Occupation	Reported Age	Reported Residence, Jan. 1, 1940. Street and Number
	F	Hayes Madeline M †	1131	stenographer	41	here
	G	Hayes Maria A †	1131	housewife	70	"
	H	Murphy Nellie A—†	1133	"	68	"
	K	Murphy William R	1133	proprietor	68	"
	L	Aglio Joseph	1137	mechanic	37	"
	M	Aglio Mary †	1137	housewife	28	"
	N	Lind Edith †	1137	laundress	43	"
	O	Moore Anna †	1137	housewife	73	"
	P	Moore Elizabeth—†	1137	stenographer	33	"
	R	Moore James	1137	electrician	42	"
	S	Abbott Alice B—†	1139	clerk	45	"
	S	Abbott Anna C—†	1139	housewife	69	"
	T	Baxter Marie †	1141	"	34	"
	U	Pepin Cora G—†	1141	clerk	30	"
	V	Pepin Francis J	1141	student	30	"
	W	Pepin Jeanette A—†	1141	librarian	26	"
	X	Pepin Nettie E—†	1141	housewife	57	"
	Y	Pepin Phillip L	1141	teacher	20	"
	Z	Ventola Genevieve—†	1145	at home	29	"
1327						
	B	Ventola Lillian—†	1145	clerk	32	"
	C	Ventola Louis	1145	retired	62	"
	D	Ventola Louis	1145	painter	25	"
	E	Ventola Michael F	1145	mechanic	23	"
	F	Ventola Patrick	1145	"	21	"
	G	Haverty Elizabeth †	1148	teacher	50	"
	H	McKenna Gertrude—†	1148	housekeeper	40	"
	K	Darcy Albina †	1149	housewife	59	"
	L	Darcy Francis	1149	retired	60	"
	M	McCarthy Dorothy M †	1149	waitress	23	"
	N	Simmons Edith A †	1149	housewife	52	"
	O	Simmons Michael J	1149	salesman	50	"
	P	Dooley Annie †	1150	housekeeper	46	"
	R	Dooley Edward J	1150	investigator	45	"
	S	Dooley James G	1150	machinist	19	"
	T	Dooley John H	1150	clerk	17	"
	U	Dooley Margaret A †	1150	secretary	50	"
	V	Piciulo Julia †	1153	stenographer	40	"
	W	Subrizi Daniel	1153	shoemaker	60	"
	X	Subrizi Minnie †	1153	housewife	41	"
	Y	Cyr Dorothy E †	1154	saleswoman	33	"

Page.	Letter	Full Name	Residence, Jan. 1, 1941	Occupation	Supposed Age.	Reported Residence, Jan. 1, 1940. Street and Number.

Hyde Park Avenue Continued

Page.	Letter	Full Name	Residence, Jan. 1, 1941	Occupation	Supposed Age.	Reported Residence, Jan. 1, 1940.
	Z	Cyr Joseph P	1154	operator	23	here
1328						
	A	Cyr Paul	1154	machinist	60	"
	B	Cyr Paul M	1154	clerk	21	"
	C	Anderson Edith—†	1154	bookkeeper	65	"
	D	Barrows Catherine E—†	1154	housekeeper	68	"
	E	Hamilton Edwin A	1154	foreman	41	"
	F	Hamilton Ethel—†	1154	housewife	41	"
	G	Starr Sarah—†	1154	at home	75	"
	H	*Finley Florence M—†	1157	housewife	38	"
	K	*Finley Frederick G	1157	machinist	48	"
	L	*Chelio Arthur	1157	merchant	27	Arlington
	M	Chelio Dita—†	1157	housewife	22	Hudson
	N	McGuire John J	1158	retired	75	here
	O	Riley Martin W	1158	"	67	"
	P	Rooney Thomas M	1158	"	63	"
	R	Sprague Annie B—†	1160	housewife	39	"
	S	Sprague Annie L—†	1160	"	60	"
	T	Sprague Georgie E—†	1160	factoryhand	27	"
	U	Sprague Laura J—†	1160	operator	30	"
	V	Sprague Thomas E, jr	1160	chauffeur	37	"
	X	Peardon Mildred G—†	1161	housewife	64	"
	Y	Peardon Noreen—†	1161	housekeeper	28	"
	Z	Peardon Percy J	1161	director	52	"
1329						
	A	*Alexander Alexander H	1164	welder	45	"
	B	Ducette Edward	1164	decorator	68	"
	C	Griggs Charles	1164	watchman	57	"
	D	Kane Eugene	1164	dyesetter	52	"
	E	Kane Rose M—†	1164	secretary	20	"
	F	Kane Sarah H—†	1164	housewife	52	"
	G	Smyth Elsa M—†	1165	"	32	"
	H	Smyth Samuel G	1165	printer	33	"
	K	Jewett Francis B	1165	engineer	40	"
	L	Jewett Sarah E—†	1165	housewife	37	"
	M	Smyth Charlotte—†	1165	"	58	"
	N	Smyth Robert	1165	molder	58	"
	O	Mahoney Francis	1168	clerk	22	"
	P	Mahoney Margaret—†	1168	superintendent	50	"
	R	Meader Edward	1168	merchant	60	"
	S	Oakes Frederick W	1168	inspector	58	"

Page	Letter	Full Name	Residence, Jan. 1, 1941	Occupation	Reported Age	Reported Residence, Jan. 1, 1940. Street and Number

Hyde Park Avenue—Continued

Page	Letter	Full Name	Residence, Jan. 1, 1941	Occupation	Reported Age	Reported Residence, Jan. 1, 1940. Street and Number
	T	Oakes Genevieve †	1168	housewife	68	here
	U	Bullard Alice G †	1172	at home	77	"
	V	Foster Alemetus †	1176	housewife	70	"
	W	Foster Andrew	1176	machinist	48	"
	X	Foster Arthur J	1176	salesman	44	"
	Y	Foster Daniel J	1176	mechanic	52	"
	Z	Foster Peter J	1176	metalworker	47	"
1330						
	A	Rocheleau Albert J	1176	mechanic	20	"
	B	Ollive Catherine V †	1180	housewife	40	"
	C	Ollive James J	1180	retired	83	"
	D	Ollive John J	1180	laborer	48	"
	P	White Margaret E †	1193	housewife	58	"
	R	White Thomas J	1193	machinist	51	"
	T	*Coyne Violet †	1195	housewife	43	13 Ingleside
	U	*Coyne William H	1195	painter	52	13 "
	W	Kelley Frank X	1197	bricklayer	72	24 Folsom
	X	Kelley Minnie †	1197	housewife	70	24 "
	Y	Walsh Mary A †	1197	"	44	here
1331						
	C	McDermott Phillip J	1210	mechanic	59	"

Lincoln Street

Page	Letter	Full Name	Residence, Jan. 1, 1941	Occupation	Reported Age	Reported Residence, Jan. 1, 1940. Street and Number
	Z	Ziino Anthony	12-14	merchant	54	here
1332						
	A	Ziino Rose †	12-14	housewife	46	"
	B	Ziino Frank	12-14	merchant	56	"
	C	*Ziino Teresa †	12-14	housewife	35	"
	D	King Edward M	15	clerk	25	"
	E	King Mark	15	mechanic	54	"
	F	King Sarah †	15	housewife	53	"
	G	Ziino Angelo	16	merchant	51	"
	H	*Ziino Rose †	16	housewife	45	"
	K	Finnigan Mary †	16	"	39	"
	L	Finnigan Thomas	16	mechanic	40	"
	M	Hannon Frank	18	inspector	44	"
	N	Hannon Katherine †	18	housewife	34	"
	O	Barry Celia A †	18	operator	35	"
	P	Barry Margaret R †	18	stenographer	37	"
	R	Barry Mary F †	18	"	25	"

Page	Letter	Full Name.	Residence, Jan. 1, 1941.	Occupation.	Supposed Age.	Reported Residence, Jan. 1, 1940. Street and Number.

Lincoln Street—Continued

Page	Letter	Full Name.	Residence, Jan. 1, 1941.	Occupation.	Supposed Age.	Reported Residence, Jan. 1, 1940. Street and Number.
	S	Barry Mary M—†	18	housewife	65	here
	T	Landt Mary A—†	20	"	85	"
	U	Landt Mary H—†	20	typist	60	"
	W	Campbell Edith M—†	21	housewife	40	"
	X	Campbell Emerson S	21	machinist	50	"
	Y	*McLean Astor B	21	carpenter	41	"
	Z	McLean Katherine H—†	21	housewife	41	"
1333						
	A	Adams Meredith W	22	musician	31	"
	B	Adams Rose B—†	22	housewife	68	"
	C	Patch George D	22	retired	71	"
	D	*Blomberg Hannah S—†	22	housewife	43	"
	E	*Blomberg Herman	22	mechanic	42	"
	F	Coleman Eva L—†	23	housewife	56	"
	G	Coleman Ira J	23	engineer	57	"
	H	Filipow John	23	mechanic	46	"
	K	Filipow Lilly—†	23	housewife	53	"
	L	Hogan Mary—†	26	housekeeper	62	"
	M	Moriarty Dorothy—†	26	operator	33	"
	N	Shea Eileen M—†	26	"	28	"
	O	Bridgman Carrie—†	27	housekeeper	70	"
	P	Butterworth Ralph W	27	guard	63	Foxboro
	R	Griffin Wallace C	27	retired	78	here
	S	Kincaide Mary—†	27	at home	75	"
	T	Stapleton J Phillip	27	machinist	22	110 Brookline av
	U	Loveland Helen H—†	29	housewife	82	here
	V	Loveland Winslow H	29	teacher	48	"
	W	Downey Edward F	41	salesman	36	"
	X	Downey Kathleen M—†	41	housewife	34	"
	Y	Daddario Frederick	42	engineer	37	"
	Z	Daddario Mary—†	42	housewife	35	"
1334						
	A	Dolbeare Helen L—†	42	"	45	"
	B	Dolbeare Howard M	42	B F D	53	"
	C	Badger Dorothy V—†	46	clerk	30	"
	D	Badger Jennie M—†	46	housewife	56	"
	E	Badger Merrill W	46	machinist	64	"
	F	Blake Mary E—†	46	clerk	55	"
	G	O'Neil Margaret—†	46	seamstress	57	"
	H	Bentley Elizabeth—†	47	housekeeper	73	"
	K	Bentley Harriet—†	47	at home	71	"

Page.	Letter	Full Name	Residence, Jan. 1, 1941	Occupation	Reported Age	Reported Residence, Jan. 1, 1940. Street and Number

Lincoln Street Continued

Page.	Letter	Full Name	Residence, Jan. 1, 1941	Occupation	Reported Age	Reported Residence, Jan. 1, 1940. Street and Number
	L	Bentley Jane—†	47	at home	70	here
	M	Lyon Blanche E—†	47	teacher	56	"
	N	Lynch Mabelle R—†	48	housekeeper	55	"
	O	Lynch Mary E—†	48	"	65	"
	P	Papasedero Frederick J	50	boilermaker	34	"
	R	Papasedero Teresa A—†	50	housewife	33	"
	S	DiGregorio Joseph	50	clerk	36	"
	T	DiGregorio Teresa—†	50	housewife	29	"
	V	Martini Americo	52	factoryhand	21	"
	W	Martini Antoinette—†	52	housewife	56	"
	X	Martini Doris—†	52	factoryhand	27	"
	Y	Martini Ida—†	52	"	24	"
	Z*	Martini John	52	molder	57	"
1335						
	A	Pino Genevieve—†	52	housewife	23	"
	B	Pino Ralph	52	chauffeur	27	Dedham
	C*	Spinelli Gabriel	52	metalworker	44	here
	D*	Spinelli Olga—†	52	housewife	34	"
	E	Brown Hattie—†	55	"	65	"
	F	Brown Robert	55	student	23	"
	G	Brown Sumner	55	attorney	29	"
	H	Brown Walter H	55	machinist	66	"
	K	McKay Etta L—†	55	housewife	33	19 Pierce
	L	McKay James R	55	coffee roaster	33	19 "
	M	Howland Allen L	60	skimaker	38	56 Brighton av
	N	Howland Marion L—†	60	secretary	35	56 "

Pierce Street

Page.	Letter	Full Name	Residence, Jan. 1, 1941	Occupation	Reported Age	Reported Residence, Jan. 1, 1940. Street and Number
	P	Mullan James C	5	operator	36	here
	R	Mullan Mary G—†	5	housewife	32	"
	S	Bowles Dorothy R—†	7	housekeeper	33	"
	T	Nabb Mabel E—†	7	"	56	"
	U	Frazier Annie A—†	7	"	67	"
	V	Cook Anna F—†	9	housewife	57	"
	W	Cook Clara V—†	9	saleswoman	22	"
	X	Cook Gerard F	9	salesman	22	"
	Y	Cook John E	9	supervisor	64	"
	Z	Corrigan Sarah A—†	9	bookkeeper	19	"
1336						
	A	Reid John P	11	carpenter	79	"

Page	Letter	Full Name.	Residence, Jan. 1, 1941.	Occupation.	Supposed Age.	Reported Residence, Jan. 1, 1940. Street and Number.

Pierce Street—Continued

Page	Letter	Full Name.	Residence, Jan. 1, 1941.	Occupation.	Supposed Age.	Reported Residence, Jan. 1, 1940. Street and Number.
	B	Reid Margaret E—†	11	housewife	72	here
	C	Norton Arthur F	11	foreman	39	"
	D	Norton Blanche A—†	11	housewife	39	"
	E	Small Luella M—†	11	housekeeper	60	329 Wood av
	F	Southwick Eugene C	11	laborer	64	here
	G	Dmohowski Anthony	11	"	20	"
	H	*Dmohowski Kozmiera—†	11	housewife	53	"
	K	Dmohowski Henry	11	gardener	22	"
	L	Dmohowski Jennie—†	11	waitress	30	"
	M	Dmohowski Joseph	11	laborer	57	"
	N	Dmohowski Josephine—†	11	waitress	24	"
	O	Spurr Sophie E—†	11	housewife	23	"
	P	Spurr William C, jr	11	guard	24	"
	R	Fuller Ralph H	11	carpenter	60	"
	S	Fuller Sadie—†	11	housewife	59	"
	T	Smiglewski Anthony	15	bartender	54	"
	U	*Smiglewski Catherine—†	15	housewife	52	"
	V	Smiglewski Francis P	15	draftsman	26	"
	W	Smiglewski Helen V—†	15	winder	28	"
	X	Frederick Edna M—†	15	housewife	30	"
	Y	*Frederick Reginald E	15	laborer	38	"
	Z	Smiglewski Anthony J	15	draftsman	31	"
1337						
	A	Smiglewski Margaret—†	15	housewife	29	"
	B	Belanger August	15	laborer	38	"
	C	Belanger Jeanne—†	15	stitcher	42	"
	D	Burke Elizabeth E—†	19	housewife	23	78 Thatcher
	E	Burke Paul E	19	custodian	28	78 "
	F	Farrell Bertha E—†	19	housekeeper	39	here
	G	Morrey Charles F	19	painter	57	"
	H	Casey Leola—†	23	bookkeeper	32	"
	K	Casey Thomas T	23	painter	31	"
	L	Harris Helen C—†	23	teacher	45	21 Business
	M	Miller Joseph A	23	pharmacist	42	here
	N	Miller Winifred L—†	23	clerk	41	"
	O	Pieczkowski Charles	25	metalworker	28	"
	P	Pieczkowski Constant	25	riveter	25	"
	R	*Pieczkowski Eleanor—†	25	housewife	62	"
	S	*Pieczkowski Frank	25	laborer	49	"
	T	Pieczkowski Stephen	25	chauffeur	38	"
	U	Jean Francis J	25	clerk	24	"

Pierce Street Continued

Page	Letter	Full Name	Residence, April 1, 1941	Occupation	Reputed Age	Reported Residence, April 1, 1940. Street and Number
	V	*Jean Minnie D †	25	cleaner	54	here
	W	Jean Wilfred X	25	"	21	"
	X	Ciardi Genevieve M †	25	housewife	23	"
	Y	Ciardi John M	25	metalworker	30	"
	Z	Lugton Agnes G †	29	clerk	44	"
1338						
	A	Lugton Walter G	29	blacksmith	74	"
	B	Bright Bertha H †	29	housekeeper	52	Milton
	C	Bright Marjorie W †	29	housewife	31	here
	D	Bright Milton G	29	assembler	29	"
	F	Abdallah Joseph	33	laborer	52	"
	G	*Abdallah Mary †	33	housewife	46	"
	H	Abdallah Victoria †	33	clerk	21	"
	L	Kotkov Benjamin	33	teacher	30	"
	M	Kotkov Sylvia †	33	housekeeper	43	"
	N	Pierce Emerson B	36	investigator	29	"
	O	Pierce Margaret G †	36	housewife	28	"
	P	Hall Florence M †	36	housekeeper	65	"
	R	Lowd Ethel †	36	housewife	61	"
	S	Lowd Ralph M	36	meter reader	33	"
	T	Ryan Thelma G †	36	secretary	24	46 McBride
	U	Ryan Thomas P	36	clerk	25	46 "
	V	Troy James G	37	"	38	here
	W	Troy Madeline J †	37	housewife	33	"
	X	McCarthy Cornelius F	37	oiler	53	"
	Y	McCarthy Elizabeth B †	37	housewife	58	"
	Z	McCarthy Jeremiah P	37	steamfitter	58	"
1339						
	A	Smith Arthur F	37	custodian	38	"
	B	Smith Gregory	37	printer	27	"
	C	Smith Henry M	37	machinist	37	"
	D	Hurlbert Ralph G	40	shipper	25	"
	E	Sweetsir Clarence H	40	carpenter	54	"
	F	Sweetsir Gladys V †	40	housewife	43	"
	G	Moran Jennie M †	40	"	61	"
	H	Moran John J	40	carpenter	58	"
	K	Corrigan Joseph L	43	merchant	37	"
	L	Corrigan Lillian M †	43	housewife	70	"
	M	Fitzgerald Mary E †	45	bookkeeper	50	"
	N	McMahon Margaret G †	45	at home	82	"
	O	McMahon Mary †	45	milliner	52	"

Page.	Letter.	Full Name.	Residence, Jan. 1, 1941.	Occupation.	Supposed Age.	Reported Residence, Jan. 1, 1940. Street and Number.

Pierce Street Continued

Page.	Letter.	Full Name.	Residence, Jan. 1, 1941.	Occupation.	Supposed Age.	Reported Residence, Jan. 1, 1940. Street and Number.
	P	Bartlett Ruth L—†	45	housewife	45	here
	R	Bartlett Samuel D	45	salesman	47	"
	S	*Fraser Joseph	49	operator	35	"
	T	Fraser Loretta—†	49	housewife	30	"
	U	Mahony Charles	49	merchant	52	"
	V	Mahony Leona M—†	49	housewife	37	"
	W	Allen Anita L—†	52	"	36	"
	X	Allen John T	52	chemist	34	"
	Y	*Adams Elizabeth K—†	52	housekeeper	53	"
	Z	*Beaton Jean—†	52	at home	82	"
1340						
	A	*Edwards Jennie S—†	52	housewife	48	79 Arlington
	B	*Edwards Robert A	52	chauffeur	20	79 "
	C	*Edwards Robert G	52	machinist	49	79 "
	D	Smigliani Charles	68	operator	31	here
	E	Smigliani Mary—†	68	housewife	26	"
	G	Smigliani Rose—†	68	"	29	"
	F	Smigliani Thomas	68	foreman	33	"
	H	Ciesielski Beatrice M—†	72	housewife	25	16 Maple
	K	Ciesielski Leo P	72	laborer	32	16 "
	L	Baker Richard H	72	roofer	22	57 Wash'n
	M	Baker Virginia—†	72	housewife	20	57 "
	N	Rimmer William S	72	carpenter	50	here
	O	Ettinger George L	74	machinist	42	"
	P	*Ettinger Violet M—†	74	housewife	41	"
	R	Brackett Mary—†	74	"	22	"
	S	Brackett Warren E	74	machinist	24	"
	T	Devlin James A	74	laborer	29	"
	U	Devlin Lillian R—†	74	housewife	29	"
	V	McDermott Mary A—†	74	housekeeper	67	"
	W	Grillo Anne C—†	78	housewife	25	238 Reservation rd
	X	Grillo Peter	78	coppersmith	26	238 "
	Y	Blais Leo	78	machinist	20	here
	Z	Blais Mary—†	78	housewife	50	"
1341						
	A	Sullivan Edward R, jr	82	upholsterer	25	29 Davison
	B	Sullivan Eileen G—†	82	nurse	22	29 "
	C	Sullivan Mary L—†	82	housewife	52	29 "
	D	Sullivan Patience M—†	82	saleswoman	26	29 "
	E	Laughlin Garrett	84	retired	78	here
	F	Laughlin Mary—†	84	housewife	78	"

Page	Letter	Full Name	Residence Jan. 1 1941	Occupation	Supposed Age	Reported Residence Jan. 1, 1940 Street and Number

Pierce Street (Continued)

Page	Letter	Full Name	Residence Jan. 1 1941	Occupation	Supposed Age	Reported Residence Jan. 1, 1940 Street and Number
	G	Zambella John	84	shoemaker	39	here
	H	Zambella Josephine—†	84	housewife	28	"
	K	Roth Emanuel J	86	clerk	18	"
	L*	Roth Ida J—†	86	housewife	46	"
	M	Toupence Eugene A	86	machinist	69	"
	N	Toupence Leah M—†	86	housewife	63	"
	O	Czarnowski Helen—†	92	factoryhand	24	"
	P	Czarnowski Joseph	92	carpenter	54	"
	R	Czarnowski Josephine—†	92	student	20	"
	S	Czarnowski Sophie—†	92	housekeeper	22	"
	T*	Czarnowski Victoria—†	92	housewife	54	"

River Street

Page	Letter	Full Name	Residence Jan. 1 1941	Occupation	Supposed Age	Reported Residence Jan. 1, 1940 Street and Number
	U	Flynn George A	1072	clerk	48	here
	V	Flynn George D	1072	attendant	21	"
	W	Flynn Mary I—†	1072	housewife	45	"
	X*	Halloran Mary A—†	1072	housekeeper	79	"
	Y	Tominey Francis J	1073	student	26	"
	Z	Tominey James	1073	baker	55	"
1342						
	A	Tominey Margaret C—†	1073	housewife	49	"
	B	Berthiaume Amelia C—†	1074	housekeeper	49	"
	C	Hoar Bernard F	1074	cashier	26	"
	D	Hoar Lauretta A—†	1074	housewife	24	"
	E	Lapham George	1074	fireman	32	"
	F	Moran Robert	1074	welder	26	28 W Milton
	G	Sanuth Barbara B—†	1074	housewife	23	here
	H	Sanuth William J	1074	clerk	28	"
	K	Sullivan Caroline—†	1074	housekeeper	62	45 Deforest
	L	Driscoll George S	1078	chauffeur	34	36 Maple
	M	Saunders Helena M—†	1078	teacher	35	here
	N	Saunders Minnie S—†	1078	housewife	68	"
	O	Meader Adelaide H—†	1078	clerk	31	California
	P	Meader Hattie M—†	1078	housewife	55	"
	R	Feinberg Michael	1081	pharmacist	28	here
	S	Feinberg Rose—†	1081	housewife	25	"
	T*	Kazin Freda—†	1081	"	46	"
	U	Kazin Harry F	1081	photographer	17	"
	V	Emanuel Angelo G	1081	proprietor	55	"
	W	Emanuel Bessie A—†	1081	housewife	45	"

Page	Letter	Full Name	Residence, Jan. 1, 1941	Occupation	Supposed Age	Reported Residence, Jan. 1, 1940. Street and Number.

River Street Continued

Page	Letter	Full Name	Residence	Occupation	Age	Reported Residence
	X	Emanuel Diana A †	1081	attendant	24	here
	Y	Emanuel George A	1081	operator	25	"
	Z	Labins Irving	1082	physician	37	"
1343						
	A	Labins Ruth H †	1082	housewife	30	"
	B	Saunders Lillian M †	1086	accountant	57	"
	C	Milne Grace L †	1086	housewife	52	"
	D	Milne James D	1086	clerk	63	"
	E	Pierce Lois G †	1086	housewife	23	"
	F	Pierce William A	1086	B F D	32	"
	G	Dunn Bartholomew	1090	retired	75	"
	H	Dunn Catherine E—†	1090	secretary	30	"
	K	Dunn Ellen—†	1090	housewife	66	"
	L	Dunn George	1090	clerk	22	"
	M	Dunn Harold B	1090	"	27	"
	N	Dunn James C	1090	chef	40	"
	O	Dunn John J	1090	woodworker	38	"
	P	Dunn Margaret—†	1090	operator	28	"
	R	Dunn Theresa A—†	1090	clerk	24	"
	S	Evans Arline L—†	1093	"	35	"
	T	Evans Charles S	1093	conductor	63	"
	U	Evans Ernest	1093	chauffeur	25	"
	V	Trayers Michael F	1093	mechanic	39	24 Summer
	W	Pierce Edwin F	1093	salesman	60	here
	X	Pierce Marion †	1093	housewife	57	"
	Y	Powers James J	1094	mechanic	53	"
	Z	Powers Mary—†	1094	housewife	54	"
1344						
	A	*Phillips Annie L—†	1094	"	76	"
	B	*Phillips Clarence M	1094	watchman	38	"
	C	Greenough Mary R—†	1098	housekeeper	56	"
	D	Habenicht Hazel L—†	1098	clerk	22	40 Berkley
	E	Hill Caroline E †	1098	housewife	42	here
	F	Hill George	1098	mechanic	32	238 Boylston
	G	Merrill William E	1098	machinist	21	here
	H	*Moyle Arthur F	1102	dairyman	56	"
	K	*Moyle Sarah A †	1102	housewife	66	"
	L	Dickinson George E	1102	teacher	68	"
	M	Dickinson Georgina E—†	1102	housewife	76	"
	N	Gleavy George F	1105	inspector	38	"
	O	Gleavy Helen C †	1105	housewife	38	"

River Street Continued

Page	Letter	Full Name	Residence, Jan. 1, 194[illegible]	Occupation	Supposed Age	Reported Residence, Jan. 1, 194[illegible] Street and Number
	P	Reardon Katherine M †	1105	housewife	62	here
	R	Reardon William J	1105	foreman	62	"
	S	McGuire Mary K †	1105	housewife	40	"
	T	McGuire William H	1105	clerk	42	"
	U	Downing Catherine J †	1106	housewife	44	"
	V	Downing John A	1106	manager	44	"
	W	Beasley Elizabeth A †	1106	teacher	51	"
	X	Beasley John H	1106	supervisor	54	"
	Y	Beasley Theresa M †	1106	housewife	77	"
	Z	Riekes Anthony	1106	laborer	53	"
1345						
	A	Riekes Helen †	1106	housewife	29	Cambridge
	B	Riekes Joseph E	1106	machinist	29	here
	C	Young Alexander J	1110	physician	31	"
	D	Young Dorothy T †	1110	housewife	29	"
	E	Desmond Mary F †	1114	"	61	"
	F	Desmond Timothy J	1114	retired	67	"
	G	Montgomery Terrance	1114	electrician	36	"
	H	Norris Herbert	1114	salesman	56	"
	K	*Allen Frances †	1114	waitress	31	"
	L	Everson Ida †	1114	at home	71	"
	N	Carroll Gertrude R †	1117	housewife	32	"
	O	Carroll Joseph E	1117	mortician	35	"
	P	Fleming David P	1122	laborer	26	34 Everett
	R	Fleming Frances J †	1122	housewife	22	34 "
	S	Larkin Helen M †	1122	"	32	Melrose
	T	Larkin James E	1122	bookkeeper	34	"
	U	Greeley Mary T †	1130	cook	43	here
	V	Nawn Bridget †	1130	housewife	39	"
	W	Nawn Dominic J	1130	finisher	43	"
	X	Whitehead Phoebe A †	1130	housekeeper	61	"
	Y	Whitehead Stanley E	1130	student	25	"
	Z	Whitehead William	1130	clerk	28	"
1346						
	B	Adams Fred L	1138	retired	80	"
	C	Carr Percy W	1138	physician	59	"
	D	Carr Sophie A †	1138	housewife	57	"
	E	Naples Lucy P †	1138	housekeeper	74	"
	F	*Carlson Gertrude A †	1138	housewife	33	Sweden
	G	Carlson William	1138	machinist	35	25 Pine
	H	Vigna John J	1138	metalworker	33	11 Atherton av

Page	Letter	Full Name	Residence, Jan. 1, 1941	Occupation	Supposed Age	Reported Residence, Jan. 1, 1940. Street and Number.

River Street—Continued

Page	Letter	Full Name	Residence, Jan. 1, 1941	Occupation	Supposed Age	Reported Residence, Jan. 1, 1940. Street and Number.
	K	Vigna Mary R—†	1138	housewife	27	11 Atherton av
	L	Chippendale Grace C—†	1140	librarian	32	here
	M	Chippendale Margaret S—†	1140	housewife	66	"
	N	Burke Bonnie B—†	1140	"	42	25 Pine
	O	Burke John J	1140	salesman	42	25 "
	P	McGuire David L	1140	clerk	36	here
	R	McGuire Paula R—†	1140	housewife	33	"
	S	Cross Alice M—†	1140	nurse	39	"
	T	Cross Norman P	1140	policeman	46	"
	U	Chalmers Irene M—†	1140	housewife	35	Methuen
	V	Chalmers Robert W	1140	supervisor	33	"
	W	Welsh Margaret K—†	1140	nurse	47	3 Chestnut
	X	Averbuck Harris	1140	attorney	33	here
	Y	Averbuck Louis L	1140	realtor	61	"
	Z	*Averbuck Rose R—†	1140	housewife	59	"
1347						
	A	Connor Charles J	1140	artist	39	"
	B	Connor Rose M—†	1140	housewife	39	"
	C	Clifford Catherine—†	1140	"	70	"
	D	Clifford Mabel B—†	1140	supervisor	40	"
	E	Clifford Myrtle E—†	1140	operator	34	"
	F	Ratner Benjamin R	1144	dentist	44	Chelsea
	G	Ratner Celia—†	1144	housewife	34	"
	H	Richard Dorothy L—†	1144	housekeeper	37	here
	K	Rogers Irene G—†	1144	housewife	31	"
	L	Rogers Russell C	1144	machinist	30	"
	U	Martyn Maria E—†	1166	housekeeper	42	"
	V	Winslow George E	1166	physician	64	"
	W	Winslow Susan C—†	1166	housewife	64	"

1348 Walter Street

Page	Letter	Full Name	Residence, Jan. 1, 1941	Occupation	Supposed Age	Reported Residence, Jan. 1, 1940. Street and Number.
	M	Kirkpatrick Bessie—†	3	housekeeper	63	here
	N	Barton Aleta—†	7	housewife	21	Northboro
	O	Barton Richard	7	draftsman	21	Upton
	P	Smith Grace I—†	7	housewife	40	here
	R	Smith Roger L	7	salesman	39	"
	S	Smith S Lawson	7	retired	74	"
	T	Casey John	8	laborer	30	"

Walter Street Continued

Page	Letter	Full Name	Residence Jan. 1, 1941	Occupation	Supposed Age	Reported Residence Jan. 1, 1940, Street and Number
	U	Nagle Margaret †	8	housekeeper	65	here
	V	O'Brien Catherine E †	8	"	80	"
	W	Zahn Martin	8	baker	50	"
	X	Putnam Helen B †	11	housekeeper	34	"
	Y	Putnam Olive C †	11	"	72	"
	Z	Strachem Christina—†	11	housewife	53	"
1349						
	A	Strachem Harry L	11	painter	56	"
	B	Strachem John M	11	student	25	"
	C	McKenna Thomas F	12	clerk	53	"
	D	Milne Margaret V—†	12	housekeeper	70	"
	E	O'Connell Patience V—†	12	housewife	40	"
	F	O'Connell Thomas F	12	salesman	20	"
	G	O'Connell Thomas W	12	clerk	46	"
	H	Rooney Alice V †	12	at home	73	"
	K	Arnold Mary A †	20	housekeeper	67	"
	L	Nourse Agnes J †	20	"	58	"
	M	Miller Leonard	24	electrician	64	"
	N	Miller Lillian —†	24	housewife	48	"
	O	McGillen John A	28	mariner	29	"
	P	McGillen Mildred J—†	28	housewife	28	"
	R	Moren Arthur L	28	tailor	58	"
	S	Moren Blanche W—†	28	housekeeper	21	"
	T	Moren Elmira M—†	28	"	26	"
	U	McGowan Edith G —†	30	stenographer	42	"
	V	McGowan Gertrude L—†	30	secretary	39	"
	W	McGowan Grace E †	30	housekeeper	35	"
	X	McGowan Margaret V †	30	"	77	"
	Y	McGowan Mary V —†	30	accountant	47	"
	Z	Campbell Ruth E †	32	housewife	51	"
1350						
	A	Campbell Walter	32	inspector	51	"
	B	Cobbett Jennie †	32	at home	78	"
	C	Goldberg Bessie—†	45	housewife	50	"
	D	Goldberg Samuel	45	factoryhand	53	"
	E	Kalen Evelyn M—†	45	examiner	38	"
	F	Morse James	45	cutter	30	"
	G	Morse Marjorie †	45	saleswoman	22	"
	H	Morse Mildred †	45	"	28	"

Page.	Letter.	Full Name.	Residence, Jan. 1, 1941.	Occupation.	Supposed Age.	Reported Residence, Jan. 1, 1940. Street and Number.

Webster Street

Page.	Letter.	Full Name.	Residence, Jan. 1, 1941.	Occupation.	Supposed Age.	Reported Residence, Jan. 1, 1940. Street and Number.
	L	Rice Audrey M—†	5	housekeeper	22	80 Patten
	M	Rice Frank L	5	mechanic	47	80 "
	N	Rice Nevada F—†	5	housewife	47	80 "
	O	Swensen Norma G—†	5	housekeeper	20	Rhode Island
	P	Brosnan Daniel J	7	clerk	42	here
	R	Paton Margaret M—†	7	housekeeper	39	"
	S	Souter Mary—†	7	"	78	"
	T	Williams Francis S	7	mechanic	21	"
	U	Williams Frederick J	7	clerk	35	"
	V	*Williams John A	7	retired	68	"
	W	Williams John A	7	laborer	27	"
	X	Williams Joseph R	7	"	24	"
	Y	*Williams Nora A—†	7	housewife	65	"
	Z	Williams Nora F—†	7	operator	32	"
1351						
	A	Littlefield Ethel G—†	9	clerk	29	"
	B	Littlefield Ethel J—†	9	housewife	54	"
	C	Littlefield Percy A	9	watchman	59	"
	D	Spencer James N	9	retired	84	"
	E	Goodwin Pauline—†	9	bookkeeper	29	"
	F	Walsh James W	15	agent	29	"
	G	Walsh Vivian—†	15	housewife	27	"
	H	Gould Charles A	15	salesman	66	"
	K	Gould Ethel—†	15	housewife	53	"
	L	Ainsworth Sarah E—†	17	at home	91	56 Central av
	M	Kohler Arthur H	17	draftsman	34	Winthrop
	N	Kohler Hazel M—†	17	housewife	27	"
	O	McDonald James	17	salesman	53	Waltham
	P	McDonald Margaret M—†	17	manager	52	"
	R	Scrivens Alfred E	17	plumber	46	here
	S	Scrivens Elizabeth J—†	17	housewife	45	"
	T	Scrivens Elwood L	17	student	21	"
	U	Avallon Alphonse A	19	laborer	23	Revere
	V	Avallon Lois J—†	19	housewife	22	N Hampshire
	W	Higgins Miriam J—†	19	secretary	38	65 Williams av
	X	King Ariel M—†	19	housewife	42	6 Loring
	Y	King Frederick D	19	carpenter	39	6 "
	Z	Alward Laura—†	21	housewife	72	here
1352						
	A	Alward Olive M—†	21	presser	36	"
	B	Wright Carol A—†	21	nurse	20	"

Page	Letter	Full Name	Residence, Jan. 1, 1941	Occupation	Supposed Age	Reported Residence, Jan. 1, 1940. Street and Number

Webster Street—Continued

Page	Letter	Full Name	Residence, Jan. 1, 1941	Occupation	Supposed Age	Reported Residence, Jan. 1, 1940. Street and Number
	C	Wright Ethel M—†	21	housewife	50	here
	D	Wright George W	21	operator	50	"
	E	Wright Laura S—†	21	student	22	New York
	F	Angell Harold E	23	manager	55	here
	G	Angell Harold S	23	salesman	25	"
	H	Angell Leona M—†	23	teacher	23	N Hampshire
	K	Angell Marjorie S—†	23	housewife	55	here
	L	Mitchell Margaret W—†	23	housekeeper	87	"
	M	Evans Emily F—†	24	"	83	"
	N	Loosen Lena S—†	24	maid	24	17 Rosa
	O	Almstedt Gustaf F	28	machinist	64	24 Winslow
	P	Lofgren Arne F	28	student	21	here
	R	Lofgren Betty A—†	28	housewife	44	"
	S	Lofgren Stephen W	28	dyer	49	"
	T	Maurer William H	28	clergyman	27	"
	U	Dray Arthur R	30	clerk	25	85 Harvard av
	V	Dray Gerald J	30	meter reader	23	85 "
	W	Dray Henry F	30	custodian	68	85 "
	X	Dray Joseph E	30	chauffeur	36	85 "
	Y	Dray Marion L—†	30	attorney	38	85 "
	Z	Dray Nora—†	30	housewife	65	85 "
1353						
	A	Dray Walter H	30	supervisor	29	85 "
	B	Haffner Jabez H	35	accountant	49	47 Warren av
	C	Haffner Mabel—†	35	housewife	49	47 "
	D	Shepherd Albert E	37	salesman	56	here
	E	Shepherd Theresa P—†	37	housewife	44	"
	F	Melanson Delphine—†	37	dressmaker	40	"
	G	Townsend Mary B—†	37	housekeeper	61	"
	H	Smith Alexander F	39	clerk	37	"
	K	Smith Esther M—†	39	housewife	29	"
	L	Brady Etta M—†	39	"	21	"
	M	Brady Eugene G	39	student	21	"
	N	Brady Harold J	39	laborer	22	"
	O	Brady Phillip	39	printer	24	"
	P	Lewis Hannah G—†	43	housekeeper	71	26 Thatcher
	R	Thayer Carrie B—†	43	housewife	65	26 "
	S	Thayer Frank	43	merchant	67	26 "
	T	Friberg Gustaf H	43	retired	65	51 Lincoln
	U	Masters Alfred E	43	painter	76	here
	V	Geary Anita M—†	45	housewife	24	1140 Hyde Park av

Page.	Letter.	Full Name.	Residence, Jan. 1, 1941.	Occupation.	Supposed Age.	Reported Residence, Jan. 1, 1940. Street and Number.

Webster Street—Continued

Page.	Letter.	Full Name.	Residence, Jan. 1, 1941.	Occupation.	Supposed Age.	Reported Residence, Jan. 1, 1940.
	W	Geary Walter J	45	gardener	24	319 Sprague
	X	Collins George E	45	painter	39	here
	Y	Collins Julia A—†	45	housewife	72	"
	Z	Kilty Alice E—†	45	secretary	49	"
1354						
	C	Ventola Alfred W	54	operator	23	"
	D	Ventola Dorothy M—†	54	housewife	23	"
	E	Dolan Thomas	54	retired	76	"
	F	Foley Mary—†	54	housekeeper	75	"

West Street

Page.	Letter.	Full Name.	Residence, Jan. 1, 1941.	Occupation.	Supposed Age.	Reported Residence, Jan. 1, 1940.
	G	Bonvie Catherine T—†	36	housewife	49	here
	H	Bonvie Charles E	36	custodian	45	"
	K	Fuller Catherine E—†	40	at home	29	"
	L	Fuller Charles E	40	laborer	28	"
	M	Fuller Helen A—†	40	housewife	52	"
	N	Fuller Helen M—†	40	stenographer	24	"
	O	Grogan Bridget M—†	40	housekeeper	79	"
	P	Downey Dorothy E—†	42	housewife	24	559 Hyde Park av
	R	Downey James W	42	mechanic	32	559 "
	S	Mackie John D	42	steelworker	31	here
	T	Mackie Pauline E—†	42	housewife	31	"
	U	Beaupre Arthur	58	upholsterer	29	19 Gordon av
	V	*Beaupre August J	58	ironworker	70	19 "
	W	Beaupre Henry E	58	rigger	37	19 "
	X	Lemire Joseph G	58	laborer	20	19 "
	Y	Lemire Mary E—†	58	housewife	46	19 "
	Z	Lasker David	60	social worker	44	here
1355						
	A	Lasker Jennie—†	60	housewife	67	"
	B	Parker Alexander P	60	draftsman	28	"
	C	Parker Mildred A—†	60	housewife	27	"
	D	*Carr Henry	62	retired	71	"
	E	Marshall Margaret—†	62	housekeeper	66	"
	F	Scott Eleanor F—†	62	"	21	"
	G	Scott John D	62	boilermaker	57	"
	H	Signori Cecelia P—†	66	housewife	28	"
	K	Signori Primo	66	foreman	31	"
	L	Parker Gordon L	66	laborer	38	"
	M	Parker Marie J—†	66	housewife	65	"

Page	Letter	Full Name	Residence	Occupation	Reputed Age	Reported Residence, Street and Number

West Street—Continued

Page	Letter	Full Name	Residence	Occupation	Reputed Age	Reported Residence, Street and Number
	N	Parker Shirley S †	66	secretary	25	here
	O	Hittinger Frances C †	68	housewife	64	"
	P	Hittinger George F	68	collector	68	"
	R	Morse Ernest C	68	retired	70	"
	S	Fahey Alice †	72	housekeeper	67	"
	T	Whalen Agnes I †	72	housewife	42	Shrewsbury
	U	Whalen William J	72	buyer	44	"
	V	Gallin Mary †	72	housekeeper	66	here
	W	Keegan Harry P	72	machinist	22	"
	X	Keegan Irene F †	72	housewife	24	"
	Y	Frazer Emily C †	74	clerk	28	"
	Z	Frazer Helen G †	74	housewife	56	"
1356						
	A	Frazer Louise A †	74	director	26	"
	B	Buttlar Henrietta E †	74	housewife	34	"
	C	Buttlar William J	74	chauffeur	33	"
	D	Forsythe Elizabeth M †	76	housewife	64	"
	E	Forsythe Esther M †	76	stenographer	36	"
	F	Forsythe Robert H	76	painter	65	"
	G	Bates Roger E	78	metalworker	63	"
	H	Byrnes Almira M †	78	housekeeper	49	"
	K	Henderson Walter	78	clerk	58	"
	L	Astley Harry E	94	retired	70	"
	M	Corbin Ardis E †	94	at home	42	"
	N	Corbin Mary B †	94	housewife	72	"
	O	*Baxter John	96	mechanic	36	"
	P	*Baxter Josephine †	96	housewife	38	"
	R	*Haines Doris †	96	"	36	"
	S	Haines William L	96	painter	35	"
	T	Barrows Helen L †	96	housewife	41	372 Cornell
	U	Barrows John O	96	clerk	45	372 "
	V	Gulesian Gladys E †	102	housewife	32	here
	W	Gulesian Philip J	102	plumber	56	"
	X	Bates Cyrus S	104	carpenter	69	"
	Y	Bates Lula M †	104	housewife	63	"
	Z	Carbee Martha B †	104	at home	88	"
1357						
	A	Derry Charles T	108	machinist	24	82 Central av
	B	Derry Louise S †	108	housewife	21	82 "
	C	Connors Constance L †	108	"	27	here
	D	Connors Joseph F	108	manager	31	"

Page.	Letter.	Full Name	Residence, Jan. 1, 1941.	Occupation.	Supposed Age.	Reported Residence, Jan. 1, 1940. Street and Number.

West Street—Continued

	E	Maguire Elizabeth R—†	110	clerk	33	here
	F	Maguire Mary T—†	110	housewife	64	"
	G	Maguire Phillip A	110	fireman	25	"
	H	McGivney Helen C—†	112	housewife	55	"
	K	McGivney Peter H	112	machinist	55	"
	L	McGivney Doris J—†	112	operator	20	"
	M	McGivney Helen R—†	112	secretary	23	"
	N	Gay Cecilia V—†	114	housewife	33	"
	O	Gay Joseph F	114	clerk	38	"
	P	Moynihan Edward B	114	salesman	32	"
	R	Stanley Signe—†	120	housekeeper	31	419 Poplar
	S	Lavelle Eva D—†	120	housewife	32	271 Gallivan Blvd
	T	Lavelle Francis G	120	chauffeur	34	271 "
	U	*Flynn Margaret E—†	120	housewife	45	here
	V	Flynn Thomas H	120	retired	57	"
	W	Rogers Alma G—†	124	housewife	68	"
	X	Rogers John W	124	manager	70	"
	Y	Cox Mary—†	142	at home	78	"
	Z	McLean Lloyd J	142	clerk	40	"
1358						
	A	McLean Mary L—†	142	housewife	32	"
	B	Dahlquist Carl H	142	boilermaker	40	124 Wood av
	C	*Dahlquist Helen E—†	142	housewife	40	124 "
	D	Grove Millicent P—†	146	"	48	here
	E	Grove Robert A	146	steamfitter	56	"
	F	Titcomb Emily E—†	146	housewife	36	"
	G	Titcomb James W	146	fireman	39	"
	H	*Lounsbury David	146	chef	35	Florida
	K	McLeod Amasa V	146	plumber	32	here
	L	*McLeod Lewis J	146	"	27	Florida
	M	*McLeod Ruth C—†	146	housewife	34	here
	N	Anderson Matilda A—†	148	operator	40	"
	O	Anderson Sarah E—†	148	at home	75	"

Winthrop Street

	P	Hartian Albert H	19	proprietor	69	here
	R	*Hartian Grace R—†	19	housewife	63	"
	S	*Hartian Morris	19	clerk	38	"
	T	Hartian Peter	19	"	22	"
	U	Allen Paul C	21	"	21	48 Maple

Page	Letter	Full Name	Residence, Jan. 1, 1941	Occupation	Age	Reported Residence, Jan. 1, 1940. Street and Number

Winthrop Street (Continued)

Page	Letter	Full Name	Residence, Jan. 1, 1941	Occupation	Age	Reported Residence, Jan. 1, 1940. Street and Number
	V	Allen Rosella A †	21	milliner	43	18 Maple
	W	Donegan Mary P †	21	clerk	23	18 "
	X	DiCesare Colette †	25	housewife	25	here
	Y	DiCesare Dominic	25	bartender	28	"
	Z*	Spadano Angelina †	25	housewife	43	"
1359						
	A	Spadano Carmen J	25	baker	21	"
	B	Spadano Eleanor F †	25	operator	22	"
	C	Spadano Joseph	25	baker	45	"
	D	Curley George E	37	clerk	20	"
	E	Curley Mary A †	37	housewife	51	"
	F	DiMarzio Alfred	37	counterman	27	"
	G	DiMarzio Theodora †	37	housewife	24	"
	H	Wolfe Edward	37	proprietor	57	"
	K	Wolfe Lillian †	37	housewife	46	"
	L	Keegan Harry P	41	trimmer	56	"
	M	Keegan Marietta R †	41	clerk	30	"
	N	Keegan Mary E †	41	housewife	57	"
	O	Keegan William A	41	carpenter	24	"
	P*	Martin Della D †	43	housewife	38	"
	R	Martin Thomas P	43	shipfitter	37	"
	S*	Trombetta Angela †	43	housewife	54	"
	T	Trombetta Mario	43	butcher	55	"
	U	Trombetta Tito	43	laborer	27	"
	V	Feeney Margaret J †	45	housewife	56	"
	W	Feeney Patrick J	45	operator	57	"
	X	Baldwin Albert C	51	lather	48	"
	Y	Baldwin Doris †	51	housewife	40	"
	Z	Boucher Bernadette †	53	"	44	"
1360						
	A	Boucher George	53	laborer	48	"
	B	Boucher Georgette †	53	housekeeper	20	"
	C	Boucher Gilbert	53	shipper	23	"
	D	Boucher Norman	53	clerk	21	"
	E	Hopkins Yvonne †	53A	sewer	33	"
	F	Rocheleau Joseph E	53A	retired	60	"

Ward 18—Precinct 14

CITY OF BOSTON

LIST OF RESIDENTS
20 YEARS OF AGE AND OVER

(NON-CITIZENS INDICATED BY ASTERISK)
(FEMALES INDICATED BY DAGGER)

AS OF

JANUARY 1, 1941

CITY OF BOSTON PRINTING DEPARTMENT

Page	Letter	Full Name.	Residence, Jan. 1, 1941.	Occupation.	Supposed Age.	Reported Residence, Jan. 1, 1940. Street and Number.
1400						
		Arlington Street				
	A	Smigliani Elizabeth †	76	housewife	26	here
	B	Smigliani Paul	76	laborer	30	"
	C	*Civitarese Anna †	76	housewife	42	"
	D	Civitarese Bernard	76	laborer	21	"
	E	Civitarese Bridget †	76	housekeeper	20	"
	F	Civitarese Dominick	76	B F D	45	"
	G	Bacon Nellie F †	78	at home	72	"
	H	Hargraves Donald S	78	investigator	47	"
	K	Hargraves Janet A †	78	housewife	44	"
	L	Cairns Ambrose	80	mechanic	63	"
	M	Cairns Cecilia G †	80	housewife	55	"
	N	Cairns Mary B †	80	stenographer	25	"
	O	Walter Annie H †	93	housewife	58	"
	P	Walter Charles M, jr	93	meter reader	30	"
	R	Walter Evelyn R †	93	housewife	27	"
	S	Coburn John H	93	draftsman	32	"
	T	Coburn Ruth H †	93	housewife	29	"
	V	Fennessy Carrie E †	97	"	52	"
	W	Fennessy Helen †	97	student	24	"
	X	Fennessy Joseph B	97	engraver	52	"
	Y	Fennessy Margaret †	97	saleswoman	24	"
	Z	Gray Dora M †	97	housewife	53	"
1401						
	A	Gray Walter H	97	retired	65	"
	B	Ruth John J	97	tire treader	23	Weymouth
	C	Ruth Mildred E †	97	housewife	23	"
	D	Stuart Frank W	100	mechanic	63	here
	E	Stuart Marguerite †	100	housewife	51	"
	F	Gilson Violette L †	100	at home	85	"
	G	Chittick Cordelia M †	102	musician	54	"
	H	Chittick Eugene G	102	plumber	57	"
	K	Chittick Susan A †	102	housekeeper	60	"
	L	Kiessling Edith R †	103	housewife	42	"
	M	Kiessling Frank E	103	electrician	43	"
	N	Kiessling Frank E, jr	103	papermaker	20	"
	O	Lunsman Etta J †	103	at home	72	"
	P	Talanian Helen †	104	housewife	32	"
	R	Talanian Richard K	104	merchant	40	"
	S	Grover John R	104	clerk	26	"
	T	Grover Lalia †	104	at home	61	"

Arlington Street—Continued

Page / Letter	Full Name	Residence	Occupation	Supposed Age	Reported Residence, Street and Number
U	Grover Olive M †	104	nurse	31	here
V	Howard Flora E †	104	housewife	52	111 Arlington
W	Howard Robert A	104	machinist	57	111 "
X	Gillis Angus S	105	carpenter	66	here
Y	Gillis Euphemia A †	105	housewife	61	"
Z	Harmon Earl	107	manager	35	"
1402					
A	Rodd Charles A	107	retired	76	"
B	Rodd Minnie E †	107	housewife	78	"
C	Rodd Dorothy M †	107	clerk	31	"
D	Rodd Jennie E †	107	housewife	51	"
E	Rodd Paul C	107	B F D	50	"
F	Griffiths Charles T	108	salesman	66	"
G	Griffiths Martha S †	108	housewife	65	"
H	Melin Marjorie †	108	"	38	"
K	Melin Otis N	108	printer	38	"
L	Kundert Shirley M †	109	housewife	30	"
M	Kundert Vinal	109	metalworker	31	"
N	Abbott Chester G †	109	"	22	"
O	Abbott Shirley †	109	housewife	21	Haverhill
P	Frazian Nicholas	109	salesman	23	923 Hyde Park
R	Frazian Rita W †	109	housewife	25	923 "
S	Boudreau Joseph J	111	pipefitter	50	here
T*	Boudreau Margaret A †	111	housewife	49	"
U	Pring Ellen V †	111	dressmaker	53	"
V	Hoar John J	111	waterproofer	28	"
W*	Hoar Mary M †	111	housewife	27	"
X	Wilson Lillian B †	117	"	30	"
Y	Wilson Nelson K	117	manager	32	"
Z	Flatley John	117	cook	33	"
1403					
A	Shanks Georgia J †	117	housewife	22	95 Wood av
B	Shanks Theodore G	117	chauffeur	29	95 "
C	DiMarzio John	118	metalworker	52	[illegible]
D	DiMarzio Mary †	118	housewife	40	914 "
E	Rizzi Anthony	118	laborer	52	914 "
F	Stidstone Marion G †	118	housewife	40	69 Arlington
G	Stidstone Wilfred L	118	salesman	40	69 "
H	Collins Sarah J †	120	at home	71	here
K	Grigg Alberta W †	120	housewife	38	"
L	Grigg Thomas J	120	electrician	34	"

Page	Letter	Full Name	Residence, Jan. 1, 1941.	Occupation.	Supposed Age.	Reported Residence, Jan. 1, 1940. Street and Number.

Arlington Street—Continued

Page	Letter	Full Name	Residence, Jan. 1, 1941.	Occupation.	Supposed Age.	Reported Residence, Jan. 1, 1940. Street and Number.
	M	Leonard Mary I †	123	clerk	54	here
	N	McGrath Charles E	123	salesman	38	"
	O	McGarth Edward	123	chauffeur	65	"
	P	McGrath Margaret E †	123	housewife	65	"
	R	Daley Margaret T †	125	"	41	"
	S	Daley William E	125	B F D	46	"
	T	Hayes Alfred	127	mechanic	55	"
	U	Hayes Alfred B	127	student	20	"
	V	Hayes Elmira M †	127	housewife	52	"
	X	Lyons Margaret E †	143	"	41	"
	Y	Lyons Thomas F	143	painter	41	"
	Z	Vogelsang Amy †	143	housewife	71	"
1404						
	A	Vogelsang Ernest F	143	painter	74	"
	B	McMullen Alexander	143	foreman	60	"
	C	McMullen Bessie †	143	housewife	53	"
	D	*DeMers Freda E †	144	"	31	"
	E	DeMers Harold T	144	merchant	32	"
	F	Clifford Arthur L	145	salesman	24	"
	G	Clifford Lillian M †	145	housewife	47	"
	H	Clifford Ralph R	145	writer	49	"
	K	Clifford Richard B	145	maint'nce man	20	"
	L	Albrecht Evelyn F †	147	waitress	21	"
	M	Albrecht William F	147	custodian	22	"
	N	Homer Alice M †	147	housewife	50	"
	O	Homer George	147	repairman	64	"
	P	Vogelsang Caroline B †	148	housewife	25	Holbrook
	R	Vogelsang Max F	148	chemist	34	"
	S	Bigelow Fred C	148	engineer	60	here
	T	Bigelow Lois G †	148	housewife	55	"
	U	Rooney Gerard	149	clerk	20	"
	V	Rooney Margaret G †	149	housewife	54	"
	W	Kinsman Esma P †	149	"	31	"
	X	Kinsman Roland J	149	policeman	38	"
	Y	Kinsman Samuel W	149	retired	68	"
	Z	Gleason Harold J	150	bricklayer	32	"
1405						
	A	Gleason Monica E †	150	housewife	35	"
	B	*Gleason Bertha F †	150	"	39	"
	C	Gleason Richard J	150	foreman	36	"
	D	Webster Florence H †	151	housewife	63	"

Page	Letter	Full Name	Residence, Jan. 1, [illegible]	Occupation	Age	Reported Residence, Jan. 1, [illegible]. Street and Number

Arlington Street—Continued

Page	Letter	Full Name	Residence	Occupation	Age	Reported Residence
	E	Webster Frank E	151	taxidermist	58	here
	F	Boultonhouse George E	154	carpenter	63	"
	G	Boultonhouse Sarah E †	154	housewife	64	"
	H	Ferrey Frank H	154	jeweler	56	"
	K	Crouse Ada H †	154	housewife	64	"
	L	Crouse William H	154	doorman	66	"

Central Avenue

Page	Letter	Full Name	Residence	Occupation	Age	Reported Residence
	N	Joyce Anna I †	94	housewife	33	here
	O	Joyce Gerard J	94	superintendent	42	"
	P	Nietzel Oscar A	100	milkman	39	"
	R	Nietzel Sophie †	100	housewife	34	"
	S	Karcher Earle C	101	accountant	42	"
	T	Karcher Irene F †	101	housewife	36	"
	U	McNamara Edward	101	retired	56	"
	V	McNamara Josephine B †	101	housewife	56	"
	W	*Forrest Agnes M †	105	"	46	"
	X	Forrest Dorothy E †	105	adjuster	21	"
	Y	Forrest Richard	105	toolmaker	46	"
	Z	Coughlin Bridget †	112	housewife	81	"
1406						
	A	Coughlin Mary I †	112	housekeeper	38	"
	B	Schiller Helen †	112	housewife	36	"
	C	Schiller Joseph	112	fireman	38	"
	D	Butler Mary †	113	housewife	70	Dedham
	E	Callahan Annie †	113	"	72	36 Maple
	F	Connolly Mary †	113	"	75	Somerville
	G	Cummings Mary †	113	"	72	"
	H	Fennell John	113	retired	80	36 Maple
	K	Hoar Regina F †	113	nurse	45	36 "
	L	Hoar William L	113	leatherworker	46	36 "
	M	Jetter Eleanor †	113	housewife	75	66 Patten
	N	Keefe Ellen †	113	"	93	36 Maple
	O	McDermott Annie †	113	"	75	36 Garfield av
	P	Mill James	113	retired	73	36 Maple
	R	Quinn Mary †	113	housewife	77	36 "
	S	Ray Alfred	113	retired	38	36 "
	T	Riley Patrick	113	"	79	New York
	U	Royle Annie †	113	housewife	54	36 Maple

Page	Letter	Name	Residence, April 1, 1943	Occupation	Supposed Age	Reported Residence April 1, 1944 Street and Number

Central Avenue—Continued

Letter	Name	Residence	Occupation	Age	Reported Residence
[illegible]	[illegible] M	128	housewife	35	70 Burrell
[illegible]	[illegible]	[illegible]	[illegible]	76	here
[illegible]	[illegible]	[illegible]	[illegible]	74	"
[illegible]	[illegible]	[illegible]	housewife	75	"
[illegible]	[illegible]	[illegible]	[illegible]	50	"

1407

Letter	Name	Residence	Occupation	Age	Reported Residence
[illegible]	[illegible]	[illegible]	[illegible]	32	"
[illegible]	[illegible]	[illegible]	[illegible]	20	"
[illegible]	[illegible]	[illegible]	[illegible]	22	"
[illegible]	[illegible]	[illegible]	housewife	53	"
[illegible]	[illegible]	[illegible]	[illegible]	21	"
[illegible]	[illegible]	[illegible]	[illegible]	25	"
[illegible]	[illegible]	[illegible]	housewife	33	"
[illegible]	[illegible]	[illegible]	[illegible]	59	"
[illegible]	[illegible]	[illegible]	[illegible]	55	"
[illegible]	[illegible]	[illegible]	housewife	37	"
[illegible]	[illegible]	[illegible]	[illegible]	36	"
[illegible]	[illegible]	[illegible]	housewife	37	"
[illegible]	[illegible]	[illegible]	[illegible]	54	"
[illegible]	[illegible]	[illegible]	housewife	57	"
[illegible]	[illegible]	[illegible]	[illegible]	71	"
[illegible]	[illegible]	[illegible]	[illegible]	71	"
[illegible]	[illegible]	[illegible]	[illegible]	33	"
[illegible]	[illegible]	[illegible]	[illegible]	39	"
[illegible]	[illegible]	[illegible]	[illegible]	23	"
[illegible]	[illegible]	[illegible]	housewife	27	"
[illegible]	[illegible]	[illegible]	[illegible]	58	"
[illegible]	[illegible]	[illegible]	housewife	55	"
[illegible]	[illegible]	[illegible]	[illegible]	55	"

1408

Letter	Name	Residence	Occupation	Age	Reported Residence
[illegible]	[illegible]	[illegible]	[illegible]	24	"
[illegible]	[illegible]	[illegible]	[illegible]	53	"
[illegible]	[illegible]	[illegible]	housewife	53	"
[illegible]	[illegible]	[illegible]	[illegible]	23	"
[illegible]	[illegible]	[illegible]	[illegible]	48	"
[illegible]	[illegible]	[illegible]	[illegible]	36	"
[illegible]	[illegible]	[illegible]	[illegible]	37	"
[illegible]	[illegible]	[illegible]	[illegible]	45	"
[illegible]	[illegible]	[illegible]	[illegible]	20	"
[illegible]	[illegible]	[illegible]	housewife	40	"

Central Avenue

M *Wagner William H [illegible]
N *Wagner William H [illegible]
O Barnes [illegible]
P Barnes [illegible]
R Barnes [illegible]
S *Johnson E [illegible]
T Johnson E [illegible]
U F [illegible]
V V [illegible]
W V [illegible]
X V [illegible]
Y V [illegible]
Z V [illegible]

1409

A V [illegible]
B MacLaren [illegible]
C MacLaren [illegible]
D MacLaren R [illegible]
E Richardson [illegible]
F Richardson [illegible] H
G *K [illegible]
H K [illegible]
K *K [illegible]
L Towers [illegible]
M Towers William [illegible]
N Garrett Mary E [illegible]
O Garrett [illegible] H
P Garrett William H [illegible]
S Brown [illegible]
R Brown [illegible] H
T *Brown N [illegible]
U Chamberlain [illegible]
V Chamberlain William [illegible]
W Dawson [illegible] F
X Dawson [illegible] F
Y Leonard [illegible]
Z Leonard [illegible]

1410

A Leonard [illegible]
B Leonard Mary [illegible]

Page.	Letter.	Full Name.	Residence Jan. 1, 1941.	Occupation.	Supposed Age.	Reported Residence, Jan. 1, 1940. Street and Number.

Elm Street

Page.	Letter.	Full Name.	Residence Jan. 1, 1941.	Occupation.	Supposed Age.	Reported Residence, Jan. 1, 1940.
	C	Weymouth Jennie M †	8	housekeeper	64	here
	D	Weymouth Lillian E †	8	"	55	"
	E	Braley Catherine R †	12	housewife	64	"
	F	Braley Frank S	12	retired	71	"
	G	Braley Louise F †	12	housewife	40	"
	H	Braley Savory C	12	salesman	39	"
	K	Breau David G	14	foreman	64	"
	L	Arnold Cora M †	18	housekeeper	71	"
	M	Noyes Edith M †	18	housewife	59	"
	N	Caflin Henry F	22	salesman	50	"
	O	Caflin Irene M †	22	housewife	50	"
	P	Berry Carroll R	24	driller	39	"
	R	House Eva G †	24	housewife	55	"
	S	House Joseph L	24	printer	59	"
	T	MacDonald Christine A †	24	housewife	55	"
	U	MacDonald E Lorraine †	24	clerk	25	"
	V	MacDonald John D	24	lineman	57	"
	W	MacDonald Madeline G †	24	stenographer	23	"
	X	McGowan Mary E †	24	nurse	22	New Jersey

Greenwood Avenue

Page.	Letter.	Full Name.	Residence Jan. 1, 1941.	Occupation.	Supposed Age.	Reported Residence, Jan. 1, 1940.
	Y	Chase Harold C	9	agent	47	here
	Z	Chase Marion B †	9	housewife	42	"
1411						
	A	Jardine George A	9	salesman	35	"
	B	Jardine Helen M †	9	stenographer	35	"
	C	*Jardine Maude A †	9	housewife	66	"
	D	Brooks Jessie M †	9	housekeeper	70	"
	E	Monarch Nettie F †	12	housewife	64	"
	F	Monarch Ralph W	12	artist	33	"
	G	Monarch William W	12	foreman	60	"
	H	Pratt Aldana E †	12	housekeeper	57	"
	K	Spaans Cornelius	12A	printer	59	"
	L	Spaans Flora M †	12A	housewife	58	"
	M	Hennessey Charles E	14	agent	49	"
	N	Hennessey Charles E	14	student	22	"
	O	Hennessey Rosa V †	14	housewife	44	"
	P	Sullivan Charles W	14	splicer	47	"
	R	Sullivan Mary R †	14	housewife	47	"
	S	*Mercer Phyllis M †	15	clerk	32	"

Page	Letter	Full Name	Residence, Jan. 1, [illegible]	Occupation	Reputed Age	Reported Residence, [illegible] Street and Number
		Greenwood Avenue—Continued				
	T	*Mercer William S	15	clerk	32	here
	U	Hyland Elizabeth M †	16	housekeeper	67	"
	V	Hyland Ruth K †	16	stenographer	37	"
	W	Freed Leon W	18 20	auditor	17	"
	X	Freed Martha H †	18 20	housewife	45	"
	Y	Freed Oscar	18 20	salesman	51	"
	Z	Bullard Bertha F †	18 20	bookkeeper	53	"
1412						
	A	Connick Frances H †	22 24	nurse	45	"
	B	Connick William J	22 24	custodian	48	"
	C	Hallett Florence E †	22 24	housewife	48	"
	D	Hallett Walter F	22 24	policeman	46	"
	E	Johnson Henry G	23	proprietor	39	"
	F	Johnson Mary C †	23	housewife	34	"
	G	Kimball Edward A	23	laborer	22	"
	H	Kimball Ethel M †	23	housewife	60	"
	K	Kimball George E	23	draftsman	63	"
	L	Kimball Helen P †	23	housewife	26	"
	M	Senger John T	26 28	breweryman	49	"
	N	Senger Lillian C †	26 28	housewife	47	"
	O	Senger Wilhelmina G †	26 28	typist	21	"
	P	Burt Arthur H	26 28	treasurer	73	"
	R	Smith Olive V †	26 28	stenographer	29	"
	S	Noble Clifford	27	steelworker	46	"
	T	Noble Vera L †	27	housewife	36	"
	U	Seavey Henrietta †	27	housekeeper	78	"
	V	Higgins Louise †	30	supervisor	45	"
	W	Lynch Eleanor H †	30	housewife	40	"
	X	Lynch Francis G	30	inspector	12	"
	Y	Lynch Jeremiah	31	retired	61	"
	Z	Lynch Mary A †	31	housewife	60	"
1413						
	A	Lynch Veronica A †	31	secretary	36	"
	B	*DeVito Domenica †	34	housewife	75	"
	C	DeVito Giacomo	34	retired	64	"
	D	Rullo Antonio	34	laborer	37	"
	E	Cummings Catherine C †	34	housekeeper	18	"
	F	Cummings Martin C	34	policeman	45	"
	G	Cummings Nora M †	34	housewife	36	"
	H	Chisholm Mary T †	35	"	56	"
	K	Chisholm Thomas	35	painter	51	"

Page	Letter	Full Name	Residence Jan. 1, 1941	Occupation	Supposed Age	Reported Residence Jan. 1, 1940. Street and Number

Greenwood Avenue—Continued

Page	Letter	Full Name	Residence	Occupation	Age	Reported Residence
	L	Kilduff Margaret J †	35	housekeeper	28	here
	M	Toomey Theresa G †	35	housewife	48	"
	N	Toomey William L	35	clerk	50	"
	P	Brown Mary †	36	housewife	62	"
	R	Brown William H	36	electrician	59	"
	S	*McGrath Joseph	36	laborer	55	"
	T	Maloy Alice M †	38	housekeeper	30	"
	U	Maloy Ruth M †	38	clerk	32	"
	V	Maloy Thomas P	38	operator	66	"
	W	Galway John L	38A	retired	74	"
	X	Galway Katherine M †	38A	housewife	65	"
	Z	Cameron Duncan	39	retired	74	"
1414						
	A	Cameron Jessie G †	39	housewife	64	"
	B	Godfrey George M	40	stenographer	37	"
	C	Godfrey Margaret M †	40	housewife	38	"
	D	Linskey Adelaide M †	40A	secretary	33	"
	E	Linskey Genevieve M †	40A	housewife	62	"
	F	Linskey Howard I	40A	operator	24	"
	G	Linskey Ruth C †	40A	secretary	21	"
	H	Linskey William J	40A	B F D	65	"
	K	Hunter John B	42	attendant	21	"
	L	Hunter Lawrence J	42	painter	57	"
	M	Hunter Lawrence J	42	"	24	"
	N	Hunter Mattie B †	42	housewife	57	"
	O	Strachan Betty F †	43	"	77	"
	P	Strachan Elizabeth M †	43	supervisor	48	"
	R	Strachan John D	43	retired	79	"
	S	Strachan Mary T †	43	secretary	50	"
	T	Freeman Lucy A †	44	housewife	69	"
	U	Freeman Marion R †	44	secretary	36	"
	V	Taylor Bertha †	45	housewife	54	"
	W	Taylor George E	45	salesman	31	"
	X	Barrett Helen M †	47–49	secretary	29	"
	Y	Barrett John F	47–49	clerk	20	"
	Z	Barrett Mary †	47–49	housewife	55	"
1415						
	A	Barrett Mary J †	47–49	waitress	24	"
	B	Barrett Michael	47–49	motorman	60	"
	C	Hinckley Charles H	47–49	clerk	44	"
	D	Hinckley Harriet M †	47–49	housewife	45	"

Page	Letter	Full Name	Residence, Jan. 1, 194[illegible]	Occupation	Reputed Age	Reported Residence, Jan. 1, 194[illegible]. Street and Number

Greenwood Avenue Continued

Page	Letter	Full Name	Residence	Occupation	Reputed Age	Reported Residence
	E	Hinckley Josephine M †	47 49	housewife	69	here
	F	Callahan George J	51 53	merchant	43	"
	G	Callahan Veronica T †	51 53	housewife	39	"
	H	Dooley James F	51 53	contractor	40	"
	K	Dooley Margaret G †	51 53	operator	38	"
	L	Driscoll Florence †	59	housewife	43	"
	M	Driscoll George L	59	secretary	54	"
	N	Panton Marjorie †	59	housekeeper	23	"
	O	Maxwell Lillian A †	60	housewife	35	"
	P	Maxwell Norman F	60	clerk	33	"
	S	Jones Francis M	62	clergyman	44	"
	T	Covell Stanley	63	manager	37	"
	U	*Covell Winifred V †	63	housewife	34	"
	V	Lenz August L	71	mechanic	41	"
	W	Lenz Bertha M †	71	clerk	43	"
	X	Lenz Emma M †	71	housewife	51	"
	Y	Lenz Robert H	71	shoeworker	53	"
	Z	Maxwell Charles F	85	janitor	36	"
1416						
	A	Maxwell Helen M †	85	factoryhand	30	"
	B	Maxwell Mary E †	85	housewife	64	"

Greenwood Circle

Page	Letter	Full Name	Residence	Occupation	Reputed Age	Reported Residence
	C	Montgomery Murdock	1	carpenter	42	here
	D	Montgomery Stella †	1	housewife	38	"
	E	Donnelly Bertha M †	2	"	57	"
	F	Donnelly Charles I	2	inspector	38	"
	G	Zwack Clement	3	goldbeater	69	"
	H	Zwack Louise †	3	housewife	69	"
	K	Mattimore Elizabeth G †	4	"	62	"
	L	Mattimore Thomas E	4	mechanic	63	"
	M	Little George T	6	guard	46	"
	N	Little Phyllis H †	6	housewife	36	"

Greenwood Square

Page	Letter	Full Name	Residence	Occupation	Reputed Age	Reported Residence
	O	Chapman Albert W	2	lawyer	40	here
	P	Chapman George L	2	teacher	44	"

Page	Letter	Full Name	Residence, Jan. 1, 1941	Occupation	Supposed Age	Reported Residence, Jan. 1, 1940. Street and Number.

Greenwood Square Continued

Page	Letter	Full Name	Residence, Jan. 1, 1941	Occupation	Supposed Age	Reported Residence, Jan. 1, 1940.
	R	Chapman Helen A †	2	housewife	39	here
	S	Hoar Mary E †	3	"	22	Dedham
	T	Hoar William K	3	chauffeur	28	95 E Glenwood av
	U	Griffin James A	3	papermaker	23	here
	V	Baronian Hagouhey †	5	housewife	41	"
	W	Baronian Murgidige	5	cutter	46	Somerville

Hilton Street

Page	Letter	Full Name	Residence, Jan. 1, 1941	Occupation	Supposed Age	Reported Residence, Jan. 1, 1940.
	Y	LePage Catherine C †	11	clerk	35	12 Harrison
	Z	LePage Catherine L †	11	housewife	65	12 "
1417						
	A	McCabe Anna †	11	"	70	here
	B	McCabe Stella †	11	weaver	65	"
	C	Ware Harriett †	11	at home	92	"
	D	Hudson Charles W	13	artist	69	"
	E	Hudson Maria A †	13	manager	73	"
	F	Collins Barbara M †	14	housewife	37	"
	G	Collins Raymond J	14	restaurateur	36	"
	H	Youngren Otto W	14	retired	70	"
	K	Laberge Eugenie B †	15	housewife	68	"
	L	Laberge Fernand	15	retired	42	"
	M	Laberge Joseph	15	operator	67	"
	N	Laberge Maurice J	15	examiner	40	"
	O	Norton Grace E †	16	housewife	32	"
	P	Norton John E	16	manager	32	"
	R	Shute Dorothy M †	16	housewife	40	"
	S	Shute Mildred A †	16	clerk	49	"
	T	Shute Stanley J	16	laborer	43	"
	U	Buckley Harry J	17	retired	65	"
	V	Rogers Alice V †	17	housewife	61	"
	W	Rogers Lillian G †	17	clerk	64	"
	X	Schultz Estella †	20	housewife	55	"
	Y	Schultz Otto	20	salesman	52	"
	Z	Donahue Catherine R †	27	operator	37	"
1418						
	A	Donahue Florence †	27	retired	77	"
	B	Donahue Margaret A †	27	clerk	44	"
	C	Donahue Martha T †	27	"	39	"
	D	Donahue Mary J †	27	housewife	74	"

Page	Letter	Full Name	Residence, Jan. 1, 1941	Occupation	Supposed Age	Reported Residence, Jan. 1, 1940. Street and Number
	G	*Gangemi Anna †	880	housewife	49	here
	H	Gangemi Anna D †	880	stitcher	23	"
	K	Gangemi Frank A	880	laborer	21	"
	L	Gangemi Joseph	880	chauffeur	25	"
	M	Gangemi Peter	880	mechanic	55	"
	N	Kallenberg Carl A	881	retired	68	"
	O	Kallenberg Herta C †	881	houseworker	29	"
	R	Wagner Minnie L †	886	housekeeper	71	"
	S	Hewitt Sarah M †	886	operator	56	918 Hyde Park av
	T	Hewitt Thomas A	886	mechanic	25	here
	U	Duff Clifton	887	laborer	26	"
	V	Duff David A	887	painter	56	"
	W	Duff Violet S †	887	housewife	49	"
	X	*Millar Alice M †	887	"	62	"
	Y	Millar John	887	laborer	22	"
	Z	Millar Robert	887	mechanic	65	"
1419						
	A	Miller Edward R	887	chauffeur	38	"
	B	Miller Grace H †	887	housewife	35	"
	C	*Lavallee Clara R †	887	stitcher	49	"
	D	Lavallee Paul C	887	carpenter	56	"
	E	Pannerot Fred M	887	painter	34	"
	F	Pannerot Henry	887	"	36	"
	G	Pannerot Jeannette †	887	houseworker	62	"
	H	Pannerot Rita M †	887	housewife	30	"
	K	Lawrence Clifton J	887	salesman	31	946 Hyde Park av
	L	Schoener Evelyn M †	887	housewife	26	here
	M	Schoener William	887	shipper	30	"
	N	*Schwinn Margaret A †	890	housewife	29	"
	O	Schwinn Robert A	890	clerk	30	"
	P	Littell Evelyn M †	890	housewife	32	"
	R	Littell James R	890	accountant	33	"
	S	Vickerson Arthur H	891	policeman	39	"
	T	Vickerson Emma †	891	housewife	65	"
	U	Jones Charles J, jr	891	operator	27	38 Rugby rd
	V	Jones Kathryn †	891	housewife	26	1123 Hyde Park av
	W	Langer Arthur	898	furrier	71	here
	X	Langer Margaretha G †	898	housewife	68	"
	Y	Pommer Frances L †	898	"	16	377 Metropolitan av
	Z	Pommer Frederick G	898	musician	57	377 "

Page	Letter	Full Name	Residence, Jan. 1, 1941	Occupation	Supposed Age	Reported Residence, Jan. 1, 1940. Street and Number

1420
Hyde Park Avenue—Continued

	D	Bradeen Lillian M †	906	housekeeper	70	here
	E	Roome John W	906	retired	81	"
	F	Sheehan Elizabeth M †	911	housewife	62	"
	G	Sheehan Mary M †	911	clerk	22	"
	H	Sheehan Timothy	911	drawtender	66	"
	K	Sullivan James F	911	serviceman	42	994 River
	L	Sullivan Theresa V †	911	housewife	38	994 "
	M	Henry Bridget †	911	"	42	here
	N	Henry Katherine †	911	cashier	21	"
	O	Henry Mary A †	911	clerk	21	"
	P	Henry Patrick J	911	custodian	47	"
	R	Carriere Anna L †	914	housewife	24	488 E Seventh
	S	Carriere Henry D	914	chauffeur	25	488 "
	T	Smith Earl H	914	messenger	54	1669 Com av
	U	Glennon Marie B †	914	housewife	23	20 Liszt
	V	Glennon Martin J	914	loftsman	22	20 "
	W	Thompson Ethel M †	914	housewife	50	here
	X	Thompson Mary A †	914	clerk	22	"
	Y	Thompson Robert M	914	metalworker	50	"
	Z	Thompson William J	914	clerk	22	"
1421						
	A	Delaney John J	915	steamfitter	53	"
	B	*Delaney Margaret T †	915	housewife	41	"
	C	Feist Adeline M †	915	"	34	"
	D	Feist Harold L	915	proprietor	35	"
	E	Ronan Alexander V †	915	bookkeeper	37	"
	F	Rosenthal Kathryn †	916	housewife	39	"
	G	Rosenthal Morris	916	salesman	43	"
	H	Deane Helen C †	916	housewife	26	"
	K	Deane Kenneth M	916	agent	30	"
	L	Kirchner Bertha †	916	tester	33	Cambridge
	M	Kirchner Philip I	916	mechanic	34	"
	N	Draper Elizabeth E †	918	housekeeper	70	here
	O	Southard Lafayette	918	painter	66	"
	P	Murphy Francis M	918	operator	28	116 Babson
	R	Murphy Margaret E †	918	housewife	33	116 "
	S	O'Connor Joseph P	918	sorter	23	1 Shepherd av
	T	O'Connor Margaret M †	918	houseworker	21	1 "
	U	O'Connor Thomas P	918	clerk	24	1 "
	V	McIntyre Joseph C	919	carpenter	51	here

**Page	Letter	Full Name	Residence, Jan. 1, 194[illegible]	Occupation	Reported Age	Reported Residence, Jan. 1, 194[illegible]. Street and Number

Hyde Park Avenue Continued

Page	Letter	Full Name	Residence	Occupation	Age	Reported Residence
	W	McIntyre Mary E †	919	housewife	49	here
	X	McIntyre Virginia M †	919	stenographer	20	"
	Y	Gigliotti George P	919	proofreader	37	"
	Z	Gigliotti Katherine J †	919	housewife	35	"
1422						
	A	Ryder Rose E †	919	"	21	59 Bradfield av
	B	Ryder Thomas F	919	painter	24	59 "
	C	Speed John J	920	mechanic	30	here
	D	Speed Lillian F †	920	housewife	30	"
	E	Brady George E	920	letter carrier	31	"
	F	Brady Margaret L †	920	housewife	36	"
	G	O'Meara James T	920	agent	41	64 Patten
	H	O'Meara Mildred M †	920	housewife	32	New York
	K	Neudeck Erwin P	922	draftsman	28	here
	L	Neudeck Yvonne A †	922	housewife	25	"
	M	Gaiser Ernest	922	baker	41	"
	N	Gaiser Kuni †	922	housewife	35	"
	O	deGuichard Anna C †	922	"	59	"
	P	deGuichard Anne M †	922	musician	30	"
	R	Lonergan Helen J †	923	housewife	38	"
	S	Lonergan Raymond T	923	electrician	42	"
	T	Lonergan William J	923	laborer	20	"
	U	Ford Florence J †	923	housewife	54	"
	V	Ford Louise D †	923	saleswoman	23	"
	X	Favor Esther R †	926	housewife	28	"
	Y	Favor Gilbert I	926	clerk	30	"
1423						
	A	Wood Albertine V †	926	dressmaker	46	Somerville
	B	Wood Dorothy A †	926	clerk	20	"
	C	Wood Everal B	926	machinist	18	"
	D	Goddard Elizabeth †	936	housewife	68	here
	E	Goddard Marjorie R †	936	investigator	32	"
	F	Goddard Samuel E	936	retired	69	"
	G	Grenier Frederick J	936	weaver	38	4 Oak
	H	Grenier Marie A †	936	housewife	38	4 "
	K	*Goodale Doris †	936	hairdresser	35	here
	L	Goodale Henry	936	machinist	62	"
	M	Goodale Margaret †	936	housewife	60	"
	N	*Mathison Lora M †	940	merchant	44	"
	O	Rasmussen Hans E	940	florist	44	"
	P	*Thorpe Ella E †	940	housewife	56	"

Hyde Park Avenue Continued

Page	Letter	Full Name	Residence, Jan. 1, 1941.	Occupation.	Supposed Age.	Reported Residence, Jan. 1, 1940. Street and Number.
	R	*Thorpe Peter S	940	retired	71	here
	S	Kelley Ellen M †	940	clerk	23	"
	T	*Petersen Minna †	940	housewife	56	"
	U	Petersen Ruth L †	940	clerk	20	"
	V	*Petersen Viggo	940	carpenter	58	"
	W	*DelSignore Diletta †	940	housewife	48	11 Delmore pl
	X	DelSignore Josephine †	940	student	20	11 "
	Y	DelSignore Oliver	940	plasterer	29	11 "
	Z	Chefitz Benjamin J	941	physician	36	here
1424						
	A	Chefitz Sylvia K †	941	housewife	31	"
	B	Draper Evelyn L †	941	houseworker	22	19 Galena
	C	Dembowski Chester P	941	salesman	24	here
	D	*Dembowski Frances †	941	housewife	45	"
	E	Dembowski Frank	941	bartender	45	"
	F	Dembowski Frank J	941	draftsman	22	"
	G	Dembowski Walter S	941	student	20	"
	H	Kenney Francis J	941	mason	42	902 Hyde Park av
	K	Kenney George L	941	policeman	40	902 "
	L	Kenney Mabel G †	941	housewife	38	902 "
	N	Bloom Fallon	943	laborer	20	here
	O	Chefitz Anna D †	943	housewife	39	"
	P	Chefitz Samuel	943	manager	39	"
	R	Maniek Charles Z	943	cobbler	41	"
	S	Maniek Virginia †	943	housewife	36	"
	T	Mosesian Higonish †	943	housekeeper	68	"
	U	Kazmerczyk Anthony	943	molder	54	"
	V	Kazmerczyk Bessie †	943	stenographer	20	"
	W	Kazmerczyk Genevieve †	943	"	24	"
	X	Kazmerczyk Helen †	943	"	28	"
	Y	Kazmerczyk Sabyna †	943	laundryworker	26	"
	Z	*Kazmerczyk Stella †	943	housewife	53	"
1425						
	A	DiCamillo Daniel	945	clerk	26	"
	B	*DiCamillo Dominick	945	"	50	"
	C	DiCamillo Maria †	945	housewife	48	"
	D	Fasano Yolanda †	945	housekeeper	24	"
	E	Franchi Giulio	945	waiter	28	Florida
	F	Franchi Julia †	945	housewife	37	here
	G	Franchi Peter B	945	butcher	42	"
	H	Donohowski Francis P	945	chauffeur	27	32 Summer

Page	Letter	Full Name	Residence, Jan. 1, 1941	Occupation	Reported Age	Reported Residence, Jan. 1, 1940. Street and Number

Hyde Park Avenue Continued

Page	Letter	Full Name	Residence, Jan. 1, 1941	Occupation	Reported Age	Reported Residence, Jan. 1, 1940. Street and Number
	K	Domohowski Ina A †	945	housewife	27	3389 Wash'n
	L	Sternfield Beatrice †	947	"	35	here
	M	Sternfield Joseph	947	salesman	42	"
	N	Rosenbaum Max	947	merchant	60	"
	O	*Rosenbaum Mollie—†	947	housewife	56	"
	P	Rosenbaum Pearl—†	947	saleswoman	30	"
	R	Laneres Jennie T †	947	housewife	35	142 Wash'n
	S	*Laneres Paul	947	barber	41	145 Fairmount
	T	Chase Amelia M—†	949	housewife	48	133 Child
	U	Chase Edward R	949	machinist	39	133 "
	V	Caggiano Angelina—†	949	housewife	28	here
	W	Caggiano Samuel	949	tailor	27	"
	X	*Grenda Martha J—†	949	housewife	42	"
	Y	Grenda Michael D	949	rubberworker	51	"
1426						
	A	Gattozzi Carmela—†	951	housewife	30	"
	B	Gattozzi Joseph A	951	draftsman	33	"
	C	*Slade John H	951	salesman	37	"
	D	Slade Julia—†	951	housewife	23	"
	E	Bandlow Esther M—†	953	"	30	11 Worcester
	F	Bandlow William E	953	steamfitter	34	11 "
	G	Budner Fay—†	953	seamstress	31	Otis
	H	Budner Simon	953	laborer	32	"
	K	Kaminsky Rae—†	953	secretary	21	"
	L	Fagone Charles C	953	machinist	22	46 N Russell
	M	Harker Henry	953	mechanic	46	here
	N	*Harker Jean—†	953	housewife	42	"
	O	*Cobb George M	953	janitor	37	"
	P	*Cobb Mary B †	953	housewife	36	"
	R	*Lundborg Reuben D	953	engineer	55	"
	S	Lundborg Sarah A—†	953	housewife	50	"
	T	Grasso Laura M—†	957	dressmaker	23	"
	U	Grasso Michael	957	laborer	27	"
	V	*Scapinaro Giovanni V	957	"	64	65 Business
	W	Riley Alice M †	957	housewife	25	Dedham
	X	Riley Stephen J	957	B F D	27	54 Rosa
	Y	Howland Grayce D †	957	biller	22	953 Hyde Park av
	Z	Howland John T	957	policeman	28	953 "
1427						
	A	Ahern Gertrude—†	957	housewife	32	here
	B	Ahern Leo	957	chauffeur	35	"

Page	Letter	Full Name	Residence, Jan. 1, 1941	Occupation	Supposed Age	Reported Residence, Jan. 1, 1940. Street and Number

Hyde Park Avenue—Continued

Page	Letter	Full Name	Residence, Jan. 1, 1941	Occupation	Supposed Age	Reported Residence, Jan. 1, 1940. Street and Number
	C	Shea George L	957	mechanic	31	121 Child
	D	Shea Loretta †	957	housewife	33	680 Hyde Park av
	E	Cataruzollo Angelo	957	sorter	27	here
	F	Cataruzollo Anne M †	957	housewife	29	"
	G	Moran Rachel E †	961	"	40	989 Hyde Park av
	H	Thomas Alexander J	961	painter	39	34 Fulton
	K	Thomas Anna K †	961	housewife	31	34 "
	L	Benjamin Ethel D †	962	"	33	here
	M	Benjamin Morris	962	dresscutter	34	"
	N	Maltzman Leo	962	draftsman	30	28 Colborne rd
	O	Maltzman Mildred †	962	housewife	32	28 "
	P	Ratner Elizabeth †	962	milliner	26	Winthrop
	R	Hoyt Liston E	965	clerk	20	1 Crosby sq
	S	Owens Adam J	965	shipper	36	here
	T	Owens Evelyn L †	965	housewife	36	"
	U	*Brodin Ernest T	966	houseman	33	"
	V	Brodin May S †	966	housewife	22	"
	W	Newell Emma C †	966	"	51	"
	X	Newell Owen	966	baker	70	"
	Y	Pearson Carl E	966	machinist	32	"
	Z	Pearson Edith E †	966	housewife	31	"
1428						
	A	Paciotti Lena †	969	student	20	"
	B	*Paciotti Mary †	969	housewife	42	"
	C	Paciotti Ralph	969	mason	48	"
	D	Macaluso Joseph	970	laborer	40	"
	E	Macaluso Sarah †	970	housewife	33	"
	F	O'Neil Florence E †	970	countergirl	26	"
	G	O'Neil George F	970	starter	32	"
	H	O'Neil John J	970	carpenter	53	"
	K	O'Neil John J, jr	970	pipefitter	24	"
	L	O'Neil Margaret G †	970	housewife	49	"
	M	O'Neil Robert E	970	student	21	"
	N	Cianca Angelina †	971	housewife	48	"
	O	Cianca Mary T †	971	factoryhand	25	"
	P	Cianca Ulysses	971	mason	53	"
	R	Massarelli Raffaella †	971	stitcher	38	"
	S	*Porzio Frank	971	retired	77	"
	T	Evans Charles H	973	bookkeeper	26	83 Arlington
	U	Evans Florence G †	973	housewife	26	83 "
	V	MacBurney Robert	973	electrician	35	83 "

Page	Letter	Full Name	Residence, April 1, 1944	Occupation	Reputed Age	Reported Residence, April 1, 1943. Street and Number

Hyde Park Avenue—Continued

Page	Letter	Full Name	Residence	Occupation	Age	Reported Residence
	W	MacBurney Sydney †	973	housewife	21	83 Arlington
	X	Podbury Hattie W †	974	"	76	here
	Y	Podbury Thomas L	974	retired	73	"
	Z	Merson Carrie †	974	housewife	55	"
1429						
	A	Merson Everett	974	patternmaker	54	"
	B	Perreault Alma L—†	978	housewife	45	"
	C	Perreault Arthur S	978	clerk	47	"
	D	Perreualt Robert F	978	timekeeper	23	"
	E	Matthews Jessie †	982	housewife	62	"
	F	Matthews Samuel	982	florist	72	"
	H	Kiederis Joseph E	989	painter	35	"
	K	Kiederis Mildred E—†	989	housewife	32	"
	L	Haigh Ethel M †	989	"	26	280 Nep[illegible]
	M	Haigh John H	989	clerk	30	280 "
	N	Henry George E	991	welder	35	here
	O	Henry Irma L †	991	stenographer	30	"
	P*	Moran Elsie C †	991	housewife	39	"
	R	Moran Martin J	991	chauffeur	39	"
	T	Staniewicz Albert C	995	welder	23	690 M[illegible]
	U	Staniewicz Gertrude M—†	995	housewife	22	690 "
	V	DiRusso Constance M—†	995	factoryhand	26	here
	W	DiRusso Dominic	995	laborer	21	"
	X	DiRusso Frank S	995	chauffeur	24	"
	Y*	DiRusso Josephine M—†	995	housewife	58	"
	Z	DiRusso Mary S †	995	houseworker	27	"
1430						
	A	DiRusso Raymond	995	merchant	58	"
	B	O'Brien Albina L—†	997	housewife	27	"
	C	O'Brien Paul J	997	operator	30	"
	D	Holt Albert	997	weaver	59	"
	E	Holt Sarah †	997	maid	79	"
	F	Hartford Catherine A—†	999	housewife	30	"
	G	Hartford James J	999	millwright	33	"
	H	Wood Margaret E †	999	at home	52	"
	K	Taber Francis R	1000	toolmaker	77	"
	L	Taber Mary E †	1000	housewife	70	"
	M	Brown Gertrude E †	1000	"	60	Squantum
	N	Brown Robert C	1000	manager	55	"
	O	McGowan Frank	1000	chemist	35	[illegible]
	P	McGowan Lois †	1000	housewife	34	1041 "

Page	Letter	Full Name	Residence, Jan. 1, 1941	Occupation	Supposed Age	Reported Residence, Jan. 1, 1940. Street and Number

Hyde Park Avenue—Continued

Page	Letter	Full Name	Residence	Occupation	Age	Reported Residence
	R	Campbell Harriett †	1001	housewife	61	here
	S	Dodson Elinor B †	1003	authoress	39	"
	T	Dodson Lillian O †	1003	housewife	65	"
	U	Dodson Oliver	1003	cleanser	67	"
	V	Dodson Rose L †	1003	artist	41	"
	W	Griffin Frank P	1004	waiter	33	607 E Seventh
	X	Griffin Leona D †	1004	housewife	30	607 "
	Y	Drea Catherine A †	1007	teacher	36	here
	Z	Drea Christine R †	1007	housewife	48	"
1431						
	A	Drea Elizabeth V †	1007	teacher	48	"
	B	Drea John J	1007	"	47	"
	C	Mazzei James	1007	clerk	31	20 Walter
	D	Mazzei Mary E †	1007	housewife	31	here
	E	Wheeler Christine J †	1009	"	38	"
	F	Wheeler Henry M	1009	B F D	47	"
	G	Wheeler Henry M, jr	1009	machinist	20	"
	H	Daigle Joseph	1011	engineer	45	"
	K	Daigle Marguerite †	1011	nurse	45	"
	L	Vattes Catherine †	1011	at home	74	"
	M	*Amara John J	1019	laborer	43	"
	N	*Amara Mary †	1019	housewife	32	"
	O	Ciesielski Harry E	1019	papermaker	20	1049 River
	P	Ciesielski Irene A †	1019	housewife	21	Chelsea
	R	Remick Frank	1022	chauffeur	35	here
	S	Remick Ruth E †	1022	housewife	30	"
	T	Hines Elizabeth A †	1022	"	28	155 Amory
	U	Hines John M	1022	cleaner	34	155 "
	V	Hoefer Albert C	1022	machinist	44	155 "
	W	Hoefer Elizabeth †	1022	housekeeper	55	155 "
	X	Richberg Edward C	1022	machinist	55	155 "
	Y	Higgins Earl S	1023	clerk	41	here
	Z	Higgins Ernest W	1023	"	63	"
1432						
	A	Higgins Irene M †	1023	painter	40	"
	B	Howlett Alice L †	1026	at home	85	"
	C	Howlett Mary L †	1026	"	92	"
	D	Reichert Albert G	1030	carpenter	50	"
	E	Reichert Blanche C †	1030	housewife	40	"
	F	Gaffey Patrick J	1033	retired	79	"
	G	Groves Madeline T †	1033	housewife	39	"

Page	Letter	Full Name	Residence, Jan. 1, 1941	Occupation	Reported Age	Reported Residence, Jan. 1, 1940. Street and Number

Hyde Park Avenue (Continued)

Page	Letter	Full Name	Residence, Jan. 1, 1941	Occupation	Reported Age	Reported Residence, Jan. 1, 1940. Street and Number
	H	Davis Edith M—†	1034	housewife	64	here
	K	Davis Willard S	1034	dentist	66	"
	M	Howden Herbert R	1038	manager	70	"
	N	Shea Dorothy M—†	1038	stenographer	33	"
	O	Shea Katherine I—†	1038	secretary	29	"
	P	Shea Katherine T—†	1038	housewife	58	"
	R	Knapp Etta M—†	1040	"	52	"
	S	Knapp Harry A	1040	clerk	51	"
	T	Damata Anthony	1041	laborer	36	34 Mt Hope
	U	Damata Mary—†	1041	housewife	26	34 "
	V	Cicchetti Alexander	1041	welder	56	here
	W	*Cicchetti Oliva—†	1041	housewife	50	"
	X	Fransoso Frank	1041	molder	45	"
	Y	*Fransoso Margaret—†	1041	housewife	35	"
	Z	Bleakney Catherine—†	1044	"	63	"
1433						
	A	Bleakney Hazel—†	1044	organist	24	"
	C	Clark Howard T	1048	chauffeur	34	"
	D	Clark Margaret—†	1048	housewife	68	"
	E	Giunta Anthony	1048	barber	31	Dedham
	F	Sherrit Susan—†	1049	housewife	59	here
	G	Sherrit William	1049	painter	58	"
	L	Walsh James	1053	"	25	"
	M	Walsh Margaret—†	1053	housewife	51	"
	N	Walsh Marie—†	1053	"	25	"
	O	Walsh Michael	1053	laborer	23	"
	P	Gill Mary—†	1054	housewife	59	"
	R	Gill Thomas	1054	foreman	59	"
	S	*Gill Catherine—†	1054	housewife	54	"
	T	Gill John J	1054	B F D	59	"
	V	Marks John H	1058	plasterer	68	"
	W	Marks Rose—†	1058	housewife	68	"
	X	Marks Rose A—†	1058	stenographer	29	"
	Y	McNulty Ellen—†	1058	nurse	65	"
	Z	Robbins Cecile—†	1058	housewife	37	"
1434						
	A	Robbins Kenneth	1058	shipper	38	"
	D	Beaulieu Albert	1062	"	44	"
	E	Beaulieu Victoren—†	1062	housewife	36	"
	F	Sowars Margaret M—†	1062	"	58	"
	G	Lavnikevich John	1062	blacksmith	57	"

Page	Letter	Full Name	Residence, Jan. 1, 1941	Occupation	Supposed Age	Reported Residence, Jan. 1, 1940. Street and Number.

Hyde Park Avenue—Continued

Page	Letter	Full Name	Residence, Jan. 1, 1941	Occupation	Supposed Age	Reported Residence, Jan. 1, 1940. Street and Number.
	L	Capobianco Elizabeth †	1066	hairdresser	35	here
	M	*Capobianco Maria C †	1066	storekeeper	55	"
	N	Capobianco Mary T †	1066	housekeeper	26	"
	O	Capobianco Frances †	1066	housewife	31	85 Harvard av
	P	Capobianco Raymond	1066	tavernkeeper	31	here
	V	Spicer Margaret J †	1072	housewife	28	"
	W	Spicer William F	1072	brakeman	28	"
	X	Jaeger Frank	1072	breweryworker	49	"
	Y	*Jaeger Nora †	1072	housewife	38	"
	Z	Jennette Henry L	1072	operator	22	144 Child
1435						
	A	Lombardi Anthony J	1072	timekeeper	32	here
	B	Lombardi Mary C †	1072	housewife	27	"
	C	Sinclair Alexander S, jr	1072	shipfitter	28	"
	D	Sinclair Helen C †	1072	housewife	22	"
	H	Doherty Frank H	1079	custodian	39	"
	K	Doherty Mae A †	1079	housewife	40	"
	L	*Ubertini Alice †	1079	"	31	"
	M	Ubertini Peter	1079	cobbler	42	"
	N	Luciano Anthony J	1079	laborer	24	"
	O	Luciano Dorothy R †	1079	housewife	24	"
	R	Bodfish Edward R	1082	salesman	43	Milton
	S	Bodfish Louise †	1082	housewife	37	"
	T	Bodfish William H	1082	retired	88	here
	U	Lombardi Joseph	1083	painter	46	"
	V	Lombardi Rena †	1083	housewife	45	"
	W	Lombardi Alexander	1083	retired	67	"
	X	Lombardi Stella †	1083	housewife	66	"
	Y	Paradee Alfred C	1083	retired	71	"
	Z	Paradee Samuel J	1083	agent	66	"
1436						
	A	Paradee Sarah M †	1083	housewife	65	"
	B	Tsetsi Stephen M	1086	barber	56	"
	C	*Tsetsi Thomasina †	1086	housewife	49	"
	D	Pezzano Joseph M	1086	mechanic	27	"
	E	Pezzano Mary †	1086	housewife	24	"
	F	Bober Rudolph J	1087	clerk	41	"
	G	Bober Ursula M †	1087	housewife	44	"
	H	MacPhee Beverly B †	1087	typist	20	"
	K	MacPhee Ethel S †	1087	housewife	50	"

Page	Letter	Full Name	Residence	Occupation	Age	Reported Residence

Hyde Park Avenue—Continued

Page	Letter	Full Name	Residence	Occupation	Age	Reported Residence
	L	MacPhee James E	1087	machinist	57	here
	M	MacPhee John S	1087	student	27	New York
	N	Doyle John	1090	metalworker	21	Haverhill
	O	Hayden Doris P †	1090	housewife	31	here
	P	Hayden William A	1090	machinist	31	"
	R	McHale Annie †	1090	housewife	33	3927 Wash'n
	S	McHale James	1090	packer	33	3927 "
	T	*Kideris Anna †	1091	housewife	66	here
	U	Kideris John G	1091	retired	76	"
	V	Simpson David B	1091	"	82	"
	W	Simpson Janet †	1091	housewife	75	"
	X	Simpson Wilhelmina M †	1091	clerk	40	"
	Y	Doherty Flora †	1092	housekeeper	41	44 Westville
	Z	Sheehan Elmer B	1092	mechanic	39	65 Templeton
1437						
	A	Burke John J	1095	clerk	22	here
	B	Burke Mary E—†	1095	housewife	53	"
	C	Dolan Frank P	1095	salesman	31	"
	D	Dolan Josephine G—†	1095	housewife	69	"
	E	Dolan Patrick F	1095	retired	68	"
	F	Hardwick Nora M—†	1096	housewife	55	"
	G	Hardwick Pliny S	1096	mechanic	56	"
	H	O'Flaherty Frances—†	1096	secretary	37	"
	K	Kiggen Florence †	1098	housewife	37	"
	L	Kiggen Joseph M	1098	clerk	39	"
	M	Bodwell Ethelind S—†	1099	housekeeper	61	"
	N	Burke Alice B †	1099	advertising	28	Winthrop
	O	Burke Ruth B †	1099	reporter	60	"
	P	Hines A Rita †	1100	housewife	21	9 Wash'n St pl
	R	Hines Edward F	1100	painter	25	9 "
	S	Kiggen Kathleen A—†	1104	housekeeper	64	here

Jefferson Street

Page	Letter	Full Name	Residence	Occupation	Age	Reported Residence
	T	Brady Edward F	30	foreman	27	32 Worcester
	U	Brady Gertrude I—†	30	housewife	26	32 "
	V	Byrnes Bernard J	30	clerk	33	here
	W	Byrnes Dorothy O †	30	housewife	33	"
	X	Barnett Irene E †	32	"	28	"
	Y	Barnett James E	32	retired	73	"

Page	Letter	Full Name	Residence, Jan. 1, 1941	Occupation	Supposed Age	Reported Residence, Jan. 1, 1940. Street and Number.

Jefferson Street—Continued

Page	Letter	Full Name	Residence	Occupation	Age	Reported Residence
	Z	Barnett James E, jr	32	electrician	27	here
1438						
	A	Barnett Mary †	32	housewife	72	"

Laval Street

Page	Letter	Full Name	Residence	Occupation	Age	Reported Residence
	B	Greene Everett S	7	engineer	43	here
	C	*Greene Mary M †	7	housewife	36	"
	D	Johnston Austin	7	salesman	39	"
	E	*Johnston Domenick	7	laborer	43	"
	F	Murray Elizabeth †	12	housewife	29	"
	G	Murray Joseph A	12	engineer	34	"
	H	Gillis Azalea W †	12	housewife	28	"
	K	Gillis John A	12	chef	33	"
	L	DiTullio Orazio	15	contractor	38	"
	M	DiTullio Philomena †	15	housewife	33	"
	N	*Ullrich Freda E †	17	"	41	"
	O	Ullrich George M	17	electrician	43	"
	P	Waller Fred R	18	painter	52	"
	R	Waller Mabel H †	18	housewife	51	"
	S	Waller Pauline M †	18	bookkeeper	21	"
	T	*Nichol Ida †	20	housekeeper	65	"
	U	Wilson Robert	20	retired	68	"
	V	Flynn Bridget T †	22	housewife	84	"
	W	Flynn James R	22	laborer	53	"
	X	Wisentainer Helen †	22	housewife	47	"
	Y	Wisentainer Louis W	22	electrician	53	"
	Z	McTiernan Charles F	23	letter carrier	36	"
1439						
	A	McTiernan Irene M †	23	housewife	29	"
	B	Petelle Ida M †	23	"	56	"
	C	Petelle Joseph G	23	machinist	57	"

Metropolitan Avenue

Page	Letter	Full Name	Residence	Occupation	Age	Reported Residence
	D	Driver Henry W	491	repairman	38	here
	E	Driver Maud S †	491	housewife	48	496 Metropolitan av
	F	Driver William H	491	retired	82	here
	G	Breen Alice †	495	housewife	27	"
	H	Breen William P	495	usher	32	"
	K	McNamara Charlotte M †	495	housewife	36	"

Metropolitan Avenue (Continued)

Page	Letter	Full Name	Residence, April 1, 1941	Occupation	Reported Age	Reported Residence April 1, 1940, Street and Number
	L	McNamara Jeremiah J	495	rigger	37	here
	M	Donaruma Anna †	499	housewife	27	"
	N	Donaruma Carmino	499	laborer	57	"
	O	Donaruma Conchetta †	499	teacher	25	"
	P*	Donaruma Consolata †	499	housewife	50	"
	R	Donaruma George	499	laborer	29	"
	S	Svendsen Anna E †	583	clerk	22	"
	T	Svendsen Elin †	583	housewife	60	"
	U	Svendsen Lawrence P	583	machinist	30	"
	V	Svendsen Sven	583	painter	66	"
	W	Svendsen Warren H	583	machinist	20	"
	X	Burns Dennis P	585	letter carrier	57	"
	Y	Burns Elizabeth A †	585	housewife	49	"
	Z*	Caldwell Elizabeth †	585	at home	73	"
1440						
	A	Oatt Ralph L	585	engineer	36	"
	B	Oatt Wilma J †	585	secretary	31	"
	C	Davies Charlotte L †	589	housewife	60	"
	D	Davies Frederick J	589	retired	72	"
	E	Davies Jane †	589	housewife	28	"
	F	Davies Leon F	589	machinist	32	"
	G	Banks Mabel E †	593	operator	27	"
	H	Banks Robert H	593	blacksmith	55	"
	K	Hersey Harriett D †	593	housekeeper	64	"
	L*	Parfumorse Anthony	597	retired	70	"
	M	Parfumorse Charles	597	clerk	33	106 Cla[illegible] av
	N	Parfumorse Ethel E †	587	housewife	30	106 "
	O	Wilder Charles H	597	salesman	35	here
	P	Wilder Helen G †	597	housewife	38	"
	R	Clancy Helen J †	601	"	35	"
	S	Clancy Henry J	601	electrician	40	"
	T	Kibler Gertrude C †	601	packer	33	"
	U	Kibler Henrietta †	601	housewife	57	"
	V	Kibler Louis D	601	mechanic	21	"
	W	Kibler Louis J	601	salesman	63	"
	X	Geyer Arthur W	605	machinist	40	"
	Y	Geyer E Louise †	605	housewife	38	"
	Z	Putman Amanda F †	605	housekeeper	75	"
1441						
	A	Daniel Hedwig E †	609	housewife	42	"
	B	Daniel William L	609	policeman	45	"

Page	Letter	Full Name	Residence, Jan. 1, 1941	Occupation	Supposed Age	Reported Residence, Jan. 1, 1940. Street and Number.

Metropolitan Avenue—Continued

	C	Foster Thelma B †	609	teacher	37	here
	D	Boone Henry A	611	accountant	31	"
	E	Boone Margaret A †	611	housewife	27	"
	F	Lapham Clarence E	611	salesman	34	Dedham
	G	Malloy Cecilia M †	611	housewife	42	101 Westminster
	H	*Halley Cecelia †	625	"	47	here
	K	*Halley James I	625	machinist	54	"
	L	Findlay David W	625	clerk	20	"
	M	Findlay Hugh	625	painter	50	"
	N	Findlay Mary F †	625	housewife	47	"

Park Street

	O	Sundell Dorothy B—†	8	housewife	33	here
	P	Sundell Harding R	8	draftsman	34	"
	R	Clarke Alice N †	8	saleswoman	36	"
	S	Flaherty Edward E	8	salesman	38	"
	T	Wood Benjamin H	9	manager	32	"
	U	Wood Marion M—†	9	housewife	30	"
	V	Hutchins Paul W	9	janitor	36	"
	W	Hutchins Thelma L—†	9	housewife	32	"
	X	Feyler Isabel M †	10	"	54	Dedham
	Y	*Feyler Margaret †	10	"	36	"
	Z	Feyler Wilbur J	10	chauffeur	31	"
1442						
	A	Feyler Wilbur W	10	retired	75	"
	B	Belcher Emerson W	11	salesman	37	here
	C	Belcher Jane B †	11	housewife	40	"
	D	Huff Katherine J †	12	"	52	"
	E	Huff Walter I	12	machinist	52	"
	F	Farrell Carrie E †	15	housewife	53	"
	G	Farrell Charles W	15	printer	24	"
	H	Farrell Margaret E †	15	clerk	21	"
	K	Farrell Raymond F	15	student	20	"
	L	Farrell William A	15	sign painter	52	"
	M	Derry Charles T	16	machinist	59	"
	N	Derry Helen C †	16	housewife	54	"
	O	Franklyn Priscilla D †	16	"	30	N Hampshire
	P	Doucette Leonard A	17	superintendent	43	here
	R	Doucette Mary A †	17	housewife	39	"
	S	Power Anna T †	18	"	53	"

Page	Letter	Full Name	Residence Jan. 1, 1941	Occupation	Supposed Age	Reported Residence, Jan. 1, 1940. Street and Number

Park Street—Continued

Page	Letter	Full Name	Residence	Occupation	Age	Reported Residence
	T	Power Edward J	18	clerk	35	here
	U	Power Francis J	18	cabinetmaker	31	"
	V	Power John J	18	clerk	56	"
	W	Power Joseph E	18	U S A	22	"
	X	Power Lawrence T	18	clerk	34	"
	Y	Carrigan John J	21	foreman	64	"
	Z	Carrigan Julia—†	21	housewife	63	"

1443 Providence Street

Page	Letter	Full Name	Residence	Occupation	Age	Reported Residence
	A	Keene Mary B—†	63	housewife	50	here
	B	Keene Virginia S—†	63	bookkeeper	23	"
	D	Gilmore Florence E—†	82	housewife	73	"
	E	Gilmore Fred A	82	cutter	72	"
	F	Gilmore Maybelle W—†	82	bookkeeper	40	"
	G	Scott Andrew A	82	laborer	27	"
	H	Scott Helen M—†	82	housewife	23	"
	K	McLane Charles N	83	rodman	49	"
	L	McLane Ida M—†	83	housewife	41	"
	M	Watt Alice M—†	83	"	30	"
	N	Watt Frederick	83	woodworker	34	"
	O	*Kucich Anthony	84	floorlayer	40	"
	P	Kucich Fortunata E—†	84	housewife	30	"
	R	Ray Blanche—†	84	housekeeper	35	"
	S	Cheney Effie M—†	85	housewife	54	"
	T	Cheney Sylvester O	85	conductor	60	"
	U	Smith Earl G	85	guard	39	"
	V	Smith Helen F—†	85	housewife	40	"
	W	Rogers George H	86	carpenter	18	"
	X	Rogers Goldie F—†	86	housewife	58	"
	Y	Camillo Joseph D	95	laborer	44	"
	Z	Piacitelli James V	95	foreman	37	"
1444						
	A	Piacitelli Jeanne—†	95	housewife	37	"
	B	Seminatore Charles	99	manager	54	220 Hanover
	C	Seminatore Rose A—†	99	housewife	52	Plymouth
	D	Gange Anna P—†	99	bookkeeper	30	here
	E	*Seminatore Fred	99	carpenter	55	"
	F	Seminatore Mary R—†	99	stenographer	31	"
	G	Seminatore Peter J	99	manager	34	"
	H	Seminatore Rose—†	99	housewife	58	"

Page	Letter	Full Name	Residence, Jan. 1, 1941.	Occupation	Supposed Age	Reported Residence, Jan. 1, 1940. Street and Number.

Providence Street Continued

Page	Letter	Full Name	Residence, Jan. 1, 1941.	Occupation	Supposed Age	Reported Residence, Jan. 1, 1940.
	K	Seminatore Salvatore	99	foreman	58	here
	L	*McNamara Bridget †	140	housewife	69	"
	M	McNamara Patrick P	140	operator	55	"
	N	O'Neill Margaret T †	140	stenographer	21	"
	O	O'Neill Nora F †	140	social worker	47	"
	P	*Rooney Timothy	140	laborer	37	"

Thatcher Street

Page	Letter	Full Name	Residence, Jan. 1, 1941.	Occupation	Supposed Age	Reported Residence, Jan. 1, 1940.
	S	Aitchison Minnie J †	3	housewife	56	here
	T	Aitchison Peter	3	boilermaker	61	"
	U	*Fenton Jean †	3	housekeeper	86	"
	V	Aitchison Agnes P †	5	housewife	31	"
	W	Aitchison Thomas	5	laborer	35	"
	X	*Smith Agnes †	5	housekeeper	54	27 Norfolk
	Y	Klock Amy L †	6	housewife	66	here
	Z	Klock Amy M †	6	secretary	32	"
1445						
	A	Klock William	6	toolmaker	62	"
	B	Waters Clark	8	painter	67	"
	C	Waters Rose E †	8	housewife	65	"
	D	Hegarty Cornelius	8	retired	77	39 Lexington av
	E	Hegarty Mary †	8	housewife	77	39 "
	F	Donlon Winifred †	9	at home	78	39 "
	G	Jurek Anna J †	9	bookkeeper	33	39 "
	H	Quinn Edward T	9	clerk	47	39 "
	K	Quinn Winifred L †	9	housewife	49	39 "
	L	Guptill George W	9	retired	73	here
	M	Guptill George W	9	clerk	28	"
	N	Guptill Nellie L †	9	housewife	63	"
	O	Guptill Veronica A †	9	"	28	371 Hunt'n av
	P	Patten Annie C †	10	"	73	here
	R	Patten Elmer W	10	machinist	37	"
	S	Patten Nathan	10	retired	79	"
	T	Patten Willa A †	10	clerk	32	"
	U	Rogers Ellis R	12–14	collector	24	"
	V	Rogers James E	12–14	salesman	41	"
	W	Rogers John G	12–14	"	34	"
	X	Rogers John J	12–14	shoemaker	63	"
	Y	Rogers Mary C †	12–14	housewife	55	"
	Z	Chaplin Edith M †	12–14	"	42	"

1446
Thatcher Street Continued

Page	Letter	Full Name	Residence, Jan. 1, 1941	Occupation	Supposed Age	Reported Residence, Jan. 1, 1940. Street and Number
1446	A	Chaplin Ernest	12 14	goldbeater	52	here
	B	Magee Charles L	16	clerk	20	218 [illegible]
	C	Magee John J	16	operator	26	218 "
	D	Magee Mary T †	16	housewife	48	218 "
	E	Brennan Arthur E	16	maint'nce man	27	19 Mayfair
	F	Brennan Marie J †	16	housewife	25	19 "
	G	Crowdis Angus	20	carpenter	43	50 Bailey
	H	Crowdis Sarah †	20	housewife	40	50 "
	K	Greeley Joseph T	20	operator	49	18 Thatcher
	L	Greeley Mary A—†	20	housewife	42	18 "
	M	Logan Magdalen M—†	20	operator	33	18 "
	N	Egan Catherine E—†	22	clerk	27	here
	O	*Egan Elizabeth—†	22	housewife	55	"
	P	*Egan Michael J	22	superintendent	56	"
	R	Olson Aleda M—†	22	housewife	60	"
	S	Olson Charles J	22	machinist	68	"
	T	McCarthy Daniel J	24	freighthandler	46	"
	U	McCarthy Mary—†	24	housewife	47	"
	V	*Grushecki Caroline—†	24	"	43	"
	W	Grushecki Charles	24	cabinetmaker	51	"
	X	Bellhumer Charles	25	retired	65	"
	Y	Bellhumer Elizabeth A—†	25	housewife	59	"
	Z	Trottier Blanche M—†	26	"	37	20 Thatcher
1447	A	Trottier Ferdinand J	26	foreman	38	20 "
	B	Bradley Eva M †	26	housewife	32	20 "
	C	Bradley Thomas F	26	policeman	34	20 "
	D	Hart Joseph F	27	"	41	83 Greenfield
	E	Hart Margaret L †	27	housewife	42	83 "
	F	Fitzpatrick Helen F †	28 30	"	34	here
	G	Fitzpatrick Joseph S	28 30	draftsman	41	"
	H	McGloin John P	28 30	pharmacist	36	"
	K	McGloin Thelma P †	28 30	housewife	32	"
	L	Newbegin Florence A—†	29	housekeeper	66	"
	N	*Carratu Grazia †	33	"	79	"
	O	Santosuosso Adeline †	33	housewife	51	"
	P	Santosuosso Alfred	33	lawyer	54	"
	R	Santosuosso Alfred, jr	33	student	22	"
	S	Welsh Frances A †	34	housewife	63	"
	T	Welsh Frances A—†	34	secretary	23	"

Page	Letter	Full Name	Residence, Jan. 1, 1941.	Occupation	Supposed Age.	Reported Residence, Jan. 1, 1940. Street and Number.

Thatcher Street Continued

Page	Letter	Full Name	Residence, Jan. 1, 1941.	Occupation	Supposed Age.	Reported Residence, Jan. 1, 1940. Street and Number.
	U	Welsh Margaret A †	34	typist	26	here
	V	Welsh Thomas F	34	machinist	29	"
	W	Welsh Walter F	34	foreman	62	"
	X	Harvey Ranson W	38	operator	35	8 Augustus av
	Y	Harvey Ruth H †	38	housewife	32	8 "

West Street

Page	Letter	Full Name	Residence, Jan. 1, 1941.	Occupation	Supposed Age.	Reported Residence, Jan. 1, 1940. Street and Number.
	Z	Hodgkinson Edward A	77	clerk	44	here
1448						
	A	Hodgkinson George F	77	mechanic	40	"
	B	Hodgkinson Thomas J	77	woodworker	50	"
	C	Olson Gertrude C †	81	housewife	61	"
	D	Olson Martin L	81	instructor	63	"
	E	Moltedo Ivy †	83	housewife	45	"
	F	Moltedo Norman	83	machinist	23	"
	G	Moltedo Theresa †	83	tailoress	61	"
	H	Badger Albert W	87	engineer	59	"
	K	Badger Ernest C	87	optometrist	57	"
	L	Milliken Olive C †	87	nurse	46	"
	M	Buckley Christine A †	103	housekeeper	22	"
	N	Silver Michael F	103	retired	68	"
	O	Black Harry B	105	salesman	56	50 Eliot
	P	Harris Lelia †	105	housewife	80	here
	R	*Wallis Mary A †	105	at home	85	50 Eliot
	S	Oliver Mary †	107	housewife	65	here
	T	Oliver William	107	machinist	68	"
	U	Goodwin Josephine G †	107	housewife	28	"
	V	Goodwin Kenneth W	107	bartender	30	"
	W	King Edith L †	111	housewife	56	"
	X	King Frank L	111	clerk	62	"
	Y	King Miriam F †	111	secretary	24	"
	Z	King Russell H	111	laborer	23	"
1449						
	A	Ciccocioppo Jennie †	117	housewife	40	"
	B	Ciccocioppo Joseph	117	laborer	46	"
	C	Esposito Mary A †	117	housewife	22	117 Hilton
	D	Esposito William	117	carpenter	26	60 Cornell
	E	Arentzen Alida G †	121	at home	61	here
	F	Arentzen Louise C †	121	"	60	"
	G	Duggan Martin J	125	retired	51	"

Page	Letter	Full Name	Residence	Occupation	Reputed Age	Former Residence

West Street (Continued)

Page	Letter	Full Name	Residence	Occupation	Reputed Age	Former Residence
	H	Duggan Martin J, jr	125	operator	22	here
	K	Duggan Nora †	125	housewife	46	"
	L	Goodfellow John R	125	machinist	54	"
	M	Johnson Agnes E †	125	clerk	35	"
	N	Johnson John A	125	woodworker	66	"
	O	King Nellie K †	125	housewife	66	"
	P	King William C	125	piano tuner	72	"
	S	Molway Eva M †	129	housewife	35	"
	T	Molway Levis J	129	machinist	45	"
	U	Grenier Elarie	129	carpenter	65	"
	V	Grenier Louis J	129	machinist	41	"
	W	Grenier Mary A †	129	housewife	31	"
	X	Grenier Oscar J	129	painter	32	"
	Y	Kaveney Francis E	131	mechanic	41	"
	Z	Kaveney Madeline A †	131	housewife	39	"
1450						
	A	Donovan Catherine †	131	operator	36	"
	B	Donovan Elizabeth E †	131	"	33	"
	C	Donovan John L	131	retired	79	"
	D	Ankudowicz Anthony	145	welder	49	"
	E	Ankudowicz Pasha †	145	housewife	47	"
	F	Crawford Catherine †	151	"	35	"
	G	Crawford Joseph R	151	chauffeur	56	"
	H	*Curry Albert G	151	retired	77	"

Westminster Street

Page	Letter	Full Name	Residence	Occupation	Reputed Age	Former Residence
	K	Jerome Caroline †	14 16	housewife	30	here
	L	Jerome James	14 16	waiter	35	"
	M	Jerome Chris P	14 16	"	27	"
	N	Jerome Domenic	14 16	"	21	"
	O	Jerome John	14 16	machinist	21	"
	P	Jerome Mary †	14 16	housewife	22	"
	R	Jerome Remage	14 16	cook	60	"
	S	Jerome Rocco	14 16	waiter	25	"
	T	Bennison Albert E	15	director	65	"
	U	Bennison Mercy R †	15	housewife	67	"
	V	Jerome Eunice L †	15	"	39	"
	W	Jerome Joseph	15	manager	36	"
	X	McCarthy Annie E †	17	housewife	58	"
	Y	McCarthy Patrick F	17	engineer	60	"

Page	Letter	Full Name	Residence, Jan. 1, 1941	Occupation	Supposed Age	Reported Residence, Jan. 1, 1940. Street and Number.

Westminster Street—Continued

Page	Letter	Full Name	Residence, Jan. 1, 1941	Occupation	Supposed Age	Reported Residence, Jan. 1, 1940. Street and Number.
	Z	Madison Bella F †	20	housewife	57	here
1451						
	A	Madison Bert J	20	ropemaker	60	"
	B	Vardaro Henry	20	machinist	27	37 Dana av
	C	*Vardaro Mary G †	20	presser	27	454 Beech
	D	Hardy Arthur J	20	salesman	27	here
	E	Hardy Dorothy K †	20	housewife	25	"
	F	Breen Alfred F	20	clerk	43	"
	G	Breen Catherine C †	20	housewife	43	"
	H	*McGrath Florence K †	20	"	27	"
	K	McGrath William	20	lineman	36	"
	L	*Ricci Anna †	20	housewife	46	"
	M	Ricci Gabriel	20	merchant	43	"
	N	Chittick Bernice E †	24	housewife	62	"
	O	Chittick John L	24	plumber	64	"
	P	Lapham Elsie M †	24	nurse	35	"
	R	MacKeen Claude E	24	engineer	40	"
	S	MacKeen Ethel B †	24	housewife	35	"
	T	Heatley Barbara L †	35–37	stenographer	21	3 Greenwood sq
	U	Heatley Frederick	35–37	salesman	53	3 "
	V	Heatley Rhena E †	35–37	housewife	50	3 "
	W	Murchie Katherine B †	35–37	"	54	here
	X	Murchie Thomas A	35–37	operator	65	"
	Y	McDonald Francis A	38	clerk	29	"
	Z	McDonald Mary E †	38	housewife	56	"
1452						
	A	Nichols Charles J	38	welder	57	"
	B	Dee Mary T †	39	housekeeper	41	"
	C	Dee Michael P	39	printer	71	"
	D	Freiburger Gerard F	39	investigator	30	"
	E	Freiburger Helen A †	39	housewife	32	"
	F	Knibel Elizabeth H †	39	"	30	"
	G	Knibel Leo F	39	pharmacist	29	"
	K	Lipson Louis E	41	merchant	41	"
	L	*Lipson Sara L †	41	housewife	37	"
	M	Browne Edward J	41	clerk	34	"
	N	Browne Mary V †	41	housewife	26	"
	O	Cole Raymond J	48	clerk	51	"
	P	Cole Rose A †	48	housewife	41	"
	R	MacGibbon Elizabeth †	48	"	76	"
	S	MacGibbon Mary I †	48	teacher	35	"

Page.	Letter	Full Name	Residence, Jan. 1, 1941	Occupation	Supposed Age	Reported Residence, Jan. 1, 1940. Street and Number

Westminster Street—Continued

Page.	Letter	Full Name	Residence, Jan. 1, 1941	Occupation	Supposed Age	Reported Residence, Jan. 1, 1940. Street and Number
	T	Carter George H	49	salesman	65	here
	U	Carter Inez M †	49	housewife	60	"
	V	Spaans Anna †	50	stenographer	61	"
	W	Spaans David	50	machinist	57	"
	X	Gallup Edward H	54	retired	72	Florida
	Y	Neal Helen W †	54	housewife	68	"
	Z	Pike Edith L †	54	housekeeper	65	"
1453						
	A	Carney James W	55	mechanic	58	here
	B	Carney Julia E †	55	housewife	56	"
	C	Carney Virginia M †	55	clerk	20	"
	D	Forbes Carolyn V †	56	banker	38	"
	E	Forbes Joseph F	56	retired	69	"
	F	Price Rita E †	56	housewife	39	"
	G	Wiedemann George O	56	manager	37	"
	H	Wiedemann Marion G †	56	housewife	37	"
	K	McIntire Mary M †	57	teacher	61	"
	L	Withington Katherine M †	57	housewife	49	"
	M	Withington Warren N	57	salesman	50	"
	N	Bryce Annie †	58	clerk	38	"
	O	Bryce Marjory †	58	housewife	71	"
	P	Bryce Robert	58	laborer	58	"
	R	Bryce Thomas F	58	machinist	60	"
	S	Walsh Katherine †	59	housewife	69	"
	T	Walsh Thomas H	59	motorman	56	"
	U	Walsh Thomas H, jr	59	chauffeur	34	"
	V	Morrison Frank J	60	attorney	37	"
	W	Morrison Mary E †	60	housewife	30	"
	X	Hastie Mary E †	60	"	65	"
	Y	Hastie Robert J	60	stereotyper	67	"
1454						
	A	Bailey Joseph	63	milkman	39	115 Clare av
	B	Wright Louise I †	63	housewife	21	Dedham
	C	Wright Marvin C	63	mechanic	26	"
	D	Baker Marion G †	63	housekeeper	21	63 Wood av
	E	Cook Elizabeth H †	65	housewife	46	here
	F	Cook Frank J	65	retired	71	"
	G	Curley Norman F	65	laborer	21	36 Water
	H	Skogstrom George B	65	shipfitter	22	11 Hillside
	K	Peroni Marjorie †	65	stenographer	26	here
	L	Peroni Thomas	65	roofer	27	"

Page	Letter	Full Name	Residence, Jan. 1, 1941	Occupation	Supposed Age	Reported Residence, Jan. 1, 1940. Street and Number.

Westminster Street Continued

Page	Letter	Full Name	Residence, Jan. 1, 1941	Occupation	Supposed Age	Reported Residence, Jan. 1, 1940. Street and Number.
	M	Barron Joseph T	65	salesman	21	43 Summer
	N	Jordan Robert E	65	chef	26	69 Westminster
	O	Wheelock Edward E	67	retired	79	here
	P	Wheelock Mabel E †	67	housewife	79	"
	R	Condy Florence B †	69	housekeeper	80	"
	S	Falconer John W	69	salesman	65	"
	T	Falconer Mary N †	69	housewife	71	"
	U	Falconer Robert N	69	laborer	43	"
	V	McMahon Alice M †	71	bookkeeper	32	"
	W	McMahon Harold J	71	student	23	"
	X	McMahon James A	71	mechanic	58	"
	Y	McMahon Winifred M †	71	housewife	53	"

Ward 18—Precinct 15

CITY OF BOSTON

LIST OF RESIDENTS
20 YEARS OF AGE AND OVER

(NON-CITIZENS INDICATED BY ASTERISK)
(FEMALES INDICATED BY DAGGER)

AS OF

JANUARY 1, 1941

JOSEPH F. TIMILTY, *Chairman*
FREDERIC E. DOWLING, *Secretary*
WILLIAM A. MOTLEY, JR.
FRANCIS B. McKINNEY
HILDA HEDSTROM QUIRK
Listing Board.

CITY OF BOSTON PRINTING DEPARTMENT

Page	Letter	Full Name	Residence, Jan. 1, 1941.	Occupation	Supposed Age.	Reported Residence, Jan. 1, 1940. Street and Number.

1500

Adams Avenue

	A	*Wysocki Helen †	10	housewife	49	here
	B	*Wysocki Walter	10	salesman	50	"
	C	Carleton Christine S †	11	housewife	39	549 E Seventh
	D	Carleton Peter E	11	carpenter	39	549 "
	E	*Madge Florence G †	14	housewife	43	here
	F	*Szlekis Beatrice †	19	"	55	"
	G	Szlekis John	19	machinist	26	"
	H	Szlekis Joseph	19	"	60	"
	K	*Harlow Harriet †	19	housewife	52	"
	L	*Harlow Morton S	19	rigger	55	"
	M	*Harlow Olive W †	19	stenographer	24	"
	N	*Kirkpatrick Harriet J †	19	housewife	73	"
	O	*Kirkpatrick Tennyson M	19	retired	74	"
	P	Baker Adelaide I †	19	housewife	41	2 Tracton av

Arlington Street

	S	Sessine Josephine V †	29	housewife	27	here
	T	Sessine Thomas P	29	laborer	31	"
	U	Glazewski Henry	29	"	20	"
	V	Glazewski John	29	"	24	"
	W	Glazewski Joseph	29	"	52	"
	X	Kowalczyk Josephine †	29	housewife	32	39 Dana av
	Y	Kowalczyk Stanley	29	laborer	32	39 "
	Z	*Labovitch Abram	32	baker	47	here
1501						
	A	*Labovitch Gertrude †	32	housewife	47	"
	C	Romines Alice †	38	housekeeper	44	"
	D	Mahan Margaret G †	38	stenographer	25	"
	E	Mahan Margaret L †	38	housewife	51	"
	F	Mahoney Catherine J †	40–42	"	29	"
	G	Mahoney Francis V	40–42	photographer	32	"
	H	Boyle Mary A †	40–42	housekeeper	67	"
	K	Dray Gertrude D †	40–42	housewife	39	"
	L	Dray Michael J	40–42	attorney	41	"
	M	Patten Mary E †	60	housewife	76	"
	N	Patten Robert	60	retired	77	"
	O	Warren Arthur R	60	machinist	63	"
	P	White Alice M †	61	housekeeper	32	"
	R	Furlong Josephine B †	63	housewife	35	"

Page	Letter	Full Name	Residence	Occupation	Age	Street and Number

Arlington Street (Continued)

Page	Letter	Full Name	Residence	Occupation	Age	Street and Number
	S	Furlong Vincent J	63	clerk	33	here
	T	Kearney Margaret †	63	housekeeper	78	"
	U	Wotton Ethel M †	63	housewife	50	"
	V	Wotton Leslie B	63	policeman	48	"
	W	Cook Arthur W	64	photographer	68	"
	X	Cook Emily A †	64	at home	91	"
	Y	Cook Luetta J †	64	housewife	66	"
	Z	Baxter Arthur	64	electrician	23	"
1502						
	A	Baxter Mary †	64	housewife	61	"
	B	Baxter Robert	64	laborer	64	"
	C	*Ogilvie Mary †	64	hairdresser	40	"
	D	Boyd Catherine W †	65	housewife	47	"
	E	Boyd P Hazen	65	salesman	48	"
	F	Gilman Arlene D †	65	secretary	20	"
	G	Ambrose Sarah W †	65	clerk	40	"
	H	Pollard Harry V	65	carpenter	70	"
	K	Pollard Margaret T †	65	housewife	72	"
	L	Newton John G	66	clerk	35	"
	M	Newton Lucy C †	66	housewife	33	"
	N	Drew Harold E	68	seaman	28	California
	O	Miller Bessie B †	68	housewife	43	here
	P	Miller Eunice C †	68	"	70	196 Colorado
	R	Miller Frank M	68	policeman	43	here
	S	Miller Frank M, jr	68	seaman	20	"
	U	Ficcichi Carmelo	70	furrier	30	"
	V	Ficcichi John	70	physician	29	"
	W	Ficcichi Mary †	70	housewife	56	"
	X	Gould Alice M †	71	housekeeper	54	"
	Y	Jefferds Lewis S	71	retired	76	"
	Z	Chasse Charles	73	engineer	32	"
1503						
	A	Greenwood Margaret E †	73	housekeeper	70	"
	B	Anderson Carl	75	machinist	45	"
	C	Beals Mira H †	75	housekeeper	80	"
	D	Ramstrom Melvin	75	draftsman	28	"
	E	Chittick Arthur B	77	architect	38	"
	F	Chittick Beverly M	77	accountant	66	"
	G	Chittick Daisy M †	77	housewife	62	"
	H	Chittick Ruth W †	77	teacher	25	"
	K	White John E	79	welder	31	61 Arlington

Page	Letter	Full Name.	Residence, Jan. 1, 1941.	Occupation.	Supposed Age.	Reported Residence, Jan. 1, 1940. Street and Number.

Arlington Street—Continued

Page	Letter	Full Name	Residence	Occupation	Age	Reported Residence
	L	White Ruth A †	79	housewife	28	61 Arlington
	M	Crowley Eleanor E †	79	stenographer	22	here
	N	Crowley Ellen A †	79	housewife	60	"
	O	Crowley Robert J	79	retired	70	"
	P	Spencer Sarah J †	81	housewife	62	"
	R	Spencer Wilson	81	metalworker	47	"
	S	Black Isabella C †	81	housewife	51	"
	T	Black John B	81	engineer	52	"
	V	*Smigliani Georgine †	83	housewife	51	3 Mason
	W	Smigliani Luco	83	laborer	61	3 "
	X	*Smigliani Peter	83	draftsman	20	3 "
	Y	Gorovitz Benjamin	87	clergyman	70	here
	Z	Gorovitz Rose †	87	housewife	70	"
1504						
	A	Gorovitz Sarah †	87	teacher	33	"

Davison Street

Page	Letter	Full Name	Residence	Occupation	Age	Reported Residence
	D	*Rizzi Angelina—†	92	housewife	47	here
	E	Rizzi Francisco	92	metalworker	47	"
	F	Rizzi Louis	92	chauffeur	20	"
	G	*Sanfilippo Gerlando	94	pedler	54	14 Stark av
	H	*Sanfilippo Jennie †	94	housewife	45	14 "
	K	Signorino Mary—†	94	mender	21	400 Hanover

Edwards Street

Page	Letter	Full Name	Residence	Occupation	Age	Reported Residence
	L	Corsi Blanche M †	9-11	housewife	33	here
	M	Corsi Mario E	9-11	builder	27	"
	N	Ciovacco Galliano	9-11	chauffeur	44	"
	O	Ciovacco Sylvia †	9-11	housewife	33	"
	P	Tolland Catherine M †	10-12	"	38	"
	R	Tolland Leo L	10-12	papermaker	39	"
	S	Redmond Jessie F †	10-12	housewife	45	"
	T	Redmond Martin J	10-12	foreman	47	"
	U	Hamlet Archie E	14-16	tel worker	49	"
	V	Hamlet Elizabeth F †	14-16	housewife	35	"
	W	Manette Douglas	14-16	chauffeur	40	"
	X	Manette Mary †	14-16	housewife	38	"

Page	Letter	Full Name	Residence, Jan. 1, 1941	Occupation	Supposed Age	Reported Residence, Jan. 1, 1940. Street and Number
		Elliot Street				
	z	Olivieri Guy J	10 12	salesman	28	here
1505						
	A	Olivieri Sylvia R †	10 12	housewife	25	"
	Y	Olivieri Anthony J	10 12	salesman	38	"
	B	Olivieri Jennie †	10 12	housewife	37	"
		Elm Street				
	C	Black Ella B †	7	waitress	46	here
	D*	Blyth Janet †	7	at home	80	"
	E	Irby Alice †	7	clerk	20	"
	F	Moynihan Eleanora L †	9	hostess	29	"
	G	Moynihan Gerard E	9	clerk	25	"
	H	Moynihan John J	9	designer	33	"
	K	Moynihan Marguerite E †	9	clerk	27	"
	L	Moynihan Mary A †	9	secretary	32	"
	M	Moynihan Michael J	9	machinist	65	"
	N	Moynihan Nora M †	9	housewife	66	"
	O*	Vokes Charles P	13	painter	64	"
	P	Vokes Rhoda I †	13	housewife	62	"
	R	Stewart Arthur H	13	chemist	40	12 [illegible]
	S	Stewart Ida †	13	housewife	35	12 "
	T	Palmer Raymond A	15	signalman	51	here
	U	Chamberlain Edward F	17	instructor	30	21 Belvedere rd
	V	Chamberlain Nora M †	17	housewife	30	21 "
	W	Quealey Kathryn M †	17	probat'n officer	52	here
	X	Hodgkinson Clara F †	21	housekeeper	62	"
	Y	Anthony Viola S †	25	housewife	41	"
	Z	Anthony Warren P	25	machinist	41	"
1506						
	A	Horner Anna †	25	stenographer	23	New York
	B	Horner Mildred K †	25	operator	28	15 Summit
	C	MacKinnon Gladstone A	27	chef	29	here
	D	MacKinnon Gladys S †	27	housewife	22	"
		Frazer Street				
	E*	Luciani Anna †	2	housewife	30	here
	F	Luciani John	2	ironworker	36	"
	G	DiStasio Carl M	2	porter	42	"
	H	DiStasio Ethel L †	2	housewife	36	"

Page	Letter	Full Name	Residence, Jan. 1, 1941	Occupation	Supposed Age	Reported Residence, Jan. 1, 1940. Street and Number

Frazer Street Continued

Page	Letter	Full Name	Residence, Jan. 1, 1941	Occupation	Supposed Age	Reported Residence, Jan. 1, 1940. Street and Number
	K	Wolffe Margaret R †	2	housewife	34	here
	L	Wolffe William	2	mechanic	36	"
	M	Gordon John M	3	carpenter	67	"
	N	*Gordon Margaret G †	3	housewife	67	"
	O	Gordon William J	3	draftsman	31	"
	P	Dudley Mary M †	3	housewife	36	"
	R	Dudley Roger W	3	salesman	36	"
	S	Smith Euphemia G †	3	operator	36	309 Wood av
	T	Shepherd Andrew W	3	retired	74	here
	U	Shepherd Georgiana †	3	housewife	72	"
	V	Nolan Harold J	32	accountant	40	40 Frazer
	W	Nolan Laura L †	32	housewife	31	40 "
	X	Kelly Frank P	34	finisher	37	here
	Y	Kelly Helen †	34	housewife	35	"
	Z	Lukow Anthony	36	machinist	59	"
1507						
	A	Lukow Frances †	36	inspector	25	"
	B	Lukow Mary †	36	housewife	61	"
	C	*Crehan Mary H †	38	"	40	"
	D	Crehan Michael F	38	waiter	43	"
	E	Doherty Bertha K †	40	housewife	32	76 Weld Hill
	F	Stephen Albert O	42	salesman	36	here
	G	Stephen Marie F †	42	housewife	25	"
	H	Huber Evelyn M †	42	"	21	"
	K	Huber William R	42	usher	23	"
	L	McGuirk Emma †	44	housewife	39	23 Harbor View
	M	McGuirk John	44	blacksmith	51	23 "
	N	Lawson Richard L	46	laborer	40	here
	O	Lawson Virginia E †	46	housewife	29	"
	P	Locke Alice E †	48	"	52	"
	R	Locke Frederick A	48	fireman	34	"

Huntington Avenue

Page	Letter	Full Name	Residence, Jan. 1, 1941	Occupation	Supposed Age	Reported Residence, Jan. 1, 1940. Street and Number
	S	Henderson Helen †	404	stenographer	43	here
	T	Henderson James H	404	clerk	45	"
	U	McMillan Ethel †	410	nurse	38	"
	V	Bilodeau Marjorie C †	411	model	31	"
	W	Cunningham John H	411	papermaker	77	"
	X	Cunningham Mary E †	411	housewife	56	"

Page	Letter	Full Name	Residence	[illegible]	[illegible]	[illegible]
		Huntington Avenue Continued				
	Y	Cass James R	412	carpenter	54	here
	Z	Mark Jesse †	412	housekeeper	62	"
1508						
	A	Leach Edward	415	contractor	43	"
	B	Leach Martha †	415	housewife	43	"
	C	Chalmers Alice †	416	clerk	28	"
	D	Chalmers Elizabeth †	416	housewife	67	"
	E	Chalmers George	416	papermaker	78	"
	F	Chalmers Margaret †	416	clerk	38	"
	G	*Gunn Benjamin	419	carpenter	69	"
	H	Gunn Frank R	419	machinist	54	"
	K	Gunn Nellie C †	419	housewife	53	"
	L	McAlpine Frank	419	clerk	20	"
	M	Stevens Bruce A	420	probat'n officer	45	"
	N	Stevens Dorothy A †	420	clerk	20	"
	O	Stevens Dorothy J †	420	housewife	44	"
	P	Clark Elizabeth W †	423	"	33	"
	R	Clark Joseph H	423	clerk	43	"
	S	Bragg Hazel J †	430	housewife	39	[illegible]
	T	Bragg Leslie	430	plumber	38	56 "
	U	Patterson Anna C †	431	nurse	63	here
	V	Roberts James S	431	painter	68	"
	W	Roberts Jennie E †	431	housewife	68	"
	X	Frazian Ann †	433	clerk	20	"
	Y	Frazian John	433	meat packer	49	"
	Z	*Frazian Mary †	433	housewife	48	"
1509						
	A	Conlin Elsie †	433	clerk	28	"
	B	Conlin J Burton	433	"	23	"
	C	Costello Elizabeth †	437	at home	79	"
	E	*Snow Anna K †	437	housewife	32	"
	D	Snow George E	437	manager	34	"
	F	Case Agnes K †	437	"	58	[illegible]
	G	Case Reider W	437	draftsman	33	here
	H	Case Theresa R †	437	housewife	33	"
	K	Holmes Harriet L †	447	at home	66	"
	L	Holmes Helen L †	447	"	64	"
	M	Goding Forest L	447	clerk	44	"
	N	Goding Marian R †	447	housewife	44	"
	O	Goding Phyllis E †	447	clerk	21	"
	P	Buntin Frances L †	448	housewife	25	"

Page	Letter	Full Name	Residence, Jan. 1, 1941	Occupation	Supposed Age	Reported Residence, Jan. 1, 1940. Street and Number

Huntington Avenue Continued

Page	Letter	Full Name	Residence, Jan. 1, 1941	Occupation	Supposed Age	Reported Residence, Jan. 1, 1940. Street and Number
	R*	Buntin Wallace A	448	salesman	24	here
	S	Thorp Aldine E †	448	housewife	22	"
	T	Thorp William W	448	teller	27	"
	U	Wickstrom Carl J	451	retired	68	"
	V	Wickstrom Emma L †	451	housewife	64	"
	W	Bramanti Charles	456	boilermaker	55	"
	X	Bramanti Rachel †	456	housewife	29	"
	Y*	Dyer Bessie †	456	at home	72	"
	Z	Dyer William C	456	fireman	48	"
1510						
	A	Hogan Charlotte †	459	housewife	37	190 Fairmount
	B	Hogan Walter C	459	guard	44	190 "
	C	Forsyth Charles F	460	lather	50	here
	D	Forsyth Florence E †	460	housewife	40	"
	E	Schwab Alexander	460	laborer	56	"
	F	Zeigler Lillian M †	460	housekeeper	58	"
	G	Vercoe Avis †	468	housewife	32	"
	H	Vercoe Laurence	468	draftsman	37	"
	K	Dalberti Alphonse	472	salesman	38	"
	L	Dalberti Christine †	472	housewife	38	"
	M	Kamp George W	476	mechanic	35	"
	N	Kamp Henrietta B †	476	housewife	35	"
	O*	Terasewicz Emily †	476	"	50	"
	P	Terasewicz Stephen	476	bartender	52	"
	R	Putnicki Catherine H †	476	housewife	29	21 Neponset av
	S	Putnicki Joseph F	476	shipfitter	29	21 "
	T	Cook Albert	479	retired	72	here
	U	Cook Sarah E †	479	housewife	69	"
	V	O'Shea Hedwig A †	480	housekeeper	35	"
	W	Grace May M †	480	housewife	69	"
	X	Grace Warren B	480	retired	72	"
	Y	Cregg Francis T	483	papermaker	21	"
	Z	Cregg Helen T †	483	operator	25	"
1511						
	A	Cregg Joseph A	483	laborer	41	"
	B	Cregg Roger E	483	retired	82	"
	C	Day Mary C †	483	housekeeper	62	"
	D	Cameron Mary E †	487	stenographer	45	"
	E	Harding Mary A †	487	at home	66	"
	G	McCabe Edward A	487	mechanic	43	"
	F	McCabe Mary T †	487	housewife	35	"

Page	Letter	FULL NAME	Residence, Jan. 1, 1941	Occupation	Reputed Age	Reported Residence, Jan. 1, 1940. Street and Number

Lexington Avenue

Page	Letter	FULL NAME	Residence	Occupation	Age	Reported Residence
	H	Carroll Margaret F †	4	supervisor	35	here
	K	Carroll Maurice A	4	foreman	70	"
	L	Lavin John	4	policeman	45	"
	M	Lavin Mary †	4	housewife	40	"
	N	Halpin Alice J †	6	"	44	"
	O	Halpin John J	6	foreman	44	"
	P	Kett Francis E	7	printer	38	"
	R	Kett Mary †	7	housewife	65	"
	S	Kett Mary E †	7	stenographer	35	"
	T	*Kett Patrick	7	engineer	75	"
	U	Kirk John N	7	molder	70	"
	V	Keck Alfred	9	student	23	"
	W	*Keck Anna †	9	housewife	48	"
	X	Keck Emily †	9	bookkeeper	24	"
	Y	Bentley Lena †	9A	housekeeper	50	40 Eldridge rd
	Z	Schemuck Mary †	9A	at home	81	40 "
1512						
	A	Wood Harry	9A	florist	63	[illegible]
	B	Merry Edgar F	10	chemist	43	here
	C	Merry Ethel B †	10	housewife	47	"
	D	Bowe Annie G †	10	"	78	"
	E	Bowe George J	10	retired	80	"
	F	Graham Ida L †	10	at home	82	"
	G	Rogers Bessie G †	11	housewife	57	"
	H	Rogers Elizabeth L †	11	secretary	33	"
	K	Rogers Harry G	11	superintendent	62	"
	L	Rogers Harry G, jr	11	bookkeeper	31	"
	P	Sullivan Kathleen D †	15	housewife	37	"
	R	Sullivan Thomas L	15	printer	39	"
	S	Attridge M Josephine †	15	housewife	39	"
	T	Attridge Thomas	15	finisher	62	"
	U	Tupper William A	15	foreman	39	"
	V	Cochrane Archie M	16	machinist	30	"
	W	Cochrane Ethel F †	16	housewife	28	"
	X	Walter George H	16	retired	68	"
	Y	Zwack Amelia L †	16	housewife	45	"
	Z	Zwack Clement C	16	gold beater	47	"
1513						
	A	Zwack Clement W	16	clerk	22	"
	B	Hipson Athelston Y	17	R F D	50	"
	C	Hipson Eva E †	17	housewife	51	"

Page	Letter	Full Name	Residence, Jan. 1, 1941	Occupation	Supposed Age	Reported Residence, Jan. 1, 1940. Street and Number

Lexington Avenue Continued

Page	Letter	Full Name	Residence, Jan. 1, 1941	Occupation	Supposed Age	Reported Residence, Jan. 1, 1940. Street and Number
	D	Foley James L	17	policeman	41	41 Warren av
	E	Foley Katherine A †	17	housewife	40	41 " "
	F	Santosuosso Henry	17	guard	50	here
	G	Santosuosso Mary V †	17	housewife	41	"
	H	Buckley Elizabeth A †	18	housekeeper	26	64 Thatcher
	K	Clark Alvina R †	18	housewife	48	64 "
	M	Clark Frances V †	18	clerk	20	64 "
	L	Clark Frank J	18	superintendent	49	64 "
	N	Cronin Francis X	18	"	20	here
	O	Cronin John J	18	guard	48	"
	P	Cronin John J, jr	18	collector	23	"
	R	Cronin Julia V †	18	housewife	48	"
	S	McIlwrath Joseph B	19	clerk	35	"
	T	McIlwrath Robert	19	watchman	61	"
	U	McIlwrath Robert J	19	clerk	24	"
	V	McIlwrath Ruth M †	19	housewife	24	"
	W	Larkin Gertrude E †	20	"	24	37 Ridlon rd
	X	Larkin Thomas T, jr	20	receiver	33	62 Seaverns av
	Y	Conlon Alice M †	20	nurse	32	32 Everett
	Z	MacLean John A	20	carpenter	59	here
1514						
	A	MacLean Margaret H †	20	housewife	63	"
	B	Marsh Agnes †	21–23	"	48	"
	C	Marsh Agnes M †	21–23	teacher	24	"
	D	Marsh Ernest J	21–23	clerk	54	"
	E	McLeod Eva M †	21–23	teacher	25	23 Everton
	F	Murphy John J	21–23	meatcutter	38	here
	G	Murphy Mary M †	21–23	housewife	36	"
	H	Crockett Edward P	25	inspector	57	16 Albion
	K	Crockett Helen R †	25	housewife	52	16 "
	L	Christian John E	25	chauffeur	28	here
	M	Christian Joseph E	25	retired	72	"
	N	Christian Margaret M †	25	housewife	56	"
	O	Porter Doris †	26	clerk	22	"
	P	Porter Earl L	26	"	24	"
	R	Felch Alice P †	26	housewife	52	"
	S	Felch Irving T	26	towerman	54	"
	T	Felch Robert I	26	student	21	"
	U	Stickney Dolly E †	26	housekeeper	72	"
	V	Drew Lillian M †	27	housewife	54	"
	W	Drew Scott E	27	clerk	56	"

Lexington Avenue—Continued

Page	Letter	Full Name	Residence, Jan. 1, 1941	Occupation	Supposed Age	Reported Residence, Jan. 1, 1940. Street and Number
	X	Anderson Agnes W †	29	housewife	54	here
	Y	Anderson Arthur W	29	machinist	20	"
	Z	Anderson Carl A	29	"	64	"
1515						
	A	Anderson Roy C	29	clerk	24	"
	B	Anderson Ruth P †	29	saleswoman	22	"
	C	Perry Alice T †	30	housewife	50	"
	D	Perry Dorothy E †	30	at home	20	"
	E	Perry Joseph A	30	mechanic	46	"
	F	Targett Alice †	30	housewife	36	49A Maywood
	G	Targett Thomas B	30	salesman	36	49A "
	H	Fink Elsie E †	30	housewife	44	here
	K	Fink Joseph H	30	chauffeur	42	"
	L	Rudolph Ernest A	30	retired	80	"
	M	Broadbent Alice E †	31	housewife	52	"
	N	Broadbent William D	31	singer	51	"
	O	Broadbent William D, jr	31	inspector	23	"
	P	Casey Joseph M	32-34	watchmaker	62	Waltham
	S	Doherty Edith C †	32-34	housewife	29	"
	R	Doherty John J	32-34	foreman	39	here
	T	Kelley Frederick	32-34	salesman	40	Cambridge
	U*	Capworitch Helen †	32-34	housekeeper	68	here
	V	O'Sullivan Anna †	32-34	housewife	37	"
	W	O'Sullivan Jeremiah J	32-34	laborer	37	"
	X	Beers Anna M †	33	waitress	59	"
	Y	Beers David	33	retired	71	"
	Z	Bolles Dorothy M †	35	housewife	37	"
1516						
	A	Bolles Emily F †	35	"	68	"
	B	Bolles Fred T	35	salesman	39	"
	C	Bolles James G	35	retired	73	"
	D	Shaw Alfred E	36	"	72	"
	E	Shaw Alice B †	36	housewife	71	"
	F	Shaw Helen I †	36	teacher	38	"
	G*	Brewer Jane †	36	housewife	56	"
	H*	Brewer Margaret D †	36	clerk	28	"
	K	Brewer William J	36	metalworker	57	"
	L	Doerfler Anna E †	38	housewife	46	"
	M	Doerfler Herbert A	38	custodian	50	"
	N	Bonn Cecil G	39	engineer	40	701 [illegible]
	O	Bonn Lania J †	39	housewife	38	701 "

Page.	Letter.	Full Name	Residence, Jan. 1, 1941	Occupation	Supposed Age.	Reported Residence, Jan. 1, 1940. Street and Number.

Lexington Avenue Continued

Page.	Letter.	Full Name	Residence, Jan. 1, 1941	Occupation	Supposed Age.	Reported Residence, Jan. 1, 1940. Street and Number.
	P	Zamborgma Anthony N	39	blacksmith	48	176 Gladstone
	R	Zamborgma Celso V	39	decorator	22	176 "
	S	*Zamborgma Louise †	39	saleswoman	44	176 "
	T	Smith Faye †	40	housekeeper	36	here
	U	Snowman Effie †	40	"	67	"
	V	Rogers Agnes C †	42	housewife	43	"
	W	Rogers Arthur L	42	supervisor	44	"
	Y	Fallon Carolyn †	43	housewife	30	113 Central av
	Z	Fallon James M	43	investigator	37	113 "
1517						
	A	Fallon Joseph A	43	mortician	25	113 "
	B	Fallon Mary G †	43	secretary	39	113 "
	C	Hallett Hattie †	44	housewife	33	here
	D	Hallett James	44	salesman	33	"
	E	Powers Flora G †	47	housewife	38	"
	F	Powers Joseph R	47	millwright	42	"
	G	Cullen Charles A	50	student	23	"
	H	Cullen Frances R †	50	"	21	"
	K	Cullen James A	50	supervisor	50	"
	L	Cullen Rose F †	50	housewife	50	"
	M	Cullen Rosemary J †	50	secretary	25	"
	N	Kelly Agnes M †	53	"	31	"
	O	Kelly Mabel C †	53	clerk	33	"
	P	Kelly Michael J	53	millwright	69	"
	R	Kelly Susan B †	53	housewife	64	"
	S	Mahon Ada E †	54	secretary	24	"
	T	Mahon Christiana †	54	housewife	57	"
	U	Mahon Christiana M †	54	clerk	21	"
	V	Mahon Clarence	54	"	36	"
	W	Mahon Sarah A †	54	supervisor	27	"
	X	Mahon Thomas	54	draftsman	56	"
	Y	Morris Edith B †	54	housekeeper	30	"
	Z	Flynn George A	55	manager	67	"
1518						
	A	Flynn Julia G †	55	housewife	68	"
	B	McCready Francis J	55	bartender	46	"
	C	McCready John R	55	"	38	"
	D	McCready Ruth A †	55	clerk	34	"
	E	Daniels John J	57	plumber	47	"
	F	Daniels Lillian Z †	57	housewife	35	"
	G	Dunn Cecilia B †	58	"	40	"

Page	Letter	Full Name	Residence Jan. 1, 1941	Occupation	Supposed Age	Reported Residence Jan. 1, 1940 Street and Number

Lexington Avenue—Continued

Page	Letter	Full Name	Residence Jan. 1, 1941	Occupation	Supposed Age	Reported Residence Jan. 1, 1940 Street and Number
	H	Dunn Dennis J	58	clerk	41	here
	K	Ljunglof Emil	59	engineer	65	"
	L	Ljunglof Selma †	59	housewife	58	"
	M	Bishop Dora A †	60	"	36	"
	N	Bishop George A	60	accountant	35	"
	O	Saunders Ernest B	61	clerk	52	"
	P	Saunders Virginia †	61	stenographer	24	"
	R	Ott Catherine †	61	housekeeper	70	"
	S	Janik Catherine T †	61	housewife	27	"
	T	Janik Chester J	61	welder	28	"

Metropolitan Avenue

Page	Letter	Full Name	Residence Jan. 1, 1941	Occupation	Supposed Age	Reported Residence Jan. 1, 1940 Street and Number
	U	Gabriel Frank M	646	carpenter	20	here
	V	Gabriel John	646	"	59	"
	W	Gabriel Kathleen †	646	nurse	27	818 Harrison av
	X	Gray Alan	650	butcher	46	here
	Z	Kukis John	650	manager	34	960 Hyde Park av
1519						
	A	Kukis Mary †	650	cashier	35	960 "
	B	Erickson Albert E	650	machinist	37	here
	C	Erickson Gertrude E †	650	housewife	35	"
	D	Casperson John H	650	painter	28	49 Clifford
	E	*Casperson Ruth E †	650	hairdresser	29	16 "
	F	DeFlurin Edward	650	tree surgeon	22	18 Rosa
	G	DeFlurin Helen M †	650	housewife	21	146 Central av
	H	Gill Annie †	654	"	62	18 Lexington av
	K	Gill Patrick F	654	lineman	63	18 "
	L	Nevells Lewis A	654	electrician	44	here
	M	Nevells Odessa I †	654	housewife	42	"
	N	Ekstrand Emmy B †	654	"	28	"
	O	Ekstrand Oscar S	654	machinist	32	"
	P	Powers Harold T	654	"	29	20 Lexington av
	R	Powers Helen V †	654	housewife	20	18 "
	S	Kane Martha M †	654	"	39	910 Harrison av
	T	Kane Walter H	654	clerk	44	1 Bulfinch pl
	U	Glennon Frances E †	654	housewife	21	here
	V	Glennon James J	654	clerk	28	"
	W	Grant James J	658	engineer	27	"
	X	Grant Leo J	658	laborer	20	"
	Y	Grant Mary V †	658	stenographer	25	"

Page	Letter	Full Name	Residence, Jan. 1, 1941	Occupation	Supposed Age	Reported Residence, Jan. 1, 1940. Street and Number

Metropolitan Avenue Continued

Page	Letter	Full Name	Residence	Occupation	Age	Reported Residence
	Z	Grant Richard F	658	clerk	23	here
1520						
	A	*Whorten Adeline V †	658	housewife	41	"
	B	Whorten Alverdo M	658	janitor	20	"
	C	Whorten Roy C	658	carpenter	46	"
	D	Gagnon George N	658	supervisor	37	"
	E	Gagnon Lillian D †	658	housewife	38	"
	F	D'Angelo Mary †	662	cleaner	26	"
	G	*D'Angelo Sophie †	662	housewife	46	"
	H	D'Angelo Vincent	662	cook	52	"
	K	Charon Adolphus P	662	retired	68	"
	L	Charon Christopher R	662	freighthandler	33	"
	M	Charon Herbert J	662	mechanic	26	"
	N	Charon Irene C †	662	at home	20	"
	O	Charon Mary A †	662	housewife	58	"
	P	Charon William L	662	painter	25	"
	R	Thompson Dorothy I †	662	housewife	30	"
	S	Thompson William E	662	repairman	30	56 Elm
	T	Chisholm William A	666	mover	47	New York
	U	Galvin Christine I †	666	housewife	44	here
	V	Galvin John T	666	watchman	49	"
	W	Galvin Mary I †	666	clerk	21	"
	X	Kelley Catherine M †	666	housewife	45	"
	Y	Kelley Edward B	666	attendant	20	"
	Z	Kelley George H	666	clerk	22	"
1521						
	A	Kelley John J	666	"	48	"
	B	Alibrande Anthony	666	engineer	49	"
	C	*Alibrande Antonina †	666	housewife	39	"
	D	Alibrande Katherine †	666	factoryhand	24	"
	E	Dubois Armand J	670	chauffeur	21	"
	F	Dubois Delia †	670	housewife	45	"
	G	LaCroix Henry	670	cashier	22	"
	H	LaCroix Mary J †	670	maid	22	"
	K	Bedard Leo E	670	engineer	33	"
	L	Bedard Olive G †	670	housewife	29	"
	M	Botteri Anthony	670	barber	37	"
	N	Botteri Jennie C †	670	housewife	32	"
	P	Hogan Evelyn F †	674	"	37	"
	R	Hogan Thomas F	674	guard	37	"
	S	Wood Lalah F †	674	housewife	41	"

Metropolitan Avenue—Continued

Page	Letter	Full Name	Residence, April 1, 1941	Occupation	Supposed Age	Reported Residence, April 1, 1940. Street and Number
	T	Wood Malcolm A	674	machinist	42	here
	U	Hain James D	686	foreman	39	"
	V	Hain Lillian V †	686	housewife	36	"
	W	Kelley George A	686	clerk	58	"
	X	Kelley Helen C †	686	operator	26	"
	Y	Kelley John J	686	clerk	25	"
	Z	Kelley Norah J †	686	housewife	56	"
1522						
	A	Garland James W	686	busboy	20	"
	B	Garland Mary †	686	housekeeper	19	"
	C	Marklis Martha †	689	housewife	51	"
	D	Marklis Paul P	689	molder	62	"
	E	Munroe Agnes †	689	operator	34	"
	F	*Munroe Bessie A †	689	housewife	59	"
	G	*Munroe David G	689	clerk	20	"
	H	*Munroe David W	689	carpenter	59	"
	K	*Munroe Hughena †	689	clerk	24	"
	L	Alexander Helen †	689	housewife	43	"
	M	Alexander Henry	689	custodian	48	"
	N	Bethge Helen M †	690	housewife	37	634 Metrop
	O	Bethge William	690	watchman	42	634 "
	P	*Ford Cornelius P	690	machinist	45	here
	R	Ford Margaret M †	690	housewife	38	"
	S	Lowe Bernard	690	retired	76	"
	T	Thompson John H	690	plumber	67	"
	U	Haas Bruno O	693	mechanic	70	"
	V	Haas Lorraine †	693	housewife	70	"
	W	Swanson Elizabeth M †	693	"	29	"
	X	Swanson Ivar J	693	clerk	30	"
	Y	Smith Alice L †	693	stenographer	36	[illegible]
	Z	Johnson Helen P †	693	housewife	88	here
1523						
	A	Ryan Mildred H †	693	waitress	54	"
	B	McCarthy Catherine †	693	operator	42	"
	C	McCarty Michael F	693	retired	74	"
	D	Vance Alice M †	693	housewife	28	"
	E	Vance Edwin F	693	manager	29	"
	F	Clements Ora E †	694	housewife	66	New Jersey
	G	Ross Ernest L	694	salesman	47	722 Metropolitan Av
	H	Ross Irene E †	694	housewife	38	722 "
	K	Coullahan Margaret L †	697	saleswoman	33	here

Page	Letter	Full Name	Residence, Jan. 1, 1941.	Occupation.	Supposed Age	Reported Residence, Jan. 1, 1940. Street and Number.

Metropolitan Avenue Continued

Page	Letter	Full Name	Residence, Jan. 1, 1941.	Occupation.	Supposed Age	Reported Residence, Jan. 1, 1940. Street and Number.
	L	Coullahan Margaret T †	697	housewife	61	here
	M	Coullahan Raymond F	697	carpenter	27	"
	N	Dooley Joseph L	700	accountant	47	"
	O	Dooley Marguerite E †	700	housewife	38	"
	P	Berube Frances H †	700	statistician	20	"
	R	Berube Helen M †	700	housewife	40	"
	S	Berube Robert V	700	trainman	46	"
	T	Welch Albert G	700	clerk	26	"
	U	Welch Loretta F †	700	nurse	37	"
	V	Tarallo Catherine T †	700	operator	26	"
	W	Tarallo Edmund R	700	teacher	24	"
	X	Tarallo Julia †	700	housewife	48	"
	Y	Tarallo Phillip	700	welder	57	"
	Z	Kristiansen Charlotte G †	701	housewife	27	35 Rockingham rd
1524						
	A	Kristiansen Rolf H	701	manager	29	35 "
	B	Myers Emily †	701	housewife	58	here
	C	Myers Mary E †	701	clerk	33	"
	D	Myers Samuel G	701	papermaker	63	"
	E	Burns Margaret G †	702	lawyer	33	1420 River
	F	O'Neil John H	702	salesman	48	here
	G	O'Neil Mary M †	702	housewife	48	"
	H	O'Neil Winifred M †	702	clerk	22	"
	K	Roman Elizabeth †	703	housewife	76	"
	L	Roman John	703	accountant	51	"
	M	Carney Daniel L	705	clerk	50	"
	N	Carney Mary J †	705	housewife	43	"
	O	*Resker Anna †	706	"	60	"
	P	Resker Francis A	706	manager	37	"
	R	Resker Gregory	706	molder	63	"
	S	Resker Joseph C	706	agent	29	"
	T	Resker Mary D †	706	secretary	33	"
	U	Resker Stephanie H †	706	bookkeeper	35	"
	V	Smart Henry M	706	machinist	47	"
	W	Smart Isabel D †	706	student	21	"
	X	Smart John	706	paperworker	22	"
	Y	Smart Margaret B †	706	housewife	47	"
	Z	Connolly Catherine A †	706	clerk	29	"
1525						
	A	Connolly John H	706	papermaker	63	"
	B	Connolly Margaret E †	706	at home	30	"

Page	Letter	Full Name	Residence, Jan. 1, 1941	Occupation	Reported Age	Reported Residence, Jan. 1, 1940. Street and Number

Metropolitan Avenue—Continued

Page	Letter	Full Name	Residence, Jan. 1, 1941	Occupation	Reported Age	Reported Residence, Jan. 1, 1940
	C	Connolly Mary H †	706	operator	26	here
	D	Connolly Rita C †	706	"	20	"
	E	Connolly Teresa F †	706	"	22	"
	F	Martin Audrey I †	707	clerk	20	"
	G	Martin Mary †	707	housewife	60	"
	H	Martin Richard	707	carpenter	61	"
	K	Weil Leopold	707	typist	29	"
	L	Weil Marjorie †	707	housewife	33	"
	M	Taber Arthur C	707	laborer	36	"
	N	Taber Josephine C †	707	housewife	34	"
	O	Powers Catherine †	709	"	75	20 Lexington st
	P	Powers James	709	paperworker	77	20 "
	R	Powers Richard K	709	retired	76	20 "
	S	Brown Arthur A	709	clerk	60	here
	T	Brown Ellen N †	709	at home	92	"
	U	Shenk Gladys E †	709	housewife	39	"
	V	Shenk William H	709	manager	43	"
	W	Neilson Douglas S	710	plumber	66	"
	X	Neilson Margaret B †	710	housewife	64	"
	Y	Neilson Margaret L †	710	clerk	32	"
	Z	Benson Jennie †	710	housewife	25	"
1526						
	A	Benson Leon	710	decorator	29	"
	B	McWhirter Alexander	710	accountant	29	"
	C	McWhirter Helen †	710	housewife	53	"
	D	McWhirter James	710	machinist	53	"
	E	Emery George W	713	guard	64	"
	F	Emery Lillian M †	713	housewife	64	"
	G	Emery May E †	713	housekeeper	55	"
	H	Smith Dora †	713	cashier	30	Revere
	K	Leighton Nellie G †	713	nurse	53	Somerville
	L	Wood Stanley C	713	printer	48	here
	M	Johnson Bernice R †	714	housewife	36	"
	N	Johnson Paul R	714	engineer	37	"
	O	Powers Richard J	714	mechanic	39	"
	P	Powers Winifred B †	714	housewife	32	"
	R	*Van Eek Caroline †	714	"	61	"
	S	Van Eek Harriet R †	714	secretary	24	"
	T	Van Eek Helen V †	714	stenographer	31	"
	U	Phelan Mabel J †	718	housewife	42	"
	V	Phelan William J	718	painter	43	"

Page	Letter	Full Name	Residence, Jan. 1, 1941.	Occupation	Supposed Age.	Reported Residence, Jan. 1, 1940. Street and Number.

Metropolitan Avenue—Continued

Page	Letter	Full Name	Residence	Occupation	Age	Reported Residence
	W	Tucker Catherine A—†	718	housewife	63	here
	X	Tucker Helen F—†	718	nurse	39	"
	Y	Tucker Herberta L—†	718	"	26	"
	Z	York Edna F—†	722	housewife	34	1032 River
1527						
	A	York Frank J	722	laborer	32	1032 "
	B	Grover Frank S	722	machinist	38	118 Arlington
	C	Grover Marguerite—†	722	housewife	38	118 "
	D	MacKeen Cecil L	722	paperworker	42	here
	E	MacKeen Thelma I—†	722	housewife	34	"
	F	Marshall Evelyn L—†	726	at home	25	"
	G	Marshall Ralph W	726	cashier	51	"
	H	Nordstrom Emil	726	tinsmith	61	"
	K	Nordstrom Ingrid—†	726	housewife	61	"
	L	Welch Douglas S	726	paperworker	36	"
	M	Welch Marion J—†	726	housewife	37	"
	N	Garrity Rosina A—†	730	"	33	"
	O	Garrity William M	730	plumber	44	"
	P	Brown Bernice—†	730	housewife	21	Maine
	R	Brown Delia E—†	730	"	60	"
	S	Brown Lester	730	paperworker	22	"
	T	Brown Woodrow	730	"	21	"
	U	Hanlon James P	730	clerk	28	1831 Hyde Park av
	V	Nyman Carl E	730	laborer	48	1831 "
	W	Nyman Susan E—†	730	housewife	48	1831 "
	X	Donavan Ellen—†	731	domestic	63	here
	Y	Donavan Mary F—†	731	housewife	27	"
	Z	Donavan Timothy J	731	clerk	34	"
1528						
	A	Moylen John F	735	therapist	49	"
	B	Moylen Lillian C—†	735	housewife	48	"
	C	Moylen Rita C—†	735	stenographer	25	"
	D	Proctor Mary E—†	735	at home	65	"

Pierce Street

Page	Letter	Full Name	Residence	Occupation	Age	Reported Residence
	G	Morse Viola M—†	63	housewife	28	here
	H	Morse William E	63	machinist	32	"
	K	O'Donnell Catherine W—†	63	housewife	29	"
	L	O'Donnell Raymond J	63	repairman	32	"

Page	Letter	Full Name	Residence, Jan. 1	Occupation	Reported Age	Reported Residence, Jan. 1, Street and Number

Pierce Street—Continued

Page	Letter	Full Name	Residence, Jan. 1	Occupation	Reported Age	Reported Residence, Jan. 1, Street and Number
	M	McMahon Helen F †	69	housewife	41	here
	N	McMahon Owen F	69	chauffeur	49	"
	O	DeLuca Claire A †	73	housewife	29	"
	P	DeLuca Michael N	73	chauffeur	30	"
	R	Brink Helen †	73	stitcher	40	"
	S	*Brink Victoria †	73	housewife	65	"
	T	Reska Frank	73	shipper	27	11 Damon [illegible]
	U	Reska Mary †	73	housewife	32	11 "
	W	Costello Bridget C †	100	"	54	here
	X	Costello Francis J	100	laborer	24	"
	Y	Costello Margaret E †	100	stenographer	26	"
	Z	Costello Mary E †	100	operator	22	"
1529						
	A	Costello Thomas H	100	laborer	67	"
	B	*Olszewski Blanche †	102	housewife	48	"
	C	Olszewski Henrietta †	102	beautician	20	"
	D	Olszewski Stanley	102	laborer	49	"
	E	*Richards Stacia M †	102	nurse	35	"
	F	McDermott Anna R †	104	stenographer	23	"
	G	McDermott Mary †	104	housewife	60	"
	H	McDermott Owen	104	retired	70	"
	K	Holmes Galen L	104	upholsterer	41	6 Dell ter
	L	Holmes Josephine †	104	housewife	30	[illegible]
	M	Glennon Elizabeth †	106	"	76	here
	N	Glennon Margaret †	106	teacher	32	"
	O	Boudrot Alice R †	109	housewife	36	"
	P	Boudrot Jeffery A	109	electrician	38	"
	R	Zambella Esther †	109	housewife	23	"
	S	Zambella John M	109	chemist	25	"
	T	Crowder Frank	111	machinist	58	"
	U	Crowder Helen F †	111	stenographer	27	"
	V	*Crowder Nellie F †	111	housewife	56	"
	W	Hamacher Virginia E †	111	"	21	Cambridge
	Y	Costello Claire E †	113	"	23	1061 River
	Z	Costello Thomas H, jr	113	electrician	28	1061 "
1530						
	A	Connors Charles F	115	chauffeur	28	here
	B	Connors Elizabeth †	115	nurse	25	"
	C	Bowes Elsa V †	115	housewife	28	"
	D	Bowes Joseph B	115	chauffeur	30	"

Page	Letter	Full Name	Residence, Jan. 1, 1941.	Occupation.	Supposed Age.	Reported Residence, Jan. 1, 1940. Street and Number.

Reddy Avenue

Page	Letter	Full Name	Residence, Jan. 1, 1941.	Occupation.	Supposed Age.	Reported Residence, Jan. 1, 1940. Street and Number.
	F	Craig Cecil V	4	policeman	49	here
	G	Craig Ethel F—†	4	housewife	38	"
	H	Bandlow Mary J—†	5	"	79	"
	K	Bandlow Walter O	5	retired	79	"
	L	Beer Clifton A	6	batteryman	38	"
	M	Beer George H	6	watchman	64	"
	N	Beer Josephine C—†	6	housewife	64	"
	O	Burke James J	7	tree surgeon	23	"
	P	Burke James P	7	electrician	53	"
	R	Burke John P	7	molder	22	"
	S	Burke Margaret M—†	7	housewife	53	"
	T	Burke Margaret T—†	7	packer	20	"
	U	Hannett Eleanor M—†	8	stenographer	26	970 River
	V	Hannett Henry D	8	stamper	24	here
	W	Hannett Leonard W	8	nurse	55	970 River
	X	Hannett Stephanie M—†	8	housewife	50	970 "
	Y	Nestor Ellen S—†	8	"	47	here
	Z	Nestor Thomas H	8	chauffeur	49	"
1531						
	A	Bolle Aurelie H—†	9	clerk	25	84 Shepton
	B	Bolle Beatrice A—†	9	housewife	49	84 "
	C	Bolle John E	9	clerk	22	84 "
	D	Hayes James J	10	attendant	23	here
	E	Hayes Jeremiah	10	manager	29	"
	F	*Hayes Katherine—†	10	housewife	56	"
	G	Hayes Katherine L—†	10	clerk	27	"
	H	Kutney Joseph N	11	manager	26	16 Radcliffe rd
	K	*Jacobanis Elizabeth B—†	11	housewife	44	Medford
	L	Jacobanis Nicholas	11	machinist	54	"
	M	Curran Eleanor T—†	12	housewife	32	here
	N	Curran Thomas C	12	agent	33	"
	O	Curran Thomas J	12	laborer	66	"
	P	Buchanan Mary E—†	13	inspector	21	"
	R	Buchanan Ruth E—†	13	housewife	46	"
	S	Buchanan Thomas	13	carpenter	44	"
	T	Seibert Charles W	15	agent	48	"
	V	Seibert George J	15	clerk	37	"
	W	Seibert Mary G—†	15	housewife	78	"
	X	Kristiansen Edwin H	16	laborer	24	"
	Y	Kristiansen Harry	16	machinist	55	"
	Z	Kristiansen Jennie M—†	16	housewife	56	"

Page	Letter	Full Name	Residence	Occupation	Age	Address

1532

Reddy Avenue (Continued)

Letter	Full Name	Residence	Occupation	Age	Address
A	Randolph Ellen A †	17	housewife	59	here
B	Randolph William E	17	foreman	61	"
C	Moriarty George N	18	brakeman	40	"
E	Neil Katherine K †	18	tailoress	49	"
D	Neil Margaret †	18	waitress	38	"
F	Rosecaln Christine D †	18	housewife	53	"
G	Rosecaln George	18	tailor	56	"
H	Griffin John W	19	machinist	21	"
K	Griffin William D	19	"	49	"
L	McAdams Irene †	19	housewife	54	"
M	McAdams Jennie M †	19	beautician	20	"
N	McAdams Marjorie E †	19	waitress	23	"
O	Dempsey Ellen †	20	housewife	50	"
P	Dempsey Mary F †	20	clerk	23	"
R	Dempsey Rita †	20	operator	22	"
S*	Dempsey Walter M	20	foreman	49	"
T	Dempsey Walter M, jr	20	U S A	21	"
U	Houlihan Mary K †	21	at home	38	"
V	Houlihan Theresa F †	21	housewife	66	"
W	Houlihan William E	21	machinist	68	"
Y*	McConnell Eliza C †	22	housewife	70	"
X	McConnell James	22	retired	75	"
Z	Nickerson Adeline M †	22	housewife	39	"

1533

Letter	Full Name	Residence	Occupation	Age	Address
A	Nickerson Sidney E	22	foreman	40	"
B	Phillips Helen W †	22	housekeeper	36	"

River Street

Letter	Full Name	Residence	Occupation	Age	Address
C	Peveronis Elizabeth †	838	packer	29	here
D	Peveronis Joseph J	838	mechanic	31	"
E	Astronski Bessie †	838	housekeeper	49	"
H*	Cyr Helen T †	861	housewife	20	[illegible]
K	Cyr Louis L	861	machinist	25	1154 "
L	Cochrane Myrtle L †	861	housewife	35	here
M	Cochrane Thomas J	861	florist	35	"
N	Carew Anna †	861	housewife	21	86 Roanoke rd
O	Carew James P	861	laborer	21	86 "
P	Cunningham Mary E †	861	housekeeper	44	here
S	Meagher Edna G †	875	clerk	20	"

Page.	Letter.	Full Name.	Residence, Jan. 1, 1941.	Occupation.	Supposed Age.	Reported Residence, Jan. 1, 1940. Street and Number.

River Street—Continued

Page.	Letter.	Full Name.	Residence, Jan. 1, 1941.	Occupation.	Supposed Age.	Reported Residence, Jan. 1, 1940.
	T	Meagher Helen L—†	875	housewife	39	here
	U	Meagher Stephen A	875	papermaker	42	"
	V	McCormick Edward J	877	electrician	36	"
	W	McCormick Kathleen E—†	877	housewife	35	"
	X	Brown Ann E—†	883	"	52	"
	Y	Brown Edward M	883	papermaker	24	"
	Z	Brown Marguerite M—†	883	papercutter	26	"
1534						
	A	Brown Russell C	883	shipper	55	"
	B	Conway Arthur T	883	laborer	49	"
	C	Christopher Joseph D	887	"	23	1 Chester pk
	D	Christopher Margaret D—†	887	housewife	20	here
	E	Griffin John J	887	foreman	50	"
	F*	Griffin Marie J—†	887	housewife	49	"
	G	Stevens Alexander	889	laborer	65	"
	H	Stevens Fannie E—†	889	housewife	72	"
	L	Tolland Emily L—†	895	operator	27	"
	M	Tolland William F	895	papermaker	52	"
	N	Brown Katherine H—†	897	housewife	47	"
	O	Brown Samuel	897	carpenter	50	"
	P	Coughlin Eugene H	897	foreman	75	"
	R	Coughlin Eugene H, jr	897	clerk	28	"
	S	Coughlin Raymond L	897	electrician	38	"
	T	MacKenzie Colin D	903	papermaker	24	"
	U	MacKenzie Jean K—†	903	housewife	52	"
	V	Delea Elsie F—†	905	"	41	Fitchburg
	W	Delea Frank J	905	mechanic	44	"
	X	Delea Mary—†	905	at home	74	"
	Y	Geisel Fred G	911	finisher	35	here
	Z	Geisel Valda E—†	911	housewife	32	"
1535						
	A*	Wiseman Minnie E—†	911A	"	49	"
	C	Wiseman Samuel	911A	proprietor	51	"
	B	Wiseman Theodore A	911A	student	21	"
	D	Wiseman William S	911A	physician	24	"
	F	Schiller Evelyn L—†	915	housewife	26	442 Dudley
	G	Schiller Henry L	915	machinist	29	5 Knight
	H	Donovan Anna D—†	915	housewife	52	here
	K	Donovan Hazel L—†	915	clerk	22	"
	L	McCarthy Charlotte F—†	943	housewife	45	"
	M	McCarthy William P	943	laborer	42	"

River Street—Continued

Page	Letter	Full Name	Residence, April 1	Occupation	Reputed Age	Reported Residence, April 1 — Street and Number
	N	Austin Arthur H	945	inspector	26	here
	O	Austin Harry L	945	retired	61	"
	P	Austin Lillian A †	945	paper sorter	33	"
	R	Kenney Edwin L	945	projectionist	29	"
	S	Kenney Elsie P †	945	housewife	35	"
	T	Dedham Alla †	946	"	39	"
	U	Dedham George F	946	engineer	43	"
	V	Yankus Anellie †	947	waitress	23	"
	W	*Yankus Anna †	947	housewife	45	"
	X	Yankus Anna †	947	maid	21	"
	Y	Yankus Vincent	947	janitor	45	"
	Z	Carbone Joseph T	947	laborer	27	"
1536						
	A	Carbone Mary E †	947	housewife	26	"
	B	Daly James F	949	laborer	39	"
	C	Daly Margaret †	949	housewife	38	"
	D	Keller Minnie †	954	"	67	"
	E	Keller Simon	954	attendant	35	"
	F	Palumbo Helen †	954	housewife	31	981 River
	G	Palumbo Louis	954	riveter	32	981 "
	H	Malone Joseph P	958	foreman	45	here
	K	Malone Margaret E †	958	housewife	35	"
	L	Malone William T	958	machinist	23	"
	M	Ashworth Gertrude E †	961	housewife	32	141 Lamartine
	N	Ashworth John C	961	merchant	22	141 "
	O	*Ashworth John J	961	laborer	51	141 "
	P	*O'Donnell Mary C †	968	housewife	32	here
	R	O'Donnell Timothy T	968	chauffeur	29	"
	S	Richardson Eleanor G †	968	housewife	50	"
	T	Richardson Florence E †	968	hairdresser	24	"
	U	Richardson George W	968	painter	54	"
	V	Richardson Kenneth G	968	clerk	29	"
	W	Rich Cora E †	968	housewife	57	"
	X	Rich Warren A	968	machinist	20	"
	Y	Rich William A	968	janitor	54	"
	Z	Cuneo Albert H	970	roofer	43	"
1537						
	A	Cuneo Annie †	970	housewife	72	"
	B	Cuneo Edward W	970	painter	37	"
	C	Gilligan Helen E †	970	seamstress	41	"
	D	McCoy Abbie †	970	saleswoman	34	"

Page	Letter	Full Name	Residence, Jan. 1, 1941	Occupation	Supposed Age	Reported Residence, Jan. 1, 1940. Street and Number.

River Street—Continued

Page	Letter	Full Name	Residence, Jan. 1, 1941	Occupation	Supposed Age	Reported Residence, Jan. 1, 1940. Street and Number.
	E	McCoy Charles F	970	clerk	20	here
	F	McCoy Helen M—†	970	operator	36	"
	G	McCoy Mary J—†	970	housewife	70	"
	H	Howland Elizabeth—†	970	paper sorter	56	905 River
	K	Howland Robert	970	laborer	22	905 "
	L	Cregg Lucy M—†	973	housewife	31	here
	M	Cregg Roger A	973	B F D	36	"
	N	Willcutt Flora L—†	973	housewife	43	"
	O	Willcutt Florence L—†	973	clerk	23	"
	P	Willcutt Francis P	973	retired	46	"
	R	Mitchell Harry T	976	mechanic	50	"
	S	Mitchell Iola E—†	976	housewife	41	"
	T	Shea Gertrude M—†	976	"	46	"
	U	Shea Warren R	976	U S A	23	"
	V	Brooks Gertrude G—†	977	secretary	52	"
	W	Greenlaw Florence K—†	977	housekeeper	54	"
	X	Lombard Mary—†	981	clerk	21	"
	Y	Lombard Philomena—†	981	housewife	53	"
	Z	Lombard Rachael—†	981	clerk	26	"
1538						
	A	*Lombard Samuel	981	laborer	59	"
	B	Lombard William	981	"	20	"
	C	Groves Mary J—†	981	secretary	26	Wellesley
	D	Groves Mary N—†	981	housewife	63	"
	E	Giles Dorothy—†	985	saleswoman	28	here
	F	*Giles Eva L—†	985	housewife	54	"
	G	Giles Marguerite—†	985	supervisor	20	"
	H	Giles Wilfred H	985	tree surgeon	24	"
	K	Sanders George	985	mechanic	57	"
	L	Sanders Nellie—†	985	housewife	54	"
	M	Sanders Paul	985	installer	24	"
	O	Butkus John	988	retired	70	"
	P	Butkus Petronella—†	988	housewife	68	"
	S	Grant Cora B—†	990	"	61	"
	T	Grant Daniel	990	janitor	60	"
	U	Grant James P	990	mechanic	24	"
	V	Grant Wilfred L	990	clerk	22	"
	W	Lawrence Helen—†	990	housewife	47	"
	X	Lawrence Willard H	990	laborer	26	"
	Y	Lawrence Willard O	990	machinist	52	"

Page.	Letter.	Full Name.	Residence, Jan. 1.	Occupation.	Age.	Reported Residence, Street and Number.

1539

River Street (Continued)

Page.	Letter.	Full Name.	Residence, Jan. 1.	Occupation.	Age.	Reported Residence, Street and Number.
1539	A	Palmer Frederick J	992	clerk	42	147 Dana av
	B	Palmer Mary C †	992	housewife	46	147 "
	C	*Pepi Esther †	992	"	28	18 Wash'n
	D	Pepi Joseph F	992	machinist	31	18 "
	E	Pierce Helen F †	992	typist	20	here
	F	Pierce James W	992	woodworker	23	"
	G	Pierce Nettie W †	992	housewife	54	"
	H	Pierce William W	992	machinist	62	"
	K	Chisholm John J	993	salesman	34	"
	L	Chisholm Susan B †	993	housewife	29	"
	M	Huelin Isaac W	994	chauffeur	39	992 River
	N	*Huelin Martha E †	994	housewife	39	992 "
	P	McCool Mary H †	995	cashier	42	here
	R	Fitzpatrick Francis J	995	millworker	54	"
	S	Fitzpatrick Louise †	995	housewife	52	"
	T	Feldman Harriett C †	996	"	20	"
	U	Feldman Samuel	996	manager	21	"
	V	McMahon Joseph P	997	printer	51	"
	W	McMahon Joseph P, jr	997	clerk	21	"
	X	McMahon Mary H †	997	housewife	46	"
	Y	Ryan Leo E	997	foreman	44	"
	Z	Pavia Ida †	998	student	20	"
1540	A	Pavia Vincent	998	chef	54	"
	B	Costello Alice F †	998	maid	20	610 River
	C	Costello Catherine M †	998	housewife	45	610 "
	D	Costello Edward M	998	printer	52	610 "
	E	Cate Helen S †	999	housewife	67	here
	F	Cate William H	999	jeweler	68	"
	G	Grenier Charles J	1000	steamfitter	27	"
	H	Honiker Alma E †	1000	housewife	60	"
	K	Honiker Joseph J	1000	laborer	62	"
	M	Vitale Dorothy R †	1000	housewife	21	"
	N	Vitale Ralph J	1000	mason	23	"
	O	*Curran Catherine M †	1001	housewife	37	"
1541	A	*Curran Coleman J	1001	finisher	42	"
	B	Feeney Edward	1001	laborer	63	"
	C	Feeney Michael P	1001	salesman	33	"

Page	Letter	Full Name	Residence, Jan. 1, 1941	Occupation	Supposed Age	Reported Residence, Jan. 1, 1940. Street and Number.

River Street—Continued

Page	Letter	Full Name	Residence, Jan. 1, 1941	Occupation	Supposed Age	Reported Residence, Jan. 1, 1940. Street and Number.
	D	*Spence Anastasia—†	1002	housewife	64	here
	E	Spence Mary E—†	1002	clerk	32	"
	F	Spence Walter D	1002	laborer	34	"
	G	*Bajko Alexander J	1002	shipper	57	"
	H	Bajko Alexander S	1002	chauffeur	25	"
	K	Bajko Estelle V—†	1002	packer	27	"
	L	*Bajko Sophie A—†	1002	housewife	54	"
	M	*Clattenburg Gertrude S—†	1004	"	49	"
	N	*Clattenburg John E	1004	machinist	56	"
	O	Clattenburg William P	1004	salesman	29	"
	R	Johnstone Isabelle G—†	1006	housewife	60	"
	P	Johnstone John C	1006	machinist	60	"
	S	Broderick Catherine M—†	1006	at home	88	"
	T	Broderick Katherine E—†	1006	housewife	65	"
	U	Kelly Mary E—†	1008	"	49	"
	V	Kelly Patrick J	1008	chauffeur	51	"
	W	Norton Owen J	1008	merchant	43	"
	X	Lawrence Edward A	1008	salesman	25	66 Harvard av
	Y	Lawrence Martha L—†	1008	housewife	25	66 "
1542						
	A	Ash Agnes A—†	1016	"	72	here
	B	Ash Henry	1016	retired	84	"
	C	Maier Herbert W	1016	mechanic	49	"
	D	Maier M Doris—†	1016	statistician	29	"
	E	Maier Mabel H—†	1016	housewife	48	"
	F	McDougald Alice—†	1017	teacher	52	"
	G	McDougald Clara—†	1017	bookkeeper	58	"
	H	Martin Francis	1020	welder	23	"
	K	Martin Josephine—†	1020	clerk	31	"
	L	Martin Raymond	1020	mechanic	25	"
	M	*Martin Sarah—†	1020	housewife	57	"
	N	Martin Stella—†	1020	clerk	21	"
	O	*Baillie Agnes—†	1020	housewife	35	"
	P	Baillie Thomas C	1020	machinist	40	"
	R	Hastings Austin P	1021	molder	67	"
	S	Hastings Sarah P—†	1021	secretary	28	"
	T	Hastings Gertrude—†	1021	at home	34	"
	U	Hastings Julia E—†	1021	housewife	59	"
	V	Coes Mabel R—†	1024	housekeeper	62	"
	W	Wilson Edith A—†	1024	at home	68	"
	X	Brooks Monica—†	1025	seamstress	34	"

Page	Letter	Full Name	Residence	Occupation	Supposed Age	Reported Residence, Street and Number
		River Street Continued				
	Y	Gibbons Dorothy A †	1025	saleswoman	27	here
	Z	Gibbons Grace M †	1025	housewife	30	"
1543						
	A	Gibbons John E	1025	policeman	30	"
	B	Gibbons Katherine V †	1025	housewife	63	"
	C	Gibbons Patrick H	1025	foundryman	68	"
	D	Kirby Helen M †	1032	housewife	34	89 Readville
	E*	Kirby Patrick E	1032	carpenter	38	89 "
	F	Curtis Alfred E	1032	clerk	34	here
	G	Curtis Alfred P	1032	printer	57	"
	H	Curtis Catherine L †	1032	housewife	57	"
	K	Curtis Paul B	1032	salesman	25	"
	L	McNulty Catherine C †	1033	housewife	56	"
	M	McNulty Francis C	1033	clerk	24	"
	N	McNulty James A	1033	sheriff	57	"
	O	McNulty James A, jr	1033	insulator	30	"
	P	McNulty John P	1033	chauffeur	28	"
	R	McNulty Joseph A	1033	oil dealer	32	"
	S	McNulty Rose M †	1033	clerk	26	"
	T	Foster Dorothy F †	1036	secretary	47	"
	U	Ticknor Marjorie P †	1036	manager	49	"
	V	Ticknor Mary H †	1036	housewife	74	"
	W	Clark Abia M †	1037	"	58	"
	X	Clark Charles W	1037	retired	58	"
	Y	Clark S Lowell	1037	machinist	28	Maine
	Z	Labree Celia †	1037	secretary	18	here
1544						
	A	Stevens Helen †	1037	"	62	"
	C	George Natalie E †	1037	hairdresser	28	"
	D	George Richard A	1037	musician	27	"
	E	Brown Bessie †	1037	housewife	48	N Hampshire
	F	Brown Clifton V	1037	clerk	50	here
	G	Kearney Edward R	1040	proprietor	50	"
	H	Kearney Gwendolyn R †	1040	technician	20	"
	K	Kearney Ruth L †	1040	housewife	40	"
	L	Thompson Crosby B	1044	clerk	60	"
	M	Thompson Fannie E †	1044	housewife	58	"
	N	Heustis Eliza J †	1044	"	72	"
	O	Heustis Frank R	1044	clerk	72	"
	P	Thompson Stephen G	1044	engineer	63	"
	R	Darling Ann E †	1045	at home	82	"

Page.	Letter	Full Name.	Residence, Jan. 1, 1941.	Occupation.	Supposed Age.	Reported Residence, Jan. 1, 1940. Street and Number.

River Street—Continued

Page.	Letter	Full Name.	Residence, Jan. 1, 1941.	Occupation.	Supposed Age.	Reported Residence, Jan. 1, 1940. Street and Number.
	S	Darling Harold D	1045	dentist	60	here
	T	Campbell Josephine A—†	1047	housewife	49	"
	U	Campbell Potter J	1047	machinist	49	"
	V	Griffin Robert D	1047	shipfitter	28	Brookline
	W	Griffin Rosemary—†	1047	housewife	25	here
	X	Schwerdtfeger Alice A—†	1048	"	26	Maine
	Y	Schwerdtfeger August R	1048	clerk	41	"
	Z	Gray Abbie A—†	1048	housewife	71	here
1545						
	A	Gray Rena M—†	1048	clerk	45	"
	B	Ciesielski John	1049	laborer	25	"
	C*	Ciesielski Pauline—†	1049	housewife	48	"
	D	Ciesielski Sophie—†	1049	inspector	22	"
	E	Ciesielski Stanley	1049	carpenter	56	"
	F*	Gaita Cira—†	1049	housewife	34	"
	G	Gaita Ciro	1049	ironworker	44	"
	H	Brigham Frances E—†	1052	at home	75	"
	K	Burnes Agnes—†	1052	housekeeper	65	"
	L	Bissell Isaac A	1056	cashier	67	"
	M	Bissell Jessie M—†	1056	housewife	64	"
	N	Wickwise Edith M—†	1056	at home	68	"
	O	Condon Alice—†	1057	paper sorter	60	"
	P	Kallenberg Margaret T—†	1057	housewife	37	"
	R	Kallenberg Oscar H	1057	painter	37	"
	S	Barnard Mary H—†	1057	at home	77	"
	T	Schluter John H	1057	baker	59	"
	U	Sukeforth Gertrude M—†	1057	housekeeper	49	"
	V	Trask Ann T—†	1060	housewife	26	72 West
	W	Trask Walter E	1060	buffer	28	72 "
	X	Maloney Catherine M—†	1060	housewife	46	here
	Y	Maloney Thomas F	1060	baker	48	"
	Z	Feeley Joseph B	1061	chauffeur	46	"
1546						
	A	Feeley Mary M—†	1061	stenographer	39	"
	B	Wall Mary A—†	1061	housekeeper	70	"
	C	Lake Arthur	1061	blacksmith	25	37 Weld Hill
	D	Lake Bertha—†	1061	housewife	26	37 "
	G*	Elliot Henry H	1065	painter	71	here
	H*	Elliot Ida M—†	1065	nurse	72	"
	K	Greenwood George C	1065	machinist	55	"

Page	Letter	Full Name	Residence, Jan. 1, 1941	Occupation	Reported Age	Reported Residence, Jan. 1, 1940. Street and Number

Riverside Square

Page	Letter	Full Name	Residence, Jan. 1, 1941	Occupation	Reported Age	Reported Residence, Jan. 1, 1940. Street and Number
	O	Curran James P	4	auto dealer	39	here
	P	Galvin Frederick P	4	agent	38	"
	R	Galvin Helen I—†	4	housewife	33	"
	S	Galvin John W	4	superintendent	74	"
	T	Galvin John W, jr	4	butcher	40	"
	U	Galvin Mary J—†	4	housewife	71	"
	V	Wallace Anna—†	9	"	39	"
	W	Wallace Merrill D	9	salesman	50	"
	X	Wallace Oscar P	9	metalworker	42	"
	Y	MacLaren Archie G	11	carpenter	45	259 Wood av
	Z	MacLaren Jennie V—†	11	housewife	45	259 "
1547						
	A	Shannon Charles B	11	laborer	24	259 "
	B	Jackson Grace—†	12	housewife	65	here
	C	Jackson Herbert I	12	draftsman	70	"
	D	Rein Martha—†	12	housekeeper	76	"
	E	Higgins Frances—†	15	housewife	56	"
	F	DeSantis Carl, jr	15	salesman	27	15 Sunnyside
	G	DeSantis Frances A—†	15	housewife	23	15 "
	H	Henderson Annie E—†	15	"	57	here
	K	Henderson Robert H	15	tailor	60	"
	L	*Allen Eva M—†	15	tube tester	45	Watertown
	M	Gale Wright B	15	pipefitter	39	"
	N	Broderick Annie L—†	16	housewife	63	here
	O	Broderick Estelle R—†	16	secretary	21	"
	P	Broderick Louis T	16	laborer	28	"
	R	Broderick Patrick J	16	clerk	63	"
	S	Shea Katherine T—†	16	housewife	25	"
	T	Shea Richard E	16	laborer	28	"
	U	Rocheleau Genevieve—†	17	housewife	25	14 Rector rd
	V	Rocheleau George R	17	electrician	25	14 "
	W	Noyes Isabelle—†	17	housewife	63	here
	X	Noyes Stewart	17	shipper	34	"
	Y	Black Sarah—†	17	housewife	71	"
	Z	Papses William P	17	boilermaker	22	"
1548						
	A	Whitaker Amelia—†	17	housewife	21	"
	B	Whitaker Richard F	17	laborer	26	"
	C	Morgan Ann L—†	18	stenographer	28	"
	D	Morgan David I	18	chauffeur	22	"

Page	Letter	Full Name	Residence, Jan. 1, 1941	Occupation	Supposed Age	Reported Residence, Jan. 1, 1940. Street and Number.

Riverside Square—Continued

Page	Letter	Full Name	Residence, Jan. 1, 1941	Occupation	Supposed Age	Reported Residence, Jan. 1, 1940.
	E	Morgan Kieran J	18	guard	60	here
	F	Morgan Leo J	18	distributor	23	"
	G	Morgan Mary J—†	18	housewife	60	"
	H	Parrott Marion E—†	20	"	31	6 Beacon
	K	Parrott Robert W	20	trimmer	35	6 "
	L	Malone Florence E—†	20	housewife	48	here
	M	Malone Thomas	20	chauffeur	52	"
	N	Richert Susan T—†	20	artist	22	"
	O	Enos John F	21	laborer	43	"
	P	Enos Theresa M—†	21	housewife	37	"
	R	Bauman Bertha S—†	21	"	53	"
	S	Bauman Earl	21	salesman	23	"
	T	Bauman Francis F	21	manager	54	"
	U	Bauman Frederick F	21	foreman	21	"
	V	Sanders Doris L—†	21	housewife	27	"
	W	Sanders Howard A	21	metalworker	28	"
	X	Chamberlain Florence I—†	24	housewife	38	"
	Y	Chamberlain Julius R	24	shipper	38	"
	Z	Pardy Alfred A	24	clerk	32	"
1549						
	A	Pardy Florence M—†	24	housewife	29	"
	B	Hayes Catherine—†	25	"	56	"
	C	Hayes James	25	retired	80	"
	D	Hayes John D	25	chauffeur	25	"
	E	Hayes Mary C—†	25	secretary	29	"
	F	Hayes Thomas P	25	clerk	27	"
	G	Duxbury Eva R—†	25	housewife	65	"
	H	Duxbury Richard	25	retired	75	"

Rosa Street

Page	Letter	Full Name	Residence, Jan. 1, 1941	Occupation	Supposed Age	Reported Residence, Jan. 1, 1940.
	K	Higgins Alice M—†	3	housewife	26	147 Minot
	L	Higgins Catherine—†	3	"	71	here
	M	Higgins Emmett J	3	salesman	29	147 Minot
	N	Higgins Michael	3	laborer	73	here
	O	Bronson Daniel	5	retired	87	30 Webster
	P	Wall Joseph A	5	operator	43	30 "
	R	Wall Mary J—†	5	housewife	42	30 "
	T	Batchelder Ezra W	7	machinist	54	here
	U	Batchelder Margaret A—†	7	clerk	22	"
	V	Batchelder Mary I—†	7	housewife	52	"

Page	Letter	Full Name	Residence		[illegible]	[illegible]	[illegible]

Rosa Street—Continued

Page	Letter	Full Name					
	W	McAdams John V		7	retired	83	here
	X	Amico Albert	8	10	cutter	30	38 Havre
	Y	Amico Rose—†	8	10	housewife	26	38 "
	Z	Lynch Anna L—†	8	10	"	40	6 Rochdale
1550							
	A	Lynch Rodman H	8	10	chauffeur	40	6 "
	B	Lynch Virginia A—†	8	10	waitress	21	6 "
	C	Hardy Caroline A—†		9	nurse	45	here
	D	Hardy Joseph		9	retired	73	"
	E	Hardy Mary A—†		9	housewife	70	"
	F	Reese Helen D—†		9	transcriber	27	"
	G	Reese Joseph D		9	chauffeur	24	"
	H	Sullivan Nora—†		9	nurse	32	"
	K	Foti Frank C	12	14	chauffeur	28	Somerville
	L	Foti Grace—†	12	14	housewife	28	"
	M	Ryan James D	12	14	editor	34	Salem
	N	Ryan Mary L—†	12	14	housewife	32	"
	O	Feeley Genevieve—†		13	"	46	here
	P	Feeley Robert J		13	pipefitter	46	"
	R	Morrell Ernest L		13	U S A	22	"
	S	Pettingell Clarence J		15	clerk	41	"
	T	Pettingell Dorothy H—†		15	housewife	33	"
	U	Pettingell Inez C—†		15	"	74	"
	V	Laughlin Bridget—†	16	18	housekeeper	80	"
	W	Ryan John T	16	18	engineer	43	"
	X	Ryan Mary H—†	16	18	housewife	42	"
	Y	DiSanto Eva—†	16	18	typist	21	321 Wood av
	Z	*DiSanto Rosaria—†	16	18	housewife	43	321 "
1551							
	A	DiSanto Salvatore	16	18	shoemaker	47	321 "
	B	*Day Hannah T—†		17	housekeeper	66	here
	C	McAvoy Julia T—†		17	at home	78	"
	D	Wintner Edward P		17	engineer	50	"
	E	Wintner Julia A—†		17	housewife	56	"
	F	Carnes Eileen G—†		19	operator	21	"
	G	Carnes Ellen T—†		19	housewife	55	"
	H	Carnes Henry F		19	serviceman	58	"
	K	Beck Margaret M—†	20	22	housewife	52	"
	L	*Beck Martin Q	20	22	fishcutter	53	"
	M	Filkins Margaret P—†	20	22	secretary	40	"
	N	Filkins Mary A—†	20	22	housekeeper	42	"

Page.	Letter.	Full Name.	Residence, Jan. 1, 1941.	Occupation.	Supposed Age.	Reported Residence, Jan. 1, 1940. Street and Number.

Rosa Street Continued

Page.	Letter.	Full Name.	Residence, Jan. 1, 1941.	Occupation.	Supposed Age.	Reported Residence, Jan. 1, 1940. Street and Number.
	O	McNamara Daniel J	21	supervisor	42	here
	P	McNamara Ethel T †	21	housewife	41	"
	R	McNamara Nora †	21	at home	76	"
	S	Halstead Benjamin G	23	clerk	26	"
	T	Halstead Ernest A	23	finisher	56	"
	U	Halstead Frank A	23	clerk	21	"
	V	Halstead Hattie H—†	23	housewife	51	"
	W	*Gaglio Anna—†	24–26	"	36	"
	X	Gaglio Antonio	24–26	barber	40	"
	Y	Irrera Antoinette—†	24–26	stitcher	21	"
	Z	Irrera Antonetta—†	24–26	"	47	"
1552						
	A	Irrera Nunzio	24–26	printer	26	"
	B	Irrera Santo	24–26	barber	49	"
	C	*Luke Jessie E—†	28–30	housekeeper	65	1331 Wash'n
	D	MacKenzie Hattie A—†	28–30	cook	39	here
	E	MacKenzie Murdock W	28–30	carpenter	43	"
	F	Hasselbrack Catherine G—†	28–30	housewife	39	"
	G	Hasselbrack Frederick J	28–30	painter	45	"
	H	Higgins Pauline—†	32–34	housewife	23	"
	K	Higgins Walter	32–34	chauffeur	32	"
	L	Cristadoro Charles E	32–34	foreman	52	"
	M	Cristadoro Emily D—†	32–34	forewoman	25	"
	N	Cristadoro Joseph	32–34	baker	21	"
	O	Cristadoro Marie—†	32–34	housewife	45	"
	P	Sullivan Catherine M—†	36–38	clerk	32	"
	R	Sullivan Ellen M—†	36–38	housewife	62	"
	S	Sullivan Margaret R †	36–38	teacher	25	"
	T	Sullivan Mary E—†	36–38	saleswoman	27	"
	U	Sullivan Michael	36–38	retired	64	"
	V	O'Rourke Andrew M	36–38	attendant	40	"
	W	O'Rourke Sadie M—†	36–38	housewife	38	"
	X	McGaw Kenneth A	40–42	laborer	38	"
	Y	McGaw Ruby B—†	40–42	housewife	38	"
	Z	Holm Henry T	40–42	chauffeur	26	93 Bloomfield
1553						
	A	Holm Julia L—†	40–42	housewife	67	93 "
	B	Powers Bernard J	40–42	finisher	43	93 "
	C	Powers Mary D—†	40–42	housewife	32	93 "
	D	Johnson Harry	44–46	brewer	39	here
	E	Johnson Irene—†	44–46	housewife	38	"

Page	Letter	Full Name.	Residence, Jan. 1, 1941.	Occupation.	Supposed Age.	Reported Residence, Jan. 1, 1940. Street and Number.

Rosa Street—Continued

Letter	Full Name	Residence	Occupation	Age	Reported Residence
F	Philbrick Margaret M—†	44-46	housewife	27	here
G	Philbrick Maurice E	44-46	clerk	38	"
H	Stracqualursi Louis	48-50	laborer	46	"
K	*Stracqualursi Urbina—†	48-50	housewife	43	"
L	Sliney Caroline A—†	48-50	student	20	"
M	Sliney Joseph E	48-50	guard	52	"
N	Sliney Mary C—†	48-50	housewife	54	"
O	Riley Catherine—†	52-54	"	49	"
P	Riley Stephen J	52-54	B F D	27	"
R	Driscoll Cornelius P	52-54	inspector	51	"
S	Driscoll Mary—†	52-54	housewife	42	"

Walter Street

Letter	Full Name	Residence	Occupation	Age	Reported Residence
T	Morse Elbert W	48	watchman	57	here
U	Morse Elbert W, jr	48	machinist	26	"
V	Morse Florence L—†	48	housewife	55	"
W	Morse Lillis P—†	48	maid	20	"
X	Cleary James	48	machinist	21	"
Y	Cleary Joseph E	48	laborer	55	"
Z	Cleary Sarah—†	48	housewife	40	"

West Street

Letter	Full Name	Residence	Occupation	Age	Reported Residence
B	Zambella Andrew	35	clerk	20	here
C	Zambella Joseph	35	shoemaker	66	"
D	*Zambella Letizia—†	35	housewife	54	"
E	Zambella Roslina—†	35	clerk	21	"
F	*Diamond Esther—†	37	housewife	67	"
G	Diamond Hyman	37	merchant	35	"
H	Diamond Samuel	37	"	37	"
K	Cairns James W	61	salesman	56	"
L	Cairns Mary E—†	61	housewife	80	"
M	Cairns Thomas H	61	painter	38	"
N	Cairns William E	61	manager	60	"
O	Heydacker Bessie L—†	63	housewife	59	"
P	Heydacker Charlotte L—†	63	stenographer	22	"
R	Heydacker Louis	63	clerk	57	"
S	Bilby Otis M	65	metalworker	40	"
T	Hain David	65	millwright	60	"
U	Hain Margaret S—†	65	housewife	60	"

Page	Letter	Full Name	Residence, Jan. 1, 1941	Occupation	Supposed Age	Reported Residence, Jan. 1, 1940. Street and Number.

West Street—Continued

Page	Letter	Full Name	Residence, Jan. 1, 1941	Occupation	Supposed Age	Reported Residence, Jan. 1, 1940
	X	Rubin Benjamin	67A	merchant	27	here
	W	Rubin Ida R—†	67A	housewife	23	"
	Y	Martin James M	67A	laborer	35	"
	Z	Martin Mary A—†	67A	housewife	35	"

1555 Westminster Street

Page	Letter	Full Name	Residence, Jan. 1, 1941	Occupation	Supposed Age	Reported Residence, Jan. 1, 1940
1555	A	Burke Genevieve G—†	85	housewife	55	here
	B	Burke John A	85	physician	27	"
	C	Burke Patrick J	85	custodian	65	"
	D	Flanagan Louise H—†	85	secretary	48	"
	E	Fletcher Dorothy—†	87	housewife	32	"
	F	Fletcher Harry M	87	surveyor	34	"
	G	Burness Florence B—†	89	housewife	28	"
	H	Burness John G	89	clerk	34	"
	K	Paris Antoinette—†	91	stenographer	22	"
	L	Paris David C	91	engineer	26	"
	M	Paris Joseph	91	salesman	56	"
	O	Paris Joseph W	91	fireman	24	"
	N	Paris Mary—†	91	housewife	47	"
	P	Wolf Alice—†	101	"	45	103 Westminster
	R	Wolf Gustav H	101	carpenter	45	103 "
	S	Wolf Gustav H, jr	101	bellhop	25	103 "
	U	Wolf John F	101	clerk	22	103 "
	T	Wolf Joseph F	101	benchworker	20	103 "

Wood Avenue

Page	Letter	Full Name	Residence, Jan. 1, 1941	Occupation	Supposed Age	Reported Residence, Jan. 1, 1940
	W	Staula Dorothy H—†	227–229	operator	24	here
	X	Staula Frank J	227–229	realtor	50	"
	Y	Staula Sarah H—†	227–229	housewife	46	"
	Z	Durkin Alice V—†	227–229	"	44	"
1556						
	A	Durkin Robert E	227–229	supervisor	44	"
	B	Brink Francis L	231–233	operator	23	"
	C	Brink Mary M—†	231–233	secretary	21	"
	D	Brink Norbert F	231–233	operator	56	"
	E	Brink Ruth C—†	231–233	housewife	46	"
	F	Lincoln Elsie H—†	231–233	"	41	"
	G	Lincoln George H	231–233	engineer	45	"
	H	Gonsalves Frank	235–237	machinist	40	"

Wood Avenue—Continued

Page	Letter	Full Name	Residence		Occupation	Age	Reported Residence Street and Number
	L	Gonsalves Hermina—†	235	237	saleswoman	35	here
	K	Gonsalves Joseph F	235	237	engineer	65	"
	M	*Kent Augusta O—†	235	237	housewife	51	"
	N	Kent Frederick S	235	237	carpenter	50	"
	O	Kent Hazel M—†	235	237	typist	22	"
	P	Kennedy Catherine—†	239	241	clerk	57	"
	R	Parker Mary E—†	239	241	housewife	46	"
	S	Parker William	239	241	chauffeur	50	"
	T	Brownson Clara M—†	239	241	at home	52	"
	U	Olssen Anton J	239	241	lamplighter	42	"
	V	Olssen Jacqueline C—†	239	241	housewife	30	"
	W	Lantz Ernest E	243	245	engineer	54	"
	X	*Lantz Georgia N—†	243	245	housewife	44	"
	Y	Seibert Chester D	243	245	proprietor	41	"
	Z	Seibert Gertrude L—†	243	245	housewife	41	"
1557							
	A	Bean Herbert A	247	249	electrician	54	"
	B	Shea Charlotte M—†	247	249	librarian	45	12 Glenside av
	C	Clark May L—†	247	249	clerk	20	Maine
	D	Znotas Frank P	247	249	agent	38	here
	E	Znotas Helen—†	247	249	housewife	33	"
	F	Stuart Elizabeth V—†	251	253	"	33	"
	G	Stuart William W	251	253	salesman	36	"
	H	*Shaughnessy Agnes—†	251	253	housewife	34	"
	K	Shaughnessy James	251	253	papermaker	39	"
	N	Fitzpatrick Elinor T—†	263	265	housewife	31	"
	O	Fitzpatrick William	263	265	engineer	41	"
	P	Coveney Alma E—†	263	265	housewife	44	"
	R	Coveney Florence M—†	263	265	clerk	20	"
	S	Coveney John	263	265	chauffeur	41	"
	T	Rayner Ann H—†	267	269	housewife	57	"
	U	Rayner John H	267	269	exterminator	60	"
	V	Rayner Ruth E—†	267	269	supervisor	26	"
	W	Rayner William F	267	269	clerk	23	"
	X	Griffin Emelie J—†	267	269	housewife	28	742 River
	Y	Griffin John F	267	269	papermaker	25	742 "
	Z	Meads Frank W	271	273	packer	55	here
1558							
	A	Meads Mabel E—†	271	273	housewife	59	"
	B	Meads Olive M—†	271	273	operator	25	"
	C	Ravida Anthony F	271	273	barber	33	"

Page	Letter	Full Name	Residence, Jan. 1, 1941	Occupation	Supposed Age	Reported Residence, Jan. 1, 1940. Street and Number

Wood Avenue—Continued

Page	Letter	Full Name	Residence	Occupation	Age	Reported Residence
	D	Ormond Donald	271–273	papermaker	34	here
	E	Ormond Genevieve †	271–273	housewife	34	"
	F	Lamothe Lillian H †	275–277	clerk	27	"
	G	Woessner Karl G	275–277	assembler	37	"
	H	Woessner Viola †	275–277	housewife	33	"
	K	*Visnick Coleman	275–277	butcher	56	"
	L	Visnick Martha †	275–277	clerk	24	"
	M	*Visnick Sarah †	275–277	housewife	53	"
	N	Bertolami Adeline †	279–281	"	55	"
	O	Bertolami Dominic	279–281	cutter	55	"
	P	Bertolami Helen †	279–281	clerk	23	"
	R	Bertolami Louis	279–281	accountant	27	"
	S	Ryan Hilda †	279–281	housewife	24	"
	T	Ryan Leo	279–281	shipper	25	"
	U	Ross Charles H	283–285	mechanic	48	"
	V	Ross Elizabeth M †	283–285	housewife	45	"
	W	Ross Herbert I	283–285	printer	22	"
	X	English Beatrice V †	283–285	wrapper	24	"
	Y	English Frank V	283–285	papermaker	56	"
	Z	English Lester V	283–285	"	22	"
1559						
	A	English Violet M †	283–285	housewife	58	"
	B	Cameron Edla M †	291–293	"	50	"
	C	Cameron Francis J	291–293	clerk	45	"
	D	Cameron Ronald B	291–293	draftsman	22	"
	E	Nester Frank E	291–293	pipefitter	52	"
	F	Nester Mary E †	291–293	housewife	50	"
	G	Shepis Joseph	295–297	upholsterer	43	193 Fairmount av
	H	Shepis Lena †	295–297	housewife	38	193 "
	K	Merlino Anthony	295–297	waiter	37	101 Lonsdale
	L	*Merlino Lena †	295–297	housewife	32	101 "
	M	DeLuca Albina M †	299–301	"	40	here
	N	DeLuca Joseph G	299–301	mechanic	46	"
	O	Guariglia Generoso A	299–301	painter	23	New York
	P	Guariglia Vincent	299–301	cutter	20	"
	R	Damiani Alfred	299–301	cabinetmaker	44	here
	S	Damiani Mary †	299–301	housewife	34	"
	T	Flaherty Edward P	303	clerk	41	"
	U	Flaherty Madeline C †	303	housewife	41	"
	V	Svenson Agda F †	303	"	69	"
	W	Svenson Sven O	303	agent	71	"

Page	Letter	Full Name	Residence, April 1, 1941	Occupation	Supposed Age	Reported Residence, April 1, 1940. Street and Number

Wood Avenue—Continued

Page	Letter	Full Name	Residence, April 1, 1941	Occupation	Supposed Age	Reported Residence, April 1, 1940. Street and Number
	X	Bohn Edna C—†	309	clerk	56	here
	Y	Bohn Emma O—†	309	housewife	60	"
	Z	Bohn Victor	309	upholsterer	63	"
1560						
	A	Malone Mildred G—†	309	housewife	22	"
	B	Malone William	309	collector	27	"
	C	Comer Frances I—†	309	housewife	26	"
	D	Comer Lawrence J	309	lather	28	"
	E	*Bulmer Eileen I—†	311	housewife	38	79 Thatcher
	F	Bulmer Roy W	311	mechanic	44	79 "
	G	Haley Elizabeth J—†	311	housewife	44	here
	H	Haley Henry V	311	signalman	45	"
	K	McDonald Edith M—†	311	clerk	43	"
	L	McDonald James	311	metalworker	71	"
	M	*Gillingham Elvira H—†	317	housekeeper	75	"
	N	Brand Owen J	317	chauffeur	22	"
	O	Gillingham Albert	317	laborer	43	"
	P	Gillingham Lena—†	317	housewife	50	"
	R	Connolly Helen E—†	317	student	21	"
	S	Connolly Helen G—†	317	housewife	44	"
	T	Connolly John B	317	papermaker	42	"
	V	Petrucci Mary—†	321	housewife	35	"
	W	Petrucci Salvatore	321	laborer	51	"
	X	McLellan Gladys M—†	321	housekeeper	47	"
	Y	Qualey Mary H—†	321	"	67	"
	Z	Flaherty John F	325	laborer	26	"
1561						
	A	Flaherty Louise D—†	325	housewife	31	"
	B	Curtis Edmond L	325	machinist	28	"
	C	Curtis Evelyn M—†	325	housewife	25	"
	D	Curtis Mary E—†	325	"	64	"
	E	Curtis Waldo I	325	steelworker	23	"
	F	*Sebetes John	325	laborer	56	"
	G	Sebetes John P	325	manager	26	"
	H	*Sebetes Margaret K—†	325	housewife	57	"
	K	Small Alice M—†	327	"	47	8 Rosa
	L	Small Arthur R	327	fireman	18	8 "
	M	McCarthy Bridget A—†	327	housewife	64	here
	N	McCarthy John E	327	millworker	28	"
	O	McCarthy Joseph J	327	sexton	29	"
	P	McCarthy Mary M—†	327	saleswoman	25	"

Page	Letter	Full Name	Residence, Jan. 1, 1941	Occupation	Supposed Age	Reported Residence, Jan. 1, 1940. Street and Number.

Wood Avenue—Continued

Page	Letter	Full Name	Residence, Jan. 1, 1941	Occupation	Supposed Age	Reported Residence, Jan. 1, 1940. Street and Number.
	R	McCarthy Patrick F	327	foreman	66	here
	S	McCarthy Rita J †	327	saleswoman	22	"
	T	*Yumansky Nellie M †	327	housewife	57	"
	U	*Yumansky William	327	laborer	53	"
	V	Heap Margaret J †	329	housewife	30	27 Dennis
	W	Heap William H	329	laborer	35	27 "
	X	Daly Christine †	329	housewife	51	here
	Y	Daly George E	329	millhand	67	"

Ward 18--Precinct 16

CITY OF BOSTON

LIST OF RESIDENTS
20 YEARS OF AGE AND OVER

(NON-CITIZENS INDICATED BY ASTERISK)
(FEMALES INDICATED BY DAGGER)

AS OF

JANUARY 1, 1941

JOSEPH F. TIMILTY, *Chairman*
FREDERIC E. DOWLING, *Secretary*
WILLIAM A. MOTLEY, JR.
FRANCIS B. McKINNEY
HILDA HEDSTROM QUIRK
Listing Board.

CITY OF BOSTON PRINTING DEPARTMENT

Page.	Letter.	Full Name.	Residence, Jan. 1, 1941.	Occupation.	Supposed Age.	Reported Residence, Jan. 1, 1940. Street and Number.

1600

Albion Street

Page.	Letter.	Full Name.	Residence, Jan. 1, 1941.	Occupation.	Supposed Age.	Reported Residence, Jan. 1, 1940. Street and Number.
	A	Thompson Anna E—†	9	teacher	45	here
	B	Thompson Florence E—†	9	housekeeper	49	"
	C	Gurney Alice M—†	13	clerk	60	"
	D	Tyler Benjamin F	13	"	29	"
	E	Dias Alice M—†	13	teacher	36	"
	F	Dias John L	13	retired	66	"
	G	Dias Letitia J—†	13	housewife	67	"
	H	Ostman Mabel D—†	13	secretary	41	"
	K	Lewis Nellie W—†	14	housewife	70	"
	L	Lewis William W	14	retired	73	"
	M	Wyatt Annie—†	14	housewife	53	"
	N	Wyatt Norman R	14	salesman	41	"
	O	Vincent Henrietta C—†	16	housewife	71	"
	P	Vincent Henry A	16	contractor	71	"
	R	Swim Edward H	16	supervisor	25	11 Wachusett
	S	Swim Eleanor R—†	16	housewife	23	Milton
	T	Lee Beatrice—†	17	"	40	here
	U	Lee Gordon J	17	agent	37	"
	V	Lee Susan L—†	17	housewife	73	"
	W	Freeman Elizabeth H—†	18	"	27	95 Sunnyside
	X	Freeman Reed	18	salesman	26	95 "
	Y	Wood Ella H—†	20	housekeeper	56	here
1601						
	A	Phinney Frank B	24	salesman	57	Harwich
	B	Phinney Sarah J—†	24	housewife	46	"
	C	Bemis Harold F	24	clerk	36	36 Manthorne rd
	D	Bemis Margaret T—†	24	housewife	25	36 "
	E	Trepanier Cecelia F—†	27	"	35	Dedham
	F	Trepanier Edgar	27	merchant	38	"
	G	Fallon Annie G—†	27	housewife	63	here
	H	Fallon Helen A—†	27	secretary	23	"
	K	Fallon John G	27	operator	28	"
	L	Dodge Edna W—†	28	housewife	53	"
	M	Dodge Ralph O	28	physician	55	"
	N	White Carrie E—†	28	at home	73	"
	O	Barry Joseph F	32	cutter	64	"
	P	Barry Katherie J—†	32	teacher	31	"

Page	Letter	Full Name				

Beacon Street

Page	Letter	Full Name				
	R	Hopkins Minerva C †	4	housewife	29	here
	S	Hopkins Orman A	4	salesman	32	"
	T	Monahan Irene F †	5	clerk	32	"
	U	Monahan Loretta M †	5	teacher	34	"
	V	Monahan Mary E †	5	housewife	62	"
	W	Monahan Veronica R †	5	teacher	29	"
	X	Higgins Della E †	6	housekeeper	73	"
	Y	Higgins Mary E †	6	housewife	32	"
	Z	Higgins Walter C	6	carpenter	32	36 Seymour
1602						
	A	Smith Joseph	7	machinist	49	here
	B	Smith Lillian †	7	housewife	46	"
	C	Briggs Ethel †	7	"	39	"
	D	Briggs John W	7	operator	54	"
	E	Gardella Mary †	9	stitcher	61	"
	F	Gardella Rose †	9	housewife	66	"
	G	Gardella Sylvester A	9	clerk	59	"
	H	Ornishi Hisa †	9	housewife	73	"
	K	Ornishi Julia M †	9	chemist	31	"
	L	Ornishi May †	9	"	36	"
	M	Ornishi Nina T †	9	clerk	31	"
	N	*O'Hanlon Elizabeth †	12	housewife	65	"
	O	O'Hanlon John T	12	shipper	28	"
	P	O'Hanlon Patrick J	12	laborer	30	"
	R	Eames Alice M †	14	housewife	49	203 D[illegible]
	S	Eames Douglas J	14	inspector	46	203 "
	T	Eames Douglas J, jr	14	laborer	20	203 "
	U	Eames Phyllis †	14	hairdresser	22	203 "
	V	Hartford Barbara A †	14	housewife	25	[illegible]
	W	Hartford Frederick F	14	electrician	26	999 "
	X	Sanseverino Concetta †	19	housewife	57	here
	Y	Sanseverino Frank	19	engineer	25	"
	Z	Sanseverino John	19	busboy	23	"
1603						
	A	Sanseverino Peter	19	tailor	57	"
	B	Sanseverino Raphael	19	busboy	33	"
	C	Sutton Clifford J	21	clerk	44	57 Austin
	D	Sutton Margaret M †	21	housewife	40	57 "
	E	Day Bridget M †	22	"	69	here
	F	Day Mary M †	22	secretary	26	"
	G	Bjork Charles J	22	shipper	55	"

Page	Letter	Full Name	Residence, Jan. 1, 1941	Occupation	Supposed Age	Reported Residence, Jan. 1, 1940. Street and Number

Beacon Street—Continued

Page	Letter	Full Name	Residence, Jan. 1, 1941	Occupation	Supposed Age	Reported Residence, Jan. 1, 1940. Street and Number
	H	Bjork Doris E—†	22	clerk	20	here
	K	Bjork Lawrence V	22	assembler	26	"
	L	Doyle George W	23	patternmaker	48	"
	M	Doyle Helen B—†	23	housewife	50	"
	N	Senior George J	23	salesman	56	"
	O	Senior Margaret L—†	23	housewife	46	"
	P	Stanley Arthur W	25	carpenter	61	"
	R	Stanley Laura F—†	25	housewife	52	"
	S	Hommel Alfred L	25	machinist	52	"
	T	Hommel Dorothy M—†	25	operator	24	"
	U	Hommel Helen A—†	25	housewife	53	"
	V	Hommel Margaret V—†	25	clerk	20	"
	W	Hommel Richard E	25	student	22	"
	X	Purdy Bruce E	25	salesman	29	Newton
	Y	Purdy Helen A—†	25	housewife	27	"
	Z	Doucette Annie M—†	26	"	31	here
1604						
	A	Doucette George R	26	machinist	39	"
	B	Pratt Estelle J—†	26	housewife	82	"
	C	Pratt Myrtle A—†	26	"	51	"
	D	Pratt Robert P	26	conductor	56	"
	E	Kirk Annie C—†	26	housewife	50	"
	F	Kirk Charles W	26	foreman	50	"
	G	Ford Anne H—†	29	housekeeper	57	"
	H	McCarthy Margaret—†	29	"	75	"
	K	Kennedy Daniel A	30	retired	70	"
	L	Kennedy Julia T—†	30	housewife	58	"
	M	Wharton Agnes D—†	33	beautician	31	"
	N	Wharton Royal S	33	carpenter	79	"
	O	Grayson Elsie A—†	34	housewife	23	"
	P	Grayson Henrietta C—†	34	"	70	"
	R	Grayson Richard D	34	electrician	29	"
	S	Grayson Richard K	34	"	70	"
	T	Shillue Anna J—†	41	housewife	45	131 Chittick rd
	U	Shillue Dennis H	41	messenger	49	131 "
	W	Colesworthy Eugenia—†	41	at home	87	1130 River
	X	Colpitt Ernest G	41	blacksmith	57	here
	Y	Colpitt Lulu E—†	41	housewife	61	"
	Z	Hill Alida T—†	42	"	79	"
1605						
	A	Hill Charles F	42	printer	80	"

Page	Letter	Full Name	Residence	Occupation	Age	Reported Residence, Street and Number

Beacon Street (Continued)

Page	Letter	Full Name	Residence	Occupation	Age	Reported Residence, Street and Number
	B	Case Horace N	46	salesman	65	here
	C	Case Rena H †	46	housewife	65	"
	D	Clapp Alice E †	50	at home	69	"
	E	Cummings Nora †	50	"	77	"
	F	Hayewell Letitia E †	50	"	86	"
	G	McNeil Catherine †	50	cook	41	"
	H	Morse Lillian K †	50	at home	70	111 Pinckney
	K	Newhall Louise C †	50	"	77	here
	L	Pownall Edna †	50	maid	43	"
	M	Stark Harriet W †	50	at home	78	"
	N	Tyler Mary †	50	matron	69	"
	O	Walker Frances N †	50	at home	82	"
	P	Alden Marion E †	51	housewife	53	"
	R	Alden Merton R	51	retired	56	"
	S	Alden Merton S	51	student	21	"
	T	Kollock Caroline B †	53	housekeeper	64	"
	U	Robson Marion J †	53	maid	45	"
	V	Tirrell Edwin Van D	60	retired	64	"
	W	Tirrell Katherine †	60	housewife	67	"
	X	MacManus Gertrude †	66	maid	48	"
	Y	Tilden Lester W	66	clerk	44	"
	Z	Tilden Mary H †	66	housewife	72	"
1606						
	A	Manchester Clara V †	71	"	61	"
	B	Manchester Erford D	71	clerk	35	"
	C	Manchester Erford J	71	secretary	63	"
	D	Manchester Fredric D	71	salesman	26	"
	E	Manchester Janice L †	71	housewife	23	"
	F	Merrow Elizabeth B †	74	teacher	23	"
	G	Merrow Harold K	74	treasurer	58	"
	H	Merrow Sally M †	74	teacher	22	"
	K	Merrow Sarah M †	74	housewife	60	"
	L	Greene Alfred R	75	auditor	51	"
	M	Greene Anna N †	75	housewife	50	"
	N	Greene Claire E †	75	clerk	26	"
	O	Greene Eleanor R †	75	social worker	30	"
	P	Cuthbertson Jane E †	76	teacher	25	"
	R	Cuthbertson Lavina E †	76	housewife	51	"
	S	Cuthbertson Robert J	76	foreman	57	"
	T	Goodby Ella †	78	housewife	68	"
	U	Goodby John	78	engraver	70	"

Page	Letter	Full Name	Residence, Jan. 1, 1941	Occupation	Supposed Age	Reported Residence, Jan. 1, 1940. Street and Number.

Beacon Street—Continued

Page	Letter	Full Name	Residence, Jan. 1, 1941	Occupation	Supposed Age	Reported Residence, Jan. 1, 1940. Street and Number.
	V	Hall Annabelle J †	78	housekeeper	57	N Hampshire
	W	Harrison Ruth †	78	secretary	43	here
	X	Hudson Mary †	79	housekeeper	67	"
	Y	Andersen Arthur P	79	chauffeur	28	"
	Z	Andersen Evelyn F †	79	housewife	32	"
1607						
	A	Sargeant Bertha A †	80	"	63	"
	B	Sargeant John L	80	salesman	34	"
	C	Sargeant Virginia †	80	housewife	37	"
	D	Sargeant William L	80	bookkeeper	66	"
	E	Welsh Mary A †	80	housewife	40	"
	F	Welsh Patrick J	80	executive	45	"
	G	Alexander Catherine A †	83	clerk	23	"
	H	Alexander Edwin J	83	mechanic	33	"
	K	Alexander Frank M	83	carpenter	21	"
	L	Alexander George H	83	conductor	64	"
	M	Alexander George H, jr	83	printer	29	"
	N	Alexander Henrietta †	83	housewife	57	"
	O	Alexander Ruth †	83	clerk	26	"
	P	Massey Archie L	85	foreman	49	"
	R	Massey Ellen G †	85	housewife	46	"
	S	Massey Emma K †	85	"	79	"
	T	Simes Amanda †	85	"	62	"
	U	Simes Ethel A †	85	"	34	"
	V	Simes Theodore H	85	clerk	22	"
	W	Norris Harry A	86	agent	72	"
	X	Norris Myra †	86	secretary	40	"
	Y	Norris Nettie B †	86	housewife	70	"
	Z	Bailey Edith H †	89	"	64	"
1608						
	A	Bailey Ruth E †	89	secretary	26	"
	B	Haskell Ruth C †	89	housekeeper	87	"
	C	Tandy Mabel H †	89	"	73	"
	D	Collins Dorothy S †	90	housewife	32	"
	E	Collins Walter R	90	engineer	29	"
	F	Powers Lavina E †	90	teacher	60	"
	G	Stewart Hamilton S	90	packer	49	"
	H	Nason Chester L	92	manager	50	"
	K	Nason Emma P †	92	housewife	48	"
	L	Nason June P †	92	clerk	23	"
	M	Emerson Donald M	94	salesman	54	"

Page	Letter	Full Name	Residence	Occupation	Age	Reported Residence, Street and Number

Beacon Street Continued

Page	Letter	Full Name	Residence	Occupation	Age	Reported Residence, Street and Number
	N	Emerson Flora B †	94	housewife	52	here
	O	Kelley Della E †	95	"	60	"
	P	Kelley Frank L	95	inspector	60	"
	R	White Flora M †	95	clerk	30	40 Vose
	S	White Isabel †	95	housewife	54	40 "
	T	White Isabel H †	95	clerk	28	40 "
	U	White Louise A †	95	housewife	22	Brookline
	V	White Robert W	95	accountant	26	40 Vose
	W	Cass Jeanette N †	97	housewife	35	86 Beacon
	X	Cass Robert L	97	checker	31	86 "
	Y	Batho Carlton J	97	clerk	31	here
	Z	Batho Etta M †	97	housewife	30	"
1609						
	A	Higbee Charles R	98	retired	65	"
	B	Higbee Emma R †	98	housewife	60	"
	C	Higbee Ruth B †	98	teacher	29	"
	D	Fogg Freda M †	99	housewife	37	"
	E	Fogg George L	99	bookkeeper	47	"
	F	Nelson Harriett D †	99	housewife	30	"
	G	Nelson William E	99	policeman	37	"
	H	Randazzo Joseph	110	salesman	51	"
	K	Randazzo Sandrina A †	110	housewife	41	"
	L	Randazzo Thomas	110	merchant	43	"
	M	Timson Barry	117	salesman	29	"
	N	Timson Herbert C	117	clerk	69	"
	O	Timson Minnie B †	117	housewife	65	"
	P	Timson Verona S †	117	secretary	62	"
	R	Timson Viola A †	117	housewife	23	"
	S	Bragg Jennie F †	120	matron	62	"
	T	Hunter Jeannette G †	120	housekeeper	53	"
	U	Timilty Harry I	120	sheriff	29	"
	V	Timilty James E	120	manager	46	"
	W	Timilty Joseph F	120	commissioner	44	"
	X	Timilty Kathleen M †	120	housewife	26	"
	Y	Mitton Sarah †	121	housekeeper	59	"
	Z	Turner Sarah J †	121	"	77	"
1610						
	A	Duffy Maurice J	122	timekeeper	36	"
	B	Leahy Agnes T †	122	bookkeeper	40	"
	C	Leahy Catherine C †	122	clerk	45	"
	D	Leahy Catherine S †	122	housewife	76	"

Page	Letter	Full Name	Residence, Jan. 1, 1941	Occupation	Supposed Age	Reported Residence, Jan. 1, 1940. Street and Number.

Beacon Street—Continued

Page	Letter	Full Name	Residence	Occupation	Age	Reported Residence
	E	Leahy Harriett M—†	122	clerk	47	here
	F	Leahy Helen E—†	122	agent	46	"
	G	Leahy Sally E—†	122	housewife	42	"
	H	Leahy Timothy F	122	inspector	44	"
	K	Ellis Frederic R	131	engineer	54	"
	L	Ellis Lucy F—†	131	housewife	58	"
	M	Kazar John D	136	engineer	66	"
	N	Kazar Marjorie S—†	136	housewife	48	"
	O	Kendall Dorothy D—†	136	secretary	50	"
	P	Morley Frank N	139	manager	65	"
	R	Morley Gertrude W—†	139	housewife	61	"
	S	Morley Robert J	139	clerk	23	"
	T	Morley Wallace G	139	salesman	33	"
	U	Kollock Annie S—†	140	housekeeper	66	"
	V	Dunton Thomas H	141	manager	44	"
	W	Dunton Wilma R—†	141	housewife	40	"
	X	Young Franz W	141	manager	71	"

Edith Street

Page	Letter	Full Name	Residence	Occupation	Age	Reported Residence
	Y	Blonquist Gustav	3	plumber	52	here
	Z	Blonquist Hulda C—†	3	housewife	52	"

1611 Fairmount Avenue

Page	Letter	Full Name	Residence	Occupation	Age	Reported Residence
	E	Atherton Mary—†	172	at home	77	here
	F	Barker Elvira—†	172	"	85	Melrose
	G	Blackmer George E	172	retired	75	here
	H	Blackmer Rosetta—†	172	housewife	63	"
	K	Bullard Mary M—†	172	at home	101	190 Fairmount av
	L	Cavanaugh Johnanna—†	172	"	84	here
	M	Clements Doris K—†	172	nurse	22	"
	N	Clements James E	172	laborer	24	"
	O	Field Ella—†	172	at home	88	N Hampshire
	P	Healy Patrick	172	retired	80	Rhode Island
	R	Hurd Margaret—†	172	at home	65	10 Faulkner
	S	*Palmer Grace—†	172	nurse	43	here
	T	Roberts Elizabeth C—†	172	at home	70	297 Poplar
	U	Whitten Amelia—†	172	"	98	here
	V	Beake Frederick A	181	millwright	44	"
	W	Beake Frederick A, jr	181	clerk	21	"

Fairmount Avenue (Continued)

Page	Letter	Full Name	Residence	Occupation	Age	Former Residence, Street and Number
	X	Beake Myrtle A †	181	housewife	41	here
	Y	Bagley George E	181	retired	77	[illegible]
	Z	Bagley Margaret E †	181	housewife	62	1138 "
1612						
	A	Cafarellam Athony	181	proprietor	56	here
	B	*Untz Amy E †	182	housewife	60	"
	C	Untz John A	182	mechanic	42	"
	D	Untz Joseph	182	retired	72	"
	E	Dinsmore Blanche G †	182	secretary	60	"
	F	Cevolani Adele †	185	clerk	23	"
	G	*Cevolani Fred	185	assembler	57	"
	H	*Cevolani Inez †	185	housewife	51	"
	K	Cevolani Romeo	185	laborer	24	"
	L	Obin Mabel A †	186	housewife	37	"
	M	Obin William	186	painter	33	"
	N	*DoPadre George G	186	repairman	40	[illegible]
	O	*DoPadre Lena G †	186	stitcher	31	1625 "
	P	Gay Mary A †	187	seamstress	28	here
	R	Lee Lillian C †	187	housewife	35	[illegible]
	S	Lee William H	187	floorlayer	35	193 "
	T	Mathey Clara E †	187	housewife	58	here
	U	Mathey Francis P	187	packer	29	"
	V	Mathey James A	187	boilermaker	70	"
	W	Mathey Joseph W	187	salesman	31	"
	X	Evans Alice S †	189	operator	33	"
	Y	*Evans Angus M	189	carpenter	64	"
	Z	*Evans Lillie †	189	housewife	103	"
1613						
	A	*Evans Margaret E †	189	"	54	"
	B	Doughty Mary I †	189	housewife	21	S Bradley
	C	Doughty Stuart V	189	clerk	31	S "
	D	Doughty Edwin W	189	carpenter	32	here
	E	Doughty Julia G †	189	housewife	36	"
	F	Henderson Arthur G	190	clerk	23	"
	G	Henderson Ella M †	190	housewife	51	"
	H	Henderson William F	190	salesman	17	"
	K	Henderson William R	190	retired	75	"
	L	Smith Elizabeth †	190	clerk	56	"
	M	Delaney Edward F	190	salesman	35	"
	N	Delaney Rilla M †	190	housewife	34	"
	O	Donlon Edward T	190	salesman	27	"

Page	Letter	Full Name	Residence, Jan. 1, 1941.	Occupation.	Supposed Age.	Reported Residence, Jan. 1, 1940. Street and Number

Fairmount Avenue Continued

Page	Letter	Full Name	Residence, Jan. 1, 1941.	Occupation.	Supposed Age.	Reported Residence, Jan. 1, 1940. Street and Number
	P	Donlon John R	190	custodian	29	here
	R	Donlon Mary A †	190	housewife	53	"
	S	Donlon Patrick J	190	molder	58	"
	T	Hackett Marjorie †	192	housewife	32	"
	U	Hackett William A	192	cashier	30	"
	V	McDermott Eleanor—†	192	housewife	24	65A Fairmount av
	W	McDermott Joseph	192	cataloguer	27	65A "
	X	Marola Gabriel—†	193	laborer	47	28 Fulton
	Y*	Marola Lillian—†	193	housewife	37	28 "
1614						
	A	MacLeod Clifton T	193½	student	21	here
	B	MacLeod John S	193½	agent	30	"
	C	MacLeod Kenneth A	193½	retired	68	"
	D	MacLeod Kenneth G	193½	dentist	27	"
	E	MacLeod Mary E—†	193½	housewife	58	"
	F	Thompson Charles B	195	retired	81	"
	G	Thompson Helen C—†	195	artist	45	"
	H	Bell Ida L †	196	housekeeper	66	"
	K	Henderson Margaret J—†	196	"	67	"
	L	Vanderlick Marion C—†	196	housewife	38	"
	M	Vanderlick Stephen J	196	attorney	42	"
	N	Norton Florence A—†	196	housekeeper	73	"
	O	Henry Norman R	196	foreman	34	"
	P	Henry Ruth E †	196	housewife	33	"
	R	Gould Anna L—†	196	"	27	102 Austin
	S	Gould James H	196	instructor	24	11 Willowdean av
	T	Smith Alice M—†	196	housewife	40	here
	U	Smith Ralph P	196	salesman	39	"
	V	West Irene A—†	196	housewife	24	"
	W	West John W	196	proprietor	27	"
	X	Bates Elizabeth W †	196	housewife	57	Brockton
	Y	Bates George W	196	salesman	69	"
	Z	Dingwell Arthur R	196	dentist	50	126 Belnel rd
1615						
	A	Dingwell Gertrude M †	196	housewife	38	126 "
	B	Beck Mary F †	197	at home	80	Canton
	C*	Costley Mary †	197	"	80	8 Friendship rd
	D	Gage Russell	197	retired	62	40 Vose av
	E	Jewett Chandler T	197	teacher	44	here
	F	Jewett Elsie K—†	197	housewife	39	"
	G*	Kaye Frederick M	197	retired	63	"

Fairmount Avenue—Continued

Page	Letter	Full Name	Residence	Occupation	Age	Reported Residence, Street and Number
	H	Lovett Alma C—†	197	at home	83	here
	K	Nicholson Mary E—†	197	"	80	172 F[illegible]
	L	Hatch Edith B—†	199	housewife	60	here
	M	Hatch Lambert W	199	custodian	68	"
	N	Fairbanks Martha A—†	199	housekeeper	36	Norwood
	O	Kammer Anna D—†	200	housewife	52	Franklin
	P	Kammer Robert R	200	superintendent	56	"
	R	Poydar Anna E—†	200	housewife	35	here
	S	Poydar Henry F	200	electrician	32	"
	T	Freeman John H	201	merchant	38	"
	U	Freeman Sarah P—†	201	housewife	39	"
	V	Curtin Eileen T—†	203	housekeeper	39	"
	W	Follansbee Catherine E—†	203	typist	23	192 Fairmount
	X	Follansbee Florence—†	203	housewife	53	192 "
	Y	Follansbee Margaret M—†	203	stenographer	21	192 "
	Z	Hayward Faustina M—†	206	housewife	58	here
1616						
	A	Hayward Herbert A	206	manager	59	"
	B	Hayward Herbert A	206	student	20	"
	C	Hayward Janet A—†	206	clerk	29	"
	E	Sloan Grace E—†	215	"	22	"
	F	Sloan Naomi H—†	215	housewife	42	"
	G	Sloan Thomas H	215	clergyman	48	"
	H	Floyd Kenneth R	217	operator	23	"
	K	Floyd Millicent J—†	217	housewife	59	"
	L*	Hussey Delia—†	220	maid	21	Cambridge
	M	May Cora L—†	220	housewife	67	here
	N	May G Byron, jr	220	treasurer	68	"
	O	Fellows John B	221	retired	74	"
	P	Fellows Mary—†	221	housewife	65	"
	R	Swale Avis L—†	221	"	28	"
	S	Swale John W	221	mechanic	38	"
	U	Colella Jessie—†	227	housewife	23	"
	V	Colella William J	227	pedler	24	"
	W*	Fagerberg Anna V—†	227	housewife	56	"
	X	Fagerberg Edgar E	227	machinist	30	"
	Y	Fagerberg Emily—†	227	housewife	22	Dedham
	Z	Fagerberg Harry	227	machinist	22	"
1617						
	A	Fagerberg Ruth—†	227	housewife	25	here
	B*	Fagerberg Solomon W	227	machinist	52	"

Fairmount Avenue Continued

Page	Letter	Full Name	Residence, Jan. 1, 1941	Occupation	Supposed Age	Reported Residence, Jan. 1, 1940. Street and Number.
	C	MacElhiney Rae W †	230	housewife	37	here
	D	MacElhiney Wallace F	230	electrician	45	"
	E	McLennan John T	230	letter carrier	41	Cambridge
	F	Puccio Daniel	230	distributor	29	here
	G	Jacobsen Bernard T	231	machinist	27	"
	H	Jacobsen Hazel W †	231	housewife	28	"
	K	Webster Alvena †	231	nurse	35	"
	L	Webster Blanche †	231	housewife	63	"
	M	Gomes Emily †	232	teacher	21	"
	N	Gomes Joaquin	223	laborer	47	"
	O	Gomes Wilhelmina †	232	housewife	41	"
	P	Carew Catherine †	235	waitress	30	Brookline
	R	Carty James	235	laborer	35	here
	S	Carty Mary J †	235	housewife	36	"
	T	Nilson Beatrice L †	235	"	42	"
	U	Nilson Carl E	235	salesman	43	"
	V	Spindler Frederck C	235	baker	67	"
	W	Russell Arthur L	237	executive	69	"
	X	Russell Isabelle M †	237	housewife	70	"
	Y	Foote Amelia H †	238	"	73	"
	Z	Foote Charles S	238	toolmaker	76	"
1618						
	A	Foote David H	238	fireman	41	"
	B	Foote Rosamond M †	238	housewife	36	"
	C	Grant Catherine C †	240	"	71	"
	D	Grant Helen G †	240	secretary	40	"
	E	Grant James D	240	retired	72	"
	F	Holland Charles J	242	"	69	"
	G	Holland Eva C †	242	clerk	28	"
	H	Holland Nora A †	242	housewife	66	"
	K	Beaudet Marion A †	245	"	23	221 Reservation rd
	L	Beaudet Roger L	245	laborer	29	221 "
	M	Kraus Benjamin F	246	engineer	48	here
	N	Kraus Dorothy F †	246	housewife	42	"
	O	Damiani Anna †	247	presser	29	"
	P	Damiani Avery	247	attendant	26	"
	R	Damiani Christine †	247	stitcher	25	"
	S	Damiani Leonido	247	carpenter	62	"
	T	Damiani Louise †	247	bookkeeper	21	"
	U	Damiani Maria †	247	housewife	59	"
	V	Raeder James R	259	architect	65	"

Page	Letter	Full Name	Residence, Jan. 1, 1942	Occupation	Age	Reported Residence, Jan. 1, 1941. Street and Number

Fairmount Avenue—Continued

Page	Letter	Full Name	Residence, Jan. 1, 1942	Occupation	Age	Reported Residence, Jan. 1, 1941. Street and Number
	W	Raeder Susan F—†	259	housewife	62	here
	X	Cafarella Domenic	260	barber	59	"
	Y	Cafarella Dorothy—†	260	housewife	23	"
	Z	Cafarella Ralph	260	machinist	20	"
1619						
	A	Cafarella Rose—†	260	housewife	57	"
	B	Brown Gilbert	265	retired	81	Danvers
	C	Contarino Anthony	265	manager	25	Haverhill
	D	Maurer Gertrude—†	265	housewife	25	here
	E	Maurer Henry	265	electrician	27	"
	F	Mooradian Aaron	265	manager	27	Haverhill
	G	Smith Catherine A—†	265	housekeeper	60	here
	H	Bush Evelyn M—†	268	housewife	51	"
	K	Bush Ralph C	268	attorney	52	"
	L	Noonan James G	268	engineer	32	10 Elven rd
	M	Noonan Lillian J—†	268	housewife	26	10 "
	N	Carr Edward F	268	photographer	24	333 Adams
	O	Carr Margaret G—†	268	housewife	26	Somerville
	P	Beyer Frederick A	272	accountant	52	here
	R	Beyer Frederick A, jr	272	clerk	23	"
	S	Beyer Marie—†	272	housewife	50	"
	T	Beyer Mary T—†	272	"	66	"
	U	Hogardt Frances A—†	272	musician	47	"
	V	Cobb Harrington	280	gardener	60	"
	W	*Cobb Mary E—†	280	housewife	41	"
	X	Geary Donald	280	salesman	28	Dedham
	Y	Graban Carl E	280	student	27	here
	Z	Graban Edith O—†	280	clerk	38	"
1620						
	A	Graban Etta G—†	280	housewife	60	"
	B	Graban Phillip L	280	retired	65	"
	C	Wells Ruth L—†	281	housewife	52	"
	D	Blum Minnie R—†	285	secretary	47	146 Spring
	E	Drake Dorothy C—†	285	teacher	27	here
	F	Drake Harold M	285	patternmaker	50	"
	G	Drake Isabel B—†	285	housewife	48	"
	H	Drake Lucille W—†	285	student	20	"
	K	Drake Sarah P—†	285	nurse	24	"
	L	Rice Alonzo H	292	investigator	46	"
	M	Rice Gladys M—†	292	housewife	40	"
	N	Rice Richard H	292	investigator	20	"

Page	Letter	Full Name	Residence, Jan. 1, 1941	Occupation	Supposed Age	Reported Residence, Jan. 1, 1940. Street and Number.
		Fairmount Avenue—Continued				
	O	Rivkin Bernard M	295	engineer	45	here
	P	Rivkin Ruth L—†	295	housewife	41	"
	R	Stone Andrew L	295	salesman	23	109 Peterboro
	S	Stone Doris E—†	295	housewife	22	109 "
	T	Faden Andrew F	303	salesman	58	here
	U	Faden Barbara—†	303	clerk	25	"
	V	Faden Paul D	303	U S A	23	"
	W	Faden Phillip W	303	painter	28	"
	X	Siebard Herman A	307	accountant	71	"
	Y	Siebard Margaretta M—†	307	housewife	69	"
		Farwell Avenue				
	Z	Moody John H	6	chauffeur	47	here
1621						
	A	Moody Theresa E—†	6	housewife	41	"
	B	Moody Theresa E—†	6	clerk	21	"
	C*	Mercer Hubert H	10	manager	34	"
	D*	Mercer Lily M—†	10	housewife	33	"
		Franklin Terrace				
	E	Beebe Grant R	4	retired	65	here
	F	Beebe Katherine M—†	4	at home	57	"
	G	Beebe Victoria C—†	4	housewife	59	"
	H	Dimmick Andrew D	6	retired	85	"
	K	Dimmick Ethel C—†	6	housewife	48	"
	L	Dimmick Herbert R	6	clerk	47	"
	M	Dimmick Herbert R, jr	6	draftsman	21	"
	N	Keefe Matilda H—†	6	housewife	78	"
	O	Hillier Albert W	12	clerk	52	"
	P	Hillier Leslie J	12	accountant	24	"
	R	Hillier Winifred E—†	12	housewife	48	"
	S	Fellows Alice Y—†	14	teacher	65	"
	T	Lugton Eunice F—†	14	clerk	40	"
	U	Lugton Louis G	14	cabinetmaker	37	"
	V	Rogers Mabel A—†	16	housewife	71	"
	W	Weil Frank T	18	clergyman	50	"
	X	Weil Hazel M—†	18	housewife	37	"

Highland Street

Page	Letter	Full Name	Residence	Occupation	Age	Reported Residence
	Y	Cox George E	38	physician	39	here
	Z	Cox Marian V †	38	housewife	35	"
		1622				
	A	Meagher Henry J	42	restaurateur	34	"
	B	Meagher Mary A †	42	housewife	77	"
	C	Meagher Mary C †	42	clerk	50	"
	D	McGrath David J	46	letter carrier	48	"
	E	McGrath John W	46	retired	81	"
	F	McGrath Mary A †	46	housewife	45	"
	G	Baxter Edward H	47	physician	88	"
	H	Collins Edward J	47	salesman	60	"
	K	Collins Harley H	47	clerk	22	"
	L	Collins Mae G †	47	housewife	45	"
	M	*Wry Walter V	47	electrician	62	12 Sumner
	N	Higgins Doris S †	54	housewife	39	here
	O	Higgins George V	54	carpenter	43	"
	P	Jordan John M	57	machinist	53	"
	R	Jordan Olive M †	57	housewife	45	"
	S	Jordan Robert H	57	machinist	23	"
	T	Whitney Jeannette M †	57	housewife	32	"
	U	Whitney Richard M	57	teacher	29	"
	V	Simonsen Agnes M †	58	housewife	50	"
	W	Simonsen Gordon A	58	clerk	24	"
	X	Simonsen Ludwig	58	chauffeur	52	"
	Y	Fahrenholt George J	58	retired	72	"
	Z	Fahrenholt Gertrude †	58	housewife	65	"
		1623				
	A	Paine Lois M †	58	"	42	"
	B	Paine Walter M	58	auditor	53	"
	C	Gross Frederick	60	fitter	44	"
	D	*Gross Myrtle †	60	housewife	38	"
	E	Potter Anna M †	60	"	43	"
	F	Potter William D	60	student	20	"
	G	Potter William T	60	superintendent	40	"
	H	Radford James E	62	draftsman	81	"
	K	Radford Paul R	62	machinist	78	"
	L	Radford Ruth H †	62	teacher	30	"
	N	Smith Inez A †	65	housekeeper	38	"
	O	Thornton Catherine †	69	at home	78	"
	P	Thornton Johanna F †	69	operator	42	"
	R	Harlow Clara A †	70	housewife	52	"

Page	Letter	Full Name	Residence, Jan. 1, 1941.	Occupation	Supposed Age.	Reported Residence, Jan. 1, 1940. Street and Number.

Highland Street—Continued

Page	Letter	Full Name	Residence, Jan. 1, 1941.	Occupation	Supposed Age.	Reported Residence, Jan. 1, 1940. Street and Number.
	S	Harlow Douglas B	70	salesman	23	here
	T	Mills Sarah S—†	70	bookkeeper	58	"
	U	Bregoli Albert L	73	machinist	30	"
	V	Bregoli Ermelindo	73	gardener	57	"
	W	Bregoli Henry	73	clerk	20	"
	X	McDonald James J	73	"	31	"
	Y	Amuzzini Emma—†	73	housewife	32	9 Fairmount ter
	Z	Amuzzini Joseph	73	bartender	34	9 "
1624						
	A	Keltie Nettie—†	75	housekeeper	65	here
	B	McCarthy Marjorie P—†	75	stenographer	21	"
	C	Byrne Catherine A—†	86	housewife	62	"
	D	Byrne James J	86	jeweler	62	"
	E	Byrne John E	86	chauffeur	28	"
	F	Happnie Catherine M—†	96	stenographer	23	"
	G	Happnie Frances T—†	96	housewife	46	"
	H	Happnie Harry G	96	carpenter	50	"
	K	*McDonald Margaret—†	96	housekeeper	30	"
	L	Bryant Annette L—†	101	technician	22	New York
	M	Bryant Clarence E	101	physician	61	here
	N	Bryant Florence M—†	101	housewife	61	"
	O	Baldwin Harry A	103	machinist	63	"
	P	Baldwin Mary M—†	103	housewife	58	"
	R	Baldwin Natalie A—†	103	clerk	21	"
	S	MacInnis Olive M—†	103	"	31	"
	T	*Cox Alice B—†	104	housekeeper	72	"
	U	Farnham Dorothy M—†	104	clerk	32	"
	V	*Farnham Jennie M—†	104	housewife	61	"
	W	*Farnham John T	104	mechanic	66	"
	X	Farnham Ruth H—†	104	clerk	21	"
	Y	Tolman Everett D	104	salesman	33	"
	Z	Tolman Ora E—†	104	bookkeeper	34	"
1625						
	A	Bowie Malcolm F	109	clerk	43	"
	B	Bowie Marion B—†	109	housewife	31	"
	D	Waldron Annie B—†	112	"	76	"
	E	Waldron Hiram E	112	realtor	84	"
	F	Waldron Marion A—†	112	teacher	47	"
	G	Upham John H	118	proprietor	34	"
	H	Upham Prudence R—†	118	housewife	34	"
	K	McNaught Margaret T—†	126	inspector	58	"

Page	Letter	Full Name	[illegible]	[illegible]	[illegible]	[illegible]

Highland Street—Continued

Page	Letter	Full Name	Residence	Occupation	Age	Reported Residence
	L	McVinney J Isadore	126	gardener	63	here
	M	Tileston Annette—†	134	at home	81	"
	N	Tileston John N	134	salesman	53	"
	O	Tileston Pauline H—†	134	housewife	55	"

Metropolitan Avenue

Page	Letter	Full Name	Residence	Occupation	Age	Reported Residence
	P	Beck Bernard B	847	clerk	25	here
	R	Beck Eleanor F—†	847	stenographer	27	"
	S	Beck Helena—†	847	housewife	50	"
	T	Neuber Clara E—†	848	"	47	"
	U	Neuber Max E	848	engineer	46	"
	V	Scheffler Albin G	848	machinist	58	"
	W	Warren Anna T—†	850	housewife	23	"
	X	Warren Maurice P	850	salesman	37	"
	Y	Gedies Francis C	854	manager	32	7 Hopewell rd
	Z	Gedies Nora S—†	854	housewife	28	7 "
1626						
	A	Taylor Elizabeth—†	854	secretary	23	here
	B	Taylor Georgianna—†	854	housewife	53	"
	C	Taylor Paul D	854	tailor	58	"
	D	McSweeney Eugene S	863	inspector	46	"
	E	McSweeney Jane F—†	863	housewife	42	"
	G	Sanborn George W	900	retired	61	"
	H	Sanborn Lillian G—†	900	housewife	59	"
	K	Topham Albert F	907	student	20	"
	L	Topham Corinne F—†	907	housewife	53	"
	M	Topham Robert A	907	contractor	58	"
	N	Wolf Bessie W—†	908	housewife	58	"
	O	Wolf Charles W	908	attendant	32	"
	P	Wolf John C	908	designer	62	"
	R	Ficicchy Adeline J—†	917	housewife	33	8 Reddy av
	S	Ficicchy James	917	hairdresser	34	8 "
	T	Harris Theresa—†	917	stitcher	23	8 "
	U	Wisbrod Elliot	917	salesman	43	California
	V	Wisbrod Rose—†	917	housewife	27	"
	W	Harlow Louise D—†	920	"	29	here
	X	Harlow William L	920	foreman	30	"
	Y	Scannell John F	921	attorney	60	"
	Z	Scannell Joseph M	921	student	20	"

Page	Letter	Full Name	Residence, Jan. 1, 1941	Occupation	Supposed Age	Reported Residence, Jan. 1, 1940. Street and Number

1627
Metropolitan Avenue—Continued

Page	Letter	Full Name	Residence, Jan. 1, 1941	Occupation	Supposed Age	Reported Residence, Jan. 1, 1940
	A	Scannell Theresa V—†	921	housewife	57	here
	B	Goodwin Edward M	933	auditor	48	"
	C	Goodwin May C—†	933	housewife	48	"
	D	George Mary E—†	934	at home	77	New York
	E	Morton Esther E—†	934	housewife	55	here
	F	Morton Harry E	934	engineer	53	"
	G	Pierce Henry G	935	artist	63	"
	H	Taylor Almira B—†	938	student	21	"
	K	Taylor Arthur B	938	salesman	51	"
	L	Taylor Mildred F—†	938	housewife	24	"
	M	Conroy Nora—†	950	maid	37	"
	N	Peabody Emma L—†	950	housekeeper	63	"
	O	Blank Frieda—†	985	typist	20	"
	P	Low Elias M	985	manager	43	"
	R	*Low Leopoldine—†	985	housewife	50	"
	S	*Low Morris	985	cashier	51	"
	T	McKenna Alma A—†	999	housewife	40	"
	U	McKenna John H	999	physician	47	"
	V	Porter Bernice E—†	999	maid	22	"

Milton Avenue

Page	Letter	Full Name	Residence, Jan. 1, 1941	Occupation	Supposed Age	Reported Residence, Jan. 1, 1940
	W	Harlow Harriet L—†	38	housewife	55	here
	X	Harlow John B	38	student	22	"
	Y	Harlow Richard F	38	"	21	"
	Z	Harlow William B	38	merchant	54	"
1628						
	A	Osborne Charles D	44	painter	34	"
	B	Osborne Frances—†	44	artist	32	"
	C	Osborne Sumner L	44	retired	73	"
	D	Vincent Harold E	45	carpenter	45	"
	E	Vincent Ivy M—†	45	housewife	44	"
	F	Coudry Blanche M—†	45	"	24	"
	G	Coudry Leo N	45	welder	30	"
	H	Barry Anna E—†	47	housewife	38	"
	K	Leonard Agnes M—†	49	"	39	"
	L	Leonard Neil F	49	mechanic	41	"
	M	Clifford Deborah M—†	52	student	20	"
	N	Clifford Helen M—†	52	housewife	54	"
	O	Dias Anne B—†	57	"	29	"

Page	Letter	Full Name	Residence, Jan. 1	Occupation	Age	Reported Residence, Street and Number
	P	Dias John L	57	operator	33	here
	R	Carlson Emil C	57	painter	58	"
	S	Carlson Emily M †	57	housewife	61	"
	T	Bradley Barbara C †	60	executive	27	"
	U	Bradley Harold L	60	merchant	60	193 C
	V	Bradley Helen M †	60	housewife	62	here
	W	Bradley Mary C †	60	clerk	25	"
	X	Hyde George E	60	"	58	"
	Z	Haslam Blanche †	75	at home	77	"
1629						
	A	Stewart Gertrude H †	75	housewife	49	"
	B	Stewart Oswald	75	U S A	23	"
	C	Stewart Oswald W	75	agent	51	"
	D	Stewart Pearson H	75	student	21	"
	E	Albee Lucy D †	79	housewife	32	"
	F	Albee Mina S †	79	"	61	"
	G	Albee Richard S	79	salesman	34	"
	H	Provost Joseph L	79	cook	30	"
	K	Malcolm Gertrude B †	82	housewife	37	"
	L	Malcolm John B	82	secretary	40	"
	M	Daly Alice M †	85	housewife	27	"
	N	Daly Francis J	85	investigator	31	"
	P	Mixer Hattie E †	92	at home	77	"
	R	Perry Edward J	92	draftsman	43	"
	S	Perry Marjorie E †	92	housewife	40	"
	T	Cunningham Frank A	100	builder	50	"
	U	Cunningham Frank A, jr	100	attendant	24	"
	V	Cunningham Mary D †	100	clerk	22	"
	W	Cunningham Rose A †	100	housewife	46	"
	X	Raynes Alfred H	103	clerk	21	"
	Y	Raynes Harriett †	103	housewife	52	"
	Z	Raynes William A	103	clerk	61	"
1630						
	A	Raynes William A, jr	103	agent	25	"
	B	Stoltz John A	108	painter	71	"
	C	Foley Gerald S	111	salesman	44	"
	D	Foley Olivia M †	111	housewife	38	"
	E	Vindetti Adeline L †	111	at home	60	"
	F	Priggen Bettina †	120	housewife	59	"
	G	Priggen George	120	contractor	65	"
	H	Koger Arabelle E †	123	housewife	45	"

Page	Letter	Full Name	Residence, Jan. 1, 1941	Occupation	Supposed Age	Reported Residence, Jan. 1, 1940. Street and Number.

Milton Avenue—Continued

Page	Letter	Full Name	Residence, Jan. 1, 1941	Occupation	Supposed Age	Reported Residence, Jan. 1, 1940. Street and Number.
	K	Koger Vivian O	123	engineer	45	here
	L	Slocum John	125	mechanic	36	"
	M	Slocum Ruth—†	125	housewife	30	"
	N	Kent Ann V—†	127	"	37	"
	O	Kent John J	127	clerk	47	"
	P	Goode Irene M—†	131	housewife	23	Belmont
	R	Goode James J, jr	131	executive	28	169 Metropolitan av
	S	Dunn Helen M—†	135	housewife	37	here
	T	Dunn William J	135	manager	41	"
	U	Staples Nellie E—†	136	housewife	61	"
	V	Staples Sherwin O	136	surgeon	34	"
	W	Dunn F Carroll	143	salesman	39	"
	X	Dunn Vivian—†	143	housewife	38	"
	Y	Coy Dorothy—†	149	"	45	"
	Z	Coy Lee F	149	dentist	49	"
1631						
	A	Freeman Margaret—†	165	housewife	58	"

Mount Pleasant Street

Page	Letter	Full Name	Residence, Jan. 1, 1941	Occupation	Supposed Age	Reported Residence, Jan. 1, 1940. Street and Number.
	B	Mason Ethel K—†	6	housewife	46	here
	C	Mason Frank A	6	engineer	47	"
	D	Countway Alden	8	artist	60	"
	E	Countway Nella—†	8	housewife	54	"
	F	Kraus Victor	8	machinist	46	"
	G	Cary Anna M—†	9	housewife	49	"
	H	Cary Ernest W	9	mechanic	50	"
	K	Cary Seth A	9	fireman	24	"
	L	Norris Clarence G	10	retired	76	"
	M	Norris Dorothy H—†	10	teacher	34	"
	N	Norris Grace H—†	10	housewife	72	"
	O	Stahl Willine C—†	10	"	41	"
	P	Sutherland Alexander K	11	mechanic	39	"
	R	Sutherland Eileen I—†	11	musician	32	"
	S	Sutherland Henrietta—†	11	housewife	69	"
	T	McIntosh Bessie—†	13	"	58	"
	U	McIntosh Thomas	13	chauffeur	54	"
	V	McIntosh Thomas J	13	accountant	22	"
	W	Ferreira Irene—†	15	housewife	23	"
	X	Ferreira Louis	15	painter	39	"
	Y	Amatucci Carlo	15	operator	40	"

Page	Letter	Full Name	Residence, Jan. 1, 1941	Occupation	Reported Age	Reported Residence, Jan. 1, 1940. Street and Number

Mount Pleasant Street—Continued

Page	Letter	Full Name	Residence, Jan. 1, 1941	Occupation	Reported Age	Reported Residence, Jan. 1, 1940. Street and Number
	Z	Amatucci Regina R †	15	housewife	35	here
1632						
	A	Quinn Emmett T	15	pinboy	32	"
	B	Quinn John P	15	machinist	77	"
	C	Quinn Mary †	15	housewife	68	"
	D	Quimby Mae B †	16	teacher	51	"
	E	Preston Caroline—†	18	housewife	87	"
	F	Walker Elizabeth P—†	18	"	51	"
	G	Walker Roger T	18	proofreader	40	"
	H	Savages Evelyn J—†	23	bookkeeper	34	"
	K	Savage Joseph V	23	accountant	32	"

New Bedford Street

Page	Letter	Full Name	Residence, Jan. 1, 1941	Occupation	Reported Age	Reported Residence, Jan. 1, 1940. Street and Number
	L	Edmonstone Charlotte S—†	14	housewife	48	here
	M	Edmonstone William M	14	teacher	50	"
	N	Leonard Mabel L—†	20	housewife	62	"
	O	Leonard Merton S	20	engineer	62	"
	P	Buckley Frank M	26	manager	43	"
	R	Buckley Sadie B—†	26	housewife	37	"
	S	Hughes Helen J—†	29	"	32	"
	T	Hughes William L	29	teacher	45	"
	U	Hughes Christopher F	32	inspector	46	"
	V	Hughes Marguerite L—†	32	housewife	41	"
	W	Bryan Dorothy F—†	36	nurse	32	"
	X	Coles Grace M—†	36	housewife	34	"
	Y	Coles Herbert B	36	mechanic	36	"

Norris Road

Page	Letter	Full Name	Residence, Jan. 1, 1941	Occupation	Reported Age	Reported Residence, Jan. 1, 1940. Street and Number
	Z	Ward Edith S—†	19	housewife	43	here
1633						
	A	Ward Roland S, jr	19	salesman	43	"

Norway Park

Page	Letter	Full Name	Residence, Jan. 1, 1941	Occupation	Reported Age	Reported Residence, Jan. 1, 1940. Street and Number
	B	Gustafson Ethel P—†	20	housewife	47	here
	C	Gustafson Herbert C	20	printer	51	"
	D	Proctor Elsie M—†	21	secretary	50	"
	E	Proctor Joseph	21	chauffeur	78	"
	F	Jennings Alma—†	21	student	21	"

Page	Letter	Full Name	Residence, Jan. 1, 1941	Occupation	Supposed Age	Reported Residence, Jan. 1, 1940. Street and Number.

Norway Park—Continued

Page	Letter	Full Name	Residence, Jan. 1, 1941	Occupation	Supposed Age	Reported Residence, Jan. 1, 1940. Street and Number.
	G	Jennings Avis †	24	housewife	23	here
	H	Jennings Crawford E	24	salesman	51	"
	K	Jennings Hope †	24	teacher	25	"
	L	Jennings Ruth H †	24	housewife	51	"
	M	Mason Miriam S †	27	housekeeper	40	"
	N	Stephan Addie S †	27	"	66	"
	O	Coburn Joseph E	30	conductor	53	"
	P	Coburn Lois †	30	housekeeper	23	"
	R	Flaherty Frank J	31	supervisor	48	"
	S	Flaherty Michael E	31	retired	38	"
	T	Flaherty Susan M †	31	housewife	42	"
	U	Hvoslef Selma L †	35	"	43	"
	V	Hvoslef Sven J	35	accountant	43	"
	W	Martin Dora F †	42	housewife	47	"
	X	Martin Weldon D	42	agent	47	"
	Y	Burke Bernard J	46	proprietor	54	"
	Z	Burke Theresa M †	46	housewife	47	"

1634 Pleasant Street

Page	Letter	Full Name	Residence, Jan. 1, 1941	Occupation	Supposed Age	Reported Residence, Jan. 1, 1940. Street and Number.
1634	A	Meldon Bertha H †	15	housewife	44	here
	B	Meldon John F	15	collector	50	"
	C	Meldon John F, jr	15	draftsman	22	"
	D	Meldon Richard W	15	salesman	21	"
	E	Esterbrook Bruce	17	clerk	27	"
	F	Esterbrook Elizabeth †	17	housewife	65	"
	G	Lyle Margaret †	17	"	60	"
	H	Lyle Robert	17	laborer	58	"
	K	Foster Marion L †	17	clerk	59	"
	L	Newcomb Charles W	27	draftsman	40	"
	M	Newcomb Ethel L †	27	housewife	40	"
	N	Petrie Anna L †	31	"	63	"
	O	Petrie Natalie C †	31	secretary	34	"
	P	Petrie Warren W	31	teacher	68	"
	R	Ellis Winifred L †	32	waitress	27	"
	S	Glover Marion E †	32	"	23	"
	T	Robertson Mary T †	32	housekeeper	70	"
	U	Coyne Margaret †	33	at home	70	55 Austin
	V	Sullivan Frank P	33	engineer	48	55 "
	W	Sullivan Michael	33	"	35	55 "
	X	Sullivan Sarah J †	33	housewife	47	55 "

Page	Letter	Full Name	Residence, Jan. 1, 1941	Occupation	Supposed Age	Reported Residence, Jan. 1, 1940, Street and Number

Pleasant Street—Continued

Page	Letter	Full Name	Residence, Jan. 1, 1941	Occupation	Supposed Age	Reported Residence, Jan. 1, 1940
	Y	Udden Elsa E—†	34	housewife	47	here
	Z	Udden John J	34	janitor	47	"
1635						
	A	Harrison Marie C—†	34	housewife	54	"
	B	Harrison Raymond C	34	operator	53	"
	C	Harrison Rosalie—†	34	clerk	22	"
	D	Carle Emma S—†	35	at home	78	"
	E	Claff Howard F	35	agent	49	"
	F	Claff Miriam—†	35	technician	21	"
	G	Claff Vera L—†	35	housewife	50	"
	H	Burtz Cecelia—†	36	maid	63	"
	K	Warren Cedric E	36	clerk	46	"
	L	Warren Georgia M—†	36	housewife	76	"
	M	Warren Helen B—†	36	secretary	53	"
	N	Allen George W	38	engineer	63	"
	O	Allen Lena B—†	38	housewife	66	"
	R	Day Clara M—†	41	"	65	"
	P	Day Clara W—†	41	secretary	35	"
	S	Day John W	41	chauffeur	67	"
	T	Dunn Charles T	42	realtor	55	"
	U	Dunn Margaret E—†	42	housewife	59	"
	V	Houston David J	42	realtor	31	"

Pond Street

Page	Letter	Full Name	Residence, Jan. 1, 1941	Occupation	Supposed Age	Reported Residence, Jan. 1, 1940
	X	Buyse Charles R	12	manager	32	here
	Y	Buyse Norma E—†	12	housewife	25	"
	Z	Curtis Roger W	12	clerk	30	"
1636						
	A	Curtis Winifred J—†	12	housewife	21	"
	B	*Copeland Emily R—†	14	nurse	39	"
	C	McPhee Bertha A—†	16	housewife	52	"
	D	McPhee Bertha E—†	16	typist	25	"
	E	McPhee George W	16	foreman	55	"
	F	Sewell Charles R	18–20	machinist	49	"
	G	Sewell Charles R, jr	18–20	clerk	23	"
	H	Sewell Hattie G—†	18–20	housewife	46	"
	K	Smith John B	18–20	machinist	58	"
	L	Smith Katherine R—†	18–20	housewife	56	"
	M	Smith Virginia M—†	18–20	stenographer	20	"
	N	McGrath Francis P	22	retired	59	"

Page	Letter	Full Name	Residence, Jan. 1, 1941	Occupation	Supposed Age	Reported Residence, Jan. 1, 1940. Street and Number

Pond Street—Continued

Page	Letter	Full Name	Residence	Occupation	Age	Reported Residence
	O	McGrath Frederick P	22	executive	57	here
	P	McGrath Margaret E—†	22	housewife	44	"
	R	Baer Charlotte H—†	24	"	37	59 Summer
	S	Baer Henry	24	polisher	43	59 "
	T	Cremin Gerald L	26	B F D	39	here
	U	Cremin Mary A—†	26	housewife	38	"
	V	Cathcart Harold M	38	optician	23	"
	W	Hewitt Amy S—†	38	housewife	40	"
	X	Hewitt Ellsworth	38	ironworker	41	"
	Y	*Nixon Lawrence	38	machinist	34	Needham
	Z	Smith Charles M	38	optometrist	73	here
1637						
	A	Smith Lucy A—†	38	housewife	63	"
	B	Parker Edna—†	38	"	29	"
	C	Parker Edwin	38	painter	34	"
	D	Henderson Ann—†	40	houseworker	23	"
	E	Henderson Annie—†	40	housewife	50	"
	F	Henderson Roy B	40	chauffeur	26	"
	G	Henderson Roy S	40	contractor	49	"
	H	Henderson Ruth—†	40	clerk	26	"
	K	Boggan Florence G—†	40	housewife	43	"
	L	Boggan William J	40	custodian	44	"

Prospect Street

Page	Letter	Full Name	Residence	Occupation	Age	Reported Residence
	M	Katzman Frederick G	11	attorney	65	here
	N	Finn Paul E	20	salesman	29	"
	O	Finn Theresa G—†	20	housewife	23	"
	R	Barbato Eugene J	rear 27	chauffeur	48	"
	S	Barbato Helen G—†	" 27	housewife	38	"
	T	Barbato John C	" 27	carpenter	22	"
	U	Barbato Phyllis R—†	" 27	secretary	21	"
	V	Goodrich Lila A—†	31	"	52	"
	W	Webber Hattie P—†	31	housekeeper	82	"
	X	Battis Annie V—†	33	housewife	42	"
	Y	Battis Karl W	33	accountant	45	"
	Z	Cristofori Amelia A—†	37	nurse	23	"
1638						
	A	Cristofori Guy	37	machinist	56	"
	B	Cristofori Hildegarde I—†	37	accountant	31	"
	C	Cristofori Mary A—†	37	fitter	27	"

Page.	Letter.	Full Name.	Residence, April 1	Occupation.	Supposed Age.	Reported Residence, April 1, Street and Number.
		Prospect Street—Continued				
	D	Corrigan John P	45	clerk	22	here
	E	Corrigan Mary H—†	45	housewife	61	"
	F	Corrigan Patrick P	45	chauffeur	62	"
	G	Cox Josephine B—†	60	at home	70	"
	H	Cox Thomas G	60	salesman	44	"
	K	Norling Alan M	60	"	30	"
	L	Norling Josephine B—†	60	housewife	32	"
		Reservoir Street				
	M	Stanley Helen M—†	9	housewife	47	here
	N	Stanley Howard P	9	salesman	49	"
	O	*Cutler Maria J—†	15	housewife	60	"
	P	Cutler Oscar H	15	clerk	30	"
	R	Cutler William H	15	chauffeur	62	"
	S	*Lee Martha—†	15	at home	66	"
	T	Wilson Harold M	30	clerk	45	"
	U	Wilson Jessie S—†	30	housewife	41	"
		Spring Hill Road				
	V	Morse Clementine E—†	9	at home	85	22 Albion
	W	Morse Ivory H	9	contractor	63	22 "
	X	Morse Sarah E—†	9	housewife	61	22 "
	Y	Morse Sarah L—†	9	secretary	20	22 "
	Z	Peterson Axel R	12	guard	63	here
1639						
	Z	Peterson Margaret R—†	12	housewife	54	"
	A	Peterson Stanley R	12	student	22	"
	B	Ford Amy S—†	19	housewife	52	"
	C	Ford Elliott T	19	clerk	53	"
	D	Ford Katherine S—†	19	at home	20	"
	E	Shreve Alfred V	19	retired	82	"
	F	Wright Marjorie F—†	19	housewife	24	"
	G	Hanson Jean M—†	22	"	53	"
	H	Hanson John A	22	agent	58	"
	K	Innes Adelaide M—†	24	clerk	20	"
	L	Innes Frederick R	24	student	23	"
	M	Innes James E	24	designer	53	"
	N	Innes Margaret L—†	24	housewife	53	"
	O	Innes Nancy C—†	24	clerk	21	"

Page	Letter	Full Name	Residence, Jan. 1, 1941	Occupation	Supposed Age	Reported Residence, Jan. 1, 1940. Street and Number.

Summit Street

Page	Letter	Full Name	Residence, Jan. 1, 1941	Occupation	Supposed Age	Reported Residence, Jan. 1, 1940. Street and Number.
	R	Rogers Augustine T	11	physician	37	here
	S	Rogers M Elizabeth †	11	housewife	37	"
	T	Kirby Louise H †	15	"	35	364 Arborway
	U	Kirby William J	15	manager	42	364 "
	V	Bergstrom Carl H	19	student	24	here
	W	Bergstrom Carl O	19	engineer	57	"
	X	Bergstrom Ruth F—†	19	housewife	53	"
	Y	Lyons Agnes †	23	"	45	Hingham
	Z	Lyons Thomas A	23	realtor	48	"
1640						
	A	Little Catherine G—†	28	housewife	43	here
	B	Little John F	28	inspector	45	"
	C	Stoltz Anna A †	33	housewife	47	"
	D	Stoltz Harold I	33	engineer	48	"
	E	Svendsen Arthur E	36	salesman	34	"
	F	Svendsen Henrietta—†	36	housewife	35	"
	G	Darville Elizabeth A—†	36	"	66	"
	H	Darville Elsie E—†	36	waitress	27	"
	K	Witherow Margaret J—†	36	at home	75	"
	L	Powell Edward J	42	cashier	23	10 Osceola
	M	Powell Pauline †	42	housewife	23	10 "
	N	Powell Leonard A	42	draftsman	50	here
	O	Powell Mabel S †	42	housewife	48	"
	P	Duffy Charles E	46	teacher	38	"
	R	Duffy Grace M †	46	housewife	36	"
	S	McDonald John D	50	installer	44	"
	T	McDonald Mary X—†	50	housewife	45	"
	U	Lynch Helena M—†	53	"	31	"
	V	Lynch John J	53	cleaner	34	"
	W	Gendron Emma A—†	54	housewife	41	"
	X	Gendron Philias A	54	salesman	38	"
	Y	Kelley Joseph F	55	watchman	24	666 Metropolitan av
	Z	Kelley Marie L †	55	housewife	26	Brookline
1641						
	A	Batho Frances H †	58	clerk	20	here
	B	Batho George H	58	"	56	"
	C	Batho Gertrude H †	58	housewife	56	"
	D	Batho Jeanne M †	58	teacher	21	"
	E	Batho William	58	retired	85	"
	F	Fogg S Elizabeth †	62	housekeeper	84	"
	G	Hull Lelia C †	62	at home	82	"

Page	Letter	Full Name	Residence, Jan. 1, 1941	Occupation	Reported Age	Reported Residence, Jan. 1, 1940. Street and Number

Summit Street Continued

Page	Letter	Full Name	Residence, Jan. 1, 1941	Occupation	Reported Age	Reported Residence, Jan. 1, 1940. Street and Number
	H	Merritt Beatrice L †	62	clerk	26	here
	K	Merritt Helen F †	62	housewife	51	"
	L	Morgan Douglas H	62	installer	23	N Hampshire
	M	Martin Evelyn E †	63	teacher	36	here
	N	Martin Mary E †	63	housewife	69	"
	O	Sullivan John J	64	gardener	54	"
	P	Sullivan John J, jr	64	musician	21	"
	R	Sullivan Katherine M †	64	housewife	52	"
	S	Gunn Hannah A †	69	"	77	"
	T	Gunn John A	69	retired	83	"
	U	Smith Clarence H	69	printer	45	"
	V	Smith Helen G †	69	housewife	45	"
	W	Taaffe Frank G	73	manager	31	"
	X	Taaffe Mary A †	73	housewife	30	"
	Y	Cross Carrie M †	76	"	64	"
	Z	Cross Harold F	76	artist	33	"
1642						
	A	Greaney Gertrude A †	76	housewife	39	"
	B	Greaney John F	76	shipfitter	43	"
	D	Crosson Margaret A †	77-79	housekeeper	56	"
	E	Grundy John J	77-79	machinist	50	Vermont
	F	Reed Frances C †	79	operator	24	here
	G	Reed Henry A	77-79	"	20	"
	H	*Neszery Ann †	77-79	housewife	24	"
	K	Neszery Earl E	77-79	operator	25	"
	L	Gardner Alexander	81	instructor	32	"
	M	Gardner Elizabeth A †	81	housewife	28	"
	N	Eriksen Ethel E †	81	"	43	"
	O	Eriksen Oscar	81	supervisor	47	"
	P	Eriksen Phyllis A †	81	librarian	20	"
	R	Eriksen Warren O	81	clerk	21	"
	S	O'Connor Cornelius	113	butler	50	"
	T	O'Connor Nora †	113	housewife	50	"
	U	Dahl Esther N †	118	"	43	"
	V	Dahl Gustave E	118	machinist	43	"
	W	O'Donnell Mary †	118	housekeeper	42	"
	X	Durfee Mildred L †	119	housewife	30	"
	Y	Durfee Norman E	119	mechanic	39	"
1643						
	A	Bodfish Margaret D †	128	secretary	42	"
	B	Bodfish Robert L	128	investigator	44	"

Page	Letter	Full Name	Residence Jan. 1, 1941	Occupation	Supposed Age	Reported Residence, Jan. 1, 1940. Street and Number.

Summit Street—Continued

Page	Letter	Full Name	Residence	Occupation	Age	Reported Residence
	C	Deagle Margaret—†	128	housewife	69	here
	D	Deagle Philip J	128	retired	79	"
	E	Labute Andrew	132	carpenter	26	"
	F	Labute Janet—†	132	housewife	24	"
	G	Card Albert B	132	realtor	59	245 Fairmount av
	H	*Card Emma M—†	132	housewife	47	245 "

Vose Avenue

Page	Letter	Full Name	Residence	Occupation	Age	Reported Residence
	K	Cross Chester D	7	carpenter	66	here
	L	Cross Mary A—†	7	housewife	60	"
	M	Coupe Elizabeth—†	7	clerk	61	"
	N	Coupe Ethel M—†	7	"	44	"
	O	Coupe Martha W—†	7	"	54	"
	P	Waldron Ralph L	14	salesman	62	"
	R	Waldron Samuel G	14	writer	23	"
	S	Thomson James M	17	examiner	45	"
	T	Thomson Mary I—†	17	housewife	41	"
	U	Jewett Edward P	18	optometrist	60	"
	V	Jewett Edward P, jr	18	clerk	21	"
	W	Jewett Ethel G—†	18	housewife	52	"
	X	Appleford Ella—†	23	"	48	"
	Y	Welliver Charles M	25	mechanic	35	"
	Z	Welliver Marion L—†	25	housewife	34	"
1644						
	A	Oldham Alice M—†	27	"	56	"
	B	Oldham Barbara B—†	27	secretary	27	"
	C	Oldham Ellen D—†	27	"	20	"
	D	Cox Catherine—†	30	clerk	62	"
	E	Hancock Alice H—†	30	housewife	59	"
	F	Holmes Fanny A—†	30	clerk	49	"
	G	Welliver Rose I—†	31	housewife	53	"
	H	Welliver Samuel	31	retired	74	"
	K	Dansie Christina—†	33	housewife	33	"
	L	Dansie Thomas C	33	chemist	34	"
	M	Galway James	33	machinist	29	"
	N	Galway Margaret J—†	33	housewife	25	"
	O	*Zambella Peter	33	retired	66	"
	P	Floyd Helene E—†	34	housewife	27	3 Pond
	R	Floyd Robert E	34	buffer	31	3 "
	S	McDonough Joseph	34	laborer	32	here

Page	Letter	Full Name	Residence, Jan. 1, 1941	Occupation	Reputed Age	Reported Residence, Jan. 1, 1940, Street and Number

Vose Avenue—Continued

Page	Letter	Full Name	Residence, Jan. 1, 1941	Occupation	Reputed Age	Reported Residence, Jan. 1, 1940, Street and Number
	T	McDonough Mary M †	34	housewife	30	here
	U	McDonough Michael	34	laborer	39	"
	V	Cox Catherine A †	rear 34	housewife	60	"
	W	Cox James J	" 34	gardener	65	"
	X	Gage Charles R	40	manager	27	"
	Y	Gage Olive A †	40	housewife	58	"
	Z	Johnson Alma J †	40	"	53	"
1645						
	A	Johnson Sven I	40	contractor	63	"

Warren Avenue

Page	Letter	Full Name	Residence, Jan. 1, 1941	Occupation	Reputed Age	Reported Residence, Jan. 1, 1940, Street and Number
	B	Tiews Charles J	5	painter	35	here
	C	Tiews Lilla V—†	5	housewife	35	"
	D	Viles Alice M—†	5	clerk	53	"
	E	Fox Ethel M—†	6	housewife	34	"
	F	Fox Thomas J	6	painter	50	"
	G	Lang Gladys V—†	21	housewife	41	186 Fairmount
	H*	Untz Dorothy M—†	35	"	41	182 "
	K	Untz George J	35	machinist	39	182 "
	L	Peterson Fannie I—†	35	housewife	41	here
	M	Peterson Walter L	35	foreman	42	"
	N	Scruton George S	37	waiter	44	41 Warren av
	O	Scruton Irene L—†	37	housewife	41	41 "
	P	Allen Alfred H	37	clerk	59	here
	R	Allen Sadie B—†	37	housewife	58	"
	S	Untz Anna E—†	39	"	40	"
	T	Untz Oswald S	39	manager	44	"
	U	Philips James B	39	repairman	25	"
	V	Philips Mary S—†	39	housewife	48	"
	W	Philips Richard P	39	chauffeur	50	"
	X	Margeson Clarence B	40	baker	24	"
	Y	Margeson Harold A	40	operator	21	"
	Z*	Margeson Seraphine—†	40	housewife	73	"
1646						
	A	Forbes Alice I—†	40	"	40	9 Cottage pl
	B	Forbes Clark J	40	rigger	42	9 "
	D	Orrock Archibald	41	driller	40	1000 River
	E	Orrock Polly—†	41	housewife	32	1000 "
	F	Hunt Bessie K—†	41	"	16	here
	G	Hunt James J	41	instructor	20	"

Page	Letter	Full Name	Residence, Jan. 1, 1941	Occupation	Supposed Age	Reported Residence, Jan. 1, 1940. Street and Number

Warren Avenue Continued

Page	Letter	Full Name	Residence, Jan. 1, 1941	Occupation	Supposed Age	Reported Residence, Jan. 1, 1940. Street and Number
	H	Barton Joseph H	44	electrician	65	here
	K	Barton Mary A †	44	housewife	63	"
	L	*Hackett Patrick J	44	carpenter	60	"
	M	Smalley Gerald P	44	clerk	21	"
	N	Toner Lena J †	44	housewife	54	"
	O	Robbins Sylvia S †	44	secretary	34	"
	P	Shepherd Clara L †	44	housewife	64	"
	R	Leadbetter Marion G †	44	"	42	"
	S	Leadbetter Stanley B	44	accountant	44	"
	T	Crosby Edith †	46	housewife	58	"
	U	Crosby Fred	46	superintendent	64	"
	V	Crosby Phyllis E †	46	secretary	23	"
	W	Hartford Lois M †	47	student	20	"
	X	Hartford Lois S †	47	housewife	85	"
	Y	Hartford Mylan O	47	musician	23	"
	Z	Hartford Olive L †	47	housewife	51	"
1647						
	A	Hartford Orville E	47	accountant	52	"
	B	Hamilton Harry R	47	steamfitter	52	"
	C	Hamilton Winifred †	47	housewife	41	"
	G	Cannell Annie M †	56	"	59	33 Charles
	H	Cannell Cecil R	56	stationer	58	33 "
	K	Cannell Francis R	56	shipper	25	33 "
	L	Ahearn Alice E †	56	housekeeper	60	here
	M	Ahearn James A	56	watchman	53	"
	N	Ahearn Patrick F	56	laborer	51	"
	P	Hoyt Norman B	60	manager	39	"
	R	Hoyt Thelma A †	60	housewife	39	"
	S	Clarke Maude E †	60	"	47	"
	T	Clarke Theodore	60	cutter	53	"
	U	*Rose Elizabeth S †	60	housewife	41	"
	V	Rose Henry	60	machinist	41	"
	W	Rose James	60	clerk	39	"
	X	Burns Thomas F, jr	70	student	20	Maine
	Y	Massey Edward M	70	mechanic	44	962 Hyde Park av
	Z	Massey Grace E †	70	housewife	42	962 "
1648						
	A	Bowley Ella A †	70	"	66	here
	B	Bowley Ernest F	70	toolmaker	68	"
	C	Bowley Lincoln E	70	carpenter	39	"
	D	Bowley Raymond F	70	teacher	43	"

Page.	Letter.	Full Name	Residence, Jan. 1, 1941	Occupation	Age	Reported Residence, Jan. 1, 1940. Street and Number

Warren Avenue Continued

Page.	Letter.	Full Name	Residence	Occupation	Age	Reported Residence
	E	Bowley Ruth T †	70	saleswoman	35	here
	G	Hanscom Elmer I	94	conductor	59	"
	H	Hanscom Elmer L	94	laborer	25	"
	K	Hanscom Isabelle D †	94	housewife	54	"
	L	Martin Annie B †	94	housekeeper	75	"
	M	Lutz Mae †	98	housewife	47	"
	N	Lutz Ralph E	98	watchmaker	48	"
	O	Lutz Robert E	98	laborer	22	"
	P	Sherlock Barbara N †	101	bookkeeper	21	"
	R	Sherlock Eloise †	101	housewife	46	"
	S	Sherlock Walter F	101	painter	49	"
	T	Vinton Frank J	102	investigator	54	"
	U	Vinton Lillian M †	102	housewife	60	"
	V	Hill James L	105	clerk	30	"
	W	Hill Kenneth L	105	gardener	26	"
	X	Hill Marguerite L †	105	teacher	33	"
	Y	Hill Mary J †	105	housewife	70	"
	Z	Hill William F	105	retired	77	"
1649						
	A	Cashman Edna M †	105	housewife	22	"
	B	Cashman Frank W	105	inspector	29	"
	C	Flaherty Joseph F	124	bookkeeper	35	"
	D	Flaherty Mildred E †	124	housewife	35	"
	E	Carey Florence E †	136	"	53	"
	F	Carey Thomas J	136	salesman	59	"
	G	Andelman Bernard	140	counterman	31	"
	H	Andelman Edward	140	"	24	"
	K	Andelman Max	140	"	55	"
	L	Andelman Rose †	140	housewife	54	"
	M	Carroll Gerald	144	machinist	22	"
	N	Carroll Grace M †	144	housewife	45	"
	O	Carroll Helen L †	144	stenographer	21	"
	P	Carroll Jeremiah C	144	engineer	47	"

Water Street

Page.	Letter.	Full Name	Residence	Occupation	Age	Reported Residence
	U	Allen Paul	18	machinist	45	here
	V	Boudreau William	18	"	50	"
	W	Sreenan Cecelia †	18	stenographer	39	"
	X	Sreenan Margaret †	18	housekeeper	44	"
	Y	Julian Amy †	20	housewife	43	"

Page	Letter	FULL NAME	Residence, Jan. 1, 1941	Occupation	Supposed Age	Reported Residence, Jan. 1, 1940. Street and Number.

Water Street Continued

Page	Letter	FULL NAME	Residence, Jan. 1, 1941	Occupation	Supposed Age	Reported Residence, Jan. 1, 1940. Street and Number.
	Z	Julian George H	20	foreman	43	here
1650						
	A	Julian Sarah A †	20	at home	79	"
	B	Reed Christopher	22	machinist	52	"
	C	Reed Margaret E †	22	housewife	51	"
	D	Reed Mildred J †	22	bookkeeper	22	"
	E	Reed Randall C	22	clerk	27	109 Arlington
	F	Reed Ruth G †	22	housewife	27	109 "
	G	*Shea Catherine †	24	"	71	here
	H	Shea John W	24	clerk	36	"
	K	Shea Mary E †	24	secretary	33	"
	L	Wood Evelyn M †	26	bookkeeper	22	"
	M	Wood Ida L †	26	housewife	51	"
	N	Wood William H	26	carpenter	64	"
	O	Connolly John J	28	electrician	28	"
	P	Connolly Martin P	28	laborer	22	"
	R	Connolly Michael	28	freighthandler	57	"
	S	Connolly Stephen P	28	laborer	53	"
	T	Connolly Stephen V	28	freighthandler	25	"
	U	Landy Coleman	28	laborer	40	"

Williams Avenue

Page	Letter	FULL NAME	Residence, Jan. 1, 1941	Occupation	Supposed Age	Reported Residence, Jan. 1, 1940. Street and Number.
	V	Callahn Richard R	10	laborer	28	198 Dana av
	W	Cleary Joseph F	10	"	65	198 "
	X	Cleary Mary E †	10	housewife	48	198 "
	Y	Iverson George G	10	contractor	49	here
	Z	Iverson George G, jr	10	"	20	"
1651						
	A	Iverson Hazel D †	10	housewife	45	"
	B	McIntyre Doris B †	10	teacher	22	"
	C	McIntyre William	10	clerk	23	53 Water
	D	Luce Frank H	12	salesman	56	here
	E	Luce Marion E †	12	housewife	56	"
	F	O'Shea Daniel J	12	cooper	27	"
	G	O'Shea Florance	12	chauffeur	55	"
	H	O'Shea Florence L †	12	teacher	22	"
	K	O'Shea Hannah †	12	housewife	54	"
	L	O'Shea James F	12	clerk	28	"
	M	O'Shea Marie K †	12	bookkeeper	25	"
	N	O'Shea Patrick F	12	operator	23	"

Williams Avenue—Continued

Page	Letter	Full Name	Residence	Occupation	Age	Reported Residence
	O	Delaney Dennis P	14	laborer	57	here
	P	Ford Ellen †	14	housewife	76	"
	R	Ford Thomas	14	retired	78	"
	S	Scherber Eben	16	lithographer	45	"
	T	Scherber Evelyn †	16	clerk	24	"
	U	Scherber Rose †	16	housewife	30	"
	V	Scherber Ruth †	16	at home	23	"
	W	*Olson Belinda M †	18	stitcher	55	"
	X	Olson John W	18	florist	25	"
	Y	*Lavangie Edla D †	20	housewife	50	"
	Z	Lavangie William H	20	floorlayer	64	"
1652						
	A	Cregg Ellen A †	20	housewife	34	"
	B	Cregg John F	20	papermaker	39	"
	C	Pritchard Thomas	20	engineer	70	"
	D	Fox Francis J	22	machinist	22	"
	E	Fox Julia C †	22	housewife	54	"
	F	Fox Mary J †	22	secretary	25	"
	G	Secher Edward M	26	bookkeeper	27	"
	H	Secher Irma W †	26	housewife	50	"
	K	Secher Lillian B †	26	"	23	"
	L	Secher Michael M	26	salesman	53	"
	M	Pulster Irving	26	plater	22	Westwood
	N	Gaumont Alphonse	30	millwright	58	here
	O	Gaumont Alphonse	30	orderly	31	"
	P	Gaumont Eli	30	clerk	21	"
	R	Gaumont Elizabeth †	30	housewife	49	"
	S	Gaumont Raymond	30	upholsterer	29	New York
	T	Gaumont Rita †	30	clerk	24	here
	U	Davis Earl L	32	farmhand	29	"
	V	Davis Elizabeth J †	32	housewife	33	"
	W	Comeau Evelyn †	32	"	36	"
	X	Comeau Leon	32	glassworker	41	"
	Y	Rockwood George	32	watchman	32	"
	Z	Rockwood Margaret R †	32	housewife	30	"
1653						
	A	Bullard Lucy B †	36	housekeeper	73	"
	B	*Skaanning Anna M †	80	housewife	49	"
	C	*Skaanning Max	80	bricklayer	48	"
	D	MacKenzie Myrtle F †	80	housewife	37	"
	E	MacKenzie Samuel	80	welder	43	"

Page	Letter	Full Name	Residence, Jan. 1, 1941	Occupation	Supposed Age	Reported Residence, Jan. 1, 1940. Street and Number

Williams Avenue—Continued

Page	Letter	Full Name	Residence, Jan. 1, 1941	Occupation	Supposed Age	Reported Residence, Jan. 1, 1940. Street and Number
	F	*Ratcliffe Margaret †	82	housewife	49	71 Sunnyside
	G	*Ratcliffe William	82	machinist	49	71 "
	H	Robinson Elizabeth R †	82	housewife	37	here
	K	Robinson Joseph S	82	writer	37	"
	L	Wilson Robert M, jr	84–86	machinist	30	9 Blanvon rd
	M	Wilson Shirley S †	84–86	housewife	30	9 "
	N	Sears Mary A †	84–86	"	30	Dedham
	O	Sears Ralph C	84–86	gardener	36	"
	P	Fopiano Henry P	88–90	clerk	34	here
	R	Gardella Natalina †	88–90	at home	91	"
	S	Landers Charles W	88–90	clerk	35	"
	T	Landers Natalie J †	88–90	housewife	35	"
	U	Strid Edna †	88–90	"	39	"
	V	Strid Henning H	88–90	welder	41	"
	W	Sweeney Allen F	100	bookkeeper	23	"
	X	Sweeney Harold R	100	mortician	45	"
	Y	Sweeney Katherine L †	100	student	21	"
	Z	Sweeney Mary J †	100	housewife	45	"
1654						
	A	Donahue Alice M †	110	housewife	51	"
	B	Donahue Frank J	110	attorney	59	"
	C	Donahue Frank J, jr	110	clerk	28	"

Ward 18—Precinct 17

CITY OF BOSTON

LIST OF RESIDENTS
20 YEARS OF AGE AND OVER

(NON-CITIZENS INDICATED BY ASTERISK)
(FEMALES INDICATED BY DAGGER)

AS OF

JANUARY 1, 1941

CITY OF BOSTON PRINTING DEPARTMENT

Page	Letter	Full Name	Residence Jan 1, 1941	Occupation	Supposed Age	Reported Residence, Jan 1, 1940. Street and Number.
1700						

Bridge Street

Page	Letter	Full Name	Residence	Occupation	Age	Reported Residence
	A	Tuffo James	43	clerk	23	here
	B	Tuffo Joseph	43	carpenter	22	"

Brush Hill Terrace

Page	Letter	Full Name	Residence	Occupation	Age	Reported Residence
	C	Cunningham Joseph M	5	merchant	32	here
	D	Cunningham Mildred F †	5	housewife	28	"
	E	Morley John F	16	attorney	30	"
	F	Morley Mary E †	16	housewife	28	"
	G	Tintle David F	20	chauffeur	26	"
	H	Tintle Helen T †	20	housewife	28	"
	K	Pace Anthony	27	merchant	30	"
	L	Pace Frances †	27	housewife	26	"

Chittick Road

Page	Letter	Full Name	Residence	Occupation	Age	Reported Residence
	M	Gaynor John F	71	retired	61	here
	N	Gaynor Joseph A	71	clerk	54	"
	O	Gaynor Margaret A †	71	housewife	58	"
	P	*MacDonald Florence †	71	housekeeper	55	"
	R	Gibson Frank G	76	clerk	34	"
	S	Gibson Gertrude S †	76	housewife	35	"
	T	Carlevale Beatrice †	76	"	45	"
	U	Carlevale Ralph	76	mason	52	"
	V	Mulhern Mary L †	92	housekeeper	55	"
	W	Mulhern Susan T †	92	housewife	46	"
	X	Mulhern William F	92	bookkeeper	54	"
	Y	*Healy Julia †	121	housewife	29	"
	Z	Healy Michael	121	machinist	38	"
1701						
	A	Walsh James E	123	boilermaker	62	"
	B	Walsh Mary A †	123	housewife	65	"
	C	Dion Ethel F †	131	"	42	"
	D	Dion Peter H	131	machinist	42	"
	E	Haskell Earle H	131	engineer	30	Mansfield
	F	Haskell Edna M †	131	housewife	23	"
	G	Laughlin Catherine †	138	"	71	here
	H	Laughlin James J	138	mortician	36	"
	K	Laughlin Mary E †	138	stenographer	42	"

Page.	Letter.	Full Name.	Residence [illegible]	[illegible]	[illegible]	[illegible]

Chittick Road (Continued)

Page.	Letter.	Full Name.	Residence	Occupation	Age	Reported Residence
	L	Slattery Mary †	139	housewife	69	here
	M	Slattery Patrick	139	boilermaker	62	"

Cottage Street

Page.	Letter.	Full Name.	Residence	Occupation	Age	Reported Residence
	N	*Foley Bridget †	10	at home	87	here
	O	Foley John J	10	retired	60	"
	P	Kerrigan Annie †	10	housekeeper	55	"
	R	Rico Gesina T †	36	"	22	"
	S	Rico Joseph	36	repairman	47	"
	T	Casciano Concetta †	38	housekeeper	40	"
	U	Ricci James	38	baker	24	[illegible]
	V	Ricci Margaret †	38	housewife	21	here
	W	Wood Artemas L	40	operator	45	"
	X	Wood Dorothy M †	40	housewife	39	"
	Y	Marino Anthony	43	chef	60	"
	Z	Marino Mabel G †	43	housewife	66	"
1702						
	A	Lange Frederick A	44	engineer	38	"
	B	English Helen T †	45	housewife	41	Mansfield
	C	English William D	45	machinist	49	"
	D	Nourse Clyde K	46	laborer	38	here
	E	Nourse John P	46	seaman	44	"
	F	Nourse Mary K †	46	housewife	23	"
	G	Nourse Elonia M †	48	"	53	"
	H	Nourse William H	48	mechanic	54	"
	L	Barry James	50	clerk	24	"
	M	Barry Mary A †	50	housewife	61	"
	N	Fiorio Ciro	53	artist	44	"
	O	Fiorio Olga †	53	housewife	44	"
	P	Boles Agnes B †	54	"	51	"
	R	Boles Ernest A	54	machinist	31	"
	S	Boles Rupert W	54	painter	55	"
	T	Brown Eileen M †	54	waitress	29	"
	U	Buckley Roberta H †	54	housekeeper	22	N Carolina
	V	Logan Francis P	59	engineer	49	here
	W	Logan Genevieve L †	59	nurse	58	"
	X	Logan William H	59	chauffeur	50	"
	Y	Tacey Bridget E †	59	housewife	60	"
	Z	Tacey George W	59	mason	59	"

Page	Letter	Full Name	Residence, Jan 1, 1941	Occupation	Supposed Age	Reported Residence, Jan. 1, 1940. Street and Number.
1703						

Dana Avenue

Page	Letter	Full Name	Residence, Jan 1, 1941	Occupation	Supposed Age	Reported Residence, Jan. 1, 1940. Street and Number.
	A	Nee Anna R—†	106	housekeeper	42	here
	B	Nee Bridget A—†	106	at home	77	"
	C	Chicketti Barbara F—†	106	housewife	20	100 W Milton
	D	Chicketti Philip L	106	machinist	22	1041 Hyde Park av
	E	Richard Joseph D	106	woodworker	36	here
	F	Richard Rose—†	106	factoryhand	30	"
	G	DiTulio Adeline—†	108	housewife	36	"
	H	DiTulio Balzarino	108	blacksmith	44	"
	K	Grasso Madeline—†	108	housewife	30	"
	L	Grasso Nicholas	108	laborer	33	"
	M	Nasuti Charles	108	student	20	"
	N	Nasuti Nicholas	108	laborer	45	"
	O	Hurst Albert	110	machinist	69	"
	P	Hurst Lillian M—†	110	housewife	66	"
	R	Hurst Marion A—†	110	clerk	36	"
	S	Sullivan Ellen M—†	110	housewife	65	"
	T	Sullivan Joseph S	110	gardener	61	"
	U	Maddestra Dominic	113	laborer	39	"
	V	Maddestra Rose—†	113	housewife	29	"
	W	Alimenti Andrew	113	painter	63	"
	X*	Alimenti Angelina—†	113	housewife	60	"
	Y	Alimenti Alfred	113	repairman	30	"
	Z	Alimenti Philomena—†	113	housewife	27	"
1704						
	A	Powers Catherine A—†	114	"	43	"
	B	Powers James E	114	chauffeur	44	"
	C	Connell Edmund A	116	agent	44	"
	D	Connell Madeline M—†	116	housewife	46	"
	E	Fennessy Isadore V	116	laborer	50	"
	F	Brown Emily M—†	118	operator	21	"
	G	Brown Margaret J—†	118	housewife	43	"
	H	Brown Sidney V	118	mover	44	"
	K	Andreozzi Frances—†	121	housewife	40	"
	L	Andreozzi Ida M—†	121	saleswoman	21	"
	M	Andreozzi Louis	121	machinist	51	"
	N	Colantoni Carmella T—†	121	housewife	22	"
	O	Colantoni Frank J	121	baker	24	"
	P	Carbone Frances—†	123	housewife	25	"
	R	Carbone Thomas J	123	machinist	32	"
	S	Barese Florindo	123	operator	48	"

Dana Avenue Continued

Page	Letter	Full Name	Residence, Jan. 1, 1941	Occupation	Reported Age	Reported Residence, Jan. 1, 1940. Street and Number
	T	Carbone Louis	123	machinist	24	here
	U*	Carbone Mary †	123	housewife	54	"
	V	Carbone Nicholette †	123	housekeeper	29	"
	W*	Carbone Rocco	123	laborer	52	"
	X*	Delgallo John	123	"	53	"
	Y*	Hughes Evangeline P †	126	at home	68	"
	Z	Jackson Richard L	126	custodian	71	"
1705						
	A	Finn James W	127	welder	22	"
	B	Finn John J	127	custodian	57	"
	C	Finn John J, jr	127	clerk	24	"
	D	Finn Mary †	127	"	20	"
	E	Finn Mary T †	127	housewife	55	"
	F	Finn Anna †	127	supervisor	30	"
	G	Finn Thomas F	127	laborer	27	"
	H	Kritzman Fannie †	128	housewife	41	"
	K	Kritzman Simon	128	merchant	49	"
	L	Kritzman William	128	mechanic	26	"
	M	Levenbaum Anna †	129	housewife	34	"
	N	Levenbaum Samuel	129	chauffeur	40	"
	O	Holt Charles W	129	clerk	31	13 Brewster
	P	Holt Frederick	129	"	55	13 "
	R	Holt Hazel F †	129	housewife	22	13 "
	S	Brophy John	130	janitor	64	here
	T	Brophy Joseph C	130	clerk	28	"
	U	Brophy Mary A †	130	housewife	26	"
	V	Barbato Angelina †	130	"	38	19 Loring pl
	W	Barbato Louis	130	laborer	45	19 "
	X	Thompson Benjamin H	132	carpenter	46	here
	Y	Thompson Mary A †	132	housewife	42	"
	Z	Inglis Edith †	132	secretary	27	"
1706						
	A	Inglis George	132	mechanic	24	"
	B	Inglis Henrietta †	132	housewife	55	"
	C	Inglis Ruth †	132	waitress	27	"
	D	McGivney James	133	retired	74	"
	E	McGivney Nellie †	133	housewife	58	"
	F	Carroll Alfred M	134	letter carrier	29	"
	G	Carroll Genevieve L †	134	operator	26	"
	H	Carroll George F	134	chauffeur	35	"
	K	Carroll Gertrude H †	134	saleswoman	27	"

Dana Avenue—Continued

Page	Letter	Full Name	Residence, Jan. 1, 1941	Occupation	Supposed Age	Reported Residence, Jan. 1, 1940. Street and Number.
	L	Carroll Herbert J	134	engineer	32	here
	M	Carroll John F	134	retired	58	"
	N	Carroll Mary M—†	134	housewife	65	"
	O	Carroll Robert J	134	U S A	23	"
	P	Femino Joseph J	135	mechanic	27	"
	R	Femino Margaret A—†	135	housewife	28	"
	S	Cheever Beatrice T—†	135	"	49	"
	T	Cheever Catherine A—†	135	stenographer	23	"
	U	Cheever John J	135	gardener	56	"
	V	Cheever John J	135	machinist	21	"
	W	Griffin James T	136	superintendent	26	58 Wash'n
	X	Griffin Madeline C—†	136	housewife	30	58 "
	Y	*Fitzgerald Annie L—†	136	"	29	here
	Z	Fitzgerald John E	136	painter	32	"
1707						
	A	*Fitzgerald Joseph W	136	machinist	60	"
	B	Jones Elizabeth A—†	137	housewife	49	"
	C	Jones John E	137	clerk	58	"
	D	*Reiser Anna F—†	137	housewife	35	"
	E	Reiser Otto T	137	mason	39	"
	F	Brolin Hazel A—†	138	housewife	32	"
	G	*Jones Albert	138	packer	65	"
	H	Swanson Elizabeth M—†	138	housewife	26	"
	K	McBride Ada V—†	138	bookkeeper	62	"
	L	McBride Estella A—†	138	housekeeper	67	"
	M	McBride Georgiana—†	138	at home	78	"
	N	Brown Edward H	138	chauffeur	49	Dedham
	O	Brown Joan R—†	138	housewife	48	"
	P	Brennan Herbert E	139	chauffeur	28	here
	R	Brennan Jean A—†	139	housewife	25	"
	S	Carlevale Angelina—†	139	"	41	"
	T	Carlevale Victor S	139	fitter	46	"
	U	Gentili Dante	141	gardener	49	38 Garfield av
	V	*Gentili Veglia—†	141	housewife	39	38 "
	W	Gibbons Francis J	141	teacher	30	here
	X	Gibbons Helen H—†	141	housewife	30	"
	Y	Pagington Edward S	142	plumber	48	"
	Z	Pagington Jane L—†	142	housewife	36	"
1708						
	A	Soares Bertha M—†	142	"	48	"
	B	*Soares Manuel F	142	foreman	46	"

Dana Avenue—Continued

Page	Letter	Full Name	[illegible]	[illegible]	[illegible]	[illegible]
	C	Linowski Helen R †	144	housewife	22	58 West
	D	Linowski John	144	metalworker	20	58 "
	E	Linowski Stanley W	144	laborer	25	58 "
	F	Lee Margaret L †	144	housewife	66	here
	G	*Gerardi Ann †	145	stitcher	28	"
	H	*Gerardi Louise †	145	housewife	57	"
	K	*Gerardi Mary †	145	stitcher	26	"
	L	*Gerardi Paul	145	machinist	20	"
	M	Colella Gennaro	145	metalworker	37	"
	N	*Colella Mamie †	145	housewife	36	"
	O	*Fiore Giacinta †	147	"	45	"
	P	Fiore Joseph	147	machinist	44	"
	R	Fiore Serafino	147	blacksmith	48	"
	S	*Fiore Stella †	147	housewife	43	"
	T	Tanzi John	147	metalworker	35	"
	U	Borsari Margaret R—†	147	housewife	21	[illegible]
	V	Borsari Mario J	147	painter	25	31 "
	W	Ginnochio Annie M—†	148	housewife	51	here
	X	Ginnochio Augustus	148	janitor	50	"
	Y	Douglass Earl B	148	millhand	29	52 Oakridge
	Z	Douglass Eleanor T—†	148	housewife	28	52 "
1709						
	A	Hall Harry H	148	molder	52	here
	B	Hall Mildred C †	148	housewife	53	"
	C	Hall Ralph E	148	foreman	30	"
	D	Willard Harold A	156	accountant	38	"
	E	Willard Lily C †	156	housewife	34	"
	F	Deacks Albert E	156	salesman	69	"
	G	Deacks Fanny L †	156	housewife	64	"
	H	*Sholds Allison F	157	clerk	20	"
	K	*Sholds Constance E †	157	housewife	56	"
	L	Sholds Fred L	157	storekeeper	57	"
	M	Bills Catherine E †	159	housewife	28	[illegible]
	N	Bills George L	159	laborer	33	106 "
	O	Colageo Anthony T	159	roofer	55	here
	P	*Colageo Nancy †	159	housewife	50	"
	R	Underhill Edward M	160	retired	78	"
	S	Underhill Elizabeth S †	160	housewife	78	"
	T	Taylor Ida L †	161	housekeeper	62	"
	U	Tucker Dorothea †	161	stenographer	23	"
	V	Tucker Frances C †	161	housewife	49	"

Page	Letter	Full Name	Residence Jan. 1, 1941.	Occupation.	Supposed Age.	Reported Residence, Jan. 1, 1940. Street and Number.

Dana Avenue—Continued

Page	Letter	Full Name	Residence Jan. 1, 1941.	Occupation.	Supposed Age.	Reported Residence, Jan. 1, 1940. Street and Number.
	W	Tucker Herbert F	164	salesman	50	here
	X	Killeen George H	165	machinist	37	"
	Y	Killeen Teresa E †	165	housewife	37	"
	Z	Bambini Anna M †	167	"	34	"
1710						
	A	Bambini Dante A	167	gardener	43	"
	B	Humora Francis	167	manager	33	"
	C	Humora Mary T †	167	housewife	32	"
	D	Bell Carleton J	168	stereotyper	32	"
	E	Bell Margaret H †	168	housewife	34	"
	F	Wheeler Eben H	171–173	salesman	40	"
	G	Wheeler Mary M †	171–173	housewife	40	"
	H	McGrath Anna E †	171–173	"	42	62 Garfield av
	K	McGrath Henry M	171–173	plasterer	42	62 "
	L	Reynolds Ann E †	171–173	at home	82	62 "
	M	McGrath Margaret †	175	housewife	45	here
	N	McGrath Patrick	175	laborer	67	"
	O	McLeod Dora A †	176	clerk	22	77 Summit
	P	Stahl Ethel H †	176	housewife	49	77 "
	R	Stahl George T	176	carpenter	59	77 "
	S	Connell James	176	molder	54	here
	T	Connell Margaret †	176	housewife	47	"
	U	Loftus Ellen F †	179	housekeeper	63	"
	V	Wall William A	179	clerk	39	"
	W	*Walsh Mary A †	180	housewife	29	"
	X	Walsh Patrick J	180	cleaner	32	"
	Y	*Marcus Beatrice M †	180	housewife	49	650 Metropolitan av
	Z	*Marcus Frank	180	laborer	52	650 "
1711						
	A	Tucci Nettie †	180	housewife	34	here
	B	Tucci Thomas	180	chauffeur	37	"
	C	Connell Patrick J	187	retired	85	"
	D	*Coombs Arthur L	187	mechanic	34	"
	E	Coombs Elizabeth H †	187	housewife	36	"
	F	Barry Edgar J	187	laborer	47	"
	G	Barry Mary E †	187	housewife	51	"
	H	Finn Owen F	188	laborer	54	"
	K	Jewett Hazel F †	188	waitress	23	"
	L	Sullivan Frederick F	198	machinist	29	"
	M	Sullivan Frederick S	188	molder	53	"
	N	Sullivan Lena A †	188	housewife	51	"

Page.	Letter	Full Name	Residence, Jan. 1, 194[illegible]	Occupation	Reputed Age	Reported Residence, Jan. 1, 194[illegible]. Street and Number

Dana Avenue—Continued

Page.	Letter	Full Name	Residence	Occupation	Age	Reported Residence
	O	Sullivan Theresa E †	188	saleswoman	20	here
	P	Kinlin Joseph E	189	supervisor	32	"
	R	Kinlin Ruth C †	189	housewife	32	"
	S	Smith Robert M	191	metalworker	30	"
	T	*Smith Sarah A †	191	housewife	25	"
	U	Zaino Angelo	191	clerk	57	"
	V	Zaino Boniface	191	machinist	23	"
	W	Zaino Caradino	191	laborer	32	"
	X	*Zaino Leonora †	191	housewife	51	"
	Y	Donovan Charles A	192	supervisor	44	"
	Z	Donovan Grace V †	192	housewife	41	"
1712						
	A	Morley Allen J	195	carpenter	36	"
	B	Morley Joseph G	195	"	31	"
	C	Morley Mary A †	195	housewife	66	"
	D	Dugan Edward M	198	retired	48	81 Richmond
	E	*Sotiros Angelina †	198	housewife	28	here
	F	*Sotiros Celia †	198	"	54	"
	G	*Sotiros Constantine	198	merchant	39	"
	H	*Sotiros Vasil	198	retired	73	"
	K	Fintle David V	199	policeman	55	"
	L	Fintle Eleanor M †	199	housewife	48	"
	M	Fintle Marie L †	199	stenographer	23	"
	N	Winchenbaugh Helen M †	202	housewife	42	"
	O	Winchenbaugh Roy A	202	decorator	45	"
	P	Fleming Katherine T †	203	housewife	30	66 Wash'n
	R	Fleming Nicholas A	203	welder	31	66 "
	S	Gleason C Arthur	207	chauffeur	27	Stoughton
	T	Gleason Pauline N †	207	housewife	24	"
	U	Reilly Claire B †	211	"	44	here
	V	Reilly John A	211	salesman	42	"
	W	*Donovan Margaret †	213	housewife	71	"
	X	*Donovan Patrick J	213	laborer	70	"
	Y	Marshall William E	213	operator	20	"
	Z	Smith Leontine E †	215	housewife	28	"
1713						
	A	Smith Robert C	215	clerk	32	"
	B	Cavanaugh Catherine H †	215	housewife	44	"
	C	Cavanaugh John J	215	chauffeur	43	"
	E	Morse Albert C	221	retired	43	"
	F	Morse Helen D †	221	at home	56	"

Page	Letter	Full Name	Residence Jan. 1 1941	Occupation	Supposed Age	Reported Residence, Jan. 1, 1940. Street and Number.

Dana Avenue—Continued

	G	Powers Nan—†	224	domestic	53	here
	H	Fleming Edward F	225	florist	42	"
	K	Fleming Mildred M—†	225	housewife	38	"
	L	Lynch Cornelius D	232	druggist	52	"
	M	Lynch Katherine G—†	232	housewife	50	"
	N	Bates Alwin M	256	clerk	21	"
	O	Bates Elizabeth H—†	256	housekeeper	49	"
	P	Bates Rachael O—†	256	nurse	24	"

Fairmount Avenue

	U	Crawford Wallace P	149	retired	61	here
	V	Mahoney Edith—†	149	domestic	46	"
	Y	McGuire Florence—†	155	housewife	31	9 Fairmount ct
	Z	McGuire Martin	155	painter	30	9 "
1714						
	A	Fitzgerald Anna A—†	157	housewife	53	here
	B	Fitzgerald Michael J	157	painter	52	"
	C	Fitzgerald Thomas J	157	"	22	"
	D	Feeney James F	157	clerk	31	Dedham
	E	Feeney Mary C—†	157	housewife	29	"
	H	Handey Jessie—†	159	laundress	60	1188 River
	K	Yong Charlie	165	laundryman	39	here

Fairmount Court

	R	Gammons Charles H	5	laborer	29	1326 River
	S	Gammons Ellen J—†	5	housewife	72	1326 "
	T	Gammons Henry A	5	laborer	38	1326 "
	U	Gammons William P	5	electrician	52	1326 "
	V	Green Bridget A—†	5	housewife	75	here
	W	Green Mary A—†	5	domestic	41	"
	X	Connolly Thomas F	5	mechanic	52	"
	Y	Connolly Winifred G—†	5	housewife	54	"
	Z	Wahl Emma F—†	5	housekeeper	46	"
1715						
	A	O'Connor John T	5	laborer	24	"
	B	O'Connor Mary T—†	5	housewife	49	"
	C	O'Connor Thomas H	5	pipefitter	50	"
	D	Delendick Sophie—†	5	housewife	38	"
	E	Delendick Stephen	5	metalworker	49	"

Page	Letter	Full Name	Residence	[illegible]	Age	[illegible]

Fairmount Court Continued

Page	Letter	Full Name	Residence	Occupation	Age	Reported Residence
	F	Donovan Clara B †	6	operator	26	here
	G	Donovan George W	6	laborer	20	"
	H	Donovan James H	6	messenger	29	"
	K	Donovan John F	6	laborer	23	"
	L	Donovan Mary A †	6	housewife	50	"
	M	Donovan Mary G †	6	weaver	31	"
	N	Leonard Charles	8	laborer	32	"
	O	Shagren Alice †	8	housewife	70	"
	P	Shagren Augustine	8	retired	83	"
	R	Taylor Esther G †	8	housewife	37	"
	S	Taylor Louis E	8	laborer	31	"
	T	Anderson Adolph C	9	carpenter	30	57 Fair[illegible]
	U	*Anderson Laura E †	9	housewife	34	157 "
	V	Shepley Mary E †	9	"	43	here
	W	Shepley Thomas W	9	painter	42	"
	X	Biegel Augustus	11	retired	76	"
	Y	Biegel Augustus G	11	upholsterer	35	"
	Z	Biegel Joseph	11	"	34	"
1716						
	A	Biegel Virginia †	11	housewife	56	"
	B	Jerzilo Bronislaw	14	laborer	50	"
	C	Jerzilo Henry	14	machinist	24	"
	D	*Jerzilo Mary †	14	housewife	47	"
	E	Jerzilo Stacia †	14	domestic	22	"
	F	*Clark John	14	laborer	43	"
	G	Fitzgerald Catherine C †	14	housewife	26	"
	H	Fitzgerald John F	14	painter	27	"

Fairmount Terrace

Page	Letter	Full Name	Residence	Occupation	Age	Reported Residence
	K	*O'Riordon Catherine †	5	housewife	56	here
	L	O'Riordon John	5	clerk	21	"
	M	Dwight Anna †	6	housewife	30	"
	N	Dwight Joseph H	6	chauffeur	37	"
	O	Eden Dorothy †	8	housewife	38	"
	P	Eden Henry D	8	machinist	39	"
	S	McDermott Esther P †	10	housewife	34	"
	T	McDermott William P	10	laborer	35	"
	U	Molinari Anna L †	11	clerk	29	"
	V	Molinari Anthony	11	laborer	64	"
	W	Molinari Esther †	11	clerk	31	"

Page	Letter	Full Name	Residence, Jan. 1, 1941.	Occupation	Supposed Age.	Reported Residence, Jan. 1, 1940. Street and Number.

Fairmount Terrace—Continued

	Y	Amuzzini Anthony	13	machinist	39	here
	Z*	Amuzzini John	13	retired	72	"
1717						
	A	Amuzzini Rose G—†	13	operator	35	"
	B	Feeney Dorothy—†	13	housewife	28	"

Floral Place

	D	Russo Angeline—†	10	housewife	32	21 Collins
	E	Russo Carmen	10	agent	40	21 "
	F	Driscoll George B	12	chauffeur	44	here
	G	Driscoll Gertrude K—†	12	housewife	46	"
	H	Bromley Elizabeth A—†	14	housekeeper	71	"
	K*	Main Christina—†	16	"	77	"
	L	Main Jane—†	16	bookkeeper	43	"

Foster Street

	M	Sheard Agnes—†	24	housewife	49	here
	N	Sheard Albert	24	ropemaker	52	"
	O	Allen Alice M—†	24	housewife	60	"
	P	Allen Stewart T	24	mover	63	"
	R	Carr Helen—†	24	housewife	40	"
	S	Carr Lawrence	24	mover	38	"
	T	Carr Robert L	24	manager	21	"
	U	Olson Hazel A—†	26	housewife	29	"
	V	Olson Jacob	26	painter	38	"
	W*	Byrnes Nellie A—†	28	housekeeper	49	"
	Y	Comer Ida A—†	41	"	62	"

Garfield Avenue

	Z	Barbuto Gaetano	2	laborer	37	here
1718						
	A	Barbuto Mary—†	2	housewife	42	"
	B*	Dolge Antonetta—†	2	"	49	"
	C	Dolge Dominic	2	operator	21	"
	D*	Dolge Salvatore	2	laborer	54	"
	E	Panciocco Evelyn—†	23	housewife	29	"
	F	Panciocco Joseph	23	repairman	56	"
	G	Panciocco Rocco	23	laborer	31	"

Page	Letter	Full Name	Residence Jan. 1, 1941	Occupation	Age	Reported Residence Jan. 1, 1940 Street and Number

Garfield Avenue Continued

Page	Letter	Full Name	Residence	Occupation	Age	Reported Residence
	H	*Pancioceo Teresa †	23	housewife	59	here
	K	Bartula Ida †	24	operator	30	"
	L	Radulski Adolph	24	machinist	58	"
	M	*Radulski Hermina †	24	housewife	52	"
	N	Radulski Wanda †	24	nurse	24	"
	O	Trocki Frank	24	attendant	27	"
	P	Trocki Rose †	24	clerk	28	"
	S	Fulton Gertrude E †	25	housewife	29	144 Dana av
	T	Fulton William M	25	painter	29	144 "
	U	Dwyer Dorothy K †	25	housewife	24	16 Child
	V	Dwyer James F	25	boilermaker	29	16 "
	W	*Amati Argene †	26	housewife	55	here
	X	Amati Richard	26	operator	22	"
	Y	*Amati Tullio	26	gardener	57	"
	Z	Gregory Arthur	26	machinist	21	"
1719						
	A	Gregory Flora A †	26	dressmaker	29	"
	B	Gregory Lucy †	26	housewife	53	"
	C	Gregory Luigi	26	laborer	59	"
	D	Gregory Viola †	26	housekeeper	27	"
	E	Denny Agnes M †	26A	housewife	36	"
	F	Denny Maurice B	26A	retired	47	"
	G	Downey Eleanor E †	27	operator	35	"
	H	Downey Gertrude A †	27	"	32	"
	K	Downey Nora E †	27	housewife	72	"
	L	Downey William J	27	janitor	73	"
	M	Ragusa Angelo	28	laborer	35	"
	N	Ragusa Nicolena †	28	housewife	32	"
	O	Pancioceo Attilio J	28	operator	28	"
	P	Pancioceo Concetta M †	28	housewife	29	"
	R	Pancioceo Frank	28	welder	21	"
	S	*Pancioceo Jennie †	28	housewife	54	"
	T	Pancioceo Louis	28	clerk	25	"
	U	Pancioceo Mary †	28	at home	23	"
	V	Towner Minnie A †	28B	housekeeper	55	"
	W	Cox Mary M †	28B	stitcher	21	Dedham
	X	Cox Roger E	28B	shipper	24	7 Roxana
	Y	Green Agnes G †	29	operator	30	here
	Z	Green John M	29	painter	11	"
1720						
	A	Green Mary A †	29	housewife	68	"

Page	Letter	Full Name	Residence, Jan. 1, 1941.	Occupation.	Supposed Age.	Reported Residence, Jan. 1, 1940. Street and Number.

Garfield Avenue—Continued

Page	Letter	Full Name	Residence, Jan. 1, 1941.	Occupation.	Supposed Age.	Reported Residence, Jan. 1, 1940. Street and Number.
	B	Green Thomas	29	retired	74	here
	C	Rich Doris M †	29	waitress	20	"
	D	Rich Esther A †	29	housekeeper	43	"
	E	Jordan Helen P †	30	stenographer	46	"
	F	Travers Theresa A †	31–33	housewife	43	"
	G	Reynolds Desire M †	31–33	"	32	"
	H	Reynolds George P	31–33	binder	34	"
	K	Gaffney Bernard P	32	chauffeur	34	"
	L	Gaffney Mary E †	32	housewife	30	"
	M	Gately Flora F †	32	"	30	36 Garfield av
	N	Gately Frederick G	32	draftsman	30	36 "
	O	Greenwood Augusta †	32	housekeeper	58	69 Water
	P	Hogan Alice C †	34	clerk	27	here
	R	Hogan Gilbert P	34	painter	59	"
	S	Hogan James F	34	clerk	24	"
	T	Hogan Mary E †	34	housewife	59	"
	U	Hogan William J	34	printer	21	"
	V	Cremin Julia †	35	housekeeper	45	"
	W	Greenan Margaret F †	35	"	52	"
	X	Shirley Alice M †	36	housewife	65	Belmont
	Y	Shirley James F	36	retired	71	"
	Z	Gately Eva H †	36	housewife	59	here
1721						
	A	Gately Thomas F	36	molder	58	"
	B	Bain Anna C †	37	housewife	38	"
	C	Bain Jeremiah A	37	metalworker	33	83 Sunnyside
	D	Cremin Dennis J	37	draftsman	43	here
	E	Cremin Helen M †	37	housewife	47	"
	F	Cremin Nora †	37	"	77	"
	G	Cremin Nora F †	37	clerk	39	"
	K	Hogan John F	38	gardener	50	"
	L*	Hogan Mary A †	38	housewife	49	"
	M	Fasolino David	39	laborer	24	"
	N	Fasolino Mary †	39	housewife	22	"
	O	Scavitto Anthony	39	chauffeur	36	"
	P	Scavitto Louise M †	39	housewife	33	"
	R	Daly Annie J †	41	"	75	"
	S	Daly Bartholomew	41	retired	78	"
	T	Daly Grace M †	41	stenographer	46	"
	U	Daly Irene E †	41	"	33	"
	V	Daly Lois A †	41	housekeeper	41	"
	W	Troy George	41	laborer	41	"

Page	Letter	Full Name	Residence	Occupation	Age	Residence (previous)

Garfield Avenue (Continued)

Page	Letter	Full Name	Residence	Occupation	Age	Residence (previous)
	x	Troy Margaret †	41	at home	70	here
	y	Andrews Arthur S	51	clerk	53	"
	z	Andrews Bruce	51	"	31	"
1722						
	A	Andrews Joseph C	51	architect	68	"
	B	*DiGregorio Domenico	52	laborer	70	"
	C	DiGregorio Mary C †	52	housewife	24	"
	D	DiGregorio Nicholas	52	machinist	31	"
	E	Casciano Antoinette †	52	housewife	40	"
	F	Casciano Armando J	52	machinist	21	"
	G	Casciano Panfilo	52	laborer	50	"
	H	Rogers Alice M †	54	clerk	40	"
	K	Rogers George A	54	"	36	"
	L	Rogers Hannah E †	54	housewife	72	"
	M	Daly John P	54	plumber	20	"
	N	Daly John T	54	installer	46	"
	O	Daly Mary A †	54	housewife	44	"
	P	Rogers James R	56	retired	86	"
	R	Rogers Katherine G †	56	secretary	40	"
	S	Rogers Sarah M †	56	housewife	72	"
	T	McCann Arthur A	56	bartender	46	"
	U	McCann Marion M †	56	housewife	30	"
	V	McGrath James G	60	retired	70	"
	W	Lynch Mary T †	62	domestic	27	"
	X	Lynch Thomas J	62	clerk	25	"
	Y	*Rowley Mary T †	62	domestic	26	"
	Z	*Rowley Sarah R †	62	housewife	64	"
1723						
	A	*Rowley Thomas J	62	machinist	20	"
	B	Rowley William J	62	janitor	60	"
	C	*Hibbert Mary †	62	housewife	45	"
	D	Hibbert Stanley	62	machinist	45	337
	E	Daly Lillian M †	66	housekeeper	39	here
	F	Daly Ruth E †	66	nurse	24	"
	G	Lyons Agnes M †	72	clerk	24	"
	H	Lyons Mary A †	72	housewife	45	"
	K	Lyons Owen F	72	watchman	50	"

Glenwood Avenue East

Page	Letter	Full Name	Residence	Occupation	Age	Residence (previous)
1	K	Strid Anna L †	79	teacher	43	here
	L	*Strid Jennie A †	79	housewife	65	"

Page	Letter	Full Name	Residence, Jan. 1, 1941	Occupation	Supposed Age	Reported Residence, Jan. 1, 1940. Street and Number.

Glenwood Avenue East—Continued

Page	Letter	Full Name	Residence, Jan. 1, 1941	Occupation	Supposed Age	Reported Residence, Jan. 1, 1940.
	M	*Strid John A	79	florist	68	here
	N	Sullivan Honora †	91	housewife	53	"
	O	Sullivan Margaret M †	91	finisher	20	"
	P	Sullivan Mary A †	91	printer	22	"
	R	Sullivan Michael J	91	porter	55	"
	S	Sullivan Michael J, jr	91	steward	23	"
	T	Hoar Anna C †	95	housewife	54	"
	U	Hoar Anna C †	95	student	20	"
	V	Hoar Frank A	95	R F D	60	"
	W	Hoar Paul F	95	laborer	23	"
	X	Watson Annie †	103	housewife	55	"
	Y	Watson David E	103	student	20	"
	Z	Watson Joseph	103	gardener	67	"
1724						
	A	Watson Thomas J	103	attendant	22	"
	C	Dolan Delia F †	104	housewife	70	"
	D	Dolan Thomas F	104	laborer	63	"
	E	Dolan Thomas P	104	bookkeeper	21	"
	F	Blivens Edith G †	111	housewife	47	"
	G	Blivens Walter	111	chauffeur	47	"
	H	Monahan William J	111	retired	85	"
	K	*Watson Gerard W	112	laborer	23	"
	L	*Watson Mary E †	112	housewife	43	"
	M	*Watson William	112	shipper	53	"

Glenwood Place

Page	Letter	Full Name	Residence, Jan. 1, 1941	Occupation	Supposed Age	Reported Residence, Jan. 1, 1940.
	N	Fleming Agnes E †	8	housewife	25	49 Cottage
	O	Fleming Kenneth A	8	operator	30	49 "
	P	Quinn Catherine †	8	housewife	50	here
	R	Quinn Edward	8	laborer	53	"
	S	Condon Anna †	11	housewife	29	"
	T	Condon John H	11	mover	29	"
	U	Giammasi Bridget †	11	housewife	39	"
	V	Giammasi John	11	toolmaker	37	"
	W	Henry Mary †	11	nurse	42	"
	X	Keefe Margaret †	15	at home	75	"
	Y	Thompson Margaret C †	15	housekeeper	39	"
	Z	Berry Louise E †	17	housewife	34	"
1725						
	A	Berry Sherman W	17	painter	32	"

Page	Letter	FULL NAME	Residence, Jan. 1, 1941	Occupation	Supposed Age	Reported Residence, Jan. 1, 1940. Street and Number

Glenwood Place—Continued

Page	Letter	FULL NAME	Residence	Occupation	Age	Reported Residence
	B	Durant David M	19	operator	46	here
	C	Durant Katherine M †	19	housewife	45	"
	D	Slattery Phyllis E †	20	"	37	"
	E	Slattery William P	20	attorney	34	"

Highland Street

Page	Letter	FULL NAME	Residence	Occupation	Age	Reported Residence
	F	Wright Harold W	7	salesman	32	here
	G	Wright Violet †	7	housewife	32	"
	H	Ewell Ethel B †	9	"	63	"
	K	Ewell John Q	9	electrician	69	"

Loring Place

Page	Letter	FULL NAME	Residence	Occupation	Age	Reported Residence
	L	Foley Walter T	11	engineer	55	here
	M	Murphy Johanna M †	11	housewife	45	"
	N	Murphy Joseph W	11	spinner	22	"
	O	Murphy Patrick J	11	retired	54	"
	P	*Smith Ellen I	14	housewife	38	"
	R	Smith Frank J	14	mechanic	35	"
	S	Stewart Gordon A	14	clerk	20	"
	T	Stewart Lila A †	14	housewife	46	"
	U	Stewart Walter C	14	engineer	33	"
	V	Adams Agnes E †	19	housewife	28	23 Bartlett
	W	Adams Ernest F	19	clerk	28	23 "

Loring Street

Page	Letter	FULL NAME	Residence	Occupation	Age	Reported Residence
	Y	Donovan John A	4	serviceman	42	here
	Z	Donovan Mary M †	4	housewife	40	"
1726						
	B	Butler Lawrence T	8	roofer	31	"
	C	Butler Rita M †	8	housewife	26	"
	D	Lambe Alice M †	17 19	"	35	"
	E	*Lambe Joseph E	17 19	shipper	37	"
	F	Sullivan Daniel F	17 19	clerk	55	"
	G	*Sullivan Melvina M †	17 19	housewife	53	"
	H	Durepo Margaret L †	21 23	"	42	"
	K	Durepo Vinal L	21 23	carpenter	43	"
	L	Scully Harold R	21 23	machinist	34	7 Roxana
	M	Scully Madeline G †	21 23	housewife	31	7 "

Page.	Letter	Full Name	Residence, Jan. 1, 1941.	Occupation	Supposed Age.	Reported Residence, Jan. 1, 1940. Street and Number.

Loring Street—Continued

Page.	Letter	Full Name	Residence, Jan. 1, 1941.	Occupation	Supposed Age.	Reported Residence, Jan. 1, 1940. Street and Number.
	N	Crowe A Ernest	25	clerk	32	here
	O	Crowe Arthur E	25	"	53	"
	P	Crowe Sarah L—†	25	housewife	51	"
	R	Habliston Mary P—†	25	clerk	39	"
	S	Haigh Laura F—†	25	housekeeper	53	"
	T	Gately John A	27	salesman	56	"
	U	Gately Rose S—†	27	housewife	52	"
	V	Maloney Agnes T—†	27	housekeeper	60	"
	W	O'Shea Cornelius P	44	attorney	47	"
	X	O'Shea Cornelius P, jr	44	student	23	"
	Y	O'Shea Daniel F	44	"	21	"
	Z	O'Shea Margaret F—†	44	housewife	45	"
1727						
	A	Fitzgerald John F	45	laborer	57	"
	B	Griffin George A	45	mechanic	46	"
	C	Griffin George W	45	machinist	21	"
	D	Griffin Lillian M—†	45	housewife	43	"
	E	Burke Joseph F	46	teacher	47	"
	F	Burke M Agnes—†	46	housewife	46	"
	G	Dray Isabelle F—†	46	clerk	26	"
	H	Reitsma Florence M—†	47	housewife	40	"
	K	Reitsma William	47	salesman	39	"
	L	*Cibotti Angelina—†	55	housewife	34	"
	M	Cibotti Ralph	55	laborer	38	"
	N	Piccirilli Salvatore	55	"	51	"
	O	*Piccirilli Susan—†	55	housewife	40	"
	P	Panciocco Clement rear	57	laborer	50	"
	R	Panciocco Mary—† "	57	housekeeper	20	"
	S	*Fasolino John	59	carpenter	52	"
	T	*Fasolino Mary—†	59	housewife	50	"
	U	Fasolino Seraphine	59	laborer	21	"
	V	Fasolino Stella—†	59	domestic	25	"
	W	Cedrone John	59	laborer	43	"
	X	*Cedrone Louise—†	59	housewife	45	"
	Y	Corscadden James B	61	clerk	48	"
	Z	Corscadden Julia E—†	61	housewife	36	"
1728						
	A	Costello Alexander J	61	laborer	41	"
	B	Costello Henry S	61	superintendent	38	"
	C	Butler John V	65	laborer	34	"
	D	*Butler Margaret M—†	65	housewife	32	"

Page.	Letter.	FULL NAME.	Residence, Jan. 1, 1941.	Occupation.	Reputed Age.	Reported Residence, Jan. 1, 1940. Street and Number.

Loring Street—Continued

Page.	Letter.	FULL NAME.	Residence, Jan. 1, 1941.	Occupation.	Reputed Age.	Reported Residence, Jan. 1, 1940. Street and Number.
	E	Nuzzo Mary C †	65	housewife	47	here
	F	Nuzzo Salvatore	65	clerk	51	"
	G	Foley George A	78	mechanic	50	"
	H	Foley Loretta M †	78	housewife	51	"
	K	Guinazzo Ellen M †	78	at home	75	"
	L	Balestra Joseph	82	molder	63	"
	M	Balestra Phyllis †	82	housewife	46	"
	N	Balestra Vincent	82	clerk	20	"
	O	Canales Emanuel J	94	manager	43	"
	P	MacDonald Anna A †	94	clerk	43	"
	R	O'Brien Alice M †	94	housekeeper	45	"
	S	Cullen George F	96	gasfitter	38	"
	T	Cullen Irene R †	96	housewife	39	"

Neponset Avenue

Page.	Letter.	FULL NAME.	Residence, Jan. 1, 1941.	Occupation.	Reputed Age.	Reported Residence, Jan. 1, 1940. Street and Number.
	U	Clark Bertha M †	3	housewife	43	59 Linden
	V	Clark Fred L	3	conductor	61	59 "
	W	Nash Elwood L	3	mechanic	24	Connecticut
	X	Woleyko Christine †	4	packer	22	here
	Y	Woleyko Frances †	4	housewife	55	"
	Z	Woleyko Lucy †	4	housekeeper	20	"
1729						
	A	Woleyko Patrick	4	molder	57	"
	B	Woleyko Victor	4	packer	25	"
	C	McQuaid Helen M †	5	saleswoman	38	"
	D	McQuaid Joseph W	5	retired	68	"
	E	McQuaid Joseph W, jr	5	steamfitter	33	"
	F	McQuaid Julia G †	5	housewife	67	"
	G	McQuaid Margaret A †	5	clerk	35	"
	H	Ritchie Harriet A †	7	housewife	78	"
	K	Ritchie Howard B	7	retired	81	"
	M	Brackett Alfred	9	machinist	27	"
	N	Brackett Josephine †	9	housewife	25	"
	O	McQuaker Alexander	9	watchman	46	"
	P	*McQuaker Elizabeth †	9	housewife	46	"
	R	Sacco Anthony	10	laborer	33	"
	S	*Sacco Josephine †	10	housewife	39	"
	T	*Mancini Alberto	10	salesman	34	7 Unity
	U	Mancini Inez †	10	housewife	29	Quincy
	V	Johanson Adeline †	11	"	55	here

Page	Letter	Full Name.	Residence, Jan. 1, 1941	Occupation.	Supposed Age.	Reported Residence, Jan. 1, 1940. Street and Number.

Neponset Avenue—Continued

Page	Letter	Full Name.	Residence, Jan. 1, 1941	Occupation.	Supposed Age.	Reported Residence, Jan. 1, 1940. Street and Number.
	W	Johanson Axel N	11	machinist	53	here
	X	Johanson Ethel M—†	11	secretary	23	"
	Y	McDermott Francis J	12	student	23	"
	Z	McDermott Mary A—†	12	housewife	51	"
1730						
	A	McDermott Michael J	12	mechanic	57	"
	B	Clark Alice M—†	12	clerk	40	"
	C	Bryant Lillian M—†	15	housewife	22	1499 Hyde Park av
	D	Bryant William F	15	laborer	24	1499 "
	E	Corsini Inez—†	15	saleswoman	21	here
	F	Good Harold S	15	electrician	26	"
	G	Good Mary A—†	15	housewife	27	"
	H	Mariano John	16	cook	50	"
	K	*Mariano Mary—†	16	housewife	50	"
	L	*Guizzardi Andrew	17	laborer	62	"
	M	*Guizzardi Dora—†	17	housekeeper	37	"
	N	Guizzardi Louis	17	laborer	26	"
	O	Guizzardi Virginia—†	17	operator	26	11 Fairmount ter
	P	Casciano Carmine	17	shipfitter	22	here
	R	Casciano Madeline—†	17	housewife	22	"
	S	Broderick Ethel R—†	18	"	46	"
	T	*Broderick Raymond	18	carpenter	55	"
	U	Holstrom John	18	engineer	77	"
	V	Richardson Gertrude E—†	18	housekeeper	44	"
	W	Meloski Frank	19	welder	22	"
	X	Meloski Mary—†	19	housewife	55	"
	Y	Meloski Stephen	19	laborer	35	"
	Z	Meloski William	19	"	25	"
1731						
	A	Stec Ignatius F	19	shipfitter	30	47 Business
	B	Stec Julia—†	19	housewife	29	47 "
	C	Bartley Frances V—†	20	"	55	here
	D	Bartley William A	20	textileworker	68	"
	E	Hassan Rose A—†	20	at home	80	"
	F	McGillivary Arthur	21	laborer	37	96 Child
	G	McGillivary Catherine—†	21	housewife	36	96 "
	H	*Potinski Anna—†	21	"	62	here
	K	*Potinski Michael J	21	chipper	62	"
	L	Schaaf Catherine W—†	22	operator	20	"
	M	Schaaf Margaret J—†	22	inspector	22	"
	N	Schaaf Margaret M—†	22	housewife	48	"

Neponset Avenue—Continued

Page	Letter	Full Name	Residence, Jan. 1, 1924	Occupation	Supposed Age	Reported Residence, Jan. 1, 1923, Street and Number
	O	Schaaf Nicholas J	22	chauffeur	61	here
	P	Mullen Jane A †	23	housewife	59	"
	R	Mullen Martin J	23	boilermaker	61	"
	S	Mullen Mary A †	23	clerk	24	"
	T	Mullen Robert P	23	teacher	22	"
	U	Mullen Thomas R	23	fireman	29	"
	V	Malley Edward A	25	conductor	46	"
	W	Malley Louis J	25	bookkeeper	59	"
	X	Battis Gladys L †	26	stenographer	36	"
	Y	Battis Lawrence L	26	salesman	42	"
	Z	Rollock Hattie L †	26	seamstress	62	"
1732						
	A	May Francis J	27	student	20	"
	B	May Martin J	27	foreman	48	"
	C	May Mary J †	27	housewife	43	"
	D	Costello James J	29	porter	38	"
	E	*Costello Jennie T †	29	housewife	37	"
	F	*Ferreira Ernestina †	30	"	33	"
	G	*Ferreira Joseph	30	machinist	43	"
	H	Romano Luigi	30	laborer	38	"
	K	Romano Cnorina †	30	housewife	28	"
	M	Ruscetti Celia †	33	"	49	"
	N	Ruscetti Dominic	33	laborer	54	"
	O	*Cook Ernest A	34	inspector	59	"
	P	*Cook Ernest A, jr	34	insulator	24	"
	R	*Cook Margaret V †	34	housewife	28	"
	S	*Cook Mary A †	34	"	21	"
	T	*Cook Mary M †	34	"	59	"
	U	Briggs Henry E	34	painter	67	"
	V	Briggs Philibert †	34	housewife	66	"
	W	Cote Edward J	34	metalworker	39	"
	X	Cote Priscilla †	34	housewife	31	"
	Y	Bailey Arthur	35	chauffeur	56	"
	Z	Brobecker Henry	35	laborer	56	"
1733						
	A	DiCarlo Alexander	35	"	50	"
	B	DiCarlo Jennie †	35	housewife	40	"
	D	*Nemiccolo Assunta †	36	"	75	"
	C	Nemiccolo Agnes †	36	"	34	"
	E	Nemiccolo Americo	36	architect	36	"
	F	Bowman Harold L	37	draftsman	32	"

Page	Letter	Full Name	Residence, Jan. 1, 1941	Occupation	Supposed Age	Reported Residence, Jan. 1, 1940. Street and Number

Neponset Avenue—Continued

Page	Letter	Full Name	Residence, Jan. 1, 1941	Occupation	Supposed Age	Reported Residence, Jan. 1, 1940. Street and Number
	G	*Bowman Viola H—†	37	housewife	24	here
	H	Curtis Irene—†	37	"	23	"
	K	Curtis Falph	37	pipefitter	27	"
	L	Elliot Ida—†	37	housekeeper	52	"
	M	Iehle Amelia—†	37	at home	79	"
	N	Smith Joseph F	39	mechanic	25	"
	O	Smith Rita B—†	39	housewife	23	"
	P	Misiewicz Michael	39	engineer	24	"
	R	*Misiewicz Nellie—†	39	housewife	43	"
	S	Misiewicz Victor	39	machinist	22	"
	T	Misiewicz Vincent	39	cook	58	"
	U	*Lucchetti Emma—†	40	housewife	45	"
	V	Lucchetti Eugene	40	gardener	43	"
	W	Peri Joseph	40	retired	71	"
	X	Peri Rose—†	40	housekeeper	29	"
	Y	Bogusiewicz Benjamin	41	butcher	40	"
	Z	Bogusiewicz Blanche—†	41	housewife	40	"
1734						
	A	Smith Margaret—†	42	housekeeper	38	"
	B	Spear Albert	42	painter	68	"
	C	Spear Edna E—†	42	housewife	73	"
	D	*Reade Carman	43–45	knitter	35	"
	E	*Reade Kathleen M—†	43–45	housewife	35	"
	F	Whelan John J	43–45	boilermaker	50	"
	G	Whelan Myrna M—†	43–45	housewife	49	"
	H	Leary Iola L—†	47–49	"	32	42 Charles
	K	Leary William F	47–49	shipper	43	42 "
	L	Schwalm Helen M—†	47–49	housewife	41	here
	M	Schwalm William E	47–49	mechanic	41	"
	N	Chadbourne Etta—†	54	at home	80	"
	O	Patrone Cass	55	adjuster	27	"
	P	*Patrone Ella—†	55	housewife	49	"
	R	Patrone Joseph	55	molder	45	"
	S	Patrone Myles	55	millworker	24	"
	T	*Patrone Anna—†	55	housewife	49	"
	U	*Patrone Joseph	55	molder	53	"
	V	Shea Eugene	56	chauffeur	60	"
	W	Shea Francis L	56	clerk	28	"
	X	Shea James D	56	"	30	"
	Y	Shea Nora—†	56	housewife	65	"
	Z	Antonucci Anthony	57	painter	29	"

Page	Letter	Full Name	Residence, Jan. 1, 1941	Occupation	Supposed Age	Reported Residence, Jan. 1, 1940. Street and Number
1735						
		Neponset Avenue Continued				
	A	Antonucci Loretta C †	57	housewife	26	here
	B	Casenza Camillo	57	laborer	42	"
	C	DiCenzo Albert P	57	"	26	"
	D	DiCenzo Maria T †	57	housekeeper	51	"
	E	Graham Florence I †	58	housewife	39	"
	F	Graham Richard	58	carpenter	51	"
	G	Hall Leonard W	58	retired	81	"
	H	Hall Percy A	58	clerk	47	"
	K	*MacLellan James	58	laborer	60	"
	L	*MacLellan Jessie †	58	housewife	58	"
	M	Kelleher John D	59	laborer	21	"
	N	*Kelleher John J	59	"	56	"
	O	Kelleher Margaret E †	59	housekeeper	23	"
	P	Lucey Dennis J	59	retired	75	"
	R	*Logue Charles A	60	baggagemaster	68	"
	S	Logue Mary M †	60	bookkeeper	38	"
	T	Logue Rose G †	60	housekeeper	32	"
	U	*Logue Theresa M †	60	housewife	72	"
	V	Mitchell Mary A †	61	"	38	"
	W	Mitchell Patrick J	61	carpenter	37	"
	X	Tarrant Charles	61	custodian	55	"
	Y	Tattant Harriet †	61	housewife	54	"
	Z	Tarrant Madeline †	61	bookkeeper	29	"
1736						
	A	*MacDonald Arabella J †	62	housekeeper	68	"
	B	*MacDonald Katherine M †	62	secretary	34	"
	C	*MacDonald Lauchlin R	62	retired	76	"
	D	*MacDonald Roy C	62	machinist	30	"
	E	McAfee Arabella C †	62	bookkeeper	36	"
	F	Marcotte Adelaide B †	63	housewife	48	"
	G	Marcotte George L	63	baker	21	"
	H	Marcotte Joseph W	63	"	18	"
	K	Welliver Caroline F †	63	housewife	50	"
	L	Welliver Willard P	63	machinist	49	"
	M	McLellan Carleton T	66	clerk	36	"
	N	McLellan Svea †	66	housewife	31	"
	O	Carlin Julia L †	66	"	60	"
	P	Carlin Thomas E	66	conductor	76	"
	R	Hodgkinson Martha E †	68	housewife	45	"
	S	Hodgkinson William J	68	policeman	50	"

Page.	Letter.	Full Name.	Residence, Jan. 1, 1941.	Occupation.	Supposed Age.	Reported Residence, Jan. 1, 1940. Street and Number.

Neponset Avenue Continued

Page.	Letter.	Full Name.	Residence, Jan. 1, 1941.	Occupation.	Supposed Age.	Reported Residence, Jan. 1, 1940. Street and Number.
	T	Kells Betty V †	70	housewife	22	1120 Hyde Park av
	U	Kells William A	70	messenger	24	1120 "
	V	Morrissey Alice M †	70	housewife	46	here
	W	Morrissey David F	70	shipfitter	21	"
	X	Morrissey Eugenia M †	70	saleswoman	20	"
	Y	Morrissey Francis J	70	machinist	46	"
	Z	Reed Annie S †	71	housewife	55	"
1737						
	A	Reed Carl O	71	painter	62	"
	B	Spence Howard C	72	operator	35	"
	C	Spence Mary A †	72	housewife	37	"
	D	Calvin Andrew	72	carpenter	43	"
	E	Calvin Janet †	72	housewife	42	"
	F	Hines Catherine F †	74	"	28	"
	G	Hines Gerard M	74	chauffeur	29	"
	H	Brown Bridget E †	74	housewife	66	"
	K	Brown Frank A	74	operator	53	"
	L	Martin Rose M †	74	housewife	27	"
	M	Martin Thomas H	74	chauffeur	30	"
	N	Lemora Gertrude †	76 78	housewife	23	"
	O	Lemora James	76 78	metalworker	28	"
	P	Costello Claire †	76 78	housewife	25	"
	R	Costello Thomas	76 78	carpenter	30	"
	S	Coddaire George H	85	salesman	28	"
	T	Coddaire Ora B †	85	housewife	30	"
	U	Fuoco Frank	85	upholsterer	39	"
	V	Fuoco Marianna †	85	housewife	39	"
	W	Bisbee Hazel M †	90	"	47	"
	X	Bisbee Howard P	90	serviceman	49	"
	Y	Peardon Barbara P †	90	housewife	23	"
	Z	Peardon Ralph J	90	mortician	25	"
1738						
	A	Zachorne Agnes C †	93	housewife	48	"
	B	Zachorne Lillian A †	93	nurse	24	Canton
	C	Zachorne William D	93	foreman	47	here
	D	Perry Edward E	94	carpenter	75	"
	E	Perry Ella F †	94	housekeeper	40	"
	F	McKinnon Daniel C	96	retired	70	"
	G	McKinnon Mary E †	96	housewife	67	"
	H	Kearney Joseph W	96	printer	41	"

Page	Letter	Full Name	Residence, Jan. 1, 1941	Occupation	Supposed Age	Reported Residence, Jan. 1, 1940. Street and Number

Neponset Avenue—Continued

Page	Letter	Full Name	Residence, Jan. 1, 1941	Occupation	Supposed Age	Reported Residence, Jan. 1, 1940. Street and Number
	K	Kearney Mary M †	96	housewife	41	here
	L	Hendry Dennis	98	retired	66	"
	M	Hendry Susan †	98	housewife	65	"
	N	McCaffrey Margaret H †	98	dietitian	39	"
	O	McCaffrey Philip F	98	compositor	35	"
	P	Campbell Elizabeth S †	99	at home	78	"
	R	Scrivens Archibald C	99	painter	56	"
	S	Scrivens Cora E †	99	housewife	60	"
	T	Scrivens George W	99	retired	86	"
	U	Scrivens Hannah L †	99	housewife	84	"
	V	Nichols Marion L †	100	housekeeper	57	Newtonville
	W	Walker Kirk W	100	draftsman	55	here
	X	*Tessier Francis A	102	chef	71	"
	Y	*Tessier Mary J †	102	housewife	57	"
	Z	Clements Eleanor C †	104	"	51	"
1739						
	A	Clements Honora E †	104	typist	22	"
	B	Welch Eleanor C †	104	clerk	26	"
	C	Appell Frank L	105	editor	26	"
	D	Appell John	105	merchant	79	"
	E	Appell Sarah A †	105	housewife	66	"
	G	Finn George R	120	superintendent	26	[illegible]
	H	Finn Marie F †	120	housewife	24	164 Beech
	K	Finn William J	120	salesman	57	here

Pond Street

Page	Letter	Full Name	Residence, Jan. 1, 1941	Occupation	Supposed Age	Reported Residence, Jan. 1, 1940. Street and Number
	L	Arnold Grace L †	3	housekeeper	64	here
	M	Nichols Edith M †	3	housewife	39	"
	N	Nichols Eugene	3	printer	37	"
	O	Gatto Ernest	3	laborer	24	Worcester
	P	Gatto Rita M †	3	housewife	22	"
	R	McDermott Jennie †	7	"	52	here
	S	McDermott Thomas	7	policeman	49	"
	T	Carr Marie C †	9	housewife	34	84 Austin
	U	Carr Matthew F	9	foreman	34	19 Chestnut
	V	McCauley Anna L †	9	housewife	65	84 Austin
	W	McCauley Catherine L †	9	secretary	24	84 "
	X	McCauley David G	9	clerk	27	84 "
	Y	McCauley Frank J	9	mechanic	31	84 "

Page.	Letter.	Full Name.	Residence, Jan. 1, 1941.	Occupation.	Supposed Age.	Reported Residence, Jan. 1, 1940. Street and Number.

Pond Street Avenue—Continued

Page	Letter	Full Name	Residence	Occupation	Age	Reported Residence
	Z	Moran Catherine G—†	11	housewife	41	here
1740						
	A	Moran Frederick L	11	teacher	40	"
	B	Wall George W	15	clerk	39	"
	C	Wall Ruth M—†	15	housewife	33	"
	D	Cole Alice S—†	15	"	39	"
	E	Cole Frederick G	15	electrician	40	"
	F	Nash Mary M—†	15	housewife	42	"
	G	Shaw Charles O	15	printer	44	"
	H	*Dattoli Isabelle—†	17	housekeeper	30	10 Williams av
	K	Black Frederick R	17	retired	74	67 Albion
	L	Spurr Mabel E—†	17	housewife	47	here
	M	Spurr William C	17	engineer	47	"
	N	Hoffman Fritz G	21	machinist	64	"
	O	Hoffman Mary E—†	21	housewife	56	"
	P	Campanelli Antonio	23	chauffeur	58	"
	R	Campanelli Armando J	23	assembler	21	"
	S	Campanelli Mario P	23	chauffeur	24	"
	T	Campanelli Serafina—†	23	housewife	50	"
	U	*Serozynski Jennie—†	33	"	45	"
	V	Serozynski Stanley	33	machinist	20	"
	W	Serozynski Vincent	33	blacksmith	55	"
	X	Thompson Catherine—†	35	housewife	53	"
	Y	Thompson John	35	instructor	54	"
	Z	Sullivan Esther M—†	35	housewife	32	"
1741						
	A	Sullivan Joseph R	35	clerk	35	"
	B	Brennan Ethel J—†	35	housewife	40	"
	C	Brennan William K	35	salesman	39	"
	D	Siracusa Mabel E—†	35	waitress	37	"

Summit Street

Page	Letter	Full Name	Residence	Occupation	Age	Reported Residence
	E	Guild Charles E	148	clerk	30	here
	F	Guild Doris M—†	148	housewife	30	"
	G	Hodgeson Lillian—†	148	housekeeper	41	"
	H	Hodgeson Miriam—†	148	secretary	20	"
	K	*Sheard Anna—†	148	clerk	48	"
	L	Collari Clara—†	149	housewife	64	"
	M	Collari Delfo	149	polisher	37	"
	N	*Collari Enrico	149	retired	69	"

Page	Letter	Full Name	Residence, Jan. 1, 1941	Occupation	Supposed Age	Reported Residence, Jan. 1, 1940. Street and Number

Summit Street—Continued

Page	Letter	Full Name	Residence, Jan. 1, 1941	Occupation	Supposed Age	Reported Residence, Jan. 1, 1940. Street and Number
	O	Collari Henry	149	machinist	28	Plymouth
	P	Collari Ida †	149	housewife	27	Everett
	R	Collari Louis	149	caretaker	32	"
	S	*Zaniboni Mary †	149	at home	79	Milton
	T	Mullen Honora †	149	housewife	27	here
	U	Mullen William J	149	mechanic	29	"
	V	Young Joseph R	151	metalworker	25	"
	W	Young Phyllis L †	151	housewife	26	"
	X	Fell Elizabeth G †	151	manager	43	"
	Y	Fell John J	151	steamfitter	52	"
	Z	Fell John J	151	machinist	22	"
1742						
	A	Crocetti Antonio	152	gardener	68	"
	B	*Luciani Adelchi	152	"	58	"
	C	Luciani Armandina †	152	housewife	48	"
	D	*Mazzoni Antonio	152	gardener	40	"
	E	Everson Betty L †	152	stenographer	22	"
	F	Everson Robert C	152	clerk	26	"
	H	Perry Eleanor M †	156	housewife	39	"
	K	Perry Raymond E	156	accountant	39	"
	L	Dowling George E	160	stockman	44	"
	M	Dowling Hilda C †	160	housewife	49	"
	N	Thayer Elmer R	160	secretary	27	15 Riverside sq
	O	Thayer Ruth A †	160	housewife	29	15 "

Tyler Street

Page	Letter	Full Name	Residence, Jan. 1, 1941	Occupation	Supposed Age	Reported Residence, Jan. 1, 1940. Street and Number
	P	Antinarelli Albert	14	foreman	44	here
	R	Antinarelli Alice C †	14	housewife	24	3270 Wash'n
	S	*Antinarelli Antoinette †	14	"	42	here
	T	Antinarelli Augustine	14	laborer	21	"
	U	Carini Anthony	15	"	27	"
	V	Carini Dominic J	15	salesman	33	159 Dana av
	W	*Carini Nancy †	15	housewife	56	here
	X	Carini Nora M †	15	"	28	159 Dana av
	Y	Carini Rose M †	15	factoryhand	21	here
	Z	Anderson Carl O	29	machinist	54	"
1743						
	A	Anderson Dorothy M †	29	bookkeeper	24	"
	B	Anderson Hannah G †	29	housewife	50	"
	C	Cullen Michael J	30	retired	80	"

Page	Letter	Full Name	Residence, Jan. 1, 1941	Occupation	Supposed Age	Reported Residence, Jan. 1, 1940. Street and Number.

Tyler Street—Continued

Page	Letter	Full Name	Residence, Jan. 1, 1941	Occupation	Supposed Age	Reported Residence, Jan. 1, 1940. Street and Number.
	D	Mola Anna T †	38	housewife	26	here
	E	Mola Primo	38	clerk	26	"
	F	*Bambini Erminia †	38	housewife	51	"
	G	Bambini Julia M †	38	operator	22	"
	H	Bambini Peter	38	gardener	52	"
	K	Burns Ann †	47	housewife	68	"
	L	Burns Barbara I †	47	stenographer	24	"
	M	Burns Nellie E †	47	matron	57	"
	N	Burns Robert	47	gardener	60	"
	O	Hartford Florence L †	55	housewife	31	"
	P	Hartford Walter R	55	plumber	31	"
	R	Lynch Julia M †	55	at home	78	"

Washington Street

Page	Letter	Full Name	Residence, Jan. 1, 1941	Occupation	Supposed Age	Reported Residence, Jan. 1, 1940. Street and Number.
	S	Abbott Eugene P	6	tester	29	here
	T	Abbott Lillian B †	6	housewife	26	"
	U	Freeman Alice C †	6	"	39	"
	V	Freeman William M	6	laborer	32	"
	W	Kelly Marie R †	6	at home	36	"
	X	Dubois Helen R †	8	housewife	25	"
	Y	Dubois Lawrence H	8	laborer	30	"
1744						
	A	Ormsby Gertrude M †	10	housekeeper	65	"
	B	Parsons Augustine G	10	retired	80	"
	C	Parsons Frank A	10	salesman	40	"
	D	Parsons Jennie A †	10	housewife	81	"
	E	Parsons Marion C †	10	domestic	42	"
	F	Parsons Ruth †	10	secretary	37	"
	G	Gallagher Raymond F	15	clerk	37	26 Charles
	H	Gallagher Ruth W †	15	housewife	33	26 "
	K	Zaitz Anna N †	15	"	49	here
	L	Zaitz Dimitri N	15	salesman	29	"
	M	Zaitz Nicholas A	15	laborer	54	"
	N	Naughmane Nellie T †	16	housekeeper	50	"
	O	Thompson Harry A	20	machinist	48	"
	P	Thompson Mary E †	20	housewife	48	"
	R	Fennessey Arthur G	20	electrician	36	"
	S	Fennessey Elizabeth S †	20	housewife	71	"
	T	Scully Kathleen E †	41	housekeeper	37	"

Page	Letter	Full Name	Residence, Jan. 1	Occupation	Supposed Age	Reported Residence, Jan. 1 Street and Number

Washington Street—Continued

Letter	Full Name	Residence	Occupation	Age	Reported Residence
U	Sullivan Charles G	41	laborer	49	here
V	*Sullivan John	41	contractor	71	"
W	Sullivan Joseph T	41	serviceman	35	"
X	Sullivan Leo J	41	laborer	29	"
Y	*Sullivan Mary A †	41	housewife	72	"
Z	McGowan Charles F	45	mechanic	41	"
	1745				
A	McGowan Edith L †	45	housewife	42	"
B	Pepi Giovanna †	48	"	55	"
C	Pepi Liberty †	48	operator	23	"
D	Pepi Sebastiano	48	tile setter	62	"
E	Pepi Susan P †	48	housewife	24	New York
F	Pepi Virgil D	48	packer	25	"
G	Hikel Richard S	52 54	photographer	28	N Hampshire
H	Hikel Virginia I †	52 54	housewife	26	"
K	Fitzpatrick Catherine G †	52 54	"	58	here
L	Fitzpatrick James F	52 54	gardener	59	"
M	Fitzpatrick Katherine J †	52 54	stenographer	23	"
N	Watson Frances M †	60 62	housewife	31	"
O	Watson Redmond M	60 62	chauffeur	44	"
P	Sieminski Mitchell A	60 62	clerk	27	"
R	Sieminski Rose T †	60 62	housewife	27	"
S	Fleming John F	64 66	clerk	32	Norwood
T	Fleming Margaret †	64 66	housewife	31	"
U	Dolan Bridget †	64 66	waitress	30	Cambridge
V	*Farmer Katherine †	64 66	housekeeper	68	130 Dana av
W	Powers Alphonse	64 66	upholsterer	34	here
X	Powers Margaret E †	64 66	housewife	37	"
Y	O'Brien Mary A †	68	"	41	"
Z	O'Brien William E	68	bailiff	47	"
	1746				
A	Meehan Joseph F	68	salesman	32	Marlboro
B	Meehan Marguerite G †	68	housewife	28	"
C	Moore Godfrey	72	molder	61	here
D	Moore Maude †	72	housewife	57	"
E	Cox Eleanor C †	80 82	"	37	"
F	Cox Frederick M	80 82	clerk	44	"
G	*Martelli Anthony	80 82	retired	75	"
H	Martelli Louis P	80 82	laborer	34	"
K	*Martelli Rose †	80 82	housewife	61	"

Page	Letter	Full Name	Residence, Jan. 1, 1941.	Occupation	Supposed Age.	Reported Residence, Jan. 1, 1940. Street and Number.

Washington Street—Continued

Page	Letter	Full Name	Residence, Jan. 1, 1941.	Occupation	Supposed Age.	Reported Residence, Jan. 1, 1940. Street and Number.
	L*	Mollo Marie A †	93	housewife	61	Rhode Island
	M	Mollo Peter G	93	chauffeur	21	49 Water
	N	Mollo Salvatore	93	laborer	63	Rhode Island
	O	Finn Anna M †	93	operator	24	here
	P	Finn Robert M	93	custodian	55	"
	R	Finn Robert M, jr	93	electrician	23	"
	T	Sullivan Elisa G †	103	attendant	36	153 Princeton
	U	Pulira Frank	107	retired	65	15 Tyler
	V	Pulira Joseph	107	carpenter	27	15 "
	W	Pulira Mary †	107	housewife	27	15 "
	X	Dolan Della S †	111	"	41	here
	Y	Dolan Joseph M	111	clerk	43	"
	Z	McMahon Agnes G †	112	operator	37	"
1747						
	A	McMahon Mary E †	112	housekeeper	74	"
	B	Holmes Clement A	118	laborer	31	"
	C	Holmes Isabelle L †	118	housewife	53	"
	D	Holmes Louise S †	118	inspector	27	"
	E	Holmes Mary E †	118	clerk	30	"
	F	Johnson Frank A	118	"	27	"
	G	Johnson Isabella F †	118	housewife	26	"
	H	Curley Charles T	139	student	22	"
	K	Healy William H	139	retired	61	"
	L	Dunn John A	147	laborer	46	"
	M	Dunn Margaret M †	147	housewife	44	"
	O	Gibbons Hannah H †	151	housekeeper	61	"
	R	Moran Mary E †	152	housewife	87	9 Wash'n St pl
	S	Moran Michael J	152	retired	60	9 "
	T	Moran Thomas H	152	laborer	58	9 "
	U	Tolland Catherine †	160	housewife	26	here
	V	Tolland William O	160	manufacturer	30	"
	W*	Panciocco Jennie †	160	housewife	45	"
	X	Panciocco Peter	160	laborer	45	"
	Y*	Giammasi Elizabeth †	162	housekeeper	49	"
	Z	Giammasi Elizabeth †	162	stitcher	25	"
1748						
	A*	Devencenzio Antonio	162	laborer	60	"
	B	Devencenzio Benjamin	162	machinist	31	"
	C	Devencenzio Irene I †	162	housewife	30	"
	D	Sparrow Celia T †	164	"	27	"

Page	Letter	Full Name	Residence	Occupation	Reputed Age	Reported Residence

Washington Street (Continued)

Page	Letter	Full Name	Residence	Occupation	Reputed Age	Reported Residence
	E	Sparrow Paul F	164	chauffeur	28	here
	F	Zaniboni Fred M	164	contractor	55	"
	G	Zaniboni Inez †	164	housewife	50	"
	H	Zaniboni William A	164	clerk	21	"

Washington Street Place

Page	Letter	Full Name	Residence	Occupation	Reputed Age	Reported Residence
	M	Guastalli Alcide	9	gardener	45	Milton
	N	Guastalli Isolina †	9	housewife	36	"
	O	*Guastalli Marie †	9	"	37	19 Loring pl
	P	Guastalli Sante	9	gardener	48	19 "
	R	*Beausang Myra †	12	housekeeper	46	here
	T	Sanuth Louis	18	laborer	58	"
	U	*Sanuth Pauline †	18	housewife	51	"
	V	*Kolava Dominick	20	laborer	65	"
	W	*Kolava Stephanie †	20	housewife	65	"
	Y	*Jurewich Eleanor †	22	"	37	"
	X	Jurewich Joseph J	22	metalworker	47	"
	Z	Kleponis Albert	22	gagemaker	21	667 E Seventh
1749						
	A	Kleponis Eleanora E †	22	housewife	20	667 "
	B	Sullivan George A	24	laborer	53	here
	C	Sullivan Nellie M †	24	housewife	51	"
	D	Sullivan Noel P	24	metalworker	21	"
	E	Novicki Anthony	26	laborer	42	"
	F	Novicki Catherine †	26	housewife	38	"
	G	Guyot Herman	30	chef	43	"
	H	Guyot Mary M †	30	housewife	45	"

Water Street

Page	Letter	Full Name	Residence	Occupation	Reputed Age	Reported Residence
	K	Hendrickson Charles A	13	steamfitter	51	here
	L	Hendrickson Ellen †	13	housewife	56	"
	M	Dionne Edward J	13	metalworker	31	[illegible]
	N	Dionne Teresa M †	13	housewife	32	1098 "
	O	Creedon Lillian M †	13	"	17	here
	P	Wilder Jeannetta D †	21	housewife	18	"
	R	Constantino Domenic	21	woodworker	29	"

Page	Letter	Full Name	Residence, Jan. 1, 1941.	Occupation	Supposed Age.	Reported Residence, Jan. 1, 1940. Street and Number.

Water Street Continued

Page	Letter	Full Name	Residence, Jan. 1, 1941.	Occupation	Supposed Age.	Reported Residence, Jan. 1, 1940.
	S	Constantino Mary M †	21	housewife	30	here
	T	Burns Rosalie M †	23	"	34	"
	U	Burns Wilfred I	23	welder	39	"
	V	Nowell Arnold P	23	machinist	20	"
	W	Nowell Edna M †	23	housewife	42	"
	X	Nowell Herbert M	23	machinist	47	"
	Y	Thomas Helen H †	25–27	housewife	40	"
	Z	Thomas Joseph J	25–27	foreman	43	"
1750						
	A	*Ryan Gertrude L †	25–27	housewife	29	"
	B	Ryan John T	25–27	machinist	35	"
	C	Piccirilli Joseph	35	laborer	41	"
	D	Piccirilli Virginia E †	35	housewife	31	"
	E	*Negrino Bernard	35	laborer	58	"
	F	Negrino Richard F	35	installer	23	"
	G	Negrino Susan A †	35	cleaner	21	"
	H	Sbardella Eleanor †	36	operator	21	"
	K	Sbardella Salvatore	36	molder	44	"
	L	*Cavaretta Frank	36	laborer	43	Newton
	M	*Cavaretta Pasquina †	36	housewife	34	"
	N	Martin Sarah †	38	"	70	here
	O	Sinclair Bessie †	38	housekeeper	70	1295 Hyde Park av
	P	Moore John D	38	stockman	63	19 Summer
	R	Moore Mary C †	38	housewife	63	19 "
	S	Curley Harold D	40	tree surgeon	27	here
	T	Curley James F	40	clerk	34	"
	U	Curley Margaret F †	40	housewife	56	"
	V	Drozdoroski Luciana †	40	"	46	"
	W	Drozdoroski Stanley I	40	clerk	21	"
	X	Braley Hugh T	41	mechanic	29	12 Elm
	Y	Braley Ruth A †	41	housewife	31	69 Water
	Z	Diamond George J	42	laborer	38	here
1751						
	A	*Diamond John W	42	"	72	"
	B	Diamond Mary C †	42	housekeeper	45	"
	C	Baril Arthur C	42	laborer	32	44 Water
	D	Baril Flora M †	42	housewife	31	44 "
	E	Tynan Blanche †	42	"	26	126 Greenfield rd
	F	Tynan Edward A	42	operator	30	126 "

Water Street—Continued

Page	Letter	Full Name	Residence, Jan. 1, 1941	Occupation	Supposed Age	Reported Residence, Jan. 1, 1940. Street and Number
	G	Valentini Florindo	43	laborer	51	here
	H	Valentini Sarah—†	43	housewife	35	"
	K	*Francisco Mary L—†	43	merchant	64	41 Water
	L	Vendette Ann—†	43	housewife	20	20 Winslow
	M	Vendette John	43	laborer	25	41 Water
	N	Daggett Catherine R—†	44	housewife	34	here
	O	Crawford Nancy R—†	44	"	27	9 Caton
	P	Crawford Ralph W	44	clerk	37	9 "
	S	Olszewski Henry S	45	presser	27	here
	T	Olszewski Jennie K—†	45	housewife	23	"
	U	Demers Sabina B—†	45	"	21	"
	V	Demers Warren A	45	chauffeur	23	"
	W	Cibotte Delia—†	46	housewife	26	"
	X	Cibotte Joseph	46	machinist	29	"
	Y	Cibotte Albert	46	driller	25	"
	Z	*Cibotte Anthony	46	retired	63	"
1752						
	A	Cibotte Arthur	46	chauffeur	24	"
	B	*Cibotte Mary—†	46	housewife	62	"
	C	Cibotte Robert	46	laborer	20	"
	D	Cibotte Viola—†	46	operator	22	"
	E	Demers Margaret M—†	47	housewife	25	"
	F	Demers Melvin E	47	carpenter	30	"
	G	Lennon James J	47	shipfitter	27	"
	H	Lennon Mary—†	47	housewife	56	"
	K	Collins Charles E	47	guard	32	"
	L	Collins Mary L—†	47	housewife	29	"
	M	Valliere Bertha—†	49	"	43	"
	N	Valliere Simeon	49	metalworker	46	"
	O	Nardi Frank V	49	merchant	43	"
	P	*Nardi Mary P—†	49	housewife	39	"
	R	*Brazil Mary A—†	49	"	34	"
	S	Brazil Thomas F	49	operator	39	"
	T	Curley Florence J	50	bricklayer	55	36 Water
	U	*O'Riorden Catherine—†	50	housewife	55	here
	V	*O'Riorden John	50	clerk	20	"
	W	Jeanetti Anthony	50	chauffeur	28	118 Dana av
	X	Jeanetti Carmello	50	laborer	56	52 "
	Y	Jeanetti Filomena—†	50	housewife	50	52 "

Page	Letter	Full Name.	Residence, Jan. 1, 1941.	Occupation.	Supposed Age.	Reported Residence, Jan. 1, 1940. Street and Number.

Water Street—Continued

Page	Letter	Full Name.	Residence, Jan. 1, 1941.	Occupation.	Supposed Age.	Reported Residence, Jan. 1, 1940.
	Z	Guinazzo Albert	50	laborer	44	here
1753						
	A	Guinazzo Theresa—†	50	housewife	35	"
	B	McIntyre Martha P—†	53	"	60	"
	C	McIntyre William A	53	foreman	64	"
	F	Hickey Dorothea R—†	69	clerk	23	"
	G	Hickey Helen I—†	69	teacher	32	"
	H	Hickey John A	69	tester	29	"
	K	Hickey John J	69	engineer	64	"
	L	Hickey Mary J—†	69	housewife	64	"
	M	Melvin Berkeley F	69	calker	33	15 Osceola
	N	Melvin Lillian M—†	69	housewife	33	15 "
	O	Hickey Elsie M—†	69	"	41	here
	P	Hickey Robert J	69	electrician	41	"
	R	Gutowski Bartholomew	70	machinist	65	"
	S	Gutowski Frank	70	"	24	"
	T	Gutowski Jennie—†	70	waitress	21	"
	U	*Gutowski Rose—†	70	housewife	55	"
	V	McGowan Andrew P	70	mechanic	31	"
	W	*McGowan Florence—†	70	housewife	41	"
	X	Kurcab Catherine—†	72	laundryworker	27	"
	Y	*Kurcab Mary—†	72	housewife	55	"
	Z	Timmons Douglas B	72	laborer	21	"
1754						
	A	Timmons Harriett A—†	72	nurse	22	"
	B	Timmons Harry G	72	laborer	42	"
	C	Mirabito Armando J	74	student	22	"
	D	Mirabito Joseph	74	laborer	57	"
	E	Mirabito Mary C—†	74	housewife	48	"
	F	Mirabito William V	74	clerk	20	"
	G	Santoro Domenica—†	74	housewife	44	"
	H	Santoro John	74	laborer	52	"
	K	Kahler Catherine R—†	78	housewife	30	"
	L	Kahler William L	78	restaurateur	35	"
	M	Gregory Hugh D	78	laborer	55	"
	N	Gregory Mary M—†	78	housewife	48	"
	O	Vardaro Bernadette L—†	82	"	27	"
	P	Vardaro Louis R	82	machinist	28	"
	R	Crowley Bridget—†	82	housewife	68	"
	S	Crowley John	82	retired	79	"

Water Street—Continued

Page	Letter	Full Name	Residence	Occupation	Age	[illegible]
	T	Enaire Arthur J	92	laborer	40	here
	U	Enaire Theresa C †	92	housewife	38	"
	V	Moynihan Ann †	92	"	78	"
	W	Moynihan Margaret M †	94	"	39	"
	X	Moynihan Maurice J	94	laborer	40	"

Williams Avenue

Page	Letter	Full Name	Residence	Occupation	Age	[illegible]
	Y	Warakouski Helen I †	9	housekeeper	21	here
	Z	Woish John S	9	bartender	27	"
1755						
	A	Woish Julius J	9	carpenter	50	"
	B	Woish Rose I †	9	housewife	47	"
	C	Keating Margaret C †	11	"	54	"
	D	Keating Michael J	11	butcher	54	"
	F	Forrest Orilla D †	19	housewife	60	"
	G	Forrest Russell E	19	merchant	62	"
	H	Forrest William E	19	chauffeur	38	"
	K	Drammis Gladys M †	19	housewife	37	"
	L	Drammis Henry M	19	machinist	39	"
	M	Hall Annie †	23	housewife	48	"
	N	Hall Walter J	23	yard master	49	"
	O	Cline Freda N †	23	housewife	51	"
	P	Cline James F	23	laborer	56	"
	R	Cline James F, jr	23	"	24	"
	S	McWhinney Bernice †	23	housekeeper	37	"
	T	Baldwin Edith A †	31	housewife	70	"
	U	Baldwin William	31	barber	76	"
	V	Barritt Addie L †	31	housekeeper	68	"
	W	Barritt Elsie I †	31	"	66	"
	X	Connell Francis J	31	butcher	43	"
	Y	Connell Mary A †	31	housewife	45	"
	Z	Leason Sybil A †	35	housekeeper	72	"
1756						
	A	Hardy Emily †	35	housewife	49	"
	B	Hardy William	35	salesman	50	"
	C	O'Connor Catherine M †	37	housewife	47	"
	E	O'Connor James F	37	student	21	"
	D	O'Connor James H	37	chauffeur	18	"
	F	Johnson Alfred P	44	retired	60	"

Page	Letter	Full Name	Residence, Jan. 1, 1941	Occupation	Supposed Age	Reported Residence, Jan. 1, 1940. Street and Number

Williams Avenue—Continued

Page	Letter	Full Name	Residence, Jan. 1, 1941	Occupation	Supposed Age	Reported Residence, Jan. 1, 1940. Street and Number
	G	*Johnson Jennie M—†	41	housewife	53	here
	H	Chaisson Joseph E	41	carpenter	44	"
	K	Chaisson Mary M—†	41	housewife	41	"
	L	Demers Anna B—†	43	housekeeper	63	"
	M	Demers Peter J	43	roofer	33	"
	N	Thoms Helen E—†	48	secretary	37	"
	O	Thoms James F	48	plumber	46	"
	P	Thoms John W	48	policeman	50	"
	R	Thoms Nora E—†	48	housewife	50	"
	S	Swanson Harriet—†	49	housekeeper	43	"
	T	Swanson Lillian V—†	49	clerk	20	"
	U	Parker Albert C	49	sorter	21	"
	V	Parker Edith S—†	49	housekeeper	58	"
	W	Whidden Aubrey J	49	operator	37	"
	X	Whidden Rebecca M—†	49	housewife	32	"
	Y	Garber Arthur E	50	installer	52	"
	Z	Garber Arthur E, jr	50	chemist	24	"
1757						
	A	Garber Irene A—†	50	housewife	47	"
	B	Carey Della J—†	rear 50	housekeeper	40	"
	C	Killilea Anna M—†	52	housewife	27	"
	D	Killilea Peter J.	52	supervisor	30	"
	E	Killilea Ann F—†	52	bookkeeper	23	"
	F	Killilea Annie F—†	52	housewife	52	"
	G	Killilea Peter J, jr	52	chauffeur	57	"
	H	Walsh Mary A—†	52	bookkeeper	22	"
	K	Williams Arthur W	53	painter	75	"
	L	Williams Ethel L—†	53	housewife	62	"
	M	Williams Vera—†	53	housekeeper	25	"
	N	Callahan Jerome	55	clerk	49	"
	O	Callahan Mary—†	55	housekeeper	68	"
	P	Manning Bernard J	56	laborer	68	"
	R	Manning Mary E—†	56	housewife	50	"
	S	Manning Regina M—†	56	student	20	"
	T	Obin Joseph A	56	painter	35	"
	U	Obin Mary D—†	56	housewife	27	"
	V	Auger Clara F—†	56	"	59	"
	W	Auger Edmond	56	molder	59	"
	X	Auger Eleanor M—†	56	clerk	21	"
	Y	Auger Joseph J	56	draftsman	29	"

Page	Letter	Full Name	[illegible]	[illegible]	[illegible]	[illegible] Street and Number

Williams Avenue—Continued

Page	Letter	Full Name	Residence	Occupation	Age	Reported Residence
	Z	Bacher George	rear 56	clerk	21	here
1758						
	A	Bacher Nellie †	" 56	stitcher	42	"
	B	Thayer George F	60	conductor	65	"
	C	Thayer Margaret R †	60	housewife	63	"
	D	Jess James H	62	chauffeur	44	"
	E	Jess Marguerite G †	62	housewife	33	"
	F	Jess Maryan G †	62	at home	79	"
	G	Kobs Anna A †	62	housewife	32	here
	H	Kobs William A	62	inspector	36	"
	K	Jansson Esther E †	64	housewife	21	Dedham
	L	Jansson Selig H	64	machinist	22	Quincy
	M	Richardson Edward A	64	assembler	26	here
	N	Richardson Frances N †	64	housewife	23	"
	O	McSweeney Charles A	65	inspector	47	24 [illegible]
	P	McSweeney Margaret E †	65	housewife	46	24 "
	R	McSweeney Margaret M †	65	student	20	24 "
	S	Hart John J	66	electrician	33	here
	T	*Hart Sophie M †	66	housewife	34	"
	U	Splitz Alice J †	66	"	40	"
	V	Splitz Stephen J	66	millhand	38	"
	W	Whiting Walter R	67	carpenter	47	"
	X	Perry Abbie W †	69	housewife	49	"
	Y	Perry Hadwen C	69	salesman	44	"
	Z	Openshaw Helen M †	69	operator	22	"
1759						
	A	Openshaw Mary B †	69	housewife	51	"
	B	Lucas Eleanor M †	73	waitress	27	"
	C	Lucas John	73	gardener	59	"
	D	*Lucas Mary A †	73	housewife	50	"
	E	Goff Annie G †	75	"	49	"
	F	Goff Frederick S	75	laborer	58	"
	G	Goff Frederick W	75	busboy	22	"
	H	Goff Irene G †	75	inspector	23	"
	K	Devlin Beatrice M †	91	housewife	[illegible]	[illegible]
	L	Devlin Paul A	91	foreman	[illegible]	[illegible]
	M	Hains Harry G	93	machinist	37	[illegible]
	N	*Hains Marjorie G †	93	housewife	[illegible]	[illegible]
	O	Ramos Bartley	93	machinist	[illegible]	[illegible]
	P	*Ramos Mary †	93	housewife	[illegible]	[illegible]

Page	Letter	Full Name.	Residence, Jan. 1, 1941.	Occupation.	Supposed Age.	Reported Residence, Jan. 1, 1940. Street and Number.

Williams Avenue—Continued

Page	Letter	Full Name.	Residence, Jan. 1, 1941.	Occupation.	Supposed Age.	Reported Residence, Jan. 1, 1940. Street and Number.
	R	Kuehn Helen M—†	95	housewife	30	here
	S	Kuehn Kenneth H	95	inspector	31	"
	T	McGunigle Mary J—†	95	housewife	27	346 Chelsea
	U	McGunigle William G	95	machinist	31	346 "
	V	Hagert Florence M—†	97	housewife	21	Foxboro
	W	Hagert George E	97	bookkeeper	23	"
	Y	Gibbs Annie M—†	107	housewife	53	here
	Z	Gibbs Charles B	107	retired	59	"
1760						
	B	Butler Charles H	163	inspector	49	"
	C	Butler Charles H, jr	163	superintendent	21	"
	D	Butler Dorothy M—†	163	clerk	23	"
	E	Butler Mildred E—†	163	housewife	43	"
	F	Jacobs Mary M—†	169	"	52	"
	G	Jacobs Ralph B	169	manager	52	"

Ward 18—Precinct 18

CITY OF BOSTON

LIST OF RESIDENTS
20 YEARS OF AGE AND OVER

(NON-CITIZENS INDICATED BY ASTERISK)
(FEMALES INDICATED BY DAGGER)

AS OF

JANUARY 1, 1941

JOSEPH F. TIMILTY, *Chairman*
FREDERIC E. DOWLING, *Secretary*
WILLIAM A. MOTLEY, JR.
FRANCIS B. McKINNEY
HILDA HEDSTROM QUIRK
Listing Board.

CITY OF BOSTON PRINTING DEPARTMENT

Page	Letter	Full Name	Residence, Jan. 1, 1941.	Occupation	Supposed Age	Reported Residence, Jan. 1, 1940. Street and Number.

1800

A Street

Page	Letter	Full Name	Residence, Jan. 1, 1941.	Occupation	Supposed Age	Reported Residence, Jan. 1, 1940. Street and Number.
1800	A	Kowalczik John	5	retired	71	here
	B	*Kowalczik Rozalia—†	5	housewife	69	"
	C	Hynes Benjamin A	5	metalworker	46	"
	D	Hynes Diana—†	5	housewife	42	"
	E	Merrell Dwight F	7	laborer	29	1410 Hyde Park av
	F	Merrell Gloria C—†	7	housewife	31	1410 "
	G	*Shea Elizabeth—†	7	"	80	here
	H	Shea John A	7	laborer	49	"
	K	*Scopa Ciriaco	7	"	55	82 Business
	L	Scopa Marion—†	7	housekeeper	30	82 "
	M	Murray Emma J—†	7	"	43	here
	N	*Cella Jacob	7	laborer	50	"
	O	Monaco Frank B	7	machinist	22	49 Business
	P	*Monaco Julia N—†	7	housewife	42	49 "
	R	Shepherd Adolph H	9	roofer	37	here
	S	Shepherd Mary G—†	9	housewife	33	"
	T	Merlo John	9	laborer	54	11 A
	U	Merlo Mary—†	9	housewife	50	11 "
	V	Green Irene A—†	9	"	37	here
	W	Green Thomas P	9	chauffeur	42	"
	X	Green Thomas P, jr	9	"	21	"
	Y	Johnson Edith—†	9	housewife	38	"
	Z	Johnson Segel	9	painter	33	"
1801	B	*Kalenda Roman	11A	laborer	65	323 Hyde Park av
	C	Ragusa Frank	11A	"	38	7 A
	D	Ragusa Josephine—†	11A	housewife	29	800 Cummins H'way
	E	Stracqualursi Edmund	11A	factoryhand	20	here
	F	Stracqualursi Frank	11A	laborer	49	"
	G	*Stracqualursi Julia—†	11A	housewife	41	"
	H	Tarallo Alexander A	15	molder	21	"
	K	*Tarallo Constance—†	15	housewife	46	"
	L	Tarallo Grace C—†	15	stitcher	24	"
	M	Tarallo Nunzio	15	laborer	55	"
	N	Tarallo Paul T	15	stripper	27	"
	O	*Sebgo John	23	laborer	55	260 Cummins H'way
	P	Yucus Stanley	23	blacksmith	52	here
	R	*Domiciewicz Alexander	25	laborer	44	"
	S	*Domiciewicz Mary—†	25	housewife	45	"

Page	Letter	Full Name				

Allen Street

Page	Letter	Full Name				
	T	Aprea Rocco J	8	machinist	23	13 Walto[illegible]
	U	Lazarovich Jeannette J †	8	housewife	25	here
	V	Lazarovich John P	8	tavernkeeper	28	"
	W	*Memmo Angelina †	8	housewife	31	"
	X	Memmo Nicholas	8	laborer	36	"
	Y	Prizio Frances A †	9	housewife	30	[illegible]
	Z	Germano Louis	9	inspector	28	here
1802						
	A	Germano Maryanna J †	9	housewife	28	"
	B	Sera Anthony	10	stonemason	52	"
	C	*Sera Mary †	10	housewife	35	"
	D	*Palumbo Augusto	10	millhand	51	"
	E	Palumbo Frank	10	upholsterer	25	"
	F	*Palumbo Marie †	10	housewife	54	"
	G	Palumbo Peter	10	gardener	20	"
	H	Palumbo Phillip	10	upholsterer	27	"
	K	Spadano Daniel	11	fireman	48	"
	L	*Spadano Nicoletta †	11	housewife	42	"
	N	*Rampini Dominica †	16	"	54	"
	O	Rampini Samuel	16	laborer	57	"

Barry Street

Page	Letter	Full Name				
	P	Plocharski Joseph S	8	machinist	55	here
	R	*Plocharski Stella A †	8	housewife	46	"
	S	Plocharski Stephen J	8	machinist	21	"
	T	Coullahan Catherine G †	18	bookkeeper	55	"
	U	Coullahan Margaret D †	18	housewife	53	"
	V	Coullahan Mary R †	18	"	57	"
	W	Jones Evelyn M †	18	"	35	"
	X	Wood Caroline E †	22	"	63	"
	Y	Wood Lloyd J	22	foreman	27	"
	Z	Rocheleau Amedee J	24	molder	50	"
1803						
	A	Rocheleau Edith R †	24	housewife	5[illegible]	"

Business Street

Page	Letter	Full Name				
	C	Jenkins Edward R	11	carpenter	42	here
	D	Jenkins Josephine V †	11	housewife	42	"

Page	Letter	Full Name	Residence, Jan. 1, 1941.	Occupation.	Supposed Age.	Reported Residence, Jan. 1, 1940. Street and Number.

Barry Street—Continued

Page	Letter	Full Name	Residence, Jan. 1, 1941.	Occupation.	Supposed Age.	Reported Residence, Jan. 1, 1940. Street and Number.
	E	White Frank J	11	machinist	65	1319 River
	F	White Margaret T—†	11	housewife	47	1319 "
	G	Strand John F	11	binder	30	here
	H	Strand Margaret L—†	11	housewife	29	"
	K	O'Brien Mary—†	11	"	30	1338 River
	L	O'Brien Terrence P	11	chemist	48	1338 "
	M	Granara Frank H	17	cutter	30	here
	N	Granara Margaret F—†	17	housewife	27	"
	O	Lambert Francis A	17	laborer	35	"
	P	Lambert Margaret—†	17	housewife	64	"
	R	Perchard Elizabeth M—†	17	"	23	79 Austin
	S	Perchard Paul A	17	clerk	26	79 "
	T	Feeney Elizabeth F—†	17	housewife	34	here
	U	Feeney Patrick J	17	bartender	44	"
	V	Allen George A	17	carpenter	40	11 Roxanna
	W	Allen Mildred C—†	17	housewife	33	11 "
	X	Walsh Margaret E—†	21	"	35	here
	Y	Walsh Thomas F	21	finisher	35	"
	Z	McDermott Francis J	21	student	20	"
1804						
	A	McDermott Johanna E—†	21	housewife	35	"
	B	Cianca Lena—†	21	"	28	Dedham
	C	Cianca Nello	21	laborer	30	"
	D	Santospirito Bartolo	21	retired	68	"
	E	MacMunn Grace A—†	21	housewife	38	1326 River
	G	Wilkins Winifred—†	24	housekeeper	45	here
	H	Brown Flora—†	24	housewife	47	29 East
	K	Brown James G	24	metalworker	22	29 "
	L	Adams Richard J	24	carpenter	40	here
	M	Adams Rita M—†	24	housewife	48	"
	N	Matthews Lillian M—†	25	clerk	54	"
	O	Bouchard Octave	25	mechanic	36	61 Gordon av
	P	*Loubier Jeannette F—†	25	stitcher	31	61 "
	R	*Loubier Philomena—†	25	housewife	67	61 "
	S	Foley Audrey E—†	25	"	23	here
	T	Foley James J	25	manager	27	"
	U	Berk Chester M	25	mechanic	29	"
	V	Berk Helen G—†	25	housewife	30	"
	W	Loubier Josephine—†	26	"	38	"
	X	Loubier Louis	26	welder	40	"
	Y	Marusa Alexander J	27	"	31	"

Business Street (Continued)

Page	Letter	Full Name	Residence, Jan. 1	Occupation	Supposed Age	Reported Residence, Jan. 1, Street and Number
	Z	Marusa Marie G †	27	housewife	26	here
1805						
	A	Bartolomeo Emilio	27	chauffeur	32	"
	B	*Bartolomeo Louis	27	finisher	60	"
	C	Finnigham Hattie †	27	housekeeper	68	"
	D	Rampino Bertha †	27	"	25	"
	E	Mitchell Ambrose	28	clerk	29	"
	F	Mitchell Marion †	28	housewife	26	"
	G	Tolland Cyril E	28	machinist	43	"
	H	Tolland Nora †	28	housewife	39	"
	K	Viscardy Charles F	29	cleaner	40	[illegible]
	L	Viscardy Elizabeth †	29	housewife	34	1479 "
	M	Russo Angelina G †	29	"	32	11 Ellis
	N	Russo Frank J	29	plumber	37	11 "
	O	Sundell Hilma †	30	housekeeper	64	here
	P	*Duguay Mary J †	30	housewife	56	"
	R	*Duguay Onesime	30	laborer	62	"
	S	Webster Assunta M †	30	housewife	21	99 Maple
	T	Webster George H	30	tender	29	99 "
	U	Abate Grace †	30	housekeeper	23	here
	V	Nee Mary E †	30	"	54	"
	W	Barsell Marguerite †	30	housewife	45	876 Harris'n Av
	X	Barsell William	30	clerk	47	876 "
	Y	Dunn Lydia M †	33	housewife	42	here
	Z	Dunn William A	33	molder	45	"
1806						
	A	Fallon Almira F †	33	housekeeper	37	"
	B	Russo Pasquale	33	painter	52	"
	C	Terry Mary †	33	housekeeper	65	"
	D	*Fortin Genevieve †	34	housewife	73	"
	E	Fortin Philias	34	laborer	77	"
	F	Carew Marie A †	34	housewife	30	"
	G	Carew Robert A	34	fireman	36	"
	H	*Demers Aristide	rear 34	mechanic	44	"
	K	*Demers Arminie †	" 34	housewife	45	"
	L	Mombourquette Frederick A	36	machinist	36	"
	M	Mombourquette Leona C †	36	housewife	33	"
	N	Deleconio Ernest	38	molder	46	"
	O	Deleconio Ernest, jr	38	plumber	21	"
	P	Deleconio Genevieve †	38	clerk	25	"
	R	Deleconio Josephine †	38	"	23	"

Page	Letter	Full Name.	Residence, Jan. 1, 1941.	Occupation.	Supposed Age.	Reported Residence, Jan. 1, 1940. Street and Number.

Business Street—Continued

Page	Letter	Full Name.	Residence, Jan. 1, 1941.	Occupation.	Supposed Age.	Reported Residence, Jan. 1, 1940. Street and Number.
	s	*Deleconio Mary—†	38	housewife	49	here
	T	*Samuelson Ina—†	38	"	35	"
	U	Samuelson Victor	38	carpenter	46	"

Central Avenue

Page	Letter	Full Name.	Residence, Jan. 1, 1941.	Occupation.	Supposed Age.	Reported Residence, Jan. 1, 1940. Street and Number.
	V	Fowler George	12A	mechanic	42	here
	W	Fowler Mary E—†	12A	housewife	41	"
	X	Chisholm Catherine—†	14	"	50	"
	Y	Chisholm Colin M	14	carpenter	56	"
	Z	Blais Imelda—†	16	bookkeeper	29	"
1807						
	A	Blais Mary H—†	16	housewife	55	"
	B	Blais Reginald	16	machinist	30	"
	C	Blais Vincent R	16	clerk	25	"
	D	Thayer Mary E—†	16	housewife	43	"

Dacy Street

Page	Letter	Full Name.	Residence, Jan. 1, 1941.	Occupation.	Supposed Age.	Reported Residence, Jan. 1, 1940. Street and Number.
	E	Martini Olive M—†	2	housewife	26	here
	F	*Martini William D	2	stonemason	36	"
	H	Paula Dominic R	8	operator	40	"
	K	*Paula Theresa—†	8	housewife	32	"

Dana Avenue

Page	Letter	Full Name.	Residence, Jan. 1, 1941.	Occupation.	Supposed Age.	Reported Residence, Jan. 1, 1940. Street and Number.
	L	Alberto John P	3	welder	25	here
	M	Alberto Mary E—†	3	housewife	23	"
	N	Cooper James	3	molder	62	"
	O	Cooper Sidney	3	machinist	32	"
	P	Cooper Sidney A—†	3	housewife	62	"
	R	Robery Ernest W	3	welder	32	28 Ottawa
	S	Robery Ruth M—†	3	housewife	22	28 "
	T	Scagnolia Lazerino	3	machinist	25	4 Glenbrook
	U	Scagnolia Mary—†	3	housewife	20	4 "
	V	Grant Florence—†	6	housekeeper	36	6 Walcott ct
	W	Peterson Edythe C—†	6A	housewife	46	1295 Hyde Park av
	X	Martell Henry	7	carpenter	23	here
	Y	Martell Margaret A—†	7	housewife	47	"
	Z	Martell Robert T	7	carpenter	47	"

1808

Dana Avenue Continued

Page	Letter	Full Name				
1808	A	Brolin Malcolm	8	clerk	20	here
	B	Brolin Malcolm F	8	machinist	42	"
	C	Brolin Mary A †	8	housewife	40	"
	D	Forrester Helen M †	8A	housekeeper	35	"
	E	Norton Gertrude M †	8A	"	47	"
	F	McCarthy Marie E †	11	housewife	26	25 Sumner
	G	McCarthy William S	11	assembler	26	25 "
	H	Ventola Anna C †	11	clerk	34	here
	K	Ventola Mary A †	11	housewife	51	"
	L	Dray Thomas L	11	retired	81	"
	M	Kilgallen Frances M †	11	housewife	28	"
	N	Kilgallen John E	11	clerk	28	"
	O	Lawlor Elizabeth A †	11	housewife	50	"
	P	Lawlor Walter J	11	clerk	53	"
	R	Goldberg Bessie †	11	housewife	40	"
	S	Goldberg Charles	11	manager	48	"
	T	Morrissey Mary T †	11	housewife	53	"
	U	Morrissey Thomas J	11	accountant	53	"
	V	Randolph Catherine A †	11	housewife	31	"
	W	Randolph William E	11	serviceman	30	"
	X	Lawler Edward F	12	clerk	40	"
	Y	Lawler Mildred M †	12	housewife	26	"
	Z	Oderman Anna †	14	"	65	"
1809	A	Oderman John F	14	manager	66	"
	B	Tooher Jane †	15	housekeeper	60	"
	C	Buckley Catherine †	24	housewife	45	"
	D	*Holmes Mary †	25	"	38	"
	E	*Kurpeski Helen †	25	"	51	"
	F	*Kurpeski Stanley	25	laborer	56	"
	G	Kurpeski Stephen	25	clerk	25	"
	H	Kurpeski Wanda †	25	"	22	"
	K	Kurpeski William	25	machinist	24	"
	L	*Sanfilippo Margaret †	26	housewife	40	"
	M	*Sanfilippo Salvatore	26	laborer	58	"
	N	Glant Armand	26	chef	30	15 Minden
	O	Glant Mary †	26	housewife	30	15 "
	P	Rooney Hugh	26	laborer	65	15 "
	R	Wills Hazel S †	27	housewife	33	here
	S	Wills James A	27	operator	30	"

Page	Letter	Full Name	Residence Jan. 1 1941	Occupation	Supposed Age	Reported Residence Jan. 1, 1940. Street and Number.

Dana Avenue—Continued

Page	Letter	Full Name	Residence Jan. 1 1941	Occupation	Supposed Age	Reported Residence Jan. 1, 1940. Street and Number.
	T	Lane Jane H—†	27	janitor	51	Somerville
	U	Lane Loretta—†	27	housewife	36	"
	V	Ginnochio Eugene	27	manager	29	here
	W	Ginnochio Evelyn—†	27	housewife	35	"
	X	Kosleika John	28	laborer	29	"
	Y	*Kosleika Katherine—†	28	housewife	54	"
	Z	Jekowski Charles	28	machinist	27	"
1810						
	A	Jekowski Edward	28	"	24	"
	B	Jekowski Frank	28	"	26	"
	C	*Jekowski Helen—†	28	housewife	58	"
	D	Hayes Sarah—†	29	clerk	57	"
	E	Paszdowski Blanche—†	29	housewife	48	"
	F	Paszdowski John	29	weaver	46	"
	G	Paszdowski Wanda—†	29	saleswoman	24	"
	H	*Tirrella Helen C—†	31	housekeeper	30	"
	K	*Tirrella Maria—†	31	housewife	86	"
	L	Tirrella Pasquale	31	engineer	57	"
	M	Ferrande Mary—†	31	housewife	32	"
	N	Grenda Adolph	32	foreman	25	"
	O	Grenda Benjamin	32	polisher	25	"
	P	*Grenda Stephania—†	32	housewife	52	"
	R	*Grenda William	32	painter	57	"
	S	Grenda William G	32	electrician	29	"
	T	Hassell Everett J	34	B F D	40	26 Harvard av
	U	Lacey Gladys—†	34	housewife	37	26 "
	V	Casciano Anthony	35	machinist	25	here
	W	Casciano Boniface	35	fireman	52	"
	X	Casciano Ettore	35	student	22	"
	Y	Casciano Margaret—†	35	clerk	20	"
	Z	Casciano Mary—†	35	"	26	"
1811						
	A	Casciano Virginia—†	35	housewife	49	"
	B	Molloy Delia—†	36	"	50	"
	C	Molloy John	36	fireman	60	"
	D	Majewski Edna—†	37	clerk	21	"
	E	Majewski Francis S	37	laborer	25	"
	F	*Majewski Josephine—†	37	housewife	40	"
	G	Vardaro Carmella—†	37	"	52	"
	H	Kowaleski Joseph	38	machinist	60	"
	K	Kowaleski Seta—†	38	clerk	20	"

Page	Letter	Full Name	Residence	Occupation	Age	Reported Residence

Dana Avenue (Continued)

Page	Letter	Full Name	Residence	Occupation	Age	Reported Residence
	L	*Adamski Catherine †	38	housewife	65	here
	M	Adamski Helen †	38	clerk	38	"
	N	Nash Anna †	rear 38	housekeeper	78	"
	O	*Lameiras Julia †	39	housewife	37	"
	P	Lameiras Julius D	39	machinist	40	"
	R	Gabriel John	39	"	25	Cambridge
	S	Gabriel Ruth †	39	housewife	24	"
	T	Gebhardt Alberta J †	41	"	38	here
	U	Gebhardt Carl G	41	laborer	38	"
	V	Hines Elizabeth C †	42	housewife	54	"
	W	Hines Helen †	42	clerk	20	"
	X	Reisert Philip	42	machinist	56	"
	Y	Spinale Mary H †	42	housewife	30	"
	Z	*Colella Gennaro	42	retired	71	78 Business
1812						
	A	Mariani Joseph	42	laborer	37	11 Allen
	B	Mariani Sally †	42	housewife	33	11 "
	C	Kwiatkowski Josephine †	43	"	43	here
	D	Kwiatkowski Walter	43	blacksmith	54	"
	E	Kwiatkowski Zenon	43	"	22	"
	F	Haudel Edna M †	43	housewife	28	"
	G	Haudel Herbert E	43	machinist	38	15 Winton
	K	Narciso Dominick A	46	clerk	26	here
	L	Narciso Helda C †	46	housewife	20	"
	M	*McGourty Mary †	46	housekeeper	67	102 Appleton
	N	Robertson Grace A †	46	"	40	here
	O	Robertson James	46	clerk	23	"
	R	Sacramone Angela †	47	housewife	29	"
	S	Sacramone James	47	clerk	30	"
	T	Bartone Francesco	48	laborer	52	"
	U	Bartone Johanna †	48	housewife	52	"
	V	Narciso Guy J	48	papermaker	29	"
	W	Narciso Stella †	48	housewife	28	"
	X	McConnon Anna L †	49	"	45	"
	Y	McConnon Joseph A	49	painter	40	"
	Z	Lucas John	49	machinist	55	"
1813						
	A	Mercaites Anthony	49	clerk	20	"
	B	*Mercaites Beatrice †	49	housewife	57	"
	C	Mercaites Francis	49	clerk	24	"
	E	Waterman Bertha R †	50A	"	22	"

Page	Letter	Full Name.	Residence, Jan. 1, 1941.	Occupation.	Supposed Age.	Reported Residence, Jan. 1, 1940. Street and Number.

Dana Avenue—Continued

Page	Letter	Full Name.	Residence, Jan. 1, 1941.	Occupation.	Supposed Age.	Reported Residence, Jan. 1, 1940. Street and Number.
	F	Waterman Harry H	50A	electrician	50	here
	G	Christensen Mary—†	52	housewife	50	71 Davison
	H	Cataloni Agnes—†	52	"	41	here
	K	Cataloni Charles	52	machinist	46	"
	N	Abramoski Aurela—†	57	inspector	22	"
	O	*Abramoski Blanche—†	57	housewife	50	"
	P	Abramoski James W	57	engineer	26	"
	R	Abramoski Louis	57	machinist	56	"
	S	*Boddie Elizabeth—†	59	housewife	59	"
	T	*Boddie Flora—†	59	housekeeper	49	"
	U	Boddie James D	59	rubbermaker	61	"
	V	Corbett Elizabeth E—†	60	superintendent	53	"
	W	Corbett Ellen B—†	60	clerk	55	"
	X	Corbett Louis F	60	"	57	"
	Y	Corbett Mary H—†	60	at home	60	"
	Z	Corbett William L	60	retired	68	"
1814						
	A	Walsh Johanna V—†	60	housekeeper	51	"
	B	Pinnel Estelle—†	61	housewife	33	"
	C	Pinnel Warren	61	carpenter	33	"
	D	Zak Bronie	61	machinist	24	"
	E	*Zak Kostanty	61	"	50	"
	F	Zak Mary—†	61	clerk	21	"
	G	*Zak Sophie—†	61	housewife	47	"
	H	Santelli Frank	63	machinist	39	"
	K	Santelli Susie—†	63	housewife	38	"
	L	*Rosenbaum Alfred	63	clerk	25	"
	M	*Rosenbaum Anna—†	63	housewife	54	"
	N	*Rosenbaum Augustine	63	tailor	54	"
	O	Tevenan Margaret T—†	65	housewife	37	"
	P	*Tevenan Patrick P	65	laborer	39	"
	R	Santospirito Geraldine—†	65	housewife	24	"
	S	Santospirito Joseph R	65	laborer	29	"

Easton Avenue

Page	Letter	Full Name.	Residence, Jan. 1, 1941.	Occupation.	Supposed Age.	Reported Residence, Jan. 1, 1940. Street and Number.
	T	White Thomas H	7	fireman	46	here
	U	White Wanda A—†	7	housewife	36	"
	V	*Budvits Barbara—†	7	"	55	"
	W	Budvits Charles	7	painter	23	"
	X	Budvits Joseph F	7	laborer	30	"

Page	Letter	Full Name	Residence	Occupation	Supposed Age	Reported Residence

Easton Avenue—Continued

Page	Letter	Full Name	Residence	Occupation	Supposed Age	Reported Residence
	Y	Budvits Joseph C	7	retired	63	here
	Z	*LeBlanc Joseph	9	painter	38	"
1815						
	A	LeBlanc Rita B †	9	housewife	32	"
	B	Tinkham Ralph E	11	painter	48	"
	C	Tinkham Viola †	11	housewife	43	"
	D	Duggan Bessie F †	12	supervisor	46	"
	E	Duggan Francis C	12	decorator	31	"
	F	Duggan Helen E †	12	housekeeper	42	"
	G	McWilliams Margaret J †	12	stitcher	37	"
	H	Scarpaci Joseph M	13	laborer	20	"
	K	Scarpaci Nellie P †	13	housewife	42	"
	L	Scarpaci Philip F	13	molder	44	"
	M	Buzzell Delia †	15	housekeeper	83	"
	N	Grenier Lester J	15	upholsterer	34	"
	O	Grenier Olive K †	15	housewife	34	"
	P	*Oleszefsky Anastasia †	15	"	78	"
	R	*Oleszefsky Benjamin	15	laborer	64	"
	S	Szymczak Jacob	15	blacksmith	51	"
	T	Szymczak Sophie †	15	housewife	40	"
	U	Ginnochio Andrew A	17	chauffeur	25	"
	V	Ginnochio Margaret M †	17	housewife	21	"
	W	Lloyd Elfrieda M †	17	"	56	60 Davison
	X	Lloyd Uriah H	17	retired	75	60 "
	Y	Logan Frances E †	19	housewife	21	[illegible]
	Z	Logan John E	19	laborer	23	59A "
1816						
	A	*Sprague Margaret M †	19	housewife	35	here
	B	Sprague Robert C	19	chauffeur	35	"
	C	Jerome Vincent W	21	machinist	24	106 Dana av
	D	Jerome Walter G	21	metalworker	29	106 "
	E	Bykowski Lucian	21	carpenter	52	here
	F	*Bykowski Mary †	21	housewife	53	"
	G	*Martino Anna L †	22	"	43	17 Grant
	H	Martino Vincent	22	molder	44	17 "
	K	Briggs Clifford E	23	painter	34	here
	L	Briggs Leah S †	23	housewife	31	"
	M	*Kodzis Adolf	23	laborer	50	"
	N	Kodzis Antonette †	23	clerk	23	"
	P	Kodzis Michael	23	laborer	24	"
	O	*Kodzis Teofila †	23	housewife	52	"

Page.	Letter	Full Name	Residence, Jan. 1, 1941	Occupation	Supposed Age.	Reported Residence, Jan. 1, 1940. Street and Number.

Easton Avenue—Continued

Page.	Letter	Full Name	Residence, Jan. 1, 1941	Occupation	Supposed Age.	Reported Residence, Jan. 1, 1940.
	R	Fox Francis E	26	painter	37	here
	S	Fox Katherine E—†	26	housewife	37	"
	T	Fitzgerald Mary E—†	26	"	24	"
	U	Fitzgerald Richard J	26	painter	24	"
	V	Lasky Alice J—†	27	housewife	23	"
	W	Lasky John V	27	laborer	26	"
	X*	Kalsevich Paul	27	"	55	21 Easton av
	Y*	Maneluk Frances—†	27	housewife	47	here
	Z	Maneluk Trofem	27	laborer	49	"
1817						
	A	Mickielevich Victoria P—†	27	hairdresser	21	"
	B	Chisholm Eleanor A—†	28	clerk	31	"
	C	Chisholm Henry G	28	chauffeur	31	11 Monponset
	D	Chisholm Howard F	28	metalworker	37	here
	E	Chisholm James W	28	retired	72	"
	F	Chisholm Jeannette A—†	28	waitress	38	"
	G	Chisholm Margaret C—†	28	houseworker	42	"
	H	Chisholm Mary L—†	28	housewife	67	"
	K	Chisholm Mary V—†	28	"	40	"
	L	Chisholm Raymond F	28	salesman	27	"
	M	Gorman Catherine A—†	29	housekeeper	55	"
	N	Rooney Katherine M—†	29	housewife	41	"
	O	Rooney Patrick H	29	supervisor	50	"
	P	Fuco Adeline—†	33	housewife	45	49 Central av
	R	Fuco Henry G	33	coach	25	49 "
	S	Fuco Joseph	33	carpenter	55	49 "
	T	Fuco Mary F—†	33	clerk	23	49 "
	U	Fuco Nancy K—†	33	"	21	49 "
	V	Mullen Margaret V—†	34	housekeeper	62	here
	W*	Markowski Joseph	35	laborer	50	"
	X*	Podworski Anthony	35	"	53	"
	Y*	Zawacki Felix	35	molder	47	"
	Z*	Fournier Alfred	35	carpenter	39	"
1818						
	A	Fournier Laura P—†	35	housewife	36	"
	B	Cibotti Donato	36	laborer	35	"
	C*	Cibotti Mary—†	36	housewife	49	"
	D	Cibotti Nicholas	36	laborer	55	"
	E	Sacramona Alice H—†	37	housewife	27	"
	F	Sacramona Thomas	37	mechanic	32	"
	G	Murphy Cecelia—†	37	housewife	38	22½ Norton

Page	Letter	Full Name	Residence, Jan. 1, 1941	Occupation	Supposed Age	Reported Residence, Jan. 1, 1940. Street and Number

Easton Avenue—Continued

Page	Letter	Full Name	Residence, Jan. 1, 1941	Occupation	Supposed Age	Reported Residence, Jan. 1, 1940. Street and Number
	H	Murphy Robert E	37	laborer	45	22½ Norton
	K	Taylor Burton M	38	clerk	30	here
	L	Taylor Margaret R †	38	housewife	29	"
	M	*Palie Anthony	38	laborer	18	"
	N	Palie Carmel	38	"	20	"
	O	Palie Julia R †	38	stitcher	21	"
	P	*Palie Mary †	38	housewife	48	"
	R	Petrillo Albert	39	chauffeur	26	"
	S	Petrillo Julia A †	39	housewife	20	"
	T	Russo Angelina †	40	"	58	37 Easton av
	U	Russo Felix	40	retired	67	37 "
	V	Russo Felix, jr	40	chauffeur	33	37 "
	W	Russo Joseph	40	clerk	23	37 "
	X	Russo Lawrence	40	laborer	31	37 "
	Y	*Benson Annie M †	42	housewife	60	21 "
	Z	Benson Francis H	42	laborer	40	21 "
1819						
	A	Benson George E	42	mechanic	24	21 "
	B	Benson Howard W	42	clerk	21	21 "
	C	Benson James T	42	laborer	32	21 "
	D	Martin Alice E †	42	housekeeper	62	21 "

Factory Street

Page	Letter	Full Name	Residence, Jan. 1, 1941	Occupation	Supposed Age	Reported Residence, Jan. 1, 1940. Street and Number
	E	Ventola Francis J	5	manager	32	here
	F	Ventola Mary C †	5	housewife	28	"
	G	Conti Frances †	5	"	28	"
	H	Conti Thomas	5	coremaker	27	"
	K	Ventola Alfred E	5	chauffeur	36	"
	L	Ventola Caroline †	5	housewife	35	"
	M	Lennon Frances J †	22	"	41	"
	N	Lennon John H	22	laborer	41	"
	O	Lynch Edward M	24	packer	58	"
	P	Lynch Isabella T †	24	housewife	54	"

1820 Fairmount Avenue

Page	Letter	Full Name	Residence, Jan. 1, 1941	Occupation	Supposed Age	Reported Residence, Jan. 1, 1940. Street and Number
1820	O	Occhiolini Augustine	65A	cabinetmaker	50	here
	P	Occhiolini Maria †	65A	housewife	40	"
	R	Rochleau Leo	65A	laborer	22	112 Gordon av
	S	Rochleau Mary †	65A	housewife	22	112 "

Page	Letter	Full Name.	Residence, Jan. 1, 1941.	Occupation.	Supposed Age.	Reported Residence, Jan. 1, 1940. Street and Number.

Fairmount Avenue Continued

Page	Letter	Full Name	Residence	Occupation	Age	Reported Residence
	T	Gauthier John W	65A	laborer	22	here
	U	McNevin Annabelle—†	65A	clerk	23	"
	V	McNevin Bertha—†	65A	housewife	50	"
	W	McNevin George	65A	laborer	52	"
	X	McNevin George M	65A	"	24	"
	Y	McNevin Helen—†	65A	clerk	21	"
	Z	Shea Lillian—†	65A	housewife	27	"
1821		**Folsom Street**				
	F	Burke Dorothy L—†	110	housewife	25	594 Canterbury
	G	Burke Frank E	110	machinist	25	594 "
	H	*McPherson Peter	110	mechanic	57	594 "
	K	Bruno Alfred	110	printer	27	here
	L	Bruno Dorothy—†	110	fitter	25	"
	M	Stade Ella M—†	110	stitcher	48	"
	N	Stade Werner W	110	mechanic	62	"
		Fulton Street				
	O	*Burak Dominick	21	retired	85	here
	P	Burak Henry	21	pinboy	22	"
	R	Marusa Bronie	22	laborer	36	"
	S	Marusa Stacia V—†	22	operator	28	"
	T	*Marusa Veronica—†	22	housewife	60	"
	U	*Kaczenas Alexander	23	retired	65	"
	V	*Kaczenas Domecella—†	23	housewife	52	"
	W	Kaczenas Helen M—†	23	operator	20	"
	X	Kaczenas Joseph J	23	machinist	22	"
	Y	Domuczicz Lydia M—†	24	housewife	23	"
	Z	Domuczicz Theodore H	24	laborer	23	"
1822						
	A	Rosen Eleanor I—†	27	housewife	27	"
	B	Rosen William J	27	clerk	27	"
	C	Haskell Dorothy E—†	28	housewife	29	40 Colorado
	D	Haskell Henry P	28	garageman	28	40 "
	E	*Elchuck Jacob J	29	laborer	43	here
	F	Elchuck Mary J—†	29	housewife	37	"
	G	*Jannette Bertha—†	30	"	44	"
	H	Jannette Biagio G	30	builder	52	"
	K	Knopf William L	30	molder	20	"

Page.	Letter	Full Name		Occupation		

Fulton Street Continued

Page	Letter	Full Name		Occupation		
	M	Valatka Alphonse G	32	clerk	28	here
	N	Valatka Anna M †	32	stenographer	23	"
	O	*Valatka Anthony M	32	laborer	60	"
	P	Valatka John J	32	draftsman	34	"
	R	Valatka Joseph A	32	laborer	21	"
	S	*Valatka Martha A †	32	housewife	57	"
	T	Trementozzi Ralph	33	finisher	46	"
	U	Trementozzi Salvatore T	33	machinist	24	"
	V	*Trementozzi Victoria M †	33	housewife	42	"
	W	Brodowski Joseph	34	mechanic	28	13 Winslow
	X	Brodowski William	34	painter	60	13 "
	Y	Lepsevich John J	35	mattressmaker	25	here
	Z	*Lepsevich Marcella †	35	housewife	54	"
1823						
	A	Lepsevich William J	35	retired	50	"
	B	Lepsevich William M	35	machinist	23	"
	C	Allenshupski Mary M †	36	housewife	31	"
	D	Allenshupski Michael J	36	shipfitter	36	"

Glenwood Avenue East

Page	Letter	Full Name		Occupation		
	E	Nasuti Antonio	1	pipelayer	43	here
	F	*Nasuti Louise †	1	housewife	38	"
	H	Rico Areoline	3	chauffeur	35	"
	K	Rico Donato †	3	at home	75	"
	L	Rico Mary R †	3	housewife	25	"
	M	Mulattieri Giovani B	5	laborer	18	"
	N	*Mulattieri Vincenza †	5	housewife	40	"
	O	Ricci Harry M	5	laborer	30	"
	P	Ricci Rose V †	5	housewife	26	"
	R	Teves Frank V	5	laborer	44	"
	S	Grasso Fiori	9	"	30	"
	T	Grasso Rose T †	9	housewife	26	"
	U	Aprea Anna L †	9	operator	24	"
	V	Aprea Ida F †	9	marker	20	"
	W	*Aprea John	9	laborer	50	"
	X	*Aprea Stella †	9	housewife	46	"
	Y	Aprea Viola B †	9	operator	22	"
	Z	*Fiore Anna †	19	housewife	18	"
1824						
	A	*Fiore Frank	19	laborer	17	"

Page	Letter	Full Name.	Residence, Jan. 1, 1941.	Occupation.	Supposed Age.	Reported Residence, Jan. 1, 1940. Street and Number.

Glenwood Avenue East—Continued

Page	Letter	Full Name.	Residence, Jan. 1, 1941.	Occupation.	Supposed Age.	Reported Residence, Jan. 1, 1940. Street and Number.
	B	Fiore Louis A	19	machinist	23	here
	C	Fiore Thomas S	19	clerk	21	"
	D	Fiore Walter S	19	chauffeur	20	"
	E	Fiore Albert	19	foreman	40	"
	F	*Fiore Laura—†	19	housewife	30	"
	G	*Fiore Mary—†	19	at home	79	"
	H	Conti John	21	laborer	30	"
	K	*Conti Mabel—†	21	housewife	29	"
	L	Diodati Amilio	21	laborer	23	Rhode Island
	N	Finingham John	22	retired	71	here
	O	Lazarovich Agnes L—†	22	housewife	33	"
	P	Lazarovich Clement J	22	grocer	37	"
	R	*McDougall Bertha E—†	23	housewife	27	"
	S	*McDougall Gabriel	23	gardener	38	"
	T	*Petrucci Angelina—†	23	housewife	43	"
	U	Petrucci Antonio	23	foreman	26	Panama
	V	*Petrucci Francesco	23	laborer	48	here
	W	Petrucci John J	23	"	20	"
	X	Petrucci Maria A—†	23	floorwoman	21	"
	Y	Chesley Albert	24	shipper	45	"
	Z	DiSanto Anna—†	27	housewife	26	"
1825						
	A	DiSanto Blais	27	machinist	24	"
	B	DiSanto Ida M—†	27	clerk	20	"
	C	DiSanto Joseph	27	proprietor	73	"
	D	*DiSanto Josephine—†	27	housewife	61	"
	E	Eisner Leroy W	39	watchman	21	Dedham
	F	*Eisner Sarah J—†	39	housekeeper	43	"
	G	Rowe Samuel A	39	collector	62	"
	K	Antinarelli Alfred	43	laborer	21	14 Tyler
	L	Lattanzio Eleanor M—†	43	operator	27	here
	M	Lattanzio Emidio J	43	mechanic	33	"
	N	Lattanzio John J	43	laborer	22	"
	O	Lattanzio William A	43	attendant	26	"
	P	Stracqualursi John	47	fireman	51	"
	R	*Stracqualursi Mary—†	47	housewife	43	"
	S	Fistola Archoline	47	attendant	26	"
	T	Fistola Ida A—†	47	stitcher	29	"
	U	Fistola Theresa—†	47	examiner	22	"
	V	Uva Alvina M—†	48	operator	25	"
	W	Uva Angelo M	48	engineer	55	"

Page	Letter	Full Name	Residence, Jan. 1, 1941	Occupation	Reputed Age	Reported Residence, Jan. 1, 1940, Street and Number

Glenwood Avenue East—Continued

Page	Letter	Full Name	Residence, Jan. 1, 1941	Occupation	Reputed Age	Reported Residence, Jan. 1, 1940, Street and Number
	X	Uva Joseph J	48	machinist	22	here
	Y	Uva Mary R †	48	examiner	26	"
	Z	*Uva Nora †	48	housewife	45	"
1826						
	A	Uva Rose M †	48	dressmaker	27	"
	B	*Schena Mary R †	48	housekeeper	73	"
	C	Barelli Adelmo P	51	clerk	21	"
	D	Barelli Eleanor C †	51	finisher	27	"
	E	Barelli Lucia †	51	housewife	56	"
	F	Barelli Nicholas A	51	chauffeur	30	"
	G	Barelli Peter	51	laborer	61	"
	H	Barelli Victor P	51	operator	27	"
	K	DiClerico Pasquale	51	laborer	47	"
	L	*DiClerico Theresa †	51	housewife	40	S Dacy
	M	Pulsone Francisco	51	retired	70	S "
	N	Lewis Florence J †	52	housewife	68	here
	O	Lewis Frank T	52	retired	78	"
	P	McCarthy Alfred O	52	laborer	23	Randolph
	R	McCarthy Mary †	52	housewife	20	"
	S	Peters Donald	52	gardener	28	1320 Hyde Park av
	T	Nolan Mary L †	52	housewife	32	here
	U	Nolan Robert J	52	laborer	38	"
	V	Rossetti Primo	55	retired	56	"
	W	Rossetti Rita †	55	stenographer	20	"
	X	Tedeschi Amato	55	molder	44	"
	Y	*Tedeschi Anna †	55	housewife	42	"

Grant Street

Page	Letter	Full Name	Residence, Jan. 1, 1941	Occupation	Reputed Age	Reported Residence, Jan. 1, 1940, Street and Number
	Z	Curley Katherine T †	15	housewife	56	here
1827						
	A	Curley Kathleen M †	15	governess	20	"
	B	Curley William M	15	molder	56	"
	C	Stack Frank C	15	proprietor	50	"
	D	Piccurello Dominic F	17	upholsterer	38	17 Roxanna
	E	Piccurello Grace L †	17	laundryworker	38	17 "
	F	Wilbur Ralph	17	laborer	23	17 "
	G	Wilbur William	17	optometrist	25	17 "
	H	*Martin Martha A †	19	housewife	37	here
	K	*Martin William	19	machinist	44	"

Page	Letter	Full Name.	Residence Jan. 1 1941.	Occupation.	Supposed Age.	Reported Residence, Jan. 1, 1940. Street and Number.

Harvard Avenue

Page	Letter	Full Name.	Residence Jan. 1 1941.	Occupation.	Supposed Age.	Reported Residence, Jan. 1, 1940. Street and Number.
	O	Churchill Gwendolyn—†	16	social worker	23	Medford
	P	Morrison Irene—†	16	housekeeper	21	N Hampshire

1828 Hyde Park Avenue

Page	Letter	Full Name.	Residence Jan. 1 1941.	Occupation.	Supposed Age.	Reported Residence, Jan. 1, 1940. Street and Number.
1828	D	Brooks Herbert M	1252	laborer	57	here
	E	*Brooks Julia—†	1252	housewife	54	"
	F	Marshall Mabel C—†	1252	"	45	"
	S	Barton Earnest R	1273	chauffeur	43	1300 Hyde Park av
	T	Collins Aubrey J	1273	physician	65	1300 "
	U	Collins Marguerite—†	1273	housewife	60	1300 "
	V	Brooks Thomas J	1273	agent	24	90 Kittredge
	W	Colford Mary—†	1273	clerk	40	here
	X	White Anna J—†	1273	housewife	37	"
	Y	Sheehan Frank	1273	machinist	37	"
	Z	Sheehan Mary E—†	1273	housewife	60	"
1829						
	A	Sheehan Patrick	1273	retired	70	"
	B	Hopkins Catherine A—†	1273	clerk	48	"
	C	Young Bessie—†	1273	housekeeper	66	"
	D	Allsop James	1273	retired	79	"
	E	Allsop Marguerite A—†	1273	housewife	80	"
	F	Downey Agnes—†	1273	"	50	"
	G	Downey Lawrence P	1273	clerk	21	"
	H	Chamberlain Mary E—†	1273	housekeeper	61	"
	K	Hay James	1273	welder	45	55 Business
	L	Packard Madge R—†	1273	housekeeper	63	here
	M	Levesque Thomas	1273	machinist	46	Cambridge
	N	Sheehan Sarah J—†	1273	organist	70	here
	O	Swinton Jessie L—†	1273	housekeeper	67	"
	P	Kelton Rufus B	1273	retired	75	"
	R	McCrillis Virginia—†	1273	housekeeper	47	"
	S	Bower Eleanor E—†	1273	housewife	52	"
	T	Bower Eleanor E—†	1273	clerk	22	"
	U	Bower George N	1273	machinist	52	"
	V	Pierce Albert D	1273	"	58	"
	W	Burnes Harry N	1273	manager	53	"
	X	Burnes Robert N	1273	student	23	"
	Y	Burnes Sara D—†	1273	housewife	50	"
	Z	Kelly Gertrude—†	1273	"	32	"

Page / Letter	Full Name	Residence	Occupation	Age	Reported Residence
1830	**Hyde Park Avenue** Continued				
A	Kelly John J	1273	policeman	36	here
S	Blanchard Clara B †	1295	housewife	29	"
T	Blanchard Edward J	1295	chauffeur	34	"
U	Obin Charles	1295	painter	33	"
V	Obin Delorez †	1295	housewife	58	"
W	Obin Edward	1295	painter	59	"
X	Obin Francis X	1295	laborer	21	"
Y	Obin Raymond	1295	painter	27	"
1831					
D	Hanlon David E, jr	1300	attorney	29	Rhode Island
E	Hanlon Mary A †	1300	housewife	56	"
F	Hanlon Rosamond M	†1300	operator	23	"
K	Padrevita Artilaro	1304	plumber	47	here
L	Padrevita Rose J †	1304	housewife	44	"
M	Capadais Beatrice †	1304	"	42	"
N	Capadais Charles	1304	chef	16	"
O	Capadais James	1304	proprietor	42	"
R	Perreault Roland A	1325	laborer	31	"
S	Perreault Sophie B †	1325	housewife	30	"
T	Lacey Margaret E †	1327	at home	74	"
U	O'Neil Bridget E †	1327	housewife	42	"
V	O'Neil Patrick J	1327	laborer	43	"
W	O'Neil Thomas E	1327	clerk	21	"
X	Bills Clara †	1327	housewife	44	"
Y	Bills Horatio	1327	stamper	49	"
Z*	Dranevich Vasili	1329	barber	48	"
1832					
C	Harper James A	1329	operator	22	527 Hyde Park Av
D	Nickerson Roberta M	†1329	housewife	22	here
E	Tately Catherine A †	1329	"	40	"
F	Tately Edward J	1329	laborer	42	"
O	Fox Louis H	1392	painter	45	59 Business
P	Fox Margaret D †	1392	housewife	35	59 "
R	Abramoski Mary †	1392	"	42	here
T	Rampino Lucy †	1394	"	25	"
U	Rampino Thomas	1394	inspector	34	"
V	Allen Joseph J	1394	waterproofer	26	"
W*	Allen Theresa M †	1394	housewife	60	"
X	Getch Charles	1394	carpenter	62	"

Page	Letter	Full Name.	Residence, Jan. 1, 1941.	Occupation.	Supposed Age.	Reported Residence, Jan. 1, 1940. Street and Number.

Hyde Park Avenue—Continued

Page	Letter	Full Name	Residence, Jan. 1, 1941	Occupation	Supposed Age	Reported Residence, Jan. 1, 1940
	X*	Juozaitis Thomas	1394	painter	81	here
	Y*	Conti Nancy—†	1400	housewife	37	"
	Z*	Jamano Alphonse	1400	laborer	60	"
1833						
	A*	Jamano Suzanna—†	1400	housewife	56	"
	B	Rampino Rosina—†	1400	"	45	"
	C	Lombardi Samuel	1400	laborer	47	"
	D*	Lombardi Theresa—†	1400	housewife	46	"
	F	Sacramona Frederick W	1408	operator	29	"
	G	Sacramona Lena—†	1408	housewife	26	"
	H	Gutowski Sophie—†	1408	"	43	"
	K	Gutowski William	1408	stripper	44	"
	M	DelSignore Frances—†	1410	housewife	31	717 Am Legion H'way
	N	DelSignore Santo	1410	chauffeur	34	717 "
	O	Abate Evelyn—†	1410	dressmaker	20	here
	P	Abate Harry	1410	laborer	50	"
	R	Abate Mary—†	1410	housewife	42	"
	S	Abate Violet—†	1410	sorter	21	"
	T	Lindquist Agnes E—†	1410	clerk	37	"
	U	Lindquist Freda—†	1410	housewife	68	"
	W	Jank Robert C, jr	1414	accountant	51	"
1834						
	A	Vialton Madeline—†	1426	housewife	32	"
	B	Vialton Samuel	1426	barber	47	"
	C	Fontenarosa Alphonso	1426	machinist	53	"
	D	Fontenarosa Anna B—†	1426	housekeeper	26	"
	E	Fontenarosa Elsie J—†	1426	storekeeper	21	"
	F	Fontenarosa Lillian M—†	1426	housekeeper	26	"
	G	Fontenarosa James	1426	machinist	34	"
	H	Fontenarosa Susan—†	1426	housewife	25	"
	N	Andreozzi Angelina—†	1433	stitcher	38	"
	O*	Andreozzi Marie—†	1433	housewife	73	"
	P*	Andreozzi Cecelia—†	1433	"	46	"
	R	Andreozzi John	1433	student	20	"
	S*	Andreozzi Sossio	1433	retired	53	"
	U	Frebria Filomena—†	1437	housewife	59	"
	V*	Pragoni Catherine—†	1437	housekeeper	58	"
	W	Prata Beatrice—†	1437	housewife	34	"
	X*	Prata Peter	1437	laborer	37	"
	Y	Santilli Antoinette—†	1437	housewife	27	"
	Z	Santilli August J	1437	winder	29	"

Page	Letter	Full Name	Residence, Jan. 1, 1947	Occupation	Reputed Age	Reported Residence, Jan. 1, 1946. Street and Number

1835
Hyde Park Avenue (Continued)

Letter	Full Name	Residence	Occupation	Age	Residence 1946
A	Cimo Rudolph	1437	metalworker	25	here
B	Cimo Teresa †	1437	housewife	23	"
C	Coviello Anthony	1440	trackman	28	"
D	Coviello Grace †	1440	housewife	27	"
F	Patrola Anthony	1441	ironworker	29	"
G	Patrola Austin	1441	machinist	26	"
H	Patrola Henry	1441	laborer	65	"
K	*Patrola Nancy †	1441	housewife	61	"
L	DiMarzio Lillian †	1442	"	31	"
M	DiMarzio William	1442	social worker	33	"
N	Menino Carl	1449	stockman	26	"
O	Menino Susan †	1449	housewife	22	[illegible]
P	*Menino Manuela †	1449	"	60	here
R	Menino Mary †	1449	winder	33	"
S	Menino Nora †	1449	inspector	30	"
T	Menino Rose †	1449	winder	22	"
U	Menino Ruth †	1449	inspector	28	"
V	*Menino Thomas	1449	retired	69	"
W	Lepori John	1453	laborer	49	"
X	*Lepori Lucy †	1453	housewife	45	"
Y	*Ruzzo Alvera †	1453	"	41	"
Z	Ruzzo Pasquale	1453	laborer	45	"

1836

Letter	Full Name	Residence	Occupation	Age	Residence 1946
A	DelZoppo Cailla	1453	"	47	"
B	*DelZoppo Philomena †	1453	housewife	46	"
C	Stragularsi Anthony	1453	blacksmith	43	"
D	*Stragularsi Elizabeth †	1453	housewife	41	"
E	Caruso Etta †	1453	"	25	[illegible]
F	Caruso Francis	1453	barber	23	52 "
G	*Cirillo Thomaso	1453	laborer	64	here
H	Ragosa Phillip	1453	"	52	9 W[illegible]
K	*Sero Frank	1453	"	54	here
L	*Luciano Bernardino	1457	"	59	"
M	*Luciano Marie †	1457	housewife	48	"
N	Luciano Nicholas	1457	welder	23	"
O	Luciano Patrick	1457	laborer	21	"
P	Malatesta Constantino	1457	carpenter	19	"
R	Carew Frank	1461	"	58	7 Adams [illegible]
S	Carew Helen †	1461	housewife	55	7 "
T	*Lazarovich Cecelia †	1461	"	69	here

Hyde Park Avenue—Continued

Page	Letter	Full Name	Residence, Jan. 1, 1941	Occupation	Supposed Age	Reported Residence, Jan. 1, 1940. Street and Number.
	U	Lazarovich Edward J	1461	merchant	40	here
	X	Moschella Edward	1472	machinist	21	"
	Y	*Moschella Jennie—†	1472	housewife	40	"
	Z	Moschella Pasquale	1472	merchant	45	"
1837						
	A	Ciardi Alfred	1478	blower	25	"
	B	*Ciardi Anthony	1478	retired	38	"
	C	*Ciardi Jennie—†	1478	housewife	61	"
	D	Ciardi Pasquale	1478	pressman	33	"
	E	Giannangelo Joseph	1479	machinist	24	"
	F	Giannangelo Philomena—†	1479	housewife	23	"
	G	*Sacchetti Angela—†	1479	"	47	17 Winslow
	H	Sacchetti Louis	1479	ironworker	49	1453 Hyde Park av
	K	Sisti John	1479	woodcarver	20	17 Winslow
	L	Amatucci Emilio	1480	laborer	45	here
	M	*Amatucci Linda—†	1480	housewife	41	"
	N	Balestra Louis	1482	milkman	23	"
	O	Germano Antoinette—†	1482	housewife	26	"
	P	Germano Blaise	1482	timekeeper	25	"
	R	Germano Frank	1482	laborer	50	"
	S	Germano Gaetano—†	1482	housewife	50	"
	T	Germano Mary—†	1482	seamstress	22	"
	U	Germano Orlando	1482	metalworker	24	"
	V	*Damata Joseph	1486	laborer	50	5 E Glenwood av
	W	*Panzino Concetta—†	1486	housewife	45	1505 Hyde Park av
	X	Panzino Vincenzo	1486	laborer	46	1505 "
	Y	Goralsky Edward	1486	counterman	29	here
	Z	Goralsky Josephine—†	1486	housewife	29	"
1838						
	A	Balestra Eugenia—†	1487	stitcher	38	"
	B	Balestra Louis	1487	mechanic	20	"
	C	McCarthy Lawrence	1487	machinist	24	"
	D	McCarthy Teresa—†	1487	housewife	20	"
	E	Cateleso Concetta—†	1488	"	36	"
	F	Cateleso Joseph	1488	chauffeur	49	"
	G	Mills Anna E—†	1492	housewife	54	"
	H	Mills William R	1492	toolmaker	33	"
	K	Petrucci Falco	1495	papercutter	48	"
	L	*Petrucci Teresa—†	1495	housewife	40	"
	N	Stone Floyd W rear	1495	retired	33	"
	O	Stone Marianna—† "	1495	housewife	29	"

Page	Letter	Full Name	Residence, Jan. 1, 1941	Occupation	Reputed Age	Reported Residence, Jan. 1, 1940. Street and Number

Hyde Park Avenue Continued

Page	Letter	Full Name	Residence, Jan. 1, 1941	Occupation	Reputed Age	Reported Residence, Jan. 1, 1940. Street and Number
	R	McCarthy Mary C †	1497	housewife	37	here
	S	McCarthy Thomas H	1497	laborer	37	53 Albemarle
	T	Vatalaso Joseph	1499	"	48	198 E Milton
	U	Vatalaso Mary †	1499	housewife	36	198 "
	V	*Pulcini Mary †	1499	"	36	8 Allen
	W	Pulicini Samuel	1499	boilermaker	45	8 "
	X	DeGrazia Carmela †	1500	housewife	26	150 Bremen
	Y	DeGrazia Pasquale	1500	chauffeur	26	150 "
	Z	Trementozzi Antonio	1500	blacksmith	72	here
1839						
	A	*Trementozzi John	1500	laborer	29	"
	B	*Trementozzi Mary S †	1500	housewife	68	"
	C	*Giannangelo Agnes †	1505	"	46	"
	D	Giannangelo Elsie †	1505	housekeeper	21	"
	E	*Giannangelo Venanzio	1505	grocer	53	"
	F	Goulart Angelina † rear	1505	housewife	22	12 Madison
	G	Goulart Anthony "	1505	chef	27	12 "
	H	Dunn Esther M †	1509	housekeeper	34	here
	K	Dunn John O	1509	retired	74	"
	L	*Memmo Anthony	1510	laborer	53	"
	M	Memmo Gerald	1510	optician	24	"
	N	*Memmo Loretta †	1510	housewife	54	"
	O	Melito Lillian †	1512	"	27	"
	P	Melito Ralph	1512	lamplighter	35	"
	R	DiCampli Benjamin	1512	boxmaker	21	"
	S	*DiCampli Bessie †	1512	housewife	41	"
	T	DiCampli Joseph	1512	carpenter	51	"
	U	Hines Agnes †	1513	student	20	"
	V	Hines John	1513	decorator	27	"
	W	Hines Mary †	1513	housewife	59	"
	X	Hines Michael	1513	welder	61	"
	Y	Cristoforo Dominic	1514	laborer	53	"
	Z	Cristoforo Josephine †	1514	stitcher	20	"
1840						
	A	Cristoforo Mary †	1514	housewife	48	"
	B	Citrano John	1514	presser	22	139 Cottage
	C	Citrano Rose †	1514	housewife	22	139 "
	D	Ciardi A Gregory	1515	stitcher	31	here
	E	*Ciardi Beatrice †	1515	housewife	61	"
	F	Ciardi Eugene	1515	assembler	26	"
	G	Ciardi Patrick	1515	engraver	38	"

Page.	Letter.	Full Name.	Residence, Jan. 1, 1941.	Occupation.	Supposed Age.	Reported Residence, Jan. 1, 1940. Street and Number.

Hyde Park Avenue—Continued

Page.	Letter.	Full Name.	Residence, Jan. 1, 1941.	Occupation.	Supposed Age.	Reported Residence, Jan. 1, 1940. Street and Number.
	H	Ciardi Salvatore	1515	machinist	33	here
	K	Rosati Adelia—†	1518	stitcher	20	"
	L	Rosati Joseph	1518	molder	50	"
	M	*Rosati Laura—†	1518	housewife	44	"
	N	Rosati Nicholas	1518	machinist	21	"
	O	Sisti Anthony	1518	"	27	"
	P	Sisti Jennie—†	1518	dressmaker	23	"
	R	*DelBianco Francisco	1519	retired	75	"
	S	White Anthony	1519	machinist	40	"
	T	White Cecilia—†	1519	housewife	30	"
	U	*Conti Louis	1521	barber	37	1392 Hyde Park av
	V	Conti Mary—†	1521	housewife	36	1392 "
	W	Porreca Eleanora—†	1524	housekeeper	53	here
	X	*Lombardi Frank	1525	laborer	55	"
	Y	*Lombardi Victoria—†	1525	housewife	59	"
	Z	Pellagrina Frank	1525	gardener	45	"
1841						
	A	Petrucci Peter	1525	molder	46	"
	B	Tanzi Samuel	1525	"	54	"
	C	Petrucci Joseph	1526	laborer	22	23 Glenwood av
	D	Petrucci Louise—†	1526	housewife	20	1410 Hyde Park av
	E	*Giannangelo Anna—†	1526	"	35	here
	F	Giannangelo Nicholas	1526	chauffeur	41	"
	G	DiMarzio William	1527	woolworker	28	"
	H	Ricottelli Alphonse	1527	clerk	22	"
	K	*Ricottelli Ginevra—†	1527	housewife	46	"
	L	Ricottelli Guido	1527	U S A	20	"
	M	Ricottelli Vincent	1527	mason	51	"
	O	Pansiocco John	1531	laborer	42	1530 Hyde Park av
	P	Adams Burtley	1531	"	40	here
	R	*Adams Mildred L—†	1531	housewife	25	"
	S	*Germano Anthony	1532	machinist	42	"
	T	Germano Philomena—†	1532	housewife	35	"
	U	*Palermo Frank	1532	retired	72	"
	V	Palermo Katherine A—†	1532	stitcher	20	"
	W	Palermo Mary—†	1532	housewife	39	"
	X	Palermo Salvatore	1532	molder	43	"
	Y	Ranieri Adeline—†	1533	housewife	33	"
	Z	Ranieri Vincenzo	1533	stonecutter	47	"
1842						
	A	DiCamillo Annunziato	1533	tailor	63	"

Hyde Park Avenue—Continued

Page	Letter	Full Name	Residence	[illegible]	[illegible]	[illegible]
	B*	DiCamillo Mary †	1533	housewife	50	here
	C	DiCamillo Nicholas	1533	machinist	20	"
	D	Viola Albert P	1540	laborer	27	"
	E	Viola Angelo	1540	"	21	"
	F	Viola Arthur	1540	plasterer	60	"
	G	Viola Dominic	1540	"	26	"
	H	Viola Louis J	1540	laborer	24	"
	K	MacNiven Leslie †	1544	factoryhand	29	"
	L	MacNiven Margaret E †	1544	housewife	25	"
	M	Welch Isabella H †	1548	"	73	"
	N	Welch Richard J	1548	coremaker	54	"
	O	Welch Robert J	1548	laborer	43	"
	P	Smith Agnes M †	1548	housewife	28	2 Blanchard
	R	Smith Thomas J	1548	millwright	31	2 "
	U	Viscardi Felix	1623	laborer	33	here
	V	Viscardi James	1623	chauffeur	28	"
	W	Viscardi Jennie †	1623	candymaker	29	"
	X	Viscardi Joseph	1623	laborer	63	"
	Y*	Viscardi Margaret †	1623	housewife	66	"
	Z	Viscardi Mary †	1623	packer	26	"
1843						
	A	Toti Dominic	1623	laborer	68	"
	B*	Toti Theresa †	1623	housewife	66	"
	C	Herbert Vino †	1625	"	56	[illegible]
	D	Herbert Walter	1625	laborer	57	198 "
	E*	Rossillo Lawrence	1625	"	50	here

Madison Street

Page	Letter	Full Name	Residence	[illegible]	[illegible]	[illegible]
	G	Conti Mary F †	1	housewife	25	here
	H	Conti Peter J	1	laborer	27	"
	K*	Haviek Anthony	3	"	65	"
	L*	Haviek Mary †	3	housewife	65	"
	M	Marusa Alexander W	3	laborer	28	"
	N*	Marusa Phillip	3	chauffeur	40	"
	O	Salvatore Albert	5	upholsterer	23	"
	P	Salvatore Anna †	5	housewife	22	"
	R*	Salvatore Carmen	5	laborer	54	"
	S*	Salvatore Mary †	5	housewife	54	"
	T	Salvatore Nicholas	5	laborer	26	"
	U	Salvatore Rose M †	5	operator	21	"

Page	Letter	Full Name	Residence Jan. 1, 1941	Occupation	Supposed Age	Reported Residence, Jan. 1, 1940. Street and Number

Madison Street—Continued

Page	Letter	Full Name	Residence Jan. 1, 1941	Occupation	Supposed Age	Reported Residence, Jan. 1, 1940. Street and Number
	V	Brauneis Blanche E—†	7	housewife	35	8 Glenwood pl
	W	Brauneis Paul	7	laborer	40	8 "
	X	*Citrone Gaetano	9	"	47	here
	Y	*Citrone Josephine—†	9	housewife	36	"
	Z	*Conti Dominick	9	laborer	58	1 Madison
1844						
	A	Tanzi Loretta—†	12	"	49	here
	B	*Tanzi Pasquale	12	clerk	20	"
	C	*Tanzi Teresa—†	12	housewife	46	"
	E	Rizzacasa Arcoline	12	timekeeper	22	"
	F	*Rizzacasa Camilla—†	12	housewife	51	"
	G	Rizzacasa Peter J	12	welder	20	"
	H	*Panzieri Amelia—†	15	housewife	55	"
	K	Panzieri Anna I—†	15	stitcher	26	"
	L	Panzieri Edna R—†	15	houseworker	24	"
	M	Panzieri Joseph	15	laborer	56	"
	N	Panzieri Victor R	15	papermaker	22	"
	O	DeBaptista Caroline—†	16	housewife	36	"
	P	DeBaptista Luigi	16	machinist	41	"
	R	Cibotti Thomas J	16	laborer	27	36 Easton av

Maple Street

Page	Letter	Full Name	Residence Jan. 1, 1941	Occupation	Supposed Age	Reported Residence, Jan. 1, 1940. Street and Number
	X	Anthony Madeline—†	39	teacher	38	here
	Y	Ashman Elizabeth F—†	39	"	46	"
	Z	Ballard Daisy—†	39	"	28	"
1845						
	A	Braddock Edna M—†	39	"	28	"
	B	Cofer Helen—†	39	"	37	"
	C	Cronan Annie—†	39	"	64	Newburyport
	D	Doherty Josephine A—†	39	"	60	here
	E	Englert Mary P—†	39	"	38	"
	F	Fahey Maria—†	39	"	44	Virginia
	G	FitzMaurice Catharine A—†	39	"	44	here
	H	Gallagher Louise E—†	39	"	25	"
	K	Grimes Mary—†	39	"	58	"
	L	Hawks Elizabeth—†	39	"	29	Ohio
	M	Kelly Margaret M—†	39	"	54	here
	N	Kelty Emma—†	39	"	40	"
	O	Loker Susan—†	39	"	30	"
	P	McEntee Catherine—†	39	"	43	"

Page	Letter	Full Name	Residence, April 1	Occupation	Age	Reputed Residence April 1, Street and Number

Maple Street Continued

Page	Letter	Full Name	Residence	Occupation	Age	Reputed Residence
	R	Purcell Ella A †	39	teacher	44	here
	S	Siebert Mary †	39	"	51	"
	T	Spalding Cecilia †	39	"	28	"
	U	Tape Laura †	39	"	45	"
	V	Tempest Mary E †	39	"	60	"
	W	Willis Angela C †	39	"	60	"
	X	*Porter Amos	40	retired	80	"
	Y	*Porter Annie L †	40	housewife	70	"
	Z	Porter Oscar F	40	laborer	36	"
1846						
	A	Kingsley Beatrice E †	40	teacher	30	"
	B	Kingsley Clarence	40	machinist	59	"
	C	Kingsley Harold R	40	clerk	31	"
	D	Kingsley Mabel D †	40	housewife	53	"
	E	Morris Fanny M †	40	housekeeper	73	"
	F	Darling Minnie A †	42	housewife	73	"
	G	Darling Willis A	42	manager	83	"
	H	Connolly John J	43	clergyman	36	"
	K	Crowley Edward F	43	"	63	"
	L	Donohue James A	43	"	48	"
	M	English Anna M †	43	housekeeper	61	"
	N	Kegan John A	43	clergyman	39	"
	O	Lennon Delia M †	43	housekeeper	55	"
	P	Mullin Mary A †	43	"	66	"
	R	O'Neill Jeremiah J	43	clergyman	35	"
	T	Davison James	47	laborer	30	"
	U	Duncan Mary R †	47	housewife	45	"
	V	Duncan Peter	47	clerk	46	"
	W	Duncan Anna †	47	housewife	56	"
	X	Duncan James	47	manager	58	"
	Y	Hill Alice V †	48	housewife	48	29 Business
	Z	Hill Earl F	48	shipper	50	29 "
1847						
	A	Hill Martin E	48	molder	26	29 "
	B	Mahoney Catherine †	18	housekeeper	75	17 Riverside sq
	C	Cardinale Anthony	18	coilmaker	33	36 Princeton
	D	Cardinale Mary †	18	housewife	29	36 "
	E	Coullahan James	48	plumber	39	30 Williams av
	F	Coullahan Rita †	48	housewife	22	32 "
	G	Callahan Rita †	51	saleswoman	21	Randolph
	H	Conlin Mary J †	51	housekeeper	65	here

Page	Letter	Full Name	Residence, Jan. 1, 1941	Occupation	Supposed Age	Reported Residence, Jan. 1, 1940. Street and Number

Maple Street—Continued

Page	Letter	Full Name	Residence, Jan. 1, 1941	Occupation	Supposed Age	Reported Residence, Jan. 1, 1940. Street and Number
	K	*Eghigian Arthur	51	chef	45	here
	L	Hanley Alice A—†	51	housekeeper	69	Randolph
	M	Topalian Edward	51	counterman	26	1144 River
	N	Gowdy Caroline—†	52	seamstress	40	1048 Hyde Park av
	O	McAllister Delia A—†	52	housewife	47	here
	P	McAllister James	52	policeman	49	"
	R	Mitchell Patrick	52	laborer	43	"
	S	Pastucha Simon	52	machinist	46	Worcester
	T	Setti Anna—†	52	housewife	30	here
	U	Setti Anthony	52	electrician	31	"
	V	Billey Frank J	56	metalworker	43	"
	W	Brennan Annie F—†	56	housekeeper	56	"
	X	Fealy Katherine E—†	56	clerk	48	"
	Y	Pearce Alice M—†	56	housewife	47	"
	Z	Pearce James A	56	electrician	47	"
1848						
	A	Staula Alfred F	62	manager	34	"
	B	*Staula Anna—†	62	housewife	74	"
	C	Staula Nicholas	62	machinist	37	"
	D	Staula Rose M—†	62	housewife	25	"
	E	Jameson Ernest W	62	machinist	42	"
	F	Jameson Mary—†	62	housewife	39	"
	G	Boyle Anthony J	65	retired	66	"
	H	Boyle Edward J	65	painter	32	"
	K	Boyle Margaret J—†	65	operator	33	"
	L	Boyle Ruth—†	65	clerk	31	"
	M	Clifford Annamarie—†	66	housewife	26	"
	N	Danielson Thyra—†	66	"	57	"
	O	Clifford Ralph	66	salesman	26	"
	P	Kelley Evangeline L—†	66	housewife	47	"
	R	Kelley William L	66	supervisor	54	"
	S	White Francis A	66	retired	65	"
	T	Young Frances—†	70	housewife	66	"
	U	Young William A	70	retired	67	"
	V	Dawes Margaret—†	71	housewife	35	"
	W	Farrington Charles J	71	retired	83	57 Highland
	X	Storrie Elizabeth E—†	71	housewife	60	here
	Y	Storrie John H	71	clerk	24	"
	Z	Storrie Margaret F—†	71	saleswoman	27	"
1849						
	A	Baxter Gertrude—†	73	clerk	33	"

Page	Letter	Full Name	Residence, Jan. 1, [illegible]	Occupation	Supposed Age	Reported Residence, [illegible] Street and Number
	B	McAuliffe Louise †	73	clerk	35	here
	C	McAuliffe Mary †	73	housekeeper	51	"
	D	Burke Emily G †	73	housewife	51	"
	E	Burke Emily G †	73	clerk	23	"
	F	Burke Mary L †	73	"	22	"
	G	Burke Thomas W	73	"	61	"
	H	Hart Clara F †	74	housewife	38	"
	K	Hart Edmund	74	accountant	36	"
	L	Muirhead John J	74	foreman	43	Dedham
	M	Muirhead Rosalie †	74	housewife	38	here
	N	Dolan Theresa †	75	"	44	"
	O	Regan Mary A †	75	housekeeper	72	"
	P	Jennings Marguerite †	79	housewife	22	47 Brookford
	R	Jennings William	79	clerk	25	21 Walton
	S	McGowan Frederick A †	79	investigator	41	here
	T	McGowan Maria D †	79	housewife	35	"
	U	Clapp Harold	81	draftsman	40	"
	V	Farrell Edmund E	81	clerk	40	"
	W	Farrell Joseph E	81	manager	73	"
	X	Smith Alexander	81	superintendent	45	"
	Y	Staula Albert	83	manager	42	"
	Z	Staula Angelina †	83	housewife	37	"
1850						
	A	Fox Annie M †	87	"	44	"
	B	Fox Frank	87	letter carrier	55	"
	C	Powers Anna †	87	housewife	45	"
	D	Powers Margaret M †	87	clerk	25	"
	E	Powers Michael	87	"	23	"
	F	Powers Richard	87	gardener	52	"
	G	Powers Richard	87	clerk	21	"
	H	Prendergast Francis	91	machinist	49	"
	K	Prendergast Marguerite M †	91	housewife	46	"
	L	Burke Mary †	91	clerk	21	"
	M	Burke Michael	91	laborer	59	"
	N	Towner Clarence S	93	shipper	58	"
	O	Towner Evelyn F †	93	clerk	23	"
	P	Towner George	93	"	20	"
	R	Towner Lillian †	93	housewife	58	"
	S	*O'Toole Edward	95	retired	75	"
	T	*O'Toole Mary †	95	housewife	78	"

Page	Letter	Full Name	Residence, Jan. 1, 1941	Occupation	Supposed Age	Reported Residence, Jan. 1, 1940. Street and Number.

Maple Street—Continued

Page	Letter	Full Name	Residence, Jan. 1, 1941	Occupation	Supposed Age	Reported Residence, Jan. 1, 1940. Street and Number.
	U	Heck Philip	97	laborer	60	here
	V	Kaiser Albert	97	retired	70	"

Margin Street

Page	Letter	Full Name	Residence, Jan. 1, 1941	Occupation	Supposed Age	Reported Residence, Jan. 1, 1940. Street and Number.
	X*	Roman Emil S	5	molder	60	here
	Y	Roman Genevieve M—†	5	housekeeper	20	"
	Z	Roman Joseph S	5	laborer	28	"
1851						
	A*	Kuzmiez Peter	13	"	60	"
	B	Stempkovski John S	13	"	31	"
	C	Stempkovski Michael	13	cementer	28	"
	D*	Urban Anna—†	13	housewife	62	"
	E*	Urban John	13	molder	52	"
	F	Stempkovski Charles J	14	painter	26	Dedham
	G	Stempkovski Mary J—†	14	housewife	23	"
	H*	Kotnick Agnes—†	15	"	52	here
	K	Kotnick Gladys B—†	15	inspector	27	"
	L	Kotnick Ignacy	15	laborer	52	"
	M	Kotnick Irene A—†	15	operator	21	"
	N	Kotnick Raymond J	15	"	23	"
	O	Russ Anna T—†	16	clerk	25	"
	P*	Russ Anna V—†	16	housewife	52	"
	R	Russ Blanche V—†	16	operator	28	"
	S	Russ Helen—†	16	assembler	21	"
	T	Russ William	16	laborer	27	"
	V*	Gray Eva—†	18	housewife	70	14 Margin
	W*	Gray Michael	18	laborer	70	14 "
	X*	Tomasaitis Anna B—†	19	housewife	52	here
	Y	Tomasaitis Anna B—†	19	operator	22	"
	Z	Tomasaitis John	19	"	20	"
1852						
	A	Tomasaitis Joseph P	19	laborer	52	"
	B*	Walters Blanche—†	20	housewife	49	"
	C	Walters John	20	laborer	37	"
	D	Walters Viola R—†	20	assembler	22	"
	E	Wharton Delina—†	37	housewife	58	"
	F	Wharton Gladys D—†	37	domestic	20	"
	G	Wharton Joseph H	37	laborer	58	"
	H	Currier Louis O	38	"	32	"

••Page	Letter	Full Name	Residence, Jan. 1	Occupation	Reputed Age	Reported Residence, Street and Number

Margin Street—Continued

••Page	Letter	Full Name	Residence, Jan. 1	Occupation	Reputed Age	Reported Residence, Street and Number
	K	Currier Marion J †	38	housewife	32	here
	L*	Kaseus Anna †	39	"	60	"
	M	Laudinsky John	39	laborer	70	"
	N*	Pescules Thomas	39	"	53	"
	O	Yucas Anastasia L †	40	waitress	25	"
	P*	Yucas Anthony J	40	laborer	64	"
	R	Yucas Anthony J	40	painter	22	"
	S*	Yucas Mary A †	40	housewife	55	"

Mason Street

••Page	Letter	Full Name	Residence, Jan. 1	Occupation	Reputed Age	Reported Residence, Street and Number
	T	Soba Frank E	3	manager	30	5 Mason
	U	Soba Wanda L †	3	housewife	30	Cambridge
	V	Sobachenski Tofil	5	molder	56	here
	W*	Sobachenski Victoria †	5	housewife	55	"
	X	Straqualursi Joseph	10	laborer	49	"
	Y*	Giovanni Mary †	10	housewife	41	"
	Z	Carlevale Constantino	12	barber	52	"
1853						
	A*	Carlevale Elvira †	12	housewife	18	"
	B	Mammone Salomina †	12	"	26	"
	C	Mammone Vincent	12	upholsterer	31	"
	D	Noyes Emily †	15	housewife	67	"
	E	Mikstas Adelia A †	15A	inspector	20	"
	F	Mikstas Alban	15A	metalworker	47	"
	G*	Mikstas Nellie F †	15A	housewife	44	"
	H	Moschella Helen L †	16	"	22	"
	K	Moschella Pasquale	16	carpenter	26	14 Moon
	L*	Serene Josephine †	16	housewife	43	here
	M	Wood Henry J	17	machinist	43	"
	N	Wood Margaret M †	17	housewife	41	"
	O	Frankino Dorothy †	17	"	31	"
	P	Frankino Samuel	17	attendant	34	"
	R	Heustis Dorothy A †	17A	housewife	29	"
	S	Heustis Ralph A	17A	machinist	38	"
	T*	Mammone Angela A †	18	housewife	36	"
	U	Mammone John	18	metalworker	36	"
	V	Poncia Lionilia M †	18	housewife	33	"
	W	Hart Francis A	19	electrician	19	"

Page.	Letter.	Full Name.	Residence, Jan. 1, 1941.	Occupation.	Supposed Age.	Reported Residence, Jan. 1, 1940. Street and Number.

Mason Street—Continued

	X	Hart Mary C—†	19	housewife	49	here
	Y	Mulgrew Bridget—†	19	"	68	"

Oak Street

	Z	Shaw Clarence	4	lather	32	50 Water
1854						
	A	Shaw Katherine—†	4	housewife	56	50 "
	B	Shaw Thomas	4	janitor	62	50 "
	C	McNeil Bernice—†	4	housewife	24	43 Sprague
	D	McNeil Murdock	4	welder	25	43 "
	E	*Stanewicz Benjamin	4	carpenter	52	690 Metropolitan av
	F	*Stanewicz Edna—†	4	housewife	45	690 "
	G	Rein Ann M—†	5	"	44	59 W Milton
	H	Rein Joseph A	5	operator	48	59 "
	K	Aspell Josephine—†	5	saleswoman	45	here
	L	Shea Catherine—†	5	housewife	69	"
	M	Shea Francis J	5	clerk	41	"
	N	Shea Joseph M	5	janitor	35	"
	O	Shea Mary E—†	5	clerk	39	"
	P	Shea Michael P	5	janitor	69	"
	R	Shea Vincent J	5	clerk	34	"
	S	*Yee Wong	6	laundryman	70	"
	T	Otis Frances T—†	10	housewife	34	"
	U	Otis George B	10	carpenter	34	"
	V	Morris George A	12	laborer	29	"
	W	Morris James L	12	retired	75	"
	X	Morris Mary A—†	12	housewife	65	"
	Y	Morris Rita E—†	12	saleswoman	24	"
	Z	Carroll Mary—†	22	mortician	55	"
1855						
	A	Thomas Alexander	22	embalmer	26	"
	B	Mulcahy Mary J—†	26	housekeeper	66	"
	C	O'Connor Louise A—†	26	"	68	"
	D	Drummey Isabel V—†	33	housewife	73	"
	E	Drummey John J	33	retired	79	"
	F	Ahearn Joseph P	33	millhand	49	"
	G	Ahearn Joseph P	33	clerk	21	"
	H	Ahearn Margaret F—†	33	"	46	"
	K	Kane James J	33	manager	30	"
	L	Kane Margaret F—†	33	housewife	23	"

Page	Letter	Full Name	Residence, Jan. 1, 1941	Occupation	Supposed Age	Reported Residence, Jan. 1, 1940. Street and Number

Oak Street Continued

Page	Letter	Full Name	Residence, Jan. 1, 1941	Occupation	Supposed Age	Reported Residence, Jan. 1, 1940. Street and Number
	M	Downey Francis E	33	laborer	35	here
	N	Downey Margaret J †	33	housewife	64	"
	O	Downey Patrick J	33	machinist	71	"
	P	O'Hare Dorothy C †	34	secretary	25	"
	R	O'Hare John J	34	attorney	59	"
	S	O'Hare Mary E †	34	housewife	56	"
	T	O'Hare Mary D †	34	secretary	39	"
	U	O'Hare Paul	34	"	26	"
	V	Lewis Elizabeth †	38	housewife	64	"
	W	Lewis Everett	38	retired	65	"
	X	McMahon Rose G †	39	housewife	29	"
	Y	O'Brien Alice A †	39	at home	71	"
	Z	O'Brien Frances B †	39	housewife	55	"
1856						
	A	O'Brien John J	39	bricklayer	59	"
	B	O'Brien Joseph F	39	teacher	27	"
	C	O'Brien Mary M †	39	clerk	53	"
	D	Nolen Delia J †	39	bookbinder	60	"
	E	Nolen John F	39	machinist	25	"
	F	Nolen Louise †	39	housewife	25	"
	G	Owen George W	40	clergyman	59	"
	H	Owen Margaret E †	40	housewife	62	"
	K	Haley Margaret A †	44	"	75	"
	L	Haley Margaret A †	44	secretary	37	"
	M	Reed Fred G	44	machinist	60	67 Westminster
	N	Reed Fred L	44	"	30	35 Davison
	O	Reed May H †	44	housewife	60	67 Westminster
	P	Reed Verna M †	44	"	23	35 Davison
	R	Bracken Anna M †	45	"	62	here
	S	Bracken Irene C †	45	bookkeeper	28	"
	T	Bracken Thomas J	45	engineer	62	"
	U	Bracken Walter W	45	manager	26	"
	V	Lavers Abby †	45	housewife	60	"
	W	Lavers Ruth †	45	bookkeeper	59	"
	X	Weston Mildred D †	48	housekeeper	49	"
	Y	Weston Samuel L	48	manager	75	"
	Z	Middleton Catherine J †	48	housewife	86	"
1857						
	A	Middleton James A	48	retired	87	"
	B	McMahon Anna M †	49	housewife	34	"
	C	McMahon James F	49	broker	35	"

Page.	Letter	FULL NAME.	Residence, Jan. 1, 1941.	Occupation	Supposed Age.	Reported Residence, Jan. 1, 1940. Street and Number.

Oak Street—Continued

Page.	Letter	FULL NAME.	Residence, Jan. 1, 1941.	Occupation	Supposed Age.	Reported Residence, Jan. 1, 1940. Street and Number.
	D	Fregeau Ellen J—†	49	housewife	63	here
	E	Fregeau Leopold I	49	musician	63	"
	F	Fregeau Marian J—†	49	clerk	25	"
	G	Frensilli John	50	"	44	"
	H	*Frensilli Regali—†	50	housewife	70	"
	K	*Frensilli Theresa—†	50	"	42	"
	M	Ide Mabel J—†	53	housekeeper	57	199 Fairmount av
	L	Phalen George	53	watchman	60	here
	N	Treworgy Effie L—†	53	at home	79	"
	P	Coleman Catherine—†	55	housewife	80	"
	R	Coleman Dennis H	55	retired	79	"
	S	Coleman Frances—†	55	housewife	35	Rhode Island
	T	Coleman Richard	55	salesman	40	"
	U	Tolland Joseph G	55	papermaker	47	here
	V	Tolland Mabel E—†	55	housewife	44	"
	W	Gray Marion E—†	58	teacher	63	"
	X	McCrillis Jenny—†	58	clerk	58	"
	Y	Farwell Chester W	59	shipper	58	"
	Z	Farwell Gretchen E—†	59	housewife	54	"
1858						
	A	Farwell Violet R—†	59	clerk	23	"
	B	Farwell Warren	59	"	29	"
	C	Lowenstein Robert	59	salesman	40	New York
	D	Wright John, jr	59	manager	25	New Jersey
	E	Coveney Beatrice D—†	60	housewife	56	here
	F	Coveney Charles L	60	clerk	45	"
	G	Coveney Leo	60	"	24	"
	H	Coveney Thomas	60	student	21	"
	K	Daley Helen G—†	60	clerk	48	Brookline
	M	Dray Henry J	62	electrician	38	here
	N	Dray Mary E—†	62	housewife	29	"
	O	Flynn Delia H—†	62	"	49	"
	P	Flynn John J	62	paperfinisher	60	"
	R	Sanderson Bertha—†	62	housekeeper	56	"
	S	MacQuarrie John H	64	metalworker	51	"
	T	MacQuarrie Lillian C—†	64	housewife	58	"
	U	Dickey Gilmore	64	manager	21	Belmont
	V	Dickey Ruth E—†	64	housewife	20	"
	W	Cardani Charles A	65	fireman	60	here
	X	Cardani Charles P	65	engineer	27	"
	Y	Cardani Rose C—†	65	housewife	51	"

Page	Letter	Full Name	Residence, Jan. 1, 194[illegible]	Occupation	Supposed Age	Reported Residence, Jan. 1, 194[illegible]. Street and Number

Oak Street—Continued

Page	Letter	Full Name	Residence	Occupation	Supposed Age	Reported Residence
	Z	McGowan David E	66	custodian	29	here
1859						
	A	McGowan James H	66	papermaker	63	"
	B	McGowan James J, jr	66	custodian	28	"
	C	McGowan Johanna C †	66	housewife	60	"
	D	McGowan Mary †	66	clerk	20	"
	E	McGowan Terrence	66	"	24	"
	F	McGowan Terrence F	66	machinist	70	"
	G	O'Brien Thomas	66	retired	70	"
	H	Dray Edward	68	"	77	"
	K	Ivers Agnes †	68	clerk	27	"
	L	Ivers Arlene M †	68	"	33	"
	M	Ivers Catherine R †	68	entertainer	21	"
	N	Ivers Evelyn M †	68	clerk	26	"
	O	Ivers Mary E †	68	housewife	58	"
	P	Collins Mary †	68	housekeeper	56	"
	R	Coleman Marian N †	70	teacher	29	"
	S	Coleman Mary E †	70	housewife	58	"
	T	Coleman Simon J	70	manager	54	"
	U	Coleman William J	70	retired	82	"
	V	Buck Dorothy †	70	teacher	33	"
	W	Buck Frank	70	retired	60	"

Pine Street

Page	Letter	Full Name	Residence	Occupation	Supposed Age	Reported Residence
	X	Corcoran Mary †	6	housewife	34	here
	Y	Corcoran Timothy D	6	gardener	38	"
	Z	Flaherty Mary J †	6	housewife	27	"
1860						
	A	Flaherty Peter A	6	clerk	30	"
	B	Rosati Nicholas G	8	machinist	40	"
	C	Rosati Theresa C †	8	housewife	36	"
	D	Haskins John H	8	retired	72	"
	E	Haskins Mary L †	8	printer	49	"
	F	Twyman Albany E	8	electrician	36	"
	G	D'Amato Hecker	8	teacher	31	"
	H	D'Amato Joseph C	8	"	33	"
	K	D'Amato Loreto	8	machinist	63	"
	L	D'Amato Mary A †	8	housewife	59	"
	M	Galaska Stanley A	10	inspector	37	176 Hunt'n av
	N	Galaska Wanda B †	10	housewife	30	176 "

Page	Letter	Full Name	Residence, Jan. 1, 1941.	Occupation.	Supposed Age.	Reported Residence, Jan. 1, 1940. Street and Number.

Pine Street—Continued

Page	Letter	Full Name	Residence, Jan. 1, 1941.	Occupation.	Supposed Age.	Reported Residence, Jan. 1, 1940. Street and Number.
	O	Jordan Alice E—†	10	housewife	44	6 Summer
	P	Jordan William B	10	clerk	46	6 "
	R	White Bessie E—†	11	housewife	53	here
	S	White Joseph	11	operator	56	"
	T	Barry Bridget M—†	11	housewife	60	"
	U	Barry John J	11	watchman	61	"
	V	McLoon James W	12	trainman	63	"
	W	McLoon M Emily—†	12	librarian	27	"
	X	McLoon Margaret G—†	12	housewife	50	"
	Y	Gelewitz Lena L—†	14	saleswoman	40	"
	Z	Gelewitz Rebecca—†	14	housewife	67	"
1861						
	A	Gelewitz Samuel S	14	clerk	46	"
	B	Anderson Arthur L	15	machinist	54	"
	C	Anderson Catherine M—†	15	housewife	55	"
	D	Anderson Dorothy G—†	15	teacher	24	"
	E	Anderson Mary M—†	15	"	31	"
	F	Connell Anastasia F—†	17	clerk	22	"
	G	Connell Anastasia M—†	17	housewife	52	"
	H	Connell Bernard D	17	clerk	21	"
	K	Connell Frederick J	17	"	28	"
	L	Connell Philip P	17	manager	27	"
	M	Connell Thomas B	17	chauffeur	24	"
	N	Crook Dorothy—†	17	clerk	20	28 Fairmount av
	O	Crook Margaret E—†	17	housewife	45	28 "
	P	Cunningham Lillian M—†	18	secretary	36	here
	R	Cunningham Lillie F—†	18	housewife	60	"
	S	Cunningham Madeline C—†	18	teacher	34	"
	T	O'Leary Margaret J—†	21	housewife	54	"
	U	O'Leary Raymond A	21	clerk	23	"
	V	Prendergast Margaret J—†	21	housewife	38	79 Maple
	W	Prendergast Patrick J	21	clerk	46	79 "
	X	Downey Joseph M	22	attorney	61	here
	Y	O'Donnell Rose A—†	22	housewife	53	"
	Z	O'Donnell Terrence	22	superintendent	57	"
1862						
	A	Codispoti Anna—†	23	clerk	26	"
	B	Codispoti Peter	23	tailor	65	"
	C	Codispoti Theresa—†	23	housewife	49	"
	D	DeFelice Joseph	23	cobbler	57	"
	E	DeFelice Mary—†	23	housewife	55	"

Page.	Letter.	Full Name.	Residence, Jan. 1, 1941.	Occupation.	Age.	Reported Residence, Jan. 1, 1940. Street and Number.

Pine Street—Continued

Page.	Letter.	Full Name.	Residence, Jan. 1, 1941.	Occupation.	Age.	Reported Residence, Jan. 1, 1940. Street and Number.
	F	DeFelice Philomena †	23	clerk	28	here
	G	Quinn Mary A †	24	housewife	76	"
	H	Quinn Richard A	24	retired	77	"
	K	Morhoff Edward	24	clerk	70	"
	L	Morhoff Ethel †	24	bookkeeper	35	"
	M	Menard Lillian G †	25	housewife	46	"
	N	Menard Mark W	25	clerk	46	"
	P	McLaughlin Charles L	29	machinist	48	"
	R	McLaughlin Helen †	29	housewife	44	"
	S	Boultenhouse Helen †	29	"	23	"
	T	Shevory Florence B †	29	"	55	"
	U	Shevory John J	29	leatherworker	27	"
	V	Shevory Orrin C	29	fireman	61	"
	W	Shevory Rita †	29	clerk	25	"
	X	Shevory Robert P	29	"	20	"

Pine Terrace

Page.	Letter.	Full Name.	Residence, Jan. 1, 1941.	Occupation.	Age.	Reported Residence, Jan. 1, 1940. Street and Number.
	Z	Martin Mary E †	1	housewife	60	here
1863						
	A	Martin Philip F	1	carpenter	64	"
	B	Coolbrith Agnes G †	1	housewife	36	"
	C	Coolbrith Edward J	1	painter	38	"
	D	Gray Annie M †	3	housewife	54	"
	E	Gray Dorothy †	3	clerk	21	"
	F	Gray Herbert J	3	foreman	54	"
	G	Gray Herbert J, jr	3	clerk	23	"
	H	Arni Harold	3	steamfitter	36	"
	K	McHugh David P	5	painter	44	"
	L	McHugh Helen †	5	housewife	41	"

Pingree Street

Page.	Letter.	Full Name.	Residence, Jan. 1, 1941.	Occupation.	Age.	Reported Residence, Jan. 1, 1940. Street and Number.
	N	Fanning John E	18	melter	25	here
	O	Fanning Mary J †	18	inspector	27	"
	P	Mahoney Mary A †	18	housewife	48	"
	R	Walsh Anna V †	18	"	28	"
	S	Walsh Joseph F	18	chauffeur	31	"
	T	Pucillo Alice †	20	housewife	33	"
	U	Pucillo Almanto	20	laborer	32	"
	V	*Vincent Mary V †	20	housewife	44	"

Page	Letter	Full Name	Residence, Jan. 1, 1941	Occupation	Supposed Age	Reported Residence, Jan. 1, 1940. Street and Number

Pingree Street—Continued

Page	Letter	Full Name	Residence, Jan. 1, 1941	Occupation	Supposed Age	Reported Residence, Jan. 1, 1940. Street and Number
	W	Vincent Mary V—†	20	houseworker	20	here
	X	Vincent Phillip	20	barber	46	"
	Y	Hurley Joseph A	20	mechanic	40	"
	Z	Hurley Ruth I—†	20	housewife	37	"
1864						
	A	Pazareskis Francis R	24	mechanic	29	1399 River
	B	Pazareskis Helen V—†	24	assembler	27	1399 "
	C	Pazareskis Joseph A	24	carpenter	55	1399 "
	D	Pazareskis Josephine A—†	24	housewife	21	1399 "
	E	Pazareskis Mary A—†	24	"	54	1399 "
	F	Brown Frederick M	24	painter	40	here
	G	Brown Margaret C—†	24	housewife	71	"
	H	Brown Michael J	24	loomfitter	70	"
	K	Brown Rose M—†	24	housewife	41	"
	L	Mulrey Alice E—†	24	houseworker	31	"
	M	Brown Mary M—†	24	housewife	40	"
	N	Brown William F	24	machinist	45	"

Radford Place

Page	Letter	Full Name	Residence, Jan. 1, 1941	Occupation	Supposed Age	Reported Residence, Jan. 1, 1940. Street and Number
	O	Purdy Doris M—†	5	clerk	33	here
	P	Purdy Loren V	5	laborer	65	"
	R	Purdy Randolph L	5	accountant	38	"
	S	Humora Alice T—†	7	clerk	22	"
	T*	Humora Catherine—†	7	housewife	50	"
	U	Humora Edward J	7	clerk	20	"
	V	Humora Max	7	janitor	50	"
	W	Humora Stella M—†	7	clerk	28	"
	X	Audette Mary J—†	9	housewife	38	"
	Y	Audette Willis J	9	burner	44	"
	Z	Jones Alicia—†	9	housewife	64	"
1865						
	A	Greene Anne A—†	10	"	45	"
	B	Greene Ralph	10	carpenter	51	"
	C	Perry John F	11	chauffeur	32	"
	D	Perry Margaret C—†	11	housewife	26	"

River Street

Page	Letter	Full Name	Residence, Jan. 1, 1941	Occupation	Supposed Age	Reported Residence, Jan. 1, 1940. Street and Number
1867						
	E	Waterman Harold L	1243	merchant	36	here
1868						
	C	Baga Lino	1326	baker	52	"

Page	Letter	Full Name	Residence, Jan. 1, 1941	Occupation	Reported Age	Reported Residence, Jan. 1, 1940. Street and Number

River Street—Continued

Page	Letter	Full Name	Residence, Jan. 1, 1941	Occupation	Reported Age	Reported Residence, Jan. 1, 1940. Street and Number
	D	Baga Mary †	1326	housewife	41	here
	F	Burke Anna †	1326	"	20	Dedham
	G	Burke Charles	1326	machinist	22	"
	H	Sanborn John E	1330	contractor	31	here
	K	Sanborn Marie J †	1330	housewife	31	"
	L	Floyd George J	1332	mechanic	34	"
	M	Floyd Helen C †	1332	housewife	30	"
	N	Cohen Goldie †	1332	"	52	"
	O	Cohen Sydney M	1332	painter	21	"
	P	Morgan James A	1334	salesman	35	"
	R	Morgan Rose E †	1334	housewife	34	"
	S	Field Alfred H	1334	milkman	43	"
	T	Field Alice A †	1334	housewife	43	"
	U	Hopkins George R	1334	chef	53	82 Central av
	V	Hopkins Harriet †	1334	housewife	54	82 "
	W	Brown Ellen M †	1334	at home	85	here
	X	Brown Katherine †	1334	waitress	48	"
	Y	Danker Annie †	1334	clerk	50	"
	Z	Foley Agnes E †	1334	housewife	28	"
1869						
	A	Foley Duncan T	1334	carpenter	30	"
	B	Faberman Arthur	1334	manager	32	"
	C	Faberman Belle F †	1334	housewife	30	"
	D	Bridges Lillian M †	1334	"	30	"
	E	Bridges Thomas A	1334	machinist	34	"
	F	Janik Edna M †	1334	housewife	32	"
	G	Janik Louis J	1334	pharmacist	37	"
	H	Law Helen E †	1334	housewife	43	"
	K	Law Raymond F	1334	inspector	43	"
	L	Raffaelle Bertrand E	1334	switchman	30	"
	M	Raffaelle Helen A †	1334	housewife	30	"
	N	Cashman Helen L †	1334	clerk	24	8 Linwood
	O	Cashman Jeremiah P	1334	"	54	8 "
	P	Cashman M Elizabeth †	1334	housewife	71	8 "
	R	Jackson Alfred	1336	mariner	67	79 Austin
	S	Jackson Joseph J	1336	clerk	26	79 "
	T	Jackson Madeline J †	1336	housewife	58	79 "
	U	Mason Ellis E	1336	engineer	51	196 Nep [illegible]
	V	Mason Sarah M †	1336	housewife	55	196 "
	W	Wright Aurilla A †	1336	"	52	here
	X	Wright Carleton L	1336	merchant	58	"
	Y	Potter Annie R †	1336	housewife	73	"

Page.	Letter.	Full Name.	Residence, Jan. 1, 1941.	Occupation.	Supposed Age.	Reported Residence, Jan. 1, 1940. Street and Number.

River Street—Continued

Page.	Letter.	Full Name.	Residence, Jan. 1, 1941.	Occupation.	Supposed Age.	Reported Residence, Jan. 1, 1940. Street and Number.
	Z	Potter Charles F	1336	superintendent	70	here
1870						
	A	Lennon Joseph A	1336	supervisor	40	4 Summer
	B	Lennon Mary M—†	1336	housewife	28	4 "
	C	Carabbio Frank J	1336	engraver	33	here
	D*	Carabbio Ida M—†	1336	housewife	33	"
	E	Conklin John J, jr	1336	draftsman	31	"
	F	Conklin Josephine R—†	1336	housewife	32	"
	G	Model Max	1336	merchant	56	"
	H	Model Rose R—†	1336	housewife	51	"
	K	West Calista A—†	1336	"	25	"
	L	West James M	1336	agent	27	"
	M	Brooks George W	1336	"	47	63 Rockdale
	N	Brooks Margaret T—†	1336	housewife	47	63 "
	O	Butterfield Claude C	1336	manager	30	here
	P	Butterfield Dorothy M—†	1336	housewife	27	"
	R	Marble Calvin A	1336	chauffeur	38	"
	S	Marble Grace E—†	1336	housewife	39	"
	T	Giles Mary M—†	1338	"	36	"
	U	Giles Thomas H	1338	tester	38	"
	V	Pascucci Edward J	1338	clerk	32	"
	W	Mintz Hyman K	1338	attorney	32	295 Fairmount av
	X*	Mintz Martha—†	1338	housewife	25	295 "
	Y	Paulsen Anna C—†	1338	housekeeper	82	1865 Hyde Park av
	Z	Specht Serena B—†	1338	domestic	67	284 Nep Valley P'kway
1871						
	A	Morrissey Henry J	1338	molder	47	here
	B	Morrissey Marguerite M—†	1338	merchant	43	"
	C	Cripps Marion L—†	1338	housewife	41	"
	D	Cripps William J	1338	policeman	45	"
	E	Bass Goldie F—†	1338	housewife	34	"
	F	Bass Harry N	1338	cutter	35	"
	G	Stack Beatrice M—†	1338	housewife	27	"
	H	Stack Joseph F	1338	bookkeeper	32	"
	K	Silverman Abraham J	1338	merchant	56	"
	L	Silverman Nettie—†	1338	housewife	46	"
	M	Conley Mae R—†	1338	clerk	48	"
	N	Boucher Joseph	1338	"	36	"
	O	Levangie Murdock	1338	machinist	52	"
	P	Cohen Joseph H	1338	manager	33	"
	R*	Cohen Regina—†	1338	housewife	29	"

Page	Letter	Full Name	Residence, Jan. 1, 1941	Occupation	Supposed Age	Reported Residence, Jan. 1, 1940. Street and Number

River Street (Continued)

Page	Letter	Full Name	Residence, Jan. 1, 1941	Occupation	Supposed Age	Reported Residence, Jan. 1, 1940. Street and Number
	S	Prior Lulu G †	1338	housewife	70	here
	T	Prior Marion G †	1338	secretary	47	"
	U	Clough Leslie R	1340	reporter	27	"
	V	Clough Margaret C †	1340	housewife	24	"
	W	Austin Walter A	1340	operator	30	"
	X	Austin Yolanda A †	1340	housewife	28	"
	Y	Pascinto Marie †	1340	"	45	"
	Z	Pascinto Salvatore R	1340	merchant	46	"
1872						
	A	*Cohen Fannie †	1340	housewife	40	"
	B	*Cohen Max J	1340	merchant	41	"
	C	Volk Henry I	1340	agent	40	"
	D	Volk Rebecca †	1340	housewife	31	"
	E	Stinson Sadie M †	1340	teacher	40	"
	F	Cogan Frederick P	1340	salesman	30	24 Rosewood
	G	Cogan Priscilla M †	1340	housewife	25	24 "
	H	Gorman Alfred C	1340	policeman	42	here
	K	Gorman Margaret H †	1340	housewife	35	"
	L	*Pichulo Florence L †	1340	"	36	"
	M	Pichulo Vincent E	1340	attorney	39	"
	N	Kelley Alice E †	1340	housekeeper	46	20 Maxwell
	O	Kelley Anna †	1340	at home	76	20 "
	P	Kisker Frederick P	1340	painter	50	20 "
	R	Logue Jeremiah	1340	chauffeur	47	here
	S	Logue Mary †	1340	housewife	47	"
	T	*Levy Barnet	1340	merchant	39	Chelsea
	U	Levy Sarah S †	1340	housewife	34	"
	V	Galiano Sarah A †	1342	cashier	51	here
	W	Andelman Evelyn M †	1342	housewife	25	"
	X	Andelman Manuel	1342	serviceman	28	"
	Y	O'Connell Bernard M	1342	boilermaker	25	1420 River
	Z	O'Connell Ruth E †	1342	housewife	21	36 Garfield av
1873						
	A	Fitzgerald Alma A †	1366	"	40	[illegible]
	B	Fitzgerald Frederick A	1366	custodian	44	6 "
	C	Cameron Isabelle F †	1368	housewife	42	here
	D	Cameron John J	1368	policeman	43	"
	E	Long Mary †	1370	housewife	36	1455 River
	F	Long Patrick J	1370	engineer	38	1455 "
	G	Waterman Edith M †	1374	housewife	36	here
	H	Waterman Herbert F	1374	salesman	38	"

Page	Letter	Full Name	Residence, Jan. 1, 1941	Occupation	Supposed Age	Reported Residence Jan. 1, 1940. Street and Number

River Street—Continued

	K	Masella Charles	1378	chef	46	here
	L	Masella Lena—†	1378	housewife	40	"

Walnut Place

	M	Barry Joseph F	8	clerk	29	here
	N	Barry Stella M—†	8	housewife	29	"
	O	McLeod Bertha C—†	8	"	69	"
	P	Barry Helen M—†	10	clerk	27	"
	R	Barry Irene R—†	10	housewife	21	"
	S	Barry Michael J	10	fireman	66	"
	T	Barry Sarah E—†	10	housewife	63	"

Walnut Street

	U	McCormack Charles E	7	retired	67	60 Walter
	V	McCormack Charles R	7	clerk	23	60 "
	W	McCormack Lida H—†	7	housewife	60	60 "
	X	Obuchon Dorothy—†	11	"	27	here
	[1]X	Obuchon Leo P	11	laborer	28	"
	Y	Calarese Carolina—†	15	housewife	42	"
	Z	Calarese Frank	15	buffer	42	"
1874						
	A	Nelson Charles W	19	clerk	24	"
	B	Nelson George E	19	"	22	"
	C	Nelson Mary—†	19	housewife	45	"
	D	Rogers Elizabeth C—†	21	"	32	"
	E	Webster Frederick B	21	laborer	31	"
	F	Webster Josephine—†	21	housewife	52	"
	K	O'Grady Dennis E	55	salesman	46	"
	L	O'Grady Edith G—†	55	housewife	40	"
	M	O'Grady Edward	55	clerk	20	"
	N	Hart William D	59	B F D	38	"
	O	Hart Winifred A—†	59	housewife	36	"
	P	Ryan Edward M	78	chauffeur	47	"
	R	Ryan Margaret T—†	78	housekeeper	50	"
	S	Faulkner Rita—†	78	housewife	79	12 Wolcott ct
	T	Faulkner Teresa—†	78	housekeeper	58	12 "
	V	Mahan Edward J	rear 85	clerk	23	here
	W	Mahan Eleanor L—†	" 85	housewife	23	"
	X	Moxhan Lillian A—†	" 85	"	61	"

Page	Letter	Full Name	Residence, Jan. 1, 1941	Occupation	Supposed Age	Reported Residence, Jan. 1, 1940. Street and Number

Wilton Street

Page	Letter	Full Name	Residence, Jan. 1, 1941	Occupation	Supposed Age	Reported Residence, Jan. 1, 1940. Street and Number
	Y	*Simoes Angelina †	9	housewife	29	here
	Z	*Simoes Manuel	9	laborer	39	"
1875						
	A	*Giammasi John	9	retired	60	"
	B	*Giammasi Louisa †	9	housewife	52	"
	C	*Rampino Domenic	10	laborer	32	"
	D	Rampino Ruth A †	10	housewife	32	"
	E	Toti Mary †	10	"	30	"
	F	Toti William	10	cobbler	35	"
	G	Rampino Columbo	10	laborer	21	"
	H	Rampino John	10	"	24	"
	K	*Rampino Peter	10	"	53	"
	L	*Rampino Susie †	10	housewife	52	"
	M	Rampino Vincent	10	laborer	27	"
	N	Piccirilli John	11	"	51	"
	O	Piccirilli Laura †	11	stitcher	20	"
	P	*Piccirilli Sarah †	11	housewife	44	"
	R	Fistola John	11	laborer	33	"
	S	*Macedo Edward	11	"	58	"
	T	*Picariello Antonio	11	farmer	62	"
	U	*Picariello Santi †	11	housewife	60	"
	V	Matukas Alfonse	12	laborer	30	"
	W	Matukas Mary H †	12	housewife	29	"
	X	McGuire Elizabeth †	12	"	56	"
	Y	McGuire Helen †	12	clerk	21	"
	Z	*Aprea Celestine †	13	housewife	48	"
1876						
	A	Aprea Frank	13	laborer	54	"
	B	Aprea Joseph	13	coremaker	24	"
	C	Aprea Rose †	13	operator	21	"
	D	Fiore Madeline M †	15	housewife	28	"
	E	Fiore Vincent	15	blacksmith	35	"

Winter Street

Page	Letter	Full Name	Residence, Jan. 1, 1941	Occupation	Supposed Age	Reported Residence, Jan. 1, 1940. Street and Number
	F	Assad Katherine T †	7	housewife	24	Medway
	G	Assad Peter	7	grinder	39	"
	H	Ricci Elizabeth T †	7	stitcher	27	here
	K	Ricci Margaret C †	7	assembler	31	"
	L	Aquilio Lena G †	8	housewife	33	"
	M	*Aquilio Nazzareno	8	machinist	48	"

Page.	Letter.	Full Name.	Residence, Jan. 1, 1941.	Occupation.	Supposed Age.	Reported Residence, Jan. 1, 1940. Street and Number.

Winter Street—Continued

Page.	Letter.	Full Name.	Residence, Jan. 1, 1941.	Occupation.	Supposed Age.	Reported Residence, Jan. 1, 1940. Street and Number.
	N	O'Rourke Bridget V—†	10	housekeeper	60	here
	O	O'Rourke Catherine T—†	10	"	64	"
	P	Lombardi Anthony D	11	laborer	20	"
	R	*Lombardi John	11	retired	70	"
	S	Lombardi Josephine M—†	11	stitcher	23	"
	T	*Lombardi Rosaline—†	11	housewife	66	"
	U	Seibetta Agnes B—†	11	"	21	625 E Fifth
	V	Seibetta Croce J	11	metalworker	22	302 "
	W	*Cotellesso Mary A—†	12	housewife	37	here
	X	Cotellesso Ralph	12	laborer	46	"
	Y	Maroncelli Frank	12	"	54	"
	Z	Maroncelli Josephine T—†	12	stitcher	23	"
1877						
	A	*Maroncelli Mary—†	12	housewife	44	"
	B	Maroncelli Vincent P	12	machinist	21	"
	C	Fitzgerald Ruth C—†	12	housewife	28	"
	D	Fitzgerald William D	12	steamfitter	30	"
	E	*Bonito Louis	13	laborer	53	"
	F	Bonito Thomas P	13	machinist	25	"
	G	Gaetani Michael J	13	metalworker	24	"
	H	Gaetani Susan V—†	13	gold stamper	23	"
	K	*Balzi Josephine—†	16	housekeeper	41	"
	L	Bielecki Adolph	16	machinist	48	"
	M	*Bielecki Julia—†	16	housewife	47	"
	N	Prohotsuk Peter	16	barber	45	"
	O	Gradzewicz Anthony	16	chef	24	"
	P	Gradzewicz Jessie S—†	16	housewife	23	"
	R	Gradzewicz John	16	counterman	22	"

Winthrop Street

Page.	Letter.	Full Name.	Residence, Jan. 1, 1941.	Occupation.	Supposed Age.	Reported Residence, Jan. 1, 1940. Street and Number.
	S	Keswick Alice W—†	20	houseworker	48	here
	T	McGuire George T	20	machinist	22	"
	U	McGuire Jessie G—†	20	housewife	50	"
	V	Padden John T	22	operator	37	"
	W	Padden Mary F—†	22	housewife	37	"
	X	Curley Mary L—†	42	"	53	"
	Y	Curley Patrick J	42	milkman	49	"
	Z	Curley Patrick J	42	janitor	28	"
1878						
	A	Curley Thomas J	42	laborer	30	"

Page	Letter	Full Name	Residence Jan. 1, 1941	Occupation	Reported Age	Reported Residence, Jan. 1, 1940 Street and Number
		Winthrop Street Continued				
	B	Petrin Eugene	42	machinist	59	here
	C	Balestra Lawrence M	44	clerk	25	[illegible]
	D	Baldwin Agnes E †	44	housewife	22	here
	E	Baldwin Robert J	44	lather	22	"
	F	Salina Benjamin	46	bartender	34	"
	G	Salina Edna †	46	cementer	23	"
	H	Salina Sophie †	46	housewife	28	"
	K	Szymanski Adam	46	millworker	46	"
	L	*Szymanski Gladys S †	46	housewife	59	"
	M	Welliver George M	46	blacksmith	78	"
	N	Welliver Margaret J †	46	housewife	74	"
		Woodland Place				
	S	Barnett Lillian A—†	20	housewife	39	here
	P	Barnett Willard E	20	electrician	41	"
	R	Barnett Willard F	20	operator	20	"

Ward 18—Precinct 19

CITY OF BOSTON

LIST OF RESIDENTS
20 YEARS OF AGE AND OVER

(NON-CITIZENS INDICATED BY ASTERISK)
(FEMALES INDICATED BY DAGGER)

AS OF

JANUARY 1, 1941

CITY OF BOSTON PRINTING DEPARTMENT

Page	Letter	Full Name	Residence, Jan. 1, 1941	Occupation	Supposed Age	Reported Residence, Jan. 1, 1940. Street and Number

Adams Street

Page	Letter	Full Name	Residence, Jan. 1, 1941	Occupation	Supposed Age	Reported Residence, Jan. 1, 1940. Street and Number
1900						
	A	Lavorgna Henry F	6	carpenter	21	here
	B	Lavorgna Immaculata M—†	6	teacher	31	“
	C	Lavorgna Joseph L	6	painter	25	“
	D	Lavorgna Lawrence T	6	U S A	25	“
	E	Lavorgna Lorenzo	6	contractor	63	“
	F	Lavorgna Maria—†	6	housewife	54	“
	G	Lavorgna Paul A	6	carpenter	32	“
	H	Lavorgna Vera J—†	6	librarian	28	“
	K	Fardy Ann M—†	9	housewife	31	1569 River
	L	Fardy William H	9	electrician	33	1569 “
	M	Petta Gerard M	9	machinist	28	33 Davison
	N	Petta Sarah A—†	9	housewife	21	33 “
	O	Casey Margaret M—†	11	“	34	here
	P	Casey Walter E	11	milkman	44	“
	R	Burke Helen—†	11	clerk	48	“
	S	Burke Margaret E—†	11	“	46	“
	T	Spencer Harold	14	engingeer	34	“
	U	Spencer Ida M—†	14	housewife	31	“
	V	Sheard Agnes M—†	18	“	39	“
	W	Sheard Arthur J	18	boilmaker	48	“
	X	Jacobson Hans J	18	engineer	30	“
	Y	Jacobson Vera L—†	18	housewife	21	“
	Z	Olson Edward M	19	machinist	46	29 Child
1901						
	A	Olson Marjorie F—†	19	housewife	38	29 “

Atherton Avenue

Page	Letter	Full Name	Residence, Jan. 1, 1941	Occupation	Supposed Age	Reported Residence, Jan. 1, 1940. Street and Number
	B	Snow Ann B—†	5	housewife	39	here
	C	Snow Walter	5	machinist	41	“
	D	Snow James L	7	checker	32	“
	E	Snow Noella M—†	7	housewife	31	“
	F	Carroll Johanna A—†	9	housekeeper	75	“
	G	Carroll Katherine V—†	9	clerk	35	“
	H	Carroll Louis R	9	machinist	41	“
	K	Carroll Robert W	9	salesman	32	“
	L	Fulceniti Arnaldo	11	metalworker	46	“
	M	Loria Rosario	11	laborer	49	“
	N	Santamaria Paul J	11	assembler	26	1854 River
	O	Santamaria Rose M—†	11	housewife	26	61 Lexington

Page	Letter	Full Name	Residence, Jan. 1, 1941	Occupation	Supposed Age	Reported Residence, Jan. 1, 1940. Street and Number

Atherton Avenue—Continued

Page	Letter	Full Name	Residence, Jan. 1, 1941	Occupation	Supposed Age	Reported Residence, Jan. 1, 1940. Street and Number
	P	Vigna Assunta—†	11	housewife	52	here
	R	Vigna Vincenzo	11	melter	52	"
	S	Blumenthal Anna—†	12	housewife	35	"
	T	Blumenthal Louis	12	salesman	35	"
	U	McNealy Helen V—†	14	housewife	43	"
	V	McNealy Henry J	14	B F D	53	"
	W*	Faherty Mary E—†	15	housewife	79	"
	X	Faherty Thomas D	15	retired	75	"
	Y	Kowalcik Joseph A	17	laborer	27	"
	Z	Kowalcik Rita F—†	17	housewife	23	"
1902						
	A	Laramie Edward P	17	shipper	28	"
	B	Petta Mary A—†	17	housewife	52	"
	C	Petta Michael J	17	machinist	54	"
	D	Snow Elizabeth V—†	17	housewife	64	"
	E	Snow Patrick F	17	retired	73	"

Baker Street

Page	Letter	Full Name	Residence, Jan. 1, 1941	Occupation	Supposed Age	Reported Residence, Jan. 1, 1940. Street and Number
	F	Archibald M Guy	5	gardener	62	here
	G	Archibald Pauline—†	5	housewife	61	"
	H	Heideloff Elizabeth—†	7	at home	76	"
	K	Heyn Herman	7	engraver	50	"
	L	Heyn Lillian C—†	7	housewife	44	"
	M	Kimball Lydia—†	9	housekeeper	65	"

Barry Place

Page	Letter	Full Name	Residence, Jan. 1, 1941	Occupation	Supposed Age	Reported Residence, Jan. 1, 1940. Street and Number
	N	Frankina Albert	35	clerk	25	35 Austin
	O	Frankina Helen—†	35	housewife	24	35 "
	P	Murray Catherine—†	35	dressmaker	60	here
	R	Murray Mary—†	35	housekeeper	81	"
	T	Diette Medora—†	37	housewife	41	"
	U	Diette Paul	37	machinist	48	"
	V	Sarro D Michael	37	bracer	32	"
	W	Sarro Susan M—†	37	housewife	32	"
	X	Rosata Angelina—†	41	"	49	"
	Y	Rosata Jeanette Y—†	41	typist	24	"
	Z	Rosata Joseph E	41	electrician	29	"

Page.	Letter.	Full Name.	Residence, Jan. 1, 1941.	Occupation.	Supposed Age.	Reported Residence, Jan. 1, 1940. Street and Number.
1903		**Barry Place—Continued**				
	A	Rosata Mary T—†	41	typist	21	here
	B	Rosata Thomas W	41	laborer	23	"
		Barry Street				
	C	Colantoni John H	7	laborer	27	here
	D	Colantoni Rose M—†	7	housewife	23	"
	E	Vittorini Henry G	7	sorter	28	"
	F	Vittorini Theresa M—†	7	housewife	25	"
	G	Conley William F	17	laborer	44	"
	H	Wallace Ellen A—†	17	housekeeper	84	"
		Blanchard Street				
	K	Malloy James	2	laborer	33	Lawrence
	L	Malloy Martha A—†	2	housewife	37	"
	M	Nedder Abraham G	2	mechanic	38	here
	N	Nedder Lily—†	2	housewife	38	"
	O	Stracqualursi Luigi	6	laborer	37	"
	P	Stracqualursi Mary—†	6	housewife	30	"
	R	Ruggiero Lena—†	16	"	25	"
	S	Ruggiero Querino	16	chauffeur	32	"
	T	*Pupi Angela—†	16	housewife	52	"
	U	Pupi August F	16	machinist	24	"
	V	Pupi Dominic L	16	"	20	"
	W	Pupi Frank	16	laborer	56	"
	X	Greathead Anna—†	17	housewife	21	65 Morton
	Y	Greathead George	17	laborer	23	65 "
	Z	Ruscito Anthony	17	"	47	here
1904						
	A	Ruscito Lucia—†	17	housewife	45	"
	B	Travers Mary M—†	19	housekeeper	41	"
	C	Gordon Leah C—†	21	housewife	32	"
	D	Gordon Patrick	21	laborer	35	"
	E	Chaisson Hugh	21	operator	22	60 Readville
	F	Salvatore Armand	21	oiler	34	here
	G	Salvatore Thelma—†	21	housewife	29	"
	H	Pasciuto Cosimo	23	laborer	58	"
	K	*Pasciuto Josephine—†	23	housewife	52	"
	L	Pasciuto Julio	23	laborer	21	"

Page.	Letter.	Full Name.	Residence, Jan. 1, 1941.	Occupation.	Supposed Age.	Reported Residence, Jan. 1, 1940. Street and Number.

Blanchard Street—Continued

Page.	Letter.	Full Name.	Residence, Jan. 1, 1941.	Occupation.	Supposed Age.	Reported Residence, Jan. 1, 1940. Street and Number.
	M	Pasciuto Anna V †	23	housewife	24	1495 Hyde Park av
	N	Pasciuto Joseph J	23	machinist	27	1495 "
	O	*Imbaro Lucy †	24	housewife	53	here
	P	Imbaro Nicholas	24	machinist	21	"
	R	*Turchetti Angelo	24	fireman	51	"
	S	Mikalauskas John	27	salesman	45	"
	T	Mikalauskas Theresa †	27	housewife	38	"
	U	Venanzi Annie †	30	"	45	"
	V	Venanzi Luigi	30	laborer	45	"
	W	Keane Margaret M—†	36	housewife	29	"
	X	Keane Thomas J	36	pipefitter	34	"
	Y	Curran Anna F †	36	stenographer	33	"
	Z	*Curran Delia †	36	housewife	65	"
1905						
	A	Curran Helen †	36	clerk	30	"
	B	Curran Julia B †	36	typist	34	"
	C	Curran Mary A †	36	operator	39	"
	D	Curran S Joseph	36	laborer	28	"
	E	Curran Sarah A †	36	stenographer	36	"
	F	Brindley Helen A †	59	clerk	42	"
	G	Conley Alice M †	59	secretary	35	"
	H	Conley Marguerite—†	59	clerk	45	"
	K	Mack Alice †	63	nurse	57	"
	L	Mack Elizabeth †	63	seamstress	62	"
	M	Mack James	63	retired	64	"
	N	Mack Mary †	63	housekeeper	66	"

Business Street

Page.	Letter.	Full Name.	Residence, Jan. 1, 1941.	Occupation.	Supposed Age.	Reported Residence, Jan. 1, 1940. Street and Number.
	O	Wood Earl F	47	laborer	25	here
	P	Wood Mildred L †	47	housewife	24	"
	R	*Monaco Benjamin	49	laborer	45	"
	T	Mutchler Margaret R †	51	housewife	36	"
	U	Mutchler Miles G	51	mechanic	43	"
	W	*Malnowski Antonina †	55	housewife	47	18 Margin
	X	Malnowski Charles	55	mechanic	22	18 "
	Y	Malnowski John	55	papermaker	47	18 "
	Z	Malnowski John, jr	55	"	25	18 "
1906						
	A	Kiehn Ella C †	55	housewife	27	here
	B	Kiehn Ellsworth F	55	electrician	38	"

Page.	Letter.	Full Name.	Residence, Jan. 1, 1941.	Occupation.	Supposed Age.	Reported Residence, Jan. 1, 1940. Street and Number.

Business Street—Continued

Page.	Letter.	Full Name.	Residence, Jan. 1, 1941.	Occupation.	Supposed Age.	Reported Residence, Jan. 1, 1940. Street and Number.
	E	Russo Anthony	57	plumber	41	here
	F	Russo Joseph	57	"	33	"
	G	*Russo Ralph	57	retired	75	"
	H	Russo Raymond	57	steamfitter	26	"
	K	*Russo Victoria—†	57	housewife	68	"
	M	*Budris Ann—†	59	"	50	"
	N	Budris Joseph	59	clerk	20	"
	O	*Vasileuski Theodore	59	laborer	45	"
	P	*Delucca Palmerosa—†	59	housewife	68	"
	R	Carreccio Alfred	61	mechanic	61	"
	S	Carreccio Benedictia—†	61	housewife	57	"
	T	Carreccio Mary—†	61	dressmaker	22	"
	U	Carreccio Nellie—†	61	"	28	"
	V	Cibotti Nancy—†	61	housewife	25	21 E Glenwood av
	W	Cibotti Patrick W	61	chauffeur	29	21 "
	Y	*Olbrys Helen—†	65	housewife	45	here
	Z	Olbrys Sofie M—†	65	operator	22	"
1907						
	A	*Olbrys Walter	65	molder	46	"
	B	*DellaGioia Albina—†	65	housewife	41	"
	C	DellaGioia Angeline I—†	65	dressmaker	20	"
	D	DellaGioia Dominic	65	laborer	48	"
	E	DellaGioia Madeline L—†	65	maid	22	"
	G	Campanello Helen G—†	68	nurse	21	"
	H	Campanello Mary—†	68	clerk	23	"
	K	Campanello Rose—†	68	housewife	50	"
	L	Nicholson Gertrude—†	68	"	45	14 Fairmount ter
	M	*Ruscito Mary—†	75	"	33	here
	N	*Ruscito Silvestro	75	laborer	39	"
	O	Mokrycki Jennie—†	76	clerk	27	"
	P	*Mokrycki Mary—†	76	housewife	64	"
	R	Mokrycki Mary—†	76	"	21	"
	S	*Mokrycki Theodore	76	machinist	54	"
	T	*Falco Anna—†	77	housewife	54	"
	U	*Falco Steven	77	laborer	58	"
	V	Mulattieri Angelo	77	painter	29	"
	W	Leoncello Jennie—†	78	housewife	43	"
	X	Keefe James T	79	chauffeur	48	"
	Y	O'Brien Alice—†	79	housewife	34	"
	Z	O'Brien Clarence W	79	chef	36	"

Page	Letter	Full Name	Residence, Jan. 1, 19[illegible]	Occupation	Supposed Age	Reported Residence, [illegible] Street and Number
1908						
		Business Street Continued				
	A	Greeley Blanche G †	81	housewife	33	here
	B	Greeley Edward H	81	policeman	44	"
	D	Frazier Albert	84	mechanic	45	"
	E	Frazier Albert, jr	84	laborer	21	"
	F	Frazier Jennie †	84	housewife	47	"
	G	*Holledanchise Anna †	84	at home	72	"
	H	*Pulsoni Jennie †	84	housewife	41	"
	K	McGowan Mary J †	85	"	71	"
	L	McGowan Thomas F	85	retired	76	"
	N	McAuliffe Bridget A †	87	housewife	72	"
	O	McAuliffe Mary †	87	"	74	"
	P	Spano Anthony	91	barber	22	"
	R	Spano Eugenia †	91	maid	24	"
	S	*Spano Ida †	91	housewife	45	"
	T	Spano Ida †	91	stitcher	20	"
	U	Spano Rocco	91	barber	54	"
	V	Fitzgerald Victoria †	95	maid	26	"
	W	*McNeil Adelaide †	95	housewife	65	"
	X	McNeil Frances †	95	"	29	"
	Y	McNeil Russell	95	foreman	29	"
	Z	Pomagzak Edward	95	laborer	35	"
1909						
	A	*Pomagzak Frances †	95	housewife	64	"
	B	Pomagzak Mary †	95	stitcher	32	"
	C	Johnson Eric R	105	clerk	37	"
	D	Richens Marie †	105	housewife	64	"
	E	*Kulpowicz Mary †	107	"	44	"
	F	Kulpowicz Peter	107	machinist	50	"
	G	Safchuk Kazimera †	109	housewife	51	"
	H	Safchuk Kazimierz	109	machinist	51	"
	L	Wysocki Anthony M	111	"	21	"
	M	*Wysocki Stella A †	111	housewife	22	"
		Charles Street				
	O	Barry George H	1	machinist	55	here
	P	Norton Bartholomew A	1	laborer	51	"
	R	Norton John T	1	molder	54	"
	S	Norton Sarah F †	1	housewife	45	"

Page	Letter	Full Name	Residence, Jan. 1, 1941	Occupation	Supposed Age	Reported Residence, Jan. 1, 1940. Street and Number.

Charles Street—Continued

Page	Letter	Full Name	Residence, Jan. 1, 1941	Occupation	Supposed Age	Reported Residence, Jan. 1, 1940.
	T	*Zella Mary—†	8	housewife	59	here
	U	Zella Michael	8	laborer	23	"
	V	Sears Frank D	14	retired	63	"
	W	Sears Mabel E—†	14	housewife	62	"
	X	Sbardello Philomena—†	17	"	51	"
	Y	Sbardello Sossio	17	laborer	52	"
	Z	Baga Guido	17	"	48	"
1910						
	A	*Baga Jennie—†	17	housewife	46	"
	B	Zaniboni Louis	17	mechanic	30	Pennsylvania
	C	Zaniboni Mina—†	17	housewife	27	here
	D	Peck Hannah C—†	20	"	64	"
	E	Peck Mary E—†	20	clerk	28	"
	F	Peck Matthias F	20	machinist	69	"
	G	Shea Anna C—†	20	housewife	23	"
	H	Shea James J	20	operator	22	"
	K	Daggett Herbert W	21	bartender	24	871 Hyde Park av
	L	Daggett Rita N—†	21	secretary	22	here
	M	McKelligan Bessie N—†	21	housewife	41	"
	N	McKelligan Frank E	21	policeman	44	"
	O	McKelligan John, jr	21	laborer	52	"
	P	Martin Mildred A—†	22–24	housewife	34	"
	R	Martin William R	22–24	draftsman	34	"
	S	Becket August J	22–24	foreman	53	"
	T	Becket Isabel N—†	22–24	housewife	42	"
	V	Sevieri Edvey M—†	26	"	42	50 Palmer
	W	Sevieri Ernest	26	shipper	49	50 "
	X	Sevieri Ernest V	26	painter	23	50 "
	Y	Faulkner Elizabeth A—†	28	housewife	49	here
	Z	Faulkner Thomas J	28	chauffeur	45	"
1911						
	A	Reilly Patrick J	28	retired	72	"
	B	Reid Ethel L—†	29	stitcher	26	1195 Hyde Park av
	C	Reid Margaret E—†	29	housewife	44	1195 "
	D	Reid Thomas E	29	chauffeur	49	1195 "
	E	Martell Mary—†	29	housekeeper	45	here
	F	Curtis Anna B—†	31	housewife	33	"
	G	Curtis Francis A	31	foreman	37	"
	H	Brady Gerald A	31	mechanic	45	"
	K	Brady Mary G—†	31	housewife	40	"
	L	Ceurvels Albert R	33	contractor	48	5 Vinton
	M	Ceurvels Anna W—†	33	housewife	48	5 "

Page	Letter	Full Name	Residence Jan. 1, 1941	Occupation	Reputed Age	Reported Residence Jan. 1, 1940. Street and Number

Charles Street Continued

Page	Letter	Full Name	Residence	Occupation	Age	Reported Residence
	N	Lawn Frances A †	33	housewife	24	354 W Third
	O	Lawn Frank T	33	leatherworker	25	354 "
	R	Ewen James	35	clerk	39	15 Lockwood
	S	Ewen Mabel N †	35	housewife	29	15 "
	U	MacInnes Archibald A	37	mechanic	30	here
	V	MacInnes Archibald W	37	R F D	53	"
	W	MacInnes Sarah N †	37	housewife	49	"
	X	MacInnes Warren R	37	plater	24	"
	Y	Dervin Catherine L †	37	housewife	46	43 Oakton av
	Z	Dervin Patrick J	37	policeman	46	43 "
1912						
	A	Elsemiller Daniel	39	trimmer	37	here
	B	Elsemiller Ethel P †	39	housewife	29	"
	C	Kelly Dora M †	39	dyer	22	"
	D	Kelly Francis J	39	machinist	45	"
	E	Kelly Lena M †	39	housewife	42	"
	F	Scanlan Daniel H	40	operator	21	"
	G	Scanlan Emma M †	40	housewife	44	"
	H	Scanlan Ralph J	40	laborer	47	"
	K	Smith Ralph H	40	chauffeur	29	"
	L	Smith Verna L †	40	housewife	24	"
	M	Grant Evelyn R †	42	cashier	20	"
	N	Grant Lillian F †	42	saleswoman	23	"
	O	Grant Nancy R †	42	housewife	44	"
	P	Grant William A	42	letter carrier	49	"
	R	Grant William A, jr	42	operator	24	"
	S	Lucas Helen A †	42	housewife	26	Dedham
	T	Lucas John G	42	mechanic	26	"
	U	Patterson Arnold M	43	engraver	22	here
	V	Patterson John G	43	foreman	50	"
	W	Patterson John G, jr	43	salesman	27	"
	X	Patterson Myrtie L †	43	housewife	52	"
	Y	Ainslie Claire G †	44	"	34	"
	Z	Ainslie James W	44	toolmaker	33	"
1913						
	A	French Arthur S	44	salesman	63	"
	B	French Margaret E †	44	housewife	60	"

Church Street

Page	Letter	Full Name	Residence	Occupation	Age	Reported Residence
	C	*Pratola Antoinette †	9	housewife	43	here
	D	Pratola Matteo	9	laborer	52	"

Page.	Letter.	Full Name.	Residence, Jan. 1, 1941.	Occupation.	Supposed Age.	Reported Residence, Jan. 1, 1940. Street and Number.

Church Street—Continued

	E	Cox Mildred I—†	9	housekeeper	46	Dedham
	F	Crawford Elizabeth—†	13	housewife	77	here
	G	Crawford John	13	retired	84	"
	H	Sullivan Henry J	15	carpenter	46	"
	K	Sullivan Mary L—†	15	housewife	45	"

Damon Place

	L*	Baressi Providence—†	8	housewife	52	here
	M	Camastro Benjamin	10	laborer	53	"
	N*	Camastro Concetta—†	10	dressmaker	22	"
	O*	Camastro Maria—†	10	housewife	48	"
	P*	Camastro Rose—†	10	dressmaker	23	"

Dedham Street

	R	Alexander Charles H	4	machinist	26	83 Beacon
	S	Alexander Margaret M—†	4	housewife	25	here
	T	Lyons Frederick	4	clerk	31	"
	U	Lyons Leon E	4	machinist	67	"
	V	Lyons Mary J—†	4	housewife	60	"
	W	Healy Catherine—†	8	clerk	23	"
	X	Healy Mary—†	8	teacher	23	"
	Y	Healy Mary E	8	housewife	48	"
	Z	Healy Ruth—†	8	nurse	20	"
1914						
	A	Healy William	8	mechanic	51	"
	B*	Drowzdowski Ignatius	9	molder	56	"
	C	Kazurny Alexander	9	rubberworker	48	"
	D*	Kazurny Veronica—†	9	housewife	47	"
	E	O'Conner Margaret M—†	10	"	41	"
	F	Berry Edward E	12	plumber	52	"
	G	Berry Mary A—†	12	housewife	51	"
	H	Coullahan Bernard	12	mechanic	48	"
	K	Nevins George L	36	retired	73	"
	L	Nevins Jessie—†	36	housewife	64	"
	M	Baessler Elizabeth—†	44	clerk	51	"
	N	Baessler Henry L	44	engraver	57	"
	O	Steward Henrietta A—†	48	housewife	75	"
	P	Steward William	48	retired	70	"
	R	Foley Ellen—†	54	housewife	71	"

Page	Letter	Full Name	Residence, Jan. 1, 1941	Occupation	Supposed Age	Reported Residence, Jan. 1, 1940. Street and Number

Dedham Street—Continued

Page	Letter	Full Name	Residence	Occupation	Age	Reported Residence
	S	Tufts Doris—†	54	housewife	30	here
	T	Martin Lillian N—†	57	"	57	"
	U	Martin Patrick H	57	policeman	62	"
	V	Nims Mildred—†	58	housewife	48	"
	W	Nims Wallace	58	mechanic	50	"

Drury Road

Page	Letter	Full Name	Residence	Occupation	Age	Reported Residence
	X	Wilson Andrew N	11	inspector	35	20 Lilac rd
	Y	Wilson Louise V—†	11	housewife	32	20 "
	Z	*Hayes Alfred	12	retired	54	here
1915						
	A	Hayes Catherine E—†	12	clerk	22	"
	B	*Hayes Mary V—†	12	housewife	44	"
	C	McGee Florence L—†	15	"	39	"
	D	McGee John T	15	teacher	42	"
	E	Riley Helen E—†	16	housewife	40	"
	F	Riley John L	16	inspector	42	"

Ellis Street

Page	Letter	Full Name	Residence	Occupation	Age	Reported Residence
	G	Daggett Harriet—†	4–6	housekeeper	82	here
	H	Foley Cornelius C	4–6	policeman	68	"
	K	Foley Margaret E—†	4–6	housewife	54	"
	L	Donovan Michael	4–6	retired	77	"
	M	*Martin Alfred J	4–6	carpenter	48	"
	N	Martin Margaret M—†	4–6	housewife	42	"
	O	Kureab Anthony	8	machinist	46	"
	P	Kureab Anthony M	8	"	21	"
	R	*Kureab Caroline—†	8	housewife	42	"
	S	Arthur Alexander A	8	foreman	45	"
	T	Arthur Edna M—†	8	housewife	40	"
	U	Belcher Charles E	8	retired	75	"
	V	King Elizabeth E—†	8	housewife	61	"
	W	King Frederick D	8	carpenter	63	"
	X	*Landolphi Antonette—†	10	housewife	52	"
	Y	Landolphi Theresa—†	10	clerk	23	"
	Z	Mazza Ferdinand	10	steelworker	26	"
1916						
	A	Mazza Iolanda—†	10	housewife	25	"
	B	Curley Agnes E—†	10	factoryhand	54	"

Page.	Letter.	Full Name.	Residence, Jan. 1, 1941.	Occupation.	Supposed Age.	Reported Residence, Jan. 1, 1940. Street and Number.

Ellis Street—Continued

	C	Curley Mary A—†	10	at home	83	here
	D	Ferris Robert	10	clerk	20	"
	E	Ferris Ruth M—†	10	"	20	"
	F	Sewall Mary E—†	10	housewife	44	"
	G	Sewall Thomas A	10	painter	43	"
	H	Delacomo Anthony	11	laborer	27	33 Business
	K	Esposito Alexander	11	"	23	22 Damrell av
	L	Esposito Mildred—†	11	housewife	22	Everett
	M	Lewis Gladys—†	12	musician	42	here
	N	Westcott Evelyn—†	12	at home	71	"
	O	Lambert Charles A	12	painter	40	"
	P	Lambert Emma R—†	12	housewife	35	"
	R	O'Brien Bernard	12	chauffeur	44	"
	S	O'Brien Elizabeth—†	12	housewife	38	"
	T	Welch Charles A	15	printer	27	Quincy
	U	Welch Margaret F—†	15	housewife	26	"
	V	Brownell Bertha W—†	17	"	34	here
	W	Brownell Irving J	17	oiler	36	"
	X	Silton Edward A	17	manager	31	"
	Y	Silton Margaret M—†	17	housewife	28	"
	Z	Chickering Herbert J	18	machinist	30	"
1917						
	A	Rocheleau Alfred O	18	welder	33	"
	B	Rocheleau Dorothy E—†	18	housewife	28	"
	C	Pinder Florence—†	20	housekeeper	53	"

Elm Place

	D	*Delgrasso Pasquale	9	retired	81	here
	E	*Sopol Mary—†	9	housekeeper	68	"
	F	*Bankowska Catherine—†	11	housewife	76	"
	G	*Bankowska Charles	11	retired	82	"
	H	*Slyva Albert	11	"	63	"
	K	*Slyva Catherine—†	11	housewife	52	"
	L	Slyva Michael	11	laborer	25	"
	M	Slyva Stella—†	11	maid	23	"

Fairview Avenue

	N	Driman Annie M—†	7	housewife	54	here
	O	Driman Francis W	7	student	21	"
	P	Driman James J	7	salesman	54	"

Page	Letter	Full Name	Residence, Jan. 1, 1941	Occupation	Supposed Age	Reported Residence, Jan. 1, 1940. Street and Number

Fairview Avenue—Continued

Page	Letter	Full Name	Residence, Jan. 1, 1941	Occupation	Supposed Age	Reported Residence, Jan. 1, 1940. Street and Number
	R	Driman Katherine L †	7	teacher	22	here
	T	Donovan Eleanor M †	45	houseworker	27	"
	U	Donovan Frances E †	45	housewife	58	"
	V	Donovan Francis L, jr	45	clerk	24	"
	W	Donovan Frank T	45	superintendent	59	"

Franklin Street

Page	Letter	Full Name	Residence, Jan. 1, 1941	Occupation	Supposed Age	Reported Residence, Jan. 1, 1940. Street and Number
	Y	*Baranowski Feliksa †	11	stitcher	53	here
	Z	Bolendz Michael P	11	machinist	41	"
1918						
	A	Bolendz Pauline R †	11	housewife	38	"
	B	Sinclair Edward J	11	machinist	29	"
	C	Sinclair Mary V †	11	housewife	28	"
	D	Gagnon Frank E	15	cleaner	41	"
	E	Gagnon Helen A †	15	housewife	39	"

Hillside Street

Page	Letter	Full Name	Residence, Jan. 1, 1941	Occupation	Supposed Age	Reported Residence, Jan. 1, 1940. Street and Number
	F	Quist Alfred	11	boilermaker	49	here
	G	Quist Catherine A †	11	housewife	40	"
	H	Quist Dorothy M †	11	clerk	21	"
	K	Haskell Ann N †	14	housewife	26	16 Hillside
	L	Haskell Charles E	14	machinist	28	16 "
	M	Haskell Elmer W	14	printer	30	here
	N	Haskell Rose L †	14	housewife	28	"
	O	Holmes Leroy C	14	machinist	43	329 Wood av
	P	Nessar Emily M †	16	housewife	42	here
	R	*Nessar George J	16	merchant	48	"
	S	*Nessar Thomas	16	millworker	52	"
	T	Avey Francis L	16	machinist	28	Somerville
	U	Avey Lillian M †	16	housewife	28	"
	V	Luurtsema Sietse E	18	printer	54	8 Thacher
	W	Luurtsema Viola †	18	housewife	58	here
	X	Campia Adeline F †	19	"	37	"
	Y	Campia Anthony W	19	molder	43	"
	Z	Patulla Antonio	19	laborer	50	"
1919						
	A	Erikson Augusta †	20	cook	62	"
	B	Nelson Carl	20	machinist	71	"
	C	Nelson Ingeborg †	20	housewife	66	"
	D	Fennessey Alice G †	21	"	44	"

Page.	Letter.	Full Name.	Residence, Jan. 1, 1941.	Occupation.	Supposed Age.	Reported Residence, Jan. 1, 1940. Street and Number.

Hillside Street—Continued

	E	Fennessey William E	21	draftsman	41	here
	F	Jones Florence—†	22	housewife	35	"
	G	Jones Peter H	22	laborer	31	"
	H	*Sorrenti Grace—†	24	housewife	45	"
	K	Sorrenti Nunzio	24	laborer	20	"
	L	*Sorrenti Samuel	24	"	54	"
	M	Kenney Emma M	28	housewife	33	"
	N	Kenney Thomas J, jr	28	timekeeper	33	"
	O	Whitney Clarence R	28	welder	37	"
	P	Whitney Elizabeth—†	28	housewife	27	"
	R	Bragg Catherine M—†	28	"	45	"
	S	Bragg Irwin	28	plumber	46	"
	T	Laramie Mitchell	28	retired	61	"
	U	Duke Charlotte I—†	30	waitress	26	"
	V	Haskell Eva B—†	30	housewife	51	"
	W	Haskell Frederick B	30	mechanic	51	"
	X	Haskell Warren H	30	salesman	20	"
	Y	Stowers Ruth M—†	30	housekeeper	28	"
	Z	Obuchon Alice L—†	30	"	25	"
1920						
	A	Obuchon Annie—†	30	housewife	52	"
	B	Obuchon George T	30	steelworker	20	"
	C	Obuchon Godfrey M	30	laborer	60	"
	D	Reynolds Frank X	30	machinist	37	"
	E	Reynolds Nora T—†	30	housewife	36	"
	F	Foley Earl S	32	machinist	22	"
	G	Foley Florence E—†	32	housewife	47	"
	H	Foley Florence S—†	32	examiner	24	"
	K	Foley Margaret E—†	32	clerk	20	"
	L	Foley Sidney J	32	gasfitter	47	"
	M	Stracqualusi John	37	machinist	48	"
	N	Stracqualusi Susan—†	37	housewife	37	"
	O	Berry Arthur D	63	accountant	59	"
	P	Berry Kathleen F—†	63	housewife	49	"
	R	Berry Richard F	63	engineer	23	"

Knight Street

	S	Schiller Amelia D—†	3	housewife	43	15 Knight
	T	Schiller Edward J	3	laborer	49	15 "
	U	Schiller George W	3	"	20	15 "

Knight Street (Continued)

Page	Letter	Full Name	Residence, Jan. 1, 1923	Occupation	Supposed Age	Reported Residence, Jan. 1, 1922. Street and Number
	V	Llewellyn Melina †	5	houseworker	43	here
	W	Schiller Charles S	5	machinist	53	"
	X	Schiller Eliza †	5	housewife	50	"
	Y	*Moses Annie †	7	"	57	"
	Z	*Moses Michael	7	watchman	52	"
1921						
	A	Johnson Gardner A	7	chauffeur	24	Sharon
	B	Johnson Helen †	7	housewife	21	"
	C	Moses Alice T †	7	houseworker	27	here
	D	Moses Sadie R †	7	operator	29	"
	E	Moses Simon J	7	mechanic	22	"
	F	Matton Henry A	7	laborer	39	"
	G	Carroll Anna M †	8	housewife	49	"
	H	Carroll John J	8	ironworker	54	"
	K	Carroll Margaret M †	8	clerk	21	"
	L	Carroll Mary R †	8	"	23	"
	M	Rousseau Isaac J	8	laborer	45	"
	N	Rousseau Lucy V †	8	housewife	33	"
	O	*Valentino Louis	11	laborer	50	"
	P	*Brousard Sarah A †	11	housewife	95	576 River
	R	Coury John	11	laborer	24	here
	S	*Coury Joseph	11	"	65	"
	T	Gilman Agnes A †	11	houseworker	23	Dedham
	U	Levasseur Emma †	11	housewife	56	here
	V	Levasseur Rose A †	11	seamstress	20	"
	W	*Costa Anthony	15	carpenter	55	5 Buckingham
	X	Costa Francis	15	mechanic	21	5 "
	Y	Costa Palmyra †	15	houseworker	27	5 "
	Z	*Costa Rose †	15	housewife	56	5 "
1922						
	A	Costa Walter	15	machinist	31	5 "
	B	Fortin Joseph P	17	foreman	51	here
	C	*Peters Harriett M †	17	housewife	55	"
	D	Peters Phillip J	17	millhand	65	"
	E	Blouin Louis E	25	laborer	41	"
	F	Blouin Rose A †	25	housewife	41	"
	G	Dumont Edward	25	laborer	34	"
	H	*Dumont Mary †	25	housewife	64	"
	K	Drolet Clarence W	27	laborer	39	84 Readville
	L	Drolet Elizabeth E †	27	housewife	36	84 "
	M	Lowell Catherine A †	29	"	29	here
	N	Lowell Paul V	29	mechanic	28	"

Page	Letter	Full Name.	Residence, Jan. 1, 1941.	Occupation.	Supposed Age.	Reported Residence, Jan. 1, 1940. Street and Number.

Norton Street

Page	Letter	Full Name.	Residence, Jan. 1, 1941.	Occupation.	Supposed Age.	Reported Residence, Jan. 1, 1940. Street and Number.
	o	*Martin Anna T—†	33	typist	27	here
	P	Martin Annie T—†	33	housewife	64	"
	R	Martin Francis J	33	carpenter	33	"
	S	Martin Lawrence H	33	machinist	29	"
	T	Martin Patrick	33	buffer	71	"
	U	Martin Patrick J	33	painter	35	"
	V	Sullivan Margaret T	34	at home	81	"
	W	Whalen Helen A—†	34	housekeeper	83	"
	X	Whalen Francis W	34	clerk	21	"
	Y	Whalen Julia L—†	34	housewife	47	"
	Z	Whalen Robert A	34	storekeeper	50	"
1923						
	A	Vogel Edward J	35	plumber	70	"
	B	Vogel Joseph L	35	machinist	37	"
	C	Vogel Mary E—†	35	housewife	70	"
	D	Lambert Grace A—†	39	"	54	"
	E	Lambert John J	39	laborer	70	"
	F	Del Conte Jennie—†	39	housewife	23	"
	G	Del Conte John	39	machinist	30	"
	H	Conley Eleanor L—†	40–42	housewife	21	"
	K	Conley James	40–42	clerk	29	"
	L	Conley Bridget T—†	40–42	housewife	53	"
	M	Conley Mary E—†	40–42	typist	26	"
	N	Conley Patrick G	40–42	machinist	61	"
	O	Conley Rita A—†	40–42	typist	24	"
	P	Cardoni Anthony	44	machinist	45	64 Stoughton av
	R	*Cardoni Lucy—†	44	housewife	50	64 "
	S	Trocchio Alfred P	44	machinist	27	64 "
	T	Falcione Constantino S	44	assembler	41	here
	U	Falcione Ida E—†	44	housewife	32	"
	V	Consalvo Pelina	44	laborer	46	"
	W	*Consalvo Philomena—†	44	housewife	39	"

Oak Place

Page	Letter	Full Name.	Residence, Jan. 1, 1941.	Occupation.	Supposed Age.	Reported Residence, Jan. 1, 1940. Street and Number.
	X	*Borghi Joseph	3	machinist	33	35 Austin
	Y	Borghi Mary—†	3	dressmaker	32	35 "
	Z	*Frankina Antonio	3	laborer	64	here
1924						
	A	Frankina Frederick	3	painter	33	"
	B	Frankina Joseph	3	clerk	22	"

Page	Letter	Full Name	Residence, April 1, 1925	Occupation	Age	Reported Residence, April 1, 1924. Street and Number
		Oak Place—Continued				
	C	Frankina Katherine †	3	dressmaker	23	here
	D	Frankina Salvatore	3	attendant	27	"
	E	*Frankina Vincenza †	3	dressmaker	47	"
	F	*Babineau Margaret †	4	housekeeper	55	"
	G	*Martyn Catherine †	4	housewife	69	"
	H	Martyn Michael	4	laborer	73	"
	K	Martyn Olga C †	4	housekeeper	29	"
	L	Papasedero Domenic J	5	clerk	32	"
	M	Papasedero Frank A	5	laborer	63	"
	N	Papasedero Rose †	5	housewife	54	"
	O	Mellea Catherine †	5	"	38	"
	P	Mellea Joseph	5	butcher	42	"
	R	DeLuca Mary †	6	housewife	48	"
	S	DeLuca Ralph	6	machinist	21	"
	T	*DeLuca Salvatore	6	laborer	50	"
	U	Altobello Edna M †	7	housewife	34	"
	V	Altobello Joseph C	7	constable	38	"
	W	*Greeley Mary †	8	housewife	81	"
	X	Greeley William	8	laborer	34	"
	Y	*Patz Catherine †	8	housewife	41	Dedham
	Z	Patz Frank	8	shoefitter	42	"
1925						
	A	Altobello Antoinette †	9	housewife	69	here
	B	Altobello Charles	9	laborer	71	"
	C	Villane Michael	9	manager	30	"
	D	Villane Susan †	9	housewife	29	"
		Readville Street				
	E	Raymond Cecelia †	7	housewife	58	here
	F	Raymond Dorothy C †	7	clerk	25	"
	G	Raymond Marion Y †	7	housewife	23	"
	H	Raymond Napoleon	7	carpenter	53	"
	K	Raymond Theodore A	7	seaman	28	Deer Island
	L	Floranzi Rose A †	9	housewife	40	here
	M	*Floranzi Samuel	9	gardener	42	"
	N	Maguire Alida †	11	housewife	40	"
	O	Maguire Francis X	11	machinist	45	"
	P	Nedder John J	13	laborer	28	"
	R	*Nedder Joseph T	13	fireman	63	"
	S	Nedder Thomas M	13	laborer	28	"

Page.	Letter.	Full Name.	Residence Jan. 1, 1941.	Occupation.	Supposed Age.	Reported Residence, Jan. 1, 1940. Street and Number.

Readville Street—Continued

Page.	Letter.	Full Name.	Residence Jan. 1, 1941.	Occupation.	Supposed Age.	Reported Residence, Jan. 1, 1940. Street and Number.
	T	DiBenedetto Giovanni	15	blacksmith	59	here
	U	DiBenedetto Ottavina—†	15	housewife	55	"
	V	Carroccio Benjamin P	17	shipper	27	"
	W	Carroccio Giovannina E—†	17	housewife	21	"
	X	Giammasi Angelo G	19	cutter	29	"
	Y	Giammasi Gina—†	19	housewife	24	"
	Z	DeSantes Andrew M	21	chauffeur	28	"
1926						
	A	*DeSantes Dominica—†	21	housewife	72	"
	B	DeSantes Thomas	21	packer	66	"
	C	*Socoloski Mary—†	23	housewife	41	"
	D	*Socoloski Napoleon	23	mason	48	"
	F	*Colella Anna—†	27	housewife	50	"
	G	Colella Bambina M—†	27	stitcher	20	"
	H	*Colella Joseph	27	repairman	61	"
	K	Colella Lena T—†	27	stitcher	22	"
	L	Colella Paul J	27	laborer	28	"
	N	Nedder Joseph J	31	superintendent	28	"
	O	Nedder Rose M—†	31	housewife	22	"
	P	Abraham James	33	chef	44	Wellesley
	R	Abraham John H	33	retired	75	here
	S	Abraham Richard	33	assembler	40	"
	T	Abraham Tamar—†	33	housewife	75	"
	U	Nedder Edward T	35	attorney	30	"
	V	Nedder Elizabeth M—†	35	housewife	24	"
	W	Nedder George T	35	barber	36	"
	X	*Nedder Helen D—†	35	housewife	25	"
	Y	Nedder Mabel—†	35	clerk	21	"
	Z	*Nedder Mary—†	35	housewife	59	"
1927						
	A	*Nedder Thomas J	35	laborer	70	"
	B	*Valenza Antonina—†	37	housewife	45	"
	C	*Valenza Cesare	37	laborer	51	"
	D	Nedder Ernest T	39	shipper	26	35 Readville
	E	*Nedder Mary K	39	housewife	32	35 "
	F	Leo Agnes D—†	41	"	40	here
	G	Leo William F	41	laborer	50	"
	H	Will James M	41	watchman	53	"
	K	Abraham Robert	43	laborer	38	"
	L	Abraham Velma E—†	43	housewife	32	"
	N	Bakula Blanche—†	49	"	49	"

Page	Letter	Full Name	Residence	Occupation	Age	

Readville Street Continued

Letter	Full Name	Residence	Occupation	Age	Reported Residence
O	Bakula Henry M	49	machinist	23	here
P	Bakula John	49	metalworker	54	"
R	McGovern George	49	laborer	56	"
S	Lasinska Edward	51	electrician	51	"
T	Lasinska Helena †	51	clerk	25	"
U	Kamarski John	53	blacksmith	55	"
V	Kamarski Minnie †	53	waitress	45	"
W	Aubin Arthur J	55	foreman	55	"
X	Aubin Evelyn C †	55	nurse	27	"
Y	Aubin Mabel †	55	housewife	57	"
Z	Doig Esther T †	55	saleswoman	25	"
	1928				
A	Schaefer Christine †	55	at home	90	"
B	Robison Elizabeth †	57	housewife	57	"
C	Robison George	57	foreman	57	"
D	McCormack Anna C †	59	housewife	42	"
E	McCormack James M	59	accountant	47	"

Reservation Road

Letter	Full Name	Residence	Occupation	Age	Reported Residence
F	*Kundy John	179	machinist	51	here
G	Kundy John J	179	clerk	28	"
H	Kundy Kate †	179	housewife	51	"
K	Scott Grace B †	181	saleswoman	22	"
L	Scott Patrick H	181	molder	61	"
M	Scott Rita F †	181	saleswoman	25	"
N	Scott Theresa M †	181	housewife	59	"
O	McElhaney John M	192	engineer	40	"
P	McElhaney M Lorraine †	192	housewife	27	"
R	Walker Albert K	192	machinist	50	"
S	Walker Alison S	192	clerk	21	"
T	*Walker Margaret T †	192	housewife	50	"
U	Walker William	192	cabinetmaker	20	"
V	Peters Gertrude M †	192	housewife	24	"
W	Peters Walter F	192	clerk	32	"
X	DeSanto Archeline	196	mechanic	31	"
Y	DeSanto Theresa †	196	housewife	58	"
Z	Gordon Thomas F	196	laborer	40	282 Silver
	1929				
A	Gelewitz Irving M	196	proprietor	45	here
B	Gelewitz Lena †	196	housewife	38	"

Page	Letter	Full Name.	Residence, Jan. 1, 1941.	Occupation.	Supposed Age.	Reported Residence, Jan. 1, 1940. Street and Number.

Reservation Road—Continued

Page	Letter	Full Name.	Residence, Jan. 1, 1941.	Occupation.	Supposed Age.	Reported Residence, Jan. 1, 1940. Street and Number.
	C	*Hokansson Ine M—†	196	housewife	36	here
	D	Hokansson Nils H	196	mason	38	"
	E	Alberto Rocco	200	engineer	29	"
	F	Alberto Stella V—†	200	housewife	31	"
	G	Jerome Joseph K	200	attorney	45	"
	H	Kurzydloski Joseph S	200	retired	70	"
	K	Kurzydloski Praxeda—†	200	housewife	65	"
	L	Tenney Florina—†	200	"	34	"
	M	Tenney William P	200	machinist	36	"
	N	Maguire Mary J—†	234	housekeeper	80	"
	O	Chludinski Adeline—†	236	housewife	48	"
	P	Chludinski Edward W	236	laborer	22	"
	R	Chludinski Frank	236	molder	51	"
	S	Chludinski Frank S	236	laborer	25	"
	T	Chludinski Lenora A—†	236	saleswoman	24	"
	U	Chludinski Philomena—†	236	inspector	20	"
	V	Ricci Dionisia—†	238	housekeeper	52	"
	W	Ricci F Alvin	238	salesman	33	"
	X	Ricci Stella F—†	238	housewife	32	"
	Y	Varone Juliet—†	238	beautician	40	221 Reservation rd
	Z	Pease Alfred E	244	draftsman	23	here
1930						
	A	Pease Edith—†	244	housewife	58	"
	B	Pease Edith L—†	244	forewoman	31	"
	C	Pease Wilbur J	244	clerk	22	"
	D	Kelly John E	262–264	plumber	30	23 Spring Park av
	E	Kelly Margaret C—†	262–264	housewife	32	23 "
	F	*Keegan Mabel—†	262–264	"	37	here
	G	Keegan Thomas H	262–264	baker	33	"
	H	Neas Agnes L—†	266–268	housewife	37	"
	K	Neas Joseph F, jr	266–268	metalworker	40	"
	L	Elder Alfred W	266–268	machinist	38	"
	M	Elder Cecelia E—†	266–268	housewife	42	"
	N	Andrews Albert L	270–272	manager	51	"
	O	Andrews Francis A	270–272	mechanic	23	"
	P	Andrews Malvina C—†	270–272	housewife	46	"
	R	Mulvey Edith W—†	270–272	waitress	27	"
	S	Chartier Edmund G	270–272	draftsman	28	Hinsdale
	T	Chartier Edna H—†	270–272	housewife	26	"

Page	Letter	Full Name	Residence, April 1	Occupation	Supposed Age	Reported Residence, April 1, Street and Number

River Street

Page	Letter	Full Name	Residence	Occupation	Age	Reported Residence
	U	Gordan Elsa †	1382	housewife	22	here
	V	Gordan Theodore	1382	machinist	23	"
	W	Nardone Joseph	1382	laborer	45	"
	X	Nardone Rose M †	1382	housewife	40	"
	Y	Nardone Joseph, jr	1384	laborer	23	1382 River
	Z	Nardone Ruth †	1384	housewife	23	13 Cottage
		1931				
	A	Abbiuso Joseph	1386	machinist	35	here
	B	Abbiuso Marion †	1386	housewife	32	"
	C	MacKay Frederick	1388	printer	37	"
	D	MacKay Violet L †	1388	housewife	33	"
	E	Grant Marjorie S †	1392	clerk	41	"
	F	Grant Mary W †	1392	housewife	73	"
	G	Grant Robert E	1392	retired	76	"
	H	Scott Annie J †	1392	cook	58	"
	L	Jeromin Amelia †	1398	housewife	51	"
	M	Jeromin Teofil	1398	machinist	54	"
	N	Pitkowski John	1398	upholsterer	22	"
	O	Foss Anna †	1398	housewife	48	"
	P	Foss Julius	1398	merchant	52	"
	R	Foss Murray F	1398	student	22	"
	S	Foss Ruth †	1398	bookkeeper	23	"
	T	Kelson Anthony	1398	machinist	43	53 Sumner
	U	Kelson Nora †	1398	housewife	38	53 "
	V	Kelson Regina H †	1398	factoryhand	20	53 "
	W	Radock Walter S	1398	accountant	34	53 "
	X	Dwyer Eleanor C †	1400	housewife	34	here
	Y	Dwyer Walter J	1400	shipper	37	"
	Z	Stack Andrew J	1400	carpenter	66	"
		1932				
	A	Stack Delia C †	1400	housewife	59	"
	B	Stack Mary C †	1400	operator	29	"
	C	MacDonald Grace †	1414	housewife	42	"
	D	MacDonald Hector K	1414	carpenter	46	"
	E	McAuliffe Elizabeth †	1414	stenographer	22	"
	F	McAuliffe Louise †	1414	"	24	"
	G	McAuliffe Mary †	1414	waitress	49	"
	H	Shute Bertha R †	1414	clerk	41	"
	K	Shute Charles W	1414	foreman	51	"

Page.	Letter	Full Name.	Residence, Jan. 1, 1941.	Occupation.	Supposed Age.	Reported Residence, Jan. 1, 1940. Street and Number.

River Street—Continued

Page.	Letter	Full Name.	Residence, Jan. 1, 1941.	Occupation.	Supposed Age.	Reported Residence, Jan. 1, 1940.
	L	Malynowski Julius	1416	chipper	52	here
	M	Malynowski Stella—†	1416	housewife	53	"
	N	Visnorvitz Francis	1416	presser	27	"
	O*	Prusik Anna—†	1418	housewife	48	"
	P	Prusik Blanche—†	1418	at home	24	"
	R	Prusik Gregory	1418	molder	48	"
	S	Prusik Sophie—†	1418	clerk	23	"
	T	O'Connell James R	1420	"	25	"
	U	O'Connell John T	1420	auditor	20	"
	V	O'Connell Lenora M—†	1420	housewife	48	"
	W	O'Connell Marion A—†	1420	stenographer	29	"
	X	O'Connell William J	1420	machinist	63	"
	Y	O'Connell William J, jr	1420	clerk	30	"
	Z*	MacDonald Anna F—†	1420	housewife	36	"
1933						
	A	MacDonald Douglas H	1420	carpenter	36	"
	B	Locke Helen M—†	1420	housewife	30	51 Fort av
	C	Locke Joseph L	1420	laborer	30	51 "
	E	Cowan Athur S	1426	retired	70	here
	F	Cowan Bertha L—†	1426	at home	46	"
	G	Cowan Elsie P—†	1426	"	43	"
	H	Cowan Hazel R—†	1426	secretary	45	"
	K	Cowan Mabel G—†	1426	"	35	"
	L	McIntire Helena G—†	1432	housekeeper	68	"
	M*	Olson Bertha M—†	1432	housewife	53	"
	N	Olson George J	1432	machinist	51	"
	O	Sullivan Frederick H	1432	"	28	Plymouth
	P	Sullivan Ruth A—†	1432	housewife	27	here
	R	Serena Anna—†	1436	"	37	"
	S	Serena Roger	1436	merchant	44	"
	T	Ciampa Louis	1436	machinist	58	"
	U	Ciampa Marie—†	1436	housewife	56	"
	V	Shempa Daniel J	1436	physician	26	"
	W	Shempa Irene—†	1436	clerk	20	"
	Z	Naguszewski Edward	1450	clergyman	35	655 Dor av
1934						
	A	O'Shea Delia M—†	1454	housekeeper	38	32 Austin
	B	Morgan Anna—†	1455	housewife	48	here
	C	Morgan Henry M	1455	machinist	49	"
	D	Smith Chester	1455	chauffeur	33	"
	E	Smith Stella—†	1455	housewife	30	"

Page	Letter	Full Name	Residence, Jan. 1, 1941	Occupation	Supposed Age	Reported Residence, Jan. 1, 1940. Street and Number

River Street—Continued

Page	Letter	Full Name	Residence, Jan. 1, 1941	Occupation	Supposed Age	Reported Residence, Jan. 1, 1940. Street and Number
	F	Richardson Arthur L	1455	painter	44	here
	G	Richardson Stella M—†	1455	housewife	39	"
	H	Sulinski Albert	1455	motorman	25	"
	K	Sulinski Barbara E—†	1455	housewife	21	"
	L	Hurd Herbert D	1455	clerk	42	"
	M	Hurd Lillian—†	1455	housewife	71	"
	N	Swale Frederick W	1455	laborer	44	221 Fairmount av
	O	Swale Margaret—†	1455	housewife	39	71 Com av
	P	Davis Arthur S	1456	baker	34	here
	R	Davis Elsie C—†	1456	housewife	34	"
	S	Hawes Clarence E	1456	painter	60	"
	T	Hawes Clarence E, jr	1456	U S A	20	"
	U	Hawes Mary A—†	1456	housewife	56	"
	V	Hawes Mary M—†	1456	stitcher	22	"
1935						
	E	Frederick Laura A—†	1481	housewife	33	"
	F	Frederick Ralph W	1481	painter	34	"
	G	Cavanaugh Joseph F	1485	social worker	38	"
	H	Cavanaugh Margaret G—†	1485	housewife	35	"
	K	Bagge Alice E—†	1487	secretary	26	"
	L	Bagge Bessie A—†	1487	housewife	55	"
	M	Bagge Francis G	1487	student	21	"
	N	Bagge Kathleen A—†	1487	operator	23	"
	O	Bagge Patrick F	1487	painter	57	"
	P	Thayer Blanche E—†	1489	housewife	52	"
	R	Thayer Everett M	1489	laborer	24	"
	S	Thayer Marion L—†	1489	clerk	27	"
	T	Fistola Joseph P	1489	ironworker	25	"
	U	Fistola Rose E—†	1489	housewife	22	"
	V	Broderick Edith L—†	1489	"	22	"
	W	Broderick William F	1489	plumber	24	"
	X	White John	1491	laborer	45	"
	Y*	White Mary—†	1491	housewife	43	"
	Z	Gattozzi Antonio C	1491	attendant	39	"
1936						
	A	Gattozzi Dominic F	1491	draftsman	41	"
	B	Gattozzi Eva—†	1491	at home	27	"
	C*	Gattozzi Maria—†	1491	housewife	68	"
	D*	Gattozzi Michael	1491	retired	69	"
	E	Gattozzi Michael	1491	draftsman	26	"
	F	Sullivan Anna R—†	1491	housewife	28	"

Page.	Letter.	Full Name.	Residence, Jan. 1, 1941.	Occupation	Supposed Age.	Reported Residence, Jan. 1, 1940. Street and Number.

River Street—Continued

Page.	Letter.	Full Name.	Residence, Jan. 1, 1941.	Occupation	Supposed Age.	Reported Residence, Jan. 1, 1940. Street and Number.
	G	Sullivan James W	1491	electrician	34	here
	H	Potinski Pauline—†	1493	housewife	26	19 Neponset av
	K	Potinski Walter L	1493	buffer	27	19 "
	L	Powers Margaret—†	1493	housewife	38	here
	M	Powers William	1493	bartender	40	"
	N	Goddard Archibald C	1493	laborer	37	34 E Dedham
	O	Goddard Earl K	1493	salesman	28	Pepperell
	P	Goddard Mabel V—†	1493	housewife	32	"
	R	Cianca Anita—†	1495	"	51	here
	S	Cianca Lena E—†	1495	"	21	Rhode Island
	T	Cianca Oscar	1495	bookkeeper	29	here
	U	Cianca Pasquale	1495	mason	56	"
	V	Mitchell John P	1495	machinist	41	"
	W	Mitchell Leona M—†	1495	housewife	37	"
	X	*Evangelist Mario	1495	upholsterer	25	"
	Y	Mazza Alfred	1495	machinist	52	"
	Z	*Mazza Mary—†	1495	housewife	47	"
1937						
	A	*Cain Everett H	1501	mechanic	42	"
	B	*Cain Florence R—†	1501	housewife	39	"
	C	*Cain Gordon E	1501	inspector	20	"
	F	DiMarzio Frank J	1515	machinist	31	"
	G	DiMarzio Margaret M—†	1515	housewife	29	"
	H	Greer Emma M—†	1515	secretary	40	"
	K	McDonough Helen G—†	1515	supervisor	63	"
	L	McDonough Lillian B—†	1515	housewife	54	"
	M	McDonough Peter J	1515	metalworker	58	"
	N	Sullivan Catherine M—†	1519	student	20	"
	O	Sullivan Dennis	1519	laborer	63	"
	P	Sullivan Eleanor—†	1519	secretary	23	"
	R	Sullivan Ellie A—†	1519	housewife	59	"
	S	Sullivan Michael H	1519	salesman	25	"
	T	LaFrance Lillian—†	1519	maid	52	"
	U	*LaFrance Nellie—†	1519	housewife	88	"
	V	Guariglia Fred R	1523	letter carrier	40	"
	W	*Guariglia Jennie M—†	1523	housewife	35	"
	Y	McLellan Arthur L	1523½	mechanic	43	"
	Z	McLellan Helen—†	1523½	housewife	34	"
1938						
	A	Patten Helen J—†	1523½	"	29	"
	B	Patten James F	1523½	painter	33	"

Page	Letter	Full Name	Residence Jan. 1 1941	Occupation	Supposed Age	Reported Residence Jan. 1, 1940. Street and Number

River Street Continued

Page	Letter	Full Name	Residence Jan. 1 1941	Occupation	Supposed Age	Reported Residence Jan. 1, 1940. Street and Number
	C	McMahon Anna †	1527	at home	81	here
	D	Walsh Elizabeth R †	1527	housewife	45	"
	E	Walsh Madeline E †	1527	bookkeeper	21	"
	F	Walsh Michael J	1527	manager	47	"
	H	Coughlin Patrick M	1531	machinist	35	"
	K	Coughlin Ruth E †	1531	housewife	36	"
	L	Tenney Frederick	1531	laborer	32	"
	M	Tenney Ralph D	1531	retired	67	"
	N	Tenney Sarah A †	1531	housewife	68	"
	O	Tenney Vincent J	1531	printer	30	"
	P	DiPietro Charles	1533	machinist	26	"
	R	DiPietro Frank	1533	clerk	21	"
	S	*DiPietro Helena †	1533	housewife	45	"
	T	DiPietro Joseph	1533	student	24	"
	U	DiPietro Nicola	1533	laborer	52	"
	V	DiPietro Raphaela †	1533	stenographer	28	"
	W	DiPietro Vincent	1533	U S A	29	"
	X	DiPietro William	1533	electrician	22	"
	Y	McGowan Albert H	1535	clerk	36	"
	Z	McGowan Mabel E †	1535	housewife	35	"
1939						
	A	Crawford Jennie †	1539	"	64	"
	B	Crawford William M	1539	laborer	65	"
	C	Kowalczik Mary L †	1539	housewife	22	"
	D	Kowalczik Stanley F	1539	laborer	25	"
	E	Burns Margaret F †	1543	housewife	45	"
	F	Burns William J	1543	policeman	45	"
	G	Driscoll Patrick	1543	retired	80	"
	H	Holland Charles R	1543	machinist	21	"
	K	Treweek Anna E †	1545	housewife	44	"
	L	Treweek William H	1545	machinist	46	"
	M	Kelley Helen L †	1545	housewife	34	"
	N	Kelley John F	1545	laborer	37	"
	R	Haefner Annetta †	1557	housewife	64	"
	S	Haefner Joseph H	1557	metalworker	55	"
	T	Roche Charles F	1559	chauffeur	29	"
	U	Roche Mary L †	1559	housewife	48	"
	V	Roche Walter M	1559	chauffeur	23	"
	W	Roche William F	1559	mechanic	49	"
	X	Roche William F	1559	chauffeur	26	"
	Y	Ambrose Glenys S †	1565	housewife	28	"

Page.	Letter	Full Name.	Residence, Jan. 1, 1941.	Occupation.	Supposed Age.	Reported Residence, Jan. 1, 1940. Street and Number

River Street—Continued

Page.	Letter	Full Name.	Residence, Jan. 1, 1941.	Occupation.	Supposed Age.	Reported Residence, Jan. 1, 1940. Street and Number
	Z	Ambrose Meredeth J	1565	manager	27	here
1940						
	A	McLellan Alan	1565	butcher	37	29 Winslow
	B	McLellan Alma—†	1565	housewife	38	29 "
	C	Tosi Emil	1565	mechanic	32	here
	D	Tosi Eunice L—†	1565	housewife	26	"
	E	DeMatteo Arthur F	1565	metalworker	28	"
	F	DeMatteo Beatrice M—†	1565	housewife	28	"
	G	DeMatteo Edward	1565	clerk	25	"
	H	DeMatteo Essie M—†	1565	housewife	27	Washington
	K	Boulanger Mary M—†	1568	"	30	here
	L	Boulanger William E	1568	factoryhand	34	"
	M	Johnston Janet H—†	1569	housewife	40	160 Summit
	N	Johnston William	1569	metalworker	44	160 "
	O	McLean Heber J	1569	fireman	67	here
	P	Riley Beulah M—†	1569	housewife	33	"
	R	Riley John H	1569	laborer	36	"
	S	Maroni Alessandro	1569	mechanic	32	"
	T	Maroni Mary—†	1569	housewife	30	"
	U	Holland Flora M—†	1570	"	59	"
	V	Holland Martin A	1570	machinist	54	"
	Y	Fennessey Margaret—†	1575	housewife	43	"
	Z	Fennessey Paul A	1575	letter carrier	43	"
1941						
	E	Connelly Frank E	1585	engineer	41	"
	F	Connelly Helen B—†	1585	housewife	34	"
	G	Andrews Susan V—†	1587	"	52	"
	H	Andrews Viola L—†	1587	houseworker	20	"
	K	Fagan Lesley I—†	1587	housekeeper	22	"
	L	McGrath Alice A—†	1589	housewife	42	"
	M	McGrath Earl F	1589	laborer	21	"
	O	McGrath William J	1589	clerk	23	"
	N	McGrath William K	1589	laborer	47	"
	P	*Jaber Sadie A—†	1591	housekeeper	62	"
	R	Randlett Elizabeth R—†	1593	housewife	45	"
	S	Randlett Percival A	1593	factoryhand	59	"
	T	Randlett Ralph W	1593	"	23	"
	U	Milloy Mary A—†	1595	housekeeper	73	"
	V	*Peterson Anne M—†	1595	housewife	43	"
	W	Peterson Ernest S	1595	carpenter	46	"
	Z	Wallace Elizabeth—†	1728	housekeeper	64	"

Page	Letter	Full Name	Residence, Jan. 1, 1941	Occupation	Supposed Age	Reported Residence, Jan. 1, 1940. Street and Number

1942

River Street Continued

Page	Letter	Full Name	Residence	Occupation	Age	Reported Residence
	A	Wallace Mary E—†	1730	housewife	40	here
	B	Wallace William L	1730	clerk	41	"
	D	O'Clare James L	1742	machinist	50	"
	E	O'Clare Medora—†	1742	seamstress	45	"
	F	*Feeney John	1742	retired	77	"
	G	Feeney Julia L—†	1742	bookkeeper	37	Wash'n D C
	H	Feeney Martin J	1742	teacher	34	here
	K	Feeney Mary J—†	1742	housewife	65	"
	L	Feeney Nicholas F	1742	draftsman	32	"
	M	Damata Dominic	1746	metalworker	44	"
	N	Dininno Albert	1746	laborer	28	"
	O	Dininno Lucy V—†	1746	housewife	24	"
	P	Renzi Eugene F	1748	salesman	21	"
	R	Renzi Joseph D	1748	laborer	26	"
	S	Renzi Luciano	1748	bartender	56	"
	T	*Renzi Mary—†	1748	housewife	46	"
	U	Renzi William P	1748	cook	23	"
	W	Bond John R	1793	merchant	64	"
	Y	McGlynn John H	1799	metalworker	42	"
	Z	McGlynn Margaret E—†	1799	housewife	35	"
1943						
	A	Mascaro Leonard	1799	retired	71	"
	B	Mascaro Leonard, jr	1799	laborer	24	"
	C	Mascaro Theresa—†	1799	housewife	51	"
	D	Snow Edward T	1808	mechanic	39	"
	E	Snow Mary K—†	1808	housewife	38	"
	F	Kelly Anne M—†	1808	secretary	36	"
	G	Kelly Mary—†	1808	housewife	75	"
	H	Kelly Morgan	1808	retired	74	"
	K	Napolitano Joseph	1812	machinist	22	"
	L	Napolitano Marco	1812	laborer	20	"
	M	*Napolitano Mary—†	1812	housewife	61	"
	N	Napolitano Thomas A	1812	laborer	63	"
	O	Donaruma Dominic J	1812	mechanic	28	24 Damrell av
	P	Donaruma Mary—†	1812	housewife	20	Dedham
	R	Corsini Fulvio P	1816	salesman	29	here
	S	Corsini Josephine P—†	1816	housewife	25	"
	T	Riccotiello Joseph	1816	laborer	25	1527 Hyde Park av
	U	Riccotiello Ruth—†	1816	operator	25	1911 River
	V	Bond Frances M—†	1817	saleswoman	30	here

Page.	Letter.	Full Name.	Residence, Jan. 1, 1941.	Occupation.	Supposed Age.	Reported Residence, Jan. 1, 1940. Street and Number.

River Street—Continued

Page.	Letter.	Full Name.	Residence, Jan. 1, 1941.	Occupation.	Supposed Age.	Reported Residence, Jan. 1, 1940. Street and Number.
	W	Bond Osie E—†	1817	nurse	38	here
	X	Bond Osie F—†	1817	housewife	61	"
	Y	Giasullo John	1817	laborer	29	"
	Z	Giasullo Mary R—†	1817	housewife	25	"
1944						
	A	Hickey Doris V—†	1817	"	22	"
	B	Hickey James W	1817	salesman	35	"
	C	Consalvo Aldemira—†	1820	housewife	49	r 75 Readville
	D	Consalvo Camillo	1820	laborer	52	r 75 "
	E	Consalvo Dante	1820	machinist	22	r 75 "
	F	Consalvo Irma—†	1820	housekeeper	24	r 75 "
	G	*DiCarlo Madeline—†	1820	at home	74	r 75 "
	H	Gentile Alphonse	1822	blacksmith	42	here
	K	Gentile Amelia—†	1822	housewife	34	"
	L	Del Conte Angelina—†	1824	clerk	23	"
	M	*Del Conte Anna—†	1824	housewife	64	"
	N	Del Conte Laura—†	1824	clerk	28	"
	O	Trocchio Attilio	1825	machinist	39	"
	P	Trocchio Frances M—†	1825	housewife	33	"
	S	*Riccio Joseph	1827	laborer	46	"
	T	*Riccio Louisa—†	1827	houswife	45	"
	U	LoConte Anna—†	1828	saleswoman	26	"
	V	LoConte Anthony	1828	fireman	32	"
	W	LoConte Mary—†	1828	clerk	29	"
	X	LoConte Rita—†	1828	housewife	24	"
	Y	LoConte Rose—†	1828	saleswoman	24	"
	Z	DeNinno Felina—†	1830	factoryhand	22	"
1945						
	A	*DeNinño Pelino	1830	laborer	58	"
	B	*Domenico Angelina—†	1830	housewife	69	"
	C	Domenico Ferzoco	1830	retired	75	"
	D	Fata Adeline—†	1832	housewife	27	"
	E	Fata Peter	1832	stockman	26	"
	F	LoConte Elizabeth T—†	1832	housewife	28	"
	G	LoConte John L	1832	merchant	30	"
	H	Saliano Ethel—†	1832	stitcher	31	"
	K	*Saliano Joseph	1832	laborer	42	"
	L	*Bartolomeo Candeloro	1834	"	62	"
	M	*Bartolomeo Josephine—†	1834	housewife	61	"
	N	*Calvani Amelia—†	1834	"	45	"
	O	*Calvani Giulio	1834	laborer	48	"

Page	Letter	Full Name.	Residence, Jan. 1, 1941.	Occupation.	Supposed Age.	Reported Residence, Jan. 1, 1940. Street and Number.

River Street—Continued

Page	Letter	Full Name.	Residence, Jan. 1, 1941.	Occupation.	Supposed Age.	Reported Residence, Jan. 1, 1940. Street and Number.
	R	Guardabascio Anthony	1837	foreman	60	here
	S	*Guardabascio Josephine—†	1837	housewife	64	"
	T	Guardabascio Michael	1837	timekeeper	27	"
	U	Bellardi Mary J—†	1837	housewife	31	"
	V	Marascio Anna—†	1838	"	36	"
	W	Marascio Onofrio	1838	laborer	42	"
	X	Pagliaro Achille	1838	retired	63	"
	Y	*Pagliaro Mary G—†	1838	at home	83	"
	Z	Ferzoco Alfred	1841	machinist	32	"
1946						
	A	Ferzoco Mary—†	1841	housewife	30	"
	B	*Perrotta Anthony	1841	retired	80	"
	C	*Galante Emma—†	1841	housewife	25	"
	D	Galante Luciano V	1841	shipper	27	"
	E	Consalvo Carmella—†	1841	cleaner	29	"
	F	Consalvo Margarino	1841	laborer	31	"
	G	Barone Frank A	1846	molder	33	"
	H	Barone Mary C—†	1846	housewife	27	"
	K	Papasodora Dominic	1846	factoryhand	26	"
	L	Galante Angelo	1851	mechanic	63	"
	M	Galante Esther—†	1851	hairdresser	26	"
	N	Galante Frank	1851	mechanic	24	"
	O	Galante George W	1851	clerk	29	"
	P	Galante Joan—†	1851	secretary	22	"
	R	Galante Julia R—†	1851	housewife	29	56 Damrell av
	S	Santamaria Jennie—†	1854	clerk	25	here
	T	Santamaria Joseph	1854	fireman	50	"
	U	Santamaria Mary—†	1854	housewife	48	"
	V	Santamaria Thomas F	1854	mechanic	20	"
	W	McGlynn Edward P	1854	machinist	40	"
	X	McGlynn Jane T—†	1854	housewife	69	"
	Y	McGlynn Michael A	1854	machinist	73	"
	Z	Howley Edward	1855	musician	27	"
1947						
	A	Howley Mary E—†	1855	housewife	55	"
	B	Howley Ulysses G	1855	chef	54	"
	C	Intonti Amelia I—†	1858	housewife	24	16 Mason
	D	Intonti Leonard	1858	laborer	29	1859 River
	E	Tucci Dominic	1858	baker	73	16 Mason
	F	Arena Angelina—†	1858	typist	25	here
	G	*Arena Annie—†	1858	at home	49	"

Page.	Letter.	Full Name	Residence, Jan. 1, 1941.	Occupation.	Supposed Age.	Reported Residence, Jan. 1, 1940. Street and Number.

River Street—Continued

Page.	Letter.	Full Name	Residence, Jan. 1, 1941.	Occupation.	Supposed Age.	Reported Residence, Jan. 1, 1940. Street and Number.
	H	Arena Placido	1858	laborer	20	here
	K	Intonti Ciriaco	1859	"	50	"
	L	*Intonti Pauline—†	1859	housewife	52	"
	M	Mercanti Francesco	1859	machinist	27	"
	N	Mercanti Rosaline—†	1859	housewife	21	"
	P	Cardinal Maria—†	1863	"	77	"
	R	Cardinal Pasquale	1863	retired	72	"
	S	Farant Genevieve—†	1863	housewife	35	"
	T	Farant George	1863	musician	36	"
	U	Cardinal Joseph	1863	chauffeur	39	"
	V	Cardinal Mary—†	1863	housewife	35	"
	X	Murray Charles F	1870	timekeeper	37	"
	Y	Murray Mary A—†	1870	housewife	68	"
	Z	Barbato Gabriel	1873	mechanic	45	"
1948						
	A	Barbato Grace R—†	1873	housewife	40	"
	B	Rogers Rosalind D—†	1873	at home	21	"
	C	Giusti Emma—†	1873	housewife	32	166 Readville
	D	Giusti Lawrence	1873	mason	41	166 "
	E	Galante Domenic	1880	metalworker	47	here
	F	Galante Elinor—†	1880	factoryhand	21	"
	G	Galante Louise A—†	1880	operator	22	"
	H	Galante Pauline—†	1880	housewife	40	"
	K	*DeAngelis Angelina—†	1883	"	65	"
	L	DeAngelis Anthony	1883	laborer	21	"
	M	DeAngelis Michael	1883	"	25	"
	N	*DeAngelis William	1883	retired	68	"
	O	*Ferraro Otino	1883	laborer	63	"
	P	Guardabascio Michael	1888	machinist	27	"
	R	Guardabascio Susan—†	1888	housewife	27	"
	S	*Bonanni Domenica—†	1888	"	63	"
	T	*Bonanni Phillip	1888	laborer	62	"
	V	*Caruso Frances—†	1892	housewife	54	"
	W	*Caruso Frederick	1892	laborer	62	"
	X	Caruso Frederick R, jr	1892	"	23	"
	Y	Caruso Mary—†	1892	stitcher	21	"
1949						
	A	*Arnestino Angelina—†	1907	housewife	63	"
	B	*Miathe Peter	1907	chauffeur	33	"
	C	*Miathe Stella—†	1907	housewife	35	"
	E	*Veleri Celia—†	1908	merchant	52	"

*Page	Letter	Full Name	Residence, Jan. 1, 1941	Occupation	Supposed Age	Reported Residence, Jan. 1, 1940. Street and Number.

River Street Continued

*Page	Letter	Full Name	Residence, Jan. 1, 1941	Occupation	Supposed Age	Reported Residence, Jan. 1, 1940. Street and Number.
	F	Veleri Daniel	1908	clerk	28	here
	H	D'Alvisio Lena B †	1911	housewife	38	"
	K	D'Alvisio Pamphia	1911	machinist	38	"
	L	D'Alvisio Elsie †	1911	hairdresser	22	"
	M*	D'Alvisio Frank	1911	retired	64	"
	N	D'Alvisio Jennie—†	1911	forewoman	30	"
	O*	D'Alvisio Laura—†	1911	housewife	59	"
	P	D'Alvisio Paul	1911	florist	24	"
	R	D'Alvisio Rose—†	1911	forewoman	28	"
	S	Laroche Hermenegilde	1913	carpenter	58	"
	T	Laroche Louise—†	1913	housewife	51	"
	U	Laroche Philip	1913	operator	23	"
	V	DiBenedetto Doris—†	1915	housewife	25	"
	W	DiBenedetto Ricco	1915	painter	26	"
	X	Infantino Philip	1915	blacksmith	55	"
	Y*	Infantino Salvatrice—†	1915	housewife	53	"
	Z	Infantino William	1915	machinist	24	"

1950 Roxana Street

*Page	Letter	Full Name	Residence, Jan. 1, 1941	Occupation	Supposed Age	Reported Residence, Jan. 1, 1940. Street and Number.
	B	Langley Albert R	7	woodworker	34	here
	C	Langley Helen F—†	7	housewife	38	"
	D	Fechiera John G	7	pressman	27	Stoughton
	E	Fechiera Linda A—†	7	housewife	25	30 Linwood
	F	Comeau Rachel M—†	7	"	29	here
	G	Comeau Stanley E	7	metalworker	28	"
	H	Garrity Joseph L	7	electrician	30	Milton
	K	Garrity Mary G—†	7	housewife	35	"
	L	Cohen Alexander P	7	tailor	61	here
	M	Cohen Bessie E—†	7	housewife	57	"
	N	Cohen Ethel G—†	7	stitcher	22	"
	O	Cohen Lillian M—†	7	at home	32	"
	P	Cohen Ruth U—†	7	packer	31	"
	R	Venskus Benjamin P	7	laborer	26	"
	S	Venskus Bertha S—†	7	housewife	28	"
	T	Wennerstrand Carl V	7	laborer	29	"
	U	Wennerstrand Mabel—†	7	housewife	26	"
	V	Robery Charles E	11	electrician	30	Dedham
	W*	Robery Eugenia M—†	11	housewife	32	144 C
	Y	Hanson Blanche D—†	11	"	24	196 Wood av
	Z	Hanson Byron R	11	mechanic	27	196 "

Page	Letter	Full Name.	Residence, Jan. 1, 1941.	Occupation.	Supposed Age.	Reported Residence, Jan. 1, 1940. Street and Number.

1951

Roxana Street—Continued

Page	Letter	Full Name	Residence	Occupation	Age	Reported Residence
	A	Pray Julia V—†	11	housewife	46	here
	B	Pray Roy H	11	steamfitter	46	"
	C	Sikora Mary P—†	11	housewife	27	"
	D	Sikora Stanley F	11	machinist	28	"
	E	Young Ann E—†	11	housewife	30	"
	F	Young Frank W	11	tester	30	"
	G	Neary Edward J	13–15	plumber	45	"
	H	Neary Mary C—†	13–15	housewife	39	"
	L	Ogonowski John S	17–19	mechanic	27	Lowell
	M	Ogonowski Mary A—†	17–19	housewife	23	Connecticut
	N	Baasner John G	17–19	shipper	68	here
	O	Baasner Margaret G—†	17–19	housewife	68	"
	P	McGuinness James A	17–19	carpenter	45	"
	R	McGuinness James E	17–19	laborer	20	"
	S	McQuarrie Evelyn F—†	17–19	housewife	29	"
	T	McQuarrie Winfred J	17–19	manager	33	"
	U	Johnson Arthur B	18	printer	38	"
	V	Johnson Violet S—†	18	housewife	35	"
	W	Wallace Elizabeth—†	18	housekeeper	73	"
	X	Wallace Lyla L—†	18	nurse	46	"
	Y	Blinstrub Mary C—†	18	housewife	39	"
	Z	Blinstrub Stanley W	18	restaurateur	43	"
1952						
	A	Prew John J	21–23	engineer	47	"
	B	Prew Mary E—†	21–23	housewife	47	"
	C	Connelly Edith L—†	21–23	"	34	"
	D	Connelly John C	21–23	policeman	40	"
	E	McGrath Ellen—†	27	housewife	61	"
	F	McGrath Nora J—†	27	bookkeeper	45	"
	G	McGrath Patrick F	27	retired	67	"
	H	Wright Frank E	29	painter	37	"
	K	Wright Janet L—†	29	housewife	29	"

Scribner Road

Page	Letter	Full Name	Residence	Occupation	Age	Reported Residence
	L	Tripp Frederick W	7	printer	30	here
	M	Tripp Jeanne F—†	7	housewife	26	"
	N	Haars Leona I—†	8	"	26	20 Westminster
	O	Haars William H	8	foreman	31	20 "
	P	Cronin John J	11	lithographer	35	here

Scribner Road—Continued

Page	Letter	Full Name	Residence, Jan. 1, 1941	Occupation	Supposed Age	Reported Residence, Jan. 1, 1940. Street and Number
	R	Cronin Mary V—†	11	housewife	31	here
	S	*Yorke Ethel L—†	12	"	35	"
	T	*Yorke Wylie H	12	salesman	38	"

Sunnyside Avenue

Page	Letter	Full Name	Residence, Jan. 1, 1941	Occupation	Supposed Age	Reported Residence, Jan. 1, 1940. Street and Number
	U	Colello Anthony	6	electrician	30	here
	V	Colello Gaetano	6	laborer	59	"
	W	Colello Giovannina—†	6	housewife	53	"
	X	Colello Guido	6	operator	20	"
	Y	Colello Guy	6	cleaner	24	"
	Z	Colello Mario	6	machinist	22	"
1953						
	A	Dinardi Concetta—†	11	housewife	39	"
	B	Dinardi Giovanni	11	laborer	46	"
	C	Hilliard Anna—†	18	housewife	31	"
	D	Hilliard Donald F	18	milkman	34	"
	E	*Fata Anna—†	20	housewife	74	"
	F	Fata Gabriel	20	carpenter	36	"
	G	Fata Gaetano	20	retired	76	"
	H	Fata Lena—†	20	housewife	37	"
	K	Barone Angelina—†	35	"	30	51 Sunnyside av
	L	Barone Thomas	35	laborer	31	51 "
	M	Tiberi Domenica—†	35	housewife	39	here
	N	Tiberi John	35	laborer	47	"
	O	Fata Arthur	37	cabinetmaker	22	"
	P	Fata Daniel	37	"	24	"
	R	Fata Gaetano	37	welder	28	"
	S	*Fata Mary—†	37	housewife	49	"
	T	Fata Peter	37	carpenter	51	"
	U	*Merlini Filomena—†	51	housewife	58	"
	V	Merlini Pietro	51	blacksmith	62	"
	X	Roy George H	51	welder	33	"
	Y	Roy Lena T—†	51	housewife	23	"
	Z	Minoie Michael J	54	machinist	24	"
1954						
	A	Minoie Salvatore	54	candymaker	59	"
	B	Panaioli Ida E—†	54	housewife	22	"
	C	*Panaioli Ostilio	54	collector	40	"
	D	Colli James C	55	painter	22	"
	E	Colli Mary M—†	55	stitcher	20	"

Page.	Letter.	Full Name.	Residence, Jan. 1, 1941.	Occupation.	Supposed Age.	Reported Residence, Jan. 1, 1940. Street and Number.

Sunnyside Avenue—Continued

Page.	Letter.	Full Name.	Residence, Jan. 1, 1941.	Occupation.	Supposed Age.	Reported Residence, Jan. 1, 1940. Street and Number.
	F	*Colli Theresa—†	55	housewife	57	here
	G	Allessi Angelina—†	55	stitcher	27	"
	H	Allessi Placido	55	chauffeur	28	"
	K	Cardillo Charles	55	attendant	21	725 Am Legion H'way
	L	Cardillo Ruth—†	55	stitcher	20	27 Callender

Sunnyside Street

Page.	Letter.	Full Name.	Residence, Jan. 1, 1941.	Occupation.	Supposed Age.	Reported Residence, Jan. 1, 1940. Street and Number.
	M	Donovan Catherine F—†	6	housewife	34	here
	N	Donovan John F	6	milkman	38	"
	O	*Cavanaugh Martin E	6	retired	73	"
	P	Cavanaugh Martin E, jr	6	machinist	37	"
	R	*Cavanaugh Mary A—†	6	housewife	64	"
	S	Cavanaugh Patrick J	6	laborer	40	"
	T	Welch Frances M—†	6	housewife	30	"
	U	Burke Mary C—†	6	"	34	"
	V	Burke Thomas H	6	bartender	35	"
	W	Mosher Damon B	7	attorney	24	"
	X	Mosher Dolores M—†	7	stenographer	25	"
	Y	Mosher Donald P	7	engineer	30	"
	Z	Mosher Louise M—†	7	housewife	60	"
1955						
	A	Mosher Percy H	7	engineer	61	"
	B	Charland Ethel I—†	7	waitress	23	"
	C	Charland Joseph F	7	molder	52	"
	D	Charland Marie N—†	7	housewife	47	"
	E	Anderson Eva M—†	10–12	"	40	"
	F	Anderson George J	10–12	policeman	45	"
	G	Hobbs James E	10–12	laborer	54	"
	H	Hobbs Louise E—†	10–12	housewife	56	"
	K	Hobbs Louise M—†	10–12	clerk	28	"
	L	Kendall Joseph R	14–16	designer	37	Lowell
	M	Kendall Viola—†	14–16	housewife	31	"
	N	DiMaggio Eva—†	14–16	"	30	here
	O	DiMaggio Peter	14–16	cutter	33	"
	P	Nannicelli Emilio	18	carpenter	29	"
	R	Nannicelli Esther—†	18	housewife	28	"
	S	Sexton Phillip F	20	accountant	37	"
	T	Sexton Stella M—†	20	housewife	36	"
	U	Vose Gertrude H—†	25	"	63	"
	V	Vose Willard B	25	retired	64	"

Page	Letter	Full Name	Residence, Jan. 1, 1941.	Occupation.	Supposed Age.	Reported Residence, Jan. 1, 1940. Street and Number

Sunnyside Street Continued

Page	Letter	Full Name	Residence, Jan. 1, 1941.	Occupation.	Supposed Age.	Reported Residence, Jan. 1, 1940. Street and Number
	W	Selander Johan A	41	carpenter	38	here
	X*	Selander Selma C †	41	housewife	42	"
	Y*	Ovesen Othilie †	42	stitcher	49	"
	Z*	Sehlin Carl	42	machinist	47	"
1956						
	A	Ceaser Anna †	42	housewife	61	"
	B*	Bornderek Adolph	44	laborer	52	"
	C*	Bornderek Felicia †	44	housewife	46	"
	D	Rosko Henry	44	laborer	24	"
	E	Rosko Jennie †	44	clerk	22	"
	F	Rosko Stanley	44	machinist	25	"
	G	Bracken Mary C †	45	housewife	38	"
	H	Bracken Thomas L	45	agent	39	"
	K	Lamb Chester A	48	rigger	29	16 Oak
	L	Lamb Dorothy L †	48	beautician	30	21 Gardner
	M	Lamb Grace H †	48	housewife	24	16 Oak
	N	Pucillo Antoinette †	48	"	57	here
	O	Pucillo James	48	clerk	20	"
	P	Pucillo Joseph	48	U S A	24	"
	R	Pucillo Michael	48	barber	59	"
	S	Pucillo Michael, jr	48	clerk	26	"
	T	McAdam Cecelia M †	49	housewife	37	"
	U	McAdam George J	49	machinist	37	"
	V	Tuzzo Elvira †	50	housewife	26	"
	W	Tuzzo Salvatore	50	shipper	33	"
	X	Galassi Edith †	50	housewife	26	"
	Y	Galassi Francis J	50	metalworker	28	"
	Z	Aquilante Frank	52	chauffeur	26	11 Waterloo
1957						
	A*	Aquilante Josephine †	52	housewife	65	17 Blanchard
	B*	Aquilante Luigi	52	retired	74	17 "
	C*	Aquilante Nellie †	52	dressmaker	25	11 Waterloo
	D	Frank Henry E	52	accountant	46	here
	E	Frank Lillian E †	52	housewife	40	"
	F	McShea Andrew E	53	clerk	45	"
	G	McShea Catherine †	53	housewife	40	"
	H	Putnam Dorothy H †	57	"	39	199 Fairmount av
	K	Putnam Wilfred F	57	manager	39	199 "
	L	Veltri Louis A	57	tailor	35	here
	M	Veltri Mary L †	57	housewife	30	"
	N	Giori Alfred	57	laborer	42	"

Page.	Letter.	FULL NAME.	Residence, Jan. 1, 1941.	Occupation.	Supposed Age.	Reported Residence, Jan. 1, 1940. Street and Number.

Sunnyside Street—Continued

Page.	Letter.	FULL NAME.	Residence, Jan. 1, 1941.	Occupation.	Supposed Age.	Reported Residence, Jan. 1, 1940. Street and Number.
	O	*Giori Anna—†	57	housewife	40	here
	P	Gage Dorothy P—†	58	"	31	Belmont
	R	Gage Russell B, jr	58	manager	33	"
	S	Munyon Albert E	58	machinist	32	here
	T	Munyon Jennie E—†	58	housewife	26	"
	U	Bigelow Arthur J	60	retired	72	"
	V	Bigelow Marie E—†	60	housewife	67	"
	W	Wallin Edith A—†	60	student	21	"
	X	Wallin Maria A—†	60	housewife	59	"
	Y	Wallin Peter B	60	machinist	62	"
	Z	Wallin Robert C	60	"	22	"
1958						
	A	*Abramczyk Alice—†	61	housewife	45	"
	B	Abramczyk Julian	61	painter	46	"
	C	Abramczyk Nora R—†	61	clerk	21	"
	D	Lockwood Elizabeth—†	62	housewife	49	"
	E	Lockwood Harold B	62	retired	54	"
	F	Lockwood Loretta M—†	62	housewife	71	"
	G	*Storm Martha—†	63	"	38	"
	H	*Storm Werner T	63	machinist	40	"
	K	Huff Joseph F	66	designer	23	12 Park
	L	Huff Rita T—†	66	housewife	25	69 Water
	M	Carpenito Antonio	66	operator	52	here
	N	Carpenito Caroline—†	66	housewife	50	"
	O	O'Brien Catherine M—†	67	"	20	Dedham
	P	O'Brien Margaret L—†	67	secretary	36	here
	R	O'Brien William P	67	retired	67	"
	S	O'Brien William P, jr	67	cleaner	34	Dedham
	T	Kelley Ann M—†	67	operator	26	here
	U	Kelley Clarence J	67	accountant	36	"
	V	Kelley David E	67	clerk	24	"
	W	Kelley Gerard M	67	social worker	31	"
	X	Kelley Hugh J	67	chauffeur	27	"
	Y	Kelley Katherine F—†	67	clerk	30	"
	Z	Williams John J	67	presser	21	"
1959						
	A	Woodlock Dorothy—†	71	housewife	26	Newton
	B	Woodlock James	71	machinist	26	"
	C	McAuley Mary V—†	72	housewife	33	here
	D	McAuley William F	72	estimator	34	"
	E	Lowney Edwin A	72	electrician	33	26 Cleveland

Page	Letter	Full Name	Residence, Jan. 1, 1941.	Occupation	Supposed Age	Reported Residence, Jan. 1, 1940. Street and Number

Sunnyside Street—Continued

Page	Letter	Full Name	Residence, Jan. 1, 1941.	Occupation	Supposed Age	Reported Residence, Jan. 1, 1940. Street and Number
	F	Lowney Simone—†	72	housewife	30	26 Cleveland
	G	Higgins Allen F	73	technician	42	here
	H	Higgins Lillian M—†	73	housewife	43	"
	K	Zwicker Mignonette D—†	73	hairdresser	45	Arlington
	L	Sawyer Charles M	75–77	manager	30	here
	M	Sawyer Genevieve L—†	75–77	housekeeper	54	Malden
	N	Sawyer Jessie P—†	75–77	housewife	30	here
	O	Huber Bertha T—†	75–77	"	60	"
	P	Huber Otto J	75–77	mechanic	60	"
	R	Griffing Carl H	76–78	chauffeur	58	"
	S	Griffing Marquita W—†	76–78	housewife	50	"
	T	Grant Edwin A	76–78	manager	36	"
	U	Grant Mildred—†	76–78	housewife	35	"
	V	Brown Frank	79–81	cook	20	"
	W	Brown Frank A	79–81	jeweler	51	"
	X	Brown Inez—†	79–81	housewife	48	"
	Y	LoConte Annette—†	79–81	"	31	"
	Z	LoConte George G	79–81	plumber	32	"
1960						
	A	Glott Louis J	80	merchant	54	"
	B	Glott Mary—†	80	clerk	27	"
	C	Glott Michael	80	"	24	"
	D	Glott Sarah—†	80	housekeeper	51	"
	E	Tucker Helen—†	80	"	37	"
	F	Andrews John V	83–85	laborer	24	"
	G	Stoddard Edna M—†	83–85	housewife	33	"
	H	Stoddard Howe M	83–85	painter	42	"
	K	Taber Harriet E—†	83–85	housekeeper	54	"
	L	Wallin Emily E—†	83–85	housewife	33	"
	M	Wallin Oscar E	83–85	patternmaker	34	"
	N	Hearn Frederick J	84	milkman	51	"
	O	Hearn Helen J—†	84	housewife	51	"
	P	Nannicelli Areoline	84	printer	20	"
	R*	Nannicelli Concetta—†	84	housewife	60	"
	S	Nannicelli Elizabeth—†	84	at home	24	"
	T	Nannicelli John	84	clerk	21	"
	U	Nannicelli Laura—†	84	"	22	"
	V	Nannicelli Nicholas	84	carpenter	60	"
	W	Schultz Barbara W—†	88	housewife	25	"
	X	Schultz Paul G	88	accountant	27	"
	Y	MacLeod Alexander J	88	clerk	33	22 Franconia

Page	Letter	Full Name.	Residence, Jan. 1, 1941.	Occupation.	Supposed Age.	Reported Residence, Jan. 1, 1940. Street and Number.

Sunnyside Street—Continued

Page	Letter	Full Name	Residence	Occupation	Age	Reported Residence
	Z	MacLeod Christine—†	88	housewife	58	22 Franconia
1961						
	A	MacLeod James A	88	operator	60	22 "
	B	MacLeod Willard K	88	clerk	31	22 "
	C	Kelley Frederick W	91–93	salesman	47	here
	D	Kelley Lillian E—†	91–93	housewife	36	"
	E	Axtman Helene E—†	91–93	"	42	"
	F	Axtman John L	91–93	attendant	44	"
	G	Arendholz Mary C—†	92	housewife	33	120 West
	H	Arendholz Mervin T	92	mechanic	35	120 "
	K	Chippendale George R	92	letter carrier	58	here
	L	Chippendale Mary E—†	92	housewife	50	"
	M	*Parlee Lula M—†	95–97	"	38	Millis
	N	*Parlee Roy C	95–97	welder	37	"
	O	Collier Chester F	95–97	motorman	48	here
	P	Collier Mary L—†	95–97	housewife	45	"
	R	Clark Charles H	96	chauffeur	48	12 School
	S	Miller Anna L—†	96	housewife	33	196 Colorado
	T	Miller Charles R	96	letter carrier	37	196 "
	U	Feeley Catherine—†	96	housewife	57	here
	V	Feeley John T	96	carpenter	28	"
	W	Feeley Patrick	96	foreman	58	"

Thompson Street

Page	Letter	Full Name	Residence	Occupation	Age	Reported Residence
	X	Lagner Joseph	5	machinist	68	here
	Y	Lagner Rose A—†	5	clerk	28	"
	Z	Lagner Rose M—†	5	housewife	63	"
1962						
	A	Costello Catherine—†	8	"	37	"
	B	Costello Lawrence	8	shipper	41	"
	C	Callan Cecelia M—†	9	clerk	42	"
	D	Callan Edward J	9	auditor	37	"
	E	Callan J Estelle—†	9	housewife	26	"
	F	Cullen Dorothy M—†	10	clerk	25	"
	G	Cullen Elizabeth G—†	10	housewife	55	"
	H	Cullen George F	10	mechanic	26	"
	K	Cullen Rita B—†	10	maid	22	"
	L	Andrews Everett S	11	salesman	41	"
	M	Swallow Bertha L—†	11	housewife	67	"
	N	Swallow Robert E	11	retired	66	"

Page	Letter	Full Name	Residence Jan. 1, 1941	Occupation	Supposed Age	Reported Residence Jan. 1, 1940 Street and Number

Thompson Street Continued

Page	Letter	Full Name	Residence	Occupation	Age	Reported Residence
	O	Ruddock Anne E †	11	housewife	67	here
	P	Ruddock Edwin N	11	shipper	67	"
	R	Ruddock Elliot T	11	clerk	31	"
	S	King Charles	13	ironworker	70	"
	T	King Dora E †	13	housewife	65	"
	U	King Dora E †	13	teacher	33	"
	V	McIntyre Mary E †	17	housewife	52	"
	W	McIntyre Michael G	17	watchman	55	"
	X	Russo Albert P	20	pipefitter	34	"
	Y	Russo Lena E †	20	housewife	29	"
	Z	Fay Agnes G †	23	"	61	"
1963						
	A	Fay Augustine P	23	retired	67	"
	B	Fay William H	23	clerk	30	"
	C	Cullen Isabelle †	23	housewife	28	"
	D	Cullen William A	23	manager	28	"
	E	DeYoung Bartholomew	25	cigarmaker	63	"
	F	DeYoung Marie †	25	stitcher	36	"
	G	Fordham Freda †	40	stenographer	21	"
	H	Fordham Frederick	40	mechanic	20	"
	K	*Fordham Leonille †	40	housewife	52	"
	L	Fordham Nancy †	40	secretary	26	"
	M	O'Neill Joseph E	43	machinist	43	"
	N	O'Neill Margaret F †	43	housewife	46	"
	O	Brink Walter	45	laborer	35	"
	P	Galanif Alexander	45	machinist	46	"
	R	Galanif Nellie †	45	housewife	42	"
	S	Gammons Phillip A	45	laborer	39	"
	T	Moray Ethel R †	45	housewife	49	"
	U	Slattery Edward J	46	clerk	45	17 Roxana
	V	Slattery Mary F †	46	housewife	45	17 "
	W	McLellan Edward	47	painter	46	here
	X	McLellan Nellie M †	47	housewife	43	"
	Y	Reilly Delia T †	48	"	44	"
	Z	Reilly Patrick J	48	painter	50	"
1964						
	A	Johnson Carl H	50	metalworker	34	"
	B	*Johnson Karen E †	50	housewife	33	"
	C	Johnson Alfred	53	manager	66	"
	D	Johnson Ellen J †	53	housewife	63	"
	E	*Guzowski Delia †	58	"	46	"

Page	Letter	Full Name.	Residence, Jan. 1, 1941.	Occupation.	Supposed Age.	Reported Residence, Jan. 1, 1940. Street and Number.

Thompson Street—Continued

Page	Letter	Full Name.	Residence, Jan. 1, 1941.	Occupation.	Supposed Age.	Reported Residence, Jan. 1, 1940.
	F	Guzowski Joseph	58	foreman	48	here
	G	Guzowski Josephine—†	58	clerk	21	"

Turtle Pond Parkway

Page	Letter	Full Name.	Residence, Jan. 1, 1941.	Occupation.	Supposed Age.	Reported Residence, Jan. 1, 1940.
	H	Kingston George A	1	repairman	29	here
	K	Kingston James A	1	millhand	32	"
	L	Kingston Mary E—†	1	housewife	69	"
	M	Kingston Celia—†	16	"	39	"
	N	Kingston Thomas J	16	chauffeur	43	"
	O	Monahan John	20	retired	77	9 Albemarle
	P	Scott Herbert F	20	machinist	45	here
	R	Scott Margaret B—†	20	housewife	44	"
	S	Mitchell Dorothy G—†	130–132	"	28	"
	T	Mitchell Henry F	130–132	clerk	30	"
	U	O'Neil Edith A—†	130–132	bookbinder	22	48 Gordon av
	V	Sprague Forest C	130–132	printer	48	48 "
	W	Sprague Madeline E—†	130–132	housewife	44	48 "

Upton Street

Page	Letter	Full Name.	Residence, Jan. 1, 1941.	Occupation.	Supposed Age.	Reported Residence, Jan. 1, 1940.
	X	Duggan June J—†	9	clerk	20	here
	Y	McGrath Margaret—†	9	housekeeper	78	"
	Z	McGrath Marion E—†	38	housewife	26	"
1965						
	A	McGrath Michael E	38	machinist	37	"

Vernon Street

Page	Letter	Full Name.	Residence, Jan. 1, 1941.	Occupation.	Supposed Age.	Reported Residence, Jan. 1, 1940.
	B	Oehme Clara—†	15	housewife	57	here
	C	Oehme Heinz	15	laborer	20	"
	D	Oehme Johannes	15	musician	37	"
	E	Oehme Otto	15	machinist	58	"
	F	Oehme Walter M	15	electrician	27	"
	G	Hansen Marie—†	17	housekeeper	64	"
	H	Hansen Ruth M—†	17	clerk	21	"
	K	Hoefel Anna W—†	22	housewife	50	"
	L	Hoefel Theodore	22	mechanic	57	"
	M	Harrington Margaret—†	42	housekeeper	40	"

Page	Letter	Full Name	Residence, Jan. 1, 1941	Occupation	Supposed Age	Reported Residence, Jan. 1, 1940. Street and Number

Weston Street

Page	Letter	Full Name	Residence, Jan. 1, 1941	Occupation	Supposed Age	Reported Residence, Jan. 1, 1940. Street and Number
	N	Assof Cecelia T †	3	housewife	42	here
	O	Assof Elrianos	3	metalworker	43	"
	P	Assof Joseph	3	laborer	20	"
	R	*Hermas Josephine †	3	laundryworker	59	"
	S	Mills Harriet R †	27	housewife	42	"
	T	Mills Walter H	27	machinist	50	"

Ward 18–Precinct 20

CITY OF BOSTON

LIST OF RESIDENTS
20 YEARS OF AGE AND OVER

(NON-CITIZENS INDICATED BY ASTERISK)
(FEMALES INDICATED BY DAGGER)

AS OF

JANUARY 1, 1941

JOSEPH F. TIMILTY, *Chairman*
FREDERIC E. DOWLING, *Secretary*
WILLIAM A. MOTLEY, JR.
FRANCIS B. McKINNEY
HILDA HEDSTROM QUIRK
Listing Board.

CITY OF BOSTON PRINTING DEPARTMENT

Page.	Letter	FULL NAME.	Residence, Jan. 1, 1941.	Occupation.	Supposed Age.	Reported Residence, Jan. 1, 1940. Street and Number.
2000						
		Albemarle Street				
	A	Chaplain David F	3	machinist	21	here
	B	Chaplain Francis A	3	draftsman	23	"
	C	Chaplain Frank E	3	policeman	45	"
	D	Chaplain Mildred E—†	3	housewife	46	"
	E	Vanuch Lillian—†	5	"	52	"
	F	Vanuch Virginia L—†	5	waitress	24	"
	G	Schiller Christine—†	5	housewife	30	"
	H	Schiller Edward	5	machinist	27	"
	K	Briggs Evangeline—†	5	housewife	34	"
	L	Briggs Harold L	5	carpenter	36	"
	M	Carlisi Alfonsina—†	rear 5	housewife	42	"
	N	Carlisi Nicholas	" 5	laborer	48	"
	O	McCarthy George P	" 5	machinist	39	"
	P	McCarthy Marie B—†	" 5	housewife	39	"
	R	Personeni Eulalie L—†	7	"	23	"
	S	Personeni Nicholas	7	laborer	31	"
	T	Rocheleau Alfred J	7	clerk	44	"
	U	Rocheleau Mary—†	7	housewife	47	"
	V	*Abbatangelo Filomena—†	7	"	55	"
	W	Abbatangelo John	7	laborer	53	"
	X	McAndrew Patrick J	9	retired	74	"
	Y	Sullivan Hannah T—†	9	housekeeper	70	"
	Z	Lombardi Louis	11	laborer	35	"
2001						
	A	*Lombardi Margaret—†	11	housewife	34	"
	B	Kingston Eleanor L—†	11	"	29	"
	C	Kingston Paul J	11	painter	31	"
		Buckingham Street				
	G	Bullman Catherine A—†	7	nurse	28	here
	H	Bullman Catherine J—†	7	housewife	69	"
	K	Bullman Clement D	7	machinist	30	"
	L	Bullman Francis J	7	clerk	32	"
	M	Bullman John B	7	mason	68	"
	N	Bullman Mary F—†	7	housekeeper	35	"
	O	O'Neil Rita A—†	7	housewife	26	22 Upton
	P	DiMarzio Maria—†	8	housekeeper	64	here
	R	Moccia Edith L—†	8	housewife	28	"
	S	Moccia William A	8	chauffeur	31	"

Page	Letter	Full Name	Residence, Jan. 1, 1941	Occupation	Supposed Age	Reported Residence, Jan. 1, 1940. Street and Number

Buckingham Street Continued

Page	Letter	Full Name	Residence, Jan. 1, 1941	Occupation	Supposed Age	Reported Residence, Jan. 1, 1940. Street and Number
	T	Chamberlain Alfred	9	seaman	36	here
	U	*Chamberlain Arthur	9	carpenter	66	"
	V	*Chamberlain Emma †	9	housewife	68	"
	W	Darcy Mary R †	9	stitcher	33	"
	X	Donohue John J	11	plumber	32	"
	Y	Donohue Mary M †	11	housewife	31	"
	Z	Butler Catherine J †	12	"	54	"
2002						
	A	Butler James F	12	agent	56	"
	B	Donohue Joseph F	12	laborer	52	"
	D	Cook Frederick V	15	"	33	"
	E	Cook Margaret M †	15	housewife	30	"
	F	Lawler Elizabeth F †	15	"	33	"
	G	Lawler Harry W	15	cutter	33	"
	H	Hannigan Catherine R †	17	housewife	29	"
	K	Hannigan John J, jr	17	electrician	31	"
	L	Donohue Daniel D	21	laborer	22	"
	M	Donohue Helen L †	21	housewife	21	"

Chester Street

Page	Letter	Full Name	Residence, Jan. 1, 1941	Occupation	Supposed Age	Reported Residence, Jan. 1, 1940. Street and Number
	N	Gardner Francis J	5	blacksmith	26	here
	O	Gardner Katherine V †	5	housewife	58	"
	P	Gardner Mildred A †	5	clerk	28	"
	R	Gardner Thomas F	5	retired	73	"
	S	Gardner Thomas R	5	paperhanger	25	"
	T	Sullivan Helen C †	5	housewife	41	"
	U	Sullivan Jeremiah F	5	superintendent	51	"
	V	DeMaina Angelo M	5	gardener	55	"
	W	DeMaina Sarah J †	5	housewife	52	"
	X	Bronsdon John P	8-10	chauffeur	33	44 Chester
	Y	Bronsdon Sarah †	8-10	housewife	38	44 "
	Z	Dean Alice C †	8-10	"	62	here
2003						
	A	Dean Henry M	8-10	attorney	63	"
	B	Fahey Francis J	9	policeman	41	"
	C	Fahey Jeannette M †	9	housewife	35	"
	D	Olson George W	9	bookkeeper	42	"
	E	Olson Gertrude †	9	housewife	40	"
	F	Olson Peter A	9	watchman	68	"
	G	King John J	15	custodian	48	"

Page.	Letter.	Full Name.	Residence, Jan. 1, 1941.	Occupation.	Supposed Age.	Reported Residence, Jan. 1, 1940. Street and Number.

Chester Street—Continued

	H	King Margaret V—†	15	housewife	45	here
	K	Pierce Eva K—†	16	"	49	"
	L	Pierce George L	16	manager	54	"
	M	Bowen Mary M—†	16	secretary	41	"
	N	Bowen Patience G—†	16	"	47	"
	O	Folan Mary L—†	16	housekeeper	49	"
	P	Quigley Clara B—†	17	housewife	50	"
	R	Quigley Henry I	17	supervisor	54	"
	S	Crowley David	19	chauffeur	47	"
	T	Crowley Mary D—†	19	housewife	49	"
	U	Donlan Thomas	19	retired	76	"
	V	Boyle Catherine C—†	39	housewife	45	"
	W	Boyle David G	39	policeman	43	"
	X	Magennis Elizabeth—†	41	housekeeper	42	"
	Y	Rooney Hannah—†	41	housewife	56	"
	Z	Rooney Joseph P	41	brakeman	66	"
2004						
	A	Rooney P Bernard	41	"	27	"
	B	McDonough John M	44	laborer	65	"
	C	McDonough Mary C—†	44	housewife	62	"
	D	Phillips Charles F	44	blacksmith	20	Quincy
	E	Phillips Helen F—†	44	housewife	21	"
	F	Hickey Agnes V—†	48	bookkeeper	27	Stoughton
	G	Hickey Mary A—†	48	housewife	67	here
	H	Hickey Robert M	48	chauffeur	34	"
	K	McGee Margaret E—†	65	saleswoman	40	"
	L	McGee Mary A—†	65	at home	75	"
	M	Stewart Anna A—†	65	housewife	38	"
	N	Stewart Chester E	65	horse trainer	38	"

Chesterfield Street

	O	Gentile Raymond	5	laborer	45	here
	P	*Gentile Vincenza—†	5	housekeeper	39	"
	R	Gentile Victoria—†	5	housewife	40	"
	S	Greto Vito	5	laborer	46	"
	T	Manganiello Gerardo	5	"	54	"
	U	*Melito Viola—†	5	housekeeper	62	"
	V	*Secondiane Anthony	5	baker	57	Dedham
	W	Grasso Pasquale	5	laborer	38	here
	X	Grasso Serafine—†	5	housewife	32	"

Page	Letter	Full Name	Residence, Jan. 1, 1941	Occupation	Supposed Age	Reported Residence, Jan. 1, 1940. Street and Number

Chesterfield Street (Continued)

Page	Letter	Full Name	Residence, Jan. 1, 1941	Occupation	Supposed Age	Reported Residence, Jan. 1, 1940
	Y	McGrath James F	6	assembler	42	here
	Z	McGrath James F, jr	6	salesman	20	"
2005						
	A	McGrath Mary M †	6	housewife	39	"
	B	Rogazzo Raymond	7	laborer	60	"
	C	Santoro Agnes †	8	dressmaker	29	"
	D	*Santoro Luigi	8	laborer	68	"
	E	*Santoro Mary †	8	housewife	66	"
	F	Gagliarde Louis	9	boilermaker	48	"
	G	*Gagliarde Pellegrina †	9	housewife	51	"
	H	*Valentini Giuseppe	9	laborer	61	"
	K	*Valentini Mary †	9	housewife	53	"
	L	*Welsh Delia †	12	"	61	Dedham
	M	Welsh James P	12	clerk	35	"
	N	Welsh Katherine B †	12	housekeeper	30	"
	O	*Welsh Michael J	12	foreman	61	"
	P	Welsh Timothy F	12	clerk	33	"
	R	Ferzoco Agnes †	13	housewife	38	here
	S	Ferzoco Alexander	13	cutter	58	"
	T	Ferzoco Anthony G	13	machinist	22	"
	U	Ferzoco Myra C †	13	housekeeper	25	"
	V	Noonan Agnes C †	16	secretary	43	"
	W	Noonan Katherine V †	16	"	44	"
	X	Noonan Margaret E †	16	"	42	"
	Y	Noonan Matthew J	16	serviceman	43	Milton
	Z	Noonan Theresa C †	16	teacher	40	here

Clifford Street

Page	Letter	Full Name	Residence, Jan. 1, 1941	Occupation	Supposed Age	Reported Residence, Jan. 1, 1940
2006						
	A	Gordon Edna D †	6	housewife	62	here
	B	Gordon G Pauline †	6	teacher	47	"
	C	Gordon Walter D	6	clerk	43	"
	D	Flaherty Mary R †	9	housekeeper	51	"
	E	Fahey Mary A †	10	housewife	68	"
	F	Leary John F	10	plumber	46	28 Clifford
	G	Lydell Kenneth	10	machinist	26	here
	H	Manning William	10	"	21	Haverhill
	K	Coughlin Arthur J	11	conductor	37	here
	L	Coughlin George E	11	storekeeper	32	"
	M	Coughlin George J	11	engineer	66	"
	N	Parker Lilla W †	14	housewife	54	"

Page	Letter	Full Name.	Residence, Jan. 1, 1941.	Occupation.	Supposed Age.	Reported Residence, Jan. 1, 1940. Street and Number.

Clifford Street—Continued

Page	Letter	Full Name.	Residence, Jan. 1, 1941.	Occupation.	Supposed Age.	Reported Residence, Jan. 1, 1940. Street and Number.
	O	Lennon Margaret N—†	15	bookkeeper	30	here
	P	Donahue Mary E—†	15A	housewife	37	"
	R	Donahue Thomas A	15A	installer	36	"
	S	Crocker Anna M—†	16	housewife	70	"
	T	Judkins Walter P	16	painter	64	"
	U	*Pickles John I	16	tailor	58	Newton
	V	O'Donnell John J	17	salesman	49	here
	W	O'Donnell Margaret F—†	17	housewife	47	"
	X	O'Donnell Mary E—†	17	at home	74	"
	Z	Flaherty Leona C—†	19	housewife	42	"
2007						
	A	Flaherty William J	19	stockman	43	"
	B	Coombs Frances R—†	21	housewife	42	"
	C	Coombs Ralph	21	salesman	46	"
	D	House Alice W—†	21	stenographer	55	"
	E	House Charles B	21	retired	58	"
	F	Arnold Frederick	22	clerk	66	14 Albion
	G	Hawley Ellen—†	22	housewife	53	9 Spring Hill rd
	H	Hawley Walter E	22	salesman	52	9 "
	K	Burns Clara M—†	24	stenographer	21	here
	L	McGrath Bernard J	24	machinist	43	"
	M	Silver Albert	24	merchant	44	"
	N	Silver Hazel M—†	24	housewife	33	"
	O	Smythe Mabel—†	24	nurse	55	"
	P	Manning Margaret G—†	26–28	winder	45	"
	R	McKenna Mary E—†	26–28	housewife	55	"
	S	McKenna Pauline M—†	26–28	operator	21	"
	T	Landry Catherine M—†	26–28	at home	24	Newton
	U	*Landry Mark J	26–28	superintendent	29	10 Clifford
	V	*Terio Assunta—†	30–32	housewife	40	here
	W	Terio Donato	30–32	foreman	45	"
	X	Gately Catherine E—†	30–32	housewife	35	654 Metropolitan av
	Y	Gately Charles L	30–32	lithographer	34	654 "
	Z	Pineault Anna W—†	34	housewife	45	here
2008						
	A	Pineault Donald H	34	conductor	46	"
	B	Noonan Anna A—†	38	housewife	54	"
	C	Noonan Anna A—†	38	secretary	22	"
	D	Noonan James P	38	conductor	54	"
	E	Noonan Matthew E	38	engineer	26	"
	F	Marden Grace—†	42	at home	81	"

Clifford Street—Continued

Page	Letter	Full Name	Residence, Jan. 1, 1941	Occupation	Supposed Age	Reported Residence, Jan. 1, 1940. Street and Number
	G	Leavitt Alfred R	44	superintendent	59	here
	H	Leavitt Doris B †	44	teacher	27	"
	K	Leavitt Flora E †	44	housewife	59	"
	L	O'Hara George F	45	carpenter	54	"
	M	O'Hara Ruth M †	45	housewife	43	"
	N	Hudson Alexander	46	retired	68	"
	O	Hudson Dorothy E †	46	clerk	23	"
	P	Jakubowski Frederick T	47	chemist	24	"
	R	Jakubowski Samuel	47	machinist	52	"
	S	*Jakubowski Sophie B †	47	housewife	48	"
	T	Leavitt Donald B	48	mechanic	26	32 Summit
	U	Leavitt Rachel P †	48	secretary	26	32 "
	V	Murphy Francis G	48	supervisor	50	here
	W	Murphy Helen B †	48	housewife	49	"
	X	Casperson Carl E	49	clerk	25	"
	Y	Casperson Hulda †	49	housewife	53	"
	Z	Casperson Maurice	49	painter	57	"
2009						
	A	Foley Alice C †	50	cook	34	"
	B	Foley Annie L †	50	candymaker	41	"
	C	Foley Esther M †	50	clerk	21	"
	D	Foley Mary M †	50	waitress	32	"
	E	Foley Theresa †	50	housewife	63	"
	F	Foley Thomas H	50	printer	68	"
	G	Foley Thomas H, jr	50	mechanic	39	"
	H	Anderson Ruth †	61	stenographer	24	"
	K	Weninger Gladys †	61	"	23	"
	L	Weninger Ruth †	61	"	47	"
	M	Whitehouse Emily L †	65	housewife	58	"
	N	Whitehouse John E	65	superintendent	60	"
	O	Whitehouse Ronald A	65	mechanic	27	"
	P	Schauman Charles W	65	salesman	41	Woburn
	R	Schauman Mary E †	65	housewife	33	"

Cross Street

Page	Letter	Full Name	Residence, Jan. 1, 1941	Occupation	Supposed Age	Reported Residence, Jan. 1, 1940. Street and Number
	S	Ferzoco Anna †	6	housewife	56	here
	T	Ferzoco Benjamin	6	laborer	25	"
	U	Ferzoco Eva †	6	examiner	22	"
	V	Ferzoco William	6	grinder	58	"

Page.	Letter.	FULL NAME.	Residence, Jan. 1, 1941.	Occupation.	Supposed Age.	Reported Residence, Jan. 1, 1940. Street and Number.

Damrell Avenue

Page.	Letter.	FULL NAME.	Residence, Jan. 1, 1941.	Occupation.	Supposed Age.	Reported Residence, Jan. 1, 1940.
	Y	Wdzienkowski Jennie M—†	6	housewife	27	here
	Z	Wdzienkowski Raymond W	6	machinist	36	"
2010						
	A	Chisholm Anne V—†	6	operator	31	"
	B	Chisholm Mary H—†	6	housewife	63	"
	C	Lennon James G	6	chauffeur	34	"
	D	Lennon Mary E—†	6	housewife	33	"
	E	Donaruma John	24	blacksmith	57	"
	F	Donaruma Mary—†	24	finisher	25	"
	G	Mattero Jennie—†	24	housewife	51	"
	H	Mattero Vincenzo	24	laborer	55	"
	K	Barone Elizabeth—†	26	stitcher	20	"
	L	Barone Joseph	26	laborer	51	"
	M	*Barone Stella—†	26	housewife	40	"
	N	Palombi Stephen	28–30	laborer	44	"
	O	*Palombi Theresa—†	28–30	housewife	40	"
	P	Abbatangelo Jennie—†	28–30	"	28	"
	R	Abbatangelo Patrick F	28–30	chauffeur	27	"
	S	*Campagnone Mary—†	32	housewife	36	"
	T	Campagnone Vito	32	laborer	49	"
	U	*Fraone Carmella—†	32	housekeeper	76	"
	V	Fraone Domenic	32	laborer	50	"
	W	Fraone Mary—†	32	housewife	37	"
	X	Burhoe Frances—†	49	"	32	"
	Y	Burhoe Ralph	49	secretary	29	"
	Z	*Donofrio Dorothy—†	53	stitcher	30	"
2011						
	A	*LaConti Carmella—†	53	housekeeper	58	"
	B	Dello Iacono Alma—†	56	cleaner	26	"
	C	Dello Iacono Anna—†	56	housewife	54	"
	D	Dello Iacono John	56	pipefitter	54	"
	E	Dello Iacono Susan—†	56	saleswoman	29	"
	F	Esposito Frank	60	machinist	51	"
	G	*Esposito Pauline—†	60	housewife	51	"
	H	Mahoney Jeremiah	60	clerk	23	9 Brainard
	K	Mahoney Marie—†	60	housewife	21	here

Eliot Avenue

Page.	Letter.	FULL NAME.	Residence, Jan. 1, 1941.	Occupation.	Supposed Age.	Reported Residence, Jan. 1, 1940.
	M	Fallavollita Louis	5	machinist	48	here
	N	*Fallavollita Susie—†	5	housewife	37	"

Page	Letter	Full Name	Residence Jan. 1, 1941	Occupation	Supposed Age	Reported Residence Jan. 1, 1940. Street and Number

Eliot Avenue—Continued

Page	Letter	Full Name	Residence	Occupation	Age	Reported Residence
	O	Ricci Domenico	5	laborer	47	here
	P*	Ragusa John	5	retired	64	"
	R	Ragusa Rita †	5	clerk	21	"
	S*	Ragusa Theresa †	5	housewife	63	"
	T	DiMarzio Ernest	7	mechanic	21	"
	U	DiMarzio Eva †	7	housewife	43	"
	V	DiMarzio James	7	supervisor	43	"
	W	Frongillo Alexander	7	laborer	55	"
	X	Mugford Lydia F †	8	housekeeper	75	"
	Y	French John L	12	painter	34	"
	Z	French Nellie H †	12	housewife	34	"

2012 Forest Avenue

Page	Letter	Full Name	Residence	Occupation	Age	Reported Residence
2012	A	Dolan John J	14	clerk	49	here
	B	Dolan Mary J †	14	housewife	49	"
	C	Brady Mary A †	26	"	42	"
	D	Brady Thomas F	26	farmer	55	"

Hamilton Street

Page	Letter	Full Name	Residence	Occupation	Age	Reported Residence
	E	McNeil Catherine E †	11	housewife	69	here
	F	McNeil George W	11	merchant	74	"
	G	Shannon Anna C †	11	housewife	50	82 Sprague
	H	Shannon Charles G	11	B F D	41	82 "
	K	Corthell Grace S †	14	housekeeper	54	here
	L	Ramsdell Lena B †	14	"	64	"
	M	Hurlbert Genevieve †	15	artist	25	40 Warren av
	N	Ramos John S	15	machinist	65	40 "
	O	Ramos Minnie D †	15	housewife	50	40 "
	P	Ferzoco Patrick H	15	instructor	36	here
	R	Ferzoco Violante †	15	housewife	29	"
	T	Cove James W	18	guard	46	64 Sprague
	U	Cove Katherine †	18	housewife	43	64 "
	V	Leary Julia †	18	at home	65	64 "
	W	Rau Avis D †	19	housewife	37	here
	X	Rau Ernest P	19	foreman	42	"
	Y*	Farrell Alice F †	24	housewife	36	"
	Z	Farrell Anthony P	24	chauffeur	36	"
2013	B	McNulty Albert J	25	salesman	55	"

Page.	Letter.	Full Name.	Residence, Jan. 1, 1941.	Occupation.	Supposed Age.	Reported Residence, Jan. 1, 1940. Street and Number.

Hamilton Street—Continued

Page.	Letter.	Full Name.	Residence, Jan. 1, 1941.	Occupation.	Supposed Age.	Reported Residence, Jan. 1, 1940. Street and Number.
	C	McNulty Albert J, jr	25	draftsman	22	here
	D	McNulty Anna T—†	25	housewife	56	"
	E	McNulty Mary E—†	25	clerk	20	"
	F	Bronsdon Annie J—†	25	housewife	70	"
	G	Bronsdon William C	25	painter	34	"
	H	Stuart Frederick A	25	laborer	20	"
	K	Grenier Ellen C—†	54	housewife	35	"
	L	Grenier William J	54	machinist	37	"
	M	Harney Claire—†	56	clerk	21	"
	N	Harney George F	56	foreman	53	"
	O	Harney George F, jr	56	machinist	23	"
	P	Harney Gertrude E—†	56	housewife	46	"
	R	Olson Mary F—†	58	"	29	"
	S	Olson William S	58	carpenter	30	"
	T	Kelley Mary A—†	60	housewife	56	"
	U	Kelley Stephen F	60	tinsmith	57	"
	V	Kelley William J	60	operator	27	"
	W	Sheehan Anna M—†	76	clerk	33	"
	X	Sheehan Fred G	76	milkman	38	"
	Y	Sheehan Lillian M—†	76	clerk	40	"
	Z	Magee Anna A—†	77	"	30	"
2014						
	A	Magee Catherine F—†	77	housewife	79	"
	B	Loughlin Thomas J	80	laborer	50	"
	C	*Walsh Ellen J—†	80	housewife	50	"
	D	Walsh Margaret A—†	80	waitress	20	"
	E	Walsh Mary E—†	80	clerk	22	"
	F	Walsh Thomas J	80	janitor	24	"
	G	Thygeson Charles E	81	salesman	44	"
	H	Thygeson Josephine G—†	81	housewife	43	"

Hawthorne Street

Page.	Letter.	Full Name.	Residence, Jan. 1, 1941.	Occupation.	Supposed Age.	Reported Residence, Jan. 1, 1940. Street and Number.
	M	Reynolds Mary—†	17	housekeeper	70	here
	N	Ahern Alice M—†	19	clerk	41	"
	O	Ahern John W	19	retired	70	"
	P	Ahern Mary A—†	19	housewife	68	"
	R	Pendergast Edward J	59	clerk	56	"
	S	Pendergast Edward J, jr	59	instructor	24	"
	T	Pendergast Eleanor T—†	59	typist	21	"
	U	Pendergast Julia V—†	59	housewife	48	"

Hyde Park Avenue

Page	Letter	Full Name	Residence, Jan. 1, 1941.	Occupation.	Supposed Age.	Reported Residence, Jan. 1, 1940. Street and Number.
	X	Williams Alice T †	rear 1819	housewife	32	here
	Y	Williams Charles R	" 1819	machinist	34	"
	Z	LeBlanc Joseph L	1823	salesman	36	"
2015						
	A	LeBlanc Mabel E †	1823	housewife	34	"
	B	Bouvier David W	1825	dyesetter	38	"
	C	Bouvier Mae P †	1825	housewife	32	"
	D	Martinson John	1825	dyesetter	67	"
	E	Charland George H	1825	laborer	27	18 Riverside sq
	F	Charland Isabella M †	1825	housewife	24	18 "
	G	McGee Francis T	1826	rigger	48	here
	H	McGee Mary L †	1826	housewife	51	"
	K	Dorgan Edward P	1826	retired	71	"
	L	Dorgan Mary A †	1826	clerk	31	"
	M	Harper James	1827	laborer	54	Dedham
	N	Smith Martha E †	1829	housewife	42	here
	O	Smith William B	1829	clerk	43	"
	P	Shaffer Annie †	1829A	housewife	48	"
	R	Shaffer James A	1829A	retired	71	"
	S	Shaffer Joseph A	1829A	clerk	23	"
	T	Colantoni Marion †	1830	housewife	33	"
	U	Colantoni Socrates	1830	laborer	43	"
	V	Kierstead Charles H	1830	retired	74	"
	W	Riva Peter E	1830	engineer	45	"
	X	McLeod Ann F †	1831	housewife	28	"
	Y	McLeod Harold E	1831	shipfitter	30	"
2016						
	A	Haley Anne E †	1833	housewife	48	"
	B	Haley John L	1833	laborer	22	"
	C	Haley William K	1833	clerk	54	"
	D	Mahoney Joseph F	1833A	machinist	28	"
	E	Malloy Mary E †	1833A	housewife	34	"
	F	Malloy Thomas J	1833A	fireman	36	"
	G	LaTora Anna †	1834	housewife	53	"
	H	LaTora Charles	1834	cobbler	59	"
	K	LaTora Guy J	1834	cutter	22	"
	L	Smith Ethel M †	1835	housewife	43	"
	M	Smith William L	1835	builder	44	"
	N	Harrington Mary E †	1835	housekeeper	46	"
	O	Sullivan Annie T †	1840	housewife	55	"
	P	Sullivan Dennis	1840	gardener	56	"

Page.	Letter.	Full Name.	Residence, Jan. 1, 1941.	Occupation.	Supposed Age.	Reported Residence, Jan. 1, 1940. Street and Number.

Hyde Park Avenue—Continued

Page.	Letter.	Full Name.	Residence, Jan. 1, 1941.	Occupation.	Supposed Age.	Reported Residence, Jan. 1, 1940.
	R	Connelly Blanche L—†	1841	housewife	45	here
	S	Connelly Dennis A	1841	B F D	56	"
	T	Hewes John R	1841	agent	67	"
	U	Hewes Mary E—†	1841	housewife	66	"
	V	Perry Helen H—†	1841	secretary	32	"
	W	Perry James A	1841	printer	33	"
	X	MacKellar Coll	1849	laborer	61	"
	Y	MacKellar Donald M	1849	"	24	"
	Z	MacKellar Dorothy S—†	1849	laundress	33	"
2017						
	A	MacKellar Sarah E—†	1849	housewife	58	"
	B	Hubbard Elizabeth—†	1849	"	47	"
	C	Hubbard William A	1849	assembler	39	"
	D	Duggan Josephine M—†	1849	housewife	38	"
	E	Duggan William F	1849	coast guard	37	"
	F	Fulton Emily E—†	1857	housewife	46	"
	G	Fulton James B	1857	shipper	21	"
	H	Fulton Wilbur H	1857	painter	52	"
	L	Paulsen Loretta A—†	1865	housewife	54	"
	K	Paulsen Paul H	1865	retired	61	"
	M	McCaffrey Charles L	1873	clerk	33	"
	N	McCaffrey Esther M—†	1873	secretary	36	"
	O	McCaffrey Helen I—†	1873	stenographer	42	"
	P	McCaffrey Mary E—†	1873	housewife	62	"
	R	McCaffrey Thomas F	1873	retired	66	"
	S	Rowan Jeremiah	1873	"	74	"
	T	McDonald Anna M—†	1873	housewife	38	"
	U	McDonald James P	1873	clerk	48	"
	V	Steffy Annie T—†	1877	housewife	67	"
	W	Steffy Genevieve R—†	1877	teacher	32	"
	X	Steffy Joseph H	1877	operator	65	"
	Y	Ready Ernest P	1877	clerk	36	"
	Z	Ready Gertrude R—†	1877	housewife	33	"
2018						
	A	Rogers Margaret R—†	1877	"	69	"
	B	Rogers Michael A	1877	retired	77	"
	C	Clark Mary E—†	1877	housewife	41	"
	D	Clark William F	1877	electrician	42	"
	E	Sutti Libertino	1885	laborer	51	68 Business
	F	Sutti Nancy—†	1885	housekeeper	22	68 "

Page.	Letter.	Full Name.	Residence, Jan. 1, 1941.	Occupation.	Supposed Age.	Reported Residence, Jan. 1, 1940. Street and Number.

Hyde Park Avenue Continued

Page.	Letter.	Full Name.	Residence, Jan. 1, 1941.	Occupation.	Supposed Age.	Reported Residence, Jan. 1, 1940.
	G	*Sutti Theresa †	1885	housewife	42	68 Business
	H	Gray Frank E	1891	printer	20	here
	K	Sinclair Jean H †	1891	housewife	44	"
	L	Sinclair Philip R	1891	mechanic	45	"
	M	Hodges Percy D	1893	author	66	"
	N	Rennie Charlotte H †	1893	housewife	33	"
	O	Rennie Matthew H	1893	pipefitter	35	"
	P	Madan Albert C	1895	clerk	69	"
	R	Madan Elizabeth F †	1895	housewife	64	"
	S	Madan Ellsworth R	1895	agent	34	"
	T	Madan May E †	1895	housewife	31	"
	U	Anthony Horace E	1899	laborer	49	1273 Hyde Park av
	V	Jenkins LeBaron H	1899	timekeeper	57	15 Hamilton
	W	Jenkins Nellie L †	1899	housewife	51	15 "
	X	Jenkins Pauline L †	1899	hairdresser	21	15 "
	Y	Parker Charlotte B †	1899	housekeeper	86	15 "
	Z	Armour Marion †	1899	"	66	here
2019						
	A	Eastman Harold F	1899	laborer	25	1273 Hyde Park av
	B	Eastman Pauline E †	1899	housewife	21	1273 "
	C	Leighton Gladys L †	1899	housekeeper	43	1273 "
	D	*Graham Catherine †	1903	housewife	59	here
	E	Graham Charles S	1903	mechanic	25	"
	F	*Graham John	1903	doorman	63	"
	G	Graham Kathryn B †	1903	bookkeeper	28	"
	H	Lewey Isaac J	1916	laborer	54	"
	K	Lewey Margaret A †	1916	housewife	56	"
	L	Lewey Margaret A †	1916	operator	20	"
	M	Lewey William J	1916	clerk	23	"
	N	Richardson Ethel M †	1919	housewife	33	"
	O	Richardson Frank	1919	machinist	39	"
	P	Barry Edward M	1919	operator	45	"
	R	Barry Mae E †	1919	housewife	45	"
	S	Barker Annie †	1923	"	61	"
	T	Barker Fred R	1923	carpenter	68	"
	U	Barker Stephen	1923	machinist	26	"
	V	O'Donnell Margaret A †	1927	housewife	43	"
	W	O'Donnell William A	1927	clerk	48	"
	X	McFarlin Dorothy J †	1928	housewife	34	"
	Y	McFarlin Vernon S	1928	engineer	31	"

Page.	Letter.	Full Name.	Residence, Jan. 1, 1941.	Occupation.	Supposed Age.	Reported Residence, Jan. 1, 1940. Street and Number.

Hyde Park Avenue—Continued

Page.	Letter.	Full Name.	Residence, Jan. 1, 1941.	Occupation.	Supposed Age.	Reported Residence, Jan. 1, 1940. Street and Number.
	Z	Sheehan Mildred M—†	1931	housewife	33	here
2020						
	A	Sheehan Paul J	1931	proprietor	34	"
	B	Beckwith Harold	1932	attendant	26	"
	C	Beckwith Josephine—†	1932	housewife	24	"
	D	McGrath Bartley	1932	retired	66	"
	E	McGrath Basil F	1932	laborer	29	"
	F	McGrath Mary T—†	1932	housewife	65	"

Irving Street

Page.	Letter.	Full Name.	Residence, Jan. 1, 1941.	Occupation.	Supposed Age.	Reported Residence, Jan. 1, 1940. Street and Number.
	G	Blomstrom Alice T—†	14	housewife	37	here
	H	Blomstrom Eskil R	14	boilermaker	38	"
	K	LeDoux Melina—†	18	housekeeper	70	"
	L	Magee James J	18	checker	65	"
	M	Magee Mary F—†	18	housewife	69	"
	N	McGrath John T	21	machinist	44	"
	O	McGrath Lena A—†	21	housewife	41	"
	P	Moore Alexander	21	shipper	62	"
	R	Moore Margaret—†	21	housewife	59	"
	S	Caldwell Augustus E	22	engineer	52	"
	T	Caldwell Frances E—†	22	housewife	48	"
	U	Caldwell Frances M—†	22	student	20	"
	V	Mahony Olive G—†	30	housewife	46	"
	W	Mahony Thomas R	30	merchant	45	"

Lakeside Avenue

Page.	Letter.	Full Name.	Residence, Jan. 1, 1941.	Occupation.	Supposed Age.	Reported Residence, Jan. 1, 1940. Street and Number.
	X	Earley Alice E—†	3	stenographer	43	here
	Y	Earley Elizabeth F—†	3	housewife	67	"
	Z	Earley James E	3	cutter	67	"
2021						
	A	Earley Mildred M—†	3	stenographer	44	"
	C	Neas Alice J—†	16	housewife	42	"
	D	Neas John H	16	boilermaker	54	"
	E	Strickland Florence P—†	16	clerk	20	"
	G	Leavitt Charlotte—†	18	housewife	38	"
	H	Leavitt William H	18	fireman	49	"

Linden Street

Page.	Letter.	Full Name.	Residence, Jan. 1, 1941.	Occupation.	Supposed Age.	Reported Residence, Jan. 1, 1940. Street and Number.
	K	Byrnes Dorcas J—†	1	bookkeeper	21	here
	L	Byrnes John T	1	retired	80	"

Page	Letter	Full Name	Residence, Jan. 1, 1941	Occupation	Supposed Age	Reported Residence, Jan. 1, 1940. Street and Number

Linden Street—Continued

Page	Letter	Full Name	Residence	Occupation	Age	Reported Residence
	M	Byrnes Julia A †	1	housewife	60	here
	N	Byrnes Paul F	1	mechanic	30	"

Manila Avenue

Page	Letter	Full Name	Residence	Occupation	Age	Reported Residence
	O	Pascucci Luigi	7	proprietor	46	here
	P	Spadoni Caroline M †	7	houseworker	27	"
	R	Spadoni Joseph A	7	timekeeper	32	"
	S	*Spadoni Julia †	7	housewife	55	"
	T	Spadoni Peter	7	foreman	59	"
	U	*Scagnoli Domenica †	11	housewife	56	"
	V	Scagnoli Joseph G	11	laborer	28	"
	W	Scagnoli Luigi	11	"	58	"
	X	Scagnoli Mary R †	11	housewife	25	"
	Y	Malloy Bartley	15	engineer	63	"
	Z	Malloy Bridget †	15	housewife	64	"
2022						
	A	Malloy Mary E †	15	clerk	30	"
	B	*Clancey James	19	laborer	60	"
	C	Padden Martin J	19	operator	47	"
	D	Padden Mary E †	19	dressmaker	40	"
	E	Padden Nora E †	19	housewife	71	"

McDonough Court

Page	Letter	Full Name	Residence	Occupation	Age	Reported Residence
	F	Scaccia Angelo	5	chauffeur	32	here
	G	Scaccia Constance J †	5	housewife	30	"
	H	*O'Neil John	7	assembler	47	"
	K	*O'Neil Julia †	7	housewife	34	"
	L	*Sullivan Elizabeth J †	8	"	40	"
	M	Sullivan Jerome F	8	machinist	40	"

Nelson Street

Page	Letter	Full Name	Residence	Occupation	Age	Reported Residence
	O	Toto Mary A †	2	housewife	29	here
	P	Toto Michael J	2	laborer	31	"
	R	Toto Salvidore	2	"	56	"
	S	*Toto Theresa †	2	housewife	51	"
	T	Moscaritolo Michael	3	laborer	27	12 Aldwin rd
	U	Moscaritolo Palmina B †	3	housewife	25	12 "
	V	Wallace Hilda T †	3	"	30	here

Page	Letter	FULL NAME.	Residence, Jan. 1, 1941.	Occupation	Supposed Age.	Reported Residence, Jan. 1, 1940. Street and Number.

Nelson Street—Continued

Page	Letter	FULL NAME.	Residence, Jan. 1, 1941.	Occupation	Supposed Age.	Reported Residence, Jan. 1, 1940. Street and Number.
	W	Wallace Samuel	3	salesman	29	here
	X	Panaioli Orfeo	5	retired	68	"
	Y	Spadoni Basil	5	metalworker	50	"
	Z	Spadoni Erice M—†	5	housewife	42	"
2023						
	A	White Anna—†	7	"	47	"
	B	White John H	7	B F D	48	"

Neponset River Parkway

Page	Letter	FULL NAME.	Residence, Jan. 1, 1941.	Occupation	Supposed Age.	Reported Residence, Jan. 1, 1940. Street and Number.
	C	*Aiello Anthony	131	laborer	56	here
	D	Aiello Antoinette—†	131	stitcher	21	"
	E	Aiello John	131	laborer	24	"
	F	Aiello Marianna—†	131	housewife	52	"
	G	*Cimo Nicholas	131	laborer	47	"
	H	Jones Arthur	131	"	27	"
	K	Jones Mary—†	131	stitcher	26	"
	L	*Grillo Angelina—†	131	housewife	62	"
	M	Grillo Carmello—†	131	"	66	"
	N	Grillo Joseph	131	machinist	41	"

Neponset Valley Parkway

Page	Letter	FULL NAME.	Residence, Jan. 1, 1941.	Occupation	Supposed Age.	Reported Residence, Jan. 1, 1940. Street and Number.
	P	Frone Frank	185A	bricklayer	53	32 Damrell av
	R	Frone Rose—†	185A	housewife	44	32 "
	S	Iencarelli Carmella—†	185A	stitcher	25	Franklin
	T	Salemme Evelyn R—†	185A	clerk	27	here
	U	*Salemme Frances M—†	185A	dressmaker	32	"
	V	Salemme Josephine M—†	185A	clerk	30	"
	W	*Salemme Mary—†	185A	housewife	60	"
	X	Salemme Raymond	185A	retired	70	"
	Y	Scott Anita W—†	198	entertainer	21	"
	Z	Scott Estelle M—†	198	operator	47	"
2024						
	A	Kane Eugene T	198	machinist	23	"
	B	Cox Evelyn P—†	198	housewife	45	148 Wash'n
	C	Cox James J	198	carpenter	46	148 "
	D	Smith Pauline J—†	198	operator	26	11 A
	F	Murphy Julia A—†	202	merchant	56	here
	H	Alimenti Augustino	208	barber	27	11 Ellis
	K	Alimenti Josephine T—†	208	housewife	27	11 "

Page	Letter	Full Name	Residence, Jan. 1, 1941	Occupation	Supposed Age	Reported Residence, Jan. 1, 1940. Street and Number

Neponset Valley Parkway—Continued

Page	Letter	Full Name	Residence, Jan. 1, 1941	Occupation	Supposed Age	Reported Residence, Jan. 1, 1940. Street and Number
	L	Sullivan Daniel F	212	clerk	23	here
	M	Sullivan Georgianna M †	212	housewife	54	"
	N	Sullivan Joseph P	212	gardener	54	"
	O	Sullivan Joseph P, jr	212	machinist	25	"
	P	Troiani Constantino	214	sprayer	32	1873 River
	R	Troiani Jessie †	214	housewife	32	1873 "
	S	Phillips Catherine I †	216	"	40	here
	T	Phillips Charles F	216	operator	41	"
	U	Delano Elizabeth E †	218	housewife	68	"
	V	Delano George W	218	retired	69	"
	W	Delano William E	218	plumber	36	"
	X	O'Connell Charles E	218	musician	30	76 Gordon av
	Y	O'Connell John D	218	starter	59	76 "
	Z	O'Connell Leo F	218	boilermaker	39	76 "
2025						
	A	O'Connell Lillian A †	218	housewife	55	76 "
	B	Wright Edgar H	218	retired	82	76 "
	C	King Charles F	218	machinist	25	here
	D	King Marion E †	218	binder	23	"
	E	King Ruth B †	218	"	22	"
	F	King Vincent P	218	clerk	21	"
	H	Kelly Mary †	220	houseworker	76	"
	K	Meyer Ella M †	220	housewife	58	"
	L	Meyer John F	220	retired	66	"
	M	Reynolds Irene L †	223	housewife	37	"
	N	Reynolds Russell E	223	machinist	41	"
	O	Sanger Nellie M †	223	housewife	71	"
	P	Murphy Helen L †	228	"	43	31 Stellman rd
	R	Murphy Jeremiah D	228	chauffeur	47	21 "
	S	Pond Jane L †	229	housewife	65	here
	T	Pond Thomas W	229	retired	84	"
	U	Tuttle Ina L †	229	at home	66	"
	V	Liddell George A	229	clerk	34	"
	W	Liddell Grace L †	229	housewife	33	"
	X	Liddell Katherine A †	229	clerk	52	"
	Y	Grady Catherine M †	235	secretary	41	"
	Z	Stirzaker Eleanor †	235	housewife	74	"
2026						
	A	Stirzaker Ernest J	235	retired	51	"
	B	Stirzaker Margaret J †	235	housewife	48	"
	C	Nutting Albert M	236	compositor	29	55 Idaho

Page.	Letter.	Full Name.	Residence, Jan. 1, 1941.	Occupation.	Supposed Age.	Reported Residence, Jan. 1, 1940. Street and Number.

Neponset Valley Parkway—Continued

Page.	Letter.	Full Name.	Residence, Jan. 1, 1941.	Occupation.	Supposed Age.	Reported Residence, Jan. 1, 1940. Street and Number.
	D	Nutting Mary E—†	236	housewife	28	55 Idaho
	E	Moran Annie—†	rear 236	"	57	here
	F	Moran John W	" 236	installer	60	"
	G	Christie David	240	machinist	36	59 Dana av
	H	Cruckshank William G	240	"	24	here
	K	Flynn Cornelius	240	boilermaker	43	"
	L	Herlihy Eugene	240	machinist	53	"
	M	Herlihy Mary A—†	240	housewife	48	"
	N	*Murphy Jeremiah	240	teamster	52	"
	O	Teed Charles A	240	painter	64	"
	P	Burns Mary A—†	244	housewife	53	"
	R	Burns Timothy A	244	operator	58	"
	S	Dooley John P	244	clerk	50	"
	T	Topham Emma G—†	247	housewife	69	"
	U	Topham Henry	247	fireman	63	"
	V	Nelson Harry M	248	barber	62	"
	W	*Nelson Jennie—†	248	housewife	56	"
	X	Bandlow George L	251	machinist	54	"
	Y	Bandlow Mary T—†	251	housewife	47	"
	Z	Kelley James J	251	attendant	40	"
2027						
	A	Verna Joseph	252	laborer	48	111 Readville
	B	Verna Leah—†	252	housewife	35	111 "
	C	Verna Luigi	252	machinist	47	111 "
	D	Sullivan John D	253	contractor	33	here
	E	Sullivan Madeline A—†	253	housewife	33	"
	F	Leary John	264	retired	69	"
	G	Mahoney Ann T—†	264	clerk	39	"
	H	Mahoney Catherine M—†	264	stenographer	43	"
	K	Mahoney Edward J	264	clerk	33	"
	L	Mahoney Grace E—†	264	houseworker	45	"
	M	Mahoney John F	264	mechanic	41	"
	N	Mahoney Mary E—†	264	housewife	72	"
	O	Bradley Alice W—†	265	"	60	"
	P	Bradley Barbara—†	265	clerk	31	"
	R	Bradley Rosamond W—†	265	typist	33	"
	S	Bradley William	265	cashier	62	"
	U	Eastman Doris C—†	284	houseworker	20	"
	V	Eastman Ida L—†	284	housewife	60	"
	W	Eastman William G	284	retired	76	"
	X	Hayward Helen M—†	284	housewife	65	65 Westminster

Page	Letter	Full Name	Residence, Jan. 1, 1941	Occupation	Supposed Age	Reported Residence, Jan. 1, 1940, Street and Number

Neponset Valley Parkway—Continued

Page	Letter	Full Name	Residence, Jan. 1, 1941	Occupation	Supposed Age	Reported Residence, Jan. 1, 1940, Street and Number
	Y	Hayward Henry	284	retired	70	65 Westminster
2028						
	A	Pearce Elsie †	292–294	housewife	51	here
	B	Pearce Thomas F	292–294	riveter	23	"
	C	Pearce William H	292–294	foreman	53	"
	D	Sheehan Michael	292–294	laborer	56	"
	E	Hagger Dorothy G †	292–294	stenographer	26	Dedham
	F	Hagger Herbert W	292–294	clerk	50	"
	G	Hagger Mary A †	292–294	housewife	47	"
	H	Hagger Richard H	292–294	student	20	"
	K	Devlin Mary A †	298	housewife	34	419 Wash'n
	L	Devlin Wallace J	298	salesman	37	419 "
	M	Littlefield Mary †	298	housewife	67	419 "
	N	Christensen Esther C †	302	bookkeeper	34	here
	O	Christensen Marie †	302	housewife	66	"
	P	Casey George E	302	operator	60	"
	R	Casey Robert M	302	trainer	30	"
	S	Casey Stella V †	302	housewife	53	"
	T	Hurst Albert W	302	underwriter	32	"
	U	Hurst Marian F †	302	housewife	30	"
	V	Watkins Alice G †	312	"	71	"

Norton Street

Page	Letter	Full Name	Residence, Jan. 1, 1941	Occupation	Supposed Age	Reported Residence, Jan. 1, 1940, Street and Number
	W	*Maria Charles	12	retired	72	here
	X	Parillo Benedetta †	12	housewife	25	"
	Y	Parillo Felix N	12	laborer	30	"
	Z	Anshewitz Helen S †	14	housewife	32	Dedham
2029						
	A	Anshewitz Theodore	14	weigher	33	"
	B	Bowley Samuel R	15	laborer	40	14 Norton
	C	Brown Bertha M †	15	housewife	45	14 "
	D	Brown Lee H	15	machinsit	49	14 "
	E	Brown Lucille H †	15	housekeeper	23	14 "
	F	Brown Quentin L	15	mover	20	14 "
	H	*Morreale Lena †	16	housewife	34	here
	K	Morreale Norfry	16	laborer	27	"
	L	Morreale Vincenzo	16	"	53	"
	M	*Molinario Assunta †	22	housekeeper	43	"
	N	McDonald Eleanor A †	22½	housewife	54	23 Vaughan
	O	McDonald Philip F	22½	laborer	52	23 "

Page.	Letter.	Full Name.	Residence, Jan. 1, 1941.	Occupation.	Supposed Age.	Reported Residence, Jan. 1, 1940. Street and Number.

Norton Street—Continued

Page.	Letter.	Full Name.	Residence, Jan. 1, 1941.	Occupation.	Supposed Age.	Reported Residence, Jan. 1, 1940. Street and Number.
	P	McDonald Philip F	22½	clerk	26	23 Vaughan
	R	Constantino Luigi	24	operator	25	here
	S	*Constantino Maria—†	24	housewife	56	"
	T	Constantino Mary C—†	24	dressmaker	23	"
	U	Constantino Salvatore	24	laborer	57	"

Prescott Street

Page.	Letter.	Full Name.	Residence, Jan. 1, 1941.	Occupation.	Supposed Age.	Reported Residence, Jan. 1, 1940. Street and Number.
	W	Barbieri Joseph P	4	gardener	39	here
	X	Barbieri Josephine—†	4	housewife	36	"
	Y	McCallion Grace C—†	4	housekeeper	48	"
	Z	Moran John	4	watchman	39	"
2030						
	A	Moran Margaret A—†	4	saleswoman	23	"
	B	Fennessey Elizabeth B—†	6	housewife	42	"
	C	Fennessey John H	6	molder	48	"
	D	Burns Hazel G—†	8	clerk	28	"
	E	Burns Helen G—†	8	operator	36	"
	F	Burns James F	8	retired	69	"
	G	Burns Mary M—†	8	operator	41	"
	H	Burns Sarah A—†	8	housewife	68	"
	K	Burns Thomas M	8	clerk	32	"
	L	Willis Adeline C—†	12	housewife	68	"
	M	Willis Walter	12	operator	36	"
	N	*Huggan Emerson W	12	mechanic	40	"
	O	*Huggan Hazel I—†	12	housewife	35	"
	P	Armour Barbara—†	12	"	24	"
	R	Armour Robert J	12	blacksmith	24	"
	S	Colleran Mary E—†	12	housewife	43	"
	T	Colleran Michael J	12	laborer	48	"
	U	*Healy Margaret M—†	14	housewife	54	"
	V	Healy Margaret M—†	14	stenographer	24	"
	W	Healy Mary M—†	14	"	29	"
	X	Healy William F	14	machinist	55	"
	Z	Bailey Jessie B—†	18	housewife	44	"
2031						
	A	Bailey Oscar R	18	mechanic	55	"
	B	Fahey Thomas B	18	oil dealer	39	"
	C	Fahey Viola O—†	18	housewife	36	"
	D	Carty Joseph	20	finisher	38	"
	E	Carty Mary C—†	20	housewife	37	"

Page	Letter	Full Name.	Residence, Jan. 1, 1941.	Occupation.	Supposed Age.	Reported Residence, Jan. 1, 1940. Street and Number.

Prescott Street Continued

Page	Letter	Full Name.	Residence, Jan. 1, 1941.	Occupation.	Supposed Age.	Reported Residence, Jan. 1, 1940. Street and Number.
	F	Hurley Arthur	20	electrician	38	here
	G	*Hurley Delia †	20	housewife	40	"
	H	*Bulman Elizabeth M †	20	"	47	1157 Hyde Park av
	K	*Berry Mary E †	20	"	38	here
	L	Berry William J	20	laborer	42	"
	M	*Grubinskas Annie †	24	housewife	51	"
	N	Grubinskas John A	24	inspector	26	"
	O	Grubinskas John C	24	machinist	49	"
	S	Bartlett Allen D	30	draftsman	36	"
	T	Bartlett Kathleen M †	30	housewife	34	"
	U	Kelley Lawrence F	30	chauffeur	25	"
	V	Kelley Mary E †	30	housewife	24	"
	X	Joyce Ella T †	32	"	36	"
	Y	Joyce Joseph F	32	laborer	38	"
	Z	Deary Francis J	32	clerk	28	"
2032						
	A	Deary Louise J †	32	housewife	24	"
	B	Freeman Alita A †	40	housekeeper	47	"
	C	*Traynor Alice †	40	housewife	32	New York
	D	Traynor Thomas J	40	clerk	33	"
	E	*Lutz Catherine S †	44	housewife	44	69 Gordon av
	F	Lutz Irene †	44	cashier	22	69 "
	G	*Lutz Walter	44	laborer	63	69 "
	H	Marchankeviez Francis S	44	"	29	here
	K	Marchankeviez Mildred N †	44	housewife	25	"
	L	*Mountain Julia †	44	"	46	"
	M	Mountain Thomas W	44	painter	55	"
	N	Olson Amelia P †	50	housewife	52	"
	O	Olson Leonard G	50	clerk	22	"
	P	*Olson William S	50	machinist	52	"
	R	Hayes Eugene O	52	laborer	53	"
	S	Hayes Gerard E	52	mechanic	27	"
	T	Hayes Robert J	52	laborer	23	"
	U	Hayes Sarah N †	52	housewife	48	"
	V	Bryant Arthur H	54	engineer	58	"
	W	Bryant Jean C †	54	housewife	65	"
	X	Keany Alfred A	56	mechanic	29	"
	Y	Keany Catherine J †	56	housewife	36	"
	Z	Keany Elizabeth A †	56	"	68	"
2033						
	A	Keany Emil F	56	mechanic	66	"

Page.	Letter.	Full Name.	Residence, Jan. 1, 1941.	Occupation.	Supposed Age.	Reported Residence, Jan. 1, 1940. Street and Number.

Prescott Street—Continued

Page.	Letter.	Full Name.	Residence, Jan. 1, 1941.	Occupation.	Supposed Age.	Reported Residence, Jan. 1, 1940. Street and Number.
	B	Cox Edward J	60	manager	46	here
	C	Cox Edward J, jr	60	clerk	20	"
	D	Cox Hilda C—†	60	housewife	47	"
	E	Clark Harry O	66	conductor	53	"
	F	Clark Ida E—†	66	housewife	82	"
	G	Clark Joseph B	66	retired	86	"
	H	Ryan Hannah T—†	73	housewife	65	"
	K	Ryan James P	73	fireman	65	"
	L	Ryan Marion R—†	73	clerk	29	"
	M	Nelson Guy S	75	milkman	52	"
	N	Nelson Guy S, jr	75	machinist	26	"
	O	Nelson Vennie T—†	75	housewife	50	"

Readville Street

Page.	Letter.	Full Name.	Residence, Jan. 1, 1941.	Occupation.	Supposed Age.	Reported Residence, Jan. 1, 1940. Street and Number.
	P	Riley Julia—†	58	housewife	82	here
	R	Riley Nora J—†	58	secretary	44	"
	S	Riley William P	58	foreman	42	"
	T	Chaisson David M	60	retired	67	"
	U	Chaisson John F	60	boxmaker	20	"
	V	Dare Florence L—†	60	housewife	36	"
	W	Dare William	60	chauffeur	38	"
	X	Langvin Antonia—†	68	housewife	81	"
	Y	Langvin Reginald J	68	carpenter	44	"
	Z	Tivnan Margaret B—†	68	housewife	32	992 River
2034						
	A	Tivnan Walter E	68	carpenter	42	992 "
	B	Holden Corinne C—†	68A	houseworker	21	here
	C	White George E	68A	watchman	69	"
	D	White Susan—†	68A	housewife	53	"
	F	DiCesare Angelina—† rear	69	"	54	"
	G	DiCesare George V "	69	laborer	21	"
	H	DiCesare John "	69	storekeeper	56	"
	K	DiCesare Julia L—† "	69	cook	23	"
	L	DiCesare Velio T—† "	69	secretary	24	"
	N	Shea Elizabeth C—†	73	housewife	33	"
	O	Shea John F	73	plasterer	44	"
	P	Fardy Catherine—†	73	housekeeper	73	"
	U	Sims Benjamin S	75B	machinist	25	"
	V	Sims J Walter	75B	printer	23	"

Page	Letter	Full Name	Residence, Jan. 1, 1941	Occupation	Supposed Age	Reported Residence, Jan. 1, 1940. Street and Number

Readville Street—Continued

Page	Letter	Full Name	Residence, Jan. 1, 1941	Occupation	Supposed Age	Reported Residence, Jan. 1, 1940
	W	Szymczak Josephine B †	75B	stitcher	28	here
	X	Szymczak Veronica P †	75B	teacher	31	"
	Y	Pasquale Joseph	75B	chef	52	"
	Z	Pasquale Velma M †	75B	housewife	33	"
2035						
	B	Colli Gaspar	75½	painter	29	496 Sumner
	C	Colli Josephine B †	75½	housewife	24	496 "
	D	Coury Ernest C	77	storekeeper	28	here
	E*	Coury Mamie B †	77	housewife	46	"
	F	Coury Nasip J	77	clerk	20	"
	G	Coury Phillip F	77	"	24	"
	H	Petrillo Camella †	78	painter	21	"
	K	Petrillo Frank	78	boxmaker	23	"
	L	Petrillo George	78	machinist	28	"
	M*	Petrillo Maria †	78	housewife	50	"
	N	Petrillo Michael	78	blacksmith	55	"
	O	Gasbarro Josephine F †	80	housewife	25	78 Readville
	P	Gasbarro Louis	80	machinist	33	78 "
	R*	Pietro Angelina †	83	housewife	37	here
	S*	Pietro Guy	83	gardener	44	"
	T*	DeFilippo Inez †	83	housewife	34	"
	U*	DeFilippo Joseph	83	millworker	46	"
	V*	Romanus Joseph	84	"	47	"
	W*	Romanus Mary †	84	housewife	50	"
	X*	Messore Concetta †	84	"	43	"
	Y	Messore Joseph A	84	laborer	23	"
	Z	Messore Pasquale	84	mason	53	"
2036						
	B*	LaConte Filomena †	85	housewife	51	"
	C	LaConte Francis D	85	chauffeur	20	"
	D*	LaConte Gerald	85	cutter	57	"
	E	LaConte Mary E †	85	seamstress	25	"
	F	Aiello Elizabeth †	85	housewife	29	1493 River
	G	Aiello Samuel	85	cementworker	31	1493 "
	H	McDonough Henry J	87	machinist	56	here
	K	McDonough Walter T	87	retired	67	"
	L*	DiLillo Angelina †	88	housewife	38	"
	M	DiLillo Gerardo	88	blacksmith	45	"
	N*	DiLillo Otto	88	retired	73	"
	O	Pinault Agnes †	88	houseworker	35	"
	P	Pinault Marie †	88	housewife	67	"

Page	Letter	Full Name.	Residence, Jan. 1, 1941.	Occupation.	Supposed Age.	Reported Residence, Jan. 1, 1940. Street and Number.

Readville Street—Continued

Page	Letter	Full Name.	Residence, Jan. 1, 1941.	Occupation.	Supposed Age.	Reported Residence, Jan. 1, 1940. Street and Number.
	R	Pinault Phillip	88	laborer	64	here
	S	*Yazback Beatrice—†	88	housewife	49	"
	T	Yazback Joseph	88	storekeeper	48	"
	U	Yazback Nassar J	88	clerk	20	"
	V	Rieger Lydia—†	89	houseworker	25	1858 River
	W	Spicer Albert W	89	machinist	34	1858 "
	X	Spicer Mary F—†	89	housewife	28	1858 "
	Y	Templeton Mary V—†	91	"	36	here
	Z	Templeton William S	91	collector	27	"
2037						
	A	Welch Francis L	91	clerk	41	"
	C	Rocheleau Helen M—†	94	housewife	49	"
	D	Rocheleau Joseph E	94	sprayer	51	"
	E	Rocheleau Robert E	94	machinist	20	"
	F	Burke Mae R—†	94	clerk	48	"
	G	Harkins Francis J	94	"	24	"
	H	Harkins Julia G—†	94	housewife	50	"
	K	Conley Nellie N—†	99	"	60	"
	L	Conley William J	99	B F D	60	"
	N	Pezzano Anthony J	104	machinist	33	"
	O	*Pezzano Catherine—†	104	housewife	32	"
	P	*Pezzano Jerry	104	retired	76	"
	R	Shepherd Doris P—†	104	housewife	23	107 Beaver
	S	Shepherd Peter E	104	roofer	33	107 "
	T	Lanciani Hugo	105	tailor	42	here
	U	Lanciani Theresa—†	105	housewife	34	"
	V	Santoro Emidio	105	salesman	36	"
	W	Santoro Rose M—†	105	housewife	29	"
	X	Blase Mary R—†	107	"	28	954 River
	Y	Blase Michael F	107	laborer	27	954 "
	Z	Scaccia Dora—†	107	clerk	24	here
2038						
	A	Scaccia Emma—†	107	"	21	"
	B	Scaccia Fred	107	laborer	54	"
	C	*Scaccia Mary—†	107	housewife	54	"
	D	Stevens Ida O—†	108	"	43	"
	E	Stevens William H	108	machinist	43	"
	F	*Sestito Elizabeth—†	111	housewife	44	162 Devon
	G	Sestito Frank	111	mason	22	162 "
	H	*Sestito Joseph	111	"	45	162 "
	K	Sestito Mary—†	111	housewife	21	Cohasset

Page	Letter	Full Name	Residence, Jan. 1, 1941	Occupation	Supposed Age	Reported Residence Jan. 1, 1940 Street and Number

Readville Street Continued

Page	Letter	Full Name	Residence, Jan. 1, 1941	Occupation	Supposed Age	Reported Residence Jan. 1, 1940 Street and Number
	L	Mahanna Alexander	111	cutter	32	135 Columbia rd
	M	Mahanna Antoinette †	111	housewife	28	135 "
	N	Lombardi Joseph	112	merchant	50	here
	O*	Lombardi Susan †	112	housewife	47	"
	P*	Verano Carmella †	112	"	33	"
	R	Verano Mario	112	laborer	34	"
	S	Elliot John J	114	superintendent	50	"
	T	Elliot Mary M †	114	housewife	48	"
	U	Elliot Robert D	114	shipper	20	"
	V	Coleman Michael J	116	watchman	69	31 Fairview av
	W	Conant Donald	116	operator	36	here
	X	Curtin John N	116	retired	79	320 Walnut av
	Y	Earley Charles E	116	laborer	36	here
	Z	Scanlon Anthony	116	"	59	"
2039						
	A	Wedding Elizabeth F †	116	housekeeper	68	"
	B*	Damelio Anna †	120	housewife	53	"
	C	Damelio Dominica †	120	student	21	"
	D	Damelio John	120	fireman	60	"
	E	Bishop Dorothy A †	122	housewife	28	"
	F	Bishop Harold E	122	custodian	29	"
	G	Bishop Helen E †	122	domestic	22	"
	H	Bishop Ida M †	122	housewife	54	"
	K*	Bishop John J	122	brakeman	57	"
	M	Guiod Emily †	124	clerk	24	"
	N*	Guiod Joseph	124	carpenter	65	"
	O	Guiod Mary †	124	domestic	20	"
	P*	Guiod Mary C †	124	housewife	50	"
	R	Lambert Raymond J	126	clerk	32	"
	S	Lambert Stella J †	126	housewife	28	"
	T	Legoski Benjamin J	126	clerk	23	"
	U	Legoski Helen F †	126	examiner	30	"
	V	Legoski Joseph S	126	laborer	25	"
	W	Legoski Josephine †	126	housewife	51	"
	X	Martin Elizabeth G †	128	"	36	"
	Y	Martin Thomas E	128	janitor	38	"
	Z	Monopoli Adeline †	135	housewife	31	"
2040						
	A	Monopoli Leonard	135	driller	35	"
	B	Cardinale Frank	135	laborer	56	"
	C	Rubino John	135	brakeman	35	"

Page	Letter	Full Name.	Residence, Jan. 1, 1941.	Occupation.	Supposed Age.	Reported Residence, Jan. 1, 1940. Street and Number.

Readville Street—Continued

Page	Letter	Full Name.	Residence, Jan. 1, 1941.	Occupation.	Supposed Age.	Reported Residence, Jan. 1, 1940. Street and Number.
	D	*Rubino Mary—†	135	housewife	31	here
	E	Mendes Christopher	135	laborer	40	"
	F	*Mendes Mary—†	135	housewife	27	"
	G	Fegan Mary L—†	139	"	20	Dedham
	H	Lanze Anthony J	139	laborer	40	here
	K	Lanze Matilda N—†	139	housewife	41	"
	L	Lanze Dominic	141	milkman	28	"
	M	*Lanze Mary—†	141	housewife	68	"
	N	*Lanze Paul	141	laborer	65	"
	O	DeSantis Alesio	144	retired	52	"
	P	*DeSantis Angelina—†	144	housewife	48	"
	R	DeSantis Joseph	144	machinist	21	"
	S	DeSantis William	144	draftsman	23	"
	U	Prianti Emma—†	146	housewife	29	"
	V	Prianti Vincent	146	laborer	37	"
	W	Valeri Guiseppe	146	"	43	"
	X	*Valeri Philomena—†	146	housewife	37	"
	Y	Colantoni Luigi	147	laborer	55	"
	Z	*Colantoni Philomena—†	147	housewife	47	"
2041						
	A	Brandano Angelina—†	147	"	52	"
	B	Brandano Salvatore	147	retired	54	"
	C	Weberson Fred	147	laborer	56	"
	D	Friedmann Catherine E—†	151	housewife	55	"
	E	Friedmann Christine T—†	151	clerk	25	"
	F	Friedmann Edward J	151	machinist	22	"
	G	Friedmann Ernest	151	plasterer	59	"
	H	Rooney Mary E—†	151	matron	62	"
	K	Haller Fred N	159	mechanic	47	"
	L	Haller Mabel R—†	159	housewife	39	"
	M	Peterson A Dorothea—†	159	at home	60	"
	N	Peterson Mildred J—†	159	clerk	30	"
	O	Maney Cora B—†	161	housewife	65	"
	P	Maney Thomas F	161	retired	78	"
	R	Halpin Delia E—†	163	housewife	68	214 Nep Valley P'kway
	S	Halpin Thomas J	163	retired	73	214 "
	T	Halpin Vincent A	163	timekeeper	24	214 "
	U	Rooney Alice M—†	163	housekeeper	29	here
	V	Rooney James	163	laborer	62	"
	W	Rooney Regina F—†	163	clerk	26	"
	X	Villa Emma—†	166	housewife	26	Malden

Page	Letter	Full Name	Residence, Jan. 1, 1941	Occupation	Supposed Age	Reported Residence, Jan. 1, 1940. Street and Number

Readville Street Continued

Page	Letter	Full Name	Residence	Occupation	Age	Reported Residence
	Y	Villa Fiorello F	166	electrician	35	Malden
	Z	Villa Olga †	166	stitcher	31	"
2042						
	A	Villa Pasquale	166	mason	63	here
	B	Logiodice Gertrude S †	170	housewife	59	"
	C	Logiodice Leonard F	170	physician	53	"

Sprague Place

Page	Letter	Full Name	Residence	Occupation	Age	Reported Residence
	D	*Binns Catherine †	41	housewife	40	here
	E	Binns Ernest J	41	laborer	40	"
	G	Puricelli Guido	43	"	44	83 Sprague
	H	Puricelli Olympia †	43	housewife	41	83 "
	K	Muirhead Eva M †	43	"	21	Norwood
	L	Muirhead Robert J	43	laborer	21	E Dedham
	M	Bacchieri Albert J	45	draftsman	23	here
	N	Bacchieri Attillio	45	laborer	45	"
	O	Bacchieri Mildred M †	45	housewife	21	Dedham
	P	Resca Alexander	49	laborer	61	here
	R	Resca Daniel J	49	operator	25	"
	S	Schiappa Joseph	49	bricklayer	54	"

Sprague Street

Page	Letter	Full Name	Residence	Occupation	Age	Reported Residence
	U	McEachern Margaret A †	43	housewife	43	here
	V	McEachern Ralph J	43	chauffeur	43	"
	W	Tully Mary F †	43	at home	80	"
	X	*Pinault Agnes †	60	"	75	"
	Y	Fortin Agnes †	60	housekeeper	50	"
	Z	Maybin Eva J †	62	housewife	47	"
2043						
	A	Maybin Mack R	62	laborer	48	"
	D	Jacobs Albert C	70	salesman	44	"
	E	Jacobs Anna M †	70	housewife	44	"
	F	Leduc Byron	70	salesman	47	"
	G	Leduc Hildegarde †	70	housewife	41	"
	H	Rogazzo Angelo	73	laborer	36	"
	K	Rogazzo Mary F †	73	housewife	30	"
	L	Schaefer Minnie C †	73	at home	78	"
	M	Holmes Louise C †	73	housekeeper	72	"
	N	Silver Mary †	74	"	49	"

Page.	Letter.	Full Name	Residence, Jan. 1, 1941	Occupation.	Supposed Age.	Reported Residence, Jan. 1, 1940. Street and Number.

Sprague Street—Continued

Page.	Letter.	Full Name	Residence, Jan. 1, 1941	Occupation.	Supposed Age.	Reported Residence, Jan. 1, 1940.
	O	Davenport Sarah E—†	78	housewife	71	here
	P	Davenport Warren J	78	retired	74	"
	R	Funk Edward D	78	machinist	23	"
	S	McGrath Helen P—†	80	housewife	27	"
	T	Phelan John J	80	attendant	23	"
	U	Phelan Susan B—†	80	housewife	51	"
	V	Phelan Walter F	80	attendant	21	"
	W	Phelan William J	80	molder	57	"
	X	Phelan David J	81	laborer	25	"
	Y	Phelan Ethel B—†	81	housewife	23	"
2044						
	A*	Parise Martin	83	machinist	40	1907 River
	B	Parise Theresa M—†	83	housewife	30	1907 "
	C	Bryett Annie L—†	86	"	60	here
	D	Bryett John T	86	machinist	59	"
	E	O'Neil Mary A—†	88	housewife	77	"
	F	O'Neil William J	88	foreman	49	"
	G	Wilson Isaac P	94	blacksmith	62	"
	H	Wilson Martha—†	94	housewife	54	"
	K*	Smith Ernest C	96	chauffeur	53	"
	L	Smith Ernest L	96	manager	23	"
	M	Smith Florence G—†	96	typist	20	"
	N*	Smith Hertha J—†	96	housewife	56	"
	O	Smith Mary C—†	96	saleswoman	21	"
	P	Driscoll Michael J	98	laborer	38	70 Sprague
	R	Driscoll Sarah L—†	98	housewife	31	70 "
	S	Johnson Grace—†	102	"	40	here
	T	Johnson Walter	102	machinist	49	"

Stanley Street

Page.	Letter.	Full Name	Residence, Jan. 1, 1941	Occupation.	Supposed Age.	Reported Residence, Jan. 1, 1940.
	U	Marchant Albert G	10	trainer	66	here
	V	Marchant Annie—†	10	housewife	58	"
	W	Grove Mary P—†	14	housekeeper	65	"
	X	Pellett Maud E—†	14	"	68	"
	Y	Folsom Charles D	16	salesman	69	"
	Z	Folsom Gertrude M—†	16	housewife	74	"
2045						
	A	Swenson Eric A	28	chauffeur	25	"
	B	Swenson Lucy A—†	28	clerk	27	"
	C	Swenson Lucy B—†	28	housewife	55	"

Page	Letter	Full Name	Residence, Jan. 1, 1941	Occupation	Supposed Age	Reported Residence, Jan. 1, 1940. Street and Number

Stanley Street—Continued

Page	Letter	Full Name	Residence, Jan. 1, 1941	Occupation	Supposed Age	Reported Residence, Jan. 1, 1940. Street and Number
	D	Kunkel Charles A	28	blacksmith	27	19 Clifford
	E	Kunkel Hazel A †	28	housewife	20	19 "
	F	Kunkel Dorothea E †	55	stenographer	24	here
	G	Kunkel Emma L †	55	housewife	56	"
	H	Kunkel Walter J	55	blacksmith	57	"

Stark Avenue

Page	Letter	Full Name	Residence, Jan. 1, 1941	Occupation	Supposed Age	Reported Residence, Jan. 1, 1940. Street and Number
	K	Qualtieri Agostino	2	laborer	55	here
	L	Qualtieri Louis M	2	"	20	"
	M	Qualtieri Rose †	2	dressmaker	23	"
	N	*Qualtieri Rosina †	2	housewife	50	"
	O	Barry Amelia †	2	"	25	"
	P	Barry Joseph	2	upholsterer	34	"
	R	Burns Edward F	8	laborer	29	"
	S	Burns Sylvia F †	8	housewife	25	"
	T	*Galdi Maria G †	8	"	52	10 Stark av
	U	Galdi Maria J †	8	dressmaker	23	10 "
	V	Galdi Victor P	8	welder	22	10 "
	W	Galdi Vito	8	laborer	55	10 "
	X	Montisano Vito	10	"	65	Dedham
	Y	Procopio Guiseppe	10	"	56	"
	Z	Procopio Nellie †	10	housewife	34	"
2046						
	A	Ferzoco Blanche †	12	dressmaker	24	53 Milton
	B	*Ferzoco Constantino	12	laborer	48	53 "
	C	*Ferzoco Frances †	12	housewife	45	53 "
	D	Ferzoco Fred	12	laborer	26	53 "
	E	Ferzoco Patrick	12	mechanic	21	53 "
	F	Marapoti Rose †	14	housewife	26	here
	G	Marapoti Rudolph	14	shoemaker	32	"
	H	Maxwell Joseph M	14	chauffeur	24	Dedham
	K	Maxwell Mary E †	14	housewife	26	"

2047 Stoughton Avenue

Page	Letter	Full Name	Residence, Jan. 1, 1941	Occupation	Supposed Age	Reported Residence, Jan. 1, 1940. Street and Number
	A	Marculaitis Agnes H †	15	housewife	48	here
	B	Marculaitis Dominic	15	machinist	45	"
	C	Marculaitis Peter J	15	"	22	"
	D	Galipeau Eugene	21	roofer	42	"
	E	Galipeau Mary †	21	housewife	38	"

Page.	Letter.	Full Name.	Residence, Jan. 1, 1941	Occupation.	Supposed Age.	Reported Residence, Jan. 1, 1940. Street and Number.

Stoughton Avenue—Continued

Page.	Letter.	Full Name.	Residence, Jan. 1, 1941	Occupation.	Supposed Age.	Reported Residence, Jan. 1, 1940.
	F	Balzarini Mary—†	23	housewife	37	here
	H	*Ravasini Gualtiero	29	baker	60	"
	K	*Ravasini Luigi	29	"	37	"
	M	Biswanger Joseph A	31	retired	78	"
	N	Biswanger Louis R	31	carpenter	35	"
	O	Biswanger Louise R—†	31	housewife	70	"
	P	Bogni Alice I—†	34	"	21	8 Oak pl
	R	Bogni Louis	34	mason	25	8 "
	S	*DiMarzio Anna D—†	34	housewife	52	here
	T	DiMarzio William	34	machinist	59	"
	U	Moran Ambrose J	37	laborer	45	"
	V	Moran Anna E—†	37	milliner	34	"
	W	Moran Helen C—†	37	at home	30	"
	X	Moran Hugh L	37	painter	38	"
	Y	Moran John M	37	bartender	30	"
	Z	Moran Philip	37	painter	26	"
2048						
	A	Moran Thomas J	37	retired	73	"
	B	Taylor John M	39	tinsmith	41	"
	C	Taylor Margaret—†	39	housewife	71	"
	D	Taylor William L	39	electrician	39	"
	E	*Abbatangelo Angelina—†	43	housewife	55	"
	F	Abbatangelo Angelo	43	laborer	54	"
	G	Abbatangelo Dominic	43	"	24	"
	H	Abbatangelo Leonard	43	"	22	"
	K	Vittorini Arthur	45	"	25	"
	L	*Vittorini Gronata—†	45	housewife	54	"
	M	Vittorini Oreste	45	laborer	46	"
	N	Vittorini Orlando	45	sorter	27	"
	O	DiPastina Nicholas	47	installer	55	"
	P	Gaetano Michael	47	laborer	55	"
	R	Scaccia Margaret—†	47	housewife	23	"
	S	Scaccia William F	47	mechanic	29	"
	T	*Micheletti Assunta—†	49	housewife	44	"
	U	*Micheletti Giovanni	49	laborer	53	"
	V	*Villa Anna—†	50	housewife	67	"
	W	Villa Christopher	50	laborer	68	"
	X	Villa John J	50	operator	26	"
	Y	Villa Palma—†	50	at home	30	"
	Z	Villa Susan—†	50	housewife	29	"

Page.	Letter.	Full Name.	Residence, Jan. 1, 1941.	Occupation.	Supposed Age.	Reported Residence, Jan. 1, 1940. Street and Number.
2049						

Stoughton Avenue—Continued

Page.	Letter.	Full Name.	Residence, Jan. 1, 1941.	Occupation.	Supposed Age.	Reported Residence, Jan. 1, 1940. Street and Number.
	A	Villa Victor J	50	operator	32	here
	B	Aloisi Elizabeth B †	61	housewife	20	"
	C	Aloisi Santo	61	butcher	20	"
	D	*Deneno Archanga †	61	housewife	43	"
	E	Deneno Felix	61	laborer	49	"
	H	Meleo Andrew	65	"	54	"
	K	*Meleo Jennie †	65	housewife	53	"
	L	*Puliafico Carmella †	65	"	38	"
	M	Puliafico Sebastiano	65	laborer	40	"
	N	Aiello Frank K	68	operator	24	1493 River
	O	Aiello Rose †	68	housewife	22	1493 "
	P	Parise Catherine †	68	"	32	here
	R	Parise Gaetano	68	laborer	40	"
	T	*Bisceglia Julia †	79	housewife	64	"
	U	Bisceglia William	79	clerk	23	"
	V	*Massimi Josephine †	79	at home	32	"
	W	Bisceglia Josephine †	79	housewife	29	"
	X	*Bisceglia Louis	79	barber	40	"
	Y	Cunningham Frances M—†	80	housewife	32	"
	Z	Cunningham Norman L	80	mechanic	32	"
2050						
	A	Flaherty Roger J	80	retired	79	"
	B	*Marapoti Agnes †	83	housewife	59	"
	C	Marapoti Claudio	83	shoemaker	55	"
	E	*Albani Filomina †	88	housewife	49	"
	F	Albani Frank	88	student	24	"
	G	Albani Jean †	88	secretary	20	"
	H	Albani Mary †	88	saleswoman	23	"
	K	*Albani Marzilio	88	metalworker	56	"
	L	Coleman Joseph W	90	mechanic	34	"
	M	Coleman Ruby †	90	housewife	28	"
	N	Ciriello Angelo	90	mechanic	23	"
	O	Ciriello Jennie †	90	housewife	43	"
	P	Ciriello Nicholas P	90	timekeeper	21	"
	R	Ciriello Vincent	90	supervisor	48	"

Vaughan Street

Page.	Letter.	Full Name.	Residence, Jan. 1, 1941.	Occupation.	Supposed Age.	Reported Residence, Jan. 1, 1940. Street and Number.
	S	Couturier Alma—†	2	housewife	38	here
	T	Couturier Rene G	2	metalworker	38	"

Page.	Letter	Full Name.	Residence, Jan. 1, 1941.	Occupation.	Supposed Age.	Reported Residence, Jan. 1, 1940. Street and Number.

Vaughan Street—Continued

Page.	Letter	Full Name.	Residence, Jan. 1, 1941.	Occupation.	Supposed Age.	Reported Residence, Jan. 1, 1940. Street and Number.
	U	Canavan Alice—†	8	housekeeper	66	here
	V	*Gasper John P	10	stockman	35	"
	W	*Gasper Nellie P—†	10	housewife	40	"
	X	Smith John T	13	laborer	21	"
	Y	Smith Norris W	13	carpenter	48	"
	Z	Smith Sarah M—†	13	housewife	43	"
2051						
	A	*Levesque Genevieve—†	14	"	53	"
	B	Levesque Joseph	14	retired	73	"
	C	Rogers Herbert	14	laborer	24	"
	D	Conley Edward J	15	painter	47	"
	E	Conley Grace E—†	15	housewife	35	"
	F	Valeri Anthony	16	laborer	43	"
	G	Valeri Domenica—†	16	housewife	36	"
	H	Campagnone Frances—†	16	"	49	"
	K	Campagnone Joseph	16	laborer	54	"
	L	Giosulli Anthony	16	"	41	104 Readville
	M	Moran Bertha H—†	17	housewife	52	here
	N	Moran Dorothy F—†	17	stenographer	22	"
	O	Moran James E	17	accountant	23	"
	P	Moran James E	17	ironworker	53	"
	R	Moran Lauretta C—†	17	stenographer	30	"
	S	Conley Mary H—†	21	at home	63	"
	T	Riley Joseph J	21	molder	57	"
	U	Riley Joseph J, jr	21	chauffeur	28	"
	V	Riley Margaret E—†	21	housewife	61	"
	W	Connolly Barbara J—†	22	"	55	"
	X	Connolly Margaret A—†	22	clerk	23	"
	Y	Connolly Mary E—†	22	"	24	"
	Z	Connolly Patrick J	22	operator	54	"
2052						
	A	McPhillips Helen A—†	rear 23	housewife	30	Rhode Island
	B	McPhillips John F	" 23	clerk	37	"

Waterloo Street

Page.	Letter	Full Name.	Residence, Jan. 1, 1941.	Occupation.	Supposed Age.	Reported Residence, Jan. 1, 1940. Street and Number.
	C	Burke Mary—†	5	housekeeper	70	here
	D	Putnicki Anthony C	5	tailor	35	"
	E	Putnicki Sophie F—†	5	housewife	28	"
	F	Taber Julia—†	5	at home	73	"
	G	Aiello Alfonsina—†	7	housewife	53	"

Page	Letter	Full Name	Residence, Jan. 1, 1941	Occupation	Supposed Age	Reported Residence, Jan. 1, 1940. Street and Number

Waterloo Street—Continued

Page	Letter	Full Name	Residence, Jan. 1, 1941	Occupation	Supposed Age	Reported Residence, Jan. 1, 1940. Street and Number
	H	*Aiello Bruno	7	laborer	63	here
	K	Filleti Mary †	7	housewife	26	"
	L	*Filleti Rocco	7	laborer	32	"
	M	*Bernasconi Angelo	9	"	51	"
	N	*Bernasconi Louise—†	9	housewife	44	"
	O	Gasbarro Frank	11	laborer	61	"
	P	*Gasbarro Josephine—†	11	housewife	54	"
	R	Gasbarro Elizabeth Y †	11	"	21	108 Readville
	S	Gasbarro Patrick A	11	laborer	23	here
	T	Manartto Anthony P	15	clerk	30	"
	U	Manartto Eliza B—†	15	housewife	28	"
	V	Spera Augusta—†	15	seamstress	49	"
	W	Spera Philip	15	retired	65	"
	X	Dugan Helen C—†	19	housekeeper	52	65 Glendale
	Y	Greer Charles J	19	salesman	38	here
	Z	Greer John P	19	machinist	40	"
2053						
	A	Vittorini Samuel	21	laborer	50	"
	B	Vittorini Victoria—†	21	finisher	36	"
	C	*Colello Anita—†	21	housewife	49	"
	D	*Colello Eugene	21	laborer	57	"
	E	Colello William	21	machinist	22	"

West Milton Street

Page	Letter	Full Name	Residence, Jan. 1, 1941	Occupation	Supposed Age	Reported Residence, Jan. 1, 1940. Street and Number
	F	Horsefield George	10	supervisor	30	here
	G	Horsefield Idella S—†	10	housewife	25	"
	H	*Frechette Blanche M †	24	"	30	"
	K	*Frechette Philip L	24	contractor	40	"
	L	Charest Everett J	24	operator	62	"
	M	Hayes Esther M—†	27	housewife	33	"
	N	Hayes Michael J	27	chauffeur	35	"
	P	Tufo Pasquale	28–30	laborer	43	"
	R	*Tufo Rose A—†	28–30	housewife	38	"
	S	Ferzoco Phyllis—†	28–30	"	30	85 Readville
	T	Ferzoco William R	28–30	boilermaker	27	85 "
	U	O'Connell James F	29	clerk	34	here
	V	O'Connell Marion C—†	29	saleswoman	26	"
	W	O'Connell Mary J—†	29	housewife	56	"
	X	*Mirabile Concetta—†	34	"	42	"
	Y	Mirabile Joseph	34	mechanic	49	"

Page.	Letter.	Full Name.	Residence, Jan. 1, 1941	Occupation.	Supposed Age.	Reported Residence, Jan. 1, 1940. Street and Number.

West Milton Street—Continued

Page.	Letter.	Full Name.	Residence, Jan. 1, 1941	Occupation.	Supposed Age.	Reported Residence, Jan. 1, 1940. Street and Number.
	Z	Cardinal Louise—†	34	housekeeper	43	here
2054						
	A	Magri Antonio	35	clerk	54	"
	B	*Magri Frances—†	35	housewife	52	"
	C	Magri Joseph	35	student	22	"
	E	Caruso Anna—†	rear 37	housewife	23	Dedham
	F	Caruso Orlando	" 37	laborer	29	"
	G	Mercanti Alexander	" 37	"	56	here
	H	Mercanti Anna—†	" 37	secretary	21	"
	K	Mercanti Filomena—†	" 37	housewife	46	"
	L	Granstrom Hulda—†	39	housekeeper	68	"
	M	O'Neil Edna—†	39	housewife	27	"
	N	O'Neil Thomas	39	machinist	27	"
	O	Villa Eva—†	41	housewife	24	"
	P	Villa Joseph	41	machinist	28	"
	S	McAvoy Catherine—†	45	housewife	25	55 Minden
	T	McAvoy Robert	45	bookkeeper	27	234 Hyde Park av
	U	Sinibaldi Antoinette—†	47	housewife	40	here
	V	Sinibaldi Mario	47	machinist	44	"
	W	Geohegan Margaret M—†	49	housekeeper	68	"
	X	Riley Anna F—†	49	"	59	"
	Y	Riley Elizabeth A—†	49	nurse	45	"
	Z	Riley Margaret E—†	49	housekeeper	61	"
2055						
	A	Riley Mary A—†	49	secretary	66	"
	B	Riley Sadie T—†	49	housekeeper	63	"
	C	Coulthurst Margaret V—†	51	housewife	63	"
	D	Coulthurst Matthew F	51	shipper	65	"
	F	Arenburg Florence A—†	56	housewife	58	"
	G	*Arenburg Herbert K	56	carpenter	75	"
	H	Hogan Thomas	56	laborer	68	400 Walk Hill
	K	Seller Oscar	56	"	58	400 "
	L	White Edward	56	"	66	here
	M	White Edward M	56	mechanic	26	"
	N	White Elsie—†	56	housewife	21	"
	O	White Mary A—†	56	"	64	"
	P	Donaldson Eugene F	57	librarian	27	"
	R	Donaldson George P	57	clerk	32	"
	S	Donaldson Sarah F—†	57	housewife	69	"
	T	Nuttall Alice C—†	58	"	45	"

Page	Letter	Full Name	Residence, Jan. 1, 1941.	Occupation	Supposed Age	Reported Residence, Jan. 1, 1940. Street and Number.

West Milton Street—Continued

Page	Letter	Full Name	Residence, Jan. 1, 1941.	Occupation	Supposed Age	Reported Residence, Jan. 1, 1940. Street and Number.
	U	Nuttall Edmund I	58	foreman	44	here
	V	Galante Dominic P	59	agent	38	1553 River
	W	Galante Edith R †	59	housewife	34	1553 "
	X	*Hamburg Burhild S †	61	"	41	here
	Y	*Hamberg Carl O	61	machinist	46	"
	Z	Cox Anna E †	63	secretary	45	"
2056						
	A	Cox Elizabeth K †	63	clerk	38	"
	B	Cox John L	63	salesman	40	"
	C	Cox John W	63	retired	76	"
	D	Cox Mary A †	63	housewife	82	"
	E	Sanders Arthur W	64	accountant	38	"
	F	Sanders James W	64	patternmaker	67	"
	G	Sanders Minnie R †	64	housewife	67	"
	H	Blatz Alice †	65	"	41	"
	K	Blatz John J	65	guard	43	"
	L	Folan Margaret J †	66	housewife	46	"
	M	Folan Patrick F	66	salesman	46	"
	N	Morrisey Mary J †	66	housekeeper	76	260 O'Callaghan way
	O	Hammel Joseph F	69	chauffeur	33	here
	P	Hammel Katherine M †	69	housewife	33	"
	R	Missler Andrew P	71	operator	35	"
	S	Missler Lillian M †	71	housewife	28	"
	T	Armour Alice W †	71	"	26	"
	U	Armour William C	71	boilermaker	28	"
	V	Blomstrom Amanda S †	72	housekeeper	65	"
	W	Blomstrom Ellen M †	72	stenographer	32	"
	X	Blomstrom Howard V	72	laborer	21	"
	Z	Slein Edward R	73	plumber	54	"
2057						
	A	Slein Mary A †	73	housewife	40	"
	B	Slein Mary C †	73	operator	24	"
	C	Ogden Albert	75	metalworker	52	"
	D	Ogden Christopher D	75	clerk	22	"
	E	Ogden Mary F †	75	housewife	48	"
	F	Noonan Anna M †	77	"	40	"
	G	Noonan John A	77	clerk	45	"
	H	Carroll Margaret †	79	teacher	42	"
	K	Clare Catherine †	79	"	42	Kentucky
	L	Hildegarde Mary †	79	"	46	here

Page	Letter	Full Name.	Residence, Jan. 1, 1941.	Occupation.	Supposed Age.	Reported Residence Jan. 1, 1940. Street and Number.

West Milton Street—Continued

Page	Letter	Full Name.	Residence, Jan. 1, 1941.	Occupation.	Supposed Age.	Reported Residence Jan. 1, 1940. Street and Number.
	M	Kamber Rose—†	79	teacher	43	here
	N	O'Connor Theresa—†	79	"	43	"
	O	Plunkett Delia—†	79	"	43	"
	P	Powers Ruth—†	79	"	32	"
	R	Whittinghill Imogene—†	79	"	35	"
	S	Lyons Nellie—†	82	housekeeper	63	"
	T	Mann Florence M—†	82	"	63	"
	U	Regan David F	82	clergyman	68	"
	V	Sennott Thomas F	82	"	31	"
	W	Hewes Dorothy F—†	85	secretary	28	"
	X	Hewes Mabel R—†	85	operator	23	"
	Y	Hewes Marion T—†	85	secretary	26	"
	Z	Hewes Mary E—†	85	housewife	58	"
2058						
	A	Hewes Walter A	85	engineer	61	"
	B	Riley George M	89	bookkeeper	79	"
	C	Wentworth Hattie L—†	89	housekeeper	47	Maine
	E	Malmquist Carl G	95	foreman	43	here
	F	Malmquist Edith B—†	95	housewife	46	"
	G	Malmquist Lorraine R—†	95	clerk	20	"
	H	Malmquist Muriel H—†	95	inspector	26	"
	K	Serror Napoleon	95	machinist	52	"
	L	Jordan Anna B—†	97	clerk	34	"
	M	Jordan Mary A—†	97	housewife	69	"
	N	Jordan William F	97	clerk	30	"
	O*	Keane Hubert	97	laborer	58	"
	P	Devlin John F	100	machinist	45	"
	R	Devlin Vesta L—†	100	housewife	44	"
	S	Diamond Samuel	101	retired	73	"
	T	Keenan Mary—†	101	housewife	54	"
	U	Keenan Peter	101	machinist	54	"
	V	Mulkern Helen M—†	105	housewife	34	"
	W	Mulkern James J	105	timekeeper	43	"
	X	Mulkern John L	105	"	46	"
	Y	Mulkern Pearl F—†	105	housewife	40	"
	Z	Kealey Beatrice—†	109	"	36	"
2059						
	A	Kealey Thomas J	109	foreman	38	"
	B	Rieger Otto J	113	laborer	22	"
	C	Veno Lena A—†	113	housewife	41	"
	D	Veno William H	113	inspector	48	"

Page	Letter	Full Name	Residence, Jan. 1, 1941	Occupation	Supposed Age	Reported Residence, Jan. 1, 1940. Street and Number

Westville Road

Page	Letter	Full Name	Residence	Occupation	Age	Reported Residence
	E	Casalis Jeanne †	25	housewife	46	here
	F	Casalis Joseph	25	toolmaker	53	"
	G	Casalis Joseph P, jr	25	machinist	22	"

Wolcott Court

Page	Letter	Full Name	Residence	Occupation	Age	Reported Residence
	L	*Pagington Charles	4	painter	65	113 Pierce
	M	Pagington George A	4	chauffeur	24	113 "
	N	*Pagington Rosalind V †	4	housewife	43	113 "
	O	Wax Ralph S	4	proprietor	22	113 "
	P	Pagington Anna J †	4	housewife	23	136 Dana av
	R	Pagington Fred T	4	plumber	28	136 "
	T	Galli Anthony	6	laborer	25	24 Prescott
	U	Galli John B	6	gardener	30	24 "
	V	*Galli Joseph	6	retired	66	24 "
	W	*Galli Loretta †	6	housewife	35	24 "
	X	*Galli Mary †	6	at home	26	24 "
	Y	McGrath Mary †	6	housewife	38	here
	Z	McGrath Robert T	6	mason	38	"
2060						
	A	McGrath James P	6	plasterer	44	"
	B	McGrath Margaret M †	6	housewife	44	"
	F	Hannon Edward	10	trainer	59	"
	G	Wright Anna C †	10	housewife	46	"
	H	Wright Francis E	10	clerk	24	"
	K	Wright Harold J	10	manager	48	"
	L	Wright Harriet J †	10	student	22	"
	M	Wright Vincent P	10	chauffeur	26	"
	N	McCallion Adelia D †	12	housewife	73	185 Nep [illegible]
	O	McCallion Peter	12	retired	73	185 "
	P	McCallion Peter W	12	machinist	33	185 "

Wolcott Square

Page	Letter	Full Name	Residence	Occupation	Age	Reported Residence
	T	O'Brien Joseph M	5	clerk	35	here
	U	O'Brien Michael J	5	retired	69	"
	V	Devine Breda A †	5	housekeeper	45	"

Wolcott Street

Page	Letter	Full Name	Residence	Occupation	Age	Reported Residence
2061						
	A	Cochrane Katherine †	16	housewife	58	here
	B	Cochrane Walter W	16	clerk	21	"

Page	Letter	Full Name.	Residence, Jan. 1, 1941.	Occupation.	Supposed Age	Reported Residence, Jan. 1, 1940. Street and Number.

Wolcott Street—Continued

Page	Letter	Full Name.	Residence, Jan. 1, 1941.	Occupation.	Supposed Age	Reported Residence, Jan. 1, 1940.
	C	Johns Eunice E—†	18	housewife	33	here
	D	Johns Harry J	18	painter	41	"
	E	Johns Julia A—†	18	housekeeper	66	"
	F	King Esther A—†	20	housewife	40	"
	G	King William J	20	chauffeur	38	"
	H	King Dorothy E—†	22	operator	32	Dedham
	K	King Nancy—†	22	housewife	72	here
	L	King Robert	22	chauffeur	35	"
	M	McNair Barbara B—†	24	housewife	28	Sharon
	N	McNair Thomas J	24	chauffeur	32	"
	O	Welliver Catherine—†	26	housewife	22	here
	P	Welliver Ray P	26	chauffeur	22	"
	R	Welliver Rhoda—†	26	housewife	54	"
	S	Welliver Staley J	26	merchant	56	"

Ward 18—Precinct 21

CITY OF BOSTON

LIST OF RESIDENTS
20 YEARS OF AGE AND OVER

(NON-CITIZENS INDICATED BY ASTERISK)
(FEMALES INDICATED BY DAGGER)

AS OF

JANUARY 1, 1941

JOSEPH F. TIMILTY, *Chairman*
FREDERIC E. DOWLING, *Secretary*
WILLIAM A. MOTLEY, JR.
FRANCIS B. McKINNEY
HILDA HEDSTROM QUIRK
Listing Board.

CITY OF BOSTON PRINTING DEPARTMENT

Page.	Letter.	Full Name.	Residence, Jan. 1, 1941.	Occupation.	Supposed Age.	Reported Residence, Jan. 1, 1940. Street and Number.

2100

Alabama Street

Page.	Letter.	Full Name.	Residence, Jan. 1, 1941.	Occupation.	Supposed Age.	Reported Residence, Jan. 1, 1940.
	A	Bennetts Alice V—†	148	housewife	41	here
	B	*Bennetts Leslie J	148	clerk	35	"
	C	*Ericson Oscar F	150	metalworker	58	"
	D	Ericson Selma E—†	150	housewife	57	"
	E	Northern Elfreda—†	154	"	44	"
	F	Northern Harry C	154	carpenter	50	"
	G	Wright Christina A—†	208	housekeeper	68	"

Babson Street

Page.	Letter.	Full Name.	Residence, Jan. 1, 1941.	Occupation.	Supposed Age.	Reported Residence, Jan. 1, 1940.
	H	Long Anna—†	85	clerk	31	here
	K	Long Francis	85	engineer	29	"
	L	McDonough Joseph	85	machinist	30	3 Whitney pk
	M	McDonough Mary M—†	85	hairdresser	22	3 "
	N	Fitzgerald Helen—†	91	housewife	65	here
	O	Fitzgerald Mary—†	91	secretary	34	"
	P	Fitzgerald Michael	91	barber	70	"
	R	Nelson Gerda—†	91	housewife	64	64 Tacoma
	S	Nelson Victor N	91	watchman	65	64 "
	T	Williams Catherine—†	91	operator	31	here
	U	Beecher Catherine—†	95	at home	77	"
	V	O'Keefe Elizabeth—†	95	housewife	74	"
	W	Warshauer Charles S	97	attorney	65	"
	X	Warshauer Gertrude—†	97	clerk	52	"
	Y	Smart Blanche—†	99	housewife	50	"
	Z	Smart Edward	99	chauffeur	50	"
2101						
	A	Smart Evelyn	99	clerk	22	"
	B	Smart Gwendolyn—†	99	"	25	"
	C	Smart Norman	99	"	20	"
	D	Fenno George	101	retired	74	"
	E	Scannell Abigail A—†	103	teacher	61	"
	F	*Scannell Marion L—†	103	"	38	"
	G	Bradley Mary E—†	109	nurse	61	Brookline
	H	Nicholson Murdock	109	contractor	60	here
	K	Conley Anna C—†	111	housewife	40	"
	L	Conley Michael	111	operator	42	"
	M	Conley Robert	111	clerk	22	"
	N	McCormack Alice G—†	111	"	31	"
	O	McCormack Catherine—†	111	housewife	61	"

Page	Letter	Full Name	Residence, Jan. 1, 194[illegible]	Occupation	Supposed Age	Reported Residence, Jan. 1, 194[illegible]. Street and Number

Babson Street—Continued

Page	Letter	Full Name	Residence	Occupation	Age	Reported Residence
	P	McCormack John E	111	seaman	32	here
	R	McCormack Mary E †	111	hairdresser	28	"
	S	McCormack Richard J	111	clerk	21	"
	T	McCormack Rita C—†	111	"	26	"
	U	McCormack Ronald A	111	doorman	66	"
	V	*McGlame James	111	plumber	50	"
	W	McGlame John	111	"	24	"
	X	McGlame Mary—†	111	clerk	26	"
	Y	*McGlame Sarah—†	111	housewife	49	"
	Z	Siegel Benjamin	113 115	merchant	45	"
2102						
	A	Siegel Rebecca—†	113 115	housewife	43	"
	B	Rais Harry A	113 115	metalworker	59	20 Fannee rd
	C	Rais Joseph	113–115	clerk	26	20 "
	D	Rais Louise	113–115	"	20	20 "
	E	Rais Margaret—†	113–115	housewife	57	20 "
	F	Dinand Augustine	117	accountant	25	here
	G	Dinand Dorothea—†	117	teacher	29	"
	H	Dinand Grace K—†	117	housewife	58	"
	K	Dinand John F	117	supervisor	64	"
	L	Dinand Joseph C	117	clerk	27	"

Blue Hill Avenue

Page	Letter	Full Name	Residence	Occupation	Age	Reported Residence
	N	Cottuli Blanche—†	1515	housewife	41	here
	O	Cottuli Edward	1515	mechanic	41	"
	P	Foley Patrick J	1515	engineer	69	"
	R	McDonald Charles	1515	tender	44	"
	S	Sheridan Agnes—†	1515	housewife	41	"
	T	Caliri Charles	1515	barber	44	"
	U	Caliri Isabelle—†	1515	housewife	40	"
	W	Flaherty Elizabeth G †	1516	"	52	"
	X	Flaherty Elizabeth G †	1516	inspector	28	"
	Y	Flaherty Margaret E †	1516	operator	31	"
	Z	Flaherty Patrick J	1516	molder	55	"
2103						
	A	McGowan Andrew	1516	clerk	50	"
	B	McGowan Molly—†	1516	housewife	43	"
	C	McGowan William	1516	baker	21	"
	D	Kramer Minnie—†	1517	housewife	61	"
	E	Pearl Benjamin	1517	mechanic	44	"

Page.	Letter.	FULL NAME.	Residence, Jan. 1, 1941.	Occupation.	Supposed Age.	Reported Residence, Jan. 1, 1940. Street and Number.

Blue Hill Avenue—Continued

Page.	Letter.	FULL NAME.	Residence, Jan. 1, 1941.	Occupation.	Supposed Age.	Reported Residence, Jan. 1, 1940.
	F	Pearl Ida—†	1517	housewife	39	here
	G	White Frances—†	1517	"	36	"
	H	White John F, jr	1517	builder	34	"
	K	Lamb Elmer	1517	chauffeur	45	"
	L	Lamb Florence—†	1517	housewife	48	"
	M	Fleming Dorothy—†	1518	clerk	30	"
	N	Fleming Julia—†	1518	housewife	62	"
	O	Fleming Timothy	1518	papermaker	33	"
	P	Fleming Walter	1518	"	26	"
	R	Kennedy Charles R	1518	U S A	22	"
	S	Kennedy Helen—†	1518	secretary	29	"
	T	Kennedy Martin F	1518	gardener	56	"
	U	Kennedy Martin J	1518	engineer	31	"
	V	Kennedy Phillip J	1518	clerk	20	"
	W	Kennedy Theresa—†	1518	housewife	54	"
	X	Melia Joseph F	1518	plumber	47	"
	Y	Murphy Daniel	1518	attendant	20	"
	Z	Murphy Mary—†	1518	housewife	51	"
2104						
	A	Lipman Benjamin	1519	salesman	51	"
	B	Lipman Henrietta—†	1519	housewife	48	"
	C	Prives Ada—†	1519	"	28	"
	D	Prives Benjamin	1519	dentist	29	"
	E	Gilmore Enid—†	1519	clerk	22	"
	F	Miller Edith—†	1519	housewife	47	"
	G	Spellman Max	1519	chauffeur	42	"
	H	Spellman Rose—†	1519	housewife	40	"
	K	Kanaris John E	1525	waiter	51	"
	L	Mastorakis Mary—†	1525	housewife	37	"
	M	Mastorakis Nickolas	1525	restaurateur	53	"
	N	Walsh Arthur J	1525	clerk	26	60 Jamaicaway
	O	Walsh Margaret M—†	1525	"	31	60 "
	P	Walsh Margaret V—†	1525	housewife	58	60 "
	R	Finnerty John J	1537	mechanic	55	here
	S	Davie Annie—†	1553	housewife	48	"
	T	Davie Thomas S	1553	plasterer	49	"
	U	Champlin Emma—†	1557	housekeeper	73	"
	V	Jones Georgia—†	1557	"	73	"
	W	Neville Minnie—†	1557	housewife	51	"
	X	Neville William J	1557	clerk	55	"
	Y	Preen Alice G—†	1557	stenographer	43	"

Page	Letter	Full Name	Residence, Jan. 1, 1941	Occupation	Supposed Age	Reported Residence, Jan. 1, 1940. Street and Number

Blue Hill Avenue—Continued

Page	Letter	Full Name	Residence	Occupation	Supposed Age	Reported Residence
	z	Preen Dorothy E †	1557	operator	39	here
2105						
	A	Ruth William F	1557	fireman	65	"
	B	Hanscom Isaiah C	1557	retired	70	"
	C	Hanscom Maude H †	1557	housewife	75	"
	R	Swenson Catherine †	1585	"	28	683 Mass av
	S	Swenson Peter	1585	mechanic	33	683 "
	U*	Gregis Louis	1589	"	49	here
	V*	Gregis Rachel †	1589	housewife	44	"
	W	Fletcher Marion †	1589	"	39	"
	X	Meagher Alice D †	1589	saleswoman	27	"
	Y	Meagher Doris V †	1589	clerk	21	"
	Z	Meagher Edward R	1589	retired	65	"
2106						
	A	Meagher Mary7†	1589	housewife	62	"
	B	Dalton Miriam †	1589	waitress	23	Milton
	C	Dalton William	1589	stockman	30	"
	D	Diemer Ada †	1589	beautician	29	19 Davison

2107 Brockton Street

Page	Letter	Full Name	Residence	Occupation	Supposed Age	Reported Residence
	P	Gusow Arthur M	6	musician	45	here
	R	Gusow Harriet †	6	housewife	47	"
	S	Stroock Louis	6	salesman	75	"
	T	Miller Celia †	6	housewife	42	"
	U	Miller Mildred †	6	stenographer	20	"
	V	Miller William	6	merchant	45	"
	W	Stoller Harry A	8	engineer	38	"
	X	Stoller Rachel †	8	housewife	37	"
	Y	Mandell Hilda S †	8	hygienist	21	"
	Z*	Mandell Jacob	8	steamfitter	49	"
2108						
	A	Mandell Mildred †	8	housewife	40	"
	B	Melone Joseph	9	mason	45	"
	C	Melone Theresa †	9	housewife	39	"
	D	Haffer Arthur	10	candymaker	36	"
	E	Haffer Hilda D †	10	housewife	32	"
	G	Singer Abraham	12	painter	38	"
	H	Singer Shirley †	12	housewife	37	"
	K	Singer Sarah †	12	housekeeper	68	"
	L	Stangel Carl	12	shipper	36	"

Page.	Letter	Full Name.	Residence, Jan. 1, 1941.	Occupation.	Supposed Age.	Reported Residence, Jan. 1, 1940. Street and Number.

Brockton Street—Continued

Page.	Letter	Full Name.	Residence, Jan. 1, 1941.	Occupation.	Supposed Age.	Reported Residence, Jan. 1, 1940. Street and Number.
	M	Stangel Edith—†	12	housewife	31	here
	N*	Murphy Bridget M—†	14	"	46	"
	O	Murphy Jeremiah F	14	chauffeur	40	"
	P	Smith Esther—†	15	housewife	25	32 Ransom rd
	R	Smith Oscar	15	manager	27	32 "
	S	Singer Frances—†	15	housewife	26	here
	T	Singer Max	15	machinist	29	"
	U	Goldstein Albert	16	merchant	37	16 Hosmer
	V*	Goldstein Helen—†	16	housewife	35	16 "
	W	Flaschner Max	16	butcher	58	here
	X	Flaschner Yetta—†	16	housewife	64	"
	Y	Kriensky Bessie R—†	17	"	26	"
	Z	Kriensky Paul J	17	salesman	29	"
2109						
	A	Levine Benjamin	17	clerk	21	"
	B	Levine Louis	17	barber	24	"
	C	Levine Rebecca—†	17	housewife	56	"
	D*	Kamenetsky Alexander	19	carpenter	42	"
	E*	Kamenetsky Frances—†	19	housewife	38	"
	F	Starr Harold H	19	salesman	35	143 Columbia rd
	G	Starr Ruth—†	19	housewife	31	143 "
	H	Cantor Adeline—†	21	"	32	here
	K	Cantor Manuel	21	merchant	35	"
	L	Zanfani Louise M—†	21	domestic	22	"
	M	Haffer Harry N	21	plumber	29	"
	N	Haffer Sadie—†	21	housewife	59	"
	O	Haffer Selma—†	21	"	29	"
	P*	Salomone Alfonso	29	chef	42	"
	R	Salomone Rose—†	29	housewife	32	"
	S	Coffin Florence A—†	30	"	49	"
	T	Coffin Robert W	30	machinist	21	"
	U	Coffin Walter S	30	"	47	"
	V*	Anderson Gertrude A—†	31	housewife	33	"
	W*	Anderson William G	31	molder	36	"

Chester Park

Page.	Letter	Full Name.	Residence, Jan. 1, 1941.	Occupation.	Supposed Age.	Reported Residence, Jan. 1, 1940. Street and Number.
	X	Lind Augustus H	1	wool sorter	56	here
	Y	Riley George	1	retired	71	"
	Z	Scholl Paul A	1	"	54	"

Page.	Letter.	Full Name.	Residence, Jan. 1, 1941.	Occupation.	Supposed Age.	Reported Residence, Jan. 1, 1940. Street and Number.
2110						
		Chester Park Continued				
	A	Scholl Victor A	1	welder	25	here
	B	Rowlands Barbara B—†	3	housewife	31	"
	C	Rowlands Grafton R	3	policeman	45	"
	D	Maguire James R	5	machinist	48	"
	E	Maguire Mary A—†	5	housewife	78	"
	F	Maguire Veronica V—†	5	clerk	40	"
		Colorado Street				
	G	*King Mary—†	161	housekeeper	76	here
	H	King Michael J	161	retired	72	"
	K	*Kallias Jerothios	170	waiter	54	37 Rexford
	L	O'Neil James	170	carpenter	68	here
	M	O'Neil Mary—†	170	housewife	71	"
	N	*Poulos Constantina—†	170	"	40	37 Rexford
	O	Poulos James	170	cook	47	37 "
	P	Johnson Anna T—†	196	housewife	42	Braintree
	R	Johnson Sigurd L	196	paperhanger	38	"
		Cummins Highway				
	S	Canniff Anne M—†	548	secretary	24	here
	T	Carew Estella E—†	548	housewife	33	"
	U	Carew John J	548	operator	34	"
	V	Foley Barbara—†	568	clerk	21	"
	W	Foley Delia—†	568	housewife	39	"
	X	Foley John	568	policeman	45	"
	Y	Libby Albert J	568	chauffeur	56	"
	Z	Libby Alice H—†	568	housewife	46	"
2111						
	A	Libby Harold E	568	optician	23	"
	B	McGarity Daniel J	586	manager	52	Maryland
	C	McGarity Ethel W—†	586	housewife	50	"
	D	Cistoldi Emilio	586	mason	60	here
	E	Cistoldi Mary—†	586	clerk	23	"
	F	Cistoldi Rita—†	586	housewife	57	"
	G	Cistoldi Francis A	586	mason	34	"
	H	Cistoldi Linda—†	586	housewife	34	"
	K	Connell James	590–592	laborer	60	"
	L	O'Brien Catherine—†	590–592	housewife	64	"

Page.	Letter.	Full Name.	Residence Jan. 1, 1941.	Occupation.	Supposed Age.	Reported Residence, Jan. 1, 1940. Street and Number.

Cummins Highway—Continued

Page.	Letter.	Full Name.	Residence Jan. 1, 1941.	Occupation.	Supposed Age.	Reported Residence, Jan. 1, 1940. Street and Number.
	M	Saef Gertrude—†	590–592	housewife	45	here
	N	Saef Leon	590–592	merchant	58	"
	O	Saef Phillip M	590–592	"	27	"
	P	Boynton Herbert	590–592	clerk	34	"
	R	Pergantides George	590–592	retired	53	"
	S	Pergantides Michael	590–592	pharmacist	27	"
	V	Frangioso Angelina—†	622	housewife	47	"
	W	Frangioso Carmino	622	contractor	53	"
	X	Frangioso Mary—†	622	clerk	23	"
	Y	Doyle Edward F	624–626	fireman	56	"
	Z	Doyle Harold G	624–626	printer	26	"
2112						
	A	Doyle Helen T—†	624–626	housewife	50	"
	B	Keenan Robert T	624–626	pressman	43	350 Cummins H'way
	C	Ferrari Josephine—†	628–630	housewife	26	here
	D	Ferrari Stephen	628–630	machinist	32	"
	E	Lavena Joseph	628–630	barber	58	"
	F	Lavena Josephine—†	628–630	housewife	60	"
	G	Wraga Agnes—†	628–630	clerk	20	"
	H	Carr Albert C	632–634	chauffeur	33	25 Charme av
	K	Carr Elizabeth—†	632–634	housewife	28	25 "
	L	Forrest Catherine—†	632–634	"	37	here
	M	Forrest Edward J	632–634	clerk	40	"
	N	O'Sullivan Mary E—†	640	housewife	36	"
	O	O'Sullivan Timothy F	640	switchman	35	"
	P	Goggin John P	640	manager	34	"
	R	Goggin Mary—†	640	housewife	33	"
	S	Padula Josephine—†	644–646	"	26	32 Weybosset
	T	Padula Pasquale	644–646	salesman	30	1 Lawrence ct
	U	Crognalo Crescenzo	644–646	engineer	43	here
	V	Frangiose Joseph	644–646	"	42	"
	W	Gelsomini Lena—†	644–646	housekeeper	60	"
	X	O'Brien Francis J	648–650	letter carrier	36	"
	Y	O'Brien Helen M—†	648–650	housewife	35	"
	Z	Burns James E	648–650	student	23	"
2113						
	A	Burns James P	648–650	clerk	55	"
	B	Burns Madeline—†	648–650	"	20	"
	C	Burns Mary—†	648–650	housewife	53	"
	D	Sullivan Michael	658	mechanic	36	"

Page.	Letter	Full Name	Residence, Jan. 1, 1941	Occupation	Supposed Age	Reported Residence, Jan. 1, 1940. Street and Number

Cummins Highway—Continued

Page.	Letter	Full Name	Residence, Jan. 1, 1941	Occupation	Supposed Age	Reported Residence, Jan. 1, 1940. Street and Number
	E	Sullivan Mildred—†	658	housewife	35	here
	F	Lynch Helen—†	658	"	26	"
	G	Lynch Herbert	658	policeman	30	"
	H	*Struch Ernest	662	laborer	39	New York
	K	*Struch Lotte—†	662	housewife	37	"
	L	DeVoe Alice—†	662	"	45	here
	M	DeVoe Henry	662	cashier	51	"
	N	Carnegie Phyllis M—†	675	clerk	40	"
	O	Gould Mary E—†	675	housewife	75	"
	P	Bradley Helen P—†	675	clerk	36	"
	R	Bradley Irma M—†	675	teacher	26	"
	S	Bradley Marguerite E—†	675	secretary	29	"
	T	Bradley Mary A—†	675	housewife	59	"
	U	Bradley Thomas	675	stonecutter	61	"
	V	Petersen Berger	677	painter	37	"
	W	Petersen Ellen E—†	677	housewife	34	"
	X	Rasmus Florence—†	677	"	37	"
	Y	Rasmus Stanley	677	draftsman	48	"
	Z	Lange Freida—†	677	housekeeper	58	"
2114						
	B	Cairns Catherine C—†	687	housewife	63	"
	C	Cairns Eleanor C—†	687	librarian	31	"
	D	Cairns Nancy J—†	687	saleswoman	22	"
	E	Cairns Norman W	687	manager	29	"
	F	Cairns Robert H	687	policeman	25	"
	G	Cairns Simon P	687	dentist	67	"
	H	Visnick Benjamin	690	mechanic	59	"
	K	Visnick Fanny—†	690	housewife	55	"
	L	Visnick Henry	690	attendant	28	"
	M	*Visnick Sylvia—†	690	housewife	23	Rhode Island
	N	*Weingeroff Fanny—†	690	"	48	"
	O	Weingeroff Morris	690	carpenter	49	"
	R	Lane Annie—†	711	at home	84	here
	S	O'Neil Marion T—†	711	housewife	48	"
	T	O'Neil Patrick F	711	B F D	52	"
	U	Kane Gertrude E—†	715	stenographer	35	"
	V	Kane William J	715	student	21	"
	W	Kane William O	715	chauffeur	50	"
	X	McLaughlin John	731	merchant	39	"
	Y	McLaughlin Sarah A—†	731	housewife	30	"

Page.	Letter.	Full Name.	Residence, Jan. 1, 1941.	Occupation.	Supposed Age.	Reported Residence, Jan. 1, 1940. Street and Number.

Cummins Highway—Continued

Page.	Letter.	Full Name.	Residence, Jan. 1, 1941.	Occupation.	Supposed Age.	Reported Residence, Jan. 1, 1940. Street and Number.
	Z	Hannon Anna C—†	731	housewife	30	here
2115						
	A	Hannon Delia A—†	731	"	62	"
	B	Hannon John J	731	gardener	71	"
	C	Hannon Thomas J	731	clerk	33	"
	D	Haines Clarence J	733	ironworker	53	"
	E	Haines Eleanor H—†	733	housewife	65	"
	F	Haines Martha W—†	733	at home	76	"
	G	King Anna—†	734–736	artist	23	188 Tudor
	H	King Catherine—†	734–736	housewife	62	188 "
	K	O'Brien James M	734–736	salesman	37	here
	L	O'Brien Mary H—†	734–736	housewife	33	"
	M	DiTullio Amadeo	734–736	painter	28	"
	N	DiTullio Annette—†	734–736	operator	29	"
	O	DiTullio Triestina—†	734–736	clerk	24	"
	P	Burns Martha—†	734–736	housewife	43	12 Hopewell rd
	R	Burns Robert	734–736	cableman	41	12 "
	S	Tagen Mary A—†	735	housewife	53	here
	T	Tagen Robert J	735	salesman	56	"
	U	Brooks Catherine—†	738–740	housewife	43	"
	V	Brooks George H	738–740	salesman	57	"
	W	Brooks George W	738–740	machinist	21	"
	X	Langlois Henry J	738–740	merchant	54	N Hampshire
	Y	Langlois Irene R—†	738–740	housewife	50	"
	Z	Langlois Walter	738–740	clerk	28	33 Lexington av
2116						
	A	McCarthy Agnes A—†	738–740	hairdresser	45	here
	B	McCarthy Cornelius	738–740	inspector	40	"
	C	Morgan Margaret—†	739	housewife	37	"
	D	Morgan William	739	policeman	40	"
	E	Meere Annie—†	739	housewife	50	"
	F	Meere Patrick	739	chauffeur	53	"
	G	Tack Dorothy—†	742–744	housewife	37	"
	H	Tack George	742–744	compositor	38	"
	K	Kostecki Fred	742–744	laborer	48	"
	L	Kostecki Joseph	742–744	baker	24	"
	M	*Kostecki Josephine—†	742–744	housewife	46	"
	S	Bennett Irene M	747	teacher	25	"
	N	Bernacky Helen—†	747	"	31	"
	O	*Bernacky Jadwiga—†	747	housewife	54	"
	P	Bernacky Stanley J	747	machinist	60	"

Page	Letter	Full Name	Residence Jan. 1, 1941	Occupation	Reported Age	Reported Residence Jan. 1, 1940. Street and Number
		Cummins Highway—Continued				
	R	Bernacky Zygmund	747	machinist	30	here
	T	Mack Lillian †	751	operator	41	"
	U	O'Brien Louise †	751	housewife	63	"
	V	O'Brien Zoe †	751	factoryhand	53	"
	W	Russell Edward	751	laborer	25	"
	X	Russell Margaret—†	751	at home	65	"
	Y	Sexton Anna E—†	754	housewife	47	"
	Z	Sexton Thomas L	754	roofer	47	"
2117						
	A	Scannell Catherine—†	754	housewife	53	"
	B	Scannell Raymond	754	student	21	"
	C	Scannell William H	754	salesman	57	"
	D	Scannell William H, jr	754	"	24	"
	G	Freaney James A	864	clerk	24	"
	H	Freaney James J	864	steamfitter	51	"
	K	Freaney May—†	864	housewife	50	"
	L	Fortin Mary E—†	864	"	42	"
	M	Fortin Perfer P	864	policeman	42	"
	N	Kalish Elizabeth—†	864	housewife	52	"
	O	Kalish Lawrence C	864	shipper	26	"
	P	Kalish Mary K—†	864	housewife	23	"
	R	Nelson Genevieve—†	864	waitress	28	"
	T	Messerli Agnes—†	876	housewife	66	"
	U	Messerli Frederick	876	realtor	66	"
	V	Hershorn Joseph	876	accountant	45	S Carolina
	W	Hershorn Wynne—†	876	housewife	40	"
	X	Heald Margaret B—†	876	teacher	37	"
	Y	Polley Edith M—†	876	"	34	"
	Z	Maus Rose—†	876	housewife	55	882 Cummins H'way
2118						
	A	Ludy Dorothy—†	876	clerk	28	592 River
	B	Ludy Marion—†	876	secretary	34	592 "
	C	Messerli Ruth—†	876	nurse	42	here
	D	Dugan Margaret—†	878	housekeeper	82	"
	E	Gavin Ruth C—†	878	clerk	34	"
	F	Ford Agnes—†	878	housewife	29	"
	G	Ford Joseph	878	attorney	26	"
	H	Hayden Elizabeth—†	878	"	72	"
	K	Hayden Harold	878	"	40	"
	L	Mahoney Ellen—†	878	housewife	77	"
	M	Mahoney Mary—†	878	clerk	37	"

Page	Letter	Full Name	Residence, Jan. 1, 1941	Occupation	Supposed Age	Reported Residence, Jan. 1, 1940. Street and Number.

Cummins Highway—Continued

Page	Letter	Full Name	Residence, Jan. 1, 1941	Occupation	Supposed Age	Reported Residence, Jan. 1, 1940. Street and Number.
	N	O'Donnell Anna—†	878	stenographer	51	here
	O	Hausding Josephine—†	878	housewife	68	"
	P	Cornell Eileen—†	878	"	36	20 Ellison av
	R	Cornell Guy	878	machinist	40	20 "
	S	Anderson Ellen—†	878	housewife	63	here
	T	Anderson Harry G	878	artist	35	"
	U	Brennan Agnes G—†	878	housewife	75	"
	V	Brennan Agnes M—†	878	clerk	32	"
	W	Brennan John A	878	retired	75	"
	X	Holland Frances—†	880	teacher	50	601 River
	Y	Kernachan Elizabeth M—†	880	librarian	43	601 "
	Z	Bruce Isabella—†	880	housewife	55	here
2119						
	A	Bruce William	880	salesman	59	"
	B	Edmonston Marjorie—†	880	clerk	28	"
	C	Herter Edith M—†	880	housekeeper	53	"
	D	Herter Lillian—†	880	teacher	52	"
	E	Sullivan Annie M—†	880	housekeeper	69	"
	F	Dunn Hannah—†	880	housewife	54	"
	G	Dunn John	880	leather sorter	53	"
	H	Brennan Agnes G—†	880	teacher	42	"
	K	Farrell Francis H	882	analyst	46	799 E Third
	L	Farrell Mary K—†	882	stenographer	45	Winthrop
	M	DeArmit Eugenie—†	882	nurse	28	876 Cummins H'way
	N	Stewart Mary—†	882	"	31	876 "
	O	Leary Adeline—†	882	housewife	65	here
	P	McCarthy Lucy—†	882	at home	80	"
	R	Brown Florence—†	882	clerk	34	"
	S	Brown Marion M—†	882	"	39	"
	T	Lyon Kathleen B—†	882	"	28	"
	U	Lyon Pauline L—†	882	librarian	30	"
	V	Lyon Sara A—†	882	"	49	"
	W	Simons Max	884	merchant	42	"
	X	Simons Ruth—†	884	housewife	29	"
	Y	Curley George A	884	physician	28	41 Mt Hope
	Z	Curley Katherine—†	884	housewife	29	6 Holborn
2120						
	A	Robinson Rudolph	884	attorney	39	here
	B	Maass Catherine—†	884	housewife	73	"
	C	Brown Henry J	884	retired	73	"
	D	Brown Katherine—†	884	housewife	73	"

Cummins Highway Continued

Page	Letter	Full Name	Residence, Jan. 1, 1941	Occupation	Supposed Age	Reported Residence, Jan. 1, 1940, Street and Number
	E	Fitzgerald Margaret—†	884	at home	65	3 Monadnock
	F	Hebert Dorothy—†	884	teacher	34	here
	G	Whitcomb Helen—†	884	"	32	"
	H	Hughes Catherine M—†	884	artist	31	New York
	K	Hughes Estella M—†	884	housewife	51	Milton
	L	Hughes Frank S	884	manager	65	"
	M	Blais Jeanne—†	884	hairdresser	40	here
	N	Casey John	886	attendant	26	"
	O	Casey Lena—†	886	housewife	26	"
	P	Shaw Laura L—†	886	"	62	"
	R	Bryan Florence M—†	886	"	57	"
	S	Bryan William	886	engraver	63	"
	T	Moran Anna M—†	886	housewife	37	"
	U	Moran Harry	886	fireman	47	"
	V	Morris Beatrice A—†	886	clerk	42	"
	W	Graham Margaret—†	886	"	48	884 Cummins H'way
	X	Fitzgerald Katherine M—†	886	"	57	here

Favre Street

Page	Letter	Full Name	Residence, Jan. 1, 1941	Occupation	Supposed Age	Reported Residence, Jan. 1, 1940, Street and Number
2121						
	E	Cohen David R	14–16	salesman	35	here
	F	Cohen Shirley—†	14–16	housewife	35	"
	G	*Anderson Alma E—†	14–16	"	52	"
	H	*Anderson Andrew	14–16	metalworker	53	"
	K	Binder Fay F—†	21	housewife	25	305 Fuller
	L	Binder Hyman	21	foreman	34	305 "
	M	*Binder Julius	21	salesman	27	305 "
	N	Gorfinkle Edna—†	21	housewife	35	here
	O	Gorfinkle George N	21	salesman	41	"
	P	Halperin Harry	25	attorney	39	"
	R	Halperin Ruth—†	25	housewife	36	"
	T	Rabinovitz Abraham J	29	attorney	32	25 Rexford
	U	Rabinovitz Esther—†	29	housewife	27	25 "
	V	Flashner Esther—†	29	bookkeeper	23	here
	W	Flashner Gertrude—†	29	housewife	40	"
	X	Flashner Samuel	29	manufacturer	54	"
	Y	Harris Bertha E—†	33	saleswoman	23	"
	Z	Harris Max S	33	merchant	49	"
2122						
	A	Harris Pearl—†	33	housewife	45	"
	B	Reynolds Lawrence W	33	salesman	33	"

Favre Street—Continued

Page	Letter	Full Name	Residence, Jan. 1, 1941	Occupation	Supposed Age	Reported Residence, Jan. 1, 1940. Street and Number
	C	*David Sarah—†	33	housekeeper	63	5 Winston rd
	D	Toeman Abraham	33	agent	36	5 "
	E	*Toeman Miriam B—†	33	housewife	31	5 "
	F	Pofcher Aaron	37	agent	35	here
	G	Pofcher Eva—†	37	housewife	32	"
	H	Bello Harry	37	merchant	41	"
	K	Bello Sara—†	37	housewife	36	"
	L	Bornstein Rose—†	41	"	43	"
	M	Bornstein Samuel	41	clerk	46	"
	P	*Koon Rose O—†	41	housekeeper	61	New York
	N	Lipson Annie—†	41	housewife	70	here
	O	Lipson Morris	41	retired	70	"
	R	Chartier Marie M—†	45	housewife	62	"
	S	Chartier Parker G	45	clerk	21	"
	T	Chartier Rosabel—†	45	stenographer	37	"
	U	Chartier Wilfred J	45	chauffeur	32	"
	V	Bello Celia—†	45	housewife	28	"
	W	Bello Jacob	45	electrician	35	"
	X	Navisky Benjamin	46	salesman	37	"
	Y	Navisky Freida—†	46	housewife	35	"
	Z	Gertel Lena—†	46	"	40	54 Winston rd
2123						
	A	Gertel Louis	46	manager	48	54 "
	B	Bello Coleman A	49	merchant	31	here
	C	Bello Rose—†	49	housewife	25	"
	D	Bello Samuel	49	merchant	29	"
	E	Bello Sarah—†	49	housewife	28	"
	F	Block David	50	foreman	38	"
	G	Block Shirley—†	50	housewife	38	"
	H	Kaplan Sally—†	50	"	25	"
	K	Kaplan Samuel	50	engineer	27	"
	L	Comi Ernest J	53	manager	35	"
	M	Comi Ines M—†	53	housewife	30	"
	N	Gorfinkle David	53	attorney	34	"
	O	Gorfinkle Helen F—†	53	housewife	33	"
	P	Feitelberg Eunice—†	54	"	34	25 Favre
	R	Feitelberg Sydney	54	pressman	38	25 "
	S	Sirk Eva—†	54	housewife	34	11 Brenton
	T	Sirk Frank A	54	salesman	34	11 "
	U	Falk Edward J	57	newsdealer	42	here
	V	*Falk Etta—†	57	housewife	39	"

Page	Letter	Full Name	Residence, Jan. 1, [illegible]	Occupation	Supposed Age	Reported Residence, Jan. 1, [illegible] Street and Number

Favre Street Continued

Page	Letter	Full Name	Residence	Occupation	Supposed Age	Reported Residence
	W	Carlin Pearl M †	57	housewife	43	here
	X	Carlin William D	57	supervisor	45	"
	Y	Messenger Esther †	57	housekeeper	48	"
	Z*	Messenger Jacob	57	retired	80	"
2124						
	A	Cantor Anna †	58	housewife	35	"
	B	Cantor Charles	58	operator	35	"
	C	Brown Samuel	58	"	55	"
	D*	Brown Sarah †	58	housewife	53	"
	E	Brown Victor	58	operator	23	"
	F	Gotthardt Celia †	61	housewife	38	"
	G	Gotthardt Emma †	61	"	72	"
	H	Gotthardt Joshua	61	salesman	44	"
	K	Mann Celia †	61	housewife	35	"
	L	Mann Lawrence	61	manager	38	"
	M	Stallions Joseph	62	superintendent	40	"
	N*	Stallions Libby †	62	housewife	38	"
	O	Mann Ida B †	62	"	40	"
	P	Mann Sumner	62	florist	41	"

Fremont Street

Page	Letter	Full Name	Residence	Occupation	Supposed Age	Reported Residence
	T*	Phillips George L	8	manager	62	here
	U	Phillips Margaret J †	8	housewife	57	"
	W	Erickson Margaret E †	8	"	34	"
	X	Erickson Sydney F	8	dispatcher	34	"
	Y	Desmond Adelaide †	8	clerk	52	"
	Z	Baker Helen A †	12	housewife	68	"
2125						
	A	Baker Helen M †	12	clerk	22	"
	B*	Crocker Barbara †	12	housewife	48	"
	C	Crocker Clarence	12	chauffeur	40	"
	D	King Doris †	12	housewife	24	28 Rexford
	E	King James	12	clerk	28	28 "
	F	Cosgrove Edward L	14	"	43	here
	G	Cosgrove Elizabeth †	14	housewife	79	"
	H	Cosgrove Frances M †	14	clerk	51	"
	L	Ellis Helen L †	14	dressmaker	45	"
	M	Ellis Helen L †	14	student	20	"
	K	Ellis James L	14	plumber	23	"

Page.	Letter.	Full Name.	Residence, Jan. 1, 1941.	Occupation.	Supposed Age.	Reported Residence, Jan. 1, 1940. Street and Number.

Greenfield Road

Page.	Letter.	Full Name.	Residence, Jan. 1, 1941.	Occupation.	Supposed Age.	Reported Residence, Jan. 1, 1940.
	N	*Homan Edna—†	69	housewife	54	here
	O	Homan Elmer	69	laborer	24	"
	P	Boccuzzi Amato	77–79	"	38	"
	R	Boccuzzi Frances M—†	77–79	housewife	32	"
	S	Colleran Eileen R—†	77–79	teacher	47	"
	T	*Fardie Donald P	81–83	machinist	24	"
	U	*Fardie Mabel I—†	81–83	housewife	50	"
	V	*Fardie William G	81–83	salesman	51	"
	W	*Fardie William H	81–83	mechanic	22	"
	X	Glynn Anne M—†	81–83	waitress	33	586 Cummins H'way
	Y	Glynn Thomas H	81–83	mechanic	40	586 "
	Z	Gunn John K	81–83	retired	67	586 "
2126						
	A	Beucler Cecilia B—†	85–87	housewife	34	here
	B	Beucler George F	85–87	bridgetender	57	"
	C	Beucler Thomas C	85–87	manager	42	"
	E	Jakubanis Felix	89	machinist	58	"
	F	*Jakubanis Stella—†	89	housewife	47	"
	G	Mahoney Edwin P	89	welder	27	Somerville
	H	Mahoney Gertrude—†	89	housewife	29	"
	K	Rosenfield Mary A—†	97	"	33	16 Miles
	L	Rosenfield Morris	97	manager	42	16 "
	M	*Chopek Josephine—†	97	housewife	50	here
	N	Chopek Stephen	97	baker	48	"
	O	McGuire Ellen R—†	117	housewife	45	"
	P	McGuire Frank J	117	welder	43	"
	R	Chopek Anna—†	117	attorney	28	"
	S	Chopek Elias	117	janitor	52	"
	T	Chopek Mary—†	117	housewife	50	"
	U	Bassett Edith T—†	125	"	55	"
	V	Bassett George E	125	foreman	55	"
	W	Coombs Isabella M—†	125	at home	86	"
	X	Sawyer Mary E—†	125	"	82	"
	Y	Moran Annie J—†	125	housewife	40	"
	Z	Moran Luke	125	policeman	41	"
2127						
	A	Thompson Alfred V	131	proprietor	43	"
	B	*Thompson Rosa D—†	131	housewife	45	"
	C	Rooney Anne M—†	131	"	35	"
	D	Rooney Francis M	131	switchman	36	"

Page	Letter	Full Name.	Residence, Jan. 1, 1941.	Occupation.	Supposed Age.	Reported Residence, Jan. 1, 1940. Street and Number.

Hallowell Street

Page	Letter	Full Name.	Residence, Jan. 1, 1941.	Occupation.	Supposed Age.	Reported Residence, Jan. 1, 1940. Street and Number.
	E	*Persico Letitia †	8	housewife	46	here
	F	Persico Peter	8	laborer	52	"
	G	*McKendall Cecilia M †	11	housewife	32	509 Park Drive
	H	McKendall William E	11	attorney	35	509 "
	K	Holtz A George	15	salesman	41	16 Abbot
	L	Holtz Anna †	15	housewife	34	16 "
	M	Eskin Rae E †	17	"	40	29 Favre
	N	Eskin Simon S	17	salesman	44	29 "
	O	Brennan Daniel J	19	mechanic	46	here
	P	Brennan Myrtle F †	19	housewife	36	"
	R	Masterson Bernard G	19	carpetlayer	48	"
	S	Masterson Josephine E †	19	housewife	46	"
	T	Svendbye Alfhild †	21	saleswoman	29	"
	U	Svendbye Henry G	21	machinist	33	"
	V	Svendbye Ingrid †	21	housewife	58	"
	W	Halperin Hannah †	21	"	21	"
	X	Halperin Joseph	21	importer	59	"
	Y	Halperin Leon T	21	clerk	23	"
	Z	Fish George H	23	supervisor	34	"
2128						
	A	Fish Mary B †	23	housewife	27	"
	B	Jensen Gunhild C †	23	"	47	"
	C	Jensen Jens B	23	painter	54	"
	D	Anderson Ann †	25	housewife	30	16 Favre
	E	Anderson Walter	25	carpenter	29	16 "
	G	Maguire Francis R	26	policeman	46	here
	H	Maguire Margaret M †	26	housewife	46	"
	K	Masterson James C	28	agent	43	"
	L	Masterson Mary M †	28	housewife	36	"
	M	Granite Edward	30	carpenter	24	"
	N	Granite Louis	30	"	48	"
	O	Granite Sigrid †	30	housewife	46	"
	P	Burke Thomas F	34	broker	43	"
	R	Burke William P	34	B F D	40	"
	S	Hurley Gerald F	34	clerk	25	"
	T	Hurley Mary E †	34	housewife	48	"
	U	Hurley Paul T	34	student	22	"
	V	Hurley Ruth K †	34	secretary	21	"
	W	Mooney Alice †	34	housewife	36	"
	X	Mooney Charles	34	buyer	40	"
	Y	O'Connor Felix A	36	underwriter	33	"

Page.	Letter.	Full Name.	Residence, Jan. 1, 1941.	Occupation.	Supposed Age.	Reported Residence, Jan. 1, 1940. Street and Number.

Hallowell Street—Continued

	Z	O'Connor Marion G—†	36	housewife	29	here
2129						
	A	Johnson Alice—†	36	"	30	"
	B	Johnson Frederick	36	machinist	34	"
	C	Nord Herlof	39	welder	35	"
	D	Nord Martha—†	39	housewife	28	"
	E	Benjaminsen Anne M—†	40	"	52	"
	F	Benjaminsen Peter	40	retired	75	"
	G	McCarthy Helen—†	40	housewife	26	"
	H	McCarthy Robert	40	laborer	29	"
	K	Neville Emma—†	44	housewife	55	"
	L	Neville Harold	44	watchman	26	"
	M	Neville John	44	fireman	54	"

Harmon Street

	N	Broderick Alice C—†	8	housewife	37	here
	O	Broderick Frederick E	8	engineer	38	"
	P	Shea Joseph W	8	attorney	34	"
	R	Shea William M	8	clerk	64	"
	S	Mason Eugene H	11	fireman	48	"
	T	Mason Margaret T—†	11	housewife	49	"
	U	Mason Paul J	11	meter reader	26	"
	V	Ellsworth Ellen—†	14	housekeeper	64	"
	W	Kenney Robert H	14	retired	73	"
	X	Westwood Jessie—†	15	housewife	79	"
	Y	Westwood Thomas H	15	retired	83	"
	Z	*Pizura Helen M—†	20	housewife	30	"
2130						
	A	Pizura William	20	clerk	29	"
	B	Pizura Bernard	20	"	24	"
	C	*Pizura Peter	20	painter	53	"
	D	*Pizura Tekla—†	20	cook	50	"
	E	Wilkinson Jennie L—†	22	housewife	60	"
	F	Wilkinson Jesse H	22	retired	63	"
	G	Prato Madeline—†	25	housewife	32	"
	H	Prato Remo	25	chef	35	"
	K	Daley Francis J	25	mechanic	28	1015 South
	L	*Daley Karen A—†	25	housewife	39	198 Hebron

Page	Letter	Full Name	Residence Jan. 1, 1941	Occupation	Supposed Age	Reported Residence, Jan. 1, 1940. Street and Number

Harmon Street—Continued

Page	Letter	Full Name	Residence Jan. 1, 1941	Occupation	Supposed Age	Reported Residence, Jan. 1, 1940. Street and Number
	M	Moran Austin W	26	curtaincutter	46	here
	N	Moran James B	26	accountant	37	"
	O	Moran Mary T †	26	housewife	75	"
	P	Moran William J	26	retired	74	"
	R	*Swidzinski Agnes †	26	cook	44	"
	S	Swidzinski Joseph	26	proprietor	50	"
	T	Pequrri Ferdinand	27	laborer	56	"
	U	*Pequrri Josephine †	27	housewife	52	"
	V	Chalmers Evelyn G †	27	"	33	146 Greenfield rd
	W	Chalmers John W	27	manager	33	17 Tremont
	X	Reilly Anne M †	30	housewife	41	79 Brookside av
	Y	Reilly Thomas H	30	agent	41	79 "
	Z	*Suchecki Katherine †	30	housewife	46	here
2131						
	A	Suchecki Stephen	30	bartender	49	"
	B	*Chepyka Helen †	33	housewife	44	"
	C	Chepyka William	33	upholsterer	46	"
	D	Marsney Mary †	33	housewife	23	"
	E	Marsney Michael	33	stripper	27	"
	F	Norton Irene M †	35	nurse	33	"
	G	Norton John J	35	shipfitter	26	"
	H	Norton Kathleen M †	35	clerk	39	"
	K	Norton Mary A †	35	housewife	59	"
	L	Norton Mary G †	35	clerk	36	"
	M	Norton Thomas	35	janitor	69	"
	N	Giovannucci Ellen M †	36	housewife	49	"
	O	Giovannucci Joseph	36	policeman	45	"
	P	Pizura Charles	39	machinist	28	"
	R	Pizura Martha †	39	housewife	24	"
	S	Huddleston Frank L	40	salesman	42	"
	T	Huddleston Inez M †	40	housewife	40	"
	U	Keating Catherine A †	44	"	75	"
	V	Keating Clotilda A †	44	clerk	33	"
	W	Keating Collette A †	44	at home	43	"
	X	Keating Irene M †	44	clerk	45	"
	Y	Keating William C	44	plasterer	74	"
	Z	Sidlowski Anastasia †	52	cook	40	"
2132						
	A	Sidlowski John	52	cabinetmaker	51	"

Page	Letter	Full Name.	Residence, Jan. 1, 1941.	Occupation.	Supposed Age.	Reported Residence, Jan. 1, 1940. Street and Number.

Harmon Street—Continued

	B	Sidlowski Michael	52	machinist	24	here
	C	Sidlowski Zofia S—†	52	at home	22	"

Harvard Street

	D	Ballantine Mabel—†	1000	attendant	50	here
	E	Flagg Eleanor—†	1000	nurse	41	"
	F	Jennings Josephine—†	1000	"	44	"
	G	Robinson George	1000	retired	76	"
	H	Spencer Iola M—†	1000	dietitian	34	"

Hebron Street

	K	Martin Toy W	83	letter carrier	47	here
	L	Martin Vera R—†	83	housewife	40	"
	M	*Birolini Ancilla—†	87	"	37	"
	N	Birolini Joseph L	87	retired	53	"
	O	*Pylypuk Mary—†	151	housewife	48	"
	P	*Pylypuk Michael	151	cook	48	"
	R	*Oas Henry	164	foreman	50	"
	S	*Oas Mathilde—†	164	housewife	47	"
	T	Oas Sophie—†	164	"	72	"
	U	Johansen Henrik K	178	molder	59	"
	V	*Strand Anna M—†	178	housewife	55	"
	W	Strand Chester R	178	mechanic	22	"
	X	Chisholm Helena J—†	179	housewife	32	"
	Y	Chisholm James W	179	policeman	35	"
	Z	Violandi Louis J	179	operator	32	"
2133						
	A	Violandi Regina B—†	179	housewife	31	"

Itasca Street

	B	*Hart Catherine A—†	196	housewife	47	here
	C	Hart Patrick	196	porter	48	"
	D	Carey Catherine V—†	198	clerk	24	"
	E	Carey Dennis	198	plasterer	67	"
	F	Carey Evelyn E—†	198	clerk	22	"
	G	Carey Mary F—†	198	"	27	"
	H	Sullivan Mary E—†	198	domestic	66	"

Page	Letter	Full Name	Residence, Jan. 1, 1941	Occupation	Supposed Age	Reported Residence, Jan. 1, 1940. Street and Number

Itasca Street Continued

Page	Letter	Full Name	Residence, Jan. 1, 1941	Occupation	Supposed Age	Reported Residence, Jan. 1, 1940. Street and Number
	K	Lynch Ann †	207	housewife	30	here
	L	Lynch Joseph F	207	plumber	32	"
	M	Barton Margaret †	208	student	21	"
	N	Barton Rose †	208	housewife	55	"
	O	Barton Rose A †	208	clerk	23	"
	P	Libby Florence E †	208	housewife	25	"
	R	Libby George A	208	clerk	28	"
	S	Reilly Beatrice †	211	housewife	48	"
	T	Reilly John	211	butcher	52	"
	U	Reilly Mary B †	211	saleswoman	24	"
	V	O'Brien Frances G †	220	housewife	35	"
	W	O'Brien Franklin J	220	pharmacist	35	"
	X	Coaker Annie H †	228	housewife	40	"
	Y	Coaker John T	228	accountant	44	"
	Z	MacDonald Arthur L	232	salesman	56	"
2134						
	A	MacDonald Arthur L, jr	232	accountant	22	"
	B	MacDonald Emily P †	232	housewife	57	"
	C	Cliggett Alfred T	243	clerk	25	"
	D	Cliggett Charlotte †	243	housewife	60	"
	E	Cliggett Charlotte M †	243	clerk	20	"
	F	Johnson Charles	243	welder	30	"
	G	Johnson Marie †	243	forewoman	29	"
	H	Stone Martha †	250	housewife	40	"
	K	Stone Max	250	letter carrier	42	"
	L	*Semchuk Anna †	255	housewife	44	"
	M	*Semchuk Michael	255	laborer	54	"
	N	Semchuk Natalka †	255	clerk	20	"
	O	Semchuk Olga †	255	secretary	25	"
	P	Semchuk Mary †	255	housewife	26	"
	R	Semchuk Walter	255	machinist	27	"
	S	*Whitman Christine †	260	housewife	80	"
	T	Webb Alfred R	268	clerk	43	"
	U	Webb Esther M †	268	housewife	41	"
	V	Masiello Barbara †	272	"	33	Canton
	W	Masiello Robert A	272	chef	31	Everett
	X	Staryk Anna †	272	housewife	45	here
	Y	Staryk Frank	272	laborer	55	"
	Z	Staryk Mary †	272	clerk	21	"
2135						
	A	Staryk William	272	chauffeur	41	"

Page.	Letter.	FULL NAME.	Residence, Jan. 1, 1941.	Occupation.	Supposed Age.	Reported Residence, Jan. 1, 1940. Street and Number.

Kennebec Street

Page.	Letter.	FULL NAME.	Residence, Jan. 1, 1941.	Occupation.	Supposed Age.	Reported Residence, Jan. 1, 1940. Street and Number.
	B	Pappalardo Sarah—†	100	housewife	36	here
	C	Pappalardo Sebastiano	100	mechanic	39	"
	D	*Slyman Bridget M—†	100	housewife	43	"
	E	Slyman Michael J	100	porter	45	"
	F	Avellino Elizabeth A—†	101	dressmaker	25	"
	G	*Avellino Josephine—†	101	housewife	82	"
	H	Avellino Josephine V—†	101	dressmaker	28	"
	K	Avellino Patricia G—†	101	housekeeper	26	"
	L	*Avellino Phillip	101	shoemaker	60	"
	M	*Avellino Sarah—†	101	housewife	53	"
	N	Davis Edward F	114	machinist	66	"
	O	Davis Irene E—†	114	waitress	21	"
	P	Davis Irving	114	machinist	27	"
	R	Davis Margaret E—†	114	housewife	63	"
	S	Gauss Lucy D—†	120	"	27	"
	T	Gauss Thomas J	120	porter	34	"
	U	Violandi Joseph P	120	carpenter	21	"
	V	*Violandi Ralph	120	laborer	60	"
	W	Donofrio Dominic	173	plasterer	48	"
	X	*Donofrio Fannie—†	173	housewife	45	"

Livermore Street

Page.	Letter.	FULL NAME.	Residence, Jan. 1, 1941.	Occupation.	Supposed Age.	Reported Residence, Jan. 1, 1940. Street and Number.
	Y	O'Connor James J	41	longshoreman	28	12 Magdala
	Z	O'Connor Joanne R—†	41	housewife	22	here
2136						
	A	*Remondi Benjamin	41	mason	62	"
	B	*Remondi Cecilia—†	41	housewife	50	"
	C	Remondi James	41	chauffeur	25	"
	D	Remondi Mary—†	41	domestic	21	"

Orlando Street

Page.	Letter.	FULL NAME.	Residence, Jan. 1, 1941.	Occupation.	Supposed Age.	Reported Residence, Jan. 1, 1940. Street and Number.
	E	Teahan Joseph F	134	electrician	45	here
	F	Teahan Winifred M—†	134	housewife	44	"
	G	Persico Frank	141	cobbler	56	"
	H	*Persico Lena—†	141	housewife	54	"
	K	Persico Olive—†	141	operator	27	"
	L	Persico Rose—†	141	"	24	"
	M	Persico Theresa—†	141	maid	30	"
	N	Keller Caroline E—†	145	housewife	41	"

Page	Letter	Full Name	Residence, Jan. 1, 1941	Occupation	Supposed Age	Reported Residence, Jan. 1, 1940. Street and Number

Orlando Street—Continued

	O	Keller George D	145	pressman	42	here
	P	Seaberg Carl R	146	clerk	36	"
	R	Seaberg Evelyn—†	146	housewife	33	"
	S	Nilsen Aagot—†	146	"	47	"
	T	Nilsen Conrad	146	foreman	46	"
	U	MacBeth Donald A	147	pressman	35	"
	V	MacBeth Nancy S—†	147	housewife	34	"
	W	McCarthy George F	151	watchman	60	"
	X	McCarthy George F, jr	151	laborer	20	"
	Y	McCarthy Mary E—†	151	housewife	49	"
	Z	*Cohen Annie—†	151	"	49	86 Ballou av
2137						
	A	*Cohen Hyman	151	salesman	49	86 "
	B	Gustafson Hedvig—†	159	housewife	43	here
	C	Gustafson Torsten	159	carpenter	45	"
	D	Fitz Celia E—†	159	cashier	59	48 Buswell
	E	Norton Norma E—†	159	housewife	27	48 "
	F	Norton William L	159	accountant	29	48 "
	G	Johnson Inez—†	163	clerk	22	here
	H	*Johnson John O	163	watchman	56	"
	K	*Johnson Olivia—†	163	clerk	54	"

Regis Road

	L	Alves Joseph F	17	mechanic	40	here
	M	Alves Mary E—†	17	housewife	45	"
	N	*Alves Rose—†	17	"	69	"
	O	McDermott Margaret J—†	17	waitress	30	"
	P	*Lundell Etta—†	19	housewife	30	Somerville
	R	*Lundell Matti J	19	shipper	31	"
	S	Holland Lela—†	19	housewife	35	here
	T	Holland Michael	19	waiter	36	"
	U	Lanata Andrew	20	engineer	68	"
	V	Lanata Andrew J	20	chauffeur	32	"
	W	Lanata Joseph J	20	"	34	"
	X	Lanata Lawrence L	20	machinist	20	"
	Y	*Lanata Louise—†	20	housewife	57	"
	Z	Guerini John	22	merchant	54	"
2138						
	A	Guerini Julia—†	22	housewife	44	"
	B	Johnson Arthur E	24	carpenter	39	"

Page.	Letter.	Full Name	Residence, Jan. 1, 1941.	Occupation.	Supposed Age.	Reported Residence, Jan. 1, 1940. Street and Number.

Regis Road—Continued

Page.	Letter.	Full Name	Residence, Jan. 1, 1941.	Occupation.	Supposed Age.	Reported Residence, Jan. 1, 1940. Street and Number.
	C	Johnson Elsa A—†	24	housewife	36	here
	D	Flaherty James B	25	manager	30	113 Babson
	E	Flaherty James M	25	cleaner	65	113 "
	F	Flaherty Margaret M—†	25	housewife	57	113 "
	G	Flaherty Mary E—†	25	clerk	27	113 "
	H	Lanata Catherine L—†	25	housewife	43	here
	K	Lanata Gladys J—†	25	"	40	"
	L	Lanata John W	25	clerk	42	"
	M	Lanata Joseph A	25	collector	50	"
	N	Cadigan Cornelius J	26	salesman	34	"
	O	Cadigan Ethel L—†	26	housewife	33	"
	P	Baker Charles E	29	machinist	33	3 Avander ct
	R	Baker Edna M—†	29	housewife	32	3 "
	S	Sheridan Lawrence	31	mechanic	43	here
	T	Sheridan Mary C—†	31	housewife	33	"
	V	Eklund Gustav T	43	leathercutter	71	"
	W	Messinger Abner G	43	agent	38	"
	X	Messinger Ebba M—†	43	housewife	39	"
	Y	Gaffey James F	62	gardener	62	"
	Z	Gaffey Margaret—†	62	housewife	62	"
2139						
	A	Rigney Peter	62	grocer	53	N Hampshire
	B	Hiltz Elizabeth F—†	62	housewife	32	here
	C	Hiltz Ralph H	62	checker	35	"
	D	Rosenfield Betty—†	67	housewife	29	"
	E	Rosenfield Harry	67	printer	35	"
	F	MacCalden Helen F—†	67	housewife	41	"
	G	MacCalden Malcolm S	67	plumber	41	"
	H	Burke Harold A	68	salesman	26	"
	K	Burke Helen C—†	68	dietitian	28	"
	L	Burke Mary B—†	68	housewife	50	"
	M	Carley Emma—†	68	housekeeper	61	591 Morton
	N	Boles Mary A—†	68	housewife	26	8 Fremont
	O	Boles Stanley L	68	painter	28	8 "
	P	Tripp Catherine A—†	68	housewife	69	8 "
	R	Tripp Charles S	68	janitor	76	8 "
	S	Bischoff Alice E—†	71	clerk	21	here
	T	Bischoff Carl C	71	waiter	53	"
	U	Bischoff Mary C—†	71	housewife	53	"
	V	Bischoff Mary M—†	71	clerk	25	"
	W	Fleming Catherine—†	71	housewife	56	"

Page	Letter	Full Name	Residence, Jan. 1, 1941	Occupation	Supposed Age	Reported Residence, Jan. 1, 1940. Street and Number

Regis Road—Continued

Page	Letter	Full Name	Residence, Jan. 1, 1941	Occupation	Supposed Age	Reported Residence, Jan. 1, 1940. Street and Number
	X	Fleming Edna †	71	housewife	27	here
	Y	Fleming Richard J	71	carpenter	25	"
	Z	Briggs Jenny L †	76	housekeeper	83	"
2140						
	A	Burke Bernard	76	clerk	28	Pittsfield
	B	*Marshall James H	76	retired	72	here
	C	*Marshall Margaret J †	76	housewife	70	"
	D	O'Donnell Margaret †	78	"	46	"
	E	O'Donnell William F	78	manager	54	"
	F	Clark Alfred B	78	"	58	"
	G	Clark Alice G †	78	housewife	58	"
	H	Leonard Alice L †	78	housekeeper	80	"
	K	Menslage Eileen †	79	housewife	32	"
	L	Menslage George	79	electrician	30	"
	M	Dillon Eliza A †	79	housekeeper	54	"
	N	Bell Benjamin	83	physician	30	"
	O	Katcher Esther †	83	housewife	32	"
	P	Katcher Philip	83	salesman	35	"
	R	Vadeboncour Bertha A †	83	housewife	34	"
	S	Vadeboncour John J	83	policeman	45	"
	T	Vitale Dennis B	83	salesman	25	"
	U	Vitale Marion R †	83	housewife	23	"

Rexford Street

Page	Letter	Full Name	Residence, Jan. 1, 1941	Occupation	Supposed Age	Reported Residence, Jan. 1, 1940. Street and Number
	V	Bartley Geraldine †	11	clerk	21	here
	W	Burgess Alexander	11	retired	70	"
	X	DeVore Everett	11	clerk	45	"
	Y	DeVore Irene †	11	"	39	"
	Z	Berg Catherine †	15	housekeeper	45	"
2141						
	A	Duffy Frank A	15	retired	81	"
	B	Duffy William F	15	clerk	22	"
	C	Maxon Mary †	16	housewife	65	"
	D	Maxon Thomas	16	retired	68	"
	E	Crangle Helen †	19	housewife	70	"
	F	Gallagher Francis	19	salesman	61	"
	G	Gillette Howard	19	plumber	46	"
	H	Gillette Isabelle †	19	clerk	25	"
	K	Lamb Arthur	22	contractor	52	"
	L	Lamb Dorothy †	22	housewife	50	"

Page	Letter	Full Name.	Residence, Jan. 1, 1941.	Occupation.	Supposed Age.	Reported Residence, Jan. 1, 1940. Street and Number.

Rexford Street—Continued

Page	Letter	Full Name.	Residence, Jan. 1, 1941.	Occupation.	Supposed Age.	Reported Residence, Jan. 1, 1940. Street and Number.
	M	Fritz Charles	22	chauffeur	47	here
	N	Fritz Charlotte D—†	22	clerk	23	"
	O	Fritz Dorothy—†	22	housewife	44	"
	P	Fitzpatrick John J	22	dentist	50	23 Oakley
	R	Fitzpatrick Margaret—†	22	housewife	42	23 "
	S	Reagan Maude—†	22	clerk	50	here
	T	Toland Patrick J	23	retired	67	"
	U	Toland Teresa M—†	23	housewife	67	"
	V	Dubb Gertrude—†	24	"	47	"
	W	Dubb Jacob	24	tailor	51	"
	X	Dubb Sylvia—†	24	clerk	21	"
	Y	Dubb Harry	24	musician	30	"
	Z	Dubb Marion E—†	24	housewife	28	"
2142						
	A	Muier Sally J—†	24	clerk	38	"
	B	Mursky Anna—†	24	housewife	66	"
	C	Mursky Helen—†	24	teacher	36	"
	D	Ross Isadore	25	painter	54	"
	E	*Ross Sadie E—†	25	housewife	50	"
	F	Barber James C	28	retired	80	"
	G	LaCasse C Raymond	28	clerk	21	"
	H	LaCasse Elizabeth—†	28	housewife	41	"
	K	LaCasse Joseph F	28	salesman	46	"
	L	Campbell Alice—†	28	saleswoman	42	"
	M	Campbell Alice M—†	28	clerk	21	"
	N	King Annie T—†	28	housewife	67	"
	O	Ney Edward	28	mechanic	42	"
	P	King Helen F—†	29	housewife	42	"
	R	King Mark J	29	operator	41	"
	T	Cullen Joseph	32	laborer	23	"
	U	Cullen Loretta M—†	32	housewife	49	"
	V	Nevins Martin	33	retired	70	"
	W	Nevins Mary—†	33	housewife	73	"
	Y	Wesson Annie—†	40	"	68	"
	Z	Wesson William C	40	B F D	45	"
2143						
	A	Fay Leonard A	40	foreman	39	"
	B	Fay Mary E—†	40	housewife	40	"
	C	Mahoney Della—†	40	"	75	"
	D	Boyle Jason A	41	foreman	58	"
	E	Donnellan Belle—†	41	housewife	65	"

Page	Letter	Full Name	Residence, Jan. 1, 1941	Occupation	Supposed Age	Reported Residence, Jan. 1, 1940. Street and Number

Rexford Street Continued

Page	Letter	Full Name	Residence, Jan. 1, 1941	Occupation	Supposed Age	Reported Residence, Jan. 1, 1940. Street and Number
	F	Donnellan Harold F	41	clerk	34	here
	G	Donnellan John	41	retired	59	"
	H	Halse Edna—†	41	bookkeeper	52	"
	K	Halse Jeannette—†	41	clerk	54	"
	L	Halse Richard	41	retired	83	"
	M	Kline Leo A	44	painter	48	"
	N	Lanata Ernestine—†	44	housewife	34	"
	O	Lanata Louis J	44	clerk	44	"
	P	Kierman Frank A	45	foreman	47	"
	R	Kierman Frank A, jr	45	manager	26	New York
	S	Kierman Lillian—†	45	housewife	47	here
	T	Beltramini Charles	46	laborer	37	Milford
	U	Beltramini Louis	46	patternmaker	32	"
	V	Beltramini Mary—†	46	housewife	29	"
	W	Purcell Catherine—†	49	clerk	47	here
	X	White Edward J	49	B F D	49	"
	Y	White James A	49	clerk	22	"
	Z	White Margaret G—†	49	housewife	49	"
2144						
	A	White William F	49	mechanic	27	"
	B	Sullivan Catherine F—†	49	clerk	24	"
	C	Sullivan Helen M—†	49	attorney	29	"
	D	Sullivan Joseph M	49	clerk	37	"
	E	Sullivan Margaret E—†	49	operator	35	"
	F	Sullivan Mary A—†	49	housewife	63	"
	G	Deely Gladys—†	51	"	43	1140 River
	H	Deely Thomas A	51	teacher	45	1140 "
	K	Banks Agnes M—†	51	housewife	76	here
	L	Banks Leonard T	51	policeman	46	"
	M	Banks Margaret P—†	51	housewife	45	"
	N	Daley John M	54	retired	69	"
	O	Follen Ellen—†	54	housewife	64	"
	P	Follen John	54	chauffeur	26	"
	R	Follen Lawrence	54	cleanser	38	"
	S	Follen Venice—†	54	housewife	25	Medford
	T	Arnold Frank	54	clerk	34	here
	U	Ostergren Ellen—†	54	housewife	74	"
	V	Murphy Anna F—†	56	"	62	"
	W	Murphy Anna G—†	56	clerk	20	"
	X	Murphy Richard H	56	policeman	65	"
	Y	Orphanos George	56	peddler	33	"

Page.	Letter.	Full Name.	Residence, Jan. 1, 1941.	Occupation.	Supposed Age.	Reported Residence, Jan. 1, 1940. Street and Number.

Rexford Street—Continued

Page.	Letter.	Full Name.	Residence, Jan. 1, 1941.	Occupation.	Supposed Age.	Reported Residence, Jan. 1, 1940. Street and Number.
	Z	Petrou George	56	inspector	33	25 Tokio
2145						
	A	Carroll Helen—†	57	housewife	35	here
	B	Carroll Mark	57	contractor	35	"
	C	Carroll Paul	57	engineer	38	"
	D	Mitchell Lois—†	57	housewife	86	890 Cummins H way
	E	Stewart Jennie—†	57	"	82	890 "
	F	Stewart Rose B—†	57	operator	54	890 "
	G	Bulger Edna—†	59	housewife	24	here
	H	Bulger Edward J	59	manager	29	"
	K	Thayer Edith—†	59	clerk	26	"
	L	Thayer Eileen—†	59	"	28	"
	M	Thayer Katherine—†	59	"	29	"
	N	Chase Howard T	59	B F D	46	"
	O	Chase Howard T, jr	59	salesman	22	"
	P	Chase Viola—†	59	housewife	46	"
	R	O'Hara Alice M—†	60	clerk	24	"
	S	O'Hara Anna M—†	60	housewife	52	"
	T	O'Hara Francis J	60	merchant	64	"
	U	O'Hara James A	60	clerk	22	"
	V	Kelly Agnes—†	61	housewife	60	"
	W	Kelly John P	61	mechanic	25	"
	X	Kelly Richard	61	clerk	62	"
	Y	Miller Frances—†	61	housewife	37	"
	Z	Miller Harold N	61	manager	37	"
2146						
	A	Flashman Bessie—†	64	housewife	28	"
	B	Flashman Sidney	64	salesman	32	"
	C	Berntson Anna—†	64	clerk	60	"
	D	Pearson Florence—†	64	buyer	46	"
	E	Pearson Grace—†	64	housekeeper	23	"
	F	Mawhinney Agnes—†	64	housewife	40	"
	G	Mawhinney James	64	janitor	41	"

Richmere Road

Page.	Letter.	Full Name.	Residence, Jan. 1, 1941.	Occupation.	Supposed Age.	Reported Residence, Jan. 1, 1940. Street and Number.
	H	Lynch John P	8	retired	71	here
	K	Lynch Mary E—†	8	housewife	69	"
	L	Rockett Edna V—†	8	"	29	"
	M	Rockett Robert E	8	clerk	29	"

Richmere Road Continued

Page	Letter	Full Name	Residence, Jan. 1, 1941	Occupation	Supposed Age	Reported Residence, Jan. 1, 1940. Street and Number
	N	Lynch Alice B †	10	housewife	41	here
	O	Lynch Charles F	10	plasterer	46	"
	P	Brady Margaret R †	11	housewife	32	"
	R	Brady Philip H	11	policeman	42	"
	S	Wilds Clarence M	15	welder	35	"
	T	Wilds Jean G †	15	housewife	36	"
	U	Goldsworthy Hollyberry †	17	"	45	"
	V	Goldsworthy Leonora †	17	waitress	20	"
	W	Goldsworthy Thomas H	17	machinist	26	"
	X	Cyr C Francis	20	realtor	35	19 Pender
	Y	Cyr Claire †	20	operator	35	19 "
	Z	Julian Caroline V †	20	housewife	35	19 "
2147						
	A	Julian James A	20	clerk	37	19 "
	B	Walsh James R	20	"	42	here
	C	Walsh Marion E †	20	housewife	38	"
	D	David Fred	28	cutter	28	16 Emerald
	E	David Sophie †	28	stitcher	25	16 "
	G	Shefranski Alexandria †	28	housewife	52	50 Angell
	F	Shefranski Anna †	28	operator	22	50 "
	H	Donahoe Edward I	38	salesman	53	374 Geneva av
	K	Donahoe Margaret G †	38	housewife	45	105 Kittredge
	L	Szydlowsky Demetro	38	cook	52	here
	M	Szydlowsky Jerry	38	U S A	22	"
	N*	Szydlowsky Mary †	38	housewife	57	"
	O	Szydlowsky Stella †	38	saleswoman	27	"
	P	Szydlowsky William	38	counterman	28	"
	R	Gallant Mary M †	47	operator	58	"
	S	Gallant Thomas J	47	"	59	"
	T	Ingersoll Orissa †	48	cashier	57	"
	U	Lynch Charles W	48	milkman	52	"
	V	Robinson Charles A	48	retired	80	"
	W	McDonnell Mary G †	59	housewife	42	"
	X	McDonnell Thomas J	59	cashier	39	"
	Y	Moran James B	59	laborer	39	"
	Z	White Ellen G †	67	teacher	32	"
2148						
	A	White Mary J †	67	housewife	68	"
	B	Butler Elizabeth G †	69	"	75	"
	C	Rowean Catherine E †	69	bookkeeper	51	46 Turner
	D	Rowean Elizabeth F †	69	clerk	60	46 "

Page.	Letter.	FULL NAME.	Residence, Jan. 1, 1941	Occupation.	Supposed Age.	Reported Residence, Jan. 1, 1940. Street and Number.

Richmere Road—Continued

Page.	Letter.	FULL NAME.	Residence, Jan. 1, 1941	Occupation.	Supposed Age.	Reported Residence, Jan. 1, 1940.
	E	Donoghue Anna B—†	80	housewife	41	here
	F	Donoghue Patrick F	80	operator	51	"

Rockingham Road

Page.	Letter.	FULL NAME.	Residence, Jan. 1, 1941	Occupation.	Supposed Age.	Reported Residence, Jan. 1, 1940.
	G	Squillace Amelia—†	6	housewife	26	6 Rocky Nook ter
	H	Squillace Anthony	6	supervisor	29	6 "
	K	Hallett Edward	10	salesman	38	here
	L	Hallett Helen A—†	10	housewife	42	"
	M	Houghton Alice M—†	10	clerk	54	"
	N	Houghton Edward T	11	retired	67	"
	O	Houghton Elizabeth L—†	11	milliner	59	"
	P	Houghton Mary T—†	11	clerk	61	"
	R	Houghton William K	11	shipper	57	"
	S	Manning Anna R—†	15	housewife	31	"
	T	Manning Frederick J	15	accountant	31	"
	U	McIver George L	17	carpenter	40	"
	V	McIver Mary S—†	17	housewife	32	"
	W	Money Isabelle S—†	17	physician	25	"
	X	Hayes Emmett J	19	letter carrier	43	"
	Y	Hayes Mary B—†	19	housewife	65	"
	Z	Seaburg George W	23	teacher	46	"
2149						
	A	Seaburg Karin R—†	23	housewife	47	"
	B	Seaburg Ruth E—†	23	student	21	"
	C	Tripp Clinton	31	machinist	52	"
	D	Tripp Priscilla—†	31	saleswoman	21	"
	F	Arata Annie—†	37	housewife	46	"
	G	MacKay Donald B	40	chauffeur	66	"
	H	MacKay Helen J—†	40	housewife	59	"
	K	MacKay Talbert M	40	accountant	26	"

Rockway Street

Page.	Letter.	FULL NAME.	Residence, Jan. 1, 1941	Occupation.	Supposed Age.	Reported Residence, Jan. 1, 1940.
	L	Dunphy Daniel	5	clerk	49	here
	M	Dunphy Mary—†	5	housewife	41	"
	N	Fitzgerald John H	7	clerk	30	"
	O	Fitzgerald Marion T—†	7	housewife	29	"
	P	Krim Frances C—†	10	"	32	"
	R	Krim John W	10	blacksmith	37	"
	S	Brennan Agnes E—†	12	housewife	39	"

Page	Letter	Full Name	Residence, Jan. 1, 1941.	Occupation	Supposed Age	Reported Residence, Jan. 1, 1940. Street and Number

Rockway Street—Continued

Page	Letter	Full Name	Residence, Jan. 1, 1941.	Occupation	Supposed Age	Reported Residence, Jan. 1, 1940. Street and Number
	T	Breman William L	12	clerk	42	here
	U	Ringler Helen M †	12	housewife	31	"
	V	Ringler Theodore A	12	mechanic	30	"

Rugby Road

Page	Letter	Full Name	Residence, Jan. 1, 1941.	Occupation	Supposed Age	Reported Residence, Jan. 1, 1940. Street and Number
	W	*Campbell Alice L †	6	nurse	50	here
	X	*Forsyth Annie C †	6	housewife	48	"
	Y	Forsyth Robert E	6	painter	50	"
	Z	Forsyth Robert L	6	clerk	22	"
2150						
	A	Whelton Ellen F †	10–12	housewife	25	"
	B	Whelton William A	10–12	chauffeur	29	"
	C	Dorsey Katherine V—†	10–12	housewife	60	Milton
	D	Dorsey Katherine V—†	10–12	social worker	27	here
	E	Dorsey Thomas F	10–12	engraver	59	Milton
	F	Wilhelm Anna E †	15	housewife	68	here
	G	Wilhelm John	15	upholsterer	68	"
	H	Wilhelm John N	15	accountant	31	"
	K	Breivogel Frank D	16	retired	77	"
	L	Breivogel Jane V—†	16	housewife	57	"
	M	Sprague Franklin	18	retired	84	"
	N	White Evelyn F—†	18	housekeeper	21	"
	O	White Nellie I †	18	housewife	55	"
	P	White Robert L	18	cutter	51	"
	R	White Rupert P	18	teacher	25	"
	S	Blugge Alice M †	19	housewife	64	"
	T	Blugge Peter C	19	painter	67	"
	U	Patterson Delia †	19	at home	78	"
	V	Shaw Harriett †	19	"	80	"
	W	Gulick Leon H	20	engineer	56	"
	X	Gulick Margaret A †	20	housewife	55	"
	Y	Patten Sarah A †	20	"	71	"
	Z	Patten William E	20	clerk	63	"
2151						
	A	Buckley Florence M †	23	housewife	32	Wollaston
	B	Buckley William A	23	printer	65	196 Fairmount av
	C	Buckley William E	23	engineer	35	Wollaston
	D	McAuley A Raymond	28	clerk	26	here
	E	McAuley George E	28	carpenter	32	"
	F	McAuley Marion E †	28	social worker	29	"

Page.	Letter.	Full Name.	Residence, Jan. 1, 1941.	Occupation.	Supposed Age.	Reported Residence, Jan. 1, 1940. Street and Number.

Rugby Road—Continued

	G	McAuley Mary E—†	28	housewife	60	here
	H	Forgeron Alice M—†	30	housekeeper	43	"
	K	Forgeron Edmund C	30	cobbler	71	"
	L	Forgeron Mildred S—†	30	clerk	44	"
	M	Kullen Anders	34	tailor	60	"
	N	Kullen Hilda—†	34	housewife	57	"
	O	Anderson Hilda—†	38	clerk	62	"
	P	Forslund Frieda A—†	38	housewife	58	"
	R	Forslund Oscar A	38	laborer	56	"
	S	Jones Charles J	38	fireman	52	"
	T	Jones Dorothy—†	38	operator	24	"
	U	Jones Sadie A—†	38	housewife	54	"
	V	Lynch Elizabeth—†	38	"	29	"
	W	Lynch Francis	38	letter carrier	33	"
	X	Jackson Alfred F	44	"	34	"
	Y	Jackson Margaret G—†	44	operator	54	"
	Z	Regan Anna V—†	44	clerk	45	"
		2152				
	A	Cox Ernest C	46	teacher	62	10 Tampa
	B	Cox Mary—†	46	housewife	55	10 "

Ruxton Road

	C	Whelan Bertha G—†	7	housewife	40	here
	D	Whelan John E	7	inspector	44	"
	E	Johnson Albert G	9	toolmaker	47	6 Ruxton rd
	F*	Johnson Constance—†	9	housewife	41	6 "
	G	Anderson Dagmar H—†	17	stenographer	36	here
	H	Anderson Knute J	17	tailor	67	"
	K	Anderson Ottilia—†	17	housewife	70	"
	L	Clark Allen T	19	fireman	22	Randolph
	M	Clark James C	19	"	20	"
	N	Clark Louis C	19	engineer	55	4 Beale
	O	Clark Rose E—†	19	housewife	48	Randolph
	P	Mungovan Florence R—†	19	"	34	here
	R	Mungovan Walter R	19	custodian	40	"

Savannah Avenue

	S	Krim Alice M—†	148	housewife	50	here
	T	Krim Evelyn M—†	148	secretary	22	"

Page.	Letter.	Full Name.	Residence, Jan. 1, 1944.	Occupation.	Supposed Age.	Reported Residence, Jan. 1, 1943. Street and Number.

Savannah Avenue—Continued

Page.	Letter.	Full Name.	Residence, Jan. 1, 1944.	Occupation.	Supposed Age.	Reported Residence, Jan. 1, 1943. Street and Number.
	U	Krim Harry T	148	salesman	52	here
	V	Lynch Dolores V †	152	dressmaker	23	"
	W	Lynch Elizabeth M †	152	housewife	50	"
	X	Lynch Michael P	152	plumber	66	"
	Y	Frangioso Domenic	155	chauffeur	31	150 Greenfield rd
	Z	Frangioso Josephine †	155	housewife	33	150 "
2153						
	A	Marshall Artisha †	156	"	63	here
	B	Marshall David	156	plasterer	68	"
	C	Marshall Violet †	156	clerk	34	"
	D	Guerini Luigi	160	contractor	43	"
	E	Guerini Vera †	160	housewife	31	"
	F	Nelson Charles	161	shipfitter	58	"
	G	Nelson Matilda †	161	housewife	50	"
	H	Lonsdale Joseph L	164	plater	35	"
	K	Lonsdale Leonard M	164	repairman	62	"
	L	Lonsdale Mary †	164	housewife	60	"
	M	Hennessy James D	164	collector	63	"
	N	Hennessy Theresa M †	164	housewife	62	"
	O	O'Farrell Eugene J	164	manager	35	"
	P	O'Farrell Monica M †	164	housewife	33	"
	R	Wolson Bernard	174	machinist	21	"
	S	Wolson Michael	174	"	51	"
	T	*Wolson Rose †	174	housewife	51	"
	V	Ferris Howard	175	carpenter	60	"
	W	Porter Carrie K †	175	housewife	56	"
	U	Porter Elwyn C	175	chauffeur	34	"
	X	Porter Pearl C †	175	housewife	32	"
	Y	Pellegrini Louis	185 187	tilesetter	35	"
	Z	Pellegrini Nancy †	185 187	housewife	30	"
2154						
	A	Baldini Irene M †	185 187	"	21	571 Cummins H way
	B	Baldini Joseph	185 187	clerk	31	208 "
	C	McCusker Bernard R	189	welder	24	here
	D	McCusker Ruth G †	189	housewife	25	"
	E	Farrell Louis	189	engineer	46	"
	F	Farrell Ruth E †	189	housewife	45	"
	G	Sheil Suzanne †	197	"	31	11 Juliette
	H	Sheil Thomas	197	superintendent	32	11 "
	K	Adams Alfred J	197	operator	47	Somerville
	L	Adams Alice K †	197	housewife	42	"

Page.	Letter.	Full Name.	Residence, Jan. 1, 1941.	Occupation.	Supposed Age.	Reported Residence, Jan. 1, 1940. Street and Number.

Savannah Avenue—Continued

Page.	Letter.	Full Name.	Residence, Jan. 1, 1941.	Occupation.	Supposed Age.	Reported Residence, Jan. 1, 1940. Street and Number.
	M	Adams Louise A—†	197	clerk	20	Somerville
	N	VanSteenbergen Alexander	203	machinist	54	here
	O	VanSteenbergen Mary—†	203	housewife	45	"
	P	Donnelly Lillian—†	203	"	45	"
	R	Donnelly Thomas H	203	coppersmith	50	"
	S	Johnson Adolph	205	machinist	52	"
	T	*Johnson Olga—†	205	housewife	50	"
	U	Jepson Berthel R	205	tailor	52	"
	V	*Jepson Marion—†	205	housewife	52	"
	W	Forrester Mary E—†	207	"	25	363 Hunt'n av
	X	Forrester Ralph V	207	agent	28	Quincy
	Y	Cunningham Alfred	207	machinist	52	here
	Z	Cunningham Caroline—†	207	housewife	54	"
2155						
	A	Kravits Mildred—†	209	"	50	"
	B	Kravits Wolf S	209	mechanic	50	"
	C	Kravits Myer	209	merchant	54	"
	D	Kravits Regina—†	209	housewife	50	"
	E	Gould Howard F	249	musician	76	"
	F	Gould Laura A—†	249	housewife	70	"
	G	Slade James	249	manager	35	"
	H	Slade Mary—†	249	housewife	26	"

Woodhaven Avenue

Page.	Letter.	Full Name.	Residence, Jan. 1, 1941.	Occupation.	Supposed Age.	Reported Residence, Jan. 1, 1940. Street and Number.
	K	Piemonte Helen M—†	14	housewife	46	here
	L	Piemonte Luigi S	14	barber	55	"
	M	Ruppersberg Mary J—†	14	housekeeper	73	"
	N	Gulesian Isabel M—†	24	secretary	40	"
	O	Veal Anna M—†	24	housewife	49	"
	P	Veal Samuel	24	lineman	70	"
	R	Allen Grace A—†	111	housewife	26	691 River
	S	Allen Wilfred W	111	salesman	28	691 "
	T	Horigan John A	113	chauffeur	37	here
	U	Horigan Mary A—†	113	housewife	57	"
	V	Horigan Michael A	113	clerk	58	"
	W	Horigan Michael J	113	laborer	35	"
	X	Horigan Thomas F	113	shipper	20	"
	Y	Horigan William J	113	chauffeur	24	"

Page	Letter	Full Name	Residence, Jan. 1, 1941	Occupation	Supposed Age	Reported Residence, Jan. 1, 1940. Street and Number

Woodhaven Avenue—Continued

Page	Letter	Full Name	Residence, Jan. 1, 1941	Occupation	Supposed Age	Reported Residence, Jan. 1, 1940. Street and Number
	z	*Camozzi Mary G †	114	housewife	34	here
2156						
	A	Camozzi Vincent	114	boilermaker	41	"
	B	Ellis Mary T †	114	housewife	25	Quincy
	C	Ellis Webster E	114	chauffeur	32	"
	D	Williams Anna M †	118	housewife	37	18 Crossman
	E	Williams George E	118	carpenter	38	18 "